SOFTWARE TOOLS FOR BUSINESS

An Information Systems Approach

ROGER HAYEN

Central Michigan University

JOHN WILEY & SONS, INC.

New York   **Chichester**   **Brisbane**   **Toronto**   **Singapore**

ACQUISITIONS EDITOR   Beth Lang Golub
MARKETING MANAGER   Debra Reigert
PRODUCTION SUPERVISOR   Deborah Herbert
DESIGN DIRECTOR   Karin Gerdes Kincheloe
TEXT DESIGNER   Lee Goldstein
MANUFACTURING MANAGER   Andrea Price
ILLUSTRATION   Sigmund Malinowski

This book was set in ITC New Baskerville by Publication Services, Inc. and printed and bound by
Courier/Kendalville. The cover was printed by Lehigh.

Recognizing the importance of preserving what has been written, it is a
policy of John Wiley & Sons, Inc. to have books of enduring value published
in the United States printed on acid-free paper, and we exert our best
efforts to that end.

Library of Congress Cataloging in Publication Data
Hayen, Roger L.
    Software tools for business : an information systems
approach / Roger Hayen.
        p.   cm.
    Includes index.

    ISBN 0-471-54694-1 (paper)
    1. Management information systems.   2. Decision support systems.
3. Business–Computer programs.   4. Data base management–Computer
programs.   5. Business report writing–Computer programs.
6. Electronic spreadsheets.   I. Title.

    HD30.213.H39   1994
    658.4′038′011–dc20
                                                    93–4642
                                                       CIP

Printed in the United States of America

10   9   8   7   6   5   4   3   2

Preface

Where to Use This Book

This book is designed for use with introductory and intermediate courses in (1) software tools, (2) information systems in business, and (3) management information systems. For a course in software tools, this would serve as the primary text, whereas it would usually be a support text for other courses. The book's design provides "hands-on" computer projects for both kinds of courses.

The book has two primary missions: (1) instruction in the fundamental mechanics of operating software tools, and (2) applying the software tools to solve realistic business problems. The basic instruction mission is addressed through the descriptions of software tool operation and the Practice Tutorials and the Practice Exercises at the end of each lesson. This level of coverage is recommended when students are first introduced to the software tools. The application mission is explored through the Comprehensive Problems and the Case Application which are also presented at the end of each lesson. This course content is suggested when students have some prior knowledge of the software tools and the focus of the course is on exploring business applications. In this situation, the descriptions of software usage serve primarily as a reference for students.

The different levels of problems included in this book allow it to be used in two different ways:

1. For each desired software tool, a course could include both instruction in tool use and problem solution assignments. The Practice Exercises and Comprehensive Problems specifically support this situation.

2. The book could be used a source of problems for hands-on projects with the instructional component of the book serving as a reference. The Case Applications facilitate this arrangement.

By selecting different levels of problems, different learning objectives may be attained for different levels of courses and even for different software tools within an individual course. Prepublication versions of this book have been used successfully in introductory spreadsheet and database courses, in introduction to information systems courses, in business software tools application courses, and in graduate-level introduction to management information systems courses. For each of these courses, different levels and combinations of problems were selected to achieve the desired learning objectives. Please refer to the Instructor's Manual for sample combinations.

Pedagogical Features

Software Tools for Business: An Information Systems Approach employs problem solving in learning the application of personal productivity software tools. The problem-solving learning objectives are supported by including the following features in the various lessons:

Content Outlines—appear for reference to indicate the topics covered in each lesson.

Margin Call Outs—highlight software tool operations and activities as a means for referencing commands in the context of their application in problem solving.

Step-by-Step Narrations—integrate concepts and keystrokes within the context of solving problems by explaining both the how and why of each activity.

Page Designs—differentiate between what is to be done and what is to be read with numerous screen shots that reinforce the results to be obtained.

Caution Alert Boxes—provide warnings of possible actions that frequently cause difficulties in using a software tool.

Keypoint Boxes—reinforce a main idea in the use or application of a software tool.

Summary Figures—provide a concise synopsis of selected software tool operations for review and reference.

When Things Go Wrong Sections—anticipate frequently occurring difficulties in using a software tool and explain suggested corrective actions.

Lesson Summary Sections—contain a review that reinforces the concepts and software tool operations presented in the lesson.

Reference Sections—provide a comprehensive summary of the commands available with each software tool.

Software Versions

The contents of this book are compatible with the following version of software tools:

Lotus 1-2-3	Releases 2.0 through 2.4 and 3.1
dBase	dBASE III+ and dBASE IV through version 2.0
WordPerfect	Versions 5.0 and 5.1
DOS	Versions 2.0 through 6.0

In a limited number of situations, the earlier version of the software tools do not contain all of the advanced features described in this book. However, earlier versions can be used to solve nearly all of the problems included in the book.

Supplements

The following supplemental materials are available to support this book:

Data Disk—includes all of the worksheet, database, and document files needed to complete the Practice Exercises and Case Application problems. Students should create their own Data Disk from the Practice Exercises and Case Applications Disk provided with this book. This will serve as a backup copy of the files, in the event of a problem with their disks, and will give students a place to store files that they create in solving problems. The data disk is available in the Instructor's Manual. Students should ask their instructors how to access this data.

Instructor's Resource Guide—includes a Solution Disk with complete answer files for the Practice Tutorials, Practice Exercises, Comprehensive Problems, and Case Applications. Teaching notes and tips provide guidance in using the Solution Disk. Transparency masters are supplied for key figures from the book.

Disclaimer

The businesses referenced in the exercises, problems, and cases of this book were selected to indicate how these businesses might use software tools. These references are *not* intended to illustrate either effective or ineffective handling of an administrative situation or of an actual software tool application by a particular business.

Acknowledgments

Many individuals have made special contributions to the successful completion of *Software Tools for Business: An Information Systems Approach*. Thanks go to each of the following reviewers for their valuable comments, suggestions, and criticisms, which helped shape this book.

Martin D. Goslar
New Mexico State University

Kenneth L. Marr
Hofstra University

Casper E. Wiggins
Texas A&M University

Marilyn Meyer
Fresno State College

Clinton P. Fuelling
Ball State University

Mary Allyn Webster
University of Florida

Frank S. Butash
University of Hartford

James Street
Merritt College

T. Grandon Gill
Florida Atlantic University

David J. Rosser
Essex Community College

Tahirih Foroughi
American Graduate School of
International Management

I am especially grateful for the many suggestions and valuable insights provided by my colleagues. Ed Fisher, Professor of Office and Information Systems, provided much needed guidance and review regarding the content of the book. Joe Dougherty, formerly of John Wiley & Sons, provided direction in the development of the case applications and management information systems framework. Beth Lang Golub, of John Wiley & Sons, gave direction in refining the content of this book. Margaret Mullen, Shelley Odelson, Scott Nelson, Andrea Brunackey, and Pete Smidt, graduate assistants, contributed to the reviewing process and furnished constant student reactions and feedback that served to enhance and to refine the content and presentation of the book. Don Nellermoe and Jim Scott, Professors of Office and Information Systems, offered encouragement and confirmed the approach used in this book. Other faculty and staff in the Office and Information Systems Department contributed to the book's formulation and development in a variety of ways. All of these efforts are greatly appreciated.

In any project of this type, "the book" overshadows many family activities. A special thanks goes to my family for their encouragement, support, and perseverance during this project.

Roger Hayen
Mt. Pleasant, Michigan

Note to the Student

Software Tools for Business: An Information Systems Approach is designed to help you prepare for a career in business by teaching you how to apply software tools to solve the business problems that actual managers of businesses often encounter. This book uses a unique approach to learning software tools—one that carefully blends software tool operations, business concepts, information systems concepts, and problem-solving techniques. It is written for those who have little or no experience with computers or business. The primary objective of this book is to assist you in developing the knowledge and skills you need to effectively use popular software tools in solving common business problems. This text will also enable you to build a solid foundation for the continued learning you will need during your future career to keep pace with the development of these software tools.

A Balanced Approach to Concepts and Hands-On Training

Businesses do not have spreadsheet, database, or word processing problems. What they have are business problems to which these tools can be applied. Real managers select and apply software tools to solve a variety of business problems. Like a mechanic learning about tools in a mechanics' toolbox, you have an equally important need to learn about the variety of situations in which software tools are used, as well as a need to master their basic operation. When you encounter a real problem in business, you need to be able to reach into your software toolbox and pick the appropriate tool for the problem at hand. The problem-solving approach of this book provides you with strong reinforcement for learning where and how software tools are used in businesses. This approach will help you to learn how to select and apply the appropriate tool in different situations. As you progress through the lessons of this book, you will be essentially a consultant to various clients as they encounter each new problem, much like an actual business analyst.

The best way to really learn how to use a software tool is to actually apply the tool in solving problems. Nearly everybody can learn how to type data into a software tool application, but learning how to properly use that tool to produce information that supports informed management decision making is more than typing. Real managers solve problems; they do not just type solutions other people develop. This book is founded on the principle of learning by doing; thus, you will be actually applying software tools to produce information in solving realistic business problems. This book provides instruction in the mechanics of operating software tools by focusing on those commands that are needed for obtaining required information rather than on covering every command in the software tool. Hands-on experience with problems that address business and information systems concepts provide learning reinforcement that goes beyond what is achieved by lecture and discussion. This kind of experience offers more than mere keystrokes for operating the software tools, because it calls for the application of critical thinking in developing problem solutions.

As appropriate, the business problems presented in this book are associated with the application of systems analysis and design techniques needed for applying the particular software tools. For example, with a spreadsheet problem using conditional logic, decision tables are used to describe the design of the logic to be implemented. And, with database programming, dataflow diagrams and structure charts are used to illustrate system components. In addition, several of the problems involve information system applications, such as estimating program development time for a custom business computer system, determining the amount of time system analysts are engaged in daily activities, managing the assignments of systems analysts, and producing computer system documentation. This exploration of generally accepted information systems concepts reinforces learning about these systems development techniques.

Many of the problems included in this book are ones that were addressed with the computer tools that were available long before spreadsheet, database management, and word processing software became available on personal computers. The hardware and software have changed significantly, but the problems managers face have remained almost the same. By applying software tools to business problems, you will learn the balanced approach of operating software tools together with the related business and information systems concepts.

Distinguishing Characteristics

This book is unique in the breadth and depth of the different business problems it offers for you to solve. Overall the book is organized as a series of lessons about each software tool with problems at the end of each lesson. These problems span levels of learning difficulty from simple tutorials to extensive case applications. This variety makes possible the flexible use of this book in meeting different learning objectives.

Practice Tutorials. The tutorials directly reinforce the software tool skills presented in a lesson by guiding you in the use of software tool operations with step-by-step instructions. These tutorials build skills in the fundamental commands used to manipulate the software tool.

Practice Exercises. The exercises support learning the tool skills of a lesson while you gain experience with a variety of business problems. These Practice Exercises are tied to an information systems framework and have approximately the same scope as Practice Tutorials, but they require critical thinking in formulating a solution.

Comprehensive Problems. The problems ask you to apply the skills of a lesson to a business problem in which you develop the entire application, in instances where problems build from one lesson to the next. In this manner, prototyping is applied in systems development, which calls for critical thinking in designing and producing the solution.

Case Applications. The applications involve the synthesis of software tool and business analysis knowledge emphsizing the problem-solving context of management information systems. These Case Applications encourage your critical thinking in the design and development of a viable solution and in making appropriate decisions by using the results.

Levels of difficulty for the end-of-lesson material are aligned with general educational objectives in the following way:[1]

Problem Group	Learning Objective
Practice Tutorials	Knowledge
Practice Exercises	Comprehension
Comprehensive Problems	Application and analysis
Case Applications	Synthesis and evaluation

Depending on the amount of time available and the level of your prior experience, a combination of Pratice Tutorials, Practice Exercises, Comprehensive Problems, and Case Applications can be used to achieve these learning objectives.

The Comprehensive Problems are self-contained and require you to build an entire solution by entering all of the data. The Practice Exercises and Case Applications make use of a Data Disk containing files with a partial solution that is accessed in solving the problem. You should see your instructor to arrange for accessing the files on the Data Disk.

The Comprehensive Problems and selected Practice Exercises are organized as spiral problems with the problems expanding or building from one lesson to the next. Spiral problems present a systems development environment similar to that of prototyping. As a result, the Comprehensive Problems for each software tool should be solved in the sequence encountered in the book. The spiral problems, which make use of results from a previous assignment, are indicated as being "continued." Each Case Application and most Practice Exercises are independent of the other assignments. As a result, Case Applications and most Practice Exercises may be solved in a sequence different from their arrangement in the text. Some problems are based on the company scenario that is described in a previous problem, but these problems do *not* require the solution of any previous assignment. Such problems are identified as a "second encounter."

Organization

The book has six parts:

Part I: Using Software Tools	Part IV: Using dBASE
Part II: Using DOS	Part V: Using WordPerfect
Part III: Using Lotus 1-2-3	Part VI: Integrating Solutions

Part I of the book contains an introduction to a management information framework and describes general terminology for interacting with software tools. Lesson T.2 in Part I is a guide to the keystroke terminology used in the book. You should read that lesson before embarking on any of the software tool lessons. Lesson T.1 in Part I introduces a management information framework for the Practice Exercises and Case Applications. This lesson should be studied before beginning the Practice Exercises or Case Applications in the Lotus 1-2-3, dBASE, or WordPerfect parts. After completing Lesson T.2 in Part I, the software tools may be explored in any desired sequence.

In Part II, the coverage of DOS is intended primarily as support for the other software tools. If you have no prior knowledge of this operating system, you should

---

[1]Benjamin S. Bloom, *Taxonomy of Educational Objectives*, New York: David McKay Company, 1956.

complete this part before you begin the lessons for the other software tools. Otherwise, you may use this part as a reference when you need it.

Parts III, IV, and V consist of lessons that contain hands-on tutorials with step-by-step instruction on how to use each of these software tools in solving a business problem together with the problems for you to solve with that tool.

Part VI explores the integration of software tools where results from two or more tools are combined in producing the desired information for decision making. Software tool integration includes information systems concepts that are useful in linking data from other computer systems, such as a general ledger system, with software tools in developing a problem solution. The design of the Comprehensive Problems and Case Applications in this part enables them to be used as *capstone problems* that encompass the review of software tool operations that are included throughout the other lessons of the book.

Learning Strategy

This book supports a learning strategy that has been applied in the "corporate world." It is based on the general concept: "Give a person a loaf of bread, and you feed them for a day. Teach a person how to grow wheat and make bread, and you feed them for a lifetime." For software tools, the general strategy is as follows:

1. Read a description of a software tool's features and operation.
2. Explore the hands-on operation of the software tool by using tutorial exercises and problems.
3. Apply the software tool to your own business problem. Reference example solutions as necessary to assist in developing your application.

In many businesses, this learning strategy is applied in a self-paced environment with individuals learning to use a software tool as they develop solutions to their own problems. Often individuals do not have time to attend a special training seminar before using each new software tool. They are provided with a book describing the software tool and are expected to learn how to effectively use the tool. The Practice Tutorials and Practice Exercises in this book specifically support this learning strategy.

This book provides you with a foundation for learning to apply software tools to solve business problems. By following the learning strategy of this book, you will experience the application of current software tools and will be ready for the new software tools of tomorrow.

R. H.

Contents

LESSON L.6 Interrogating Spreadsheet Models with Data Tables L-163

LESSON L.7 Applying Functions L-185

LESSON L.8 Preparing Forecasts with Regression Analysis L-212

LESSON L.9 Automating Solutions with Macros L-235

LESSON L.10 Consolidating Results with Combine L-276

LESSON D.9   Processing with Menu Programs   D-204

Reference   D-230

PART V   USING WORDPERFECT

LESSON W.1   Creating and Printing Documents   W-1

LESSON W.2   Modifying and Correcting Documents   W-26

LESSON W.3   Formatting Documents   W-54

Using
Software
Tools

Management Information System Framework

CONTENT

- Information Systems Characteristics
- Management Activity Levels
- Business Functions
- Management Functions
- Application Framework

T.1.1 Introduction

"Welcome back Brenda. How was your four-day workshop in Lotus 1-2-3? Now that you've graduated from 'Lotus University,' you should be ready to forge ahead with the development of our corporate planning and budgeting system," said Greg, Brenda's manager. Brenda is apprehensive about the lead role Greg expects her to take in the creation of this important management information system (MIS) for supporting corporate decision making. As a junior financial analyst, she has had limited experience in preparing department budgets, but no experience in developing an entire corporate plan. At the workshop, Brenda explored the operation of Lotus 1-2-3 and learned many of its menus and commands. With her degree in finance and her newly acquired knowledge of 1-2-3 spreadsheets, everyone seems to expect that building a corporate planning and budgeting system will be a snap. Moreover, Brenda is concerned because Greg now thinks of her as the company's champion of planning and budgeting. After all, she has learned how to manipulate the rows and columns of a spreadsheet. How can she fulfill the expectations of her manager? Brenda thinks, "How, indeed?"

Like Brenda, virtually everyone who works, works for some kind of business—businesses that do *not* have spreadsheet problems, database problems, or word processing problems. What they have are business problems to which personal productivity software tools—Lotus 1-2-3, dBASE, and WordPerfect—may be applied in obtaining solutions. Without the underlying business problems, there is little need for any of these software tools.

Brenda has learned that business problems do not wear labels: "I'm a spreadsheet problem, won't you please use Lotus 1-2-3 to solve me?" Instead, they appear as business problems, such as, "We need to borrow money to pay our suppliers by Friday. Where can we get it?" You, the user of a software tool, must determine whether this is a problem to be attacked with a personal productivity software tool, such as a spreadsheet, database, or word processor. Or, perhaps, *no* software tool is necessary at all—just better management practices. Software tools are not a panacea for solving all management problems.

Often workshops, like the one that Brenda attended, focus on the mechanics and structure of a software tool. But if you know only keystroke operations, this does not ensure that you can effectively and efficiently use software tools in solving everyday business problems. Brenda believes that she could master every command in Lotus 1-2-3 and still not be able to apply this software tool in solving her planning and budgeting problem. Merely knowing menu selections and commands does not mean that you know how to create solutions to business problems. And if you are not going to solve problems, there is little reason to learn how to operate software tools. With software tools, two types of learning are involved: (1) operating the software tool and (2) applying the tool in solving business problems. Although related, these are two separate and distinct learning objectives. To the novice software tool user, the selection of commands to solve everyday business problems is like French cuisine to a short-order cook. Learning only software tool commands does not automatically give you the ability to carry out the expected business analysis.

T.1.2   Software Tool Learning Components

In learning about personal productivity software tools, you need to gain an understanding of the *what*, *where*, and *when* of applying a software tool, as well as learning *how* to drive the tool by selecting and executing its commands. You need to know both the *mechanics* of operating a software tool and the *context* in which that tool is applied in solving common business problems. You need to know the context in which different tools are best used—because if the only tool you learned how to use was a hammer, the whole world would look like a nail. As with any other tool, in learning to use software tools, you need to comprehend the business situation in which that tool is typically applied.

A relation between software tool operation and business problem solving is illustrated in Figure T.1, with each type of learning divided into low and high categories. Without learning about the application of software tools in business problem solving, you are merely moving along the horizontal axis from low to high. To *effectively* use software tools in a business environment, which you surely want to do, your learning needs to proceed along the diagonal from low–low to high–high. How can this be accomplished? By learning the mechanical operation of software tools together with an introduction to widely accepted business applications. Brenda's stress level was elevated because her manager expected her to learn how to solve common business problems, whereas her workshop concentrated on learning the mechanics of operating the software.

Learning about a word processor provides you with a standard of comparison for looking at other software tools. With word processing, you have a broad foundation in writing skills and a good understanding of the business problem—putting words on paper to support communication activities. In learning about a word processor, you would typically concentrate on the mechanics of capturing words electronically and manipulating them into the proper form. This learning is usually centered on how to run the software tool to create documents, perform corrections, carry out cut-and-paste operations, and print documents.

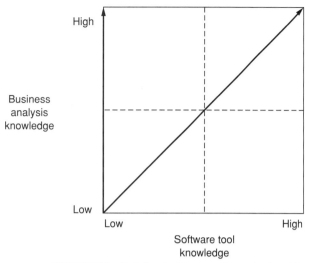

FIGURE T.1. Relation between software tool and business analysis knowledge.

Does learning how to operate a word processor increase your knowledge of sentence structure and grammar or how to write business correspondence? By learning all the features of a word processor, do you automatically become a fluent writer of novels? Are users with prior experience in writing only letters and memos expected to write a technical reference manual on learning how to use a word processor? In general, learning how to use a word processor typically allows you to better perform your *current* writing activities. Learning to run a word processor does not automatically improve your writing ability. To improve skills in business writing, separate courses are frequently required, for instance, technical writing, business correspondence, or writing computer-user manuals. Usually, learning the operation of a word processor is *not* expected to impart these writing skills. However, when you are learning the use of a software tool, you can gain an appreciation for its application by solving typical problems attacked with the tool. For instance, when entering an example business letter into a word processor, you gain an understanding of what a business letter is like. A similar situation exists with other software tools, for instance, the general characteristics of the typical problems tackled with a spreadsheet or database tool.

T.1.3   Information Systems Characteristics

Information systems characteristics supply a framework for business problems that will provide you with a solid foundation for learning about the application of personal productivity software tools. The framework represents a structured approach to learning common software tool applications and will help your learning progress along the vertical axis of Figure T.1 from low to high.

What is an appropriate framework of management information systems characteristics that supports learning the operation of personal productivity software tools in solving typical business problems? Generally accepted information systems characteristics (identified in textbooks such as Davis and Olson [2], Schultheis and Sumner [6], Laudon and Laudon [4], Kroenke [3], and McLeod [5]) include management activity levels, business functions, and management functions. Although other characteristics exist, these three are sufficient in providing you with a broad-based framework of typical business problems.

By solving a variety of problems within this framework, you gain a better understanding of the appropriate use of software tools as well as where you might best apply each tool in developing management information to solve generally recognized business problems. This framework of management information systems characteristics is used with the Practice Exercises and Case Application problems in this book to provide you with an understanding of the *context* in which software tools are used in business problem solving. This should help you to avoid the kind of false expectations encountered by Brenda. Overall, the framework acts as a springboard into more complex business analysis with personal productivity tools. Each of the characteristics is examined individually so that you can become familiar with their particular attributes.

T.1.4 Management Activity Levels

Because of different job functions and management responsibilities, business activities can be categorized into organizational levels. Software tools are applied to serve these different organizational levels. Employing the broadly accepted framework developed by Anthony [1], the levels within an organization can be classified by the management activities that typically occur at each level. These management activity levels, illustrated in Figure T.2, are described as follows:

> *Strategic planning.* The process of determining organizational objectives that encompass the definition of goals, policies, and general guidelines charting a course for an organization. This activity level includes making changes in these objectives and allocating resources to attain them. The characteristics of an organization are matched to its environment. This level focuses on those activities that are usually performed by top management.
>
> *Managerial control.* The process by which managers ensure that resources are obtained and used effectively and efficiently to achieve an organization's objectives.

FIGURE T.2. Management activity levels.

This activity level includes the establishment and monitoring of budgets. It is also known as *tactical* planning and control. This level is typically concerned with those activities that are carried out by middle management.

Operational control. The process of ensuring that specific tasks are carried out in attaining organizational objectives. Criteria of task completion are established and evaluated. Existing facilities and resources are applied to accomplish day-to-day activities effectively and efficiently within budget constraints. Activities at this level are frequently performed by first-line management.

T.1.5   Business Functions

The basic business functions carried out by nearly all businesses are often grouped to include the areas of (1) finance, (2) production/operations, (3) marketing, and (4) human resources. Examples of common applications in each of these areas are listed in Figure T.3; this list is not exhaustive, but merely reflects common and frequently occurring systems in nearly all business enterprises. Some business functions may be unique to a particular industry, whereas other functions are more universal. The functions delineated in Figure T.3 are representative of the major information systems of many business organizations.

Production/operations tends to be a more diverse, less well-defined business function than the other three, because some businesses manufacture products whereas others provide services. The activities involved in producing or delivering a service are often categorized as the **operations** function. For example, in the airline transportation industry, their operations encompass passenger reservations, crew scheduling, and aircraft scheduling. These operations are the primary activities undertaken by this type of industry in producing a service. For our purposes, a broad definition of production/operations is applied that includes those activities that are carried out by both manufacturing and nonmanufacturing businesses in producing goods or delivering services.

Finance Systems
Budget
Cost Accounting
Funds Management
Billing
Accounts Receivable
Accounts Payable
General Ledger
Credit Analysis
Financial Analysis
Financial Planning
Capital Requirements Planning

Production Systems
Shipping and Receiving
Purchasing
Material Requirements Planning
Production/Operation Scheduling
Crew Scheduling
Inventory
Distribution
Quality Control
Engineering

Marketing Systems
Marketing Research
Pricing
Product Development
Product Planning
Advertising and Promotion
Sales Management
Sales Order Entry
Sales Forecasting
Customer and Sales Analysis

Human Resource Systems
Payroll
Labor Relations
Compensation Planning
Employee Benefits
Human Resource Requirements Planning
Human Resource Actions
Human Resource Records
Training

FIGURE T.3. Functional business systems.

Each of these four primary business functions is described as follows:

Finance. This business function encompasses the legal and historical record-keeping activities and yields accurate financial statements that support managers in financial decision making and in the allocation and control of financial resources. This function supports the creation of planning information for anticipated future business conditions. An organization's financial health is monitored and analyzed through accounting systems that are responsible for the preparation of financial statements and reports.

Production. This function is concerned with the planning and control of processes that produce goods or deliver services, including the control of inventories, the scheduling of activities, and the movement of goods and/or services; it is also known as the operations function.

Marketing. This function is concerned with the selling of goods and/or services to customers to meet their needs and wants. This includes the planning, promotion, and sale of existing products or services in current markets, together with the development of new products and new markets to better serve present and potential customers. This business function provides for effectively pricing, promoting, and distributing a company's goods and services.

Human resources. This function is involved in the recruitment, placement, evaluation, compensation, and development of the employees in an organization. This includes the implementation and reporting requirements of federal, state, and local laws and regulations.

Each of these business functions transcends the management activity levels as they are portrayed in Figure T.4. That is, each business function occurs at each of the activity levels. The pyramid in Figure T.4 indicates that the volume of activity typically increases in moving from the strategic planning level to the operational control level. As a result, you might anticipate more opportunities for using software tools in addressing operational control problems than in addressing strategic planning problems.

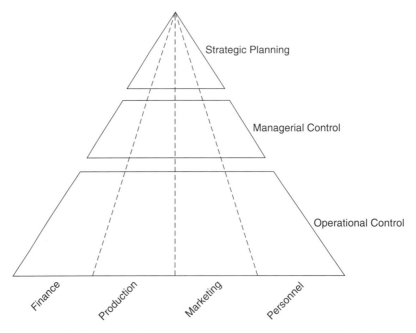

FIGURE T.4. Functional business systems across management activity levels.

T.1.6   Management Functions

Management is the process of directing tasks and of organizing resources to achieve organizational goals. The basic functions of management performed by managers in nearly all business enterprises, according to Henri Fayol and others, are often delineated by the four activities of (1) planning, (2) organizing, (3) directing, and (4) controlling. These management functions are interrelated is as illustrated in Figure T.5. Each function can be described, in general, as follows:

Plan. Determine what is to be done, how it will be done, when it will be done, and who will do it by setting objectives and determining the resources and courses of action needed to meet those objectives.

Organize. Establish structure to permit implementation of the plan by setting up or identifying departments or other organizational entities responsible for carrying out their designated tasks. Organizing is the process of dividing work into tasks and coordinating those tasks to achieve one or more objectives. Necessary resources are acquired, including human resources. The best individuals are found, hired, and trained for the tasks that have been identified.

Direct. Provide guidance in carrying out tasks that work toward achievement of the plan.

Control. Monitor activities by measuring actual performance to determine if the designated objectives have been attained. Actual results are compared with intended results with variance reports and corrective actions taken when necessary.

Good management is the process of carrying out these four functions so that a business can achieve its goals. All managers perform these functions, regardless of their level in an organization or their particular business functional area. Managers require information systems that support these primary management functions across activity levels and business functions. This information may be furnished through the application of personal productivity software tools.

T.1.7   Application Framework

Information is required at the various management activity levels, across business functions, and to support management functions. Personal computer productivity software tools can be applied to supply information in support of these requirements

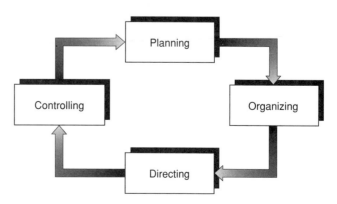

FIGURE T.5. Management functions.

in managing a business enterprise. The interrelationship of management activity levels, business functions, and management functions is illustrated by the management characteristics cube in Figure T.6. Although each characteristic is present, its extent tends to vary depending on each individual business situation.

The information systems framework provides a foundation for gaining the business analysis knowledge indicated in Figure T.1. This application framework is explored in this book as a series of organized lessons. Each lesson contains a description of specific software tool operations followed by Practice Tutorials, Practice Exercises, Comprehensive Problems, and a Case Application, as appropriate for the particular software tool lesson.

Practice tutorials. These tutorials directly reinforce the software tool skills presented in a lesson. They provide a convenient means for you to increase your understanding of a software tool's operation before undertaking the exercises, problems or cases that follow.

Practice exercises. These exercises support learning the tool skills of the lesson while expanding your experience with a variety of business problems. These are stand-alone business problems that focus on a combination of management information systems characteristics.

Comprehensive problems. These problems apply the skills of a lesson to a business problem in which you develop the entire application. These problems build from one lesson to the next, a process similar to carrying out the development of an information system by using a prototyping approach, where your solution is iteratively refined.

Case applications. These applications involve the integration of the software tool and business analysis knowledge, emphasizing the problem-solving context of the management information system foundation. Case Applications are more comprehensive than Practice Exercises and require additional effort in identifying and solving the particular business problem.

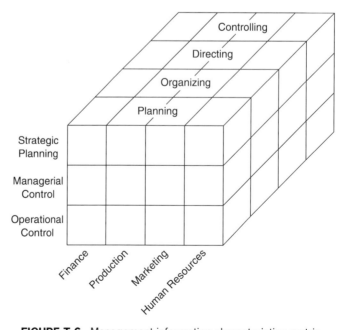

FIGURE T.6. Management information characteristics matrix.

The Practice Tutorials, Practice Exercises, Comprehensive Problems, and Case Applications are specifically designed to increase your knowledge of business problems. The anticipated outcome of each of these end-of-lesson sections in enhancing your business analysis knowledge is expected to follow the course shown in Figure T.7. This figure indicates how solving these different configurations of business problems helps your learning progress along the vertical axis of business analysis knowledge from low to high. You should gain a better understanding of the functional business areas, management functions, and management activity levels from these business problems. In this manner, software tools are integrated with management information system characteristics.

The Practice Exercises and Case Applications in this book have been carefully selected to reinforce the application framework. Figure T.8 illustrates one combination of typical business problems that can be placed within the information systems grid of management activity levels and functional business areas. The arrangement indicated in Figure T.8 is drawn from the Practice Exercises and Case Applications included in this book. Indeed, you could consider your role as that of a "consultant" for various "clients" as you move from problem to problem, much as a business analyst might.

To assist you in relating this MIS framework to personal productivity software tools, each Practice Exercise and Case Application is clearly identified by the primary characteristics of management activity level and business function. In addition, the Case Applications are related to the management functions appearing in the case. Each of these primary characteristics is incorporated in, at least, one of the cases. The particular mix of management skills and software tool skills are indicated at the beginning of each Practice Exercise or Case Application.

Practice Exercises and Application Cases make use of files that have been partially developed and are provided to you on a Data Disk. Your task as a "business consultant" is to complete the Practice Exercise or Case Application by applying the software tool skills included in the particular lesson.

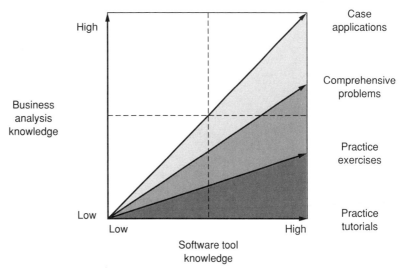

FIGURE T.7. Relation between software tool and business analysis knowledge from different problem solution options.

	Finance	Production	Marketing	Human Resources
Strategic Planning	Financial ratio analysis	Break-even analysis	Market forecasting	Labor forecasting
	Variance reporting	Project feasibility	Contract tracking	Labor negotiations
Managerial Control	Project investment analysis	Production scheduling	Advertising and sales planning	Staff planning
	Portfolio management	Material requirements planning	Advertising media scheduling	Skills inventory
Operational Control	Financial reporting	Inventory control	Sales support system	Payroll register
	Checkbook ledger	Project tracking	Direct-mail marketing	Job placement

FIGURE T.8. Integration of management functions with information characteristics matrix.

T.1.8 Learning How to Learn About Software Tools

The actual software that you will use in the future with business problems is very likely to be different than that explored in learning the functional capabilities of software tools in this book. Few people who are learning how to use Lotus 1-2-3 today remember even hearing about VisiCalc, which was the first spreadsheet program developed for use on a personal computer. Furthermore, changes in software tools are likely to accelerate. However, future business problems are likely to be similar to many of today's problems. For example, the need for computing a loan payment or creating a budget has not changed in the last century, but the tools for generating these solutions have undergone dramatic changes. Therefore, in learning about software tools, you need to learn about the *context* in which different tools are applied in solving common business problems, since this is more enduring than the specific menu selections and commands of a particular software tool. As the Lotus 1-2-3 of today becomes the VisiCalc of tomorrow, you need to be prepared to move on to the next generation of software tools.

What is the general procedure for learning about software tools? If you give someone a loaf of bread, you feed him for a day. If you show him how to grow wheat and make bread, you feed the person for a lifetime. In learning software tools, you need to *learn how to learn* to use new software tools so that you will be prepared for the next upgrade of Lotus 1-2-3, dBASE, WordPerfect or, perhaps, their replacements. The mission of this book is to help you learn how to learn. In accomplishing this objective, these are the steps you should learn to follow:

1. Read the description of operating the software tool in each lesson.
2. Increase your understanding of the software tool operation by working the tutorial examples.

3. Gain experience and learn the context of using the software tool by solving other problems, such as those included in the Practice Exercises, Comprehensive Problems, and Case Applications.

4. Apply the software tool in producing information to solve your own problems.

5. Reference the lesson descriptions and examples as necessary to assist you in using the software tool with your own problems.

This approach to learning to use software tools in producing solutions to practical, everyday business problems goes beyond just learning about the software tools in this book. By becoming comfortable with the method of learning supported by this book, you will be better prepared to learn how to operate and where to apply the future software tools that you may encounter. When presented with a new software tool, this approach should help you avoid Brenda's situation of elevated anxiety because of her manager's expectations.

T.1.9 Lesson Summary

- Lotus 1-2-3, dBASE, and WordPerfect are personal productivity software tools that can be applied in obtaining management information.

- The management information system (MIS) environment is described by key characteristics that often include (1) management activity levels, (2) business functions, and (3) management functions.

- Management activity levels form a hierarchy that consists of (1) strategic planning, (2) managerial control, and (3) operational control.

- Typical business functions can be delineated in the areas of (1) finance, (2) production/operations, (3) marketing, and (4) human resources.

- The generally accepted management functions consist of (1) planning, (2) organizing, (3) directing, and (4) controlling.

- These characteristics can be arranged as a matrix that provides a framework for applying personal productivity software tools in solving business problems.

- Case Applications and Practice Exercises furnish a means for exploring personal productivity software tools skills in the context of a broad framework of generally accepted management information system characteristics.

- *Learning how to learn* about software tools furnishes you with a basis for learning about future software tool enhancements and replacements.

T.1.10 References

1. Anthony, Robert N., *Planning and Control Systems: A Framework for Analysis,* Cambridge, Mass.: Harvard University Graduate School of Business Administration, 1965.

2. Davis, Gordon B., and Margrethe H. Olson, *Management Information Systems: Conceptual Foundations, Structure, and Development,* 2nd ed., New York: McGraw-Hill, 1985.

3. Kroenke, David, *Management Information Systems,* 2nd ed., New York: McGraw-Hill, 1992.

4. Laudon, Kenneth C., and Jane Price Laudon, *Management Information Systems: A Contemporary Perspective,* 2nd ed., New York: Macmillan Publishing, 1991.

5. McLeod, Raymond, *Management Information Systems: A Study of Computer-Based Information Systems,* 4th ed., New York: Macmillan Publishing, 1990.

6. Schultheis, Robert, and Mary Sumner, *Management Information Systems: The Manager's View,* 2nd ed., Homewood, Il: Irwin, 1991.

LESSON T.2

Software Navigation Guide

CONTENT
- Keystroke Terminology for Using Software Tools
- Key Names for Using Software Tools

T.2.1 Introduction

As you embark on your journey through the utilization of management information software tools, an introduction to the keystroke terminology deployed in this lesson is appropriate. The lessons on Using Lotus 1-2-3, Using dBASE, and Using DOS are designed as guided activities that may be (1) read and used as examples in working with each software tool or (2) followed in a hands-on manner as various commands and activities are presented and illustrated. To observe the actual operation of each tool, the hands-on manner is suggested; however, either approach can be used.

T.2.2 Keystroke Terminology for Using Software Tools

In learning Lotus 1-2-3, dBASE, and DOS, a number of different tasks are performed. To assist in carrying out these tasks, the various activities that you perform in operating each software tool are indicated by key manipulation words: **press**, **enter**, **type**, **select**, **move to**, **click**, **double-click**, **drag**, and **action**. *Whenever a line BEGINS with one of these words, perform that designated activity as follows:*

Keystroke	Directions
Press	Press or strike the specified key or keys. It is used primarily with cursor movement keys, special keys, function keys, and the \<return\> or \<Enter\> key. It is often used when only a single key is to be pressed. However, sometimes two keys must be pressed simultaneously.
Enter	Type the specified text by pressing one or more keys *followed* by the \<Enter\> key.

Type   Type the specified text by pressing one or more keys but do *not* follow the text with <Enter>. This is usually used when several keys are to be pressed.

Select   Choose a command from a *menu*. Usually the menu selection or pick is made by stiking the appropriate key or by moving the cursor to the desired command and pressing <Enter>. Move the menu cursor using the cursor directional keys or the mouse pointer.

Move to   Reposition the pointer or cursor to a specified place on the screen.

Click   Press and release the mouse button. This is the left mouse button unless otherwise indicated. Usually a menu selection is made with this activity.

Double-click   Click the mouse button twice without changing your selection.

Drag   Press the mouse button and hold it down while moving the mouse. This is the left mouse button unless otherwise indicated.

Action   Perform the necessary activities to complete the requested task(s). Action requires the application of commands that have been previously described in detail.

Keypoint!   Press, strike, enter, type, select, move to, click, double-click, drag, and action are keywords that are used in describing the operation of Lotus 1-2-3, dBASE, and DOS. They are *not* commands for these software tools!

T.2.3   Key Names for Using Software Tools

Special keys on your computer's keyboard are referenced by name, rather than by using distinctive symbols to designate these keys. The name of a key is enclosed with the symbols < > to indicate it is an individual key, for example, <Home>, <End>, <PgUp>, <PgDn>, <PrtSc>, <F1>. Key names are those defined for a typical IBM personal computer keyboard. If you have a different keyboard, you will need to make the necessary revisions for the key-naming convention to match those for your computer.

A plus (+) is used whenever two or more keys must be pressed *simultaneously*, such as <Ctrl>+<Break> or <Ctrl>+<Alt>+<Del>.

The names used to describe special keys on keyboards that have only a symbol reference are as follows:

Key	Action
<Enter>	enter or return
<Return>	return or enter
<backspace>	backspace
<left>	cursor left
<right>	cursor right
<up>	cursor up
<down>	cursor down
<shift>	shift
<Tab>	tab
<Ctrl>	control
<Esc>	escape

Caution Alert!

On some keyboards, pressing the cursor movement keys may result in typing a number. If this occurs and the cursor does not move, then press the <Num Lock> key and try again!

T.2.4   Lesson Summary

- Key words are deployed to indicate the various activities that are to be performed in manipulating the software tools. These are **press**, **enter**, **type**, **select**, **move to**, **click**, **double-click**, **drag**, and **action**.

- The **action** key word designates carrying out a series of steps that have been previously described.

- Special keys, identified on your keyboard with a distinctive symbol, are referenced by name, for example, the cursor movement keys of <left>, <right>, <up>, and <down>.

- The plus (+) symbol is used to indicate pressing two or more keys concurrently, such as <Ctrl>+<Break> or <Alt>+<P>.

Using
DOS

LESSON

0.1

Accessing and Applying Essential Commands

CONTENT

- What Is an Operating System?
- Human Operating Systems
- Personal Computer Operating Systems
- The Versions of IBM DOS
- Naming DOS Files
- About DOS Commands
- Starting DOS
- The DOS Prompt
- Revising Date and Time
- Listing Files
- Formatting a Data Disk
- Displaying a File's Content
- Duplicating Files
- Checking Disk Usage
- Removing Unwanted Files
- Recovering Deleted Files
- When Things Go Wrong

0.1.1 What Is an Operating System?

Operating systems are the fundamental language of the computer. An operating system is *required* for nearly all computers: personal computers, minicomputers, and mainframes. It is virtually impossible to perform any significant useful business computing without an operating system. For example, an operating system is necessary for an ordinary person to perform any operations with a computer's disk drive.

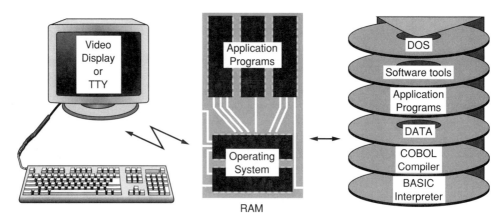

FIGURE O.1. Operating system resides in RAM.

Operating systems are part of what is known as **systems software**. Systems software is a collection of **programs** that are used to start up the computer, to load, execute, store, and retrieve application programs, to store and retrieve files, and to perform a series of utility operations.

As shown in Figure O.1, the operating system (O/S) program must be placed in random access memory (RAM) and resides there while the computer is in operation. The operating system sits between the hardware or the personal computer itself and your software tool or application program. One of its primary functions is to allow application programs and data to be accessed and stored on disk. As illustrated, the operating system reduces the amount of RAM that is available for application programs. When a computer is turned on, the first step is to place or load the operating system into RAM. This loading process is referred to as **booting** the computer and must be performed regardless of whether it is a personal computer or a mainframe computer. The primary difference is that with a personal computer, you, the end user, are responsible for loading the operating system, whereas on a mainframe, it is performed for you by the data processing operations staff.

Keypoint! An operating system is *required* for any ordinary person to perform any activities with a computer's disk drives!

0.1.2 Human Operating Systems

Consider how language is used by people. Language represents a human "operating system." Think about these languages:

English	Spanish
Danish	Finnish
French	Japanese
German	Chinese
Sign language	Braille

Is one better than the other? Is one more popular? Is the most popular language the "best" language?

You must know, at least, one language to function in our society. However, people can learn different languages. You need to know a language before you can pursue any career, including that of an accountant, pharmacist, physician, teacher, or attorney. Like people, computers usually must have an operating system before they can perform any useful activities. Several different operating systems can be used on the same computer, just as different languages are used by people.

0.1.3   Personal Computer Operating Systems

A number of operating systems are available for the IBM and compatible personal computers, including the following:

DOS

PC-DOS	All three of these are essentially synonyms for the same operating
MS-DOS	system developed by Microsoft, although to a computer scientist
IBM-DOS	there may be important differences.

CP/M-86

UCSD p-system

UNIX or XENIX

OS/2

DOS, which stands for **D**isk **O**perating **S**ystem, is *not* considered to be the "best" operating system by many computer scientists. Even so, it is the *most* popular and has become the current de facto standard because most business application software tools run under DOS.

The current popularity of DOS stems, at least partially, from the fact that initially DOS only cost $40, whereas CP/M-86 was priced at $250. If you wanted to run dBASE, you could get a version of dBASE that would run under either CP/M-86 or DOS, but not under both operating systems. The price difference was a major factor in making DOS the more popular personal computer operating system, because CP/M-86 did not provide any significant improvements in functionality or performance, in spite of its higher price.

DOS on a personal computer is *not* the first variation of a DOS created to control a computer. The very first DOS was written for an IBM mainframe computer in 1969. Mainframe DOS was produced as an entirely separate development from creating the variation of DOS that runs on a personal computer. They share the same name because a primary feature of both mainframe and personal computer DOS is the ability to manipulate data stored on disks, regardless of the computer's size. Today, when people think of DOS, they are usually thinking of the operating system that runs on a personal computer.

Most people using a personal computer use DOS because this operating system permits them to use Lotus 1-2-3, WordPerfect, dBASE, and other application programs. If a company wanted to use an accounting system that ran only under the UNIX operating system, then it would obtain UNIX. The software tool or application program you want to run will usually determine the operating system required.

An important feature of UNIX and OS/2 is that these operating systems are specifically designed to function in a computer network (a collection of personal computers connected so that they can interact with each other and, when available, with a mainframe). Applying complex communications, users can readily share processing activities, such as might occur when several users are all performing order entry at the same time.

OS/2 is a more recently developed operating system for personal computers and has been designed to facilitate running DOS application programs. That is, a DOS application can be run when OS/2 is the primary operating system on a personal computer. This permits using application software developed for either operating system. However, if the application program does not make use of the advanced features of an operating system, such as OS/2, then it may not be beneficial to use the advanced operating system.

MS-DOS, which is the Microsoft version of DOS, runs on a number of different brands of computers, which include but are not limited to the following:

Epson	Texas Instruments
Compaq	Wang
NEC	AT&T
Tandy	Panasonic
Zenith	Dell

The versions of DOS on these brands of computers are often not identical with the version of DOS that runs on the IBM PC. That is, although most of the operating systems commands are identical, some are not. A computer is said to be 100 percent compatible when the IBM PC version of DOS can be loaded and executed on another brand of computer. Although few 100 percent compatible brands exist, today most brands are considered compatibile, since all the popular application software that runs on an IBM personal computer can run on the other brands.

Keypoint! Most application programs are developed for use with a particular operating system. An application program designed to run under one operating system cannot usually run under a different operating system. To use a specific application program, you need to use the operating system for which it was designed. In most situations you have *no* choice on the operating system: you make the decision on the software tool and the operating system is decided for you.

Keypoint! Disk files written with one operating system may *not* be readable by another operating system or may require a conversion to be performed to be used with the other operating system. In general, it is best *not* to use more than one operating system on a microcomputer!

0.1.4 The Versions of IBM DOS

DOS is available in several different versions. Each version represents an expansion of the capabilities of DOS. Consequently, when one is considering the use of DOS, it is necessary to answer the question: Which DOS? For example, Lotus 1-2-3 Release 1 was designed to work with DOS 1.1, whereas Lotus 1-2-3 Release 1A was designed for DOS 2.0, and Lotus 1-2-3 Release 2.4 runs under DOS 2.1 or higher.

The "D" in DOS is for disk operations performed by this operating system. As disk technology has advanced and new versions of DOS have been developed, these upgraded versions of the operating system have supported the use of improved disk storage technology. Although other features have been added from one version of DOS to the next, the different versions of DOS can be classified by enhancements in disk drive capabilities. Changes in the functional features of DOS that distinguish the various versions are as follows:

DOS Version	Disk Drive Capability or Enhancement
1.0	Single-sided 5.25-in. disks
1.1	Double-sided 5.25-in. disks
2.0	PC/XT hard disk
2.1	Portable PC and PCjr half-height drives
3.0	PC/AT high-capacity floppy and hard disks
3.1	Network support
3.3	3.5-in. disks, multiuser
4.0	Larger disk files and expanded memory
5.0	Higher density 3.5-in. disks, improved memory usage, and file undelete capability

The versions of DOS are distinguished by differences in disk drives; therefore, you need to determine the kind of floppy disk drive available on your computer. The most frequently used choices are listed here:

- 5.25-in. double-sided, double-density   (2S/2D)   (360KB)
- 5.25-in. double-sided, high-density   (2S/HD)   (1.2MB)
- 3.5-in. double-sided, double-density   (2S/2D)   (720KB)
- 3.5-in. double-sided, high-density   (2S/HD)   (1.44MB)

where KB = kilobytes and MB = megabytes.

Double-density disks can usually be used in a high-density disk drive of the same size, but high-density disks *cannot* be used in double-density disk drives. Determine the type of floppy disk drive available on your personal computer and use disks appropriate for your disk drive.

> Floppy disks required for my disk drive:
> _____

Keypoint! Your version of DOS must support the hardware and application programs you are using. A new version of an application program may require a new version of DOS!

Keypoint! When purchasing software, be sure the floppy disks containing the software are the same size and density as the floppy disk drives of your computer!

0.1.5   Naming DOS Files

The fundamental unit of storage of data on disks is a **file**. You store files of data on a disk and retrieve files of data from a disk. Files can contain either an applications program, such as Lotus 1-2-3, dBASE, WordPerfect, or data, such as a letter you wrote using WordPerfect. Each file stored on a disk *must have a unique name*. Files have a "first name," which will be designated as the **filename**, and they have a "last name," which will be referred to as the **extension**. The format for naming a file is

filename.extension

Notice that the dot separates the filename from the extension. For example, the files named **MYFILE.ONE** and **MYFILE.TWO** are two distinct files because they have different extensions.

DOS filenames are *one to eight* characters long, and the extension is *zero to three* characters in length. The extension is optional, whereas the filename is required. When no extension is used, the dot is omitted. The characters that can be used in creating filenames and extensions are

- the letters of the alphabet
- the numbers or digits 0 through 9
- the special characters

$$ \$ \ \# \ \& \ @ \ ! \ \% \ (\ ) \ - \ \{ \ \} \ ' \ \_ \ ` \ \hat{} \ \sim $$

Notice that the space or a blank is *not* a legal character in naming files, nor are special characters, such as [ ] / \ | ? *

Examples of legal names of files are as follows:

To name files saved on a disk

MYFILE	BUDGET94	94BUDGET
94BUDGET.#19	TRASH.MOR	PROFIT.PGM
PROFIT.DAT	READ_ME.DOC	NEW&OLD.4

These examples illustrate that the use of an extension is optional. If you choose to use an extension, you must specify it when you refer to the file. You will find that most application packages have special extensions that are used in naming files. Some of the standard file extensions are

.BAS	BASIC program file
.BAT	Batch file
.COM	Command program file
.EXE	Executable program file
.SYS	System configuration or device driver file

Other special extensions may be used in conjunction with language compilers and commercial software products, such as Lotus 1-2-3, dBASE, and WordPerfect. Examples of some of these are

.BAK	Backup file
.C	C language source file
.DAT	Data file
.DBF	dBASE database file
.DOC	Document file
.HLP	Help file
.OVL	(Also .OVR) Program overlay file
.PAS	Pascal source program
.PIC	Lotus 1-2-3 graph file
.TXT	ASCII text file
.WK1	Lotus 1-2-3 worksheet file

When a file is requested or specified to DOS, the request can contain a disk drive designator in addition to the name of the file. In DOS, the disk drive designator or specifier is a single letter identifying the drive followed by a colon. It specifies the disk drive where DOS is to look for the file. This means you could have two files with the same name, on each of two different drives, and DOS can clearly distinguish between them. An example file specification including a drive specifier is

To name a file including its disk drive specifier

B:PROFIT.PGM

The general form of identifying a file in DOS is

d:filename.ext

where

d: is the drive specifier (such as **A:**, **B:**, or **C:**)

filename   is the primary name of the file

.ext   is the file extension

To find out which files are stored on a given disk, the DIR (directory) command allows you to see a list of the files. The DIR command is described in a later section, entitled Listing Files.

Keypoint!

> If your personal computer has two disk slots side by side, usually the one on the left is drive **A** and the one on the right is drive **B**. If the computer has two slots, one above the other, usually the top one is drive **A** and the bottom one is drive **B**. Drive **C** is typically the designator of the first (and usually only) hard disk drive.

0.1.6 About DOS Commands

DOS commands are similar to commands used with other operating systems for personal computers and mainframes. For the most part, they consist of regular, Englishlike words, such as COPY, ERASE, and PRINT—all activities you would like to perform with files stored on disk. The actions that can be performed are the same regardless of the size of the computer. By learning the commands for PC DOS, you will have learned the fundamental operating system commands available with most operating systems.

DOS does not exist as a single file, but rather it is a family of associated files. The fundamental reason for this division of DOS into a number of component files is that if all of the DOS instructions in the DOS family of files were loaded into RAM, then there would *not* be any RAM remaining for application programs. The execution of each DOS command requires a number of computer instructions to be processed. Those commands that contain the most instructions (this is reflected in the large size of a file for a DOS command) and/or those that are used infrequently are stored on disk as a file until they are needed. For these DOS commands, when you enter the command, the file is first loaded into RAM and then the instructions of the command are carried out. The following files are usually part of the DOS family of associated files:

To determine if a file is one of these selected DOS files consult this list

COMMAND.COM	IBMBIO.COM	IBMDOS.COM
ANSI.SYS	FORMAT.COM	CHKDSK.COM
SYS.COM	DISKCOPY.COM	COMP.COM
EDLIN.COM	MODE.COM	FDISK.COM
BACKUP.COM	RESTORE.COM	PRINT.COM
RECOVER.COM	ASSIGN.COM	TREE.COM
GRAPHICS.COM	SORT.EXE	FIND.EXE
MORE.COM	DISKCOMP.COM	

The file COMMAND.COM is the main DOS file. This file and the two files IBMBIO.COM and IBMDOS.COM make up the component of DOS that *must* always be stored in RAM for DOS to operate. (Non-IBM personal computers have similar files.) If any of these three files is removed from your disk, DOS is no longer available, and the disk will fail to boot.

DOS commands are divided into two categories—internal and external—which identify where the instructions of the command reside. The DOS commands that do *not* require a special file to be loaded into RAM from disk for their execution are known as **internal** commands. The other DOS commands that are stored as *separate files* are known as **external** DOS commands. When you boot DOS, all internal commands are available. To use an external DOS command, the DOS disk must be inserted into the appropriate disk drive, usually drive A: for a floppy disk personal computer. For a hard disk personal computer, DOS is usually installed on the hard disk, making all DOS commands available for immediate access without inserting a disk. With a hard disk, a common practice is to place all the external DOS files in a separate area on the disk known as a **directory**. This directory is frequently named DOS or BIN.

Since FORMAT.COM was one of the DOS family of associated files, FORMAT is an external command. This means that to format a new disk, you must have your DOS disk containing the FORMAT.COM file in a disk drive *before* the command can be executed.

Because COPY is not included in the list of DOS files, COPY is an internal command. There is no COPY.COM file. The DOS disk does *not* need to be inserted into a disk drive to execute the COPY command. Once DOS has been loaded into the computer's memory, all the internal commands are then available to you, even if the DOS disk is not in a disk drive.

The concept of internal and external commands is most important when your computer has only floppy disk drives. In this situation, the appropriate DOS disk *must* be inserted into a disk drive, usually drive A:, to access the external DOS commands. With a hard disk drive, DOS is usually stored on the hard disk, so that the difference between internal and external commands is unimportant. The distinction is important only with a hard disk drive when you enter a DOS command and receive the error message:

Bad command or filename

This signals that either the particular DOS file has not been placed on the hard disk, an incorrect command name was entered, or the path to a directory containing your DOS commands is not properly defined. (The PATH command is described in the next Lesson.)

Keypoint!

> **Internal** DOS commands can be executed from the DOS prompt *without* the DOS disk in a disk drive!
>
> **External** DOS commands *require* that the DOS disk be placed in a disk drive or that the commands reside on the hard disk drive to execute the desired command at the DOS prompt!

0.1.7   Starting DOS

There are fundamentally two methods for booting DOS, which causes the primary DOS file COMMAND.COM to be loaded into the computer's main memory. The method used depends on whether your computer has its power already turned on.

The exact procedure for starting DOS may vary depending on the particular hardware configuration and the manner in which DOS has been set up on either floppy disks or the computer's hard disk drive.

To get ready to start your computer	**Action:** Determine whether your personal computer:

        (*a*)   has only floppy disk drives (one or two)

        (*b*)   has a hard drive (with one or more floppy disk drives)

        (*c*)   is connected to a network

Action: If your computer has only floppy disk drives, obtain a copy of the DOS disk. Place the disk in drive A (the left or top drive on most IBM personal computers).

Action: If your computer has a hard disk drive, usually DOS is already available. Do nothing. Do *not* put a DOS disk in drive A unless it is required for a special application. Do *not* put a data disk or an application disk in drive A until after the system has been booted.

Action: If your computer is connected to a network and requires a start-up disk, obtain a copy of that disk. Place the disk in drive A (the left or top drive on most IBM personal computers).

To load DOS performing a cold boot	**Action:** If the *power is turned off* (cold boot), boot the DOS operating system by simply turning on the power to the personal computer system unit. Be sure that the power to your display monitor and printer is also on. To avoid potential problems with different hardware configurations, turn on the power to your peripherals first!

As part of a "cold boot," most brands of personal computers perform a test on RAM memory chips, known as a power on self-test (POST). This checking process takes some time to conduct. The amount of time depends on the particular model of personal computer and the amount of memory. For early personal computers, the POST can take several minutes. You need to wait patiently while this test is performed. If any defective chips are detected, an error message, such as PARITY ERROR 1, is displayed, and the booting process is terminated.

To load DOS performing a warm boot	**Action:** If the *power is already on* (warm boot), boot the operating system by pressing <Ctrl>+<Alt>+<Del>.

A complete POST is not carried out when a "warm boot" is performed.

When the operating system is booted or loaded into RAM, the programs in the IBMBIO.COM, IBMDOS.COM, and COMMAND.COM files are placed in memory and executed. If a CONFIG.SYS file, which describes the use of special devices, is present, its information is also loaded with DOS. Then, if an AUTOEXEC.BAT file is present, the commands in that file are executed. Execution of the AUTOEXEC.BAT file could automatically load the date and time from a computer's on-board clock and could initiate execution of an application software tool, such as Lotus 1-2-3. If your personal computer does not have an on-board clock, the date and time should be entered when the operating system is loaded. The date is entered in the form of month-day-year, where each is a number and the year may be either two digits or four digits. The time is entered in the form of hour:minute:second using a 24-hour clock with 2:15 P.M entered as 14:15. The entry of seconds is optional.

If requested when you boot your computer, enter the date and time in this manner:

To enter date and time during booting	**Enter:** `10-26-92`	That is, MM-DD-YY using the current date
	Enter: `14:15`	That is, HH:MM using the current time

If an error message such as this appears when you boot DOS:

Non-System disk or disk error
Replace and press any key when ready

It means that the disk in drive A does not contain the three main DOS files IBM-BIO.COM, IBMDOS.COM, and COMMAND.COM. As indicated by the error message, remove the disk in drive A and replace it with a disk that does contain DOS. Or, if you have a personal computer with a hard disk, remove the disk from drive A and press any key.

When DOS has been loaded successfully, and after the date and time have been entered, any one of several things will happen, depending on how your particular computer is set up. These differences include the following potential alternatives:

- The DOS prompt appears, usually **A>** or **C>** or **A:\>** or **C:\>**.
- The DOS Shell is activated, as illustrated in Figure O.2.
- A customized menu is displayed, like that in Figure O.3.
- The WINDOWS environment is accessed with a display like that in Figure O.4.
- An application software tool is activated.

The display of a customized menu frequently occurs when DOS is accessed on a network. WINDOWS is a graphical user interface (GUI) that facilitates the execution or launching of application programs and the movement of information among applications. When one application, such as WordPerfect or Lotus 1-2-3, is used frequently, a common practice is to initiate its execution as an integral part of booting DOS.

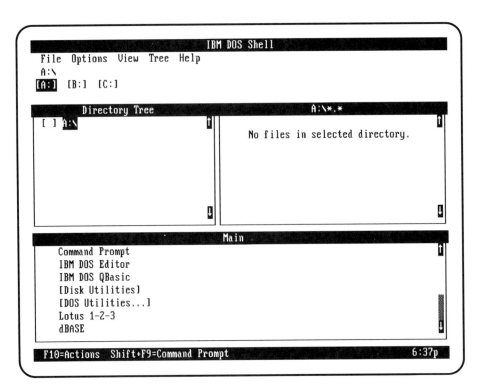

FIGURE O.2. DOS Shell.

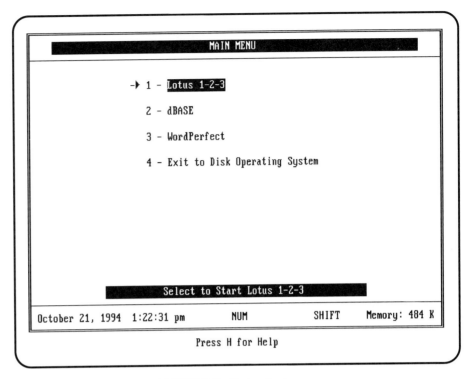

FIGURE O.3. Customized menu.

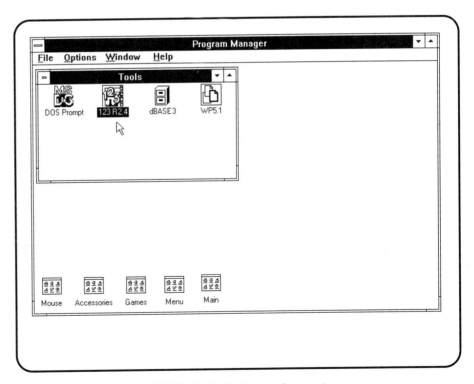

FIGURE O.4. Windows environment.

If your procedure for initializing DOS is different from that described, enter the specific instructions here:

My procedure to start DOS:

_____

_____

_____

_____

0.1.8   The DOS Prompt

Unless your personal computer has a special configuration at startup, the DOS prompt appears in the form:

A>   or   **A:\\>**   (for floppy disks)

or

C>   or   **C:\\>**   (for hard disks)

The appearance of this **prompt** signals that DOS is patiently waiting for you to enter a command. This could be a DOS command or it could be the name of an application program or software tool that you want to begin executing. In the DOS prompt example, the letter "A" tells you which disk is the active or **default** disk drive. With this as the default, the default drive is *assumed* to be the drive on which the command is to be executed, unless the letter for a different disk drive is entered with your command. The default drive is changed in this manner, from the DOS prompt:

To change the default disk drive

Enter: B: This specifies drive B as the default disk drive for future DOS commands

Keypoint!   A default disk drive is the drive accessed when the disk drive letter is *not* specified in a DOS command!

If the message

Place disk B in drive A:.
Press any key when ready.

appears on your screen, your hardware configuration contains only one floppy disk drive. Drive **A** is assumed to perform *double duty* and also to operate as disk drive **B**. In this situation you should proceed as follows:

Action: Place a disk in drive A as requested.
Press: <Enter>

Then the DOS prompt appears in the form: **B>** or **B:\>** Disk drive B is now indicated as the default disk drive.

When you boot DOS, if the DOS Shell shown in Figure O.2 appears, then

To obtain the DOS prompt from the DOS Shell	**Move to:**	Command Prompt	Use the cursor direction keys to move to the desired selection
	Press:	`<Enter>`	

You exit from the DOS Shell and obtain the DOS prompt.

If a customized menu, similar to that in Figure O.3, appears, then

To obtain the DOS prompt from a customized menu	**Select:**	Exit to DOS	Or a similar selection, which terminates the menu and transfers to DOS

The DOS prompt will appear. You are now ready to begin entering DOS commands.

If WINDOWS is automatically accessed when you boot DOS, you can exit to DOS by selecting the DOS icon.

To obtain the DOS prompt from WINDOWS	**Move to:**	DOS icon	Position the mouse pointer on the DOS icon, usually identified by "DOS"
	Double-click:	`<left mouse button>`	

You access the DOS prompt from WINDOWS. Usually a message is displayed informing you of how to return to WINDOWS.

Both the DOS Shell and WINDOWS facilitate performing many of the same activities as those carried out directly with DOS. You may want to pursue the use of these tools. In many ways, they represent an extension of DOS. However, the fundamental disk storage activities accomplished with these tools are exactly the same as those executed directly in DOS. The DOS Shell and WINDOWS just provide a different method for executing the DOS commands. The operation of the DOS Shell and WINDOWS are beyond the scope of this book. However, by learning the DOS commands, you will have a fundamental understanding of disk storage actions that can be performed, regardless of the user interface.

0.1.9   Revising Date and Time

If the date and time were not requested when DOS was booted, they can be displayed for your review and changed whenever desired. With the DOS prompt displayed, proceed in this manner:

To change the computer's date	**Enter:**	`DATE`	Request a change in the computer's date

DOS responds with the current date:

Current date is Mon 10-26-1994
Enter new date (mm-dd-yy):

A new date can now be entered, or the current date may be accepted as the desired date.

	Press:	`<Enter>`	Accept the current date as the desired date

To change the computer's time	**Enter:** TIME	Request a change in the computer's time

Now DOS displays the current time in this manner:

Current time is 14:15:30.30
Enter new time:

Like the date, a new time can be entered or the current time may be accepted as the correct time.

	Press: <Enter>	Accept the current time as the desired time

    The DATE and TIME commands can be used to change the current values for the computer's clock. A personal computer with an on-board clock may require additional steps for these values to be stored when the computer is turned off. If your changes to DATE and TIME are not "remembered" when you turn off or reboot your computer, then additional steps are required. In this situation, you may want to seek assistance.

0.1.10   Listing Files

Where did my file go? Which disk is it on? You know you created that file, but you can't remember its name. This is one of the most frequently occurring situations encountered when using a personal computer. How do you track down or locate your file stored on your disk? The DIR (directory) command provides the ability to obtain a listing of the files placed on a disk.

Action: Make sure your computer is turned on and DOS has been booted.

    If your computer has only floppy disk drives, then proceed in this manner:

Action:	If necessary, place the DOS disk in drive A:	
Enter:	A:	Make drive A the active disk drive; the DOS prompt appears as **A>** or **A:\>**

Or if your computer has a hard disk drive or is connected to a network, then proceed as follows:

Enter:	C:	Or the drive letter for your hard disk, if it is different

Now that you have specified the default disk drive, proceed as described.

To obtain a listing of the files on your default disk drive	**Enter:** DIR	Obtain directory of files on DOS disk

A listing of files is displayed on your screen, similar to that shown in Figure O.5. As illustrated for each file, the directory listing contains the filename, the file extension, the size of the file in number of characters or bytes, and the date and time the file was last changed. A file is changed only when it is *written* to the disk. A file can be read as many times as you like without being changed.

```
Volume in drive A has no label
Volume Serial Number is 3D63-15D8
Directory of A:\

AUTOEXEC BAT       592 12-09-92  11:37p
ANSI     SYS      9018 05-09-91  12:00p
COMMAND  COM     47987 05-09-91  12:00p
CONFIG   SYS       177 10-10-92   2:08p
COUNTRY  SYS     17686 05-09-91  12:00p
DISKCOPY COM     11793 05-09-91  12:00p
DISPLAY  SYS     15781 05-09-91  12:00p
DRIVER   SYS      5398 05-09-91  12:00p
FASTOPEN EXE     12034 05-09-91  12:00p
FDISK    COM     57304 05-09-91  12:00p
FORMAT   COM     32911 05-09-91  12:00p
KEYB     COM     15163 05-09-91  12:00p
KEYBOARD SYS     38206 05-09-91  12:00p
KEYBGK   COM     15880 05-09-91  12:00p
MODE     COM     23585 05-09-91  12:00p
PRINT    COM     15624 05-09-91  12:00p
PRINTER  SYS     18804 05-09-91  12:00p
REPLACE  EXE     20210 05-09-91  12:00p
SETVER   EXE     12001 05-09-91  12:00p
Press any key to continue . . .
```

FIGURE 0.5. Listing of files with DIR command.

To get a list of files with a pause when the screen is full	**Enter:**	DIR/P	Obtain directory of files with a pause once the display screen is filled
	Press:	<Enter>	As requested to advance to the next screen
	Action:	Repeat <Enter>, if necessary	

| To get a list of files in the wide arrangement | **Enter:** | DIR/W | Obtain directory in wide arrangement |

With this "wide" display, file names are listed in five columns without the file size and date information. This permits the display of more file names on a single screen.

| To list files with the same extension | **Enter:** | DIR *.COM/P | Obtain directory of any file with the COM extension with a pause (/P) for a full-screen display |

| To determine if a single file is on your disk | **Enter:** | DIR COMMAND.COM | Obtain the directory listing for the file COMMAND.COM, verifying the existence of this file on your disk |

| To clear your screen | **Enter:** | CLS | Clear the screen before you continue |

| To obtain a list of the files beginning with a specified letter | **Enter:** | DIR C*.* | Obtain the directory of *all* files that begin with the letter C, regardless of the extension |

The asterisks (*) are used as "wildcard" or global characters and mean that any characters are acceptable for the remaining characters in the filename or extension.

Action: Check to see that the printer is connected and the power is on.

To print the contents of your current screen	**Press:**	`<Shift>+<PrtSc>`	Print the contents of the screen
	Action:	Advance the paper on the printer to a new page.	
	Enter:	`DIR *.COM`	Obtain the specified directory listing for files with the COM extension only
	Press:	`<Shift>+<PrtSc>`	Print the contents of the screen

| To produce a listing of files directly on your printer | **Enter:** | `DIR > PRN` | Send the listing of files directly to your printer [PRN] *without* displaying the list on your screen |
| | **Action:** | Advance the paper on the printer to a new page and rip it off. | |

Here, the "greater than" symbol (>) is used to *redirect* the output of the DIR command to the printer, which is specified as the PRN device. Redirection provides a more convenient method of obtaining a hard copy listing of the files, rather than performing a series of print screens with the <Shift>+<PrtSc>. Redirection may be used with any DOS commands that display information on your screen.

| To observe the response from entering a nonexistent DOS command | **Enter:** | `LIST` | Attempt to obtain a listing of files |

The response is the error message:

Bad command or file name

If you enter an incorrect or nonexistent DOS command, this error message is displayed. Should this occur, merely reenter the desired DOS command.

The DIR command gives you the ability to obtain a variety of listings of the files stored on a disk. The list can be an individual file, a group of files with similar file names, or all the files on the disk. These listings allow you to verify the existence of files on your disk as you track down the name of a file or determine its location on a particular disk.

Key	Action
<Ctrl>+<Break>	Terminates execution of command
<Pause>	Causes the output displayed to pause when information is displayed too fast to read (restart output by pressing <Enter>)
<Ctrl>+<S>	Temporarily stops output to the screen so it can be read (restart output by pressing any key)
<Ctrl>+<PrtSc> or **<Ctrl>+<P>**	Toggles on/off "echo" printing of information displayed on screen
<Esc>	Cancels the currently displayed command without processing it
<F1>	Displays the last command typed one character at a time
<F2>	Displays the last command typed up to the character you type after pressing <F2>
<F3>	Displays the entire last command typed
<F4>	Displays the last command typed deleting all the characters before the character you typed after pressing <F4>
<Shift>+<PrtSc> or **<PrtSc>**	Causes the content of the current screen to be printed

FIGURE 0.6. Selected special-purpose DOS key.

0.1.11   Formatting a Data Disk

Different operating systems arrange the storage of data on disks differently. Before a disk, whether it is a floppy disk or a hard disk, can be used, it must be set up to receive the files from a specific operating system. This process of setting up the disk is known as initializing or formatting the disk. The FORMAT command is used to initialize a disk so that DOS can write files on it. During formatting, each surface of the disk is set up as a series of concentric circles called *tracks*, with each track divided into segments, which are called *sectors*. A sector is the smallest unit of storage on the disk. A directory area and file allocation table are established in the outermost track for storing the names and locations of files on the disk. If you attempt to store data on a disk that has *not* been formatted, you will receive the error message:

General failure reading drive; B
Abort, Retry, Fail?

In which instance, you should:

Press: A   That is, select abort

You are returned to the DOS prompt where you can then proceed to format the disk.

Caution Alert!

> FORMAT destroys all existing files containing either programs or data on a disk! Use FORMAT only on brand new disks or on old disks when you want to wipe out all the files on the disk!

Caution Alert!

> Inadvertently formatting a hard disk has been a significant problem in losing programs and data! Be very careful that you DO NOT FORMAT your hard disk instead of your floppy disk.

To FORMAT a disk, use the following procedures:

To format a disk

1. **Action:**   Be sure the computer is turned on and the operating system has been booted. You should have either the **A>** or **C>** DOS prompt on your screen, depending on whether your personal computer has floppy disk drives or a hard disk drive.

2. **Action:**   Check to see that the DOS disk is in drive A, if your computer has only floppy disk drives. This is necessary because FORMAT is an external DOS command.

3. **Action:**   Place the disk to be formatted in drive B.

4. **Enter:**   FORMAT B:

5. When these messages appear

   Insert new diskette in drive B:
   and press ENTER when ready . . .

   Press: <Enter>

6. *If* this message is displayed:

   Volume label (11 characters, ENTER for none)?

   Press: <Enter>

7. When asked if you want to format another disk,

   Enter: N   This terminates formatting and displays
                                            the DOS prompt

8. Your formatting is completed (Figure O.7).

   Action: Remove either or both disks.

Some versions of DOS display a message on the screen indicating the progress of the format. When the FORMAT process has been completed, you are ready to proceed to your next task, where data can now be stored on your freshly formatted disk.

Keypoint!

> The UNFORMAT command may allow you to recover data from a disk that was "erased" by the FORMAT command! The UNFORMAT must be used on the disk *before* any new files are written to the disk. UNFORMAT is available beginning with DOS version 5.0.

```
A:\=>FORMAT B:
Insert new diskette for drive B:
and press ENTER when ready...

Checking existing disk format.
Formatting 360K
Format complete.

Volume label (11 characters, ENTER for none)?

    362496 bytes total disk space
    362496 bytes available on disk

      1024 bytes in each allocation unit.
       354 allocation units available on disk.

Volume Serial Number is 3A61-16CD

Format another (Y/N)?
```

FIGURE O.7. Formatting a disk.

0.1.12 Displaying a File's Content

The data or programs residing in a disk file may be stored in several different ways. Two of the more common arrangements of data and/or programs in files are ASCII (American Standard Code for Information Interchange) and binary. ASCII files are frequently used in transferring information between a variety of applications. For example, ASCII files can be read into Lotus 1-2-3, dBASE, and WordPerfect. These software tools can also output ASCII files. An ASCII text file produced by Lotus 1-2-3 can be transferred into WordPerfect for inclusion in a WordPerfect document. Binary files are in a form that facilitates loading programs or data directly into RAM without the need to convert the contents of the file. Binary files are usually unique to different operating systems. ASCII files can be used to pass data between different operating systems, whereas binary cannot. For example, an ASCII file produced with a mainframe computer could be transferred to a personal computer that uses DOS, and the file could be read directly into WordPerfect or Lotus 1-2-3.

Action: Make the disk drive containing DOS your default disk drive.

Action: Place your formatted Data Disk in drive B, if you have two floppy disk drives, or in drive A if you only have one disk drive.

To create an ASCII text file containing a list of your files	**Enter:** `DIR > B:MYFILE.TXT`	Use redirection to place a listing of your directory in the file named MYFILE.TXT on the B disk drive as an ASCII text file; if you have only one disk drive, allow it to be used as drive B

In this example, the extension TXT is used as a convenient means of indicating that the file contains text information. This extension is not required for creating an ASCII text file; any extension may be used.

To display the contents of an ASCII file	**Enter:** `TYPE > B:MYFILE.TXT`	Display the ASCII file on your screen
	Action: Check that your printer is turned on.	
	Press: `TYPE > B:MYFILE.TXT`	Capture the screen in hard copy form
To attempt to display the contents of a binary file	**Enter:** `TYPE COMMAND.COM`	Ask to have the main DOS file displayed. Notice the junk that appears. This is because COMMAND.COM is a BINARY file and *not* an ASCII file.

From the foregoing use of the TYPE command, you can really see the difference between an ASCII text file and a BINARY or machine language file. ASCII files can be printed and you can read them directly.

Action: Check to see if the printer is attached to your computer and that it is turned on.

To directly print an ASCII file	**Enter:** `PRINT B:MYFILE.TXT`	PRINT is an external DOS command

When asked for the device for printing,

	Press: `<Enter>`	Indicates that your printer (PRN) is the appropriate device for printing

The file is printed. If you had several files to print, you could immediately enter a print command for the next file. A print queue of up to 10 files is permitted. Each file would then be printed until all files in the print queue have been printed. However, they must be ASCII text files in order for you to read them.

A common practice with application software is to provide a file with a title like READ.ME or README.DOC, which contains instructions for using the application software. These are usually ASCII files and can be printed by using this DOS PRINT command.

The AUTOEXEC.BAT and CONFIG.SYS files are two special files that are utilized when the operating system is booted. These files contain processing instructions that you could enter and/or modify and, as a result, are ASCII text files. You can look at these files, *if they exist on your DOS disk,* in this manner:

To look at the contents of your AUTOEXEC.BAT file	**Enter:**	TYPE AUTOEXEC.BAT	Display the contents of the AUTOEXEC.BAT file, if it exists
To look at the contents of your CONFIG.SYS file	**Enter:**	TYPE CONFIG.SYS	Display the contents of the CONFIG.SYS file, if it exists
	Action:		If you have an AUTOEXEC.BAT and/or a CONFIG.SYS file, create a hard copy printout of these files.
	Action:		Examine the commands contained in these two files.

The content of an ASCII text file can be displayed on your screen or printed for your use. A binary file is useful for loading application programs into RAM, but you cannot directly read it.

0.1.13   Duplicating Files

Duplicate copies of files can be made by using the COPY command. Therefore, you can make and use copies of your data files and can back up your application software programs. You may have a file on one disk that you would like to transfer to another disk drive. Frequently, you might create a file with an application program and would then like to revise a copy of the file, leaving the original file untouched. The purpose of the COPY command is to let you make an exact duplicate of a file with a different file name on the same disk or with any desired file name on a different disk.

Action: Verify that your computer is turned on, DOS has been booted, and your Data Disk is located in drive B. The DOS disk does *not* need to be in drive A, because COPY is an internal DOS command. If your computer has only floppy disk drives, you may leave your DOS disk in drive A.

To make a copy of a file	**Enter:**	COPY B:MYFILE.TXT B:MYFILE.TWO	
	Enter:	DIR B:	Both files are displayed in the directory of drive B
	Enter:	B:	Make drive B the default drive
To make copies of all the files with the same filename but different extensions	**Enter:**	COPY MYFILE.* YOURFILE.*	Both files are copied with the extension of TXT and TWO
	Enter:	DIR	Obtain another directory listing

To change the name of a file	**Enter:**	RENAME MYFILE.TXT MYFILE.ONE
		Change the name of the file
	Enter:	DIR Verify the new name of the file
	Enter:	DIR/W > PRN Obtain a hard copy listing of your file names by using redirection to send it directly to your printer

The COPY command allows you to make duplicate copies of one or more files with different names on the same disk or with the same or different names on another disk. Both data and application program files can be copied. Groups of files are copied by using the asterisk (*) wildcard character. (*All* the files on the disk in drive A can be copied to a disk in drive B with the command: COPY A:*.* B:) The name of a file may be changed either by copying the file or by directly renaming the file. With the RENAME command, the file resides in exactly the same location on a disk, but it has a new name.

0.1.14   Checking Disk Usage

The current usage of a disk's storage space and status of the computer's memory can be reviewed with a check disk (CHKDSK) command. Execution of this command produces a report that lists the following information:

- Bytes of total disk space
- Bytes occupied by hidden or system files
- Bytes occupied by user files
- Bytes in bad sectors, if any
- Total usable bytes on disk
- Bytes of total RAM
- Bytes of available RAM

An example of a hidden file is the IBMDOS.COM file. This resides on the DOS disk, but does not usually appear when a DIR command is issued. Files are hidden because they are special files that users should not normally access or directly use. A bad sector is a defective area on a disk that cannot be used to store data. Bad sectors are identified when the disk is formatted, and no data will be stored on this area of the disk. A few bad sectors do not mean that the disk is totally defective. In fact, even on hard disks of large mainframe computers, the occurrence of a few bad sectors is quite normal. Hard disks are often manufactured with more storage capacity than a stated capacity, such as 60 megabytes (MB). That is, a 60-MB hard disk might be manufactured with a 63-MB capacity. The difference would be an "allowance" for bad sectors. In any event, the check disk (CHKDSK) command provides this information for you.

Action: Be sure that your computer is turned on, DOS has been booted, and your Data Disk is in drive B, and drive B is the default disk drive.

To check the status of a disk's usage	**Enter:**	A:CHKDSK B: If DOS is on a different disk than A, enter that disk identifier in place of that for A

Since drive B was the default drive and CHKDSK is an external command, it was necessary to use the drive identifier as part of the file name for the CHKDSK command. Figure O.8 illustrates a typical output from the CHKDSK command.

```
C:\=>CHKDSK A:
Volume Serial Number is 3D63-15D8

   1457664 bytes total disk space
    499712 bytes in 29 user files
    957952 bytes available on disk

       512 bytes in each allocation unit
      2847 total allocation units on disk
      1871 available allocation units on disk

    655360 total bytes memory
    514016 bytes free

C:\=>
```

FIGURE O.8. Report from CHKDSK command.

Press: <Shift>+<PrtSc>   Print the screen

CHKDSK provides a report on the status of an entire disk instead of examining information describing individual files. The report indicates the amount of RAM that is available for executing programs and the amount of memory occupied by the COMMAND.COM portion of DOS.

O.1.15 Removing Unwanted Files

When a file is no longer required, it can be deleted from a disk. This frees up the disk space for use by another file. Files are deleted or erased in this manner:

	Action:	Verify that B is your default disk drive and your printer is turned on.	
	Enter:	DIR/W > PRN	Obtain a hard copy list of the current files
To delete a single file	**Enter:**	DEL MYFILE.TWO	Remove this file from your Data Disk
	Enter:	DIR	File MYFILE.TWO should be gone
To delete all files with the same filename regardless of the extension	**Enter:**	ERASE YOURFILE.*	Both files will be removed; ERASE is a synonym for DEL
	Enter:	DIR	Confirm that the files have been deleted
	Enter:	DIR/W > PRN	Obtain a hard copy list of the remaining files

An individual file or a group of files may be removed from disk storage with the DEL (delete) or ERASE command. The DIR command is useful in verifying the removal of files. Be careful not to delete any important files!

Caution Alert!	When the asterisk (*) wildcard character is used in the DEL command, a group of files is deleted at one time. Be *very* careful to make sure that you want to delete every one of the files affected by applying the wildcard characters! The command **DEL *.*** will delete all your files. Be careful in using this command. You could accidentally wipe out all of the files on a disk!
Keypoint!	When you delete a file, such as MYFILE.TWO, DOS changes the file name to ?YFILE.TWO, which makes the disk space available for storing another file. A file that has been deleted inadvertently may be recovered, as long as the recovery is attempted *before* any other files are written on the disk for storage. A special purpose utility program, such as PC TOOLS or NORTON UTILITIES, is required to perform this task with DOS version 4.0 and earlier. Beginning with DOS version 5.0, the UNDELETE command lets you recover a deleted file. If you accidentally delete a file, take action to recover it immediately!

0.1.16 Recovering Deleted Files

When you delete a file, DOS does not actually delete your data in the file. Instead, it *marks* the file as deleted in the disk's table of contents, the File Allocation Table (FAT), so the area occupied by the deleted file can be reused the *next time* DOS *writes* data to the disk. The old data remain on the disk until DOS writes any other file to the same area of the disk. This could be one of your data files or any other temporary work file used by DOS or an application program. DOS marks a deleted file in the FAT by replacing the first character of the file name with a question mark (?). That is, when you delete MYFILE.TWO, DOS changes the file name to ?YFILE.TWO.

Because the data in a deleted file remain intact until another file is written to the disk, a file that was accidentally deleted may be recovered by using the UNDELETE command that is available beginning with DOS version 5.0. To ensure a successful recovery of a deleted file, the UNDELETE command should be used *before* any other files are written to the disk.

The MYFILE.TWO and YOURFILE.* files, which were deleted in the previous section, Removing Unwanted Files, can be recovered by proceeding as follows at the DOS prompt:

Action:		Verify that B is your default drive and contains the same Data Disk that you used in the previous section.
Enter:	`DIR`	Verify deletion of the files because they are not listed with this command
Enter:	`UNDELETE /LIST`	Request a list of the deleted files on your default disk drive

To get a list of previously deleted files

DOS responds by producing a list of deleted files, as shown in Figure O.9. This output illustrates how DOS has marked the files for deletion and indicates whether the deleted file can be recovered. Because no other files were written to the disk after these files were deleted, DOS indicates that all three files can be successfully recovered.

```
B:\>UNDELETE /LIST

Directory: B:\
File Specifications: *.*

    Deletion-tracking file not found.

    IBM DOS directory contains 3 deleted files.
    Of those, 3 files may be recovered.

Using the IBM DOS directory.

    ?YFILE   TWO 1073 10-21-94 2:10p ...A
    ?OURFILE TXT 1073 10-21-94 2:10p ...A
    ?OURFILE TWO 1073 10-21-94 2:10p ...A

B:\>
```

FIGURE O.9. List of deleted files.

Caution Alert!

> Once you delete a file from your disk, you may not be able to recover it. The UNDELETE command can recover a deleted file only if no other files have been created or changed on your disk. If you accidentally delete a file, stop what you are doing and immediately use the UNDELETE command to recover the file!

When recovering a deleted file, you need to provide DOS with the first character of the file name. The deleted files in Figure O.9 can be recovered in this manner:

To recover a previously deleted file

| **Enter:** | UNDELETE | Initiate recovery of all the deleted files on the default disk drive |

In carrying out the UNDELETE, DOS proceeds through the list of deleted files one at a time. You are asked whether you want to undelete the file and then are requested to enter the first character of the file name. The undelete operation continues. In response to

Undelete (Y/N)?

| **Enter:** | Y | Specify, Yes |

When requested to

Please type the first character for ?YFILE .TWO:

Enter:	M	First character of file name
Action:	Complete the recovery of the other two deleted files.	
Enter:	DIR > PRN	Obtain a hard copy list of all file names, including the recovered ones

The complete dialog of the UNDELETE operation for these three files is shown in Figure O.10. This dialog contains the message "Deletion-tracking file not found." Deletion-tracking is an advanced feature of DOS that is used with other special DOS commands, as is described in the *DOS Reference Manual*. For your purposes in recovering deleted files, the absence of a deletion-tracking file does not cause any difficulties in

```
B:\>UNDELETE

Directory: B:\
File Specifications: *.*

    Deletion-tracking file not found.

    IBM DOS directory contains 3 deleted files.
    Of those, 3 files may be recovered.

Using the IBM DOS directory.

    ?YFILE TWO 1073 10-21-94 2:10p ...A Undelete (Y/N)?Y
    Please type the first character for ?YFILE .TWO: M

File successfully undeleted

    ?OURFILE TXT 1073 10-21-94 2:10p ...A Undelete (Y/N)?Y
    Please type the first character for ?OURFILE.TXT: Y

File successfully undeleted

    ?OURFILE TWO 1073 10-21-94 2:10p ...A Undelete (Y/N)?Y
    Please type the first character for ?OURFILE.TWO: Y

File successfully undeleted

B:\>
```

FIGURE O.10. Recovering deleted files.

executing the UNDELETE command. All of the deleted files were recovered, as is indicated in Figure O.10 and is verified with the DIR command.

In general, you are urged to use caution in deleting files. However, if a file you want was accidentally deleted, then by immediately using UNDELETE, you should be able to recover the file.

0.1.17 When Things Go Wrong

A number of different conditions may occur while you are trying to use DOS commands. Some of the more common difficulties and the ways to recover from them are described here.

1. You entered a DOS command such as **DIRMYFILE. TWO** instead of **DIR MYFILE.TWO** and the error message "Bad command or file name" appeared on your screen. This error often occurs when you have *not* used the appropriate spacing within a DOS command.

   a. Review the spacing required for the DOS command's syntax.

   b. Reenter the DOS command by using the appropriate spacing. You may use the <F3> to recall your command and then to modify it before pressing <Enter> to execute the command.

2. You entered a DOS command such as **FORMAT B:** and the error message "Bad command or file name" was displayed. You know the command name and the syntax are correct. This error usually occurs when an external DOS command has been removed from the DOS disk or, with a hard disk, when the external DOS command resides in a directory not specified by the PATH command. (The PATH command is described in the next Lesson.)

   a. Make the DOS disk your default drive.

   b. Use DIR to obtain a listing of files on the DOS disk. Confirm that the file for the external command is not in this file listing.

   c. If you are accessing DOS from a floppy disk, obtain another copy of the DOS disk and verify that it contains the desired file for your DOS command.

   d. If you are accessing DOS from a hard disk or network, seek assistance in locating the external DOS commands for your particular hardware environment. You will learn how to track down the location of files on a hard disk in the next Lesson. Seeking assistance is the best procedure for now.

   e. Reissue your DOS command once you have verified the existence of the file containing the external DOS command.

3. Everything that is displayed on your screen goes to the printer. If you are using a shared printer, the printer is tied up by the output from your computer and no one else is able to print. This can be caused by toggling on the "echo" printing of information displayed on your screen with either the <Ctrl>+<PrtSc> or <Ctrl>+<P> special-purpose DOS keys.

   a. Press <Ctrl>+<PrtSc> or <Ctrl>+<P> once. Because this is a toggle to turn "echo" print on and off, be sure you press these keys only once.

   b. Issue the DIR command to confirm that output occurs only on your screen and is not echo printed.

0.1.18 Lesson Summary

- An operating system is a collection of programs used to start up a computer; load, execute, store, and retrieve application programs; store and retrieve files; and perform a series of utility operations.

- One of the primary functions of an operating system is the manipulation of files stored on a disk.

- DOS is one of the most popular operating systems for personal computers.

- A number of different versions of DOS exist. The version of DOS must match an application program's requirements.

- DOS files are identified in the form of **d:filename.ext**, where **d:** is the drive identifier, **filename** is the primary name of the file, and **.ext** is the file extension.

- DOS commands are organized as internal and external commands. Internal commands are stored in RAM when the operating system is booted, whereas external commands are obtained from disk storage as the command is being executed.

- DOS may be started with either a "cold boot" or a "warm boot."

- A date and time for the computer's clock may be entered either when DOS is booted or when desired with the DATE and TIME commands.

- The DOS prompt (that is, **A>** or **C>**) is your signal that DOS is waiting for a command to be entered. It indicates the current default disk drive.

- The DIR (directory) command is used to obtain a listing of files stored on a disk. The listing is usually displayed on the screen but can be printed with a <Shift>+<PrtSc> or by redirection. Some PCs print the screen with only the <PrtSc> key depressed.

- The FORMAT command prepares a new disk for use. This is an external DOS command, and therefore the FORMAT.COM file must be available for execution. If a disk containing programs or data is formatted, existing information on the disk will be destroyed.

- If you accidentally FORMAT a disk containing files that you want, the UNFORMAT command in DOS version 5.0 or later may be able to restore your disk.

- The contents of a file can be displayed on your screen with the TYPE command. A hard copy can be obtained with the PRINT command. In general, TYPE is used with ASCII text files, because these files are stored in a form that you can read.

- A file can be duplicated with the COPY command, and a new name can be assigned to a file with the RENAME command.

- The status of disk storage space can be reviewed with the CHKDSK command.

- Unwanted files are removed with either the DEL or ERASE commands. Use caution when you delete groups of files.

- A deleted file can be recovered with the UNDELETE command in DOS version 5.0 or later. UNDELETE should be performed *before* any new files are written to your disk.

0.1.19 Practice Tutorial

Your understanding of operating systems is reinforced by exploring the DOS commands that are described in this Lesson as a guided activity in a hands-on manner. As you do these tasks, remember the usage of Enter, Type, Press, and Action as described in Lesson T.1, Software Navigation Guide.

Task 1: Obtain a diskette that can be formatted. Be sure that this disk matches your hardware. This will be your Data Disk.

Task 2: Boot the operating system, if necessary.

Task 3: Carry out the activities as described in Sections O.1.9 through O.1.15, taking care to produce each of the requested printing tasks. If you are using DOS version 5.0 or higher, perform the UNDELETE activities in Section O.1.16.

Task 4: Organize your printouts and label them with the title of each section.

Time Estimates

Novice: 90 minutes

Intermediate: 60 minutes

Advanced: 45 minutes

0.1.20 Practice Exercises

Build your expertise with DOS by applying several of the more frequently used commands. In preparation for this exercise, obtain a diskette that can be formatted and boot DOS. Determine the appropriate commands required for each task and write them in the space provided before you turn on your computer and begin executing them.

Task 1: Format your diskette, which will be your Data Disk. The DOS command is:

> _____

Task 2: Produce a hard copy listing of all files on your DOS disk that have extensions of EXE, SYS, or BAT. (*Note:* Your DOS disk may not have files with all of these extensions. Produce a listing of those that are available on your disk.) The DOS commands are:

> _____

> _____

> _____

Task 3: Create a file with the name MYDOS.TXT on your Data Disk. It should contain a listing of all of the files with the COM extension that reside on your DOS disk. Obtain a hard copy listing of this file. The DOS commands are as follows:

> _____

> _____

Task 4: Copy the file MYDOS.TXT to MYDOS.TWO on your Data Disk. Then copy the file MYDOS.TWO to MYDOS.DOC on your Data Disk. Produce two hard copy listings of the directory of your Data Disk. The first listing is to contain all those files with extensions beginning with the letter T, and the second listing should display the names of all files on the disk. The DOS commands are:

> _____

> _____

> _____

> _____

Task 5: Change the name of MYDOS.DOC to README.DOC. Output a hard copy listing of the directory of files. The DOS commands are:

> _____

> _____

Task 6: Remove the file MYDOS.TWO from your Data Disk. Confirm its removal with a hard copy listing of the resulting directory. The DOS commands are:

> _____

> _____

Task 7: (*Optional*)   If you are using DOS version 5.0 or later, use the UNDELETE command to restore the MYDOS.TWO file. Confirm the success of your undelete operation with a hard copy listing of the directory. The DOS commands are:

> _____

> _____

Task 8: Check the usage of the storage space on your Data Disk and the current usage of RAM. Create a hard copy of this output. The DOS commands are as follows:

> _____

> _____

Task 9: Organize the output listings from Tasks 2 through 8 by labeling each output with the task number.

Time Estimates

Novice: 90 minutes

Intermediate: 60 minutes

Advanced: 45 minutes

Working with Directories and Special Files

CONTENT

▓ **What Is a Directory?**
▓ **Creating and Using Directories**
▓ **Exploring Special Files**
▓ **Creating and Modifying Special Files**
▓ **When Things Go Wrong**

0.2.1 What Is a Directory?

Every disk must have a **directory,** which is like a table of contents that describes the files stored on a disk. As is illustrated in Lesson O.1, the DIR (Directory) command produces a listing of this information about the files on your disk. Every disk must have, at least, one directory, known as the *root directory,* which is set up when your disk is formatted. Besides the root directory, other user-defined directories are *optionally created* to better manage large numbers of files stored on the same disk. A user-defined directory is just a named area that you set up in your disk's table of contents for maintaining a list of files. The concept of user-defined directories is not unique to personal computers. With many mainframe computers, each user is assigned a separate disk storage area or directory identified by a unique user name. The ability of DOS to work with user-defined directories was introduced in DOS 2.0, the first version of DOS that supported a hard disk.

Consider an office filing cabinet as the physical analogue of a large-capacity computer disk. Imagine a file cabinet with only one drawer that is about a mile long. You could place many files in this drawer, but it would be a real pain to try to find any specific file. A set of file cabinets with a number of separate drawers provides much more convenient access to information. One drawer might be designated for human resource information, whereas a second drawer would house purchase orders, and a third would contain customer data. When human resource data are required, the human resource file drawer is accessed and the desired file is extracted or inserted. Assigning each file drawer to a different business function helps keep the data that are stored in them better organized.

Disk storage on a computer can be organized, arranged, and managed like information stored in a file cabinet. A hard disk with 40, 60, 120, or more MB of storage is like a huge file drawer. As the user of a personal computer, you have the choice of one huge drawer or a number of small drawers. Like drawers in a typical file cabinet, a large disk can be divided into areas that are designated and labeled for a particular function. When a file drawer contains so much information that you can no longer easily find what you want, you can subdivide it. In the same way, when a directory contains too many files, it can be subdivided into several user-defined directories. These directories, other than the root directory, are also known as *subdirectories,* because they are at lower levels. User-defined subdirectories give you the same ability to manage your files as the drawers of a file cabinet.

User-defined directories can be established on both floppy disks and hard disks. Floppy disks hold considerably less data, and so the use of directories on them is infrequent. With a hard disk, the amount of data storage usually requires user-defined directories. Keeping track of 50 files on a floppy disk is relatively easy compared with managing 1000 or more files on a hard disk. Another reason for setting up user-defined directories is that the number of files that can be entered in the *root directory* is limited as follows:

Disk Size	File Entries
360 KB 5.25 in.	112
720 KB 3.5 in.	112
1.2 MB 5.25 in.	224
1.44 MB 3.5 in.	224
Fixed disk	512

Although you may have unused storage space on your disk, once you reach the maximum number of entries in the root directory, you cannot store any more files. This limitation forces the use of user-defined directories with hard disks; directories are not merely a convenient alternative.

The *root directory* is referenced by specifying the disk drive designator. Thus, **B:** identifies the root directory on drive B. Each user-defined directory is identified by a unique directory *name.* The rules for naming directories are the same as those that are used for filenames: up to eight characters in the directory name. A user-defined directory name can have an extension, but generally does not. For ease and clarity of use, extensions should be used only in naming individual files.

Keypoint!

> The *root directory* is the *highest* level directory and is always present on every disk! This directory is established when a disk is formatted!

The levels of directories and files are often considered to be organized like a tree. The files are the leaves of the tree and the directory branches are *paths* to get to each leaf (file). Some paths have more branches than others, and some branches have more leaves than others. Visualize a big oak tree. The disk itself, the root directory, is like the trunk of the oak. The user-defined directories are branches. Then at the end of the branches, the leaves are the individual files. Consider the file structure as illustrated in Figure O.11, where each directory contains one or more files identified by a DAT extension. The root directory is the directory available when a disk is initially specified as the default disk drive. All other directories are user-defined and must be set up before a file can be placed in them. You will learn how to create user-defined directories in the next section of this Lesson.

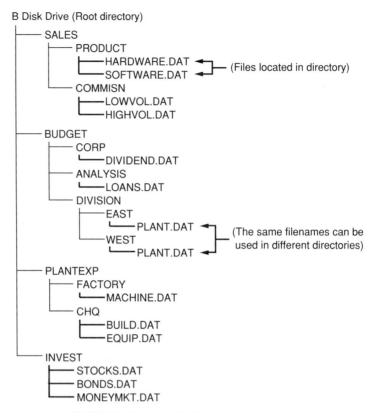

FIGURE O.11. Example directory tree structure.

Keypoint!   A user-defined directory must be set up *before* any files can be stored in it!

Examples of specifying files residing in the directories illustrated in Figure O.11 are as follows:

To specify files located in a
user-defined directory

```
B:\BUDGET\CORP\DIVIDEND.DAT

B:\BUDGET\DIVISION\WEST\PLANT.DAT

B:\BUDGET\DIVISION\EAST\PLANT.DAT

B:\INVEST\STOCKS.DAT

B:\INVEST\BONDS.DAT

B:\PLANTEXP\CHQ\BUILD.DAT
```

Each user-defined directory level is separated from others in the file specification by a backslash (\), with the series of directory names and backslashes leading from the disk drive identifier to the desired file. This specification is vital in indicating the **path** to the desired file. File specifications like these can be used in any DOS command where a file name has previously been used, such as with the COPY, RENAME, DEL, and DIR commands.

Keypoint!   A file specification that includes a directory reference can be used in place of any file name in a DOS command!

If drive B were the currently active drive, then the file specification could proceed like this:

| To specify files located in a user-defined directory of the default disk drive

```
\BUDGET\CORP\DIVIDEND.DAT
\BUDGET\DIVISION\WEST\PLANT.DAT
\BUDGET\DIVISION\EAST\PLANT.DAT
```

Here, the first backslash (\) indicates that the file specification *begins* from the root directory level.

If the \BUDGET\DIVISION directory on drive B were the currently active directory, then the files could be referenced in this manner:

To specify files located within the current user-defined directory

```
WEST\PLANT.DAT
EAST\PLANT.DAT
```

When *continuing* with a file specification in the currently active directory, a back-slash (\) should *not* be used at the beginning of the file specification, because a backslash at the beginning means that a file's specification starts from the root directory. As a consequence, an error message is produced by a file specification of **\WEST\PLANT.DAT,** when **\BUDGET\DIVISION** on drive B is the currently active directory. The WEST directory does not branch from the root directory, and so it is not a valid *path* specification.

Figure O.11 represents a project-oriented directory arrangement. In a similar manner, user-defined directories can be established for a group of different users. Suppose that in an office, three people, Beth, Harry, and Jim, will be working with Lotus 1-2-3 on the *same* personal computer with a hard disk or on a network file server where they all access the same disk. Keeping each person's files separated from those of the other people helps to avoid the confusion or conflict that might occur when both Beth and Jim have files containing different data that are given the *same name*. A separate user-defined directory for each person would help to avoid this problem. A common practice would be to create the following directories:

```
C:\LOTUS\BETH
C:\LOTUS\HARRY
C:\LOTUS\JIM
```

When Beth creates a BUDGET worksheet in Lotus 1-2-3, the full name of the file would then be

```
C:\LOTUS\BETH\BUDGET.WK1
```

Five basic DOS commands are used in managing and working with user-defined directories:

- MD (Make directory)
- RD (Remove directory)
- CD (Change directory)
- TREE (Display directory arrangement)
- PATH (Establish directories to be searched for a command when it is *not* found in the current directory.)

The operation of each of these DOS commands is explored in the next section.

> *Keypoint!* | Directories below the root directory level are optional. You must set up and manage the user-defined directories on your personal computer!

O.2.2 Creating and Using Directories

Figure O.12 contains a directory structure that might be established when DOS, Lotus 1-2-3, dBASE, and WordPerfect all reside on the same disk. A common practice in organizing files on a hard disk is to create a separate user-defined directory for each software tool, as demonstrated by the structure of Figure O.12. This structure is used in the following discussion of creating, accessing, and removing directories.

Action: Place your Data Disk in drive B and make sure that DOS is available on another disk drive. (If you have a hard disk drive, you may use drive A, rather than drive B for the following activities.)

Action: Make drive B your default disk drive.

| To create a user-defined directory with the name of DOS | **Enter:** | MD \DOS | Create a directory with the name of DOS |

| To create another directory with the name of LOTUS | **Enter:** | MD \LOTUS | Create a directory with this name |

| To create a lower level directory within an existing higher level directory | **Enter:** | MD \LOTUS\DATA | Establish a directory with the name of DATA within the \LOTUS directory |

```
B:\=>TREE
Directory PATH listing
Volume Serial Number is 2322-12FF
B:.
    ├───DOS
    ├───LOTUS
    │   └───DATA
    ├───DBASE
    │   └───DATA
    └───WP
        ├───LETTERS
        └───MEMOS

B:\=>
```

FIGURE O.12. Directory tree structure for Data Disk.

Each of these three user-defined directories is now created and ready for storing files.

Enter: MD \DBASE\DATA   Attempt to establish the \DBASE\DATA
                                        directory before creating the \DBASE
                                        directory

The error message "Unable to create directory" appears to inform you that you cannot create this directory. The \DBASE directory must be established before the lower level subdirectory is created, since \DATA is underneath the \DBASE directory.

Caution Alert!

> When several levels of directories are used, a higher level directory must be set up *before* a lower level subordinate directory can be created!

Action: Establish the other remaining directories as indicated in Figure
                O.12, including the \DBASE\DATA directory.

Enter: DIR > PRN   Produce a hard copy listing of the file and
                                        directory entries at the *root level* on driveB

Action: Examine the resulting directory listing.

The DIR command displays only the directories available at the next *immediately* lower level. The "<DIR>" in the listing indicates which entries are user-defined directories. As a result, the DATA directories under both LOTUS and DBASE, and the LETTERS and MEMOS directories, are *not* included in the listing from the DIR command. Your output should be similar to Figure O.13, which shows several files stored at the root directory level, as well as the remaining directory entries.

```
B:\=>DIR

 Volume in drive B has no label
 Volume Serial Number is 2322-12FF
 Directory of B:\

COMMAND  COM    37637 06-17-88  12:00p
CONFIG   SYS      113 08-28-90   8:02p
AUTOEXEC BAT       85 11-20-90   5:54p
DOS          <DIR>      11-06-90  12:19p
LOTUS        <DIR>      11-06-90  12:19p
DBASE        <DIR>      11-06-90  12:20p
WP           <DIR>      11-08-92   9:09p
         7 file(s)     37835 bytes
                      208896 bytes free

B:\=>
```

FIGURE O.13. Root directory listing with file names and user-defined directories.

To change your current default directory	**Enter:**	CD \WP	Issue a change directory command to make \WP the current directory

Unless your computer has been set up in a special manner, the DOS prompt is still **B>,** indicating drive B is the default disk drive. There is no indication to you that **WP** is the current directory.

To establish a DOS prompt that specifies your default directory	**Enter:**	PROMPT PG	Modify the DOS prompt

This PROMPT command causes the current directory name consisting of the default disk drive identifier and its path to be displayed as part of the DOS prompt in the form **B:\WP>.** When you are working with directories, you are strongly urged to use this PROMPT command to provide you with a constant reminder of the current default disk drive and directory. A PROMPT command is almost always included in the AUTOEXEC.BAT file. If you enter just the PROMPT command without any of the parameters, the DOS prompt is returned to its original form of the default disk drive letter only.

	Enter:	DIR > PRN	Output a hard copy listing of the directories that reside within the WP directory

Your directory listing, like the one shown in Figure O.14, contains two special files with the names of dot (·) and dot-dot (··), which are flagged with "<DIR>" in the column for file size. These two special files hold information that describes the table of contents for your user-defined directory. They are created when the MD (make directory) command is executed and are not actually directories.

```
B:\WP=>DIR

 Volume in drive B has no label
 Volume Serial Number is 2322-12FF
 Directory of B:\WP

 .              <DIR>      11-08-92    9:09p
 ..             <DIR>      11-08-92    9:09p
 LETTERS        <DIR>      11-08-92    9:09p
 MEMOS          <DIR>      11-08-92    9:09p
         4 file(s)            0 bytes
                        208896 bytes free

 B:\WP=>
```

FIGURE O.14. Directory listing with special <DIR> files.

To return to the root directory	**Enter:**	CD \	Return to root directory
	Enter:	DIR	Confirm your directory listing at the root level
	Action:	Make your disk drive containing DOS your default drive.	
	Enter:	COPY COMMAND.COM B:	Copy this file to the root directory for your data disk
	Action:	*If they exist,* copy your CONFIG.SYS and AUTOEXEC.BAT files to the root directory of your Data Disk on drive B.	

To copy a file to a user-defined directory named DOS	**Enter:**	COPY FORMAT.COM B:\DOS	
			Copy this file to the \DOS directory of your Data Disk on drive B, if this file is available on your computer

~~~~~~~~
Caution Alert!
~~~~~~~~

> If the message "File not found" appears when this COPY command is executed, the FORMAT.COM file is not located in the root directory of your disk containing DOS. Most likely, your computer has a hard disk with the DOS files stored in a different directory. If this error occurred, make the directory containing FORMAT.COM and the other DOS files your active directory. Then, reissue the COPY command.

Action: If you can access them on your computer, copy the files EDLIN.COM, CHKDSK.COM, TREE.COM, SORT.EXE, GRAPHICS.COM, and ANSI.SYS to the same \DOS directory on your Data Disk in drive B.

To get a file listing of the user-defined directory named DOS	**Enter:**	DIR B:\DOS	Obtain a listing of the files in the \DOS directory on drive B
	Action:	Make drive B your default drive.	
	Enter:	CD\DOS	Make DOS your current directory
	Enter:	DIR > PRN	Produce a hard copy listing of the files in your \DOS directory

The resulting list of DOS files, which you copied to the \DOS directory on your data disk, should be similar to Figure O.15.

To back up to the root directory	**Enter:**	CD \	Return to the root directory of your Data Disk
	or		
	Enter:	CD ..	

To produce a tree diagram or listing of your user-defined directories	**Enter:**	TREE	Produce a tree diagram of the directories below the root directory

A tree diagram displays the arrangement of directories on a disk, as illustrated in Figure O.12. This tree diagram is available with DOS version 4.0 or higher. Earlier versions of DOS produce only a list of the directory contents. A similar directory tree is also available when using the DOS Shell, as shown in Figure O.16. This underscores the equivalence of the information available either directly with a DOS command or with the DOS Shell.

```
B:\DOS=>DIR

 Volume in drive B has no label
 Volume Serial Number is 2322-12FF
 Directory of B:\DOS

.               <DIR>      11-06-90   12:19p
..              <DIR>      11-06-90   12:19p
CHKDSK   COM    17771 06-17-88   12:00p
EDLIN    COM    14249 06-17-88   12:00p
FORMAT   COM    22923 06-17-88   12:00p
DISKCOPY COM    10428 06-17-88   12:00p
MORE     COM     2166 06-17-88   12:00p
SYS      COM    11472 06-17-88   12:00p
TREE     COM     6334 06-17-88   12:00p
SORT     EXE     5914 06-17-88   12:00p
ANSI     SYS     9148 06-17-88   12:00p
        11 file(s)      100405 bytes
                        208896 bytes free


B:\DOS=>
```

FIGURE O.15. Listing of files copied to \DOS directory.

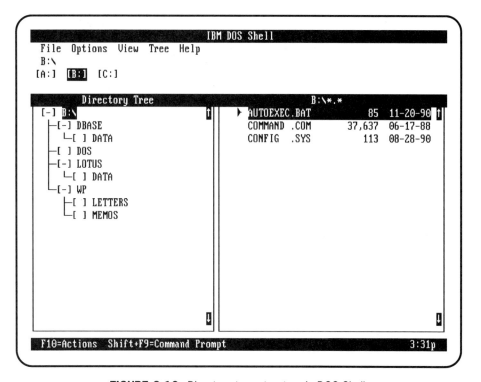

FIGURE O.16. Directory tree structure in DOS Shell.

| To produce a tree diagram or listing that includes the files in each directory | **Enter:** | TREE /F > PRN | Produce a hard copy listing of the tree diagram and list the files within each directory |

The **/F** parameter used with the TREE command causes a *full* listing of the *files* to be displayed as part of the three diagram.

Action: Create the directory \DOS2 on your Data Disk.

| To copy all the files from one directory to another directory on the same disk | **Enter:** | COPY \DOS*.* \DOS2 | Copy *all* the files from the \DOS directory to the \DOS2 directory |

Wildcard or *global characters* can be included in the file specifications that are used when designating files that are stored in directories. Files can be copied to different directories on the same disk, or to the same or different directories on another disk.

| | **Enter:** | CD \WP | Make WP your current directory |
| | **Enter:** | TREE | Produce a tree diagram for the directories below the WP directory |

To remove a directory from within the current directory	**Enter:**	RD LETTER	Remove this directory
	Enter:	DIR	Confirm the removal of the directory
	Enter:	CD \	Return to the root directory level
	or		
	Enter:	CD ..	
	Enter:	RD \ DOS2	Attempt to remove the \DOS2 directory

This message appears:

Invalid path, not directory,
or directory not empty

The \DOS2 directory is not "empty." All files must be deleted or erased from a directory before it can be removed.

To delete all the files in a directory	**Enter:**	DEL \DOS2*.*	Delete all the files in the \DOS2 directory
	or		
	Enter:	DEL \DOS2	
	Enter:	Y	Yes, you want to delete all the files in the directory

Use of the *.* wildcard causes all the files in the specified directory to be erased. All the files on the entire disk are *not* deleted by using this wildcard, only those in the specified directory.

| | **Enter:** | RD \DOS2 | Now, remove the unwanted directory |
| | **Enter:** | TREE /F > PRN | Obtain a hard copy listing of the remaining directories and files on the disk in drive B |

Keypoint!   All the files *must* be deleted from a directory *before* the directory can be removed!

To establish a search path for your executable files	**Enter:**	PATH=B:;B:\DOS;B:\LOTUS;B:\DBASE;B:\WP

Establish a sequence of directories to be searched in looking for an executable file

The PATH command specifies a series of directories to be searched when a command does *not* exist in the *active* directory. In the foregoing PATH command, the directories are searched in sequence from left to right. That is, after the current directory is searched, the root directory on drive B is searched, then the \DOS directory on drive B, then the \LOTUS directory on drive B, and so on.

When a new application software tool, such as Lotus 1-2-3 or WordPerfect, is installed on a hard disk, the installation programs for these packages will frequently modify the PATH command in the AUTOEXEC.BAT file located in the root directory of the hard disk. The name of the directory housing the software tool is added to those already listed in an existing PATH command. (The AUTOEXEC.BAT file is described in more detail in the next section.)

Enter:	CD \WP\MEMOS	Switch to the \WP\MEMOS directory on your Data Disk
Enter:	CHKDSK B:	CHKDSK command is obtained from the \DOS directory on your Data Disk and executed even though \WP\MEMOS is the active directory

To display your currently active PATH	**Enter:**	PATH	List the currently active PATH command

Caution Alert!

> If your computer has a hard disk, a PATH command may have been invoked when you booted your computer. If necessary, return to this initial PATH command by (1) rebooting your computer or (2) accessing the root directory on your hard disk and entering AUTOEXEC.

User-defined directories are an important mechanism for dividing disk storage into manageable chunks. These directories are named to facilitate their reference as an integral part of the name for a file stored in a particular directory. A file's name, including the directory specification, is used in a variety of DOS commands, such as DIR, COPY, DEL, and RENAME. The primary DOS commands used to manage user-defined directories are MD (make directory), RD (remove directory), CD (change directory), TREE, and PROMPT. The detailed syntax for each of these commands is described in the Using DOS Reference section. In general, user-defined directories are more important in administering files stored on hard disks, rather than on floppy disks.

O.2.3 Exploring Special Files

When DOS is booted, the COMMAND.COM, IBMBIO.COM, and IBMDOS.COM programs are executed and loaded into RAM, as described in Section O.1.6 of Lesson O.1. Thus, DOS searches for a CONFIG.SYS file to obtain information for setting up DOS to work with different devices. Finally, the commands residing in an AUTOEXEC.BAT file are executed. CONFIG.SYS and AUTOEXEC.BAT are two special files that are important in the operation and use of a personal computer.

Setup information for a number of different hardware characteristics may reside in a CONFIG.SYS file. Two of the more important ones are the number of **files** and the number of **buffers.** The number of files specifies how many "open" files DOS can work with at any one time. An **open file** is one with a link established by DOS that enables the reading or writing of information to the file. You might envision an open file as similar to a telephone call. If you had 8 telephones, you could dial up 8 of your friends. Then, at any point in time, you could be talking with one of them. However, if you had a total of 20 friends, but only 8 phones, you would be limited to carrying on conversations with only 8 friends at a time. The FILE command in DOS establishes the maximum limit of the number of files that are "open" for reading and writing. This is similar to the number of telephones you might have. When counting the number of files, applications programs, such as dBASE and WordPerfect, are included in the count, because one or more application programs are accessed while you are using this software.

The default value for the quantity of open files automatically assigned by DOS is eight (8) files. For many applications this is sufficient. However, for some applications, particularly dBASE, this number of files can be exceeded. For example, dBASE makes use of several program files, database files, index files, report files, and command files, which can all be active or "open" at one time. If you attempt to use more files than have been established with the FILE command in the CONFIG.SYS file, dBASE generates the following error message:

Too many files open

The command being executed is then aborted.

What does this "Too many files open" error message mean to you? If the error message appears, you need to either "close" files you are not using or modify the CONFIG.SYS file so that more files can be "open." One solution is to set the number of FILES in the CONFIG.SYS to a very large value. However, a fixed amount of RAM is reserved for each of these files. Hence, specifying a large number of files uses RAM that is unavailable for your application software. Selecting the proper number of files is a balancing act. You want sufficient files to run your software application. But you do not want to use too much RAM, so that you have more room for your application. For dBASE, a common number of files that is specified is 20. This number also serves very well for Lotus 1-2-3 and WordPerfect.

Keypoint!   Many software tools include an indication of the minimum number of files that should be set up when the software is installed! If you experience the "Two many files open" error message, check the requirement for your application software tool!

An example CONFIG.SYS file appears as Figure O.17. The FILES command specifies the number of "open" files at any one time, whereas the BUFFERS command indicates the number of buffer areas to be established for reading and writing files. DEVICE furnishes information to establish the appropriate settings for special hardware usage. BREAK turns on/off the extended checking feature of the <CTRL>+

```
FILES = 20
BUFFERS = 20
DEVICE = C:\MOUSE\MOUSE.SYS
DEVICE = C:\NET\NETWORK.SYS
DEVICE = C:\DOS\ANSI.SYS
DEVICE = C:\DOS\HIMEM.SYS
DEVICE = C:\DOS\EMM386.EXE  FRAME = D000
DEVICE = C:\DOS\SMARTDRV.SYS
BREAK = ON
LASTDRIVE=Z
```

FIGURE O.17. Typical CONFIG.SYS file.

<C> for stopping a program's execution, whereas LASTDRIVE specifies the maximum number of drives you can access by setting up the letter for this last valid disk drive identifier.

A **buffer** is an intermediate data storage area set aside in RAM by DOS. As information is read from disk, written to disk, or printed, it is *temporarily stored* in a buffer. The reason for this is that RAM operates at a much faster speed than the input and output devices. A buffer acts as a cushion in adjusting for the different speeds. More buffers provide a bigger cushion and can increase the overall performance in reading and writing large files. The more buffers DOS has, the more data there are in memory. However, each buffer may use up to 532 bytes of RAM, reducing the amount of RAM available to the application software. Establishing the number of buffers is a balancing act, like allocating the number of open files. The default number of buffers is often only two or three, depending on your particular hardware configuration. Database applications, like dBASE, read and write a lot of data to and from disk. For these applications, their performance can be improved by allocating more buffer storage in RAM. Typically, 10 to 20 buffers provides the best results.

Recent releases of Lotus 1-2-3 support the use of expanded memory. This is RAM beyond the 640KB of RAM normally used by DOS 5.0 and all earlier versions for executing application programs. When expanded memory is used with Lotus 1-2-3, larger spreadsheet applications can be created and manipulated. The portion of the spreadsheet that exceeds the 640KB DOS limit is stored in the expanded memory. To use expanded memory, you must set up memory for access by DOS and Lotus 1-2-3. Special DOS "device" commands are employed to activate this expanded memory. EMM386.EXE is a DOS 5.0 program provided with IBM versions of DOS for setting up expanded memory. The DOS DEVICE command is used to execute this program and to establish the expanded memory for use by Lotus 1-2-3. Device drivers like these are invoked by commands in the CONFIG.SYS files. If your release of Lotus 1-2-3 supports the use of extended memory and you have expanded memory hardware available on your computer, determine the necessary device drivers and include them in your CONFIG.SYS file as appropriate for your hardware environment.

Keypoint!

> The CONFIG.SYS file is processed only when DOS is booted. If you revise your CONFIG.SYS file, you will have to reboot DOS *before* the new configuration is available for your applications!

An AUTOEXEC.BAT file contains DOS commands, like those illustrated in Figures O.18 and O.19. Once DOS has been loaded and the CONFIG.SYS conditions have been set, then the DOS commands in the AUTOEXEC.BAT file are executed. As shown in Figures O.18 and O.19, typical commands included in the AUTOEXEC.BAT file are PATH, PROMPT, CD (change directory), and program execution commands, such as LOTUS, DBASE, and WP. The AUTOEXEC.BAT file in Figure O.18 sets up the PATH and PROMPT, and then initiates the execution of the LOTUS.COM file, which activates the Lotus Access System program. When you exit from Lotus 1-2-3, AUTOEXEC.BAT returns processing to the root directory and clears the screen. The AUTOEXEC.BAT file in Figure O.19 establishes the PATH and PROMPT,

```
PATH=C:;C:\DOS;C:\LOTUS;C:\DBASE;C:\WP
PROMPT $P$G
CD C:\LOTUS
LOTUS
CD C:\
CLS
```

FIGURE O.18. AUTOEXEC.BAT file to initiate execution of Lotus 1-2-3.

```
PATH=C:;C:\DOS;C:\LOTUS;C:\DBASE;C:\WP
PROMPT $P$G
CD\DOS
DOSSHELL
CD\
```

FIGURE O.19. AUTOEXEC.BAT file to initiate execution of DOS Shell.

and then activates the DOS Shell, which produces the display screen shown previously in Figure O.2. From the DOS Shell, you could then select the desired application program you want to execute, such as Lotus 1-2-3, dBASE, or WordPerfect.

The CONFIG.SYS and AUTOEXEC.BAT files are usually modified only when new application software is installed on your personal computer. Because of the importance of these files, you should understand their basic function and monitor their contents when installing a new application software package.

Keypoint!

> The AUTOEXEC.BAT can be executed *at any time* from the DOS prompt by entering: AUTOEXEC. You do not need to reboot your computer, although you may do so!

O.2.4   Creating and Modifying Special Files

DOS provides two methods for creating and editing special files like CONFIG.SYS and AUTOEXEC.BAT: copying input from your keyboard directly to a file or editing input by using a text editor. The COPY CON command copies information input at your keyboard into a specified file, where the CON means your keyboard console. A major limitation of using COPY CON is that an existing file *cannot* be revised; only *new files* can be created, and mistakes cannot be corrected once a line has been completed. EDLIN and EDIT are text editors furnished as part of DOS. They can be used to create or revise any ASCII text file. EDLIN supports line-at-a-time editing, whereas EDIT lets you do full-screen editing similar to that available with a word processor like WordPerfect. That is, you typically make changes to only a single line at a time with EDLIN. When the changes on that line are completed, then another line can be edited. The full-screen EDIT was added to DOS beginning with version 5.0. Because the most frequent use of DOS editors is creating and modifying the CONFIG.SYS and AUTOEXEC.BAT files, editing capabilities are examined with examples of these files.

O.2.4.1.   Using the COPY CON Command

The creation of a CONFIG.SYS file, consisting of selected commands from Figure O.19, proceeds as described below using the COPY CON command. Until you press <Enter> at the end of each line or the <F6> at the end of the last line, you may <Backspace> or cursor <left> to make revisions to the line. However, once you press <Enter> or <F6>, you cannot go back and revise a line. Your only option is to reenter the file completely. For this reason, COPY CON is typically used with files that contain only a limited number of command lines.

Action: Place your Data Disk in drive B and make drive B your default disk drive.

To create a CONFIG.SYS file by using the COPY CON command

Enter:	COPY CON CONFIG.SYS	Initiate execution of the copy and specify the destination file name
Enter:	FILES = 20	Enter the desired commands for this file

Enter:	BUFFERS = 20	
Enter:	DEVICE=C:\DOS\ANSI.SYS	
Enter:	BREAK = ON	Only type the next command, do *not* press <Enter> at the end of the line
Type:	LASTDRIVE = Z	This is the last command in the file
Press:	<F6>	Signal termination of keyboard entry, ˆ**Z,** that is, <Ctrl>+<Z> appears in response to pressing <F6>
Press:	<Enter>	Terminate execution of the copy and save the text in the specified file
Enter:	TYPE CONFIG.SYS	Display the contents of the newly created file
Action:	Produce a hard copy listing of this CONFIG.SYS file.	

O.2.4.2. Using EDLIN

The EDLIN text editor is used to create the AUTOEXEC.BAT file shown in Figure O.18 and to store it on your Data Disk. EDLIN is an external DOS command that must be accessed from your DOS disk.

Action: Keep your Data Disk in drive B and make the disk containing DOS your default disk drive.

Prepare for creating a new AUTOEXEC.BAT by ensuring that any existing AUTOEXEC file has been erased from drive B by proceeding like this:

Enter:	DEL B:AUTOEXEC.BAT	If the file already exists on the disk in drive B, then delete the file

If you receive the message "File not found" when you execute the DEL command, then the file did not exist. Otherwise, the file was deleted. In either situation, an AUTOEXEC.BAT file does *not* exist in the root directory of the disk in drive B, and you are ready to begin to create this file as described below with the dialog from EDLIN as shown in Figure O.20.

To use EDLIN to create an AUTOEXEC.BAT file		
Enter:	EDLIN B:AUTOEXEC.BAT	
		Activate EDLIN and specify the name of the file to be created or modified; the asterisk (*) EDLIN command prompt appears
Enter:	I	Issue the EDLIN Insert command that allows you to enter new lines in the text file
Enter:	PATH=C:;C:\DOS;C:\LOTUS;C:\DBASE;C:\WP	
Enter:	PROMPT PG	
Enter:	CD C:\LOTUS	
Enter:	LOTUS	
Enter:	CD C:\	
Enter:	CLS	
Press:	<F6>	The <F6> function key displays ˆ**Z,** indicating that you want to terminate Insert

```
B:\=>EDLIN B:AUTOEXEC.BAT
New file
*I
        1:*PATH=C:;C:\DOS;C:\LOTUS;C:\DBASE;C:\WP
        2:*PROMPT $P$G
        3:*CD C:\LOTUS
        4:*LOTUS
        5:*CD C:\
        6:*CLS
        7:*^Z
*4
        4:*LOTUS
        4:*123
*L
        1: PATH=C:;C:\DOS;C:\LOTUS;C:\DBASE;C:\WP
        2: PROMPT $P$G
        3: CD C:\LOTUS
        4:*123
        5: CD C:\
        6: CLS
*E

B:\=>
```

FIGURE O.20. Dialog in EDLIN to create AUTOEXEC.BAT file.

	Press:	`<Enter>`	Execute the <Ctrl>+<Z>, which terminates inserting lines into the file and returns to the EDLIN command prompt
To edit an existing line in a file while in EDLIN	**Enter:**	4	Request editing of line 4 and obtain the EDLIN line edit prompt; line 4 is displayed and ready for editing
	Enter:	123	Change LOTUS to 123, that is, specify execution of 123.EXE instead of LOTUS.COM by the AUTOEXEC.BAT file; return to the EDLIN command prompt
To list the contents of a file while in EDLIN	**Enter:**	L	List the contents of this text file
To exit from EDLIN	**Enter:**	E	This ends the EDLIN editor and saves the file to your disk as AUTOEXEC.BAT

Keypoint!   Before you end EDLIN, you may make revisions to any line in the file by specifying the line's number and entering the desired text!

The text file you just created, which is an ASCII text file, can now be displayed on the screen. EDLIN has many other commands for text editing. However, EDLIN is not as easy to use as EDIT nor as powerful as a word processor. It provides only some fundamental editing capabilities.

Enter: TYPE B:AUTOEXEC.BAT

The file's contents are displayed

Action: Produce a hard copy listing of this AUTOEXEC.BAT file.

Enter: DIR B: Display a directory listing of files and confirm the existence of the AUTOEXEC.BAT
file

To use EDLIN to revise an
existing file

Enter: EDLIN B:AUTOEXEC.BAT

Prepare to revise an existing file

At the EDLIN prompt,

Enter:	L	List the file
Enter:	4	Line 4 will be revised
Enter:	LOTUS	Change 123 to LOTUS
Enter:	L	List the file again
Enter:	E	End EDLIN and save the file
Enter:	DIR B:	Obtain a directory list of drive B

The directory listing contains two AUTOEXEC files. One has the BAT extension as
you entered it, the other has the BAK extension. When EDLIN is used to modify
an existing file, a copy of the file is created with the BAK extension. That is, the
old version of the file is automatically backed up and identified with this BAK
extension.

Enter: TYPE B:AUTOEXEC.BAT

Display the revised file

Enter: TYPE B:AUTOEXEC.BAK

Display the backup copy of the file

Action: Produce a hard copy of the directory listing for drive B and of the
revised AUTOEXEC.BAT file.

Although the CONFIG.SYS file was created using the COPY CON command, this
is also an ASCII text file that can be modified by using EDLIN.

Action: Using EDLIN, access the CONFIG.SYS file on drive B and change the number
of files to 25; then obtain a hard copy listing of the revised file.

In addition to the EDLIN commands I, L, and E demonstrated above, a number of
other editing commands are available in EDLIN. Some of the more frequently used
commands are shown in Figure O.21. Other commands are described in the *DOS
Reference Manual.*

O.2.4.3. Using EDIT

The DOS Editor, available beginning with DOS 5.0, provides an alternative means for
creating the AUTOEXEC.BAT file shown in Figure O.19. EDIT is an external DOS
command that is accessed from the EDIT.COM file and also requires a second file
QBASIC.EXE. Both the EDIT.COM and QBASIC.EXE files *must* be available on your
DOS disk and accessible in the current directory or through your search path.

Edit Command	Action
line-1,line-2,line-3C	Copy the group of lines beginning with line 1 and ending with line 2 immediately ahead of line 3
D	Delete the current line
line-1,line-2D	Delete the group of lines beginning with line 1 and ending with line 2
line	Edit the specified line, making revisions to this selected line
I **lineI**	Insert lines immediately before the current line or before the specified line
L **line-1,line-2L**	Display a group of lines before and after the current line or from line 1 through line 2
line-1,line-2,line-3M	Move the group of lines beginning with line 1 and ending with line 2 immediately ahead of line 3
<F6> **<Ctrl>+<Break>**	Terminate inserting (I) lines or editing a selected line
E	Ends EDLIN and saves the edited file
Q	Ends EDLIN without saving any changes in the edited file

FIGURE O.21. Selected EDLIN commands.

Caution Alert!

The DOS Editor does not work if the QBASIC.EXE file is not in the current directory, the search path, or the same directory as the EDIT.COM file. If you delete QBASIC.EXE from your hard disk to save space, you cannot use the DOS Editor!

Action: Keep your Data Disk in drive B and make the disk containing DOS your default disk drive.

Get ready for creating a new AUTOEXEC.BAT file by ensuring that any existing AUTOEXEC files have been erased from drive B by continuing in this manner:

Enter: DEL B:AUTOEXEC.*   Delete any existing files on the disk in drive B

In the event the message "File not found" appears, then there were no existing AUTOEXEC files. Otherwise, the files were deleted. For either situation, the AUTOEXEC files have been removed and you are ready to begin creating a new AUTOEXEC.BAT file, instead of revising an existing file. EDIT is used to create the AUTOEXEC file of Figure O.19 as described below.

To use EDIT to create an AUTOEXEC.BAT file

Enter: EDIT B:AUTOEXEC.BAT

Active EDIT and specify the name of the file to be created or modified

A full-screen text entry window appears, as illustrated in Figure O.22, and you are ready to begin entering the commands for the AUTOEXEC.BAT file.

Action: Enter the AUTOEXEC.BAT commands as shown in Figure O.22. At the end of each line, use <Enter> to advance to the next line. Use <Del>, <Backspace>, and <Ins> to correct any of your typing errors. Refer to Figure O.23 for a list of some of the more frequently used special keys in the DOS Editor, as necessary, in making corrections.

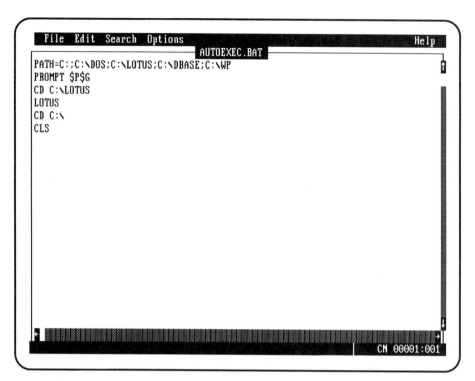

FIGURE O.22. EDIT full-screen window for creating AUTOEXEC.BAT file.

Once you have entered the file, you need to save the file before you exit from EDIT. Continue as follows:

To save your file created with EDIT	**Press:**	`<Alt>`	Access the EDIT menu in the bar at the top of the EDIT screen
	Select:	`File`	Press <F> or <Enter> when the menu cursor is positioned on **File**
	Select:	`Sav`	Save the file to disk
To exit from EDIT	**Press:**	`<Alt>`	Access the menu again

Key	Action
<Ins>	Toggle insert/overtype on or off
<Del>	Delete character at cursor location or selected text
<Backspace>	Delete character to left of cursor location
<Ctrl> + <Y>	Delete current line containing cursor
<Enter> or **<Ctrl> + <N>**	Insert new line at cursor location
<Shift> + <arrow>	Select text by holding down <Shift> and using cursor keys to mark the desired text
<Shift> + <Del>	Cut selected text and save to Clipboard for future use
<Ctrl> + <Ins>	Copy selected text and save to Clipboard for future use
<Shift> + <Ins>	Paste text from Clipboard into file at cursor location
<F1>	Request Help

FIGURE O.23. Selected special-purpose DOS EDIT keys.

Select: File   Another File activity is desired

Select: Exit   Press \<X\> or move cursor to Exit and
                                        press \<Enter\> to leave EDIT

Processing returns to the DOS prompt. You are ready to continue with any other desired activity.

Action: Obtain a hard copy of the AUTOEXEC.BAT file produced with EDIT by using either the DOS PRINT command or the DOS TYPE command with redirection.

Unlike EDLIN, EDIT does not automatically create a backup copy of a file that is modified. You must perform your own backups.

Action: Make a backup copy of your AUTOEXEC.BAT file on drive B by copying it to AUTOEXEC.BAK on the same disk.

Your AUTOEXEC.BAT file can now be revised by proceeding as follows at the DOS prompt:

To use EDIT to revise an existing file

Enter: EDIT B:AUTOEXEC.BAT Access this existing file for modification

Action: Using the DOS Editor special keys, revise the line that contains *only* LOTUS by changing LOTUS to 123. That is, have the AUTOEXEC.BAT file execute 123.EXE instead of LOTUS.COM.

Action: Save the revised file.

Instead of exiting from EDIT to obtain a hard copy of this ASCII text file, you can do this from within EDIT in this manner:

To print a copy of your file while in EDIT

Press: \<Alt\>   Access EDIT menu

Select: File   Desired option

Select: Print   Desired activity

Press: \<Enter\>   Confirm printing of complete document

Action: Exit from EDIT and use the DIR command to confirm the existence of both the modified and backup AUTOEXEC files.

This completes the creation of the AUTOEXEC.BAT file as a "plain" ASCII text file using EDIT.

Caution Alert!

> Word processing programs can also be used to create CONFIG.SYS and AUTOEXEC.BAT files. These programs often insert special control characters into the files they create and must be used following special procedures in preparing these ASCII text files to ensure that they contain only text and no unwanted control characters!

Special-purpose files, such as CONFIG.SYS and AUTOEXEC.BAT, may be created or modified by using either the COPY CON command, the EDLIN line-at-a-time text editor, or the EDIT full-screen text editor. These capabilities are provided as an integral part of DOS. They produce "plain" ASCII text files, which do not contain any special control characters that might affect the execution of the commands contained in these special-purpose files. EDLIN and EDIT work best for creating and modifying files that consist of several command lines, because the lines can be entered and edited as desired. EDIT is the most convenient means provided by DOS for both entering and revising ASCII text files.

0.2.5 When Things Go Wrong

You may encounter a variety of difficulties in working with directories and in creating special-purpose files. Some of the more common situations and how to approach them are described here:

1. You created a user-defined directory for storing your data, but you don't remember its name.

   a. Use CD\ to access the root directory level.

   b. Use DIR to obtain a list of directories and files stored at the root level.

   c. Inspect the list to determine if your directory exists at this level. If it does, then you have found the user-defined directory name.

   d. If the desired user-defined directory was not found, use the TREE command to obtain a directory diagram (DOS 4.0 or later) or a directory list (DOS 3.3 or earlier).

   e. Locate the desired user-defined directory name and use it as appropriate.

2. You created a file and placed it in a user-defined directory. You don't remember the exact name of the file or the directory.

   a. Use the TREE /F command to obtain a directory and file diagram or list, depending on your version of DOS.

   b. Identify the desired file including its user-defined directory and use the file as desired.

3. You issued a DOS command and received the error message "Bad command or file name." This usually indicates that the file is not in the current director or is not in a directory specified with the PATH command.

   a. Verify that you used the correct spelling of the file name.

   b. Use DIR to verify that the desired command is not in the current directory, but with a slightly different spelling.

   c. Examine the PATH to determine what other directories DOS would search for the command.

   d. Use either the CD command to access the desired directory containing the file to be executed or the PATH command to change the directories to be searched.

4. You used the COPY CON command to create an ASCII text file, but incorrectly entered one or more commands.

   a. Access the file to be corrected by using either EDLIN or EDIT.

   b. Correct the desired commands.

   c. Save the modified file and use it as desired.

0.2.6 Lesson Summary

- Directories are used in organizing and managing a large number of files stored on a disk.

- The root directory is the "highest" level directory, exists on every disk, and is specified by the disk drive letter identifier.

- Directories below the root directory are optional. They are created and named by the user.

- Directory names follow the same rules as those for file names.
- A file is the basic unit of storage in a directory, regardless of whether it is the root directory or a user-defined directory.
- Once created, a file stored in a directory is referenced by including the directory name as part of the file name.
- The TREE command produces a diagram of directories on a disk.
- The PATH command specifies a series of directories to be searched when a command or executable file cannot be found in the current active directory. Executable files include those with extensions .COM, .EXE, and .BAT, but do not include your own data files.
- CONFIG.SYS is a special file that contains the information used by DOS to establish the number of open files and buffers that are available when running an application program.
- The FILES command in the CONFIG.SYS files determines the maximum number of files that can be open. If this value is set too low, the error message "Too many files open" may be encountered when using dBASE.
- Special files, such as CONFIG.SYS and AUTOEXEC.BAT, can be created with the COPY CON command, EDLIN, or EDIT. They all produce "plain" ASCII text files without any special control characters.
- EDLIN is a line-at-a-time text editor that can be used to modify or create "plain" ASCII text files, such as CONFIG.SYS and AUTOEXEC.BAT.
- EDIT is a full-screen text editor that can be used with "plain" ASCII text files.

0.2.7   Practice Tutorial

Your understanding of operating systems is reinforced by exploring the DOS commands described in this Lesson as a guided activity in a hands-on manner. As you embark on these tasks, remember the usage of Enter, Type, Press, and Action as described in Lesson T.2, the Software Navigation Guide.

Task 1: Carry out the activities as described in Sections 0.2.2 and 0.2.4, taking care to produce each of the requested printing tasks.

Task 2: Organize your printouts and label them with the title of each section.

Time Estimates

Novice: 60 minutes

Intermediate: 45 minutes

Advanced: 30 minutes

0.2.8   Practice Exercises

Expand your capabilities with DOS by working with directories and special files. Be sure that you create all these directories and store all the special files produced on your Data Disk.

Task 1: Create the directories shown in this directory diagram:

```
            Disk Drive (Root directory)

         ┌───── BIN
         ├───── 123
         │        ┌─── DATA
         │        │      ┌── HERBIE
         │        │      └── PATTIE
         │        └─── BUDGET
         ├───── DB
         │        ┌─── PAYROLL
         │        └─── PERSONNEL
         └───── DOC
                  ┌─── HERBIE
                  └─── PATTIE
```

Task 2: Produce a hard copy listing of the tree diagram for the directories created in Task 1. The DOS commands are:

> _____

> _____

Task 3: Copy the COMMAND.COM, FORMAT.COM, and EDLIN.COM files to the BIN directory. Produce a hard copy listing of the files in this directory and of the tree diagram with the files shown. The DOS commands are:

> _____

> _____

> _____

> _____

Task 4: Remove the BIN directory and produce a hard copy listing of the tree diagram after this change. The DOS commands are:

> _____

> _____

> _____

Task 5: Create a CONFIG.SYS file containing these commands:

```
BREAK=ON
BUFFERS=20
FILES=15
LASTDRIVE=E
DEVICE=C:\DOS\ANSI.SYS
DEVICE=C:\DOS\VDISK.SYS 1024 512 256 /X:8
INSTALL=C:\DOS\FASTOPEN.EXE
COUNTRY=045,865 C:\DOS\COUNTRY.SYS
```

Produce a hard copy listing of the file. The DOS command to begin editing is:

> _____

Task 6: Create an AUTOEXEC.BAT file containing these commands:

```
@ECHO OFF
PATH C:;C:\DOS
PROMPT $P$G
C:\DOS\GRAPHICS
VER
DATE
TIME
DOSSHELL
```

Produce a hard copy listing of the file. The DOS command to begin editing is:

> _____

Task 7: Organize your printouts from Tasks 2 through 6 by labeling each output with the task number.

Time Estimates

Novice: 60 minutes

Intermediate: 45 minutes

Advanced: 30 minutes

Reference

CONTENT

- Loading DOS
- Command Summary

0.3.1 Loading DOS

The procedure for loading DOS into memory may vary, depending on your particular hardware and software configuration. In particular, many local area networks (LAN) have special procedures for using DOS. This section describes two of the more common methods of loading DOS when your hardware is configured with either floppy disks or a hard disk and is not hooked up on a LAN.

0.3.1.1. Two Floppy Drives

Obtain a disk containing DOS. This may be a "DOS disk" that contains only DOS files or an application software tool, such as WordPerfect, which contains the DOS COMMAND.COM file and the hidden DOS files IBMBIO.COM and IBMDOS.COM.

1. Place the DOS disk in drive A:
2. Load DOS:

   A Perform a cold boot by turning on the power switch to your personal computer. If your monitor and printer are not turned on, turn these on before you turn on the power to your system unit. Enter the date and time, if requested.

   or

   B Perform a warm boot by pressing <Ctrl>+<Alt>+<Del> all together. Enter the date and time, if requested.

   or

   C With your computer already turned on and at the DOS prompt (usually, **A>** or **A: \>**),

> **Enter:**   COMMAND
>
> Enter the date and time, if requested.

3. DOS is now loaded and ready for your use.

0.3.1.2. Hard Disk Drive

With a hard disk drive, DOS usually resides on the hard disk. The procedures for loading DOS are as described below.

1. Load DOS:

> **A** Perform a cold boot by turning on the power switch to your personal computer. Enter the date and time, if requested.
>
> **or**
>
> **B** Perform a warm boot by pressing <Ctrl>+<Alt>+<Del> all together. Enter the date and time, if requested.
>
> **or**
>
> **C** With your computer already turned on and at the DOS prompt (usually, **C>** or **C: \>**),
>
> **Enter:**   COMMAND
>
> Enter the date and time, if requested.

2. DOS is loaded and ready for your use.

If the error message "Non-system disk" appears when you boot DOS, then either the hard disk does not contain DOS or a data diskette has been inadvertently left in the A disk drive. When booting a computer with a hard disk, the usual procedure is for the computer to attempt to obtain DOS from the A disk drive before looking at the C disk drive. This feature lets you boot DOS in the unlikely event that your hard disk is damaged. Therefore, if a data diskette is in the A disk drive, remove it and boot the computer by using one of the methods described above. If the hard disk does not contain DOS, then load DOS by using the Two Floppy Disk method described in Section O.3.1.1.

0.3.2 Command Summary

In this section, selected DOS commands are presented in alphabetical order for ease of reference. The most frequently used commands are presented here, along with the most often used form of the command. Parameters enclosed in brackets are optional. For a complete reference, you should see a *Disk Operating System Reference Manual.* Although many of these DOS commands are the same for an earlier version of DOS as for the most recent version of DOS, some of the commands can be used only under the most recent versions. Use the VER command described below to check the version of DOS loaded on your personal computer.

Although the commands listed here are for the IBM version of DOS, you should keep in mind that the functions carried out by these commands are present with nearly all versions of DOS, as well as most other microcomputer and mainframe operating systems. The exact syntax of the commands may be different with other operating systems. However, for some commands, such as the COPY command, you will find that they are often very similar.

The commands presented here can be classified into the following categories:

1. Internal DOS command
2. External DOS command
3. Language processor
4. Special-purpose file

Language processors and special-purpose files are included as examples of frequently encountered files other than the external DOS commands. For each command type presented here, its classification is specified. Several symbols are used in specifying the syntax of DOS commands. These symbols are a notation convention applied with this command summary.

Conventions	Meaning
lowercase characters	User-supplied information
UPPERCASE CHARACTERS	DOS command word or parameter
< >	Indicates the user-supplied information is required
[ ]	Specifies optional portion of DOS command

Commands

ATTRIB (Attribute)

Purpose: Displays, sets, or removes the read-only, archive, system, and hidden attributes assigned to files.

Format:
ATTRIB [+R| − R] [+A| − A] [+S| − S] [+H| − H] [[drive:] [path] filename] [/S]

where

+R sets attribute to read-only
−R clears read-only attribute
+A sets attribute to archive
−A clears archive attribute
+S sets attribute to system file
+H sets attribute to hidden
−H clears hidden file attribute
/S changes attributes of all files in the current directory and all of its subdirectories

Examples:
ATTRIB MYFILE.TXT
Causes the current attributes of MYFILE.TXT to be displayed.

ATTRIB +R MYFILE.TXT
Changes the attribute of MYFILE.TXT to read-only so you cannot replace the file by writing a new version of the file over the current version of the file.

ATTRIB +R A:*.*
Changes the attributes of all files in the current directory on disk drive A to read-only.

Command type: External

Commands

AUTOEXEC.BAT File

Purpose: The AUTOEXEC.BAT file is a special file that is automatically executed whenever DOS is booted. This allows many application package programs to be self-starting. For example, when DOS is booted with the Lotus 1-2-3 system disk in drive A, the AUTOEXEC.BAT file is executed, causing Lotus to be loaded and executed. Because of this special use, it is listed here with the DOS commands.

Command type: Special-purpose file

Example AUTOEXEC.BAT file:

```
DATE
TIME
CD\LOTUS
LOTUS
```

This AUTOEXEC file prompts for the date and time and then changes the default directory to LOTUS and causes the LOTUS program to be executed.

BACKUP

Purpose: Used to back up one or more files from a fixed disk to diskettes. Files that have been backed up can be *restored* only to the fixed disk for later use.

Format:
BACKUP [drive:] [path] [source] [.ext] < drive :>[/S]

where
    source is the source file name and
    /S causes the files in all directories to be backed up

Command type: External

Remarks: The disk(s) receiving the backup files must be formatted before the BACKUP command is initiated.

Examples:
BACKUP C:\A:/S
Causes all the files on the fixed disk to be backed up.

BACKUP C:\WP*.* A:
Causes all files in the WP directory on drive C to be backed up to the disk in drive A.

BASIC

Purpose: Access IBM Disk BASIC. (May not be available on other brands of personal computers.)

Format:
BASIC

or

BASIC [drive:]<filename.ext>

Command type: Language processor

Commands

Remarks: BASIC has been replaced with QBASIC beginning with DOS version 5.0.

Examples:
BASIC
Causes Disk BASIC to be loaded into memory.

BASIC A:MORTGAGE.BAS
Causes BASIC to be loaded and then the BASIC language program MORTGAGE to be loaded from drive A and executed immediately.

BASICA

Purpose: Access IBM Advanced BASIC stored on disk (may not be available on other brands of personal computers).

Format:
BASICA

or

BASICA [drive:] <filename.ext>

Command type: Language processor

Remarks: BASICA has been replaced with QBASIC beginning with DOS version 5.0.

Examples:
BASICA
Causes Advanced BASIC to be loaded into memory.

BASICA B:MORTGAGE.BAS
Causes Advanced BASIC to be loaded and then the BASIC language program MORTGAGE to be loaded from drive B and executed immediately.

CHDIR or **CD** (Change Directory)

Purpose: Changes the current directory of either the specified drive or the default drive or displays the current directory.

Format:
CHDIR [[drive:]path]

or

CD [[drive:]path]

or

CD

Command type: Internal

Remarks: The current directory is where DOS looks to find files when file names are entered without a directory specification. Before attempting to change the current directory, it must be created with the Make Directory (MD) command.

Commands

Examples:
CHDIR\
Causes the current directory to be the root directory of the default drive.

CD B:\BUDGET\DIVISION
Causes the current directory to be the DIVISION directory on drive B.

CD B:EAST or CD EAST
Causes the current directory to be the existing path plus EAST. Notice the omission of the " \" before the user-defined directory name.

CD
Causes the name of the current directory to be displayed.

CHKDSK (Check Disk)

Purpose: Produce a status report on the disk and memory space for a designated or default drive.

Format:
CHKDSK [drive:]

Command type: External

Remarks: CHKDSK processes the disk loaded in the designated or default drive. The disk must be placed in the drive before you issue the CHKDSK command.

Example:
CHKDSK A:
Causes the disk in drive A to be checked.

CLS (Clear Screen)

Purpose: Clears the screen and positions the DOS prompt in the upper left-hand corner of the screen.

Format:
CLS

Command type: Internal

CONFIG.SYS

Purpose: Provides DOS with setup information for hardware and operating characteristics. When DOS is booted, the information in this file is used in configuring DOS. Because of this special use, it is listed here with the DOS commands.

Command type: Special-purpose file

Example file:

FILES=15
BUFFERS=20
DEVICE=MOUSE.SYS

This CONFIG.SYS file sets the number of FILES and BUFFERS and then activates the MOUSE driver.

Commands
_____

COPY

Purpose: To copy one or more files from one disk to another disk or to copy one or more files on a disk to the same disk but with a different name. This command is used frequently in making backup copies of your files.

Format:

Option 1—Copy with different name (General form of command)

COPY [drive:] [path] <source>[.ext] [drive:] [path] <target>[.ext][/V]

where
    source   is the source file name
    target   is the target file name
       /V   causes a verify to be performed on the copy

Option 2—Copy with same name

COPY [drive:] [path] <source>[.ext][/V]

Copies the source file to a file with the same name in the current directory of the default drive. Notice that in this form of the COPY command, no target file is specified, and so DOS defaults to a file with the same name on the default drive and directory.

or

COPY [drive:] [path] <source>[.ext] <drive:> [path] [/V]

Copies the source file to a file of the same name, but to the specified drive and directory since no target file name is specified.

Command type: Internal

Remarks: Global Character or Wild Card Character of * and ? can and are frequently used in the filename and extension specification of the COPY command. This facilitates copying several files at one time. See Global File Characters below for a description of their use.

Examples:
COPY B:MYFILE
Causes the source file MYFILE on drive B to be copied to a target file named MYFILE on the default drive.

COPY *.* B:
Causes all the files on the default drive to be copied to drive B.

COPY MYFILE.ABC B:*.XYZ /V
Cause the source file MYFILE.ABC on the default drive to be copied to drive B and given the filename MYFILE.XYZ.

DEL (Delete) [See ERASE]

DIR (Directory)

Purpose: Provides a listing of the files in a specified directory. This command is frequently used to determine which files are contained on a particular disk.

Commands

Format:
DIR [drive:] [path] [filename[.ext]] [/P] [/W]

where
    /P   causes the display to pause when the screen is full
    /W   causes a wide display listing of the filenames

Command type: Internal

Examples:
DIR
Creates a listing of all files in the current directory.

DIR B:/W
Creates a listing of all file names on the disk in drive B to be listed in a wide display.

DIR B:*.ABC/W
Creates a listing of all files on the disk in drive B with the extension of ABC to be listed in a wide display.

DIR C:\LOTUS*
Creates a listing of all files in the \LOTUS\directory on drive C.

DISKCOMP

Purpose: Compares the contents of a *floppy* disk in one drive to that of a disk in another drive. More often used after a DISKCOPY to ensure that the copy is identical to the original. This command is used only with floppy disks.

Format:
DISKCOMP [drive:] [drive:]

Command type: External

Remarks: This command produces an error message if used with a fixed disk. It is to be used only with floppy disks.

Example:
DISKCOMP A: B:
Compares the disk in drive A to the one in drive B.

DISKCOPY

Purpose: Copies the contents of the entire disk in the source drive to the target drive. This command is frequently used to make a backup copy of an entire disk. This command is used only with *floppy* disks. Your source and target disks must be the same size and density.

Format:
DISKCOPY [drive:] [drive:]

Command type: Internal

Remarks: This command produces an error message if used with a fixed disk. It is to be used *only* with floppy disks.

Commands
_____

Example:
DISKCOPY A: B:
Copies the entire disk in drive A to the disk in drive B including any operating system and
hidden files.

EDIT

Purpose: Access the DOS full-screen editor.

Format:
EDIT [drive:] [path] [<filename>[.ext]]

Command type: External

Remarks: This command is available beginning with DOS version 5.0.

EDLIN

Purpose: Access the DOS line-at-time editor.

Format:
EDLIN [drive:] [path] [<filename>[.ext]]

Command type: External

ERASE (Delete)

Purpose: Delete files with the specified file name.

Format:
ERASE [drive:] [path] [<filename>[.ext]]

or

DEL [drive:] [path] [<filename>[.ext]]

Command type: Internal

Examples:
ERASE MYFILE.ABC
Erases the file MYFILE.ABC from the current directory of the default drive.

DEL A:*.ABC
Erases all files with the extension ABC on drive A.

ERASE A:*.*
Erases all files on the disk in drive A. Be careful when you use this form of the command
because it causes all the files to be destroyed.

FORMAT

Purpose: Prepares or initializes a floppy disk to accept program and data files. A disk must
be formatted before any files can be stored on it. Formatting causes all files residing on a
disk to be destroyed.

Format:
FORMAT [<drive:>] [/S][/V]

Commands

---

where
  /S   causes the DOS operating system to be copied to the disk being formatted
  /V   permits a user-supplied label to be entered for identifying the disk

Command type: External

Examples:
FORMAT B:/S
Causes the disk in drive B to be formatted, with DOS placed on the disk.

FORMAT B:/S/V
Causes the same action as above and places a volume label on the disk.

FORMAT
Causes the disk in the default drive to be formatted.

Global File Characters

Purpose: Provides for specifying groups of files with the same filename, extension or part of a filename or extension.

Format:
?
A question mark (?) in the filename or extension signifies that any character may occupy that position.

*
An asterisk (*) in the filename or extension signifies that any character can occupy that position and all remaining positions to the right of the asterisk in the filename or extension where it appears. When an asterisk is used to specify the entire filename or extension, it specifies *all* files regardless of the filename, extension or both, depending on where the asterisk is used in specifying files.

Examples:
DIR B:123??BUD.*
Causes all files to be listed with filenames that begin with 123, have any characters in positions four and five, and contain BUD in positions six through eight. Files with these filenames and any extension are listed. The * signifies all extensions.

COPY *.* B:
Causes all files to be copied from the active drive to the disk in drive B.

GRAPHICS

Purpose: Allows the contents of a graphics display screen to be printed on a printer when a color/graphics monitor adaptor is installed.

Format:
GRAPHICS [/R]

where the /R causes black to print as black and white to print as white. If the /R is omitted, the default is to print black as white and white as black.

Command type: External

Remarks: The GRAPHICS command is usually executed before you initiate the execution of any application programs.

Commands

LABEL

Purpose: Allows a volume label to be placed on a disk.

Format:
LABEL [drive:] [volume label]

Command type: External

Example:
LABEL B: LOTUS_DATA

MIRROR

Purpose: Creates a file containing information describing the contents of a disk for use in recovering files with the UNDELETE and UNFORMAT commands. A file is created that contains a snapshot of the file allocation table and the root directory of the specified disk.

Format:
MIRROR [drive:]

Command type: External

Remarks: An image of the system area of the designated disk is saved in the file MIRROR.FIL. If this file exists from a prior execution of MIRROR, the old version of the file is saved as the MIRROR.BAK file. This command is available beginning with DOS version 5.0.

Example:
MIRROR B:

MKDIR (Make Directory)

Purpose: Creates a directory on the specified disk. This command is particularly useful in dividing a fixed disk into directories for use with different application programs. It may also be used with floppy disks.

Format:
MKDIR [drive:]<path>

or

MD [drive:]<path>

Command type: Internal

Example:
MD C:\LOTUS\DATA
Creates the directory \LOTUS\DATA on drive C.

MORE

Purpose: Causes one screen of output to be displayed at a time. Output to the screen is temporarily halted until you press a key to advance to the next screen. This command is used frequently with other DOS commands that send output to your display screen.

Format:
MORE < [drive:] [path]<filename>

Commands

──

other-DOS-command | MORE

Command type: External

Remarks: With the first form of the command, the contents of a file are redirected (<) to MORE for display. The second form of the command pipes (|) the output of the DOS command through MORE for display to your screen.

Example:
MORE < A:MYFILE.ABC

TYPE A:MYFILE.ABC | MORE

DIR A: | MORE
This use of MORE is similar to the DIR /P command.

PRINT

Purpose: Prints a file directly to your printer from DOS.

Format:
PRINT

or

PRINT [drive:] [filename.ext]

When using this command you will be asked to indicate the printer you want to use. Just press <Enter> to use the printer attached to your personal computer.

Command type: External

Remarks: Once the command has been entered for one file, it may be entered for additional files while the first file is being printed. A print queue of up to 10 files is permitted as the default for this command.

Example:
PRINT B:MYFILE.DOC
Causes the contents of MYFILE.DOC to be printed.

PROMPT

Purpose: Allows the user to define a new DOS prompt.

Format:
PROMPT [prompt-text]

Command type: Internal

Remarks: Prompt-text can be any desired text string or special metastrings.

Example:
PROMPT pq$g
Causes the following DOS prompt to be displayed if the current directory and path on drive A: is \LOTUS:

    A:\LOTUS = >

Other metastrings that may be included in the PROMPT are $d for date and $t for time.

Commands
_____

QBASIC

Purpose: Start IBM DOS QBASIC (may not be available on other brands of personal computers).

Format:
QBASIC

or

QBASIC [drive:] <filename.ext>

Command type: Language processor

Examples:
QBASIC
Causes QBASIC to be loaded into memory.

QBASIC B:MORTGAGE.BAS
Causes QBASIC to be loaded and then the QBASIC language program MORTGAGE to be loaded from drive B.

RENAME

Purpose: Allows the name of a file to be changed.

Format:
RENAME [drive:] [path]<source>[.ext] <target>[.ext]

or

REN [drive:] [path]<source>[.ext] <target>[.ext]

where
      source is the old filename and
      target is the new filename

Command type: Internal

Examples:
REN MYFILE YOURFILE
Causes the name of MYFILE to be changed to YOURFILE in the directory on the default drive.

RENAME B:\LEVEL1\MYFILE.* YOURFILE.XYZ
Causes the file MYFILE on drive B in the directory LEVEL1, regardless of its extension, to be named YOURFILE with an XYZ extension.

RESTORE

Purpose: Used to restore one or more files that have been previously backed up to diskettes from a fixed disk.

Format:
RESTORE <source-drive:> [drive:] [path] [filename[.ext]][/S]

Command type: Internal

Commands

Remarks: The drive specified immediately after RESTORE is the source drive that contains the file to be RESTORED from the BACKUP. The filename indicates the target drive and files that are to be RESTORED. The /S indicates that all files in the directories are to be RESTORED.

Example:
RESTORE A: C:*.* /S
Restores all files including those in the directories from diskettes in drive A: to a fixed disk in drive C:.

RMDIR (Remove Directory)

Purpose: Removes the directory from the disk in the specified drive.

Format:
RMDIR [drive:] <path>

or

RM [drive:] < path >

Command type: Internal

Remarks: The directory must be empty before it can be removed. That is, all the files in the directory must be deleted and all lower level subdirectories must be removed before this command is issued.

Examples:
RM B:\LEVEL2\LEVEL3
Causes LEVEL3 to be removed from LEVEL2.

SORT

Purpose: Causes the specified input to be arranged in sequence and output to your display screen, a file, or another specified device such as your printer.

Format:
other-DOS-command | SORT [/R][+n] [> [drive:][path]filename]

where
    /R   reverses the sort sequence, that is, the sort order is from Z to A and then 9 to 0
    /+n   specifies that column n is used for the sort; otherwise the default is to sort on column 1, the left-most column

Command type: External

Remarks: The output from the DOS command is piped (|) through the SORT process and redirected to the specified file or device.

Examples:
DIR | SORT > PRN
Creates a hard copy listing of the directory, sorted by the first character of the filename.

TYPE MYFILE.TXT | SORT > A:MYFILE.ABC
Sequences the contents of MYFILE.TXT and places the result in MYFILE.ABC.

DIR | SORT | MORE
Displays a sorted listing of the current directory on your screen, with a pause as each screen, of information is displayed.

Commands

SYS (System)

Purpose: Transfers the main DOS operating system files (COMMAND.COM, IBMBIO.COM, and IBMDOS.COM) from one disk to another disk.

Format:
SYS <drive:>

Command type: External

Remarks: **drive**: specifies the target drive to which the files will be transferred. The disk in the target drive must be formatted but should *not* contain any files.

TREE (Display Directory)

Purpose: Displays all the directory paths found on the specified drive and, if requested, the files residing in those directories.

Format:
TREE [drive:] [/F]
where the /F requests the names of the files to be displayed.

Command type: External

Example:
TREE B:/F

TYPE

Purpose: Causes the contents of the designated file to be displayed on the screen.

Format:
TYPE [drive:][path]<filename>[.ext][| MORE]

where the | MORE causes a pause after one full screen of output at a time and any key is pressed to obtain the next screen.

Command type: Internal

Remarks: The file must be an ASCII text file for you to be able to read the file that is displayed. A binary file, such as one with a COM extension, will be displayed as what appears as a bunch of random garbage characters.

Example:
TYPE B:MYFILE.DOC

UNDELETE

Purpose: Allows previously deleted files to be recovered.

Format:
UNDELETE [[drive:][path]filename[.ext]] [/LIST|/ALL]

where
        /LIST   produces a list of files that can be recovered
        /ALL   recovers all files without prompting by replacing the first character of the
                 filename with a number sign (#)

Commands

Command type: External

Remarks: This command is available beginning with DOS version 5.0.

Example:
UNDELETE /LIST
Causes a list of deleted file to be produced.

UNDELETE A:MYFILE.TXT
Allows this particular file to be recovered.

UNFORMAT

Purpose: Allows a disk erased by the FORMAT command to be recovered.

Format:
UNFORMAT [drive:] [/TEST]

where
    /TEST   describes how UNFORMAT would recreate the information on this disk, but
            does not actually perform the unformat operation

Command type: External

Remarks: This command is available beginning with DOS version 5.0.

Example:
UNFORMAT/TEST
Causes a description of how the unformat would be performed.

UNFORMAT A:
Performs an unformat on the disk in drive A.

VER (Version)

Purpose: Causes the version number of DOS to be displayed on the screen.

Format:
VER

Command type: Internal

VOL

Purpose: Causes the volume label of a specified disk drive to be displayed.

Format:
VOL [drive:]

Command type: Internal

XCOPY

Purpose: Copies groups of files from multiple directories, which can include lower level
directories.

Commands

Format:
XCOPY <source-path> <target-path> [/S] [/E] [/P] [/D:date]

where
    source-path   specifies the source disk drive and/or directory and
    target-path   specifies the destination disk drive and/or directory
          /S   causes all files and lower-level directories to be copied
          /E   causes empty directories to be included in the copy
          /P   prompts you to confirm the creation of each destination file
          /D   causes files to be copied that have been modified on or after the specified
               date

Command type: External

Remarks: This command is available beginning with DOS version 3.2.

Examples:
XCOPY C:\DATA B:\DOC
Causes all files in the DATA directory to be copied to the DOC directory on the B disk drive.

XCOPY C:\MEMOS B:\ /S /E /D:04/11/93
Causes all the files and directories within the MEMOS directory to be copied, beginning at the root directory on the B disk drive, including any empty directories when the file was modified on or after 04/11/93.

PART

III

Using
Lotus 1-2-3

Creating a Worksheet

CONTENT

L.1.1   What Is Lotus 1-2-3?

Lotus 1-2-3 is what is known as an electronic spreadsheet, which is one of the most popular microcomputer software tools. There are a number of 1-2-3 work-alikes, such as Quattro Pro, Twin, and GoldStar, which run on microcomputers, and other look-alikes, such as 20/20, which run on mainframe and minicomputers.

These software tools are known as **electronic spreadsheets** because they emulate electronically the familiar accounting spreadsheets that have been prepared by hand for years, like that shown in Figure L.1 for the four-year plan at Good Morning Products. This tool received its name from these manual, paper accounting spreadsheets. Spreadsheets are often used for business modeling, where what-if analysis is performed. A **business model** is a mathematical description of a business problem that usually states

GOOD MORNING PRODUCTS
PROJECTED INCOME STATEMENT

	YEAR 1	YEAR 2	YEAR 3	YEAR 4
SALES	1305000	1566000	1879200	2255040
COST OF SALES	887400	1064880	1277856	1533427
GROSS PROFIT	417600	501120	601344	721613
SALARIES	39000	42120	45490	49129
BENEFITS	7410	8003	8643	9334
ADMIN EXPENSE	30015	36018	43222	51866
DEPRECIATION	8000	8000	9000	9000
INTEREST	1600	1600	1600	1600
TOTAL EXPENSES	86025	95741	107954	120929
EARNINGS BEFORE TAX	331575	405379	493390	600684

FIGURE L.1. Accounting spreadsheet.

the assumptions and relationships among the variables that make up the model, such as the four-year plan for Good Morning Products. A **what-if** is performed whenever a data value is revised and the entire spreadsheet is *recalculated*. For example, a what-if analysis is performed by changing the SALES in YEAR 1 from $1,305,000 to $1,500,000 and recalculating the entire four-year plan. A series of different what-if alternatives can be produced very easily once a spreadsheet has been created. The application of a spreadsheet software tool to solving business problems is nearly limitless.

In Lotus 1-2-3, the accountant's spreadsheet is called a worksheet and is used to produce spreadsheet reports like that for Good Morning Products, shown in Figure L.2. While you are creating a 1-2-3 worksheet, it is displayed as an arrangement of **rows** and **columns** with the rows numbered and the columns lettered, as illustrated with the accounting spreadsheet in Figure L.3. Each row and column intersection in the worksheet is known as a **cell**. A cell is the basic unit of a worksheet in which you store data. Lotus 1-2-3 is a very large spreadsheet. It has 256 columns and 8192 rows, with the columns lettered beginning with A and ending with IV, and the rows numbered starting with 1.

It is impossible to view all these rows and columns of a football-field-size spreadsheet on your display screen at one time. Hence, your screen becomes a window allowing you to look at a portion of this huge spreadsheet. Think of your screen as moving about the large Lotus 1-2-3 worksheet to display a single view of rows and columns at any one time.

Cells are named by specifying the column letter followed by the row number. For example, **D11** is the **cell name** of the cell located at the intersection of column **D** and row **11**, that is, **D11** is the cell's **address**. In Figure L.3, the cell **D11** contains the amount of SALARIES for YEAR 3.

Lotus 1-2-3 allows you to place a **value** or a **label** in each cell as the cell's **content**. A **value** may be a constant number or it may be an equation or formula that produces a numeric result. A **label** is alphanumeric data, such as a name or address. A key

```
                        GOOD MORNING PRODUCTS
                      PROJECTED INCOME STATEMENT

                      YEAR 1      YEAR 2      YEAR 3      YEAR 4
                   -----------------------------------------------
SALES              $1,305,000  $1,566,000  $1,879,200  $2,255,040
COST OF SALES         887,400   1,064,880   1,277,856   1,533,427
                   -----------------------------------------------
   GROSS PROFIT       417,600     501,120     601,344     721,613

SALARIES               39,000      42,120      45,490      49,129
BENEFITS                7,410       8,003       8,643       9,334
ADMIN EXPENSE          30,015      36,018      43,222      51,866
DEPRECIATION            8,000       8,000       9,000       9,000
INTEREST                1,600       1,600       1,600       1,600
                   -----------------------------------------------
   TOTAL EXPENSES       86,025      95,741     107,954     120,929
                   -----------------------------------------------
EARNINGS BEFORE TAX  $331,575    $405,379    $493,390    $600,684
                   ===============================================
```

FIGURE L.2. Lotus 1-2-3 accounting spreadsheet report.

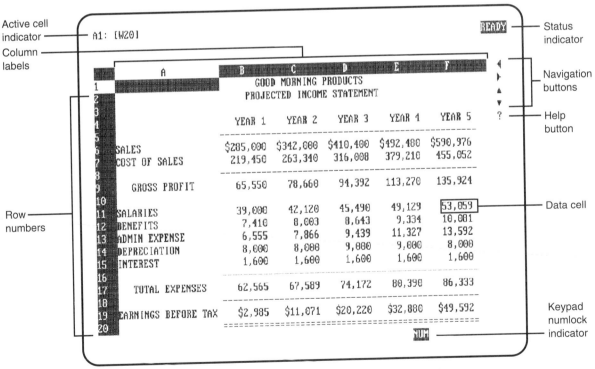

FIGURE L.3. Accounting spreadsheet as entered in 1-2-3.

distinguishing feature of labels is that you cannot perform any arithmetic with them. If used in arithmetic calculations, labels have a value of zero (0).

Keypoint!

> Each **cell** in Lotus 1-2-3 contains either a **value** or a **label**! If it does NOT contain a value or label, then it is **blank**!

Formulas are used to calculate data values that are displayed in many of the cells of a worksheet. Formulas are constructed by combining numeric constants, cell names, and arithmetic operators to define your calculation. It's this feature of 1-2-3 that sets it apart from other software tools such as word processor. If all you wanted to do was merely type a table of data like the accounting spreadsheet shown in Figure L.2, then there would be little advantage to using a spreadsheet program like 1-2-3. But when the spreadsheet has many of its values calculated, then you are using 1-2-3 as it was designed to be used. For example, in Figure L.4, the shaded values are all cells that have their value calculated by using formulas for the Good Morning Products Projected Income Statement. The other numeric data values are input as constants. This is a common situation for many 1-2-3 applications.

Although you could do all of the calculations by hand and then just type them into the cells of your 1-2-3 worksheet, this really defeats the purpose for using a spreadsheet software tool. You want the spreadsheet tool to do the arithmetic for you. Examples of 1-2-3 cell contents are summarized in Figure L.5.

In Figure L.5, the apostrophe preceding the cell content of COST OF SALES is a signal that this cell contains a label. Notice that with text and numeric values, a cell's content and display are identical. With formulas, the content is the equation, and the calculated outcome of the formula is displayed together with any specified formatting, such as commas and currency symbols. For example, the COST OF SALES for YEAR 1 in Figure L.3 is calculated by the formula **+B6*0.68**, which is the SALES

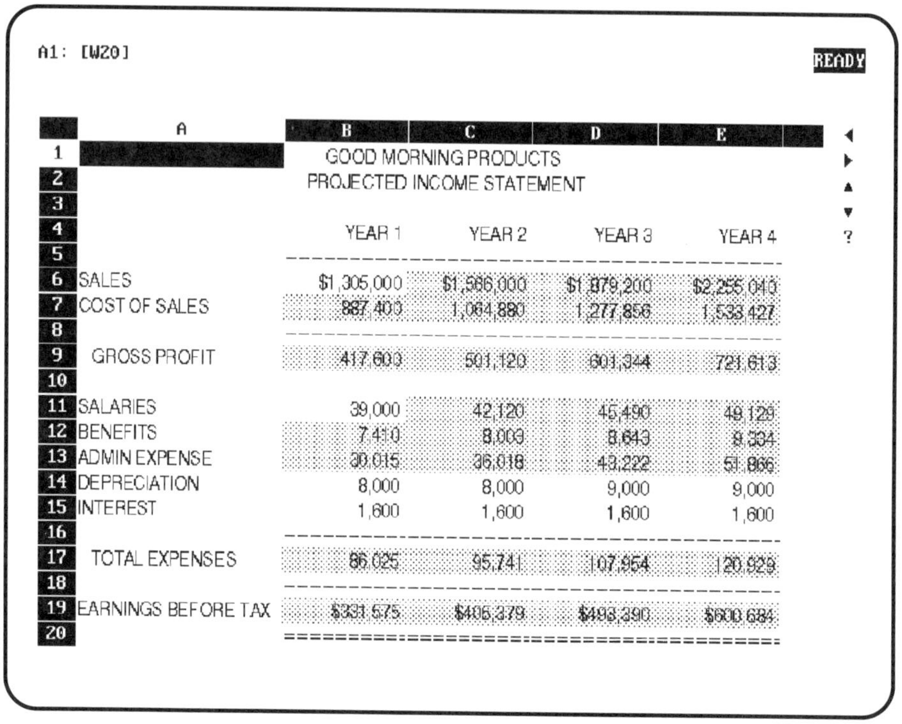

FIGURE L.4. Typical use of formulas in a spreadsheet.

Cell Name	Cell Content	Cell Display	Cell Use
A7	'COST OF SALES	COST OF SALES	Label
B6	1305000	$1,305,000	Value—Constant
B7	+B6*0.68	887,400	Value—Formula

FIGURE L.5. Examples of using cells.

amount for YEAR 1 in cell **B6**, multiplied by 0.68 (68%), which is the COST OF SALES percent of SALES. Used in this manner, cells are like mailboxes. The cell name is like the address on your mailbox, whereas the cell content is like the mail deposited in your mailbox. Your mailbox has only one address, but it may have many different contents, or it could be empty. However, unlike your mailbox, which may contain many pieces of mail at once, *a cell may contain only a single value.* When entering text, values, and formulas, the results end up displayed in the cells on your screen similar to an accountant's paper spreadsheet and ready for printing as a report to support your information requirements for decision making.

Keypoint! | You really harness the power of 1-2-3 by using formulas in your worksheet to calculate the data values displayed on your screen!

L.1.2   The 1-2-3 Worksheet Display

When you create a 1-2-3 worksheet, you enter labels and values into the cells of your worksheet to produce a report that you can either view on your display screen or print as a paper copy. During this process, you are typing the worksheet contents *arranged in the same manner as they are to be printed*, as shown in Figures L.2 and L.3. The arrangement of information on your display screen as it is to be printed is, in general, known as a **WYSIWYG** (What You See Is What You Get) approach to creating a report. This approach is used with a number of different computer software tools, including many word processing programs, as well as spreadsheet programs like 1-2-3. VisiCalc, the first spreadsheet program, used this method of displaying worksheet information on a screen arranged as it is to be printed.

Beginning with Release 2.3 of 1-2-3, Lotus Development included a special feature in 1-2-3 known as the WYSIWYG Add-In. **Add-Ins** are special programs created by Lotus Development and other software developers that you can run while you are using 1-2-3. Add-Ins provide 1-2-3 with additional capabilities, since they actually become part of 1-2-3 when you use them. The WYSIWYG Add-In allows you to enhance the appearance of your worksheet by including spreadsheet publishing features, such as underlines, bold characters, italics, special fonts, shading, and cell outlines. However, these enhancements *do not change* the location or arrangement of information on your spreadsheet. They only *enhance* the appearance of information you have already entered into your worksheet. You still need to *place data at cell locations to produce the desired reporting arrangement*, which is similar to creating a document using a word processor.

The basic 1-2-3 worksheet in Figure L.2 can be enhanced with the Lotus WYSIWYG Add-In to produce the worksheet shown as a screen display in Figure L.6 and as a final printed report in Figure L.7. Notice that the quality of the printed report in Figure L.7

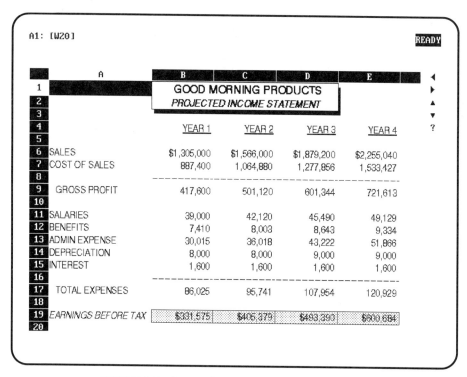

FIGURE L.6. Screen display using WYSIWYG features.

is better than the screen display of Figure L.6. Some of the key 1-2-3 WYSIWYG Add-In features illustrated in Figure L.6 include the following:

1. A report heading displayed using two different sizes and styles of fonts.
2. An outline and drop shadow box around the two-line report heading.
3. Column titles that are underlined.
4. An outline box surrounding the EARNINGS BEFORE TAX data values.
5. Light shading applied to the EARNINGS BEFORE TAX data values.
6. EARNINGS BEFORE TAX displayed in italics.

GOOD MORNING PRODUCTS *PROJECTED INCOME STATEMENT*			
	YEAR 1	YEAR 2	YEAR 3	YEAR 4
SALES	$1,305,000	$1,566,000	$1,879,200	$2,255,040
COST OF SALES	887,400	1,064,880	1,277,856	1,533,427
GROSS PROFIT	417,600	501,120	601,344	721,613
SALARIES	39,000	42,120	45,490	49,129
BENEFITS	7,410	8,003	8,643	9,334
ADMIN EXPENSE	30,015	36,018	43,222	51,866
DEPRECIATION	8,000	8,000	9,000	9,000
INTEREST	1,600	1,600	1,600	1,600
TOTAL EXPENSES	86,025	95,741	107,954	120,929
EARNINGS BEFORE TAX	$331,575	$405,379	$493,390	$600,684

FIGURE L.7. Printed report using WYSIWYG features.

Use of the WYSIWYG Add-In to perform this spreadsheet publishing is described in Lesson L.12, Enhancing Appearance with WYSIWYG.

Just because Lotus Development decided to name their spreadsheet publishing feature WYSIWYG does not mean that they have the exclusive use of this term in describing the overall operation of a spreadsheet, word processor, or other software tool. You should remember that **WYSIWYG** is a general concept that can be applied to many software tools where the screen display matches what is to be printed.

Keypoint!

> WYSIWYG has two meanings when creating a Lotus 1-2-3 worksheet:
>
> 1. The general *arrangement* of information on your display screen as that information is viewed and/or printed.
> 2. A special Add-In feature that *enhances the appearance* of the data as viewed and/or printed.

The 1-2-3 worksheet display screen is your window into an electronic copy of your report. Once you have the report displayed on your screen, in the manner you want it to appear on paper, the document can be printed. Overall, you create a 1-2-3 worksheet display by entering labels and values to produce your report as you want it to appear in printed form and then you print it.

The description of Using Lotus 1-2-3 in this book focuses on creating business models with data arranged for printing, but without the enhancements for spreadsheet publishing, since these are usually applied after you have the right arrangement of information. The emphasis is one of *obtaining the right data* before you are concerned with enhancing its appearance. Because if you have the wrong information, all of the available spreadsheet publishing enhancements are of little good to you.

L.1.3   Starting 1-2-3

The exact procedure for starting Lotus 1-2-3 will vary depending on your particular hardware configuration and the manner in which 1-2-3 has been installed on either floppy disks or the computer's fixed disk. The procedures will vary for floppy disk usage depending on whether DOS has been placed on the Lotus 1-2-3 SYSTEM Disk. For older releases of 1-2-3, a "key" disk may be required when you run it from a fixed disk. If you are using 1-2-3 on a network, a menu may be provided for starting 1-2-3. The procedures described here are general procedures. You will need to check on the exact procedures for the computer that you are using.

These procedures assume that you will be storing the 1-2-3 worksheet files that you create on your own floppy disk. If your worksheet files will be stored on the computer's fixed disk, you should investigate the specific procedures for this on your particular computer.

Before you begin you will need a formatted floppy disk on which you will store your 1-2-3 worksheet files. This disk will be called your **Data Disk**. If you do not know how to format a new Data Disk, follow the procedure described in the Using DOS section.

The standard method to activate Lotus 1-2-3 is to proceed at the DOS prompt:

To start Lotus 1-2-3   **Enter:**   LOTUS

If your procedure is different, enter the instructions here:

My procedure to start Lotus 1-2-3:

_____

_____

_____

_____

L.1.4   The 1-2-3 Access System

The Access System is the gateway to the set of programs that comprise Lotus 1-2-3. The heart or main program is the 1-2-3 Lotus Spreadsheet/Graphics/Database program. This is the one you will use most of the time. The other programs are auxiliary programs to perform other activities in support of this program. The PrintGraph program produces hard copy printed graphs. Without PrintGraph, graphs could only be displayed on your screen. Some, more advanced, releases of Lotus 1-2-3 integrate the printing of graphs with the other printing activities. Different releases of Lotus 1-2-3 have different Access Menu choices and, therefore, your menu choices may vary somewhat from those listed here. The menu selections and their actions are summarized in Figure L.8.

As illustrated in Figure L.9, beginning with Release 2.3, the second line of the menu area is a list of the available menu choices or commands. The first line is a one-line description of the menu choice that is highlighted by the menu cursor or pointer. You can think of this as a one-line HELP message. In earlier releases of 1-2-3, the Access System menu choices appear on the top line, whereas the help description is on the second line.

L.1.5   Menu Selection in 1-2-3

You can select a command from 1-2-3 menus in one of three ways. The first two methods are available with all releases of 1-2-3, and mouse support is available beginning with Release 2.3. Selections are made like this:

1. Strike the *capital* or *first* letter of the desired command.

   or

2. Move the menu cursor using <left>, <right>, <Home>, and <End> to the command of your choice and press <Enter>. As you move the menu cursor you can read the one-line description or help message.

   or

3. Point to the menu command of your choice using the mouse and click the <left button> to make your selection.

Lotus 1-2-3 has a feature described by computer software designers as ring menus. **Ring menus** are circular in their operation. That is, if your menu cursor is at the rightmost menu choice and you press <right>, the menu cursor will go to the left end of the menu. If your cursor is located at the left end and you press <left>, the menu cursor is positioned at the very right end of the menu.

Menu Selection	Action
1-2-3	Enter the 1-2-3 worksheet program
PrintGraph	Enter the graphics printing program
Translate	Enter program to translate files from other programs, such as DBASE, to Lotus 1-2-3
Install	Enter the install procedure to initialize or change the hardware configuration
Exit	Leave the Access System and return to DOS

FIGURE L.8. Lotus 1-2-3 Access System menu choices.

To access the main 1-2-3 worksheet program	**Select:**	1-2-3	Desired menu choice for main worksheet program

To proceed to the Lotus 1-2-3 spreadsheet program from the Access System, you selected **1-2-3**. (When a Lotus 1-2-3 "key" disk is required, the SYSTEM Disk *must* remain in drive A: until after you have selected **1-2-3** from the Access System Menu.)

L.1.6   The 1-2-3 Worksheet Screen

The Lotus 1-2-3 worksheet now appears on your screen. The highlighted **cell pointer** is at cell **A1**, which is in the upper-left corner of the worksheet area. The cell pointer indicates the **current cell** location on the worksheet where any data value or formula you enter is stored.

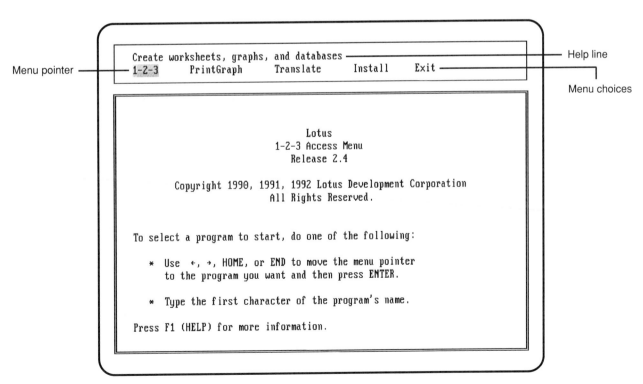

FIGURE L.9. Lotus 1-2-3 access screen and menu.

To move the cell pointer to another cell location

Action: Move the cell pointer about your screen using the cursor control keys: <left>, <right>, <up>, <down>, <PgUp>, <PgDn>, <Home>, <Ctrl>+<right>, <Ctrl>+<left>, <Tab>, and <Shift>+<Tab>. <End> can be pressed and then followed with <left>, <right>, <up>, and <down>. <left button> can be used to position the cursor with a mouse.

As you move the cell pointer around your screen, notice how the cell name of the pointer location is displayed in the very upper-left corner of the screen.

The 1-2-3 worksheet screen is arranged as illustrated in Figure L.10. The areas of the screen are described as follows:

Control panel. Top three lines of the screen.

Line 1. Location of cell pointer and content of the cell. A **cell's content** is the data that you enter into a cell.

Line 2. Edit line or first line of menu. This line serves a dual purpose.

Line 3. Blank or single-line description or help message. This line also serves a dual purpose.

Mode indicator. This is the word in the upper-right corner. The **mode indicator** specifies the current processing **mode**, or state, of 1-2-3. Figure L.11 is a list of some of the more frequently occurring mode indicators. Watch the mode indicator as you use 1-2-3.

Worksheet area. When data values and labels are entered into cells, the labels and results of the formulas appear in this part of your screen using the WYSIWYG method of displaying results in the worksheet area arranged for future printing.

Key indicator panel. Located in the lower-right corner of the screen, this indicates which "lock" keys have been toggled on and advises you of other advanced

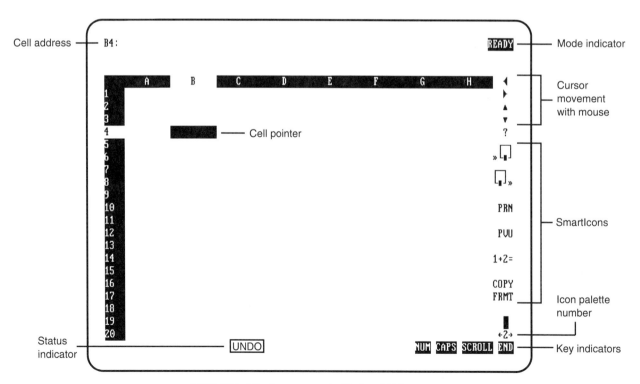

FIGURE L.10. Arrangement of Lotus 1-2-3 screen.

Mode Indicator	Description
READY	1-2-3 is ready for you to enter data, locate the cell pointer, or select a command.
WAIT	1-2-3 is carrying out a command that requires additional time for processing.
LABEL	1-2-3 detected that you are entering a Label as a cell's content.
VALUE	1-2-3 detected that you are entering a Value (numeric constant or formula) as a cell's content.
MENU	1-2-3 recognized that you have caused a menu to be displayed for choosing a command.
EDIT	You issued a request to edit a cell's contents or 1-2-3 detected an error in a cell formula and wants you to correct it.
POINT	1-2-3 wants you to specify a cell range or you are entering data in a cell using the cell pointer to specify cell names.
ERROR	1-2-3 is displaying an error message. Selecting HELP will display the 1-2-3 Help screen related to the message. Pressing <Esc> or <Enter> clears the error message.

FIGURE L.11. Selected mode indicators.

conditions in 1-2-3. For example, a CALC indicator signals that a solution of the spreadsheet needs to be computed, because a label or value has been placed in the worksheet since the last calculation of the results. The UNDO indicator identifies that the Undo feature has been turned on or enabled for your use. You will learn about some of the other status indicators in these Using Lotus 1-2-3 lessons.

Scroll arrows. These are used with a mouse to move the cell pointer by clicking on the arrow indicating the desired direction of movement. Scroll arrows are available beginning with Release 2.3.

SmartIcons. A **SmartIcon** is a small picture representing a 1-2-3 command. They provide a short-cut method to execute many commonly used 1-2-3 commands by using the mouse and clicking the desired icon. SmartIcons are available beginning with Release 2.4. They require the use of the SmartIcon Add-In. If this Add-In was previously attached, they may appear automatically each time you start 1-2-3.

In Release 2.4, if the WYSIWYG and SmartIcon Add-Ins are attached automatically when you start 1-2-3, then your screen may appear like that shown in Figure L.12. Because WYSIWYG controls the appearance of the cell pointer and borders, your screen may look somewhat different than that in Figure L.12.

Now let's see how the indicator keys operate.

To toggle the CAPS indicator on or off

Press: <Caps Lock>   The CAPS indicator toggles on or off

Keypoint!

If something goes wrong, don't panic! Help is only a keystroke away. Just press the <F1> function key and the 1-2-3 help menu will appear. You can obtain information on many of 1-2-3's features!

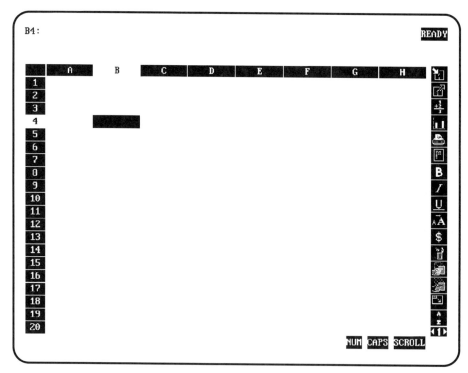

FIGURE L.12. Arrangement of Lotus 1-2-3 screen with WYSIWYG and SmartIcon Add-Ins attached.

L.1.7   Accessing the Main 1-2-3 Menu

Lotus 1-2-3 is a menu driven program. Other than entering labels and values, you give 1-2-3 commands by selecting them from a menu. A menu does not immediately appear on entering the 1-2-3 Spreadsheet. You need to request 1-2-3 to display the menu choices on your screen.

To display the main 1-2-3 menu

Press: /   Access main menu

Or, with mouse support, merely position the mouse pointer in the control panel area:

Move mouse   (Control Panel)   Access main menu by positioning mouse
pointer to: pointer

The Main 1-2-3 Menu appears on your screen as shown in Figure L.13. At this top level menu, the choices available are as described in Figure L.14. The worksheet commands are displayed on a second menu when this command is selected.

To display the worksheet commands

Select: Worksheet

Remember, this menu operates just like the 1-2-3 Access System Menu. Notice that the Mode Indicator now displays MENU, indicating that you are in the menu mode of operation. The Worksheet menu appears as shown in Figure L.15. From the Worksheet menu, another menu selection can be made to obtain a list of the global menu commands.

To display the global commands

Select: Global

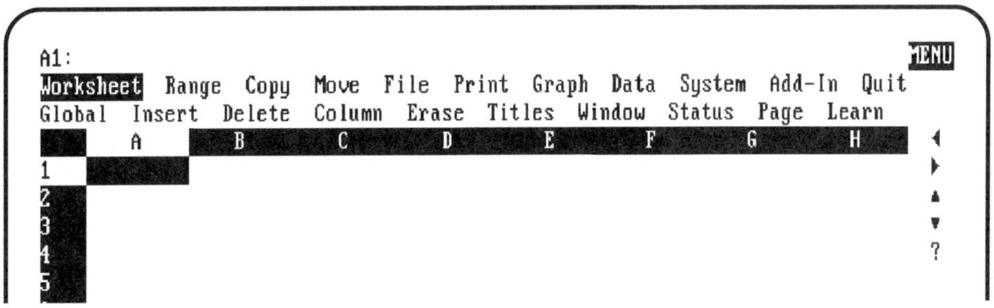

FIGURE L.13. Main 1-2-3 menu.

The next menu appears as shown in Figure L.16 with a Setting Sheet replacing the worksheet area for Release 2.2 or higher, while the worksheet area remains displayed for earlier releases. A **setting sheet** provides information on current parameter settings, such as that for the Global Column Width or Format. Like the other Worksheet selections, the **Global** commands affect the *entire* worksheet. *Portions* of the worksheet are operated on by using the **Range** menu selection.

Keypoint!

> **Worksheet** and **Global** are commands that affect the entire worksheet.
>
> **Range** is a command that affects a specified portion of the worksheet!

Setting sheets and **dialog boxes**, an extension to the setting sheet, use the following components to described the currently selected settings:

- *Option button.* Specifies the selection of one option from a group of options. An option is selected when an * (asterisk) appears in parentheses next to the option.

Menu Selection	Activity
Worksheet	Commands that affect the *entire* worksheet.
Range	Commands that affect *a specified portion* of the worksheet.
Copy	Operation that makes a copy of the cell contents from one location at another location.
Move	Operation that moves the cell contents from one location to another location.
File	Operations that load and save disk files, as well as change the default disk drive.
Print	Commands that print all or part of the worksheet.
Graph	Commands that display a graph on a graphics screen and save the image for later printing.
Data	Commands that manipulate data in a 1-2-3 database.
System	Command to leave 1-2-3 temporarily and use the operating system at DOS prompt.
Add-In	Command that permits separate special programs to be activated.
Quit	Command to leave the 1-2-3 worksheet and return to the 1-2-3 Access System.

FIGURE L.14. Main 1-2-3 menu choices.

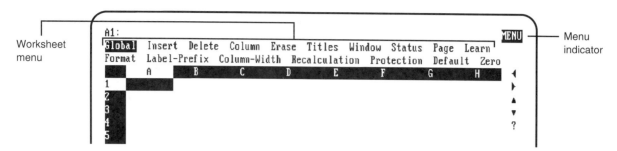

FIGURE L.15. Worksheet menu.

- *Check box.* Indicates an option is selected when an X appears in brackets next to the options. The check box is used to toggle the option on or off as desired.
- *Text box.* Contains a value that you entered to establish a desired setting.
- *Popup dialog box.* An extension of the settings sheet that appears on top of the setting sheet to provide additional options. Popup dialog boxes (Figure L.17) appear by pressing F2 (EDIT) and then typing the highlighted letter of the option or by clicking on the option with the mouse pointer.

The Lotus 1-2-3 menu commands and command paths are arranged as shown in Figure L.18. The exact set of commands may vary somewhat from one release of Lotus 1-2-3 to another. However, Figure L.18 (on pages L-16 and L-17) illustrates the primary commands and menu choices.

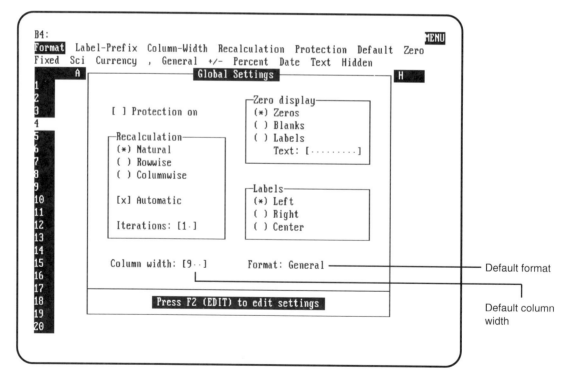

FIGURE L.16. Worksheet global menu with setting sheet.

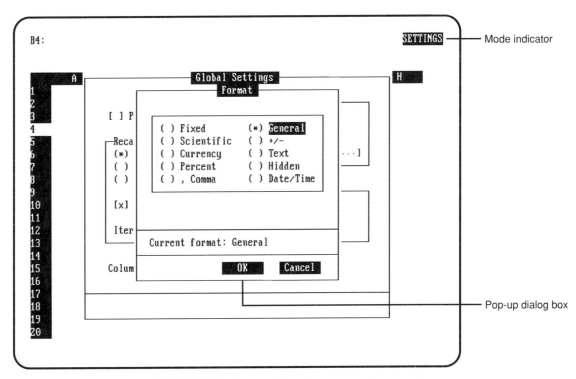

FIGURE L.17. Popup dialog box for changing format.

L.1.8 Reversing Menu Choices

The <Esc> key is used to "undo" or "back up" from the last menu selection or entry. With the Global menu displayed in the Control Panel, you can proceed to back up to the prior menu choice. Let's see how this is performed.

To return to the previous menu or READY mode	**Press:**	<Esc>

To back up one more level in the 1-2-3 menus	**Press:**	<Esc>

From the Global menu, you are now back at the READY mode. You can move your cell pointer about the worksheet in the READY mode. In summary,

1: To back up one level in the menu structure, press <Esc>.

- Each time you strike <Esc>, you back up one level until you exit from the top-level menu to the READY mode.

2. To get to the READY mode from ANY level in the menu structure, press <Ctrl>+<Break>.

- Remember, <Ctrl>+<Break> means to hold down the <Ctrl> key like a <shift> key and strike the <Break> key.

L.1.9 1-2-3 Menu Command Notation

In 1-2-3, you construct a command, which the computer can execute, by making a series of menu choices. Some commands require more menu choices than others. For

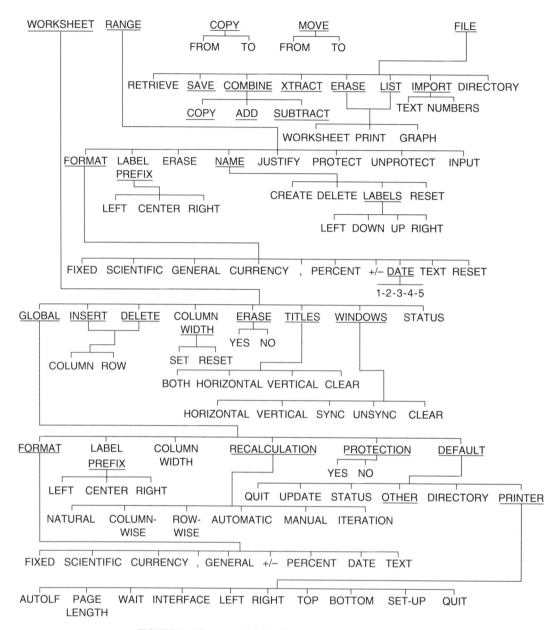

FIGURE L.18. Lotus 1-2-3 selected command menu map.

example, to change the width of each column on the worksheet, make these menu selections and entries:

To change the column width of all worksheet columns

Press:	/	Access main menu

(or move mouse pointer to Control Panel)

Select:	Worksheet	
Select:	Global	Effect entire worksheet
Select:	Column-Width	Desired activity
Enter:	12	Friendly reminder, press <Enter> after you type 12

This command causes columns **G** and **H** to disappear from your screen, since the width of each column is such that only six columns now fit across the worksheet area.

FIGURE L.18. (Continued)

This entire group of menu selections and entries makes up *one command* that 1-2-3 can execute. In addition to listing each selection and entry as illustrated earlier, there are two other "standard" methods for indicating a series of menu selections and entries. One spells out the menu selections, whereas the other utilizes the first letter of the selection (that is, the letter you would type to make the menu selection). For example, the foregoing command could be listed as either:

/Worksheet Global Column-Width 12

or

/WGC12

Throughout most of this description of 1-2-3, the individual menu selections and entries will be used to help you understand the operation of 1-2-3.

Before you continue, let's return the column width to its original or default width of 9 spaces. A **default** is the value that 1-2-3 assumes before you have entered any other specific value. The column is returned to the original starting width in this manner:

To return the column width to the initial 1-2-3 default setting			

Press:	/	Access main menu
Select:	Worksheet	
Select:	Global	Effect entire worksheet
Select:	Column-Width	Desired activity
Enter:	9	Desired column width

And columns **G** and **H** are again displayed on your screen.

Keypoint! **Default** values are those assumed by 1-2-3 when this application software tool is initiated. They remain in effect until changed! Examples are default column width and disk drive.

L.1.10   Creating and Using a Spreadsheet: Good Morning Products

Good Morning Products in an international bottler and distributor of the Liquid Gold brand of fresh orange juice. Good Morning Products, located in Citrus Grove Valley, California, was established in 1919 by Charles "Frosty" Frost. Frosty now serves as the Chairman of the Board of Good Morning Products. The business is family owned and operated with Matthew "Crush" Frost as President and Chief Executive Officer (CEO), Kimberly Frost-Moore as Vice President and General Manager, Christopher Frost as Treasurer and Jennifer Frost-Krone as Secretary. Kim and Chris are working on next quarter's budget. They have estimated that sales will be $289,500 and that cost of sales are 68% of sales. They want to begin their plan with a 1-2-3 worksheet, which contains planning accounts computed as indicated below:

Sales = 289500
Cost of Sales = 68% * Sales
Gross Profit = Sales − Cost of Sales

Chris will set up this worksheet with the account names starting in cell **A1**. The 1-2-3 formulas are then

Cell	Equation	
B1	input amount	(entered directly)
B2	.68*B1	
B3	+B1−B2	

After this worksheet is created for the first quarter, it will be extended into other quarters with a plan prepared for the entire year. Figure L.19 illustrates the completed worksheet for the first quarter.

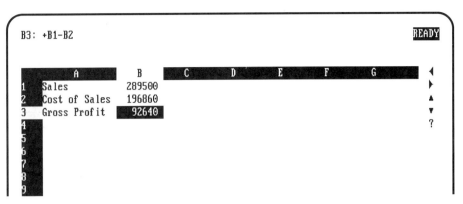

FIGURE L.19. Good Morning Products first quarter worksheet.

L.1.11 Building a 1-2-3 Worksheet

Chris constructed the worksheet in Figure L.19 by entering labels and values like this:

Action: Verify you are at the READY mode. If necessary, use <Esc> to get to READY.

| To enter a label | **Press:** | <Home> | Position worksheet cursor at **A1** |
| | **Enter:** | Sales | |

Notice that when you press <S>, the mode indicator immediately switches to LABEL. Lotus 1-2-3 has detected from the *first* character typed that a *label* will be entered.

As you type **Sales** it appears on the Edit Line. When you press <Enter>, what is on the Edit Line is moved to the Cell Content. If you make a mistake while typing **Sales**, you may <backspace> to remove any unwanted characters and then type the desired characters.

Once a value has been entered into a cell, the contents of the cell appear both as the cell content and in the worksheet area. The cell content is: '**Sales**. Lotus 1-2-3 places the apostrophe to the left of **Sales** to specify that this is a label. Several other characters besides the apostrophe may be used. These are explored later.

| To enter a constant numeric value | **Move to:** | **B1** | Location for next cell entry |
| | **Enter:** | 289500 | Desired value |

Notice that when you press <2>, the mode indicator immediately switches to VALUE. Again, the *first* character typed has identified this Cell Content characteristic.

Next, *Cost of Sales* is calculated by using a formula. *Cost of Sales* is assumed to be 68 percent of *Sales*. That is, the formula **.68 * Sales** will be used to have 1-2-3 calculate the desired result. Now enter the label and equation as follows:

| To enter another label | **Move to:** | **A2** | Location of account name |
| | **Enter:** | Cost of Sales | |

| To enter a formula that calculates a value | **Move to:** | **B2** | Location of account value |
| | **Enter:** | .68*B1 | |

Notice that the formula appears as the Cell Content in the Control Panel and the result of the formula appears in the worksheet area. Here, the asterisk (*) indicates

Operator	Symbol
Add	+
Subtract	−
Multiply	*
Divide	/
Exponentiation	^
Group Calculations	( )

FIGURE L.20. Arithmetic operators.

multiplication. The arithmetic operators in Lotus 1-2-3 are shown in Figure L.20. These are similar to those used in other software tools such as dBASE.

The **Cost of Sales** label displayed in **A2** has been chopped off and now reads **Cost of S**, as shown in Figure L.21. This is because the default column width in 1-2-3 is 9 characters. Cell **A2** still contains **Cost of Sales**. It is just that there is only room for **Cost of S** in the worksheet area. Be patient. This will be corrected in due time. But first the other labels and equations will be entered.

Now let's enter the *Gross Profit* information.

To enter the third label	**Move to:** **A3**	Location of account name
	Enter: Gross Profit	

Like *Cost of Sales*, **Gross Profit** is cut off and displayed as **Gross Pro** (Figure L.21) Accept this for now and continue by entering the desired formula.

To attempt to enter a formula that references other cells to calculate a value	**Move to:** **B3**	
	Enter: B1-B2	Location of account value
	What appears in cell **B3**? _____	

Lotus 1-2-3 has interpreted your entry as a LABEL, since the formula begins with a letter.

To actually enter a formula that references other cells to calculate a value	**Enter:** +B1-B2

The desired result is obtained as shown in Figure L.21. The plus sign (**+**) in the formula of cell **B3** signals 1-2-3 you are entering a formula, which can be observed with

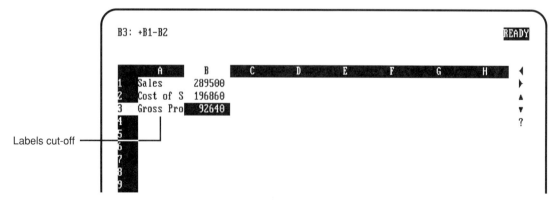

FIGURE L.21. Chris's initial worksheet for the first quarter.

the VALUE Mode Indicator. In 1-2-3, a value or formula must begin with a numeric digit or one of these special characters:

+   −   .   (@   # $

Frequently, a + or (is used to begin a formula since neither alters the mathematical result.

Now you are ready to print this result.

| To obtain a printed copy of your 1-2-3 screen | **Action:** Obtain a hard copy of your 1-2-3 worksheet with a <Shift>+<PrtSc> screen dump. |

Keypoint!

> The screen dump with <Shift>+<PrtSc> may NOT work if you are using Release 2.3 or later and your screen is set to the Graphics selection, rather than the default Text option. If nothing prints, obtain assistance with your particular release and installation of Lotus 1-2-3!

L.1.12 Changing Appearance with Column Width

Now let's adjust the width of column **A**, since Kim wants to display the entire labels contained in both cells **A2** and **A3**. Here, the width of *only* column **A** is to be revised, *not* all columns in the worksheet, as shown in Figure L.22.

To change the width of a single selected column

Move to:	A3	Any cell in column **A**, which is the column to be widened
Press:	/	Access main menu
Select:	Worksheet	
Select:	Column	For some releases of 1-2-3, you select Column-Width
Select:	Set-width	
Press:	<right>	Column width is increased by one space
Press:	<right>	Another space
Press:	<right>	Keep going

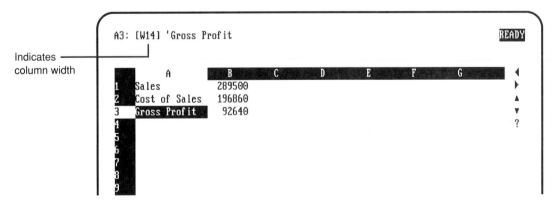

FIGURE L.22. Chris's completed worksheet for the first quarter.

Press:	`<right>`	
Press:	`<right>`	The column is now 14 characters wide and all labels are completely visible
Press:	`<Enter>`	Complete column width specification

By using the <left> and <right> cursors, you can **preview** the width of the column before making your final choice for the column width. Of course, if you knew 14 was the desired width, you could have entered 14 immediately by typing that value.

The **[W14]** following the cell name in Line 1 of the Control Panel indicates that the column width of column **A** has been set to 14. *Only* the column width of **A** has been set, the other columns (**B** through **IV**) remain at the default width of 9. Please notice, you did *not* type the **[W14]** on the Cell Content line. Lotus 1-2-3 placed it there as a result of executing the / Worksheet Column Set-Width 14 (/WCS14) command. Some earlier releases of 1-2-3 do not display the **[W14]** column width specification.

Action: Obtain a hard copy of your 1-2-3 worksheet with the revised column width using a <Shift> + <PrtSc> screen dump.

Caution Alert!   You DO NOT type the column width specification as part of the cell content! This is entered by the / Worksheet Column Set-Width command (/WCS)!

L.1.13 Saving a 1-2-3 Worksheet File

Before you save your file, it is necessary to make sure the file will be written to or placed on your Data Disk. This is accomplished by setting your default disk drive.

To set your default disk drive

Press:	`/`	Access main menu
Select:	`File`	Choose File option
Select:	`Directory`	Desired action
Enter:	`A:` or `B:`	Drive identifier of the drive where your Data Disk is located

If your drive for storing worksheet files is different or if a subdirectory is used for storing these files, enter your drive and/or subdirectory here:

My storage drive/directory for worksheet files:

_____

Once the drive identifier and/or subdirectory name has been entered, it remains in effect until either you change it or you Quit the 1-2-3 worksheet. In fact, your copy of 1-2-3 may be set up so that the drive identifier is automatically set to the one you want. If **A:**\or **B:**\appeared when you entered the / File Directory (/**FD**) command, and if this is the correct drive, then you do not need to specify this each time you access 1-2-3.

Now you are ready to save a copy of your worksheet. Your 1-2-3 worksheet is only in your computer's memory until you save it to your Data Disk. If your computer was accidentally turned off before you saved your worksheet file, your entire worksheet could be lost. Your worksheet is saved by writing a copy of it to your Data Disk.

To save your 1-2-3 worksheet file	**Press:**	/	Access main menu
	Select:	File	
	Select:	Save	Desired file activity
	Enter:	PLAN	Name of your worksheet file, a DOS file name limited to a maximum of 8 characters

When your worksheet file is saved, 1-2-3 identifies it with the extension of WKS, WK1, or WK3, depending on your release of 1-2-3. WKS identifies release 1x worksheets, WK1 specifies release 2.x worksheets (Figure L.23), and WK3 denotes release 3.x worksheet files. For each release, Lotus 1-2-3 stores the file contents in a different manner. However, files for an earlier release of 1-2-3 are "upward compatible" with newer releases. Therefore, a WKS worksheet can be read and used with release 2.x of 1-2-3, which normally stores its worksheet files with the WK1 extension.

After saving your worksheet file for the very first time, then for the second and all other times the file is saved, the worksheet file on your Data Disk is **updated** with new information by writing over the top of your old file. Once a file is saved, if you make any additional revisions to your worksheet, it is necessary to save the file after the revisions; otherwise, the revisions would be lost. This requires that the old file contents be replaced by the new information. That is, the new file is written over the old file. Thus, for the *second and all other* file saves, the menu command sequence is as follows:

To save a 1-2-3 worksheet file for the second and all other times	**Press:**	/	Access main menu
	Select:	File	
	Select:	Save	Desired file activity
	Press:	\<Enter\>	Use suggested file name
	Select:	Replace	Existing file is written over with the new information

Lotus 1-2-3 displays the Replace/Cancel/Backup menu choices only when the file already exists and when the copy you are saving will be written over the existing file. When 1-2-3 suggests a file name, you may enter a new file name, if desired. Only if the new name matches an existing file will the Replace/Cancel/Backup menu appear.

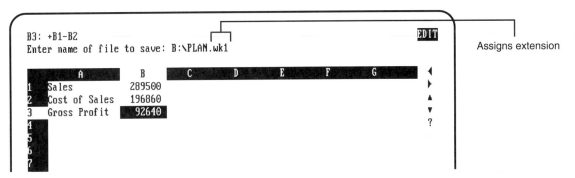

FIGURE L.23. Worksheet file named with release 2.x WK1 extension.

Keypoint!

Be sure to Save your worksheet file on your Data Disk before you leave 1-2-3. Once you Quit 1-2-3, the electronic copy in the computer's memory is lost!

L.1.14   Leaving Lotus 1-2-3

When your work in 1-2-3 is finished and you are ready to exit from this software tool, use the Quit command as described in the discussion that follows. Be sure that you are ready to leave 1-2-3 before entering this command. Otherwise, you will need to restart Lotus 1-2-3.

To exit from 1-2-3

Action: Verify that you are at the READY mode.

Press: /   Access main menu

Select: Quit   Desired option

You are returned to the 1-2-3 Access System screen. Continue like this:

Select: Exit   Desired activity

And you have successfully terminated the Lotus 1-2-3 application.

Caution Alert!

Always Quit 1-2-3 and Exit from the Access System. Do *not* just shut off your computer. If you did *not* save your worksheet file, most releases of 1-2-3 remind you of the need to perform a save when you select Quit!

L.1.15 When Things Go Wrong

Several conditions may occur while you are attempting to initially enter your business model into Lotus 1-2-3. Some of the more common difficulties and how to approach them are described below:

1. A wrong label or value has been entered in a cell. You want to replace this with a different cell content.

   a. Position the worksheet cell pointer on the cell containing the unwanted label or value.

   b. Enter the desired cell contents. The old content is replaced by the new content. You do NOT need to remove the old content prior to entering the new content.

2. You have made several menu selections and accessed an unwanted lower-level menu. You want to return to the READY mode to start over with your command.

   a. Press <Ctrl>+<Break> to exit from any level in the menu structure.

   b. You are returned to the READY mode for your next activity.

3. You are saving your worksheet file (/FS) and notice that the disk drive for storing the file is NOT the one you want.

   a. Use <Esc> or <Backspace> to remove the unwanted disk drive identifier.

   b. Enter your file name prefixed with the desired disk identifier. For example, you might enter **B:PLAN** to specify storing file **PLAN** on disk drive **B.**

L.1.16 Lesson Summary

- A Lotus worksheet is arranged as a matrix of cells into which labels and values are placed.
- The 1-2-3 Access System is the gateway to the family of programs that comprise Lotus 1-2-3.
- The main parts of the worksheet screen are the control panel and the worksheet area.
- WYSIWYG describes the manner in which you enter information on a worksheet as you want it to appear on paper. It also specifies the use of a special 1-2-3 Add-In that enchances the appearance of the data you have placed in your worksheet.
- The first character of a cell entry indicates whether the cell contains a value or a label.
- Column widths can be revised either individually or globally.
- Always save your work on your Data Disk before you Quit 1-2-3.

L.1.17 Practice Tutorial

Develop the PLAN worksheet described in this Lesson as a guided activity in a hands-on manner starting at Section L.1.10. If necessary, clear your 1-2-3 worksheet before you begin. Remember the use of the keywords as described in Lesson T.2 of the section Using Software Tools.

Task 1: Print the results as illustrated in Figure L.8 by using <Shift>+<PrtSc>

Task 2: Save this as worksheet file MYPLAN on your Data Disk.

Time Estimates

Novice: 45 minutes

Intermediate: 30 minutes

Advanced: 20 minutes

L.1.18 Practice Exercises

(1) Case: Inland Container

Business Problem: Pricing proposal
MIS Characteristics: Marketing
                    Managerial Control

Inland Container designs and manufactures custom corrugated boxes for packaging
a variety of products. Recently, Mary Montoya, a sales representative for Inland, was
contacted by Richard Rielly from Rydder Truck Rental to prepare a bid proposal
for supplying packing cartons. Rydder Truck sells cartons to their customers for use
in packing their household goods in preparation for moving. Mary decided that
a spreadsheet would be useful in developing this pricing proposal and prepared a
worksheet design by sketching out the labels and equations for her RYDDER worksheet
as follows:

	A	B	Formula Description
1	Units Sold	187300	
2	Price per Unit	3.19	
3	Sales	+B1*B2	(Units Sold*Price per Unit)
4	Cost of Sales	.73*B3	(.73*Sales)
5	Gross Profit	+B3−B4	(Sales−Cost of Sales)

Carry out the following tasks in producing Mary's RYDDER worksheet:

Task 1: If necessary, before you begin, clear the worksheet with these commands:
          / Worksheet Erase Yes (/WEY).

Task 2: Enter the labels and formulas provided by Mary's worksheet design.
          Quick check answer: Gross Profit = 161321.

Task 3: Obtain a hard copy of your result using <Shift>+<PrtSc>.

Task 4: Save this as worksheet file RYDDER on your Data Disk.

Time Estimates

Novice: 45 minutes

Intermediate: 30 minutes

Advanced: 20 minutes

(2) Case: Grant Jefferson PC

Business Problem: Expense report
MIS Characteristics: Finance
                    Operational Control

Larissa Minto is a personnel recruiter for Grant Jefferson PC certified public accountants. She travels to college campuses throughout the area to interview prospective

graduates. Last week she conducted interviews on the campus of Central State University. After each trip, Larissa completes an employee expense report. She has found that a spreadsheet provides a convenient way for preparing her report, since she can enter each individual expense and have them summed. As an example, Larissa sketched out a design of her TRAVEL expense worksheet for last week in this manner:

	A	B	C	D
1		Expense Report		
2		Thursday	Friday	Total
3	Meal Cost	8.75+15.90	5.65+6.25+12.80	+B3+C3
4	Lodging	77.85	77.85	+B4+C4
5	Mileage	.35*211	.35*215	+B5+C5
6	Telephone	6.45	11.35	+B6+C6
7				
8	Total	+B3+B4+B5+B6	+C3+C4+C5+C6	+D3+D4+D5+D6

Look at how Larissa entered the amount of each meal and the calculation of her mileage as cell formulas. She is reimbursed at the rate of 35 cents per mile for driving her own car. By entering the amount for each meal, she let 1-2-3 do her arithmetic. Then, if she happened to incorrectly enter a value, it could be more readily detected and revised.

Carry out the following tasks in creating Larissa's TRAVEL worksheet:

Task 1: If necessary, before you begin, clear the worksheet with these commands: / Worksheet Erase Yes (/WEY)

Task 2: Enter the labels, values, and formulas provided by Larissa's worksheet design.

> *Quick check answer:* Total [Total] = 372

> (*Hint:* Let 1-2-3 control the number of decimal places displayed. You will learn how to control this in Lesson L.3.)

Task 3: Obtain a hard copy of your result using <Shift>+<PrtSc>.

Task 4: Save this as worksheet file TRAVEL on your Data Disk.

Time Estimates

Novice: 45 minutes

Intermediate: 30 minutes

Advanced: 20 minutes

(3)   Case: Carnival Cruise

> Business Problem: Recruitment planning
> MIS Characteristics: Human Resources
>   Managerial Control

Carnival Cruise has experienced continuing growth during the past several years as this form of vacationing has increased in popularity. Carnival's Human Resource (HR) Department recruits employees from four sources: newspapers, radio, walk-ins, and referrals. All recruits are interviewed (unless the prospective recruit declines) and a selection decision is made. Brenda Ramereiz, the HR Department's recruiting manager, monitors the number of interviews conducted by recruitment source. She wants to know which source yields the most hires and the average cost per hire to assist her in planning future recruiting activities. Brenda prepared a worksheet design by sketching out the labels, values, and formulas for her RECRUIT worksheet as follows:

	A	B	C	D	E
1		Newspaper	Radio	Walk-ins	Referrals
2	Interviews	1260	930	330	710
3	Offers	318	142	80	276
4	Hires	226	96	46	262
5	Total Cost	73080	89280	11380	27680
6					
7	Percent Offers	+B3/B2	+C3/C2	+D3/D2	+E3/E2
8	Yield Ratio	+B4/B2	+C4/C2	+D4/D2	+E4/E2
9	Cost/Interview	+B5/B2	+C5/C2	+D5/D2	+E5/E2
10	Cost/Hire	+B5/B4	+C5/C4	+D5/D4	+E5/E4

Perform the following tasks in developing Brenda's RECRUIT worksheet:

Task 1: If necessary, before you begin, clear the worksheet with these commands: / Worksheet Erase Yes (/WEY)

Task 2: Set the column width to 14 spaces with the command: / Worksheet Global Column-Width 14 (/WGC14)

Task 3: Enter the labels and formulas provided by Brenda's worksheet design.

Quick check answer: Yield Ratio [Referrals] = .369

(*Hint:* Let 1-2-3 control the number of decimal places displayed. You will learn how to control this in Lesson L.3.)

Task 4: Obtain a hard copy of your result using <Shift> + <PrtSc>.

Task 5: Save this as worksheet file RECRUIT on your Data Disk.

Time Estimates

Novice: 45 minutes

Intermediate: 30 minutes

Advanced: 20 minutes

(4)   Case: Taco Grande

Business Problem: Materials purchasing
MIS Characteristics: Production/Operations
Operational Control

Taco Grande is a fast-food restaurant with Mexican cuisine that provides dine-in, carry-out, and delivery service. Each Tuesday, the restaurant's manager, Don Chilito, prepares an order for the number of pounds of meat and cheese he wants delivered from their supplier, Mid-Central Sysco Food Services. Don has developed a method of tracking and forecasting the number of each menu item they expect to sell during the next week for use in planning his order. The amount of meat and cheese used as ingredients in preparing each item is indicated in this table:

Item	Units	Meat	Cheese
Taco	1740	3 oz	1.25 oz
Burrito	940	5 oz	1.5 oz
Enchilada	700	4.5 oz	1.25 oz
Tostado	500	2.5 oz	.75 oz
Tamale	620	3.5 oz	1.25 oz

Don wants to prepare a spreadsheet to assist him in determining the number of pounds of meat and cheese to order each Tuesday. He prepared a worksheet design by sketching out the labels and equations for his TACO worksheet as follows:

	A	B	C	D
1	Item	Units	Meat	Cheese
2	Taco	1740	3*B2	1.25*B2
3	Burrito	940	5*B3	1.5 *B3
4	Enchilada	700	4.5*B4	1.25*B4
5	Tostado	500	2.5*B5	.75*B5
6	Tamale	620	3.5*B6	1.25*B6
7				
8	Total oz		+C2+C3+C4+C5+C6	+D2+D3+D4+D5+D6
9				
10	Total lb		+C8/16	+D8/16

Observe the manner in which Don included the recipe for each item in his worksheet, and then review how he converted his order to pounds in cells **C10** and **D10**.

Perform the following tasks in developing Don's TACO worksheet:

Task 1: If necessary, before you begin, clear the worksheet with these commands: /Worksheet Erase Yes (/WEY)

Task 2: Enter the labels and formulas provided by Don's worksheet design.

Quick check answer: Total lb [Cheese] = 350.625

Task 3: Obtain a hard copy of your result using <Shift>+<PrtSc>.

Task 4: Save this as worksheet file TACO on your Data Disk.

Time Estimates

Novice: 45 minutes

Intermediate: 30 minutes

Advanced: 20 minutes

L.1.19 Case Application

Case: Thornton Wilder & Company PC

Business Problem: Audit report preparation

MIS Characteristics: Finance

                    Operational Control

Management Functions: Controlling

Tools Skills: Labels

          Values

          Formulas

Thornton Wilder & Company (TWC) is an international public accounting firm with offices in most major metropolitan areas. One of the primary business services provided by TWC is conducting accounting audits for clients. These audits consist of an independent examination of the accounting records and other evidence relating to the operations of a client's business to support the expression of an impartial expert opinion about the reliability of the client's financial statements. The purpose of an audit is to determine whether the financial statements of the client company have been presented in accordance with generally accepted accounting principles.

Charles Zinger is the TWC manager in the Houston office, who is in charge of the audit team conducting an audit for Desert Energy, Inc. Desert Energy is a pioneer in the independent power industry specializing in "clean coal" gasification and gas-turbine powered cogeneration of electrical and steam energy. Gas-fired cogeneration is highly efficient because it uses waste energy and saves fuel, while it is environmentally clean and operationally flexible. Desert Energy has a total capacity of approximately 960 megawatts of electricity and two million pounds per hour of steam. This is a uniquely vertically integrated company with all the skills necessary to run power plants for the long term, from initial development to ownership and operation.

Charlie's responsibilities include reviewing and approving the workpapers prepared by the Desert Energy audit team. Workpapers serve as the means of recording the field work performed in obtaining the audit evidence. Charlie has assigned Julia Schultz, an audit associate, the task of developing workpapers that summarize Desert's operations. Julia has been performing audits since she joined TWC four years ago and recently completed the requirements for her CPA. When she first joined WTC, her orientation including learning the specific audit procedures used at WTC and the use of a personal computer in preparing audit workpapers. Each audit associate is provided with a personal computer which they take with them to their client to assist in workpaper preparation through the engagement.

Julia uses a 1-2-3 spreadsheet in producing financial statement workpapers. As she examines a client's records, the evidence collected, such as Net Sales or Administrative Expenses, is entered in her spreadsheet. If further examination should produce a different value than the one initially entered, this can be readily revised in her 1-2-3 worksheet.

In preparing for the Desert Energy audit, Julia obtained the layout of a Statement of Earnings from the illustrative financial statements in Thornton Wilder's *Accounting and Auditing Manual*. Although she has participated in a number of audits, the procedures of TWC require this review to ensure that their audit standards are being followed. The layout she selected with Charlie's assistance for use with Desert Energy is this:

Example Company, Inc.
STATEMENT OF EARNINGS
(Dollars in thousands)

	19X2	19X1	Increase
Net sales	XXXXXX	XXXXXX	XXXXXX
Cost of sales	XXXXXX	XXXXXX	XXXXXX
Gross Profit	XXXXXX	XXXXXX	XXXXXX
Operating expenses			
Marketing	XXXXXX	XXXXXX	XXXXXX
Research and Develop	XXXXXX	XXXXXX	XXXXXX
Administrative	XXXXXX	XXXXXX	XXXXXX
Operating Profit	XXXXXX	XXXXXX	XXXXXX
Other income	XXXXXX	XXXXXX	XXXXXX
Earnings before tax	XXXXXX	XXXXXX	XXXXXX
Income tax	XXXXXX	XXXXXX	XXXXXX
NET EARNINGS	XXXXXX	XXXXXX	XXXXXX

During the past several weeks, Julia has been collecting evidential matter through inspection, observation, and inquires. Following TWC's preferred report layout, she has sketched out her 1-2-3 worksheet design in this manner:

	A	B	C	D
1			' Desert Energy, Inc.	
2			'STATEMENT OF EARNINGS	
3			' (Dollars in thousands)	
4		"19X2	"19X1	"Increase
5		"_ _ _ _ _	"_ _ _ _ _	"_ _ _ _ _
6	'Net sales	727551	606184	+B6−C6
7	'Cost of sales	506839	420871	+B7−C7
8		"_ _ _ _ _	"_ _ _ _ _	"_ _ _ _ _
9	' Gross Profit	+B6−B7	+C6−C7	+D6−D7
10	'Operating expenses			
11	' Marketing	89790	73308	+B11−C11
12	' Research and Develop	20285	13886	+B12−C12
13	' Administrative	52358	41762	+B13−C13
14		"_ _ _ _ _	"_ _ _ _ _	"_ _ _ _ _
15	' Operating Profit	+B9−(B11+B12+B13)	+C9−(C11+C12+C13)	+B15−C15
16	'Other income	9653	2559	+B16−C16
17	' Earnings before tax	+B15+B16	+C15+C16	+D15+D16
18	'Income tax	30389	28637	+B16−C18
19		"_ _ _ _ _	"_ _ _ _ _	"_ _ _ _ _
20	' NET EARNINGS	+B17−B18	+C17−C18	+D17−D18

In this worksheet design, the dollar amounts are those that Julia has collected as a part of her audit activities, whereas the formulas are those generally accepted accounting equations applied in computing these selected financial statement accounts. Julia is ready to enter this worksheet into 1-2-3 and to produce a hard copy of the workpaper for her scheduled weekly review with Charlie.

Tasks

1. In preparation for entering the labels, values, and formulas for the Statement of Earnings, make sure you clear your worksheet. Then, set the global column width to 14 and the column width for column **A** to 24.

2. Construct the audit worksheet by entering the labels, values, and formulas provided by Julia.
   (*Hint:* The apostophe (') causes labels to be left-justified within a cell, whereas the quote (") causes labels to be right-justified. You'll learn more about this in Lesson L.3.)
   Quick check answer: NET EARNINGS [Increase] = 7264.

3. Produce a hard copy of your results by using <Shift>+<PrtSc>.

4. Save this as worksheet file DESERT on your Data Disk.

5. Review your output and determine which operating expense increased the most. Circle this expense on the hard copy of your results.

6. (*Optional*) Write a short narrative describing how you might improve the audit report by adding one or more columns to determine where the *most significant* changes occurred.

Time Estimates

Novice: 90 minutes

Intermediate: 60 minutes

Advanced: 45 minutes

Building and Printing Worksheets

CONTENT

- Loading a 1-2-3 Worksheet File
- Clearing the 1-2-3 Worksheet
- Building Equations by Pointing
- Cell Ranges
- Printing 1-2-3 Results
- Printing 1-2-3 Cell Formulas
- Using SmartIcons to Retrieve Files and Print Worksheets
- When Things Go Wrong

L.2.1 Loading a 1-2-3 Worksheet File

The PLAN worksheet file that Chris constructed and saved for Good Morning Products can be retrieved and reloaded into 1-2-3 for continued use. An existing worksheet file is loaded from your Data Disk in this manner:

Action: Start 1-2-3, if necessary, and proceed to the READY mode.

Action: Set your default disk drive/directory with the / File Directory (/FD) command, as required.

To load or retrieve an existing worksheet file

Press:	/	Access main menu
Select:	File	
Select:	\<Retrieve\>	Desired file activity

When you retrieve an existing file, 1-2-3 presents you with a list of available worksheet files (Figure L.24). You then select the desired file from this list in this manner:

| **Move to:** | PLAN | File name of desired file |
| **Select:** | \<Enter\> | Select file |

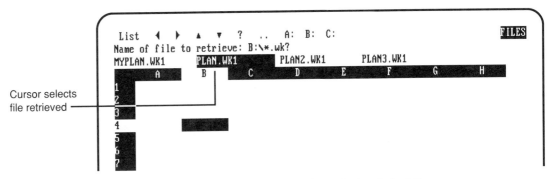

Cursor selects
file retrieved

FIGURE L.24. List of available files for retrieving desired file.

This / File Retrieve (/FR) command loads your selected worksheet file into the memory of 1-2-3 and makes it ready for your use.

L.2.2 Clearing the 1-2-3 Worksheet

When you build a 1-2-3 worksheet, it is stored in your computer's memory. Lotus 1-2-3 provides you with the ability to clear or to erase your current worksheet so that you can immediately begin work on another one. This is the equivalent of leaving 1-2-3 with the Quit command and then restarting it to obtain a completely new worksheet. A new worksheet is obtained in this manner:

Action: Make sure you are at the READY mode and you have the PLAN worksheet loaded.

To clear or erase your current worksheet		
Press:	/	Access main menu
Select:	Worksheet	Menu containing desired command
Select:	Erase	Desired action
Select:	Yes	Confirmation to really perform the erase

The worksheet is blanked out or deleted from the memory of your computer. It still exists on your Data Disk, as long as you performed a / File Save (/FS) prior to issuing the / Worksheet Erase Yes (/WEY). You now have a new, "clean" worksheet with the column width and all other characteristics set to the 1-2-3 default values.

Caution Alert! Be sure that you have saved your worksheet file (/FS) before you perform a / Worksheet Erase Yes (/WEY). If you have not saved it, you will need to reenter it!

L.2.3 Building Equations by Pointing

Lotus 1-2-3 allows you to create equations either by typing them, as you have done thus far, or by entering cell names into equations by **pointing** to them with the cell pointer. Let's rebuild the Good Morning Products worksheet by using pointing to create the formulas. This method may also be used to change or to revise the contents of cells.

Action: Verify that you have a new, "clean" worksheet with the /WEY command and then set the width of column **A** to 14 spaces.

Action: In cells **A1** through **A3** enter each label in its designated cell:

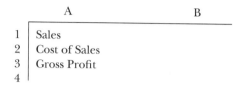

	A	B
1	Sales	
2	Cost of Sales	
3	Gross Profit	
4		

When building a worksheet like this, a common practice is to enter the labels in column **A,** before you begin to enter your formulas in column **B.** This helps to ensure that you are building correct formulas in the desired cell locations. This method of worksheet development is strongly suggested, although 1-2-3 does *not* require this approach.

Action: Place the value 289500 in cell **B1.**

To build an equation using pointing			
Move to:	**B2**		Location of formulas when completed
Type:	.68*		Begin formula
Press:	<up>		

Observe that the cell pointer moves to cell **B1. B1** appears as part of the equation on the Edit Line. The Status Indicator displays POINT, as portrayed in Figure L.25.

Press:	<Enter>	Complete specifying formula

The equation is entered as the cell content and the result appears in the worksheet. The cell pointer has returned to cell **B2,** where the equation was being entered.
Now let's build the next formula using pointing.

To build a formula containing only cell names using pointing		
Move to:	**B3**	Location of next formula
Press:	+	Plus is used to specify that a value or formula is being entered
Press:	<up>	Edit line displays: +B2
Press:	<up>	Edit line displays: +B1
Press:	–	Desired arithmetic operator

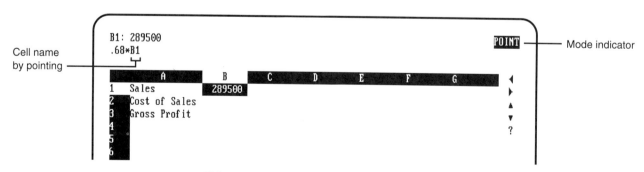

FIGURE L.25. Building a formula with pointing.

Notice that the cell pointer returns to cell **B3**.

Press:	<up>	Point to next part of formula
Press:	<Enter>	Complete specifying formula

The equation **+B1 − B2** has been placed into cell **B3**.

Caution Alert!

> Before you begin to enter an equation by pointing, be sure that the cell pointer is located *at the cell where you want the formula when you are finished!*

If you have mouse support, you may use your mouse to point to the desired cell when building equations by pointing. Merely move the mouse pointer to the cell to be included in your formula and click the <left button>. You still need to type the arithmetic operators before pointing to the desired cell using your mouse. Clicking the <left button> a second time, after selecting a cell for inclusion in your formula, completes the specification of the formula in the same manner as pressing <Enter>. If you have a mouse, let's build the formula in cell **B3** by pointing with the mouse.

To build a formula by pointing with a mouse

Click:	**B3**	Location of next formula
Press:	+	Plus is used to specify that a value or formula is being entered
Click:	**B1**	Edit line displays: +B1
Press:	−	Desired arithmetic operator

Notice that the cell pointer returns to cell **B3**.

Click:	**B2**	Point to next part of formula
Double-Click:	<left button>	Complete specifying formula

Again, the equation **+B1−B2** has been placed into cell **B3**.

Pointing is the *preferred method* of building equations. In general, it *reduces your chances of committing an error*. For example, it is very easy to type **D21** when you mean **D12**. It is much more difficult to point to the wrong cell.

Action: Save this second creation of the worksheet for Good Morning Products as the file PLAN. You will need to replace the old version of PLAN with this new version.

Keypoint!

> Equations can be created either by *typing* the equation or by *pointing* to cell names. Pointing to cell names usually *reduces your chances of making an error* in the cell name!

L.2.4   Cell Ranges

When building or modifying a worksheet, you will frequently want to operate on a group of cells, rather than on the entire worksheet. For example, with the Good Morning Products PLAN worksheet occupying only three rows and two columns, you do *not* want to print all 256 columns and 8192 rows of the 1-2-3 worksheet when producing a printed report of these results. (Imagine the amount of paper that would be wasted.) In 1-2-3 a group of cells is known as a **range** of cells. Lotus 1-2-3 provides a method for readily referencing cell ranges by using a shorthand, convenient notation. A **range** of cells is any **rectangular** group of cells, such as that shown in Figure L.26. Examples are

- A single row of cells
- A single column of cells
- A rectangular block of cells composed of many rows and columns
- A single cell

Keypoint!   A range of cells MUST be a *rectangular* block!

A range of cells is described by its upper-left corner and lower-right corner. Examples of ranges are

- A1..D1   Row of cells
- A1..A20   Column of cells
- A1..D20   Rectangular block of cells
- A1..A1   Single cell

The ellipsis (..) means "through." That is, **A1..D20** means cells **A1** through **D20.** The ellipsis is also used in 1-2-3 to indicate that a range is **anchored**. Once the cell pointer has been **anchored,** then it can be expanded or stretched over any desired range of cells. The cell range is highlighted in the worksheet area, as illustrated in Figure L.26, to visually indicate the specified cell range. Anchoring can be removed by pressing <Esc> to allow a new cell to be specified as the beginning location for expanding the cell pointer. Anchoring is explored in the next section. For now, remember that the ellipsis means "through" and is used to denote anchoring.

Keypoint!   An anchored cell pointer, such as **A1..A1,** can be expanded or stretched over a desired range of cells!

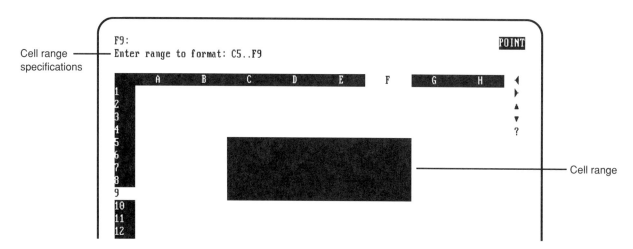

FIGURE L.26. Range of cells C5..F9.

L.2.5   Printing 1-2-3 Results

Lotus 1-2-3 incorporates the WYSIWYG (What You See Is What You Get) method of reporting as described in the previous lesson. Your report needs to appear on your screen in *exactly* the same *arrangement* as you want it printed. That is, you need to enter labels, values, and formulas into cell locations that occupy the desired position for your final output report. In this lesson, the WYSIWYG approach is used to indicate the general procedure of arranging labels and values in cells in the desired location for printing them as a management-style report.

Let's look at how Chris can obtain a hard copy printout of the PLAN worksheet for Good Morning Products. The first step is to specify the range of cells to be printed. The second step is actually to print the desired worksheet area.

Action: Be sure that PLAN is your active worksheet and that you are in the READY mode.

To access the Print menu	**Press:**	/	Access main menu
	Select:	Print	General activity to be performed

The Print menu appears with two choices: Printer and File. By selecting Printer the report is directed to your printer. If you select File, the report is written as a text file to disk. You could then use the DOS Print command to have it printed or you might load the text print file into your word processing program, make any desired changes, and then print it from your word processor.

Continue with the printing operation like this:

To request hard copy, printed output	**Select:**	Printer	Choose sending output directly to printer

When you select Printer, a Print Settings dialog box (Figure L.27) appears if you have Release 2.2 or higher. This dialog box provides a summary of all the current printing options you have specified, such as the range of cells to be printed.

Now let's actually request the cell range to be printed for the hard copy report.

To specify the cell range for printing	**Select:**	Range	Specify the area of the worksheet to print
	Press:	<Home>	Position cell pointer at the upper-left corner of the range to be printed
	Press:	.	The period anchors the cell pointer
	Move to:	F7	Position cell pointer at the cell in the lower-right corner of the print range
	Press:	<Enter>	Complete range specification

Observe that the cell pointer expanded over your selected range of cells, as illustrated in Figure L.28.

Keypoint!	With the keyboard, a cell range is *anchored* by pressing the period key <.>. A previously anchored range is *unanchored* with the <Esc> to allow the beginning location of the range to be changed before anchoring the cell range!

If you have mouse support, after selecting Range, you may specify a range of cells by highlighting it. A cell range is **highlighted** by moving the mouse pointer to the upper-left corner of your cell range. Press and hold the <left button> while you drag

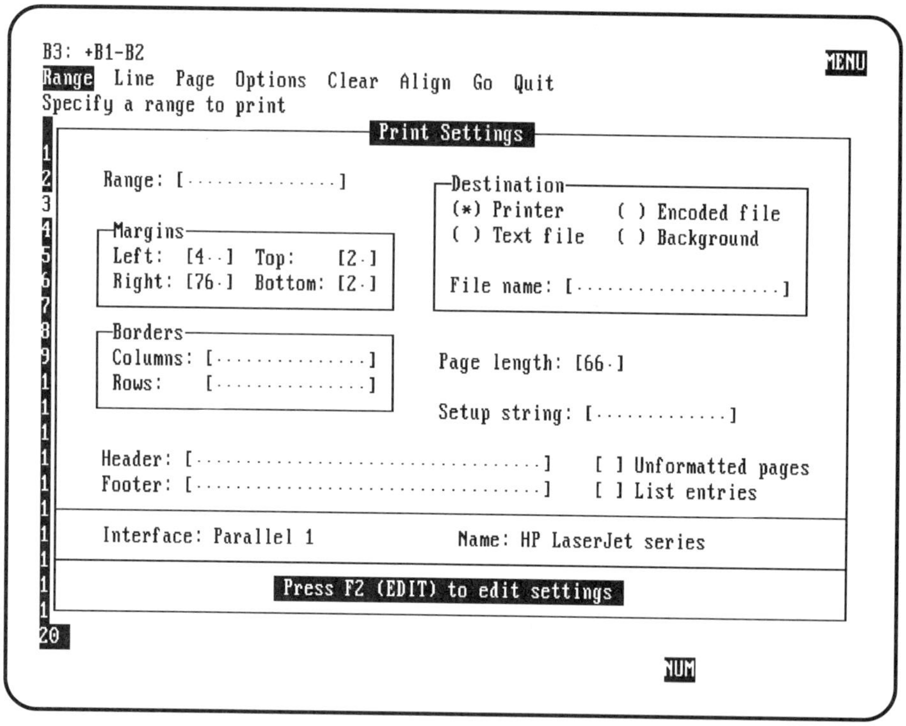

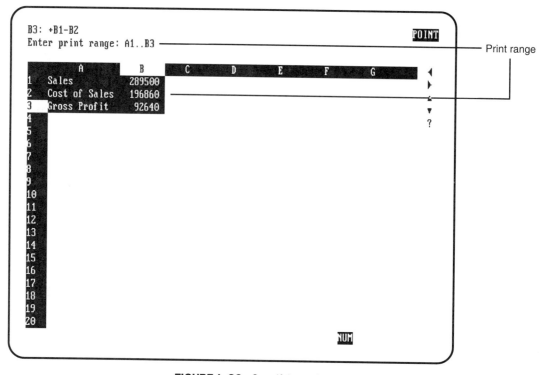

FIGURE L.27. Print settings dialog box.

FIGURE L.28. Specifying print range.

the mouse pointer to the lower-right corner of your range. Release the <left button>. Then click the <left button> to indicate completion of your range specification. Clicking the <right button> is equivalent to pressing <Esc> and cancels the current command. For example, if you release the <left button> before completely identifying the range, clicking the <right button> would allow you to proceed to reenter the range specification.

If you have a mouse available, let's specify the cell range for printing using your mouse.

To specify a cell range for printing using a mouse	**Select:**	Range	Specify the area of worksheet to print
	Move mouse pointer to:	**A1**	Position *mouse* pointer at the upper-left corner of the range to be printed
	Drag to:	**F7**	Hold down the left mouse button while you drag the cell pointer with the mouse
	Click:	<left button>	Complete range specification

When you complete the range specification, you are returned to the Print menu (Figure L.27). You do *not* return to READY. This is your first encounter with this type of 1-2-3 menu. Also, observe how this menu contains the command Quit. Selecting Quit here means to quit or leave *this menu*, and *not* 1-2-3. In 1-2-3, menus that operate in this manner are known as **sticky menus**. Lotus 1-2-3 uses **sticky menus** because it assumes that you will want to make *additional selections from the same menu*. Selecting Quit from a sticky menu causes you to back up one level in the menu structure. From the Print menu, selecting Quit would return you to the READY mode.

Keypoint!	Lower level command menus in 1-2-3 that contain QUIT are **sticky menus.** You will return to this menu to select additional commands until you either select QUIT or press <Esc>, which backs you up one level in the menu hierarchy!

Action: Before your report is actually printed, you need to set up your printer. Make sure that it is attached to your computer, is turned on, and has paper. If you have a dot matrix or similar printer, adjust the perforation to the silver bar or print head of your printer. This will be the top of the page. If you are using a laser or inkjet printer, make sure that it is set to begin printing on a new page.

To actually print a specified cell range	**Select:**	Align	Advise 1-2-3 that the print head is at the top of a new page
	Select:	Go	Cause printing to take place
	Select:	Page	Advance paper to the top of the next page
	Select:	Page	Advance paper a second time; this option ejects an additional page so that you can easily rip it off your printer; select this command only if necessary
To exit from the Print menu and return to the READY mode	**Select:**	Quit	Leave the Print menu

Although you might use the form feed button on your printer to advance the page, it is suggested that you do *not*. Lotus 1-2-3 does *not* know that you pushed the form feed, but it does remember the Page command. If you push the form feed button, you will need to keep manually adjusting the top perforation of the paper. The resulting

Sales	92640
Cost of Sales	196860
Gross Profit	289500

FIGURE L.29. Printed results.

report for PLAN is illustrated in Figure L.29. This procedure for printing your 1-2-3 solution is summarized in Figure L.30.

Action: Save your PLAN worksheet file, which will store these print settings as part of the saved worksheet file.

Keypoint! | Use the Page command to eject the paper in your printer to a new page. Lotus 1-2-3 keeps track of pages when you use this command!

L.2.6   Printing 1-2-3 Cell Formulas

Lotus 1-2-3 displays the formula only for *one cell at a time in the control panel*. This makes it difficult for you to review all your formulas to ensure that they are correct. If the formulas are in error, your printed results are useless. By printing the cell formulas you can obtain a listing of all of the cell contents at one time. This allows you to *document* the formulas used in obtaining the results displayed in your reports. You can more readily answer questions about how cell formulas were computed. Also, by documenting your worksheet with a listing of the labels and formulas in the worksheet, you have a backup copy in the event that the copy of the worksheet file on your Data Disk is damaged or destroyed.

Let's obtain a listing of the cell contents for Chris's PLAN worksheet.

To initiate printing

Press:	`<Ctrl>+<Break>`	Make sure you are at READY
Press:	`/`	Access main menu
Select:	`Print`	Desired activity
Select:	`Printer`	Specify destination of output

To review the cell range for printing

Select:	`Range`	Identify area to print

1. Initiate printing from the READY mode with: / Print Printer
2. Specify range of cells to print
   a. **Select:** `Range`   (Desired option)
   b. **Action:** Stretch cell pointer over range to be printed
3. Setup printer, as appropriate
   a. Make sure printer is attached to your computer
   b. Turn the printer ON
   c. Adjust the perforation to the top of page
   d. **Select:** `Align`   (Cause 1-2-3 to recognize top of new page)
4. Print report, **select:** `Go`   (Cause printing of report)
5. Advance paper or eject page from printer, select: Page (you may need to repeat this to sufficiently advance the paper for your printer)
6. Exit from the Print menu, **select:** `Quit`

FIGURE L.30. Summary of printing Lotus 1-2-3 solution.

```
A1:       'Sales
B1:       289500
A2:       'Cost of Sales
B2:       0.68*B1
A3:       'Gross Profit
B3:       +B1-B2
```

FIGURE L.31. Cell-Formula listing.

The Range you previously entered for printing the solution results should appear. This Range is stored with the worksheet when you performed a Save. The same Range remains in effect until you perform a / Worksheet Erase Yes (/WEY), until you / Quit (/Q) from 1-2-3, or until you change it.

Press:	`<Enter>`	Accept indicated cell range

Select:	`Options`	Get desired menu
Select:	`Other`	Obtain menu for selecting printing option
Select:	`Cell-Formulas`	Specifies that cell formulas will be printed instead of the results as displayed on the screen
Action:		Make sure the printer is still attached and turned on. If the paper is not appropriately positioned as described above, position the paper.
Select:	`Quit`	Return to Print menu

To request printing of all formulas

Select:	`Go`	Cause cell formulas to print
Select:	`Page`	Advance paper
Select:	`Page`	Again, advance paper so that it can be easily removed, if necessary
Select:	`Quit`	Leave Print menu

To actually print the cell formulas

The list of cell formulas for PLAN is produced as portrayed in Figure L.31.

The selection of the Cell-Formulas is a toggle switch. Once you have selected this command, it *remains in effect* until you change it. Hence, if you request another printing of the report, you will again obtain the cell formulas unless you select the As-Displayed command instead of the Cell-Formulas command. Figure L.32 describes the Print Option Other menu choices, while Figure L.33 summarizes the steps used to obtain a report of your cell formulas.

Menu Selection	Action
As-Displayed	Prints the data as it appears on your screen
Cell-Formula	Prints the cell contents of each nonblank cell in the print range
Formatted	Prints output with page breaks, headers, and footers
Unformatted	Prints a continuous output *without* page breaks, headers, or footers; often used when printing a text file where you do not want blank lines in the file for page breaks

FIGURE L.32. / Print printer options other menu choices.

1. Initiate printing with: / Print Printer (you may skip this step if you are already at the Print menu)
2. Specify range of cells to print
   a. **Select:**   `Range`   (Desired option)
   b. **Action:**   Stretch cell pointer over range to be printed
3. Specify that cell formulas are to be printed
   a. **Select:**   `Options`   (Obtain desired menu)
   b. **Select:**   `Other`   (Choose menu for desired printing)
   c. **Select:**   `Cell-Formulas`   (Desired choice)
   d. **Select:**   `Quit`   (Return to Print menu)
4. Set up printer, as appropriate
   a. Make sure printer is attached to your computer
   b. Turn the printer ON
   c. Adjust the perforation to the top of page
   d. **Select:**   `Align`   (Cause printing of report)
5. Print report, **select:**   `Go`   (Cause 1-2-3 to recognize top of new page)
6. Advance paper or eject page from printer, **select:**   `Page`   (you may need to repeat this to sufficiently advance the paper for your printer)
7. Reset printing to your solution results to avoid accidentally printing cell formulas in your next report
   a. **Select:**   `Options`   (Obtain desired menu)
   b. **Select:**   `Other`   (Choose menu for desired printing)
   c. **Select:**   `As-Displayed`   (Desired choice)
   d. **Select:**   `Quit`   (Return to Print menu)
8. Exit from the Print menu, **select:**   `Quit`

FIGURE L.33. Summary of printing 1-2-3 cell contents.

Keypoint!   The / Print Printer Options Other Cell-Formulas (/PPOOC) command is used to *document* the contents of your worksheet for reference and backup!

L.2.7   Using SmartIcons to Retrieve Files and Print Worksheets

SmartIcons provide a shortcut method to execute many commonly used 1-2-3 commands by merely using the mouse to click the desired icon. These SmartIcons are available beginning with Release 2.4 as an Add-In. If your release of 1-2-3 does not include this Add-In, you may still want to read this section to get an overview of its use. When it is available, this Add-In must be attached before the SmartIcons are displayed on your screen for selection using your mouse. When the SmartIcon Add-In is attached, an **icon palette** appears along the right side of your 1-2-3 worksheet area, as illustrated previously in Figure L.10. If the WYSIWYG Add-In is also attached, then different pictures are used for the SmartIcons, as illustrated in Figure L.12.

Caution Alert!   The SmartIcon Add-In uses memory space. When SmartIcons are attached, the maximum size of your worksheet is reduced. Attaching this Add-In may also limit the use of other Add-Ins or the Undo feature at the same time!

If a SmartIcon palette does not appear with your 1-2-3 worksheet, then you need to attach or activate this feature. Let's see how this is accomplished by starting from the READY mode.

To attach the SmartIcon palette	**Press:**	/	Access main menu
	Select:	Add-In	Desired action
	Select:	Attach	Desired activity
	Select:	ICONS.ADN	Desired Add-In
	Select:	No-Key	Desired option

When an Add-In is attached, 1-2-3 allows you to assign it a hot-key. Hot-keys allow you to use the <Alt> and a function key to execute the Add-In once it has been attached. The No-Key option is selected because it is not required with your use of this Add-In.

| **Select:** | Quit | Complete Attaching Add-In and return to the READY mode |

The SmartIcon palette should now appear with your worksheet.

Lotus 1-2-3 actually provides more than one icon palette. Ten different pages or palettes are available. (When WYSIWYG is used with SmartIcons, then only seven palettes are available.) Each icon palette is identified by page number at the bottom of the palette. Different palettes contain different combinations of the 1-2-3 SmartIcons. Let's see how you can change the icon palette displayed by using your mouse.

| To display a different SmartIcon palette | **Move to:** | <right icon arrow> | Position your mouse pointer on the arrow to the right of the icon palette page number |
| | **Click:** | <right icon arrow> | Desired activity |

This causes the second SmartIcon palette to appear. Now continue to review the other icon palettes.

Click:	<right icon arrow>	Desired activity
Click:	<right icon arrow>	Desired activity
Action:		Using the <right icon arrow> and the <left icon arrow>, scroll through your entire set of different icon palettes. When you have finished looking at the different palettes, return to icon palette one (1).

The SmartIcons explored in this Lesson are the File Save, File Retrieve, and Print icons, as shown in Figure L.34. Lotus 1-2-3 provides you with a means to determine the action of each SmartIcon by displaying a description of a selected icon's action (Figure L.35). Let's look at the description for the File Retrieve icon.

SmartIcon	WYSIWYG SmartIcon	Command	Description
		File Save	Saves the current worksheet file.
		File Retrieve	Retrieves the current worksheet file.
PRN		Print	Print the current range or a highlighted range.

FIGURE L.34. SmartIcons used in this lesson.

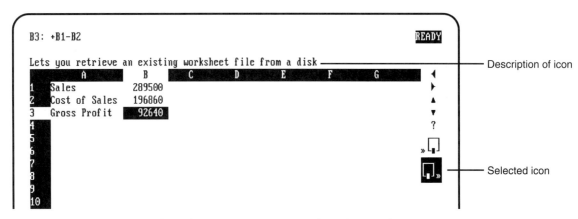

FIGURE L.35. Display Description of File Retrieve SmartIcon.

To display the description of a SmartIcon	**Move to:**	File Retrieve SmartIcon
		That is, position the mouse pointer on this icon
	Press and hold:	<right mouse button>
		The desired description is displayed as long as you keep your mouse button depressed
	Action:	Display the description of the File Save and Print icons. Then look at the descriptions of several other icons of your choice.

L.2.7.1. Retrieving and Saving Worksheets

The File Save and File Retrieve SmartIcons let you quickly perform these activities. Let's learn how they are used.

Action: To get ready to use these SmartIcons, make sure the PLAN worksheet with the print settings is your currently active worksheet file.

To save a worksheet file using a SmartIcon	**Move to:**	File Save SmartIcon Position the mouse pointer on this icon
	Click:	<left mouse button> Select the icon
	Select:	Replace The file already exists

Your current worksheet file with the same file name is stored to your Data Disk. This or any other worksheet file can be retrieved from your Data Disk.

To retrieve a worksheet file using a SmartIcon	**Move to:**	File Retrieve SmartIcon
		Position the mouse pointer on this icon
	Click:	<left mouse button> Actually select the icon

This causes a list of available worksheet files to be displayed (Figure L.36).

	Move to:	PLAN Desired worksheet file
	Click:	<left mouse button> Select the file

The PLAN worksheet is retrieved as your current worksheet file and ready for your use.

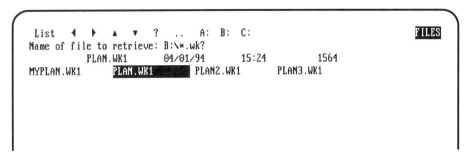

FIGURE L.36. List of available worksheet files.

L.2.7.2. Printing Worksheets

The Print SmartIcon lets you print your worksheet in two different ways:

1. Print the current range established previously with the / Print Printer Range (/PPR) command.
2. Print a highlighted range changing your previously established range.

Other than changing the print range, all other print settings remain the same as those selected under the / Print Printer (/PP) command. Selecting the Print SmartIcon is like selecting Go from the Print menu. Let's examine the use of the Print SmartIcon.

To print the current range using the Print SmartIcon		

Move to: Print SmartIcon   Position the mouse pointer on this icon

Click: <left mouse button> Select the icon

The worksheet is printed. However, since the print range does not print an entire page, the page is not ejected.

Action: Eject the page using the / Print Printer Page (/PPP) command or by manually ejecting the page from your printer.

A desired cell range may be printed regardless of the range previously established with the 1-2-3 print command. This is accomplished by highlighting the desired cell range before selecting the Print icon. You **highlight** a cell range by positioning the mouse pointer at one corner of the range and dragging the pointer to the opposite corner of your cell range while you press and hold the <left mouse button>.

To print a highlighted cell range using the Print SmartIcon

Move to: **A1**   Position mouse pointer for highlighting desired range

Drag to: **B3**   Use mouse to highlight desired range

Select: Print SmartIcon   Desired activity

Action: Eject page from your printer to obtain the printed copy.

SmartIcons provided a shortcut method for performing these file and print activities. If you have SmartIcons available, choose either the SmartIcon or keyboard command method of carrying out these activities in 1-2-3, since they are merely alternative ways of performing the same actions.

Action: If desired, you may now Quit from 1-2-3.

L.2.8   When Things Go Wrong

Several situations may arise while you are building formulas and printing results. Some of the more common difficulties and how to recover from them are described below:

1. When you issue the / File Retrieve (/FR) command, the desired worksheet filename does not appear in the list of files.

   a. Use <Ctrl> + <Break> or <Esc> to exit from the /FR command.

   b. Verify that you have your Data Disk inserted in the desired disk drive.

   c. Use the / File Directory (/FD) command to check your default directory. If this is not the correct directory, set the desired drive/directory.

   d. Reissue the / File Retrieve (/FR) command and select the desired file.

2. The formula you were building by using pointing ended up in the wrong cell. This occurs when your worksheet cell pointer was at the wrong location as you *started* building the equation.

   a. Position the cell pointer on the cell containing the unwanted formula.

   b. Remove the unwanted formula with the command / Range Erase <Enter> (/RE) or by pressing <Delete> (Release 2.3 or higher). Because the cell pointer was located at the unwanted cell, you do not need to change the range to be erased.

   c. Position the cell pointer at the cell location where you want the formula.

   d. Reenter the equation by using either pointing or typing, as desired.

3. You performed a print and the cell formulas were printed when you wanted your solution printed. The / Print Printer Option Other (/PPOO) has been set to Cell-Formulas. This is a toggle setting, with the last setting remaining in effect until it is changed.

   a. Access the Print Option Other (/PPOO) menu and select As-Displayed.

   b. Reissue the commands to print your report.

4. When you print your report several blank pages are printed. This usually occurs when the print range is larger than necessary and includes a number of blank cells.

   a. Change your print range so that it does *not* include extra blank rows and columns.

   b. Reissue the commands to print your report.

L.2.9   Lesson Summary

- An existing 1-2-3 worksheet file is loaded into memory with the / File Retrieve (/FR) command. A list of existing worksheet filenames appears for your selection.

- The / Worksheet Erase Yes (/WEY) command is used to initialize a blank worksheet with default settings without leaving 1-2-3.

- Always be sure that your work is saved on your Data Disk before you perform a / Worksheet Erase Yes (/WEY).

- Formulas can be created by either typing cell names or by pointing at desired cells.

- Building formulas by pointing is usually less error prone than typing them.

- A range of cells is any rectangular group of cells, such as a range of cells to be printed as a report.

- When using the keyboard, a cell range is anchored by using the period (.) so that the cell pointer can be expanded over the desired range of cells.

- Cell contents and cell formulas may be printed by using the Print menu.

- SmartIcons provide a shortcut method of executing commands, such as those for saving and retrieving files and for printing a cell range.

L.2.10 Practice Tutorial

Develop the PLAN worksheet described in this Lesson as a guided activity in a hands-on manner. Clear your 1-2-3 worksheet before you begin. Remember the utilization of the keywords as described in Lesson T.2 of the section Using Software Tools.

Task 1: Print the results as illustrated in Figure L.29.

Task 2: Print the cell formulas as shown in Figure L.31.

Task 3: Save this as worksheet file MYPLAN2.

Time Estimates

Novice: 45 minutes

Intermediate: 25 minutes

Advanced: 15 minutes

L.2.11 Practice Exercises

(1) Case: Inland Container (revisited)

Mary Montoya has reviewed her pricing proposal worksheet design for Rydder Truck Rental. She is comfortable with her design, but would like to obtain a printed report rather than a screen dump to send to Richard. Mary's design remains as follows:

	A	B	Formula Description
1	Units Sold	187300	
2	Price per Unit	3.19	
3	Sales	+B1*B2	(Units Sold*Price per Unit)
4	Cost of Sales	.73*B3	(.73*Sales)
5	Gross Profit	+B3−B4	(Sales−Cost of Sales)

Task 1: Rebuild the RYDDER worksheet by using pointing to create the equations. Be sure to clear the worksheet before you begin entering the labels and equations.

Quick check answer: Gross Profit = 161321

Task 2: Print the solution results as a Lotus 1-2-3 report.

Task 3: Print the cell formulas.

Task 4: Save this as worksheet file RYDDER2.

Time Estimates

Novice: 45 minutes

Intermediate: 25 minutes

Advanced: 15 minutes

(2)   Case: Ebony & Hatcher Housewares Group

Business Problem: Financial reporting
MIS Characteristics: Finance
                              Managerial Control

Ebony & Hatcher Housewares Group is a worldwide manufacturer and distributor of household appliances like toasters and coffee makers. Crystal Somozas is the financial analyst for the Group who is responsible for compiling the quarterly statement of operating income by geographical region. Crystal has obtained the Operating Income for each geographical region and entered it in the EHGROUP.WK1 worksheet file. She still needs to compute the totals for the quarter. Crystal wants you to continue developing the worksheet in this manner:

Task 1: Retrieve the EHGROUP.WK1 worksheet file from your Data Disk and review the labels and values that have already been entered.

Task 2: Set the global column width to 12 and the column width for column **A** to 20.

Task 3: Develop and enter formulas to compute the totals for each geographical area for the quarter and for each month of the quarter. The Total column should contain the company's total operating income for the quarter. Use pointing to create your formulas.

  Quick check answer: Total [Total] = 168219

Task 4: Print the solution results as a Lotus 1-2-3 report.

Task 5: Print the cell formulas.

Task 6: Save this as worksheet file EHGROUP.

Time Estimates

Novice: 30 minutes

Intermediate: 20 minutes

Advanced: 15 minutes

(3)   Case: Bradley Blackstone Consulting

Business Problem: Human Resource Planning
MIS Characteristics: Human Resources
                              Strategic Planning

Bradley Blackstone Consulting (BBC) specializes in the development and installation of custom computer software systems for business and government. BCC has experienced rapid growth that is expected to continue at a rate of 20 percent per year for the next several years. Their Vice President for Human Resources, Karla Paredes, is responsible for preparing a human resources plan for the software engineering staff necessary to support their anticipated growth. From historical data, Karla determined the number of scheduled retirements and the retention rate of current employees. She needs to determine the number of systems engineers they need to plan to hire for each of the next three years. Karla has already entered the labels and values in her BBCHIRES worksheet while she sketched out the required formulas as follows:

	A	B	C	D
	A	B	C	D
4		Year 1	Year 2	Year 3
5		$-----$	$-----$	$-----$
6	Target Staff Level		+B6*1.2	+C6*1.2
7				
8	Beginning Staff Level		+B15	+C15
9				
10	Retirements			
11	Retention Rate			
12	Turnover Losses	(B8−B10)*(1−B11)	(C8−C10)*(1−C11)	(D8−D10)*(1−D11)
13	New Hires	+B6−B8+B10+B12	+C6−C8+C10+C12	+D6−D8+D10+D12
14				
15	Ending Staff Level	+B8−B10−B12+B13	+C8−C10−C12+C13	+D8−D10−D12+D13

Karla wants you to continue developing her human resource planning worksheet in this manner:

Task 1: Retrieve the BBCHIRES.WK1 worksheet file from your Data Disk and review the labels and values that have already been entered.

Task 2: Set the global column width to 14 and the column width for column **A** to 24.

Task 3: Enter the formula in each cell as determined by Karla. Use pointing to create your formulas.

   Quick check answer: New Hires [Year 3] = 490

Task 4: Print the solution results as a Lotus 1-2-3 report.

Task 5: Print the cell formulas.

Task 6: Save this as worksheet file BBCHIRES.

Time Estimates

Novice: 45 minutes

Intermediate: 30 minutes

Advanced: 20 minutes

(4)   Case: First United National Bank

   Business Problem: Waiting line analysis
   MIS Characteristics: Production/Operations
            Strategic Planning

Shawn Somerville is a senior vice president responsible for teller operations at First United National Bank. Shawn is considering opening a drive-in window to enhance customer service at the Meridian Road branch. He had a study conducted that estimated that customers will arrive at the rate of 15 per hour or one every four minutes, which is an arrival rate (a) equal to 15. The associate who would staff the window can service customers at the rate of one every three minutes, which is a service rate (s) of 20. To evaluate this idea, Shawn decided that these waiting line factors should be evaluated:

Average Utilization of Teller $= a / s$
Average Number in System $= a / (s - a)$
Average Waiting Time in Line $= a / (s * (s - a))$
Average Waiting Time in System $= 1 / (s - a)$

Here, the utilization rate indicates the amount of time the teller is busy servicing a customer, while a customer's waiting time in the system includes the waiting time in line and the time for service by the teller. These times are computed in hours, which can be converted to minutes by multiplying by 60.

Shawn has started the FUNBANK worksheet for carrying out his analysis. He wants you to complete the analysis by entering the necessary formulas in the worksheet. In preparation for completing the worksheet, your first step is to organize the formulas that you will be using on the SPREADSHEET PLANNING FORM below. The Cell column indicates the cell name in which the formula will be entered. In the Cell Formula column, you should write out the cell formula to be entered using 1-2-3 cell names.

SPREADSHEET PLANNING FORM

Account Name	Formula Description	Cell	Cell Formula
Arrival Rate (a)	Input data value	B4	15
Service Rate (s)	Input data value	B5	20
Avg Utilization	a/s	B7	
Avg Number in Systems	$a/(s - a)$	B8	
Avg Wait Time in Line (in hours)	$a/(s * (s - a))$	B9	
Avg Wait Time in System (in hours)	$1/(s - a)$	B10	
Avg Wait Time in Line (in minutes)		D9	
Avg Wait Time in System (in minutes)		D10	

You are ready to continue developing the worksheet in this manner:

Task 1: Retrieve the FUNBANK.WK1 worksheet file from your Data Disk and review the labels and values that have already been entered.

Task 2: Enter the formulas from the PLANNING FORM using pointing to create them.

Quick check answer: Avg Waiting Time in System = 12 minutes

Task 3: Print the solution results as a Lotus 1-2-3 report.

Task 4: Print the cell formulas.

Task 5: Save this as worksheet file FUNBANK.

Time Estimates

Novice: 50 minutes

Intermediate: 30 minutes

Advanced: 20 minutes

L.2.12 Comprehensive Problems

This is the beginning of the Comprehensive Problems for Lotus 1-2-3. After these problems are started in this Lesson, they are continued in the following Lessons. The problems in those Lessons build on the solution you develop in this Lesson and the subsequent Lessons.

(1)   Case: Woodcraft Furniture Company

Business Problem: Profit planning
MIS Characteristics: Production/Operations
                                  Strategic Planning

The Woodcraft Furniture Company is an established manufacturer of home furniture. Woodcraft, founded in 1955, is located in the heart of the hardwood forest country. The company's initial market was local; it has since expanded into a 15-state regional market. Woodcraft's president, Joe Birch, an MBA graduate from Harvest University, has repositioned his company from the twentieth to the largest furniture maker in the region. Joe has achieved this remarkable task within his three-year tenure at Woodcraft. He attributes this success to his fine staff and their active management style. To further improve operations, he recently hired you to head the strategic planning department. Your primary task is to coordinate the financial planning and budgeting operations. Joe has asked you to prepare a financial forecast for next year's income before tax (IBT).

Woodcraft produces three products: tables, chairs, and sofas. Martha Goodguess, the director of marketing, has compiled the results of her market research for next year. She expects 10,600 tables to be sold. For each table sold, on the average, five chairs are sold. She expects the sale of 7067 sofas. The price schedule for these is as follows:

Product	Price
Tables	$510
Chairs	110
Sofas	400

Martha has planned an advertising expenditure of 10 percent of total sales.

Ray Jointer, production manager, expects to produce these units with 157 production line employees at an average salary of $11.70 per hour. Last year, the average hours worked per employee were 2080. Ray expects the same number of hours this year. A check of Ray's records indicates that the raw materials cost is 26 percent of total sales. The factory overhead charge is 58 percent of the cost of raw materials.

In the finance department, Talbert "Tall" Pine, the treasurer of Woodcraft, has reviewed the production forecast and believes that no new external financing is required. A review of last year's financial statements with "Tall" produces the following estimates:

1. Total debt is $1,960,000 at an average interest rate of 9.5 percent.

2. Insurance expense is 3 percent of total sales.

3. Management salaries will be $876,000.

4. General and administrative expenses will be $310,000.

After a meeting with Joe, you've settled on a planning report format like this:

WOODCRAFT FURNITURE
Pro Forma Income Statement

	Next Year
Production:	
(in units)	
Tables sold	XXXXXX
Chairs sold	XXXXXX
Sofas sold	XXXXXX
Revenues:	
Tables sales	XXXXXX
Chairs sales	XXXXXX
Sofa sales	XXXXXX
Total sales	XXXXXX
Cost of sales:	
Raw materials	XXXXXX
Labor	XXXXXX
Overhead	XXXXXX
Cost of Sales	XXXXXX
Gross Profit	XXXXXX
Operating Expenses:	
Advertising	XXXXXX
Insurance	XXXXXX
Management salaries	XXXXXX
General and administrative	XXXXXX
Operating Expenses	XXXXXX
Operating Profit	XXXXXX
Interest Expense	XXXXXX
Income Before Taxes	XXXXXX
Return on Sales	XXXXXX

You now have all of the preliminary data required to prepare a forecast for next year. In preparation for creating this spreadsheet, you pull out your list of useful accounting identities for reference:

Gross Profit = Total Sales − Cost of Sales
Operating Profit = Gross Profit − Operating Expenses
Interest Expense = Total Debt ∗ Interest Rate
Income Before Taxes = Operating Profit − Interest Expense
Return on Sales = Income Before Taxes / Total Sales ∗ 100

Your first step is to organize the input data values and formulas that you will be using on the SPREADSHEET PLANNING FORM below. By organizing your spreadsheet like this, you will have the formulas needed for entry into 1-2-3. Under the Formula Description column, write out the equation in English. Then in the Cell column indicate the cell name in which the formula will be located. In the Cell Formula column, write out the cell formula using 1-2-3 cell names. With this Spreadsheet Planning Form, entering these formulas in 1-2-3 is greatly simplified.

SPREADSHEET PLANNING FORMS

Account Name	Formula Description	Cell	Cell Formula
Tables Sold			
Chairs Sold			
Sofas Sold			
Tables Sales			
Chair Sales			
Sofa Sales			
Total Sales			
Raw Materials			
Labor			
Overhead			
Cost of Sales			
Gross Profit			
Advertising			
Insurance			
Management Salaries			
General and Admin			
Operating Expenses			
Operating Profit			
Interest Expense			
Income Before Taxes			
Return on Sales			

You are ready to embark on the following tasks:

Task 1: Construct this spreadsheet for Woodcraft.

Task 2: Print the results.

Task 3: Print the cell formulas.

Task 4: Save this as worksheet file WOOD.

Quick check answers: Income Before Taxes = 1264686
Return on Sales = .0899 or 8.99%

Time Estimates

Novice: 75 minutes

Intermediate: 60 minutes

Advanced: 45 minutes

(2)   **Case: Midwest Universal Gas**

Business Problem: Corporate planning
MIS Characteristics: Finance
Strategic Planning

Midwest Universal Gas (MUG) is a diversified energy company serving the energy needs of business and industry throughout mid-America. Recently, the company has experienced a shift in demand for natural gas. This is partly due to changing economic activity, climatic conditions, and energy conservation. The director to MUG's gas division, Mary Derrick, has just called you to her office. Mary is concerned that her division's after-tax return on investment might fall below 12 percent. She instructs you to coordinate the compilation of next year's pro forma or projected income statement for the gas division.

Your first task is to establish a demand forecast for natural gas in your markets for next year. Francis Foresight, the director of marketing, said that last year's production and sales were 715 billion cubic feet (BCF). He also reported that this year's demand has decreased to an annual rate of 700 BCF, because of economic and conservation activities. Francis believes that, given the proper budget, his department will be able to add several accounts to the 341 communities currently being served. Traditional marketing and selling expenses have been between 10 and 14 percent of sales. Francis asked for an increased level of 14.4 percent of sales to support a more aggressive marketing effort. In addition to the predicted new accounts, Francis anticipates an expansion in industrial accounts. After considering all these conditions, he expects next year's volume to be 732 BCF. Based on an analysis of prior years' sales, he expects revenues to be generated in this manner:

Volume Sold	Next Year's Rate
22% Retail	$350,000 per BCF
78% Wholesale	$286,000 per BCF

Given this forecast of demand for next year, you decide to check with the production department to ensure Midwest's ability to meet the demand. Petro Newgas, or "Pete," reports no problem in satisfying this demand and the company has sufficient pipeline capacity to transport the gas. Pete discusses a variety of sources and costs for next year's production with you. After three hours of looking at reports and tables, the numbers almost become a blur! Pete finally indicates that he expects the average cost of gas to be 61 percent of total sales revenue.

Having secured the demand and production forecast, your next encounter is with Sam Wright, the division controller. Sam has reviewed the operating budget and concludes that with anticipated salary increases and other price adjustments, next year's general administrative expenses will be $16,250,000. Also, Sam expects to be able to charge off 8.6 percent of the division's investments to depreciation. With the adjustment for new plant and equipment, next year's divisional investments will total $102,400,000. Midwest has $39,200,000 in long-term debt at an average interest rate of 10.5 percent. In addition to this long-term debt, Midwest has outstanding $13,933,000 of short-term debt at an average interest rate of 12 percent. Sam expects federal, state, and local taxes to be at the rate of 46 percent. Sam works with you in laying out this format for the pro forma statement:

MIDWEST UNIVERSAL GAS

Pro Forma Income Statement
(Dollars in thousands)

	Next Year
Production:	
(in BCF)	
Retail gas sold	XXXXXX
Wholesale gas sold	XXXXXX
Total Gas Sold	XXXXXX
Revenues:	
Retail sales	XXXXXX
Wholesale sales	XXXXXX
Total Sales	XXXXXX
Expenses:	
Cost of sales	XXXXXX
Marketing and selling	XXXXXX
General and administrative	XXXXXX
Depreciation	XXXXXX
Total Expense	XXXXXX
Operating Income	XXXXXX
Interest Expense	XXXXXX
Income Before Taxes	XXXXXX
Income Taxes	XXXXXX
Net Income	XXXXXX
Return on Investment	XXXXXX
Supporting Balance Sheet Items:	
Investments	XXXXXXXX
Short-term debt	XXXXXXXX
Long-term debt	XXXXXXXX

You now have all of the preliminary data required to prepare next year's forecast. Remember, the *Pro Forma Statement is in dollars in thousands*, so drop three zeros on *all* input *dollar amounts*. In preparation for constructing this spreadsheet, you reference your list of useful accounting identities and financial ratios:

Depreciation = Investments * Depreciation rate
Operating income = Total sales − Total expense
Interest expense = Short-term debt * Short-term interest rate +
    Long-term debt * Long-term interest rate
Income taxes = Income before taxes * Tax rate
Return on investment = Net income / Investments * 100

Your first step is to organize the input data values and formulas that you will be using on the Spreadsheet Planning Form below. By organizing your spreadsheet like this, you will have the formulas needed for entry into 1-2-3. Under the Formula

Description column, write out the equation in English. Then in the Cell column indicate the cell name in which the formula will be located. In the Cell Formula column, write out the cell formula using 1-2-3 cell names. With this Spreadsheet Planning Form, entering these formulas in 1-2-3 is greatly simplified.

SPREADSHEET PLANNING FORMS

Account Name	Formula Description	Cell	Cell Formula
Retail Gas Sold			
Wholesale Gas Sold			
Total Gas Sold			
Retail Sales			
Wholesale Sales			
Total Sales			
Cost of Sales			
Marketing & Selling			
General Admin.			
Depreciation			
Total Expense			
Operating Income			
Interest Expense			
Income Before Taxes			
Income Taxes			
Net Income			
Return on Invest			
Investments			
Short-term Debt			
Long-term Debt			

You are ready to launch into the following tasks:

Task 1: Construct this spreadsheet for Midwest Universal Gas.

Task 2: Print the results.

Task 3: Print the cell formulas.

Task 4: Save this as worksheet file MUG.

> *Quick check answers:* Net Income = 12523(000's)
> Return on Investment = .1223 or 12.23%

Time Estimates

Novice: 75 minutes

Intermediate: 60 minutes

Advanced: 45 minutes

L.2.13   Case Application

Case: Advanced Mobile Communications
Business Problem: Financial ratio analysis
MIS Characteristics: Finance
　　　　　　　　Strategic Planning
Management Functions: Controlling
Tools Skills: Reporting Formulas

Advanced Mobile Communications (AMC) manufactures and markets a variety of electronic equipment which includes cellular car telephones, portable phones, two-way radios, beepers, citizen-band radio, and radar detectors. Founded in 1966 by James Wu, AMC recently moved its cellular phone manufacturing into a new plant nearby its Cincinnati headquarters in the Executive Plaza. Jimmy still serves as the company's President and Chief Executive Officer. Carol Ann Lopez was recently promoted to the position of Vice President of Finance after Martin Rydder's retirement last year. Carol Ann and Jimmy regularly monitor the financial health of AMC, with review meetings scheduled monthly.

AMC just finished closing its book for last year. Carol Ann is interested in preparing a comparison of AMC's performance to that of other companies in the same industry. She knows that this can be done by comparing financial ratios for AMC against those for the same industry segment. Carol Ann recently received a report of industry ratios from the Electronic Manufacturers', Association.

Carol Ann is preparing for her monthly review meeting with Jimmy and AMC's executive committee next Tuesday. She has assembled AMC's income statement and balance sheet (or statement of financial position) data and entered it in a worksheet together with ratio data from the Electronic Manufacturers Association.

An income statement or statement of operations details the revenues and expenditures, such as sales, cost of sales, administrative expenses, wages and salaries, and advertising expenses. This statement shows the net profit or earnings of the organization for a specified period of time. These earnings may be distributed to shareholders or owners as a dividend, or they may be retained by the firm for investment in other business activities.

A balance sheet or statement of financial position delineates the assets and liabilities of an organization at a particular time, such as the end of a quarter or a year. Liabilities represent the proportion of the business financed by a firm's suppliers and creditors. The difference between a firm's assets and liabilities is the owners' equity or the owners' share of the firm.

Carol Ann knows that a performance ratio report for AMC's overall business assists in monitoring and controlling their operations. These performance ratios can be measured against an external industry standard. The ratios are computed using data from the general ledger and other accounting systems. These performance measurements vary from one industry to another. Some of the more popular ratios, and those used by AMC, are as follows:

1. *Liquidity ratios.* These ratios describe the ability of an organization to pay its financial obligations when they are due.

   - *Current ratio*, a measure of the ability of a firm to cover its short-term debt with assets readily converted to cash:

     Current ratio = Current assets / Current liabilities
     (A ratio greater then 1.0 is usually desired.)

   - *Quick ratio*, a measure of the ability of a firm to pay off its short-term obligations without relying on the sale of its inventories:

     Quick ratio = (Current assets − Inventories) / Current liabilities

2. *Asset management ratios.* These ratios provide a signal of how effectively a firm is managing its assets.

   - *Inventory turnover*, a measure of how rapidly goods are being purchased and sold as they move through inventory:

     Inventory turnover = Cost of good sold / Inventory

   - *Average collection period*, a measure of the level of accounts receivable:

     Average collection period = Accounts receivable / Average sales per day
     where average sales per day = sales / 360

- *Total asset turnover*, a measure of the utilization of all the assets of a firm:

  Total asset turnover = Sales / Total assets

3. *Debt management ratios.* These ratios impart an indication of the extent to which a firm uses debt financing. Debt financing allows owners to maintain control of a firm with a limited investment. When a firm earns more with borrowed funds than it pays in interest, the return to the owners is greater than if no borrowing had been used.

   - *Debt ratio*, a measure of the total funds provided by creditors:

     Debt ratio = Total debt / Total assets

   - *Times-interest-earned (TIE) ratio*, a measure of a firm's ability to meet interest payments when they are due:

     TIE = Earnings before interest and taxes / Interest

4. *Profitability ratios.* These ratios supply information about a firm's overall operating performance, which reflects the effectiveness of a firm's management.

   - *Return on sales (ROS)*, a measure of the amount of profit or profit margin generated from each dollar of sales:

     ROS = Net income / Sales

   - *Return on total assets (ROA)*, a measure of the profit generated by the assets of the company:

     ROA = Net income / Total assets

   - *Return of equity (ROE)*, a measure of the profit generated by the investment of the owners:

     Return on equity = Net income / Stockholders' equity

5. *Market value ratios.* These ratios furnish an indication of a company's past accomplishments and of its investors' outlook for future performance.

   - *Earnings per share*, a measure of the earnings for each share of common stock:

     Earnings per share = Net income / Number of common stock shares

   - *Price/earnings (P/E) ratio*, a measure comparing the price of a share of common stock to the earnings for a share:

     Price/earnings ratio = Price per share / Earnings per share

Tasks

1. Examine last year's income statement and balance sheet for AMC by loading the worksheet file RATIO.WK1 from your Data Disk. All dollar amounts and the number of shares of common stock are entered in thousands, except the stock price, which is entered in dollars.

2. Print the financial statements and the areas set up for the ratio analysis. Review these and notice that Carol Ann has already entered the industry ratios.

3. Create the formulas to compute each of the 12 ratios. (*Hint:* You may want to use pointing together with the <PgUp> and <PgDn> to locate the desired cells for each formula.)

4. The COMMENT column of the ratio analysis provides an indication of the possible evaluation from comparing AMC's ratios to those of the industry. Make your own comparison for these ratios. From the list of possible evaluations, enter yours in the COMMENT column.

5. Print the completed financial ratio analysis and save your complete worksheet file.

6. Review your report and determine the one or two ratios that appear as areas of concern where AMC's management should focus their attention. Write a short narrative describing your analysis of the ratios and the area of greatest potential distress.

Time Estimates

Novice: 90 minutes

Intermediate: 60 minutes

Advanced: 45 minutes

Copying Cells and Producing Reports

CONTENT

- Expanding the Basic Worksheet
- Using Edit to Revise a Cell's Content
- Removing or Blanking Out a Cell's Content
- Adding Formulas to the Worksheet
- Building the Worksheet by Copying Cell Contents
- Changing Appearance with Global Column Width and Format
- Adding Rows for Growth Rates and Ratios
- Relative and Absolute Addressing
- Including a Total Column
- Using UNDO to Correct Errors
- Report Column Headings and Underlines
- Label Prefixes
- Presentation Quality Reporting
- Using SmartIcons to Copy Cell Contents and Enhance Worksheets
- When Things Go Wrong

L.3.1 Expanding the Basic Worksheet

Kim and Chris desire to expand the worksheet model to one that encompasses four quarters, as shown in Figure L.37. The formulas used to produce the results in Figure L.37 are written out in Business English, as shown in Figure L.38. For their quarterly report, columns **B**, **C**, **D**, and **E** each contains the forecast for one quarter.

In this worksheet, Sales are specified as an input value of 289,500 in the first quarter. They are projected to grow at a rate of 9 percent each quarter. The Sales amount in the second quarter is computed by multiplying the first quarter Sales by 1.09, that is, by 109 percent. Sales in the third and fourth quarters are computed in

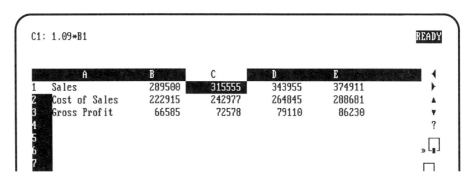

FIGURE L.37. Four-quarter worksheet.

a similar manner by using the Sales amount from the previous quarter. The Cost of Sales is expected to be 77 percent of Sales in each quarter. Gross Profit is still the difference between Sales and Cost of Sales. The worksheet in Figure L.37 is produced as described in the following sections of this Lesson.

L.3.2 Using Edit to Revise a Cell's Content

The first step is to retrieve the PLAN worksheet file, since it contains desired labels and formulas.

Action: Use the /FR command to retrieve the PLAN worksheet file.

You are now ready to continue creating the four-quarter worksheet. First, the formula in cell **B2** is revised, and then the other formulas are added to the worksheet.

| To position the cell pointer at the cell to be revised | **Move to:** | **B2** | Use cursor movement keys, press <F5>, and enter **B2,** or click with mouse |

Pressing the <F5> (GOTO) function key and entering the cell address is known as a "goto cell address" action in 1-2-3. This is an alternative method for moving the cursor directly to a desired cell location from anywhere on the worksheet.

Now let's actually revise the formula in cell **B2.**

| To revise or change a cell's content | **Press:** | <F2> | Activate EDIT mode |

This <F2> (EDIT) function key activates the EDIT mode so that the *existing* content of a cell can be modified. The formula is copied from the cell content line to the edit line (Figure L.39), where the revisions are displayed as they take place.

| | **Press:** | <Home> | Position EDIT cursor |

The edit cursor moves to the left end of the edit line.

Sales = 289500, PREVIOUS Sales * 1.09 FOR 3 columns
Cost of Sales = Sales * .77 FOR 4 columns
Gross Profit = Sales - Cost of Sales FOR 4 columns

FIGURE L.38. Formulas for four-quarter worksheet in Business English.

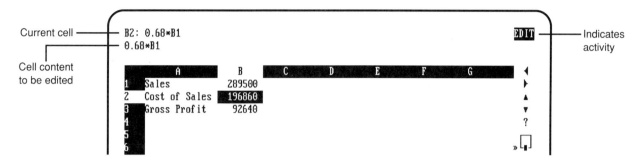

FIGURE L.39. Cell content displayed for editing.

Press:	<right>	Move to character for editing
Press:	<right>	Position EDIT cursor on six [6]
Press:	<Del>	Remove unwanted character
Press:	<Del>	Remove one more character
Type:	77	Desired new value
Press:	<Enter>	Complete EDIT revision

In summary, <F2> (EDIT) activates the EDIT cell content line. Use <left>, <right>, <Home>, and <End> to move the edit cursor. Type the characters to be inserted. Use <Del> or <backspace> to remove unwanted characters. <Del> removes the character *at* the cursor location, whereas <backspace> removes the character immediately to the *left* of the edit cursor. The procedure for revising a cell's content is summarized in Figure L.40.

L.3.3   Removing or Blanking Out a Cell's Content

To completely remove the content of a cell so that it contains absolutely nothing, the cell's content must be erased. Unwanted labels or values in an individual cell or a cell range are eliminated with the / Range Erase (/RE) command. Beginning with Release 2.3, an unwanted data value in an individual cell may be removed by pressing the <Delete> key. The procedure for erasing cell contents is summarized in Figure L.41. Use this procedure as necessary in creating your 1-2-3 worksheets.

Method 1

1. Position cell pointer on cell to be changed.
2. Enter desired cell content.
   - The OLD content is replaced with the NEW content that you entered.

Method 2

1. Position the cell pointer on the cell to be changed.
2. **Press:** <F2> activate EDIT mode
3. Edit cells's content.
4. **Press:** <Enter> Complete edit

FIGURE L.40. Summary of revising a cell's content.

1. Move to:	cell or upper-left corner of group of cells whose contents you want to eliminate
2. Press:	/
3. Select:	Range
4. Select Erase:	An unanchored range appears as denoted by the ellipsis [··]
5. Action:	Stretch the cell pointer over the range to be erased using the cursor control keys. As you move the cursor, the cell pointer expands over the range of cells.
6. Press:	<Enter> Unwanted cell contents are deleted

FIGURE L.41. Summary of removing a cell's content.

Caution Alert!

Do NOT blank out cells by placing a <space> in them. If you do, *they contain LABELS.* The LABELS just happen to be spaces. Although the cells appear to be blank on the worksheet, they will contain space characters. To find out if you have this situation, move your cursor to a cell and inspect the cell content for the existence of an apostrophe ('). Cells containing spaces as LABELS can occasionally create difficulties in 1-2-3!

L.3.4 Adding Formulas to the Worksheet

Kim and Chris have placed their desired formulas in column **B** for creating the worksheet in Figure L.37. Now the formulas in columns **C, D,** and **E** are ready to be added to their worksheet. First, let's add a growth rate formula for the second quarter Sales in **C1.** Adding a formula to an existing worksheet is the same as initially entering a formula in a new worksheet.

To add a formula to an existing worksheet			
Move to:	**C1**	Desired location
Type:	1.09*	
Press:	<left>	Point to cell **B1**
Press:	<Enter>	Complete formula

Look at the 1-2-3 cell formulas displayed in Figure L.42. Notice that the formulas in cells **D1** and **E1** are the same as those in **C1** with the exception of the *column letters.* The formulas in cells **D1** and **E1** could be entered like cell **C1** by creating each formula individually. If this were a 12-month plan rather than one with four quarters, it would be necessary to enter the formula 10 times. Lotus 1-2-3 provides a shortcut

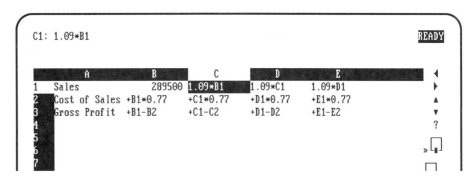

FIGURE L.42. Lotus 1-2-3 formulas for four-quarter worksheet.

method for copying formulas from one cell into other cells. But 1-2-3 does NOT make an *exact* copy. Lotus 1-2-3 *adjusts* column letters or row numbers depending on how you perform the copy. When you copy cells from one column to another column, the column letter(s) is revised while the row number(s) remains unchanged. On the other hand, when cells are copied from one row to another row, the row number(s) is revised while the column letter(s) remains unchanged. In performing a copy, 1-2-3 lets you copy **FROM** a source range of cells **TO** a target range of cells.

L.3.5   Building the Worksheet by Copying Cell Contents

The general scheme of copying formulas in the Good Morning Products worksheet is shown in Figure L.43, where formulas are copied from cells **C1, B2,** and **B3.**

Let's look at how the copy is performed for the Sales formulas.

To copy a formula from one cell to other cells			
Move to:	**C1**		Cell **from** which formula will be copied
Press:	/		Access main menu
Select:	Copy		Desired activity

The Copy command is specified in two parts. The first part indicates the source range of cells or **what** you want to copy **from.** The second part of the Copy command specifies the target range of cells **where** you want them copied **to.** An <Enter> is used to switch from the first part to the second part of the command.

Since only one cell is to be copied and the worksheet cursor was located at this cell, **C1** is the suggested cell whose content is to be copied. This is the desired cell, so the **from** specification is completed like this:

Press:	<Enter>	Complete specification of **from** range

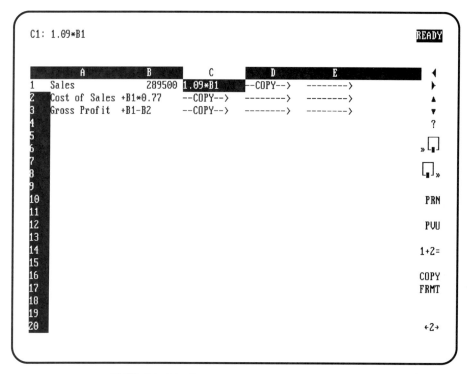

FIGURE L.43. Scheme for copying cell contents.

The **to** range is now specified in this manner:

Move to:	**D1**	Upper-left corner of the range **to** which formula will be copied
Press:	.	Yes, you press the period

Notice that pressing the period once caused two (··) to be displayed. You have **anchored** the cursor as indicated by the ellipsis. Once a range has been anchored, the cursor is stretched over the desired range of cells with the cursor control keys.

Move to:	**E1**	Lower-right corner of range **to** which formula will be copied

The cell pointer **expands** to cover the entire range **to** which the formula will be copied, highlighting the cell range.

Press:	<Enter>	Complete Copy command

When you press <Enter>, the formula is copied from **C1** into **D1** and **E1.**

If you have mouse support, you may use the mouse to specify the desired range of cells by clicking on the upper-left corner of the range and dragging the cursor to the lower-right corner.

Now you are ready to copy the formulas from both cells **B2** and **B3** at the same time, because they can be specified as a cell range.

To copy formulas from several cells in a range at one time

Move to:	**B2**	Desired starting location
Press:	/	Access menu
Select:	Copy	Desired activity
Press:	<down>	Expand already anchored cell pointer

The cursor is expanded over cells **B2** and **B3,** since the formulas from both cells will be copied at one time.

Press:	<Enter>	Complete **from** range specification
Move to:	**C2**	Beginning cell of destination range
Press:	.	Anchor unanchored cell pointer
Move to:	**E2**	Stretch pointer to specify top row of destination range
Press:	<Enter>	Complete copy

The formulas are copied into cells **C2** through **E3,** as desired. When copying a cell range to another cell range only the top row or leftmost column of the **to** or **destination** range needs to be specified.

Action: Move your cursor about this range of cells and look at the formulas that have been copied. Notice that 1-2-3 *automatically adjusted the column letter* in performing the copy. In 1-2-3, cells that are copied like this and have their column letter(s) and row number(s) adjusted during the copy are **relatively referenced.** This procedure for copying cell contents is summarized in Figure L.44.

Copying Cell Contents

1. Action:	Place cell pointer on upper-left cell of **FROM** range	
2. Press:	/	Access main menu
3. Select:	Copy	Desired activity
4. Action:	Expand already anchored cell pointer over **FROM** range Note: If cursor is at WRONG cell location, unanchor **FROM** range by pressing <Esc> or <Backspace>, position cursor, and anchor it.	
5. Press:	<Enter>	Complete **FROM** specification
6. Action:	Move cell pointer to upper-left cell of **TO** range	
7. Press:	.	Anchor unanchored cell pointer
8. Action:	Expand cell pointer over **TO** range	
9. Press:	<Enter>	Complete **TO** specification and perform copy

Moving Cell Contents

1. Action:	Place cell pointer on upper-left cell of **FROM** range	
2. Press:	/	Access main menu
3. Select:	Move	Desired activity
4. Action:	Expand already anchored cell pointer over **FROM** range Note: If cursor is at WRONG cell location, unanchor **FROM** range by pressing <Esc> or <Backspace>, position cursor and anchor it.	
5. Press:	<Enter>	Complete **FROM** specification
6. Action:	Position cell pointer at upper-left cell of **TO** range	
7. Press:	<Enter>	Complete **TO** specification and perform move

FIGURE L.44. Summary of copying or moving cell contents.

L.3.6 Changing Appearance with Global Column Width and Format

The appearance of the Good Morning Products worksheet can be improved by adjusting the width of *all* columns other than column **A** and by establishing the display of numbers as integers. First, let's set the column widths.

To set the global column width

Press:	/	Access main menu
Select:	Worksheet	

Although the Worksheet menu displays the Column command, you do NOT want to choose this command at this time! Selecting Column from the Worksheet menu will only allow you to change the width of the *current* column!

Select:	Global	Change width of *all* columns
Select:	Column-Width	Desired activity

By choosing the Column-Width command from the Global menu, you change the width of *all* columns that do not have their column width set individually with the / Worksheet Column Set-Width (/WCS) command.

Press:	<right>	Preview column width

Notice that the width of the columns is increased from 9 spaces to 10 spaces, which allows you to preview the effect of setting the column width. Continue changing the column width like this:

Press:	`<right>`	
Press:	`<right>`	Column width is now at 12
Press:	`<right>`	Column **F** disappears from the screen
Press:	`<left>`	Cause column **F** to reappear
Press:	`<Enter>`	Complete column width command

The column width has been set to 12 spaces.

Now let's change the format to remove the decimals *from the display*. The decimals are still used in the calculations; they are just NOT displayed!

Keypoint!
> Format changes the number of decimals displayed on the screen, but it does NOT change the number of decimals used in the calculations!

To change the format for displaying numbers

Press:	`/`	Access main menu
Select:	`Worksheet`	
Select:	`Global`	Change entire worksheet
Select:	`Format`	Desired activity
Select:	`Fixed`	Type of format
Enter:	`0`	Number of decimal places

Thus, the format for displaying the numbers is changed.

Action: Print the revised worksheet and save this as the PLAN2 file.

In addition to this Fixed Format, 1-2-3 allows you to display numbers by using many different formats. Examples of some of the more commonly used formats are illustrated in Figure L.45.

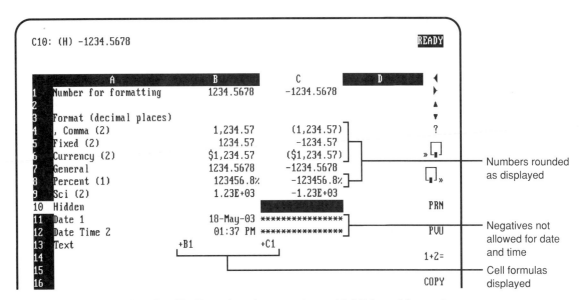

FIGURE L.45. Examples of commonly used 1-2-3 format for numbers.

> *Keypoint!* | The selection of Worksheet Global results in commands that apply to the entire worksheet, except those characteristics set separately with the Range or Column commands!

> *Keypoint!* | The selection of Range results in commands that apply to any range of cells in the worksheet, rather than the entire worksheet!

L.3.7   Adding Rows for Growth Rates and Ratios

Chris and Kim want to enhance the business model portrayed in Figure L.37 by entering the *Sales Growth Rate* and *Cost Percent* as separate values as, illustrated in Business English in Figure L.46. This allows these values to be readily reviewed and revised. A different value can be used in each of the columns of the model. Business models frequently use growth rates and ratios, as shown in Figure L.47. These growth rates and ratios embody managerial assumptions of future business operations. Figure L.47 illustrates the resulting 1-2-3 worksheet, whereas Figure L.48 shows the cell formulas.

Assumption variables, such as the *Sales Growth Rate* and *Cost Percent*, may be placed at the top or bottom of a worksheet. You should consider their placement depending on where you would like them printed in your final output report.

> *Keypoint!* | Place key assumption variables in your worksheet where you want them to print in your final report, such as at the top or bottom of the report!

Now let's continue with PLAN2. The first step is to add blank rows at the top of the worksheet so that there is room to place these assumption variables.

Action: Make sure PLAN2 is your active worksheet.

To insert blank rows in an existing worksheet			
Move to:	D1	This could be any cell in row **1**	
Press:	/	Access main menu	
Select:	Worksheet		
Select:	Insert	Desired activity	
Select:	Row	Type of insert	
Press:	<down>	Expand cursor	

This expands the cell pointer so that it is two (2) rows high. The height of the cell pointer indicates the number of rows that will be inserted *above* the cell pointer.

Press:	<Enter>	Complete inserting rows into worksheet

Sales Growth Rate = 0.08, 0.09, 0.11, 0.09
Cost Percent = 0.77, 0.76, 0.74, 0.72
Sales = 289500, PREVIOUS Sales * (1 + Sales Growth Rate) FOR 3 columns
Cost of Sales = Sales * Cost Percent FOR 4 columns
Gross Profit = Sales - Cost of Sales FOR 4 columns

FIGURE L.46. Formulas for four-quarter worksheet in Business English with growth rate and ratio.

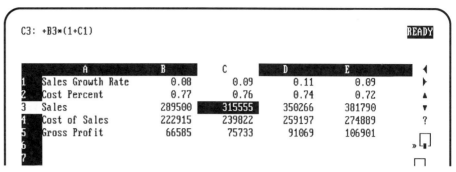

FIGURE L.47. Four-quarter worksheet with separate growth rate and ratio.

In a similar manner, rows and columns may be removed from your worksheet with the / Worksheet Delete (/WD) command.

The values for the *Sales Growth Rate* are now added to the worksheet.

Move to:	**A1**
Action:	Add the *Sales Growth Rate* label and its data values from Figure L.46.

When you initially enter these *Sales Growth Rate* data values, they appear as a zero. This is because the cells have been formatted as Fixed with no decimal places (/WGFF0). These cells should be formatted with two places to the right of the decimal, while the other cells remain as integers. This is accomplished with a Range Format.

To format a selected range of cells

Move to:	**B1**	Desired location
Press:	/	Access main menu
Select:	Range	Only selected range of cells revised
Select:	Format	Desired activity
Select:	Fixed	Type of format
Press:	<Enter>	Accept 2, which is the suggested number of decimal places
Move to:	**E1**	Anchored range starting in **B1** is displayed when number of decimals is input, so only cursor needs to be expanded over desired range

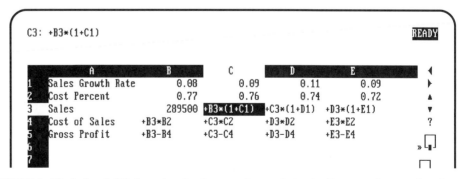

FIGURE L.48. Lotus 1-2-3 formulas for four-quarter worksheet with separate growth rate and ratio.

The **Sales Growth Rate** in **A1** currently appears as **Sales Growth R** because column **A** is too narrow now that you have entered data in column **B.**

Action: Increase the width of column **A** by four (4) characters using the /Worksheet Column Set-Width (/WCS) command.

Continue developing the Good Morning Products quarterly worksheet by entering the *Cost Percent* in this manner:

Move to: **A2**   Desired location

Action: Add the *Cost Percent* label and its data values from Figure L.46.

This time each of these data values appears as a one (1).

Action: Use the /Range Format Fixed 2 (/RFF2) command to change the format of those cells containing these data values.

Although the *Sales Growth Rate* data values are entered in cells **B1..E1,** the formulas for calculating *Sales* do not make use of these *Sales Growth Rates.* The formulas for calculating *Sales* need to be modified so that the growth rates are used. Let's inspect the current formulas and modify them so that they use the *Sales Growth Rate* and *Cost Percent.*

| To inspect cell formulas changed by inserting rows | **Move to:**   **B4**   Desired location |

Notice that the row number was revised when the rows were inserted so that the formula is now **.77 * B3.**
    Now let's add the growth rate formula in cell **C3.**

Move to: **C3**   Next cell location

This formula needs to be modified so that the growth rate formula will be **+B3*(1+C1).** That is, the Sales Growth Rate is obtained from cell **C1.** The general formula for a growth rate is

Prior value * (1 + growth rate amount as a decimal)

Action: Revise the contents of cell **C1** so that it contains the growth rate formula for calculating Sales.

Move to: **D3**   Next cell location

Notice that this cell still contains the same old formula.

Keypoint!   Once you have performed a COPY, 1-2-3 does NOT remember that a formula was placed into a cell by copying!

Action: Copy the formula from **C3** into **D3** and **E3.**

Action: Modify the formula in **B4** so the *Cost Percent* is obtained from cell **B2.**

Action: Copy this formula into cells **C4** through **E4.**

Once again, 1-2-3 will automatically adjust the column letter in performing the copy, since these cells are **relatively referenced.**

Action: Wrap up the development of this quarterly worksheet by performing these tasks:

1. Print the worksheet.
2. Print the worksheet's cell formulas.
3. Save this worksheet as PLAN3.

L.3.8   Relative and Absolute Addressing

Rather than using a different growth rate or ratio in each column, Chris and Kim would like to revise their Good Morning Products model so that the *same* growth rate and ratio are used in *all* columns. That is, only one cell is used for each growth rate and ratio, as illustrated in Figure L.49. When the formula in cells **C3** and **B4** are copied, the columns letters are automatically revised. Of course, the formulas in cells **D3, E3, C4, D4,** and **E4** could each be entered individually. However, by using **absolute referencing,** cell formulas can be copied *without* revising the column letter or row number. The currency symbol ($) is used in a cell name to specify if the cell is **absolutely referenced.** For example, in the formula **+B3 ∗ (1+$B$1)** the cell **B1** is absolutely referenced. A cell may have a mixed reference like **$B1.** In this case, the row number would change but the column letter would not, when a copy is performed. In a similar fashion, **B$1** would change column letters but not row numbers.

An absolute cell reference may be entered by typing the currency symbols, or its reference can be changed by using the <F4> (ABS) key. Pressing this key repeatedly will modify a cell reference from relative to absolute to mixed. The <F4> (ABS) may be used when a formula is being typed or built by pointing or when a formula is being edited.

Keypoint!

> Absolute referencing and relative referencing make a difference only when cell formulas are *copied!*

Let's modify the PLAN3 worksheet for Good Morning Products so that it contains a **single** *Sales Growth Rate* and *Cost Percent* ratio used across all columns.

To change relative reference to absolute reference by editing a cell's content	**Action:**	Make sure PLAN3 is your currently active worksheet.
	Move to: C3	Cell to be revised
	Press: <F2>	Activate EDIT mode
	Move to: C	in cell name **C1**
	Press: <del>	Delete the C

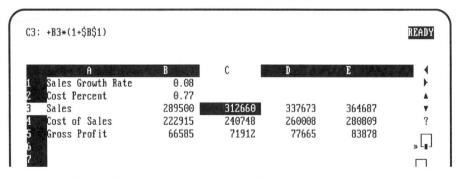

FIGURE L.49. Four-quarter worksheet with single growth rate and ratio.

Press:	B	Change column to B
Press:	<F4>	Cell's reference is changed to absolute
Press:	<Enter>	Complete command

To change another relative reference to absolute reference by editing a cell's content

Move to:	**B4**	Next cell location
Press:	<F2>	Activate EDIT mode
Move to:	B	in cell name **B2**
Press:	<F4>	Cell's reference is changed to absolute
Press:	<Enter>	Complete command

Once the cell formulas are revised with absolute references, they are ready for copying into the cells of the other quarters. Let's do this copying.

Action:	Copy the cell formula in **C3** into **D3** and **E3.**
Action:	Copy the cell formula in **B4** into **C4** through **E4.**
Move to:	**C1** — Next cell location
Action:	Erase the cell values in **C1** through **E2,** because they are no longer needed.

Your result should appear as shown in Figure L.49, with the cell formulas illustrated in Figure L.50. If ZEROS occur in cells **C5** through **E5,** or if you get the same values in all four columns, then your absolute referencing was not successful. Try it again! By now you should be very familiar with the Copy command and should begin to realize its importance in creating business models.

Action: Complete the development of this worksheet by carrying out these tasks:

1. Print the worksheet.
2. Print the worksheet's cell formulas.
3. Save this worksheet as PLAN4.

L.3.9 Including a Total Column

Chris and Kim want to enhance their worksheet by including a total column to produce the result illustrated in Figure L.51.

To add the four quarters to obtain the total for the year, the formula in cell **F3** could be **+B3+C3+D3+E3.** This would work all right, since there are only four

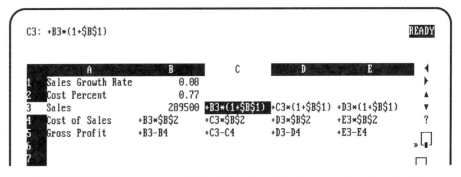

FIGURE L.50. Four-quarter worksheet formulas with single growth rate and ratio.

columns. If the columns were months, the formula would become rather lengthy. Lotus 1-2-3 provides a more convenient manner of writing the formula by using the **@SUM** function. Functions are a compact method of requesting frequently performed computations. Lotus 1-2-3 has a large variety of different functions. All 1-2-3 functions begin with the @ symbol. The Help file, accessed with the <F1> function key, provides a convenient list and description of the available 1-2-3 functions by selecting @Functions from the Help Index.

Let's include a total column in the Good Morning Products worksheet by using the @SUM function to add the data values for the four quarters.

Action:	Continue from PLAN4. Retrieve this worksheet file, if necessary.	

To use @SUM to total the four quarters

Move to:	**F3**	Cell where SUM will reside
Type:	@SUM(	Here the parenthesis is part of the function
Move to:	**B3**	You are in the point mode
Press:	.	Anchor cell pointer to specify range of cells to be added
Move to:	**E3**	Stretch cursor over desired cell range
Type:	)	Again the parenthesis is part of the function
Press:	<Enter>	Complete entering formula

The desired sum is thus calculated. If desired, you may also use your mouse to specify this cell range for the @SUM function.

Action: Repeat this procedure for cells **F4** and **F5.**

Keypoint! | All Lotus 1-2-3 functions begin with the @ symbol! |

One of the biggest sources of errors in using the @SUM function is when the cell is added into itself. That is, the cell that contains the total is included in the cell range specified in the @SUM. This would occur if you had moved the cursor to **F1** instead of **E1** with the formula in cell **F1** being **@SUM(B1..F1)**. If this happened, the **CIRC** status indicator appears when <Enter> is pressed. Each time a new label or value is entered into the worksheet, the sum is added to itself; it keeps getting bigger and

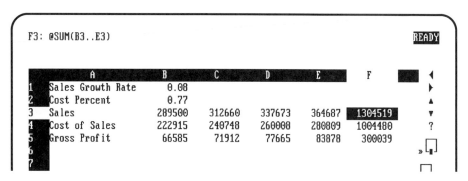

FIGURE L.51. Four-quarter plan with total column.

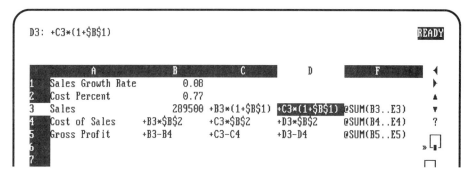

FIGURE L.52. Selected four-quarter plan worksheet formulas with sum functions.

bigger. Hence, if **CIRC** (the Circular equation indicator) appears, *immediately* reenter the cell formula, being careful to avoid this condition of **circular equations,** which exists when a cell formula references itself in performing a calculation.

Caution Alert!

> Expanding the cell pointer over the cell into which the current formula is being entered is a frequent source of circular equation errors. Be careful in specifying the range for an @SUM function!

When the total column, column **F,** is displayed on the worksheet, column **A** disappears. All six columns, **A** through **F,** can be viewed at one time on your screen by adjusting the column width.

Action: Change the global column width to 10 spaces (Figure L.51), print this result, and save the worksheet as the PLAN5 file.

L.3.10   Using UNDO to Correct Mistakes

What would you do if you accidentally typed over, erased, or copied over an important cell formula? Of course, you could figure out the formula and reenter it. The Undo feature is an important safeguard against these time-consuming mistakes. When the Undo feature is turned on or **enabled,** you can press <Alt> + <F4> (UNDO) almost any time 1-2-3 is in the READY mode and cancel the most recent operation that changed worksheet data and/or settings since the previous READY mode. With Release 2.4, an UNDO SmartIcon is also available for executing the Undo command. Undo cannot cancel all changes. For example, you cannot Undo changes made to files stored on your Data Disk by using the / File Save (/FS) command.

Before the Undo feature can be used it must be **enabled.** The 1-2-3 default is for Undo to be turned off or **disabled.** The appearance of the Undo status indicator as illustrated previously in Figure L.10 and below in Figure L.53 signals that this feature has been turned on. The best situation for using the Undo feature is to turn it on when you first enter 1-2-3. If your 1-2-3 Undo has not been enabled, then let's see how it can be turned on by using the / Worksheet Global Default Other Undo Enable (/WGDOUE) command.

To enable the Undo feature

Action: If necessary clear your worksheet with the / Worksheet Erase Yes (/WEY) command.

Press: /   Access main menu

Select: Worksheet

Select:	Global	
Select:	Default	Undo is a default
Select:	Other	
Select:	Undo	Desired command
Select:	Enable	Desired activity
Select:	Quit	Return to READY mode

Undo is enabled, and the UNDO status indicator is displayed. Undo may be used to cancel a previous action or command. However, turning off Undo is not an action that can be reversed with Undo.

Once Undo has been enabled, you can access an existing worksheet and use this feature as desired. Let's see how Undo works by making an intentional mistake and using Undo to cancel that previous erroneous action.

To make the intentional mistake

Action:		Retrieve your PLAN5 worksheet for testing the Undo feature.
Move to:	**B5**	Cell where error is to be placed
Enter:	\=	Enter repeating label in place of formula, as shown in Figure L.53

The mistake has been entered and can now be *immediately* corrected before any other cell contents are entered or other 1-2-3 commands are executed.

To Undo a mistake

| **Press:** | <Alt>+<F4> | Desired Undo activity |

With the SmartIcons of Release 2.4, clicking the UNDO icon causes the same action as pressing <Alt>+<F4> (UNDO). The contents of cell **B5** are returned to the formula

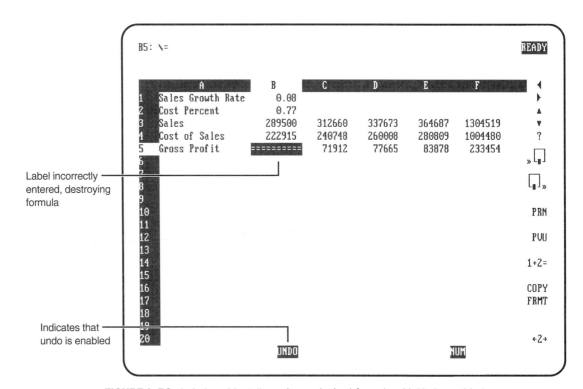

FIGURE L.53. Label accidentally replaces desired formula with Undo enabled.

that resided in the cell before the mistake was made. In this manner, you can use the Undo feature to assist you in recovering from mistakes when you are building and revising your worksheets.

Keypoint!

> The Undo feature requires that a portion of memory be reserved to store the previous copy of your worksheet. This reduces the amount of memory available for your worksheet or attaching Add-Ins. When attaching Add-Ins or creating very large worksheets, if the message "out of memory" appears on your screen, you may want to *disable* the Undo feature!

L.3.11   Report Column Headings and Underlines

Now let's add headings and underlines to produce the report shown in Figure L.54 for Good Morning Products. The first step is to add blank rows so that there is room for these management style report features.

Action: Verify that PLAN5 is your currently active worksheet file.

To add blank lines for the report heading

Move to:	D3	This could be any cell in row 3
Press:	/	Access main menu
Select:	Worksheet	
Select:	Insert	Desired activity
Select:	Row	Type of insertion
Press:	<down>	Beginning drawing cursor over number of rows to be inserted
Press:	<down>	Cursor is three rows high
Press:	<Enter>	Three rows are inserted into worksheet
Move to:	D8	Desired location for inserting another row
Press:	/	Access main menu
Select:	Worksheet	
Select:	Insert	Desired activity
Select:	Row	Type of insert
Press:	<Enter>	Complete activity inserting one row

Another row is inserted for the underlining.

Action: Move the cell pointer about the worksheet and observe that 1-2-3 once again changed the row numbers in the formulas to adjust for the rows that were inserted.

Now let's add the column headings to the worksheet.

To add column headings to a worksheet report

Move to:	B4	Desired location of first heading
Enter:	"1st QTR	Desired heading

The quote (") specifies this is a LABEL, which is to be RIGHT-justified in the cell. That is, the "R" in QTR will be flush with the right edge of the cell.

```
Sales Growth Rate      0.08
Cost Percent           0.77

                     1ST QTR   2ND QTR   3RD QTR   4TH QTR     TOTAL
                     -------   -------   -------   -------   -------
Sales                 289500    312660    337673    364687   1304519
Cost of Sales         222915    240748    260008    280809   1004480
                     -------   -------   -------   -------   -------
Gross Profit           66585     71912     77665     83878    300039
```

FIGURE L.54. Report with column headings and underlines.

Action:	Enter the other column headings in the same manner.	
Move to:	**B5**	Desired location for underlining
Enter:	" -------	Desired underlining as label

This will give you a right-justified underline. The dash or hyphen is used instead of the underscore key to make the underline appear correctly.

Action: Copy **B5** to **C5..F5** to complete the underlining.
Action: Copy **B5..F5** to **B8.**

This produces the entire underline in row **8** in one operation.

Action: Print this report and save the result as PLAN5.

L.3.12 Label Prefixes

Lotus 1-2-3 uses **label prefixes** to identify the positioning of a label within a cell. The apostrophe (') is the default prefix that is inserted by 1-2-3 if you do not type one as the first character of the label. When a *label begins* with a numeric digit, you must type the label prefix. For example, the label "123 Main Street" would require that you type an apostrophe as the first character. Otherwise, 1-2-3 would assume that you were trying to enter a value and would beep at you because this is not a formula it can understand. However, remember that a label has a value of zero, so you cannot perform any arithmetic on numbers entered as labels. The label prefixes in Lotus 1-2-3 are shown in Figure L.55.

Prefix	Description
'	left-justified
"	right-justified
^	center
\	repeat character fills entire cell with a string of the single character immediately following the \<backslash\>

FIGURE L.55. Label prefixes.

L.3.13 Presentation Quality Reporting

You are nearing the completion of preparing next year's budget for Good Morning Products. Your task is to complete the management style report with headings, underlines, and so on as portrayed in Figure L.56. Notice that this report contains the date on which the report was produced. This date was obtained from the computer's clock using the @NOW or @TODAY function together with a / Range Format Date 1 (/RFD1) as illustrated in the cell content of **F1** in Figure L.57. Here, your column width must be 10 spaces or greater to provide room for the date to be displayed.

Each of the main report heading lines is a **long label** entered in column **B,** as illustrated in Figure L.57. Since the *columns to the right are blank,* these long labels are extended over the blank cells. If the cells to the right were not **blank,** the display of the long label would be chopped off.

The heading is centered over the width of the report. Lotus 1-2-3 does *not* have a command that permits you to center a long label over several columns. The label prefix ^ only lets you center a label *within* a column. You must *manually center* a heading like

```
                                                        21-Oct-94

                           GOOD MORNING PRODUCTS
                      PRO FORMA PROFIT AND LOSS STATEMENT
                      ------------------------------------

      Sales Growth Rate      0.08
      Cost Percent           0.77

                           1ST QTR   2ND QTR   3RD QTR   4TH QTR    TOTAL
                           -------   -------   -------   -------   -------
      Sales                 289500    312660    337673    364687   1304519
      Cost of Sales         222915    240748    260008    280809   1004480
                           -------   -------   -------   -------   -------
      Gross Profit           66585     71912     77665     83878    300039
                           =======   =======   =======   =======   =======
```

FIGURE L.56. Report with headings.

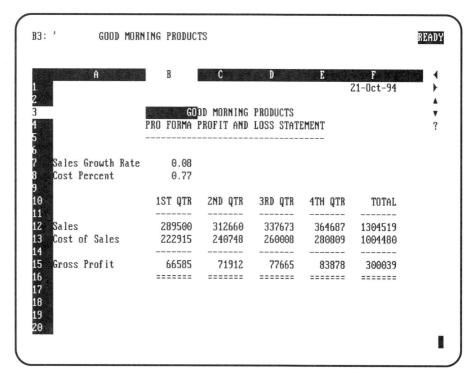

FIGURE L.57. Heading entered as a long label in **B3**.

this when it extends over several columns. Therefore, when entering each long label, include a sufficient number of spaces between the apostrophe and the first character of the title to appropriately center the main report heading. Eight (8) spaces are used in cell **B3**. If your centering is off with your first try, edit the cell using <F2> (EDIT) and add or remove spaces to obtain the desired positioning of the report heading.

Action: Revise the four-quarter report to add the desired headings and underlines.

| To include the date from the computer's clock on your report

Action: Enter the @NOW or @TODAY function in the desired cell to obtain the current date in the report. Format this cell as /RFD1. Other selected Date Formats are available, as illustrated in Figure L.58.

Lotus 1-2-3 contains a number of functions in addition to the @NOW and @SUM functions. Functions are available for performing mathematical, logical, financial, date, statistical, database, and special operations. Selected 1-2-3 functions are explored in Lesson L.7. Also, see the *Lotus 1-2-3 Reference Manual* or access HELP with <F1> for a complete list of functions and their computational operations.

L.3.13.1. Adjusting Margins

Before the report is actually printed, you need to check the print margins to determine if the report will fit across your page as desired. The Print Settings dialog box shown in Figure L.59 indicates changes to the current default settings of:

Left Margin = 4
Right Margin = 76

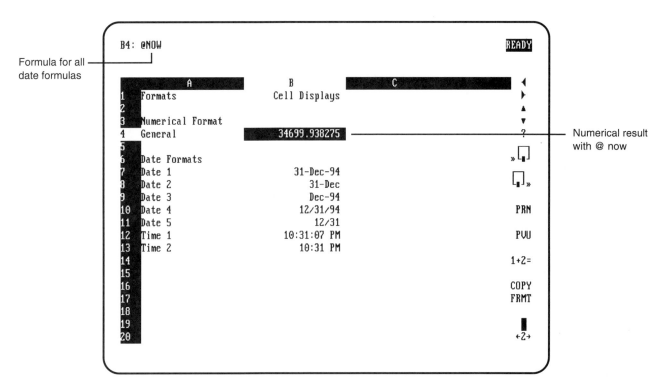

Formula for all date formulas

B4: @NOW   READY

	A	B	C
1	Formats	Cell Displays	
2			
3	Numerical Format		
4	General	34699.938275	
5			
6	Date Formats		
7	Date 1	31-Dec-94	
8	Date 2	31-Dec	
9	Date 3	Dec-94	
10	Date 4	12/31/94	
11	Date 5	12/31	
12	Time 1	10:31:07 PM	
13	Time 2	10:31 PM	

Numerical result with @ now

PRN

PVU

1+2=

COPY
FRMT

←2→

FIGURE L.58. Selected date and time formats.

B3: '   GOOD MORNING PRODUCTS   MENU
Header Footer Margins Borders Setup Pg-Length Other Quit
Left Right Top Bottom None
┌──────────────────────── Print Settings ────────────────────────┐

    Range: [A1..F20········]   ┌─Destination─────────────────┐
                                  │ (*) Printer   ( ) Encoded file │
    ┌─Margins────────────┐   │ ( ) Text file ( ) Background │
    │ Left: [4··] Top: [2·] │   │   │
    │ Right: [83·] Bottom: [2·] │ │ File name: [·················] │
    └────────────────────┘   └──────────────────────────────┘

    ┌─Borders────────────┐
    │ Columns: [·············] │   Page length: [66·]
    │ Rows: [·············] │
    └────────────────────┘   Setup string: [\027\018·····]

    Header: [··························]   [ ] Unformatted pages
    Footer: [··························]   [ ] List entries

    Interface: Parallel 1   Name: HP LaserJet series

              Press F2 (EDIT) to edit settings

FIGURE L.59. Print setting sheet with margins and setup.

Although this Left Margin is usually satisfactory, the Right Margin frequently requires adjusting. Your 1-2-3 screen displays up to 72 characters. Typical computer paper is 85 characters wide. If the Right Margin is set too small, it will result in the rightmost column being printed *below* the other columns, as illustrated in Figure L.60. Although your computer paper is physically wide enough for this column, the Right Margin specification prevents it from being printed in the desired location. The Right Margin is modified in this manner from the Print Printer menu (/PP).

To adjust the right margin for printing

Action:		Continue with the worksheet containing the headings, and access the Print Menu with the /PP command.
Select:	Options	Menu choice to change margins
Select:	Margins	Desired activity
Select:	Right	Desired margin
Enter:	83	Desired position for Right Margin
Select:	Quit	Leave Options "sticky" menu and return to Print menu

The Default Right Margin in 1-2-3 is 76 characters. This is the appropriate width that exactly matches your 1-2-3 display screen. If you designed all of your reports to be the exact width of your display screen, you would not need to adjust the margins. However, to use the entire width of a typical $8\frac{1}{2}$-in.-wide piece of paper, this adjustment is usually required.

A wide-carriage printer frequently allows 132 characters to be printed across a page. This requires an adjustment in the Right Margin so that printing will take place across the entire page. Otherwise, printing would be like that shown in Figure L.60, although your printer is much wider.

```
Sales Growth Rate      0.08
Cost Percent           0.77

                    1ST QTR   2ND QTR   3RD QTR   4TH QTR
                    -------   -------   -------   -------
Sales                289500    312660    337673    364687
Cost of Sales        222915    240748    260008    280809
                    -------   -------   -------   -------
Gross Profit          66585     71912     77665     83878
                    =======   =======   =======   =======


      TOTAL
      -------
      1304519
      1004480
      -------
       300039
      =======
```

FIGURE L.60. Printing with right margin set too small.

L.3.13.2.   Compressed Printing

Many printers have a compressed print mode that allows more characters to be printed per inch across a page. Typically, 10 characters are printed per inch with up to 85 characters across an $8\frac{1}{2}$-in.-wide page. With compressed print, 16 characters can be printed per inch on many dot matrix and laser printers. This lets you print up to 136 characters across an $8\frac{1}{2}$-in.-wide page and even more characters with a wide-carriage printer. Compressed print is frequently used for reports consisting of 12 monthly columns. The / Print Printer Options Setup (/PPOS) command is used to specify printer Setup codes that control compressed and normal printing. These Setup codes consist of three-digit ASCII code numbers preceded by a backslash, which are obtained from the user manual for each printer. Three-digit ASCII codes are used, since the characters used to control this operation of a printer are often special characters that do not have keys on a typical personal computer keyboard. For several different brands of dot matrix printers, the Setup strings are as follows:

Setup	Setup String
Compressed print	\027\015
Normal print	\027\018

In these Setup strings, the \027 represent an <Escape>. It is used with some printers, but is not required for all printers. If these Setup strings fail to control your printer, you will need to check out your specific codes in your printer's reference manual. If your Setup strings are different, enter them here for your future reference:

My Setup Strings for Lotus 1-2-3:

Compressed Print _____

Normal Print _____

_____

_____

Let's look at how the Setup printer control string is modified.

Action:	Access the Print menu with the /PP command.	
Select:	Setup	Specification to be revised
Enter:	\027\015	Set compressed print
Select:	Quit	Leave Options "sticky" menu and return to Print menu

To change the printer setup control string

You are now ready to print your report.

Action: Print the report in compressed print.

Action: Change the Setup to normal print.

Action: Make the necessary menu selections and entries to perform these activities:

1. Print the Good Morning Products management style report.

2. Print the cell formulas.

3. Save the completed report as PLAN6.

~~~~~~
Caution Alert!
~~~~~~

> When you print the As-Displayed report, if the TOTAL column appears on a separate page, it is because either the column width is too wide or the right margin has not been set or both. Revise the default global column width and be sure that the Right Margin has been set!

If you performed the print expecting the results to be output and cell formulas happen to be displayed, you will need to reset the option to AS-DISPLAYED using the Print Printer Options Other As-Displayed (/PPOOA) command.

Keypoint!

> The Options Other command is a toggle that switches between As-Displayed and Cell-Formulas. Once the Print Printer Options Other (/PPOO) has been established, it remains in effect until you change it!

L.3.14   Using SmartIcons to Copy Cell Contents and Enhance Worksheets

Let's explore several 1-2-3 SmartIcons that are useful in building worksheets and preparing reports, which are available beginning with Release 2.4. Some of the more frequently used SmartIcons and those examined in this lesson are shown in Figure L.61.

SmartIcon	WYSIWYG SmartIcon	Command	Description
DEL		Erase Range	Erases cell contents in the highlighted range.
COPY		Copy Range	Copies a selected range to another specified range.
MOVE		Move Range	Moves a selected range to another specified range.
REP DATA		Repeat Data	Copies content of cell in upper-left corner of highlighted range to all cells in the selected range.
1 + 2 =		Sum Values	Sums values in highlighted range, when you include empty cells to the right of or below the range.
+ROW		Insert Rows	Inserts one or more rows above highlighted rows.
−ROW		Delete Rows	Delete all rows in the highlighted range.
+COL		Insert Columns	Inserts one or more columns to the left of the highlighted columns.
−COL		Delete Columns	Deletes all columns in the highlighted range.
UNDO		Undo	Cancels previous action or command when Undo feature is enabled.

FIGURE L.61. Selected SmartIcons for this Lesson.

Action: Make sure that the SmartIcon Add-In has been attached. If necessary, attach this Add-In as described in the previous Lesson.

Action: Retrieve your PLAN4 worksheet file and set the Global Column-Width to 10. This will allow columns **A** through **F** to be displayed for both copying cell contents for the four quarters and including the **TOTAL** column.

L.3.14.1. Erasing Cell Contents

Cell contents can be erased by using a SmartIcon by highlighting the cell range to be erased and then clicking the Erase Range SmartIcon (Figure L.61). Let's learn how this can be used to remove the contents of two different cell ranges.

Action:	Highlight the cell range **D3..E3.**	
Action:	Scroll to SmartIcon page 5, which contains the Erase Range (DEL) icon.	
Click:	Erase Range SmartIcon	Desired activity
Action:	Highlight the cell range **C4..E5.**	
Click:	Erase Range SmartIcon	Desired activity

The cell contents of the appropriate cells are erased. Your worksheet appears as in Figure L.62 with the labels, data values, and formulas before any copying was done. You may erase any selected range of cells from your worksheet using this Range Erase SmartIcon.

L.3.14.2 Copying Cell Contents

Lotus 1-2-3 provides two different SmartIcons for copying the contents of a single cell or a cell range into other cells:

1. The Copy Range (COPY) SmartIcon copies any selected cell range into any other cell range, located anywhere on your worksheet.

2. The Repeat Data (REP DATA) SmartIcon is more limited. It allows you to copy a single cell into an adjacent cell range. However, this is most useful when a cell's content is copied across a row or down a column.

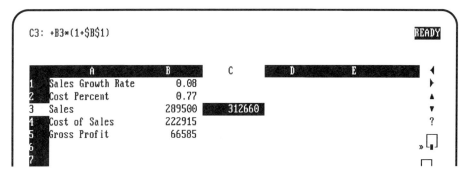

FIGURE L.62. Worksheet remaining after erasing selected cells.

Since the Copy Range SmartIcon is more general, let's see how this is used to copy the formulas for the other quarters of the Good Morning Products worksheet. First, copy the *Sales* formula from the second quarter into the third and fourth quarters.

To copy a cell's contents using the Copy Range SmartIcon			
Click:	C3		Position cell pointer and specify the copy **from** range
Action:	Scroll to SmartIcon page 4, which contains the Copy Range (COPY) icon.		
Click:	Copy Range SmartIcon		Desired activity
Highlight:	D3..E3		Specify the copy **to** range by using the mouse pointer [Figure L.63]
Click:	<left mouse button>		Cause copy to be performed

Now you are ready to copy the formulas for both *Cost of Sales* and *Gross Profit* into the cells of the next three quarters at the same time.

To copy a selected cell range using the Copy Range SmartIcon		
Highlight:	B4..B5	Select the **from** cell range
Click:	Copy Range SmartIcon	Desired activity
Highlight:	C4..E4	Specify the **to** cell range
Click:	<left mouse button>	Complete copy command

The formulas are copied into the desired cells, with the worksheet appearing like that shown previously in Figure L.49. Whether SmartIcons or keyboard commands are used to perform a copy, the cells contain the same formulas and display the same results.

Action: Move the cell pointer about the area where you copied the formulas and verify that they are indeed the same formulas.

For a worksheet like Good Morning Products Pro Forma Profit and Loss Statement with the columns as time periods that contain similar formulas, the Repeat Data (REP DATA) SmartIcon is a convenient way for copying each row of formulas, one row at a time.

Action: To prepare for using the Repeat Data SmartIcon, you need to erase the formulas so that you can copy them by using this SmartIcon. That is, erase the cell contents in the cells **D3..E3** and **C4..E5.** This is performed as described in the previous section.

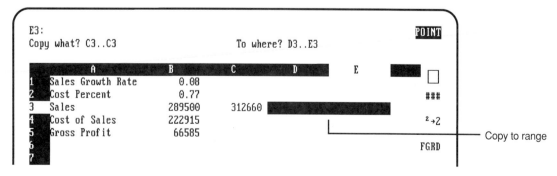

FIGURE L.63. Highlighted copy TO specification with the Copy Range SmartIcon.

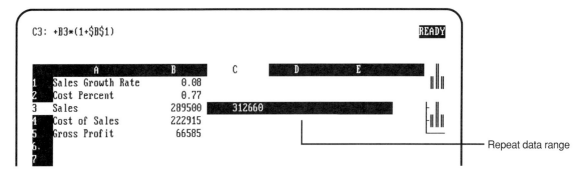

FIGURE L.64. Highlighted range for use with Repeat Data SmartIcon.

Now you are ready to use the Repeat Data SmartIcon to carry out the copy operations. With this SmartIcon, you highlight the cell containing the formula to be copied **from** *and* the cells where the formula is to be copied **to** as *one cell range* (Figure L.64). The cell to be copied **from** *must* be in the upper-left corner of the selected cell range. Let's see how this copy is done.

To copy a cell's contents into adjacent cells using the Repeat Data SmartIcon	**Highlight:**	**C3..E3**	The cell range in the row where you want the formula, including the formula
	Action:	Scroll to SmartIcon page 8, which contains the Repeat Data (REP DATA) icon.	
	Click:	Repeat Data SmartIcon	Desired activity

The formula is copied into the specified cells. Now continue with the next formula.

Highlight:	**B4..E4**	The next formula and its cell range
Click:	Repeat Data SmartIcon	Desired activity
Highlight:	**B5..E5**	The next formula and its cell range
Click:	Repeat Data SmartIcon	Desired activity

The formulas are again copied into the desired cells, with the worksheet appearing like that shown in Figure L.49. With the Repeat Data SmartIcon, only one formula or data value may be copied at a time. To copy different formulas, the Repeat Data SmartIcon is used with each formula.

L.3.14.3. Summing Cell Contents

Now, let's add a total column to the worksheet to obtain the total for the year using the Sum Values SmartIcon. This SmartIcon creates a formula containing the @SUM function in the selected cells. These cells are located either (1) immediately to the right of or (2) immediately below the cells whose values you want summed. The @SUM function may be applied to a series of rows or columns in the specified cell range at one time. Here's how the SmartIcon can be used.

To total selected cells using the Sum Values SmartIcon	**Highlight:**	**B3..F5**	Cells to be summed including cells where total is desired to the right of the cells containing values (Figure L.65)
	Action:	Scroll to SmartIcon page 2, which contains the Sum Values (1 + 2 =) icon.	
	Click:	Sum Values SmartIcon	Desired activity

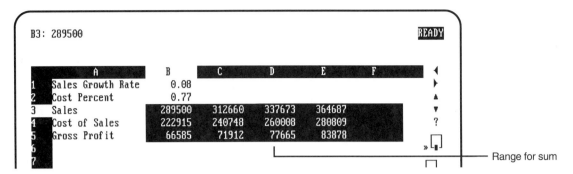

FIGURE L.65. Highlighted range for summing with the Sum Values SmartIcon.

The summation is performed as illustrated in Figure L.66. Now you can verify the use of the @SUM function.

Action: Position the cell pointer on each of the cells **F3, F4,** and **F5** to verify that these cells contain the @SUM function resulting from using the Sum Values SmartIcon.

Action: Save this as the PLAN5A worksheet file.

L.3.14.4. Moving Cell Contents

In preparation for creating a presentation quality report, the key assumptions of *Sales Growth Rate* and *Cost Percent* can be relocated on the worksheet at row **11** so that they are below the main body of the report. This makes the key assumptions available for review, but places them out of the way from the main report. This can be accomplished with the Move Range SmartIcon.

To move a selected cell range using the Move Range SmartIcon

Highlight:	**A1..B2**	Select the **from** cell range
Click:	Move Range SmartIcon	Desired activity; as necessary locate the icon page containing this icon
Click:	**A11**	Specify the upper-left corner of the **to** cell range
Click:	\<left mouse button\>	Complete copy command

The cell contents are moved to the specified worksheet location. Whether SmartIcons or keyboard commands are used to perform a move, the same result occurs.

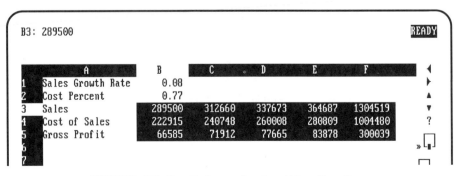

FIGURE L.66. Results from using Sum Values SmartIcon.

L.3.14.5.   Inserting Rows and Completing the Report

The presentation-quality report can be completed by inserting several rows and adding labels to produce the report shown in Figure L.67. Additional rows may be inserted by using the Insert Rows (+ROW) SmartIcon.

First, five (5) rows need to be added above the current cells containing the *Sales* information. Then, a row is inserted between the *Cost of Sales* and *Gross Profit* information. Let's see how this is accomplished for the Good Morning Products report.

To insert several rows by using the Insert Rows SmartIcon	**Click:**	**B1**	This could be any cell in row **1**
	Highlight:	**B1..B5**	Specify that 5 rows are to be inserted
	Click:	Insert Rows SmartIcon	Desired activity; as necessary locate the icon page containing this icon
To insert a single row using the Insert Rows SmartIcon	**Click:**	**B10**	Location for inserting next row
	Click:	Insert Row SmartIcon	Desired activity

Rows are inserted *above* the cell pointer with the height of the cell pointer specifying the number of rows to be inserted. You have the necessary blank rows for adding the report heading, column titles, and underlining. You are ready to complete this report so it appears as shown in Figure L.67.

Action: Enter the report heading as long labels in cell **B2..B4.**

Action: Enter the column headings as right-justified labels in cells **B6..F6.**

Action: Enter the underline in cell **B7** as a right-justified label that is a series of minus signs.

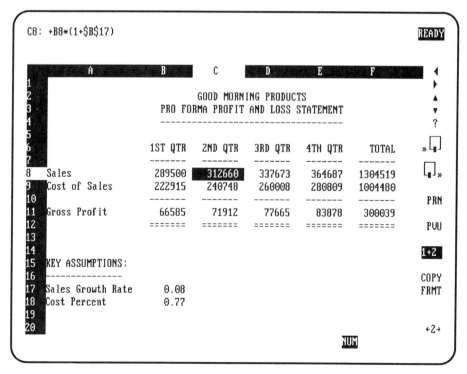

FIGURE L.67. Complete management style report.

Action: Use the Repeat Data SmartIcon to copy the underline into cells **C7..F7.**

Action: Use the Copy Range SmartIcon to copy the underline from cells **B7..F7** to cell **B10.**

Action: Add the double underline in cells **B12..F12** by using the equal sign for the label in cell **B12** and then copy it with the Repeat Data SmartIcon.

Action: Add the labels in cells **A15..A16** to identify the key assumptions.

Action: Print the complete presentation-quality report and save this as the PLAN6A worksheet file on your Data Disk. Be sure to set the margins before printing your report.

Action: If desired, you may now Quit from 1-2-3.

L.3.15 **When Things Go Wrong**

A variety of difficulties may be encountered while you are changing column widths, copying cell contents, and creating management style reports. Some of the more common situations and how to approach them are described here:

1. Asterisks (*) have appeared in one or more cells that should contain a numerical value. This usually occurs when the column width is too narrow.

    a. Position the cell pointer on one of the cells filled with asterisks.

    b. Review the cell's content to ensure that you have the desired value and/or formula.

    c. Check the cell's content to determine if the column's width is controlled by the global column width or by an individual column width setting.

    d. Use the / Worksheet Global Column-Width (/WGC) or / Worksheet Column Set-Width (/WCS) command, as appropriate. Adjust the column width using <right> to expand the width until the asterisks disappear.

2. For some unknown reason, all of the numerical values in the worksheet area are displayed with two places to the right of the decimal. This usually occurs when the <Enter> key is pressed repeatedly after the main menu is accessed with the slash (/). Continually pressing <Enter> results in execution of the / Worksheet Global Format Fixed 2 (/WGFF2) command.

    a. Position the cell pointer on one of the cells displayed with two places to the right of the decimal.

    b. Check the cell's content to determine if the cell's format is controlled by a global or range format.

    c. Use the / Worksheet Global Format (/WGF) or / Range Format (/RF) command, as appropriate. Revise the cell's format to the General format or so that the desired number of decimals are displayed.

3. You entered a decimal number less than one, such as .19 or .87, as a value in a cell and a zero (0) or one (1) appeared in the worksheet area. This usually indicates that the cell has been given a format that displays only integer numbers.

    a. Position the cell pointer on the cell displaying the zero or one.

    b. Review the cell's content to ensure that a number less than one has been entered in the cell.

    c. Check the cell's content to determine if the cell's format is controlled by a global or range format.

    d. Use the / Worksheet Global Format (/WGF) or / Range Format (/RF) command, as appropriate. Modify the cell's format so that the desired number of decimals are displayed.

4. When you performed a copy, the values in cells that have been copied are all zeros. This may be caused by using relative referencing when absolute referencing should have been used.

    a. Position the cell pointer on the cell containing a zero that should have a nonzero value. This is a cell whose content was copied from another cell.

    b. Review the cell to determine whether relative or absolute referencing has been used and which should be used.

   c. Edit the cell from which the formula was copied, changing the appropriate relative references to absolute references.

   d. Carry out the copy a second time to place the corrected formula into the desired cells.

5. When you add a series of numbers that you have entered on your worksheet, you get a result of zero. This usually occurs when numbers have been entered as labels, rather than values.

   a. Position the cell pointer on the cells containing the numbers that have been summed.

   b. Check the cell's content to determine if the number was entered as a label; if so, a label prefix is present.

   c. Edit each cell and remove the label prefix so that the cell contains a value rather than a label.

6. You completed entering a formula containing an @SUM function and the CIRC indicator appeared. This usually results when the @SUM function contains the cell name of the cell where the @SUM has been placed so that the sum is added to itself.

   a. Position the cell pointer on the cell containing the @SUM function that was just entered and where the CIRC first appeared.

   b. Review the cell's content to determine if the sum range includes the cell where the formula has been placed.

   c. Edit the cell to correct the range of cells in the @SUM function so that it excludes the cell where the formulas resides.

7. You have printed a report and the output appears with a larger than desired right margin. This frequently occurs when the right margin has not been appropriately set.

   a. Check the setting of the right margin with the / Print Printer Options Margins (/PPOM) command.

   b. Set the right margin to match the desired printing width for your printer.

L.3.16 Lesson Summary

- A cell's content can be revised by editing or by replacement.
- The Copy command provides a convenient method for duplicating cell formulas.
- Global commands control the appearance of cell formats and column widths.
- Cell formulas readily accommodate growth rate and ratio logic.
- Relative and absolute cell addressing assist in copying similar formulas from one cell to another cell.
- The @SUM function is useful in creating total columns.
- Report headings, column headings, and underlines are added to reports to produce presentation-quality management reports.
- Label prefixes determine the location of a label within an individual cell.
- The current date can be obtained from the computer's clock for inclusion in a report.
- Margins and Setup strings control the appearance of reports printed on paper.
- SmartIcons provide an alternative method for erasing, copying, moving, and summing cell ranges. They let you insert and delete worksheet rows and columns.

L.3.17 Practice Tutorial

~~~~~~~~
Caution Alert!

Be sure to save the current worksheet to your Data Disk before you begin another exercise or problem!
~~~~~~~~

Develop the PLAN6 worksheet described in this Lesson as a guided activity in a hands-on manner. Use your PLAN worksheet from the Practice Tutorial in Lesson L.1 as a starting point for this exercise.

Task 1: Access your PLAN worksheet and review it.

Task 2: Carry out the activities described in this Lesson to produce the PLAN6 worksheet.

Task 3: Print the results as illustrated in Figure L.53.

Task 4: Print the cell formulas.

Task 5: Save this as worksheet file MYPLAN6.

Time Estimates

Novice: 75 minutes

Intermediate: 60 minutes

Advanced: 45 minutes

L.3.18 Practice Exercises

(1) Case: Inland Container (continued)

Mary Montoya needs to revise her worksheet for evaluating the pricing proposal for Rydder Truck Rental. Richard wants a monthly proposal for supplying cartons during the next quarter. After visiting with Richard, Mary is ready to extend her worksheet as a three-month plan for April, May, and June with a total column for the quarter using the following assumptions and worksheet design:

1. Units Sold increase by 3 percent per month.

2. The Units Sold Growth Rate is contained in a single, separate cell and referenced using absolute referencing.

3. Price per Unit increases by $0.20 in the third month.

4. The worksheet model is designed to accept an input Price per Unit increase in any or all of the three months.

5. The Percent Cost of Sales is revised from 73 percent to 67 percent beginning in the first month, and remains the same for all three months.

6. The Percent Cost of Sales is contained in a single, separate cell and is referenced using absolute referencing.

7. A report is created with column headings and underlines.

8. The date of the report is included in its upper-right corner.

9. The report title is
   PROJECTED INCOME FROM RYDDER TRUCK CONTRACT
   which is underlined.

Carry out these tasks to review Mary's worksheet:

Task 1: Access your RYDDER worksheet from Practice Exercise 1 in Lesson L.2 as your beginning point for this exercise.

Task 2: Build this worksheet incorporating Mary's revisions.

Task 3: Print the results.

Task 4: Print the formulas.

Task 5: Save this as worksheet file RYDDER2.

> *Quick check answer:* Gross Profit [Total] = 622550

Time Estimates

Novice: 60 minutes

Intermediate: 45 minutes

Advanced: 30 minutes

(2)   Case: Truck-Lite

> Business Problem: Budget variance analysis
> MIS Characteristics: Finance
>   Managerial Control

Kevin Kotsi is Vice President of Marketing for Truck-Lite Group. Truck-Lite produces automotive tail lamp assemblies and related plastic molded parts. A state-of-the-art distribution center has contributed to their continued growth in the automotive market. Kevin is concerned with monitoring Truck-Lite's marketing expenses. He received a worksheet from the Accounting Department that contains the budget and actual expenses for the last year. The Accounting Department prepared Kevin's worksheet by extracting the data from their general ledger system and writing it directly as a 1-2-3 worksheet file. Kevin wants a variance analysis included as part of the expense report to determine those accounts that may require further investigation. For each account, he wants to see the variance as a dollar amount and as a percentage. These are computed as follows:

Variance = Budget − Actual
Percent Variance = Variance / Budget

The TRUCK.WK1 worksheet Kevin received from Accounting already has the column headings set up for the Variance and Percent Variance. He would like you to complete this report.

Task 1: Retrieve the TRUCK worksheet file from your Data Disk and review its contents.

Task 2: Enter the formulas to compute the variance and percent variance for the *first* expense in the worksheet.

Task 3: Copy these formulas for each of the other expense items and for the total Marketing Expenses. [*Hint:* Any rows that do not contain data should not include a formula. If you accidentally copy the formula to these rows, then erase the cell contents.]

Task 4: Set a Range Format for the Percent Variance column as Percent with one place to the right of the decimal.

Task 5: Print Kevin's variance analysis as a Lotus 1-2-3 report.

Task 6: Print the cell formulas as documentation of the cell contents.

Task 7: Save this as the worksheet file TRUCK.

Task 8: (*Optional*)   Review the variance calculations. Which three accounts had the largest variance and which had the largest percent variance? Is a positive variance good or bad? Why? Write a paragraph explaining your answer. Use salaries and automobile expenses to illustrate your interpretation.

Time Estimates

Novice: 45 minutes

Intermediate: 30 minutes

Advanced: 20 minutes

(3)   Case: Biogenetic Laboratories

Business Problem: Compensation planning
MIS Characteristics: Human Resources
                              Managerial Control

Biogenetics Laboratories is a medium-sized pharmaceutical company that has produced several block-buster products through genetic engineering. Top management at Biogenetics realizes that their success is tied to the quality of information processing that supports their research and production operations. Daryl Kent, Manager of Information Systems Development, believes that rewarding good job performance makes it easier to retain key personnel. Biogenetics provides monetary rewards that are a combination of cost of living adjustments (COLA) and merit pay increases. Although everyone receives the same COLA percent increase each year, merit pay rewards are based on an employee's performance rating. Biogenetics uses a five-point scale for rating job performance, with a five as the best rating. For next year, the company has set the COLA increase at 3 percent. Daryl has been allocated a fixed amount of $35,000 for merit pay increases in his department. Following company guidelines, he needs to assign merit pay increases based on performance rating. He has decided that the best procedure for his I/S Department is to compute the merit increase for each employee as follows:

(Individual rating) / (Sum of all ratings) * (Merit dollars)

The new salary for each employee is computed as the sum of the current salary plus the COLA increase plus the merit increase. Daryl has started developing the BIOGEN worksheet, which contains the COLA percent and merit amount together with a listing of the department's employees, including their current salary and performance rating. He wants you to complete the development of the compensation planning worksheet as follows:

Task 1: Retrieve the BIOGEN.WK1 worksheet file from your Data Disk and review the data that have been entered. Observe that the COLA and Merit values have been placed in individual cells.

Task 2: Using appropriate absolute and relative referencing, create the formulas for the COLA Increase, Merit Increase, and New Salary for the first employee.

Task 3: Copy the formulas for the COLA Increase, Merit Increase, and New Salary for each of the other employees. Be careful not to copy the Current Salary or Performance Rating. Also, exercise care that you do not destroy the formulas for total compensation.

Task 4: Print the solution results as a Lotus 1-2-3 report.

Task 5: Print the cell formulas.

Task 6: Save this as your worksheet file BIOGEN.

Time Estimates

Novice: 60 minutes

Intermediate: 45 minutes

Advanced: 30 minutes

(4)   Case: Dial America Telemarketing

Business Problem: Capacity Planning
MIS Characteristics: Production/Operations
Strategic Planning

Dial America Telemarketing serves a variety of businesses that use 800-Service for receiving customer orders. In response to a television, magazine, or newspaper advertisement, a customer dials 1-800-ORDER-IT to reach a telemarketing associate at Dial America. As a telemarketing service organization, Dial America does order entry for more than 50 different businesses, with each business contracting with Dial America for its order entry services. Dial America is experiencing explosive growth as the number of orders processed increases each quarter. Scott Silvenis, Dial America's Manager of Information Systems Operation, is concerned with the ability of its current local area network (LAN) to handle the increase processing requirements. The current network is limited in the number of workstations and available disk storage capacity. Scott needs to know when the capacity of the current LAN will be exceeded so that he can plan to upgrade the system. Scott has started creating the DIAL worksheet with his computer system capacity plan. He arranged the worksheet with separate areas for "ASSUMPTIONS" and "PROJECTIONS." Scott has entered the values and formulas for the first quarter of his eight-quarter plan. He wants to you complete the development of his capacity planning worksheet in this manner:

Task 1: Retrieve the DIAL.WK1 worksheet file from your Data Disk and review Scott's work. Assoc Hours per Month are computed based on an eight-hour workday and 22 work days per month. The eight-hour day is adjusted for personal time and related work breaks. Observe the use of absolute and relative referencing in the formulas for the first quarter of the projections.

Task 2: Using appropriate relative and absolute reference, create the formula for the Number of Orders in the second quarter of year 1. This is a growth rate formula that uses the Order Growth rate provided as an assumptions.

Task 3: Copy the growth rate formula for the Number of Orders into the cells for the other six quarters.

Task 4: Copy the other formulas and values for the projections from the first quarter of the plan into the other seven quarters.

Task 5: Set a Range Format for Capacity Utilization as Percent 1.

Task 6: Print the capacity plan as a hard copy report.

Task 7: Document the worksheet by printing the cell formulas.

Task 8: (*Optional*)   Review the results. Based on this plan, when will Scott first need to add workstation capacity and/or disk storage capacity? If expansion takes place in increments of the current Design Capacity, will further expansion be required? If so, when? For which computer resource(s)? Write a paragraph explaining your answers.

Time Estimates

Novice: 60 minutes

Intermediate: 45 minutes

Advanced: 30 minutes

(5)   Case: Horizon Industries, Ltd.

Business Problem: Financial statement reporting
MIS Characteristics: Finance
                     Strategic Planning

Horizon Industries, Ltd., manufactures a broad range of residential carpet marketed worldwide through specialty retailers, department stores, and wholesale distributors. Their product line includes a uniquely styled collection of wool carpet for the high-end residential market. Alexis Cameron is Horizon's senior accountant responsible for preparing the Statement of Earnings for inclusion in Horizon Industries' annual report to shareholders. Alexis has compiled the basic financial data and began entering them in the HORIZON.WK1 worksheet file. For each account in her worksheet, she still needs to compute the change between this year and last year and needs to include formulas to calculate the Percent of net sales. The formula for the "Increase" is

Amount [19X2] - Amount [19X1]

The formula for the "Percent of net sales" for each year is

Account amount / Net sales amount * 100

The multiplication by 100 will display the percent amounts in the desired form. Alexis prefers this method for positioning the decimal rather than using 1-2-3's percent format. She does not want the percent symbol displayed with each computed value because Percent is already specified by the column title.

Alexis has sketched out the final report design with the desired report heading as shown here:

Horizon Industries, Ltd.
STATEMENT OF EARNINGS
(Dollars in thousands)

	19X2	19X1	Increase	Percent of Net Sales 19X2	19X1
Net Sales	XXX,XXX	XXX,XXX	XXX,XXX	XXX.XX	XXX.XX
Cost of Sales	XXX,XXX	XXX,XXX	XXX,XXX	XXX.XX	XXX.XX
Gross Profit	XXX,XXX	XXX,XXX	XXX,XXX	XXX.XX	XXX.XX
Operating Expenses					
Marketing	XXX,XXX	XXX,XXX	XXX,XXX	XXX.XX	XXX.XX
Research and develop.	XXX,XXX	XXX,XXX	XXX,XXX	XXX.XX	XXX.XX
Administrative	XXX,XXX	XXX,XXX	XXX,XXX	XXX.XX	XXX.XX
Operating Profit	XXX,XXX	XXX,XXX	XXX,XXX	XXX.XX	XXX.XX
Other (Income) Deductions					
Royalty income	XXX,XXX	XXX,XXX	XXX,XXX	XXX.XX	XXX.XX
Interest income	XXX,XXX	XXX,XXX	XXX,XXX	XXX.XX	XXX.XX
Interest expense	XXX,XXX	XXX,XXX	XXX,XXX	XXX.XX	XXX.XX
Miscellaneous	XXX,XXX	XXX,XXX	XXX,XXX	XXX.XX	XXX.XX
Other Deductions	XXX,XXX	XXX,XXX	XXX,XXX	XXX.XX	XXX.XX
Earnings before tax	XXX,XXX	XXX,XXX	XXX,XXX	XXX.XX	XXX.XX
Income Tax	XXX,XXX	XXX,XXX	XXX,XXX	XXX.XX	XXX.XX
NET EARNINGS	XXX,XXX	XXX,XXX	XXX,XXX	XXX.XX	XXX.XX

Task 1: Retrieve the HORIZON.WK1 worksheet file from your Data Disk and review its contents.

Task 2: Enter the formula to compute the Increase or variance between the dollar amounts for Net sales for this year and last year. Use copying to place this formula in the other cells in the Increase column. Set the Global Format to comma with no decimals.

Quick check answer: NET EARNINGS [Increase] = 33,530

Task 3: Enter the formula for computing the Percent of net sales for each of the two years. Use absolute referencing in the cell name for Net Sales in the denominator of these formulas. Copy these formulas to the other cells in the Percent of net sales columns. Set the Range Format for these two columns to comma with two places to the right of the decimal.

Quick check answer: NET EARNINGS [19x2 Percent] = 11.47

Task 4: Complete a management style report for Alexis by adding the report heading and underlining as indicated in her report design sketch.

Task 5: Print the completed report.

Task 6: Print the cell formulas.

Task 7: Save this as the HORIZON worksheet file.

Time Estimates

Novice: 60 minutes

Intermediate: 45 minutes

Advanced: 30 minutes

(6)   Case: Austin Antares Consulting

Business Problem: Estimating program development time

MIS Characteristics: Human Resources

Managerial Planning

Austin Antares Consulting (AA) specializes in the development and implementation of custom business computer system applications. The firm provides the expertise for a complete systems development effort including systems analysis, systems design, programming, hardware selection, and installation. AA signed an engagement letter with Northland Industries for the development of a Sales Order Processing system. The project has been assigned to Claude McMillan's development team. During the New System Design phase, Claude worked with his team in producing a dataflow diagram of the proposed system, as shown in Figure L.68.

In preparing for next week's review with Northland's project sponsor, Claude needs to refine AA's cost estimate for the New System Build phase in which his staff will undertake writing the computer programs specified by the processes in their dataflow diagram. At the meeting with the project's sponsor, Claude expects a Go/No-Go decision for continuing with the system's development. The standard practice at AA is to estimate the amount of programming time for building a system using this formula:

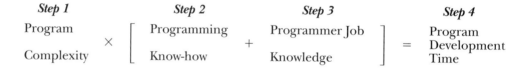

Step 1		*Step 2*		*Step 3*		*Step 4*
Program Complexity	×	[Programming Know-how	+	Programmer Job Knowledge]	=	Program Development Time

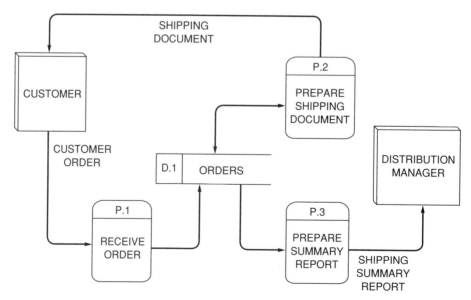

FIGURE L.68. Dataflow diagram of proposed system.

Over the years, AA has collected data on various computer development projects. These data have been compiled and refined to provide the factors used in the Program Development Time formulas. Claude refers to these tables in making his estimates:

Programmer Know-how	Weighting Points
Analyst/Programmer III	0.75
Analyst/Programmer II	1.00
Analyst/Programmer I	2.00

Programmer Job Knowledge Available	Required	
	Much	Some
Detailed	0.75	0.25
General	1.25	0.50
None	2.00	1.25

Programming Function	Program Complexity		
	Simple	Complex	Very Complex
Data retrieval	1	2	4
Data presentation	1	3	5
Data edit checking	2	4	7
Calculate	1	2	4

Claude created his ESTIMATE.WK1 worksheet file by selecting the appropriate factors from these tables for the Sales Order Processing system. He has entered these values in the worksheet and is ready to finish the estimate of program development time and cost for the meeting with the project's sponsor at Northland Industries. Claude wants you to complete the worksheet as follows:

Task 1: Retrieve the ESTIMATE.WK1 worksheet file from your Data Disk and review the data Claude has entered for each of the three processes specified by the dataflow diagram.

Task 2: Create the formulas to compute the Program Development Time for each Processing Function and the Total for each process.

Task 3: Create a formula for the **Total program development time in days.** This should be the summation of the **Total** for each of the three processes.

Quick check answer: Total program development time in days = 28.25

Task 4: AA's engagement letter with Northland provides for these daily billing rates:

	Daily Rate
Analyst/Programmer III	$800
Analyst/Programmer II	600
Analyst/Programmer I	600

Create a formula that computes the **Estimated program development cost** using these billing rates for each of the three analyst/programmers on Claude's team. Format this cell as Currency 0.

Task 5: Print the solution results as a Lotus 1-2-3 report.

Task 6: Print the cell formulas to document the worksheet.

Task 7: Save this as your ESTIMATE worksheet file.

Time Estimates

Novice: 60 minutes

Intermediate: 45 minutes

Advanced: 30 minutes

L.3.19   Comprehensive Problems

(1)   Case: Woodcraft Furniture Company (continued)

Joe Birch wants you to extend Woodcraft's income statement model to be a monthly projection with a column of quarterly totals. He wants you to sum only those variables that are additive. For those variables that cannot be summed, their weighted average should be calculated for the quarter. Joe has indicated that the weighted average should be used for the Table Price, Chair Price, and Sofa Price. For example, the weighted average Table Price is the total Tables Sales divided by the Tables Sold. The Return on Sales in the total column must be computed using the totals for the quarter, since this cannot be summed. In general, growth rates and ratios like this cannot be summed in the total column, but must be computed separately.

"Tall" Pine has assisted you in collecting the following data for your use in extending the worksheet:

	July	August	September
Table Price	$510	$510	$525
Chair Price	110	110	120
Sofa Price	400	420	420
Employees	157	160	165
Hourly Rate	9.60	9.60	9.60
Hours Worked per Employee	174	174	174
Tables Sold	850	900	970
Sofas Sold	561	594	627
Management Salaries	73000	73000	73000
General and Administrative	24000	25000	26000

The percents and ratios used to determine the Cost of Sales, Overhead, Advertising, and Insurance are the same for this monthly projection as they were for the annual projection. The annual interest rate is divided by 12 to obtain the monthly rate. Joe wants you to be sure to include a report heading, column headings, and underlines.

Your tasks for developing this projection for Woodcraft are as follows:

Task 1: Construct this quarterly spreadsheet for Woodcraft.

Task 2: Print the result.

Task 3: Print the cell formulas.

Task 4: Save this worksheet file as WOOD2.

> *Quick check answers:* Income Before Taxes [Total] = 545767
> Return on Sales [Total] = .1482 or 14.82%

Time Estimates

Novice: 75 minutes

Intermediate: 60 minutes

Advanced: 45 minutes

(2)   Case: Midwest Universal Gas (continued)

Midwest Universal Gas (MUG) operates and plans their fiscal year by quarter. This is important for MUG, since the volume of gas sold varies with the weather from quarter to quarter. Mary Derrick wants you to revise the MUG projection to be a quarterly projection with an annual total. Those planning items that can be summed for the annual total, such as expenses and revenues, should be summed. Any items that cannot be summed should have their weighted average calculated in the total column, if appropriate. Sam has assisted you in collecting the following data for each quarter:

	1st Quarter	2nd Quarter	3rd Quarter	4th Quarter
Total Gas Sold	228 BCF	201 BCF	82 BCF	221 BCF
General Admin.	$4,465,000	$3,740,000	$3,980,000	$4,065,000

Other planning items are calculated based on the same assumptions as in the annual projection. Sam has advised you that the annual interest rate can be converted to a quarterly rate by merely dividing by 4. Similarly, annual depreciation can be revised to quarterly depreciation. Mary has suggested that the Retail and Wholesale Prices for gas and the average cost of gas should be included as separate assumptions so that they can be readily printed out in their report. Since these prices and cost rates remain the same for the entire year, Mary wants them to appear only once. No additional debt borrowing or repayment is planned during the year, and so this balance will remain constant. Similarly, no new investments are currently planned during the next year. Like the annual plan, this plan will also be prepared as dollars in thousands.

Your tasks for developing Mary's requested projection for MUG are as follows:

Task 1: Construct this annual plan by quarter for MUG.

Task 2: Print the result.

Task 3: Print the cell formulas.

Task 4: Save this worksheet file as MUG2.

> *Quick check answers:* Net Income [Total] = 12523(000's)
> Return on Investment [Total] = .1223   or   12.23%

Time Estimates:

Novice: 75 minutes

Intermediate: 60 minutes

Advanced: 45 minutes

L.3.19 | Case Application

Case: Rolling Stones Tire Center

Business Problem: Payroll register
MIS Characteristics: Human Resources
                         Operational Control
                         Implementation
Management Functions: Controlling
Tools Skills: Formulas
              Copying
              Absolute/relative referencing
              Reporting

The Rolling Stones Tire Center located at the intersection of Highway 20 and Bannister Road provides complete tire service for passenger cars, truck fleets, and farms. Rolling Stones was founded by "Dusty" Rhodes in 1946 and specializes in selling the Road Runner brand of tires; however, they also serve as a dealer for most major brands of tires. The longstanding motto of providing outstanding customer service has contributed to the success of Rolling Stones. This is a family-owned business, which is currently managed by Dusty's two children, Kari and Rusty. Last year, Rolling Stones had gross sales in excess of $2 million. In addition to Kari and Rusty, the Tire Center has 10 hourly employees. Kari and Rusty receive a monthly salary, together with a year-end bonus, depending on their profits for the year.

Rusty manages the shop operations, while Kari is the office manager, who is responsible for preparing the weekly payroll. Until recently, she has been manually preparing the payroll. The hours worked are obtained from each employee's time card. She combines these data with the pay rate for each employee to compute the gross pay and deductions. Kari then writes each of the checks for distribution on Thursday. Last month, Kari was late in getting the checks computed and written, because she was so busy processing customer orders. The paychecks weren't available for distribution until Friday, and their employees were quite upset.

Kari believes that she could create a worksheet for computing gross pay, deductions, and net pay. This would reduce the chances of making a math error with a calculator and would speed up the process. The worksheet could also compute the total deductions so Kari could make these deposits on time. She embarked on setting up her payroll register on the file PAYROLL.WK1.

The payroll register is designed to be used each week. Kari collects the time cards, enters the regular and overtime hours worked, revises any pay rates, and computes the payroll. Since pay rates change infrequently, the primary data to be entered each week are only the hours worked.

Your task is to complete the payroll register worksheet for the Rolling Stones Tire Center. From the Data Disk, load the PAYROLL.WK1 file, which contains the layout of the payroll register and all the data for the current week's payroll. These data for each employee include name, social security number, pay rate, regular hours worked, and overtime hours worked. From this, calculations can be performed for gross pay, federal withholding tax, state withholding tax, FICA (Social Security contribution), health insurance, and net pay. A total for each of these payroll items can be obtained for use in completing the payroll processing.

Kari has specified the following calculations for items in the payroll register:

Weekly Gross Pay. Multiply the pay rate by the regular hours worked plus one and a half times the overtime hours.

Federal Withholding Tax. 16% of the weekly gross pay for each employee.

State Withholding Tax. 6% of the weekly gross pay for each employee.

FICA. 7.5% of the weekly gross pay.

Health Insurance. $25 per employee per week.

Although health insurance is the same amount for all employees, Kari is in the process of negotiating a new health care insurance policy. This policy would result in a different cost depending of the type of coverage selected. As a result, Kari wants to set up the worksheet so that it would handle this anticipated modification by merely entering the necessary data.

Tasks

1. Format all the numbers and percentages. All columns containing dollar amounts should be formatted with two decimal places. The columns containing the hours worked should be formatted with one decimal place. Withholding tax rates and the FICA rate are values of common factors that should be formatted as percentages with one decimal place.

2. Since tax rates that apply to all employees should be entered only one time, an area for these factors is provided at the top of the worksheet. This permits additional employees to be added to the payroll register without changing the location of these values. Also, the values are readily printed with the weekly payroll register. Enter the appropriate values for each rate.

3. Create formulas to compute gross pay, each deduction except health insurance, and net pay. Be sure these formulas reference the rate input in the common factor area. Input the health insurance amount for each employee. Develop formulas which total the hours worked, gross pay, each deduction, and net pay.

4. Print the completed worksheet. This should fit on a single page if you have a wide carriage printer or if you have a narrow printer and use compressed print.

5. Save your completed worksheet.

6. Kari needs to deposit the federal withholding taxes and the FICA at her bank for payment to the Internal Revenue Service. What is the amount of the check she needs to write this week?

7. Write a brief summary describing the following characteristics of the completed worksheet:

   (a) Why are the social security numbers entered as labels? What would happen if they were not labels?

   (b) Why does column K need to be at least 10 spaces wide?

   (c) Which function is used to include the date on the Payroll Register report?

   (d) What feature of labels is used with the report heading?

Time Estimates:

Novice: 75 minutes

Intermediate: 60 minutes

Advanced: 45 minutes

Interrogating Spreadsheet Models

CONTENT

▦ Spreadsheet Model Interrogation
▦ What If with 1-2-3
▦ Goal Seeking with 1-2-3
▦ Using Backsolver for Goal Seeking
▦ Doing Windows
▦ When Things Go Wrong

L.4.1 Spreadsheet Model Interrogation

One of the main reasons Kim purchased Lotus 1-2-3 for Good Morning Products was 1-2-3's ability to quickly perform what-if analysis. Through model interrogation, a variety of spreadsheet solutions can be readily explored to obtain information to support decision making. What-if analysis and goal-seeking analysis are two of the key features for interrogating a spreadsheet model. What if and goal seeking are *not* new Lotus 1-2-3 commands or menu selections. They are the use of formulas and values in worksheets to develop alternative solutions that support business decision making. Data values and/or formulas are revised in examining these alternatives. Often, a spreadsheet is built with the very idea that a number of what-if alternatives will be explored.

Crush, Good Morning Products' CEO, has meetings scheduled with the firm's accountant, management committee, and banker. Before the meetings, Crush would like to see an evaluation of the following potential courses of action:

1. What is **Gross Profit [Total],** that is, the **Gross Profit** in the **Total** column, when the **Sales Growth Rate** is changed to 9 percent per quarter?

2. What is **Gross Profit [Total]** when **Sales [1ST QTR]** are increased by 11 percent over the original or base amount and the growth rate is increased to 12 percent for each of the other three quarters?

3. When **Sales** are increased, it is expected that the **Cost of Sales** will decrease. Kim anticipates that the **Cost Percent** would now be 75 percent. With the first quarter increase and the 12 percent **Sales Growth Rate** as in (**2**), what is **Gross Profit [Total]**?

4. With the 12 percent **Sales Growth Rate** as in (**2**) and the **Cost Percent** as in (**3**), what amount of **Sales [1ST QTR]** are necessary to reach a goal of $500,000 **Gross Profit [Total]**, that is, the **Gross Profit** for the entire year?

Before you embark on the evaluation of each of these alternative courses of action, you should perform a File Save on the original or **base** worksheet solution. Then, after modifying the worksheet in conducting these evaluations, you can always use File Retrieve to return to the base worksheet.

Keypoint!

> Perform a / File Save (/FS) *before* you begin what-if and goal-seeking interrogation, since you are making *permanent* changes to the cells in your current worksheet!

L.4.2   What If with 1-2-3

The first three alternatives on Crush's lists require a what-if analysis. Let's see how Chris proceeds to evaluate each alternative.

1. This what if can be computed by changing a data value, since the **Sales Growth Rate** was set up using a separate cell. (How convenient.)

To perform a what if by changing a data value

Move to:	B7	Desired location for what if
Enter:	.09	What if data value

The solution is recalculated with the result
Gross Profit [Total] = 304502

Action: Print this worksheet containing the revised what-if result.

The result of this what-if analysis is illustrated in Figure L.69, with the **Gross Profit [Total]** computed using the formula **@SUM(B15..E15)**.

2. This is a what if that can be evaluated by revising a cell formula and changing a data value. First the formula is revised.

To perform a what if by modifying a cell formula

Move to:	B12	Desired location for increase percent
Press:	\<F2\>	Initiate edit cell's content
Type:	*1.11	Here, 1.11 is an 11 percent increase
Press:	\<Enter\>	Complete edit

Next, the cell's data value is revised to the desired 12 percent increase in quarters two through four.

To change a data value for a what if

Move to:	B7	Desired location for revised growth rate
Enter:	.12	Revised what-if data value

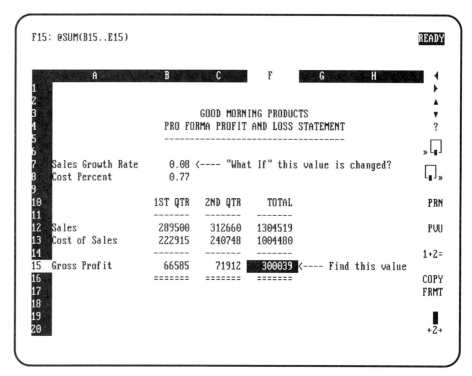

FIGURE L.69. What-if analysis with input data value revised.

The solution is recalculated with the result

Gross Profit [Total] = 353237

Action: Print your worksheet containing this what-if result.

As illustrated in this example, the formula in **B12** was revised to **289500*1.11.** Lotus 1-2-3 immediately performed the calculation in this cell as well as the other cells of the worksheet. If the **Sales** increase amount had been set up in a separate cell like the growth rate in cell **B7,** then the data value for the increased amount could merely have been revised rather than editing the formula. However, since the increase was not placed in a separate cell, the edit procedure was used. As you can see, if a value is to undergo a number of changes, the preferred method of performing what-if analysis is to establish a separate cell to hold these data values. This example has illustrated both the *separate cell* and *modify formula* approaches to performing what-if calculations.

Keypoint!

> When a what if involves changing an existing data value by a percentage or by adding a fixed amount, let 1-2-3 do this arithmetic. Avoid the temptation of reaching for your calculator. After all, 1-2-3 is a "big" calculator! Furthermore, the revised cell formula is helpful in remembering your assumptions for these what-if values!

3. This what-if alternative is evaluated by changing another data value.

To perform a what if by changing a data value

Move to:	**B8**	Desired location
Enter:	.75	Revised what-if data value

The solution is recalculated with the result

Gross Profit [Total] = 383953

Action: Print your worksheet with this what-if solution.

Keypoint!

Data values that may be interrogated using a what-if analysis should be set up as *separate cells*. If the spreadsheet model had not been designed with the *Sales Growth Rate* and the *Cost Percent* as separate cell values, then these what-ifs would have required you to modify cell formulas for *Sales* and *Cost of Sales*. These modified formula would then need to be copied into the other columns of the worksheet model!

L.4.3   Goal Seeking with 1-2-3

The last alternative on Crush's lists requires a goal-seeking analysis. Goal seeking is also known as a backward solution. You know the desired value for a cell *calculated by a formula,* such as **Gross Profit [Total],** and you want to find the value for an **input cell,** such as **Sales Growth Rate.** This **input** cell usually *contains a constant.* You want to find a new value for this **input** constant that will produce the desired or target value for the cell calculated by the formula, as illustrated with the goal seek in Figure L.70 for the **Sales Growth Rate** when the desired **Gross Profit [Total]** is 310000. The **Sales Growth Rate** is found by using a trial-and-error procedure. Different values for the **Sales Growth Rate** input cell are entered until the desired goal is attained. Although this is not an elegant process, it does produce the desired output *without* rewriting any formulas. With some practice, goal seeking by trial-and-error provides a convenient method for interrogating a spreadsheet model.

Chris proceeds to evaluate Crush's last alternative in this manner:

4. This is a goal-seek analysis that makes use of the changes from alternatives (**2**) and (**3**) above. If you did not want those revisions, you would need to change the formulas back to their original values, or you could retrieve your original worksheet. In goal seeking, you know the value you want to end up with in a particular cell: the **goal** cell. To obtain this value, you need to change the value in another cell: the **adjust** or input cell. Although you might like to, you can*not* move to cell **F15** and enter the value 500000 and automatically have the value computed for cell **B12** that produces this result. This is the meaning of a "backward" solution of the worksheet. In 1-2-3, you can*not* obtain this solution directly. If you move to **F15** and enter 500000, of course, this value will appear in the cell; however, the value in **B12,** and all other cells, would remain *UN*changed. Let's evaluate Chris's last alternative using goal seeking that is performed by the "trial-and-error" method.

To perform goal seeking using the trial-and-error method			
Move to:	B12		Cell whose value you want to find
Enter:	350000		Gross Profit [Total] = 418191
Enter:	500000		Gross Profit [Total] = 597416
Enter:	450000		Gross Profit [Total] = 537674
Enter:	425000		Gross Profit [Total] = 507804
Enter:	420000		Gross Profit [Total] = 501829, this is close enough, so stop [Figure L.71]

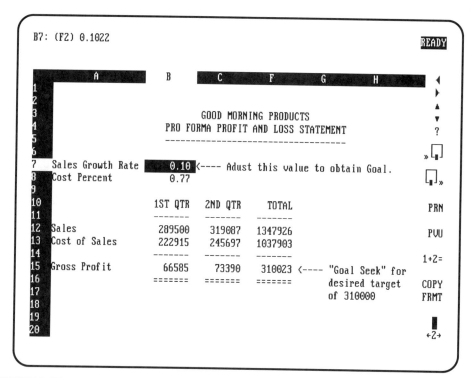

FIGURE L.70. Example goal-seek analysis of sales growth rate for desired target value of formula.

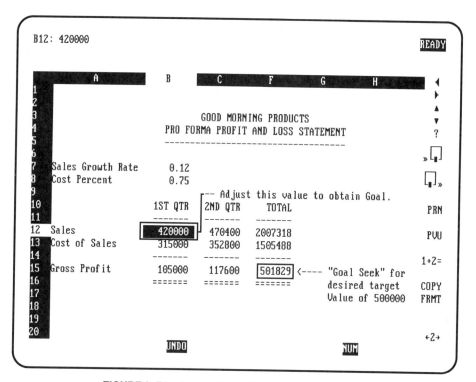

FIGURE L.71. Goal-seek result for first-quarter sales.

Of course, you could have tried other values. Although this is not an elegant way to perform goal seeking, it is one method for arriving at the desired solution *without* rewriting all the formulas in your worksheet. Lotus 1-2-3 does allow you to obtain an organized series of solutions using the / Data Table 1 (/DT1) command, which is explored in Section L.6.2.

Action: Print a report of this alternative and save the worksheet with the what-if and goal-seeking data as file PLAN7.

You now have the information Crush wants for the meeting with Good Morning's accountant tomorrow afternoon. What if and goal seeking were a great team for evaluating these alternatives.

L.4.4 Using Backsolver for Goal Seeking

The Backsolver Add-In, available beginning with Release 2.4, provides a convenient means for directly performing a goal-seeking analysis or backward solution. (If you are using an earlier release of 1-2-3 than Release 2.4, then just read this section to gain an appreciation for this feature.) Backsolver can be used in place of the trial-and-error method of goal seeking. When Backsolver produces a solution, it automatically carries out the equivalent of the trial-and-error substitution of solution values that you would have entered until you obtained the desired goal value.

Because Backsolver is an Add-In, it must be attached before it becomes available for your use. Like other Add-Ins, Backsolver takes up memory space, so you may need to detach other Add-Ins or disable the Undo feature to attach this Add-In. When you attach Backsolver, no status indicator or other screen display appears to advise you that this Add-In is attached. You just need to remember that you have attached it.

Backsolver is started or **invoked** each time you want to use it to perform a goal seek. This Add-In can be invoked by either selecting Invoke from the Add-In menu or by setting up a function key. Because a function key provides the most convenient way to start Backsolver, it is the method demonstrated in this lesson. The function key for invoking Backsolver is set up when this Add-In is attached. Let's see how this Add-In is attached and assigned a function key.

Action: If necessary, clear your current worksheet using the /WEY command. Because the Backsolver requires some memory space, it is usually best to attach this Add-In before you have loaded a worksheet.

To attach the Backsolver Add-In			
Press:	/	Access main menu
Select:	Add-In	
Select:	Attach	Desired activity
Select:	BSOLVER.ADN	Choose Backsolver Add-In
Select:	9	Specify <Alt>+<F9> as the function key for starting Add-In
Select:	Quit	Complete selection of Add-In and return to the READY mode

The Backsolver Add-In is now available for your use.

Now let's load the PLAN7 worksheet that was used previously for your spreadsheet model interrogation.

Action: Retrieve the PLAN7 worksheet for performing goal seeking with Backsolver.

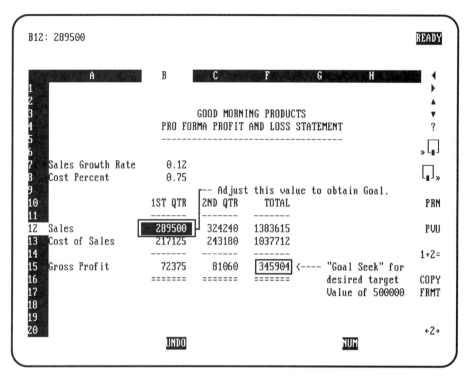

FIGURE L.72. The PLAN7 worksheet *before* goal-seek analysis using Backsolver Add-In.

For this goal-seeking alternative, the **Sales Growth Rate** and **Cost Percent** are set to the values described in Crush's alternatives (2) and (3). In preparation for exploring the use of Backsolver, the **Sales [1ST QTR]** should be set to its initial value of 289500.

Action: Verify and change any of the input values for **Sales Growth Rate, Cost Percent,** and **Sales [1ST QTR],** as necessary, in preparation for doing this goal seek. Your worksheet's solution values should be the same as those shown in Figure L.72.

The goal seek that is Crush's alternative (4) is to be carried out as indicated in Figure L.72. Let's use Backsolver to do the goal seek or backward solution.

| To goal seek using the Backsolver Add-In | **Press:** | <Alt>+<F9> | Invoke Backsolver using the previously selected function key |

The Backsolver menu appears, as shown in Figure L.73. These menu choices are summarized in Figure L.74.

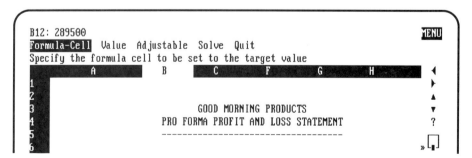

FIGURE L.73. Backsolver menu.

Menu Selection	Action
Formula-Cell	Specify the cell containing the formula that will be set to the target value.
Value	Specify the desired result value for the formula cell.
Adjustable	Specify the input cell to be changed to obtain the target value in the formula cell.
Solve	Cause the goal-seek solution to be calculated.
Quit	Return to the READY mode without solving the goal seek.

FIGURE L.74. Backsolver menu choices.

Select:	Formula-Cell	Prepare to specify cell with known value
Enter:	F15	Specify the desired cell that contains the formula; may also be indicated by pointing
Select:	Value	Prepare to specify the known value for the formula
Enter:	500000	Specify the known value
Select:	Adjustable	Prepare to specify the cell whose value will be changed or adjusted
Enter:	B12	Specify the desired cell that is to be adjusted; may also be indicated by pointing
Select:	Solve	Cause the goal seek to be performed and return to READY mode

When Solve is selected, 1-2-3 calculates the goal-seeking solution, with the results displayed in the specified cells in your worksheet (Figure L.75). In this manner, the

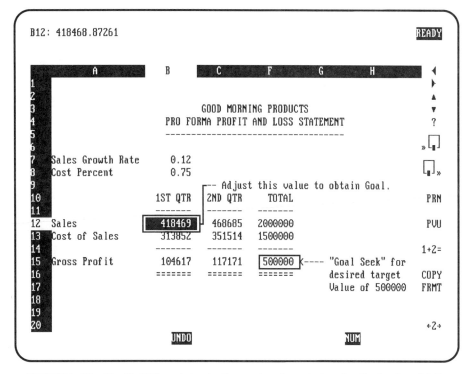

FIGURE L.75. The PLAN7 worksheet *after* goal seek analysis using Backsolver Add-In.

Backsolver Add-In can be used to perform your goal-seeking analysis. If the Undo feature is enabled, you may use <Alt>+<F4> (UNDO) to return to your initial solution, the one you had before you performed the goal seek by using Backsolver. When the Backsolver is no longer required, you may detach it from the Add-In menu.

Action: Position the cell pointer at cell **F14** and verify that this cell still contains its original formula.

Caution Alert!

When using Backsolver, the cell specified as the **Adjustable** cell must contain a data value and not a formula. If it contains a formula, an error message is displayed. This helps to avoid accidentally destroying your cell formulas when using the Backsolver!

L.4.5 Doing Windows

The worksheet model Chris and Kim have been evaluating fits nicely on one display screen. With large models, the cell that is being revised and the cell containing the value being observed in a what-if or goal-seeking analysis often do not fit on the same screen. When this happens, 1-2-3 allows you to divide your screen into two windows, with each window containing a selected group of rows and columns. For example, when exploring a what-if situation where the *Sales Growth Rate* is revised and the *Gross Profit [Total]* is observed, the display screen might be split horizontally, as illustrated in Figure L.76, or vertically, as illustrated in Figure L.77.

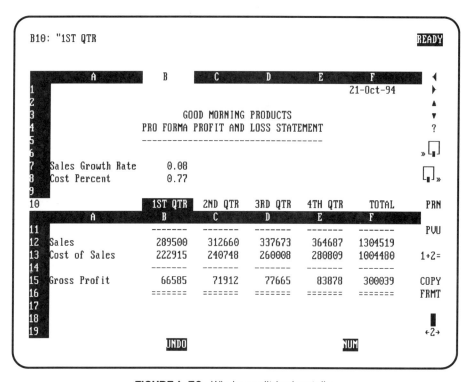

FIGURE L.76. Window split horizontally.

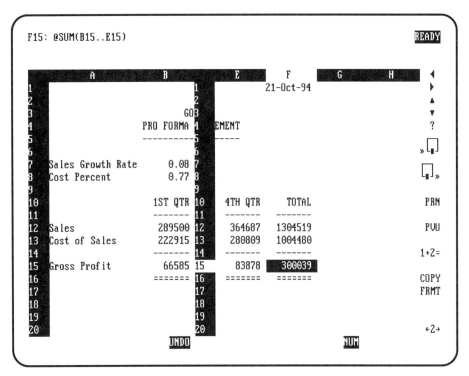

FIGURE L.77. Window split vertically.

Let's see how the worksheet area display can be divided horizontally into two windows.

To split the worksheet area horizontally	**Move to:**	B11	Or any cell in row **11**; the position of the cursor determines where the split will occur
	Press:	/	Access main menu
	Select:	Worksheet	
	Select:	Window	Desired activity
	Select:	Horizontal	Type of split desired

The window is split horizontally. Now, the cell pointer is toggled between the two windows using the <F6> (WINDOW) key.

| To move the cell pointer from one window to another window | **Press:** | <F6> | Cursor jumps to other window |

In addition to viewing two areas of your worksheet during model interrogation, windowing is also useful when building larger worksheets. You may use the <F6> (WINDOW) to move from one window to the other while building formulas by the pointing method. The Windows menu contains several available menu selections, which are summarized in Figure L.78.

Keypoint!

Lotus 1-2-3 Worksheet Windows allow you to view and work with two different areas of a worksheet at one time. This is helpful when performing interrogation and when building larger worksheet models!

Menu Selection	Action
Horizontal	Split the screen horizontally at the row where the cell pointer is located.
Vertical	Split the screen vertically at the column where the cell pointer is located.
Sync	Synchronize the scrolling of windows so that the rows or columns displayed in each window are coordinated as the cell pointer is moved at the edge of the displayed area.
Unsync	Scroll the windows independently so that the rows or columns displayed in each window are not coordinated.
Clear	Return the display to a single window. (Use to switch from horizontal to vertical or remove windows.)

FIGURE L.78. / Worksheet Window menu choices.

Caution Alert!   Lotus 1-2-3 allows a maximum of only two windows to be used at one time!

L.4.6   When Things Go Wrong

Several difficulties may be encountered while you are performing what-if and goal-seeking analyses. The best protection is to have saved a copy of your worksheet file *before* you started on your spreadsheet interrogation. Common difficulties and how to approach them are described as follows:

1. You discovered that you modified the wrong cell in performing your what-if analysis. This occurs when the worksheet cursor was positioned at the wrong location when you began editing with <F2> (EDIT).

    a. If the Undo feature is enabled, merely press <Alt>+<F4> (UNDO) to cancel the change to the cell formula.

    b. If the Undo feature is disabled, perform a / File Retrieve (/FR) to load the saved version of your original or base worksheet; otherwise, you need to reenter the formula in the cell.

    c. Carefully position the worksheet cursor at the desired location and edit the cell's contents for the what if.

2. In performing a goal seek, you happened to enter the desired value in your goal cell and destroyed the cell's formula.

    a. If the Undo feature is enabled, then press <Alt>+<F4> (UNDO) to cancel your previous action; otherwise, perform a / File Retrieve (/FR) to return to your original or base version of your worksheet.

    b. Carefully position the worksheet cursor at the cell whose value you want to find.

    c. Use the trial-and-error method to enter data values until the desired value is obtained for the goal cell containing the formula. Alternatively, use Backsolver, if available, to perform your goal seek.

L.4.7   Lesson Summary

- Spreadsheet model interrogation explores a variety of solutions to obtain information for decision making.

- A key reason for building a spreadsheet model is to permit the evaluation of alternative solutions.

- What if and goal seeking are two primary methods of interrogating a spreadsheet model.

- A what-if analysis frequently involves changing the data value in a cell and observing its impact on the solution.

- During what-if analysis the data values may be changed or formulas can be modified.

- A goal-seeking analysis is the backward solution of a spreadsheet model, where the value of a formula is known and a data value in another cell is adjusted by using a trial-and-error procedure until the desired target value is obtained.

- If available, the Backsolver Add-In allows you to perform a goal-seeking analysis directly. This Add-In must be attached before you can invoke or use it. A function key provides the most convenient method for invoking this Add-In.

- Lotus 1-2-3 worksheet windows allow two different areas of a spreadsheet to be viewed concurrently. This supports both model-interrogation and model-building activities.

L.4.8   Practice Tutorial

Carry out the spreadsheet model interrogations described in this Lesson as a guided activity in a hands-on manner. Access your MYPLAN6 worksheet from the Practice Tutorial 1 in Lesson L.3 as a starting point for this exercise.

Task 1: Develop and print the results for each of the three what-if alternatives.

Task 2: Produce and print the results for the goal-seeking alternative. Do both the trial-and-error method and the Backsolver solution, if you have this Add-In available.

Time Estimates

Novice: 60 minutes

Intermediate: 45 minutes

Advanced: 30 minutes

L.4.9   Practice Exercises

(1)   Case: Inland Container (continued)

After further discussions with Richard Rielly at Rydder Truck, Mary Montoya realized that a number of different situations might occur. She wanted to explore these alternative scenarios as part of her pricing proposal preparation. Mary wants you to evaluate the following potential courses of action:

(a) What is the Gross Profit [Total] when the Unit Sold Growth Rate is increased to 7 percent per month?

(b) What are the Sales [June] when the Units Sold [April] are increased by 6 percent over the original or base amount and the Unit Sold Growth Rate is 0 percent for each of the other remaining months?

(c) When the Sales are revised as in (b) above, the Percent Cost of Sales is expected to decrease to 63 percent. What are the Sales [Total] and Gross Profit [Total] under these assumptions?

(d) With the Units Sold Growth Rate, Percent Cost of Sales, and Units Sold [April] reset to their base or original values, what are Sales [Total] and Gross Profit [Total] when the Price per Unit Increase is $0.15 in May and June?

(e) With the Price per Unit Increase and other assumptions as in (d) above, what Unit Sold Growth Rate is necessary to obtain a Gross Profit [Total] of 660000?

Task 1: Access your RYDDER2 worksheet from Practice Exercise 1 in Lesson L.3 as your starting point for this exercise.

Task 2: Prepare a solution for each of the what-if alternatives and print the results.

Task 3: Produce a solution for the goal-seeking alternative and print the results.

Quick check answers: (a) Gross Profit [Total] = 648037

(b) Sales [June] = 673044

(c) Sales [Total] = 1939716
Gross Profit [Total] = 717695

(d) Sales [Total] = 1935322
Gross Profit [Total] = 638656

(e) Gross Profit [Total] of 659969 is close enough for finding the desired Units Sold Growth Rate.

Time Estimates

Novice: 60 minutes

Intermediate: 45 minutes

Advanced: 30 minutes

(2)   Case: Frontier Datatran Services

Business Problem: Production planning
MIS Characteristics: Production/Operations
Managerial Control

Frontier Datatran Services is a service bureau that specializes in contract data entry. They provide key entry and processing of customer orders. The clients of Frontier are small businesses that do not want to maintain the computer operations necessary to enter and process customer orders. Frontier picks up their clients' orders from the post office, enters the data, produces the shipping documents, and delivers them to their clients in the greater metropolitan area. The shipping documents are delivered to clients on a regular schedule, with larger clients receiving several batches each day.

Heather Stallings manages Frontier's on-line data entry services, which is managed as a separate profit center. She created the FRONTIER.WK1 worksheet to evaluate next year's operations. Heather is considering several changes in their data entry processing and wants you to do an analysis to address these questions:

(a) What will happen to **Gross profit** if the number of **Orders entered** increases to 180,000 per year?

(b) Heather believes that the fee collected for each order processed might be increased to $3.49 for next year. If the number of **Orders entered** remains at the volume specified in (a) above, what **Gross profit** can she expect?

(c) In setting profit goals for next year, Heather and her manager would like to reach a **Gross profit** of $50,000. With a **Fee per order** set at the initial or base price of $3.19, how many orders need to be entered to attain their goal?

(d) The breakeven number of Orders entered is the number that results in a **Gross profit** of zero. Heather wants to know this breakeven volume when the **Fee per order** is at the base price of $3.19.

(e) Heather believes in paying a fair wage rate to her employees. If she increases the **Wage rate** to $12.00 per hour, what volume of orders needs to be entered for breakeven?

(f) Heather is considering installing an upgraded computer system that will *increase* the annual computer expense by $15,000. This upgrade will *reduce* the **Standard time per order** by 2 minutes. The Standard time per order is the average allotted time for processing each order, as determined by conducting a time study in Heather's department. She wants to do her evaluation using the initial or base **Wage rate** so that the upgrade's effect can be compared to current operations. If Frontier installs this upgrade, what volume of orders needs to be entered for a breakeven **Gross profit?**

(g) If Heather has the upgrade installed as described in (f) above, what is the **Gross profit** with the base volume of **Orders entered?**

Task 1: Access the FRONTIER worksheet file from your Data Disk. Print this initial or base solution. Review the contents of the worksheet.
(*Optional*)   Print the cell formulas for use in your review.

Task 2: Prepare and print a solution for each of Heather's alternatives. [*Hint:* As you prepare each alternative, save your worksheet file as FRONT1, FRONT2, and so forth. This will allow you to reaccess any of your alternatives, if necessary.]

Task 3: Clearly identify the changes in each of your alternative reports by circling or highlighting the cells you modified.

Task 4: (*Optional*)   Heather's best estimate of the volume of **Orders entered** to be processed next year is 150,000. Based on this expectation and the original **Fee per order** of $3.19, perform the analysis and write a paragraph describing whether the upgrade should be made and why.

Quick check answers: (a) Gross profit = 55,392

(b) Gross profit = 109,392

(c) (One of these is close enough.)
Orders entered = 158817
169718
173652

(d) (One of these is close enough.)
Orders entered = 71,932
73,689
74,371

(e) (One of these is close enough.)
Orders entered = 115932
116767
118301

(f) (One of these is close enough.)
Orders entered = 48,921
53,116
55,747

(g) Gross profit = 91,300

Time Estimates

Novice: 60 minutes

Intermediate: 45 minutes

Advanced: 30 minutes

(3)   Case: Meridian Manufacturing Company

Business Problem: Collective Bargaining
MIS Characteristics: Human Resources
Strategic Planning

Meridian Manufacturing specializes in the production of exercise equipment that includes treadmills, rowing machines, and ski machines. Cheryl Love, Vice President of Human Resources, heads the bargaining team for Meridian in its contract negotiations with Local 319 of the United Machine Workers (UMW). In the 10-year history of Local 319, no strikes or lost production days have occurred. The demand for home exercise equipment has been growing steadily and is expected to continue increasing at about 10 percent per year. Officials of Local 319 have presented their demands to Meridian's management for the next three years' labor contract. In preparation for the next bargaining session, Cheryl wants to evaluate several alternatives:

(a) What is the **Total contract cost** when wages are increased at the rate of 7 percent, 6 percent, and 5 percent, respectively, for each of the next three years? [*Hint:* These increases are specified by the **WAGE INCREASE DEMAND.**]

(b) Although Cheryl expects the Legally required indirect benefits, such as social security and worker's compensation, to be increased by 1 percent beginning with the first year of the contract, there is a chance that this increase may not take place. With the wage increases as in (a) above, what is the **Total contract cost** if the **Legally req'd** continues at the 9 percent rate for the duration of this contract?

(c) The current proposal contains medical and dental insurance costs for the "Low" coverage plan. A "High" coverage plan, with reduced employee deductibles, is being considered by Cheryl. The cost of the "High" coverage Medical insurance in the first year of the new contract would be $2800, and the Dental insurance would be $420. The increases in each of the insurance plans after the first year of the contract are expected to be the same as for the "Low" option. Cheryl believes that with this "High" insurance option, Local 319 might agree to a 5 percent wage increase in each of the three years of the contract. Under this alternative, Cheryl expects that the **Legally req'd** indirect benefit will remain as specified in (b) above. What is the **Total contract cost** for this wage and benefit package?

(d) With the "Low" insurance option and the **Legally req'd** at Cheryl's initial estimate of 10 percent, she would like to know what wage increase percentage in each of the three years would limit the **Total contract cost** to $1,200,000. [*Hint:* Since the same amount is used in all three years, use a formula in **Year 2** and **Year 3** that references the desired wage increase percentage in **Year 1.**]

In setting up her worksheet, Cheryl included **Current** wage and benefit data for this year so that data for the next three years of the contract can be compared to these data. Because the contract is under negotiation for the next three years, Cheryl wants the changes for all her alternatives made only in **Year 1, Year 2,** and **Year 3** of the new contract.

Task 1: Access the BARGAIN worksheet file from your Data Disk. Print this initial or base solution. Review the contents of the worksheet.

(*Optional*)   Print the cell formulas for use in your review. Notice that Cheryl set up the data for the **Current** year and the three contract years under negotiation.

Task 2: Prepare and print a solution for each of Cheryl's alternatives. Remember, her alternatives change data only in the three years of the new contract, not in the **Current** year. [*Hint:* As you prepare each alternative, save your worksheet file as BARGAIN2, BARGAIN3, and so forth. This will allow you to reaccess any of your alternatives, if necessary.]

Task 3: Clearly identify the changes to the cells you modified for each of your alternative reports by circling or highlighting them on your printed solution.

Task 4: (*Optional*)   Formulate your own collective bargaining alternative and develop the solution for it. Print this solution. Write a short narrative description detailing the changes in your alternative and summarizing the results obtained.

Quick check answers: (a) Total contract cost = 1,233,986

(b) Total contract cost = 1,181,461

(c) Total contract cost = 1,214,574

(d) Wages Increase Demand of .058 or 5.8 percent is close enough for finding the desired Total contract cost.

Time Estimates

Novice: 60 minutes

Intermediate: 45 minutes

Advanced: 30 minutes

L.4.10 Comprehensive Problems

(1) Case: Woodcraft Furniture Company (continued)

Woodcraft's quarterly management meeting is about to start. Joe Birch and the other operating managers have gathered for your presentation of the next quarter's anticipated financial performance. These meetings are held in the Board Room, which contains a workstation connected to a large full-screen full-color projector. This permits managers to ask questions and immediately review the possible impacts during the meeting. Once you conclude your presentation, the questions begin:

(a) Martha Goodguess is considering lowering the product prices. What will the **Return on Sales** be if *only* prices on all three products are reduced by 5 percent and no other changes are made? That is, these revisions are to Woodcrafts's original quarterly projection. [*Hint:* Multiply by .95 to obtain a 5 percent decrease in prices.]

(b) Joe Birch would like to know the consequence of a drop in table demand by 7 percent in each month, if there are *no other changes to their projection*. What is **Return on Sales** and **Income Before Tax** with these **Tables Sales**?

(c) If table demand should drop by 7 percent as determined in (b) above, what **Table Price** is necessary to maintain the "base case" **Return on Sales** of 14.82 percent? Assume that the same price is charged for tables in all three months of the quarter.

(d) Ray Jointer is concerned that a strike is imminent unless concessions are made to union demands. Ray would like to see the financial consequences of increasing the number of planned production employees by three for each month during the quarter and increasing all base wages to $12.50 starting in July, if there are *no other changes* to the projection. [*Hint:* Access the original worksheet to obtain the "base" values.]

(e) Joe then asks you how much prices must increase to achieve the same "base case" **Return on Sales** of 14.82 percent if the union demands in (d) above are met. [*Hint:* Create a new cell for the PRICE ADJUSTMENT and modify each of the prices so that each is a formula that uses this cell in its computation.]

(f) What prices are necessary for Woodcraft to achieve breakeven under the conditions of union demand specified in (d) above? Breakeven occurs when the Return on Sales is zero. [*Hint:* Use the PRICE ADJUSTMENT in (e) above to assist in finding these breakeven prices.]

Task 1: Access the WOOD2 spreadsheet file as the "base solution" and reaccess this file each time you need to return to the "base solution."

Task 2: Prepare and print the results for each alternative.

Task 3: Clearly identify the changes to the cells you modified for each of your alternative reports by circling or highlighting them on your printed solution.

Task 4: Save the worksheet from (f) as file WOOD3.

Quick check answers: (a) Return on Sales [Total] = .1318   or   13.18%

(b) Income Before Taxes [Total] = 451062
Return on Sales [Total] = .1297   or   12.97%

(c) Return on Sales [Total] = .1482
is obtained with the desired Table Price.

(d) Income Before Taxes [Total] = 282974
Return on Sales [Total] = .0768   or   7.68%

(e) (One of these is close enough.)
Price Adjustment = .187   or   18.7%
.229   or   22.9%
.243   or   24.3%

(f) (One of these is close enough.)
Price Adjustment = −.089   or   −8.9%
Table Price [July] = 465
Chair Price [August] = 100
Sofa Price [September] = 383

Price Adjustment = −.113   or   −11.3%
Table Price [July] = 452
Chair Price [August] = 98
Sofa Price [September] = 373

Price Adjustment = −.167   or   −16.7%
Table Price [July] = 425
Chair Price [August] = 92
Sofa Price [September] = 350

Time Estimates

Novice: 60 minutes

Intermediate: 45 minutes

Advanced: 30 minutes

(2)   Case: Midwest Universal Gas (continued)

At Midwest Universal Gas, Mary Derrick has reviewed your projections for next year. She is quite pleased that your expected return on investment will be 12 percent. However, she did not get to the top by accepting everything at its face value. Therefore, she instructs you to generate the following what-if analyses:

(a) What will happen to the **Return on Investment** if Francis achieves a volume sold of 25 percent in **Retail Sales?** [*Hint:* Remember, when **Retail Sales** are 25 percent, then **Wholesale Sales** must be 75 percent.]

(b) Petro Newgas from production has always predicted costs of production within a percent or two of actual. If the **Cost of Sales** should go up to 65 percent of **Total Sales** and there are no other changes to their projection, what is the **Return on Investment**? [*Hint:* Access the original worksheet to obtain the "base" values.]

(c) Prices may swing as much as 10 percent greater than expected owing to various legislation. If both retail and wholesale prices are increased by 10 percent and there are *no other changes* in their projection, what is the Return on Investment?

(d) If the mix of sale volumes is changed to 25 percent retail and 75 percent wholesale, as in (a) above, and if the same portion of gas is sold in each quarter, how many BCF of gas must be sold to achieve a 15 percent **Return on Investment**? [*Hint:* The **Total Gas Sold [Total]** in BCF should be a *constant data value* (not a formula), with the BCF for each quarter calculated using this same cell value. Calculate the **Total Gas Sold [1st Qtr]** = 228/732 * **Total Gas Sold [Total],** and similarly for the other three quarters. **Total Gas Sold [Total]** is adjusted in carrying out this goal seek.]

(e) If the **Cost of Sales** should go up to 65 percent as indicated in (b) above, what is the required demand for the year in BCF to achieve a 12 percent **Return on Investment**? Assume that the same portion of gas is sold in each quarter as in (d) above and that the original mix of sales volumes is used.

(f) If prices are increased by 10 percent as indicated in (c) above and the sales volumes are as specified in (a) above, what demand in BCF is necessary to reach a 12 percent **Return on Investment**? [*Hint:* Use the same method as in (d) above.]

Task 1: Access the MUG2 spreadsheet file as the "base solution" and reaccess this file each time you need to return to the "base solution."

Task 2: Prepare and print the results for each alternative.

Task 3: Clearly identify the changes to the cells you modified for each of your alternative reports by circling or highlighting them on your printed solution.

Task 4: Save the worksheet from (f) as file MUG3.

Quick check answers: (a) Return on Investment [Total] = .1241   or   12.41%

(b) Return on Investment [Total] = .0760   or   7.60%

(c) Return on Investment [Total] = .1508   or   15.08%

(d) (One of these is close enough.)
BCF [Total] = 696   798   849

(e) (One of these is close enough.)
BCF [Total] = 648   710   867

(f) (One of these is close enough.)
BCF [Total] = 532   656   784

Time Estimates

Novice: 60 minutes

Intermediate: 45 minutes

Advanced: 30 minutes

L.4.11 Case Application

Case: Global Electric Products

Business Problem: Advertising and sales planning
MIS Characteristics: Marketing
                    Managerial Control
Special Characteristic: International
Management Functions: Planning
Tools Skills: Formulas
              What if
              Reporting

Global Electric Products (GEP) manufactures and markets a variety of electrical appliances for personal and home use including hair dryers, telephones, blenders, toasters, mixers, coffee makers, food processors, and related household appliances. Thomas "Gus" Gustafson is the Vice President of Sales and Marketing for Global Electric. Gus is engrossed in the process of preparing the advertising and sales plan for next year.

The products manufactured by Global Electric are produced at 23 assembly plants located throughout the United States, Mexico, and the Pacific Rim. Most products are manufactured in, at least, two locations. This helps assure a continuous supply of products under unstable conditions such as labor strikes or political turmoil.

Global Electric's sales and marketing effort is divided into four primary market territories: the United States, Mexico, Australia, and Japan. A sales manager is responsible for each territory. These territories are organized into two regions of responsibility. Samuel "Sam" Ling is the Director of North America Sales, which includes the United States and Mexico. Linda "LJ" Jecker is the Director of Worldwide Sales, which includes Australia and Japan. Global Electric defines Worldwide Sales as all sales territories other than those in North America. Their reporting relationship is illustrated by this organization chart:

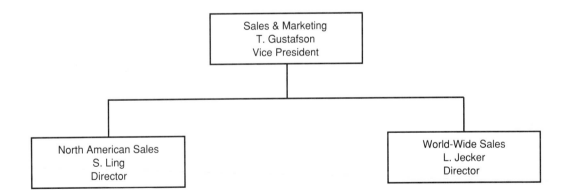

Gus, Sam, and LJ are engaged in developing next year's sales and advertising budget arranged by quarter by marketing area. Gus had his research assistant prepare an analysis of advertising expenditures per quarter. This analysis underscores the seasonality of Global Electric's sales. The analysis relates advertising in the first quarter to that of each of the other quarters with the following advertising factors derived from historical data:

	1st Qtr	2nd Qtr	3rd Qtr	4th Qtr
Advertising factor	1.00	0.80	1.20	1.10

For each sales and marketing territory, Global Electric plans the sales in both local currency and U. S. dollars (USD). This assists each of the area managers with their planning activities. After Gus, Sam, and LJ complete their overall plan, each director will work with the lower level managers in developing more detailed plans for advertising in magazines, newspapers, television, radio, direct mail, and other media. The managers will then finalize their plans as they begin translating them into specific media campaigns.

When planning sales, Global Electric's analysis of past years of data indicate a close relationship between advertising expenditures and sales revenue. Gus has developed an advertising-driven sales forecast. For each territory, the sales generated per dollar (USD) of advertising expenditure has proved to be an effective method for forecasting sales. His analysis has established the following relationship:

	United States	Mexico	Australia	Japan
Sales per $ Ad	8.25	7.50	9.10	7.40

They have determined that the "what's left over" method of planning advertising in the United States is appropriate for next year. With this method, the percentage of advertising (Percent Ad) for the United States is computed by adding all of the percentages for the other sales areas and then subtracting this from 100 percent to obtain the value for the United States.

Brian Page, Director of Financial Planning, provided an analysis of the best estimate for expected exchange rates for next year for each sales territory. This exchange rate converts U. S. dollars to the local sales territory currency, by multiplying the exchange rate times the U. S. dollar amount.

Gus, Sam, and LJ have started their advertising and sales planning worksheet, which is stored as file ADPLAN.WK1 on the Data Disk, in preparation for developing a series of alternatives, which they will discuss at their planning retreat in Grand Cayman next week. Thus far, they have entered the formulas for the North America operations.

Tasks

1. Print the budget and the formulas for computing the Sales amounts. Review these as a guide to completing the formulas for the remaining sales areas.

2. Complete the formulas for the Worldwide territories, a total for each of the Sales for the year, and a total for all sales in U. S. dollars. The row names have been set up to assist you in this activity.

3. Print the completed "base case" report and save your worksheet file.

4. Gus, Sam, and LJ are interested in exploring several alternatives for their advertising and sales plan. Use what-if and/or goal-seeking interrogation techniques to generate the results for each of the following alternatives:

(a) Australia is an expanding market area. LJ believes that the next year represents an opportunity for Global Electric to increase its sales. What are **Total Sales [Total]** in U. S. dollars (USD) when the **Percent Ad** for Australia is increased to 20 percent? What are the total Australian sales in local currency for the entire year? All other ratios and amounts remain at their "base values."

(b) Sam believes that next year has considerable potential for food processor products. He is proposing a $50,000 increase in the advertising budget in the *first quarter,* with related increases in each of the other three quarters. What are **Total Sales [Total]** in USD with this increase in advertising? What is **Advertising [Total]** in USD for these sales? All other ratios and amounts remain at their "base values."

(c) Gus reviewed their production capacities and distribution channels. He believes that Global Electric has the capacity to handle Total Sales of $20 million for next year. What advertising budget is required to attain this level of sales? [*Hint:* Determine the value for the first quarter. The Total is then computed using this value.]

Time Estimates

Novice: 90 minutes

Intermediate: 60 minutes

Advanced: 45 minutes

Graphing Results

CONTENT

- Introduction to Graphing
- Fundamentals of 1-2-3 Graphs
- Creating a Bar Graph
- Using a Mouse for Graph Settings
- Saving Graph Settings
- Producing a Stack Bar Graph
- Producing a Line Graph
- Producing Pie Charts
- Creating an *XY* Graph
- Accessing Named Graphs
- Graph Building Command Summary
- Printing Graphs
- Using SmartIcons to Create Graphs
- When Things Go Wrong

L.5.1 Introduction to Graphing

Kim and Chris want to obtain several graphs of their next year's budget for review by Good Morning Products' management committee before they meet with their banker. Like other business people, they realize that individuals who view graphs find the material more interesting, grasp the message more quickly, and remember the information longer than those who view numbers alone. Graphs support this visual communication, helping you communicate more effectively. Research, common sense, and experience affirm that presentations that include graphs are more effective and persuasive than speeches without graphs. A graph converts a boring table of numeric data from your 1-2-3 worksheet into an attention-getting display that lets you compare data visually and immediately. Some examples of what a graph can do are as follows:

- Make your message more powerful, clear, and persuasive.
- Present your message in an interesting and pleasing form.

- Make viewers grasp your point faster and remember it longer.
- Summarize large quantities of complex data.
- Discover new relationships among your data.

Businesses like Good Morning Products usually measure and plan events at *regular time intervals*. They analyze their data to find trends and detect irregularities. **Time series** graphs display such data in meaningful patterns or **trends.** Data that change with time are often identified by key words such as days, weeks, months, quarters, years, and annual.

The graphs used in business often deal with three basic situations: (1) showing trends (how do conditions change over time?), (2) comparing components and relative amounts (what proportion is each individual component of the total amount?), and (3) showing the relationship between two variables (how are the two variables related?). You need to determine your particular situation in selecting the graph that is best for communicating your point of view. Figure L.79 summarizes typical situations and frequently used graphs.

Lotus 1-2-3 lets you prepare several different types of graphs from the data values in your worksheet. These include the graph types shown in Figure L.80. The general characteristics of each of these popular 1-2-3 graphs are listed here.

- *Bar.* (Figure L.80*a*). Consists of a series of vertical or horizontal bars. Each bar in the graph represents a single data value from a series of data values, such as the sales in a particular quarter from the sales for all four quarters of a year. The height or length of each bar is a measure of the data value that is readily compared with the other data values. When data are compared over time, the *x* axis usually indicates the time period, while the *y* axis shows the quantity being measured, such as dollars, units sold, or number of employees. When more than one data series are included in the graph, the data values are clustered together by time period in a side-by-side arrangement. Bar graphs are most useful when there are a limited number of data series to be compared.
- *Line.* (Figure L.80*b*). Consists of one or more series of data points that are connected with a straight line. Each line represents one series of data values, such as revenues or expenses. When data are compared over time, the *x* axis usually indicates the time period, while the *y* axis shows the quantity being measured. Line graphs are most useful for illustrating conditions where there are many data values in each series of data values, such as illustrating the number of employees over a 20-year time period.
- *Pie.* (Figure L.80*c*). Shows each data value as a relative measure to the whole amount for the entire data series. A pie chart is limited to comparing the components of a single data series. One or more segments of a pie chart may be **exploded**, or displayed separately from the other segments of the pie chart, as a means of emphasizing that segment.
- *Stack Bar.* (Figure L.80*d*). Consists of related data values from different data series that are stacked on top of each other to form a single bar. Each segment

Situation	Graph Type
Showing trends	Bar graph, line graph
Comparing components	Pie chart, exploded pie chart, stacked-bar graph
Showing relationships	*XY* graph

FIGURE L.79. Choosing a graph type.

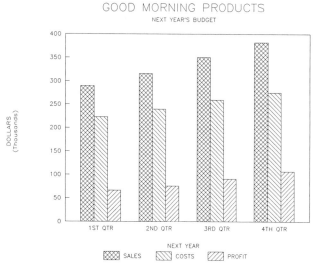

FIGURE L.80a. Bar graph.

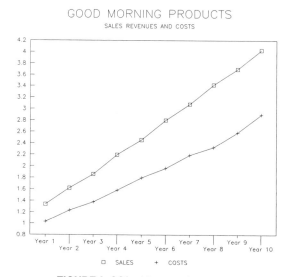

FIGURE L.80b. Line graph.

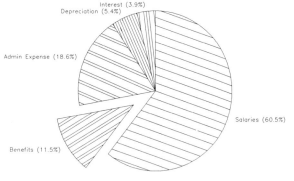

FIGURE L.80c. Pie chart.

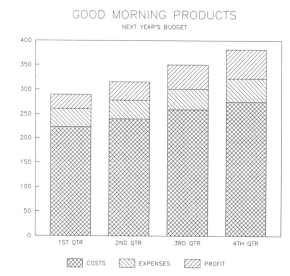

FIGURE L.80d. Stack-bar graph.

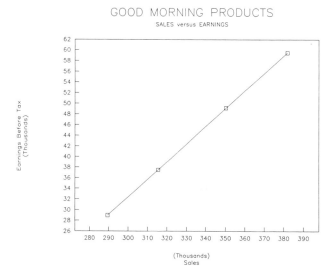

FIGURE L.80e. XY graph.

of the bar shows an individual data value for a different data series, while the overall bar height shows the total for all the data series. For example, each segment could be a separate cost category; then the entire bar would be the total costs for the time period. This graph lets you compare both a total and the components that make up that total over several time periods or several different alternatives.

- *XY.* (Figure L.80*e*). Shows the relationship between two or more data series. One data series is selected for the *x* axis and the other data series are displayed on the *y* axis. Frequently a line connects the points of the data values in each data series. An *XY* graph is most useful when the *x* axis data are not units of time, but represent some other condition, such as number of units produced or sales revenue in dollars.

L.5.2   Fundamentals of 1-2-3 Graphs

Kim and Chris want to compare **Sales, Cost of Sales,** and **Gross Profit** for the four quarters of their budget year. After considering the different types of graphs, they believe a bar graph is best for showing this comparison. When completed, their bar graph will be like that shown in Figure L.81. This graph illustrates several features that are specified in creating a 1-2-3 graph:

1. Data ranges selected for display on the graph. Lotus 1-2-3 allows up to six different ranges.
2. Two lines of titles appear at the top of the graph.
3. A title appears on the *Y* axis.

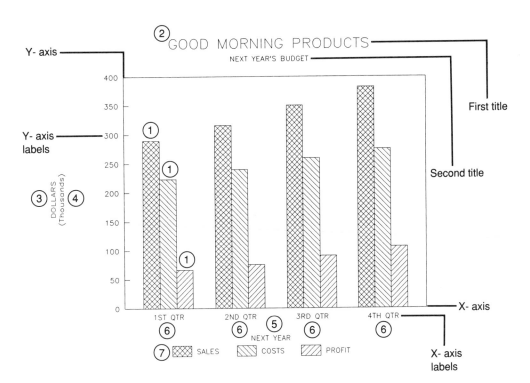

FIGURE L.81. Bar graph.

4. Lotus 1-2-3 scales the *Y* axis.

5. A title appears on the *X* axis.

6. Each group of bars is identified with an *X* axis label.

7. A legend appears at the bottom of the graph.

These characteristics are designated as the graph is built by selecting the appropriate command from a Graph menu. In addition to these characteristics, Lotus 1-2-3 graphs may include several other features that are described after the creation of this basic 1-2-3 bar graph is explored.

With 1-2-3 Release 2.4 and earlier releases, graphs like Figure L.81, are created and previewed on your display screen in the main 1-2-3 program and then are printed with a separate PrintGraph program. This requires that you save a *snapshot* or *image* of your graph as it appears on your display screen for printing. The general relationship of the 1-2-3 and PrintGraph programs is illustrated in Figure L.82. From the 1-2-3 program, you issue commands that create an *.PIC file, which is the "snapshot" of your graph. Later, after you exit from the 1-2-3 program, you use the Printgraph program to print this "snapshot." The *.PIC file is a *separate file* from your worksheet file. With Release 3.x of 1-2-3, the printing of graphs is included in the main 1-2-3 program and appears as a menu choice on the Print menu. The examples explored here are printed with the separate PrintGraph program.

L.5.3   Creating a Bar Graph

After Kim and Chris determined that a bar graph was the most appropriate choice for comparing **Sales, Cost of Sales,** and **Gross Profit** for the four quarters of their budget, they were ready to create, preview, and save their bar graph (Figure L.81) for printing. In Figure L.81 the bars for each data value appear next to one another. This arrangement of bars is known as a **side-by-side** bar graph. Notice that the graph does *not* include the **Total** column with the sum for the four quarters. Because they

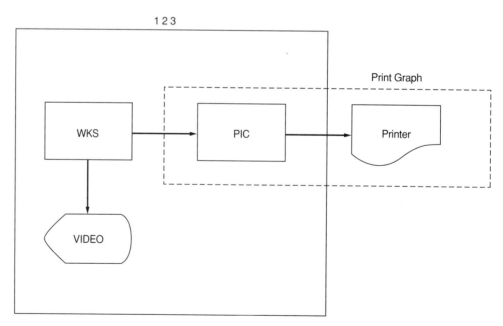

FIGURE L.82. Graph file saved for separate printing.

wanted to compare the data for the four quarters, they realized that including the **Total** column would distort and distract from this comparison. As a result, they limited their graph to the data for just the four quarters. Let's examine the process for creating this bar graph.

Action: Be sure that PLAN6 is your currently active worksheet file. Now the Graph menu is accessed and the graph type specified beginning from the READY mode.

To access the Graph menu

Press:	/	Access main menu
Select:	Graph	This is a sticky menu and causes the Graph Settings sheet to be displayed

As many of the graph characteristics are specified, they appear in the Graph Setting dialog box (Figure L.83) that appears when the Graph command is selected. (The Graph Settings are displayed beginning with Release 2.2). Watch this dialog box as you specify each characteristic of the bar graph.

Each of the bar graph's characteristics is specified by making various choices from this Graph menu. First, the type of graph is selected.

To choose a graph type

Select:	Type	Indicate that you want to specify a graph type
Select:	Bar	Type of graph desired

Before the data values are specified for this bar graph, the name for each group of bars along the X-axis is established from a range of cells in the worksheet. You may use either the keyboard or a mouse, if available, to specify this and other graph ranges.

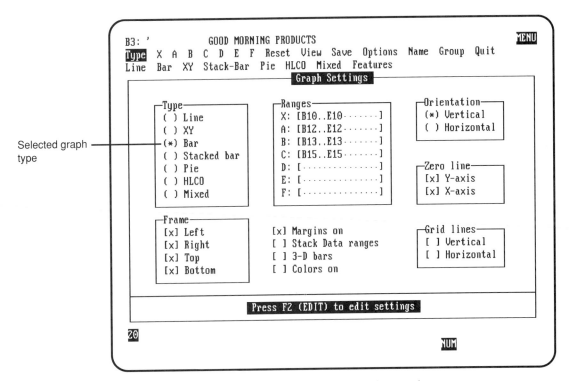

Selected graph type

FIGURE L.83. Graph settings dialog box for bar graph.

To specify the X-axis names for each cluster of bars for each time period	**Select:**	X	This cell range contains the names for each cluster of bars
	Move to:	**B10**	Beginning cell containing names for bar clusters
	Press:	.	Anchor the range
	Move to:	**E10**	Stretch worksheet cursor to define cell range
	Press:	<Enter>	Complete *X* axis range specification

Next, the data values for each of the three data series that make up the bars are specified, with the selections appearing in the Graph Settings dialog box (Figure L.83). Each data series to be displayed on your graph is obtained from a data range in the worksheet. This is usually a row or a column of data. The best procedure in Lotus 1-2-3 is to use these ranges starting with **A,** then using **B, C,** and so on.

To specify the A-range data values for graphing	**Select:**	A	This data range will contain the data for **Sales**; a single graph can contain up to six data ranges identified as "A" through "F"
	Move to:	**B12**	Beginning cell of **Sales** data series in the "A" data range
	Press:	.	Anchor the range
	Move to:	**E12**	Other end of the **Sales** data in the "A" data range
	Press:	<Enter>	Complete data range specification, which now appears as a Graph Setting [Figure L.83]

Keypoint! | For each data range, the data to be graphed *must be in adjacent cells* in that row or column. If you include blank cells, their values will be considered as zeros!

Keypoint! | Each data range produces one set of bars, one line, or a pie chart on a Lotus 1-2-3 graph. To graph three lines, three data ranges must be used!

Action: Repeat the foregoing procedure for data ranges "B" and "C." In data range **B,** identify the cells as **B13..E13** for **Cost of Sales,** and in data range **C,** specify cells **B15..E15** for **Gross Profit.**

Now let's take a look at the graph by previewing it on your display screen.

To preview a graph by displaying it on your screen	**Select:**	View	The graph appears
	Action:		Inspect the resulting bar graph and notice how each cluster of bars for each quarter contains a single data value from each of the three data ranges that were specified for display in the graph. Your cluster of bars should be like those shown in Figure L.81.

When you have finished inspecting your work, return to the graph menu and graph setting sheet.

To terminate viewing a graph and return to the Graph menu with the Graph Settings dialog box	**Press:**	<Esc>	Or any other key

~~~~~~~~
Caution Alert!
~~~~~~~~

Your computer must be equipped with a graphics adapter to preview a graph on your display screen.

~~~~~~~~
Caution Alert!
~~~~~~~~

If your display screen goes blank when you select view, then either you do NOT have a graphics adapter or you need to run the Install program because 1-2-3 does NOT recognize your current graphics adapter. Pressing <Esc> will return you to the Graph menu!

Next, let's add the titles at the top of the graph, a title along the Y-axis, a title along the X-axis, and a legend, as illustrated in Figure L.81. These titles can be entered one after the other until all these graph options are specified.

| To begin adding titles to a graph | **Select:** | Options | Selected from the Graph menu |
| | **Select:** | Titles | Desired option |

When you choose Titles, a Graph Legends & Titles dialog box appears so that you can see the current setting for these graph specifications (Figure L.84). You are ready to add the first title.

| To specify the first title of the graph | **Select:** | First | This is the topmost line of the title |
| | **Enter:** | Good Morning Products | |

To add the second title to the graph	**Select:**	Title	Since you were returned to the Options menu
	Select:	Second	This is a command under the Title menu
	Enter:	Next Year's Budget	

To specify the Y-axis title	**Select:**	Title	Desired option
	Select:	Y-Axis	
	Enter:	Dollars	Desired title

To specify the X-axis title	**Select:**	Title	Choose desired option
	Select:	X-Axis	
	Enter:	Next Year	Desired title

This completes the specification of all the titles for the bar graph. They should be the same as those shown in Figure L.84.

The legend for the graph is specified from the same Options menu as the Titles. Now let's add the legend for each of the data ranges at the bottom of the graph. You continue with the Options menu by entering the desired legend.

To add the A-range legend for **Sales**	**Select:**	Legend	Desired option
	Select:	A	Corresponds to the "A" data range specified above for **Sales**
	Enter:	Sales	Word to appear in legend

To add the B-range legend for **Cost of Sales**	**Select:**	Legend	Desired option
	Select:	B	Matches the "B" data range of graph
	Enter:	Costs	Word to appear in legend

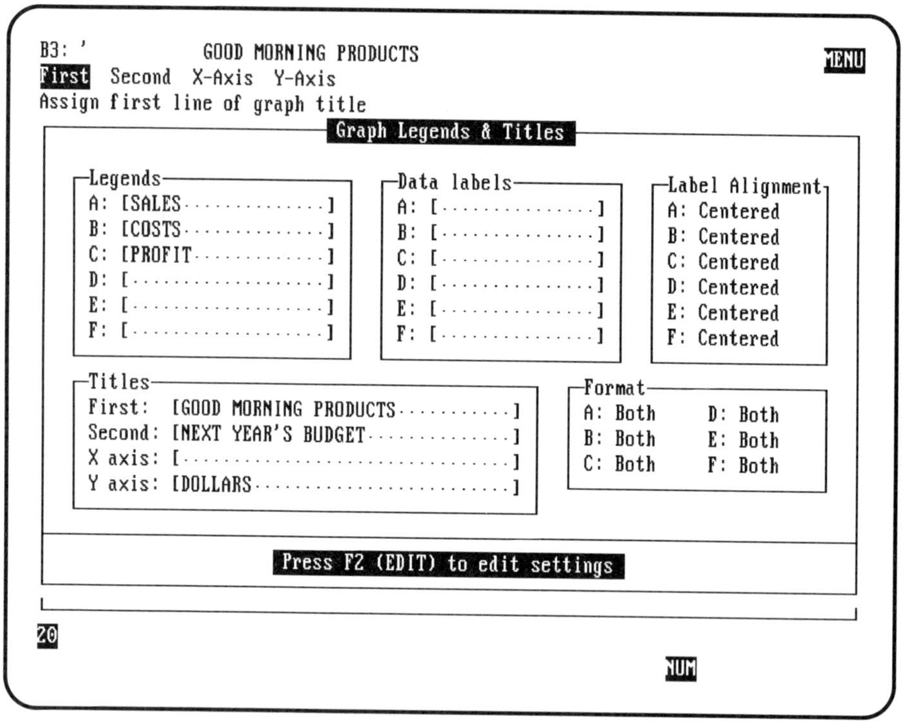

```
B3: '          GOOD MORNING PRODUCTS                          MENU
First Second X-Axis Y-Axis
Assign first line of graph title
                    ┌──────── Graph Legends & Titles ────────┐
  ┌─Legends─────────────┐  ┌─Data labels─────────┐  ┌─Label Alignment─┐
  │ A: [SALES·········] │  │ A: [·············] │  │ A: Centered     │
  │ B: [COSTS·········] │  │ B: [·············] │  │ B: Centered     │
  │ C: [PROFIT········] │  │ C: [·············] │  │ C: Centered     │
  │ D: [·············] │  │ D: [·············] │  │ D: Centered     │
  │ E: [·············] │  │ E: [·············] │  │ E: Centered     │
  │ F: [·············] │  │ F: [·············] │  │ F: Centered     │
  └─────────────────────┘  └─────────────────────┘  └─────────────────┘
  ┌─Titles──────────────────────────────────┐  ┌─Format──────────────┐
  │ First:  [GOOD MORNING PRODUCTS········] │  │ A: Both    D: Both  │
  │ Second: [NEXT YEAR'S BUDGET···········] │  │ B: Both    E: Both  │
  │ X axis: [·····························] │  │ C: Both    F: Both  │
  │ Y axis: [DOLLARS·····················] │  └─────────────────────┘
  └──────────────────────────────────────────┘

              ▐ Press F2 (EDIT) to edit settings ▌

  └───────────────────────────────────────────────────────────────┘
  20
                                                              NUM
```

FIGURE L.84. Graph Legends & Titles dialog box for bar graph.

To add a C-range legend for **Gross Profit**

Select:	Legend	Desired option
Select:	C	Match the "C" data range
Enter:	Profit	Word to appear in legend
Select:	Quit	Leave this sticky menu

Now let's preview the complete bar graph with its titles and legend.

To preview the completed graph

Select:	View	From the Graph menu
Press:	<Esc>	Complete preview of graph and return to the Graph menu

The Graph Setting and Graph Legend & Titles dialog boxes contain information on a number of additional graph setting that you can make. You may explore these as desired or consult a *Lotus 1-2-3 Reference Manual*.

Keypoint!   A Graph Settings dialog box appears only with Releases 2.2 and later of 1-2-3.

Before this graph can actually be printed, it needs to be saved in an *.PIC file for later use by the 1-2-3 PrintGraph program. Let's save the bar graph for printing.

To save a graph as an *.PIC file for printing

Select:	Save	From the Graph menu
Enter:	Bar	File name for the graph

The graph is written to the file BAR.PIC on your default disk drive for later use in printing. Before printing this graph, let's create several other graphs and save them. Then, they can all be printed at one time.

Keypoint!   To create an *.PIC file containing the graph "snapshot" or image, a SAVE must be performed from the *Graph Menu* once a graph has been completed. This file is required to print the graph!

Keypoint!   Even if you do NOT have a graphics adapter, you may still print your graph using the PrintGraph program. Just save it to an *.PIC file. In this case, exercise extra care to ensure that you have made all the correct entries for your graph, because you would need to return to the 1-2-3 program to make any changes in data ranges, titles, legends, and so on!

L.5.4   Using a Mouse for Graph Settings

When mouse support is available, you may use the mouse to specify Graph Settings. The mouse is used to (1) select option buttons (only one option is selected at a time), (2) mark check boxes (select as many options as desired), (3) and select text boxes (Figure L.85). The dialog box is activated by clicking anywhere in the box with the mouse or by pressing <F2> (EDIT). The mode indicator changes to SETTINGS and the Graph menu disappears to advise you that setting can be specified directly in the dialog box. For text boxes, you select the text box and then type the desired settings. When you finish your graph specifications, select OK to return to the MENU mode.

The Graph MENU mode is often more convenient than the SETTING mode for specifying data ranges, because you can using pointing to define your data ranges. However, 1-2-3 also allows you to make changes directly on the Setting Sheet. You should use the method you like best.

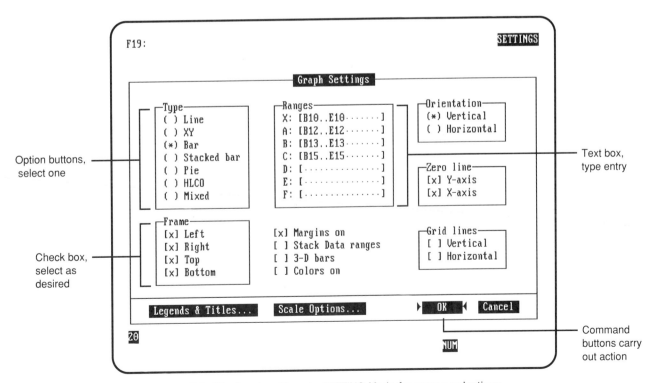

FIGURE L.85. Graph settings in SETTING Mode for mouse selections.

L.5.5   Saving Graph Settings

The graph **settings** that you completed for the bar graph, and whose specifications appears in the Graph Settings dialog box, can be saved with your 1-2-3 worksheet file. This permits a graph's settings to be readily accessed for future use, such as when data are revised for a what-if analysis. In fact, 1-2-3 allows you to create and store several different graph settings with an individual worksheet. Then, after revising data for a what-if, you can easily view *any* of the graphs that you have already defined.

When storing several graph settings as part of your 1-2-3 worksheet, each graph is given a distinct name. A convenient naming scheme for graph settings is to use the same name for the settings as you use for the *.PIC file for printing the graph. Let's name the current graph setting for Good Morning Products as the BAR graph for future reference. This is accomplished beginning from the Graph menu.

To name a graph setting that is saved with the worksheet file			
Select:	Name	Desired activity for naming graph
Select:	Create	Name is being assigned to your graph
Enter:	Bar	Desired name of graph setting

Your graph setting is assigned the name BAR, and you are ready to continue with any other graphing activity. After several additional graph settings have been developed, you will then see how to recall this BAR graph's settings.

L.5.6   Producing a Stack Bar Graph

Kim and Chris want to consider several other graphs that they may want to use in supporting different viewpoints during their presentation to the management committee. Kim suggested the use of a stack bar graph to show how **Sales** were divided between **Cost of Sales** and **Gross Profit** for each of the four quarters of their plan. They want to continue their graphing activities by changing their side-by-side bar graph into the stacked bar graph, as portrayed in Figure L.86. This is an easily performed activity, since the *same data ranges* will be considered; only their presentation is revised. Let's change the graph type, starting from the Graph menu.

To change a graph type			
Select:	Type	From the Graph menu
Select:	Stacked-Bar	Desired chart type

To preview the revised graph			
Select:	View	Graph is displayed
Press:	<Esc>	When you have finished looking at the graph to return to the Graph menu

Although it was very easy to switch from the side-by-side bar graph to this stack bar graph, what is wrong with the graphical presentation of the data? As Kim explains to Chris, the total height of the bar for each quarter should represent the **Sales** for that quarter. However, **Sales** are included as one of the data ranges in the graph. Lotus 1-2-3 will graph your data by using whatever graph type you specify, regardless of whether it makes sense to display the data using that graph type. Kim wants to use a stack bar graph in their presentation, but does not want it to include the separate range of data for **Sales**. How can this be corrected? Let's look at this modification by continuing from the Graph menu.

To remove an unwanted data range from a graph setting			
Select:	Reset	Prepare to remove unwanted data range
Select:	A	Desired range containing **Sales** data

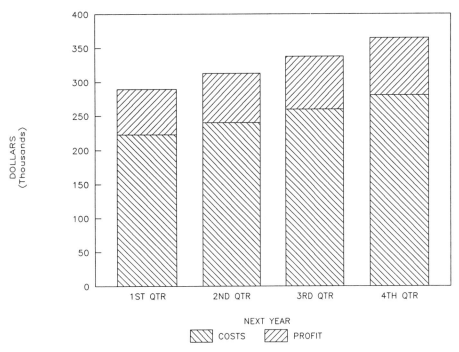

FIGURE L.86. Stacked bar graph.

Select:	Quit	Return to main Graph menu
Select:	View	Preview the revised graph
Press:	<Esc>	When you are done viewing the graph

Chris and Kim now have the graph they want (Figure L.86). The titles and legend remained from the side-by-side bar graph, so these did not need to be entered.

Like the side-by-side bar graph, the settings for this stack bar graph can be named for future reference, and the image can be saved for later printing. Let's perform these activities.

	Select:	Save	Create a file for printing
To save this graph as a file for future printing	**Enter:**	stack	*.PIC file is written to disk
	Action:		Give these graph settings the name STACK for future reference.

L.5.7   Producing a Line Graph

In reviewing their bar graphs, Kim points out to Chris that a line graph might provide a better picture of the increasing trends in **Sales, Cost of Sales,** and **Gross Profit** from quarter to quarter. They agree that a line graph is useful for their presentation to emphasize these conditions. Let's explore the development of their line graph, as shown in Figure L.87. Because this graph contains nearly the same data that were included in their stack bar graph, they can continue from the stack bar graph settings in defining the settings for this graph.

Action: Because the **Sales** data in the A-range were deleted from the stack bar graph, specify the **Sales** data in **B10..E10** for the A-range.

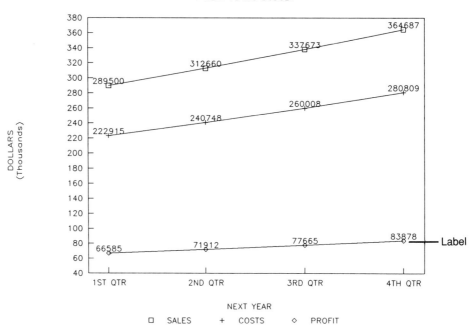

FIGURE L.87. Line graph with data labels.

Now let's change this to a line graph and preview the result.

To change the graph type to line	**Select:**	Type	From the Graph menu
	Select:	Line	Desired chart type
	Select:	View	Preview the revised graph
	Press:	<Esc>	When finished viewing graph

As shown in Figure L.87, 1-2-3 lets you include data labels with each of the data points on the line. By specifying the data values plotted in the graph, it is easy to read the actual value that was plotted. Of course, 1-2-3 allows you to specify any cell range you want for data labels. The data labels for the line graph are an option that can be added to this graph.

To initiate the specification of data labels	**Select:**	Options	This will allow data labels to be added
	Select:	Data-Labels	This allows data labels to be specified for each data range

To select the cell range containing the data labels for the A-range	**Select:**	A	Choose the "A" data range
	Move to:	**B12**	Beginning of "A" range
	Press:	.	Anchor range
	Move to:	**E12**	End of the "A" range
	Press:	<Enter>	Complete "A" range specification
	Select:	Above	Choose location of data labels

To specify the data labels for the other data ranges

Action: Repeat the foregoing procedure for data ranges "B" and "C." In data range **B,** identify cells **B13..E13** for **Cost of Sales,** and in data range **C,** specify cells

B15..E15 for **Gross Profit.** Select the Above option for the location of these data labels.

To complete the data label specification and preview the graph	**Select:**	Quit	Leave Data-Labels menu
	Select:	Quit	Return to Graph menu
	Select:	View	Display the line chart
	Press:	<Esc>	When finished viewing graph
	Action:	Save the image of this graph as the LINE.PIC file for later printing.	
	Action:	Give these graph settings the name LINE for future reference if modifications should be necessary.	
	Select:	Quit	Leave the Graph menu and return to READY mode
	Action:	Save the worksheet file as PLAN7.	

When you save the worksheet file, the *graph settings* that you have entered are *saved as part of your worksheet file.* These graph definitions are the commands you entered and *not* a copy of the actual graph. The image or "snapshot" of the actual graph was saved in the *.PIC file in preparation for printing the graph.

L.5.8   Producing Pie Charts

Chris and Kim would like to create a graph that shows the proportion of the total **Sales** for the year that are expected each quarter. That is, this graph will show the percent of **Sales** attained in each quarter. These data for Good Morning Products can be displayed as a pie chart like that in Figure L.88. Pie charts are different from line and bar graphs, because only an "A" data range is displayed on a pie chart. The

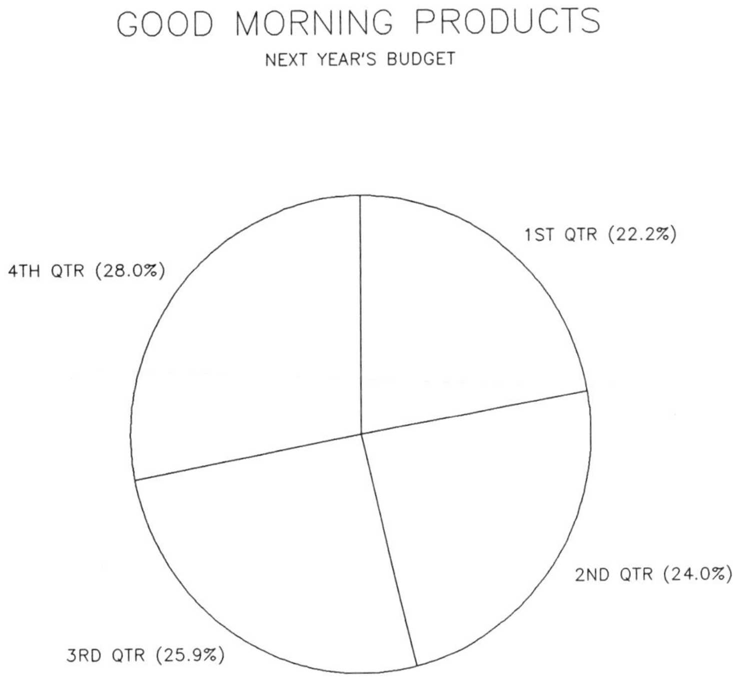

GOOD MORNING PRODUCTS
NEXT YEAR'S BUDGET

1ST QTR (22.2%)

4TH QTR (28.0%)

2ND QTR (24.0%)

3RD QTR (25.9%)

FIGURE L.88. Pie chart.

"B" data range can be used to specify cross-hatching or shading and explosion of the various pie slices, whereas the other data ranges are not used with a pie chart.

A plain pie chart can be created from the Graph menu. Let's see how this is accomplished.

Action: Access the Graph menu and review the settings that remain from the line graph.

To specify a pie type graph

| **Select:** | Type | From the Graph menu |
| **Select:** | Pie | Desired chart type |

Because the data in graph ranges B and C are not used with this pie chart, these settings need to be removed. The other settings for the X-range, A-range, and titles can still be used in this graph. Unwanted graph settings are removed using the Reset command.

To remove the unwanted graph settings

Select:	Reset	Prepare to remove B-range
Select:	B	Desired range to be reset
Action:	Also, reset the C-range, since this is *not* used with your pie chart.	
Select:	Quit	Return to main Graph menu

By resetting the B-range, you avoid a potential mess with your graph, since the data in the B-range would be used to specify options for your pie chart. Now, look at your graph.

To display the pie chart

Select:	View	Graph is displayed
Press:	<Esc>	When finished viewing graph
Action:	Name this the PIE graph and save it as the PIE.PIC file for printing.	

Since the graph titles have already been entered, they were used in displaying this pie chart in the same manner as they had been used with the bar, stack bar, and line graphs. Once you begin entering a graph description, the settings remain the same until you either change them or select the Reset command. Reset discards your active graph settings. The Reset Graph command removes *all* settings from your current graph definition creating a "clean" settings sheet.

Keypoint! | Graph settings remain as specified until a setting is either changed or all settings are discarded with the Reset command!

An exploded pie chart has one or more slices of the pie moved outward for emphasis, as illustrated in Figure L.89. Usually explosion is used to highlight selected variables that make up the pie chart. Along with exploding the pie slices, cross-hatching patterns can be selected. Data values are recorded in a *separate range of cells* to specify exploding and cross-hatching.

Action: For Good Morning Products, enter these values in the indicated cells:

Cell	B20	C20	D20	E20
Contents	107	3	5	1

GOOD MORNING PRODUCTS
NEXT YEAR'S SALES BUDGET

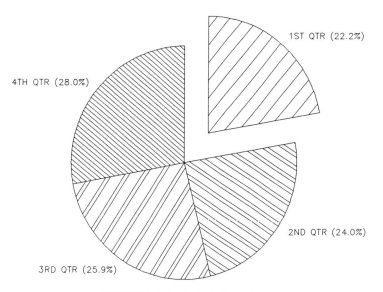

FIGURE L.89. Exploded pie chart.

Eight (8) different cross-hatching patterns are available, which are designated with a number from 0 to 7. Zero has no cross-hatching, but each of the other numbers produces a different pattern, as illustrated in Figure L.90. Adding 100 to the cross hatching data value causes that slice to be displayed as exploded. For the Good Morning Products pie chart, the data values describing cross-hatching and exploding were stored in cells **B20** through **E20,** a convenient location out of the way of the main

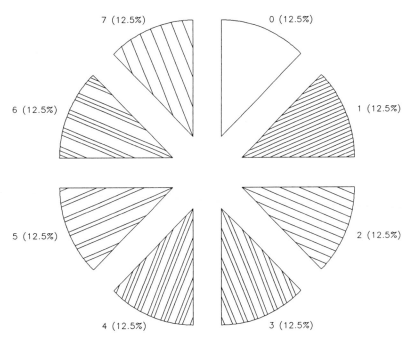

FIGURE L.90. Cross-hatch shading for pie charts.

worksheet area. In general, these values should be stored in a row if the graph "A" range data is in a row.

Let's produce the cross-hatched and exploded pie chart for **Sales** by quarter at Good Morning Products.

Action: Access the main Graph menu.

To specify the B-range for the cross-hatching and explosion	**Select:**	B	This data range will contain the cross-hatching and explosion specifications
	Move to:	**B20**	Begin the "B" data range
	Press:	.	Anchor range
	Move to:	**E20**	End "B" data range
	Press:	<Enter>	Complete data range specification
To look at the revised pie chart	**Select:**	View	Graph is displayed
	Action:		Exit from the View, and then name this as the EXPIE graph and save it in the file EXPIE.PIC for printing.

L.5.9   Creating an XY Graph

Chris and Kim would like a graph for their management committee review that shows the relationship between **Sales** and **Gross Profit.** That is, they want a graph that portrays the change in **Gross Profit** as **Sales** change, regardless of the time period. In 1-2-3, the XY graph type is used to illustrate this relationship. One data series is selected for the X-axis and one or more data series are plotted on the Y-axis. The desired XY graph of **Sale** versus **Gross Profit** appears as Figure L.91. A point is plotted on the graph for each (X,Y) coordinate formed by a pair of data values from the two data series. Let's look at how this graph is created.

Action: Access the Graph menu, if necessary.

Because the other graphs for Good Morning Products have been created already, the Graph Settings dialog box contains the specification for the last graph you defined. A "clean" Graph Settings is desired for specifying this XY graph.

To remove all the previously specified Graph Settings from the current dialog box	**Select:**	Reset
	Select:	Graph

Now the desired graph is specified, beginning with the XY graph type.

To select the XY graph type	**Select:**	Type
	Select:	XY

The **Sales** data are selected for display as the X-range and appear on the X-axis because **Gross Profit** is usually caused by **Sales.** Then the **Gross Profit** is assigned to the A-range.

To specify the X-range data series for display on the X-axis	**Select:**	X
	Action:	Specify the X-range as the quarterly **Sales** data in **B12..E12.**
To specify the A-range data series for display on the Y-axis	**Select:**	A
	Action:	Specify the A-range as the quarterly **Gross Profit** data in **B15..E15.**

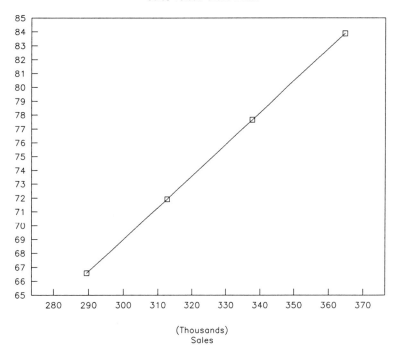

FIGURE L.91. XY graph of sales versus gross profit.

Because the Reset command removed *all* the Titles specifications, these need to be entered, including the first title line. The scaling of the X-axis and Y-axis are performed and displayed automatically by 1-2-3. You do *not* need to enter this scaling as part of the title. Now let's complete this graph and view it.

Action: Specify the titles as shown in Figure L.91

Action: Preview the graph. If you detect any errors, correct them.

Action: Name this as the XY graph and save it as the XY.PIC file for printing.

Action: Save the worksheet file as PLAN8. This also saves all your *graph settings* in the same worksheet file.

Although there are several additional activities that can be performed from the Graph menu, you have examined the primary ones by building this set of six graphs for Good Morning Products. You may want to explore some of the other aspects of graphing when you have time available.

The current graph specifications, as indicated in the Graph Settings dialog box, and each of the named graph settings are saved when a worksheet file is saved. These settings describe how to create a graph from a worksheet's data. The *.PIC files, which are a snapshot of the graph as displayed on your screen, are saved for printing. This *.PIC image is all that is processed by the PrintGraph program.

Keypoint!

> 1. The Graph Settings are stored with the worksheet file for use with other future data!
>
> 2. The "snapshot" image is stored as an *.PIC file for printing. This image cannot be modified; it can only be re-created!

L.5.10 Accessing Named Graphs

The graph settings that Kim and Chris have created and named can be recalled as desired to view these graphs and then to make any desired changes to these existing graph definitions. Let's recall a graph setting.

Action: Access the main Graph Menu.

Select:	Name	Desired option
Select:	Use	Command to access previously defined graph settings with a list of named graphs appearing for your selection
Select:	BAR	Desired graph

To access a named graph setting

The selected bar graph appears on your display screen.

Press:	\<Esc>	Return to the graph settings for the selected named graph
Action:		Review at least two of your other graph settings by recalling them and then return to the READY mode.

In this manner, any of the graphs you have defined and named can be viewed and, if desired, revised. If you wanted to produce a "screen show" of all five of your graphs, you could proceed to select each graph in turn with this / Graph Name Use (/GNU) command.

Action: Run through a "screen show" of the six graphs you have developed for Good Morning Products by selecting and displaying each graph with the / Graph Name Use (/GNU) command.

L.5.11 Graph Building Command Summary

Graphs are constructed by selecting commands from the main Graph menu and from the graph Options menu. Those commands not illustrated above may be explored as desired. The commands for each of these menus are summarized in Figures L.92 and L.93.

L.5.12 Printing Graphs

To print a graph, it is necessary to leave the main 1-2-3 program and access the PrintGraph program. Let's see how this is accomplished, beginning from the READY mode after you have saved your current worksheet file.

To leave the main 1-2-3 program in preparation for printing graphs

Press:	/	Access main menu
Select:	Quit	
Select:	Y	Yes, you do want to leave 1-2-3

You are returned to the 1-2-3 Access System, where you can now activate the PrintGraph program.

Graph Menu Selection	Activity
Type	Style of graph is selected from among alternatives, which include Line, Bar, XY, Stacked Bar, and Pie. Some releases of 1-2-3 include additional graph types.
X	"X" data range provides labels for X-axis or data values for an XY graph.
A B C D E F	Data ranges to be included on graph, with a maximum of six different data ranges permitted.
Reset	Removes all or selected settings for a graph.
View	Causes graph to be displayed on your screen for previewing.
Save	Stores a "snapshot" or image of the graph in an *.PIC file for printing.
Options	Allows specification of other graph characteristics.
Name	Permits a graph setting to be named for future reference when several graphs are created within a single worksheet.
Group	Specifies the X-range and the A–F data ranges all at once when the data to be graphed are located in adjacent rows or columns with the X-range as the topmost row or leftmost column of data.
Quit	Leave the Graph menu and return to the READY mode.

FIGURE L.92. Graph menu choices.

Options Menu Selection	Activity
Legend	Specify legend identification for each of the A–F data ranges.
Format	Select lines and symbols for displaying data.
Titles	Enter titles of up to 39 characters for the two lines at top, the Y-axis, and the X-axis.
Grid	Add horizontal or vertical grid lines to graph.
Scale	Control the X-axis and Y-axis scales.
Color	Causes display of graph in color (when color display is available).
B & W	Causes display of graph in black and white (usually best when graph is printed in black and white).
Data-Labels	Identify data labels for points or bars in a graph.
Quit	Leaves the Options menu and returns to the main Graph menu.

FIGURE L.93. Graph options menu.

To initiate execution of the
PrintGraph program

Select: PrintGraph   This is selected from the main access
menu of 1-2-3

Or, from the DOS prompt:

Enter: PGRAPH   This method is typically used with some
Student Releases of 1-2-3

A PrintGraph setting sheet appears when you have successfully accessed the
PrintGraph program, as illustrated in Figure L.94. Under the HARDWARE SETTINGS,
check the Graphs directory and the Fonts directory. The Graphs directory should be
set to the disk drive where you stored the *.PIC files, and the Fonts directory should be
set to the same disk drive and directory where your Lotus 1-2-3 programs are stored. If
these are not correct, revise them to reflect the appropriate directories. For example,
assume that your *.PIC files are located on drive B:, then the Graphs directory should
be set to this disk drive.

To set the Graphs directory
for the *.PIC files

Select: Settings   Desired activity
Select: Hardware   These are the ones to be revised
Select: Graphs-Directory   Specific setting to be changed
Enter: B:\   Change directory
Select: Quit   Backup one sticky menu
Select: Quit   Return to main PrintGraph menu

If you need to change any other setting, use the procedure as described above.
Now the graph image *.PIC files can be selected for printing. Let's see how this is
done, starting from the main PrintGraph menu.

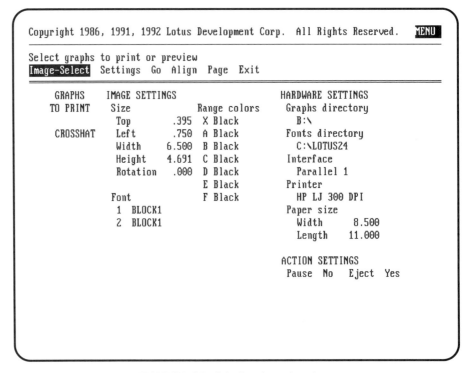

FIGURE L.94. PrintGraph setting sheet

To select graph images (*.PIC) files for printing	**Select:**	Image-Select	This causes a list of graph files to be displayed, as shown in Figure L.95
	Press:	<space>	Select the BAR graph, as indicated by # symbol at the left of the filename
	Press:	<down>	Move to next graph
	Action:		Continue selecting each graph by pressing <space> until they are all selected. (This will allow you to print all of them at once.)

If you wanted to print only a single graph, it could be selected individually. Pressing <space> is a toggle that "marks" a graph for printing. Notice that you can preview each graph by pressing the <F10> (GRAPH) key before you mark it. When your selection of graphs is complete, you return to the main PrintGraph menu.

To return to the main PrintGraph menu	**Press:**	<Enter>	Return to main PrintGraph menu

You are now ready to print your graphs. The Align, Go, and Page commands on the main PrintGraph menu perform the same functions as those on the Print menu in 1-2-3. Let's proceed to print the selected *.PIC graphs.

To actually print the selected graphs	**Select:**	Align	Be sure paper is at top of a new page in your printer
	Select:	Go	Cause graphs to actually be printed
	Select:	Page	Eject the last page printed

Thus, your graphs are printed. This may take several minutes. Because printing graphs is a slow process, you will need to wait while 1-2-3 prints your selected graphs.

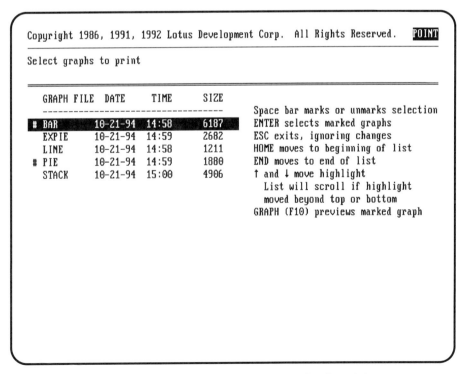

FIGURE L.95. List of available graph image files for printing.

Keypoint!

If any data or titles are incorrect, you need to return to the 1-2-3 program to change them and then repeat the process for printing your graph! The desired Graph Setting can be selected from your worksheet with the / Graph Name Use (/GNU) command.

Caution Alert!

Your printer must have been installed to work with 1-2-3 in printing your graphs. If a bunch of weird characters appear instead of your graph, Lotus 1-2-3 needs to be reinstalled with your printer identified as the one for printing graphs. Note that some printers do NOT allow graphics to be printed. You may want to verify that your printer is a graphics printer! If necessary, you may want to seek assistance with this process.

When you have printed all your graphs, then you are ready to leave the PrintGraph program.

| To exit from the PrintGraph program | **Select:** | Exit | Leave PrintGraph |
| | **Select:** | Yes | You really want to when you are done |

This returns you to the Lotus 1-2-3 Access Menu, where you can then make your next desired selection.

L.5.13   Using SmartIcons to Create a Graph

A Graph SmartIcon is available that lets you create a Quick Graph. This icon is useful when the data that you want to graph are located in consecutive or adjacent rows or columns. The data range for graphing includes the X-range together with the A–F data ranges. Data values for the X-range must be located in the top row or in the left column of the data range for your graph, depending on whether the data are organized rowwise or columnwise. The PLAN6 worksheet file in Figure L.96 is revised so the column titles, **Sales, Cost of Sales,** and **Gross Profit** are all in *one data range.* This arrangement is produced by deleting the rows of underlines from the worksheet to illustrate the consecutive rows of data (a rowwise arrangement) required for using the Graph SmartIcon. When you have data arranged like this, then you may use the Graph SmartIcon (Figure L.97) to produce a Quick Graph. This is similar to using the keyboard command / Graph Group (/GG).

Using the consecutive rowwise data range in Figure L.96, the bar graph in Figure L.98 is created by using the Graph SmartIcon. Let's see how this is accomplished.

Action: Access your PLAN6 worksheet file and use / Worksheet Delete Row (/WDR) to remove the rows containing the underline. This produces the necessary consecutive arrangement of the rows of data for graphing (Figure L.96).

Now you are ready to actually create the graph.

| To create a graph using the Graph SmartIcon | **Action:** | Highlight the cell range **B10..E13** containing the data range for the graph (Figure L.96). |
| | **Click:** | Graph SmartIcon   Desired activity |

The QuickGraph Setting dialog box appears as illustrated in Figure L.99. Your default settings may be different from those shown in this figure.

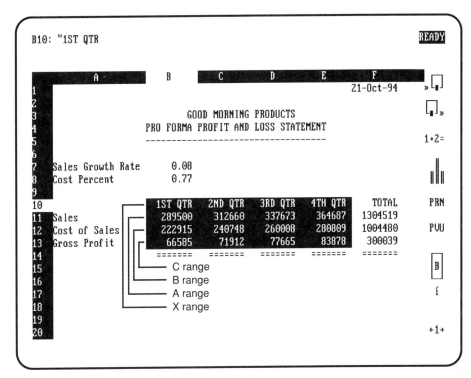

FIGURE L.96. Consecutive rowwise data arrangement for Graph SmartIcon.

SmartIcon	WYSIWYG SmartIcon	Command	Description
		Graph	Produce Quick Graph of the highlighted range.

FIGURE L.97. Graph SmartIcon.

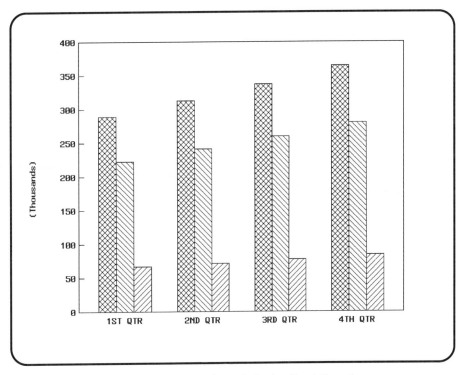

FIGURE L.98. Bar graph created using Graph SmartIcon.

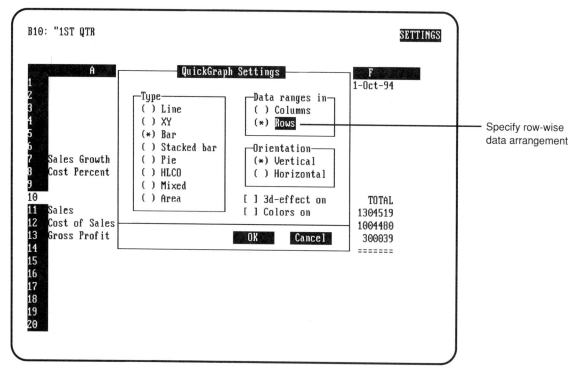

FIGURE L.99. QuickGraph Settings dialog box.

Action:	Use your mouse to select the QuickGraph Settings, as indicated in Figure L.99.	
Click:	OK	Complete graph settings and cause graph to be displayed, as shown in Figure L.98
Press:	<Esc>	When finished viewing graph and return to READY mode

The Graph SmartIcon lets you quickly create a graph that you can display on your screen. However, you must still use the keyboard for the other Graph commands that add Titles and Legends or that Name and Save the graph for printing.

Action: Using keyboard commands, name this graph QUICK and save it as the QUICK.PIC file for printing. Save your worksheet file with these graph settings as PLAN6QG. Then print this graph.

L.5.14 When Things Go Wrong

Several conditions may occur while you are defining and printing graphs. Some of the more common difficulties and how to approach them are described below:

1. You have just completed printing your graph and discover an error in the data displayed or the title used for the graph. When using the separate PrintGraph program, this requires that you exit from that program and reaccess your worksheet containing the graph definitions.

   a. Select Exit from the main PrintGraph Menu to return to the Lotus 1-2-3 Access System or the DOS prompt.

   b. Initiate execution of the 1-2-3 worksheet program.

   c. Retrieve your worksheet file containing your data together with the graph definitions.

   d. Employ the / Graph Name Use (/GNU) command to recall the desired graph definition.

   e. Modify your graph to correct the errors.

   f. View the modified graph to confirm that the errors have been corrected.

   g. Save the graph in an *.PIC file.

   h. Save your worksheet file containing the revised graph definition.

   i. Exit the 1-2-3 program and execute the PrintGraph program.

   j. Select and print the revised graph.

2. You are producing a pie chart or other graph and the ranges you have selected contain unwanted data values. That is, you want to produce a graph from data values that are not adjacent to one another. A limitation of producing a 1-2-3 graph is that each data series graphed must be in *one cell range*.

   a. As necessary, proceed to the READY mode.

   b. Locate a convenient, out of the way area of your worksheet for placing the data to be graphed. For the PLAN8 worksheet, this might be the cells **G25..I28,** as shown in Figure L.100.

   c. Create cell formulas that reference the cells containing the values to be graphed, such as **+A12** in cell **G25** to place the value for cell **A12** in cell **G25.** Do this for each of the cells you want to include in the range to be graphed, as illustrated in Figure L.100. Notice that you can use formulas to obtain values for labels as well as numeric data values.

   d. Create your graph definition by specifying these cells for the X-range and data ranges of your graph.

   e. Complete the graph definition and perform a view; then name and save this graph in the same manner as you would for any other graph.

L.5.15 Lesson Summary

- A graph is created by selecting up to six data ranges for display on a single graph.
- A pie chart is limited to displaying only one data range.
- Several different types of graphs can be produced, including bar, stacked-bar, line, and pie.
- In the 2.x releases of Lotus 1-2-3, an image of a graph is saved to be printed later using a separate PrintGraph program.

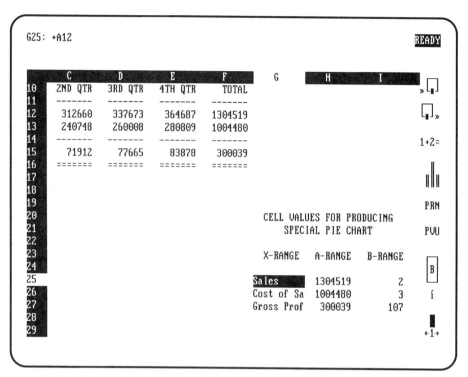

FIGURE L.100. Rearranging cell values into ranges for graphing.

- The appearance of a graph is enhanced with titles, legends, labels, and cross-hatching.

- A graph can be previewed on your display screen prior to saving the image or selecting an image for printing.

- The Install program is used to describe your specific hardware configuration to 1-2-3. If graphs do not display on your screen or cannot be printed, Lotus 1-2-3 may need to be reinstalled.

L.5.16 Practice Tutorial

Create the graphs described in this Lesson as a guided activity in a hands-on manner. Access your MYPLAN6 worksheet from the Practice Tutorial in Lesson L.3 as a starting point for this exercise.

Task 1: Create each graph, name the graph settings, and save each image as an *.PIC file for printing

Task 2: Print each of these graphs.

Task 3: Save the MYPLAN6 worksheet file with its named graph settings.

Time Estimates

Novice: 60 minutes

Intermediate: 45 minutes

Advanced: 30 minutes

L.5.17 Practice Exercises

(1) Case: Inland Container (continued)

Mary Montoya is finalizing her monthly proposal for Rydder Truck Rental. She is scheduled to review the proposal with Inland's district marketing manager tomorrow, before sending it to Richard. Mary wants to create the following graphs in preparation for her review:

(a) Bar graph of **Sales, Cost of Sales,** and **Gross Profit** for the three months, April, May, and June. Include titles and a legend, as appropriate. Name this graph as RTR_BAR for future reference.

(b) Line graph of **Units Sold** for the three months. Include labels of the number of units sold and place a title on the Y-axis. Give this graph the name RTR_LINE.

(c) Pie chart of **Cost of Sales** and **Gross Profit** in the Total column. This chart show how much of every sales dollar goes to each of these two components. [*Hint:* Create a separate range containing just these two data values, which are placed in the new range with these formulas. For example, the formulas might be: +E14 and +E16] Assign this graph the name RTR_PIE.

(d) Modify the pie chart from (c) above so that the two areas are cross-hatched and the **Gross Profit** slice is exploded. Name this graph as RTR_P_E.

Produce each of these graphs by performing the following tasks:

Task 1: Access your RYDDER2 worksheet from Practice Exercise 1 in Lesson L.3 as your starting point for this exercise.

Task 2: Create each graph, view the graph to confirm its content, name the graph for future reference, and save each graph image as an *.PIC file for printing.

Task 3: Save the RYDDER2 worksheet file with its graph settings.

Task 4: Print each of these graphs.

Time Estimates

Novice: 60 minutes

Intermediate: 45 minutes

Advanced: 30 minutes

(2) Case: Safety-Kleen Corporation

Business Problem: Annual report
MIS Characteristics: Finance
Strategic Planning

Safety-Kleen Corporation provides fluid recovery services to a variety of businesses, primarily those that generate relatively small quantities of hazardous fluid waste. Customers include auto repair facilities, auto body repair shops, fleet maintenance operations, dry cleaners, and manufacturing plants. Allan Brinckman, Safety-Kleen's Chief Financial Officer, is preparing a set of graphs for inclusion in their Annual Report. Under Allan's direction a table of Selected Financial Data has already been developed for the report. Allan wants you to generate the following set of graphs:

(a) Bar graph of **Revenue** for five years. Title the graph "Revenues" and place "Dollars in Millions" on the Y-axis. Name this graph REVENUES for future reference.

(b) Bar graph of **Net earnings** for five years. Title this graph "Earnings" and use the same "Dollars in Millions" title for the Y-axis as in (a) above. Name this graph EARNINGS for future reference.

(c) Bar graph of **Total assets** for five years. Title this graph "Total Assets" and use "Dollars in Millions" as the Y-axis title. Name this graph ASSETS for any future use.

(d) Bar graph of **Shareholder's equity** for the last five years. Title this graph "Shareholders' Equity" and use "Dollars in Millions" as the Y-axis title. Name this graph EQUITY for future use.

(e) Bar graph of **Cash dividends per share** and **Earnings per share** for the past five years. The bars for **Cash dividends per share** are to be located to the left of the **Earnings per share.** Use "Earnings per Common Share" as the title for this graph. Create a legend that identifies **Cash dividends per share** as "Dividends" and **Earnings per share** as "Earnings." Place the title "$ per Share" on the Y-axis. Name this graph SHARE_B for future reference.

(f) Line graph of **Cash dividends per share** and **Earnings per share.** Other than the type of graph, this graph is the same as that in (e) above. Name this graph SHARE_L for future reference.

Produce each of these graphs by performing the following tasks:

Task 1: Access the KLEEN.WK1 worksheet file from your Data Disk and review the table of Selected Financial Data for the Annual Report data contained in this worksheet.

Task 2: Create each graph, view the graph to confirm its contents, and save these graph images as *.PIC files for printing.

Task 3: Save your KLEEN.WK1 worksheet file containing the graph settings.

Task 4: Print each graph.

Task 5: (*Optional*)   Using the Selected Financial Data, add a **Retained earnings per share** account to the worksheet. This is computed for each year as follows:

Earnings per share − Cash dividends per share

Create a stack-bar graph that contains the **Retained earnings per share** and the **Cash dividends per share.** Use the same graph titles as in (e) above. Set up an appropriate legend for your graph. Name this graph SHARE_S for future reference. Print a hard copy of the graph. Write a short paragraph describing why you do not need to include the **Earnings per share** data as a separate component of your graph.

Time Estimates

Novice: 60 minutes

Intermediate: 45 minutes

Advanced: 30 minutes

(3)   Case: State Mutual Insurance

Business Problem: Work Sampling
MIS Characteristics: Human Resources
Managerial Control

Akio Kosai is the systems manager for the Policy Management System (PMS) at State Mutual Insurance. Akio is exploring methods to enhance the productivity of his staff of 10 systems analysts. To help him find areas where changes might be made, a work sampling study was conducted to determine how each analyst spends a typical workday. Work sampling is a procedure in which an individual's activities are recorded at random times throughout the day to determine the relative amount of time spent on each activity. Data were collected over a two-week period in March and summarized for each systems analyst. Akio just received the SMI.WK1 worksheet file that contains the summary from the work sampling. He wants to compare the results for each systems analyst and obtain an overall understanding of the analysts' daily activities. Akio would like you to prepare two graphs for his review:

(a) Bar graph showing the results for each systems analyst for each of the six categories measured by work sampling. The X-axis should contain the name of each analyst and have the title "Systems Analyst." The Y-axis should be titled "Percent of Day." The graph should have the title "Typical Workday." A legend should identify each of the six work activities observed.

(b) Pie chart displaying the **Average** portion of the day spent on each activity by all the analysts assigned to this system. Title this graph "Typical Workday." Obtain the labels for each slice of the pie from the second row of the column headings that identify each work activity. Apply cross-hatching to all slices of the pie. (Do not use cross-hatch zero, since this does not cause cross-hatching.)

Produce each of these graphs by performing the following tasks:

Task 1: Access the SMI.WK1 worksheet file from your Data Disk and review the table of results for the work sampling study. Print a hard copy of the worksheet for your reference as you build these graphs. Look at the six categories observed in this study.

Task 2: Create the bar graph that compares the components of the typical workday for each systems analyst. Name this the ANALYSTS graph for future reference. View the graph to make sure it's appropriately specified and save this graph image as an *.PIC file for printing.

Task 3: Develop Akio's pie chart that summarizes an **Average** workday for all systems analysts. Name this the WORKDAY graph for future reference. View the graph to check it out and then save the graph image in an *.PIC file for printing.

Task 4: Save your SMI.WK1 worksheet file containing the graph settings.

Task 5: Print each graph.

Task 6: (*Optional*)   Akio is considering adopting a new software engineering tool that promises to reduce programming/coding time by 10 percent. If this efficiency gain can be realized, what percentage of a typical workday would become available for other system development activities? Write a paragraph explaining your answer based on the information presented in the pie chart for a typical workday of a systems analyst.

Time Estimates

Novice: 60 minutes

Intermediate: 45 minutes

Advanced: 30 minutes

(4)   Case: Dow Chemical Company

Business Problem: Strategic sector analysis
MIS Characteristics: Marketing
        Strategic Planning

Sam Wyman, a vice president for worldwide operations at Dow Chemical, has a meeting scheduled next Monday with Dow's Management Committee to review current performance and long-term strategies for growth. The current strategy that guides Dow's allocation of resources is to direct resources toward specialty product areas, with a goal of a balanced company that has equal sales coming from three strategic sectors: basics, industrial specialties, and consumer specialties. Sam wants to explore several alternative graphs so that he can select the most appropriate for his presentation. In preparing for the meeting, he would like you to produce the following graphs:

Graph Type	Performance Measure	Time Period	Graph Name
Stack-bar	Sales by sector	All	SALES_B
Stack-bar	Operating income by sector	All	INCOME_B
Line	Sales by sector	All	SALES_L
Line	Operating income by sector	All	INCOME_L
Pie	Sales by sector	19x5	S_P_X5
Pie	Sales by sector	19X9	S_P_X9
Pie (exploded)	Sales by sector	19X9	S_P_X9_E

Task 1: Retrieve the DOWCHEM.WK1 worksheet from your Data Disk and review the **Sales** and **Operating income** data by strategic sector.

Task 2: Develop the stack-bar and line graphs as described in Sam's list. Save these graph images as *.PIC files for printing. Use either "SALES" or "OPERATING INCOME" for your graph title, as appropriate. On the Y-axis, use "$ in billions" as the title. Each graph should have a legend containing the sectors designators of "Basics," "Industrial," and "Consumer." View each graph to verify its content and identify the graph with the name provided by Sam.

Task 3: Produce the pie charts in Sam's list and save these graph images as *.PIC files for printing. Use "SALES" as each graph's main title. Include a subtitle to indicate the pie chart's contents. Identify each strategic sector by specifying the appropriate labels from the table of data. For the exploded pie chart, explode all the slices and select cross-hatching codes other than zero. View each graph to confirm that you have the desired graph. Name each graph for future reference using the names in Sam's list.

Task 4: Save your DOWCHEM.WK1 worksheet file, which contains your graph settings.

Task 5: Print each graph.

Task 6: (*Optional*)   Compare the stack-bar, line, and pie graphs for Sales. Write a paragraph explaining which graph(s) provide the most easily understood picture of sales by sector.

Task 7: (*Optional*) Add a section to the bottom of the current worksheet area that computes the Percentage of Sales by sector. That is, for each year, compute the percentage of sales for each strategic sector by dividing the Sales for that sector by the Total Sales. Create a stack-bar graph with the percentage of sales for each sector for all five years. Include titles and a legend similar to those used above. Name this as graph PCT_SALE. Save the graph in an *.PIC file and produce a hard copy of your graph. Write a paragraph that describes how this graph helps to understand how well Dow Chemical is doing in moving toward its diversification goal of equal sales in each strategic sector.

Time Estimates

Novice: 60 minutes

Intermediate: 45 minutes

Advanced: 30 minutes

(5) Case: Napa Valley Wooden Box

Business Problem: Profit planning
MIS Characteristics: Finance
                                      Strategic Planning

John Rensneaker is the operations manager of Napa Valley Wooden Box, a maker of attractive, well-made wooden cases for fine-quality wines. The firm specializes in producing six-bottle gift boxes. John has been working on a pro forma income statement containing their profit plan for the next three years. The plan is nearly complete, and he is preparing to present it to the owners at their regular monthly meeting on Monday. John wants these graphs for the meeting:

(a) Stack-bar comparing the three components that make up **Cost of goods** for the three years of the profit plan. Title the graph the same as that included on the worksheet. Title the Y-axis as "Dollars" and identify each bar by year. Include a legend that indicates each component of the stack-bars.

(b) Stack-bar comparing the three components that comprise **Cost of goods** and the components that make up **Operating expenses.** Use the same titles and a similar legend for this graph as for (a) above.

(c) Pie charts for each of the three years showing the distribution of each sales dollar as the three components of **Cost of goods, Operating Expenses,** and the **Earnings before tax.** Title the graph with the firm's name and "Distribution of Sales Dollar, 19X1." Identify each pie chart by its appropriate year in the graph's title. Use cross-hatching for each of the slices of the pie. The same cross-hatching arrangement may be used for all three graphs. Use the name of the items included in the pie chart to identify each slice.

Produce each of these graphs by performing the following tasks:

Task 1: Retrieve the NAPA.WK1 worksheet file from your Data Disk and review the Proforma Income Statement for the next three years' profit plan. Print a hard copy of the worksheet for your reference.

Task 2: Create John's stack-bar graph described in (a) above. View this graph, save the graph's image as an *.PIC file for printing, and name the graph CST_GOOD for your future reference.

Task 3: Develop the stack-bar graph described in (b) above. View it, save its image in an *.PIC file, and name the graph CST_EXP for future reference.

Task 4: Produce John's three pie charts described in (c) above. View them and save their images in *.PIC files. Name each graph SALES for the specific year such as SALES_1. [*Hint:* Create a separate area of your worksheet that contains the data and labels for the pie charts since these values are not all adjacent to one another in the current worksheet report.]

Task 5: Save the NAPA.WK1 worksheet file with these graph settings.

Task 6: Print each of these graphs.

Task 7: (*Optional*)   Write a paragraph explaining why the Distribution of Sales Dollar graph could be produced as a pie chart, but not as a stack-bar graph.

Time Estimates

Novice: 60 minutes

Intermediate: 45 minutes

Advanced: 30 minutes

(6)   Case: Advanced Micro Chips

Business Problem: Total quality management
MIS Characteristics: Production/Operations
Operational Control

Advanced Micro Chips emphasizes product quality through a Total Quality Management (TQM) program. In managing the production of computer memory chips, Alberto Mendoza uses a control chart for TQM monitoring. As each batch of memory chips is produced and tested, Alberto collects data on the portion of defectives in the batch. These data are plotted on a control chart to determine if any significant changes have occurred in the quality of the chips produced. If a change is detected, Alberto can take corrective actions in their manufacturing process. The control chart used by Alberto is a plot of three lines. Two of these, the Upper Control Limit (UCL) and Lower Control Limit (LCL), remain constant while the fraction of defectives in each batch is plotted. Alberto identifies each batch with a number. The UCL and LCL are computed using a common statistical formula for control charts that provides a measure of the expected deviation of the fraction of defectives. Alberto use his control chart to try to spot a trend in the number of defectives. Whenever the fraction of defectives falls outside the upper and lower control limits, this is a red flag to Alberto, indicating that corrective action may be required.

Alberto collected the data and updated his AMC.WK1 worksheet with the fraction of defectives. He has included the statistical formulas for computing the UCL and LCL. Alberto wants you to produce his control chart from these data by proceeding as follows:

Task 1: Retrieve the AMC.WK1 worksheet file from your Data Disk and review its contents. Page to the right to see all the data entered for the control chart.

Task 2: Create Alberto's control chart for the memory chip production with these characteristics:

(1) Line graph containing **UCL, LCL,** and **Fraction defective.**

(2) X-range containing the Batch numbers.

(3) Graph title: Control Chart of Memory Chip Production

(4) Y-axis title: Fraction of Batch Defective

(5) X-axis title: Batch Identification Number

Task 3: View this graph to verify its contents. Name the graph CONTROL and save the graph image as an *.PIC file for printing.

Task 4: Save your AMC.WK1 worksheet file containing the graph settings for the control chart.

Task 5: Print the graph.

Task 6: (*Optional*)   Review the control chart. Does Alberto appear to have a problem with the memory chip manufacturing process? Write a summary indicating whether a problem exists. Explain your interpretation of the control chart.

Time Estimates

Novice: 45 minutes

Intermediate: 30 minutes

Advanced: 20 minutes

L.5.18 Comprehensive Problems

(1)   Case: Woodcraft Furniture Company (continued)

Joe Birch of Woodcraft Furniture likes to see visual presentations of data. Although you have produced an impressive array of management reports, he has requested that you create several graphs. Joe is considering having these graphs added to the "Briefing Book" prepared for each of Woodcraft's quarterly management meetings. Martha, Ray, and "Tall" have requested these graphs:

(a) A stack-bar graph of Sales by product for three months in the quarter. "Tall" has indicated that the height of each bar will also indicate the Total Sales. Include titles and a legend for this graph.

(b) A line graph comparing **Total Sales, Cost of Sales, Operating Expenses,** and **Income Before Taxes** for the three months in the quarter. Include appropriate titles and a legend.

(c) A bar graph of the number of units of **Tables, Chairs,** and **Sofas** sold for the three months in the quarter. Include appropriate titles and a legend.

(d) A pie chart of **Cost of Sales, Operating Expenses, Interest Expense,** and **Income Before Tax** for the **Total** quarter. This pie chart will show Joe and Ray the breakdown of each dollar of Sales.

(e) A pie chart of Sales by product for the entire quarter with Sofa Sales exploded and each slice cross-hatched.

Produce each of these graphs by performing the following tasks:

Task 1: Access the WOOD2 spreadsheet file for creating these graphs.

Task 2: Create each graph, name the graph, and save each image as an *.PIC file.

Task 3: Print each of these graphs.

Task 4: Save the WOOD2 worksheet file with its graph settings.

Time Estimates

Novice: 60 minutes

Intermediate: 45 minutes

Advanced: 30 minutes

(2)   Case: Midwest Universal Gas (continued)

At Midwest Universal Gas, Mary Derrick and Sam Wright have reviewed the various management reports you have produced. To better understand the relationships underlying their pro forma financial statement, they have requested the preparation of several graphs. As an integral component of their annual review, they are considering including the following graphs:

(a) A stack-bar graph of the **Retail** and **Wholesale Gas Sold** for the four quarters in the year. The height of each stack-bar will also indicate **Total Gas Sold.** Include titles and a legend on the graph.

(b) A line graph comparing **Total Sales, Total Expense, Interest Expense,** and **Net Income** for the quarters. Include appropriate titles and a legend.

(c) A bar graph of the **Return on Investment** for each quarter. Include appropriate titles and a legend.

(d) A pie chart of **Cost of Sales, Marketing and Selling, General Admin,** and **Depreciation** for the year. This pie chart will show Mary and Sam the breakdown of each dollar of **Total Expenses.**

(e) A pie chart of **Total Expense, Interest Expense, Income Tax,** and **Net Income** for the year with **Net Income** exploded and each slice cross-hatched.

Produce each of these graphs by performing the following tasks:

Task 1: Access the MUG2 spreadsheet file for creating these graphs.

Task 2: Create each graph, name the graph settings, and save each image as an *.PIC file.

Task 3: Print each of these graphs.

Task 4: Save the MUG2 worksheet file with its graph settings.

Time Estimates

Advanced: 30 minutes

Intermediate: 45 minutes

Novice: 60 minutes

L.5.19   Case Application

Case: Oil Patch Machine Tool

> Business Problem: Breakeven analysis
> MIS Characteristics: Production
> > Strategic Planning
>
> Special Characteristic: International
> Management Functions: Planning
> > Organizing
> Tools Skills: Graphing
> > Reporting

Oil Patch Machine Tool (OPM) manufactures a variety of specialized oil field processing equipment, which is used in extracting and processing oil before it is sent to a refinery. This equipment is marketed worldwide. Wherever oil production takes place and international trade agreements permit, Oil Patch is there with its hardware.

Oil Patch was founded by Jack B. Long in 1943. Jack serves as president and chief executive officer, while Jack, Jr., is the chief operating officer of the company. Since its founding, the company's growth has paralleled that of worldwide oil production and now has more than 5000 employees.

Because of their international market, Jack, Jr., has established manufacturing facilities for their hardware in several different strategic locations, often nearby to key oil-producing areas, which include plants in Pasadena, Texas; Calgary, Alberta; Riyadh, Saudi Arabia; Valencia, Venezuela; Singapore; Copenhagen, Denmark; Adelaide, Australia; and Monterey, Mexico.

Oil Patch has developed a new JB-7 valve, which is used in pumping and collecting oil for processing. This valve will be produced under the direction of Robert "Rob" Billesbach, Senior Vice President of Manufacturing. Rob and Jack, Jr., have determined that Oil Patch has the capacity to manufacture their new JB-7 valve at either their Pasadena, Texas, or Singapore plants. The Pasadena plant is more automated than the Singapore plant.

The Pasadena facility exploits flexible manufacturing systems (FMS), which integrate machining centers and robots with computerized parts transfer, in an "automatic factory." They combine FMS with computer-aided design. This contributes to their opportunity to go from a new design to full-scale production virtually overnight. The plant located in Singapore is not as automated. It makes use of islands of automation with numerically controlled machine tools, robots, automated storage/retrieval, systems, and machining centers. However, this automation is not as integrated and requires additional labor in fabricating products.

Numerically controlled (NC) machine tools are operated under the direct control of a digital computer. NC programs guide the movement of a machine tool to produce a desired part. For example, consider a wing support for an airplane that is cut from a large block of aluminum. The NC program would control the cutting of the desired shape; or in an similar manner, fabric could be cut to the desired pattern for a coat or dress.

The capabilities of a machine center surpass those of a NC machine. With a machine center, a machine is automatically controlled with automatic tooling changes. For example, if a part requires holes of several different diameters, the machine center would automatically change the drills used for the different size holes as each individual hole is drilled. On the other hand, an NC machine would require an operator to make a tool change.

Jack, Jr., determined that each JB-7 valve can be sold at a price of $300. Rob determined that semiautomatic NC machines are available at the Singapore plant, whereas the Pasadena site has a machine center available for manufacturing the JB-7. Rob and his staff have pulled together the following manufacturing costs:

	Pasadena	Singapore
Setup Cost (one time, fixed setup expense)	$420,000	$200,000
Labor per Unit	8	83
Material per Unit	10	12
Packaging per Unit	2	5

Note: All amounts are stated in U.S. dollars.

Jack, Jr., has gathered information from marketing that indicates that Oil Patch might sell as many has 3000 JB-7 valves. However, after their last planning meeting, Rob and Jack, Jr., have decided that they should select the plant location by evaluating sales from 500 to 3000 units. For their decision choice, they rely on breakeven analysis, which is a standard approach for choosing among manufacturing processing alternatives. This method is most suitable when a manufacturing process entails a large initial investment (fixed setup cost or expense) and also has variable costs. Rob has started to lay out their analysis in the BREAK.WK1 file on the Data Disk in preparation for selecting a plant location.

Tasks:

1. Access the BREAK.WK1 worksheet file and examine it. Notice that Rob has laid out the number of units for evaluating each alternative.

2. Enter formulas to calculate (a) the total revenue, (b) the total costs for the machine center at the Pasadena plant, and (c) the total costs for the semiautomatic NC machine processing at the Singapore plant for *each of the specified number of units between 500 and 3000.*

3. Determine the breakeven point for each plant location by developing a line graph consisting of three lines: (a) the total revenue, (b) the total costs for the Pasadena machine center, and (c) the total costs for the Singapore NC machines. Use the number of units produced as the X-axis. The breakeven points on the graph occur where the total costs line for each plant intersects the total revenue line. Give the graph a title that identifies this as the JB-7 Valve that is a Breakeven Analysis for Plant Location Selection. Provide titles for both the X-axis and the Y-axis. Include a legend to identify each of the three lines on the graph. Save this graph in an *.PIC file and create a hard copy using the PrintGraph program. (*Hint:* Wait until you complete Task 5 before you print this graph.)

4. Rob has indicated that breakeven points can be computed directly using the breakeven formula:

$$\text{Breakeven units} = \frac{\text{Fixed setup expense}}{(\text{Unit selling price} - \text{Unit cost})}$$

Use this formula to compute the breakeven points you determined above in the graphical solution. Enter these formulas in the cells indicated on the BREAK.WK1 worksheet file. Enter only one breakeven formula for each plant, not one for each of the alternative number of units produced.

5. Print a report of the results and save the worksheet file. The report should fit on a single page if you have a wide-carriage printer or if you use compressed print on a narrow printer. Print the breakeven graph.

6. Review your output. On the breakeven graph, when total revenues are greater than total costs, the distance between the cost line and the revenue line is an indication of the amount of profit. In choosing an alternative it is desirable to maximize this distance between cost and revenues. Write a short summary analyzing the results of this breakeven analysis. Based on estimated sales of 3000 units, at which plant should Oil Patch manufacture the JB-7 valve and why?

Time Estimates

Novice: 75 minutes

Intermediate: 60 minutes

Advanced: 45 minutes

LESSON

L.6

Interrogating Spreadsheet Models with Data Tables

CONTENT

- Model Interrogation with Data Table
- Data Table 1
- Data Table 2
- Applying Data Table to Breakeven Analysis
- When Things Go Wrong

L.6.1 Model Interrogation with Data Tables

The what-if analysis capability of 1-2-3 is enhanced with the Data Table commands. Data tables let you obtain results for a set of what-if alternatives all at one time. You can conduct a sensitivity analysis by exploring an output table of the results for the series of what-if input data values. In general, **sensitivity analysis** is the study of model output results when key input values vary. That is, how sensitive is output to changes in input values? For example, if a price per unit increase of 1 percent causes a return on sales increase of 5 percent, then return on sales is sensitive to a price per unit increase. On the other hand, if a price per unit increase of 1 percent causes little or no change in return on sales, then return on sales is not sensitive to a price per unit increase.

A **data table** is a convenient cell range in your worksheet setup to show the results that a formula generates each time a solution is calculated by using one of a series of different input data values. That is, the data tables show a whole series of what-if results at one time. Lotus 1-2-3 supports the development of two kinds of tables that capture these series of what-if results. A Data Table 1 allows you to change one input data value and capture calculated values from one or more different formulas in your worksheet. A Data Table 2 lets you change two input data values and display the calculated results from a single formula.

At Good Morning Products, Kim and Chris would like to prepare a what-if analysis that examines a series of different data values as they evaluate alternative courses of action. PLAN5 is used to perform this analysis.

Action: Access PLAN5 as your current worksheet file in preparation for this analysis.

The questions to be addressed are:

1. What are **Sales [Total]** and **Gross Profit [Total]** when **Sales** are increased by a series of **Sales Growth Rates** ranging from 7 percent to 15 percent?
2. When the **Cost Percent** is 71 percent, which combinations of **Sales Growth Rates** in (1) and of **Sales [1ST QTR]** between $300,000 and $400,000, produces a **Gross Profit [Total]** of, at least, $500,000?

L.6.2   Data Table 1

The first potential actions to be examined by Chris and Kim for Frosty involve determining the **Sales [Total]** and **Gross Profit [Total]** when **Sales** are varied by a series of Growth Rates. This what-if evaluation is conducted by using a Data Table 1. You first need to select an area of your worksheet to hold the table. For this example, an area immediately below the Pro Forma Statement will be used. The resulting data table is portrayed in Figure L.101.

In general, a Data Table 1 is arranged as illustrated in Figure L.102. The table resides in a convenient range of cells with a series of input values in the leftmost column of the table. The top row of the table contains one or more formulas that are evaluated using each input value. The upper-left corner of a Data Table 1 may either be blank or may contain any convenient label for documentation. Use of this cell is not required for a Data Table 1. When the Data Table 1 commands are executed, 1-2-3 places each of the input values into a single designated input cell in an application area of the worksheet and calculates the entire worksheet. Hence, there is a solution calculated for *each of the input data values.* The results of each of the designated formulas are then stored in a row of the computed results area of the data table range portrayed

```
A11: [W18] 'Sales Growth Rate                                    READY

          A              B        C        D        E        F      ◄
1   Sales Growth Rate    0.08                                       ►
2   Cost Percent         0.77                                       ▲
3                                                                   ▼
4                      1ST QTR  2ND QTR  3RD QTR  4TH QTR   TOTAL    ?
5                      -------  -------  -------  -------  -------
6   Sales               289500   312660   337673   364687  1304519
7   Cost of Sales       222915   240748   260008   280809  1004480
8                      -------  -------  -------  -------  -------
9   Gross Profit         66585    71912    77665    83878   300039
10
11  Sales Growth Rate  +F6      +F9
12              7%     1285363   295634
13              8%     1304519   300039
14              9%     1323921   304502
15             10%     1343570   309021
16             11%     1363467   313597
17             12%     1383615   318232
18             13%     1404016   322924
19             14%     1424671   327674
20             15%     1445582   332484
```

FIGURE L.101. Interrogation with Data Table 1.

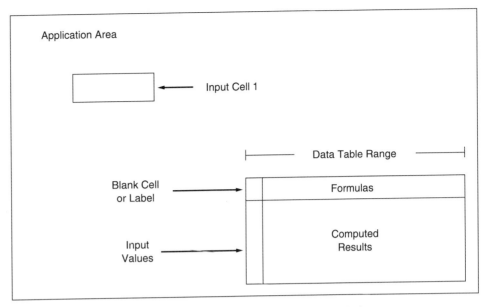

FIGURE L.102. General layout of Data Table 1.

in Figure L.102. Each row in a Data Table 1 holds the solution calculated using the input data value in the leftmost column of the data table for that row. When the Data Table 1 command is executed, you are prompted for the data table range and the input cell. As a result, the input data values and output formulas need to be established *before* the Data Table 1 command is executed.

Let's begin constructing a Data Table 1 to address the first question, with the *Sale Growth Rate* varying from 7 percent to 15 percent by placing a descriptive label in the upper-left corner of the data table.

To label the left column for documentation			
Move to:	**A11**	Cell at upper-left corner of Data Table
Enter:	Sales Growth Rate	Label to indicate data stored in this column of data table

Next the *Sales Growth Rate* data values are placed in the leftmost column using the / Data Fill (/DF) command. This is a convenient method for entering a regular series of data values like those for this growth rate.

To use Data Fill to enter input data values for the Data Table 1			
Move to:	**A12**	Position cursor to enter series of What-If values
Press:	/	Access main menu
Select:	Data	Begin data operations
Select:	Fill	This command allows the series of **Sales Growth Rate** data values to be created
Press:	.	Drop anchor
Move to:	**A20**	End of range
Press:	\<Enter\>	Complete range specification
Enter:	.07	Starting data value in series
Enter:	.01	Step increment
Enter:	.16	Stopping ending value; this value will not be displayed

Did all your data values happen to appear as zeros? If this occurs, then you need to change the format of these cells in this column to / Range Format Percent 0 (/RFP0).

Action: Perform a / Range Format Percent 0 on cells **A12** through **A20**.

If you examine the values in **A12** through **A20,** you will find that they are all constant values and not formulas. Of course, you could have typed each data value individually. Data Fill is just a convenient method of entering a series of constant data values like this.

Now that the input values for **Sales Growth Rate** have been established, let's set up the remainder of the data table.

To enter formulas for calculating results that appear in the data table	**Move to:** B11	Position cursor in the cell of the topmost row of the data table
	Enter: +F6	Cell that defines the output or computed value for **Sales [Total],** which is desired for the What-If analysis
	Move to: C11	Position cursor to define next data table output
	Enter: +F9	Cell that defines the output value for **Gross Profit [Total]**

The cell formulas **+F6** and **+F9** provide a convenient method for collecting the desired data values from the application area of the worksheet. Cells **B11** and **C11** currently display the **data value** calculated by the formulas in these cells. As a reminder of the formulas in these cells, you need to change the format to / Range Format Text (/RFT).

To display formulas in the top row of the data table	**Action:** Perform a / Range Format Text (/RFT) on cells **B11** and **C11** so that the formula is displayed for your reference.

The entire data table is now set up and ready to receive the calculated results. Let's actually calculate the results and have them displayed in the data table.

To calculate and place results in the data table	**Move to:** A11	Cell in the upper-left corner of Data Table 1 area
	Press: /	Access Main Menu
	Select: Data	Desired activity
	Select: Table	Desired option
	Select: 1	There is only one input cell whose value is changed
	Press: .	Anchor range at cell **A22**
	Move to: C20	Highlight Data Table 1 area by moving cell pointer to the lower-right corner
	Press: <Enter>	Complete range specification
	Move to: B1	This is the single input cell that is given the series of input data values from the leftmost column of the data table
	Press: <Enter>	Complete Data Table 1 command calculating the results and placing them in the results area of the data table

Cell **B1** already contains a value used in computing the initial solution of the worksheet prior to carrying out the creation of the data table. When the data table is performed, this cell is temporarily given each of the data values from the series of values in cells **A12** through **A20** as the results are calculated for storage in the rows of the data table. Each *row* in the data table is one complete solution of the entire worksheet using the appropriate input data value in cell **B1.**

This completes the creation of the series of what-ifs. Kim and Chris can now evaluate and compare these results in formulating their plan for next year.

Action: Print a report of both the Pro Forma Statement area and the data table.

Action: Print a list of cell formulas.

Action: Save this as PLAN9.

Keypoint!

> A Data Table 1 permits the calculation of a number of output results that will appear immediately to the right of the input column. The input column must be on the left side of the Data Table range. The formulas to be evaluated and stored in the table must be in the top row of the Data Table range!

L.6.3   Data Table 2

The second alternative question to be scrutinized by Kim and Chris for Crush involves the evaluation of the **Gross Profit [Total]** at a series of **Sales Growth Rates** *in combination with* a series of **Sales [1st Qtr]** values. This what-if evaluation involves *two input data values.* The results are generated with a Data Table 2 yielding the data table shown in Figure L.103.

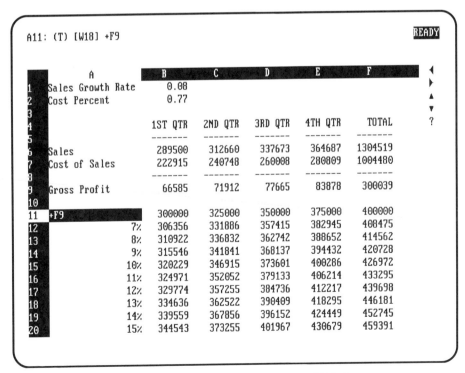

FIGURE L.103. Interrogation with Data Table 2.

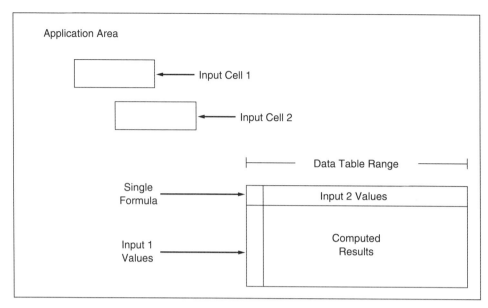

FIGURE L.104. General layout of Data Table 2.

In general, a Data Table 2 is arranged as illustrated in Figure L.104. The table resides in a range of cells, with one series of input data values in the leftmost column of the table and the other set of input data values located in the table's top row. The upper-left corner of a Data Table 2 holds a *single* formula, the results of which are recorded in the data table *for each pair of inputs* from the left column and the top row. When the Data Table 2 commands are executed, 1-2-3 places each pair of the input values into the designated input cells in an application area of the worksheet and calculates the entire worksheet. That is, a solution is calculated for each pair of input data values. The results of the single formula are then placed in the computed results area of the data table range portrayed in Figure L.104. When the Data Table 2 command is executed, you are prompted for the data table range and each of the two input cells in your application area. The values in the left column go into input cell 1, whereas those in the top row are placed into input cell 2. The input data values and single output formula need to be laid out in the data table range *before* the Data Table 2 command is executed.

Chris and Kim are ready to create their Data Table 2. They will use the same area as that for the Data Table 1, with changes made to modify the table from exploring question (1) above, since the same **Sales Growth Rates** are employed. The values of **Sales [1st Qtr]** will be changed in increments of $25,000. Although a smaller increment can be used, this one will provide a general view of the impact of changing **Sales**.

Action: Verify that the just completed PLAN9 worksheet is your currently active worksheet file.

Since question (2) is a combination of a traditional what-if analysis together with a Data Table 2, the what-if data value is entered as the next step. This illustrates how traditional what-if analysis is used in conjunction with data tables.

To enter a what-if data value for use with a data table	**Move to:**	**B2**	**Cost Percent** to be revised prior to performing data table operations.
	Enter:	.71	New what-if value for **Cost Percent**

Now the data table can be set up for the second series of input data values for the **Sales [1st Qtr]** by using the / Data Fill (/DF) command.

To use Data Fill for the second series of input data values			
Move to:	**B11**	Cell location where the Sales values will be placed using Data Fill
Press:	/	Access main menu
Select:	Data	Desired activity
Select:	Fill	Desired option
Press:	<Esc>	Unanchor this previously defined range
Move to:	**B11**	Beginning of Data Fill range
Press:	.	Drop anchor
Move to:	**F11**	Highlight Data Fill range
Press:	<Enter>	Complete range specification
Enter:	300000	Starting value
Enter:	25000	Increment value
Enter:	400000	Ending value, complete Data Fill

Next the formula for the computed results is entered in the upper-left corner of the data table range.

To enter the single formula for the computed results			
Move to:	**A11**	Cell location of formula for computing results in data table
Enter:	+F9	Formula referencing cell containing **Gross Profit [Total]**, which is to be computed for each pair of **Sales Growth Rates** and **Sales [1st Qtr]** data values
Action:		Perform a / Range Format Text (/RFT) on cell **A11** so that the formula is displayed.

This completes the setup of the Data Table 2. The table is ready for calculating the results.

To calculate and store results in the data table			
Action		Verify that your cell pointer is located at **A11,** which is the upper-left corner of the Data Table 2 area.
Press:	/	Access main menu
Select:	Data	Desired activity
Select:	Table	Desired option
Select:	2	Type of Data Table
Move to:	**F20**	Expand the cursor over the entire Data Table
Press:	<Enter>	Complete range specification
Move to:	**B1**	If necessary, this is the input cell for the **Sales Growth Rate** values located in **A12..A20**
Press:	<Enter>	Complete specifying first input cell
Move to:	**B6**	Input cell for the **Sales [1st Qtr]** located in **B11..F11**
Press:	<Enter>	Complete Data Table 2 command calculating the results and placing them in the results area of the data table

The Data Table of Figure L.103 is complete. Inspecting the table, you can see that **Sales [1st Qtr]** of $350,000 with a 15 percent **Sales Growth Rate** are required to meet the required target value. Other combinations exist with Sales of $375,000 and $400,000. In general, the table shows a greater sensitivity to the selected values of **Sales [1st Qtr]** than to the **Sales Growth Rates** specified in this analysis.

Action: Print a report of both the Pro Forma Statement area and the data table.

Action: Print a list of cell formulas.

Action: Save this as PLAN10.

Keypoint! A Data Table 2 permits the evaluation of only a single cell formula, which must be located in the upper-left-hand corner of the Data Table range!

L.6.4   Applying Data Table to Break-Even Analysis

Break-even analysis is frequently applied in evaluating alternative business opportunities with spreadsheet models. A spreadsheet may be created with formulas that specifically calculate break-even volumes and prices. Another approach to break-even analysis is the utilization of a pro forma financial statement worksheet that has been created to project revenues and expenses. Rather than rewriting the formulas, a Data Table can be used to perform this evaluation. Consider an expanded pro forma financial statement for Good Morning Products shown in Figure L.105, which contains both variable and fixed costs. This model contains cells for both the number of **Bottles** produced and the **Price per Bottle.**

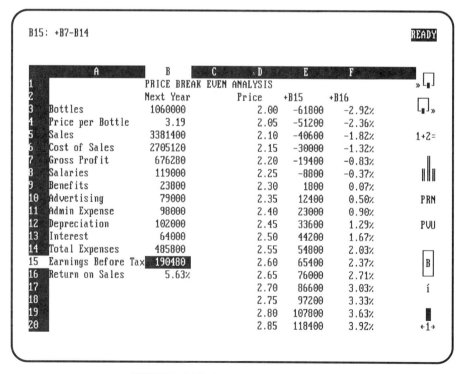

FIGURE L.105. Break-even Data Table 1.

The Data Table in Figure L.105 shows the impact on **Earnings Before Tax** and **Return on Sales** when the **Price per Bottle** is incremented by $0.05. The results in this Data Table indicate that the break-even Price is about $2.30 per bottle, because this is where Earnings switch from negative to positive. A second solution of this table using Prices from $2.25 to $2.30 would find that the exact break-even price is $2.30 per bottle, since $2.29 produces a loss of $320.

Keypoint!

Data Table facilitates conducting a breakeven analysis from a pro forma statement model WITHOUT rewriting any formulas in the model!

A Data Table 2 can be used to evaluate combinations of break-even prices and volumes, as illustrated in Figure L.106. For each specified volume, break even occurs when **Earnings Before Tax** switches from negative to positive. This analysis can now be plotted as shown in Figure L.107 on page 172. Since break even was not attained with 750,000 bottles this is not included in the graph.

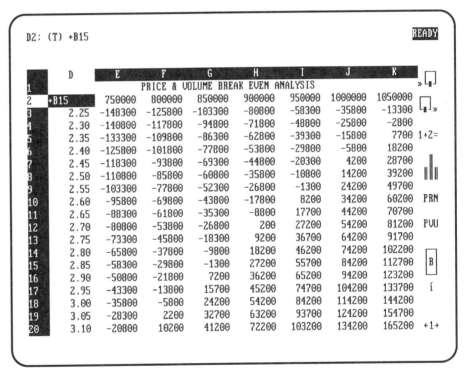

FIGURE L.106. Break-even Data Table 2.

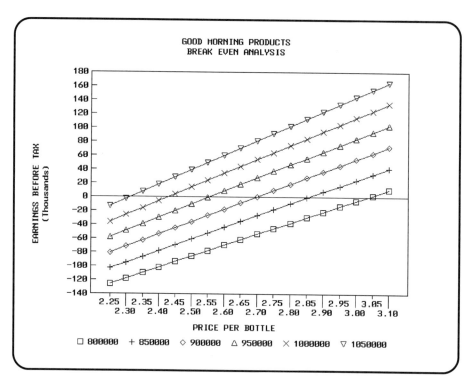

FIGURE L.107. Break-even Graph.

L.6.5   When Things Go Wrong

Several situations may be encountered while you are interrogating a worksheet model using data tables. Some of the more frequently occurring difficulties and how to approach them are described here:

1. You just completed executing your Data Table command and realize that you specified the wrong input cell(s). This may occur because you either typed the wrong cell name or pointed to the wrong cell.

   a. Review your interrogation to determine the desired cell(s) to be used in the analysis.

   b. Reissue the Data Table command and specify the correct input cell(s). Pointing is usually the best method to use for this because it reduces the chance of indicating the wrong cell. When you reissue the Data Table commands, any old values in the data table range are replaced with new values.

2. All zeros appeared in your data table area when you executed the Data Table command. This may occur when the formulas are not included in the data table range as the top row for a Data Table 1 or as the upper-left corner for a Data Table 2.

   a. Review the layout of your data table to carefully determine the top row and left column.

   b. Reissue the Data Table command.

   c. Unanchor the already specified data table range and change it to the correct table range.

   d. Complete the execution of the Data Table command.

3. Values in your data table appear as zeros or ones, or they are not displayed with the desired number of decimals. The occurrence of zeros and ones usually results when the values in the data table are less than one and an integer global format is in effect. Values in the table without the desired number of decimals are usually caused by an unwanted global format.

   a. Review the columns of your data table where the difficulty exists.

   b. Use the Range Format command to change the column(s) to the desired format with the appropriate number of decimals. It may be necessary to set individual Range Formats for the columns of a Data Table 1.

L.6.6   Lesson Summary

- Data Table supports performing a series of what-if analyses with specified data values and obtaining an output table of the results.

- With Data Table 1, the series of data values are used in only one cell, and computed results for several cells are placed in an output table.

- With Data Table 2, a series of data values are used in each of two input cells, and computed results for a single cell are placed in the output table. A result is calculated for each combination of data values in the two input data series.

- For a what-if analysis that requires the revision of data values in more than two cells, any additional cells need to be manually revised before the data table is calculated.

- Data table is a convenient method for carrying out break-even analysis without the need to rewrite the formulas of a pro forma financial statement spreadsheet model.

L.6.7   Practice Tutorial

Develop the Data Table 1 and Data Table 2 as described in this Lesson in Sections L.6.2 and L.6.3 as a guided activity in a hands-on manner. Access your MYPLAN6 worksheet from the Practice Tutorial in Lesson L.3 as a starting point for this exercise.

Task 1: Create the Data Table 1.

Task 2: Print this Data Table.

Task 3: Save this as worksheet file MYPLAN9.

Task 4: Create the Data Table 2.

Task 5: Print this Data Table.

Task 6: Save this as worksheet file MYPLAN10.

Time Estimates

Novice: 60 minutes

Intermediate: 45 minutes

Advanced: 30 minutes

L.6.8   Practice Exercises

(1)   Case: Inland Container (continued)

After Mary Montoya reviewed the Rydder Truck Rental proposal with her district manager, she returned to her office with several additional alternatives that need to be explored. Before finalizing the proposal for Richard, she wants a more in-depth analysis of selling **Price per Unit** and the number of **Units Sold.** She wants you to perform this investigation by carrying out the following Data Table analyses:

(a) What are the **Sales [Total]** and **Gross Profit [Total]** when the **Price per Unit [April]** ranges from $3.15 to $3.30 in increments of $0.01?

(b) What are the **Units Sold [Total], Sales [Total],** and **Gross Profit [Total]** when the **Units Sold** are increased by a series of **Units Sold Growth Rates** that range from 2 percent to 18 percent in increments of 1 percent?

(c) What is the **Gross Profit [Total]** when the **Price per Unit [April]** described in (a) is combined with the **Units Sold Growth Rates** in (b)?

Prepare each of these data table analyses by doing these tasks:

Task 1: Access your RYDDER2 worksheet from Practice Exercise 1 in Lesson L.3 as your starting point for this exercise. Review the worksheet's contents.

Task 2: Create the Data Table for each alternative.

Task 3: Print the results for each alternative.

Task 4: Save the worksheet from (c) as file RYDDER10.

Time Estimates

Novice: 60 minutes

Intermediate: 45 minutes

Advanced: 30 minutes

(2)   Case: Abacus Computer Systems

Business Problem: Product pricing
MIS Characteristics: Marketing
                                Managerial Control

Abacus Computer Systems, owned and operated by Herbert and Patricia Wattsun, is a full-service personal computer outlet. It provides total system support, selling turn-key systems to business and government. Each system sold includes hardware, software, installation, and training. Herbie and Pattie specialize in the Abacus line of computers. Next year they expect to sell 73 systems at an average price of $7500 per system. Herbie thinks that Abacus may not make sufficient profit at this expected level of sales and wants to consider other alternatives to make the company more profitable. After discussing their plans for next year, Pattie and Herbie formulated the following potential courses of action to be evaluated with a Data Table analysis:

(a) What is the **EBT** (Earnings Before Tax) and **ROS** (Return On Sales) when the number of **Systems Sold** ranges from a low of 60 to a high of 77?

(b) What is the **ROS** when the number of **Systems Sold** is as described in (a) and the **Price per System** ranges from $6000 to $8000 in increments of $500?

Prepare each of these data table analyses by doing these tasks:

Task 1: Retrieve the ABACUS.WK1 worksheet file from your Data Disk and review Herbie and Pattie's planning model for Next Year.

Task 2: Produce the Data Table for alternative (a). Format the cell formulas in the top row of your Data Table as Range Text so that you can easily verify the formulas. Format the ROS results column in the Data Table as Percent 2. Print the completed Data Table. Save this as the ABACUS1 worksheet file.

Task 3: Pattie wants you to inspect your computed results and determine the break-even number of Systems Sold. Circle this value together with its **EBT** and **ROS** on your printout.

Task 4: Retrieve the ABACUS.WK1 worksheet file so that you can start over from scratch. Produce the Data Table for alternative (b). Format the **ROS** data values in the Data Table as Percent 2. Print the completed Data Table. Save this as your ABACUS2 worksheet file.

Task 5: Herbie wants you to determine the combinations of break even for the number of **Systems Sold** and the **Price per System** included in your Data Table 2. Inspect your results and circle each of these break-even combinations on your printout.

Task 6: (*Optional*)   To help Pattie and Herbie understand their alternatives, create a break-even analysis graph from the results of the Data Table 2. Use the **Price per System** as your X-axis.

Time Estimates

Novice: 60 minutes

Intermediate: 45 minutes

Advanced: 30 minutes

(3)   **Case: Sparrow Memorial Hospital**
Business Problem: Project feasibility
MIS Characteristics: Production/Operations
Strategic Planning

Heidi Firchau is the assistant hospital administrator of Sparrow Memorial Hospital. Sparrow is a privately owned, 400-bed acute care facility. Because heart disease is a major cause of death among the residents in Sparrow's market area, the hospital administrator is interested in increasing its cardiac care delivery by establishing an open-heart surgery facility with support units for related cardiac care procedures. Currently, the cardiac care hospital located nearest to Sparrow has a waiting period of nearly two months for patients requiring open-heart surgery. In addition to weighing the social responsibility issues from the hospital engaging in open-heart surgery, Heidi needs to determine the economic viability of this proposed project. She has developed the SPARROW.WK1 worksheet model for computing the **Contribution margin** from open-heart surgery. Her worksheet contains four profit centers involved in an open-heart surgery procedure:

Open-Heart Surgery. Operating room and related equipment for actually performing the surgery.

Surgical ICU. Intensive care unit immediately following surgery.

Progressive Care Unit. Step-down care unit following the ICU providing reduced levels of care as the patient recovers.

Cardiac Cath. Cardiac catheterization and angioplasty procedures used in diagnosis for open-heart surgery and related cardiac care.

For each open-heart procedure, Heidi has entered the **Number of procedures** for Open-Heart Surgery (usually, only one) and Cardiac Cath (usually, more than one). For the Surgical ICU and Progressive Care Unit, she has entered the average duration of the stay in each unit as a number of **Patient days.** The revenues and costs for each procedure or day are entered. Costs are divided into two categories: Contract services and Variable costs. Contract services or a contract service agreement (CSA) constitutes the services provided by physicians. For CSA expenses, the hospital acts as the billing agent. As a result, Heidi entered these costs separately. The Variable costs are all the costs incurred directly by the hospital. Heidi's worksheet computes the **Contribution margin** for each profit center based on an expected number of open-heart **Surgeries each year.** These are summed to provide an overall **Contribution margin.** For a hospital the size of Sparrow, Heidi has determined that up to 260 open-heart procedures could be carried out each year in the facility that is being proposed. She needs to review the feasibility of this project with the hospital executive management committee next Tuesday. In preparation for this meeting, she wants to evaluate these alternatives:

(a) What is the **Contribution margin [Total]** when the number of **Surgeries per year** ranges from a low of 230 to a high of 270? What number of **Surgeries per year** is necessary for break even?

(b) What is the **Contribution margin [Total]** when the number of **Surgeries per year** is as described in (a) and the **Patient day [Progressive Care Unit]** varies from a low of 10 to a high of 15? What is the break-even number of **Surgeries per year** for each length of stay in the **Progressive Care Unit?**

Prepare each of these data table analyses by doing these tasks:

Task 1: Retrieve the SPARROW.WK1 worksheet file from your Data Disk and review Heidi's feasibility study.

Task 2: Produce the Data Table for alternative (a). Format the cell formula(s) in the top row of your Data Table as Text to improve readability. Print the completed Data Table. Save this as your SPARROW1 worksheet file. Circle the number of **Surgeries per year** for break even. Based on Heidi's estimated market and ability to deliver 260 open-heart **Surgeries per year,** is this project economically feasible?

Task 3: Retrieve the SPARROW.WK1 worksheet file again so that you can start over with the next analysis. Produce the Data Table for alternative (b). Format the formula as Text. Print the completed Data Table. Save this as your SPARROW2 worksheet file. Where break even occurs, circle the break-even point combinations on your printout.

Task 4: (*Optional*) Review your Data Table from Task 3. Would you say that the project's economic feasibility is sensitive to the number of **Patient days** in the **Progressive Care Unit?** Why? Write a paragraph explaining your interpretation.

Task 5: (*Optional*) To help Heidi understand the alternatives in preparation for her meeting, create a break-even analysis graph from the results of the Data Table 2 for alternative (b).

Time Estimates

Novice: 75 minutes

Intermediate: 50 minutes

Advanced: 30 minutes

(4) Case: Hawaiian Electric Industries

   Business Problem: Training benefits
   MIS Characteristics: Human Resources
                        Managerial Control

Constance Watanabe manages the Information Center within the Information Systems Department of Hawaiian Electric. She is considering expanding the services provided in the Information Center to include additional training in personal computer software tools such as presentation graphics and desktop publishing. Her proposed facility would accommodate up to 12 participants in one training class. An evaluation of training effectiveness is an important aspect of human resource management for any training program like Connie's. She wants to evaluate her proposed program using a cost/benefit analysis. Training costs for her program include instructors, equipment, materials, facilities, and the time of participants. Potential training benefits include the dollar value of productivity increases, turnover rates, and absenteeism rates. In order to obtain approval for her training program, the benefits must be greater than the costs. Connie has developed the TRAIN.WK1 worksheet containing the cost/benefit analysis for next year's operation of the training program. Although she has carefully estimated the costs and benefits, these may vary owing to changes in business conditions. Connie wants to obtain a better understanding of her analysis by developing these data tables:

   (a) What are the **TOTAL COSTS, TOTAL BENEFITS,** and **NET BENEFITS** when the **Number of trainees** ranges from 24 to 48?

   (b) What are the **TOTAL COSTS, TOTAL BENEFITS,** and **NET BENEFITS** when the **Training days per trainee** ranges from 10 to 20?

   (c) What are the **NET BENEFITS** when the **Number of trainees** described in (a) is combined with the **Training days per trainee** in (b)?

Prepare each of these data table analyses by doing these tasks:

Task 1: Retrieve the TRAIN.WK1 worksheet file from your Data Disk and review Connie's cost/benefit analysis.

Task 2: Produce the data table for alternative (a). Print the completed data table. Save this as the TRAIN1 worksheet file.

Task 3: Connie wants you to identify the minimum **Number of trainees** that are required for **TOTAL COSTS** to exceed **TOTAL BENEFITS**. Circle this value on your printout.

Task 4: Create the data table for alternative (b). Print this table and save your results as the TRAIN2 worksheet file.

Task 5: Find the minimum **Training days per trainee** that are required to obtain a positive **NET BENEFITS.** Circle this value on your printout.

Task 6: Access the TRAIN.WK1 worksheet file so that you can begin with a completely new data table. Develop the data table for alternative (c). Print the resulting table.

Task 7: For each combination of **Number of trainees** and **Training days per trainee** determine the pairs that are required to just achieve a positive **NET BENEFITS.** Circle these values on your printed report.

Task 8: (*Optional*)   To help Connie understand her cost/benefit analysis, create a graph using the results of the data table from alternative (c) that you developed in Task 6. Select the **Training days per trainee** for the options of 10, 12, 14, 16, 18, and 20 days as your six data ranges on the graph. Write a paragraph describing why it was necessary to make this selection. Is this a limitation of Lotus 1-2-3 graphs?

Time Estimates

Novice: 75 minutes

Intermediate: 50 minutes

Advanced: 30 minutes

L.6.9   Comprehensive Problems

(1)   Case: Woodcraft Furniture Company (continued)

Joe Birch, Martha Goodguess, Ray Jointer, and "Tall" Pine have studied your presentation of Woodcraft's financial plan at the last operating managers meeting. They would like to obtain more information concerning several additional alternatives:

(a) Ray Jointer is still concerned about the imminent strike and the current union demands. In preparation for the next negotiation meeting, Ray would like a table of alternatives for next quarter's plan that displays **Labor [Total]**, **Income Before Taxes [Total]**, and **Return on Sales [Total]** when the **Hourly Rate** ranges from $9.75 to $12.50 in increments of $0.25. Then, as a different wage rate is negotiated, the bargaining team will have an idea of the impact on Woodcraft's financial performance. No other changes are made to this projection; all other data values are at their original or "base" values as saved in the WOOD2 worksheet file.

(b) Martha Goodguess is also on the bargaining team with Ray. She has suggested exploring an increase in the number of hours worked each quarter as an alternative concession. She would like to explore **Hours Worked** ranging from 174 hours to 202 hours in increments of 4 hours. Martha would also like a table of alternatives for next quarter's plan, which displays **Labor [Total]**, **Income Before Taxes [Total]**, and **Return on Sales [Total]**. Prepare this table using the original **Hourly Rate** of $9.60. Martha has suggested to Ray that it would be better for Woodcraft to settle for 190 hours per month at the original **Hourly Rate** of $9.60 than it would to increase the **Hourly Rate** to $11.00 with the original **Hours Worked** of 174 hours per month. Ray has pointed out that the additional hours would satisfy the work speed-up concern of the union, and it should improve quality. Do you agree with Martha? Why or why not?

(c) Joe would like to maintain Woodcraft's profitability and feels that a **PRICE ADJUSTMENT** is an appropriate strategy in responding to the union demands. Considering the union's demand, Joe feels that $11.00 per hour is likely to result from the current negotiations. At this hourly wage, he would like to explore a series of **PRICE ADJUSTMENTS** ranging from 2 percent to 12 percent in increments of 1 percent. "Tall" reminds you that worksheet WOOD3 includes a revision that incorporates a **PRICE ADJUSTMENT** cell. You concur that you can begin your analysis using that worksheet. Joe would like to have a table that shows **Total Sales [Total]**, **Income Before Taxes [Total]**, and **Return on Sales [Total]** at each of these **PRICE ADJUSTMENTS**.

(d) After further discussions with Ray and Martha, Joe would like to explore Woodcraft's profitability for a variety of combinations of **PRICE ADJUSTMENTS** and **Hourly Rates**. They want you to revise the table from (c) above with **Hourly Rates** from (a) above placed in a row at the top of the table. They want the table to contain the **Return on Sales [Total]** for each of these combinations of **PRICE ADJUSTMENTS** and **Hourly Rates**.

Prepare each of these data table analyses by doing these tasks:

Task 1: Access the WOOD2 spreadsheet file as the "base solution" and create the data tables for (a) and (b).

Task 2: Print the results for each alternative.

Task 3: Save the worksheet from (b) as file WOOD4.

Task 4: Access the WOOD3 spreadsheet file as the beginning point and create the data tables for (c) and (d).

Task 5: Print the results for each alternative.

Task 6: Save the worksheet from (d) as file WOOD5.

Quick check answers: (a) Return on Sales [Total] = .1163   or   11.63% at Hourly Rate = 11.00

        (b) Return on Sales [Total] = .1180   or   11.80% at Hours Worked = 198

        (c) Return on Sales [Total] = .1403   or   14.03% at Price Adjustment = .09   or   9%

        (d) Return on Sales [Total] = .1403   or   14.03% at Price Adjustment = .09   or   9% and at Hourly Rate = 11.00

Time Estimates

Novice: 60 minutes

Intermediate: 45 minutes

Advanced: 30 minutes

(2)   Case: Midwest Universal Gas (continued)

Mary Derrick, Francis Foresight, and Sam Wright have carefully considered the alternatives you explored for them concerning the Midwest Universal Gas financial plan. They would like to examine several additional alternatives:

(a) Francis and Mary have been working on a rate increase proposal for the State Utility Commission. This proposal would allow MUG to increase the price of gas to its wholesale customers. The Commission has recently been more favorable to these rate increases as a means of promoting the development of alternative energy sources by major corporations. In preparing their proposal, Francis would like to obtain a table of alternatives for next year's plan displaying **Total Sales [Total]**, **Net Income [Total]**, and **Return on Investment [Total]** when the **Wholesale Rate** for gas ranges from the current $286,000 per BCF to $300,000 per BCF in increments of $1000 per BCF. That is, they want to explore the sensitivity of **Return on Investment [Total]** to the **Wholesale Rate** for gas. No other changes are made to this projection; all other data values are at their original or "base" values as saved in the MUG2 worksheet file. [*Hint:* Remember, your spreadsheet is in thousands of dollars; therefore, the **Wholesale Rate** should range from 286 to 300 in increments of 1.]

(b) Petro Newgas from production is concerned about the **Cost of Sales** because the worldwide demand for natural gas has been increasing faster than new gas fields have been found and developed. To analyze the sensitivity of the profitability of MUG to increasing costs of natural gas, Pete would like a table of alternatives for next year's plan showing **Cost of Sales [Total]**, **Net Income [Total]**, and **Return on Investment [Total]** when the **Cost of Gas percent** ranges from the current value of 61 percent to 70 percent in increments of 1 percent. All other data values are at their base amounts. Does this table support Pete's concern that **Return on Investment** is sensitive to the **Cost of Gas percent?**

(c) Mary and Francis remain confident that they can obtain a 10 percent price increase from the State Utility Commission. They would like to explore the sensitivity of next year's plan to changes in the total volume of gas sold. Mary reminds you that your spreadsheet model in file MUG3 included a 10 percent price increase and was set up to examine different volumes of gas sold. The table they want contains the **Total Sales [Total]**, **Net Income [Total]**, and **Return on Investment [Total]** when the **Total Gas Sold [Total]** ranges from 700 BCF to 800 BCF in increments of 10 BCF. You retrieve the MUG3 file and begin to prepare this analysis.

(d) As a final analysis in preparing their proposal, Pete has recommended to Mary and Francis that they should review the impact of increasing costs of natural gas together with changes in the volume of gas sold to explore the potential impact on **Return on Investment** for the year. They all agree that this analysis should be performed using the 10 percent price increase in the same manner as (c) above. The complete table is to contain the **Return on Investment [Total]** evaluated when the **Cost of Gas percent** ranges from 61 percent to 70 percent in increments of 1 percent in combination with **Total Gas Sold [Total]** ranging from 700 BCF to 800 BCF in increments of 10 BCF. [*Hint:* Yes, you can use the MUG3 file from (c) as a starting point for developing this table.]

Prepare each of these data table analyses by doing these tasks:

Task 1: Access the MUG2 worksheet file as the "base solution" and create the data tables for (a) and (b).

Task 2: Print the results for each alternative.

Task 3: Save the worksheet from (b) as file MUG4.

Task 4: Access the MUG3 worksheet file as the beginning point and create the data tables for (c) and (d).

Task 5: Print the results for each alternative.

Task 6: Save the worksheet from (d) as file MUG5.

Quick check answers: (a) Return on Investment [Total] = .1290   or   12.90%
at Wholesale Rate = 295 (000's)

(b) Return on Investment [Total] = .0644   or   6.44%
at Cost of Gas = .66   or   66%

(c) Total Sales [Total] = 255794
at Total Gas Sold [Total] = 770 BCF

(d) Return on Investment [Total] = .1116   or   11.16%
at Total Gas Sold [Total] = 760 BCF and
at Cost of Gas = .65   or   65%

Time Estimates

Novice: 60 minutes

Intermediate: 45 minutes

Advanced: 30 minutes

L.6.10 Case Application

Case: Godfather's Pizza

> Business Problem: Staff planning
> MIS Characteristics: Human Resources
>   Managerial Control
> Management Functions: Staffing
>   Organizing
> Tools Skills: Data Table
>   Graphing

Marquetta Garcia is the owner of a chain of Godfather's Pizza Restaurants. She operates six restaurants in the suburban area. Marquetta obtained her franchises from Willy Theisen, after a visit to Omaha when her relatives introduced her to Willy and his popular pizza.

Godfather's evolved out of a beer joint that opened in southwest Omaha, Nebraska, in 1973. The pizza served at Wild Willy's was so popular that founder Willy Theisen opened a separate restaurant and named it after the popular gangster movie of that time. The growth of Godfather's was explosive. Willy opened more restaurants in Omaha and Lincoln, Nebraska, and suddenly people started calling him about franchises. Marquetta was among this early group of Godfather's enthusiasts and obtained the exclusive right to operate restaurants in her area.

Kevin Porter is the manager of the Bannister Mall restaurant. He has been working with Marquetta in preparing a staffing plan by quarter for the next year. Kevin's analysis of weekly sales by quarter has confirmed the seasonality of these sales. Kevin contacted F. Charles Walden, the director of MIS at Godfather's Investment, the company that now manages Godfather's franchises and company-owned restaurants. Chuck described to Kevin that they used **Sales per Employee Hour** as a key factor in planning and budgeting for the approximately 200 company-owned restaurants. Chuck's recent analysis had revealed that the current **Sales per Employee Hour** is about $28. Kevin examined available data for the Bannister Mall restaurant and found that their value was very close to that obtained from Chuck.

Kevin and Marquetta are concerned with establishing a target staffing level so that they will be better prepared to hire staff. In addition to Kevin, staffing at the Bannister Mall restaurant includes 2 full-time equivalent (FTE) assistant managers and 8 full-time equivalent (FTE) associates. Including Kevin, current staffing is 11 FTE. Marquetta and Kevin use FTEs in their planning because a number of their associates are part-time employees. Their current staffing level of 11 FTE is achieved with a total of 23 employees.

Chuck explained to Kevin the method used to determine the number of **Weekly Hours** for staffing. The **Weekly Hours** are obtained by dividing the **Weekly Sales** by the **Sales per Employee Hour.** Since the **Weekly Sales** vary from quarter to quarter, **Weekly Hours** can be determined for each quarter individually, and an average **Weekly Hours** can be computed for the year (that is, **Weekly Hours [Average]** where **[Average]** indicates the column). To determine the number of **FTE Associates** required, the **Manager Hours per Week** and **Asst Mgr Hours per Week** are subtracted from the **Weekly Hours.** The remaining hours are those that are staffed by associates. By dividing these remaining hours by the **Assoc Hours per Week,** the number of **FTE Associates** can be obtained. Kevin and Marquetta are interested in the **FTE Associates** per quarter and the average for the year in formulating their staffing plan.

In addition to obtaining the results for the "base case," Marquetta and Kevin would like to obtain more information concerning the design of alternative staffing arrangements:

(a) Kevin is concerned about the **Sales per Employee Hour.** Although Chuck's value for Godfather's Investment is nearly identical to the value he obtained with his analysis, Kevin thinks that this value could well vary over a range from $25 to $30. If this would occur, he would like to know the potential impact on the number of **FTE Associates** by quarter and the average for the year. The average is important to Kevin and Marquetta since they attempt to maintain as stable a level of staffing as possible. Kevin is reluctant to lay off good employees during the quarters with lower sales because he is aware of the difficulties that are often encountered in replacing these associates.

(b) Marquetta realizes that another staffing option is to adjust the **Assoc Hours per Week** to accommodate anticipated variations in **Weekly Sales.** They might employ more associates for fewer hours per week or fewer associates with increased hours. They could, for example, employ sufficient **FTE Associates** to cover their peak quarter with increased hours and cut back the hours as the **Weekly Sales** change from quarter to quarter. To assess these options, Marquetta has suggested that Kevin explore alternative staffing designs that vary the **Assoc Hours per Week** from 36 to 46 hours in increments of 2 hours with the **Sales per Employee Hour** at Chuck's value of $28. They want to review the potential impact on the number of **FTE Associates** by quarter and the average for the year.

(c) Marquetta and Kevin have been discussing the impacts of **Sales per Employee Hour** and **Assoc Hours per Week.** They recognize that they can control the

Assoc Hour per Week with their staffing plan. However, they can only react to anticipated **Weekly Sales.** Although some special promotions can be used to influence Weekly Sales, they cannot control their customers' appetite for Super Combos. Marquetta has suggested that Kevin explore the **FTE Associates [Average]** when **Sales per Employee Hour** vary from $25 to $30 while **Assoc Hours per Week** vary from 36 to 44 in increments of 2 hours, as in (b) above. This analysis should provide insight into alternative staffing designs that would permit adjusting **Assoc Hours per Week** in response to varying **Sales per Employee Hour.**

(d) Kevin has indicated that they may want to use the assistant managers as a cushion for variations in **Sales per Employee Hour.** With the **Assoc Hours per Week** fixed at their initial planning level, the **Asst Mgr Hours per Week** could be varied from 40 to 48 in increment of 2 hours, while the **Sales per Employee Hour** vary from $25 to $30. The **FTE Associates [Average]** furnishes the information for assessing this option.

Kevin is concerned with a sensitivity measure for the alternatives. Although he could just use the "eyeball" method of comparing a change in one variable with that of a second variable, Kevin would like a better measure. He consulted with Chuck to determine a sensitivity measure they might use. Even though more sophisticated procedures could be applied, Chuck has recommended a simple ratio that measures the relative change between two variables. Chuck has assured Kevin that this ratio is appropriate for their analysis.

$$\text{Relative change} = \frac{(\text{Ending value} - \text{Beginning value})}{\text{Sum(all values)} / \text{Number of values}}$$

This relative change can be computed for each variable, such as **Sales per Employee Hour** and **FTE Associates [Average].** Chuck suggested using relative change like this, since the magnitude of the variable is removed from the comparison and the result may be readily stated as either a decimal ratio or a percentage relationship. A sensitivity measure would then be:

$$\text{Sensitivity measure} = \frac{\text{Relative change in } \textbf{FTE Associates [Average]}}{\text{Relative change in } \textbf{Sales per Employee Hour}}$$

For this sensitivity measure, notice that relative change of the values from the input cell of the data table is used as the denominator. When used with a / Data Table 1, this is the preferred method for computing the sensitivity measure. The closer the value of this measure is to zero, the less "sensitive" the variable in the numerator is to the one in the denominator. A negative sensitivity measure indicates that as one variable increases, the other decreases. Still, the closer to zero, the less sensitive the variable in the numerator is to changes in the denominator.

Tasks

1. Access the STAFF.WK1 worksheet file and examine it. Review the manner in which Kevin has laid out the columns for use with **Weekly Sales, Weekly Hours,** and **FTE Associates.**

2. Enter the formulas to compute **Weekly Hours** and **FTE Associates. Weekly Hours** should be computed from **Weekly Sales** and **Sale per Employee Hour. FTE Associates** should be computed from the hours available for associates and the **Assoc Hours per Week,** where the hours available for associates are those that remain after deducting manager hours and assistant manager hours from the Weekly Hours.

3. Develop a data table for alternative staffing arrangement (a) above. This table should display the **FTE Associates** for each quarter and for the average. Format each of the **FTE Associate** values in your table as Fixed 1. Include formulas to compute the relative change in **Sales per Employee Hour** and the **FTE Associates [Average].** Format these relative changes as Percent 1. Calculate the Sensitivity Measure in the indicated cell and format this as Fixed 2. Print a copy of the finished report and save this file as STAFFA.WK1.

4. Develop a data table for Kevin's alternative staffing arrangement (b) above. Calculate relative changes in **Assoc Hour per Week** and **FTE Associates [Average].** Revise the label for relative change to be **Assoc Hours per Week,** and then calculate the Sensitivity Measure. Format the cells for the data table, relative changes, and sensitivity measure as indicated in Task 3 above. Print a copy of the finished report and save this file as STAFFB.WK1. Compare the sensitivity measure from Task 3 using the **Sales per Employee Hour** to the one for this task, using **Assoc Hours per Week.** Write a brief summary describing which is more sensitive. Why?

5. Develop a data table for alternative staffing requirement (c) above. Format the **FTE Associates [Average]** in the data table as Fixed 1. Print a report of the results. Create a line graph with the **Sales per Employee Hour** on the X-axis and each of the alternative **Assoc Hours per Week** as a line on the graph. Label the X-axis as "Sales per Employee Hour," and the Y-axis as "FTE Associates." Include a legend that identifies each line on the graph. Place an appropriate title on this graph. Save the graph as STAFFC.PIC and then save your worksheet file as STAFFC.WK1. Complete Task 6 before you Quit 1-2-3 and print this graph.

6. Develop a data table for alternative staffing requirement (d) above. Format the cells of the data table as indicated in Task 5 above. Print a report of the results. Create a line graph similar to that of Task 5 with the **Sales per Employee Hour** on the X-axis and each of the alternative **Asst Mgr Hours per Week** as a line on the graph. Add labels for the axes, legend, and titles. Save the graph as STAFFD.PIC and the worksheet file as STAFFD.WK1. Print both of these graphs. Review the graphs and provide Marquetta with your interpretation of the sensitivity of these two staffing alternatives. Include in your summary an indication of why you view one as more sensitive than the other. [*Hint:* Use the "eyeball" method and compare your two graphs. Lines on the graph that are close together are less sensitive than those that are further apart.]

Time Estimates

Novice: 120 minutes

Intermediate: 90 minutes

Advanced: 60 minutes

LESSON

L.7

Applying Functions

CONTENT

- Introduction to Functions
- @IF—Building in Decisions
- Table Lookup of Values
- Well Rounded Numbers with @ROUND
- @PMT for Loan Payment Calculation
- Other Selected Functions
- When Things Go Wrong

L.7.1 Introduction to Functions

Functions are used to perform special-purpose computations. They represent a short-hand method of having quite complex calculations performed for you by Lotus 1-2-3. For example, functions are available to calculate loan payments, depreciation, net present value, and internal rate of returns. You have already used the @SUM function as a shortcut method of adding a series of data values. Functions are usually used in expressions that appear as part of a cell formula. Each function produces a single output value for the formula in a cell. Functions are available to perform several different categories of computations, including the following:

- Financial
- Mathematical
- Statistical
- Date and time
- Logical
- Database

In this Lesson, several of these functions are examined to provide you with a general idea of the use and application of 1-2-3's many functions.

L.7.2 @IF—Building in Decisions

Kim and Chris met with the production manager at Good Morning Products to review the cost of producing Liquid Gold. They were informed of a changing **Cost Percent.** For **Sales** of $325,000 or less in any one quarter, the costs are 77 percent, whereas for **Sales** of more than $325,000, the costs are 73 percent. Because of the processing used, these **Cost Percents** apply to all of the **Sales** in all four quarters. Kim sketched out the following table relating **Sales** and **Percent Costs;** tables like this are known as **decision tables:**

IF CONDITIONS: Sales	THEN ACTIONS: Cost Percent
$325,000 or less	77%
More than $325,000	73%

This decision table can be implemented by using the @IF function that has this general form:

@IF(expr-1 relational-operator expr-2, true-expr, false-expr)

where the relational operators are listed in Figure L.108. "Expr" indicates an expression that could be a formula or value. Values may include text strings, such as "yes" or "no."

An @IF function is evaluated by 1-2-3 in this manner:

1. Compute the values for expr-1 and expr-2.
2. Compare the results of expr-1 and expr-2 obtaining either a "true" or "false" outcome.
3. If the outcome is "true," compute and display the true-expr.
4. If the outcome is "false," compute and display the false-expr.

Examples of several @IF functions and their components are illustrated in Figure L.109.

The decision table for Good Morning Products can be implemented using the PLAN6 worksheet as the starting point. Let's look at how the @IF function is used to include the decision table in this worksheet.

Action: Access the PLAN6 worksheet.

Action: Revise the global cell format to be **Comma 0.** This will make the dollar amounts more readable.

Operator	Symbol
Equal to	=
Not equal to	<>
Less than or equal to	<=
Less than	<
Greater than or equal to	>=
Greater than	>

FIGURE L.108. Relational operators.

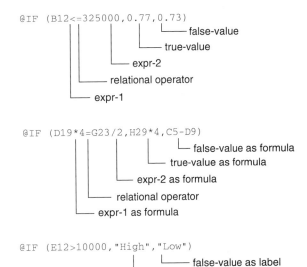

FIGURE L.109. Example @IF functions.

Now the cells are set up that contain the **Cost Percents** used in the @IF function. This makes them easier to change and display for reference.

To set up data values in separate cells for use in the true and false expressions	**Move to:**	**B8**	Desired location for lower limit
	Enter:	.73	Specify the low value limit
	Move to:	**C8**	Desired location for upper limit
	Enter:	.77	Specify the high value limit

Next the @IF function is entered for the first quarter.

To enter the @IF function as part of a cell formula	**Move to:**	**B13**	Cell where the formula will reside
	Enter:	`@IF(B12<=325000,$C$8,$B$8)*B12`	

Pointing may be used to reference the cell names in this formula as it is entered. The cell **C8** provides the true-condition value whereas cell **B8** contains the false-condition value. The @IF function produces the desired **Cost Percent,** which is then multiplied by **Sales** to calculate the **Cost of Sales** in cell **B13** (Figure L.110). This illustrates how a function can be used as part of a more complex formula.

Why does the @IF function contain only one comparison when two conditions exist for the Good Morning Products' decision table? When one condition is true, the other condition has to be false. As a result, it is necessary to test for only one condition. In general, a decision table can be implemented by using one fewer comparison than the number of conditions in the decision table.

Now let's copy the formula with the @IF function into the other three quarters of the plan.

To place the @IF function in the cells for the other three quarters

Action: Copy the formula from **B13** into **C13..E13.** Absolute referencing was used when the formula was entered in cell B13 so that this copying could be performed. The results are illustrated in Figure L.110.

A **Cost Percent Used** has been added as row 20 in the worksheet of Figure L.110 for your reference in observing the operation of the @IF. This row shows which

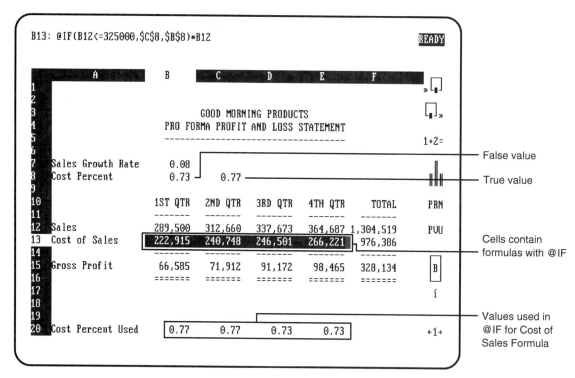

FIGURE L.110. Results with decision table.

Percent was actually selected by the @IF function for use in calculating the **Cost of Sales** amount.

Action: Print a report of the Pro Forma Statement.

Action: Print a list of cell formulas.

Action: Save this as PLAN11.

Application of the @IF can be extended to more complex situations. Kim and Chris reviewed the results with the production supervisor. After considerable discussion and additional analysis of production costs, this revised decision table was created:

IF CONDITIONS:	THEN ACTIONS:
Sales	Cost Percent
$250,000 or less	77%
More than $250,000 and $350,000 or less	75%
More than $350,000	73%

@IF functions can be used to implement this decision table. Because this decision table contains three conditions, two @IF functions are necessary for its implementation. The third condition occurs when the other two conditions are both false. The decision table is implemented with one fewer @IF function than the number of conditions. For Good Morning Products, the PLAN11 worksheet can be modified to include this decision table. First these new **Cost Percents** are set up:

Cell	**B8**	**C8**	**D8**
Contents	73%	75%	77%

To set up cells containing **Cost Percent** for use with @IF

Action: Enter these values in cells **B8..D8.**

Next let's enter a new formula for the **Cost of Sales.**

To enter @IF functions as part of a cell formula to implement the decision table

Move to: **B13**   Desired location for @IF

Enter: @IF(B12<=325000,$D$8,@IF(B12<=350000,$C$8,$B$8))*B12

In this formula, the second @IF function with **B12 <= 350000** is used as the false-value for the first @IF function. Lotus 1-2-3 permits this use of a function within a function. The second @IF function is evaluated only after the first @IF is evaluated as false. This means that the **Sales** amount in cell **B12** has to be greater than **325000** for the second @IF to be evaluated. For this reason, it is not necessary to include a test for **B12>325000** in the second @IF. Also, when the second @IF is evaluated as false, then the **Sales** amount in **B12** has to be greater than **350000**; hence, a separate test for this is not required.

Now the formula for this decision table can be placed in the cells for the other three quarters.

To place the decision table formula in other cells

Action: Copy the contents of **B13** to **C13..E13** to place the formula in the cell for the other three quarters.

This produces the result shown in Figure L.111 and illustrates the application of @IF functions to implement a decision table with more than two conditions. In Figure L.111

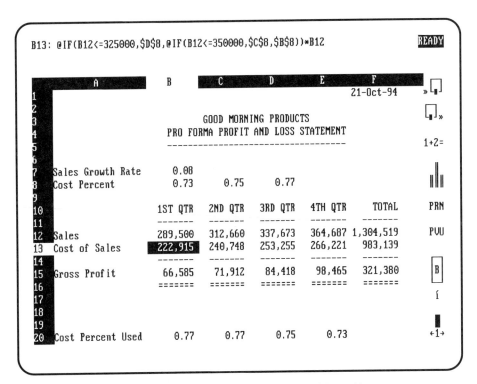

FIGURE L.111. Results for expanded decision table.

Operator	Action
#AND#	Both conditional expressions must be true for "true" result
#OR#	One conditional expression must be true for "true" result
#NOT#	Reverse the result so "true" becomes "false" and similarly for "false."

FIGURE L.112. Logical operators.

the **Cost Percent Used** in each column is displayed for your reference to reinforce the operation of the @IF functions. Although the formula in cell B20 could have been

@IF(B12<=325000,$D$8,@IF(B12<=350000,$C$8,$B$8))

a different formula was used in this cell to show an alternative method of implementing the decision table:

@IF(B12<=325000,$D$8,0) + @IF(B12>325000#AND#B12<=350000,$C$8,0) + @IF(B12>350000,$B$8,0)

This formula uses three @IF functions. Each @IF tests for only one of the conditions in the decision table. If the test is true, a **Cost Percent** value is selected. If the test is false, a value of zero results for that @IF. The results from the three @IF are then added together to calculate the value displayed in cell **B20.** Since the conditions are **mutually exclusive,** that is, only one condition can be true at a time, the correct **Cost Percent** is calculated for this cell. In this manner, one value is selected from the series of three data values.

Look at the second @IF used in the formula for cell **B20.** It uses an #AND# logical operator in testing *both* the upper and lower limits of the value contained in **B12. Logical operators** are used to combine two or more comparisons like these. The #AND# logical operator requires both conditions to be satisfied or to be "true." The cell name **B12** had to be *repeated* in each part of the conditional expression. The logical operators used in 1-2-3 to specify complex conditions are shown in Figure L.112. When implementing a decision table you should consider your options in specifying the conditions being evaluated. Then select the method that is easiest for you understand.

Keypoint! | When using the logical operator #AND# or #OR# in an @IF where the *same cell name* is referenced, the cell name must be *repeated* in each conditional expression!

Action: Print a report of the Pro Forma Statement.

Action: Print a list of cell formulas.

Action: Save this as PLAN12.

L.7.3   Table Lookup of Values

Kim and Chris have met with the production manager to further review and refine the costs associated with producing Liquid Gold. Their prior decision table has been expanded as follows:

IF CONDITIONS: Sales	THEN ACTIONS: Cost Percent
$250,000 or more and Less than $300,000	77%
$300,000 or more and Less than $325,000	76%
$325,000 or more and Less than $350,000	75%
$350,000 or more and Less than $380,000	74%
$380,000 or more and Less than $410,000	73%
$410,000 or more and Less than $450,000	72%
$450,000 or more	71%

This table is a series of step changes, as illustrated in Figure L.113. A decision table like this could be implemented by using **nested** @IF functions with a second @IF function as the false-value for a first @IF function. A total of six @IF functions would be required, one fewer than the total number of conditions. This would be a rather complex formula to set up. Lotus 1-2-3 provides another method for implementing a decision table like this one. A table of values, known as a **lookup table,** is entered in a convenient cell range. Lotus 1-2-3 then uses the **Sales** amount to **look up** the **Cost Percent** in the table. When you have a number of conditions like this, a table arrangement is often easier to create and modify than a lengthy cell formula.

Let's get ready to implement this lookup table in 1-2-3.

Action: Retrieve file PLAN12, if necessary.

Action: Erase the **Cost Percent Used** cell contents row since this is no longer needed for this example, if necessary.

Now the values from the decision table can be entered at a convenient location in the worksheet.

To set up the data values for a lookup table

Action: Enter the **Sales** versus **Cost Percent** lookup table in cells **A18..B26,** as illustrated in Figure L.114.

Action: Range Format cell **B20..B26** as Percent 0.

The cells **A20..B26** contain the decision table described above as the lookup table illustrated in Figure L.114. To look up the desired **Cost Percent** value when you know a **Sales** value, you go down column "A" until you find a **Sales** value that is *equal to or just less than* your value. Then, you obtain the desired **Cost Percent** from the adjacent column to the right, column "B." In 1-2-3, finding a value in a table like this is known as

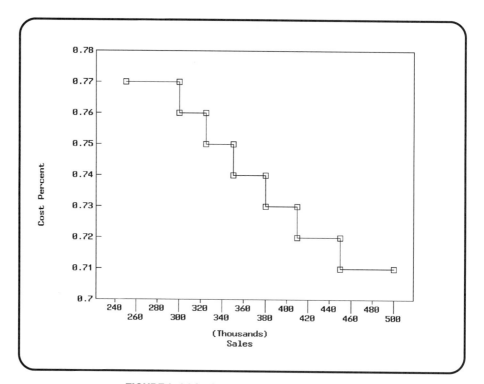

FIGURE L.113. Step changes in cost percent.

```
B8:  (F2) @VLOOKUP(B12,$A$20..$B$26,1)                              READY

        '        A           B         C         D         E         F
7   Sales Growth Rate      0.08
8   Cost Percent           0.77      0.76      0.75      0.74
9
10                        1ST QTR   2ND QTR   3RD QTR   4TH QTR    TOTAL
11                        -------   -------   -------   -------   -------
12  Sales                 289,500   312,660   337,673   364,687 1,304,520
13  Cost of Sales         222,915   237,622   253,255   269,868   983,660
14                        -------   -------   -------   -------   -------
15  Gross Profit           66,585    75,038    84,418    94,819   320,860
16                        =======   =======   =======   =======   =======
17
18              Sales    Cost %
19          ----------------------------------------------
20             250000      77%
21             300000      76%
22             325000      75%
23             350000      74%
24             380000      73%
25             410000      72%
26             450000      71%
```

FIGURE L.114. Lookup table for cost percent.

a **table lookup.** This is performed with the @VLOOKUP function. The "V" (vertical) indicates that the table is organized in a series of columns as in this example. A companion function @HLOOKUP (horizontal) permits the table to be organized as a set of rows.

When the **Cost of Sales** amounts are calculated, the **Cost Percent** for each quarter is obtained from the cells in row **8.** Each of these values is obtained by a separate lookup in the table. Let's see how the @VLOOKUP is implemented in obtaining these data values.

To set up the **Cost of Sales** formula for use with **Cost Percent** from the lookup table			
	Move to:	**B13**	Desired location for formula
	Action:	Enter the formula **B8*B12,** which calculates the **Cost of Sales.**	
	Action:	Copy the formula from **B13** into **C13..E13**	

To use @VLOOKUP in a formula			
	Move to:	**B8**	Desired location for @VLOOKUP
	Action:	Enter the formula **@VLOOKUP(B12,$A$20..$B$26,1).** The absolute references are used to facilitate copying of this cell.	
	Action:	Copy the formula from **B8** into **C8..E8.**	

The general arrangement of the @VLOOKUP function is defined as:

@VLOOKUP(expression,lookup-table-range,table-column)

In the example for Good Morning Products, 1-2-3 obtains the "input" or "lookup" value for **Sales** from cell **B12,** since this cell name is the entire expression. Lotus 1-2-3 searches down the leftmost column in the defined table range until it finds a cell that is *equal to or just smaller* than this input value. The result for the @VLOOKUP function is then obtained from the first column to the right, since a table-column or offset of 1 is specified. A lookup table can have as many columns as you choose, but the first column must contain the classification scheme, and the first column of the table is always known as column zero (0), regardless of where you place it in your worksheet.

In addition to the decision table for Good Morning Products, @VLOOKUP can be used for other similar tables such as a tax table or a sales commissions table.

Action: Print a report of the Pro Forma Statement.

Action: Print a list of cell formulas.

Action: Save this as PLAN13

L.7.4 Well Rounded Numbers with @ROUND

Chris and Kim were reviewing the results in Figure L.111 and discovered that some of the arithmetic appears as if it is in error. In cell **F12,** the total of the four quarters of **Sales** should be 1,304,520 and not 1,304,519. This total is off by one. Similarly, in cell **E15,** the **Gross Profit** for the 4th Quarter should be 98,466 and not 98,465. Of course, Chris and Kim could have changed the cell format so that two places were displayed to the right of the decimal. In this example, the amount of the error would be 0.01 instead of one. Moving the decimal does not remedy this condition, but merely moves the decimal location.

This appearance of arithmetic errors stem from how rounding is handled within 1-2-3. For the Good Morning Products report, the numbers displayed on the screen are rounded *as they are displayed* by the / Worksheet Global Format Fixed 0 (/WGFF0) command, and *not when they are calculated.* For this format, the digits to the right of the decimal are still *stored and used in computing other cell values*. Merely changing the cell format does not eliminate this rounding problem. For a 12-month plan that is summed for the year's total, *the difference could be as great as six*. Rounding differences often cast doubt on the integrity of a report and should be avoided. They occur most frequently when summing across rows and totaling columns. The 1-2-3 @ROUND function provides a means of addressing this problem. In a worksheet, consider using the @ROUND function when a formula contains:

1. A multiplication by a fraction
2. A division
3. An exponentiation
4. Use of another function that may have a fractional result

Since addition and subtraction of integers results in integers, those cell formulas that contain only addition and subtraction do not require rounding. Although the application of @ROUND makes a formula look as if it is more complex, this is required to avoid the appearance of an error caused by rounding.

Keypoint!

> The rounding problem is *not* unique to Lotus 1-2-3 and other spreadsheets; it exists universally throughout all computing applications. The @ROUND function is a convenient method for addressing this problem in 1-2-3!

The worksheet in Figure L.111 can be modified with rounding by adding the @ROUND function to the cells **C12..E12** and **B13..E13**. For example, the cell formula in **C12** would be modified as

@ROUND(B12*(1+$B$7),0)

In general the @ROUND function has two arguments: (1) the formula to be calculated and (2) a formula specifying the number of decimal places. These arguments are *separated by a comma*. Thus, the general form of the function is

@ROUND(formula to be calculated, formula for decimal places)

When an integer number is desired, the number of decimal places is set to zero.

Action: Continue with the PLAN12 worksheet file. Access this worksheet file, if necessary.

To apply the @ROUND function to cell formulas

Action: Modify cells **C12..E12** and **B13..E13** by adding the @ROUND function (Figure L.115). Use <F2> to edit the cells in revising the formulas.

Action: Print a report of the Pro Forma Statement.

Action: Print a list of cell formulas.

Action: Save this as PLAN14.

L.7.5   @PMT for Loan Payment Calculation

Matt and Kim have recently returned from the international Juicers and Processors Equipment Fair in London. They became quite interested in a new juicing machine that would allow them to increase their production capacity by 25 percent and also cut the cost of oranges per bottle by 10 percent. Chris estimates the cost of this equipment

Round function added to formula

Integer displayed

Values changed by rounding

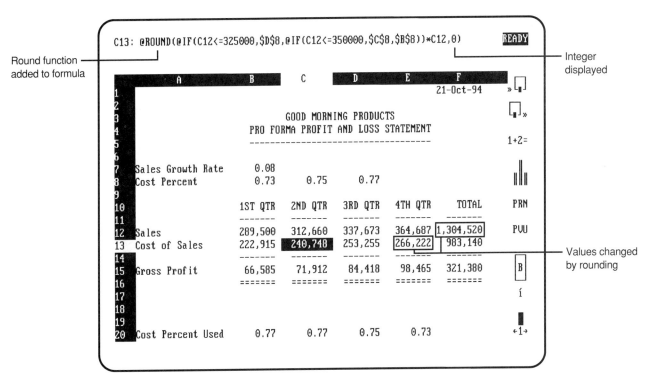

FIGURE L.115. Pro forma statement with rounding.

to be $500,000. Good Morning Products can finance 80 percent ($400,000) with a loan from the Last National Bank of Walnut Creek. With a 20 percent down payment, Last National will provide the loan at an interest rate of 10 percent with financing for 10 years. Kim wants to know the amount of the loan payment required for repayment of this loan if the payment is made at the end of each month or at the end of each year (that is, one annual loan payment).

The loan payment is computed with the 1-2-3 @PMT function. The general form of the function is

@PMT(loan amount, interest rate, number of periods)

where the interest rate must be specified as a period interest rate. That is, for a monthly loan the interest rate is a monthly rate and the number of periods is in months. The

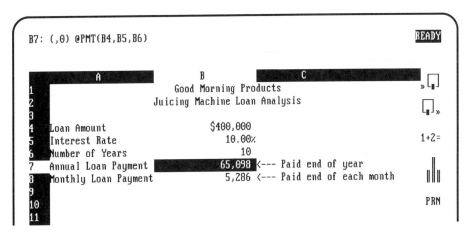

FIGURE L.116. Loan payment calculation with @PMT function.

loan payment analysis for Good Morning Products new juicer is shown in Figure L.116. The loan payments are computed in this manner:

Time Period	Cell Name	Cell Content	Cell Display
Annual	B7	@PMT(B4,B5,B6)	65,098
Month	B8	@PMT(B4,B5/12,B6*12)	5,286

Notice that for cell **B8** the annual interest rate is converted to a monthly rate by dividing by 12, and the term is stated in months by multiplying the number of years by 12.

Keypoint!

You, the end user, must be sure you **match up** the interest rate period with the number of periods in the @PMT function. This situation also occurs for all other financial functions that use interest rates and time periods!

After reviewing the results in Figure L.116, Kim and Chris decided on the annual loan payment because of the cyclical nature of their business. They could make the payment after their big crop had been processed each year. Chris wants to create a loan payment table like that illustrated in Figure L.117. The formulas for this table are shown in Figure L.118. Notice that the amount of interest, principal reduction, and loan balance are calculated for each year. The @PMT function is used only once, in cell **B7,** to determine the amount of the payment. The 1-2-3 loan function com-

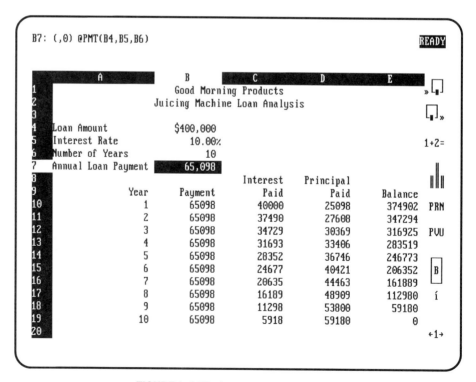

FIGURE L.117. Loan payment schedule.

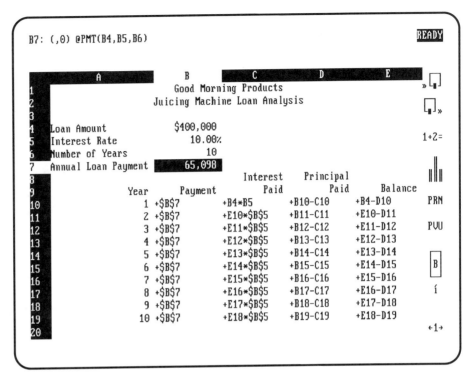

FIGURE L.118. Loan payment schedule formulas.

putes only the payment amount, so you must supply the formulas for calculating the other values. When other financial functions and depreciation functions are used in 1-2-3, similar computations would be required to produce a depreciation schedule.

To use the @PMT function for a loan payment schedule

Action: Create and print the loan payment schedule shown in Figures L.117 and L.118. Save this as the LOANPAY worksheet file.

L.7.6   Other Selected Functions

Lotus 1-2-3 contains about 100 different functions. Some of the more frequently used functions include the following:

Function	Action
@ABS(expression)	Absolute value of an expression
@AVG(range)	Computes average of values
@COS(expression)	Calculates cosine of expression
@COUNT(range-list)	Counts nonblank cells in list or range of values
@DATE(year,month,day)	Number of days since the beginning of the century; the number 1 = 01 Jan 1900
@DATEVALUE(character-string)	Converts a character string into its equivalent date number, for example "26-Oct-92" is converted to the date number 33903.
@DAY(date)	Day number of date
@DDB(cost,salvage,life,period)	Double-declining balance depreciation

Function	Action
@EXP(expression)	Computes *e* (2.7182818 . . .) to the power of the expression
@FV(payment,int-rate,period)	Future value of a series of equal payments
@HLOOKUP(expr,table-range,offset)	Horizontal table lookup in the row of the range specified by the offset with result based on the value of the expression
@IF(condition,true-exp,false-exp)	Selects an action from two available actions
@INT(expression)	Integer portion of expression value
@IRR(guess,range)	Internal rate of return for a series of cash flows
@LENGTH(string)	Counts number of characters in string
@LN(expression)	Natural logarithm (base *e*) of expression
@LOG(expression)	Common logarithm (base 10) of expression
@LOWER(string)	Converts all alphabetic characters in a string to lowercase
@MAX(range-list)	Finds maximum in list of values
@MIN(range-list)	Finds minimum in list of values
@MONTH(date)	Month number of date
@NOW	Obtains the current date and time from the computer's clock
@NPV(interest-rate,range)	Net present value of a series of cash flows
@PI	The constant 3.1415926536
@PMT(principal,int-rate,period)	Loan payment calculation
@PV(payment,int-rate,period)	Present value of a series of equal payments
@RAND	Produces a random number between 0 and 1
@ROUND(expr,decimal-expr)	Rounds to specified decimal places
@SIN(expression)	Calculates sine of expression
@SLN(cost,salvage,life)	Straight-line depreciation
@SQRT(expression)	Positive square root of expression
@STD(range-list)	Computes standard deviation of list or range of values
@SUM(range-list)	Adds the list or range of values
@SYD(cost,salvage,life,period)	Sum-of-the-year's digits depreciation
@TAN(expression)	Calculates tangent of expression
@TODAY	Today's date as an integer number from the computer's clock, same as @INT(@NOW)
@UPPER(string)	Converts all alphabetic characters in a string to uppercase
@VAR(range-list)	Computes population variance of list or range of values
@VLOOKUP(expr,table-range,offset)	Vertical table lookup in the column of the range specified by the offset with result based on the value of the expression
@YEAR(date)	Year number of date

For additional functions and their description, see the *Lotus 1-2-3 Reference Manual.*

L.7.7 When Things Go Wrong

When using functions, several different conditions may occur that cause you difficulties. Some of the more common obstacles and how to approach them are discussed here:

1. Your @IF function does not seem to be operating properly, but you cannot immediately detect the difficulty. Moreover, your @IF refers to comparison values that you have placed in separate cells, like those shown in Figure L.110.

    a. Temporarily change all of the values in the referenced cells to zeros, except the value in a selected cell; set its value to 1.

    b. Observe the result. You should now get a familiar data value.

    c. Selectively place the 1 in your referenced cells and observe the results obtained.

    d. By observing the results of the @IF, determine which part is not operating as desired.

    e. Correct and test your @IF function.

    f. Place the original values back into the referenced cells to produce the final calculated results.

2. Your @PMT or other financial function produces a value that appears to be too large or too small. This usually occurs when the function is used to compute a result for some time period other than years.

    a. Review the interest rate and term parameters of your financial function. Have you matched up the interest rate and term so that they are for the same time period?

    b. Correct the interest rate and term, as necessary, so that their time periods match up. If these are calculated values, such as those obtained by dividing and multiplying by 12, you may want to locate this arithmetic in separate cells. This would permit you to view the values used in the computation of the financial function. Then, in your financial function, such as the @PMT, use a formula like **+B5** to reference the calculated value.

L.7.8 Lesson Summary

- Functions provide a shorthand method for performing more complex computations.

- Functions are used in cell formulas. A function produces a single calculated value within a cell.

- The @IF function selects one of two values based on whether a condition is evaluated to be either true or false.

- A decision table is a general method for describing conditional logic.

- The @IF function may be used to implement a decision table.

- Rounding differences are common to computations performed with a computer.

- The @ROUND function provides a means of rounding numbers to a desired precision as they are calculated, instead of rounding them as they are displayed.

- The @PMT function is an example of the financial functions in Lotus 1-2-3. This function computes the amount of a loan payment when the amount of the loan, the interest rate, and the time period of the loan are known.

- When using Lotus 1-2-3 financial functions, the interest rate and time period must be matched up. That is, a monthly interest rate is required when the duration of a loan is entered in months to compute a monthly payment.
- The @VLOOKUP and @HLOOKUP functions facilitate the use of a table included in your worksheet to determine a value for use in a formula, like those for taxes and sales commissions.
- Lotus 1-2-3 contains more than 100 different functions that can assist in developing formulas for more complex calculations.

L.7.9   Practice Tutorial

Develop the @IF, @ROUND, and @VLOOKUP worksheets as described in this Lesson in Sections L.7.2, L.7.3, and L.7.5 as a guided activity in a hands-on manner. Access your MYPLAN6 worksheet from Practice Exercise 1 in Lesson L.3 as a starting point for this exercise.

Task 1: Create the two @IF worksheets.

Task 2: Print the results for each @IF.

Task 3: Save these worksheets as MYPLAN11 and MYPLAN12.

Task 4: Modify your MYPLAN12 worksheet by including @ROUND.

Task 5: Print this worksheet.

Task 6: Save this as worksheet file MYPLAN13.

Task 7: Add the @VLOOKUP to your MYPLAN13 worksheet.

Task 8: Print this worksheet.

Task 9: Save this as worksheet file MYPLAN14.

Time Estimates

Novice: 45 minutes

Intermediate: 30 minutes

Advanced: 20 minutes

L.7.10   Practice Exercises

(1)   Case: Inland Container (continued)

In reviewing the Rydder Truck Rental proposal with her district manager, Mary Montoya wanted to make a couple more changes before sending the proposal to Richard:

(a) She wanted to provide a price break to Rydder Truck based on the number of units they purchased. The **Cost of Sales** is calculated by using a **Percent** cost of sales as specified by this decision table:

Units Sold	Cost Percent
190,000 or less	67%
More than 190,000	64%

(b) Mary did not want any rounding differences in the proposal she was going to submit to Richard. She wanted to include the @ROUND function in her worksheet model, as appropriate, so that **Units Sold, Sales, Cost of Sales,** and **Gross Profit** would be rounded as integers when their values were calculated. This would ensure that all her totals would add across the rows and her computations in each column would be correct.

Develop a solution for each of the alternatives by performing these tasks:

Task 1: Retrieve your RYDDER2 worksheet from Practice Exercise 1 in Lesson L.3 as your starting point for this exercise. Review the contents of your worksheet model.

Task 2: Revise Mary's RYDDER2 worksheet to implement the decision table for the selection of the **Percent** cost of sales as indicated in (a) above.

Task 3: Print the result of this worksheet and inspect it for rounding differences. Circle each total that you identify as an apparent error caused by rounding.

Task 4: Modify the RYDDER2 worksheet to include rounding as described in (b) above.

Task 5: Print the results with rounding. Did you correct all the rounding differences that you detected?

Task 6: Print the results with both rounding and the decision table.

Task 7: Print the formulas.

Task 8: Save this worksheet as RYDDER11.

Quick check answers: (a) Cost of Sales [Total] = 1225293
(b) Cost of Sales [Total] = 1225294
Gross Profit [Total] = 661220

Time Estimates

Novice: 30 minutes

Intermediate: 20 minutes

Advanced: 10 minutes

(2) Case: Dust Busters

Business Problem: Loan payment schedule
MIS Characteristics: Finance
Managerial Control

Jean Marie Herdzina manages the local franchise of Dust Busters janitorial services. She is considering the purchase of a new van in order to expand her business in the metroplex. She plans to borrow $18,000 at 12 percent interest per year for a period of four years. What is Jean Marie's monthly payment?

Task 1: Build a worksheet that produces a *payment schedule* for this loan. Construct the worksheet so that Jean Marie can easily enter the loan amount and interest rate to explore other loan alternatives as she shops for the best deal.

Task 2: Print the results.
Quick check answer: Monthly payment = $474.01

Task 3: Print the formulas.

Task 4: Save this as worksheet file PAYMENT.

Task 5: (*Optional*)   For Jean Marie's loan, the interest rate could vary from 8 percent to 14 percent in increments of 0.5 percent. Create a separate worksheet containing a table that displays the payment at each of these interest rates. [*Hint:* Consider using a data table to produce this table of results.] Print the results, print the formulas, and save this as worksheet file PAYMENT2.

Time Estimates

Novice: 30 minutes

Intermediate: 20 minutes

Advanced: 10 minutes

(3)   Case: Dust Busters (second encounter)

Business Problem: Depreciation schedule
MIS Characteristics: Finance
                          Operational Control

Jean Marie purchased the new van described in Problem 2 above. After she uses it in her business for the next five years, she expects to sell it for $4000. Her accountant has suggested that, for her income statement, she should depreciate the van using the straight-line method.

Task 1: Build a worksheet that uses the appropriate depreciation function to compute the annual depreciation amount for the new van.

Task 2: Print the result.

Quick check answer: Annual depreciation = $2800

Task 3: Print the formula.

Task 4: Save this as worksheet file DEPREC.

Time Estimates

Novice: 30 minutes

Intermediate: 20 minutes

Advanced: 10 minutes

(4)   Case: Abacus Computer Systems (second encounter)

Business Problem: Profit analysis
MIS Characteristics: Marketing
                          Managerial Control

At Abacus Computer Systems, Herbie and Pattie Wattsun, the owners and operators of this full-service computer outlet that sells turn-key systems to business and government, are preparing to take another look at their profit plan for next year. On returning from a visit with their accountant, they knew they had to refine their plan. Abacus was expecting to undergo considerable growth and change during the upcoming year. Their accountant suggested that Pattie and Herbie prepare a quarterly budget with an annual total. Herbie made these revisions on their ACS.WK1 worksheet and asked Pattie to review the results. She has suggested these additional modifications to Herbie:

(a) Include the @ROUND function in the worksheet model because several of the numbers do not cross-total or foot correctly.

(b) Include a decision table for the **Cost Percent.** They discovered that their **EBT** (Earnings Before Tax) was quite sensitive to changes in **Cost Percent.** Pattie obtained additional data from their suppliers for this decision table:

Units Sold	Cost Percent
18 or less	81%
More than 18	76%

Develop a solution for each of the alternatives by doing these tasks:

Task 1: Retrieve the ACS.WK1 worksheet file from your Data Disk and review Pattie and Herbie's quarterly profit plan for next year.

Task 2: Print the solution of the worksheet. Review each of the cross-totals, that is, the sum across each row that resides in the **Total** column. Circle each value that appears as an error because the cross-total is incorrect. Review the footing of each of the **Total Exp** amounts for each quarter, that is, the adding of the individual expenses items into the **Total Exp** account. Circle each value that appears to be in error because the numbers do not foot correctly.

Task 3: Pattie wants you to add rounding to your worksheet model as described in (a) above. Print this result and save your worksheet as the ACS2 file. (*Hint:* Did you remember to copy your revised formulas so that all cells that need to be rounded have rounding included?)

Task 4: Compare your worksheet from Task 2 with that in Task 3. Have the rounding problems been corrected?

Task 5: Now Pattie wants you to revise the worksheet with rounding to include the decision table she developed as described in (b) above. Print this result and save your worksheet as the ACS3 file.

Time Estimates

Novice: 60 minutes

Intermediate: 45 minutes

Advanced: 30 minutes

(5) Case: Buffalo Computer Systems

Business Problem: Time study
MIS Characteristics: Production/Operations
Operational Control

Buffalo Computer Systems produces and markets desktop computers. Most sales are made directly to their customers, with each computer system assembled to the customer's specific order. The assembly of Buffalo computers takes place under a quality of work life (QWL) program, with the entire assembly of a computer system performed by one employee.

Susan Dell, one of Buffalo's systems analysts, is responsible for upgrading their Production Information System (PIM). PIM provides assembly employees with the information necessary to complete each order. The PIM system makes use of several paper copy reports and an on-line inquiry system to check the location of the parts used in each computer. To help Susan determine the benefits from redesigning their PIM system, she teamed up with Karl Goodwin, Buffalo's work standards engineer, to conduct a time study that measures the amount of time required for each job element in the final assembly of a computer system. While Karl determined the standard time to assemble one computer system, he also recorded the amount of time an employee spent looking up information and filing documents. Karl observed the completion of 10 computer systems and recorded this information in the BUFFALO.WK1 worksheet file. Job elements 1, 2, 3, 9, and 10 involve the retrieval of information or the completion of documents from the PIM system as part of the assembly process. Job element 3 is performed with an on-line system, whereas the other elements are carried out by using paper documents. Susan and Karl want you to complete the time study computations as follows:

Task 1: Retrieve the BUFFALO.WK1 worksheet file and review its content. This is a standard format that Karl uses for recording time study data. Look at the columns that have been established for the total time for the 10 observations (SUM), the average time for each element (AVG), and the standard deviation of the time for each element (STD).

Task 2: Enter functions in the appropriate columns to compute the total time, average time, and standard deviation for each of the job elements.

Task 3: Enter a function in cell **M17** that computes the total of the average time per job element. This is the average time to assemble one computer system.

Task 4: Print your completed time study analysis.

Task 5: Save the completed BUFFALO worksheet file.

Task 6: Karl has established an allowance of 22 percent of the normal cycle time for activities that include personal time and work area cleanup. He has included this calculation in his time study analysis to arrive at the standard time for the assembly of one computer system. What is this standard time?

Task 7: (*Optional*)   Prepare a pie chart comparing the average time for each job element. Explode those slices that comprise the information processing activities for Susan's review in her analysis of upgrading the PIM system.

Time Estimates

Novice: 45 minutes

Intermediate: 30 minutes

Advanced: 20 minutes

(6)   Case: Brush Creek Heating & Cooling

Business Problem: Payroll withholding tax
MIS Characteristics: Human Resources
                              Operational Control

Juanita Fiori is responsible for preparing the weekly payroll report for Brush Creek Heating & Cooling. Since employees earn different weekly wages, Juanita needs to apply different tax rates to calculate the amount of federal and state withholding payroll taxes. She uses the BRUSH.WK1 worksheet file for computing her payroll each week. Juanita just received the appropriate tax tables from her accountant and needs to include these in calculating the withholding taxes for her weekly payroll. The withholding taxes are as follows:

Gross Pay	Federal Tax Rate	State Tax Rate
Less than $100	5%	0%
$100 or more and Less than $200	10%	2%
$200 or more and Less than $300	11%	3%
$300 or more and Less than $500	12%	4%
$500 or more and Less than $700	14%	5%
$700 or more and Less than $1000	16%	6%
$1000 or more	18%	8%

Develop a solution that implements this decision table by carrying out these tasks:

Task 1: Access the BRUSH.WK1 worksheet file on your Data Disk and review Juanita's payroll register. Observe that she has completed all of the formulas for calculating her payroll except those for the federal and state withholding taxes.

Task 2: Juanita wants you to add the withholding tax table to her payroll worksheet.

Task 3: Add formulas to the worksheet that compute the federal and state withholding tax by looking up the tax rates in this table. (*Hint:* Use the table-column number or offset to select the federal or state tax rate for the respective calculation.)

Task 4: Print the completed payroll register for Juanita.

Task 5: Print the withholding tax table as a separate report.

Task 6: Save the completed BRUSH worksheet file.

Task 7: (*Optional*)   For Juanita's withholding, the same weekly gross pay amounts provide a single table containing both the federal and state withholding tax rates. If these weekly gross pay amounts were different for the state withholding tax than for the federal withholding, what change might be made to the tax rate table to accommodate this situation? Write a paragraph describing the approach you would take.

Time Estimates

Novice: 45 minutes

Intermediate: 30 minutes

Advanced: 20 minutes

L.7.11 Comprehensive Problems

(1) Case: Woodcraft Furniture Company (continued)

Ray Jointer, production manager of Woodcraft, has analyzed the **Labor** required to meet production requirements and has developed this decision table:

Total Sales	Hours Worked
1,250,000 or less	174
More than 1,250,000	190

Ray and Joe would like to have you modify their monthly plan for the next quarter to include this decision table in the computation of the Labor expense for each month.

Task 1: Access the WOOD2 spreadsheet file for inclusion of the decision table.

Task 2: Revise the worksheet to include this decision table.

Task 3: Print the results.

Task 4: Save the worksheet as file WOOD6.

   Quick check answer: Labor [Total] = 830477

Time Estimates

Novice: 30 minutes

Intermediate: 20 minutes

Advanced: 10 minutes

(2) Case: Midwest Universal Gas (continued)

Francis Foresight has reviewed the pricing structure at Midwest Universal Gas for retail customers. The State Utility Commission has developed a pricing structure that requires a discount when larger volumes of gas are consumed. After some investigation of historical data, Francis has developed this decision table:

Retail Gas Sold	Retail Rate
0 BCF or more and Less than 35 BCF	350
35 BCF or more and Less than 50 BCF	338
50 BCF or more	322

Francis and Sam would like to revise next year's plan by quarter to include this decision table in the computation of **Retail Sales.**

Task 1: Access the MUG2 spreadsheet file for inclusion of the decision table.

Task 2: Revise the worksheet to include this decision table.

Task 3: Print the results.

Task 4: Save the worksheet as file MUG6.

> *Quick check answer:* Retail Sales [Total] = 53845

Time Estimates

Novice: 30 minutes

Intermediate: 20 minutes

Advanced: 10 minutes

(3)   Case: Woodcraft Furniture Company (continued)

After Joe Birch reviewed your reports for Woodcraft Furniture prepared in case 1 above, he asked for some revisions to the model. To be sure that the quarterly totals add and report correctly, Joe wants all revenue and expense amounts, which are calculated by multiplying by a rate or ratio, to be rounded to the nearest whole dollar.

Task 1: Access the WOOD6 spreadsheet file.

Task 2: Revise the worksheet to include this rounding.

Task 3: Print the results.

Task 4: Print the cell formulas.

Task 5: Save the worksheet as file WOOD7.

Time Estimates

Novice: 30 minutes

Intermediate: 20 minutes

Advanced: 10 minutes

(4)   Case: Midwest Universal Gas (continued)

Francis Foresight has requested the application of rounding to next year's financial plan for Midwest Universal Gas. Use the @ROUND function on those revenue and expense line items that might produce fractional results.

Task 1: Access the MUG6 spreadsheet file.

Task 2: Revise the worksheet to include this rounding.

Task 3: Print the results.

Task 4: Print the cell formulas.

Task 5: Save the worksheet as file MUG7.

Time Estimates

Novice: 30 minutes

Intermediate: 20 minutes

Advanced: 10 minutes

(5)   Case: Woodcraft Furniture Company (second encounter)

Woodcraft Furniture is considering the modernization of its painting and finishing operations. Ray Jointer has recommended the installation of a new electrostatic painting process. This painting and drying process is computer controlled and would provide an improvement in the quality and durability of the finish on all of Woodcraft's painted furniture. The equipment, including its installation, would cost Woodcraft $1,200,000. Talbert Pine has suggested that Woodcraft could finance this with $200,000 from current cash reserves and a loan of $1,000,000 for seven years at an interest rate of 10.5 percent. The loan would be repaid in monthly installments. What is Woodcraft's monthly payment? "Tall" wants you to create a loan payment schedule containing the interest paid, the principal paid, and the ending balance for each month.

Task 1: Build this worksheet.

Task 2: Print the results.

Task 3: Print the cell formulas.

Task 4: Save the worksheet as file WOOD8.

> *Quick check answer:* Monthly Payment = 16860.67

Time Estimates:

Novice: 45 minutes

Intermediate: 30 minutes

Advanced: 15 minutes

(6)   Case: Midwest Universal Gas (second encounter)

Francis Foresight and Mary Derrick have been reviewing Midwest's marketing plans. Midwest has an opportunity to extend its services into Fountain Hills, a major new housing development and office park. This extension would require the purchase and installation of $43,000,000 worth of plant and equipment. Sam Wright has explored several alternatives and suggests that Midwest could finance this expansion with a bond issue. An 11 percent interest rate is available on the 20-year bonds Sam has recommended. Midwest would make annual payments of principal and interest. Sam and Mary want to know Midwest's annual payment for this bond issue.

Task 1: Build this worksheet.

Task 2: Print the results.

Task 3: Print the cell formulas.

Task 4: Save the worksheet as file MUG8.

> *Quick check answer:* Annual Payment = 5399.752 (000s)

Time Estimates

Novice: 30 minutes

Intermediate: 20 minutes

Advanced: 10 minutes

L.7.12   Case Application

Case: **Falcon Industries**

Business Problem: Inventory control

MIS Characteristics: Production
Operational Control

Management Functions: Directing
Controlling

Tools Skills: Formulas
Functions

Falcon Industries (FI) produces process control computers used in production control applications, such as plywood manufacturing, plate glass manufacturing, and steel rolling. These process control computers are specifically designed to operate processes that require the thickness of products made in large sheets to be monitored.

Founded in 1982 by Kurt Bohnhoff, Falcon Industries has experienced rapid growth derived from increasing automation and robotics in manufacturing. Kurt currently serves as the President and Chief Executive Officer of Falcon. As a result of Falcon's explosive growth, Kurt recently embarked on the installation of a new accounting system that includes modules for inventory control and purchasing. However, these two systems will be the last ones installed.

Carlos Mendez, the manufacturing superintendent, is responsible for the final assembly of the line of RB3 process controllers. The RB3 is assembled from parts that are purchased from a variety of suppliers. One of the major problems Carlos faces is having the correct parts on hand for building these computers. Last week, Carlos had to limit production to four hours per day on both the first and second shifts because of a shortage of parts.

Sonja Dalton, the purchasing manager, is responsible for ordering the parts used in the RB3 process controller. Carlos met with Sonja to review the problems he has encountered with stockouts, which require curtailing the assembly operation. Sonja pledged to place orders for items each day, if Carlos would advise her of which ones should be ordered and the appropriate order quantity. They both agreed that orders should be placed to attempt to minimize costs. While the purchase order and inventory control systems were being installed, Carlos consented to creating a spreadsheet for managing the inventory of the most critical items. Each day he would have Sharon Yin, a production expediter, update the current inventory and determine the items to be ordered. Sharon would send a copy of the report to Sonja with the items marked or flagged for reorder. Sonja would then place the necessary orders. That is, Carlos would deploy the worksheet to furnish Sonja with a "programmed decision" of the items to order and their order quantity. Ordering items for manufacturing processes like that of Falcon Industries is a structured or programmed decision that Carlos can implement in an inventory management worksheet.

To assist Carlos in setting up this inventory management system, Sonja organized data on the cost of each item, the number of days for delivery, and the cost of preparing each order. From their annual production plan, Carlos acquired data on the total number of each item that they expected to consume during the next year. He contacted Sarah Wasson in finance and obtained a cost of carrying items in inventory. Sarah's carrying cost considers the costs of borrowing money, providing floor space, obsolescence, and pilferage.

Falcon Industries exploits two general types of inventory management systems—(1) fixed-order quantity and (2) fixed-order interval—described as follows:

- *Fixed-Order Quantity (also known as the economic order quantity).* An order is triggered by the "event" of reaching a specified reorder level. This event takes place at any time, depending solely on when the trigger level of inventory occurs. Fixed-order quantity is a perpetual inventory system that requires continual monitoring of the current level of inventory. Overall, the order quantity is fixed whereas the time between orders varies.

- *Fixed-Order Interval (also knows as fixed-time period, periodic system, and periodic review system).* An order is triggered by the passage of time. At the end of a predetermined time period, an order quantity is computed to bring the inventory up to a required level. An order is then placed for this quantity. The inventory quantities are assessed only at the end of the review period. Overall, the time between orders is fixed, whereas the order quantity varies. This method usually results in larger inventories and their associated costs.

Sonja has been using the fixed-order interval method with the items for the RB3. Once a month she receives a report from the current inventory system and orders parts for the next month. As a result of her meeting with Carlos, she switched to the fixed-order quantity method for the major components of the RB3. This inventory method is the same as that being implemented with their new accounting system.

Carlos and Sonja discussed how maintaining inventory is a balancing act. Ordering in large quantities reduces the cost of ordering, but increases the cost of holding items in inventory. With small orders, the cost of holding items in inventory is reduced, but the cost of ordering is increased. For the fixed-order quantity method, they summarized the cost of inventories as described by the following formula:

$$
\begin{matrix}
\text{Total} & & \text{Annual} & & \text{Annual} & & \text{Annual} \\
\text{annual} & = & \text{cost of} & + & \text{ordering} & + & \text{carrying} \\
\text{cost} & & \text{units} & & \text{cost} & & \text{cost}
\end{matrix}
$$

or

$$
TC = DU + \frac{D}{Q}F + \frac{Q}{2}CU
$$

where

TC = Total annual cost
D = Demand (annual in units)
U = Unit cost
Q = Quantity to be ordered (economic order quantity, EOQ)
F = Fixed cost of placing an order
C = Carrying cost as a percent of unit cost

With this inventory method, the reorder point or level of inventory that triggers an order is

$$
R = dL
$$

where

d = Average daily demand = $D/360$
L = Lead time in days for delivery of an order

The economic order quantity (EOQ), which minimizes the total annual cost, is

$$
Q = \sqrt{\frac{2FD}{CU}}
$$

Carlos agreed to compute this EOQ and reorder point in a worksheet and furnish this to Sonja for issuing the orders. Carlos and Sonja were both confident that their worksheet would solve the problem with stockouts until the new accounting system had been completely installed.

Tasks:

1. Access the EOQ.WK1 worksheet file and examine the data. Review the manner in which Carlos and Sharon laid out the columns for computing the **Daily Demand, Reorder Point, Quantity Available, Reorder Quantity** (EOQ), and **Place Order.** Observe the cells in the upper left area of the worksheet, which contain the **Ordering cost** and **Carrying cost** that apply to all items.

2. Enter formulas for computing the **Daily Demand**, **Reorder Point**, and **Quantity Available**. Carlos wants you to compute the **Daily Demand** based on a 360 day year and rounded to the nearest whole unit. The **Quantity Available** is obtained by adding the **Quantity On-hand** and the **Quantity On-order**. The **Reorder Point** is computed using the equation for this as Carlos had explained it to Sonja.

3. Enter formulas for computing the Reorder Quantity (EOQ). This is computed using the EOQ equation, when the Quantity Available is less than or equal to the Reorder Point; otherwise, the value is set to zero.

4. Enter a formula in the **Place Order** column which displays the label "Y" if an order is placed. Otherwise, a blank is displayed. This allows Sonja to review the report quickly and order the necessary items.

5. Print the report of the results and save the worksheet file. The report should fit on a single page if you have a wide carriage printer or if you use compressed print on a narrow carriage.

6. Write a short summary suggesting improvements to this inventory management system and indicating how this report might be used to explore what-if situations.

Time Estimates

Novice: 75 minutes

Intermediate: 60 minutes

Advanced: 45 minutes

Preparing Forecasts with Regression Analysis

CONTENT

- Regression Analysis for Forecasting
- Performing Regression Analysis
- A Growth Rate Representational Model
- When Things Go Wrong

L.8.1 Regression Analysis for Forecasting

Chris and Kim want to extend the business plan for Good Morning Products to be a five-year plan. They have been discussing how they might determine the number of bottles of Liquid Gold that would be sold in each of the next five years. If they could determine this sales forecast, then it could be used as the base for expanding their business plan. First, they need to analyze past sales to create a **representational model** of sales in bottles. Second, the representational model can be used to forecast future sales. Lotus 1-2-3 provides them with these capabilities by using the Data Regression commands.

Regression analysis is a statistical technique that "fits" a straight line to a series of historical or actual data values. With regression, you "discover" a straight line that best matches your actual or observed data. This linear regression produces an equation that can be used as a representational model to project estimates of possible future results. The general equation for a simple linear regression line is

$$Y = mX + b$$

where Y = dependent variable
X = independent variable
m = slope of line
b = intercept constant

For their analysis, Kim and Chris have identified annual sales in bottles as the dependent variable. This is the one they would like to project into the future. They

YEAR	SALES (liters in thousands)
1	294
2	311
3	333
4	346
5	362
6	397
7	422
8	436
9	475
10	489

FIGURE L.119. Historical data collected for analysis.

will use time in years as the independent variable. So their general regression line equation is

$$\text{SALES} = m * (\text{YEAR}) + b$$

with b — independent variable, SALES — dependent variable

Chris compiled data on **SALES** of Liquid Gold during the past 10 years (Figure L.119). These data for Good Morning Products are used to discover the slope (m) and intercept (b) of a regression line, which is then applied to forecast future sales.

L.8.2   Performing Regression Analysis

Chris and Kim will analyze the data for yearly **SALES** shown in Figure L.119 as a means of forecasting future **SALES.** In performing their analysis, they will fit a straight line to these data. A key question they need to answer is how closely does the fitted regression line match their data. Although Kim and Chris realize that the **R-squared** value of a regression analysis indicates this fit, Frosty needs a picture to show him how well the calculated or estimated regression line matches the actual data. Chris will produce a graph as part of this analysis so that he can review the quality of the line with Frosty. Since Chris and Kim are interested in a five-year projection, they will include these data in the initial data setup shown in Figure L.120.

Chris considers the activities that are necessary to carry out this regression analysis and prepares his work plan.

1. Enter actual historical data in the worksheet.

2. Perform the regression analysis, calculating the slope (m) and intercept (b).

3. Calculate estimated values using the slope (m) and intercept (b) from the regression results.

4. Graph the actual and estimated data values to visually review the regression results.

5. Calculate the five-year forecast using the regression equation.

6. Graph the actual data together with the five-year forecast to view the historical and anticipated future sales.

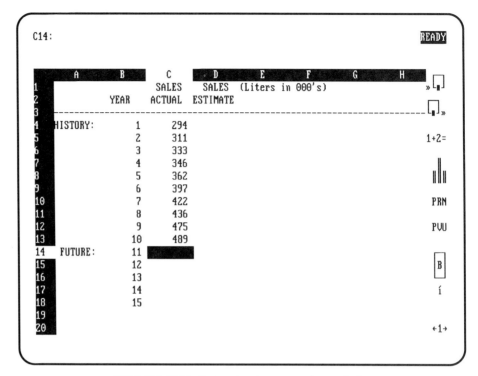

FIGURE L.120. Data setup for regression analysis.

Let's do each of these activities to perform the analysis for Chris and Kim. The first step is to enter the actual historical data in the worksheet. The data in Figure L.119 are entered into a worksheet, as illustrated in Figure L.120.

To set up the worksheet with data for the regression analysis	**Action:** Obtain a "clean" worksheet.
	Action: Enter the data values and labels as illustrated in Figure L.120.

The second step is to actually carry out the regression analysis on their data.

To perform the regression analysis	**Press:** /	Access main menu
	Select: Data	Desired activity
	Select: Regression	Desired option

A Regression Settings dialog box appears (Figure L.121) to display the current settings for the regression analysis. Let's specify these settings.

Select:	X-Range	Specify *independent* variable **YEAR**
Move to:	**B4**	Top of range
Press:	.	Anchor
Move to:	**B13**	Expand highlight to specify range
Press:	\<Enter\>	Complete X-Range specification
Select:	Y-Range	Specify *dependent* variable **SALES**
Move to:	**C4**	Top of range
Press:	.	Anchor

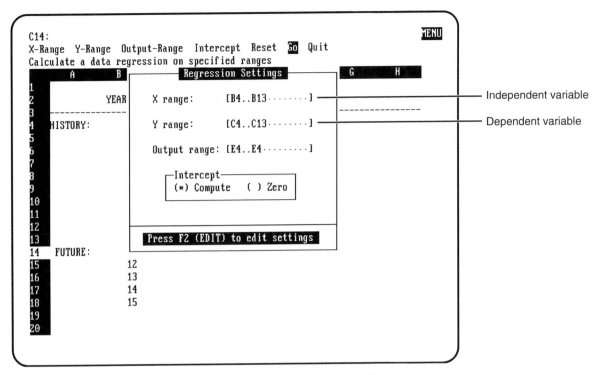

FIGURE L.121. Regression settings.

Move to:	C13	Expand highlight to specify range
Press:	\<Enter\>	Complete Y-Range specification
Select:	Output-Range	This is the upper-left corner of range where results of regression analysis will be placed by 1-2-3
Move to:	E4	Upper-left corner cell of location; this should be an empty area
Press:	\<Enter\>	Complete specification

This completes the specification of the input data and where the regression results will be placed.

Now the regression can be performed on the selected data.

To cause the regression to be calculated and the results displayed

Select:	Go	Regression is processed

Results of this regression are shown in Figure L.122 in the range **E4..H12**. The "Constant" of **263.8** is the intercept (*b*), while the "X Coefficient" of **22.30909** is the slope (*m*) of the line. The "R-Squared" of **0.988953** indicates a very, very good match between the actual data and the regression line, since 1.000 represents a perfect match and zero indicates no match at all.

The third step is calculating the **SALES ESTIMATE** column by using the intercept (*b*) and slope (*m*) determined from the regression. This will allow them to plot the data for Frosty's inspection. Let's calculate the **SALES ESTIMATE** by using the regression equation.

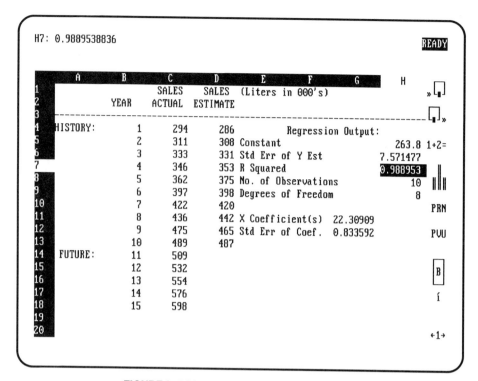

FIGURE L.122. Results of regression analysis.

To develop the formula for calculating the estimate for YEAR 1	**Move to:**	**D4**
	Enter:	@ROUND(+$G$11*B4+$H$5,0)

This is the equation using the slope from **G11** and the intercept from **H5**; the absolute references to these cells will assist in copying them for use with the other years of the forecast

The @ROUND is used so that all values are computed and displayed as integers. Also, these integer values are more readily used as data labels on a graph. For these reasons, Chris and Kim prefer to use the @ROUND function rather than the / Range Format Fixed 0 (/RFF0) command.

To calculate the **SALES ESTIMATE** for the other years	**Action:** Copy the formula in **D4** into **D5..D13** for the estimates.

The fourth step is to create a graph that compares the **SALES ACTUAL** to the **SALES ESTIMATE** as a means of reviewing the quality of the regression line to forecast future sales. Now let's develop this graph.

To create a graph that compares the actual and estimated **SALES** for the past 10 years	**Action:** Create a graph as defined by the Graph Settings in Figure L.123. Include the titles on this graph as shown in the completed graph in Figure L.124.

The graph in Figure L.124 shows the relationship between the **SALES ACTUAL** and the **SALES ESTIMATE.** Because these two lines closely match, Frosty is convinced that the regression line provides a good representational model for projecting the future **SALES** of Liquid Gold.

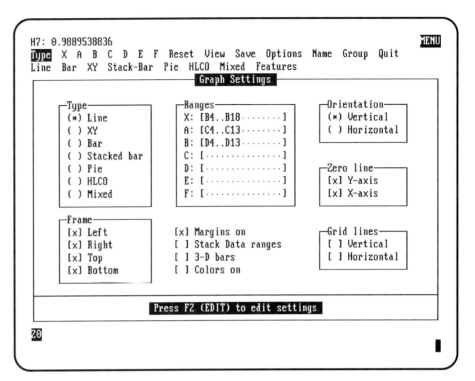

FIGURE L.123. Graph settings for results of regression analysis.

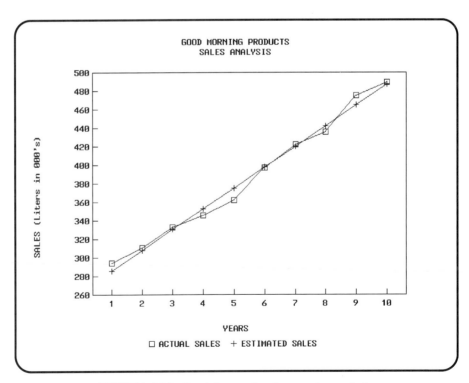

FIGURE L.124. Graph for results of regression analysis.

The fifth step can now be performed by calculating the forecast **SALES** for years 11 through 15. These estimates of the future **SALES** are placed in the same column as the **SALES ACTUAL** for the prior 10 years. This will allow Kim and Chris to develop a graph that is *a single line* that combines the 10 years of historical data with the 5-year forecast. It is necessary to place these data in the same column so that they are located in the *same data range* for graphing as a single line. Let's enter the formulas for calculating the forecast **SALES.**

<table>
<tr><td>To calculate the **SALES** for the first year of the forecast</td><td>**Move to:**</td><td>**C14**</td><td>First year of forecast</td></tr>
<tr><td></td><td>**Enter:**</td><td>@ROUND(+$G$11*B14+$H$5,0)</td><td></td></tr>
</table>

This is the equation using the slope from **G11** and the intercept from **H5**

To calculate the forecast **SALES** for the next four years

Action: Copy the formula in **C14** into **C15..C18** for next four years of the forecast.

When these estimates are placed in column **B** with the **SALES ACTUAL,** the data are arranged for creating a graph with a single line. This permits Kim and Chris to develop a graph that combines the historical data with the forecast data, as portrayed in Figure L.125.

The sixth step is actually creating the graph of actual and future **SALES** as a *single line.* Let's prepare this graph.

To produce the graph combining actual and future **SALES**

Action: Create a graph with a single line showing the **SALES ACTUAL** for the first 10 years and SALES FORECAST for the next 5 years, as defined by the Graph Settings in Figure L.126. Include the titles on this graph as shown by the graph in Figure L.125.

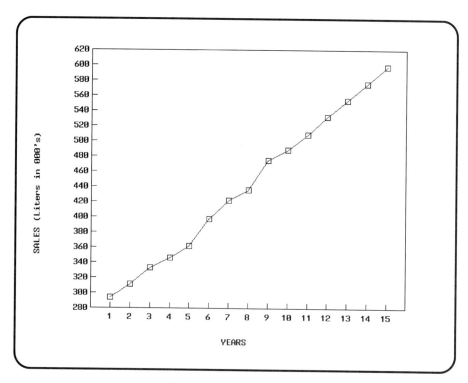

FIGURE L.125. Sales forecast.

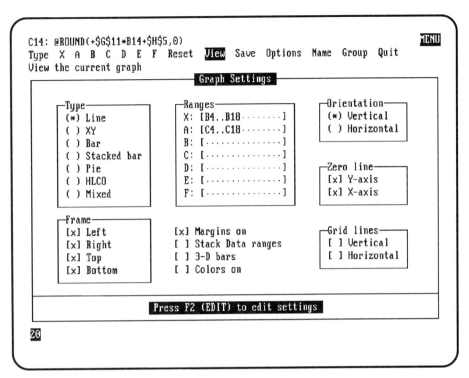

```
C14: @ROUND(+$G$11*B14+$H$5,0)                                    MENU
Type  X  A  B  C  D  E  F  Reset  View  Save  Options  Name  Group  Quit
View the current graph
                          ┌─────Graph Settings─────┐
  ┌─Type──────────┐  ┌─Ranges───────────┐  ┌─Orientation──┐
  │ (*) Line      │  │ X: [B4..B18·······] │  │ (*) Vertical │
  │ ( ) XY        │  │ A: [C4..C18·······] │  │ ( ) Horizontal│
  │ ( ) Bar       │  │ B: [··············] │  └──────────────┘
  │ ( ) Stacked bar│ │ C: [··············] │
  │ ( ) Pie       │  │ D: [··············] │  ┌─Zero line────┐
  │ ( ) HLCO      │  │ E: [··············] │  │ [x] Y-axis   │
  │ ( ) Mixed     │  │ F: [··············] │  │ [x] X-axis   │
  └───────────────┘  └──────────────────┘  └──────────────┘

  ┌─Frame─────┐
  │ [x] Left  │    [x] Margins on         ┌─Grid lines───┐
  │ [x] Right │    [ ] Stack Data ranges  │ [ ] Vertical │
  │ [x] Top   │    [ ] 3-D bars           │ [ ] Horizontal│
  │ [x] Bottom│    [ ] Colors on          └──────────────┘
  └───────────┘

            ┌──Press F2 (EDIT) to edit settings──┐

 20
```

FIGURE L.126. Graph settings for sales forecast.

Chris and Kim have completed the analysis they need to establish a representational model for preparing the **SALES** forecast for Good Morning Products.

Action: Print a report of the regression analysis.

Action: Print a list of cell formulas.

Action: Save this as PLAN15.

Action: Name, save, and print both of these graphs containing the actual, estimated, and future sales.

L.8.3   A Growth Rate Representational Model

Kim and Chris selected a business model with a constant amount of increase each year (also known as a linear change) for their initial analysis. That is, the same increase amount is added to each prior year's estimated value to arrive at the next year's estimated value, as illustrated in Figure L.127. After further discussion with

Projection

	YEAR 1	YEAR 2	YEAR 3	YEAR 4	YEAR 5
SALES	100	110	120	130	140

Equation

SALES = 100, PREVIOUS SALES + 10 FOR 4 columns

FIGURE L.127. Constant amount (linear) change projection technique.

Projection

	YEAR 1	YEAR 2	YEAR 3	YEAR 4	YEAR 5
SALES	100	110	121	133	146

Equation

SALES = 100, PREVIOUS SALES * (1 + .10) FOR 4 columns

FIGURE L.128. Constant growth rate projection technique.

Frosty, they believe that a growth rate model, as illustrated in Figure L.128, may be a better representation. A **growth rate** is a compounded increase from year to year. Many business situations are described by growth rates. These include salary increases, interest rates, and inflation rates. A comparison of a growth rate of 10 percent to a linear increase of $10 is illustrated in Figure L.129.

To obtain a growth rate representational model, Kim and Chris need to use natural logarithms. The regression is performed on the natural logarithm of the sales data. Then estimated values are determined by using the regression equation. Since these estimates are a natural logarithm, they must be converted back to regular scalar data values of the **SALES ESTIMATE.** The @LN and @EXP functions provide Chris with a convenient method of converting the initial sales data to natural logarithms and then converting them back to the desired estimated sales values. Chris carried out these operations to produce the worksheet shown in Figure L.130, which makes use of the equations displayed in Figure L.131.

Chris performed the regression using the year in column **A** as the **independent** variable and the LN(SALES) in column **C** (the natural logarithm of the sales) as the **dependent** variable. The LN(SALES) ESTIMATE in column **D** is computed by using the regression equation Constant (*b*) and X Coefficient (*m*) in the same manner as

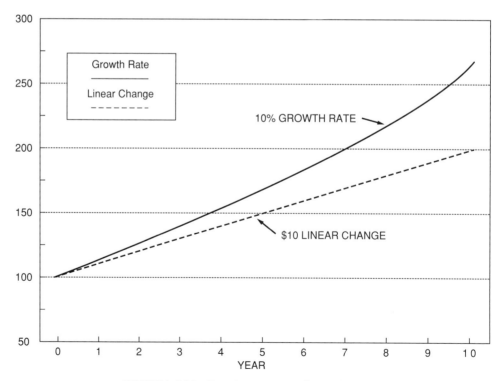

FIGURE L.129. Growth rate versus linear change.

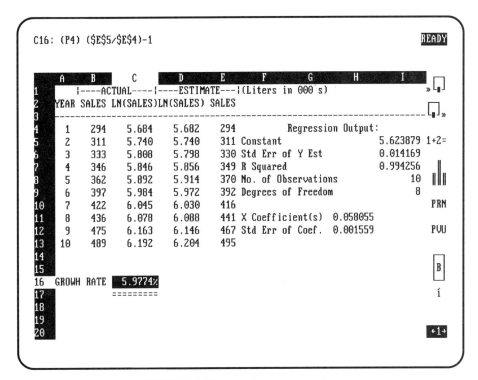

FIGURE L.130. Growth rate regression.

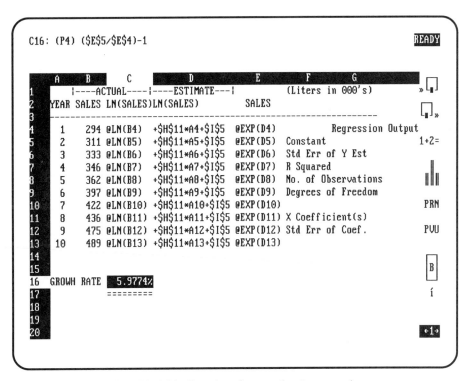

FIGURE L.131. Equations for growth rate regression.

for the linear analysis described in the previous section. These natural logarithms are converted to the ESTIMATED SALES by using the @EXP function. The key equations are as follows:

Cell	Formula	Description
C4	@LN(B4)	Log transformation
D4	+$ H$11*A4+$I$5	Regression line equation
E4	@EXP(D4)	Scalar transformation
C16	(E5/E4) − 1	Growth rate equation

The equation in **C16** is used to obtain the growth rate as a ratio between the **SALES ESTIMATE** data values of two adjacent years. The value one (1) is subtracted to obtain the growth rate from the multiplier applied from one time period to the next.

Chris summarized a work plan for performing the regression analysis to determine the annual growth rate in **SALES.**

1. Enter actual historical data in the worksheet.
2. Transform the linear **ACTUAL SALES** data to natural logarithms by using the @LN function.
3. Perform the regression analysis with **YEARS** as the independent variable and the natural log of **ACTUAL SALES** as the dependent variable to calculate the slope (m) and intercept (b).
4. Calculate the **ESTIMATED SALES** values as natural logarithms by using the slope (m) and intercept (b) from the regression results.
5. Transform the natural log **ESTIMATED SALES** values to linear **ESTIMATED SALES** values using the @EXP function.
6. Calculate the **GROWTH RATE** by using any two adjacent linear **ESTIMATED SALES** values.

Let's perform each of these activities in determining the **GROWTH RATE** of **SALES** for Liquid Gold. The first step is to enter the actual historical data in the worksheet.

To set up the worksheet data for the regression analysis

Action: Obtain a "clean" worksheet. Using Figure L.130, enter the labels in rows **1** through **3**. Then enter the data values in columns **A** and **B**. If desired, you may access your PLAN15 worksheet and modify it as necessary.

Now do the second step and perform the natural log transformation.

To transform the linear actual sales to natural logarithms

Action: Enter the formula **@LN(B4)** in cell **C4** and then copy this formula into cells **C5..C13.**

The third step does the regression analysis on the transformed sales data.

To perform the regression analysis

Action: Specify the X-range, Y-range, and Output range as shown by the Regression Settings in Figure L.132. If you accessed PLAN15 as your starting point, then use the / Data Regression Reset (/DRR) command to remove your previous Regression Settings before you enter the new settings. When you have the Regression Settings specified, then select Go to calculate the regression results.

The fourth step is calculating the **LN(SALES)** by using the intercept (b) and the slope (m) determined from the regression analysis.

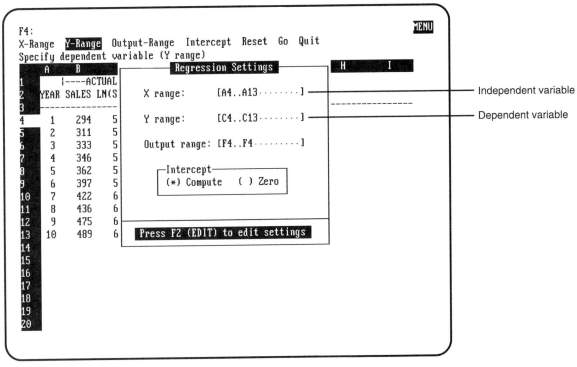

FIGURE L.132. Regression settings for growth rate.

To calculate the LN(SALES) using the regression equation

Action: Enter the formula **+$H$11 ∗ A4 + $I$5** in cell **D4** and then copy this formula into cells **D5..D13.**

The fifth step transforms the natural log values for the **SALES ESTIMATE** to linear data values.

To transform the natural log sales estimates to a linear scale

Action: Enter the formula **@EXP(D4)** in cell **E4** and then copy this formula into cells **E5..E13.**

The sixth step calculates the growth rate by using the **SALES ESTIMATE** in any two adjacent years.

To calculate the growth rate

Action: Enter the label **GROWTH RATE** in cell **A16.** In cell **C16,** enter the formula **(E5/E4) −1,** which calculates the sales growth rate by using the **ESTIMATED SALES** data values for the first two years.

Your results should be the same as those in Figure L.130. The growth rate model produces a higher "R-squared," indicating that this is a better "fit" or representation of the sales relationship. Kim and Chris are convinced that the growth rate model is the better representation for the sales forecast. Frosty concurs with this assessment and supports their decision to use this growth rate of 5.9774 percent for their sales forecast for the next five years.

L.8.4   When Things Go Wrong

Some difficulties may occur when you are performing regression analysis and computing estimated values. Some of the more common situations are described here.

1. You just finished calculating the regression and discover that you used the **wrong** range for the independent or dependent variable. The wrong column or row of data is easily selected when your worksheet contains several columns or rows of data.

   a. Reexecute the / Data Regression (/DR) command.

   b. Carefully specify the desired ranges of data. Pointing should be used to help ensure that the correct data ranges are specified.

   c. Use the same output range. No change is required.

   d. Select Go to compute your regression. Lotus 1-2-3 replaces the old results with your new results. You do not need to erase the old results before you redo the regression.

2. You added the formulas to your worksheet to compute the estimated values by using your regression equation. The value appears correct in the cell where you entered the formula for calculating the estimate. However, in the cells where you copied the formula, these other estimated values appear to be wrong and a number of them are zeros. This usually occurs when you have used relative referencing in the formula for the estimated value, rather than absolute referencing.

   a. Inspect the cell where you entered the initial formula for calculating an estimated value by using the regression equation. Confirm the use of relative referencing.

   b. Edit the formula for computing the estimated value, changing the references to absolute for cells containing the slope (m) and intercept (b) of the regression equation.

   c. Copy the formula with absolute referencing into the other cells where you want the estimated values to reside.

L.8.5   Lesson Summary

- Regression analysis is a statistical technique in which a straight line is "fitted" to a series of data points. The line is described by its slope (m) and intercept (b).

- Separate data ranges are identified for the dependent and independent variables of the regression equation.

- Results of the regression analysis are stored in an output range, which is a convenient blank area of your worksheet.

- The "R-squared" value of the regression analysis indicates how well the computed regression line matches up with the actual data values. A value of 1.000 indicates a perfect match, whereas a value of zero indicates that a line cannot be "fitted" to the data values. The closer an "R-squared" is to one, the better the "fit."

- The slope (m) and intercept (b) obtained from a regression analysis provide a representational model that can be applied to forecast future results.

- A growth rate representational model is an alternative for "fitting" a series of data points to a line that represents compound growth from one time period to the next.

- A growth rate regression requires a transformation that is implemented by the application of natural logarithms using the @LN function. The @EXP function is used to obtain the antilogarithm.
- A growth rate often yields a better representational model that matches the manner in which managers frequently think about changes into the future when planning and discussing sales increases, salary increases, interest rates, and price changes.

L.8.6   Practice Tutorial

(1)   Develop the PLAN15 worksheet with the linear regression described in this Lesson in Section L.8.2 as a guided activity in a hands-on manner.

Task 1: Create the worksheet and perform the regression analysis.

Task 2: Print the results, as illustrated in Figure L.122.

Task 3: Save this as worksheet file MYPLAN15.

Time Estimates

Novice: 35 minutes

Intermediate: 25 minutes

Advanced: 15 minutes

(2)   Develop the growth rate worksheet described in this Lesson in Section L.8.3.

Task 1: Create the worksheet and perform the regression analysis.

Task 2: Print the results, as illustrated in Figure L.130.

Task 3: Save this as worksheet file MYPLAN16.

Time Estimates

Novice: 45 minutes

Intermediate: 30 minutes

Advanced: 20 minutes

L.8.7   Practice Exercises

(1)   **Case: Inland Container (second encounter)**

Mary Montoya reviewed her customer accounts and discovered that U-Stor-It seemed to have similar requirements and business plans as those for Rydder Truck Rental. By analyzing U-Stor-It's sales, Mary believes that she can determine the demand pattern for Rydder Truck. Mary extracted and recorded the data for U-Stor-It as follows:

CONTRACT MONTH	UNITS SOLD	CONTRACT MONTH	UNITS SOLD	CONTRACT MONTH	UNITS SOLD
1	119302	6	140239	11	166518
2	128058	7	144796	12	174944
3	130959	8	153924	13	173221
4	131796	9	154061	14	179168
5	141810	10	157418	15	187258

> *Task 1:* Build the worksheet containing Mary's data for U-Stor-It. Perform a regression analysis for a linear model.
>
> *Task 2:* Print the results. Circle the R-squared value. Is this a "good" representation model? Why?
>
> *Task 3:* Save this as worksheet file STLINE.
>
> > *Quick check answers:* Intercept = 115545.7
> >
> > Slope = 4585.7

Time Estimates

Novice: 45 minutes

Intermediate: 30 minutes

Advanced: 20 minutes

(2)   Case: Inland Container (continued)

Mary thinks that a growth rate for U-Stor-It's Units Sold may provide a better representational model. Using the data in Case 1 above, determine the growth rate for **Units Sold.**

> *Task 1:* Modify the STLINE worksheet and perform the regression analysis for a growth rate model. Include a cell in your worksheet that contains the growth rate determined from this representational model.
>
> *Task 2:* Print the results. Circle the R-squared value. Is this better or worse than that for the linear change model? Why?
>
> *Task 3:* Save this as your GROWTH worksheet file.
>
> > *Quick check answer:* Growth Rate = 3.0738%

Time Estimates

Novice: 45 minutes

Intermediate: 30 minutes

Advanced: 20 minutes

(3)   Case: Inland Container (continued)

Mary's divisional manager has asked her to explain the representational model for U-Stor-It from the regression analysis in case 1 above. To do this, she needs to compute the estimated number of units sold for each month by using the regression equation determined in case 1. Then, she can prepare a graph that contains a plot of the Actual and Estimated Units Sold. This should help her explain to her manager how well the regression line matches up with the actual data.

> *Task 1:* Access your STLINE worksheet file from (1) above.
>
> *Task 2:* Add a column to the worksheet that contains the calculated estimates by using the regression equation.
>
> *Task 3:* Print the results showing both the actual and estimated **Units Sold.**
>
> *Task 4:* Create a graph containing the actual and estimated **Units Sold.** Use titles to appropriately identify your graph. Print a hard copy of the graph.
>
> *Task 5:* Save this as worksheet file REGPLOT.

Time Estimates

Novice: 45 minutes

Intermediate: 30 minutes

Advanced: 20 minutes

(4)   Case: Wheels In Motion Manufacturing

Business Problem: Cost analysis

MIS Characteristics: Finance

Managerial Control

Wheels In Motion Manufacturing (WIMM) produces custom aluminum wheels for sport/utility vehicles and light trucks. Jackie Wright, a senior cost analyst, is preparing a report for WIMM's comptroller, describing the behavior pattern of maintenance costs. As a common practice, Jackie uses the equation of a straight line as one method for determining the fixed and variable cost components for manufacturing wheels. The intercept of the line represents the fixed costs, and the slope of the line indicates the variable cost per unit of production. Jackie has gathered data regarding the **Machine Hours** of production, the number of **Units Produced,** and the **Maintenance Costs** each month for the past 20 months. She entered this data in the WHEELS.WK1 worksheet file for her analysis of maintenance costs. The comptroller asked her to perform the cost analysis for review at next Wednesday's meeting with the vice president of manufacturing.

Task 1: Retrieve the WHEELS.WK1 worksheet file from your Data Disk and review Jackie's data for her cost analysis.

Task 2: Using the **Machine Hours** as the independent variable and the **Maintenance Costs** as the dependent variable, carry out the regression analysis. Save this as the WHEELS1 worksheet file.

Task 3: Print the results containing both Jackie's input data and your regression. What is the fixed cost? What is the variable cost per **Machine Hour?** How well does this straight-line equation explain the **Maintenance Costs?** Circle and identify these three values on your printout.

Task 4: Using the **Units Produced** as the independent variable and the **Maintenance Costs** as the dependent variable, carry out the regression analysis. Save this as the WHEELS2 worksheet file.

Task 5: Print the results for this second analysis displaying both Jackie's input data and your regression. What is the fixed cost? What is the variable cost per **Unit Produced?** How well does this straight-line equation explain the **Maintenance Costs?** Circle and identify these three values on your printout.

Task 6: (*Optional*)   Write a paragraph describing which cost analysis provides the "best" estimate of the fixed and variable **Maintenance Costs.**

Task 7: (*Optional*)   Create a graph of the **Maintenance Costs** and the **Machine Hours.** Retrieve the WHEELS1 worksheet file as your starting point. Add a column to your worksheet that contains the estimated Maintenance Costs which are calculated from the equation of the straight line. Prepare an *XY* graph with the **Machine Hours** as the X-range, the Actual **Maintenance Costs** as the A-range, and the Estimated **Maintenance Costs** as the B-range. Set the Graph Options Format A to Symbols; otherwise, these points on your graph will be connected by a strange-looking line that seems to zigzag randomly about your graph. Label the X-axis as "Machine Hours" and the Y-axis as "Maintenance Costs." Place the title "MAINTENANCE COST

ANALYSIS" at the top of your graph. Save the *.PIC file. Save this revised WHEELS1 worksheet file. Produce a hard copy of your graph.

Task 8. (*Optional*)   Create a second graph of the **Maintenance Costs** and **Units Produced.** Retrieve the WHEELS2 worksheet file as your starting point. To this worksheet, add a column with the Estimated **Maintenance Costs** computed from the equation of the straight line. Prepare an *XY* graph like that in Task 7 above, but with the X-range assigned the **Units Produced.** Title the X-Range "Units Produced" and use the other titles as indicated above. Save this modified WHEELS2 worksheet file. Save the *.PIC file for the graph and produce a hard copy of your graph.

Time Estimates

Novice: 90 minutes

Intermediate: 60 minutes

Advanced: 45 minutes

(5)   Case: Outback Electronics Manufacturing

Business Problem: Production forecasting
MIS Characteristics: Production/Operations
Strategic Planning

Outback Electronics Manufacturing (OEM) produces a variety of personal consumer electronic products. One of their hottest selling items is the Gran Sport portable stereo radio and cassette tape player for joggers. The Gran Sport is extremely lightweight and durable. It readily withstands the jolting abuse of the most serious joggers.

Nina Kim is the production manager responsible for manufacturing the Gran Sport. OEM's production line has the capacity for producing up to 12,000 Gran Sports per month before a second production line would need to be added. The Gran Sport was first marketed at the beginning of the year, and demand has remained strong for the past 12 months. Nina is concerned that, if demand continues to increase, OEM will exceed its production capacity. To analyze her situation, she has gathered data on the number of Gran Sports produced in each of the past 12 months and entered this in her OEM.WK1 worksheet.

Task 1: Access the OEM.WK1 worksheet file from your Data Disk and review Nina's production data for the past 12 months.

Task 2: Using regression analysis, develop a linear change representational model. Use the equation of the straight line for this regression to calculate the **Estimated Production** in units for the past 12 months. Then, apply the same equation to project the expected production for each of the next 12 months. What is the expected number of Gran Sports that need to be produced in December 19X2? What is the R-squared for this representational model? Will OEM exceed its production capacity by the end of 19X2?

Task 3: Print the results for your linear change representational model. Save this as the OEM_LC worksheet file.

Task 4: (*Optional*)   Develop a graph that compares the **Actual Production** in units to the **Estimated Production** in units for the past 12 months. Include appropriate titles on your graph. Identify this graph with the range name LASTYR. Print a hard copy of the graph.

Task 5: (*Optional*)   Develop a graph that contains a single line showing the past 12 months of production and the expected production for the next 12 months. Identify this graph with the range name NEXTYR. Print a hard copy of the graph. Save your worksheet as the OEM_LC file.

Task 6: (*Optional*)   Retrieve the OEM.WK1 worksheet for a fresh start. Using regression analysis develop a growth rate representational model. Use the equation from this regression to calculate the **Estimated Production** in units for the past 12 months. Then, compute the compounded growth rate from any two appropriate estimates. Apply your computed growth rate to obtain the expected production for each of the next 12 months. Print a report of the results and save this as the OEM_GR worksheet file. What is the expected number of Gran Sports that need to be produced in December 19X2? What is the R-squared for this representational model? Is it better or worse than that for the linear change representational model? If OEM's production growth follows this model, will they exceed their production capacity by the end of 19X2?

Task 7: (*Optional*)   Develop a graph that compares the **Actual Production** in units to the **Estimated Production** in units for the past 12 months for your growth rate representation model. Identify this graph with the range name LASTYR_G. Print a hard copy of this graph.

Task 8: (*Optional*) Develop a graph that contains a single line showing the past 12 months of production and the expected production for the next 12 months based on your growth rate model. Identify this graph with the range name NEXTYR_G. Print a hard copy of the graph. Save your worksheet as the OEM_GR file.

Time Estimates

Novice: 90 minutes

Intermediate: 60 minutes

Advanced: 45 minutes

(6)   Case: Barney, Upjohn and Moody Investments

Business Problem: Stock performance beta
MIS Characteristics: Finance
                              Strategic Planning

Ricardo Sussman is a rising star portfolio analyst at Barney, Upjohn and Moody Investments. Ric uses the beta coefficient as a measure of relative performance of the stocks selected for inclusion in the portfolio he manages. A stock's beta is a number that compares the stock's return to those of a broad-based market index of stocks. When a line is plotted with the Market Index as the independent variable and an individual stock's return as the dependent variable, the beta is the slope of the line. A stock's return includes both its dividend yield and its price appreciation. A beta of 1.0 indicates that the returns on an individual stock are exactly the same as those for the market index. A beta of 0.5 indicates that the individual stock's return increases (decreases) one half as fast as the market index. That is, a 10 percent increase in the market index return would result in a 5 percent increase in the return of the individual stock. On the other hand, for a stock with a beta of 2.0, a 10 percent increase in the market index return is expected to produce a 20 percent increase in the return on the individual stock.

Although *Value Line Investment Surveys* regularly compute and publish individual stock beta estimates, Ric has a special need to determine the beta for Ford Motor. His sense of the stock market in preparing special analyses such as this has been a key factor in his success at Barney, Upjohn and Moody. Ric collected the **Percentage Rate of Return** data for both the **Ford Motor** Company and the Standard and Poor's

500 **Market Index.** He entered this year-end data for each of the last 10 years in his BETA.WK1 worksheet file in preparation for computing Ford Motor's beta.

Task 1: Retrieve the BETA.WK1 worksheet file from your Data Disk and review Ric's data of the **Percentage Rate of Return** for **Ford Motor** and the S&P 500 **Market Index.**

Task 2: Using the **Market Index** as the independent variable and the **Ford Motor** return as the dependent variable, perform the regression analysis.

Task 3: Print the results containing both Ric's input data and your regression. What is Ford Motor's beta? Circle this on your printout. (*Hint:* The beta is the slope of the regression line.)

Task 4: (*Optional*)   Continuing with the **Market Index** as the independent variable, compute the expected percentage rate of return for Ford Motor by using the regression equation. That is, each data value of the Market Index is used to compute a corresponding expected rate of return for Ford Motor. Locate these Estimated rates of return to the right of the **Market Index** column in your worksheet. Prepare an *XY* graph of these results with the **Market Index** as the X-range, the *actual* **Ford Motor** rates of return as the A-range, and the *estimated* **Ford Motor** rates of return as the B-range. Set the Graph Options Format A to Symbols; otherwise, the points on your graph will be connected by a line and your graph will look like a plate full of spaghetti. Label the X-axis "Percentage Rate of Return (Market Index)" and the Y-axis "Percentage Rate of Return (Ford Motor)." Place "CHARACTERISTIC LINE FOR FORD MOTOR" as a title at the top of your graph. Save the *.PIC file and the BETA.WK1 file. Produce a hard copy of this graph.

Time Estimates

Novice: 60 minutes

Intermediate: 45 minutes

Advanced: 30 minutes

L.8.8   Comprehensive Problems

(1)   Case: Woodcraft Furniture Company (second encounter)

Martha Goodguess, the director of marketing at Woodcraft, has collected data on the annual number of households nationwide and Woodcraft's sales of tables. She would like you to analyze these data for developing a forecast of future tables sales.

HOUSEHOLDS (in millions)	TABLES SOLD
39.2	5505
40.8	5911
40.9	6603
41.6	6711
41.7	6924
42.0	7803
42.2	8221
42.9	8423
43.0	9321
43.3	9924

(a) Martha wants you to perform a regression analysis on these data to develop a representational model that can be applied to forecast future table sales. Is this a "good" representational model? Why or why not?

(b) To assist Joe Birch in understanding this representational model, Martha wants you to calculate the estimated tables sold from the regression equation, and then graph the actual tables sold and the estimated tables sold. (*Hint:* Use an *XY* graph with households as the X-Range.)

(c) Martha has obtained the following estimates of the number of households for the next five years from the Data Resources Institute. She wants you to apply the regression model from (a) to forecast table sales for each of the next five years.

HOUSEHOLDS
(in millions)

44.6
45.9
47.3
48.7
50.2

Analyze the historical data and prepare a forecast by performing these tasks:

Task 1. Construct a worksheet containing the actual data.

Task 2. Perform the regression analysis described in (a).

Task 3. Produce the graph (*optional*) and the forecast as requested in (b) and (c).

Task 4. Print the results and the graph.

Task 5. Save this as worksheet file WOOD9.

> *Quick check answers:* (a) Intercept $= -38168.7$
> Slope $= 1094.4$
>
> (c) Estimated Tables Sold [50.2] $= 16772$

Time Estimates

Novice: 60 minutes

Intermediate: 45 minutes

Advanced: 30 minutes

(2) Case: Midwest Universal Gas (second encounter)

Francis Foresight, the marketing director at Midwest Universal Gas, has collected the following data on the Total **Gas Sales** during the past 10 years. He would like you to analyze these data and develop a representational model of **Gas Sales** that can be used to forecast future **Gas Sales.**

YEAR	GAS SALES (in BCF)[a]	YEAR	GAS SALES (in BCF)[a]
1	457	6	586
2	498	7	636
3	511	8	651
4	527	9	663
5	541	10	719

[a]BCF = billions of cubic feet.

(a) Francis wants you to perform a regression analysis on these data to develop a forecast model that can be applied to future Gas Sales. Is this a "good" representational model? Why or why not?

(b) To assist Mary Derrick and Sam Wright in understanding this representational model, Francis wants you to calculate the estimated **Gas Sales** from the regression equation and graph the actual **Gas Sales** with the estimated **Gas Sales** for the 10-year period.

(c) Now Francis and Mary want you to apply the regression model from (a) to forecast **Gas Sales** for each of the next five years.

(d) Sam would like you to use regression analysis to determine the **growth rate** of **Gas Sales** for the last 10 years. Is this a "better" representational model than that from (a)? Why or why not?

Analyze the historical data and prepare a forecast for Midwest Universal Gas by performing these tasks:

Task 1. Construct a worksheet containing the actual data.

Task 2. Perform the regression analysis as described in (a).

Task 3. Produce the graph and the forecast as requested in (b) and (c).

Task 4. Print the results and the graph.

Task 5. Save this as worksheet file MUG9.

Task 6. Use the @LN and @EXP functions and regression analysis to determine the growth rate as described in (d).

Task 7. Print this result.

Task 8. Save this as worksheet file MUG9GR.
  Quick check answers: (a) Intercept = 426.1
                              Slope = 27.8

  (c) Estimated Gas Sales [year 15] = 843

  (d) Growth rate = .0493   or   4.93%

Time Estimates

Novice: 60 minutes

Intermediate: 45 minutes

Advanced: 30 minutes

L.8.9   Case Application

Case: Northwest Orient Airlines

  Business Problem: Forecasting
  MIS Characteristics :Marketing
                    Strategic Planning
  Management Functions: Planning
                    Organizing
  Tools Skills: Regression analysis
                    Graphics

Northwest Airlines (NWA) has been expanding its hub operations at the Kansas City International Airport (MCI) during the past dozen years. The location of Kansas City in the heartland of the United States makes it a desirable location for connecting flights for both east–west and north–south air traffic. Jonathan "Jon" Swanberg, Director of Marketing Analysis, is assessing the future demand for airport services that would support the continuation of expanding aircraft operations through this airport. Scott Govin, NWA's Vice President of Marketing, has requested that Jon assess the possibilities of MCI's capacity and expansion, which have impact on marketing and route expansion plans for all of NWA. At MCI the average delay per aircraft has only been two to three minutes since NWA started this hub operation. This is considerably less than at many other airports and contributes to NWA's on-time performance record.

Airport capacity and the associated delays are becoming increasingly important to the Federal Aviation Administration (FAA) as well as to NWA. NWA, like most other airlines, has adopted the "hub" concept since the deregulation of aviation in 1979. Under the hub concept, the aircraft for a particular airline tend to converge on an airport at the same time. Passengers get off one aircraft and get on another to continue their journey. Hubs have added to the traffic saturation at most larger airports, resulting in airlines exceeding airport capacity, experiencing delays, and increasing airborne holding time.

Jon uses NWA's and the FAA's definition of capacity and demand for the purposes of analysis:

Capacity. A measure of the maximum number of aircraft operations (takeoffs and landings) that can be accommodated at an airport during a specified time period.

Demand. The magnitude of aircraft operations (takeoffs and landings) to be accommodated in a specific time period.

User demands on airports, such as MCI, have remained relatively unconstrained by the FAA, so reductions in aircraft delays can best be achieved by increasing capacity through airport improvements. Airport improvements range anywhere from the construction of an entirely new airport, like the Denver Regional Airport, to new ways of handling air traffic, such as the Precision Runway Monitor Program (PRM), which facilitates simultaneous independent Instrument Flight Rules (IFR) approaches to parallel runways less than 4,300 feet apart, in use at the Memphis Airport.

Annual aircraft operations demand data during the past 12 years have been collected by Jon and his staff. They have studied the fundamental economics of air traffic and are confident the NWA operations at MCI during the next five years can expand in a manner consistent with their past experience.

MCI has a current capacity of 650,000 aircraft operations per year. Expansion through computer-assisted air traffic management systems can be installed in two to three years, while runway construction requires five to six years. The capacity can be increased by 200,000 aircraft operations per year by installing a Precision Runway Monitor Program system. Jon wants to address several questions: Is this capacity at MCI sufficient to sustain NWA's anticipated growth? Does NWA need to explore growth at other airports or begin negotiations with airport management to expand the capacity of the present facility? Does Jon need to alert Scott and to encourage NWA management to initiate additional capacity expansion at MCI during the next year?

Beside these questions, Scott specifically requested that Jon develop information so NWA can determine its preference among several strategic planning alternatives, including the following:

(a) Continue the same airport configuration with no changes required.

(b) Develop approach aids, runway extensions, and crossover taxiways to increase capacity.

(c) Construct additional runways to increase capacity.

Tasks

1. Access the FORECAST.WK1 worksheet and explore the data it contains. Notice that the 1900 was dropped from the year number. This scale adjustment will affect only the intercept of a regression line. Jon has laid out the worksheet with the actual historical data and provided a place for estimated and forecast values.

2. Jon wants you to perform a regression analysis on these data to develop a representational model that can be applied to forecast future aircraft operation demand on MCI. Select the year as the independent variable (X-Range) for the regression analysis. Is this a "good" representational model? Why or why not?

3. To assist in understanding this relational model, Scott wants you to calculate the estimated aircraft operation demand for the 12 years of historical data by applying the regression equation. Graph both the actual demand and the estimated demand for the 12 years of historical data. Use years as the X-axis for your line graph. Visually compare the actual data to the estimated data. Explain how the graph reinforces your interpretation of whether this is a "good" representational model.

4. Jon wants you to apply the regression model from Task 2 to forecast aircraft operation demand for the next five years. Prepare a line graph that portrays the actual demand and the forecast demand as a single line. Jon has already set up your worksheet so that you can place the data in a single column for plotting. Does demand exceed the current capacity of MCI during this time period?

5. If demand does not exceed capacity within the five-year forecast period, extend the forecast a sufficient number of years to determine when the capacity would be exceeded.

6. Print the report of your results, save the two graphs in *.PIC files for printing, and save the worksheet file. Then print the two graphs.

7. Write a short summary of your analysis. Based on the information provided by this forecast, does NWA need to undertake capacity expansion activities during the coming year? Why or why not?

Time Estimates

Novice: 75 minutes

Intermediate: 60 minutes

Advanced: 45 minutes

LESSON

L.9

Automating Solutions with Macros

CONTENT

L.9.1 What Are 1-2-3 Macros?

A 1-2-3 **macro** is like automatic typing. Macros help you automate your work during a 1-2-3 session. Instead of entering 1-2-3 commands manually, one at a time at the keyboard, a series of 1-2-3 commands can be stored in a range of cells. Any time you want this series of commands executed, you can request 1-2-3 to begin executing them. For example, at Good Morning Products, Chris can set up a macro that contains the commands to print the Pro Forma Profit and Loss Statement report. Then, any time Kim makes a change to their plan, all she needs to do to obtain another copy of the report is to execute the macro.

L-235

Macros may contain some special commands that can be executed only as a macro command. For example, a special "macro only command" would allow you to turn off the beep or computer's bell when it would have usually sounded, such as when you try to move the cursor past the left side of the worksheet. After you have entered and named a macro, you can **invoke** or **execute** it. When you execute the macro, 1-2-3 reads the instructions and performs the specified tasks. When 1-2-3 finishes executing the macro, you return to the READY mode to continue working with your 1-2-3 worksheet.

Macros are automatic typing of *any* sequence of keystrokes in your 1-2-3 worksheet. They have these characteristics:

1. Sequence of macro keystrokes is entered into cells as labels.
2. Macro keystrokes are executed when desired as many times as desired.
3. Keystrokes may be
   - Menu selection commands
   - Any cell entry
   - Any other entry
   - Special macro only commands

Macros are most useful for the following:

- Printing several reports from one worksheet.
- Developing customized worksheets for someone who is not familiar with 1-2-3.
- Automating frequently used 1-2-3 commands.
- Typing the same label many times in different locations throughout a worksheet.
- Performing any repetitive procedure that requires a series of sequential commands.
- Storing selected range(s) of cells in a file.
- Combining ranges(s) of cells in several worksheet files.

The general concept of macros is not unique to 1-2-3. Many software packages have this capability. For example in dBASE, a command or program file provides this ability to store and execute commands when desired. Macros and command files provide the ability to defer the execution of commands. In 1-2-3 this is accomplished by placing the commands in a convenient range of cells where they can be reviewed and edited. Then, when desired, the macro is executed. It can be reused as many times as you want.

Like most command languages, 1-2-3 macros are **procedural.** They start at the top and execute sequentially down the column where the macro is stored. Branching and looping commands similar to those in third-generation computer languages like BASIC provide a means for controlling the sequence of execution of 1-2-3 macro commands.

L.9.2   When to Use Macros

There are a number of situations where macros can be used to automate worksheet activities. Here are several of the most common uses:

1. Are reports and graphs produced by someone not trained in the use of 1-2-3? Use macros to guide users in the printing of reports and displaying graphs.

2. Does your report consist of several reports to be printed, with each report having different print specifications? If so, a macro can be used to store the different specifications and to facilitate printing of the desired report.

3. Are data input by someone not trained in the use of 1-2-3? Use macros to prompt the user for the data and store it in the proper location.

4. Do you expect to use a multikeystroke command sequence more than 10 times in the development of your worksheet? For example, /RE <Enter> or /WIR <ENTER>. If so, macros can be used to simplify these commands.

5. Will you type the same label in one worksheet more than 10 times? If so, consider creating a macro to enter the label.

L.9.3 Creating Macros

There are three essential components to the use of a 1-2-3 macro:

1. Create the macro commands.
2. Name the macro.
3. Execute the macro.

Before a macro can be executed, it must be created *and* named. A macro is developed in five steps:

1. Plan your macro and go through the steps of your task manually.
2. Enter the macro as one or more labels in a column.
3. Name the macro, giving it a range name.
4. Document the macro with comments for future reference.
5. Save the macro by saving the worksheet file.

Before entering a macro in worksheet cells, plan the steps necessary to accomplish the desired task. When you have a good idea of all of the required processing steps, go through each keystroke manually, writing down each key that you press. (This is sometimes known as the **dry run.**) Check the sequence to be sure that it is correct. You are then ready to enter the macro.

To assist in developing his macro, Chris completed a Macro Planning Form (Figure L.133) for printing the Good Morning Products report. A Macro Planning Form like this provides a convenient means for recording the steps from your dry run before you enter them as labels in your worksheet.

MACRO PLANNING FORM

Macro Name	Macro Command	Descriptive Comment
\P	/pprA1.F16<Enter>	Specify print range
	omr83<Enter>q	Set right margin
	agpq	Align, Go, Page, Quit
		Blank cell to end macro

FIGURE L.133. Macro Planning Form for dry run of printing report.

L.9.4   Special Key Indicators for Macros

In 1-2-3 special keyboard keys, such as <left>, <right>, <Home>, <Esc>, <Del>, and <F2>, are specified by a literal key name enclosed within { } (braces) so that they can be used in macros. If you press any of these special keys while you are actually entering a macro, their action is *carried out immediately,* rather than storing the keystroke as part of your macro. Naming special keys provides a means for including these keystrokes in your macro where their actions are *deferred until the macro is executed.* Special macro key indicators are as listed in Figure L.134.

L.9.5   Entering Macros

Locate an unused, out-of-the-way area on your worksheet where you can place the macro. Each of the macro commands is stored in a cell as a **label.** These may be long labels, with their display extended into the columns to the right. Lotus 1-2-3 starts executing the macro at the top of the column of the designated range and continues sequentially down the column until it encounters a blank cell.

Keypoint!

> Macro commands are arranged in a single column, one command immediately under another command! A blank cell indicates the end of a macro!

Key Indicator in Macro	Substitute for This Key
~	<Enter>
{left or left n}	<left> cursor movement one or n cells
{right or right n}	<right> cursor movement one or n cells
{up or up n}	<up> cursor movement one or n cells
{down or down n}	<down> cursor movement one or n cells
{bigleft}	<Ctrl>+<left>
{bigright}	<Ctrl>+<right>
{home}	<Home>
{end}	<End>
{pgup}	<PgUp>
{pgdn}	<PgDn>
{menu}	/ (slash) access main menu key
{bs}	<Backspace>
{esc}	<Esc>
{del}	<Del>
{edit}	<F2> edit function key
{name}	<F3> name function key
{abs}	<F4> absolute cell reference function key
{goto}	<F5> goto function key
{window}	<F6> window function key
{query}	<F7> query function key
{table}	<F8> table function key
{calc}	<F9> calculate function key
{graph}	<F10> graph function key

FIGURE L.134. Special macro key names.

Some key points in entering macro commands into cells are as follows:

1. Do *not* leave any spaces when typing in a macro *instruction*. Spaces are guaranteed to cause errors, unless they are part of a text entry, such as "Good Morning Products."

2. Begin each macro instruction with an apostrophe (') label prefix. Although this is not always required, it is a good practice and helps avoid errors. Remember: when you type the **/,** the command is *executed immediately*. By starting with **'/,** you are creating a label so that the command is *not* executed immediately.

Caution Alert!   Most keyboards include a left single quote mark ('). This is not the apostrophe ('). Be careful to use the apostrophe to start entering each macro command as a label!

---

3. Type the entries for a macro in any column of cells. You may type more than one instruction or command sequence in the same cell.

4. Macro instructions may include any of the standard keyboard characters (for example, h, 9 , +), as well as any of 1-2-3's special keys.

5. A macro instruction in a cell may be as short as a single keystroke or as long a 240 characters.

6. To help avoid pitfalls, try to terminate each macro instruction cell entry with a tilde (~), Quit, or cell pointer movement key: left, right, up, or down. The tilde character (~) is used to indicate <Enter>.

7. Leave the cell below the macro blank to ensure termination of execution of the macro.

Caution Alert!   Missing **TILDES** (~) are the greatest source of error in entering macro instructions!

In deciding where to place a macro on your worksheet, consider these guidelines:

1. Locate a macro so that modifying it does not interfere with the application area of the worksheet. Watch the location so that inserting and deleting rows and columns in either the macro or application area will not cause difficulties (Figure L.135).

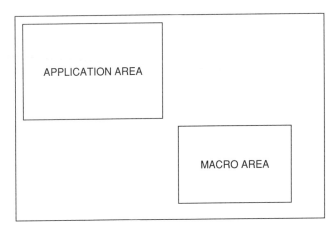

FIGURE L.135. Locating macros in the worksheet.

2. When using several macros in one worksheet, arrange them so that they are "stacked" one above the other in your worksheet.

3. If possible, reserve at least three columns in your macro area for (1) the macro range name, (2) the macro commands, and (3) comments describing the macro.

Caution Alert! A blank row inserted in the middle of a macro will cause it to terminate execution!

L.9.6   Macros for Producing Reports

Macros are a convenient method for storing different report specifications so that several reports can readily be printed from the same worksheet. Figure L.136 shows a macro Chris created for printing the range **A1..F16** containing the Pro Forma Statement report for Good Morning Products. He placed the macro commands in cells **C17..C20,** which are *below* the report in an out-of-the-way location that permits rows to be inserted into the report without disturbing the macro. Cell **B17** contains the name of his macro, while cells **E17..E20** contain comments describing the macro's action. Only the actual macro commands in cells **C17..C20** are required. The macro name in cell **B17** and the comments in cells **E17..E20** provide a convenient method of remembering the macro name and the purpose of each macro command; this is **documentation** for the macro. Notice that the commands in cells **C18** and **C19** have a "q" at the end. Since the "q" signifies a quit (i.e., leave the current menu), it is not necessary to have a tilde (~) for an <Enter> following the quit.

The macro in Figure L.136 causes the report to be printed "As-Displayed" following the Lotus 1-2-3 general WYSIWYG approach to reporting. This macro can be modified

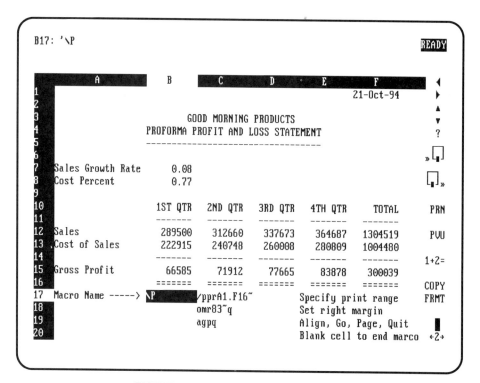

FIGURE L.136. Macro for printing report.

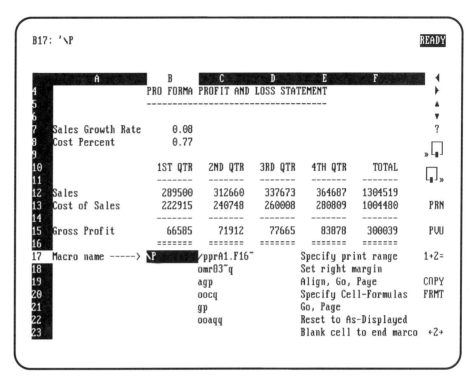

FIGURE L.137. Macro for printing report and cell formulas.

as illustrated in Figure L.137 so that the report will be printed both "As-Displayed" *and* with the "Cell-Formulas."

Keypoint!

> Lotus 1-2-3 does *not* require the documentation of macros. In Figures L.136 and L.137, the range name in cell **B17** and the descriptions in cells **E17..E22** are documentation. You could remove these labels and the macro would still execute as desired. However, this documentation makes it easier for you to understand the action of the macro!

For some reporting requirements, you may want to select several different areas of the worksheet for printing. For example, the report Chris printed in Figure L.138 has the rows containing the assumptions for **Sales Growth Rate** and **Cost Percent** *eliminated* for this "management" report. This is accomplished by printing *two separate areas* of

```
                                                   21-Oct-94

                         GOOD MORNING PRODUCTS
                 PRO FORMA PROFIT AND LOSS STATEMENT
                 ------------------------------------

                   1ST QTR   2ND QTR   3RD QTR   4TH QTR    TOTAL
                   -------   -------   -------   -------   -------
Sales               289500    312660    337673    364687   1304519
Cost of Sales       222915    240748    260008    280809   1004480
                   -------   -------   -------   -------   -------
Gross Profit         66585     71912     77665     83878    300039
                   =======   =======   =======   =======   =======
```

FIGURE L.138. Report from two different work areas.

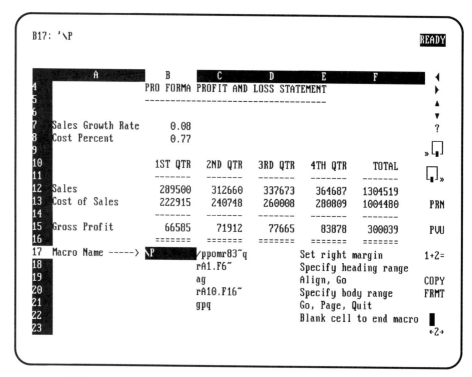

FIGURE L.139. Macro for printing report with two areas of worksheet.

the report using the macro shown in Figure L.139. After the heading area is printed, the print range is changed to the body of the report for printing. A macro provides a very convenient mechanism for selecting and printing these two or more separate areas of the worksheet as one report.

Figures L.136, L.137, and L.139 illustrated three different macros that may be used in printing reports. For now, let us create the macro for printing the Good Morning Products Pro Forma Statement report in Figure L.138 by entering the macro commands and documentation from Figure L.139. Later this macro will be named and then executed.

Action: Retrieve the PLAN6 worksheet file.

To create macro commands

Move to:	**B17**	Location of cell range where macro will reside
Action:	Enter the macro name, macro commands, and comment statements as label in the cells **B17..E22** as shown in Figure L.139.	

This macro is now ready to be named and executed.

L.9.7   Naming Macros

A preferred **macro name** is the <backslash> followed by any single letter of the alphabet (A thru Z), such as \A or \Z, since this provides the simplest way to run a macro. However, with Lotus 1-2-3 Release 2.2 and higher, macro names may be any combination of up to 15 characters. A macro occupies a range of cells going down a single column. The *topmost cell* in this range is assigned the macro's range name.

A **named range** is any 1-2-3 cell range to which you assign a **range name,** which may be up to 15 characters. The range name provides a convenient means of referencing this cell range and is the method used to name macros. Let's assign \P as the range name for the macro that prints the Pro Forma Statement for Good Morning Products.

Action: Verify that the PLAN6 worksheet file with the macro command is your currently active worksheet.

To name a macro	**Move to:**	C17	Top cell of macro commands in the column where macro has been entered, that is, the first cell containing the macro (Figure L.139.)
	Press:	/	Access main menu
	Select:	Range	Desired activity
	Select:	Name	Desired option
	Select:	Create	Type of naming action
	Enter:	\P	Name of macro (Figure L.140)
	Press:	<Enter>	Worksheet cursor should already be positioned at desired cell

Here, the \P macro name is a good name for a print macro, and \W is a good name to use for a what-if macro. Choose any letter that helps you remember the name of the macro and use the command / Range Name Create (/RNC) command to assign the range name. Once a macro is created and named, it can be saved in your worksheet file. This is similar to saving Graph Settings with your worksheet. Let's save the worksheet, which also saves the macro.

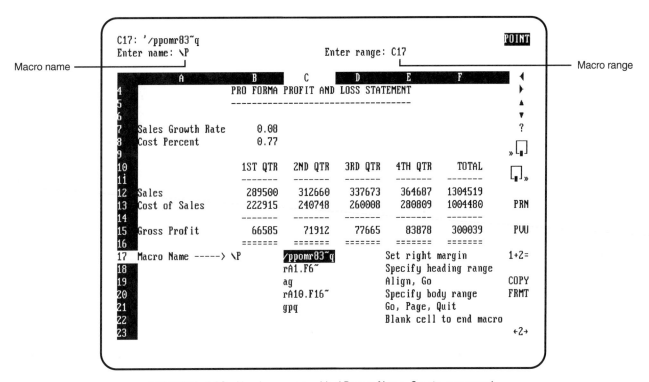

FIGURE L.140. Naming macro with / Range Name Create command.

| To save a macro with the worksheet | **Action:** Save this worksheet file as PLAN16. |

Keypoint!

> To save a macro once it has been completed, save the current worksheet file! In some releases of 1-2-3, such as 3.x, macros may be saved as separate files.

L.9.8   Executing a Macro

Once a macro has been entered on the worksheet and has been named, then it is ready to be invoked or executed. A macro is executed by pressing the <Alt> key and striking the single letter of the macro name while the <Alt> is depressed. Let's execute the \P macro in Figure L.139, which causes the printing of Kim's report for Good Morning Products.

| To execute a macro | **Press:** | <Alt>+<P> | Execute macro\P |

Now any time that Kim or Chris revises any of the data in their Pro Forma Statement for Good Morning Products, they can quickly obtain another copy of this report by merely executing their \P macro.

Because the Pro Forma Statement is a small worksheet model, you can see both the application area and macro area at the same time. This makes it relatively easy for you to know that the macro name is \P. What if this were a larger worksheet so that both the application area and macro area were not visible at the same time? Lotus 1-2-3 provides an alternative method for executing macros in which a list of available macro names is displayed. You can then selected the desired name from this list of available macros. Let's execute the \P macro by selecting its name from a list.

| To execute a macro by selecting the name from a list | **Press:** | <Alt>+<F3> | List of available macros is displayed Figure L.141 |
| | **Select:** | \P | Desired macro |

The macro is executed and produces that same report for Good Morning Products.

When macros are named with the <backslash> and a single letter, you can execute them by using either the <Alt>+<single-letter> or the <Alt>+<F3> with a selection from a list of available macros. You may use either method. Pick the method you like the best.

L.9.9   Macros for Data Entry and What-If

Let us consider another use of macros to provide users with **guided data entry** in which the worksheet cursor is automatically positioned for inputting each data value. This is most useful when several different what-if alternatives are being explored. The macro orchestrates data entry so that values are entered in the desired cells. For example, consider the loan analysis for the new juicing machine at Good Morning Products. As Chris and Kim evaluate purchasing this machine, they would like to perform several what-if evaluations with different loan amounts, interest rates, and number of years. Chris suggested that they should create a macro that would guide the entry of data for each what-if analysis they performed. This would help ensure that the correct data are entered in the appropriate cells. He developed the worksheet in Figure L.142, which contains a macro in cells **E11..E15** that allows them to conduct their what-if analysis

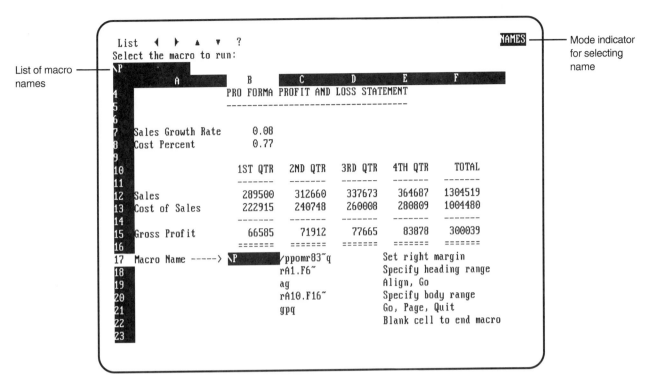

FIGURE L.141. Execute macro by selecting name from list.

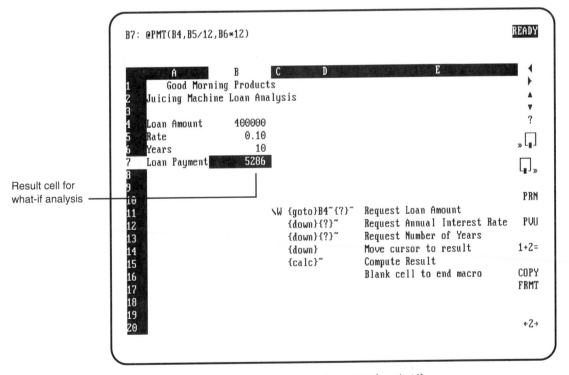

FIGURE L.142. Macro for guided data entry for what-if.

for different loan alternatives. This macro is placed in the lower-right corner of the spreadsheet, an out-of-the-way location that *allows either rows or columns to be added* to the main worksheet area without affecting the macro, as illustrated previously in Figure L.135.

When the macro in Figure L.142 is executed, the worksheet area is positioned so that Kim can readily view the entire data entry area, regardless of the location of the worksheet cursor prior to executing the macro. Then, the cursor moves to cell **B4** and pauses. The {?}~ allows Kim to enter a number for the amount of the loan, and the cursor moves down to cell **B5.** Another number is entered for the interest rate, and the cursor moves to cell **B6.** After the last value is entered for the number of years, the cursor moves to cell **B7,** where the result is located. Positioning the cell pointer at this location accentuates the result, which is computed with the @PMT function. Lotus 1-2-3 is then specifically directed to recalculate the worksheet.

Let's create the worksheet with the macro for this guided data entry for the what-if analysis of the loan payment for Good Morning Products. First, the application and macro areas are set up.

Action: Use /WEY to obtain a "clean" worksheet. Set the Global Column Width (/WGC) to 12. Set the width of columns **C** and **D** to 3 and 15, respectively. This establishes the desired column widths for the macro. Enter the labels and data values for the application area as shown in Figure L.142. Enter the @PMT formula in cell **B7.**

To create the macro commands

Action: Enter the macro commands in the macro area **C11..E17,** as shown in Figure L.142. Be sure to enter each of the tildes.

Now let's range name this macro and save the worksheet file.

To range name the macro

Action: Use the / Range Name Create (/RNC) command to range name cell **D11** of the macro as \W.

Action: Save this as the PMTMAC1 worksheet file, which saves the entire worksheet including the macro.

Next, this what-if macro is executed and data for another alternative are entered. Let's execute the macro.

To execute the macro

Press: <Alt>+<W>   Cause macro to begin execution

The "CMD" indicator at the bottom of Figure L.143 signals that 1-2-3 is in the process of executing a macro while the cell pointer is located at cell **B4** for entering the new loan amount.

Now the new data values are entered as the cursor is automatically positioned at each cell.

To enter data at each cell location

Enter: 420000   New loan amount
Enter: .11   New interest rate
Enter: 12   New term of loan

Execution of the macro is complete with the cell pointer located at cell **B7,** and the READY mode appears.

When the macro in Figure L.142 is executed, the location of the cell pointer moves to each cell to indicate the data values that are to be input. Lotus 1-2-3 provides an alternative method for entering data when performing a what-if analysis using a macro. Figure L.144 illustrates a macro that is used to perform the same what-if analysis as that of Figure L.142. The Figure L.144 macro makes use of an "x" command, which

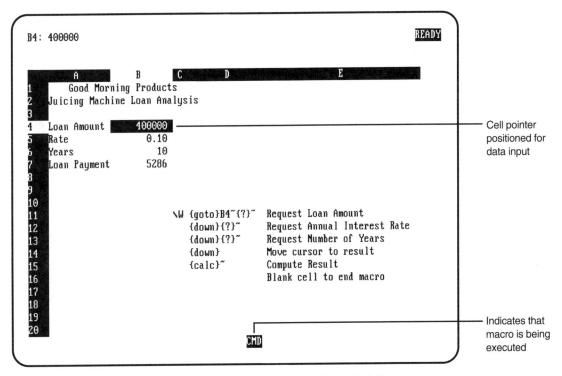

FIGURE L.143. Execution of macro for guided data entry.

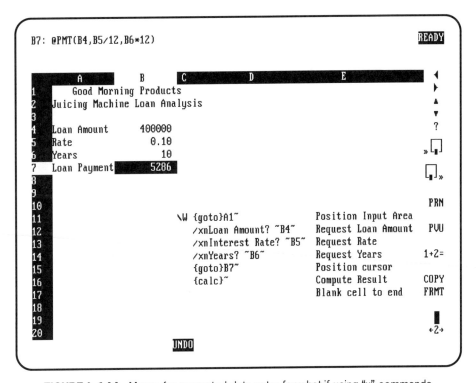

FIGURE L.144. Macro for prompted data entry for what-if using "x" commands.

can be used only in a macro. You cannot execute it manually with direct input to the keyboard. The **/xn** command generates a **prompt message** in the control panel, allows you to enter a number, then places that number in the designated cell, which is **B4** for this example. During execution of the macro command, "Loan Amount?" is the message displayed in the edit area of the control panel as a prompt for the data to be entered (Figure L.145).

Let's modify the guided data entry macro in Figure L.142 so that it will do the prompted data entry using the "x" commands in Figure L.144.

To modify the macro for prompted data entry	**Action:** Verify the PMTMAC1 file is your current worksheet.

Action: Revise the macro commands and the descriptive comments in cells **D11..E17** as illustrated in Figure L.144. Change the width of column **D** so that the entire command in each cell is visible.

Since the macro has already been named, it is not necessary to name the macro again. As long as the macro name is not deleted with a / Range Name Delete (/RND) command, the same range name remains assigned to the first cell at the top of the macro. The prompted data entry macro is ready for execution.

Action: Save this as the PMTMAC2 worksheet file before you execute it.

To execute the prompted data entry macro

Press: <Alt>+<W>   Execute macro

The prompt message appears in the control panel (Figure L.145), and 1-2-3 waits for the Loan Amount to be entered. Let's enter the data for this prompt and each of the other two prompts.

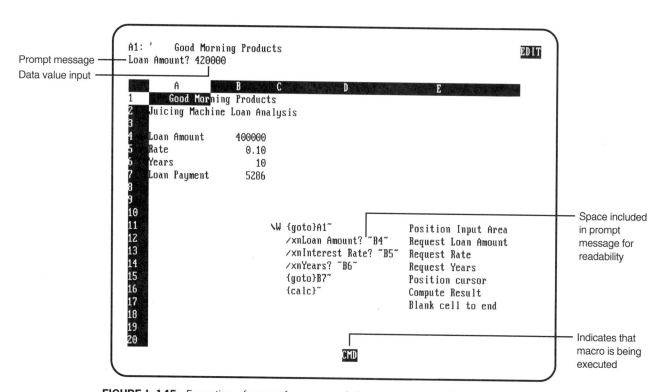

FIGURE L.145. Execution of macro for prompted data entry for what-if using "x" commands.

To enter data at each prompt	**Enter:**	400000	New loan amount
	Enter:	.12	New interest rate
	Enter:	10	New term of loan

Again, execution of the macro is complete with the cell pointer located at cell **B7,** and the READY mode appears.

Now let us execute this macro one more time to see how the /xn command *edits the input data,* allowing only a numeric constant to be entered.

To execute the macro and detect invalid data input	**Press:**	<Alt>+<W>	Execute the \W macro
	Enter:	xxxx	Enter characters as data values

The error message shown in Figure L.146 is displayed. Earlier releases of 1-2-3 display this error message in the status line at the bottom of the screen. The /xn macro allows the input of only a numeric constant. Lotus 1-2-3 detected that you attempted to enter a label and displayed the "Invalid Number Input" error message and the ERROR mode indicator. Now continue data entry by removing the error message.

To cancel the input error message	**Press:**	<Esc>	The error message disappears

The Loan Amount is still requested so that the value can be entered as a number. Let's reenter the data.

	Enter:	420000	New loan amount
	Enter:	.11	New interest rate
	Enter:	12	New term of loan

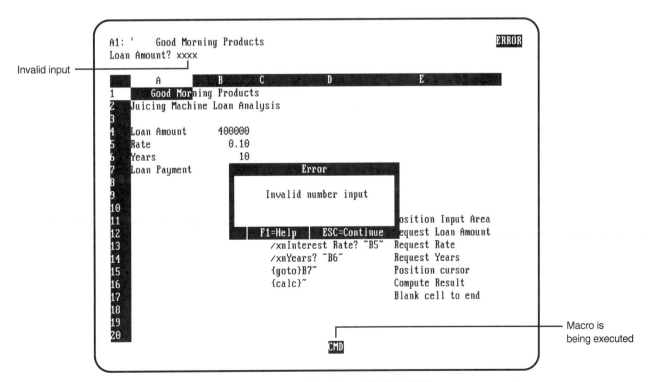

FIGURE L.146. Data entry error with /XN or {GETNUMBER} macro command.

In this manner, the /xn command **edits data** on input and allows the input of numeric values only. With this macro, when Kim and Chris are doing their loan analysis, 1-2-3 ensures that only numbers are entered. This helps prevent data entry errors that might occur if they use the macro in Figure L.142, which allows any cell entry to be made.

Lotus 1-2-3 contains several additional "x" macro commands. Some of these commands are the following:

/X Macro Command	Action
/XGcell-location~	Go to cell-location to continue processing macro commands.
/XIformula~more-macro-commands~	If formula or condition is true, then execute more-macro-commands; otherwise continue executing the macro in the next cell.
/XLprompt-message~cell-location~	Displays a prompt-message, waits for a response, and enters input as a label.
/XNprompt-message~cell-location~	Displays a prompt-message, waits for a numeric response, and enters input as a value.
/XQ	Quit executing macro commands.

Lotus 1-2-3 contains a number of advanced **keyword macro commands.** The keyword tells 1-2-3 what action is to be performed. Keywords help provide a clear understanding of the action performed by the macro command. For example, the "xn" macro command illustrated in Figure L.144 can be replaced by the {GETNUMBER} keyword command as portrayed in Figure L.147. The action of the {GETNUMBER}

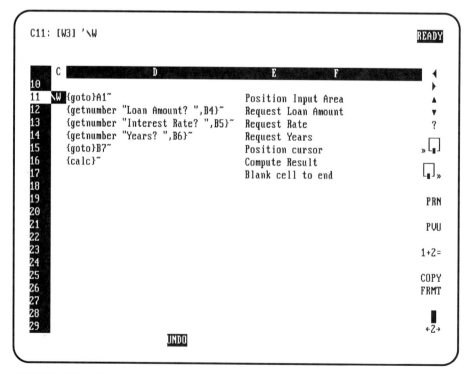

FIGURE L.147. Macro for prompted data entry for what-if using {GETNUMBER} commands.

command is *exactly the same* as that of the "xn" command and produces the same prompt message in the control panel as shown previously in Figure L.145. The general form of the {GETNUMBER} command is

{GETNUMBER "prompt-message",cell-location}

A similar {GETLABEL} command can be used in place of the /XL command.

Lotus 1-2-3 contains about 50 advanced keyword macro commands. These macro commands support the development of very complex macro programs. Some of the more commonly used commands are as follows:

Keyword Macro Command	Action
{BEEP}	Sounds the computer's bell.
{BLANK location}	Erases a cell or range of cells.
{BORDERSOFF}	Turns off the display of the worksheet frame of column letters and row numbers.
{BORDERSON}	Turns on the display of the worksheet frame of column letters and row numbers.
{BRANCH location}	Go to cell location to continue processing macro commands.
{BREAK}	Cause a <ctrl>+<break>, which returns 1-2-3 to the READY mode.
{GETLABEL "prompt",location}	Displays a prompt message, waits for a response, and enters input as a label.
{GETNUMBER "prompt",location}	Displays a prompt message, waits for a numeric response, and enters input as a value.
{IF condition}	Evaluates a condition to determine which macro instruction is executed next, allowing branching within a macro.
{INDICATE "message"}	Changes the mode indicator in the upper-right corner of the screen.
{LET location,formula}	Enters a label or number in a cell.
{PANELOFF}	Turns off the display of the control panel. Used so that macro commands do not flash across control panel as they are executed.
{PANELON}	Turns on the display of the control panel.
{QUIT}	Terminates execution of a macro, returning keyboard control to a user.
{WAIT time-number}	Suspends macro execution for a specified duration.

For additional advanced keyword macro commands and their descriptions, see the *Lotus 1-2-3 Reference Manual.*

Let's modify the prompted /xn data entry macro for the Good Morning Products loan analysis to use the {getnumber} keyword command as shown in Figure L.147.

To modify the macro for prompted data entry to use keyword commands	**Action:** Verify that the PMTMAC2 file is your currently active worksheet.
	Action: Revise the macro commands in **D12..D14** so that they include the {getnumber} keyword command as shown in Figure L.147. Change the width of column **D** so that the entire command in each cell is visible.

To range name the macro	**Action:** Because cell **D11** is already range named as \W, nothing needs to be done. If desired, you may use the / Range Name Create (/RNC) command to verify that **D11** is named \W.
	Action: Save this as the PMTMAC3 worksheet file.

Now this keyword macro is ready for execution.

To execute the keyword command macro	**Action:** Use <Alt>+<W> to execute this macro and use the test data values 420000, .11, and 12 as the loan amount, interest rate, and term of the loan, respectively.
	Action: Print a hard copy of the entire worksheet for documentation that includes both the application and macro areas.

As illustrated in this section for Good Morning Products, 1-2-3 macros provide a convenient way to perform data entry for what-if analysis.

L.9.10   Executing Macros Automatically

Lotus 1-2-3 supports the application of an **auto execute** macro. If Chris set up an auto execute macro for the Good Morning Products loan analysis, then when Kim retrieved the worksheet, she would *immediately* be prompted to enter the data. The 1-2-3 auto execute macro is assigned the special range name of \0 (zero). When a worksheet is retrieved and loaded into 1-2-3, the \0 (zero) macro is executed automatically. This feature is particularly useful in creating spreadsheet applications that are to be operated by individuals not familiar with using 1-2-3. An auto execute macro would usually guide the user in data entry and report generation as a "canned" computer application. Since the \0 (zero) macro executes only as the worksheet is retrieved, it would have to be assigned a second range name of \A through \Z if you want to be able to execute it with the <Alt>+<letter> keys from the READY mode.

Let's modify the prompted data entry macro so that it is automatically executed when the worksheet is retrieved.

To modify the macro for automatic execution	**Action:** Verify that the PMTMAC3 file is your currently active worksheet. If not, make it your current worksheet.
	Action: Range name cell **D11** as \0.
	Action: Save this as the PMTMAC4 worksheet file and clear your worksheet with the /WEY command.

Now the worksheet file can be retrieved, causing the \0 macro to be executed.

To run the auto execute macro	**Action:** Retrieve the PMTMAC4 worksheet file. When prompted, use these values as your test data: 420000, .09, 8. The first prompt is for the new loan amount, as shown previously in Figure L.145.

Because this macro is also named \W, its execution can be initiated with the <Alt>+<W> keys from the READY mode as shown previously. Let's see how this works after the auto execute macro was run.

To execute the same macro using \W range name	**Action:** At the READY mode, use the <Alt>+<W> to execute the macro. When prompted, use these values as your test data: 390000, .11, 12.

As demonstrated with this example, a macro can be executed automatically when a worksheet is retrieved and also executed from the READY mode as desired.

L.9.11 Interrupting and Debugging Macros

Execution of a macro may be interrupted at any time by pressing <Ctrl>+<Break> and then <Esc> to get rid of the ERROR indicator. Macro execution is terminated, and you are returned to the READY mode. Let's run the \W macro in the PMTMAC3 worksheet file to see how execution of this macro is interrupted.

Action: If necessary, retrieve the PMTMAC3 file as your currently active worksheet.

Press: <Alt>+<W>   Execute the \W macro

When you are prompted to enter any of the data values, execution of the macro can be stopped. Let's terminate execution when prompted for the Loan Amount.

To terminate a macro during execution	**Press:** <Ctrl>+<Break>	Stops macro and displays error message (Figure L.148)
	Press: <Esc>	Return to READY

When a macro is being executed, an error may occur that causes the macro to stop execution or that causes the wrong result. Because a macro is executed so quickly

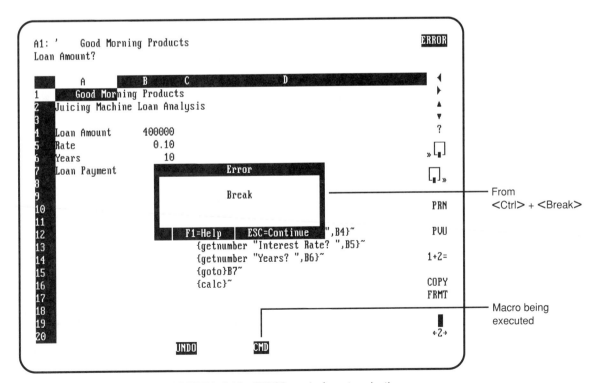

FIGURE L.148. ERROR mode from terminating macro.

by 1-2-3, it is difficult to know exactly which keystroke caused the error. Lotus 1-2-3 has a special feature to help you debug macros by tracking down these errors so that they can be corrected. The **STEP mode** feature lets you run the macro one keystroke at a time. You see the result of each keystroke and can locate the exact place where the error was detected by 1-2-3. This allows you to determine the difficulty with the macro and to correct it. The STEP mode is toggled on by pressing < Alt > + < F2 > before the macro is executed. A status indicator appears (Figure L.149) to advise you that the STEP mode is turned on. Pressing < Alt > + < F2 > a second time at the READY mode toggles the STEP mode off. When the STEP mode is turned on and a macro is executed, each keystroke of the macro is executed one at a time by pressing <space>.

Let us execute the \P macro that prints the report for Good Morning Products with the STEP mode turned on so that you can observe its operation.

Action: Make the PLAN16 file containing the \P macro for Good Morning Products your currently active worksheet.

To toggle on the STEP mode	**Press:**	<Alt>+<F2>	Turn on the STEP mode
To run the macro	**Press:**	<Alt>+<P>	Begin running the \P macro
To execute the individual macro keystrokes	**Press:**	<space>	Execute the first keystroke of the macro command
	Action:	Press <space> eight times and watch the control panel and the status line as each keystroke of the macro is executed. Thus far the right margin is specified as shown in Figure L.150.	
	Action:	Continue to press <space> until you return to the READY mode. Watch the action on your screen as each keystroke of the macro is entered. This underscores the automatic typing characteristic of 1-2-3 macros.	
To toggle off the STEP mode	**Press:**	<Alt>+<F2>	Turn off STEP mode

Now let's see how the STEP mode works when there is an error in a macro. This requires a macro that contains an error. The \P macro can be modified to contain an *intentional error* so that you can observe what happens. Because missing tildes (~) are one of the primary causes of macro errors, let's create this as an intentional error.

To create an intentional error with a missing tilde (~)	**Move to:**	C18	Cell to be modified
	Press:	<F2>	Edit cell's content
	Press:	<backspace>	Remove tilde
	Press:	<Enter>	Complete edit

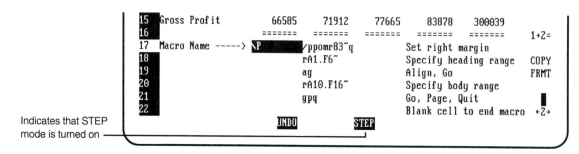

Indicates that STEP mode is turned on

FIGURE L.149. STEP mode toggled on.

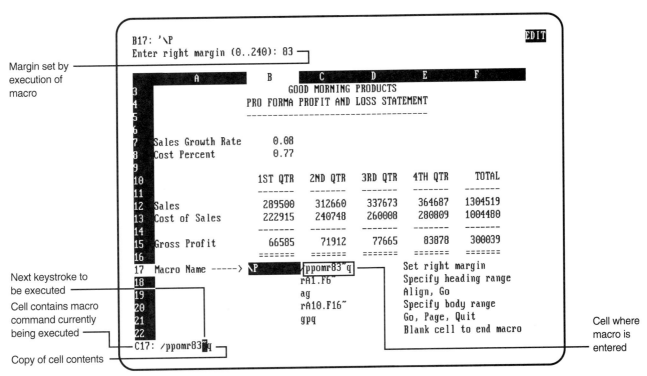

FIGURE L.150. Execution of macro in STEP mode.

First, let's execute this macro *without* the STEP mode to observe what happens when this error is encountered.

To execute the \P macro containing an error	**Press:** \<Alt>+\<P>	Execute macro

When 1-2-3 encounters this error, the message shown in Figure L.151 appears. The CMD indicator is displayed while the macro is being executed.

To clear error message and return to READY mode	**Press:** \<Esc>	The READY mode appears

Did 1-2-3 actually detect the error as the missing tilde in cell **C18**? By using the STEP mode, the exact location where 1-2-3 detected the error can be determined. Let's use the STEP mode to find that location.

To toggle on STEP mode	**Press:** \<Alt>+\<F2>	Turn on STEP mode

To run macro	**Press:** \<Alt>+\<P>	Run \P macro

To find location where error is detected	**Action:**	Press \<space> until the ERROR mode occurs. Watch the status line as the macro command in each cell is processed one keystroke at time. The keystroke executed when the error message appears is the one *where the error is detected*. The SST indicator is displayed (Figure L.152) to signal the occurrence of an error in the STEP mode.

For this example, the error is detected when the tilde in cell **C20** is the keystroke that is executed. However, the error occurred prior to this keystroke. You need to inspect the series of keystrokes executed *before* this last keystroke to determine the exact

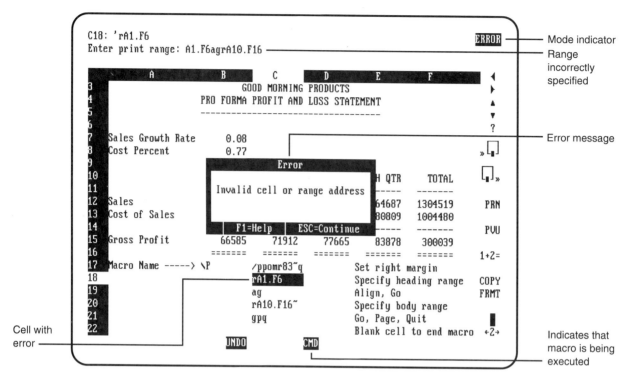

FIGURE L.151. Error in macro execution.

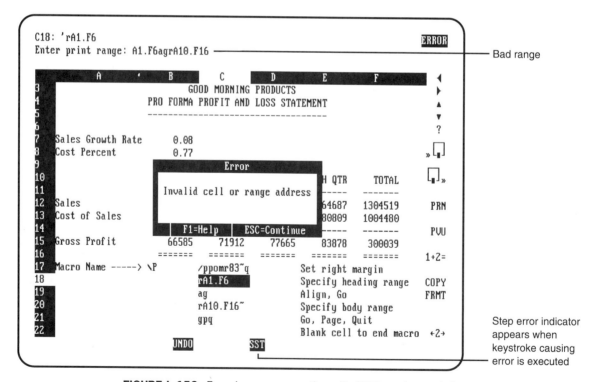

FIGURE L.152. Error in macro execution with STEP mode toggled on.

location of the error, rather than where 1-2-3 stopped execution because of an error. By carefully inspecting cells **C20, C19,** and **C18** together with the print range displayed in the control panel, you can see that the error is the missing tilde in cell **C18.** The STEP mode is useful in tracking down errors in macros. However, the *keystroke where an error is detected by 1-2-3 may be several keystrokes after the actual error.* Once you know the location, you need to carefully examine the preceding keystrokes. Also, carefully performing a *dry run* before entering a macro can help to avoid errors that will need to be tracked down and corrected.

Keypoint!

> The macro command keystroke where an error is detected by 1-2-3 may be several keystrokes *after* the occurrence of the actual error. You need to examine your macro keystrokes working backward from where the error is detected in locating the actual cause of the error!

Now let's correct this error in the macro and rerun it.

Action: Correct the error in cell **C18** by using Edit (<F2>) and adding the missing tilde.

Action: Execute the macro and use <space> to execute each keystroke. The macro should now execute without any errors.

Action: Toggle off the STEP mode.

The STEP mode provides a mechanism for tracking down errors in a macro as that macro is executed. This helps you in debugging your macros.

L.9.12 Using the LEARN Mode

In 1-2-3, the LEARN mode captures keystrokes as you type them and stores them in a designated range as macro commands. You can then execute these macro commands like those you manually enter. In the LEARN mode, only the keystrokes you type are stored. If you want to develop a macro that uses keyword macro commands, these keyword commands must be typed directly in each macro command. They cannot be stored using the LEARN mode.

At Good Morning Products, Chris would like to create a macro for Kim that saves the current worksheet file. Because this macro does not use any keyword commands, it can be created by using the LEARN mode. After determining that he wants a macro that saves the current worksheet, Chris plans out the remaining steps for using the LEARN mode:

1. Decide the cell range where the macro will be located.
2. Specify the LEARN range using the / Worksheet Learn Range (/WLR) command.
3. Turn on the LEARN mode to start recording all keystrokes.
4. Carry out the task to be stored as macro commands.
5. Turn off the LEARN mode to stop recording keystrokes.
6. Range name the top cell of the stored macro commands.
7. Run the macro.

The macro for saving the Good Morning Products worksheet can be added to the PLAN16 worksheet that prints the Pro Forma Statement report. A good location for this macro is at cell **C24,** which is below the print macro. Let us specify this as the location for the macro and use LEARN to create and store it.

Action: If necessary, retrieve the PLAN16 file as your currently active worksheet.

To specify the LEARN range	**Move to:**	**C24**	Location where macro will be stored
	Press:	/	Access main menu
	Select:	Worksheet	
	Select:	Learn	Desired activity
	Select:	Range	Desired option
	Press:	<Enter>	Cursor is already at desired location

| To toggle on the LEARN mode | **Press:** | <Alt>+<F5> | Toggle on the LEARN mode and cause the LEARN indicator to be displayed (Figure L.153) |

Now the command can be entered to save the file, and these keystrokes will be stored in the LEARN range at cell **C24.** Let's type these keystrokes.

To store keystrokes as macro commands	**Type:**	/FS	/ File Save command
	Press:	<Enter>	Accept current filename
	Type:	R	Choose Replace option

This completes the keystrokes for saving the current worksheet file. The LEARN mode is toggled off to stop recording keystrokes.

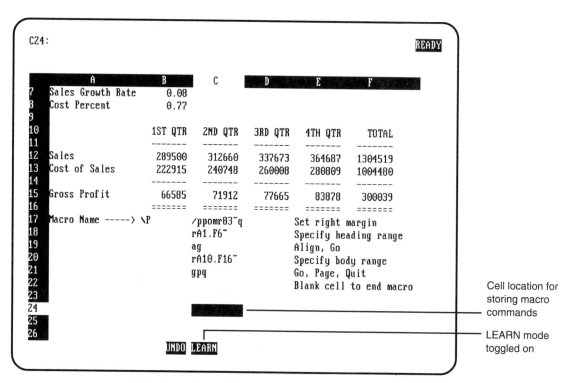

FIGURE L.153. LEARN mode toggled on for creating a macro.

| To toggle off the LEARN mode | **Press:** | <Alt>+<F5> | Toggle off the LEARN mode and cause the CALC indicator to appear |
| | **Press:** | <Enter> | The CALC indicator disappears and the keystrokes appear in cell C24 (Figure L.154) |

Once the macro command is stored in cell **C24** it is ready to be named and executed like a macro command that is typed directly into the cell.

Caution Alert!

> Every keystroke you type is recorded in the LEARN mode. If you change the command by using <Esc>, <Backspace>, or <Delete>, these keystrokes are also recorded and will be executed each time the macro is run (Figure L.155). Be careful when using the LEARN mode to avoid these errors. For this reason, a *dry run* should be performed before using the LEARN mode to record keystrokes for a macro!

To name and execute the macro stored using LEARN

Action: Range name cell **C24** as \S, since this is a good name for a macro that saves the current worksheet file. Add documentation for the macro by entering the label \S in cell **B24** and the descriptive comment "Save current worksheet" in cell **E24**.

Action: Execute the macro using <Alt>+<S>. The worksheet is saved including this newly created macro.

Keypoint!

> For each macro you create using the LEARN mode, the / Worksheet Learn Range (/WLR) command is used to set up a separate range for storing the macro commands!

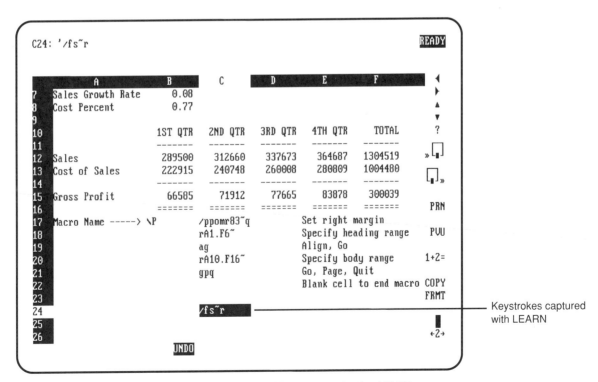

FIGURE L.154. Macro created using LEARN.

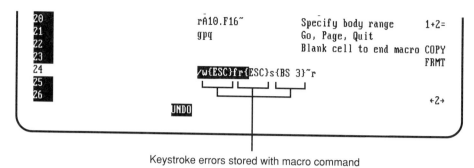

Keystroke errors stored with macro command

FIGURE L.155. Errors stored in macro command from LEARN.

Keypoint!   To use LEARN to store macro commands in a range that already contains macro commands, old macro commands must be erased before you toggle on the LEARN mode!

L.9.13 Utility Macros

When you are creating a Lotus 1-2-3 worksheet, several macros may be exploited to assist with repetitive operations such as erasing the contents of cells, inserting or deleting rows, saving the current worksheet file, and creating formulas for several projection techniques. Figure L.156 contains a sample of some of these macros. You may want to develop your own file of utility macros and save it for use in building your worksheets. The macros in Figure L.156 can provide a start for your own library of utility macros.

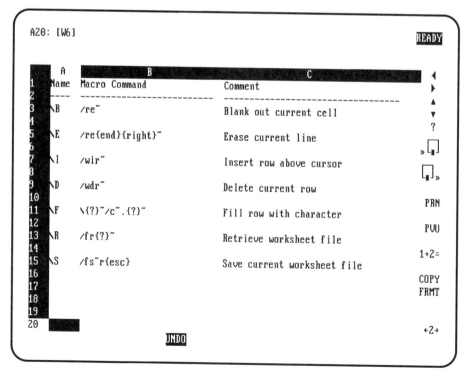

FIGURE L.156. Selected utility macros.

L.9.14   Using SmartIcons with Macros

SmartIcons are available beginning with Release 2.4 for use in executing macros as shown in Figure L.157. Macros are created and named as described previously in this lesson. These SmartIcons only provide an alternative method for executing the macro. Let's see how these SmartIcons are used in executing macros.

Action: If necessary Attach the SmartIcon Add-In.

Action: Verify that the PLAN16 file is your currently active worksheet containing the \P macro for printing the report for Good Morning Products. Make sure you are at the READY mode.

To execute the \P macro using the RUN SmartIcon	**Click:** RUN SmartIcon	Desired activity
	Select: \P	List of macro names is displayed for your selection, as shown previously in Figure L.141

The macro is executed in the same manner as if you had initiated execution with the keyboard command.

Now let's explore the use of the STEP SmartIcon.

To toggle on the STEP mode using a SmartIcon	**Click:** STEP SmartIcon	The STEP mode is turned on
To execute the macro using the STEP feature	**Click:** RUN SmartIcon	The macro is ready for execution one keystroke at a time
	Action: Press <space> to execute the macro in the STEP mode. The macro is executed in the STEP mode in the same manner as when execution is initiated from the keyboard.	
To toggle off the STEP mode using a SmartIcon	**Click:** STEP SmartIcon	The STEP mode is turned off

Use these SmartIcons as desired when you execute macros as an alternative to the keyboard commands.

Action: If desired, you may now Quit from 1-2-3.

SmartIcon	WYSIWYG SmartIcon	Command	Description
RUN		Run macro	Select and run a macro
STEP		STEP mode	Toggle on/off STEP mode of macro execution

FIGURE L.157. Selected SmartIcons for this Lesson.

L.9.15   When Things Go Wrong

A number of difficulties may be encountered when you start to run your macros. Remember, missing tildes (~) are the most frequent cause of macro errors. Some of the more common situations and how to approach them are as follows:

1. You attempt to run a macro by pressing <Alt> and the letter assigned to your macro. Lotus 1-2-3 beeps at you and nothing else happens. This usually occurs when you have not named your macro or you have pressed the wrong letter.

   a. Use / Range Name Create (/RNC) to obtain a list of range names and determine whether you have named your macro. If you have already named it, then verify the name. With version 2.2 and higher, you may also use < Alt >+< F3 > to obtain a list of macro names for execution.

   b. If your macro was not named, then assign it your desired name. If you used < Alt >+< F3 > to obtain the list of macro names and the one you want is not on the list, press <Esc> twice to return to the READY mode before you proceed to name your macro.

   c. Execute the macro using the appropriate name.

2. You initiated the execution of your macro and the ERROR mode indicator flashed on, signaling an error condition. This happens whenever a syntax error is detected during macro execution.

   a. Press <Enter> or <Esc> to terminate execution of your macro.

   b. Press < Alt >+< F2 > to activate the STEP mode of macro execution. STEP appears in the status indicator area of your screen as a reminder that you are in the STEP mode. This lets you execute your macro one keystroke at a time.

   c. Initiate execution of your macro.

   d. Repeatedly press <Enter> to step through the macro one keystroke at a time and to observe its operation. Input any values in response to a prompt. Lotus 1-2-3 requests this input with an SST in the status indicator area.

   e. When your macro encounters the error condition, it stops execution, ERROR is displayed as the worksheet mode indicator, and an error message is displayed identifying the problem with your macro. You have found the general location of your error.

   f. Press <Enter> or <Esc> to return to the READY mode.

   g. Determine the cause of your error and correct it. The error may reside in the cell above the location where execution of the macro actually stopped. This depends on the particular cause of your error.

   h. Rerun the macro to test your correction.

   i. Use < Alt >+< F2 > to toggle off the STEP mode of macro execution when your macro works correctly.

L.9.16   Lesson Summary

- Macros are like automatic typing. Menu selection commands and data entry keystrokes are stored for execution on demand.

- Macros are useful for performing any repetitive series of sequential 1-2-3 commands.

- A macro consists of a series of commands stored as labels in a column of the worksheet. An individual cell may contain a macro command up to 240 characters long.

- The tilde ($\sim$) is used in place of the $<$Enter$>$ in a macro.

- Macro execution is terminated when a blank cell is encountered.

- In addition to the macro commands, a macro may be documented by using a cell to store the macro name and a column to hold comment statements describing the intended action of each macro command. This documentation is not required, but greatly enhances understanding macros.

- /X macro commands are commands that are used only in macros. They cannot be executed interactively from the keyboard. These commands are retained from early releases of 1-2-3, and all have keyword macro commands that are their equivalents.

- Advanced keyword macro commands extend the capabilities of macros and permit the creation of third-generation-like programs within 1-2-3.

- Macros executed from the keyboard are named by using any single letter of the alphabet. A macro executed automatically when retrieving a worksheet is named 0 (zero).

- A macro is executed by pressing $<$Alt$>$ and the letter of the macro.

- Macro execution can be terminated by pressing $<$Ctrl$>+<$Break$>$.

- Special keyboard keys are assigned names for their reference in a macro.

- The LEARN mode records keystrokes as they are actually executed in a designated cell range. These keystrokes can then be range named and run as a macro.

- Utility macros assist in the creation of worksheets and can be used in the construction of many different worksheets.

- SmartIcons provide a convenient alternative for running a macro, including use of the STEP mode of execution.

L.9.17 Practice Tutorial

(1) Develop the PLAN16 worksheet with a macro for printing a report as described in this Lesson in Sections L.9.6, L.9.7, and L.9.8 as a guided activity in a hands-on manner.

> *Task 1:* Access the PLAN6 worksheet and add the macro illustrated in Figure L.141.
>
> *Task 2:* Name the macro.
>
> *Task 3:* Execute the macro that prints the results.
>
> *Task 4:* Save this as worksheet file MYPLAN17.

Time Estimates

Novice: 45 minutes

Intermediate: 30 minutes

Advanced: 20 minutes

(2) Develop the loan payment worksheet and macros for guided data entry and for prompted data entry described in this Lesson in Section L.9.9.

> *Task 1:* Create the Loan Analysis (Figure L.142).
>
> *Task 2:* Add the guided data entry macro, name it, and execute it.
>
> *Task 3:* Print the results.
>
> *Task 4:* Save this as the worksheet file LOAN1.

Task 5: Revise the macro for prompted data entry and execute it. (Use either "X" commands or keyword commands.)

Task 6: Print the results.

Task 7: Save this as worksheet file LOAN2.

Time Estimates

Novice: 45 minutes

Intermediate: 30 minutes

Advanced: 20 minutes

L.9.18. Practice Exercises

(1)   Case: Inland Container (continued)

In carrying out her analysis of the Rydder Truck Rental proposal, Mary Montoya has prepared a variety of different plans. Mary is convinced that macros could be added to her RYDDER2 worksheet file to help with her analysis as she prepares several additional alternatives for presentation to her district marketing manager. Mary knows that by adding macros to her worksheet, she can easily use the worksheet with other proposals. Mary wants to make these enhancements to her worksheet:

(a) Develop a macro (\P) for printing the entire report.

(b) Create a macro (\F) for printing all the cell formulas to document her worksheet.

(c) Build a macro (\M) that prints a managerial report. This report includes only a report heading and the projected values by month. The Unit sold growth rate, Price per unit increase, and Percent cost of sale data are *not* printed.

(d) Create a macro (\G) that *guides* data entry for the Unit sold growth rate, Price per unit increase, and Percent cost of sales. For the Price per unit increase, the macro should allow a value to be entered for each month.

(e) Prepare a macro (\D) that *prompts* data entry for the Unit sold growth rate, Price per unit increase, and Percent cost of sales. The macro should request a new value of Price per unit increase for each of the three months.

Before you begin entering your macros in Mary's worksheet, plan your macros by doing a *dry run* and writing down the necessary keystrokes in this Macro Planning Form.

MACRO PLANNING FORM

Macro Name	Macro Command	Descriptive Comment

Task 1: Retrieve Mary's RYDDER2 worksheet file and review it.

Task 2: Create the \P macro described above in (a). Enter, range name, and run this macro.

Task 3: Add the \F macro from (b) to Mary's worksheet. Execute this macro.

Task 4: Include the \M macro from (c) in the worksheet. This macro prints two separate areas of the worksheet as a single report. Run this macro.

Task 5: Include the \G macro described in (d) in this worksheet. Test the macro using these data:

	April	May	June
Units sold growth rate	.05		
Price per unit increase	.02	.01	.03
Percent cost of sales	.64		

Once you have entered the data by running this macro, use the \M macro to obtain a copy of the results. Save this as your INLAND2 worksheet file.

Task 6: Implement the \D macro that requests data as indicated in (e). Test the macro by using the data provided in Task 5. Use the \M macro to print a report with these results. Save this revision of your INLAND2 worksheet file.

Task 7: Print the area of your worksheet containing these macros.

Time Estimates

Novice: 60 minutes

Intermediate: 45 minutes

Advanced: 30 minutes

(2)   Case: Homestead Saving & Loan

Business Problem: Loan amortization schedule
MIS Characteristics: Finance
Operational Control

Donna Carter is a senior loan officer at Homestead Savings & Loan. As she meets with each of her customers, Donna prepares one or more loan payment schedules for their review and use. She created the HSLOAN.WK1 worksheet file that contains her loan payment schedule to help her prepare these schedules. One of the features of Donna's payment schedule is that it can be used for any number of years, up to 30 years, with the payment schedule computed for only the number of years she specifies. Donna wants you to enhance the operation of her worksheet by including several macros.

Before you start to create Donna's macros, plan your macros by performing a *dry run* and recording the desired keystrokes in this Macro Planning Form.

MACRO PLANNING FORM

Macro Name	Macro Command	Descriptive Comment

Task 1:   Access Donna's HSLOAN.WK1 worksheet file and review its contents. Notice that the interest rate is entered as a decimal, but displayed in a Percent 2 format.

Task 2:   Create a macro (\P) that prints Donna's Loan Payment Schedule. Perform the *dry run* and record the macro keystrokes. Enter, range name, and execute this macro.

Task 3:   Create a macro (\F) that prints the formulas in the Loan Payment Schedule. Perform the *dry run* and record the macro keystrokes. Enter, range name, and execute this macro. Be sure that this macro resets the print option to As-Displayed for any subsequent printing activities.

Task 4:   Devise a macro (\G) that *guides* data entry for the **Loan Amount, Interest Rate,** and **Number of Years.** Test your macro using these data:

	Loan 1	Loan 2
Load Amount	120000	180000
Interest Rate	.085	.105
Number of Years	15	25

After entering the data for each loan, use your print macro to obtain a hard copy of the results. Save this as your HSLMAC worksheet file.

Task 5: Develop a macro (\ D) with *prompted* data entry for the **Loan Amount, Interest Rate,** and **Number of Years.** Test this with the same data provided above in Task 4. Obtain a printed report of the results using your print macro. Save this version of your HSLMAC worksheet file.

Task 6: Print the area of your worksheet file containing your macros.

Time Estimates

Novice: 60 minutes

Intermediate: 45 minutes

Advanced: 30 minutes

(3)   Case: First Overland Bank

Business Problem: Employee benefit selection
MIS Characteristics: Human Resources
                                  Managerial Control

Kerri Zinn is a human resource benefits specialist at First Overland Bank. The Bank's dental insurance coverage is about to expire. Kerri is responsible for selecting a new dental insurance plan. Proposals from three insurance carriers are under evaluation. The elements from each plan must be compared, weighing the components of each plan against one another. Although many factors are included in each proposal, Kerri has narrowed the list of key elements to eight:

- Number of doctors in the plan
- Percentage of dollar amount of preventive procedures covered
- Age limit at which orthodontic procedures are covered
- Maximum annual total dollar amount of orthodontics coverage
- Maximum annual total dollar amount of coverage for a family
- Maximum annual total dollar amount of coverage for an individual
- Annual deductible dollar amount
- Monthly cost of the plan per employee

To organize her evaluation, Kerri developed a point-scoring method to compare these very different elements of the plan. She uses a 10-point scale for each component, with 10 as the highest score. Kerri collects the data for each component and then uses a **Conversion Factor** to produce the point score. For example, the **Number of Doctors,** such as 3500, is divided by her conversion factor of 1100 to yield a score of 3.18. Some components of the plan are more important than others. Kerri assigns an **Importance Weight** to each element. The highest **Importance Weight** is 1.00. This weight is multiplied by the score to produce the final **Plan Scoring** for each element of the plan. For example, her **Importance Weight** for **Number of Doctors** is 0.20, whereas that for **Monthly Cost per Employee** is 0.70. Using these values, the **Plan Scoring** for the **Number of Doctors** is 0.64.

Kerri has entered the **Conversion Factors, Importance Weights, Plan Characteristics,** and **Plan Scoring** in her FOB.WK1 worksheet file. The **Plan Characteristics** are the data submitted by each insurance carrier in their proposals. In preparing for a review with the Bank's benefits committee next Thursday, Kerri would like to enhance her worksheet as follows:

(a) Develop a macro (\P) for printing a management report consisting of the report heading, the **Plan Characteristics,** and **Plan Scoring.**

(b) Develop a macro (\F) for printing the formulas in her worksheet to maintain her documentation.

(c) Create a macro (\D) that guides data entry of a new set of **Importance Weights.**

Before you begin to create these macros for Kerri, plan your macros by performing a *dry run* and recording the desired keystrokes in this Macro Planning Form.

MACRO PLANNING FORM

Macro Name	Macro Command	Descriptive Comment

Task 1: Retrieve Kerri's FOB.WK1 worksheet file and review its contents. Notice how Kerri organized the worksheet as three screens; consequently, you can use <PgDn> and <PgUp> to easily move from one section of her report to another.

Task 2: Create the macro described above in (a). The report heading includes rows 1 through 6. Perform the *dry run* and record the macro keystrokes. Enter, range name, and execute this macro.

Task 3: Review Kerri's initial Point Scoring Analysis. Since the plan with the highest **Total Plan Score** is the "best" plan, which plan is best? Circle this value on your printed report.

Task 4: Develop the macro described above in (b). Kerri wants to print only the formulas contained in the Plan Scoring section of her worksheet.

Perform the *dry run* and record the macro keystrokes. Enter, range name, and execute this macro. Be sure this macro resets the print option to As-Displayed for any subsequent printing activities.

Task 5: Create the macro described above in (c). Perform the *dry run* and record the macro keystrokes. Enter, range name, and execute this macro. Test the macro by changing these data:

Number of Doctors	0.15
Monthly Cost per Employee	0.80

Task 6: Execute the appropriate macro to produce a copy of the report containing the results for the revised data values entered in Task 5.

Task 7: Review the revised results from the report generated in Task 6. Which plan is "best" with these revised **Importance Factors?** Circle the "best" **Total Plan Score** on your output report.

Task 8: Print the area of your worksheet file containing these macros.

Task 9: Save this as the FOBMAC worksheet file.

Time Estimates

Novice: 60 minutes

Intermediate: 45 minutes

Advanced: 30 minutes

L.9.19 Comprehensive Problems

(1) Case: Woodcraft Furniture Company (continued)

Martha Goodguess and Joe Birch have been examining the collection of what-if analyses you generated at Woodcraft's last quarterly management meeting. They envision that these analyses will continue for future management meetings. At your weekly project development review meeting with "Tall" Pine, a consensus was reached to enhance the pro forma financial statement planning system by automating several of its repetitive processes so that Debbie Young, an administrative assistant in your department, can support the monthly analysis and reporting process. Your work plan to augment this system consists of these enhancements:

(a) Develop a macro for printing the report.

(b) Create a macro to print the worksheet formulas so that current documentation can be maintained.

(c) Develop a macro that prompts data entry for the **Hourly Rate** and **Hours Worked.** Test the macro with these data:

Hourly Rate	11.00
Hours Worked	190

(d) Devise a macro that guides data entry for the **Tables Sold** and **Sofas Sold** during each month of the quarter. Test the macro with these data:

	July	August	September
Tables Sold	876	924	992
Sofas Sold	541	603	630

(e) Create a set of four macros to change the column headings for each quarter. That is, July, August, and September would be revised to October, November, and December, and similarly for each of the other two quarters.

In your discussions with "Tall," the decision was made to locate these macros below and to the right of the main application area. This will permit the use of <PgDn>, <PgUp>, <Tab>, and < Shift >+< Tab > to move between the application area and the macro area.

Before you begin to enter your macros into the worksheet, plan these macros by performing a *dry run* and record the desired keystrokes in this Macro Planning Form.

MACRO PLANNING FORM

Macro Name	Macro Command	Descriptive Comment

Task 1: Access the WOOD2 worksheet file.

Task 2: Perform a *dry run* and record the necessary macro keystrokes.

Task 3: Name each macro and execute it.

Task 4: Print each macro and its results.

Task 5: Save this as the worksheet file WOOD10.

Quick check answers: (c) Income before taxes = 343519
Return on sales = .0933   or   9.33%

(d) Income before taxes = 580110
Return on sales = .1544   or   15.44%

Time Estimates

Novice: 60 minutes

Intermediate: 45 minutes

Advanced: 30 minutes

(2)   Case: Midwest Universal Gas (continued)

Mary Derrick, Francis Foresight, and "Pete" Newgas have examined the collection of what-if analyses you compiled for Midwest Universal Gas. They anticipate that many of these analyses will continue as an integral part of MUG's planning process. Sam Wright's administrative assistant, Herbie Loo, has been assigned the task of supporting your analysis activities. A review of the current system has convinced Sam and Mary that it should be modified to include these enhancements:

(a) Create a macro for printing the entire report.

(b) Develop a macro for printing a management summary report containing the same report heading and these selected line items: **Total Gas Sold, Total Sales, Total Expense, Operating Income, Interest Expense, Income Before Taxes, Income Taxes, Net Income,** and **Return on Investment.**

(c) Develop a macro to print the worksheet formulas so that current documentation can be maintained.

(d) Create a macro with prompted data entry for the **Retail Rate, Wholesale Rate,** and **Cost of Gas** percent. Test the macro with these data:

Retail Rate	385
Wholesale Rate	315
Cost of Gas	65%

(e) Construct a macro that guides data entry for the **Total Gas Sold** during each quarter of the year. Test the macro with these data:

	1st Qtr	2nd Qtr	3rd Qtr	4th Qtr
Total Gas Sold	264	221	85	243

(f) Create either a single macro or a set of four macros to change the column headings for each quarter. MUG engages in preparing a "rolling" plan each quarter. For example, for the second quarter the column heading would be 2nd, 3rd, 4th, and 1st; and these heading change in a similar manner for each of the other two quarterly planning periods. These macros change only the column headings. They should *not* move any of the columns of data.

In your discussions with Sam and Mary, the decision was made to locate these macros below and to the right of the main application area. This will permit the use of <PgDn>, <PgUp>, <Tab>, and < Shift >+< Tab > to move between the application area and the macro area.

Before you begin to enter your macros into the worksheet, plan these macros by performing a *dry run* and record the desired keystrokes in this Macro Planning Form.

MACRO PLANNING FORM

Macro Name	Macro Command	Descriptive Comment

Task 1: Access the MUG2 worksheet file.

Task 2: Perform a *dry run* and record the required macro keystrokes.

Task 3: Name each macro and execute it.

Task 4: Print each macro and its results.

Task 5: Save this as the worksheet file MUG10.

Quick check answers: (d) Net income   = 10248 (000's)
Return on investment = .1001   or   10.01%

(e) Net Income   = 15752 (000's)
Return on investment = .1538   or   15.38%

Time Estimates

Novice: 60 minutes

Intermediate: 45 minutes

Advanced: 30 minutes

L.9.20   Case Application

Case: First Bank of America

Business Problem: Project Investment Analysis
                 Capital Budgeting

MIS Characteristics: Finance
                     Management Control

Management Functions: Planning
                      Organizing

Tools Skills: Financial functions
              Macros
              What-if
              Reporting

The First Bank of America of Broken Spoke is a full-service bank that serves a variety of commercial and individual customers. The First Bank of America (FBA) was founded in 1804 by John J. Green. Today, John J. Green, III, is the Bank's Chairman and Chief Operating Officer. The innovation of the three J. J. Greens has kept First Bank profitable when other banks or savings and loans have fallen on hard times. To maintain the bank's competitive advantage, J. J. has been a leader in implementing computer technology. He recently attended a meeting of bank executives where he learned about advances in return item processing. A return item is a check that has been sent back to the bank where it was deposited because of insufficient funds in the account at the bank on which it was drawn. The return item must be debited from the depositor's account and the check sent to the depositor. This return item processing requires special handling that is different from that of other checks processed in the bank's demand deposit accounting system. J. J. learned that return items could be processed off-line from the normal demand deposit accounting transactions using a special-purpose minicomputer or a personal computer local area network (PC LAN) system. His bank could anticipate a considerable saving with this return item processing. J. J. chatted with several vendors of return item processing systems, collecting their brochures and business cards before returning to Broken Spoke.

On his return, J. J. called in his comptroller, Carrie Campbell, and assigned her the project of conducting an analysis of return item processing systems. She was to prepare a recommendation for the acquisition of the most cost-effective system.

Carrie recognized that her analysis was a capital budgeting decision with mutually exclusive projects. That is, either a minicomputer-based system or a PC LAN–based system could be selected. However, First Bank would not acquire both systems. Carrie sifted through the material J. J. had gathered at the bankers' meeting. She made telephone calls to several vendors and their customers. In each instance, Carrie was interested in a turnkey return item processing system. That is, the vendor would supply the hardware, software, and training all in one complete package. Fundamentally, all First Bank would need to do would be to plug in the computer and run the program.

Carrie has narrowed the field to two different systems. One, available from Great Western Systems (GWS), runs on a minicomputer, and the other, supplied by Data Management Products (DMP), runs on a PC LAN. She has computed the annual net cash flows for both systems. The annual net cash flows include depreciation expenses and the saving from current processing methods. For this type of investment, J. J. and

Carrie have established a five-year life. Changes in computer technology make it risky to consider a useful life longer than this. During the second and each following year, the net cash flows for the minicomputer are expected to increase by $2000, whereas those for the PC LAN are anticipated to increase by $3000. This differential stems from the expectation that the PC LAN will require somewhat less systems management support than the minicomputer.

First Bank of America uses the net present value (NPV) method of project selection. The net present value of each project is computed by using the bank's anticipated cost of capital, discount rate, or interest rate for funds invested in plant and equipment. The project with the largest positive net present value is selected, because this represents the greatest return on the bank's investment. Net present value is a discounted cash flow technique that recognizes that a dollar received in year 1 of an investment is worth more than a dollar received in year 4 of the investment. The cost of capital is used in determining the present value of funds received in the future.

Carrie knows that net present value is easy to compute by using Lotus 1-2-3 because the function @NPV is designed to perform this computation. However, to get the *net* present value, it is necessary to include the cost of the investment as a cash outflow, which is indicated by making the purchase price a negative value in the net cash flow stream. For purposes of her net present value analysis, Carrie will assume that the purchase of the computer system occurs at the end of year 0, which is equivalent to the beginning of year 1. However, this lets Carrie enter the purchase price separately from the other cash flows for year 1. She will apply the @NPV function to net cash flows in years 1 through 5 because the purchase price should not be discounted. Her calculation for net present value for each computer system will be the negative of the purchase price plus the net present value of the stream of cash flows in years 1 through 5.

The NPVs for the minicomputer system by Great Western Systems and for the PC LAN system by Data Management Products can be computed. A programmed decision for making the choice between the two systems can be included in the worksheet. This decision incorporates logic that picks the system with the largest NPV. Carrie wants to have the label "Minicomputer" or "PC LAN" displayed on the worksheet, depending on which system has the greatest NPV.

As result of this analysis, Carrie can provide J. J. with a worksheet that includes the recommended decision. However, Carrie knows that J. J. may want to explore some other possibilities. He is likely to want to evaluate several what-ifs with different costs of capital, purchase prices, and net cash flows. She will set up the worksheet so that she is ready to prepare these additional alternatives, if J. J. poses such questions. Then J. J. and Carrie can make their final selection of return item processing systems.

Tasks:

1. Access the CAPBUD.WK1 worksheet file and review its contents. Notice that Carrie has set up a single assumption cell for the cost of capital. The years 0 through 5 have been established with year 0 containing the purchase price and each of the other five years containing values for the system's operation. For each system, Carrie has already included the purchase price and the first year's net cash flow. She has placed the label "Choice → " in column **A,** with the idea that you will place the programmed decision next to it in column **B.**

2. Enter the equations to compute the Net cash flow for years 2 through 5 using the increases for each computer system from Carrie's analysis as described before.

3. Enter the equation to compute the NPV for each system in the cell immediately to the right of the "Net present value" label. (*Hint:* Remember that the @NPV function is used only for the cash flows in years 1 through 5; the purchase price in year 0 is included in your formula, but not in the @NPV function.)

4. Enter an @IF function in the cell next to "Choice" to display either the "Minicomputer" or "PC LAN" label.

5. Carrie expects that she will need to run several different analyses for J. J., and so she wants you to create a macro, with the name \P, for printing the report. Carrie wants to place all macros below and to the right of the current worksheet area. (*Hint:* Use <Tab> and <PgDn> to get to the location for your macros.) Execute this macro and then save your worksheet file.

6. With the number of changes that might occur to the worksheet, Carrie would like you to create a macro named\S to use for saving the worksheet. That is, every time this macro is executed, the current worksheet is saved. Execute this macro. If desired, set up this macro so that the user is prompted for a different worksheet file name each time the file is saved.

7. So that Carrie is well prepared to address different alternatives that J.J. might want to consider, she wants you to create a macro that will guide data entry for several key variables. Each time the macro is executed, J. J. will be guided in entering new data for (1) cost of capital, (2) minicomputer purchase price, (3) minicomputer net cast flow in year 1, (4) PC LAN purchase price, and (5) PC LAN net cash flow in year 1. Name this macro\W and execute it with a different set of test data; you invent them. Then execute it a second time with the original data. Use the \P macro to print the worksheet and then the\S macro to save it.

8. Perform a what-if analysis and determine the cost of capital that would reverse the investment choice.

9. (*Optional*)   Although First Bank applies the net present value technique in capital budgeting, J. J. would like to know the payback period for each alternative. The payback period is the amount of time it takes for the net cash inflows to be equal to the purchase price. That is, the payback period addresses the issue of how long it will take to recover the purchase price. Payback is not a discounted cash flow technique, and hence a dollar received in year 3 is considered to have the same value as a dollar received in year 1. Carrie knows that the payback period can be readily assessed from a graph of the cash flows. For each investment alternative, add a row to the worksheet that contains the "Sum-Net cash flow" where this sum is the purchase price in year 0, the purchase price plus the year 1 net cash flow in year 1, the purchase price plus the sum of the year 1 and year 2 cash flows in year 2, and so on for the other three years. Create a line graph with Year as the X-axis and the "Sum-Net cash flow" for each of the two investments plotted in the **A** and **B** ranges. The payback period is where these lines cross the zero line displayed on your graph. Label your graph with a title for the graph and titles for each of the axes. Save the *.PIC file of your graph and print it. What is the approximate payback period for each investment alternative?

10. Carrie is concerned about the documentation of the worksheet. Print the cell formulas for the worksheet and be sure to include those for the macros.

11. Write a brief summary of your NPV analysis. Indicate any suggestions that you might have to improve this worksheet or revise it for use with any other set of mutually exclusive project investment decision choices.

Time Estimates

Novice: 120 minutes

Intermediate: 90 minutes

Advanced: 60 minutes

Consolidating Results with Combine

CONTENT

- **What Is Consolidation?**
- **Expanding the Budget Worksheet Model**
- **Preparing a Business Unit Worksheet for Consolidation**
- **Preparing the Second Worksheet for Consolidation**
- **Setting Up the Consolidation Worksheet**
- **Consolidating Worksheets Using Named Ranges**
- **Alternative Processing for Consolidation**
- **Preparing Business Unit Worksheets for File Xtracts**
- **Extracted Data Values**
- **Consolidating Worksheets Using Xtract Files**
- **When Things Go Wrong**

L.10.1 What Is Consolidation?

For business modeling with worksheets, **consolidation** is the process of adding the results from several different worksheets. Each of several individual worksheets might contain the data for a separate business entity, such as a department or division. A consolidation would provide a summary of data for an entire group of departments or divisions.

Consolidation is one component of multidimensional worksheet modeling. Typically, business consolidations employ the three dimensions of (1) variables, planning items, or accounts, (2) time periods, and (3) business units, as illustrated in Figure L.158. The worksheet is usually organized with the variables and time periods placed in the rows and columns of a worksheet, while the third dimension of business units is implemented with multiple spreadsheets. In Lotus 1-2-3 Release 2.4 and earlier, each worksheet is physically stored in a separate disk file. With Release 3.x, Lotus 1-2-3 has been enhanced to accommodate multiple worksheets within a single worksheet file stored on disk. This enhancement in Release 3.x underscores the importance of

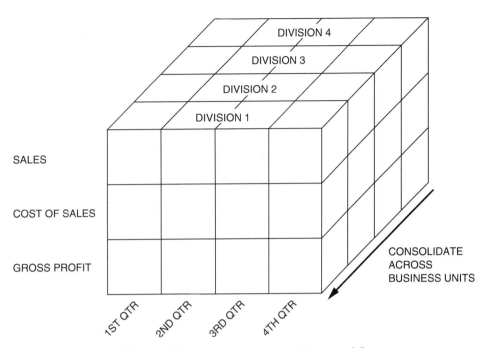

FIGURE L.158. Multidimensional worksheet modeling

multidimensional modeling in the solution of a variety of business problems. This Lesson explores the implementation of multidimensional modeling by using multiple worksheet files for consolidation. This strategy can be used across all releases of Lotus 1-2-3.

Consider the situation at Good Morning Products. Because of the success with operations in California, the Board of Directors decided to build a second plant in Florida to expand the production of Liquid Gold. Crush and Kim worked for several months in finalizing the arrangement for this expansion. With two plants, each organized as a separate business unit, the organization structure of Good Morning Products appears as shown in Figure L.159.

Under this organization structure, a budget is prepared for each of the two divisions. Then, to obtain the budget for the corporation, Kim needs to consolidate or add the results from each of the two divisions. As illustrated in Figure L.160, a

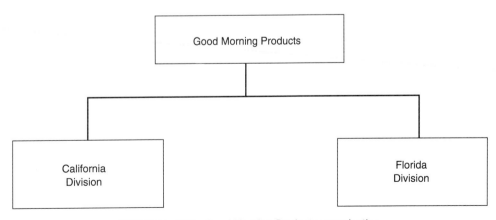

FIGURE L.159. Good Morning Products organization

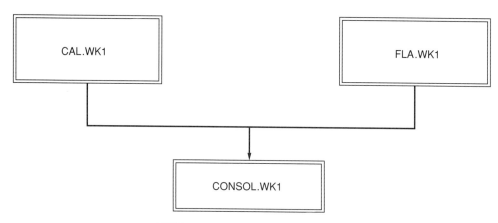

FIGURE L.160. Consolidation system

budget worksheet is prepared for each of the California (CAL) and Florida (FLA) Divisions. These results are then consolidated in a corporate (CONSOL) worksheet to generate the consolidated corporate report. Figure L.161 is a dataflow diagram (DFD) that depicts the overall planning process, including the consolidation. Here, the dataflow diagram illustrates the interactions among processes, files, and dataflows, such as reports. Figure L.161 shows the use of the worksheet files in the preparation of the division and corporate reports, which goes beyond merely creating the individual worksheet files as shown in Figure L.160. As depicted in the DFD, budget preparation takes place in the two processes described as follows:

> *P.1—Prepare Division Budget.* Data are obtained for each division and entered into that division's worksheet to produce the division's budget report. Worksheet files (F.1 and F.2) containing the formulas and report layout are accessed in preparing these reports.

> *P.2—Prepare Corporate Budget.* Data are consolidated from the individual divisions to generate the consolidated corporate report. A worksheet file (F.3) provides the framework for carrying out the consolidation and producing the report.

This reflects a common practice in the consolidation of business results, which follows a two-step process of

1. Prepare the results for each individual business entity, such as a department or a division.
2. Add or consolidate the individual business unit results to obtain a corporate result.

If an organization had three levels rather than just two, this processing could be performed across each level. That is, departments could be consolidated into divisions, and then the divisions could be consolidated to the corporate level.

L.10.2 Expanding the Budget Worksheet Model

Besides **Sales, Cost of Sales,** and **Gross Profits,** Kim and Crush want their budget model to include several additional planning items or variables. They have expanded the worksheet to include the expense items, **Earnings Before Tax** and **Return On Sales,** as illustrated in Figure L.162. Chris and Frosty are interested in including the **Return On Sales** ratio, since this provides a measure of the profitability on each dollar of Liquid Gold sold.

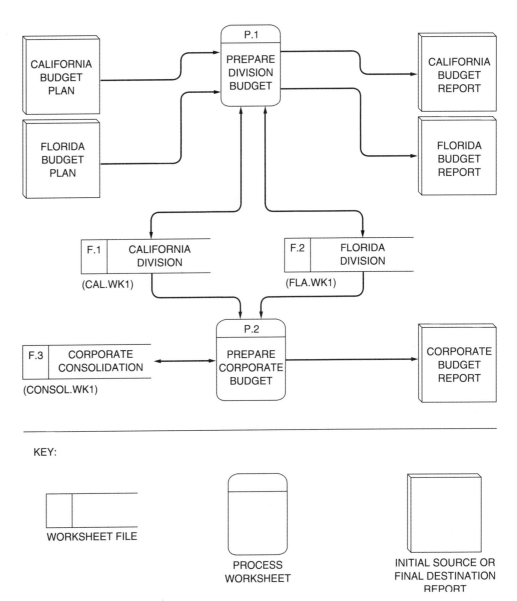

FIGURE L.161. Dataflow diagram (DFD) of consolidation processing

Kim and Chris expanded the budget model for the California Division of Good Morning Products by carrying out several modifications.

To expand the budget model to include additional planning items

Action: Retrieve the worksheet file PLAN6.WK1 in preparation for modifying the budget to include additional planning items.

Action: Delete the top two rows of the PLAN6.WK1 worksheet. This removes the date and one blank line at the top because they are not required with this worksheet.

Action: Add the @ROUND function to the calculation of the **Sales** and the **Cost of Sales** variables for the four quarters.

Action: Add the equations described by the business model logic contained in Figure L.163 to the PLAN6.WK1 worksheet. Place these formulas in the cell locations and include underlining as illustrated in Figure L.162. Be sure to use the @ROUND function on any values that might compute to a decimal fraction.

```
F25: (P1) +F23/F10                                              READY

                A          B         C         D         E        F
8                       1ST QTR   2ND QTR   3RD QTR   4TH QTR   TOTAL
9                       -------   -------   -------   -------   -------
10  Sales               289500    312660    337673    364687   1304520
11  Cost of Sales       222915    240748    260008    280809   1004480
12                      -------   -------   -------   -------   -------
13  Gross Profit         66585     71912     77665     83878    300040
14
15  Salaries             23000     23000     25000     29000    100000
16  Benefits              4370      4370      4750      5510     19000
17  Admin Expense         6659      7191      7766      8388     30004
18  Depreciation          2000      2000      2500      2500      9000
19  Interest              1600      1600      1600      1600      6400
20                      -------   -------   -------   -------   -------
21  Total Expenses       37629     38161     41616     46998    164404
22
23  Earnings Before Tax  28956     33751     36049     36880    135636
24
25  Return On Sales      10.0%     10.8%     10.7%     10.1%     10.4%
26                      =======   =======   =======   =======   =======
27

                        UNDO
```

FIGURE L.162. Modified budget worksheet for California division

Keypoint! The numbers in the worksheet model are rounded so that they will cross-total and foot correctly. Also, if the numbers are *not* rounded here, other rounding difficulties will be encountered when the consolidation is performed!

Action: For each of the new planning items, except **Return On Sales,** compute the **Total** column by adding the values across each row.

Action: Use the same formula for **Return On Sales** in the **Total** column as that used in the other four quarters. Format the **Return On Sales** row as a Percent with one decimal.

Caution Alert! A ratio such as **Return On Sales** *cannot* be summed for the four quarters. It must be computed separately in a column like the **Total** column! Be careful to add only those numbers that have meaning when added!

		1st Qtr	2nd Qtr	3rd Qtr	4th Qtr
Salaries	=	23000	23000	25000	29000
Benefits	=	Salaries * .19 FOR 4 columns			
Administrative Expense	=	Sales * .023 FOR 4 columns			
Depreciation	=	2000	2000	2500	2500
Interest	=	1600 FOR 4 columns			
Total Expenses	=	SUM (Salaries THRU Interest)			
Earinings Before Tax	=	Gross Profit − Total Expenses			
Return on Sales	=	Earnings Before Tax/Sales			

Figure L.163. Additional equations for budget worksheet in Business English.

```
                              CALIFORNIA PLANT
                    PRO FORMA PROFIT AND LOSS STATEMENT
                    -----------------------------------


Sales Growth Rate          0.08
Cost Percent               0.77

                        1ST QTR   2ND QTR   3RD QTR   4TH QTR    TOTAL
                        -------   -------   -------   -------   -------
Sales                    289500    312660    337673    364687   1304520
Cost of Sales            222915    240748    260008    280809   1004480
                        -------   -------   -------   -------   -------
Gross Profit              66585     71912     77665     83878    300040

Salaries                  23000     23000     25000     29000    100000
Benefits                   4370      4370      4750      5510     19000
Administrative Expense     6659      7191      7766      8388     30004
Depreciation               2000      2000      2500      2500      9000
Interest                   1600      1600      1600      1600      6400
                        -------   -------   -------   -------   -------
Total Expenses            37629     38161     41616     46998    164404

Earnings Before Tax       28956     33751     36049     36880    135636

Return on Sales           10.0%     10.8%     10.7%     10.1%     10.4%
                        =======   =======   =======   =======   =======
```

FIGURE L.164. Budget report for California division.

Action: Print the results for the California Division as illustrated in Figure L.162 and then save this as worksheet file CAL. A report of the resulting budget worksheet model is shown in Figure L.164.

L.10.3 Preparing a Business Unit Worksheet for Consolidation

When the results from one worksheet are transferred to another worksheet in a consolidation, a common practice is to transfer a selected range of cells, rather than the entire worksheet. For example, with Good Morning Products, the range **B10..E23,** as illustrated in Figure L.162, contains the results that are to be consolidated. Only these cells need to be summed. To transfer the results from an individual business entity worksheet to a consolidation worksheet, the worksheet for the individual business entity must be set up to accommodate this transfer of a range of data.

In Lotus 1-2-3, the / Range Name Create (/RNC) command is a convenient method for defining the range of cells that will be transferred when performing a consolidation. By naming a range of cells, that range is then referenced by name rather than by specific cell names. When integrating results among several worksheets, **Range Names** are a preferred method of referencing. This allows the location of the cells for the consolidation to be modified without changing its range name reference. Specific cell names do not accommodate these revisions. Range names reduce modifications and help avoid errors caused by specifying an incorrect range of cells.

Keypoint!

> **Range names** facilitate changing the specific location of a ranges of cells in one worksheet *without* changing the reference to that range of cells in another worksheet!

For the California Division, Kim and Chris want to use a Range Name for their consolidation. Let's give this range for the consolidation the name BUDGET.

Action: Be sure the CAL worksheet is the currently active file.

To range name a worksheet area			
Move to:	**B10**	Upper-left corner of the range to be named, which contains **Sales** for the 1st Qtr	
Press:	/	Access main menu	
Select:	Range	Only a portion of the worksheet is to be named	
Select:	Name	Desired activity	
Select:	Create	Specific action	
Enter:	budget	User-supplied name of the range of cells	

The range of cells is already anchored. With the cell cursor located in the upper-left corner, the range can be defined by expanding the cell pointer as illustrated in Figure L.165.

Move to:	**E23**	Highlight cells by expanding pointer to lower-right corner of the range being named, as shown in Figure L.165	
Press:	<Enter>	Complete specification of the range name and return to READY mode	
Action:	Save the CAL worksheet file with the range name definition.		

Keypoint!   Range name definitions are saved when you save your worksheet file!

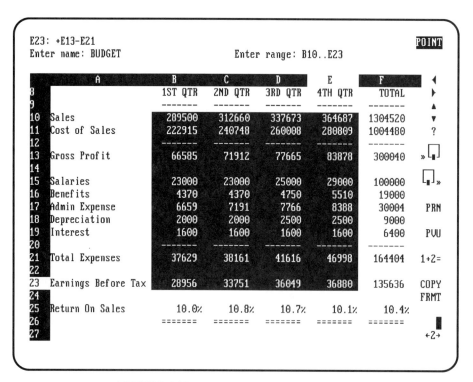

FIGURE L.165. BUDGET range name definition.

The BUDGET range name is ready for use in the consolidation process once it has been defined in this manner. When a worksheet file is saved, the range name definition is saved as part of the worksheet file.

L.10.4 Preparing the Second Worksheet for Consolidation

For Good Morning Products, like many other businesses, once a worksheet has been created for one business unit, it can be "cloned" for other business units. With a standard budget that uses the same line items or planning variables for all business units, the differences between the business unit plans are the input or assumption data, which are unique to each business unit. This is the situation for the Florida Division of Good Morning Products.

One of the primary reasons that Good Morning Products acquired the Florida plant was that it could produce Liquid Gold more efficiently. The **Cost Percent** at this plant is only 71 percent of **Sales**. Also, the **Sale Growth Rate** at this facility is expected to be 14 percent each quarter during the coming year, with **Sales** in the first quarter of $117,000. These planning data and the other data unique to the Florida Division are shown in Figure L.166. The budget for this Division can be prepared for Crush and Kim by cloning it from the CAL worksheet file.

Let's use the CAL file for creating the FLA worksheet.

To clone a worksheet from a file for another business unit

Action: Retrieve the CAL worksheet file containing all the desired formulas for the Pro Forma Profit and Loss Statement.

Action: *Immediately* save this as the FLA worksheet file. This will help to ensure that the CAL worksheet is not inadvertently replaced with the modified FLA file and is a primary step in cloning the FLA worksheet from the CAL worksheet.

Action: Revise the **Sale Growth Rate, Cost Percent, Sales [1st QTR], Salaries, Depreciation**, and **Interest**, as indicated by the data provided in Figure L.166.

Action: Print the resulting budget report (Figure L.167) for the Florida Division and save the modified FLA worksheet file, completing this cloning operation.

Once the **BUDGET** named range is established in the CAL worksheet file, it remains defined in Kim and Chris's FLA worksheet for Good Morning Products. Let's confirm the use of the BUDGET range name.

To check a range name specification

Press:	/	Access main menu
Select:	Range	Only part of the worksheet is named
Select:	Name	Desired activity
Select:	Create	Specific action

		1st Qtr	2nd Qtr	3rd Qtr	4th Qtr
Sales Growth Rate	= 0.14				
Cost Percent	= 0.71				
Sales	=	117000			
Salaries	=	14000,	14000,	15000,	18000
Depreciation	=	3000 FOR 4 columns			
Interest	=	1800 FOR 4 columns			

Figure L.166. Data for Florida division.

```
                              FLORIDA PLANT
                   PRO FORMA PROFIT AND LOSS STATEMENT
                   ------------------------------------


        Sales Growth Rate          0.14
        Cost Percent               0.71


                          1ST QTR   2ND QTR   3RD QTR   4TH QTR    TOTAL
                          -------   -------   -------   -------   -------
        Sales              117000    133380    152053    173340    575773
        Cost of Sales       83070     94700    107958    123071    408799
        Gross Profit        33930     38680     44095     50269    166974
                          -------   -------   -------   -------   -------
        Salaries            14000     14000     15000     18000     61000
        Benefits             2660      2660      2850      3420     11590
        Administrative Expense  2691      3068      3497      3987     13243
        Depreciation         3000      3000      3000      3000     12000
        Interest             1800      1800      1800      1800      7200
                          -------   -------   -------   -------   -------
        Total Expenses      24151     24528     26147     30207    105033

        Earnings Before Tax  9779     14152     17948     20062     61941

        Return on Sales      8.4%     10.6%     11.8%     11.6%     10.8%
                          =======   =======   =======   =======   =======
```

FIGURE L.167. Budget report for Florida division.

A list of named ranges is displayed, continue like this:

Select:	budget	This named range is displayed, as indicated by the expanded cell pointer
Press:	\<Enter\>	Accept current definition

The appearance of the same named range confirms that it remains defined and is ready for use in consolidation processing.

Keypoint! When creating worksheets for multiple business units, completely develop the worksheet for an individual business unit including all range names and graphs. Verify the contents of this worksheet. Then "clone" the worksheet for use with the other business units. Include any unique formulas after copying the worksheet. This helps to avoid errors in formulas across the entire set of worksheets for all of the business units!

L.10.5 Setting Up the Consolidation Worksheet

When a consolidation is performed, a good strategy to deploy with Lotus 1-2-3 is to set up a separate worksheet into which the data from each business unit are added as the consolidation is carried out. Typically, this worksheet would contain the report heading, column headings, account or planning item names, and any formulas used to calculate special columns or rows, such as a total column, or a growth rate or ratio row. These special rows and columns need to be established in such a manner that the formulas are correctly calculated when the consolidation is performed.

At Good Morning Products, Chris designed the CONSOL worksheet shown in Figure L.168 for performing the consolidation. Notice that the planning items and columns are set up as an *exact image* of the CAL and FLA worksheets. This is necessary

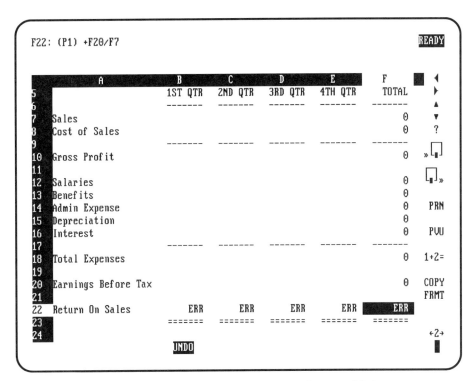

FIGURE L.168. CONSOL worksheet set up for consolidation.

because the range of cells from the two individual division worksheets will be placed into the CONSOL worksheet. If the CONSOL worksheet contained additional rows, then the data from the individual divisions would not match up with the desired rows in the CONSOL worksheet. Unless each row is individually consolidated, this match between the worksheets of the individual business units and the consolidation worksheet is required.

Keypoint!

> The range of cells summed in the consolidation worksheet should be an *exact image* of the cells in the individual business unit worksheets!

Figure L.169 shows the formulas Chris wants to use in the consolidation worksheet to calculate the **Total** column and the **Return On Sales** variable. Let's set up this consolidation worksheet for Good Morning Products.

To set up the consolidation worksheet

Action: Retrieve the CAL worksheet file. (The FLA file could also be used.)

Action: *Immediately* save this as the CONSOL worksheet to avoid inadvertently destroying the CAL worksheet.

Action: Remove rows 4, 5, and 6, which contain the **Sales Growth Rate, Cost Percent,** and a blank line. These rows are not required for the consolidated results and are *not* included as part of the range of data that will be consolidated.

Action: *Carefully* erase the data and formulas in the **1st Qtr** through the **4th Qtr** for all variables except **Return On Sales**. Do *not* erase the equations in the **Total** column or the underlining because these are used with the consolidated results. The revised worksheet appears as shown in Figure L.169.

Action: Save this revised CONSOL worksheet file.

This completes arranging Chris's CONSOL worksheet for performing the consolidation with data from the division worksheets.

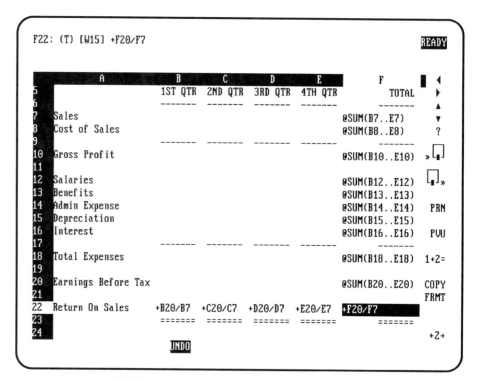

FIGURE L.169. Equations in CONSOL worksheet.

L.10.6   Consolidating Worksheets Using Named Ranges

In Lotus 1-2-3, consolidation is carried out with the / File Combine Add (/FCA) command. This command requests the source file and, if desired, the range of the data to be combined. The / File Combine command has three available options, as described in Figure L.170.

The Add command is used to perform the consolidation. The Subtract command could be used to compute the differences between two worksheets, such as might be performed for a financial variance analysis between actual and forecast results. The Copy command is a convenient means of moving complex formulas from one worksheet to another one.

When a / File Combine is carried out, the location of the incoming data is determined by *the position of the worksheet cell pointer.* This designates the upper-left-hand corner of the range where the data will be located. If the cursor is *not* positioned correctly, the incoming data will *not* be placed in the desired location on the current worksheet.

Caution Alert!

> The worksheet cell pointer *must* be carefully positioned in the upper-left-hand corner of the desired location for the incoming data!

Command	Action
Add	Numeric values are added to constants or blank cells in the current worksheet.
Copy	Formulas, data, and labels are copied to the current worksheet.
Subtract	Numeric values are subtracted from constants or blank cells in the current worksheet.

FIGURE L.170. File Combine menu choices.

Because a consolidation requires the careful positioning of the worksheet cursor and the specification of the file and range from which data will be obtained, a macro provides a convenient and safe way to specify the commands necessary for performing the consolidation. Also, by using a macro, the consolidation can be readily repeated for any revisions in the worksheet files of any of the business units.

Chris planned the macro for the consolidation of Good Morning Products with a "*dry run*" (Figure L.171).

Notice that each of the areas in the worksheet where data are to be added is erased before the / File Combine is executed. This preserves the underlining while ensuring that these cells contain blanks when the consolidation process is initiated. Also, this allows Chris to save the consolidated results in the CONSOL worksheet file for his reference, while still initializing the designated worksheet cells each time the consolidation is carried out. Figure L.172 portrays this macro in the CONSOL worksheet. Of course, if you wanted to, you could execute each of these commands manually, rather than placing them in a macro.

Let's develop Chris's CONSOL worksheet macro.

To enter and execute the consolidation macro	**Action:** Make sure the CONSOL worksheet is the currently active file.

Action: Make sure the CONSOL worksheet is the currently active file.

Action: Enter the consolidation macro, as shown in Figure L.172. Remember to use / Range Name to assign the range name \C to the cell containing { **home**}.

Action: Review the macro and correct any errors. Save this version of the CONSOL worksheet file.

Action: Execute the \C macro with <Alt>+<C>.

Action: Review the consolidated results. If you have any errors, correct them and repeat the execution of the \C macro.

Action: Print the consolidated results, which should match those illustrated in Figure L.173.

Action: (*Optional*) Save the CONSOL worksheet file with the consolidated results. This would save the results of the most recent consolidation.

This completes the consolidation process for the California and Florida Divisions of Good Morning Products. Chris has developed the information Kim and Frosty wanted for their planning by following the steps summarized in Figure L.174. Frosty has his eye on another plant in Arizona. What changes would Chris need to make to accommodate another division?

MACRO PLANNING FORM

Macro Name	Macro Command	Descriptive Comment
\C	{home}	Position cursor to view consolidate
	/reB7.E8~	Remove prior data, if existing
	/reB10.E16~	Continue removing old data
	/reB18.E20~	Continue removing old data
	{goto}B7~	**Position cursor for combine**
	/fcanBUDGET~	File Combine Add Named-Range
	CAL~	File to combine
	/fcanBUDGET~	File Combine Add Named-Range
	FLA~	File to combine

Figure L.171 Macro Planning Form for consolidation.

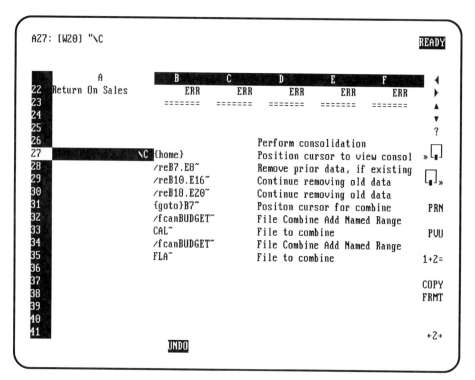

FIGURE L.172. Macro for consolidating worksheets.

Caution Alert!

The / File Combine Add (/FCA) command places incoming data in the currently active worksheet beginning at the current location of the cell pointer. To avoid possible data loss from combining files incorrectly, save your current worksheet file before executing this command!

```
                          GOOD MORNING PRODUCTS
                    PRO FORMA PROFIT AND LOSS STATEMENT
                    ------------------------------------

                        1ST QTR   2ND QTR   3RD QTR   4TH QTR    TOTAL
                        -------   -------   -------   -------   -------
Sales                    406500    446040    489726    538027   1880293
Cost of Sales            305985    335448    367966    403880   1413279
                        -------   -------   -------   -------   -------
Gross Profit             100515    110592    121760    134147    467014

Salaries                  37000     37000     40000     47000    161000
Benefits                   7030      7030      7600      8930     30590
Administrative Expense     9350     10259     11263     12375     43247
Depreciation               5000      5000      5500      5500     21000
Interest                   3400      3400      3400      3400     13600
                        -------   -------   -------   -------   -------
Total Expenses            61780     62689     67763     77205    269437

Earnings Before Tax       38735     47903     53997     56942    197577

Return on Sales            9.5%     10.7%     11.0%     10.6%     10.5%
```

FIGURE L.173. Consolidated budget report for Good Morning Products.

1. Create the Business Unit Files
   a. Enter the formulas and labels for the worksheet.
   b. Define the range of data for consolidation with the / Range Name Create (/RNC) command.
   c. Save the worksheet file.
   d. Clone the file for each additional business unit.
2. Create the Consolidation File
   a. Clone the variable names and column headings from the business unit file.
   b. Erase the cell contents of those cells whose values are to be consolidated.
   c. Enter the macro for performing the consolidation.
   d. Save this consolidation worksheet file.
3. Perform the Consolidation
   a. Execute the consolidation macro.
   b. Print any desired reports and/or graphs.

FIGURE L.174. Summary of named range consolidation processing.

L.10.7 Alternative Processing for Consolidation

When conducting consolidation by using named ranges, each of the business unit worksheet files must be accessed and the cell formulas must be computed before the range is added into the current worksheet. If these are large business unit files with many formulas, a significant amount of time may be required to calculate each one. Also, consider the situation in which a consolidation is being conducted for 20 business units. Suppose a consolidation has already been carried out for an initial budget. Then, the budget is revised for two of the business units. The / File Combine Add Named-Range (/FCAN) command would require that all 20 of the business unit worksheets be calculated as the consolidation is performed. Because this may take a significant amount of processing time, Lotus 1-2-3 provides another method for performing consolidations. The results for each business unit can be stored in a separate worksheet file (Figure L.175). When the / File Combine Add (/FCA) is executed, the values can be added immediately without calculating the formulas for the business unit worksheet. Then, if only 2 worksheets of the 20 business units were revised, only those 2 would need to be recalculated in repeating the consolidation.

The calculated values for a section of a worksheet file can be placed in a *separate file* with / File Xtract Values (/FXV). These data values can subsequently be accessed with the / File Combine Add (/FCA) command when performing a consolidation. Once created with the / File Xtract command, the separate file is just a regular worksheet file and can be used like any other 1-2-3 worksheet file. The / File Xtract command has two available options, as described in Figure L.176. The primary distinction between Values and Formulas is whether the calculated value of a formula is to be stored as a numeric constant or the formula, itself is stored in the designated worksheet file.

The application of / File Extract Values (/FXV) can be readily explored with the Good Morning Products corporate consolidation. When a / File Xtract is deployed, the interaction among the worksheet files appears as illustrated in Figure L.175. The dataflow diagram (DFD) for the processing of this consolidation for Good Morning Products is portrayed in Figure L.177. Here, the P.1—Prepare Division Budget and the P.2—Prepare Corporate Budget involve processing similar to that used with the Named Range approach. The difference is the intermediate storage of data in the two Xtract files. Also, for this processing, the corporate report is written to both the printer and *a file*.

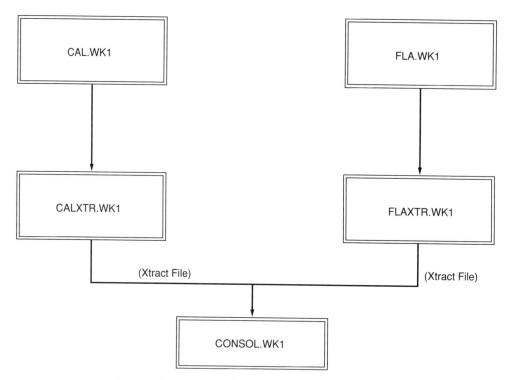

FIGURE L.175. Consolidation system with File Xtracts.

> *Keypoint!*   The / File Xtract Values (/FXV) command stores worksheet results in a *separate file* that can be accessed when conducting a consolidation. When revising a consolidation, you need only to recalculate the worksheets for those affected business units before redoing the consolidation!

L.10.8   Preparing Business Unit Worksheets for File Xtracts

A / File Xtract Values (/FXV) is performed on each of the individual business unit worksheet files for Good Morning Products to produce an Xtract file for each business unit. Although a / File Xtract can be executed manually, a macro can be used to carry out these activities. Of course, with a macro, the command sequence can be edited and is reusable. For these reasons, macros are frequently used for this activity.

As he did with the other macros, Chris planned the extraction of data for individual business units with a *dry run* for the California Division (Figure L.178).

Command	Action
Values	Labels, constant numbers, and numeric values located in a specified cell range of the current worksheet are stored to another worksheet file on disk with all the worksheet settings.
Formulas	Formulas, constants, and labels located in a specified cell range of the current worksheet are stored to another worksheet file on disk with all the worksheet settings.

FIGURE L.176. File Xtract menu choices.

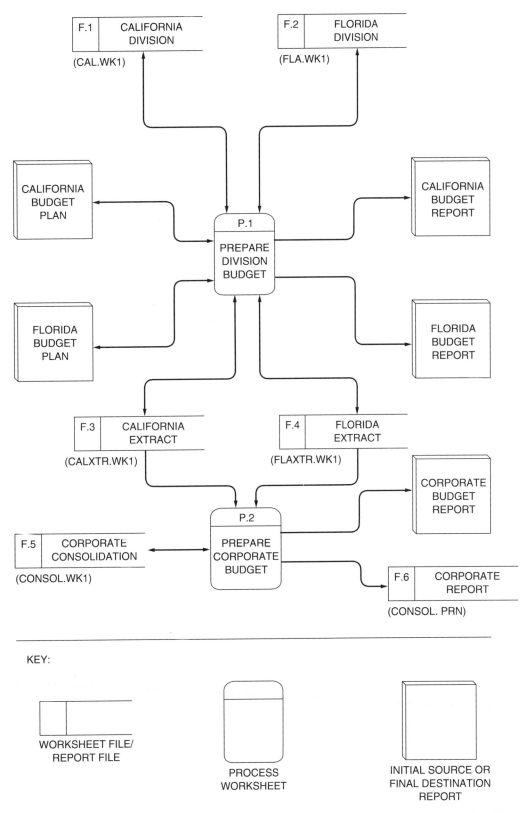

FIGURE L.177. Dataflow diagram (DFD) of consolidation processing with Xtracted intermediate files.

MACRO PLANNING FORM

Macro Name	Macro Command	Descriptive Comment
\X	{goto}A10~	Position the cursor to view extract
	/fxvCALXTR~	Extract values for file CALXTR.WK1
	B10.E23~	Range to extract
	R	Replace file CALXTR.WK1 if existing
	{esc}	Discard Replace command if first time file CALXTR.WK1 is saved

Figure L.178. Macro Planning Form for File Extract.

Here, he assigned the Xtract File the name of CALXTR. The range to be extracted was specified with the specific cell names **B10..E23.** He could have also used the previously assigned range name of BUDGET instead of these specific cell names. The Replace command is used when a copy of the file already exists on disk. If CALXTR is being created for the very first time, then the Replace command is not needed. The {esc} discards the "R" for the Replace command in this situation; otherwise, the {esc} is ignored.

Caution Alert!

> When a file is saved for the very first time, a Replace command is not used. For the second time and all other Saves, the Replace is required. The macro command sequence $R\{esc\}$ supplies the Replace command when needed, but discards it when the file does *not* exist!

Let's modify the CAL worksheet file for Chris's processing at Good Morning Products.

To modify an individual business unit worksheet to include a File Xtract macro using specific cell referencing

Action: Access the CAL worksheet as the currently active file.

Action: Enter the File Xtract macro as shown in Figure L.179 and assign this macro the**X** range name.

Action: Review your macro and correct any errors. Save this version of the CAL worksheet file.

Action: Execute the**X** macro.

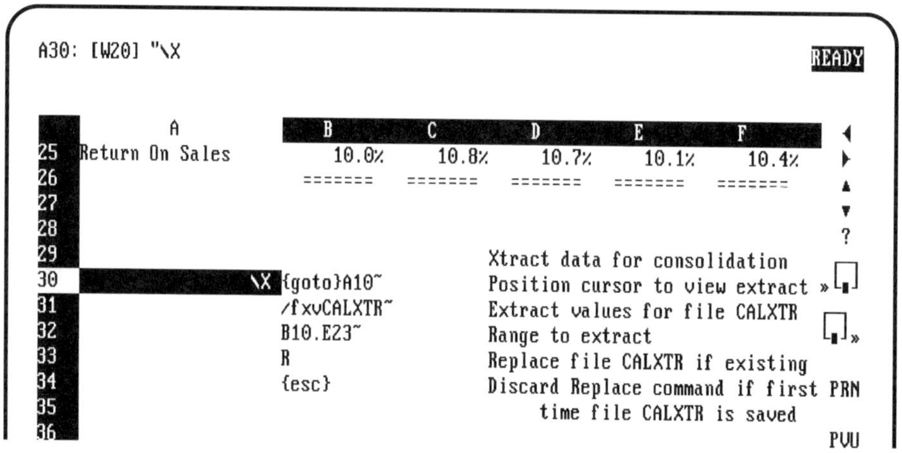

FIGURE L.179. Macro in CAL worksheet for performing extract.

Now let us modify the FLA worksheet file for the Florida Division.

To modify a second
business unit worksheet to
include a File Xtract macro
using a range name

Action: Access the FLA worksheet as the currently active file.

Action: Enter the File Xtract macro as shown in Figure L.179 and assign this macro the \ **X** range name. In place of the specific cell range **B10..E23,** use the **BUDGET** range name. Change the name of the Xtract file to FLAXTR instead of CALXTR.

Action: Review your macro and correct any errors. Save this version of the FLA worksheet file.

Action: Execute the \ **X** macro.

If the \ **X** macro had been included in the CAL worksheet file *before* it was cloned to the FLA worksheet, then only the Xtract file name would have needed to be modified. All the rest of the macro included in the cloned file for the Florida Division would have contained the desired commands. Execution of these two File Xtracts produces the desired intermediate files for use in the consolidation processing of Good Morning Products.

L.10.9 Extracted Data Values

When the / File Xtract Values (/FXV) commands are executed, the data values for the designated ranges are stored in the specified files on disk. Because these Xtract Files are the same as any other 1-2-3 worksheet file, they can be viewed, printed, or edited like any other worksheet.

Let's examine the contents of the extracted files for the California and Florida Divisions of Good Morning Products.

To examine the contents of
an extracted worksheet file

Action: Retrieve the CALXTR worksheet file and examine its contents, which should be the same as those illustrated in Figure L.180. Notice that the upper-left-hand corner of the worksheet is positioned at cell **A1** and that all the cells contain numeric values, *not* formulas. If desired, print this worksheet.

Action: Retrieve the FLAXTR worksheet file and examine its contents, which should be like those portrayed in Figure L.181. Print this worksheet, if desired.

Chris has the desired Xtract files ready for the consolidation processing of Good Morning Products.

L.10.10 Consolidating Worksheets Using Xtract Files

Consolidation with Xtract Files proceeds in much the same manner as that for the Named Range method. The difference is specifying that the entire file is to be combined.

For the Good Morning Products consolidation, a macro is employed as a convenient method for making these commands reusable. The *dry run* for this macro is shown in Figure L.182.

Look at the commands in the last four lines of this macro. Chris wants a copy of the report stored as ASCII text in the file CONSOL.PRN. This saves the report in a form for printing additional copies outside of Lotus 1-2-3 or for use with a word processor, such as WordPerfect. When a report is saved in a file like this, Lotus 1-2-3 automatically assigns the file extension *.PRN, which identifies it as a PRiNt file.

```
A1: 289500                                                          READY

          A          B          C          D        E      F      G      ◄
1       289500     312660     337673     364687                          ►
2       222915     240748     260008     280809                          ▲
3       -------    -------    -------    -------                          ▼
4        66585      71912      77665      83878                           ?
5
6        23000      23000      25000      29000                          » ⌑
7         4370       4370       4750       5510
8         6659       7191       7766       8388                          ⌑ »
9         2000       2000       2500       2500
10        1600       1600       1600       1600                          PRN
11       -------    -------    -------    -------
12       37629      38161      41616      46998                          PVU
13
14       28956      33751      36049      36880                          1+2=
15
16                                                                       COPY
17                                                                       FRMT
18
19
20                                                                       ←2→
                               UNDO
```

FIGURE L.180. Extracted CALXTR worksheet file for California division.

```
A1: 117000                                                          READY

          A          B          C          D        E      F      G      ◄
1       117000     133380     152053     173340                          ►
2        83070      94700     107958     123071                          ▲
3       -------    -------    -------    -------                          ▼
4        33930      38680      44095      50269                           ?
5
6        14000      14000      15000      18000                          » ⌑
7         2660       2660       2850       3420
8         2691       3068       3497       3987                          ⌑ »
9         3000       3000       3000       3000
10        1800       1800       1800       1800                          PRN
11       -------    -------    -------    -------
12       24151      24528      26147      30207                          PVU
13
14        9779      14152      17948      20062                          1+2=
15
16                                                                       COPY
17                                                                       FRMT
18
19
20                                                                       ←2→
                               UNDO
```

FIGURE L.181. Extracted FLAXTR worksheet file for Florida division.

MACRO PLANNING FORM

Macro Name	Macro Command	Descriptive Comment
\C	{home}	Position cursor to view consolidate
	/reB7.E8~	Remove prior data, if existing
	/reB10.E16~	Continue removing old data
	/reB18.E20~	Continue removing old data
	{goto}B7~	**Position cursor for combine**
	/fcaeCALXTR~	File Combine Add Entire File
	/fcaeFLAXTR~	File Combine Add Entire File
	/pfCONSOL~	Write report to the file CONSOL.PRN
	r	Replace old file, if existing
	rA1.F24~	Desired report range
	agq	Complete report

Figure L.182. Macro Planning Form for File Combine of extracted worksheets

Let's include this macro in the consolidation file for Good Morning Products.

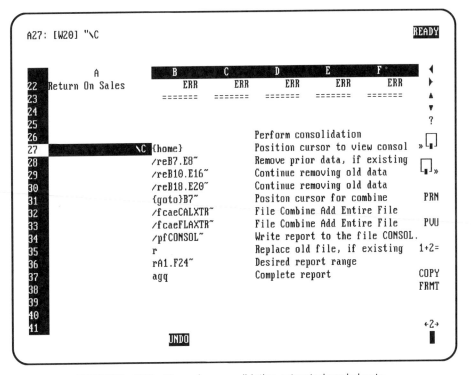 *To modify the macro for consolidating extracted worksheet files and saving report files*

Action: Retrieve the CONSOL worksheet as the currently active file.

Action: Immediately give this file a new name by saving it as the CONSOL2 worksheet.

Action: Enter the macro as illustrated in Figure L.183. The existing macro used with the CONSOL worksheet may be modified, if desired.

Action: Save this version of the CONSOL2 worksheet file and execute the \C macro. [*Note:* When this macro is executed for the very first time, an error will occur, since the CONSOL.PRN file does *not* exist. Just execute the macro a second time.]

Action: Review the consolidated results, which should be the same as those obtained with the Named Range consolidation as shown in Figure L.173.

FIGURE L.183. Macro for consolidating extracted worksheets.

1. Create the Business Unit Files

   a. Enter the formulas and labels for the worksheet.

   b. Enter the / File Xtract (/FX) command in a macro to guide the file extract operation; a range name may be used to designate the selected cell range to be extracted.

   c. Save the worksheet file.

   d. Execute the / File Xtract macro.

   e. Clone the file for each additional business unit.

2. Create the Consolidation File

   a. Clone the variable names and column headings from the business unit file.

   b. Erase the cell contents of those cells where the consolidated values will be placed.

   c. Enter the macro for performing the consolidation.

   d. Save this consolidation worksheet file.

3. Perform the Consolidation

   a. Execute the consolidation macro.

   b. Print any desired reports and/or graphs.

FIGURE L.184. Summary of Xtract File consolidation processing.

The consolidated results have been produced for Good Morning Products using the procedure summarized in Figure L.184. Chris and Kim can use either (1) the Xtract File method or (2) the Named Range method of consolidation. Based on the current size of their budget, Chris prefers to use the Named Range procedure. However, Kim envisions an expanded budget arrangement that would be best processed by using the Xtract File strategy. Keep both strategies in mind as you design your consolidation applications.

L.10.11 When Things Go Wrong

A number of difficulties may be encountered when you are consolidating worksheets. Some of the more frequently occurring situations and how to approach them are as follows:

1. Unexpected results were obtained in the consolidation worksheet with blank cells occurring where numerical values should have been and numerical values appearing where blank cells should have been. This condition usually takes place when the worksheet cell pointer is positioned in the wrong location *prior* to performing the / File Combine Add.

   a. Review your macro used to perform the consolidation and examine the macro command that positions the worksheet cell pointer.

   b. Determine the correct position for locating the worksheet cell pointer and revise the macro with the correct location.

   c. Reexecute your consolidate macro and review the results.

2. When your consolidation is performed, the values for a variable or account, such as Sales, appear on different rows rather than being added. This usually occurs when the worksheets being consolidated are *not exact images*.

   a. Examine the worksheets for each of the business units to determine the location of each variable or account being consolidated.

   b. Compare the locations of each variable for each worksheet to identify any variables that are not positioned at exactly the same location. Cloning worksheets helps to avoid this potential difficulty.

   c. Rearrange the accounts or variables of your worksheet so that they are exact images.

   d. Access your consolidation worksheet and reexecute the consolidation.

3. When you execute the macro to perform the consolidation, an ERROR occurs. An error in a consolidation macro is the same as an error in any other 1-2-3 macro.

   a. Press <Alt>+<F2> to toggle on the STEP mode of macro execution.

   b. Execute your macro and observe its operation. This also provides a convenient method to watch each file as it is added with the / File Combine Add command.

   c. Locate the error condition in your macro and correct it.

   d. Test the change to your macro with the STEP mode still turned on.

   e. Toggle off the STEP mode with <Alt>+<F2>.

   f. Reexecute your consolidation macro.

L.10.12 Lesson Summary

- Consolidation is the process of adding the results for several different business units to obtain corporate results.

- Consolidation is one component of multidimensional worksheet modeling. Recent enhancements to Lotus 1-2-3 are specifically designed to accommodate multidimensional modeling.

- The primary steps in consolidation are (1) to prepare the results of each individual business unit and (2) to perform the consolidation of the results to obtain a corporate total.

- An individual business unit worksheet may be readily cloned by copying one business unit's completed worksheet file for use with the data of a second business. This helps ensure that the same formulas are used in both worksheets.

- The / Range Name Create (/RNC) command is used to identify the range of cells in each individual business unit worksheet that will be consolidated at the corporate level.

- The consolidation worksheet for the corporate total is designed as an "exact image" of the range of data to be summed from each individual business unit.

- The / File Combine Add Named-Range (/FCAN) command is used with each business unit to sum its results in the consolidation worksheet. Execution of this command causes the worksheet of the business unit to be calculated as the File Combine is performed.

- A macro is a convenient method of arranging the commands for performing a consolidation. This makes it easy to repeat the consolidation as needed.

- The / File Xtract (/FX) command provides an alternative method for implementing consolidation processing. With this command, the results for each business unit are stored in an intermediate file. The primary worksheet file for each business unit *does not need to be calculated* as the consolidation is performed.

- The / File Xtract (/FX) command is executed for each of the individual business units to create the intermediate worksheet files. This extract can be readily performed with a macro.

- The / File Combine Add Entire File (/FCAE) command is used to consolidate the results for each of the individual business units that have been stored in a separate extract file.

- An ASCII text file of a report can be written to a file for printing additional copies of a report outside of Lotus 1-2-3 or for use with word processing software such as WordPerfect.

L.10.13 Practice Tutorial

(1)   Carry out the Range Name method of business consolidation as described in this Lesson in Sections L.10.2 through L.10.6 as a guided activity in a hands-on manner.

> *Task 1:* Access the PLAN6 worksheet and modify it, creating the CAL worksheet, and print the California results.
>
> *Task 2:* Clone the FLA worksheet from the CAL worksheet and print the Florida results.
>
> *Task 3:* Develop the CONSOL worksheet including the consolidation macro.
>
> *Task 4:* Perform the consolidation and print the consolidated results and the cell formulas.

Time Estimates

Novice: 90 minutes

Intermediate: 60 minutes

Advanced: 45 minutes

(2)   Conduct the File Xtract method of business consolidation as described in this Lesson in Sections L.10.7 through L.10.10 as a guided tutorial activity in a hands-on manner.

Task 1: Modify the CAL worksheet created in Practice Tutorial 1 to contain the File Xtract macro and execute this macro.

Task 2: Modify the FLA worksheet to include the File Xtract macro and execute this macro.

Task 3: Revise the CONSOL worksheet macro for the consolidation of extracted files and save this as the CONSOL2 worksheet file with the results printed as a report and stored in an ASCII file for printing outside of Lotus 1-2-3.

Task 4: Carry out the consolidation and print the cell formulas for the consolidation worksheet in addition to the results printed by the macro.

Time Estimates

Novice: 60 minutes

Intermediate: 45 minutes

Advanced: 30 minutes

L.10.14 Practice Exercises

(1)   Case: Inland Container (continued)

Mary Montoya's divisional manager asked her to prepare a consolidated plan including the proposals for both Rydder Truck Rental and U-Stor-It. This would let them review the combined results from the acceptance of both proposals.

Task 1: Retrieve the RYDDER11 worksheet file and examine its contents. Then, save this as the RTR worksheet file.

Task 2: Modify the worksheet by assigning the range name INCOME to the data values of **Units Sold**, **Price per Unit, Sales, Cost of Sales,** and **Gross Profit** for the three months of Mary's plan. (*Hint:* This is to be only one range that is named INCOME.) Save this again as your RTR worksheet file.

Task 3: Retrieve the USI.WK1 worksheet file and inspect its contents. Mary cloned this from a version of her RYDDER worksheet files and entered U-Stor-It's data.

Task 4: Revise this worksheet by assigning the range name INCOME to the same data values as described in Task 2. Save this USI worksheet file.

Task 5: Access the INLDCONS.WK1 worksheet file that Mary created for use with her consolidation. Review the contents of this worksheet. Notice that the planning accounts or items included in this worksheet are an exact image of those in her RTR and USI worksheet file. Also, Mary wants to have the average **Price per Unit** computed from the consolidated values for **Sales** and **Units Sold**. She has included the formula for this calculation in her worksheet. Initially this contains "ERR" because of a division by zero. However, once the consolidated data are placed in the worksheet, this value will then be computed. Mary knows that her consolidation will not destroy these formulas, so the correct results will be computed.

Task 6: Add a macro (\ C) to the INLDCONS worksheet file to perform Mary's consolidation of the RTR and USI proposals using the Named Range method. Design this macro to erase any old data values for **Units Sold, Sale, Cost of Sales,** and **Gross Profit** before the consolidation is performed. Execute this macro and print the combined results for Mary's divisional manager.

Quick check answer: Gross Profit [Total] = 1392154

Task 7: Print the worksheet area containing the macro. Save this INLDCONS worksheet file.

Task 8: (*Optional*) Mary wants you to explore the File Xtract method of consolidation. Modify the RTR and USI worksheet files by adding a macro (\ X) that saves the results of each proposal in the RTRXT and USIXT files, respectively. Print the area of these two worksheet files containing your macro commands. Access the INLDCONS worksheet file and change its name by saving it as the INLDCNXT file. Include a macro (\ C) in this INLDCNXT file to perform the consolidation by using your RTRXT and USIXT files. This macro should erase any old data values before the consolidation is carried out. Execute this macro and print a report of the resulting consolidation. Print the area of the worksheet containing your \ C macro. Save your revised INLDCNXT worksheet file containing your macro.

Time Estimates

Novice: 90 minutes

Intermediate: 60 minutes

Advanced: 45 minutes

INLAND CONTAINER
MACRO PLANNING FORM

Macro Name	Macro Command	Descriptive Comment

(2) Case: Pure H2O

Business Problem: Aggregate planning
MIS Characteristics: Production/Operations
                     Managerial Planning

Pure H2O is a worldwide leader in water quality improvement systems. They manufacture an industrial purification system that soften, filters, deionizes, and reclaims
water. Pure H2O operates manufacturing facilities in the United States, England, and
Brazil. Carlos Hernandez, a senior production planner, is responsible for planning
and coordinating production of the Commander 2001 purification system. He has
recieved an aggregate production plan from the production planners at each of Pure
H2O manufacturing facilities. Carlos needs to consolidate these plans to produce their
Corporate Aggregate Plan. He received copies of these worksheet files:

Division	Lotus 1-2-3 File
U.S.	H2O_US
England	H2O_GB
Brazil	H2O_BR

Carlos started setting up the H2O_CORP.WK1 as his consolidation worksheet file.
This file contains the desired planning items with formulas to calculate the overall
Total for the year. He removed all of the data values from this file in preparation for
performing his consolidation.

Task 1: Retrieve each of the H2O division worksheet files and review their content.
Print a copy of the Aggregate Plan for each division. In preparation for
carrying out the consolidation, assign the Range Name PLAN to the cells
containing the quarterly data values for the planning items from **Beginning
Inventory** through **Employees Req'd**. Save each of these worksheet files.

Task 2: Retrieve the H2O_CORP.WK1 worksheet and review its contents. Observe
that the planning items or accounts in this worksheet are an *exact image* of
those in the individual division worksheets. Notice the formulas Carlos has
placed in the **Total** column to calculate these values after the consolidation
is performed.

Task 3: Develop and add a macro (\ C) to the H2O_CORP worksheet file to
perform Carlos's consolidation of the data for the three divisions by using
the Named Range method. Design this macro to remove any old values
for the quarterly data before the consolidation is performed. Execute this
macro and print the consolidated results for Carlos's use.

Quick check answers: Demand forecast [Total] = 124,700
                         Production requirement [Total] = 123,900
                         Production hours req'd [Total] = 558,390

Task 4: Print the area of the H2O_CORP worksheet containing the macro and
save this file.

Task 5: (*Optional*)   Carlos would like you to try out the File Xtract method of consolidation. Modify each of the three division files by adding a macro (\X)
that saves the results for each division in the H2O_USXT, H2O_GBXT,
and H2O_BRXT files. Retrieve the H2O_CORP worksheet file and change
its name by saving it as the H2O_CPXT file. Add a macro (\ C) to this
file that does the consolidation using the H2O_USXT, H2O_GBXT
and H2O_BRXT files. This macro should erase any old data values as the

first step in doing the consolidation. Execute this macro and print the resulting report. Print the area of the worksheet containing your \C macro commands. Save this revised H2O_CPXT file with your macro.

Time Estimates

Novice: 90 minutes

Intermediate: 60 minutes

Advanced: 45 minutes

PURE H2O MACRO PLANNING FORM

Macro Name	Macro Command	Descriptive Comment

(3)   Case: Mountain State Corporation

Business Problem: Consolidated variance analysis
MIS Characteristics: Finance
Strategic Planning

Mountain State Corporation's (MSC) business activities include petroleum exploration, production, refining, marketing, and related manufacturing operations. MSC is organized into three business segments: Refining and Marketing group, Oil and Gas Production group, and Truck-Lite group. The Refining and Marketing group refines crude oil into blended motor oils and gasoline. The Gas and Oil Production group owns working interests in more than 2,100 oil and gas wells. This group operates pipelines for transporting gas and oil. The Truck-Lite group produces automotive tail lamp assemblies and related plastic molded parts.

Homer Conrad, a financial analyst, is responsible for preparing a Variance Report of MSC's Consolidated Statement of Operating Income. Homer received the financial data from the three groups and created a worksheet for each one as follows:

Group	Lotus 1-2-3 File
Refining and Marketing	MSREFINE
Oil and Gas Production	MSOIL
Truck-Lite	MSLITE

Homer began developing the MSCORP.WK1 worksheet file for his consolidated report. This file consists of the desired line items with formulas to compute the **Variance** and **Percent Variance** columns and the various subtotal line items. In preparing the MSCORP.WK1 file for consolidation processing, he removed all of the data values from this worksheet.

Task 1: Retrieve the worksheet for each of MSC's groups and review their content. Print a copy of the Variance Report for each group. To get ready for the consolidation, assign the Range Name VARIANCE to the cells containing the **Budget** and **Actual** data values for the planning items from **Net Sales** through **Miscellaneous**. The remaining line items are calculated after the consolidation is completed. Save each of these worksheet files.

Task 2: Retrieve the MSCORP.WK1 worksheet file and examine its contents. Observe the arrangement of the planning items in this worksheet as an *exact image* of those in the group worksheets. Look at the formulas for computing the **Variance** and **Percent Variance** columns.

Task 3: Create a macro (\ C) in Homer's MSCORP.WK1 worksheet to perform the consolidation of the three groups using the Named Range method. This macro should remove any old data values, but not any formulas, before the consolidation is performed. Execute this macro and print the CONSOLIDATED STATEMENT OF OPERATING INCOME Variance Report.

Quick check answer: Net earnings [Variance] = 4,482

Task 4: Print the area of the MSCORP worksheet containing your consolidation macro and save this file.

Task 5: (*Optional*) Homer would like you to experiment with the File Xtract method of consolidation. Modify each of the three group files by adding a macro (\ X) that saves the results of each group in the files: MSREFXT, MSOILXT, and MSLITXT. Retrieve the MSCORP worksheet file and change its name by saving it as the MSCORPXT file. Modify the macro (\ C) in this file to carry out the consolidation using the Xtract files for the three groups. This macro should erase any old data values before beginning the consolidation of the group files. Execute this macro and print the resulting report. Print the worksheet area that contains the \ C macro command. Save this modified MSCORPXT worksheet file.

Task 6: (*Optional*) The Oil and Gas Production Group sells most of its petroleum feedstocks to the Refining and Marketing Group. Refining and Marketing, in turn, sells some of its products to the Truck-Lite Group. The STATEMENT OF OPERATING INCOME Variance Report for each group includes these intracompany sales and related expenses. Homer must eliminate these intracompany amounts in the final preparation of the CONSOLIDATED STATEMENT; otherwise, the consolidated amounts will be overstated. He collected all the intracompany sales and expenses, and he recorded them in the MSELIM.WK1 worksheet file. Prepare the consolidated statement with the intracompany amounts eliminated.

(a) Retrieve Homer's MSELIM worksheet and review its contents. Assign the Range Name VARIANCE to this worksheet in the same manner as you did for the group worksheets.

(b) Create a new macro (\E) that performs all the same steps in consolidating the three groups using the Named Range method. Then, this macro is to *subtract* the MSELIM data values, rather than add them. (*Hint 1*: You may copy the commands from the \C macro for use with this \E macro.) (*Hint 2*: Choose the Subtract option when performing the File Combine for this MSELIM worksheet.)

(c) Execute this macro, print the results, print the macro commands and save your worksheet file.

Quick check answer: Net earnings [Variance] = 3,493

Time Estimates

Novice: 90 minutes

Intermediate: 60 minutes

Advanced: 45 minutes

MOUNTAIN STATE CORPORATION
MACRO PLANNING FORM

Macro Name	Macro Command	Descriptive Comment

L.10.15 Comprehensive Problems

(1)   Case: Woodcraft Furniture Company (continued)

At Woodcraft Furniture, Joe Birch, Martha Goodguess, and "Tall" Pine just returned from Ashville, West Virginia, where they completed negotiations for the pur-

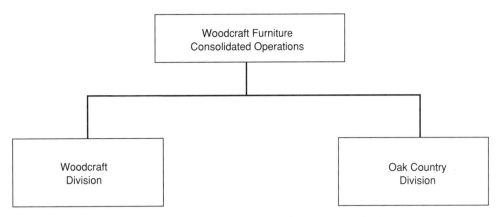

FIGURE L.185 Woodcraft Furniture Company organization.

chase of Oak Country Products, a furniture business specializing in manufacturing oak furniture. With this acquisition, Joe and "Tall" have organized Woodcraft Furniture Corporation as shown in Figure L.185. The Woodcraft Division is Woodcraft's main business unit before the acquisition.

Joe is concerned about controlling the entire business operation. He wants you to create a Pro Forma Income Statement for the Oak Country Division just like that of the Woodcraft Division. These results from the Oak Country Division can be consolidated with the old Woodcraft Division to produce the corporate plan for the quarter. "Tall" and Martha have assembled the following data for the Oak branch:

	July	August	September
Table Price	$450	$450	$470
Chair Price	100	110	110
Sofa Price	350	350	350
Employees	30	40	50
Hourly Rate	9.60	9.60	9.60
Hours Worked per Employee	174	174	174

	July	August	September
Tables Sold	170	227	285
Sofas Sold	112	150	188
Management Salaries	9000	9000	9000
General and Administrative	3500	4500	5500

Because of the quality of oak used in the furniture at the Oak Country Division, the **Cost of Sales Percent** is 28 percent of **Sales**. However, this operation has less **Overhead** with an **Overhead Ratio** of 40 percent of **Raw Materials**. The **Advertising** and **Insurance** expenses are the same percent of **Total Sales** as for the Woodcraft Division. Woodcraft borrowed $360,000 at an annual interest rate of 9.8 percent for use in purchasing Oak Country. Oak Country is expected to pay the **Interest Expense** on this loan in a manner similar to that of the Woodcraft Division.

Joe and "Tall" have analyzed their requirements for a corporate consolidation. They have determined that the planning items or variables to be consolidated should include the following:

Tables Sold	Cost of Sales
Chairs Sold	Gross Profit
Sofas Sold	Advertising
Table Sales	Insurance
Chair Sales	Management Salaries
Sofa Sales	General and Administrative
Total Sales	Operating Expenses
Raw Materials	Interest Expense
Labor	Income before Taxes
Overhead	

Once these items have been consolidated, then the **Total** for the quarter is to be computed. For the **Return On Sales**, this ratio is to be calculated for each month and for the quarter **Total**.

Joe believes that the Named-Range consolidation method can be used to produce the corporate consolidation. Your tasks for developing the consolidated corporate projection for Woodcraft are as follows:

Task 1: Access the WOOD2 worksheet file from Lesson L.3 and modify it by adding the appropriate **BUDGET** named range. Modify the worksheet by adding rounding to the appropriate formulas. Change the report title to "Woodcraft Division."

Task 2: Print the result and save this as worksheet file WOOD11.

Task 3: Clone the WOOD11 worksheet into the OAK11 worksheet by making the changes for the Oak Country Products Division. Change the report title to "Oak Country Division." Verify the inclusion of the **BUDGET** range name. Print the results and be sure to save this file.

> *Quick check answers:* Income before taxes [Total] = 150175
> Return on sales [Total] = .1795   or   17.95%

Task 4: Set up a WOODCONS worksheet file for performing the consolidation. Include a macro in this file to carry out the consolidation of the two divisions (a Macro Planning Form is provided for your use). Do not include the unit prices, employees, hourly rate, or hours worked in the consolidated report; these rows should be removed from the worksheet. Change the report title to "Woodcraft Consolidated Operations." Save this worksheet file, execute the macro, and print the corporate results. Also print the cell formulas for those cells containing the macros.

> *Quick check answers:* Income before taxes [Total] = 695941
> Return on sales [Total] = .1540   or   15.40

Task 5: (*Optional*)   Prepare user documentation that describes the operation of the system. These instructions should include both the preparation of the individual business unit reports and the consolidated corporate report.

Task 6: (*Optional*)   Prepare a dataflow diagram (DFD) of Woodcraft's planning and budgeting system for inclusion in the system's documentation.

Task 7: (*Optional*)   Describe the changes to this system that would be necessary if Woodcraft purchased another division, such as Lazy Days Rocker, or if they created a new division.

Task 8: (Optional)   Joe believes that the File Xtract method may provide a better means of performing their consolidation. He wants you to modify the WOOD11, OAK11, and WOODCONS worksheets to perform this consolidation by using macros. Save the business unit file under the same file names, but save the consolidation file as the WOODCONX worksheet. The macro in the WOODCONX worksheet is to save the results in an ASCII file for printing outside of Lotus 1-2-3. Execute the macro to print the results for the consolidation and then print the macro for each worksheet.

Time Estimates

Novice: 150 minutes

Intermediate: 120 minutes

Advanced: 90 minutes

WOODCRAFT FURNITURE MACRO PLANNING FORM

Macro Name	Macro Command	Descriptive Comment

(2)   Case: Midwest Universal Gas (continued)

Under Mary Derrick's guidance, MUG has experienced a period of relatively good earnings. Francis Foresight and Petro Newgas have worked with Mary in convincing the Board of Directors to acquire Blue Flame Natural Gas. Blue Flame is located in the same general geographical area and serves customers similar to those of MUG. With this acquisition, Mary has organized MUG as illustrated in Figure L.186. Sam Wright has recommended a planning system to Mary that will allow them to control the entire business operation. They want you to prepare a projection for Blue Flame similar to that for the MUG Division, which was MUG's primary business unit before the acquisition was made. The results from the Blue Flame Divisions can be consolidated

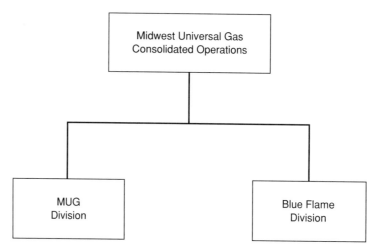

FIGURE L.186. Midwest Universal Gas corporate organization.

with the MUG Division to provide the plan for next year for MUG's consolidated operations. Mary has requested the assembly of the following data for the Blue Flame Division:

	1st Quarter	2nd Quarter	3rd Quarter	4th Quarter
Total Gas Sold	82 BCF	63 BCF	29 BCF	56 BCF
Retail Volume Ratio	43%	43%	43%	43%
General Administrative	$990,000	$990,000	$990,000	$990,000
Investments	$35,000,000	$35,000,000	$35,000,000	$35,000,000
Short-term Debt	$0	$0	$0	$0
Long-term Debt	$25,000,000	$25,000,000	$25,000,000	$25,000,000

Francis reviewed the gas rates for Blue Flame and has determined that next year they will be the same as those currently used in the plan for the MUG Division. Sam examined the other expenses for the Blue Flame Division. Those that are the same as the MUG Division's are the **Cost of Sales Percent, Marketing and Selling Percent**, the **Depreciation Rate**, the **Short-**and **Long-term Interest Rates**, and the **Tax Rate**. As indicated in the foregoing data for the Blue Flame Division, MUG borrowed $25,000,000 to acquire Blue Flame at a cost of $35,000,000. This financing was all in the form of long-term debt.

Mary, Sam, and Francis have reviewed their requirements for a consolidated statement of operations. They have determined that the planning items or variables to be consolidated should include the following:

Retail Gas Sold	Total Expense
Wholesale Gas Sold	Operating Income
Total Gas Sold	Interest Expense
Retail Sales	Income Before Taxes
Wholesale Sales	Income Taxes
Total Sales	Net Income
Cost of Sales	Investments
Marketing and Selling	Short-term Debt
General Administrative	Long-term Debt
Depreciation	

Once these variables have been consolidated, then the **Totals** for the year are to be calculated. For the **Return on Investment,** this ratio is to be calculated for each quarter and for the annual **Total**.

Sam believes that the Named-Range consolidation method can be used to produce their corporate projection. Your tasks for developing the consolidated statement of operations for MUG are as follows:

Task 1: Access the MUG2 worksheet file from Lesson L.3 and modify it by adding the appropriate **BUDGET** named range. Modify the worksheet by adding rounding to the appropriate formulas. Change the report title to "MUG Division." (*Hint:* Remember that the Pro Forma Statement is in dollars in thousands, and so three zeros are dropped on all input dollar amounts.)

Task 2: Print the result and save this as worksheet file MUG11.

Task 3: Clone the MUG11 worksheet into the BFN11 worksheet by making the changes for the Blue Flame Natural Gas Division. Change the report title to "Blue Flame Division." Verify the inclusion of the **BUDGET** range name. Print the results and be sure to save this file.

> *Quick check answers:* Income before taxes [Total] = 4389(000's)
> Return on investment [Total] = .1254   or   12.54%

Task 4: Set up a MUGCONS worksheet file for performing the consolidation. Include a macro in this file to carry out the consolidation of the two divisions (a Macro Planning Form is provided for your use). Do not include the **Retail Rate**, **Wholesale Rate**, **Cost of Gas Percent**, or any other input percents or rates in the consolidated report; these rows should be removed from the worksheet. Change the report title to "Midwest Universal Gas Consolidated Operations." Save this worksheet file, execute the macro, and print the corporate results. Also print the cell formulas for those cells containing the macros.

> *Quick check answers:* Net income [Total] = 16912(000's)
> Return on investment [Total] = .1231   or   12.31%

Task 5: (*Optional*) Prepare user documentation that describes the operation of the system. The instructions should describe both the preparation of the individual business unit reports and the consolidated statement of operations.

Task 6: (*Optional*) Prepare a dataflow diagram (DFD) of MUG's planning and budgeting system for inclusion in the system's documentation.

Task 7: (*Optional*) Describe the changes to this system that would be necessary if MUG acquired another division, perhaps by purchasing Northern Natural Gas.

Task 8: (*Optional*) Sam believes that the File Xtract method may provide a better means of performing the consolidation. He wants you to modify the MUG11, BFN11, and MUGCONS worksheets to perform this consolidation using macros. Save the business unit file under the same file names, but save the consolidation file as the MUGCONX worksheet. The macro in the MUGCONX worksheet is to save the results in an ASCII file for printing outside of Lotus 1-2-3. Execute the macro to print the results for the consolidation and then print the macro for each worksheet.

Time Estimates

Novice: 150 minutes

Intermediate: 120 minutes

Advanced: 90 minutes

MIDWEST UNIVERSAL GAS
MACRO PLANNING FORM

Macro Name	Macro Command	Descriptive Comment

L.10.16 Case Application

Case: **SeaWest**

Business Problem: Multinational financial reporting
MIS Characteristics: Finance
                              Operational Control
Special Characteristic: International
Management Functions: Directing
                              Controlling
Tools Skills: Formulas
            Copying
            Import data
            Reporting
            Extract data
            Consolidation
            Macros

SeaWest manufactures, constructs, and manages wind farms. Their wind turbine generators churn silently in a breeze, producing electricity that is sold to electric utilities, such as Pacific Gas & Electric (PG&E), Southern California Edison (SCE), and Florida Power & Light (FP&L). A typical wind farm consists of several hundred wind turbine generators that are connected to a substation where the electricity passes into a utility's electrical distribution grid for lighting cities and turning the wheels of industry. SeaWest recently completed construction of a wind farm in Tehachapi, California which, at the time of completion, was the largest single wind project of its kind.

SeaWest's chief executive officer, Charles "Chuck" Davenport, manages the company's operations from corporate offices in San Diego, California. He has organized the company into business units for each of the functions of construction, manufacturing, and management of wind farms, as portrayed in Figure L.187. The manufacturing operations are organized in two divisions: Micon Wind Turbines (MWT) Division located in Copenhagen, Denmark, and Wind Energy Turbines (WET) Division located in Maracaibo, Venezuela. Both of these manufacturing divisions operate as autonomous enterprises under the direction of a local manager. The locations in Denmark and Venezuela evolved with the development of the wind turbine manufacturing industry. Each manufacturing facility was initially established as a joint business partnership to take advantage of the technologies originated by the business partners. Recently, SeaWest bought the remaining interest in these businesses, making them wholly owned subsidiaries, and organized them as operating divisions.

Niels Rydder, Vice President and Chief Financial Officer of SeaWest, has established a manual system for preparing the quarterly financial statements for the Wind Turbine Manufacturing (WTM) Business Unit while a computer-based system is developed. Last quarter, the financial statements were not completed until a month after the end of the quarter. As a result, Niels and Chuck could not review them at their monthly board of directors' meeting. Niels wants to accelerate development of the computer-based system to avoid this situation next quarter. He has directed Sheila Norgaard, SeaWest's controller, to expedite development of the computer-based system.

SeaWest makes use of a unified chart of accounts so that each division reports data for the same set of accounts. However, each of the manufacturing divisions maintains its own accounting system in the local currency; the Micon Wind Turbines Division accounting records are in Danish Krone (DKK), and the Wind Energy Tur-

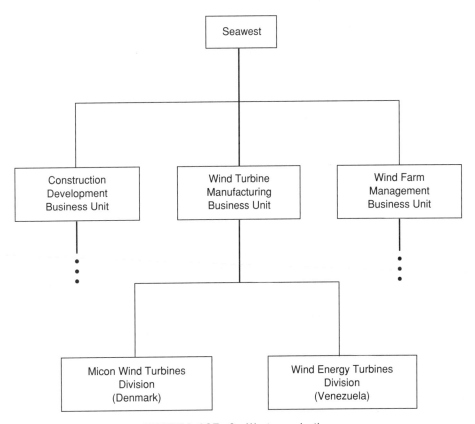

FIGURE L.187. SeaWest organization.

bines Divisions are in Venezuelan Bolivar (VZB). The divisions are committed to "close" their books (accounting records) by the seventh working day following the end of a quarter. With each division operating autonomously, there are no sales or material transfers between them. The consolidation to obtain the Wind Turbine Manufacturing Business Unit operating results is performed by adding the results for the two divisions together, with no intracompany eliminations necessary. All debt borrowing takes place at the corporate level, and therefore the divisions and business units do not include an interest expense in their statement of financial operations.

SeaWest makes use of electronic mail (E-mail) for sending messages between the manufacturing divisions and the corporate headquarters in San Diego, including the transfer of financial data.

Sheila just finished a preliminary system design review with Niels for producing the consolidated financial reports for the Wind Turbine Manufacturing Business Unit. On the morning of the eighth business day, each division will transmit a summary file from their general ledger system to the corporate headquarters. The file transmitted will contain both budget and actual data for the quarter. Since the divisions keep their accounting records in local currency, the current currency exchange rate will be included in the file transmitted by E-mail. A template worksheet will contain columns for Budget, Actual, Variance, and Percent Variance in the manner specified by Niels. The ASCII text files transmitted by E-mail will be loaded into the worksheet and a division report produced in U.S. dollars (USD). Sheila will then save a separate worksheet file for each division holding the Budget and Actual dollars. Once the division reports have been printed, she will consolidate the results for the two divisions to produce the report for the business unit. The results for the business unit will be written as a report to a file so that they can be included in SeaWest's quarterly report to management. In this report, the business unit information is integrated with that of other business units and narrative explanations are added.

In preparing the financial reports, a local currency per U.S. dollar conversion exchange rate, such as 5.698 DKK per USD, is applied to obtain USD from local currency. The conversion is achieved by *dividing* the local currency amount by the exchange rate. For example

100 DKK / 5.698 DKK per USD = 17.55 USD

Niels has specified these computations for the reports

Variance = Actual − Budget

$$\text{Percent variance} = \frac{\text{Variance}}{\text{Budget}}$$

After her review with Niels, Sheila sketched out the financial reporting system, as illustrated by the file interaction diagram in Figure L.188. The processing steps are delineated with the dataflow diagram (DFD) portrayed in Figure L.189. The MWT.DOC (F.1) and WET.DOC (F.2) files are the ASCII files received via E-mail. These are brought into the FINRPT.WK1 (F.3) worksheet file, which is a template worksheet, where the local currency budget and actual values are converted to USD, and the variance and percent variance are computed. A report is printed for each division, and the budget and actual amounts in USD are stored in the MWTUSD.WK1 (F.4) and WETUSD.WK1 (F.5) files for performing the consolidation. The consolidation is carried out by using the same FINRPT.WK1 (F.3) template worksheet file. The report is written for the WTM business unit, and an ASCII text file of the report (F.6) is created for use in preparing the quarterly management report.

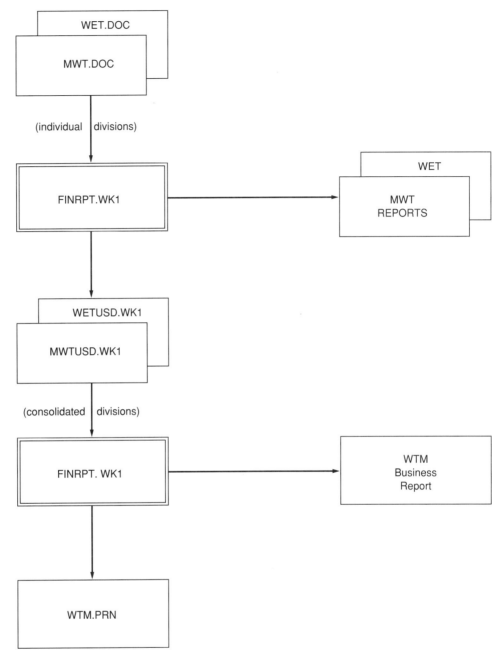

FIGURE L.188. Financial reporting system.

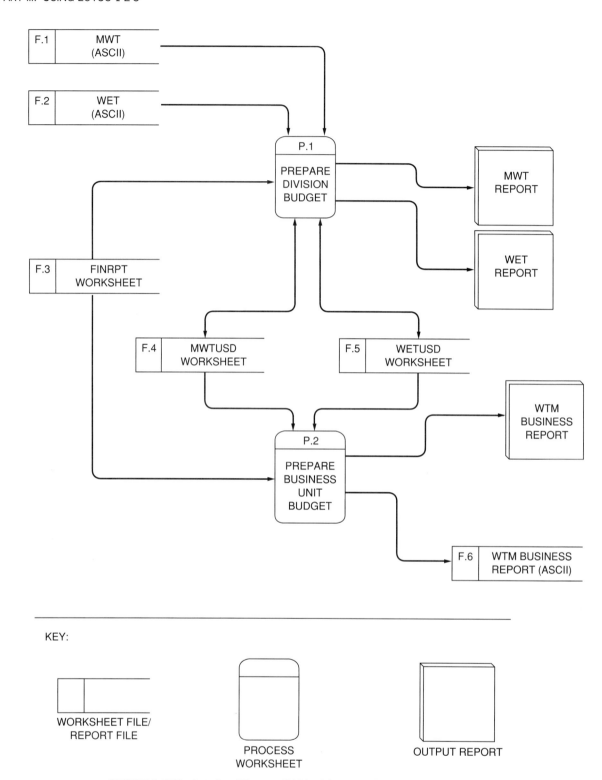

FIGURE L.189. Dataflow Diagram (DFD) of SeaWest financial reporting system.

Sheila began developing the FINRPT worksheet. She decided on the following column usage:

Column	Use
A	Budget amount in local currency
B	Actual amount in local currency
C	Account name in English
D	Budget amount in USD
E	Actual amount in USD
F	Variance amount in USD
G	Percent variance

Columns **A** and **B** are used as an input area to receive the ASCII text files. Columns **C** through **G** contain the report that is to be printed. The overall column arrangement is

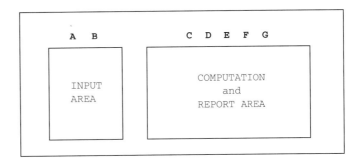

Thus far, Sheila has entered the account names and column headings in the FIN-RPT.WK1 worksheet. The remainder of the system needs to be completed.

Tasks

1. Before you enter 1-2-3 and access the worksheet, look at the MWT.DOC and WET.DOC files by using the TYPE command at the DOS prompt. Notice that the "Exch Rate" appears as the first line in each file and that the data values are separated by commas to facilitate their direct input to a 1-2-3 worksheet file.

2. Access the FINRPT.WK1 worksheet and review the arrangement of the columns. Notice that columns **A** and **B** are blank, because they are reserved as an input area for the ASCII text files.

3. Produce the report for the Micon Wind Turbine Division. At cell location **A4**, import the MWT.DOC file using the / File Import Numbers (/FIN) command. The File Import Numbers command is similar to the File Combine Add Entire File, but the input file is an ASCII text file rather than a 1-2-3 worksheet file. Be sure that the amount rows match up with the account names in column **C**. Enter equations that compute the **Budget**, **Actual**, **Variance**, and **Percent Variance** in USD. The formulas for **Budget** and **Actual** should round the values to the nearest integer. The **Percent Variance** should be formatted as a Percent 1. Print this report and save your worksheet in the FINRPT.WK1 file. Store only the **Budget** and **Actual** USD columns in the file MWTUSD.WK1. The range you store in this file may include a line that contains the words "Budget" and "Actual."

4. Generate the report for the Wind Energy Turbines Division by using the WET.DOC file for the input data and the FINRPT.WK1 file containing the

equation entered in Task 3. Store the **Budget** and **Actual** USD columns in the file WETUSD.WK1 in the same manner as those for the MWTUSD.WK1 file. Notice that this application of the / File Xtract command permits the same FINRPT.WK1 file to be used for both divisions. What would need to be done to use the Named-Range method of consolidation?

5. Develop the report for the Wind Turbine Manufacturing Business Unit. Consolidate the MWTUSD.WK1 and WETUSD.WK1 files by using the FINRPT.WK1 worksheet. Include the equations to compute the **Variance** and **Percent Variance.** (*Hint*: Since this file contains data in the **Budget** and **Actual** columns, use the / File Combine Copy (/FCC) command with the MWTUSD.WK1 file and then use the / File Combine Add (/FCA) command for consolidating the WE-TUSD.WK1 data. With this method, the existing data in the Budget and Actual columns do not need to be erased before you begin the consolidation.) Produce the report for the Wind Turbine Manufacturing Business Unit and store the report in the WTM.PRN print file. Do *not* save the resulting FINRPT.WK1 file. If you do you will destroy the formulas for computing the **Budget** and **Actual** values from the input data in local currency amounts. You may want to save a backup copy of the FINRPT.WK1 worksheet in a file, such as FINRPTBK.WK1, before you begin this consolidation. That way, if you accidentally destroy your formulas, you can easily recover them.

6. (*Optional*)   Access the FINRPT.WK1 worksheet file from Task 3 which contains the formulas for computing **Budget, Actual, Variance,** and **Percent Variance.** Create a macro that performs all of the activities in Tasks 3 through 5, except saving the FINRPT.WK1 file. Have the macro place the title "Micon Wind Turbines Division," "Wind Energy Turbines Division," or "Wind Turbine Business" on the line below the title "SeaWest Quarterly Financial Report" for each respective report. *Save the file and then execute your macro.* (*Hint*: If your macro does not work correctly the first time, be sure to reaccess the FINRPT.WK1 file *before* you modify the macro and *always save* the file *before* you test the macro. This is necessary because you destroy the formulas for **Budget** and **Actual** in USD when you execute the macro.)

7. SeaWest is considering establishing a third manufacturing division located in southern California to engage in the assembly of Mitsubishi wind turbines. This division would purchase all the subassemblies from Mitsubishi and then assemble them into a completed wind turbine unit. Niels and Chuck have evaluated the business opportunity and determined that this would enhance SeaWest's profitability. What changes would need to be made to the current financial reporting system that you completed in Task 6 to incorporate the reporting for this third division? How could the currency exchange rate be handled, since this division would keep its books in USD? Write a short summary report for Niels and Sheila responding to these questions.

8. Write a paragraph describing how you might revise this financial reporting system so that the division reports would be produced in *both* local currency and USD.

Time Estimates

Novice: 180 minutes

Intermediate: 150 minutes

Advanced: 90 minutes

SEAWEST MACRO PLANNING FORM

Macro Name	Macro Command	Descriptive Comment

Managing Data

CONTENT

- Data Management
- Arranging Data with Sort
- Using SmartIcons with Sort
- Setting up Data Ranges for Queries
- Finding Selected Data in the Input Range
- Extracting a Report of Selected Data
- Performing Complex Queries
- When Things Go Wrong

L.11.1 Data Management

Chris and Kim have been experimenting with the use of 1-2-3 to maintain the checkbook ledger for Good Morning Products. They are in the process of revising their general ledger and accounting software. The checkbook ledger in 1-2-3 can provide them with temporary processing while the new software is being installed and tested. Chris set up the checkbook ledger as the 1-2-3 database shown in Figure L.190. This database is organized as a table consisting of rows and columns. A database table like this may be located in any desired cell range of your worksheet. Each row in the table is a **record** that contains the data for an individual transaction. Each column is a **field** that contains data for a characteristic or attribute of the transaction, such as the account number or amount of the transaction. These characteristics placed in fields are also known as **data items** or **data elements.** With Lotus 1-2-3, the worksheet area containing the database *must be organized* so that the fields are in columns, while the records are entered in rows. Lotus 1-2-3 does *not* permit you to reverse this arrangement of column and row usage for a database. Also, since a 1-2-3 worksheet has more rows than columns, this arrangement helps ensure that your database is set up to accommodate the maximum number of records. For a 1-2-3 database, the field names are placed in the top row of the database range, with the records located immediately below these field names (Figure L.190).

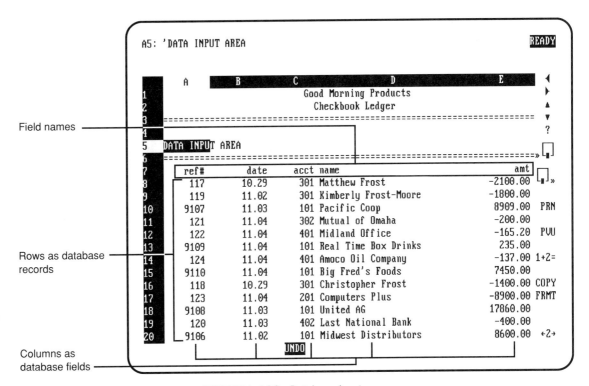

FIGURE L.190. Database input area.

Keypoint!   A 1-2-3 database *must* be arranged so that the columns contain fields and the rows consist of records!

When you create a 1-2-3 database, remember these rules:

- The first row of the database must contain the field names. Subsequent rows contain the records. Do *not* insert any blank rows or divider lines between the field names (first row) and the records.

- The entries in a field must be either all labels or all values. Do *not* enter values in some records and labels in other records for the same field.

- Field names in a database must be unique.

Before Chris could enter any data in the Good Morning Products checkbook ledger database, he and Kim needed to design it by identifying the various fields. Kim described the fields for the database by preparing the **data definition** in Figure L.191. In this design, they decided to enter data for the "amt" field with deposits as positive numbers and expenses as negative numbers, because this allows them to calculate the current balance by adding all of the data in this column. Good Morning Products uses a **chart of accounts** in Figure L.192 to classify each of their checkbook ledger transactions. Using their data definition, the next step is to plan the size of each field and specify those fields that contain numeric data values. They wrote out their design by using the Database Planning Form shown in Figure L.193. From this Database Planning Form, they determined the settings for column widths and formats for each field as indicated in Figure L.194. This completed their database design. They are now ready to begin entering the database in a 1-2-3 worksheet.

Field Name	Description
ref#	Reference number of check or deposit
date	Date of check or deposit as month and day
acct	Chart of account number for transaction
name	Name of person or company describing transaction
amt	Amount of transaction (positive number is deposit; negative number is expense)

FIGURE L.191. Database definition.

The worksheet area where records are entered in a database is known as the DATA INPUT AREA, as shown in Figure L.190. Let us set up the DATA INPUT AREA for the checkbook ledger database and enter data in it.

To set up a 1-2-3 database for entering data

Action: Set up the checkbook ledger as shown in Figure L.190.

1. Enter the heading as shown in rows **1** through **6** of Figure L.190.
2. Enter the field names as defined in Figure L.191 and illustrated in Figure L.190.
3. Set the column widths as specified in Figure L.194.
4. Set the range formats for the data as specified in Figures L.193 and L.194. Range format the columns of the database in rows **8** through **50.** By extending these formats for extra rows, the database is ready for entering additional records.

Now the database records can be entered.

To enter database records

Action: Enter the records as shown in Figure L.190. For this database, all numeric data are entered as values as specified in the Database Planning Form in Figure L.193.

Action: Print a hard copy of the database and save this worksheet as the CKBOOK1 file.

Once a 1-2-3 database is set up, various activities can be carried out by using these data. Several of the more common activities are the following:

- *Sorting.* Arranges the records in a database in a desired sequence based on the data stored in a field that you select, such as the account number or date of a transaction. These data may be arranged in either an ascending or descending sequence.

Acct	Account Name
101	Sales Revenue
201	Cost of Sales
301	Salaries
302	Benefits
401	Admin. Expense
402	Interest
410	Depreciation

FIGURE L.192. Chart of accounts.

DATABASE PLANNING FORM

Data Name	Data Type	Column Width for Largest Value	Decimal Places
ref#	Value	9	0
date	Value	12	2
acct	Value	9	0
name	Label	30	
amt	Value	12	2

FIGURE L.193. Database Planning Form for the checkbook ledger.

- *Finding.* Allows you to look at selected records by highlighting them where they occur in the database. The records are selected by matching a condition or **criteria** that you specify, such as viewing all of the 101 accounts.
- *Extracting.* Copies selected records to another range in your worksheet for preparing **exception reports.** The records are selected by matching a condition or **criteria** that you specify. Because the records are copied to another range, you can then print a report that contains only the selected records.

Each of these common activities is examined using the Good Morning Products database in the sections that follow in this Lesson.

L.11.2 Arranging Data with Sort

The ledger transactions for Good Morning Products shown in Figure L.190 were *not* entered in date order. Kim would like this list organized in date sequence. Whenever two or more items occur on the same date, the "ref#" field serves as a tiebreaker in determining the sequence within a particular day. This can be accomplished with the / Data Sort (/DS) commands of 1-2-3. The desired Data Sort is specified as shown in the Sort Settings dialog box in Figure L.195.

Let's arrange these data by the fields **date** and **ref#**.

Action: Verify that CKBOOK1 is your currently active worksheet.

To use Data Sort to arrange a database

Press:	\<Home\>	Position screen for viewing DATA INPUT AREA
Press:	/	Access main menu
Select:	Data	Desired activity

Column Widths

Global	9
Column B	12
Column D	30
Column E	12

Cell Formats

Global	G
Column B	F2
Column E	F2

FIGURE L.194. Column width and format settings for the database.

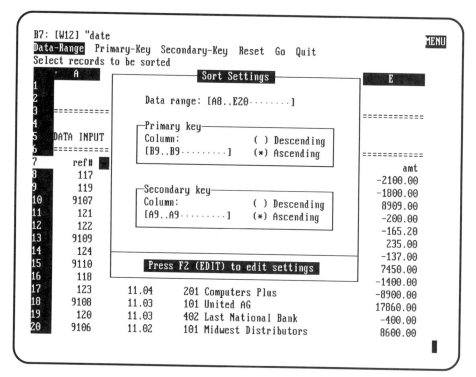

FIGURE L.195. Sort Settings dialog box.

Select:	Sort	Desired option
Select:	Data-Range	Specify area to be sorted, which is the INPUT AREA
Move to:	**A8**	Top-left corner of range
Press:	.	Anchor
Move to:	**E20**	Highlight range by moving cell pointer to bottom-right corner of range
Press:	<Home>	Complete range specification
Select:	Primary-Key	This is the main field for sorting
Move to:	**B9**	Or any row in column **B,** which is the column containing the field that is the primary key
Press:	<Enter>	Complete primary key specification
Select:	A	Choose ascending sorting sequence
Select:	Secondary-Key	This is the tiebreaker
Move to:	**A8**	Or any row in column A
Press:	<Enter>	Complete secondary key selection
Select:	A	Again, choose ascending sort order
Select:	Go	Cause the sort to be performed

The sort is carried out and the records appear in the requested sequence, as illustrated in Figure L.196.

Keypoint!   The Data Sort commands may be used on any range of data. It is NOT limited to a 1-2-3 database table!

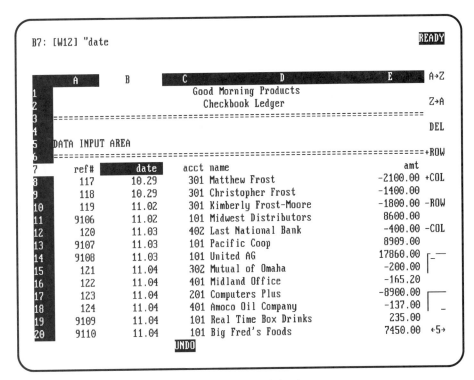

FIGURE L.196. Sorted database.

Caution Alert!

1. Do NOT include any blank rows in your sort data range. Blanks always come first when you specify ascending order. If any blank rows were included in the sort data range, you will have that number of blank rows at the top of your sorted data!

2. Do NOT include the field names in the Data Range. If you do 1-2-3 will treat that row as if it were any regular record and change its location during the sort!

Keypoint!

Use the / Data Fill (/DF) command to enter a field or record number in a database before you do the / Data Sort (/DS). Then include this field with the record number in the sort data range. If you need to re-sort the records back to their original sequence, you can use the field that contains these numbers as the primary sort key!

L.11.3   Using SmartIcons with Sort

SmartIcons are available beginning with Release 2.4 for use in specifying the sort sequence of a database, as shown in Figure L.197. These icons provide an alternative for indicating the sort sequence for a **single field** when the database to be sorted is separated from any other ranges in a worksheet by at least two blank rows and columns. The Sort Settings established with the / Data Sort command are ignored when using the Sort SmartIcons.

Let's see how these SmartIcons are used in sorting the database by the account number.

Action: Make sure CKBOOK1 is your currently active worksheet file.

SmartIcon	WYSIWYG SmartIcon	Command	Description
A → Z		Sort ascending	Sorts database in ascending order using the current column
Z → A		Sort descending	Sorts database in descending order using the current column

FIGURE L.197. Selected SmartIcons for this Lesson.

To attempt to sort the database using a selected field	**Click:**	**C10**	Position the cell pointer in the desired *sort field* of any record in the database
	Click:	Sort Ascending SmartIcon	Desired activity

The QuickSort dialog box appears as shown in Figure L.198. Because the database *does not begin* in row **1** or have, at least, two blank rows above it, 1-2-3 *assumes* that the database begins in row **1** and that row **1** contains the field names. The sort range of **A2..E20** is suggested. However, this is *not* the desired sort range.

Click: Cancel   Abort the sort

So let's fix the database range so that the SmartIcon can be used for the sort.

To position the database to enable the use of the Sort SmartIcon

Action: From the READY mode, insert two rows above the current row **7,** containing the field names of the database. You may use the Insert Row SmartIcon.

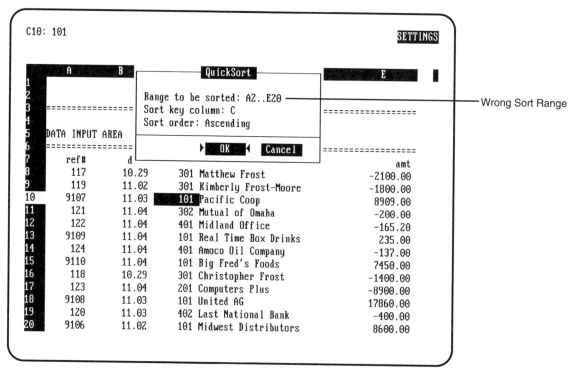

FIGURE L.198. QuickSort dialog box.

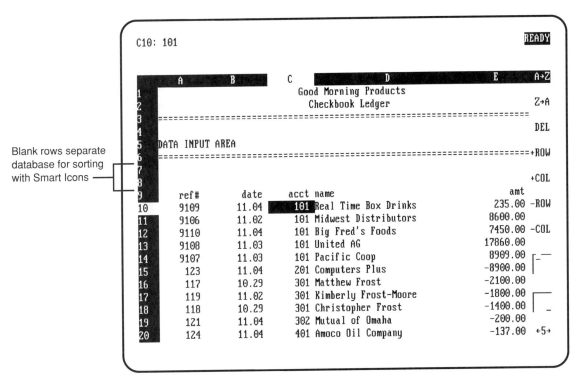

Blank rows separate database for sorting with Smart Icons

FIGURE L.199. Sorted database using SmartIcon.

Now the sort can be performed using the SmartIcon.

To actually sort the database using a selected field	**Click:**	**C10**	Select sort field
	Click:	Sort Ascending SmartIcon	
			Desired activity
	Click:	OK	Accept the sort range of **A10..E22**

The sort is performed, with the result shown in Figure L.199. Use these SmartIcons as desired when you arrange a database as an alternative to the keyboard commands. When you use the Sort SmartIcons, be careful to surround your database with sufficient rows and columns so that only the database is sorted.

Action: Using the Sort Descending SmartIcon, arrange the database on the amount (amt) field.

Action: Print this arrangement of the database and save the worksheet as the CKBOOK2 file. If desired, you may now Quit from 1-2-3.

L.11.4   Setting Up Database Ranges for Queries

To enable Kim and Chris to perform find and extract queries on the checkbook ledger database, they need to identify several areas for use with their 1-2-3 database. The Query Find command allows them to look at desired records or rows in their database that match specified conditions, such as the account ("acct" field) number. A range is designated to hold these conditions. The Query Extract command copies desired records to a separate worksheet range. To accommodate this database processing, the three areas that must be established are the **input** data area, the **criteria** data area, and the **output** data area. The CRITERIA and OUTPUT ranges are the supporting areas for query finds and extracts performed on a database that resides in the INPUT range. These three worksheet ranges or areas serve the following purpose:

> *INPUT.* Contains the data as they are input for manipulation with database commands. The first or topmost row of this range contains *labels* that identify the fields of the database.
>
> *CRITERIA.* Contains selection or search criteria that act like a filter when extracting and finding data. The first row of this range contains labels that identify the fields of the database to which the criteria are matched. Values in the criteria range indicate what you are searching for in the INPUT area.
>
> *OUTPUT.* Contains copies of data values from the INPUT area that match the criteria when an extract is performed. That is, the criteria act as a filter in copying *matching* records from the INPUT area, whereas the OUTPUT area serves as a depository for the information extracted from the database.

When Chris initially developed the checkbook ledger, he created the INPUT DATA AREA. The other two areas still need to be set up by entering labels to indicate their location, as shown in Figure L.200. The settings for column widths and cell formats used with the CRITERIA and OUTPUT ranges are specified in Figure L.201. They are the same as those used with the corresponding fields in the INPUT range. As a result, the design for the INPUT area is applied to these CRITERIA and OUTPUT areas. In addition, the rows of the CRITERIA area are formatted as Text so that any formulas entered in this range are displayed. The field names in the topmost row of the INPUT, CRITERIA, and OUTPUT ranges must be spelled *exactly* the same. The safest way to

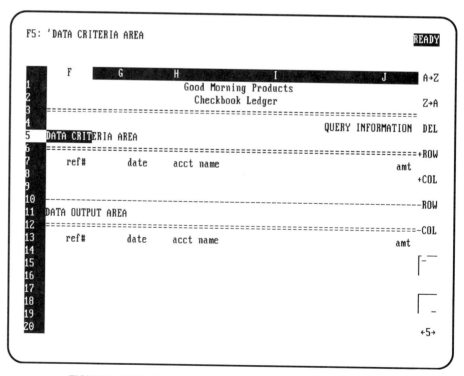

FIGURE L.200. Database support areas for queries and extracts.

Column Widths

Column G	12
Column H	30
Column I	12

Cell Formats

Column G	F2
Column J	F2
Range F8..J8	T

FIGURE L.201. Additional column width and format settings for database support areas.

accomplish this is to enter the field names for the INPUT area and then *copy* them to each of the other areas.

Let us set up these two support areas for use with the Good Morning Products database.

Action: Retrieve the CKBOOK1 file as your currently active worksheet. This is the desired starting point for defining the support areas.

To set up the labels describing the CRITERIA and OUTPUT areas

Action: Copy the field names from **A7..E7** to **F7..J7** for the CRITERIA area and then copy them to the **F13..J13** for the OUTPUT area, as shown in Figure L.200.

Action: Set the column widths and formats as specified in Figure L.201.

Action: Enter the other labels for headings and underlines as shown in Figure L.200.

Look at how the INPUT, CRITERIA, and OUTPUT areas are arranged in the worksheet (Figures L.190 and L.200). The column widths were carefully selected so that the database INPUT area fills a single screen, with the CRITERIA and OUTPUT areas located to the right of the INPUT area. This design makes it easy to move from the DATA INPUT AREA in columns **A** through **E** to the DATA CRITERION AREA and DATA OUTPUT AREA in columns **F** through **J** by using the "BIG RIGHT" and "BIG LEFT" cursor movements (<Ctrl>+<right> or <Tab> and <Ctrl>+<left> or <Shift>+<Tab>). That is, BIG RIGHT and BIG LEFT move one window to the right or left. You should consider designing your 1-2-3 database areas to make use of these convenient cursor movements. However, one limitation of this side-by-side design is that you need to exercise additional care if you insert or delete any rows in the DATA INPUT AREA, so that the support areas are not accidentally modified. If you add all new records to the bottom of your database and then use / Data Sort (/DS) to arrange it, you avoid this potential problem.

Before a find or extract is performed, the ranges occupied by the INPUT, CRITERIA, and OUTPUT areas *must be specified for use with these Data Query commands.* Merely entering the field names does not specify these ranges for use as database ranges for the Query commands. The desired settings for the three database ranges are summarized in the Query Settings dialog box shown in Figure L.202.

Let's specify each of these three database ranges for actually conducting queries. First the / Data Query command is used to access the menu for specifying each range.

Action: Make sure CKBOOK1 is still your current worksheet.

To access the menu for specifying database ranges

Press:	/	Access main menu
Select:	Data	Desired activity
Select:	Query	Desired option

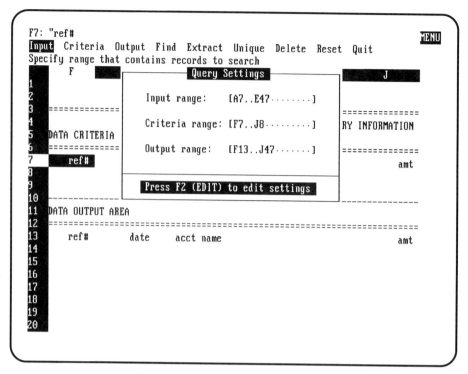

FIGURE L.202. Query Setting dialog box.

Now each of the ranges is specified.

To specify the INPUT range	**Select:**	Input	INPUT area will be established
	Move to:	A7	Upper-left-hand corner of the INPUT area, including the row of field names
	Press:	.	Anchor
	Move to:	E47	Highlight the range by moving the cell pointer to the bottom-right corner of the INPUT area. This range has more rows than currently required, which permits additional rows to be entered later.
	Press:	<Enter>	Complete INPUT range specification
To specify the CRITERIA range	**Select:**	Criteria	CRITERIA area will be set up
	Move to:	F7	Upper-left-hand corner of range
	Press:	.	Anchor
	Move to:	J8	Lower-right-hand corner of range to highlight desired range
	Press:	<Enter>	Complete CRITERIA range specification

Because this criteria range contains two rows, it provides for at most *one* matching condition for each of the database fields.

To specify the OUTPUT range	**Select:**	Output	OUTPUT area will be set up
	Move to:	F13	Upper-left-hand corner of range
	Press:	.	Anchor

Move to:	**J47**	Lower-right-hand corner of range to highlight desired range
Press:	\<Enter\>	Complete OUTPUT range specification

The OUTPUT area should be set up with sufficient rows to handle the maximum number of rows that could be copied during an extract.

    Now let us return to the READY mode before carrying out any other database activities.

Action: Return to the READY mode.

Keypoint!   The INPUT, CRITERIA, and OUTPUT data ranges must be set up under the / Data Query (/DQ) *before* an Extract or Find command may be executed!

L.11.5 Finding Selected Data in the Input Range

Kim would like to inspect all the **401,** Admin Expense, transactions by looking at them in the INPUT area. By using the / Data Query Find (/DQF) command she can view each transaction where it resides in the INPUT area and look at the record as it was entered. By reviewing the transaction records in this manner, Kim can audit them inspecting each record for any error or omissions. Because the data are viewed in the INPUT area, Kim will *not* be using the OUTPUT area for her audit review. First let's actually enter the CRITERIA for reviewing the **401,** Admin Expense, transactions (Figure L.203).

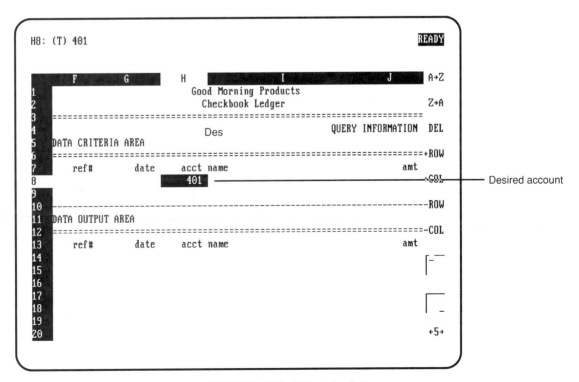

FIGURE L.203. Criteria for find.

Action: Verify that CKBOOK1 is still your current worksheet.

<table>
<tr><td>To establish criteria for a Query Find</td><td>**Move to:**</td><td>**H8**</td><td>The "acct" field in the CRITERIA area</td></tr>
<tr><td></td><td>**Enter:**</td><td>401</td><td>Desired account number</td></tr>
</table>

You may enter either a constant, like the **401,** or a 1-2-3 formula when specifying a value in the CRITERIA area. Once Kim's desired value is placed in the CRITERIA area, the **401** transactions can be inspected in the INPUT area.

<table>
<tr><td rowspan="4">To use Find to look at matching records in the INPUT area</td><td>**Press:**</td><td>/</td><td>Access main menu</td></tr>
<tr><td>**Select:**</td><td>Data</td><td>Desired activity</td></tr>
<tr><td>**Select:**</td><td>Query</td><td>Desired option</td></tr>
<tr><td>**Select:**</td><td>Find</td><td>Desired action</td></tr>
</table>

A worksheet cursor appears in the INPUT range at the first record from the top of the database containing the **401** account number, as illustrated in Figure L.204. The Find command permits Kim to change any of the data values in these selected records, if she wants to revise them.

Now let's examine the other **401** transactions.

<table>
<tr><td rowspan="2">To Find the next matching record in the INPUT range</td><td>**Press:**</td><td><down></td><td>Cursor moves to the next matching record</td></tr>
<tr><td>**Press:**</td><td><down></td><td>BEEP sounds indicating that this is the last row in the database containing the desired value</td></tr>
</table>

The cursor direction keys <up> and <down> can be used to *browse* through the rows in the INPUT area that match the values entered in the CRITERIA area.

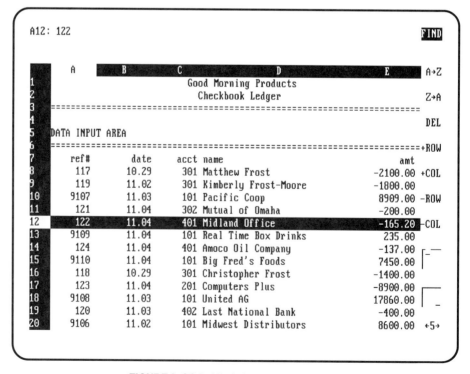

FIGURE L.204. Worksheet cursor for find.

Press:	<Esc>	Terminate the Find command and return to the Data Query menu
Action:		Return to the READY mode.

Because the OUTPUT area is not used with the Find command, the contents of that area are ignored with the Find. It could be blank or it might contain any values placed there for use with another Data Query command.

Keypoint! | The OUTPUT data range is ignored when using the / Data Query Find (/DQF) command!

L.11.6 Extracting a Report of Selected Data

Chris would like a special report of the **101**, Sales Revenue, accounts. That is, he wants the **101** accounts displayed in a separate area of his worksheet so that he can print them as a 1-2-3 report. To accomplish this, he wants to copy the records for the **101** account into the OUTPUT area for printing. First, the CRITERIA are specified for the desired condition.

Action: Make sure that your current worksheet is CKBOOK1.

To specify CRITERIA for Query Extract

Action:		Return to the READY mode
Move to:	**H8**	The "acct" field in the CRITERIA area
Enter:	101	Desired account number

By placing the account number **101** in the CRITERIA area and leaving the other fields blank, Chris has set up the CRITERIA so that those records with account number **101** will be selected regardless of the values in the other fields of these records. In this manner, a blank CRITERIA value has a special purpose, which is to accept *any* value in that field, rather than to accept only blank values. With the CRITERIA established, let's proceed to obtain Chris's desired listing of selected records.

To copy selected records from the INPUT range into the OUTPUT range

Press:	/	Access main menu
Select:	Data	
Select:	Query	
Select:	Extract	Desired action

Rows with the matching account number are copied from the input area to the output area, with the result as illustrated in Figure L.205.

Action: Return to the READY mode

Action: Print the INPUT area and the OUTPUT area as two separate reports.

Action: Save your worksheet as the CKBOOK3 file.

Keypoint! | In the CRITERIA range a missing or null data value means that *any* and *all* values in that field are acceptable!

Once a Data Query command has been executed, 1-2-3 provides a convenient method for redoing the same command with a different set of CRITERIA values. After

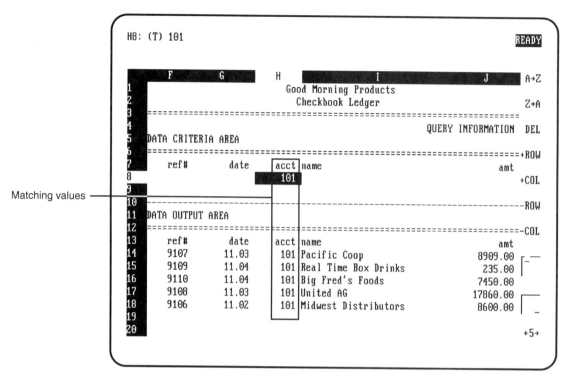

FIGURE L.205. Worksheet produced with Extract.

Chris completed his Sales Revenue report, he wanted a schedule of Salaries, account number **301.** Let's produce this Query Extract by proceeding from the READY mode.

To specify new CRITERIA	**Move to:**	**H8**	CRITERIA area cell contains "acct" field value
	Enter:	301	Desired account number

To redo the Data Query Extract command with the new criteria	**Press:**	<F7>	Cause the last Data Query activity to be performed again
	Action:		Position the worksheet area to view your OUTPUT area.

The schedule of Salaries now appears in the OUTPUT area. You could use the <F7> (QUERY), since a Data Query Extract was the last Data command executed. Lotus 1-2-3 remembers the most recent command and allows you to execute the same command with different CRITERIA values with the <F7> (QUERY) key.

Chris wants to produce a third exception report that lists those Sales Revenues exceeding $8000. A 1-2-3 formula specifies the condition for selecting the desired records. Let's prepare Chris's exception report.

To specify the desired CRITERIA

Action: Erase the account number from cell **H8,** since any account number is valid for Chris's report.

Action: In cell **J8** enter this formula: **+E8 > 8000**

In this formula, the **+E8** references the topmost cell in the INPUT area *immediately under* the "amt" field name. (Figure L.206). By referencing the "amt" field in this way, the / Data Query Extract checks *each value* in the records in the INPUT area to determine which records are to be copied to the OUTPUT area. Formulas like this can be used to specify any of the selection conditions in the CRITERIA area.

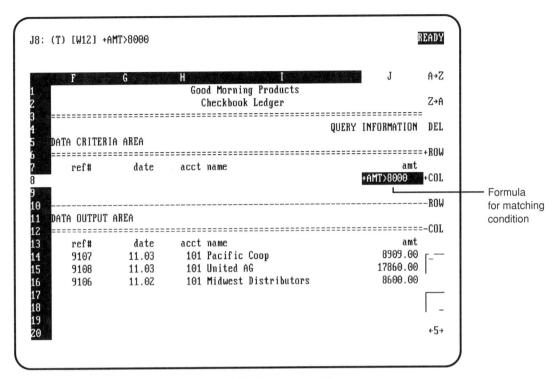

FIGURE L.206. Formula-specified criteria.

Action: Execute the / Data Query Extract command to generate the desired exception report. You may be able to use the <F7> (QUERY) key to repeat this command.

Action: Produce a hard copy of this exception report.

A variation on the Extract command is the Unique command. This performs the same action of copying matching records from the INPUT area to the OUTPUT area. However, if two or more records are identical in ALL fields, only one copy is made in the OUTPUT area. This results in Unique values in each row of the OUTPUT area.

L.11.7 Performing Complex Queries

Lotus 1-2-3 provides the ability to carry out more complex queries. Consider the situation in which Chris would like to prepare a report of the Salaries (account **301**) and Benefits (account **302**). That is, he wants a report of the records containing account **301** *OR* account **302**. Although Chris could do two Extracts, one for each desired account number, he would like one report with both account numbers. When Kim and Chris set up the CRITERIA area, they made it two rows high. The top row contains the field names and the second row holds the data values. But this arrangement allows only one value to be entered for each field at a time. Additional matching data values can be specified for an individual field by adding rows to expand the size of the CRITERIA range (Figure L.207).

Let's carry out an Extract on the Salaries and Benefits to produce Chris's report.

Action: Verify that CKBOOK3 is your current worksheet.

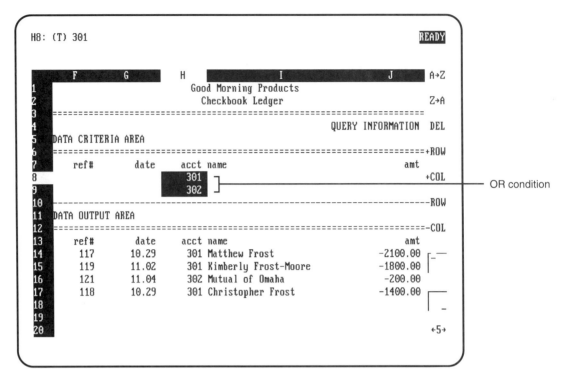

FIGURE L.207. CRITERIA setup for OR query.

To specify matching values for an OR condition as the desired CRITERIA	**Move to:**	**H8**	Location for first "acct" value
	Enter:	301	Desired value for Salaries
	Move to:	**H9**	Location for second "acct" value
	Enter:	302	Desired value for Benefits

To expand the CRITERIA range for the OR condition	**Press:**	/	Access main menu
	Select:	Data	
	Select:	Query	Desired activity
	Select:	CRITERIA	Worksheet cursor expands to indicate *current* CRITERIA range
	Press:	<down>	Expand cell pointer to include *second* row of data values
	Press:	<Enter>	Complete range specification
	Action:	Return to the READY mode.	
	Action:	From the READY mode, execute the / Data Query Extract command to produce the schedule of Salaries and Benefits in the OUTPUT area.	
	Action:	Produce a hard copy report of the Salaries and Benefits schedule.	

Kim has been examining the Sales Revenue (account **101**) and needs to produce a report of those revenues with a date of **11.04.** That is, the account number is **101** *AND* the date is **11.04.** Whenever data values are placed in more than one field of the CRITERIA area, 1-2-3 treats these as an *AND* condition in which *all* of the values must match before a record is selected (Figure L.208).

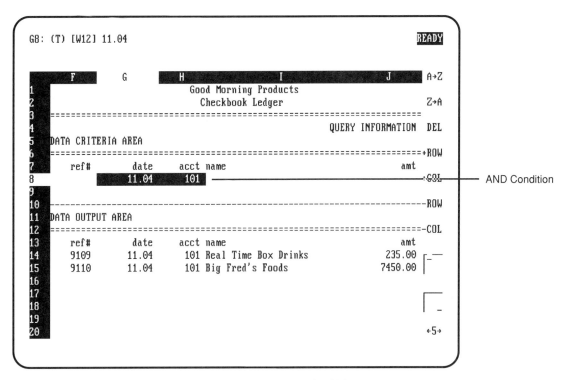

FIGURE L.208. CRITERIA for AND query.

Let us proceed to develop Kim's special report.

Action: Make sure that CKBOOK3 is still your current worksheet.

To specify an AND condition
as the desired CRITERIA

Action: Revise the CRITERIA range so that it is only *two* rows high, with the field names in the topmost row. This is necessary, since Kim has only one set of conditions for her CRITERIA.

Action: Place the value **101** in cell **H8** for the **acct** field and the value **11.04** in cell **G8** for the **date** field. You may erase the value in cell **H9,** since it is not used with this Query.

Action: Carry out the Data Query Extract. You may use <F7> (QUERY) if an Extract was the most recently performed Data Query command.

Action: Print Kim's special report.

Action: Save this worksheet as the CKBOOK3 file.

Lotus 1-2-3 supports the use of the AND and OR logical operations on a database by placing several data values in the CRITERIA area. An OR operation requires the use of more than one row for specifying data values. When a row is no longer required for specifying the conditions of a Data Query, the CRITERIA range needs to be adjusted to eliminate this unwanted row.

Keypoint!   Blank rows must be removed from the CRITERIA area, since they cause *all* rows to be selected with the Data Query Extract and Find commands!

L.11.8   When Things Go Wrong

Several situations may cause difficulties when you are manipulating data with / Data Sort or / Data Query commands. Some of the more frequently occurring conditions and how to approach them are as follows:

1. You just completed performing a sort in ascending sequence and a bunch of blank lines appeared at the top of your sorted data range. When sorting in ascending order, a blank character comes before any numbers or alphabetic characters in the sort sequence. The result is that records containing blanks are sorted to the *top* of the data range. This usually occurs when the data range for the sort was extended beyond those rows that *actually contain* data so that blank rows were included in the sort data range.

   a. Use the / Move command to reposition those rows containing data so that the blank rows are eliminated. When using the / Data Sort with a database, other columns of the worksheet often contain data that you still want. Using a / Worksheet Row Delete command could wipe out these data. For this reason, the / Move command is usually the best procedure.

   b. Use the / Data Sort Data-Range command to specify the desired data range without any blank lines. This will set up the correct range for use with your next / Data Sort operation.

2. You attempt to perform a / Data Query Find or / Data Query Extract, but 1-2-3 just beeps at you. This happens when any of the INPUT, CRITERIA, and OUTPUT ranges have not been set up.

   a. Use the / Data Query command to determine the current setting for the INPUT, CRITERIA, and OUTPUT ranges. Review these to determine which one has not been set.

   b. Set the INPUT, CRITERIA, and OUTPUT areas to the desired cell ranges.

   c. Reexecute your Find or Extract command.

3. You executed the / Data Query Find or / Data Query Extract command and all the records in the INPUT area were selected even though you selected records by placing the desired data values in the CRITERIA range. This usually occurs when the CRITERIA range is defined to be more than two rows high. In this case, the other rows contain blanks that cause *all* of your records to be selected.

   a. Verify that you have entered the correct data values and/or formulas in your CRITERIA range. Make any necessary corrections.

   b. Use the / Data Query Criteria command to review your current CRITERIA range.

   c. Redo the CRITERIA range to eliminate any blank rows.

   d. Reexecute your Find or Extract command.

L.11.9   Lesson Summary

- A database may be set up in 1-2-3 that is arranged so that the columns contain fields and the rows consist of records.
- Field names are placed in the first or topmost row of the database area.
- The / Data Sort (/DS) facilitates the sorting of the rows in a data range. Blank rows always appear at the top when an ascending sort is performed.

- If a database is set up surrounded by at least two blank rows and columns, the Sort SmartIcons can be used to arrange the database using a single sort field.

- A database query requires that the user define three ranges of a database: input, criteria, and output.

- The criteria range acts as a filter for selecting specified records from the input range.

- The Find command allows a user to review selected records in the INPUT range and, if desired, change the data values for these records.

- An output range is a depository for selected database records when an Extract is performed.

- The Unique command produces a separate copy of the selected records with exact duplicates of the records eliminated. Therefore, the records displayed in the OUTPUT range each contains a unique set of data values.

- The Find command provides a review of your records where they reside in the INPUT range, whereas the Extract command produces a separate listing in the OUTPUT range of only those records matching the selection CRITERIA.

L.11.10 Practice Tutorial

(1) Develop the CKBOOK1 worksheet described in this Lesson as a guided activity in a hands-on manner.

(a) Carry out the Sort, Find, and Extract.

(b) Calculate the checkbook ledger balance with an @SUM function in cell **E5.**

Task 1: Build the database worksheet.

Task 2: Print the initial database, the result of the sort, and the result of the extract.

Task 3: Add the @SUM function to the worksheet.

Task 4: Save this as worksheet file CKBOOK4.

Quick check answer: (b) Balance = 27951.80

Time Estimates

Novice: 60 minutes

Intermediate: 45 minutes

Advanced: 30 minutes

L.11.11 Practice Exercises

(1) **Case: Inland Container (second encounter)**

Mary Montoya tracks the monthly sales to each of her customers so that she can analyze them. She uses these results to guide her in contacting customers and to provide information in preparing proposals for supplying additional packing cartons. To assist her in these analyses, Mary has designed a database containing fields described by this data dictionary:

Field Name	Description
PARTNO	Container product identification/catalog number
CUSTNO	Customer identification number
CNAME	Customer name
QUANT	Quantity sold during previous month
PRICE	Product selling price per container
SALES	Sales revenue from products sold (QUANT * PRICE)
PERCENT	Percent of total SALES for all products (SALES each product / TOTAL sales all products)

Mary created the INLAND.WK1 worksheet file for her database. She wants you to carry out these tasks in updating and analyzing her Sales Analysis database:

Task 1: Retrieve the INLAND.WK1 worksheet file containing Mary's database and inspect its layout and contents. Notice that she has entered values for all columns (database fields) except SALES and PERCENT. Mary knows that the values for these two fields can be computed from her input data. Print a copy of the DATA INPUT AREA for your use.

Task 2: Add these records to the bottom of the DATA INPUT AREA in Mary's database:

partno	custno	cname	quant	price
38192	23931	MOVING EXPERIENCE	145880	1.77
37374	37689	STORAGE INN	122440	1.96
31453	58711	U-STOR-IT	193400	3.19
31601	73459	STOR-N-LOCK	125800	2.24
34307	57276	GENERAL MOVERS	124800	2.41

Task 3: Add equations to calculate SALES as described by Mary's data definition.

Task 4: Add a formula in cell **F5** to compute the TOTAL sales.

Quick check answer: TOTAL [SALES] = 4,989,234

Task 5: Add equations to calculate the PERCENT of total sales as defined in the data definition. Range Format this column as Percent 2. Print a copy of the DATA INPUT AREA and save this version of the INLAND worksheet file.

Task 6: Arrange the database in descending order with "sales" as the primary sort key. Print a report of the resulting INPUT DATA AREA. (*Hint:* Be sure to include all the database columns in your sort range, but do not include any blank rows.)

Task 7: Using the report from Task 6, draw a line across your report to separate the "sales" into two groups. The first group should be those with the largest percents that make up the top 20 percent of sales. The second group contains the smallest percents and makes up the remaining 80 percent of sales. How many customers are in the group that makes up the top 20 percent of Mary's sales? Which ones are they?

Task 8: Produce an exception report containing customers with the "largest" SALES—that is, those with SALES greater than $200,000. Implement this as an extract that includes only the PARTNO, CNAME, SALES, and PERCENT. Place your DATA OUTPUT AREA and CRITERIA AREA in a convenient location on your worksheet. Use range names to identify each area. Print your DATA OUTPUT AREA as a report and save the modified INLAND worksheet file.

Task 9: (*Optional*)   Make these changes to the records in Mary's database:

(1)   Change the QUANT sold to **ANOTHER ATTIC** to 72960.

(2)   Change the QUANT sold to **PACKAGING STORE** to 102480.

(3)   Change the PRICE for all records with PARTNO **34307** to 2.39

Print a report of the revised DATA INPUT AREA and save the revised worksheet file. (*Hint:* Use the Find command to locate these records and make these changes while executing the Find command.)

Time Estimates

Novice: 60 minutes

Intermediate: 45 minutes

Advanced: 30 minutes

(2)   Case: Best Buy Products

Business Problem: ABC inventory analysis
MIS Characteristics: Production/Operations
Managerial Control

Stewart Kassen is the merchandising manager at Best Buy Products. Best Buy is a catalog showroom that provides its customers with high-quality, name brand merchandise at discount prices. Each year, Best Buy produces a catalog from which customers select their merchandise. Customers may shop in person at a catalog showroom, may phone their order to a store, or may order by mail. Stewart is responsible for both managing Best Buy's inventory and preparing its annual catalog. To assist in these efforts, he has designed a database that contains fields described by the following data dictionary definitions:

Field Name	Description
PRODUCT	Product identification/catalog number
DESCRIPT	Product description
QTY	Quantity sold during previous year
PRICE	Product selling price per unit
COST	Product cost per unit
CONTRIB	Contribution margin or profit per unit (PRICE - COST)
PROFIT	Total profit for year from product (QTY * CONTRIB)
PERCENT	Percent of total profit for all products (PROFIT each product / PROFIT all products)

Best Buy regularly adds new products and removes obsolete products from its available catalog merchandise. Stewart uses ABC Inventory Analysis as a guide in reviewing product additions and deletions. The ABC approach divides products into three groups by their total profit: A items constitute roughly the top 20 percent of the items, B items the next 30 percent, and C items the last 50 percent. This method of inventory analysis shows that a small number of products usually account for a large dollar volume and that a large number of products frequently account for a small dollar volume. Stewart gives more attention to the products in his groups of A and B items. He wants you to perform the following tasks in updating their inventory database:

Task 1: Retrieve the BESTBUY.WK1 worksheet file containing Stewart's database and review its contents. Observe that he has entered values for all columns (database fields) except CONTRIB, PROFIT, and PERCENT. Print a copy of his DATA INPUT AREA for your reference.

Task 2: Add these records to the bottom of the DATA INPUT AREA in Stewart's database:

product	descript	qty	price	cost
519510B	SHARP 13 COLOR TV	103	218.85	142.25
564508A	SONY REMOTE RACK SYSTEM	41	499.75	379.81
564672A	MAGNAVOX RACK SYSTEM	47	479.80	331.06
5149918	SANYO VCR	91	269.85	164.61

Task 3: Add equations for the CONTRIB, PROFIT, and PERCENT fields to the database as described in Stewart's data definition. Print a copy of the DATA INPUT AREA and save this version of the BESTBUY worksheet file.

Quick check answer: TOTAL [PROFIT] = 132,463.90

Task 4: Sort the database in descending sequence with "percent" as the primary sort key. Print a report of this arrangement of the database. (*Hint:* Be sure to include all the database columns in your sort range.)

Task 5: (*Optional*)   Add a column at the right side of your DATA INPUT AREA that computes the *accumulated* PERCENT. That is, the **percent** from the first row is added to that of the second row and so on for the other rows in the database. Range Format this columns as Percent 2. Print a report of these results.

Task 6: Using the report from either Task 4 or Task 5, draw a line across the report to separate the inventory into the A items, B items, and C items based on the rough percentages Stewart uses for each of these item groups. On your report, write a comment to specify each of the three inventory groups for Stewart.

Task 7: Produce a report containing the "high" PRICE items—those with a PRICE greater than $400. Do this as an extract that includes only the PRODUCT, DESCRIPT, PRICE, and PROFIT columns. Lay out a DATA OUTPUT AREA and a CRITERIA AREA in a convenient location on your worksheet. Use a range name to identify each area. Print your completed report and save your worksheet file.

Task 8: (*Optional*)   Use the Find command to locate the record in the DATA INPUT AREA for **product** number **519510B**. Produce a hard copy of this screen using <Shift>+<PrtSc>. What is the price of this product?

Time Estimates

Novice: 60 minutes

Intermediate: 45 minutes

Advanced: 30 minutes

(3)   Case: Bull and Bear Investment Group

Business Problem: Stock fund management
MIS Characteristics: Finance
                    Managerial Control

Julian Soros is the fund manager for Bull and Bear Investment Group's (BBIG) Emerging Growth Fund. The Fund aggressively targets stocks of companies expected to achieve accelerated growth in earnings or revenues. Julian scans stocks traded in the over-the-counter (OTC) market in search of additions to the Fund. He regularly adds new stocks and removes underperforming stocks from the Fund. In evaluating a prospective stock, he reviews a company's performance and assesses how well it has performed relative to the overall stock market. Julian uses return on assets (ROA), return on equity (ROE), and a stock's beta in evaluating a stock for inclusion in the Fund. He knows that the beta relates the change in the stock's price to that of the overall market. A stock with a beta of one tends to increase or decrease in price as the overall market changes, while a stock with a beta of two tends to change twice as fast as the overall market. Julian usually prefers stocks with betas greater than one.

Julian has designed a database to assist him in evaluating the performance of prospective stocks that contains fields described by the following data dictionary definitions:

Field Name	Description
SYMBOL	Stock trading symbol
COMPANY	Company name
SALES	Net sales revenue
INCOME	Net income
ASSETS	Total assets
EQUITY	Stockholder's equity
BETA	Stock's beta value
ROA	Return on total assets (INCOME/ASSETS)
ROE	Return on stockholder's equity (INCOME/EQUITY)

Task 1: Retrieve Julian's BBIG.WK1 worksheet file containing his database and review its contents. Observe how Julian entered values for all columns in the database except ROA and ROE. Print a copy of the DATA INPUT AREA for your reference.

Task 2: Add these records to the bottom of the DATA INPUT AREA in Julian's database:

symbol	company	sales	income	assets	equity	beta
TYSNA	TYSON FOODS	3825	120.0	2501	663	0.85
UCIT	UNITED CITIES GAS	220	3.4	341	71	0.37
VALM	VALMONT INDUSTRIES	874	15.5	351	112	1.24
VELCF	VELCRO INDUSTRIES	105	7.2	119	65	0.35
YELL	YELLOW FREIGHT	2302	65.3	1116	469	1.08

Task 3: Add equations for the ROA and ROE fields to the database as described in the database definition. Range Format these two columns as Percent 2. Print another copy of the DATA INPUT AREA and save this revised BBIG worksheet file.

Task 4: Sort the database in descending sequence with the "beta" as the primary sort key and the "roe" as the secondary key. Produce a hard copy report of this database. (*Hint:* Be sure to include the appropriate columns in your sort range.) Which five stocks tend to experience price increases and decreases at about the same rate as those for the overall stock market? Circle these on your printout.

Task 5: Sort the database in descending sequence with the "roe" as the primary key and the "beta" as the secondary key. Generate a report of this arrangement of the database. Which stocks have the best return on stockholder equity? On your printout, circle those with a ROE of 25 percent or better.

Task 6: Produce a report containing the "best" prospects—those stocks with an ROE greater than 15 percent *and* a beta greater than 1.00. Prepare this as an extract that includes only the SYMBOL, COMPANY, SALES, ROE, and BETA columns. Place your DATA OUTPUT AREA and CRITERIA AREA in a convenient location on your worksheet. Use a range name to identify each area. Print your completed report and save your modified worksheet file.

Task 7: (*Optional*)   Use the Find command to locate the record for the stock with the symbol of **DBRN** in the INPUT DATA AREA. Obtain a copy of this result with the <Shift>+<PrtSc>. What are the **beta** and **roe** for this stock?

Time Estimates

Novice: 60 minutes

Intermediate: 45 minutes

Advanced: 30 minutes

L.11.12 Comprehensive Problems

(1)   Case: Woodcraft Furniture Company (second encounter)

At Woodcraft Furniture, Martha Goodguess has recommended that Ray Jointer use Lotus 1-2-3 to develop a prototype database for producing several inventory reports. Ray intends to use these reports in preparing his weekly production plan. Martha described to Ray how the data could be arranged in different sequences and how he could prepare special reports containing selected data. To test their application, Ray has compiled the following data:

part#	type	desc	quant	price
37896	chair	Country	127	115
38962	sofa	Traditional	41	427
35621	chair	Queen Anne	111	98
32711	sofa	Contemporary	17	459
35623	table	Queen Anne	19	488
31924	sofa	European	63	377
37895	table	Country	23	525
39829	sofa	Leisure World	28	519
32944	sofa	Futon	37	401
33117	chair	Shaker Farmhouse	151	103
32141	chair	Queen Anne	47	132
34911	table	Shaker Farmhouse	54	527

Task 1: Build the database worksheet using Ray's field names and the data he provided.

Task 2: Print a report of the initial database with the data arranged in the sequence as collected by Ray. Include the company name and "INVENTORY REPORT" as the title for this report.

Task 3: Sort the database with product "type" as the primary sort key and the product "part#" as the secondary key. Print a report of the database arranged in this sequence.

Task 4: Produce a report with an extract for the sofa products. This report is to include all the fields.

Task 5: Save this database as worksheet file WOODDB1.

Task 6: (*Optional*)   Add an "amt" field to the database where

amt = quant * price

This field indicates the total value of each product held in inventory. Add a cell above the "amt" field that contains the total inventory value. Why is it desirable to locate this cell above the input area of the database? Print this revised worksheet and then save this database as worksheet file WOODDB2.

Quick check answer: Total amt = 175475

Time Estimates

Novice: 90 minutes

Intermediate: 75 minutes

Advanced: 40 minutes

(2)   Case: Midwest Universal Gas (second encounter)

At Midwest Universal Gas, Sam Wright is exploring the use of Lotus 1-2-3 to develop a prototype database for producing several special reports from accounts receivable information. Francis Foresight intends to use these reports in preparing marketing plans. Sam described to Mary Derrick how he could create reports arranged in different sequences and how he could prepare special reports that contain only selected data for Francis. The following data have been collected for use in testing this database application:

cust#	type	name	address	zip	amt
35711	r	Mike Segalo	777 N Chevrolet	59901	142.80
33429	w	JD Automotive	11729 N Mission	59903	496.23
26727	r	Brian Duddles	511 S Franklin	59902	76.21
37924	r	Maria Rossi	427 E Oak St	59902	87.43
31184	w	Allied Engineering	1005 E Corporate Dr	59907	573.92
35707	r	Autumn Viviano	1100 S Appian Way	59905	162.31
36308	r	Mark Wing	3190 N Salem Blvd	59901	66.89
34795	r	Bruce Peralez	8585 S Whiteville	59902	83.72
34251	w	First of America	2165 Commerce Dr	59903	411.27
34129	w	Action Auto World	1170 N Broadway	59907	391.73
36924	r	Clint Landiz	4196 N Lincoln	59905	54.54
34911	r	Chad Horvath	931 S Gulley	59901	87.11

Task 1: Build the database worksheet using the field names and data provided by Sam.

Task 2: Print a report of the initial database with the data arranged in the sequence as collected by Sam. Include the company name and "ACCOUNTS RECEIVABLE" as the title for this report.

Task 3: Sort the database with customer "type" as the primary sort key and the "cust#" as the secondary key. Print a report of the database arranged in this sequence.

Task 4: Produce a report with an extract for the "w" (wholesale) customers. This report is to include all the fields of the database.

Task 5: Save this database as worksheet file MUGDB1.

Task 6: (*Optional*)   Add a cell above the "amt" field that contains the total amount of accounts receivable. Why is it desirable to locate this cell above the input area of the database? Print this revised worksheet and then save this database as worksheet file MUGDB2.

Quick check answer: Total amt = 2634.16

Time Estimates

Novice: 90 minutes

Intermediate: 75 minutes

Advanced: 40 minutes

L.11.13 Case Application

Case: Deerfield Fabrication

Business Problem: Production scheduling
MIS Characteristics: Production/Operations
                          Managerial Control
Management Functions: Directing
                        Controlling
Tools Skills: Data sort
           Database query
           Macros
           Reporting

Deerfield Fabrication produces customized equipment for the restaurant industry. It specializes in kitchen and food handling equipment manufactured from high-quality stainless steel. The high quality of their equipment sets the standard by which other manufacturers are gauged. The equipment Deerfield produces is used by most major fast food restaurants. Deerfield's growth has paralleled that of the fast food industry, expanding with the market for "food away from home."

Vince Robertson, Deerfield's president and chief executive officer, founded the company in 1966. Deerfield recently relocated its operations to a modern plant facility with more than 2 million square feet of floor space. Deerfield uses a number of special-purpose machines in the manufacture of it products. Many of these were originally designed by Vince.

Deerfield custom builds each order. Although many parts are similar, the exact dimensions and specifications will change from one order to the next. As a result, the complexity and scope of an order causes the amount of processing time to vary. Each order is produced using a job shop production configuration. In this arrangement, an order or job is assigned to a work center for completion. When one job is finished, the next job is started.

The growth of customer orders is straining the production capacity of Deerfield and has created a number of problems. The number of customers complaining about late orders has increased 50 percent. One major customer, Hot Stuff Now, with a chain of several hundred restaurants had to delay the opening of 10 restaurants because Deerfield could not deliver equipment on time. Hot Stuff Now's president called Vince and is threatening to stop ordering equipment from Deerfield. Vince has summoned Margaret "Maggie" Kim, Deerfield's superintendent of manufacturing, to his office to discuss the problem.

Recently Maggie attended an Operations/Production Management Seminar on Job Shop Production Scheduling conducted by Chase, Aquilano and Associates. At the seminar, Richard "Rich" Chase explained that priority rules are applied as guidelines for selecting which job is started first in job shop manufacturing. A number of rules exist for evaluating different performance conditions. Three of the more common scheduling rules are these:

(a) First-come, first-served (FCFS). Orders are processed in the sequence in which they arrive.

(b) Shortest operation time (SOT). Orders are processed in an inverse sequence to the time required to process each order. This is the same as the shortest processing time (SPT) rule.

(c) Earliest due date (EDD). Orders are processed with the earliest due date first.

Rich described how the quality of a schedule can be assessed by several different measures of performance. Two of the more frequently applied measures for evaluating priority scheduling rules are

(a) Meeting due dates of customers.

(b) Minimizing flow time (the time a job spends in the shop).

Flow time is the time a job spends in the shop both waiting to be processed and being processed. The mean flow time is an average for all the jobs waiting to be processed. An optimal schedule is one that minimizes the mean flow time.

Rich reviewed the benefits of each scheduling rule. First, the FCFS method is usually not the best method for scheduling because the sequence in which orders arrive has no relation to either due date or processing time for the order. Second, the SOT method provides for completing the greatest number of orders during a schedule period. SOT may help improve cash flow because orders can be shipped and billed as they are completed. However, this may provide only an illusion of improved cash flow, since these orders might be those with the smallest dollar values and lowest profitability. Third, the EDD method concentrates on customer satisfaction by meeting as many due dates as possible during a schedule period.

After her return from the seminar, Maggie began to develop a database table in 1-2-3 that contains a list of jobs awaiting processing. She explained to Vince that she could include the flow time per job, as proposed by Rich, in her report. With this analysis they should be able to better control their scheduling and increase the number of jobs completed on schedule. In addition to her actions, Maggie also suggested that the sales staff should be informed of the growing backlog of orders and should advise customers of increased ordering time for the production of their orders.

Maggie devised their production scheduling database table with the following fields:

Field Name	Description
job#	A unique number assigned to each job scheduled for production.
cust#	A unique number assigned to each customer. A customer may have more than one scheduled job.
order	The date of the order, entered in the form "mm.dd" as a number, such as "3.15," and formatted as Fixed 2.
due	The due date of the order, entered in the same form as the order date.
description	A description of the product being fabricated for the order.

Maggie decided to use a number with two places to the right of the decimal for entering the date because this is a convenient method that avoids the use of more complex date functions in 1-2-3.

The 1-2-3 database should provide Maggie and Vince with the information they require to better direct and control the job shop schedule. They are both hopeful that they can satisfy the requirements for their major customer, Hot Stuff Now.

Tasks

1. Access the PRODSCH.WK1 worksheet file and inspect its contents. An INPUT AREA has been created and Deerfield's orders entered. Suggested locations for the CRITERIA and OUTPUT AREAS have been identified to the right of the INPUT AREA. A column has been established to hold the Flow Time per Job and a cell setup for the Mean Flow Time. (*Hint:* Use <Tab> and <Shift>+<Tab> to move right and left between the INPUT AREA and the other areas.)

2. Add equations to calculate the Flow Time per Job and the Mean Flow Time. For the first job, the flow time is just the **days** needed to complete the job. For all other jobs, the flow time is the immediately preceding job's flow time plus the **days** for completion. The mean flow time is the average flow time for all the jobs on the schedule. (*Hint:* Use a function to compute the average flow time.)

3. Add column titles for the CRITERIA AREA and the OUTPUT AREA. (*Hint:* The safest method for accomplishing this is to copy the labels from the INPUT AREA. This ensures that the titles are spelled the same way.) Format the second row of the CRITERIA AREA using / Range Format Text so that the equations entered in this area will be displayed. Execute the commands necessary for defining the INPUT, CRITERIA, and OUTPUT areas for use with a 1-2-3 database.

4. Before exploring the scheduling rules, Maggie and Vince want to query the database, looking at selected records and printing several special reports as follows:

   (a) Browse through the database and look at the orders that are **due** on 4.15. Use the FIND command to locate these records.

   (b) Produce a list of all of the orders for **cust#** 5055. Extract these records and print a report for Maggie.

   (c) Prepare a list of the jobs **due** on 6.01. Extract these records and print a report.

(d) Create a list of orders for the "beverage" product. Extract these records and print a report. (*Hint:* The **description** "beverage" in the CRITERIA AREA must exactly match the spelling in the INPUT AREA of the database. If a label contains spaces, the spacing must also exactly match in both areas.)

(e) Develop a list of the jobs **due** during May and June. Extract these records and print a report. (*Hint:* So that the fields in the INPUT AREA can be referenced in an equation by name, place the cursor on the cell containing "job#" in the INPUT AREA and perform a / Range Name Label Down on all the field names through the "description" in the INPUT AREA. This allows the fields in the INPUT AREA to be referenced by their names rather than by cell names. In the **due** date field in the CRITERIA AREA, enter the formula: +**due** > **5.** Now complete the Extract.)

(f) Produce a list of all the jobs **due** in April. Extract these records and print a report. [*Hint:* Use the #AND# logical operator in this manner: +**due** > **4**#AND#**due** < **5.**]

5. Now Vince and Maggie want to explore the EDD and SOT production scheduling methods as follows:

(a) Sort the data in the INPUT AREA by **due** date and print a report. When sorting by **due** date, use the **days** field as a tiebreaker. [*Hint:* Flow Time Per Job is NOT part of the INPUT AREA and should NOT be sorted.]

(b) Sort the data by **days** and print a report. Use the **due** date field as a tiebreaker. [*Hint:* Again, the Flow Time Per Job should NOT be sorted.]

(c) Write a summary comparing the two schedules. Which has the smaller mean flow time? What do you see as the advantages or disadvantages of each schedule? Considering the current problem facing Vince and Maggie, which schedule do you recommend?

6. As Deerfield processes orders, new orders will be added to the production schedule and completed orders removed. After Maggie has made these revisions, she would like to produce both an Earliest Due Date report and a Shortest Operation Time report. Create a macro that will produce both these reports. The macro should place the title "Earliest Due Date" or "Shortest Operation Time" immediately below the current "Production Schedule" title before the report is printed. Within the macro, the Sorts should be performed to compute the flow times as each report is prepared. For sorting, use the tiebreakers specified previously. Save the file that includes this macro.

7. (*Optional*)   Maggie has studied the results of the output for the Earliest Due Date and the Shortest Operation Time. In addition to the mean flow time, she would like to compare the scheduling rules by calculating the number of days late for each order. To accomplish this, Maggie will need to revise the dates so that she can perform date arithmetic in 1-2-3. She has created the PROD-SCH2.WK1 worksheet file with the dates entered using the @DATEVALUE function. Each date is displayed with the Date 2 format. A "schedule start" date has been added to her report. The "start" date and "stop" date for each job can then be computed. For the first job in the schedule, the "start" date is the same as the "schedule start" date. For the second and all other jobs, the "start" date is the "stop" date of the previous job plus 1. The "stop" date for all jobs is the "start" date plus the number of "days" minus 1. The number of days "late" is the "stop" date minus the "due" date. If this result is negative, a zero is displayed, because the job is not late; otherwise the number of days "late" is displayed. The "flow" days are computed as described before. The average days late ("avg days late") is computed using the data values in the "late" column. Enter the formulas to calculate values for the start, stop, late,

and flow columns. Enter formulas for the **mean flow time** and **avg days late.** Sort the data for both schedule rules and print the reports using a macro like that from Task 6. Save your worksheet file. Compare the results and write a summary of the effect of these two schedule rules. Do you still recommend the same schedule as in Task 5? Why or why not?

Time Estimates

Novice: 120 minutes

Intermediate: 90 minutes

Advanced: 60 minutes

Enhancing Appearance with WYSIWYG

CONTENT

- **What Is WYSIWYG?**
- **Attaching WYSIWYG**
- **Accessing the Main WYSIWYG Menu**
- **Using SmartIcons with WYSIWYG**
- **Enhancing a Worksheet's Appearance**
- **Saving Format Specifications**
- **Printing an Enhanced Worksheet**
- **Adding a Graph to a Worksheet**
- **Enhancing Graphs**
- **When Things Go Wrong**

L.12.1 What Is WYSIWYG?

Chris and Kim just returned from their weekly review meeting with Frosty. He is pleased with their work in developing the Pro Forma Profit and Loss Statement (Figure L.209) for Friday's meeting with Good Morning Products' Board of Directors. Frosty indicated his approval of the content and layout of the report. However, because of the importance of this meeting, he would like to have the appearance of the report enhanced to provide additional impact when he presents it to the Board. During their meeting Kim and Chris talked to Frosty about how they could improve the appearance of the report by using spreadsheet publishing features.

WYSIWYG is a Lotus 1-2-3 Add-In that is available beginning with Release 2.3. It lets you enhance a 1-2-3 worksheet by using **spreadsheet publishing** features. With spreadsheet publishing the appearance is improved by adding features like boldface, italics, underlines, and outlines to a basic 1-2-3 worksheet. However, cell contents

```
                                                          21-Oct-94

                         GOOD MORNING PRODUCTS
                  PRO FORMA PROFIT AND LOSS STATEMENT
                  ------------------------------------

    Sales Growth Rate       0.08
    Cost Percent            0.77

                         1ST QTR  2ND QTR  3RD QTR  4TH QTR    TOTAL
                         -------  -------  -------  -------   -------
    Sales                 289500   312660   337673   364687  1304519
    Cost of Sales         222915   240748   260008   280809  1004480
```

FIGURE L.209. Worksheet before enhancing appearance.

(labels and values) are not revised with WYSIWYG. Only the appearance of what is *already* stored in the cells is improved. The actual cell contents are entered and/or revised in the same manner, regardless of whether WYSIWYG is used to enhance their appearance.

Kim and Chris explained the spreadsheet publishing features to Frosty and described how their final worksheet would be enhanced, as shown in Figure L.210. Their worksheet includes many of the more commonly used spreadsheet publishing features and are as follows:

1 Boldface type style.

2 Italics type style.

3 Larger 14-point font size.

4 Underline style.

5 Double underline style.

6 Outline around range.

7 Grid lines applied to range.

8 Double line across range.

9 Shading applied to range.

10 Drop shadow applied to range.

11 Graph added to worksheet for printing.

12 Text added to graph.

13 Ellipse added to graph.

14 Rectangle added to graph.

15 Arrow added to graph.

In this lesson, you will explore the use of each of these features in taking Good Morning Products' basic 1-2-3 worksheet of Figure L.209 and turning it into the more professional-looking document of Figure L.210.

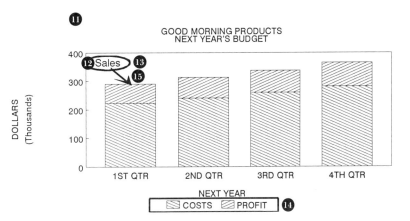

FIGURE L.210. Printed worksheet with enhanced appearance.

Keypoint!

WYSIWYG changes only the *appearance* of cell contents. It does *not* change the actual label, data value, or formula stored in a cell!

One of the most common enhancements to a worksheet like that for Good Morning Products is to change the fonts used in displaying and printing results, as shown in Figure L.210. Lotus 1-2-3 lets you use several different fonts with a worksheet. A **font** is the overall appearance of letters, numbers, and symbols. Fonts are distinguished by their typeface and type size. A **typeface** is the particular graphical design of the printed or displayed characters. Each typeface has a distinct appearance, with all of the characters in the typeface sharing a common design. For example, Dutch and Swiss are two families of typefaces used with WYSIWYG. The type size is a measurement of the height of the characters that is usually specified in points, where a **point** is approximately 1/72 of an inch. Bold, italics, and bold italics are alternative versions of a single type design. Hence, a 14-point bold italic Swiss typeface is one specific font. The default fonts furnished with 1-2-3 and available for use with WYSIWYG are shown in Figure L.211. Unless you change the font, Swiss 12-point is the default font automatically used with WYSIWYG. Boldface and/or italics may be applied to the seven character typefaces to provide these enhanced versions of the basic fonts supplied with 1-2-3. Besides these fonts, you could purchase other Bitstream fonts and use them with 1-2-3. This lesson is limited to the standard WYSIWYG fonts provided by Lotus Development with 1-2-3.

Default Character Fonts	Bold Fonts
Swiss 12 Point	**Swiss 12 Point**
Swiss 14 Point	**Swiss 14 Point**
Swiss 24 Pt	**Swiss 24 Pt**
Dutch 6 Point	**Dutch 6 Point**
Dutch 8 Point	**Dutch 8 Point**
Dutch 10 Point	**Dutch 10 Point**
Dutch 12 Point	**Dutch 12 Point**

Italics Fonts	Bold Italics Fonts
Swiss 12 Point	***Swiss 12 Point***
Swiss 14 Point	***Swiss 14 Point***
Swiss 24 Pt	***Swiss 24 Pt***
Dutch 6 Point	***Dutch 6 Point***
Dutch 8 Point	***Dutch 8 Point***
Dutch 10 Point	***Dutch 10 Point***
Dutch 12 Point	***Dutch 12 Point***

Default Special Font

Xsymbol 12 Point

➡①②③④⑤⑥⑦⑧⑨⑩❶❷❸❹❺❻❼❽❾❿➔
♥♣♦♠

FIGURE L.211. Standard fonts available with WYSIWYG.

L.12.2 Attaching WYSIWYG

The WYSIWYG feature of 1-2-3 is an Add-In, similar to SmartIcons and Backsolver, and is available beginning with Release 2.3. It must be attached before you can use it to enhance a worksheet like that developed by Chris and Kim for Good Morning Products. Because Add-Ins take up additional computer memory, you may *not* be able to use SmartIcons, Backsolver, WYSIWYG, and Undo all at the same time. In the event that you try to attach WYSIWYG and the "Not enough memory for graphics mode" message appears, you will need to detach other Add-Ins or disable Undo. Usually, with most hardware configurations, sufficient memory is available so that you can use both WYSIWYG and SmartIcons at the same time.

Keypoint!

> You may not have sufficient computer memory to use both WYSIWYG and Undo at the same time. You will probably want to disable Undo before using WYSIWYG!

When you attach WYSIWYG, the appearance of the worksheet changes, with all of your data displayed initially in the Swiss 12-point font. So that you can see this affect on your worksheet, let's retrieve the PLAN8 worksheet for Good Morning Products you developed in Lesson L.5 *before* attaching WYSIWYG.

Action: Retrieve your PLAN8 worksheet file (Figure L.212) in preparation for enhancing it by using WYSIWYG spreadsheet publishing features.

Now let us see how WYSIWYG is attached starting from the READY mode.

To attach the WYSIWYG spreadsheet publishing Add-In			
Press:	/	Access main menu
Select:	Add-In	Desired action
Select:	Attach	Desired activity
Select:	WYSIWYG.ADN	Desired Add-In
Select:	No-Key	Desired option

Because WYSIWYG has its own special method for conveniently accessing the WYSIWYG menu, a hot-key is *not* required for using this Add-In.

Select: Quit   Complete Attaching Add-In and return to the READY mode

When WYSIWYG is attached, the worksheet is displayed as shown in Figure L.213 by using the Swiss 12-point font. If SmartIcons are also attached, their display changes as well (Figure L.213).

Besides manually attaching WYSIWYG each time you start 1-2-3, you may establish a default setting that causes WYSIWYG to be automatically attached each time you start 1-2-3. This is indicated by the Default Setting dialog box shown in Figure L.214. The default is established as described in Figure L.215. Regardless of the method

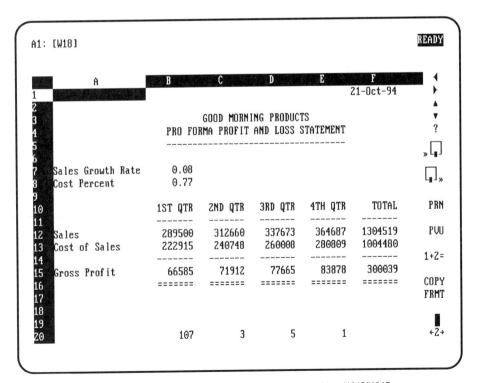

FIGURE L.212. Worksheet display before attaching WYSIWYG.

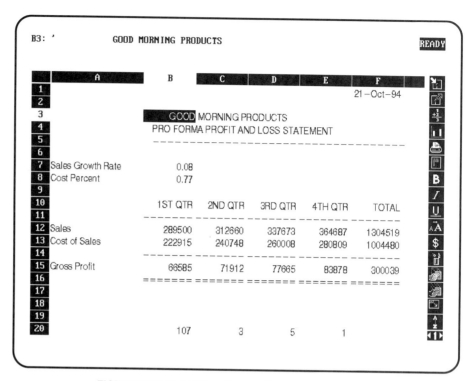

FIGURE L.213. Initial worksheet display with WYSIWYG.

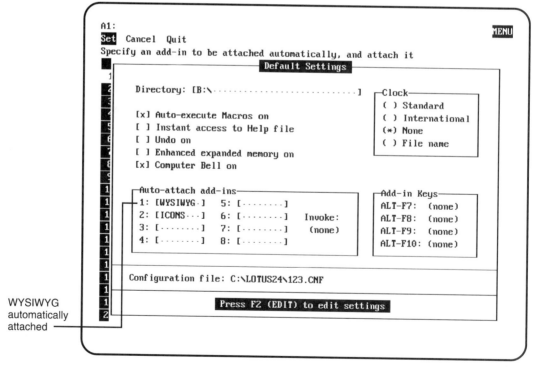

FIGURE L.214. Default Settings dialog box.

1. Initiate default setting changes from the READY mode with
   / Worksheet Global Default Other Add-In
2. Specify setting of Add-In:
   a. Select: `Set`   Desired option
   b. Select: `1`   WYSIWYG is assigned as first auto-attach Add-In
   c. Select: `WYSIWYG.ADN`   Desired Add-In
   d. Select: `No-Key`   Desired option
   e. Select: `No`   Do *not* display the WYSIWYG menu when starting 1-2-3
   f. Select: `Quit`   Complete this setting
3. Request updating of the 1-2-3 configuration file that contains this and other default settings:
   a. Select: `Update`   Desired activity
   b. Select: `Quit`   Return to READY mode

FIGURE L.215. Setting auto-attach for WYSIWYG.

employed, once WYSIWYG is attached, you are ready to enhance the appearance of a
worksheet and graph like that for Good Morning Products.

Keypoint!   When WYSIWYG is attached and a mouse is installed, the mouse pointer appears as an
arrow instead of a small rectangle!

L.12.3 Accessing the Main WYSIWYG Menu

The method of accessing the Main WYSIWYG menu is similar to that used to access
the Main 1-2-3 menu. From the READY mode, the Main WYSIWYG menu is accessed
by pressing the <colon> (:). Let's access this WYSIWYG menu.

To access the Main   **Press:**   :   Use the colon to access this menu
WYSIWYG menu

The menu appears as shown in Figure L.216.
   At this top-level menu, the choices available are as described in Figure L.217. For
now, let's return to the READY mode.

To return to the READY   **Select:**   `Quit`   Menu selection to leave menu
mode from the WYSIWYG   or
menu   **Press:**   `<Esc>`   Return to READY from top level menu

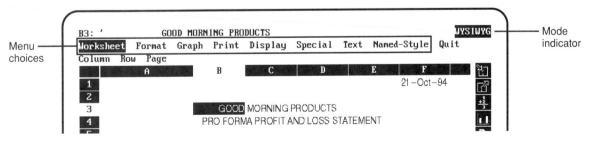

FIGURE L.216. Main WYSIWYG menu.

Menu Selection	Activity
Worksheet	Sets column widths, row heights, and page breaks.
Format	Controls the appearance of your worksheet as displayed on your screen and when printed, including specifying fonts, boldface, and italics.
Graph	Allows you to add, edit, and save graphics, including objects such as arrows, rectangles, and text.
Print	Creates printed copies of your worksheet that include all the spreadsheet publishing enhancements done with WYSIWYG commands.
Display	Controls the display of your worksheet on the screen, including colors and image size.
Special	Operations that copy and move WYSIWYG formats from one cell range to another, including obtaining formats and graphics from other files.
Text	Supports entering and editing text in a worksheet range as though the words are paragraphs in a word processor.
Named-Style	Supports naming a WYSIWYG cell format so that format can be applied to other cells in the current worksheet.
Quit	Leaves WYSIWYG menu and returns to READY mode.

FIGURE L.217. Main WYSIWYG menu choices.

If you have mouse support, you can use your mouse to access either the Main WYSIWYG menu or the Main 1-2-3 menu as described in Figure L.218.

L.12.4 Using SmartIcons with WYSIWYG

SmartIcons provide a shortcut method to execute many of the commonly used WYSIWYG commands by merely using the mouse to click the desired icon. These SmartIcons are available beginning with Release 2.4 as an Add-In. This Add-In must be attached together with the WYSIWYG Add-In to use SmartIcons with WYSIWYG. The procedure for attaching the SmartIcons is summarized in Figure L.219, and the SmartIcons used with WYSIWYG are as indicated in Figure L.220. Because SmartIcons simplify many of the WYSIWYG activities, you should consider using them when enhancing your worksheet with spreadsheet publishing features, like those demonstrated with the Good Morning Products report (Figure L.210).

Keypoint!

> SmartIcons simplify applying many of the WYSIWYG spreadsheet publishing features to your worksheet!

Using a mouse with the WYSIWYG menu

1. Move the mouse pointer to any location in the Control Panel to display either the 1–2–3 or WYSIWYG menu, depending on which you accessed most recently.
2. If the menu displayed is *not* the one you want, then switch to the other menu.

   Click: `<right mouse button>`
3. Position the mouse pointer on the desired command and select it.

   Click: `<left mouse button>`

FIGURE L.218. Using a mouse with the WYSIWYG menu.

1. Initiate attaching the SmartIcons with: / Add-In Attach
2. Select the desired Add-In: ICONS.ADN
3. Because a hot-key is *not* needed, select: No-Key
4. Return to the READY mode, select: Quit

FIGURE L.219. Attaching the SmartIcon Add-In.

WYSIWYG SmartIcon	Command	Description
	Print	Print the current range or a highlighted range.
	Preview	Display preview of the current range or a highlighted range.
	Bold	Bold or clear bold from a range.
	Italics	Italicize or clear italics from a range.
	Clear Attributes	Clear all WYSIWYG attributes from a specified cell range.
	Single Underline	Single underline or remove underline from a range.
	Double Underline	Double underline or remove double underline from a range.
	Change Font	Cycle through available fonts for a range.
	Change Color	Cycle through available colors for a range.
	Change Background	Cycle through available background colors for a range.
	Drop Shadow	Add or remove drop shadow from a range.
	Outline	Cycle through available outlines for a range.
	Shading	Cycle through available shading for a range.
	Circle	Draw circle around selected cell range.
	Add Graph	Add current graph to selected cell range.
	Copy Attributes	Copy WYSIWYG attributes from current range to another range.
	Align Across	Align text across a column range.
	Row Page Break	Insert page break in current row.
	Column Page Break	Insert page break in current column.

FIGURE L.220. SmartIcons used with WYSIWYG.

L.12.5   Enhancing a Worksheet's Appearance

Once WYSIWYG is attached, you are ready to enhance the Good Morning Products Pro Forma Profit and Loss Statement that Kim and Chris want for their Board of Directors meeting. Each of the commonly used enhancements illustrated in Figure L.210 are added to the basic 1-2-3 worksheet file. The first step is to access the basic worksheet file and make some minor changes in preparation for adding these enhancements.

Action: Verify that file PLAN8 is your currently active worksheet.

As shown previously in Figure L.213, the underlines obtained with the minus (−) and equal (=) signs have a different appearance with WYSIWYG because the width of these characters is increased. With WYSIWYG, characters are usually displayed and printed with **proportional spacing,** where characters take up different amounts of space depending on the particular character. For example, the letter I takes up less space than the letter W. Because the minus (−) and equal (=) are proportionally spaced, they take up more space as WYSIWYG characters provided with 1-2-3. This results in the display shown in Figure L.213 and is why it is desired to remove the old-style underlining. Let's remove the old underlining so that it can be replaced using WYSIWYG alternatives.

| To remove basic worksheet attributes in preparation for using their WYSIWYG enhancements | **Action:** Use the / Range Erase (/RE) command to remove the underlines in the cells **B5, B11..F11, B14..F14,** and **B16..F16.** |

The cells **B20..E20** contain data values for cross-hatching and explosion used with the pie chart. Let's hide these so that they are not displayed or printed with this report.

| To hide data values | **Action:** Use the / Range Format Hidden (/RFH) command to hide cells **B20..E20.** |

For the completed report, Kim wants the numeric data formatted using commas. Let's make this change to the format.

| To change the Global Format to commas | **Action:** Use the / Worksheet Global Format <comma> 0(/WGF,0) command to place commas in the numeric data values. |

The revised worksheet (Figure L.221) is now ready for adding the desired spreadsheet publishing enhancements. Whenever you have included underlining in a basic worksheet, you may want to remove it when using WYSIWYG for enhancing the appearance of these report characteristics.

L.12.5.1   Changing Fonts

The first enhancement that Chris and Kim want to make to their Good Morning Products report is the addition of boldface, as illustrated previously in Figure L.210, ❶. Let's add boldface to *Gross Profit*.

To boldface cell contents	**Move to:**	A15	Desired cell
	Press:	:	Use colon to access menu
	Select:	Format	Desired activity
	Select:	Bold	Desired option
	Select:	Set	Add boldface
	Press:	<Enter>	Accept specified cell range

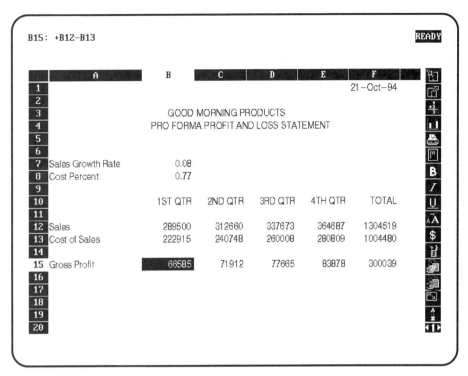

FIGURE L.221. Worksheet revised in preparation for spreadsheet publishing enhancements.

Or with mouse support and SmartIcons, add boldface.

Click:	**A15**	Desired cell
Click:	`Bold SmartIcon`	Desired option
Action:	Add boldface to the Good Morning Products report heading in cell **B3.**	

When a WYSIWYG format is added to a cell, a format code appears in the cell contents area to indicate the application of this format, for example, the "{Bold}" format code in Figure L.222. You do *not* type this as part of the cell contents. It is displayed like range formats and individual column widths as a reminder that these attributes are applied to the cell.

Second, let's add italics to *Sales Growth Rate* in their report, as shown previously in Figure L.210, ❷.

To italicize cell contents

Move to:	**A7**	Desired cell
Press:	:	Use colon to access menu

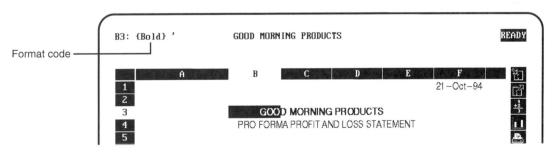

FIGURE L.222. Bold format code displayed with cell contents.

Select:	Format	Desired activity
Select:	Italics	Desired option
Select:	Set	Add italics
Press:	<Enter>	Accept specified cell range

Or with mouse support and SmartIcons, add italics.

Click:	**A7**	Desired cell
Click:	Italics SmartIcon	Desired option
Action:	Add italics to the Pro Forma Profit and Loss Statement report heading in cell **B4**.	

Now let's select a different typeface and change the point size of the Good Morning Products report heading, as shown previously in Figure L.210, ❸.

To change the typeface and point size of a font

Move to:	**B3**	
Press:	:	Use colon to access menu
Select:	Format	Desired activity
Select:	Font	Desired option

The Wysiwyg Font Selection dialog box appears (Figure L.223), indicating that Swiss 12 Point, the default, is the current font.

Select:	2	Choose Swiss 14 Point font
Press:	<Enter>	Accept specified cell range

Or with mouse support and SmartIcons, change the font.

Click:	**A7**	Desired cell
Click:	Change Font	Each click cycles to the next SmartIcon available font, with Swiss 14 Point selected with one click

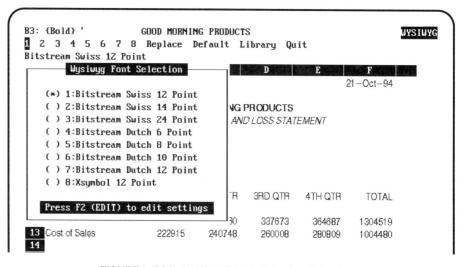

FIGURE L.223. WYSIWYG Font Selection dialog box.

Action: Change the font for the Pro Forma Profit and Loss Statement report heading in cell **B4** to Swiss 14 Point and retain the italics style.

L.12.5.2 Preselecting a Range

When using commands that affect a range of cells, you usually specify the range as an option *during execution* of the command. If you want to use several different commands with the same range, you need to enter the range with each command. For example, if you wanted to apply bold, italics, and Swiss 14-point font to the same range, you would need to specify that range with each Format command. Lotus 1-2-3 provides an alternative method of specifying or **preselecting** the range *before* you start to execute a command. When a range is preselected, 1-2-3 skips the prompt that requests the range or displays this as the current range in a dialog box. This allows you to specify the range once and issue several commands without indicating the range for each command. Let us preselect the column titles for each of the four quarters.

To preselect a range of cells			
Move to:	**B10**	Position cell pointer at corner of cell range
Press:	<F4>	Activate range selection in the POINT mode
Move to:	**E10**	Position cell pointer at opposite corner of cell range (Figure L.224)
Press:	<Enter>	Complete range selection

Or with mouse support a range can also be preselected.

Click:	**B10**	Position cell pointer
Drag to:	**E10**	Highlight desired cell range

Once preselected, a cell range remains selected until you either move the cell pointer or press <Esc>. Let's cancel this preselection.

To cancel a preselected cell range			
Press:	<Esc>	Range selection is removed

Keypoint!

> When a single cell is the desired range, merely moving the cell pointer to that location preselects it, making it the suggested range. However, in this situation, you are still prompted for the range when executing the command and need to press <Enter> to accept this single cell as your range!

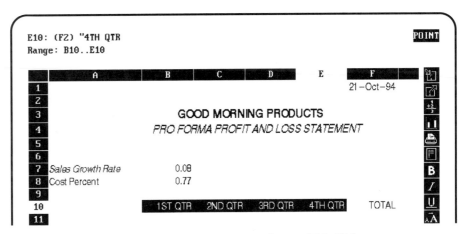

FIGURE L.224. Preselecting cell range **B10..E10**.

L.12.5.3 Underlining Cell Contents

Kim and Chris want to add underlining to their Pro Forma Profit and Loss Statement, as shown previously in Figure L.210, **4**. Let us underline the column titles for each of the four quarters and the annual total with a single underline.

<table>
<tr><td>To underline cell contents
with a single underline</td><td>**Action:**</td><td></td><td>Preselect the range **B10..F10.**</td></tr>
</table>

Press:	:	Use colon to access menu
Select:	Format	Desired activity
Select:	Underline	Desired option
Select:	Single	Desired underline

Or with mouse support and SmartIcons, add the underlines after preselecting the range.

Click:	Single Underline SmartIcon	
		Desired option

Now let's remove or clear the single underline applied to the column title of the *TOTAL* column, because a different attribute is desired.

To clear an underline from cell contents

Move to:	**F10**	Desired cell
Press:	:	Use colon to access menu
Select:	Format	Desired activity
Select:	Underline	Desired option
Select:	Clear	Desired underline
Press:	<Enter>	Complete command

Or with mouse support and SmartIcons, clear an existing underline from a cell.

Move to:	**F10**	Desired cell
Click:	Single Underline SmartIcon	
		Desired option

When SmartIcons are used to specify an underline, bold, or italics, clicking the icon on a cell that *already contains* this format feature causes that format feature to be removed or cleared.

Because Kim really wants a double underline for the **TOTAL** column, let's add it to that column title (Figure L.210, **5**).

To underline cell contents with a double underline

Move to:	**F10**	Desired cell
Press:	:	Use colon to access menu
Select:	Format	Desired activity
Select:	Underline	Desired option
Select:	Double	Desired underline
Press:	<Enter>	Complete command when an individual single cell is formatted

Or with mouse support and SmartIcons, add a double underline to a cell.

Move to:	**F10**	Desired cell
Click:	Double Underline SmartIcon	
		Desired option

L.12.5.4 Outlining Cell Contents

An **outline** is a line or border that surrounds one or more cells in a worksheet. Outlines may be applied to any or all sides of a cell, as desired. Chris wants to use outlines to highlight key results in the Good Morning Products report. Let's place an outline around the cells that contain the data values for *Gross Profit*, as shown previously in Figure L.210, ❻.

To outline cells placing a border around the entire cell range	**Action:**		Preselect the range **B15..F15.**
	Press:	:	Use colon to access menu
	Select:	Format	Desired activity
	Select:	Lines	Desired option
	Select:	Outline	Desired line arrangement

Or with mouse support and SmartIcons, add the outline after preselecting the range.

	Click:	Outline SmartIcon	Desired option

When the SmartIcon is used, continued clicking of this icon cycles through the several line types available for outlining, including removing the outline.

Let's create a grid around the cells containing the *Sales Growth Rate* and *Cost Percent* assumptions (Figure L.210, ❼).

To add a grid around the cells in a range	**Action:**		Preselect the cell range **A7..B8.**
	Press:	:	Use colon to access menu
	Select:	Format	Desired activity
	Select:	Lines	Desired option
	Select:	All	Line location

A SmartIcon is *not* available for creating this grid.

Next let's add a double line between the *Cost of Sales* data values and the *Gross Profit* data values, as shown previously in Figure L.210, ❽. This is accomplished by using a double outline applied to the top of the cells in row **14.**

To create a double line at the top of a cell range	**Action:**		Preselect the cell range **B14..F14.**
	Press:	:	Use colon to access menu
	Select:	Format	Desired activity
	Select:	Lines	Desired option
	Select:	Double	Desired line type
	Select:	Top	Desired line position
	Press:	<Enter>	Complete command

There is *no* equivalent SmartIcon available for adding this line.

L.12.5.5 Shading Cell Contents

In the Good Morning Products report, Kim wants to use shading to draw attention to the *TOTAL Sales* amount (Figure L.210, ❾). Let's add shading to the data value for *Sales* in the *TOTAL* column.

To add shading to cell contents			
Move to:	B12	Desired location
Press:	:	Use colon to access menu
Select:	Format	Desired activity
Select:	Shade	Desired option
Select:	Light	Desired shading density
Press:	<Enter>	Complete command

Or with mouse support and SmartIcons, shading is added to a cell.

Move to:	F10	Desired cell
Click:	Shading SmartIcon	Desired option

When the SmartIcon is used, continued clicking of this icon cycles through the available shading densities, including removing the shading.

L.12.5.6   Adding a Drop Shadow

Chris and Kim want to add emphasis to their report heading. Let's add a drop shadow around the report heading in cells **B3..F4** to accentuate this report feature (Figure L.210, **10**).

To add a drop shadow			
Action:	Preselect the cell range **B3..F4**.
Press:	:	Use colon to access menu
Select:	Format	Desired activity
Select:	Lines	Desired option
Select:	Shadow	Desired line arrangement
Select:	Set	Add drop shadow
Press:	<Enter>	Complete command

Or with mouse support and SmartIcons, add the drop shadow after preselecting the range.

Click:	Drop Shadow SmartIcon	Desired option

When the SmartIcon is used, clicking this icon removes the drop shadow when the range already has the format applied to it.

L.12.5.7   Changing Column Width and Row Height

Kim believes that increasing the amount of white space on a page often makes the page easier to read. For their Pro Forma Profit and Loss Statement, she wants to explore increasing the width of the *TOTAL* column and changing the height of a row containing the report heading to see if this improves the report's appearance.

Let's increase the width of the *TOTAL* column using WYSIWYG commands.

To increase the column width using WYSIWYG			
Move to:	F6	Or any other cell in column **F**
Press:	:	Use colon to access menu
Select:	Worksheet	Desired activity

Select:	Column	Desired option
Select:	Set-Width	Desired operation
Press:	<Enter>	Accept current column for change
Press:	<right><right>	Increase column width and observe change
Press:	<Enter>	Complete change in column width

Or with mouse support the column width is revised by using the mouse to indicate the desired change.

Action:		Position the mouse pointer in the column letter border at the right edge of column **F** (Figure L.225).
Click:		Edge between column **F** and column **G**
		Mouse pointer changes to double-headed arrow [Figure L.225]
Drag:		Mouse pointer to right and release
		Increase the column width as desired [Figure L.225]

When the column width is changed using WYSIWYG commands, this change modifies the column width in your basic worksheet in the same manner as using the / Worksheet Column Set-Width (/WCS) command. The major difference with WYSIWYG is the ability to use the mouse pointer to change the column width.

Now let's increase the spacing between the two title lines by changing the height of the row **4,** containing PRO FORMA PROFIT AND LOSS STATEMENT.

To increase the row height using WYSIWYG

Move to:	A3	Or any other cell in row **3**
Press:	:	Use colon to access menu
Select:	Worksheet	Desired activity
Select:	Row	Desired option
Select:	Set-Height	Desired operation
Press:	<Enter>	Accept current row for change
Enter:	24	Desired height in points, or use <down> to increase the height one point at time

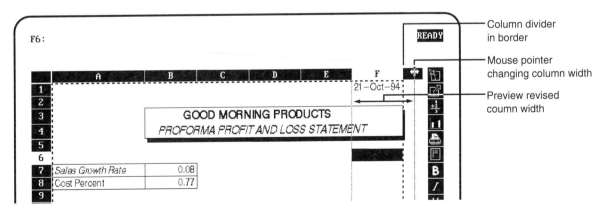

FIGURE L.225. Using the mouse pointer to change column width.

Or with mouse support the row height is revised by merely using the mouse to specify the desired height.

Action: Position the mouse pointer in the row number border between rows **3** and **4** (Figure L.226).

Click: Divider between row **3** and row **4**

Mouse pointer changes to double-headed arrow (Figure L.226)

Drag: Mouse pointer down to desired height and release

Increase the row height desired (Figure L.226)

The Good Morning Products report with the revised column width and row height is shown in Figure L.227.

Because row heights cannot be specified in a basic 1-2-3 worksheet, a modified row height is available only with WYSIWYG. Unlike the column width, the row height specification is stored only with the WYSIWYG format.

After reviewing the changes in Figure L.227, Kim and Chris decide that the initial column width and row height provide sufficient white space on their report. They want to set the width of column **F** and height of row **3** to their initial sizes. First let's reset the column width.

To reset the column width using WYSIWYG

Action: Move to any row in column **F.** Use the : Worksheet Column Reset-Width (:WCR) command to reset the column width. Or, with mouse support, use the mouse to click the column divider in the border and drag the mouse pointer to the left until the desired column width is obtained. However, when using the mouse pointer, the column width is *not* reset to the global default, but remains specified individually at the desired size.

Next let's reset the row height in a similar manner.

To reset the row height using WYSIWYG

Action: Move to any column in row **3.** Use the : Worksheet Row Auto (:WRA) command to reset the row height. Or with mouse support, use the mouse in the row border between rows **3** and **4** to click and drag the row to the desired height. However, when using the mouse pointer, the row height is *not* returned to the default value for the font displayed in that row, which is the situation when Auto is selected.

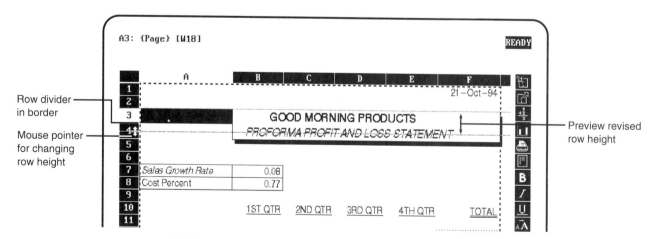

FIGURE L.226. Using the mouse pointer to change row height.

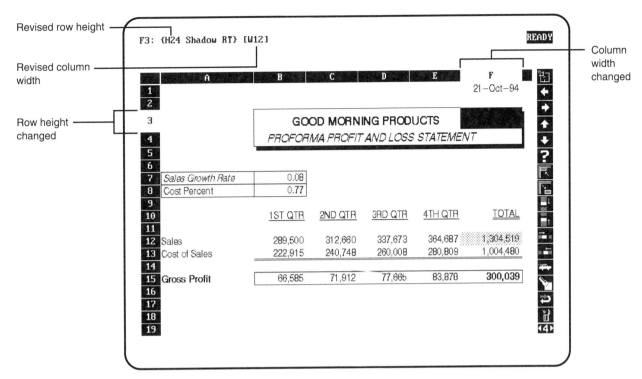

Revised row height

Revised column width

Row height changed

Column width changed

FIGURE L.227. Revised Good Morning Product report.

Kim and Chris have returned to their initial worksheet as displayed in Figure L.210. They are confident that this meets Frosty's requirement for their presentation to the Board of Directors.

L.12.6 Saving Format Specifications

The special WYSIWYG format features added to enhance a worksheet, like that for Good Morning Products, are stored in a *separate* computer file from your *.WK1 file. When you use WYSIWYG and save your worksheet file, 1-2-3 stores your basic worksheet in the *.WK1 file, while the WYSIWYG format is stored in a file with the FMT extension. For example, when a / File Save (/FS) is performed for a worksheet with a filename of PLAN17, the basic worksheet is stored in the PLAN17.WK1 file, and the WYSIWYG format specifications are stored in the PLAN17.FMT file. Let's save the Good Morning Products worksheet and format files.

To save a worksheet file and its WYSIWYG format file

Press:	/	Access main menu
Select:	File	
Select:	Save	Desired activity
Enter:	PLAN17	Name for both worksheet and format files

Or with mouse support and SmartIcons, the files are saved by merely selecting an icon.

Click:	File Save SmartIcon	
Action:	For the second and all other files saves performed for these files, select Replace when this option is requested.	

Keypoint!	WYSIWYG *must* be attached in order to save an *.FMT file when performing a / File Save (/FS)!

After a worksheet is saved with its associated WYSIWYG format file, WYSIWYG must be attached when loading the file with / File Retrieve (/FR) so that the enhanced format features appear on your screen. If you retrieve the worksheet file without WYSIWYG attached, the format features do not appear until this Add-In is attached.

L.12.7 Printing an Enhanced Worksheet

Once the Good Morning Products worksheet is enhanced with 1-2-3's spreadsheet publishing features, this enhanced worksheet is ready for printing. Because the printing process with the many enhanced features is usually much slower than printing without the enhancements, 1-2-3 provides you with the ability to **preview** or look at the layout of your report before you actually print it. Then, if you detect the need to make any changes, these revisions can be made before the worksheet is printed. Let us preview Kim's Good Morning Products report before it is printed.

To preview an enhanced report prior to printing

Action: Preselect the range **A1..F18** for previewing and printing.

Press: :   Use colon to access menu

Select: Print   Desired activity

The Wysiwyg Print Setting dialog box appears as shown in Figure L.228. The preselected Print Range needs to be added to this Print Setting before previewing the report layout.

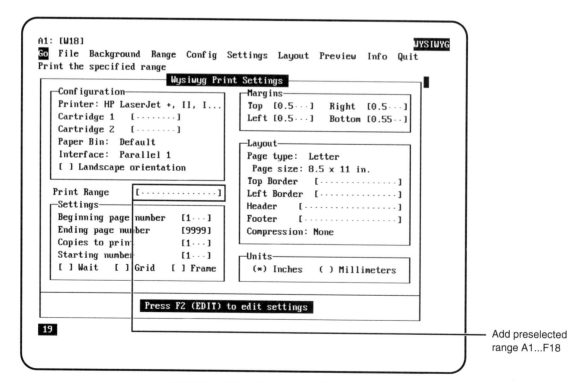

FIGURE L.228. Wysiwyg Print Setting dialog box.

Let's add the preselected range to the WYSIWYG Print Setting.

Select: Range   Desired option

Select: Set   Accept the preselected print range

Select: Preview   Desired option to view layout

The page layout appears as shown in Figure L.229. The purpose of this report preview is to help you determine if the general arrangement of the report meets your requirements. If you detect any errors or omissions, then you can change them before printing the report.

Now let's return to the WYSIWYG Print menu.

| To return to the WYSIWYG Print menu from the Preview

Press: \<Enter\>   Or press any other convenient key

If any corrections are necessary, you need to Quit from this Print menu to make those revisions.

When the Print Range is set and you are ready to actually produce a hard copy of the report, printing is requested with the Go command. Let's print the enhanced worksheet report by continuing from the WYSIWYG Print menu (: Print).

| To print an enhanced report

Select: Go   Desired activity

The hard copy report is produced, and you automatically return to the READY mode. Lotus 1-2-3 adds a dashed line around the print range to indicate that this area is the "page" that was printed (Figure L.230).

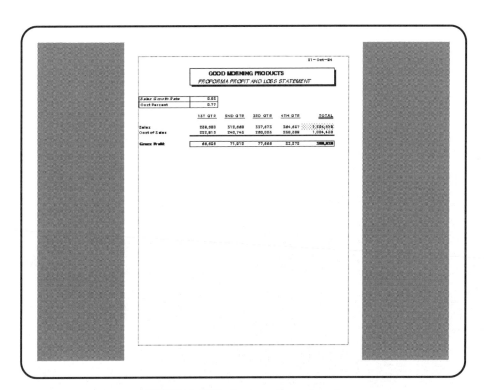

FIGURE L.229. Preview of page layout.

Format code ——

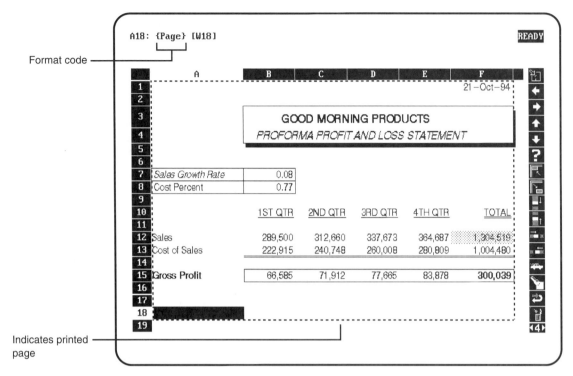

Indicates printed page ——

FIGURE L.230. Page indicated for printing.

When mouse support and SmartIcons are available, the Preview and Print process is simplified. Let's carry out these activities by using the SmartIcons, if they are available.

To preview and print with SmartIcons	**Action:**	Preselect the range **A1..F18** for previewing and printing.
	Click:	Preview SmartIcon	Action for Preview
	Click:	<left mouse button>	Return to READY mode
	Click:	Print SmartIcon	Action to Print report

While the Print SmartIcon can be used either with or without WYSIWYG, the Preview SmartIcon can be used only with WYSIWYG.

L.12.8 Adding a Graph to a Worksheet

With WYSIWYG, a graph is printed as part of a report. A separate PrintGraph program is *not* required or used. Kim wants to include the STACK bar graph in the report for the Board of Directors, as shown previously in Figure L.210. Let's add the STACK bar graph to the Good Morning Products report. First make this the current or active graph for the worksheet by selecting it from the available named graphs stored with the worksheet, because this is the easiest way to work with the graph.

| To choose a named graph in preparation for adding it to the worksheet | **Action:** Select the desired STACK graph with the / Graph Name Use (/GNU) command. Verify that this is the desired graph (Figure L.231) and return to the READY mode. |

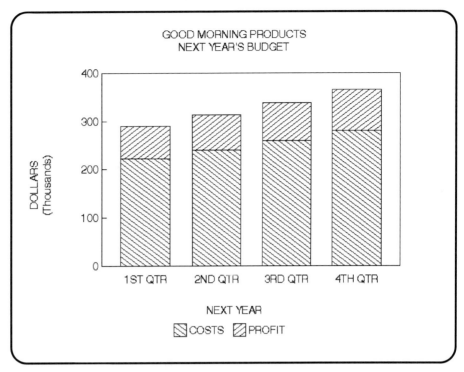

FIGURE L.231. Desired STACK bar graph.

Second the graph is actually added to the worksheet in preparation for printing it (Figure L.210 **11**). The size of the range specified for the graph determines the size of the graph's image as it is both displayed and printed.

Keypoint!	The size of your preselected cell range determines the size of the graph displayed in the worksheet!

Now let's place the graph in the Good Morning Products worksheet.

To add the current graph to the worksheet	**Action:**	Preselect the range **A21..F36** where the graph will be placed.
	Press:	: Use colon to access menu
	Select:	Graph
	Select:	Add Desired activity
	Select:	Current Desired option
	Select:	Quit Complete graph activities

Or with mouse support and SmartIcons, add the graph to the worksheet *after* preselecting the range.

Click: Add Graph SmartIcon   Desired activity SmartIcon

Action: Preview and print the enhanced worksheet with this graph by specifying a print range that includes both the main worksheet area and the graph area. The printed copy should appear similar to that in Figure L.210, but without the special notations added to the basic 1-2-3 graph.

Action: Save the worksheet and format as the PLAN17 file.

L.12.9   Enhancing Graphs

A basic 1-2-3 graph is enhanced with WYSIWYG by editing the graph to add features such as special text, geometric shapes, and arrows (Figure L.210; features **12**, **13**, **14** and **15**. Kim and Chris want these features added to their basic graph for Good Morning Products to enhance its appearance.

L.12.9.1   Adding Text to a Graph

By adding the text "Sales" to their STACK bar graph, Kim and Chris can specifically identify the meaning of the entire height of the bar (Figure L.210, **12**). First let's choose the graph to be revised with editing.

To choose a graph for editing

Action:	Place the worksheet cursor in any cell, such as **A21,** where the graph is located on the worksheet for specifying this as the graph that will be changed.	
Press:	:	Use colon to access menu
Select:	Graph	
Select:	Edit	Desired activity
Press:	<Enter>	Cell pointer is located at desired graph for editing

The worksheet disappears from the screen, with a copy of the graph filling almost the entire screen (Figure L.232) and with the Graph Edit menu, a sticky menu,

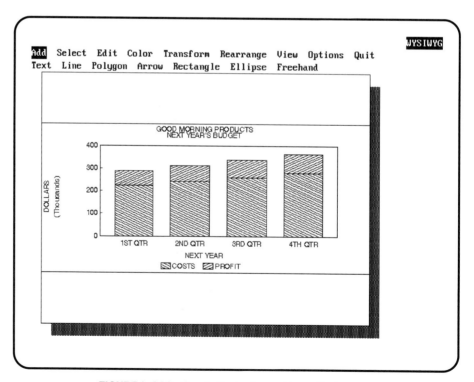

FIGURE L.232. Graph display for making edit changes.

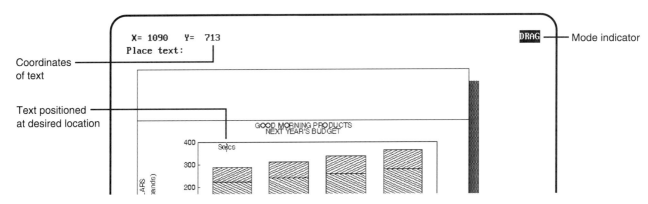

FIGURE L.233. Positioning text in graph.

appearing for your menu selections. This enlarged image makes it easier for you to add enhancements to the graph.

Now the text "Sales" can be placed on the graph. Let's add this enhancement.

To add text to a selected graph	**Select:**	Add	Desired activity
	Select:	Text	Desired option
	Enter:	Sales	Desired text

The text appears on the screen, with a cross-hair indicating the center of the text, and the mode indicator changes to DRAG to identify that the text can be positioned as desired on the graph (Figure L.233). The exact position of the cross-hair is specified by the *X* and *Y* coordinates in the upper-left-hand corner of the display.

Action: Position the text at coordinates $X = 1090$ and $Y = 709$ by using either the cursor movement keys or the mouse, if available.

Press: <Enter> Complete adding text and return to Graph Edit menu

The completed entry is surrounded by a set of eight small squares, indicating that this is a **selected object** on the graph (Figure L.234). A selected object is one that can be moved or revised.

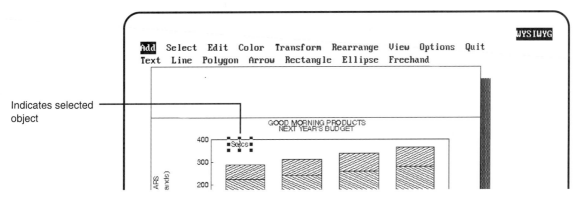

FIGURE L.234. Selected graph object.

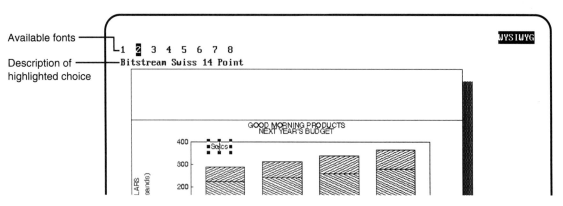

Available fonts

Description of
highlighted choice

FIGURE L.235. Font revised to Swiss 14 point for text object added to graph.

When text is added to a graph, the default Swiss 12-point font is applied to this text. This can be changed, since the object is already selected, by continuing with the Edit Text commands. Let's revise the font applied to "Sales."

To change the font of a selected text object

Select:	Edit	Desired activity
Select:	Font	Desired option
Select:	2	Desired Bitstream font (Figure L.235)

"Sales" appears in Swiss 14 point on the graph.

L.12.9.2 Adding Geometric Objects to a Graph

Because of the importance of "Sales" on the graph, Kim wants to increase the reader's attention to this message, as shown in Figure L.210, **13**. First let's add an ellipse around "Sales" to emphasize this text.

To add an ellipse to a graph

Action:		Verify that the STACK bar graph is still displayed with the : Graph Edit (:GE) menu, as shown previously in Figure L.232.
Select:	Add	Desired activity
Select:	Ellipse	Desired option
Move to:	X=778 Y=514	Upper-left-hand corner
Press:	<Enter>	Anchor beginning point

Or with mouse support

Click:	<left mouse button>	
Move to:	X=1403 Y=958	Stretch box to specify size (Figure L.236)
Press:	<Enter>	Specify ending point

Or with mouse support

Click:	<left mouse button>	

The width of the line forming the ellipse can be increased to make this feature stand out even more. Let's increase the line's width.

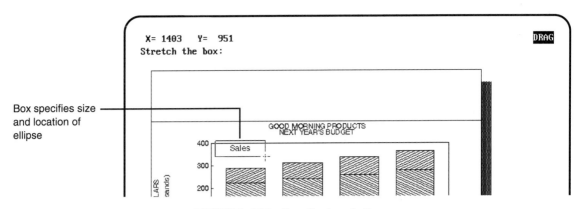

FIGURE L.236. Specify size of ellipse.

To change the width of a line for an object	**Action:**	Verify that the ellipse just added to the graph is a selected object and that the : Graph Edit (:GE) menu is the current menu.
	Select:	Edit	Desired activity
	Select:	Width	Desired option
	Select:	Narrow	Next width size

The width of the line forming the ellipse increases and now appears as shown in Figure L.210, **13**.

The next object Chris wants to add to the Good Morning Products graph is a box surrounding the legend to set this off from the rest of the graph (Figure L.210, **14**). Let's add a rectangle as the desired box.

To add a rectangle to a graph	**Action:**	Verify that the STACK bar graph is still displayed with the : Graph Edit (:GE) menu, as shown previously in Figure L.232.
	Select:	Add	Desired activity
	Select:	Rectangle	Desired option
	Move to:	X=1299 Y=3795	Upper-left hand corner
	Press:	<Enter>	Anchor beginning point
	Or, Click:	<left mouse button>	
	Move to:	X=2653 Y=4078	Stretch box to specify size (Figure L.237)
	Press:	<Enter>	Specify ending point
	Or, Click:	<left mouse button>	
	Action:	Change the width of the line forming the rectangle to narrow.

Now let's complete the enhancements to the Good Morning Products graph by adding an arrow that points to the top of the stack bar for the first quarter (Figure L.210, **15**).

To add an arrow to a graph	**Action:**	Verify that the STACK bar graph is still displayed with the : Graph Edit (:GE) menu, as shown previously in Figure L.232.
	Select:	Add	Desired activity
	Select:	Arrow	Desired option
	Move to:	X=1050 Y=993	Upper-left-hand corner
	Press:	<Enter>	Anchor beginning point
	Or, Click:	<left mouse button>	

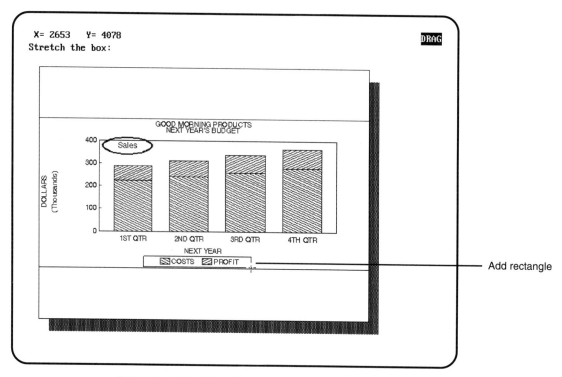

Add rectangle

FIGURE L.237. Using the mouse pointer to change column width.

Move to:	X=1250 Y=1206	Stretch line to specify size
Press:	<Enter>	Specify ending point
Or Click:	<left mouse button>	
Action:	Change the width of the line forming the arrow to narrow.	
Action:	Print the enhanced worksheet with its graph to produce the final report for Good Morning Products.	
Action:	Save the worksheet and format as the PLAN17 files.	

Kim and Chris have their complete report (Figure L.210) for submission to Good Morning Products' Board of Directors. The WYSIWYG Add-In let them enhance this report with a number of spreadsheet publishing features. Lotus 1-2-3 proved itself as a powerful software tool that enabled them to create a professional-quality business document.

L.12.10 When Things Go Wrong

Several situations may arise when you are enhancing your worksheet and graph using the WYSIWYG Add-In. Some of the more common difficulties and how to approach them are described as follows:

1. You applied several WYSIWYG attributes to a cell range and want to remove them.
   a. Preselect the cell range where you want to remove all the attributes.
   b. Use the : Format Reset (:FR) command to remove all the attributes at one time.

2. You added a graph to your worksheet, but you placed it at the wrong location.
   a. Position your cell pointer on the graph or preselect the graph you want to relocate.
   b. Use the : Graph Move (:GM) command to move your graph to the desired location.

3. You added an object to a graph, such as a text or a geometric shape, that you want to remove.
   a. Position the cell pointer on the graph and use : Graph Edit (:GE) to select the graph to be changed.
   b. From the : Graph Edit (:GE) menu, use Select One to choose the desired object.
   c. Use Rearrange Delete to actually remove the object from your graph.

L.12.11 Lesson Summary

- WYSIWYG is a spreadsheet publishing Add-In for 1-2-3 that is used to improve the appearance of a worksheet by adding features such as boldface, italics, underlines, outlines, shading, and graphic objects.

- WYSIWYG does not change the contents of any cells but merely displays the contents by using spreadsheet publishing enhanced attributes.

- WYSIWYG uses additional computer memory. The Undo feature may need to be disabled in order to have sufficient memory to use WYSIWYG.

- A separate menu is used with the WYSIWYG commands. This menu is accessed by pressing the <colon> (:).

- When available, SmartIcons simplify the use of many of the WYSIWYG commands.

- A preselected range provides a convenient way to add several WYSIWYG attributes to the same cell range.

- The WYSIWYG format specifications are saved in a separate file with the FMT extension. This allows you to access the worksheet file without using WYSIWYG.

- An enhanced printed report is obtained by using the WYSIWYG print (: Print) command. Use of the / Print command causes a report to be output *without* the WYSIWYG attributes.

- A graph is printed with WYSIWYG by adding the graph to the worksheet. Several graphs may be added to one worksheet. Once added, the graph is printed with the rest of worksheet. A separate program is not required for printing graphs.

- Text and geometric objects may be added to a graph for emphasis. They are then printed with the graph.

L.12.12 Practice Tutorial

(1) Develop the PLAN17 enhanced worksheet and graph described in this Lesson as a guided activity in a hands-on manner. Use your PLAN8 or MYPLAN6 worksheet from the Practice Tutorial in Lesson L.5 as a starting point for this exercise. If you have not completed that exercise, then develop that worksheet before you begin this exercise.

> *Task 1:* Access your PLAN8 or MYPLAN6 worksheet file and review it.
>
> *Task 2:* Attach WYSIWYG and SmartIcons, if available.
>
> *Task 3:* Carry out the activities described in this Lesson to produce the enhanced PLAN17 worksheet and graph.
>
> *Task 4:* Print the enhanced report as illustrated in Figure L.210.
>
> *Task 5:* Save this as worksheet file MYPLAN17.

Time Estimates

Novice: 60 minutes

Intermediate: 45 minutes

Advanced: 30 minutes

L.12.13 Practice Exercises

(1)   Case: Inland Container (continued)

Mary Montoya is finalizing her monthly proposal for Rydder Truck Rental. She is scheduled to review the proposal with Inland's district marketing manager tomorrow. Mary wants to enhance the appearance of her report by using spreadsheet publishing as follows:

> *Task 1:* Access your RYDDER2 worksheet from Practice Exercise 1 in Lesson L.5 as your starting point for this exercise.
>
> *Task 2:* Add these spreadsheet publishing features to the report:
>
>   (1) Remove the underlining with the minus (−) in preparation for using an enhanced form of underlining.
>
>   (2) Boldface the report title and "Gross Profit."
>
>   (3) Italicize "Units Sold" and "Price per Unit."
>
>   (4) Change the typeface to Swiss 14 point for the title line.
>
>   (5) Use a single underline with the column titles for the three months and the **Total** for the quarter.
>
>   (6) Place a single line across the row between **Cost of Sales** and **Gross Profit** that is located at the top of the cells in this range.
>
>   (7) Add light shading to the **Sales** amounts for each of the months and the quarter total.
>
>   (8) Place an outline around the **Gross Profit** amounts for each of the three months and the total.
>
>   (9) Surround the title line with a drop shadow. Remove any blanks from the beginning of this labels and use the : Text Align Center (:TAC) command to center the label *across* columns.
>
>   (10) Add the RTR_BAR graph to the worksheet for printing. Place this in a convenient range below the data.

(11) Add the text "GOOD GROWTH" in Swiss 14 point to the graph with an arrow that points to the bar for **Sales** in the third month. Set the width of the arrow to narrow.

Task 3: Preview the report with the graph on your screen. Make any necessary modifications. Then print this report containing both the data and the graph.

Task 4: Save your RYDDER2 worksheet and format files.

Task 5: Write a short paragraph describing several other spreadsheet publishing enhancements that you might use with Mary's report and indicate why you would want to make these improvements.

Time Estimates

Novice: 30 minutes

Intermediate: 20 minutes

Advanced: 10 minutes

(2)   Case: Safety-Kleen Corporation (continued)

In finalizing information for inclusion in Safety-Kleen's Annual Report, Allan Brinckman, the Chief Financial Officer, wants to improve the appearance of this information for the stockholders. Allan wants you to perform the following spreadsheet publishing tasks:

Task 1: If you have *not* completed Practice Exercise 2 in Lesson L.5, then complete that exercise before enhancing the report for Safety-Kleen using 1-2-3's spreadsheet publishing features.

Task 2: Access the KLEEN.WK1 worksheet file from your Data Disk and review the data and graphs contained in this worksheet.

(1) Remove the underlining with the minus (−) in preparation for using an enhanced form of underlining.

(2) Boldface "SAFETY-KLEEN," "Income Statement Data," and "Balance Sheet Data."

(3) Italicize "Selected Financial Data" and "(Expressed in millions, except per share amounts)."

(4) Change the typeface to Swiss 14-point for the two title lines.

(5) Use a single underline with the column titles for the five years.

(6) Add light shading to the **Earnings per share** amounts for each of the five years.

(7) Place an outline around the **Total assets** amounts for each of the five years.

(8) Surround the two title lines with a drop shadow in columns **A** through **C.** Remove the blanks from the beginning of each of these labels and use the : Text Align Center (:TAC) command to center these labels across the columns **A** through **C.**

(9) Place a double line across row **3,** located at the bottom of the cells in this range.

(10) Add the REVENUES graph in the range **A24..B34.**

(11) Add the EARNINGS graph in the range **C24..F24.**

(12) Add the text "OUTSTANDING GROWTH" in Swiss 14-point to the EARNINGS graph with an arrow that points to the bar for the fifth year. Set the width of the arrow to narrow.

Task 3: Preview the report with the two graphs on your screen. Make any necessary corrections. Then print this report containing both the Selected Financial Data and the two graphs.

Task 4: Save your KLEEN worksheet and format files.

Task 5: Write a short paragraph describing, at least, three other spreadsheet publishing enhancements that you might use with Allan's graph and indicate why you would want to use them.

Time Estimates

Novice: 45 minutes

Intermediate: 30 minutes

Advanced: 20 minutes

(3)   Case: State Mutual Insurance (continued)

Akio Kosai, the systems manager for the Policy Management System (PMS), is preparing to present the results of PMS's work sampling study to State Mutual's Director of Human Resources. He wants to prepare a professional-quality report for this presentation. Akio wants you to complete these tasks to enhance his report:

Task 1: If you have *not* completed Practice Exercise 3 in Lesson L.5, then complete that exercise before applying spreadsheet publishing to enhance the report for State Mutual Insurance.

Task 2: Access the SMI.WK1 worksheet file from your Data Disk and review the data and graphs that are included in this worksheet.

   (1) Remove the underlining with the minus (−) in preparation for using an enhanced form of underlining. Hide the data in cells **B22..G22** that are used with the pie chart.

   (2) Boldface "STATE MUTUAL INSURANCE," "Work Sampling Activities," and "Average."

   (3) Italicize "SYSTEMS ANALYSTS' TYPICAL WORK DAY" and "Average."

   (4) Change the typeface to Swiss 14 point for the two title lines.

   (5) Use a single underline with the column titles for each of the work sampling activities.

   (6) Add light shading to the amounts in the **Program/Coding** column of the activities for each of the systems analysts.

   (7) Place an outline around the **Average** amounts for each of the work sampling activities.

   (8) Surround the two title lines with a drop shadow in columns **A** through **F.** Remove the blanks from the beginning of each of these labels. Then use the : Text Align Center (:TAC) command to center these labels across the columns **A** through **F.**

   (9) Place a double line across row **5,** located at the top of the cells in this range.

   (10) Add the ANALYSTS graph in the range **A24..G38.**

   (11) Add a rectangle around the legend of that graph with a line width of narrow.

   (12) Add the text "MOST PROGRAMMING" in Swiss 14 point to this graph. Add an arrow that points to the bar for Program/Coding for Lisa. Set the width of this arrow to narrow.

Task 3: Preview the report with the bar graph on your screen. Make any corrections needed. Then print this report containing both the Work Sampling Activities Data and the graph.

Task 4: Save your SMI worksheet and format files.

Task 5: Write a short paragraph describing, at least, three other spreadsheet publishing enhancements that you might use with Akio's graph and indicate why you would want these features.

Time Estimates

Novice: 45 minutes

Intermediate: 30 minutes

Advanced: 20 minutes

(4)   Case: Dow Chemical Company (continued)

Sam Wyman is preparing for his meeting with Dow's Management Committee to review current performance and long-term strategies for growth. Sam wants a professional appearance for his report for this meeting. He would like you to carry out these tasks in enhancing his report:

Task 1: If you have *not* completed Practice Exercise 4 in Lesson L.5, then complete that exercise before enhancing the report for Dow Chemical Company using the spreadsheet publishing features of 1-2-3.

Task 2: Retrieve the DOWCHEM.WK1 worksheet file from your Data Disk and examine the data and graphs that are included in this worksheet.

(1) Remove the underlining with the minus ($-$) and equal ($=$) in preparation for using an enhanced form of underlining.

(2) Boldface "THE DOW CHEMICAL COMPANY," "Sales," "Operating Income," and "Percent Sales."

(3) Italicize "STRATEGIC SECTORS" and "In billions."

(4) Change the typeface to Swiss 14 point for the two title lines.

(5) Use a double line across the top of the cells in columns **A..F** of rows **5, 13, 21,** and **29.**

(6) Place a single line across the top of the cells in columns **A..F** of rows **11, 19,** and **27.**

(7) Use a single underline in the cells with the column titles for the five years in rows **6, 14,** and **22.**

(8) Add light shading to the amounts for **Total Sales** for each of the five years.

(9) Place an outline around the **Total Operating Income** amounts for the five years.

(10) Surround the two title lines with a drop shadow in columns **A** through **E.** Remove the blanks from the beginning of each of these labels and use the : Text Align Center (:TAC) command to center these labels across the columns **A** through **E.**

(11) Add the SALES_B graph in the range **A30..F46.**

(12) Add a rectangle around the legend of the graph with a line width of narrow.

(13) Add the text "TOTAL SALES" in Swiss 14 point to the graph. Next add an arrow that points to the top of the bar for the last year. Use a narrow width for this arrow.

Task 3: Preview the report and its bar graph on your screen. Make any necessary changes. Then print this report containing both the Strategic Sector data and the graph.

Task 4: Save your DOWCHEM worksheet and format files.

Task 5: Write a short paragraph that describes, at least, three other spreadsheet publishing features that you might use with Sam's report and indicate why you would want these enhancements.

Time Estimates

Novice: 45 minutes

Intermediate: 30 minutes

Advanced: 20 minutes

(5)   Case: Napa Valley Wooden Box (continued)

John Rensneaker is preparing for his presentation to the owners at their regular monthly meeting on Monday. John wants to improve the professional appearance of his report for this meeting. He wants you to enhance his basic worksheet and graph by performing the following tasks:

Task 1: If you have *not* completed Practice Exercise 5 in Lesson L.5, then complete that exercise before enhancing the report for Napa Valley Wooden Box by using spreadsheet publishing features.

Task 2: Retrieve the NAPA.WK1 worksheet file from your Data Disk and examine the data and graphs that are included in this worksheet.

   (1) Remove the underlining with the minus (−) and equal (=) in preparation for using an enhanced form of underlining. Hide the data in cells **A31..E40** that are used with the graphs.

   (2) Boldface "Napa Valley Wooden Box," "Net sales," and "Return on sales."

   (3) Italicize "Pro Forma Income Statement" and "Earnings before tax."

   (4) Change the typeface to Swiss 14 point for the two title lines.

   (5) Use a single underline in the cells with the column titles for the three years in row **4.**

   (6) Place a single line across the top of the cells in columns **B..D** of rows **15, 17,** and **24.**

   (7) Use a double line across the top of the cells in columns **B..D** of rows **19** and **26.**

   (8) Add light shading to the amounts for **Return on sales** for each of the three years.

   (9) Place an outline around the **Earnings before tax** amounts for the three years.

   (10) Surround the two title lines with a drop shadow in columns **A** through **D.** Remove the blanks from the beginning of each of these labels. Now use the : Text Align Center (:TAC) command for centering these labels across the columns **A** through **D.**

   (11) Add the CST_EXP graph in the range **A32..D50.** Yes, the graph may be placed on top of the cells containing the hidden data values.

   (12) Add a rectangle around the legend of the graph with a line width of narrow.

(13) Add the text "TOTAL COSTS" in Swiss 14 point to the graph. Add an arrow that points to the top of the bar for the last year. Set the width of this arrow to narrow.

Task 3: Preview the report with its stack bar graph on your screen. Make any necessary changes. Then print this report containing both the Pro Forma Income Statement data and the graph.

Task 4: Save your NAPA worksheet and format files.

Task 5: Write a short paragraph that describes, at least, three other spreadsheet publishing features that you might use with John's report and indicate why you would want these enhancements.

Time Estimates

Novice: 45 minutes

Intermediate: 30 minutes

Advanced: 20 minutes

L.12.14 Comprehensive Problems

(1) Case: Woodcraft Furniture Company (continued)

Joe Birch of Woodcraft Furniture is preparing for Woodcraft's quarterly management meeting. He wants to improve the appearance of his worksheet by using 1-2-3's spreadsheet publishing features by performing these tasks:

Task 1: If you have *not* completed Comprehensive Problem 1 in Lesson L.5, then complete that problem before using spreadsheet publishing with Woodcraft Furniture Company's report.

Task 2: Access the WOOD2 worksheet file from your Data Disk and review the data and graphs that you included in this worksheet.

(1) Remove the underlining with the equal (=). Then replace the underlining with the minus (−) with a single line at the top of those cells, except for the column titles, where the underline is just removed.

(2) Boldface the company name and account names for **Total Sales, Gross Profit, Income Before Taxes,** and **Return on Sales.**

(3) Italicize "Pro Forma Income Statement" and each of the subheadings for assumptions, production, revenues, cost of sales, and operating expenses that you have included in your report.

(4) Change the typeface to Swiss 14 point for the report title lines.

(5) Use a single underline in the cells with the column titles for the three months of the quarter and the **Total.**

(6) Add light shading to the amounts for **Income Before Taxes** for each of the three months and the total for the quarter.

(7) Place an outline around the amounts for **Return on Sales** for the three months and their total.

(8) Surround the report title lines with a drop shadow. Remove the blanks from the beginning of each of these labels, and using the : Text Align Center (:TAC) command, center these labels.

(9) Add the stack-bar graph of Sale by product for the three months to a worksheet range for printing.

(10) Add a rectangle around the legend of this stack-bar graph with a line width of narrow.

(11) Add the text "Total Sales" in Swiss 14 point to this stack-bar graph. Add an arrow that points to the top of the bar for the last month. Set the width of this arrow to narrow.

(12) Add the pie chart of Sales by product for the quarter total to a worksheet range for printing.

Task 3: Preview the report with the stack-bar graph and pie chart on your screen. Make any necessary revisions. Then print this report containing both the Pro Forma Income Statement data and the graphs.

Task 4: Save your WOOD2 worksheet and format files.

Task 5: Write a short paragraph that describes, at least, four other spreadsheet publishing features that you might use with Joe's report and indicate why you would want to use them.

Time Estimates

Novice: 50 minutes

Intermediate: 30 minutes

Advanced: 20 minutes

(2)   Case: Midwest Universal Gas (continued)

At Midwest Universal Gas, Mary Derrick and Sam Wright have reviewed the various management reports that you have produced. In preparation for their annual review, they want you to improve the appearance of their report by adding these spreadsheet publishing features:

Task 1: If you have *not* completed Comprehensive Problem 2 in Lesson L.5, then complete that problem before enhancing the report for Midwest Universal Gas.

Task 2: Access the MUG2 worksheet file from your Data Disk and review the data and graphs that you included in this worksheet.

(1) Remove the underlining with the equal (=). Then replace the underlining with the minus (−) with a single line at the top of those cells, except for the column titles, where the underline is merely removed.

(2) Boldface the company name and account names for **Total Sales, Total Expense, Operating Income, Income Before Taxes,** and **Return on Investment.**

(3) Italicize "Pro Forma Income Statement" and each of the subheadings for assumptions, production, revenues, and expenses that you have included in your report.

(4) Change the typeface to Swiss 14 point for the report title lines.

(5) Use a single underline in the cells with the column titles for the four quarters and the **Total.**

(6) Add light shading to the amounts for **Net Income** for each of the four quarters and the **Total.**

(7) Place an outline around the amounts for **Return on Investment** for the four quarters and their total.

(8) Surround the report title lines with a drop shadow. Remove the blanks from the beginning of each of these labels and use the : Text Align Center (:TAC) command to center these labels.

(9) Add the stack-bar graph of Sales by type of Gas Sold for the four quarters to a worksheet range for printing.

(10) Add a rectangle around the legend of this stack-bar graph with a line width of narrow.

(11) Add the text "Total Gas Sold" in Swiss 14 point to this stack-bar graph. Add an arrow that points to the top of the bar for the last quarter. Set the width of this arrow to narrow.

(12) Add the pie chart of expenses and net income for the year to a worksheet range for printing.

Task 3: Preview the report with the stack-bar graph and piechart on your screen. Make any necessary changes. Then print this report containing both the Pro Forma Income Statement data and the graphs.

Task 4: Save your MUG2 worksheet and format files.

Task 5: Write a short paragraph that describes at least four other spreadsheet publishing enhancements that you might use with Mary's report, indicating why you would want to use them.

Time Estimates

Novice: 50 minutes

Intermediate: 30 minutes

Advanced: 20 minutes

L.12.15 Case Application

Case: Oil Patch Machine Tool (continued)

Business Problem: Breakeven analysis
MIS Characteristics: Production
Strategic Planning
Special Characteristic: International
Management Functions: Planning
Organizing
Tools Skills: Spreadsheet Publishing

At Oil Patch Machine Tool (OPM), Robert "Rob" Billesbach, Senior Vice President of Manufacturing, is preparing for another meeting with Jack, Jr., OPM's chief executive officer. Rob wants to make a professional presentation for this important plant location decision for the JB-7 valve. He knows that the appearance of the report will assist him in selling his idea to Jack. He wants to improve the look of this report by using 1-2-3's spreadsheet publishing features.

Tasks

1. If you have *not* completed the Case Application in Lesson L.5, then complete that case before enhancing the report for Oil Patch Machine Tool's breakeven analysis.

2. Access and review the BREAK.WK1 worksheet file. Examine the breakeven graph.

3. Enhance the basic report by using each of these spreadsheet publishing features as you determine appropriate: boldface, italics, Swiss 14-point font,

single underline, single line across cell range, double line across cell range, light shading, outline around range, and drop shadow around range.

4. Add the breakeven graph to the worksheet for printing with the data. Include these features on this graph: rectangle around the legend, circle around each breakeven point, the text "Breakeven," and an arrow from the text "Breakeven" pointing to each of the breakeven points on the graph. [*Hint:* Use the Ellipse option to create the circles.]

5. Preview and print the report including the graph. [*Hint:* If your printer has the capability, use a Landscape Orientation with Automatic Compression to print your report and graph on the same page.]

6. Review your output. Write a short summary describing any other enhancements that you could make to further improve the appearance of your report and indicate why you would use them.

Time Estimates

Novice: 50 minutes

Intermediate: 30 minutes

Advanced: 20 minutes

REFERENCE

CONTENT

- Starting Lotus 1-2-3
- 1-2-3 Command Summary
- WYSIWYG Command Summary

L.13.1 Starting Lotus 1-2-3

Lotus 1-2-3 may be started in a number of different ways depending on your particular hardware configuration. When 1-2-3 is installed on a local area network (LAN), a different start-up procedure may be used. This section describes two of the more common methods of starting 1-2-3.

L.13.1.1 Two Floppy Drives

To get ready, obtain the Lotus 1-2-3 SYSTEM Disk with DOS installed on it. Be sure that the Lotus 1-2-3 SYSTEM Disk has been set up for your hardware configuration. If it has not, you will need to perform the Install procedure. It is best to get some help with this step from your resident 1-2-3 expert, or you should see the Lotus 1-2-3 *Getting Started* manual. With your disk in hand, you are now ready to proceed:

1. Place the 1-2-3 SYSTEM Disk in drive A:.
2. Place your Data Disk in drive B:.
   A Perform a COLD BOOT by turning on the power switch to your personal computer.
      Enter the date and time, if requested.

      or

   B Perform a WARM BOOT by pressing <Ctrl>+<Alt>+<Del> all together.
      Enter the date and time, if requested.

      or

    C At the DOS prompt (usually, **A>**),

Enter: LOTUS

or

Enter: 123   for the Student Version

3. The Lotus Access System Menu appears on your screen.

Select: 1-2-3   by pressing <Enter> or < 1 >

You are ready to make your desired menu selections and worksheet entries.

If you are using a Student Version of Lotus 1-2-3, then in step **2A** above entering **123** causes the immediate access of the worksheet component, and you are ready to make your desired menu selections or worksheet entries. Booting your computer with the Student Version results in this same access of the worksheet component of Lotus 1-2-3.

L.13.1.2   Hard Disk Drive

Before you are ready to start up Lotus 1-2-3, you need to answer these questions:

1. Has Lotus 1-2-3 been installed on the hard disk? _____
2. Does the version of Lotus 1-2-3 installed on the hard disk require the use of the SYSTEM Disk as a "key" disk to get Lotus started? _____

If the answer to question 1 is *no,* see your Lotus 1-2-3 expert.

If the answer to question 2 is *yes,* obtain the copy of the Lotus 1-2-3 SYSTEM Disk.

If the computer is not turned on, turn it on and enter the date and time, if requested.

Make sure that you are at the DOS prompt (that is, **C>**). Drive C: is usually the default disk drive for a computer equipped with a hard disk. You should verify this, since yours may be identified by a different letter.

1 Place the Lotus 1-2-3 SYSTEM Disk in drive A:, if the answer to question 2 was yes; otherwise, you may skip placing the SYSTEM Disk in drive A:.

Enter: LOTUS

2 The Lotus Access System Menu appears on your screen.

Select: 1-2-3   by pressing <Enter> or < 1 >

3 Remove the SYSTEM Disk from drive A:, if one was used.

Place your Data Disk in drive A:.

You are ready to make your desired menu selections and worksheet entries.

L.13.2   1-2-3 Command Summary

Many of the more frequently used Lotus 1-2-3 menu commands are summarized in the following table. The purpose is to provide a quick reference review of these menu selections. The menu commands are arranged in the sequence in which they are encountered within the Lotus 1-2-3 menus. These menu selections are for Release 2.4 of Lotus 1-2-3. Earlier releases have similar menu choices and, when the menu choice is available, perform the same action. Release 3.x does not make use of a separate PrintGraph program, but includes this activity within the Print menu selections. The detailed action of each menu command may be obtained with the <F1> help key or reviewed in the *Lotus 1-2-3 Reference Manuals.* The first character in each menu choice indicates the key used for selection.

L.13.2.1 1-2-3 Worksheet Commands

Menu Selections	Action
/Worksheet	
Global	
Format	Selects the appearance of a data value in a cell from among the available choices. The Global Format is applied to all cells that are *not* formatted with a Range Format.
Fixed	
Sci(entific)	
Currency	
,	
General	
+/−	
Percent	
Date	
Text	
Hidden	
Label-Prefix	Sets the label alignment for all future label entries.
Left	
Right	
Center	
Column-Width	Sets the column width of all columns *not* specified by a separate column width for a range of columns.
Recalculation	Specifies the recalculation order, whether or not recalculation takes place automatically or when <F9> (CALC) is pressed, and the number of times the recalculation is to be performed. Natural invokes nonprocedural calculation in Lotus 1-2-3.
Natural	
Columnwise	
Rowwise	
Automatic	
Manual	
Iteration	
Protection	Turns protection on or off for cells *not* protected as a separate range.
Enable	
Disable	
Default	Changes default settings, such as the default directory and printer. Changes can be saved with Update for future access.
Printer	
Directory	
Status	
Update	
Other	
International	
Punctuation	
Currency	
Date	
Time	
Negative	
Help	
Clock	
Undo	
Beep	
Add-In	
Expanded-Memory	
Autoexec	
Zero	Specifies how a numeric value of zero is displayed. Label permits the use of a characters string such as N/A for not available.
No	
Yes	
Label	
Insert	Inserts one or more blank rows or columns in the worksheet.
Column	
Row	

Menu Selections	Action
/Worksheet	
Delete	Deletes one or more rows or columns from the worksheet.
Column	
Row	
Column	Sets the width of a single column or range of columns; resets one or more columns to the global width. An individual column may be hidden or displayed.
Set-width	
Reset-width	
Hide	
Display	
Column-Range	
Set-width	
Reset-width	
Erase	Deletes the entire worksheet.
Titles	Freezes rows and/or columns along the top and at the left edges of the worksheet so that they can be viewed when the worksheet area is scrolled.
Both	
Horizontal	
Vertical	
Clear	
Window	Splits the window into two areas and turns on or off synchronized scrolling.
Horizontal	
Vertical	
Sync	
Unsync	
Clear	Returns to a single window area.
Status	Displays information about the current global setting of a worksheet such as available memory, recalculation method, and circular references.
Page	Inserts a row in the worksheet that triggers a page break or skips to the top of a new page when the worksheet is printed.
Learn	Records keystrokes as macro instructions in a range of cells as they are entered and executed.
Range	
Cancel	
Erase	
Yes	
No	
/Range	
Format	Specifies the format for a range that overrides the global format. When hidden, the data do not appear in the cells, but appear in the control panel.
Fixed	
Sci(entific)	
Currency	
,	
General	
+/−	
Percent	
Date	
Text	
Hidden	
Reset	Turns off the range format and returns format to global setting.
Label	Changes the alignment of labels in the indicated range.
Left	
Right	
Center	
Erase	Deletes the data in the specified range of cells. Does *not* change a range format or protection status.

Menu Selections	Action
/Range	
Name	Identifies a range with a name up to 15 characters
Create	in length that can be used instead of cell names.
Delete	
Labels	Assigns labels as range names using the specified
Right	location of label names to the cells to be
Down	named.
Left	
Up	
Reset	Deletes all range names in worksheet.
Table	Creates a cross-reference table of range names and
	cell names.
Justify	Rearranges a column of labels as a paragraph,
	making them equal lengths.
Prot(ect)	Specifies a range of cells to be protected when
	global protection is activated.
Unprot(ect)	Specifies a range of cells that are *not* protected
	when global protection is activated.
Input	Creates an input data form that limits movement
	of the cursor to unprotected cells.
Value	Copies the value of a formula from one range to
	another range. The cell contents are converted
	from formulas to specific values in the copy
	process.
Trans(pose)	Copies data from one range to another with the
	rows transposed to columns in the copy process.
Search	Locates character strings in labels or formulas in
Formulas	the specified range.
Labels	
Both	
Find	
Replace	
/Copy	Duplicates cell contents from one cell range to
	another cell range. Formulas may have their row
	number and/or column letter revised in the
	copy depending on whether the cell formulas
	use absolute or relative referencing.
/Move	Transfers the cell contents from one cell range to
	another cell range.
/File	
Retrieve	Loads the specified worksheet file into memory,
	replacing any current worksheet file.
Save	Saves the current worksheet file to disk. An
Cancel	existing file may be replaced or a backup copy
Replace	may be created.
Backup	
Combine	Integrates data from another *worksheet* file on disk
	into the current worksheet file.
Copy	Duplicates data from a specified worksheet file in
Entire-File	the current worksheet.
Named/Specified-Range	
Add	Adds numeric values from a specified file to
Entire-File	numbers in the current worksheet.
Named/Specified-Range	
Subtract	Subtracts numeric values in a specified file from
Entire-File	numbers in the current worksheet.
Named/Specified-Range	

Menu Selections	Action
/File	
Xtract	Saves a specified cell range as a worksheet file on
Formulas	disk as either cell formulas or cell values.
Cancel	
Replace	
Backup	
Values	
Cancel	
Replace	
Backup	
Erase	Deletes the specified file from disk.
Worksheet	
Print	
Graph	
Other	
List	Displays a list of files of the specified type.
Worksheet	
Print	
Graph	
Other	
Linked	
Import	Loads data from an ASCII text file on disk into
	the current worksheet.
Text	Loads each line as a long label in a single column.
Numbers	Loads each number or character string enclosed in
	quotes in a line in the import file into a separate
	column. Adjacent columns are filled from left
	to right for each line of the import file.
Directory	Changes the default directory for the current
	session in the Lotus 1-2-3 worksheet.
Admin(istration)	Produces a table of information about files,
Reservation	updates links to worksheet files, and controls
Get	access to a worksheet file's reservation, which is
Release	shared.
Table	
Worksheet	
Print	
Graph	
Other	
Linked	
Link-Refresh	
/Print	
Printer	Sends designated output report to printer.
(same choices as / Print File)	
File	Causes designated output report to be sent to a
	file for later use or printing.
Range	Specifies range to be printed.
Line	Causes paper to advance one line.
Page	Causes paper to be ejected to top of a new page.
Options	
Header	Specifies header line for each page.
Footer	Specifies footer line for each page.
Margins	Specifies page margins.
Left	
Right	
Top	
Bottom	
None	

Menu Selections	Action
/Print	
File	
Options	
Borders	Establishes borders at top and on left of each
Columns	page. Used to repeat heading when a report is
Rows	several pages long.
Setup	Establishes setup character string for printer.
Pg-Length	Specifies page length in number of lines.
Other	Specifies display of cell contents.
As-Displayed	
Cell-Formulas	
Formatted	
Unformatted	
Clear	Returns current print settings to their default
All	settings.
Range	
Borders	
Format	
Align	Establishes top of page for printer.
Go	Causes printing to be performed.
/Graph	Specifies the kind of graph to be created.
Type	
Line	
Bar	
XY	
Stack-Bar	
Pie	
HLCO	
Mixed	
Features	Changes the horizontal or vertical orientation of
Vertical	the Y axis; adds or removes special features.
Horizontal	
Stacked	
Frame	
3D-Effect	
X	Specifies the range of data for the X axis of the
	graph or the labels for slices of pie chart.
A .. F	Specifies up to six ranges of data to be graphed.
	Data are graphed on the Y axis. Only data in
	the A-range are used with a pie chart.
Reset	Changes all or selected graph settings, returning
Graph	them to their default settings.
X	
A .. F	
Ranges	
Options	
View	Causes the current graph to be displayed.
Save	Saves the graph as an image for printing.
Cancel	
Replace	
Options	
Legend	Specifies the legend for each range.
A .. F	
Range	

Menu Selections	Action
/Graph	
Options	
Format	Specifies the use of lines and/or symbols in plotting graph.
Graph	
A .. F	
Lines	
Symbols	
Both	
Neither	
Titles	Specifies titles for graph and/or each axis.
First	
Second	
X-Axis	
Y-Axis	
Grid	Causes a grid to be added to or removed from a graph.
Horizontal	
Vertical	
Both	
Clear	
Scale	Specifies the scaling method and format for each axis.
Y-Scale	
(same as X-Scale)	
X-Scale	
Automatic	
Manual	
Lower	
Upper	
Format	
Fixed	
Sci(entific)	
Currency	
,	
General	
+/−	
Percent	
Date	
Text	
Hidden	
Indicator	
Yes	
No	
Color	Causes graph to be displayed in color on a color monitor.
B&W	Causes graph to be displayed in black and white, regardless of use of a color monitor.
Data-Labels	Specifies range containing labels to be displayed at the points or bars on a graph.
A .. F	
Group	
Name	Identifies a name for the graph and preserves the graph setting under the specified name. Produces a table listing of available named graphs.
Use	
Create	
Delete	
Reset	
Table	
Group	Specifies multiple graph data ranges in adjacent rows or columns.
Columnwise	
Rowwise	

Menu Selections	Action
/Data	
Fill	Enters a sequence of data values in a specified range. Identifies range for values, and specifies start, step (or increment), and stop values.
Table	Performs "what-if" or "sensitivity" analyses by
1	computing a series of solutions with one or two
2	data values revised for each solution. Results are
Reset	stored as a table in a specified range.
Sort	Arranges rows or records in a range in the
Data-Range	sequence specified by the key columns or fields.
Primary-Key	
Secondary-Key	
Reset	
Go	Causes specified sort to be performed.
Query	Locates and edits selected rows or records in a database range.
Input	Specifies range containing database rows or records.
Criteria	Specifies range containing matching data values for query.
Output	Specifies range where data are copied when performing an extract or unique query.
Find	Locates records or rows in the input area that match the values in the criteria area.
Extract	Causes columns or fields to be copied to the output area that match the specified criteria.
Unique	Causes columns or fields to be copied to the output area that match the specified criteria and eliminates any duplicates.
Delete	Removes records in the input area that match the
Cancel	specified criterion.
Delete	
Reset	Clears the input, criteria, and output range specification.
Distribution	Computes a frequency distribution of data values in a specified range.
Matrix	
Invert	Performs a matrix inversion.
Multiply	Multiplies the columns of a matrix in one data range with the row of a matrix in a second data range to produce a result in a third data range.
Regression	Performs a statistical regression analysis on the specified dependent and independent variables in a data range.
X-Range	Specifies one or more independent variables.
Y-Range	Specifies the dependent variable.
Output-Range	Indicates output range for regression results.
Intercept	Controls the intercept when performing the
Compute	regression.
Zero	
Reset	Clears the regression specifications.
Go	Causes the specified regression to be performed.
Parse	Converts long labels in a single column into a
Format-Line	range of numeric data values and/or labels.
Create	
Edit	

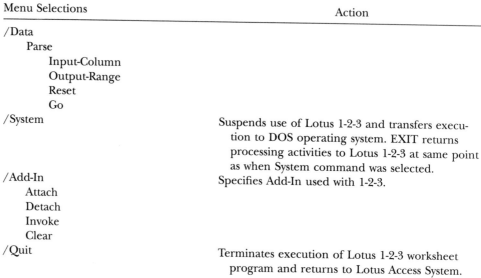

Menu Selections	Action
/Data	
Parse	
Input-Column	
Output-Range	
Reset	
Go	
/System	Suspends use of Lotus 1-2-3 and transfers execution to DOS operating system. EXIT returns processing activities to Lotus 1-2-3 at same point as when System command was selected.
/Add-In	Specifies Add-In used with 1-2-3.
Attach	
Detach	
Invoke	
Clear	
/Quit	Terminates execution of Lotus 1-2-3 worksheet program and returns to Lotus Access System.

L.13.2.2 PrintGraph Commands

Menu Selections	Action
Image-Select	Designates one or more graph files (*.PIC) for printing. Use <F10> (GRAPH) to preview image of graph during selection.
Settings	Controls settings for printing graph.
Image	
Size	Specifies the size, position, and rotation (portrait or landscape) of graph.
Full	Causes graph printing as full page.
Half	Causes graph printing as half page. Two graphs may be printed on one page.
Manual	
Top	
Left	
Width	
Height	
Rotation	
Font	Indicates the typeface of the printed characters.
1	
2	
Range-Colors	Assigns colors to data ranges in graphs for printing in color.
X	
A .. F	
Hardware	Specifies printer, printer interface, paper size, and location of graph (*.PIC) files and font files. If you are using Lotus 1-2-3 on a LAN, check with the LAN manager before making changes to any of these settings.
Graphs-Directory	
Fonts-Directory	
Interface	
Printer	
Size-Paper	
Length	
Width	
Action	Controls actions between printing graphs when two or more graphs have been selected.
Pause	
Eject	
Save	Saves the current PrintGraph settings configuration for future use.

Menu Selections	Action
Settings	
Reset	Returns all the PrintGraph settings to those in the configuration file.
Go	Causes the selected graphs to be printed.
Align	Specifies the top of the page to the printer.
Page	Advances paper to top of the next page.
Exit	Terminates execution of PrintGraph program.

L.13.3 WYSIWYG Command Summary

Menu Selections	Action
:Worksheet	Establishes column widths, row heights, and page breaks.
Column	
Set-Width	
Reset-Width	
Row	
Set-Height	
Auto	
Page	
Row	
Column	
Delete	
:Format	Controls the appearance of the worksheet as displayed on-screen and when printed.
Font	Selects the font for current cell range and requests changes and updates to available fonts.
1 .. 8	
Replace	
1 .. 8	
Default	
Restore	
Update	
Library	
Retrieve	
Save	
Erase	
Bold	Adds or removes boldface to specified cell range.
Set	
Clear	
Italics	Adds or removes italics to specified cell range.
Set	
Clear	
Underline	Adds or removes desired underlining from specified cell range.
Single	
Double	
Wide	
Clear	
Color	Specifies colors for a selected cell range.
Text	
Normal	
Red	
Green	
Dark-Blue	
Cyan	
Yellow	
Magenta	
Background	
(same choices as Text)	

Menu Selections	Action
:Format	
Color	
Negative	Set colors for negative values.
Normal	
Red	
Reverse	Reverse background and text colors.
Lines	Adds or removes single, double, or wide lines to a selected cell range.
Outline	
Left	
Right	
Top	
Bottom	
All	
Double	
Outline	
Left	
Right	
Top	
Bottom	
All	
Wide	
(same choices as Double)	
Clear	
(same choices as Double)	
Shadow	Adds or removes drop shadow to selected cell range.
Set	
Clear	
Shade	Adds or removes shading from cell range.
Light	
Dark	
Solid	
Clear	
Reset	Removes all special format attributes from the cell range, returning them to the default format.
:Graph	Adds, edits, or saves graphics in the format file associated with the worksheet.
Add	Adds a graphic to a specified cell range.
Current	
Named	
PIC	
Metafile	
Blank	
Remove	Removes a graphic from a specified cell range.
Goto	Moves the cell pointer to the selected graphic.
Settings	Changes characteristics of a graphics display on the worksheet, including replacing it and specifying automatic updating when data change.
Graph	Replace one graphic in worksheet with another graphic.
Range	Moves a graphic to a different cell range or changes its size.
Sync	Turns on or off automatic updating of a graph.
Yes	
No	
Display	Turns on or off the display of selected graphics.
Yes	
No	
Opaque	Hides worksheet data under graphic.
Yes	
No	

Menu Selections	Action
:Graph	
Move	Moves a graphic from one cell range to another in the worksheet.
Zoom	Displays a full-screen view of a selected graphic.
Compute	Recalculates worksheet and redraws graph.
View	Displays a full-screen view of a graph file (*.PIC)
PIC	or metafile (*.CGM) without adding it to the
Metafile	worksheet.
Edit	Adds and modifies text, objects, and other enhancements to graphics.
Add	
Text	
Line	
Polygon	
Arrow	
Rectangle	
Ellipse	
Freehand	
Select	Selects graphics object(s) for editing.
One	
All	
None	
More/Less	
Cycle	
Graph	
Edit	Modifies selected object.
Text	
Centering	Aligns a text object.
Left	
Center	
Right	
Font	
1 .. 8	
Line-Style	Specifies appearance of lines for selected object.
Solid	
Dashed	
Dotted	
Long-Dash	
Chain-Dotted	
Chain-Dashed	
Hidden	
Width	Specifies line width of object.
Very-Narrow	
Narrow	
Medium	
Wide	
Very-Wide	
Arrowheads	Adds or removes arrowheads from lines.
Switch	
One	
Two	
None	
Smoothing	Converts corners of selected lines and polygons to curves or changes smoothed curves to straight corners.
None	
Tight	
Medium	

Menu Selections	Action
:Graph	
Edit	
Color	Specifies display colors for selected objects.
Lines	
Black	
White	
Red	
Green	
Dark-Blue	
Cyan	
Yellow	
Magenta	
Hidden	
Inside	Specifies color inside an object such as an ellipse
(select from	or a rectangle.
color palette)	
Text	
(same as Lines)	
Map	Specifies available color choices in the color
1 .. 8	palette.
Background	
(select from	
color palette)	
Transform	Repositions selected object by changing its
Size	rotation or orientation.
Rotate	
Quarter-Turn	
X-Flip	
Y-Flip	
Horizontal	
Vertical	
Clear	
Rearrange	
Delete	Removes selected object(s) from graphic.
Restore	Restores the most recently deleted object(s).
Move	Relocates selected object.
Copy	Duplicates selected object.
Lock	Protects selected object from changes.
Unlock	Removes change protection from selected object.
Front	Places selected object in front.
Back	Places selected object in back.
View	Changes size and selects area of graphic displayed.
Full	
In	
Pan	
+	
−	
Up	
Down	
Left	
Right	
Options	Changes the display of grid lines, graph cursor
Grid	size, and font size of all text in a graphic.
No	
Yes	
Cursor	
Small	
Big	
Font-Magnification	

Menu Selections	Action
:Print	
Go	Causes printing of worksheet that includes the WYSIWYG features.
File	
Background	Sends copy to an encoded file that is printed while you continue other activities with 1-2-3.
Range	Specifies cell range for printing.
Config	Specifies printer information.
Printer	
Interface	
1st-Cart	
2nd-Cart	
Orientation	Specifies arrangement on paper.
Portrait	
Landscape	
Bin	Specifies selection of printer paper.
Reset	
Single-Sheet	
Manual	
Upper-Tray	
Lower-Tray	
Settings	Specifies page numbers and copies for printing.
Begin	
End	
Start-Number	
Copies	
Wait	
Grid	
Frame	
Reset	
Layout	Specifies paper size and related characteristics.
Page-Size	
Letter	
A4	
80X66	
132X66	
80X72	
Legal	
B5	
Custom	
Margins	
Left	
Right	
Top	
Bottom	
Titles	
Header	
Footer	
Clear	
Borders	
Top	
Left	
Clear	
Top	
Left	
All	
Compression	Changes size of printed image for fitting it on one printed page.
None	
Manual	
Automatic	

Menu Selections	Action
:Print	
Layout	
Default	Replaces or saves the current page layout as the default.
Restore	
Update	
Library	Retrieves or saves a page layout stored in a file.
Retrieve	
Save	
Erase	
Preview	Displays the selected range as a page layout for review prior to actual printing.
Info	Removes or displays Wysiwyg Print Settings dialog box.
:Display	Controls how 1-2-3 displays the worksheet on the screen.
Mode	Switches the screen display among the graphic and text modes.
Graphics	
Text	
B&W	
Color	
Zoom	Changes the sizes of the displayed cell contents.
Tiny	
Small	
Normal	
Large	
Huge	
Manual	
Colors	Specifies colors for the screen display.
Background	
(same colors as Text)	
Text	
Black	
White	
Red	
Green	
Dark-Blue	
Cyan	
Yellow	
Magenta	
Unprot(ected)	
(same colors as Text)	
Cell-Pointer	
(same colors as Text)	
Grid	
(same colors as Text)	
Frame	
(same colors as Text)	
Neg(ative)	
(same colors as Text)	
Lines	
(same colors as Text)	
Shadow	
(same colors as Text)	
Replace	Modifies the palette of eight available colors.
(same colors as Text, unless modified)	

Menu Selections	Action
:Display	
Options	Specifies how the screen is displayed, including page breaks and grid lines.
Frame	
1-2-3	
Enhanced	
Relief	
Special	
Characters	
Inches	
Metric	
Points/Picas	
None	
Grid	
No	
Yes	
Page-Breaks	Displays page-break in worksheet.
Yes	
No	
Cell-Pointer	
Solid	
Outline	
Intensity	
Normal	
High	
Adapter	
Auto	
1 .. 8	
Blink	
Yes	
No	
Font-Directory	Specifies directory where 1-2-3 fonts are located.
Rows	Specifies number of rows displayed.
Default	Changes default display settings.
Restore	Replaces current setting with stored setting.
Update	Stores current setting in the WYSIWYG.CNF file.
:Special	Copies and moves WYSIWYG formats from one cell range to another or saves them in a file for use with another worksheet.
Copy	
Move	
Import	
Export	
:Text	Enters and edits text in a worksheet range as though the words are paragraphs in a word processor.
Edit	
Align	
Left	
Right	
Center	
Even	
Reformat	
Set	
Clear	
:Named-Style	Names a collection of WYSIWYG formats from a single cell for use with other cell ranges.
1 .. 8	
Define	

PART

IV

Using dBASE

Creating a Database

CONTENT

- Starting dBASE
- Creating and Using a Database
- Planning the Database
- Operating dBASE
- Command Mode Versus Menu Mode
- Setting the Default Disk Drive
- Establishing a dBASE Catalog
- Creating the WINES Database
- Using a Mouse with dBASE IV
- Viewing or Correcting Data
- Reviewing or Changing a Structure
- Leaving dBASE
- When Things Go Wrong

D.1.1 Introduction

A database management system (DBMS) is one of the more popular microcomputer application software packages used for record-keeping activities. dBASE has been the best-selling microcomputer DBMS. Both dBASE IV and dBASE III+ are widely used versions of this popular DBMS, which evolved from dBASE II, the first version of this DBMS. There are several database packages that are similar to dBASE, such as Paradox and FoxPro. They are known as database management systems since their primary purpose is to store data for access and use in supporting a variety of business requirements.

dBASE has been the leader in these microcomputer database systems with the language of both dBASE IV and dBASE III+ recognized as a standard followed by other software developers. As each of these other developers has extended the features of the dBASE language, the various forms of this DBMS language have come to be known as XBase. Each implementation of XBase includes new commands that extend the capabilities of the DBMS from a particular software developer. However, by learning the fundamentals of the dBASE language, you will not only have an understanding of the operation of this DBMS but you will also have a fundamental understanding of the operation of the various XBase DBMSs.

These database management systems implement what is commonly known as a relational database model. A relation model is a simple arrangement of data as a table with a series of rows and columns, as is illustrated in Figure D.1 for a simple wine list. A relational database table holds the data describing an *object* or *entity,* such as customers or products, like bottles of wine. Each row stores the data for an individual *occurrence* of an entity. Each column is a *field* that contains information describing an *attribute* or *characteristic* of the entity, such as name, identification number, or price. In dBASE IV, a table may be up to 255 fields or columns wide by an unlimited number of rows, while dBASE III+ is limited to 128 fields or columns. (However, the student version of dBASE IV is limited to 120 rows, whereas that for dBASE III+ may contain only 31 rows.)

A table arrangement of data like this makes it easier for end users to visualize associations among the data stored in it. An **end user** is an individual who actually uses the information produced from an application to support the decision-making activities of the job function. Frequently, a separate table is created for each object about which data are recorded; such an application of tables is known as object oriented.

Keypoint!

> An entity is an object, event, or person about which an organization stores data, such as products, customers, employees, orders, and shipments. Data describing entity occurrences are stored in a database table or relation!

Like most database management systems, dBASE provides for three primary tasks:

- *Database Creation.* The content, relationship, and structure of data in a database are defined. This is the data definition capability of a DBMS that is performed with the **data definition language** (DDL).

- *Database Interrogation.* Data in a database can be accessed and displayed as management information to assist in answering questions and in satisfying reporting requirements. This is the data manipulation capability of a DBMS, which is accomplished with the **data manipulation language** (DML).

WINES Database File (Relation or TABLE)

NAME	MAKER	YEAR	PRICE
COUNTRY CHABLIS	ALMADEN	1983	9.00
STRAWBERRY HILL	BOONE'S FARM	1989	5.24
VINO BLANCO	MOGEN DAVID	1988	3.00
BLANC DE BLANC	FETZER VINOS	1982	19.00
VIN ROSE	GEYSER PEAK	1985	9.50

Records (rows or occurrences)

Fields (columns, attributes, data elements, or data items)

FIGURE D.1. Database as a relational table.

- *Data maintenance.* Data need to be added, updated, corrected, and deleted from the database. This is the data-entry feature of a DBMS that is also implemented by using the DML.

In learning about the operation of dBASE, those features are explored that permit each of these tasks to be carried out.

Keypoint!

> Data definition language (DDL) is used to describe the fields contained in a database!
>
> Data manipulation language (DML) is applied to enter and revise data and to access and display requested information!

D.1.2 Starting dBASE

The exact procedure for starting dBASE will vary depending on your particular hardware configuration and the manner in which dBASE has been installed on either floppy disks or the computer's fixed disk. Although the full version of dBASE IV must be installed on a fixed disk, dBASE III+ can be run from floppy disks. The procedures will differ for floppy disk usage depending on whether DOS has been placed on the dBASE disk. There are a number of different configurations for installing and running dBASE that depend on whether dBASE is accessed by using a local area network (LAN). The procedure described here is a general procedure. You will need to check on the exact procedure for the computer that you are using.

The procedure assumes that you will be storing the dBASE application files that you create on *your own floppy disk*, the data disk. If your dBASE application files will be stored on the computer's fixed disk, you should investigate the specific procedures for this on your particular computer.

A standard method to activate or launch dBASE is to proceed at the DOS prompt in this manner:

To start dBASE

Enter:　　　DBASE

If your procedure is different, enter the instructions here:

> My procedure to start dBASE:
>
> _____
>
> _____
>
> _____
>
> _____

D.1.3 Creating and Using a Database: Golden Gourmet Wine Management

The Golden Gourmet features elegant dining with a distinctive cuisine. The Golden Gourmet restaurant was established in 1957 by Augustus "Auggie" and Angela "Angie" Capriccio. Auggie and Angie now serve as the host and hostess greeting each customer as they arrive and making them feel welcome. The business is organized as a closely held family owned corporation. Auggie and Angie's four children handle the day-to-day operations of the restaurant. Delbert "Bert" Capriccio is the general manager, directing the restaurant's overall operation. Luigi "Lou" Capriccio is in charge of food preparation, Elizabeth "Beth" Capriccio-Goodrich directs the servers, and Anastasia "Annie" Capriccio-Santa Fe is the head cashier. Bert and Beth would like to create a wine management system (WMS) for the Golden Gourmet, which would enhance customer service. This system would improve supervision of the wine cellar by using a database to produce a series of management reports.

Bert and Beth just completed a user-requirements analysis of the restaurant's wine cellar. Their analysis revealed a need for maintaining the following information about each wine:

Information	Example/Description
NAME OF THE WINE	MONTEREY BURGUNDY
WINE MAKER	ALMADEN VINEYARDS
YEAR	1982
BIN NUMBER	C10 (this tells you where it is stored)
PRICE PER BOTTLE	$6.95 (highest price is less than $100.00)
QUANTITY ON HAND	45 bottles (never more than 100 bottles of any wine)
LAST ORDER DATE	10/28/88 (mm/dd/yy when order placed)
CHILL	Yes or no, true or false (temperature for serving)
TYPE	Type of wine: red, white, or rosé

Beth and Bert presented the system's functional requirements to Auggie. They described how they would produce a wine list by using this database. The wine list should list the wine name, wine maker, year, and price for each wine in stock. Auggie supported their idea and suggested that the wine list should be arranged so that all red wines are grouped together, and similarly for the white, and rosé wines, since this is the customary practice in the restaurant business.

Beth would like to be able to produce a second report from the database to be used by the servers. The servers need to know whether the wine is to be chilled before serving. The serving list should be arranged in bin number order and should contain the bin number, the wine name, the wine maker, and whether the wine needs to be chilled.

The wine management system is to be used to help Bert in ordering wines. The quantity of each wine on-hand will be updated daily. Then a listing of all wines with stock levels below a certain amount (a **programmed decision**) can be prepared for ordering (an exception report). Beth described to Auggie how an **exception report** allows them to focus their attention only on those items that require immediate action. Also, Bert would like to produce ad hoc exception reports that list all wines with stock levels above certain quantities. He will use this list when he is trying to figure out which wines to offer as specials.

The itemization of information required for this wine database and the descriptions of how the database will be used provide important information for the design of a **database structure.** The database needs to be carefully designed so that it contains all of the information necessary to produce the desired listings and reports.

D.1.4   Planning the Database

Beth and Bert know the importance of planning their database before they fire-up dBASE and begin entering data. As part of their functional requirements, they have prepared the following information for setting up the database design for the Golden Gourmet:

1. Decide how many fields or columns are needed and what data should be stored in each of the fields.
2. Decide on the label for each field—a dBASE field name may be up to 10 characters long. It must begin with a letter and may contain letters, digits, and underscores.
3. Decide how wide to make each field—to allow for the largest data value.

A data type needs to be selected for each field. The primary types of data in dBASE are:

CHARACTER	Alphanumeric data.
NUMERIC	All positive and negative numbers.
DATE	Date in the form mm/dd/yy.
LOGICAL	True or false, yes or no; has only one of these values.

A CHARACTER type field accepts alphabetic, numeric, and special characters, whereas a NUMERIC type field allows only numbers to be entered.

A database plan or design lists the field names, sizes, and data types that describe the entity about which data are to be stored. A Database Planning Form is useful to you in creating a design for a database *before* you attempt to enter it in dBASE. Beth reviewed the information requirements for Golden Gourmet's wine management system and developed the Database Planning Form shown here.

DATABASE PLANNING FORM

Data Name	Data Type	Number of Characters for Largest Value	Dec(imal) Places
NAME	Character	15	
MAKER	Character	12	
YEAR	Character	4	
BIN	Character	3	
PRICE	Numeric	5	2
ON_HAND	Numeric	3	0
L_ORDER	Date	8	
CHILL	Logical	1	
TYPE	Character	5	

D.1.5 Operating dBASE

dBASE is fundamentally a command-driven software package. As a user, you enter commands such as

USE B:WINES	Activates the WINES database file on disk drive B:

or

DISPLAY ALL	Causes all the records in the active database file to appear on the display screen

dBASE commands may be entered in either upper- or lowercase letters. These commands are entered at what is known as the **DOT prompt** in dBASE. To help users construct commands, dBASE has a function known as the CONTROL CENTER mode [dBASE IV] or ASSIST mode [dBASE III+]. In the CONTROL CENTER/ASSIST mode, a menu is displayed and commands are created by making a series of menu selections. The purpose of the CONTROL CENTER/ASSIST mode is to present you with a menu of available dBASE commands. Once you have a basic understanding of dBASE commands, the CONTROL CENTER/ASSIST mode is a useful reminder in helping you construct or select your commands for execution.

The CONTROL CENTER menu screen for dBASE IV is shown in Figure D.2, while that for the ASSIST menu screen of dBASE III+ is shown as Figure D.3. These screens usually appear automatically when entering dBASE. You may exit from the CONTROL CENTER/ASSIST mode in this manner:

| To exit from the Control Center/Assist Mode | **Press:** | <Esc> | |
| | | | |

And, if requested,

| | **Select:** | Yes | Confirm exit from Control Center |

At the DOT prompt, you may enter the CONTROL CENTER/ASSIST mode like this:

| To access the Control Center/Assist Mode | **Press:** | <F2> | Enter Control Center/Assist mode from Dot prompt |
| | **Action:** | Return to the dot prompt. | |

Navigation through the CONTROL CENTER/ASSIST menus is described at the bottom of these screens in the **navigation line,** as illustrated in Figures D.2 and D.3.

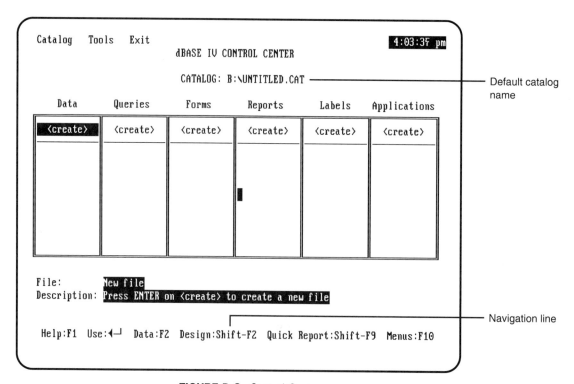

FIGURE D.2. Control Center menu screen.

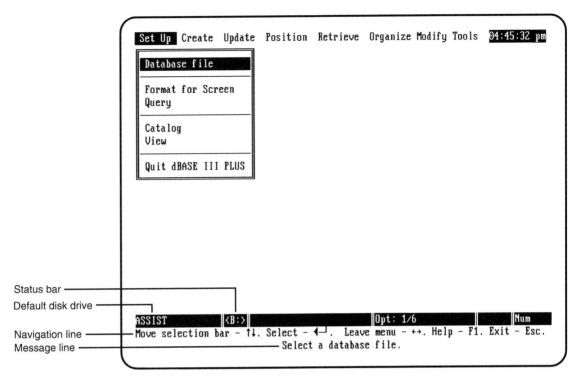

FIGURE D.3. Assist menu screen.

This line shares the bottom of the screen with the **status bar** and **message line.** Each of these lines is displayed by dBASE as appropriate for the current screen—they do not appear on all screens. When they are displayed, the information they contain is described as follows:

> *Status Bar.* Displays information that includes the current command being executed, the default disk drive, the active database file, the current record number in the database or option number from a menu, whether the insert (Ins) or delete (Del) option is in effect, and the status of the <Caps Lock> key.
>
> *Navigation Line.* Displays instructions for moving from one CONTROL CENTER/ASSIST menu to another or for moving within a menu.
>
> *Message Line.* Displays an explanation of the current menu option or any other action that may be taken.

In the explanations that follow in these dBASE lessons, the differences between version III+ and IV of dBASE are specifically indicated when they occur. Usually, this is designated with [version III+] and [version IV], respectively. You should follow those commands that match your version of dBASE. A review of the commands for the other version will help you gain an understanding and appreciation for some of the differences and similarities among the dBASE versions.

The dBASE command **USE B:WINES** is formed in the CONTROL CENTER mode of dBASE IV with several menu selections. It is first necessary to set the default disk drive to B: and then to access the file. This could be accomplished beginning from the main CONTROL CENTER screen as follows (DO NOT execute these commands; *only read them* to obtain an overview of using the CONTROL CENTER):

Press:	<F10>	Access menu
Move to:	Tools	Choose Tools option
Select:	DOS utilities	Desired option
Press:	<F10>	Access DOS utilities menu, with menu choice of DOS
Select:	Set default drive:directory	
Type:	B:	The desired disk drive identifier
Action:	Remove any unwanted characters with <Del>.	
Press:	<Enter>	
Press:	<F10>	Access menu
Select:	Exit	Return to CONTROL CENTER

From the main CONTROL CENTER screen, the desired database file could now be activated with this command:

Select:	WINES	Desired data file

The same dBASE command **USE B:WINES** is formed in the ASSIST mode of dBASE III+ by these menu selections (DO NOT execute these commands; *only read them* to obtain an overview of using ASSIST):

Select:	Setup	
Select:	Database File	Desired option
Select:	B:	Desired disk drive
Select:	WINES	Designated database file name

For a number of the commands you will be exploring in dBASE, the command line form is more convenient to list and describe than a series of menu selections. Some dBASE activities require the menu mode of operation, whereas others are performed only in the command line mode. Throughout this description of dBASE, the most convenient form for describing commands will be used. You may then decide to use either the command line entry or the CONTROL CENTER/ASSIST menu mode of operation, when a choice is available.

Keypoint!

> If something goes wrong, don't panic! Help is only a keystroke away. Just press the <F1> function key and the dBASE help menu appears (Figure D.4). You can obtain information on many of dBASE's features!

D.1.6 Command Mode Versus Menu Mode

As illustrated above, dBASE can be operated from either the command mode or the menu mode. Although the command mode of operation from the dot prompt is the same in both dBASE IV and dBASE III+, the menu mode of operation is considerably different. Thus, if you learn only the menu selections in dBASE III+, then learning the menu mode in dBASE IV is almost like learning an entirely different database management system.

dBASE commands are upward compatible with newer versions, including the commands from prior versions. Borland International, the software development

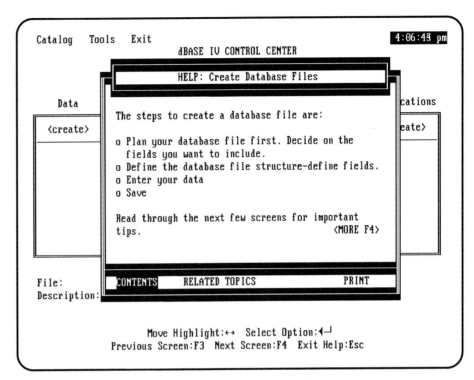

FIGURE D.4. Example HELP screen.

company that sells dBASE, has indicated their support for continued compatibility of new versions of dBASE with the current dBASE III+ and dBASE IV "standard"—a standard achieved through the command mode of operation. Those developers who have evolved the XBase standard have produced this standard from the command mode of operation, not the menu selections from either the CONTROL CENTER or the ASSIST mode of operation. What this means to you is that by learning the command mode of dBASE operation, you should be in the best position to work with future upgraded versions of dBASE or the other XBase work-alikes.

A number of dBASE commands are not available in the menu mode of operation. They can be accessed only from the dot prompt in the command line mode of operation. Thus, the command mode of operation allows the use of many additional dBASE commands, whereas the menu mode of operation is limited to only a subset of the dBASE commands.

The command mode supports dBASE programming, which is similar to Lotus 1-2-3 macros, but is more powerful and flexible than 1-2-3. Most applications that are used on a regular basis—daily, weekly, or monthly—make use of dBASE programs. The easiest way to build user-specific applications programs in dBASE is to write programs using the commands entered at the dot prompt. Menu mode selections cannot be readily included in dBASE programs. By learning to operate dBASE in the command mode, you have a better foundation for creating dBASE programs. Thus, learning the command mode of operation prepares you for creating these programs, which are the focus of the last two dBASE lessons in this book.

The command mode has a "history" feature that makes commands readily available for reuse. If a series of menu selections is not correct, a new set of menu choices is usually required. With the command mode, the incorrect command can be accessed and the error can be corrected with editing. This is a very convenient method for correcting errors or for repeating a series of commands that are similar.

In summary, reasons for you to learn the command mode of operation of dBASE include the following:

- Supports standard, upward-compatible language.
- Provides use of a number of commands not available from a menu.
- Allows some operations to be performed more quickly than selecting from menus.
- Supports dBASE programming.

D.1.7   Setting the Default Disk Drive

Beth and Bert have completed their database plan, and are now ready to create their database. Before they enter the database, they want to establish the default disk drive. Then, as they access their various dBASE files, they will *not* need to include the disk drive letter with each filename. This is accomplished as follows:

Action: Activate dBASE using your start-up procedure.

To set the default disk drive

Press:	<Esc>	Exit from the CONTROL CENTER/ ASSIST mode
Select:	Yes	If requested

At the dot prompt, proceed as follows:

Enter:	SET DEFAULT TO B:	Specify the default disk drive; use the appropriate letter for your computer system

D.1.8   Establishing a dBASE Catalog

Bert knows that most dBASE applications make use of a number of separate computer files. Several database files may be used with one application. In addition, dBASE deploys a number of other files to describe reports and to arrange these data. Thus, a dBASE application is usually not a single file, but rather it is a set of related files, such as all of the files for the payroll application, the inventory application, the general ledger accounting application or, in Bert's situation, the wine management system. A **catalog** is a dBASE feature that helps you to organize the various dBASE files into a logically related application group. dBASE then knows how to work with only the files within the catalog. Since only one catalog may be in use at a time, dBASE can limit the use of the files in the catalog to the application that is currently active.

The catalog for Bert and Beth's wine management system is set up in this manner:

To set a CATALOG

Enter:	SET CATALOG TO GOLDEN	

When prompted with the message "Create new file catalog? (Y/N)"

Press:	<Y>	Confirm new file catalog
Action:	Wait for "Enter title..." prompt.	
Enter:	WINE MANAGEMENT SYSTEM	
		Provide catalog description

Here, GOLDEN is a DOS file name and is limited to the rules for naming files under DOS. dBASE responds with the "File catalog is empty" message and returns to the dot prompt. The "get ready" actions in dBASE have been completed. Bert and Beth can now proceed in creating their database.

Although dBASE IV requires the use of a CATALOG, this is optional in dBASE III+. In dBASE IV, if you do not create a catalog, dBASE automatically generates an "UNTITLED" CATALOG for your use. Because a catalog helps in organizing your files, be sure to create a catalog to hold your dBASE applications as described here.

Keypoint!

After activating dBASE, the first two commands you enter should usually be:

```
SET DEFAULT TO B:        or your disk drive
SET CATALOG TO GOLDEN    or your catalog name
```

D.1.9   Creating the WINES Database

With their database plan ready and dBASE activated, Bert and Beth's next step in creating the WINES database is to describe the fields or structure of the database using the data definition language (DDL) of dBASE. This step takes the fields identified in their database plan and enters them into dBASE. dBASE employs a fill-in-the-blank DDL with the information for each field entered on a database structure form.

Let's create the database for the WINES management system.

To CREATE a new database file

Press:	<Esc>	If you are at the CONTROL CENTER/ ASSIST and need to exit to the dot prompt
Select:	Yes	If requested, confirm exit
Enter:	CREATE WINES	Specify database file name

Here, WINES is a DOS file name and must follow the file naming conventions.

dBASE IV

Or from the CONTROL CENTER panel, proceed in this manner:

| **Select:** | <create> under Data | The file name is specified on completion of the <create> operation |

dBASE III+

Or from the ASSIST menu, make these selections:

Select:	Create	Desired action
Select:	Database File	
Enter:	WINES	Specify database file name

Caution Alert!

The database name, such as WINES, is a DOS filename that must *not* exceed eight (8) characters in length. If you enter a file name that is more than eight (8) characters long, only the first eight (8) characters will be used!

By entering either the CREATE command or making the menu selections and entries, you are placed in the CREATE database mode of dBASE, as indicated in the Status Bar. Your database structure is entered as shown in Figure D.5. Use <Enter> or <right> to move to the next item in the structure. The cursor control keys <left>,

<right>, <up>, and <down> can be used to move the cursor for revising entries. The data TYPE can be selected by using <space> to toggle through the available choices until the desired Field Type appears, as indicated by the instruction displayed in the Navigation Line.

Let's enter the structure for the WINES database.

To define a character database field

Enter:	NAME	
Press:	<Enter>	Character is the desired data type
Enter:	15	Specify field width

VERSION IV

Press:	<Enter>	Skip to the next field

When the field width is entered, dBASE III+ automatically advances to the next Field Name definition, whereas dBASE IV requires an <Enter> to skip by the Index definition in advancing to the next Field Name definition.

Action: Complete the definition for the fields MAKER, YEAR, and BIN by proceeding in a similar manner.

Notice how Beth specified YEAR as a Character type field, since she does not plan to perform any arithmetic using the values in this field. *When no computations are planned, numbers may be placed in either a Character or Numeric type field.* The postal zip code is another example of field usually filled with numbers that may be defined as character type data, at least, for those in the United States.

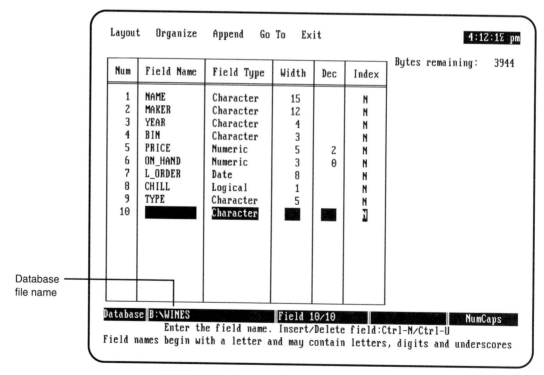

Database file name

FIGURE D.5. Structure for WINES database.

~~~~~~
Caution Alert!
~~~~~~

> When things go wrong, don't panic! You may use <Esc> to exit from entering the structure or data. This will allow you to start over. Or you may continue entering the structure and data. You can then make revisions as described in the sections "Viewing or Correcting Data" and "Reviewing or Changing a Structure." Refer to those sections if you find yourself in trouble entering the structure and data!

Now continue entering the data definition.

To define a Numeric field			
Enter:	PRICE	
Press:	<Space>	Toggle to the Numeric data type
Press:	<Enter>	Select the Numeric data type
Enter:	5	
Enter:	2	Places to the right of the decimal

VERSION IV			
Press:	<Enter>	Advance to the next field definition
Action:	Enter the definition for the ON_HAND field in a similar manner.	

To define a Date field			
Enter:	L_ORDER	
Select:	Date	Use the <space> to toggle to the desired field type and press <Enter>

Since the Width of the Date type of field is always automatically set to eight characters, you are not requested to enter a Width specification.

VERSION IV			
Press:	<Enter>	Advance to the next field definition

To define a Logical field			
Enter:	CHILL	
Select:	Logical	Toggle to the desired Field Type and press <Enter>

In a similar manner, since the Width of the Logical type of field is always automatically set to one character, you are *not* requested to enter it.

Action: Enter the data definition for the wine TYPE field.

Action: Review your complete data definition structure. If any entries are not correct, use the cursor to move to the part of the definition that needs to be corrected and change it.

When you have completed entering the structure,

Move to:	the last field that is blank	
		Field number is 10 for this data definition
Press:	<Enter>	Complete data definition

If a confirmation is requested,

Press:	<Enter>	Confirm request

If a database file name is requested,

VERSION IV			
Enter:	WINES	Specify name of database file

If a "Title for file WINES.dbf" is requested,

Enter: WINE MANAGEMENT DATABASE

To begin entering database records when a database is created

When prompted by the "Input data records now?(Y/N)" message,

Press: <Y>   Indicate that you want to begin entering data records

dBASE will display its EDIT data-entry screen, as illustrated in Figure D.6, and allow you to immediately begin entering your data records. Beth assembled the data records in Figure D.7 for entry into the database.

Keypoint!

> The structure of a database must be entered before any records can be placed into the database!

Caution Alert!

> Toggle on your CAPS LOCK key and enter all data in uppercase. This will help avoid potential difficulties in using this database to explore other features of dBASE. dBASE differentiates between uppercase and lowercase characters. By entering all your data in uppercase, you will not need to be concerned with this differentiation as you work through these dBASE lessons!

With the cursor located in the NAME field, continue like this:

To enter a database record

Type: COUNTRY CHABLIS

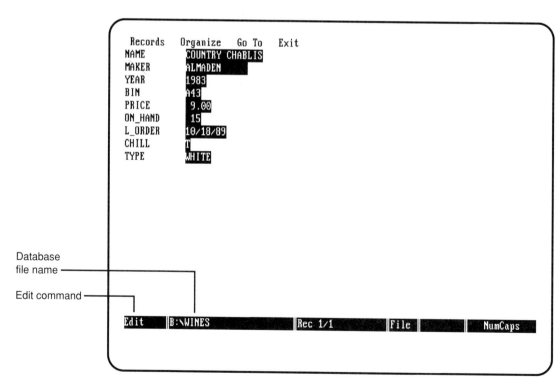

Database file name

Edit command

FIGURE D.6. EDIT screen for entering data.

NAME	MAKER	YEAR	BIN	PRICE	ON_HAND	L_ORDER	CHILL	TYPE
COUNTRY CHABLIS	ALMADEN	1983	A43	9.00	15	10/18/89	.T.	WHITE
STRAWBERRY HILL	BOONE'S FARM	1989	C14	5.24	48	09/16/92	.T.	RED
VINO BIANCO	MOGEN DAVID	1988	B20	3.00	50	11/25/91	.F.	RED
BLANC DE BLANC	FETZER VINOS	1982	D23	19.00	21	11/20/90	.T.	WHITE
VIN ROSE	GEYSER PEAK	1985	C15	9.50	24	11/05/91	.T.	ROSE
RIPPLE	HOOTCH HUT	1989	C28	2.50	64	06/30/92	.F.	RED
MOREAU ROUGE	J. MOREAU	1982	D12	18.50	15	05/25/90	.F.	RED
TORRES DE CASTA	M. TORRES	1985	B15	5.24	10	07/15/91	.T.	ROSE
MAD DOG 20/20	MOGEN DAVID	1989	B20	3.00	50	11/02/92	.F.	RED
EXTRA DRY WHITE	RIVERSIDE	1986	A25	12.76	48	11/19/91	.T.	WHITE
VINO ROSA	WENTE BROS	1989	B34	7.50	24	11/29/92	.T.	ROSE
ZINFANDEL	TAYLOR FARMS	1989	A22	6.50	10	11/29/93	.F.	RED

FIGURE D.7. Data entered in WINES database.

Notice how COUNTRY CHABLIS fills the entire NAME field. Typing the "S" causes dBASE to automatically "beep" and advance to the MAKER field. dBASE takes this action whenever you completely fill a field with a data value. Data values in other fields will result in the same action.

Type: ALMADEN

Press: <Enter>   Advance to the next field

Since ALMADEN does not occupy the entire field, an <Enter> is used to advance to the next field.

Type: 1983   Field is filled, you advance to the next field

Type: A43   Again, field is filled

Type: 9.00

Notice how pressing the decimal causes the 9 to be automatically positioned in the field. You do not need to use the <space> to position numbers within the Numeric type field. The two zeros then complete filling the field.

Type: 15

Press: <Enter>   Complete entry since value does not fill the field

Type: 101889   Enter the date

Notice that when you enter this date, you do *not* type the slash (/) as part of entering the date. You only type the digits for the month, day, and year. Since the entire field is filled, you automatically advance to the next field.

Type: Y   Enter value for CHILL and advance to the next field using Y or T for true

Type: WHITE   Complete the last field of this record

Notice that when you fill the last field with WHITE, dBASE *automatically* advances to the *next* record. A new empty EDIT form is displayed on the screen and the record number in the Status Bar is incremented. If the value in the last field contained less than five characters, an <Enter> would cause the advance to the next record.

Action: Complete entering the data for the other wines provided in Figure D.7.

When you have entered your last record:

To exit from data entry

Move to: the first blank field of the next new record
Press: <Enter>

This will terminate your data entry.

dBASE stores *both* your structure and data in the *same* database file with a file extension of DBF. This storage of the data definition with the data, as illustrated in Figure D.8, is a key feature of a DBMS like dBASE. This makes the data readily available for use with a number of different application programs.

Keypoint!   dBASE stores your data in the .DBF database file in the sequential order in which you initially entered each data record!

D.1.10   Using a Mouse with dBASE IV

Beginning with Version 1.5 of dBASE IV, you can use a mouse for many operations. You can use a mouse to select commands from a menu, select an item from a list, and position the cursor. If a mouse is installed on your computer, after you load dBASE IV, a **mouse pointer** appears on your screen as a small rectangle (Figure D.9). As you move the mouse around on your desktop, the mouse pointer moves on your screen in exactly the same motion. For example, moving your mouse to the left causes the mouse pointer to move to the left.

The key manipulation words **click, double-click,** and **drag,** as defined in Lesson T.2 "Keystroke Terminology in Using Software Tools," apply to your use of the mouse in carrying out the various mouse-enabled activities in dBASE IV.

D.1.11   Viewing or Correcting Data

Once you have entered all of your data and returned to the dot prompt, you can view and/or correct the data you have entered. This is done with the EDIT feature of dBASE. A hard copy of any of the records can be obtained by displaying that record on your screen and then using the <Shift>+<PrtSc> to dump a copy of the screen to your printer.

Beth wants you to change the bin number for STRAWBERRY HILL to C22. From the command line:

To change a record

Enter: EDIT   Access the Edit screen
Action: Use <PgUp> and/or <PgDn> to display the record for STRAW-
               BERRY HILL on your screen.

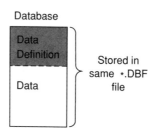

FIGURE D.8. Data definition and data stored together in database file with extension .DBF.

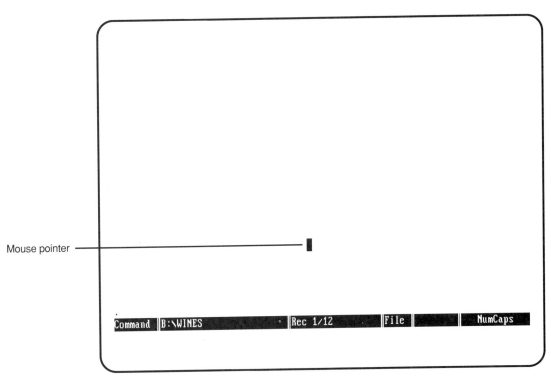

Mouse pointer

Command B:\WINES   Rec 1/12   File   NumCaps

FIGURE D.9. Mouse pointer for use with dBASE IV.

Watch the Status Bar as you use <PgUp> and <PgDn>. This contains the number of the record displayed on your screen. "Rec 2/12" indicates you have record 2 displayed and there are 12 records in your database. With the record for STRAWBERRY HILL displayed on your screen,

| **Move to:** | the BIN field | Use cursor or mouse |
| **Type:** | C22 | Enter the new bin number |

The new value automatically replaces the old value. You do *not* need to remove the old value before you enter this new value.

Action: Use <PgUp> and <PgDn> to review the other data. If you discover any other errors, correct them.

Action: Use <Shift>+<PrtSc> to print the EDIT screen of several database records.

To exit from EDIT and save changes to the database

| **Press:** | <Ctrl>+<End> | Exit from Edit *and* save your changes |

If you need to add more records to your database, dBASE IV allows you to do this with the "Add new records? (Y/N)" prompt whenever you attempt to go to the next record with a <PgDn>, <down>, or <Enter>. For dBASE III+, you need to enter the APPEND command at the dot prompt in order to add records onto your existing database. See Figures D.10 and D.11 for EDIT activities.

D.1.12 Reviewing or Changing a Structure

Once a database structure has been created, it can be reviewed and revised. Since the CREATE command is used only for a *new* database, changes must be made using a modify command in dBASE. Let's review the WINES database structure.

Special Keys	Action
\<PgUp\>	Backward one record
\<PgDn\>	Forward one record
\<up\>	Backward one field
\<down\>	Forward one field
\<Ctrl\> + \<Y\>	Delete current field
\<Ctrl\> + \<U\>	Delete/undelete record (a toggle)
\<Ctrl\> + \<End\>	Exit EDIT *and* save changes
\<Esc\>	Exit EDIT and do *not* save changes

FIGURE D.10. Special EDIT keys.

From the command line:

To look at a database structure

Enter: DISPLAY STRUCTURE

dBASE IV

Or, from the CONTROL CENTER mode:

Move to: Data (if necessary)

Select: WINES   Desired database file

Select: Modify structure/order
                         Desired activity

Press: \<Esc\>   Remove Organize menu from display to
                                            view structure

When you have finished viewing this structure, return to the Control Center in this manner:

Press: \<Esc\>

Select: Yes   when requested

dBASE III+

Or, from the ASSIST menu:

Select: Tools

Select: List Structure   Desired activity

Enter: N

The DISPLAY STRUCTURE command displays the data definition on your screen as shown in Figure D.12. You may obtain a hard copy of this structure with a \<Shift\>+\<PrtSc\> screen dump.

The MODIFY command is used to change an existing structure. If you happened to make a mistake in originally entering your structure, make use of MODIFY. If there are no corrections, then just remember that MODIFY is available for changing an existing structure when the need should arise.

Operation	Action
Move cursor to a field	Click the field
Move cursor to a position in a field	Click the position
Open a menu on the menu bar	Click the menu name
Close menu	Click outside the menu

FIGURE D.11. Mouse actions in EDIT.

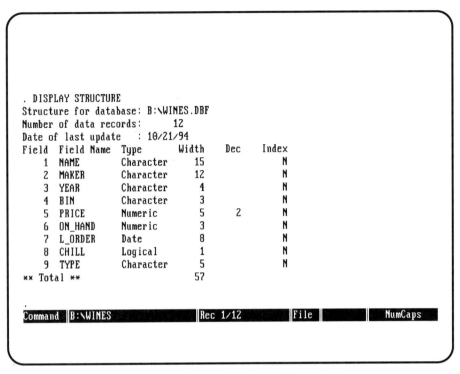

```
. DISPLAY STRUCTURE
Structure for database: B:\WINES.DBF
Number of data records:     12
Date of last update   : 10/21/94
Field  Field Name  Type        Width   Dec   Index
    1  NAME        Character      15            N
    2  MAKER       Character      12            N
    3  YEAR        Character       4            N
    4  BIN         Character       3            N
    5  PRICE       Numeric         5     2      N
    6  ON_HAND     Numeric         3            N
    7  L_ORDER     Date            8            N
    8  CHILL       Logical         1            N
    9  TYPE        Character       5            N
** Total **                      57
.
```

FIGURE D.12. Structure listing for WINES database.

To change your structure from the command line:

To change a database structure

Enter: MODIFY STRUCTURE   Desired activity

dBASE IV

Or, from the Control Center mode:

Move to: Data (if necessary)

Select: WINES   Desired database file

Select: Modify structure/order

Press: <Esc>   Remove Organize menu from display and position cursor in structure

dBASE III+

Or, from ASSIST:

Select: Modify   Desired activity

Select: Database File

After making any changes under MODIFY STRUCTURE, exit in the same manner as you did for creating the structure:

To exit from modifying a structure

Move to: last blank Field Name

Press: <Enter>

Or with the cursor located anywhere in the data definition:

Press: <Ctrl>+<End>

Keypoint!   Use the MODIFY STRUCTURE command to revise the fields, their size, or type (see Figures D.13, D.14, and D.15). Fields may be added to or removed from a database using MODIFY STRUCTURE!

Special Keys	Action
\<up\>	Backward one field
\<down\>	Forward one field
\<Ctrl\> + \<Y\>	Erase current value from field
\<Ctrl\> + \<U\>	Delete current field from definition
\<Ctrl\> + \<N\>	Add field above current field
\<Ctrl\> + \<End\>	Exit EDIT *and* save changes
\<Esc\>	Exit EDIT and do *not* save changes

FIGURE D.13. Special MODIFY STRUCTURE keys.

Operation	Action
Move cursor to a field	Click the field
Move cursor to a position in a field	Click the position
Cycle through choices in field type	Click field type option until desired choice appears.
Open a menu on the menu bar	Click the menu name
Close menu	Click outside the menu

FIGURE D.14. Mouse actions in MODIFY STRUCTURE.

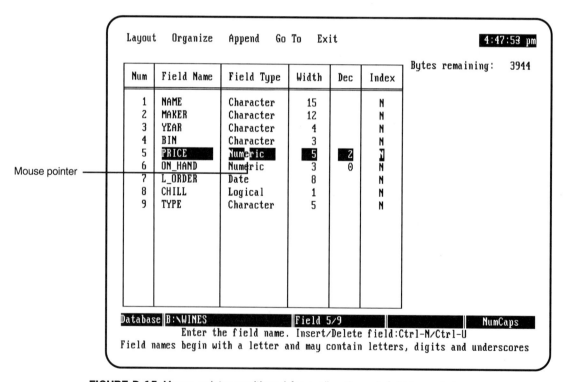

FIGURE D.15 Mouse pointer positioned for cycling through field type choices.

D.1.13 Leaving dBASE

When you need to exit from dBASE after you have completed all of your work, use the QUIT command as described below. Be sure you are ready to leave dBASE before entering this command. Otherwise, you will need to restart dBASE.

To leave dBASE, enter the command like this:

To exit from dBASE	**Enter:**	Quit	

dBASE IV	Or, from the Control Center mode,		
	Press:	<F10>	Access Menu
	Move to:	Exit	Choose Exit option
	Select:	Quit to DOS	Desired action

dBASE III+	Or, from the ASSIST menu,		
	Select:	Set Up	
	Select:	Quit dBASE III PLUS	Desired action

Caution Alert! Always be sure to QUIT from dBASE, since this closes your database files in a way that causes dBASE to perform housekeeping activities. Do NOT just shut off your computer as this might cause a loss of data in your dBASE database!

D.1.14 When Things Go Wrong

A variety of different conditions may occur while you are initially attempting to enter your structure and data. Some of the more common difficulties and how to recover from them are described here:

1. The field width is too small for my data values when entering data.
   a. Use <Ctrl>+<End> to Exit from data entry.
   b. Use MODIFY STRUCTURE to access the data definition.
   c. Change the Width of the field(s).
   d. Exit from the STRUCTURE definition form.
   e. Use EDIT or APPEND to continue entering your data.

2. A field is missing from my structure.
   a. Use MODIFY STRUCTURE to access the data definition.
   b. Position your cursor in the field *below* the location where you want a new field to be added.
   c. Use <Ctrl>+<N> to insert a new field.
   d. Enter the specification for the new field.
   e. Exit from the STRUCTURE definition form.
   f. Use EDIT to enter data values to the newly created field in all the records in your database.

3. The wrong data values have been entered for one or more records in the database.
   a. Use EDIT to view the records.
   b. Use <PgUp> and/or <PgDn> to locate the desired record(s).
   c. Enter the new data values, replacing the old data values.

4. You had to Quit dBASE before you had all your data entered.
   a. Use SET DEFAULT TO . . . and SET CATALOG TO . . . to get ready.
   b. **Enter**:   USE ?   Request a list of database files to be displayed
   c. **Select**:   < your database file from the list provided >
   d. Use EDIT and/or APPEND to continue entering data in your database.

D.1.15 Lesson Summary

- Database relations store data describing entities such as products or customers.
- dBASE IV and dBASE III+ are widely used versions of the dBASE database management software.
- A data definition language is used to describe the fields contained in a database, whereas a data manipulation language is applied to enter, revise, access, and display these data.
- A database plan is a mechanism to organize the fields that will be contained in a database prior to entering a database definition into a DBMS such as dBASE.
- The primary types of data that can be stored in a dBASE database are character, numeric, date, and logical.
- dBASE is a command-driven software package. Commands may be entered directly at the dot prompt on the command line or selected from a menu by using the CONTROL CENTER/ASSIST mode of operation.

- The command mode supports the "standard" upward-compatible features of the dBASE language.
- The CREATE command is used to access the fill-in-the-form DDL of dBASE where the database definition is entered.
- Data records may be viewed and corrected using the EDIT command.
- A database definition is reviewed with a DISPLAY STRUCTURE command and revised with a MODIFY STRUCTURE command.
- The mouse can be used to position the cursor and to make menu selection. This capability is available beginning with dBASE IV Version 1.5.
- The QUIT command is used to terminate dBASE and to close the active database file.

D.1.16 Practice Tutorial

Develop the Wine Management System for the Golden Gourmet. You will be entering the commands and data as provided in this Lesson as a guided hands-on activity. By following the steps described in this Lesson, you should obtain a better understanding of the operation of dBASE.

Task 1: Create the GOLDEN catalog for coordinating the files of the Wine Management System.

Task 2: Create the WINES database and define its structure.

Task 3: Print the structure with <Shift>+<PrtSc>.

Task 4: Enter the data provided in Figure D.7.

Task 5: Print the data for several wines from the EDIT data-entry screen with <Shift>+<PrtSc>.

Task 6: Exit dBASE, which will save your file.

Time Estimates

Novice: 90 minutes

Intermediate: 60 minutes

Advanced: 30 minutes

D.1.17 Practice Exercises

(1) **Case: Ray's Used Cars**

Business Problem: Inventory Management
MIS Characteristics: Operational Control
Production/Operations

Ray's Used Cars salvages wrecked vehicles recycling their reusable parts. Ray stores some vehicles in his salvage yard in the condition in which they are received. For some of those with more popular parts, Ray dismantles them, storing them in his warehouse. Ray decided a database would be useful in tracking his inventory. He prepared a database plan and assembled the following test data:

DATABASE PLANNING FORM

Data Name	Data Type	Number of Characters for Largest Value	Dec(imal) Places
MAKE	Character	10	
MODEL	Character	10	
YEAR	Numeric	2	0
PART	Character	15	
PN	Numeric	7	0
PRICE	Numeric	6	2
LOC	Character	3	
ON_CAR	Logical	1	

Here, Ray has used PN to indicate the part number, LOC indicates the location in the salvage yard or warehouse, and ON_CAR specifies whether the part is on the vehicle or has been disassembled.

MAKE	MODEL	YEAR	PART	PN	PRICE	LOC	ON_CAR
CHEVROLET	CAVALIER	85	LF FENDER	978653	65.00	A11	Y
FORD	ESCORT	89	HOOD	78563	90.00	J21	N
HONDA	CIVIC	91	FRONT BUMPER	765392	110.00	F37	Y
DODGE	SHADOW	90	RR DOOR	571329	125.00	B12	Y
FORD	F150	91	GRILL	675398	87.50	C14	N
JEEP	CJ5	87	TRANS 5 SPS	356841	255.00	J22	Y
BUICK	PARK AVE	88	WINDSHIELD	889761	89.00	B29	N
CHEVROLET	S10 BLAZER	84	REAR DOOR	461378	159.00	C19	Y

Carry out the following tasks in developing this database:

Task 1: Create a CATALOG named RAYS. The dBASE command is

_____

Task 2: Create the database USEDCARS with the structure as defined above. The dBASE command is

_____

Task 3: Print the structure with <Shift>+<PrtSc>.

Task 4: Enter the test data provided by Ray.

Task 5: Print the data for several parts in the database from the EDIT data-entry screen by using <Shift>+<PrtSc>.

Task 6: Exit dBASE, which will save your file. The dBASE command is

_____

Time Estimates

Novice: 90 minutes

Intermediate: 60 minutes

Advanced: 30 minutes

(2)   Case: First American National Bank

Business Problem: Loan Portfolio
MIS Characteristics: Finance
Operational Control

Melissa LeBlanc is a personal banker at the First American National Bank. She is responsible for a portfolio of loans to small construction businesses. To help Melissa track her loan portfolio, she considered her information requirements and designed a database. Her database plan and test data are provided as follows:

DATABASE PLANNING FORM

Data Name	Data Type	Number of Characters for Largest Value	Dec(imal) Places
LOAN	Numeric	8	0
CUSTOMER	Character	24	
AMOUNT	Numeric	10	2
BALANCE	Numeric	10	2
RATE	Numeric	5	2
CREDIT	Logical	1	

Here, Melissa used RATE to indicate the interest rate as a percent, and CREDIT specifies whether or not the credit status is satisfactory.

LOAN	CUSTOMER	AMOUNT	BALANCE	RATE	CREDIT
90768895	BORCHMANN CONSTRUCTION	355000.00	342789.28	9.25	Y
90866534	KNUDSEN CONSTRUCTION	1250000.00	987850.55	9.10	Y
90563982	NEBRASKA BUILDERS	555000.00	433007.21	9.45	Y
90784431	FOUR SQUARE BUILDERS	321000.00	299788.43	8.75	Y
90677892	MOOSE BUILDERS	458000.00	239458.89	9.15	Y
90553371	METROPOLITAN BUILDERS	2030000.00	1988564.31	8.45	Y
90779872	PAYLESS CONSTRUCTION	980000.00	1112290.45	9.25	N
90637553	RESTORATION CONSTRUCT	267000.00	129867.73	8.45	Y
90663785	KASTLE CONSTRUCTION	375000.00	251891.31	9.15	Y
90638925	ATLAS BUILDERS	432000.00	501532.49	9.00	N

Perform the following tasks in developing this database:

Task 1: Create a CATALOG named BANKER. The dBASE command is

.
_____

Task 2: Create the database LOANS with the structure as defined above. The dBASE command is

.
_____

Task 3: Print the structure with <Shift>+<PrtSc>.

Task 4: Enter the test data provided by Melissa.

Task 5: Print the data for several customers in the database from the EDIT data-entry screen by using <Shift>+<PrtSc>.

Task 6: Exit dBASE, which will save your file. The dBASE command is

.
_____

Time Estimates

Novice: 90 minutes

Intermediate: 60 minutes

Advanced: 30 minutes

(3)   Case: Gaslight Realtors

Business Problem: Multiple Listings
MIS Characteristics: Production/Operation
Operational Control

Rumaldo Hernandez manages the multiple listings for residential real estate at Gaslight Realtors. Rumaldo wants to maintain all of Gaslight's listings in the firm's own database. Margarita Glasnapp, Gaslight's managing broker, believes this separate database would provide Gaslight with a competitive edge in marketing real estate listed with the firm. Once a week the new entries in the database would be uploaded to the multiple listing database maintained by the Greater Metro Realtors Association. Rumaldo and Margarita sketched out a database design that contains the fields described by the following data dictionary definition:

Field Name	Description
MLS_NO	Multiple listing identification number
ADDRESS	Property street address
SQ_FT	Total square feet of finished living area
STY	Number of stories
AGE	Approximate age of property
BRM	Number of bedrooms
BATH	Number of bathrooms
AC	Indicator of whether or not the dwelling has central air conditioning
FPL	Indicator of whether or not the dwelling has a fireplace
FRM	Indicator of whether or not the dwelling has a family room
PRICE	Price of property
L_DATE	Listing date

From this data dictionary definition, Rumaldo prepared this database plan:

DATABASE PLANNING FORM

Data Name	Data Type	Number of Characters for Largest Value	Dec(imal) Places
MLS_NO	Character	5	
ADDRESS	Character	14	
SQ_FT	Numeric	4	0
STY	Numeric	1	0
AGE	Character	3	
BRM	Numeric	1	0
BATH	Numeric	3	1
AC	Logical	1	
FPL	Logical	1	
FRM	Logical	1	
PRICE	Numeric	6	0
L_DATE	Date	8	

Then, he assembled the following test data:

MLS_NO	ADDRESS	SQ_FT	STY	AGE	BRM	BATH	AC	FPL	FRM	PRICE	L_DATE
19742	1420 WARD	1200	1	20+	2	1.0	.F.	.F.	.F.	46900	02/24/94
22312	1180 BANNISTER	2600	2	5	4	2.5	.T.	.T.	.T.	176000	02/14/94
23675	9624 STATE AV	1800	1	2	3	2.0	.T.	.F.	.T.	102500	03/11/94
23676	3001 SOUTHWEST	1600	1	7	3	1.5	.T.	.F.	.F.	98000	02/28/94
22706	8021 WORNALL	3200	2	6	5	3.5	.T.	.T.	.T.	240000	03/19/94
28277	8011 TRUMAN	2100	2	10	4	2.5	.T.	.T.	.T.	149500	02/17/94
22352	1024 SANTA FE	2300	1	8	4	2.5	.T.	.T.	.T.	169500	02/19/94
23820	632 WALNUT	1550	1	2	2	1.5	.T.	.F.	.F.	105500	02/15/94
23517	534 OAK GROVE	2900	2	20+	6	3.0	.T.	.T.	.T.	201500	02/14/94
23758	2542 JUNCTION	1900	2	18	3	2.5	.T.	.T.	.T.	99500	02/16/94
18897	1109 ARLINGTON	1400	1	3	2	2.0	.T.	.F.	.F.	86000	02/21/94
23655	2411 HOLMES	1550	1	14	2	1.5	.F.	.F.	.F.	88500	03/21/94
24164	8150 BLUE PKWY	1700	1	11	3	1.5	.T.	.F.	.T.	119500	02/28/94
17997	2601 BARRY	2600	2	16	4	2.5	.T.	.F.	.T.	158000	03/04/94
27575	3201 BROADWAY	1450	1	20+	3	1.5	.F.	.F.	.F.	68500	02/11/94
23636	9850 QUIVIRA	1600	1	15	3	1.5	.T.	.F.	.F.	92500	02/04/94
25664	6753 GARFIELD	3600	2	7	5	3.5	.T.	.T.	.T.	276500	02/14/94
23680	1512 ATLANTIC	1450	1	5	2	2.0	.T.	.F.	.F.	78500	02/02/94
27419	4528 BELLEVIEW	2100	2	6	4	2.5	.T.	.T.	.T.	159500	02/07/94
25777	4501 FAIRMONT	2200	2	4	4	2.5	.T.	.T.	.T.	179000	02/07/94

Develop this database for Gaslight Realtors by performing the following tasks:

Task 1: Create a CATALOG named HOMES. The dBASE command is

_____

Task 2: Create the database GASLIGHT with the structure as defined above. The dBASE command is

_____

Task 3: Print the structure with <Shift>+<PrtSc>.

Task 4: Enter the test data provided by Rumaldo.
The dBASE command to enter data is

_____

Task 5: Print the data for several homes in the database from the EDIT data-entry screen by using <Shift>+<PrtSc>.

Task 6: Exit dBASE, which will save your file. The dBASE command is

_____

Time Estimates

Novice: 90 minutes

Intermediate: 60 minutes

Advanced: 30 minutes

D.1.18 Comprehensive Problems

(1) **Case: Yen To Travel**

Business Problem: Sales Support
MIS Characteristics: Marketing
Operational Control

Yen To Travel is a travel booking agency that specializes in selling packaged tours to clients. Established in 1966 by Brenda Esprit, Yen To is one of many travel agencies that serve as a tour broker. The tours are conducted by independent tour agents. Yen To is allocated a number of spaces on each tour. Sara McGill, the office manager of Yen To, would like to maintain a record of tour packages and to produce various management reports that would provide information to better manage their booking agency. Ashley Valley serves as Yen To's booking agent. She works with the independent tour agents to set up tour packages and obtains Yen To's allocations of seats on each tour.

Recently, Yen To overbooked their popular Las Vegas tour, because their records overstated the number of available seats. Brenda and Sara want to avoid this situation in the future. They believe a database could be used to develop a tour management system (TMS) that would provide the necessary information in a timely manner.

Ashley analyzed Yen To's requirements for tour management and identified the following information that needs to be maintained for each tour:

Information	Example/Description
NAME OF TOUR	WHITEWATER RAFT
TOUR AGENT	BIG SKY TOUR
TOUR CODE	R43
DEPARTURE DATE	10/21/90
NUMBER OF DAYS	12 (always less than 100 days for any tour)
PRICE PER PERSON	$1595 (the highest price is less than $10,000)
SEATS SOLD	21 (always less than 100 seats for any tour)
SEATS OPEN	12 (always less than 100 seats for any tour)
TYPE	Type of tour: air, sea, bus
PASSPORT	Yes or no, is passport required

Sara and Brenda would like to be able to produce a Tour List using this database.

Tour List

The *Tour List* should list the tour name, tour agent, departure date, and price for each tour. Sara would like the tour list *arranged* so that tours are grouped together *by type*.

Brenda has suggested that a second report (the Representatives List) be produced from the database for the travel representatives. Each representative needs to know whether or not a passport is required.

Representatives List

The *Representatives List* should contain the tour code, tour name, tour agent, price, number of days, and whether a passport is required.

The Tour Management System (TMS) is to be used to help Brenda and Ashley with their seat allocation. The number of seats sold and open will be updated each day. Then a listing of all tours with a seat level below a certain amount (a Seat Request List) can be prepared for requesting additional seats. Ashley can use this list to contact the independent tour agents. The number of open seats can also be used to determine if a special discount should be offered on selected tours.

Seat Request List

Ashley wants this *Seat Request List* to contain the tour code, tour name, agent, seats sold, seats open, and price for the selected tours.

Sara and Ashley have worked with their travel representatives to assemble data for input to the database for the following tours:

TOUR	AGENT	CODE	DEPART	DAYS	PRICE	SOLD	OPEN	TYPE	PASS
JAMAICA COOLER	WILD ADVENT	C14	01/10/91	7	1490	16	3	SEA	Y
WHITE WATER RUN	SNAKE RIVER	A23	05/18/91	3	358	3	11	BUS	N
BAJA FISHING	WILD ADVENT	F12	06/18/91	10	1250	5	1	AIR	Y
WHALE WATCH	SEA WATCH	W19	02/19/92	4	455	2	23	SEA	N
AFRICAN SAFARI	WILD ADVENT	H92	07/10/92	14	4580	1	6	AIR	Y
CHERRY BLOSSOM	GRAY LINE	W63	04/14/91	5	476	15	3	BUS	N
LONDON TOWER	HMS TOURS	W73	09/05/91	11	2179	4	5	AIR	Y
OUTBACK	HMS TOURS	A78	11/12/91	12	2395	5	2	SEA	Y
SUPER BOWL	WILD ADVENT	B29	01/18/92	3	875	25	12	AIR	N
LAS VEGAS	WILD ADVENT	G53	01/05/92	4	349	7	21	AIR	N
GRAND CANYON	GRAY LINE	W43	06/21/91	7	370	3	14	BUS	N

Brenda has obtained a Database Planning Form for your use in designing the database in preparation for setting it up in dBASE.

DATABASE PLANNING FORM

Data Name	Data Type	Number of Characters for Largest Value	Dec(imal) Places
_____	_____	_____	_____
_____	_____	_____	_____
_____	_____	_____	_____
_____	_____	_____	_____
_____	_____	_____	_____
_____	_____	_____	_____
_____	_____	_____	_____
_____	_____	_____	_____
_____	_____	_____	_____
_____	_____	_____	_____

Brenda wants you to create a TMS for Yen To by carrying out the following tasks:

Task 1: Sketch out your database design with the database planning form before you access dBASE and begin defining its structure.

Task 2: Create a CATALOG named YENTO for organizing the files for this problem. The dBASE command is

.
_____

Task 3: Create the TOURS database. The dBASE command is

.
_____

Task 4: Enter the data provided for the database.

Task 5: Print the data for several TOURS from the EDIT data entry-screen with <Shift>+<PrtSc>

Time Estimates

Novice: 90 minutes

Intermediate: 60 minutes

Advanced: 45 minutes

(2)   Case: Silver Screen Video
      Business Problem: Inventory Management
      MIS Characteristics: Production/Operations
                           Operational Control

Silver Screen Video specializes in selling home video tapes of popular movies. Ernest "Ernie" Kasper opened the doors of Silver Screen in 1984. While Ernie directs the overall activities, Amy Lighthart manages the day-to-day operations of Silver Screen. Amy first started with Silver Screen in 1986 as a part-time sales associate and rapidly progressed to her current position of Operations Manager. Todd Powers is Silver Screen's assistant manager. Todd's duties include the acquisition of new video tapes. Ernie and Amy want to improve their system for keeping track of movies by using a database for producing several management reports.

Amy and Todd conducted an analysis of Silver Screen's requirements for movie management and determined that the following information needs to be maintained for each movie:

Information	Example/Description
NAME OF MOVIE	HORROR ON ELM ST
FILMMAKER	DISNEY FILMS
MOVIE LOCATION CODE	R43
YEAR PRODUCED	1989
PRICE PER MOVIE	$29.95 (the highest price is less than $100)
QUANTITY ON HAND	21 (always less than 100)
LAST ORDER DATE	10/10/89 (mm/dd/yy when order placed)
TYPE	Type of movie: comedy, drama, suspense, horror. The type is coded by the first three letters COM, DRA, SUS, HOR.
RATING	MPAA rating: G, PG, R, X, NR (not rated)
TV	Yes or no, whether or not movie has been shown on television

Amy and Ernie would like to be able to produce a Movie List using this database.

Movie List

The *Movie List* should list the movie name, filmmaker, year produced, type, rating, and price for each movie. Amy would like this movie list *arranged* so that movies are grouped together *by type*.

Amy has suggested that a second report (the Sales List) be produced from the database for use by the sales staff. The sales associates need to know the location of each movie.

Sales List

The *Sales List* should contain the location code, movie name, filmmaker, price, type, and rating.

The Movie Management System (MMS) is to be used to help Todd in ordering movies. The quantity of each movie on hand will be updated daily. Then a listing of all movies with stock levels below a certain amount (*Order List*) can be prepared for ordering.

Order List

Todd wants the Order List to contain the movie name, filmmaker, year produced, quantity on hand, last order date, and type.

Ernie and Amy also want to be able to list all the movies that have been shown on television to determine the use of special discounts and to make adjustments to order quantities.

TV List

This TV Listing should contain the movie name, year produced, price, type, rating, and whether or not the movie has been shown on TV. Amy obtained a Database Planning Form for your use in designing this database in preparation for setting it up in dBASE.

DATABASE PLANNING FORM

Data Name	Data Type	Number of Characters for Largest Value	Dec(imal) Places

Todd organized and collected data for input to the database for the following movies:

MOVIE	MAKER	LOC	YEAR	PRICE	QTY	L_ORDER	TYPE	RATE	TV
ROMANCE THE STONE	LUCAS FILMS	C14	1983	29.95	3	01/10/91	DRA	G	Y
NIGHTMARE ELM ST	TOUCH STONE	B21	1986	24.95	15	11/19/90	HOR	PG	N
WITNESS	TRI STAR	R16	1981	25.95	13	12/16/91	DRA	R	Y
RAINMAN	UNITED ARTS	D52	1988	49.95	16	02/21/90	DRA	R	N
HELLRAISER	PARAMOUNT	A02	1987	19.95	2	06/15/90	HOR	R	N
PET CEMETERY	KING FILMS	C16	1989	29.95	2	03/14/91	HOR	R	N
DRAGNET	HANKS FILMS	F25	1988	27.95	9	08/21/90	COM	PG	Y
PUNCHLINE	MGM FILMS	P49	1988	21.95	8	12/31/90	COM	PG	Y
JAWS IV	PARAMOUNT	S69	1987	29.95	9	07/02/91	SUS	R	N
TEMPLE OF DOOM	LUCAS FILMS	E20	1983	24.95	5	05/23/90	SUS	PG	Y
MONEY PIT	HANKS FILMS	L42	1982	29.95	6	01/20/90	COM	G	Y
TOP GUN	TRI STAR	H45	1986	19.95	14	10/11/91	DRA	PG	Y
DUNE	TOUCH STONE	M23	1984	17.95	2	09/25/90	SUS	G	N
DEAD POETS SOC	PARAMOUNT	I36	1989	39.95	14	08/01/91	COM	R	N
E T	LUCAS FILMS	N29	1980	16.95	16	04/03/90	SUS	G	Y

Ernie and Amy have assigned you the task of setting up this database and developing the desired reports as described below:

Task 1: Sketch out your database with a database planning form before you access dBASE and begin defining its structure with dBASE's DDL.

Task 2: Create a CATALOG named SILVER for organizing the files for this problem. The dBASE command is

Task 3: Create the MOVIES database. The dBASE command is

_____

Task 4: Enter the data furnished for the database.

Task 5: Print the data for several MOVIES from the EDIT data-entry screen with <Shift>+<PrtSc>

Time Estimates

Novice: 90 minutes

Intermediate: 60 minutes

Advanced: 45 minutes

D.1.19 Application Case

Case: Prestige Motor Center

Business Problem: Sales Support System

MIS Characteristics: Marketing

Operational control

Management Functions: Directing

Controlling

Tools Skills: Database design

Database creation

Data entry

Prestige Motor Center (PMC) is a supermarket for quality automobiles of distinction for discriminating customers. PMC holds the exclusive franchise for the automobiles from several manufacturers: Acura, Audi, BMW, Buick, Cadillac, Infiniti, and Porsche. Founded in 1973 by Jorge Haas, PMC recently moved into new quarters in the Regency Auto Mall located just off the interstate highway in the exclusive suburb of Bloomfield Hills, home to many successful business executives and community leaders. Jorge remains at the helm of PMC, serving as President and Chief Executive Officer. In relocating to the new facility, he organized PMC with three separate showrooms that specialize in American, German, and Japanese nameplate autos. One service department provides service to all the different nameplates. However, within service, Jorge arranged the mechanics by their specialization. When a customer's vehicle needs service, PMC's service department handles all their requirements from warranty service and routine maintenance to tires, batteries, and body shop repairs.

PMC established its reputation as a leader in providing customer service, as indicated by their motto:

"We don't sell automobiles, we provide trouble-free luxury personal transportation!"

Recently, *Automotive News* featured an article on PMC's success in marketing prestige automobiles. Jorge learned from his early experiences that selling luxury automobiles requires considerable personal attention. Whereas other dealers strive to merely sell automobiles, PMC focuses on selling the continued, uninterrupted use and service of a fine automobile. This is a relationship that begins before the sale and continues throughout the customer's ownership of a vehicle. For nearly every make of automobile sold by PMC, the level of service furnished to their customers exceeds that of the manufacturer's warranty.

As described by Daniel "Dan" Birge, the Sales Manager, "PMC values its customers and strives to maintain an ongoing relationship with them. Busy executives don't have the time to repeatedly return an automobile to the dealership for warranty service or routine maintenance." For these customers, PMC established a Gold Key Preferred Customer Service plan.

PMC's dedication to service is demonstrated by Edwin Kaufman's experience last week. Mr. Kaufman encountered difficulty in starting his Infiniti. He called Geraldine Jarvis, his personal account associate at PMC. (A personal account associate not only sells the vehicle but is responsible for arranging all subsequent service.) Gerri arranged to have Mr. Kaufman's car picked up at his office. The problem was diagnosed and corrected, and the car returned so Edwin could make his 4 P.M. meeting across town. Mr. Kaufman has come to expect and appreciate this level of service from PMC. As a Gold Key Preferred Customer, he has usually taken delivery of a new auto in the fall of each year for the past 15 years. Like Mr. Kaufman, many of PMC's customers are repeat customers as a result of the courteous service provided by their personal sales associates.

PMC offers Gold Key Preferred Customer Service on all the nameplates it sells. When a Gold Key Preferred Customer experiences difficulty, PMC will pick up the auto, service it, and return it, as illustrated by Mr. Kaufman's experience. If the service is expected to take more than a day, PMC supplies a substitute vehicle of equal or better quality, while their auto is being serviced or repaired. Gold Key Preferred Customers like to be well treated and are willing to pay for this attention. Popularity of the Gold Key Preferred program is reflected by its steady growth, with more than 1200 customers currently enrolled in this program.

Jorge and Dan want to ensure that the high level of customer satisfaction is continued. They believe that an information system to support their personal account associates would be beneficial in maintaining the desired level of customer satisfaction. By establishing a customer sales support database, information could be maintained on customer purchases and sales contacts. For this reason, the preliminary ideas for the database were discussed with PMC's personal account associates at their last weekly sales review meeting. Dan asked the account associates to describe how they might use such a database. Speaking for the associates, Gerri described how knowing information about the current vehicle owned by a customer and a customer's preference for the next auto would be beneficial in contacting customers and following up on sales leads. The account associates pointed out that knowing the date of the customer's last purchase would further their efforts in maintaining customer contacts and guide them in pursuing customers who might want to replace their current vehicle. Jorge and Dan described how the database should identify the account associate responsible for contacting each customer. Since account associates are expected to contact customers periodically, Dan wanted the database to contain a date of last contact for monitoring these activities.

Dan and Jorge discussed the development of a prototype database with the personal account associates. A prototype would contain the desired data fields, but would not have all of the data entered or instructions completed for using all aspects of the database. However, the prototype could be quickly developed so that they could begin working with it. This would allow them to examine the database and explore its operation before they finalized its development and implementation. If they should discover a significant deficiency in using the database, this could be readily corrected, resulting in a more useful information system for sales support.

After their meeting Dan and Jorge sat down and summarized their anticipated use of the database, which encompassed these activities:

- Contacting customers to follow up on satisfaction and anticipated automobile needs.
- Contacting customers for special preferred showings of new models.
- Reviewing personal account associate customer contacts for the account associate of the month award.

- Listing of customer with last contact date and account associate to monitor customer follow-up activities.

- Listing customers by account associate so each associate has a list of customers for which they are responsible.

- Listing customers by vehicle make so information furnished by the manufacturers can be passed on to the customer.

- Exploring trends in the nameplates of vehicles purchased by customers.

Jorge asked Melissa Prezzato, his Administrative Assistant, to pull together samples of the data that they would include in their prototype database. These records are as follows:

CUSTOMER NAME	PHONE NUMBER	MAKE LAST AUTO BOUGHT	PURCHASE DATE	PRICE OF AUTO	NEXT AUTO PREFERS MAKE	LAST CONTACT DATE	PERSONAL ACCT ASSOC ID
WILLY THEISEN	333-2020	AUDI	09/30/94	38300	INFINITI	10/04/94	JJH
LORI KARWACKI	445-6781	BMW	06/15/93	41500	PORSCHE	07/07/94	GHJ
APRIL YOUNG	321-9006	ACURA	04/21/93	28200	INFINITI	10/16/94	AMS
THELMA PORRECA	765-8721	BUICK	01/23/92	19100	CADILLAC	05/01/94	AMS
DEANNA STOEY	878-3356	AUDI	03/21/93	26300	BMW	06/18/94	GHJ
CHERYL NORTH	332-4591	PORSCHE	10/26/92	35200	PORSCHE	10/04/94	JJH
COREY WHITE	321-3554	CADILLAC	11/11/93	29600	CADILLAC	10/21/94	CAS
MARI MARTINEZ	447-5190	PORSCHE	12/03/93	65000	INFINITI	03/31/94	GHJ
DEBBIE GOMEZ	765-5212	BMW	01/23/92	23100	AUDI	04/11/94	CAS
MARK MOLONEY	333-5014	ACURA	02/14/93	26700	CADILLAC	09/09/94	AMS
ANDREW WARNER	322-2530	AUDI	03/11/92	22100	BMW	09/21/94	JJH
LANDIS BRZENK	447-4865	AUDI	09/26/93	21300	CADILLAC	10/07/94	CAS

DATABASE PLANNING FORM

Data Name	Data Type	Number of Characters for Largest Value	Dec(imal) Places

Tasks

1. Design the sales support database for PMC. Examine the example records to determine the size and type of each field. Use the Database Planning Form provided.

2. Access dBASE and create the database designed in Task 1. Use <Shift>+ <PrtSc> to produce a hard copy of the database structure.

3. Enter the data compiled by Melissa into the database. Use <Shift>+<PrtSc> to print, at least, three input records of your choice.

4. Review the prototype database created for PMC and suggest fields that should be added to this database. Write a summary describing these fields and explaining why each field should be included in the database. Consider any additional reports that might be produced from this database and include their description in your summary.

Time Estimates

Novice: 90 minutes

Intermediate: 60 minutes

Advanced: 45 minutes

LESSON

D.2

Reviewing and Modifying Data

CONTENT

- Accessing an Existing Database
- Reviewing and Changing Data
- Looking at Data
- Adding Records
- Deleting Records
- Obtaining a Hard Copy of a Database File
- Using History
- Abbreviated Commands
- When Things Go Wrong

D.2.1 Accessing an Existing Database

Once the WINES database has been created, the *next* time you enter dBASE you can access this as an existing database. Let's access the WINES database.

To access an existing database file

If you are at the CONTROL CENTER/ASSIST screen,

| **Press:** | `<Esc>` | Proceed to the DOT prompt |
| **Select:** | `Yes` | If requested, confirm exit |

From the dot prompt continue in this manner:

Enter:	`SET DEFAULT TO B:`	Set the default disk drive, if necessary
Enter:	`SET CATALOG TO GOLDEN`	
		Activate desired catalog
Enter:	`USE WINES`	Activate desired database file

Or specify the disk drive with the file name like this:

Enter: USE B:WINES   Activate desired database file

The USE command allows you to *access an existing database*. This command can be employed on entering dBASE or at the dot prompt any time you want to switch from one database file to another. The drive identifier for your data disk may be established automatically to the appropriate drive when you enter dBASE, as indicated in the Status Bar. If not, the SET DEFAULT TO command is recommended so you do not need to enter the letter identifying the disk drive every time you create or access a file, since the default drive is assumed if one is not specifically entered with a file name.

D.2.2   Reviewing and Changing Data

Data can be reviewed and/or changed by looking at either one record at a time or by looking at a screen full of records at once. The EDIT command is used to review and/or change an individual record at a time. The BROWSE command is used to view a screen full of records at one time. Any field may be changed in either EDIT or BROWSE by moving your cursor to the desired field and changing the value.

To edit individual records one at a time, from the dot prompt,

| To EDIT an individual record |

Enter: EDIT

Action: Using EDIT, find TAYLOR FARMS ZINFANDEL and change the price to 7.50. After entering the EDIT mode, use <PgDn> or <PgUp> to locate the desired record. Then use <up> or <down> to move to the PRICE field.

To exit from EDIT,

| To complete the edit activity and return to the dot prompt |

Press: <Ctrl>+<End>

To exit from the EDIT screen and save your changes to the data, the <Ctrl> + <End> is used. (In dBASE III+, the ˆ or hat character in the Help Area is used to indicate the use of the <Ctrl> key.)

To review a screen full of records at a time, from the dot prompt,

| To edit several records |

Enter: BROWSE

Action: Using BROWSE, find TAYLOR FARMS ZINFANDEL and change the price to 6.50. After entering the BROWSE mode, use <up> or <down> to locate the desired record. Then use <Enter>, <Tab>, <Shift>+<Tab>, <right>, or <left> to move to the desired field and character position within a record, or use the mouse pointer as described in Figure D.16.

An example of the screen displayed with the BROWSE command is illustrated in Figure D.17.

To exit from BROWSE,

Press: <Ctrl>+<End>   Exit from BROWSE and save any changes

Caution Alert!

When you exit from EDIT or BROWSE:

<Ctrl> + <End> saves any changes that were made!
<Esc> causes any changes to be lost!

Operation	Action
Move cursor to a field	Click the field
Move cursor to a position in a field	Click the position
Move highlight right or left one field	Click right or left browse table border
Move highlight to far right or far left field	Double-click right or left browse table border
Move highlight to preceding or following record	Click top or bottom browse table border
Move highlight up or down one page	Double-click top or bottom browse table border
Size the current column	Drag the right column border of that column to the left or right
Open a menu on the menu bar	Click the menu name
Close menu	Click outside the menu

FIGURE D.16. Mouse actions in BROWSE.

D.2.3 Looking at Data

Once data have been entered in a database, you can look at it on your screen. From the dot prompt proceed with the following command:

To DISPLAY data

Enter: DISPLAY ALL OFF

This instructs dBASE to display all records in your database file, as shown in Figure D.18. The OFF indicates that the record numbers, automatically assigned by dBASE, are not to be displayed.

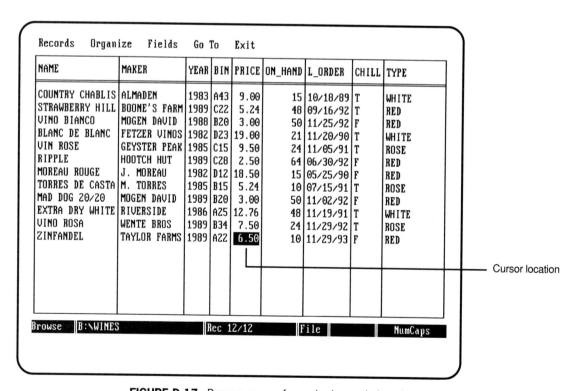

FIGURE D.17. Browse screen for reviewing and changing data.

No record numbers —

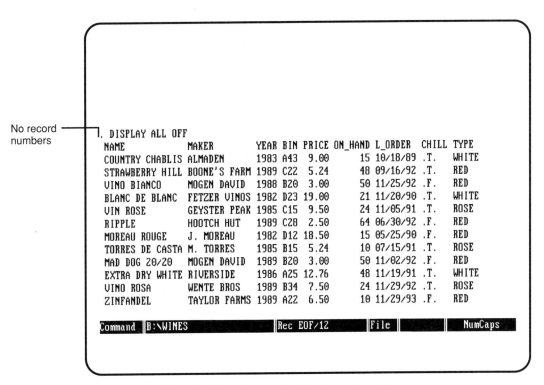

```
. DISPLAY ALL OFF
  NAME            MAKER        YEAR BIN PRICE ON_HAND L_ORDER  CHILL TYPE
  COUNTRY CHABLIS ALMADEN      1983 A43  9.00      15 10/18/89 .T.   WHITE
  STRAWBERRY HILL BOONE'S FARM 1989 C22  5.24      48 09/16/92 .T.   RED
  VINO BIANCO     MOGEN DAVID  1988 B20  3.00      50 11/25/92 .F.   RED
  BLANC DE BLANC  FETZER VINOS 1982 D23 19.00      21 11/20/90 .T.   WHITE
  VIN ROSE        GEYSTER PEAK 1985 C15  9.50      24 11/05/91 .T.   ROSE
  RIPPLE          HOOTCH HUT   1989 C28  2.50      64 06/30/92 .F.   RED
  MOREAU ROUGE    J. MOREAU    1982 D12 18.50      15 05/25/90 .F.   RED
  TORRES DE CASTA M. TORRES    1985 B15  5.24      10 07/15/91 .T.   ROSE
  MAD DOG 20/20   MOGEN DAVID  1989 B20  3.00      50 11/02/92 .F.   RED
  EXTRA DRY WHITE RIVERSIDE    1986 A25 12.76      48 11/19/91 .T.   WHITE
  VINO ROSA       WENTE BROS   1989 B34  7.50      24 11/29/92 .T.   ROSE
  ZINFANDEL       TAYLOR FARMS 1989 A22  6.50      10 11/29/93 .F.   RED
```

| Command | B:\WINES | | Rec EOF/12 | File | | NumCaps |

FIGURE D.18. Data displayed without record numbers.

The following command tells dBASE to display the records with the record numbers:

Enter: DISPLAY ALL   Desired activity

Or

VERSION III+

from the ASSIST menu, pick these options:

Select: Retrieve
Select: Display
Select: Specify scope
Select: ALL
Select: Execute the command

A similar display mode is *not* available from the Control Center of dBASE IV, but requires the use of a dBASE report, which will be described with other report writing features in subsequent lessons. In [VERSION IV], the Display Data option from the Control Center takes you to either the EDIT or BROWSE screen for viewing data by selecting these options:

VERSION IV

Select: WINES **under** Data   Desired database file
Select: Data Display   Desired option
Press: <F2>   Toggle between EDIT and BROWSE screens
Press: <Esc>   Exit from Data Display

An alternative to the DISPLAY command for looking at the data is to use the LIST command in this manner:

To display data using LIST	**Enter:**	LIST ALL OFF

The LIST command operates in the same manner as the DISPLAY command, except if you have more than one screen of data, LIST will *not* stop until the last record has been displayed. Some records may scroll off the top of your screen.

dBASE stores records in the order in which they are initially entered into the database. Each record is assigned a record number starting with 1. (dBASE uses record numbers merely as a mechanism for keeping track of records.) The OFF parameter indicates that record numbers are not to be displayed. dBASE allows you to position a record pointer that can be used in displaying or listing records in this manner:

To position the record pointer	**Enter:**	GO TOP	Position pointer at record number 1
	Enter:	DISPLAY	Look at record 1
	Enter:	GO BOTTOM	Position pointer at last record
	Enter:	DISPLAY	Look at last record
	Enter:	GO 5	Position pointer at record number 5
	Enter:	DISPLAY	Look at record 5

The commands

	Enter:	GO 6	Position record pointer
	Enter:	DISPLAY NEXT 3	Look at records

move the pointer to record number 6 and then display the next three records. These commands allow a group of records to be displayed or listed.

D.2.4 Adding Records

Records can be added to the database file using either the APPEND or BROWSE commands. APPEND permits entry of one record at a time using the same screen display as that used with EDIT. BROWSE allows records to be added to the bottom of the file using the BROWSE screen display.

To add records to a database file using APPEND	**Enter:**	APPEND
	Action:	Add these two records to the database:

NAME	MAKER	YEAR	BIN	PRICE	ON_HAND	L_ORDER	CHILL	TYPE
NAPA BURGUNDY	TAYLOR FARMS	1989	A23	6.50	24	07/17/93	.F.	RED
CABERNET	TAYLOR FARMS	1988	A25	7.00	24	11/29/91	.F.	RED

If your cursor is located at a blank EDIT screen,

	Press:	<PgUp>	Move to last record with data before leaving APPEND

To complete adding records and return to the dot prompt	Now, to exit from APPEND,		
	Press:	<Ctrl>+<End>	Return to the dot prompt

If you issue the <Ctrl> + <End> while your cursor is located at a blank record in APPEND, *this blank record is added to your database although you do not want it.* (See Section D.2.9 for a description of how to remove a blank record.)

Records may also be added to your existing database using the BROWSE screen. At the dot prompt,

To add records to a database file with BROWSE	**Enter:**	BROWSE	
	Action:	Using the cursor, move to the bottom of the file.	
	Press:	<down>	Attempt to go past the bottom
	Enter:	<Y>	When requested
	Action:	Now, add these two records to the database:	

NAME	MAKER	YEAR	BIN	PRICE	ON_HAND	L_ORDER	CHILL	TYPE
RED TABLE WINE	TAYLOR FARMS	1989	A26	4.76	11	11/29/93	.F.	RED
BOONE'S FARM	SMOTHERS BRO	1988	A88	13.80	10	05/08/92	.F.	ROSE

Action: Move to a nonblank record before leaving BROWSE.

To complete adding records and return to the dot prompt	Now, exit from BROWSE.		
	Press:	<Ctrl>+<End>	Return to the dot prompt

As with APPEND, if you issue the <Ctrl> + <End> while your cursor is located at a blank record in BROWSE, this blank record is added to your database although you do not want it.

Caution Alert!	Do *not* issue <Ctrl> + <End> to exit from APPEND or BROWSE when your cursor is located on a *blank record,* since this blank record will be included in your database!

D.2.5 Deleting Records

Records can be marked for deletion under either the EDIT or BROWSE mode of data display. With EDIT, you use <PgDn> and <PgUp> to move to the record you want to delete. With BROWSE, <up> and <down> can be used to position the cursor at the record you want to mark for deletion.

Action: EDIT the database and move to BOONE'S FARM, the desired record for deletion.

To mark a record for deletion	**Press:**	<Ctrl>+<U>	DEL appears in the Status Bar to indicate the record is "marked for deletion."
	Action:	Exit from the EDIT mode of data display.	
	Action:	Access the database with BROWSE and move to BOONE'S FARM, the desired record.	

To undelete a record previously marked for deletion	**Press:**	<Ctrl>+<U>	DEL disappears in the Status Bar to indicate the record is no longer "marked for deletion."

Keypoint!   Delete is a toggle! Pressed the first time it marks the record for deletion. The second time it "undeletes" the records!

Action: Select a couple of other records; then delete *and* undelete them.

Watch DEL appear/disappear in the Status Bar when a record is toggled between the marked/unmarked for deletion status (Figure D.19).

To permanently delete database records

Records are permanently removed from the database file with the PACK command. Any records marked for deletion are removed when the PACK command is entered at the dot prompt. Until then, they can be undeleted. You may invoke EDIT and BROWSE as many times as you want before issuing the PACK command.

Action: Since you will want to use all of the records you have entered for other queries on the WINES database, be sure *no* records are marked for deletion when you exit from EDIT or BROWSE.

Keypoint!   Records marked for deletion may be *undeleted* until the PACK; command has been executed to *permanently remove* the records marked for deletion from the database!

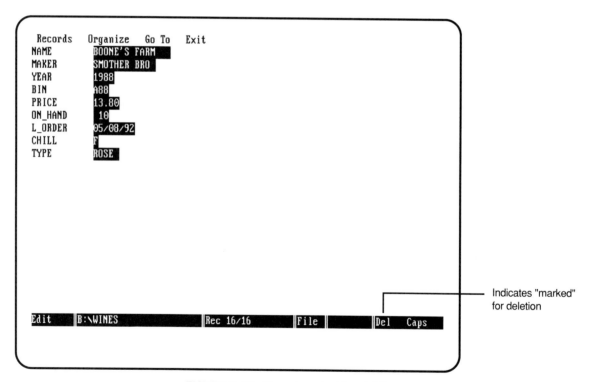

FIGURE D.19. Record marked for deletion.

D.2.6   Obtaining a Hard Copy of a Database File

To obtain a hard copy, of your data use this command:

To produce a hard copy list	**Enter:**	LIST ALL OFF TO PRINT

Here the TO PRINT will cause the data to be written to the printer.
Use this command to advance the page after printing:

To advance page after printing	**Enter:**	EJECT

The TO PRINT may also be used with the DISPLAY command in directing the results of the DISPLAY to your printer as they are shown on your screen.

The EJECT command can also be used when you are doing a screen dump with the <Shift>+<PrtSc>. That is, after you press the <Shift>+<PrtSc> to capture your screen, then enter the EJECT command to advance the paper to the top of a new page. By using EJECT, you do not need to manually advance the page.

D.2.7   Using History

History is a dBASE feature that stores your previously executed dot prompt commands, but not your menu choices, for *reuse*. History normally keeps a list of up to the last 20 commands that you have entered and executed in a **buffer** or storage area. At the dot prompt, you can scroll through this list of commands using the <up> and <down> keys. Let's use the history feature by first executing a series of commands.

Enter:	USE WINES	
Enter:	DISPLAY ALL OFF	
Enter:	GO TO 6	
Enter:	DISPLAY NEXT 3	
Enter:	BROWSE	
Action:	Exit from BROWSE	

After you exit from the BROWSE and return to the dot prompt, the history buffers can be accessed. Now let's use history.

To look at commands stored in history buffer	**Press:**	<up>	BROWSE is displayed
	Press:	<up>	NEXT 3 is displayed
	Press:	<up>	GO TO 6 is displayed
	Press:	<down>	NEXT 3 is displayed
	Press:	<down>	BROWSE is displayed
	Press:	<Enter>	BROWSE is executed

If you enter a command incorrectly, such as:

To use history	**Enter:**	DIPSALY ALL OFF

Then, <up> would redisplay the command.

Press:	<up>	
Action:	Make edit changes to the command and re-execute it.	

Or after executing a command such as:

Enter: LIST ALL OFF   List only to your screen

You could use history to recall the command and add TO PRINT at the end of the command in this manner:

Press: <up>   Display previous command

Move to: cursor to left of OFF

Type: TO PRINT

Press: <Enter>   Execute the revised command producing a
                                             hard copy

And the revised command is executed. Using history, *you only need to type the change* to this command rather than the entire command.

Keypoint! | History is a convenient method of recalling a previously executed command for reuse!

D.2.8   Abbreviated Commands

dBASE permits the use of shortened commands. Only the first four (4) characters are required for a command, since they uniquely identify the command word.
The command: DISPLAY ALL OFF

To use abbreviated
commands

Can be entered as: DISP ALL OFF
Or the command: MODIFY STRUCTURE
Can be entered as: MODI STRU
     Make use of abbreviated commands to reduce your typing effort and also to reduce spelling errors when you are entering your dBASE commands.

D.2.9 When Things Go Wrong

Several situations may occur when you are revising and displaying data. A couple of the more frequent difficulties and how to recover from them are described here.

1. For some reason you were returned to the dot prompt before completing your EDIT, APPEND, or BROWSE operations to change data.

   a. Reissue the EDIT, APPEND, or BROWSE command. This may be accomplished using history.

   b. Review your data to be sure that no changes were lost.

   c. Continue making changes to your data.

2. One or more records with no data appear in your database when you use the DISPLAY, LIST, BROWSE, or EDIT operations, as illustrated in Figure D.20. This indicates that you have a record where, at least, one of the character fields contains the character <space>, while the other fields contain *no* data. This makes the entire record appears as if it contains *no* data, but dBASE interprets a <space> as a legal character.

   a. Use EDIT or BROWSE and move to the "blank" record.

   b. Use <Ctrl>+<U> to "mark" the record for deletion.

   c. Exit from EDIT or BROWSE with <Ctrl>+<End>.

   d. Use PACK to permanently remove this unwanted record from your database.

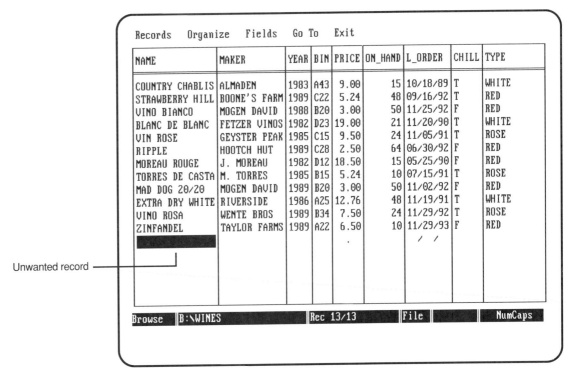

Unwanted record

FIGURE D.20. Unwanted blank record at bottom of database.

D.2.10   Lesson Summary

- An existing database file is accessed with the USE command.
- The SET DEFAULT TO command is used to establish the desired disk drive of your data disk when the drive letter is not entered with the file name.
- The SET CATALOG TO command activates the desired catalog for your application.
- Records can be reviewed and revised with the EDIT and BROWSE commands. EDIT displays one record at a time, whereas BROWSE presents a screen full of records.
- DISPLAY and LIST cause database records to be displayed on the screen. Record numbers are suppressed with the OFF option.
- Records can be added to an existing database with APPEND, BROWSE, or EDIT.
- In the EDIT and BROWSE modes, records can be marked for deletion. However, they remain in the database until the PACK command is executed.
- A hard copy of data can be obtained by using TO PRINT with the LIST command.
- History stores up to the last 20 commands you have executed. These commands may be accessed for reuse. A command containing an error can be accessed and edited before reexecuting it.
- Only the first four (4) characters of a dBASE command word need to be entered.

D.2.11   Practice Tutorial

Look at and revise data in the Wine Management System by entering the commands and data as described in this Lesson as a guided activity in a hands-on manner. Using your Data Disk, access the WINES database before you begin.

Task 1: Look at the data with the DISPLAY, LIST, EDIT, BROWSE, and GO to commands.

Task 2: Add the four (4) records for Napa Burgundy, Cabernet, Red Table Wine, and Boone's Farm.

Task 3: Produce a hard copy listing of all the records in the database file by listing them to the printer.

Time Estimates

Novice: 60 minutes

Intermediate: 45 minutes

Advanced: 30 minutes

D.2.12   Practice Exercises

(1)   **Case: Best Buy Products**

Business Problem: Merchandising Management

MIS Characteristics: Marketing

Managerial Control

Stewart Kassen is the merchandising manager at Best Buy Products. Best Buy is a catalog showroom that provides its customers with high-quality, name-brand merchandise at discount prices. Each year, Best Buy produces a catalog from which customers select their merchandise. Customers may shop in person at a catalog showroom, may phone their order to a store, or may order by mail. Stewart is responsible for both managing Best Buy's inventory and preparing its annual catalog. To assist in these efforts, he designed a database that contains fields described by the following data dictionary definition:

Field Name	Description
PRODUCT	Product identification/catalog number
DESCRIPT	Product description
LOC	Warehouse location
QTY	Current inventory quantity
LPRICE	Product list price
SPRICE	Product selling price
SHIP	Indicator of whether or not a mail order item can be shipped to the customer or must be picked up
L_ORDER	Date last order received from manufacturer

Best Buy regularly adds new products and removes obsolete products from its available catalog merchandise. Stewart wants you to perform the following tasks in updating their database:

Task 1: Access the BESTBUY.DBF database file in the EXERCISE catalog. After reviewing the structure and data, produce a hard copy listing of the database structure for your reference. The dBASE commands are

- _____

- _____

- _____

Task 2: On Stewart's return from the semiannual consumer's electronics show and convention, he ordered several new products to be added to Best Buy's catalog merchandise. Add the records for these products to the database:

PRODUCT	DESCRIPT	TYPE	LOC	QTY	LPRICE	SPRICE	SHIP	L_ORDER
441546C	SONY DISCMAN	AUD	B027	4	229.95	199.85	.T.	08/27/95
514696A	GOLDSTAR VCR	TV	B008	4	279.95	238.75	.T.	08/18/95
841358B	STEALTH CD CARRIER	MISC	A072	10	29.95	25.85	.T.	10/04/95
519278B	RCA 13 COLORTRACK TV	TV	A096	23	329.95	299.90	.T.	08/22/95

My dBASE command to begin entering data is

- _____

Task 3: Several products have been discontinued. Stewart wants you to delete the records from the database for the following PRODUCT numbers:
514733C   514865A   519510B   519715A
Permanently remove these records from Best Buy's database. The dBASE commands are

- _____

- _____

- _____

Task 4: Produce a hard copy listing of all the remaining records in the database. My dBASE command is

.

_____

Time Estimates

Novice: 90 minutes

Intermediate: 60 minutes

Advanced: 45 minutes

(2)   Case: Rent-A-Worker

Business Problem: Temporary Employment Services

MIS Characteristics: Human Resources

Managerial Control

Rent-A-Worker is an employment contractor providing temporary help to a variety of businesses, such as banks, insurance companies, medical services, and government offices. Their specialized services are grouped into four major categories:

OFF—office services, clerical, secretarial, word processing

IND—light industrial, laborers

MAR—sales clerks, marketing demonstration, telemarketing

IDP—data entry, information specialist, data processing operators

Lorna Zomer, director of employee placement, maintains a database of their temporary employees. Their database contains fields as described by this data dictionary definition:

Field Name	Description
SSN	Social security number
LNAME	Last name
FNAME	First name
MI	Middle initial
PHONE	Phone number
SKILL	Skill category: OFF, IND, MAR, IDP
RATE	Pay rate per hour
EXP	Experience in years
DOH	Date of first hire
JOB	A status indicator of whether or not the individual is currently on a job assignment

Rent-A-Work has experienced some turnover in its employees. Lorna wants you to carry out the following tasks in updating their database:

Task 1: Access the RENTWORK.DBF database file in the EXERCISE catalog. Review the structure and data. Then produce a hard copy listing of the database structure for your reference. The dBASE commands are

.

_____

.

_____

.

_____

Task 2: Lorna has signed employment agreements with several additional individuals. Add the records for these temporaries to the database:

SSN	LNAME	FNAME	MI	PHONE	SKILL	RATE	EXP	DOH	JOB
101446287	MAJERLE	LIONEL	H	756-3889	IDP	19.00	8.0	05/23/84	.T.
429611238	QUASARANO	KRISTIN	L	287-6207	MAR	11.50	3.5	10/10/89	.T.
219683383	MIOTKA	RYAN	A	289-5023	OFF	12.00	3.5	09/09/89	.T.
337056876	ORTEGA	CARA	N	756-6011	MAR	10.00	1.0	07/10/93	.F.

My dBASE command to begin entering data is

. _____

Task 3: Several temporaries have found permanent employment. Lorna wants you to delete the records from the database for individuals with the following LNAME:

AGOSTA   BONINI   MOJICA   SCHEMBRI

Permanently remove these records from Rent-A-Worker's database. The dBASE commands are

. _____

. _____

. _____

Task 4: Produce a hard copy listing of all of the remaining records in the database. My dBASE command for this is

. _____

Time Estimates

Novice: 90 minutes

Intermediate: 60 minutes

Advanced: 45 minutes

(3)   Case: Overland Trucking

Business Problem: Shipment Tracking
MIS Characteristics: Production/Operations
Operational Control

Debra Mendoza manages the dispatch operations of Overland Trucking. Whenever customers want to check on the status of a shipment, they phone the dispatch office. Fred Marcini and Stuart Varney, Overland's dispatchers, use their shipment tracking database to determine the status of the customer's shipment. Fred and Stuart worked with Debbie in designing their database, which contains the fields described by this data dictionary definition:

Field Name	Description
S_ID	Shipment tracking identification number
CUSTOMER	Name of customer receiving shipment
SENT_FROM	Origination city of shipment
SENT_TO	Destination city of shipment
TRUCK	Identification number of truck hauling shipment
WEIGHT	Weight of shipment
SHIP_DATE	Planned date for shipment to leave the origination city
TARIFF	Shipment fee
PRE	Indicator of whether or not the tariff was prepaid
HAZ	Indicator of whether or not the shipment contains hazardous materials

Perform the following tasks in modifying the content of Overland's database:

Task 1: Access the OVERLAND.DBF database file in the EXERCISE catalog and review the structure and data. Produce a hard copy listing of the database structure for your reference. The dBASE commands are

. _____

. _____

. _____

Task 2: Fred scheduled several additional shipments. Add the records for these shipments to the database:

S_ID	CUSTOMER	SENT_FROM	SENT_TO	TRUCK	WEIGHT	SHIP_DATE	TARIFF	PRE	HAZ
7699	GOLD COAST	BOSTON	ALBANY	3741J	2590	11/25/93	527.00	.F.	.F.
7711	OLD MARKET	NEW YORK	BOSTON	3741J	280	11/21/93	133.00	.T.	.F.
7821	LAZY LEOPARD	ATLANTA	MIAMI	3855J	300	11/19/93	99.00	.T.	.F.
7637	GREEN ONION	OMAHA	DALLAS	3987J	1100	11/21/93	372.50	.T.	.F.

My dBASE command to start entering these data is

. _____

Task 3: Stuart wants you to delete the records from the database with the following S_ID:

7625   7764   7802   7809

Permanently remove these records from Overland's database. The dBASE commands are

. _____

. _____

. _____

Task 4: Produce a hard copy listing of all the remaining records in the database. The command for this listing is

. _____

Time Estimates

Novice: 90 minutes

Intermediate: 60 minutes

Advanced: 45 minutes

D.2.13 Comprehensive Problems

(1)   Case: Yen To Travel (continued)

Brenda and Ashley have made arrangements to add several tours to those available from Yen To Travel. These tours, which Sara wants included in the database, are as follows:

TOUR	AGENT	CODE	DEPART	DAYS	PRICE	SOLD	OPEN	TYPE	PASS
ROCKY MTN HIGH	WILD ADVENT	D80	01/15/92	7	750	6	2	BUS	N
HOLLYWOOD STAR	GRAY LINE	R54	06/23/91	12	1375	21	9	AIR	N
FRENCH RIVIERA	WILD ADVENT	M48	06/19/92	10	2356	29	1	SEA	Y
BIG APPLE	SEA WATCH	A59	04/22/92	10	566	14	5	BUS	N

Task 1: Access the database file in the YENTO catalog. The dBASE commands are

.

_____

.

_____

Task 2: Look at the data with the DISPLAY, LIST, EDIT, BROWSE, and GOTO commands. Screen print the results of the DISPLAY and BROWSE commands.

Task 3: Add the four (4) records provided above to the database. My dBASE command to begin entering data is

.

_____

Task 4: Produce a hard copy listing of all records in the database. My dBASE command is

.

_____

Time Estimates

Novice: 90 minutes

Intermediate: 60 minutes

Advanced: 45 minutes

(2)   Case: Silver Screen Video (continued)

Todd recently received a shipment for Silver Screen Video containing several new movies. Amy wants you to include these movies in their database:

MOVIE	MAKER	LOC	YEAR	PRICE	QTY	L_ORDER	TYPE	RATE	TV
MOONSTRUCK	KING FILMS	J91	1987	29.95	10	05/05/90	DRA	PG	Y
THE ACCUSED	TRI STAR	J88	1988	27.95	7	06/02/91	DRA	R	N
SEVENTH SIGN	LUCAS FILMS	K72	1987	22.95	8	09/11/90	DRA	R	Y
ABOUT LAST NIGHT	TRI STAR	P39	1985	21.95	4	10/04/90	COM	R	N

Task 1: Access the database file in the SILVER catalog. The dBASE commands are

· _____

· _____

Task 2: Look at the data with the DISPLAY, LIST, EDIT, BROWSE, and GOTO commands. Screen print the results of the DISPLAY and BROWSE commands.

Task 3: Add the four (4) records provided above to the database. My dBASE command to begin entering data is

· _____

Task 4: Produce a hard copy listing of all records in the database. My dBASE command is

· _____

Time Estimates

Novice: 90 minutes

Intermediate: 60 minutes

Advanced: 45 minutes

D.2.14 Application Case

Case: Good Morning Products

  Business Problem: Checkbook Ledger
  MIS Characteristics: Finance
                  Operational Control
  Management Functions: Controlling
  Tools Skills: Displaying data
        Printing data
        Entering data
        Revising data

Good Morning Products (GMP) is an international bottler and distributor of the Liquid Gold brand of fresh orange juice. Good Morning Products, located in Citrus Grove Valley, California, was established in 1919 by Charles "Frosty" Frost. Frosty has served as the Chairman of the Board of Good Morning Products for the past 15 years. The business is family owned and is operated with Matthew "Crush" Frost as President and Chief Executive Officer (CEO), Kimberly Frost-Moore as Vice President and General Manager, Christopher Frost as Treasurer, and Jennifer Frost-Krone as Secretary.

The Board of Directors of Good Morning Products had decided to build a branch plant in Florida to expand their production of Liquid Gold. The demand from their international operations has increased substantially and this location facilitates their export activities.

Last month, Chris spent the better part of one week "closing" the books on the prior month and reconciling their bank statement. He is convinced that there is a better method for tracking Good Morning's revenues and expenses.

With the expansion of Good Morning's operations, Chris and Kim are exploring alternatives for maintaining their checkbook ledger. This ledger contains a listing of all cash transactions conducted by the company. With the expansion of the Florida plant, a checkbook ledger will need to be maintained in both locations. Chris wants to explore the use of a prototype ledger system before arranging for its implementation at both locations.

Kim and Chris have reviewed the chart of accounts used by Good Morning Products and determined that it is adequate to meet the management reporting requirements of both plants. Their chart of accounts is as follows:

Account Number	Description
101	Sales Revenue
201	Cost of Sales
301	Salaries
302	Benefits
401	Administrative Expense
402	Interest
410	Depreciation

Before they go "live" with their system, Chris would like to take a more conservative approach by building a prototype of the system that he could examine and fine-tune. This would give him the opportunity to enter data into the checkbook ledger and to explore making any necessary changes and revisions. Chris wants to try out the system with data for the last couple of months which Jennifer has assembled and loaded into their prototype database, LEDGER.DBF.

Tasks

1. Access the LEDGER.DBF database file in the CASES catalog and review its structure. Use <Shift>+<PrtSC> to obtain a hard copy of the structure.

2. Display all the records in the database on your screen and then produce a hard copy listing of the records.

3. Generate another hard copy listing of the database after adding these records to it:

REF_NO	DATE	ACCT	NAME	AMT
9111	11/09/92	101	Hinky Dinky Foods	3210.00
126	11/10/92	201	Down River Growers	−4712.00
127	11/11/92	401	Turkey Express	−411.70
9112	11/11/92	101	Bag 'N' Save	1107.90

4. Modify records in the database as follows:

   (a) For record number 5, change the amount (AMT) to: −423.00

   (b) For the record with account (ACCT) number 201, change the name from

   Computers Plus

   to

   Golden Triangle Orchards

   (c) For record number 14, Chris wants to change the account (ACCT) number to A41. What happens when you attempt this revision? If the account (ACCT) number is *not* accepted, then leave the old account number.

   (d) Produce a hard copy listing of the revised database.

5. Remove records from the database as follows:

   (a) Mark record number 9 for deletion.

   (b) Mark the records for account (ACCT) number 401 for deletion.

   (c) Produce a hard copy listing of this database.

   (d) Enter the command SET DELETE ON and produce a second hard copy listing of the database.

   (e) What is the difference between the listing produced in (c) and that created in (d)?

   (f) Perform a PACK on the database, enter the command SET DELETE OFF, and produce a hard copy listing of the database.

   (g) What is the difference between the listing produced in (d) and the output realized in (f)?

6. (*Optional*)   Compare this database developed in dBASE for this lesson to that illustrated in "Using Lotus 1-2-3," Lesson L.11. Write a summary describing the similarities and differences between this application implemented in dBASE and that created in Lotus 1-2-3.

Time Estimates

Novice: 90 minutes

Intermediate: 60 minutes

Advanced: 45 minutes

Querying a Database

CONTENT

- Using a Database to Answer Questions
- Accessing an Existing Database with Prompting
- Displaying Selected Records
- Summing Values in a Field
- Counting Database Records
- Computing the Average of Values in a Field
- Using Memory Variables in Computations
- Revising Values in a Field
- When Things Go Wrong

D.3.1 Using the Database to Answer Questions

At Golden Gourmet, Bert, Annie, Beth, and Lou have formulated a number of questions they would like to address by using their WINES database. These questions underscore the reasons for which data are stored in a database. Some of the potential management questions that can, in general, be explored with a database are illustrated by these examples.

Keypoint!
> A primary reason for maintaining a database is to obtain management information by querying the database!

The questions to be addressed with the Golden Gourmet's wine management system include the following:

1. What red wines do they have in stock?
2. How much is the VIN ROSE?
3. Which wines have to be chilled before serving?
4. Which wines should be reordered? (Wines with less than 24 bottles on hand.)

5. What RED wines do they have for less than $10 a bottle?

6. Which WHITE wines are more than $10 a bottle *and* which ROSE wines are less than $8 a bottle? (Produce a single display showing the results of this query).

7. How many bottles of wine do they have on hand?

8. What is the total investment in wines?

9. What is their investment in white wines?

10. How many different types of red wine do they have?

11. What is the average number of bottles in inventory?

12. What is the average price of a bottle of wine on the menu?

13. What is the average price of a bottle of wine in the wine cellar?

14. Increase the price of all wines by $1 per bottle.

15. Have a sale (special) on red wines of $1 off per bottle.

Each of these questions is addressed individually in demonstrating the operation and capabilities of dBASE's data manipulation language (DML).

D.3.2 Accessing an Existing Database with Prompting

When you go to access a previously created catalog or database file, you may not remember the names you assigned to these files. dBASE provides a means for you to obtain a list of the existing catalogs and/or database files from which you can then pick the desired file. To access the GOLDEN catalog and WINES database file using menu prompting, you should proceed in this manner:

To obtain a list of available catalogs

Action:	Activate dBASE and obtain the dot prompt.	
Enter:	`SET DEFAULT TO B:`	Specify your default disk drive
Enter:	`SET CATALOG TO ?`	Request list of available catalogs

The "?" causes a screen to appear, as illustrated in Figure D.21, with a selection window containing a list of the available catalog files.

Move to:	`GOLDEN`	Desired catalog
Press:	`<Enter>`	Select catalog

To obtain a list of available database files

Enter:	`USE ?`	Request list of available database files in the active catalog

Again, the "?" causes another screen to appear, as shown in Figure D.22, with a window containing a list of the database files that belong to the selected catalog. The name of the catalog appears at the top of the selection window for your reference.

Move to:	`WINES`	Desired database file
Press:	`<Enter>`	Select database file

The desired database is activated, as indicated in the Status Bar.

The "?" in the SET CATALOG TO and the USE commands provides a convenient method for determining which catalog and database files are available on your disk. Make use of this form of these commands whenever you need to be prompted with a list of available files.

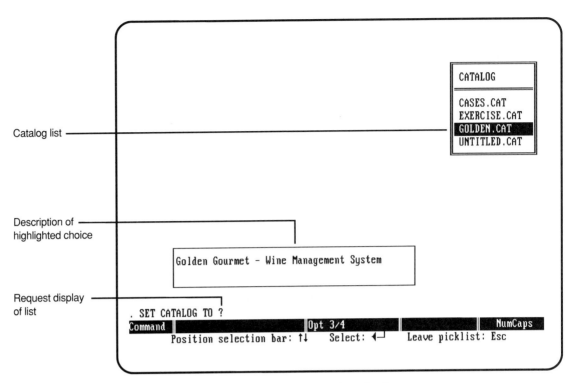

Catalog list

Description of highlighted choice

Request display of list

FIGURE D.21. List of catalogs for selection.

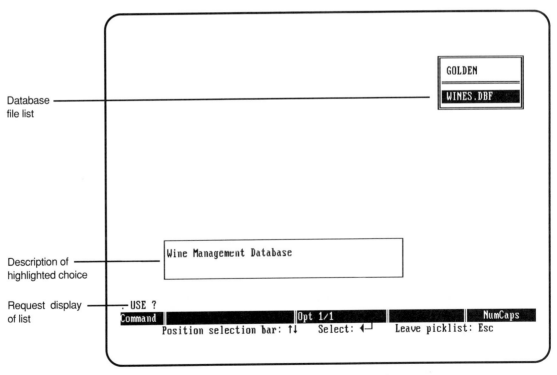

Database file list

Description of highlighted choice

Request display of list

FIGURE D.22. List of database files for selection.

D.3.3   Displaying Selected Records

As each question is explored, the CLEAR command may be used to clear your screen before you execute the commands for the next query. Also, remember that a hard copy of the output results can be sent directly to your printer by including *TO PRINT at the end of either a DISPLAY or LIST command*. The questions for the Golden Gourmet are explored in this manner:

1. What red wines do they have in stock?

   Enter: `DISPLAY ALL OFF FOR TYPE = 'RED'`

   Or if you only want to display the NAME, MAKER, YEAR, PRICE, and TYPE fields, use this command:

   Enter (this command must be typed all on one line):

   `DISPLAY ALL NAME, MAKER, YEAR, PRICE, TYPE FOR TYPE = 'RED'`

   Here, RED is enclosed in apostrophes because it is CHARACTER type data. The result is shown in Figure D.23.

> **To display selected records for a character field**

> **To display selected fields for selected records**

> *Keypoint!*   CHARACTER data in a FOR condition are enclosed in either apostrophes or quotes! The choice is yours, just be consistent within a command!

> *Caution Alert!*   CHARACTER data must have the upper- and lowercase letters matched. *RED, Red,* and *red* are all different character values. No result will be displayed if you enter "Red" or "red" when the value is "RED" in your database!

2. How much is the vin rosé?

   Enter: `DISPLAY ALL OFF NAME, PRICE FOR NAME = 'VIN ROSE'`

   The output is

NAME	PRICE
VIN ROSE	9.50

```
. DISPLAY ALL NAME, MAKER, YEAR, PRICE, TYPE FOR TYPE = 'red'
. (note -- no records displayed)
.
. DISPLAY ALL NAME, MAKER, YEAR, PRICE, TYPE FOR TYPE = 'RED'
Record#  NAME           MAKER          YEAR PRICE TYPE
      2  STRAWBERRY HILL BOONE'S FARM  1989   5.24 RED
      3  VINO BIANCO    MOGEN DAVID    1988   3.00 RED
      6  RIPPLE         HOOTCH HUT     1989   2.50 RED
      7  MOREAU ROUGE   J. MOREAU      1982  18.50 RED
      9  MAD DOG 20/20  MOGEN DAVID    1989   3.00 RED          Desired value
     12  ZINFANDEL      TAYLOR FARMS   1989   6.50 RED
     13  NAPA BURGUNDY  TAYLOR FARMS   1989   6.50 RED
     14  CABERNET       TAYLOR FARMS   1988   7.00 RED
     15  RED TABLE WINE TAYLOR FARMS   1989   4.76 RED
.
Command  B:\WINES              Rec EOF/16       File           NumCaps
```

FIGURE D.23. Red wines in stock.

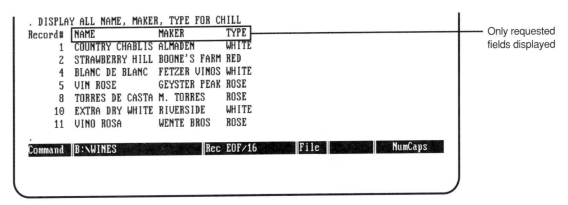

FIGURE D.24. Chilled wines.

3. Which wines have to be chilled before serving?

Enter:	DISPLAY ALL NAME, MAKER, TYPE FOR CHILL

To display selected records for a logical field

This yields the display in Figure D.24.

  Since CHILL is a logical field, specifying FOR CHILL indicates dBASE is to find *all records where CHILL is true or yes.* Only the field name of a logical field is specified in the condition—no relational operator or comparison value is included. This is because *a logical field already has a value of "true" or "false."* All other conditions require an evaluation to determine if they are either "true" or "false."

  To find all wines that do *not* need to be chilled, a display is requested in this manner:

Enter:	DISPLAY ALL NAME, MAKER, TYPE FOR .NOT. CHILL

4. Which wines should be reordered? (Wines with less than 24 bottles on hand.)

Enter:	DISPLAY ALL OFF NAME, MAKER, ON_HAND FOR ON_HAND<24

To display selected records for a numeric field

The result appears in Figure D.25. In this command, notice how the ON-HAND field is listed both as a field to be displayed' *and* as a field in the FOR CONDITION. Whenever fields are requested by listing them, the field involved in the FOR CONDITION needs to be included in the list *if you want to see the values used in testing the FOR CONDITION.*

5. What red wines do they have for less then $10 a bottle?

Enter:	DISPLAY ALL OFF FOR TYPE = 'RED' .AND. PRICE < 10

To display selected records using two field values

The selected wines are displayed as shown in FigureD.26.

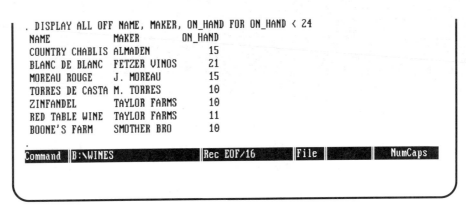

FIGURE D.25. Wines to be reordered.

```
. DISPLAY OFF FOR TYPE = 'RED' .AND. PRICE < 10
NAME            MAKER        YEAR BIN PRICE ON_HAND L_ORDER CHILL TYPE
STRAWBERRY HILL BOONE'S FARM 1989 C22 5.24      48 09/16/92 .T.   RED
VINO BIANCO     MOGEN DAVID  1988 B20 3.00      50 11/25/92 .F.   RED
RIPPLE          HOOTCH HUT   1989 C28 2.50      64 06/30/92 .F.   RED
MAD DOG 20/20   MOGEN DAVID  1989 B20 3.00      50 11/02/92 .F.   RED
ZINFANDEL       TAYLOR FARMS 1989 A22 6.50      10 11/29/93 .F.   RED
NAPA BURGUNDY   TAYLOR FARMS 1989 A23 6.50      24 07/17/93 .F.   RED
CABERNET        TAYLOR FARMS 1988 A25 7.00      24 11/29/91 .F.   RED
RED TABLE WINE  TAYLOR FARMS 1989 A26 4.76      11 11/29/93 .F.   RED
.
Command ‖B:\WINES            ‖Rec EOF/16    ‖File ‖      ‖   NumCaps
```

FIGURE D.26. Red wines under $10.

6. Which white wines are more than $10 a bottle and which rose wines are less than $8 a bottle? (Produce a single display showing the results of this query.)

To display selected records using several logical operators

Enter (this command must be typed all on one line):

```
DISPLAY ALL OFF FOR (TYPE = 'WHITE' .AND. PRICE > 10)
              .OR. (TYPE = 'ROSE' .AND. PRICE < 8)
```

Observe the use of parentheses to group the two conditions. This ensures that white *and* greater than $10 are evaluated separately from rose *and* less than $8. When several conditions are used in a single query like this, parentheses should be included to specify their order of evaluation, with conditions inside the parentheses evaluated first. The selected wines satisfying this query appear as shown in Figure D.27.

The DISPLAY command is used to select a specified set of rows and/or columns from the database relation.

A general form of the DISPLAY command is

To display records— reference

DISPLAY [scope] [ON/OFF] [expression list] [FOR condition] [TO PRINT]

where **scope** is the set of records such as ALL, 15, or NEXT 3

ON/OFF indicates the display of record numbers

expression list is the set of fields

FOR condition is a comparison to specified values

TO PRINT is an option to direct the output to your printer

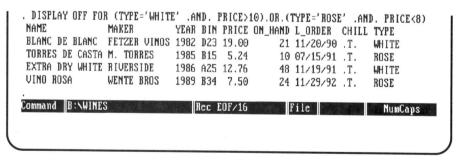

```
. DISPLAY OFF FOR (TYPE='WHITE' .AND. PRICE>10).OR.(TYPE='ROSE' .AND. PRICE<8)
NAME            MAKER        YEAR BIN PRICE ON_HAND L_ORDER CHILL TYPE
BLANC DE BLANC  FETZER VINOS 1982 D23 19.00     21 11/20/90 .T.   WHITE
TORRES DE CASTA M. TORRES    1985 B15 5.24      10 07/15/91 .T.   ROSE
EXTRA DRY WHITE RIVERSIDE    1986 A25 12.76     48 11/19/91 .T.   WHITE
VINO ROSA       WENTE BROS   1989 B34 7.50      24 11/29/92 .T.   ROSE
.
Command ‖B:\WINES            ‖Rec EOF/16    ‖File ‖      ‖   NumCaps
```

FIGURE D.27. White wines over $10 and rosé wines under $8.

Operator	Symbol
Equal to	=
Not equal to	<>
Less than or equal to	<=
Less than	<
Greater than or equal to	>=
Greater than	>

FIGURE D.28. Relational operators.

The FOR condition is used to select the desired rows from the database table. The general form of the condition is

field-name relational-operator comparison-value

Where the relational operators are as indicated in Figure D.28.
A **compound condition** is created with two or more individual conditions by using logical operators to associate them. The logical operators are summarized as described in Figure D.29.

Keypoint!   When using the logical operators .AND. and .OR. in a comparison where the *same field name* is referenced, the field name *must be repeated* in each conditional expression!

D.3.4   Summing Values in a Field

Several questions that Bert and Beth want to explore involve the summation of one or more selected fields across all or a designated set of records in the WINES database. In dBASE the SUM command is used to add numeric fields for a specified group of records. Let's see how this is applied in addressing the questions for the Golden Gourmet.

7. How many bottles of wine do they have on hand?

Enter: SUM ON_HAND

The solution is

ON_HAND
    448

To sum a numeric field

Operator	Action
.AND.	Both conditional expressions must be true for "true" result.
.OR.	One conditional expression must be true for "true" result.
.NOT.	Reverse the result so "true" becomes "false" and "false" becomes "true."

Note: Each logical operator is surrounded by periods!

FIGURE D.29. Logical operators.

Keypoint!

> Your sum may be different than the 448. If this occurs, the usual cause is that you have different values for ON_HAND in your database as a result of entering and revising the data in the previous lessons. Accept whatever summation is obtained. It is *not* necessary for you to go back and correct your data!

Keypoint!

> You may *not* use TO PRINT with the SUM command to direct the result to the printer. Use <Shift> + <PrtSc> to obtain a hard copy of your result!

8. What is the total investment in wines?

To sum a value calculated from several numeric fields

Enter: SUM PRICE*ON_HAND

The outcome is

PRICE*ON_HAND
            3175.26

As indicated in this example, an asterisk is the arithmetic operator that causes the value in field PRICE to be multiplied by the value in field ON_HAND for each record. This result is calculated for each record, which is then added with the SUM command. The arithmetic operators used in dBASE are shown in Figure D.30. These are the same as those used in Lotus 1-2-3, as well as with many other computer languages.

9. What is their investment in white wines?

To sum a calculated value for selected records

Enter: SUM PRICE*ON_HAND FOR TYPE = 'WHITE'

The resulting output is

PRICE*ON_HAND
            1146.48

The SUM command is used to sum a specified set of rows and/or columns from the database relation. A general form of the SUM command is

To SUM records—reference

SUM [scope] [expression list] [TO memvar list] [FOR condition]

Where **scope** is the set of records such as ALL, 15, or NEXT 3
      expression list is the set of fields, which may be equations
      TO memvar list is a list of memory variables where the result
          may be placed for future reference (memory variables
          are described in a following section of this Lesson)
      FOR condition is a comparison to specified values, as described
          in detail earlier

Notice that the SUM command does *not* include the TO PRINT option. For now, <Shift>+<PrtSc> is the best method of capturing this output as hard copy.

Operator	Symbol
Add	+
Subtract	−
Multiply	*
Divide	/
Exponentiation	^
Group Calculation	()

FIGURE D.30. Arithmetic operators.

D.3.5   Counting Database Records

One of the questions posed by Lou requires a count of the number of records in the WINES database that satisfy a specified condition. In dBASE the COUNT command is used to determine how many records match a desired condition. Let's explore this question.

10. How many different types of red wine do they have?

To count the number of selected records

Enter: COUNT FOR TYPE = 'RED'

With the result being

9 records

The COUNT command is used to tally the number of rows in the data base relation that meet a specified condition.
A general form of the COUNT command is

To COUNT records— reference

COUNT [**scope**] [**expression list**] [**TO memvar list**] [**FOR condition**]

where **scope** is the set of records such as ALL, 15, or NEXT 3
      expression list is the set of fields, which may be equations
      TO memvar list is a list of memory variables where the result
         may be placed for future reference
      FOR condition is a comparison to specified values, as described
         in detail earlier

Again, the COUNT command does *not* include the TO PRINT option.

D.3.6   Computing the Average of Values in a Field

Some of the questions that Beth and Bert want to examine involve obtaining an average for the values stored in a numeric field of the WINES database. In dBASE the AVERAGE command calculates this result across a set of selected records. Now let's look at how this is carried out in answering questions for the Golden Gourmet.

11. What is the average number of bottles in inventory?

To calculate the average of the data values in a numeric field

Enter: AVERAGE ON_HAND

The output is

16 records averaged
ON_HAND
     28

12. What is the average price of a bottle of wine on the menu?

Enter: AVERAGE PRICE

Which yields this answer:

16 records averaged
PRICE
   8.36

The AVERAGE command is used to perform both a SUM and a COUNT for a field. The sum is divided by the count to compute the average. A general form of the AVERAGE command is

To AVERAGE numeric values—reference

AVERAGE [**scope**] [**expression list**] [**TO memvar list**] [**FOR condition**]

Where **scope** is the set of records such as ALL, 15, or NEXT 3

expression list is the set of fields, which may be equations

TO memvar list is a list of memory variables where the result may be placed for future reference

FOR condition is a comparison to specified values, as described in detail earlier

The AVERAGE command does *not* include a TO PRINT option.

D.3.7   Using Memory Variables in Computations

Several of the questions Bert and Beth want to explore require the calculation and storage of an intermediate numeric result that is subsequently used in performing another arithmetic calculation. In dBASE memory, variables allow a value to be calculated and stored for later use. With a memory variable the value is stored separately from the data in the database records. Let's learn how this is applied in addressing questions with the WINES database.

13. What is the average price of a bottle of wine in the wine cellar?

| To store a calculated result in a memory variable

Enter: SUM PRICE * ON_HAND TO mINVEST

16 records summed
PRICE * ON_HAND
     3175.26

Enter: SUM ON_HAND TO mBOTTLES

16 records summed
ON_HAND
     448

| To perform calculations with values stored in memory variables and display the result

Enter: ? mINVEST /mBOTTLES

With the final result of
     7.09

Here, mINVEST and mBOTTLES are memory variable, where these two values are stored in a "scratch pad" work area that can be envisioned like this:

Memory Variable Name	Memory Variable Contents
mINVEST	3175.26
mBOTTLES	448

To assist in distinguishing memory variables from field names, the "m" is used as a prefix on the memory variable name. This convention is frequently employed by developers of dBASE applications. Although this convention is *not required*, it helps in separating memory variable names from field names. This convention is continued throughout these dBASE lessons.

In dBASE, memory variables are similar to cells in a Lotus 1-2-3 worksheet. That is, mINVEST is the name of a cell for storing a value similar to a Lotus 1-2-3 cell with the name of D23. But in dBASE, cell names are *not* predefined by row and column designators, like those in a spreadsheet.

Here, the "?" indicates that the results of the arithmetic are to be displayed on your screen. This average needs to be computed in two steps like this because the number of bottles of wine ON_HAND for each wine is different. The computation of the average by this method provides an average that reflects the number of different bottles ON_HAND for each wine.

Memory variables are stored in a work area that is separate from the database table. Unless special actions are taken, these values are lost when you exit from dBASE, since they are *not* stored in the database file.

Caution Alert!

Memory variables are stored separately from a database file. Their values are lost when you QUIT dBASE!

D.3.8   Revising Values in a Field

Two of the questions posed by Lou required the revision of a numeric value in a selected field of a set of records. An old value is replaced by a new value. In dBASE the REPLACE command permits a numeric value to be calculated using a formula and the result placed in a specified field. Now let's explore this method of updating numeric fields in the designated records in the WINES database.

14. Increase the price of all wines by $1 per bottle.

To replace field values with new field values

Enter: `REPLACE ALL PRICE WITH PRICE + 1`

The results of the revised PRICE are viewed by using the DISPLAY command, as shown in Figure D.31.

Caution Alert!

REPLACE *permanently* changes the values in your database file. You may want to create a backup copy of your database *before* using the REPLACE command!

15. Have a sale (special) on RED wines of $1 off per bottle.

To replace field values with new values for selected records

Enter: `REPLACE ALL PRICE WITH PRICE - 1 FOR TYPE = 'RED'`

The outcome is illustrated in Figure D.32.

The REPLACE command is used to provide new values for a specified set of rows in a designated column of the database relation. A general form of the REPLACE command is

To REPLACE field values—reference

REPLACE [scope] <field> WITH [expression] [FOR condition]

where **scope** is the set of records such as ALL, 15, or NEXT 3
        field is the database field that is to be changed
        expression is the equation used to determine the new value
        FOR condition is a comparison to specified values

The data values are modified with the REPLACE command. However, *to view the results of a REPLACE operation*, the DISPLAY, LIST, EDIT, or BROWSE commands are used to actually look at the revised values.

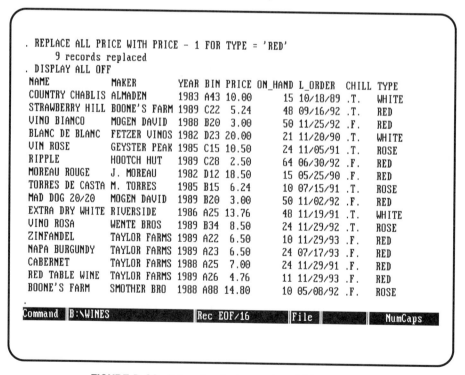

. REPLACE ALL PRICE WITH PRICE + 1
    16 records replaced
.DISPLAY ALL OFF
NAME   MAKER   YEAR BIN PRICE ON_HAND L_ORDER   CHILL TYPE
COUNTRY CHABLIS ALMADEN   1983 A43 10.00   15 10/18/89 .T.   WHITE
STRAWBERRY HILL BOONE'S FARM   1989 C22 6.24   48 09/16/92 .T.   RED
VINO BIANCO   MOGEN DAVID   1988 B20 4.00   50 11/25/92 .F.   RED
BLANC DE BLANC FETZER VINOS   1982 D23 20.00   21 11/20/90 .T.   WHITE
VIN ROSE   GEYSTER PEAK   1985 C15 10.50   24 11/05/91 .T.   ROSE
RIPPLE   HOOTCH HUT   1989 C28 3.50   64 06/30/92 .F.   RED
MOREAU ROUGE   J. MOREAU   1982 D12 19.50   15 05/25/90 .F.   RED
TORRES DE CASTA M. TORRES   1985 B15 6.24   10 07/15/91 .T.   ROSE
MAD DOG 20/20   MOGEN DAVID   1989 B20 4.00   50 11/02/92 .F.   RED
EXTRA DRY WHITE RIVERSIDE   1986 A25 13.76   48 11/19/91 .T.   WHITE
VINO ROSA   WENTE BROS   1989 B34 8.50   24 11/29/92 .T.   ROSE
ZINFANDEL   TAYLOR FARMS   1989 A22 7.50   10 11/29/93 .F.   RED
NAPA BURGUNDY   TAYLOR FARMS   1989 A23 7.50   24 07/17/93 .F.   RED
CABERNET   TAYLOR FARMS   1988 A25 8.00   24 11/29/91 .F.   RED
RED TABLE WINE TAYLOR FARMS   1989 A26 5.76   11 11/29/93 .F.   RED
BOONE'S FARM   SMOTHER BRO   1988 A88 14.80   10 05/08/92 .F.   ROSE
.
Command ▐B:\WINES   ▐Rec EOF/16   ▐File ▐   ▐   NumCaps

Request display of replace result

FIGURE D.31. Price increase of $1 per bottle.

. REPLACE ALL PRICE WITH PRICE - 1 FOR TYPE = 'RED'
     9 records replaced
. DISPLAY ALL OFF
NAME   MAKER   YEAR BIN PRICE ON_HAND L_ORDER   CHILL TYPE
COUNTRY CHABLIS ALMADEN   1983 A43 10.00   15 10/18/89 .T.   WHITE
STRAWBERRY HILL BOONE'S FARM   1989 C22 5.24   48 09/16/92 .T.   RED
VINO BIANCO   MOGEN DAVID   1988 B20 3.00   50 11/25/92 .F.   RED
BLANC DE BLANC FETZER VINOS   1982 D23 20.00   21 11/20/90 .T.   WHITE
VIN ROSE   GEYSTER PEAK   1985 C15 10.50   24 11/05/91 .T.   ROSE
RIPPLE   HOOTCH HUT   1989 C28 2.50   64 06/30/92 .F.   RED
MOREAU ROUGE   J. MOREAU   1982 D12 18.50   15 05/25/90 .F.   RED
TORRES DE CASTA M. TORRES   1985 B15 6.24   10 07/15/91 .T.   ROSE
MAD DOG 20/20   MOGEN DAVID   1989 B20 3.00   50 11/02/92 .F.   RED
EXTRA DRY WHITE RIVERSIDE   1986 A25 13.76   48 11/19/91 .T.   WHITE
VINO ROSA   WENTE BROS   1989 B34 8.50   24 11/29/92 .T.   ROSE
ZINFANDEL   TAYLOR FARMS   1989 A22 6.50   10 11/29/93 .F.   RED
NAPA BURGUNDY   TAYLOR FARMS   1989 A23 6.50   24 07/17/93 .F.   RED
CABERNET   TAYLOR FARMS   1988 A25 7.00   24 11/29/91 .F.   RED
RED TABLE WINE TAYLOR FARMS   1989 A26 4.76   11 11/29/93 .F.   RED
BOONE'S FARM   SMOTHER BRO   1988 A88 14.80   10 05/08/92 .F.   ROSE
.
Command ▐B:\WINES   ▐Rec EOF/16   ▐File ▐   ▐   NumCaps

FIGURE D.32. Price of red wines reduced $1 per bottle.

D.3.9 When Things Go Wrong

Different situations may arise when you are querying a database that result in wrong data being displayed or in an error message. Two of the more frequently occurring difficulties and how to recover from them are described here:

1. The command produced the wrong results, such as displaying the wrong set of fields or listing records with a PRICE less than $10 when you wanted those more than $10.

   a. Reissue the desired command with the revised fields or comparison values. This may be accomplished with history.

   b. Review the result to determine if it matches your request.

2. The command you entered resulted in a syntax error, as illustrated in Figure D.33 for dBASE VI and in Figure D.34 for dBASE III+. dBASE IV only informs you of the occurrence of the syntax error. dBASE III+ points to the location of the error, with the "?" indicating the point in the command where the error was detected.

   a. Use history to recall the command on the Edit line. In dBASE VI, this may also be accomplished by selecting Edit from the error message screen.

   b. Make edit changes to correct the error.

   c. Execute the revised command. With a DISPLAY command, you may want to avoid using the TO PRINT option until after you have verified your query. Then, using history, add the TO PRINT option and reissue the command.

   d. Review the result to verify that it satisfies your query.

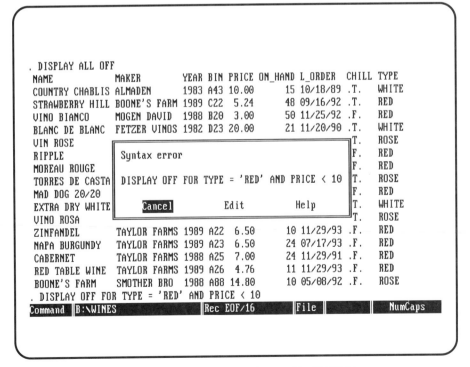

FIGURE D.33. Syntax error detected in dBASE IV.

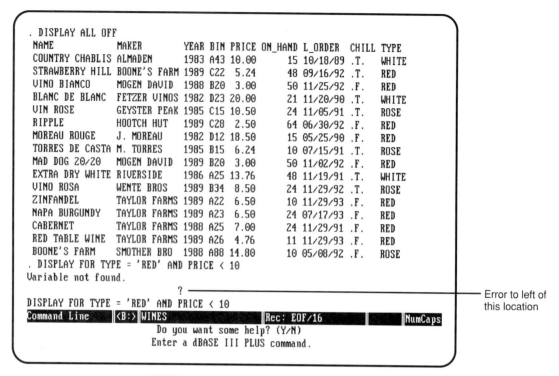

```
. DISPLAY ALL OFF
NAME             MAKER         YEAR BIN PRICE ON_HAND L_ORDER CHILL TYPE
COUNTRY CHABLIS  ALMADEN       1983 A43 10.00      15 10/18/89 .T.   WHITE
STRAWBERRY HILL  BOONE'S FARM  1989 C22  5.24      48 09/16/92 .T.   RED
VINO BIANCO      MOGEN DAVID   1988 B20  3.00      50 11/25/92 .F.   RED
BLANC DE BLANC   FETZER VINOS  1982 D23 20.00      21 11/20/90 .T.   WHITE
VIN ROSE         GEYSTER PEAK  1985 C15 10.50      24 11/05/91 .T.   ROSE
RIPPLE           HOOTCH HUT    1989 C28  2.50      64 06/30/92 .F.   RED
MOREAU ROUGE     J. MOREAU     1982 D12 18.50      15 05/25/90 .T.   RED
TORRES DE CASTA  M. TORRES     1985 B15  6.24      10 07/15/91 .T.   ROSE
MAD DOG 20/20    MOGEN DAVID   1989 B20  3.00      50 11/02/92 .F.   RED
EXTRA DRY WHITE  RIVERSIDE     1986 A25 13.76      48 11/19/91 .T.   WHITE
VINO ROSA        WENTE BROS    1989 B34  8.50      24 11/29/92 .T.   ROSE
ZINFANDEL        TAYLOR FARMS  1989 A22  6.50      10 11/29/93 .F.   RED
NAPA BURGUNDY    TAYLOR FARMS  1989 A23  6.50      24 07/17/93 .F.   RED
CABERNET         TAYLOR FARMS  1988 A25  7.00      24 11/29/91 .F.   RED
RED TABLE WINE   TAYLOR FARMS  1989 A26  4.76      11 11/29/93 .F.   RED
BOONE'S FARM     SMOTHER BRO   1988 A88 14.80      10 05/08/92 .F.   ROSE
. DISPLAY FOR TYPE = 'RED' AND PRICE < 10
Variable not found.
                       ? ─────────────────────────────────────
DISPLAY FOR TYPE = 'RED' AND PRICE < 10
┌─────────────┐ ┌────────┐                ┌──────────┐ ┌─────────┐
│Command Line │ │<B:>│WINES              │Rec: EOF/16│ │ │NumCaps │
└─────────────┘ └────────┘                └──────────┘ └─────────┘
           Do you want some help? (Y/N)
           Enter a dBASE III PLUS command.
```

Error to left of this location

FIGURE D.34. Syntax error detected in dBASE III+.

D.3.10 Lesson Summary

- The DML of dBASE allows management questions to be addressed by formulating database queries.

- The FOR condition can be included with the DISPLAY or LIST command to select records from the database.

- Compound FOR conditions may require the use of parentheses to group expressions with a field name repeated when it is used in more than one comparison.

- The SUM, COUNT, and AVERAGE commands perform these actions on selected records within a designated field. Equations combining data from two or more fields may be used with the SUM or AVERAGE commands.

- Memory variables store data values in a work area outside of the database. They are used for computations of values that are not included as rows or columns in the database.

- The values stored in a database field can be revised with the REPLACE command. This command permits the values in all rows or selected rows of the table to be changed simultaneously with one single command.

D.3.11 Practice Tutorial

The Wine Management System can be exploited to respond to a variety of database queries as described in this Lesson. Formulate these queries as a guided activity in a hands-on manner.

Task 1: Access the WINES database in the GOLDEN catalog on your data disk before you begin.

Task 2: Produce the responses to database questions 1 through 15. Use <Shift> + <PrtSc> and TO PRINT to obtain hard copies of each of these results.

Task 3: Label each of your results with the question number of the query you performed.

Time Estimates

Novice: 60 minutes

Intermediate: 45 minutes

Advanced: 30 minutes

D.3.12 Practice Exercises

(1) Case: County Line Baskets

Business Problem: Inventory Control
MIS Characteristics: Production/Operations
Operational Control

Melissa Wetherbee, the owner and manager of County Line Baskets, sells basket kits to a variety of basket weavers. Melissa's baskets are made of different materials and designed for different levels of difficulty. Some of the more specialized basket designs require the use of a form or mold to shape the basket during weaving. Melissa uses a database to keep track of her inventory and respond to questions from customers. She designed her database containing the fields as described by this data dictionary definition:

Field Name	Description
ID_NO	Basket pattern identification number
NAME	Basket pattern name
SIZE	Basket size in inches indicated as length × width × height or diameter × height
MATERIAL	Material from which basket is made
MOLD	Indicator of whether or not a mold is used
DIFF	Difficulty level of basket, designated as follows: BEG = beginner, INT = intermediate, ADV = advanced, ALL = any level
PRICE	Selling price of basket kit
QTY	Quantity currently held in inventory

Task 1: Access the BASKET.DBF database file in the EXERCISE catalog and review the structure and data. Produce a hard copy listing of the database structure for documentation and reference. The dBASE commands are

· _____

· _____

· _____

Task 2: Produce responses to the following management questions, using <Shift> + <PrtSc> and TO PRINT to obtain hard copies:

(1) Which INTermediate baskets are available?

· _____

(2) Which BLACK ASH baskets have a BEGinner difficulty level?

.
_____

(3) How much is BERRY PICKER?

.
_____

(4) How many baskets are of ADVanced difficulty?

.
_____

(5) Which basket kits should Melissa reorder? (Kits whose quantity in inventory is less than 12.)

.
_____

(6) How many baskets kits does Melissa currently have in inventory?

.
_____

(7) What is the total investment in basket kits? The value of investment is indicated as the PRICE * QTY for each kit.

.
_____

(8) What is the average price of a basket kit?

.
_____

(9) Melissa wants you to increase the price of each basket kit by $2.50. Produce a listing showing the increased prices.

.
_____

.
_____

Task 3: Label each of your results with the question number of the query you performed.

Time Estimates

Novice: 90 minutes

Intermediate: 60 minutes

Advanced: 45 minutes

(2)   Case: United Marketing Services

Business Problem: Media Analysis
MIS Characteristics: Marketing
                          Strategic Planning

United Marketing Services is a mail-order direct-marketing firm that sells its products by using a variety of advertising media. Mary Montoya, manager of marketing effectiveness, is responsible for monitoring the success of United's advertising. To track customer responses, Mary developed a database containing fields described by the following data dictionary definitions:

Field Name	Description
PN	Product identification number
PRODUCT	Product name
QTY	Quantity sold
PRICE	Selling price of product
MEDIA	Advertising media from which customer order was placed designated as follows: RADIO, TV, DMAIL = direct mail, NEWSP = newspaper
DATE	Date of advertisement
AREA	Geographical area or region of customer order and advertisement
PREV	Indicator for previous order from customer

Task 1: Access the UNITED.DBF database file in the EXERCISE catalog and review the structure and data. Produce a hard copy listing of the database structure for documentation and reference. The dBASE commands are

- _____
- _____
- _____

Task 2: Produce responses to the following management questions, using <Shift>+<PrtSc> and TO PRINT to obtain hard copies:

(1) Which orders resulted from DMAIL advertisements?
- _____

(2) Which products were ordered from the SOUTH area?
- _____

(3) What is the total quantity of products sold by NEWSP advertisements?
- _____

(4) Which orders were from customers who had previously ordered from United Marketing?
- _____

(5) How many RIPSAWs were ordered from RADIO advertisements?
- _____

(6) How many RIPSAWs were ordered from the SOUTH area?
- _____

(7) What is the average number of items per order? Each database record is one order.
- _____

(8) What is the value of all the orders? The value of an order is the PRICE * QTY for that order.
- _____

    (9) What is the value of the orders from TV advertisements?

    .

_____

    (10) A $2 shipping and handling fee is added to the price for each item ordered. Since the current prices do NOT include this fee, increase the prices of all items ordered to include the fee. Produce a hard copy listing with these increased prices.

    .

_____

    .

_____

    (11) (*Optional*) How many items were sold as a result of advertisements appearing on 08/11/94? [*Hint:* Use the FOR condition: DATE = CTOD("08/11/94")] where CTOD() is a dBASE function that converts character data to a date value.]

    .

_____

    .

_____

Task 3: Label each of your results with the question number of the query you performed.

Time Estimates

Novice: 90 minutes

Intermediate: 60 minutes

Advanced: 45 minutes

D.3.13   Comprehensive Problems

Case: Yen To Travel (continued)

At Yen To Travel, Brenda and Ashley have formulated a number of questions that they want to answer by interrogating the database of their Tour Management System.

Task 1: Access your database file in the YENTO catalog.

    .

_____

Task 2: Produce responses to the following management questions, using <Shift>+<PrtSc> and TO PRINT to obtain hard copies:

    (1) Which SEA tours are available?

    .

_____

    (2) How much is the WHALE WATCH?

    .

_____

    (3) How many tours require a passport?

    .

_____

    (4) For which tours should additional seats be requested? (Tours with less than 10 seats open.)

    .

_____

(5) Which SEA tours are less than $1000?

.
_____

(6) How many open seats are available?

.
_____

(7) What is the total revenue from seats that have been sold? (Where the revenue from each tour is the number of seats sold * price per seat.)

.
_____

(8) What is the total revenue from BUS tours?

.
_____

(9) How many different AIR tours do they have?

.
_____

(10) What is the average number of seats sold?

.
_____

(11) What is the average price of a tour?

.
_____

(12) What is the average price of a seat that has been sold?

.
_____

.
_____

(13) Increase the price of all tours by $100 per tour.

.
_____

.
_____

(14) Have a sale (special) on BUS tours of $50 off per seat.

.
_____

.
_____

Task 3: Label each of your results with the question number of the query you performed.

Time Estimates

Novice: 90 minutes

Intermediate: 60 minutes

Advanced: 30 minutes

(2)   Case: Silver Screen Video (continued)

Amy and Ernie have been reviewing the information they want to obtain from the database of their movie management system for Silver Screen Video. They have formulated a number of questions that they would like to have answered by interrogating their database.

Task 1: Access the database file in the SILVER catalog.

.
_____

Task 2: Produce responses to the following management questions, using <Shift>+<PrtSc> and TO PRINT to obtain hard copies:

(1) Which DRAma movies are available?

  .

_____

(2) Which HORror movies are rated PG?

  .

_____

(3) How much is TOP GUN?

  .

_____

(4) How many movies are rated R?

  .

_____

(5) Which movies have been shown on television?

  .

_____

(6) Which movies should be reordered? (For movies shown on TV this is less than 7, whereas for movies that have *not* been shown on TV this is less than 15.) [*Hint:* You may produce two separate lists of movies.]

  .

_____

  .

_____

(7) Which suspense movies are less than $20?

  .

_____

(8) How many movies do we have on hand?

  .

_____

(9) What is the total investment in movies?

  .

_____

(10) What is the total investment in movies shown on TV?

  .

_____

(11) How many different suspense movies do we have that are rated PG or R?

  .

_____

(12) What is the average number of movies on hand?

  .

_____

(13) What is the average price of a movie?

  .

_____

  .

_____

(14) What is the average price of a suspense movie *not* shown on TV?

  .

_____

(15) Increase the price of all movies by 10 percent.

  .

_____

  .

_____

(16) Have a sale (special) on horror movies of $2 off per movie.

. _____

. _____

Task 3: Label each of your results with the question number of the query you performed.

Time Estimates

Novice: 30 minutes

Intermediate: 60 minutes

Advanced: 90 minutes

D.3.14 Application Case

Case: Management Development Institute

Business Problem: Inventory Control

MIS Characteristics: Production

                           Managerial Control

Management Functions: Organizing

                             Controlling

Tools Skills: Queries

                Memory variables

                Displaying data

                Printing data

Management Development Institute (MDI) was founded in 1974 by Harry D. Cougar to deliver quality continuing education to managers and business leaders. Harry continues to serve as MDI's President and Chief Operating Officer, directing operations from the company's modest headquarters located at the foot of the Rocky Mountains in Golden, Colorado. MDI's seminars are presented at a variety of locations across North America and in Europe and Japan, wherever a management training need exists.

MDI delivers training to help people manage more intelligently by giving them practical skills, knowledge, and techniques that really pay off back on the job. The key to an organization's competitiveness is its superior management. To achieve that payoff in today's demanding world, managers need more knowledge and sharper skills than ever before. MDI's seminars are geared to helping managers cope with today's unique problems.

To accomplish its educational objectives, Management Development Institute promises to:

- Limit the class size to guarantee more individualized instruction.
- Use only the most current and authoritative textual material on the subject.
- Deliver industry experts who present concise, accurate, and real life answers to participants' concerns.
- Keep the workshop practical.
- Provide generous reference materials that include lecture notes, case studies, guidelines, and checklists.

As a service-oriented business, MDI relies on production/operations management techniques to control its activities. Harry considers their operations management function as encompassing the management of the resources required to produce their service of management training seminars. He views MDI's inventory as seats it schedules and sells in management seminars, since seminar seats are the primary resource used to produce revenue. From this perspective, Harry envisions the inventory control problems encountered by MDI as similar to those of the airline industry, which has an inventory of seats on scheduled flights. Once a seminar has started, the seat is either occupied or not. Seminar seats are a perishable commodity. They cannot be held in inventory indefinitely until they are purchased, since the date of the seminar determines when the service will be provided. And, like an airline scheduling a plane that accommodates a certain number of passengers, once a facility of a specified size has been booked for a seminar, a larger or smaller facility cannot be readily arranged. MDI's inventory control is concerned with effectively and efficiently managing this inventory.

Daniel "Dan" MacFadden, MDI's Vice President of Operations, has overall management responsibility for developing seminars, scheduling seminars, recruiting and assigning instructors, arranging facilities, and monitoring activities. For each seminar, Ingrid Olson, the Seminar Coordinator, arranges a facility where the seminar is conducted. She frequently rents meeting space at popular and readily accessible hotels in each city where a seminar is scheduled. Ingrid knows the importance of reserving quality space, since an uncomfortable environment can have significant impact on the quality of a seminar.

Dan has arranged for the granting of Continuing Education Units (CEUs) to each participant of an MDI seminar. These are useful to a number of different certified business professionals in meeting their continuing educations requirements, such as those for a certified public accountant (CPA), certified systems professional (CSP), certified management accountant (CMA), and one holding a certificate in data processing (CDP).

During their recent management retreat in Breckenridge, Harry, Dan, and Ingrid discussed the possibility of establishing a database to provide them with better information for managing their operations. Dan described to Harry and Ingrid how a Seminar Management System (SMS) could be used to address a number of ad hoc questions concerning their seminars, including those concerned with monitoring and controlling their seat inventory. Ingrid described the embarrassment of MDI last week when she discovered that a seminar had been overbooked, because she did not have an accurate count of seats sold. Since MDI highly values its customer relations, both Harry and Dan hoped they could avoid this situation in the future. Harry supported Ingrid's concern for better inventory control information. It seemed that Dan's proposal for a Seminar Management System would meet their requirements.

Dan worked with Ingrid in designing their database, which includes the following fields:

Field Name	Description
ID	Identification number uniquely designating each seminar
NAME	Name of seminar
LOCATION	City where seminar is to be held
DATE	Beginning date of seminar
PRG	Program group of seminar
DUR	Duration of seminar in days
CEU	Number of Continuing Education Units
SEAT	Total number of seats for seminar (seminar capacity)
SOLD	Number of seats sold
FEE	Seminar fee or price
ARRG	Whether or not facility arrangements have been completed

To assist in the marketing and coordination of MDI's seminars, Ingrid grouped them by program (PRG) categories, which she has classified as follows:

Program Designator	Program Name
FIN	Finance and Accounting
HRS	Human Resource
MGT	Management
MIS	Management Information Systems

Tasks

1. Access the SEMINAR.DBF database of MDI's Seminar Management System in the CASES catalog and review its structure and content. Obtain a hard copy of the structure.

2. Harry, Dan, and Ingrid have formulated a number of questions that they want to address with the MDI's Seminar Management System. These questions represent typical ad hoc queries for which responses can be obtained from a database. To test the query capabilities of their database, they want you to issue queries with dBASE's DML to extract information to answer these questions:

   (a) Which management seminars are scheduled? Generate a hard copy list of these seminars.

   (b) How much is the COMMUNICATIONS SKILLS seminar?

   (c) Which seminars do *not* have the local arrangements completed? Produce a hard copy list of these seminars.

   (d) How many seminars have their local arrangement completed? Produce a hard copy list of these seminars.

   (e) Which MIS seminars are available for a FEE of less than $800? Generate a hard copy list of these seminars that includes only the seminar NAME, LOCATION, and FEE.

   (f) How many seats have been sold for all of the currently scheduled seminars?

   (g) What is the total revenue that is received if *all* seminar seats are sold?

   (h) What is the total revenue if *all* the seats in the finance seminars are sold?

   (i) How many MIS seminars are included in this schedule?

   (j) What is the average number of seats available per seminar?

   (k) What is the average number of seats that have been sold per seminar?

   (l) What is the average fee for a seminar?

   (m) What is the average duration of a seminar?

   (n) What is the average number of CEUs for these seminars?

   (o) What is the average price of the seminar seats that have been sold?

   (p) How many seats remain to be sold? [*Hint:* Have all computations performed with dBASE commands.]

   (q) Increase the fee for all seminar seats by $25. Produce a list of the seminars that includes the NAME, LOCATION, DATE. and FEE fields.

   (r) Decrease the fee for each seminar by $50 for those seminars with a fee greater than $900 and less than 10 seats sold. Generate a list of the NAME, LOCATION, DATE, and FEE for these seminars.

3. Label each of your results with the question number of the query you performed.

4. The current database design could be expanded to include other fields, such as that for instructors. What additional fields might MDI want to incorporate in their database? What types of queries could be addressed with these fields? Why is it important to consider the potential queries to be conducted on a database when it is being designed? Write a summary addressing these questions.

Time Estimates

Novice: 120 minutes

Intermediate: 90 minutes

Advanced: 45 minutes

Printing Hint!

In the event that your output is more than 80 characters wide and you do not have a wide-carriage printer, you may want to use compressed printing with dBASE. This is accomplished by sending a character string to the printer that controls its operation. These character strings vary from one brand and/or model of printer to the next. You may need to check on the control characters for your particular printer.

These examples illustrate the character strings for IBM and Epson dot matrix printers and for Hewlett Packard LaserJet printers. Proceed in the desired manner described below.

IBM and Epson

SET PRINT ON	(Direct output to printer)
??CHR(027)+CHR(015)	(Request compressed print)
or	
??CHR(027)+CHR(018)	(Request regular print)
SET PRINT OFF	(Halt all output to printer)

HP LaserJet

SET PRINT ON	(Direct output to printer)
??CHR(027)+"E"+CHR(027)+"(s16.66H"	(Compressed print)
or	
??CHR(027)+"E"	(Regular print)
SET PRINT OFF	(Stop all output to printer)

If your printer control characters are different, enter yours here:

Compressed print: _____

Regular print: _____

LESSON
D.4

Arranging and Listing a Database

CONTENT

- Producing Management Listings with Index
- Producing Management Listings with Sort
- Producing Listings for Wine Management System
- Using INDEXED Databases
- When Things Go Wrong

D.4.1 Producing Management Listings with Index

As Beth and Bert embarked on the development of the Wine Management System for the Golden Gourmet, they identified several key listing of information they wanted to obtain. They have considered their initial user requirements, and Beth decided that they would begin by creating the following listings:

1. A wine list with the wines arranged by type.
2. A server list with the wines arranged by bin.
3. A wine list with the wines arranged by both wine type and wine name.
4. A price list with wines arranged by price so the higher priced wines are listed first.

Beth accessed the WINES database in their GOLDEN catalog and began producing these listings.

1. List the wines by type—all reds together, all whites, and so on.

Enter:	`INDEX ON TYPE TO WINETYPE`
	Create a sequenced index of the database
Enter:	`SET INDEX TO WINETYPE`
	Activate the index
Enter:	`DISPLAY ALL OFF` View the sequenced records

To INDEX on a single character field

The result is illustrated in Figure D.35.

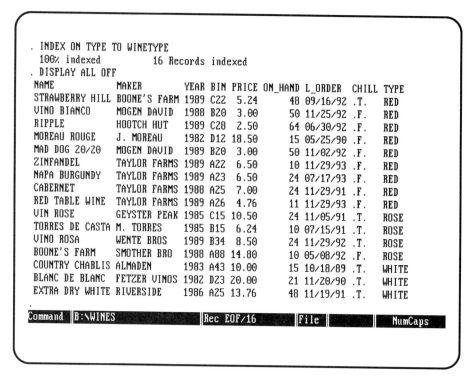

. INDEX ON TYPE TO WINETYPE
   100% indexed   16 Records indexed
. DISPLAY ALL OFF

NAME	MAKER	YEAR	BIN	PRICE	ON_HAND	L_ORDER	CHILL	TYPE
STRAWBERRY HILL	BOONE'S FARM	1989	C22	5.24	48	09/16/92	.T.	RED
VINO BIANCO	MOGEN DAVID	1988	B20	3.00	50	11/25/92	.F.	RED
RIPPLE	HOOTCH HUT	1989	C28	2.50	64	06/30/92	.F.	RED
MOREAU ROUGE	J. MOREAU	1982	D12	18.50	15	05/25/90	.F.	RED
MAD DOG 20/20	MOGEN DAVID	1989	B20	3.00	50	11/02/92	.F.	RED
ZINFANDEL	TAYLOR FARMS	1989	A22	6.50	10	11/29/93	.F.	RED
NAPA BURGUNDY	TAYLOR FARMS	1989	A23	6.50	24	07/17/93	.F.	RED
CABERNET	TAYLOR FARMS	1988	A25	7.00	24	11/29/91	.F.	RED
RED TABLE WINE	TAYLOR FARMS	1989	A26	4.76	11	11/29/93	.F.	RED
VIN ROSE	GEYSTER PEAK	1985	C15	10.50	24	11/05/91	.T.	ROSE
TORRES DE CASTA	M. TORRES	1985	B15	6.24	10	07/15/91	.T.	ROSE
VINO ROSA	WENTE BROS	1989	B34	8.50	24	11/29/92	.T.	ROSE
BOONE'S FARM	SMOTHER BRO	1988	A88	14.80	10	05/08/92	.F.	ROSE
COUNTRY CHABLIS	ALMADEN	1983	A43	10.00	15	10/18/89	.T.	WHITE
BLANC DE BLANC	FETZER VINOS	1982	D23	20.00	21	11/20/90	.T.	WHITE
EXTRA DRY WHITE	RIVERSIDE	1986	A25	13.76	48	11/19/91	.T.	WHITE

```
Command  B:\WINES              Rec EOF/16      File            NumCaps
```

FIGURE D.35. Wines sequences by type.

The INDEX command is employed to obtain a display of the database sequenced by the type of wine, with all the RED wines first, the ROSE second and the WHITE wines last. With the INDEX command, a separate table is created that contains *only the desired sequence of record numbers.* This table enables the database to be displayed in the desired sequence. A second copy to the database file is *not* required to obtain this desired sequence when an INDEX is used. The database file remains in its original sequential order. The INDEX is called on when the data are displayed. In dBASE, the INDEX is *stored in a separate file* so it can be used when desired. dBASE identifies these INDEX files with a file extension of NDX. You can think of the index file as a cross-reference table like this:

Index Sequence Number	Database Record Number	Index Sequence Number	Database Record Number
1	2	9	15
2	3	10	5
3	6	11	8
4	7	12	11
5	9	13	16
6	12	14	1
7	13	15	4
8	14	16	10

2. List the wines by bin number.

Enter: INDEX ON BIN TO WINEBIN

Create a second index

Enter: DISPLAY ALL OFF

This yields the display in Figure D.36.

3. A list of the wines arranged by wine type and wine name.

Enter: INDEX ON TYPE + NAME TO TYPENAME

Create an index using two fields

Enter: DISPLAY ALL OFF

Here, the "+" is used to form an index from the values stored in two or more fields. The "+" operator performs a **concatenation** on the data values from the two character type data fields with the characters from the second field placed to the right of those from the first field. This forms a value that is a combination of the values in the two fields, such as WHITE COUNTRY CHABLIS. In this arrangement, the second field acts as the *tiebreaker*. Whenever values in the first field are identical, the characters from the second field determine the indexing sequence. This concatenated field is used to create the desired index for this listing, with the output shown in Figure D.37.

Whenever two or more fields are used to form an index, they must be of the *same data type*. That is, all fields of the index must be of the character data type or they must be of the numeric data type. However, when two or more numeric fields are used for the index, the "+" operator is treated as an arithmetic operator that *adds* the values in the numeric fields and then uses the result for building the index. In the event you want to form an index that uses both a character type field and a numeric type field, then the numeric field may be converted to character type data for building the index

To index on more than one character field

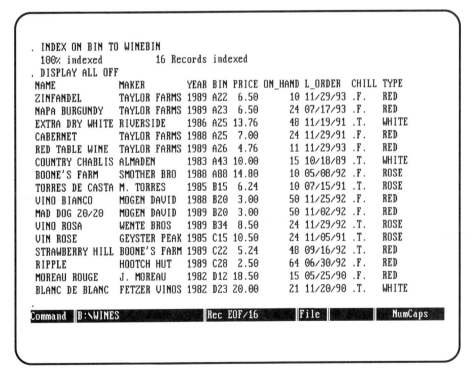

FIGURE D.36. Wines sequenced by bin.

```
. INDEX ON TYPE + NAME TO TYPENAME
  100% indexed           16 Records indexed
. DISPLAY ALL OFF
  NAME            MAKER         YEAR BIN PRICE ON_HAND L_ORDER  CHILL TYPE
  CABERNET        TAYLOR FARMS  1988 A25  7.00      24 11/29/91 .F.   RED
  MAD DOG 20/20   MOGEN DAVID   1989 B20  3.00      50 11/02/92 .F.   RED
  MOREAU ROUGE    J. MOREAU     1982 D12 18.50      15 05/25/90 .F.   RED
  NAPA BURGUNDY   TAYLOR FARMS  1989 A23  6.50      24 07/17/93 .F.   RED
  RED TABLE WINE  TAYLOR FARMS  1989 A26  4.76      11 11/29/93 .F.   RED
  RIPPLE          HOOTCH HUT    1989 C28  2.50      64 06/30/92 .F.   RED
  STRAWBERRY HILL BOONE'S FARM  1989 C22  5.24      48 09/16/92 .T.   RED
  VINO BIANCO     MOGEN DAVID   1988 B20  3.00      50 11/25/92 .F.   RED
  ZINFANDEL       TAYLOR FARMS  1989 A22  6.50      10 11/29/93 .F.   RED
  BOONE'S FARM    SMOTHER BRO   1988 A88 14.80      10 05/08/92 .F.   ROSE
  TORRES DE CASTA M. TORRES     1985 B15  6.24      10 07/15/91 .T.   ROSE
  VIN ROSE        GEYSTER PEAK  1985 C15 10.50      24 11/05/91 .T.   ROSE
  VINO ROSA       WENTE BROS    1989 B34  8.50      24 11/29/92 .T.   ROSE
  BLANC DE BLANC  FETZER VINOS  1982 D23 20.00      21 11/20/90 .T.   WHITE
  COUNTRY CHABLIS ALMADEN       1983 A43 10.00      15 10/18/89 .T.   WHITE
  EXTRA DRY WHITE RIVERSIDE     1986 A25 13.76      48 11/19/91 .T.   WHITE
  .
```

| Command | B:\WINES | | Rec EOF/16 | | File | | | NumCaps |

FIGURE D.37. Wines arranged by type and name.

with a dBASE function known as the STR( ) or string function. It would be used like this:

To index on character and numeric fields

Enter: `INDEX ON MAKER + STR(PRICE) TO MKRPRICE`

Keypoint!

> When creating an index from two or more fields, the data type of all the fields must be the same. The STR( ) function can be used to convert Numeric type data to characters or the DTOC( ) function can be used to convert Date type data to characters!

The INDEX ON command is used to order the records in the database relation in the designated sequence of the index.

A general form of the INDEX command is

To INDEX records—reference

INDEX ON <key expression> **TO** <filename>

where **key expression** identifies the fields used for the index

   filename specifies the file where the index is stored

When an index is created with the INDEX ON command, your database may be immediately viewed, arranged in the sequence of the INDEX. However, if you have a previously created INDEX that you would like to use, this may be achieved with the SET INDEX TO command that makes the previously created INDEX your *currently active* INDEX.

The SET INDEX TO command is used to activate an existing index for use with the database relation. A general form of the SET INDEX TO command is

To set an existing INDEX—reference

SET INDEX TO <index file(s)>

where **index file** is the name of the index file or files that are to be activated; when no index file name is specified, all indexing is turned off.

D.4.2   Producing Management Listings with Sort

Beth needed to sort the database file to produce the last of their desired listing. She continued in this manner:

> **4.** List the wines by price so the higher priced wines are listed first, and then the lower priced wines.

To arrange a database file with SORT

> **Enter:**   SORT ON PRICE/D TO WINPRICE
> Sequence the database
>
> **Enter:**   USE WINPRICE   Access the sorted copy of the database
>
> **Enter:**   DISPLAY ALL OFF   Look at the sorted data
>
> The result is shown in Figure D.38.

The SORT command *makes a copy of the entire database file* and arranges the file in the specified sequence. In dBASE, the SORT command provides one method for arranging a listing in descending sequence. The /D parameter following PRICE specifies a descending sequence.

The SORT command is used to order the records in the database relation and store the sorted records in a *second database relation.* A general form of the SORT command is:

To SORT a database file—reference

SORT ON <**field(s)**> **TO** <**filename**>

where **field** identifies the field used for the sort with /A or /D specifying an
   ascending or *descending* order for the sort
   filename specifies the file where the *sorted* database is stored.

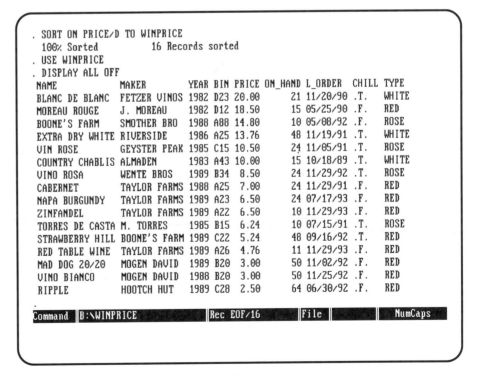

```
. SORT ON PRICE/D TO WINPRICE
  100% Sorted          16 Records sorted
. USE WINPRICE
. DISPLAY ALL OFF
NAME            MAKER        YEAR BIN PRICE ON_HAND L_ORDER  CHILL TYPE
BLANC DE BLANC  FETZER VINOS 1982 D23 20.00      21 11/20/90 .T.  WHITE
MOREAU ROUGE    J. MOREAU    1982 D12 18.50      15 05/25/90 .F.  RED
BOONE'S FARM    SMOTHER BRO  1988 A88 14.80      10 05/08/92 .F.  ROSE
EXTRA DRY WHITE RIVERSIDE    1986 A25 13.76      48 11/19/91 .T.  WHITE
VIN ROSE        GEYSTER PEAK 1985 C15 10.50      24 11/05/91 .T.  ROSE
COUNTRY CHABLIS ALMADEN      1983 A43 10.00      15 10/18/89 .T.  WHITE
VINO ROSA       WENTE BROS   1989 B34  8.50      24 11/29/92 .T.  ROSE
CABERNET        TAYLOR FARMS 1988 A25  7.00      24 11/29/91 .F.  RED
NAPA BURGUNDY   TAYLOR FARMS 1989 A23  6.50      24 07/17/93 .F.  RED
ZINFANDEL       TAYLOR FARMS 1989 A22  6.50      10 11/29/93 .F.  RED
TORRES DE CASTA M. TORRES    1985 B15  6.24      10 07/15/91 .T.  ROSE
STRAWBERRY HILL BOONE'S FARM 1989 C22  5.24      48 09/16/92 .T.  RED
RED TABLE WINE  TAYLOR FARMS 1989 A26  4.76      11 11/29/93 .F.  RED
MAD DOG 20/20   MOGEN DAVID  1989 B20  3.00      50 11/02/92 .F.  RED
VINO BIANCO     MOGEN DAVID  1988 B20  3.00      50 11/25/92 .F.  RED
RIPPLE          HOOTCH HUT   1989 C28  2.50      64 06/30/92 .F.  RED
.
Command  B:\WINPRICE              Rec EOF/16      File            NumCaps
```

FIGURE D.38. Wines sorted by price.

Unlike the INDEX command, the SORT command does *not* require the sort fields to be of the same data type. All you need to do is list the sort fields, separated by commas. That is, you may perform a SORT with different data types in this manner:

To perform a sort on fields of different data types

Enter: `SORT ON TYPE, PRICE TO TPRICE`

where **TYPE** contains character type data
   PRICE contains numeric type data

Action: Look at the contents of the TPRICE file using the DISPLAY command.

Keypoint!

> SORT creates a *duplicate* copy of the database arranged in the desired sequence. This is a separate database file that increases the amount of disk space consumed to store the data! A database sorted in five different sequences would take up five times as much disk storage space as the original database file!

D.4.3   Producing Listings for Wine Management System

Thus far, the prototype listings produced by Beth and Bert have displayed all the fields for all the records from the Golden Gourmet's WINES database. Beth reviewed their original user requirements for the Wine Management System. They were particularly interested in preparing three lists:

1. Wine list
2. Serving list
3. Order list

These listings, containing selected fields that she specified with Bert's assistance, were reviewed by Lou and Annie. The Order List was to contain only selected rows. After experimenting with the listings produced using the INDEX and SORT commands, Beth was ready to create these three listings.
   Beth created the wine list using these commands:

To output a listing arranged with an index and containing selected fields

Enter: `INDEX ON TYPE TO WINETYPE`
Enter: `SET INDEX TO WINETYPE`
Enter: `LIST ALL OFF NAME, MAKER, TYPE, YEAR, PRICE TO PRINT`
Enter: `EJECT`

This report is shown in Figure D.39.
   Then she produced the serving list using these commands:

To output another listing arranged in a different sequence

Enter: `INDEX ON BIN TO WINEBIN`
Enter: `SET INDEX TO WINEBIN`
Enter: `LIST ALL OFF BIN, NAME, MAKER, CHILL TO PRINT`
Enter: `EJECT`

This list appears as Figure D.40.

NAME	MAKER	TYPE	YEAR	PRICE
MOREAU ROUGE	J. MOREAU	RED	1982	18.50
CABERNET	TAYLOR FARMS	RED	1988	7.00
NAPA BURGUNDY	TAYLOR FARMS	RED	1989	6.50
ZINFANDEL	TAYLOR FARMS	RED	1989	6.50
STRAWBERRY HILL	BOONE'S FARM	RED	1989	5.24
RED TABLE WINE	TAYLOR FARMS	RED	1989	4.76
MAD DOG 20/20	MOGEN DAVID	RED	1989	3.00
VINO BIANCO	MOGEN DAVID	RED	1988	3.00
RIPPLE	HOOTCH HUT	RED	1989	2.50
BOONE'S FARM	SMOTHERS BRO	ROSE	1988	14.80
VIN ROSE	GEYSER PEAK	ROSE	1985	10.50
VINO ROSA	WENTE BROS	ROSE	1989	8.50
TORRES DE CASTA	M. TORRES	ROSE	1985	6.24
BLANC DE BLANC	FETZER VINOS	WHITE	1982	20.00
EXTRA DRY WHITE	RIVERSIDE	WHITE	1986	13.76
COUNTRY CHABLIS	ALMADEN	WHITE	1983	10.00

FIGURE D.39. Wine list.

Finally, she generated the order list using these commands:

To output a listing with selected fields and records

Enter: SET INDEX TO   Turn off use of all indexes

Enter (this command must be typed all on one line):

    LIST ALL OFF NAME, MAKER, ON_HAND FOR ON_HAND < 24 TO PRINT

Enter: EJECT

The requested list, which is an *exception report* containing only those records that meet the reorder criteria, is contained in Figure D.41.

Beth obtained the desired sequence with the INDEX command and then used the LIST command to direct the output to the printer, since she wanted to create a hard copy of each report.

A general form of the LIST command is

To list selected fields and selected records—reference

LIST [**scope**] [**ON/OFF**] [**expression list**] [**FOR condition**] [**TO PRINT**]

BIN	NAME	MAKER	CHILL
A22	ZINFANDEL	TAYLOR FARMS	.F.
A23	NAPA BURGUNDY	TAYLOR FARMS	.F.
A25	EXTRA DRY WHITE	RIVERSIDE	.T.
A25	CABERNET	TAYLOR FARMS	.F.
A26	RED TABLE WINE	TAYLOR FARMS	.F.
A43	COUNTRY CHABLIS	ALMADEN	.T.
A88	BOONE'S FARM	SMOTHERS BRO	.F.
B15	TORRES DE CASTA	M. TORRES	.T.
B20	VINO BIANCO	MOGEN DAVID	.F.
B20	MAD DOG 20/20	MOGEN DAVID	.F.
B34	VINO ROSA	WENTE BROS	.T.
C15	VIN ROSE	GEYSER PEAK	.T.
C22	STRAWBERRY HILL	BOONE'S FARM	.T.
C28	RIPPLE	HOOTCH HUT	.F.
D12	MOREAU ROUGE	J. MOREAU	.F.
D23	BLANC DE BLANC	FETZER VINOS	.T.

FIGURE D.40. Serving list.

NAME	MAKER	ON_HAND
COUNTRY CHABLIS	ALMADEN	15
BLANC DE BLANC	FETZER VINOS	21
MOREAU ROUGE	J. MOREAU	15
TORRES DE CASTA	M. TORRES	10
ZINFANDEL	TAYLOR FARMS	10
RED TABLE WINE	TAYLOR FARMS	11
BOONE'S FARM	SMOTHERS BRO	10

FIGURE D.41. Order list.

where **scope** is the set of records such as ALL, 15, or NEXT 3

ON/OFF indicates the display of record numbers

expression list is the set of fields

FOR condition is a comparison to specified values

TO PRINT indicates the list is to be sent to the printer

D.4.4　Using INDEXED Databases

An INDEX file permits a database to be accessed in the order of the index. However, the index is stored in a separate file. Whenever an indexed database file is *updated* by adding or deleting records, *the index must also be updated.* If more than one index is associated with a database, each index must be changed. This can be accomplished by one of two methods:

1. Always INDEX the database before using the INDEX. If the database is already indexed, its index will be changed.

2. Activate *all* the associated INDEX files *before* making any updates to the database.

The first method is safe, but it requires the most computer processing time. The second method makes the revisions to the INDEX, but you must be careful to be sure *all* the INDEX files are active.

All the INDEX files may be activated when the USE command is entered. For the WINES database, the INDEX files for the wine list and serving list may both be activated with the command:

To activate one or more index files with the USE command	**Enter:**　　USE WINES INDEX WINETYPE, WINEBIN

The database records will be displayed in the sequence specified by the *first* index file in the list. For this example, it is the WINETYPE INDEX.

The SET INDEX TO command may also be used to specify the active index files as follows:

To activate one or more existing index files with SET INDEX TO command	**Enter:**　　SET INDEX TO WINEBIN, WINETYPE

This command causes the database records to be displayed in the order of the WINEBIN index. However, the WINETYPE index is *also updated* when changes are made to the database file by adding new records or by deleting existing records.

So whenever INDEX files are to be updated at the same time as changes are made to the database, be sure to activate *all affected INDEX files* with either the USE command or the SET INDEX TO command.

Keypoint!　　Whenever INDEX files are to be updated at the same time as changes are made to the records in your database, be sure to activate *all* affected INDEX files with either the USE command or the SET INDEX TO command!

D.4.5   When Things Go Wrong

Several situations often cause difficulties when you are arranging and listing a database. Four of the more common difficulties and how to approach them follow.

1. Your data are not arranged in the desired sequence because you issued an INDEX or SORT command using the wrong field(s).

   a. Reissue the INDEX or SORT command. This may be carried out by using the history feature.

   b. When the "File already exits" message appears, specify that you want to overwrite the existing file. This will replace the old file, which was in error, with your newly designated sequence.

   c. Use the DISPLAY, LIST, or BROWSE command to view the data in your newly designated arrangement.

2. You performed a SORT on the correct data fields. However, when you DISPLAY the data they are *not* in the sort sequence, but remain in the same sequence as before the sort was performed.

   a. Check the Status Bar to determine if the sorted database file is your *active database*.

   b. If your active database file *is* the sorted file, then activate the *original* database with the USE command and reissue the SORT command. Something went wrong with your SORT. You may use history in modifying and reissuing your SORT command.

   c. If the active database file is *not* the sorted file or you just performed the SORT in the prior step (b), then employ the USE command to activate your newly created and sorted database file. Once a database has been sorted, the new database file must be activated with the USE command *before* you can view the data in the sorted arrangement.

   d. Make use of the DISPLAY, LIST, or BROWSE commands to view your sorted database file.

3. When performing an INDEX, you receive the "Data type mismatch" message, as illustrated in Figure D.42 for dBASE IV and in Figure D.43 for dBASE III+. This message indicates that the data types for the specified fields are different.

   a. Use history to recall the command at the dot prompt for editing. In dBASE IV, this may also be accomplished by picking Edit from the error message screen.

   b. Make edit changes that add the STR( ) function to your numeric fields.

   c. Execute the revised command.

   d. Use the DISPLAY, LIST, or BROWSE command to review the sequence of your data.

4. You know you have created several INDEX files, but you can't remember their names. You want to activate a previously created INDEX file for use with your database.

   a. **Enter:**   SET INDEX TO ?   Request list of available INDEX files in *your current catalog*

   The "?" causes a screen to appear, as shown in Figure D.44, with a window containing a list of INDEX files available for use with your database. A second window appears that indicates the fields used for arranging the INDEX.

To request a list of INDEX files

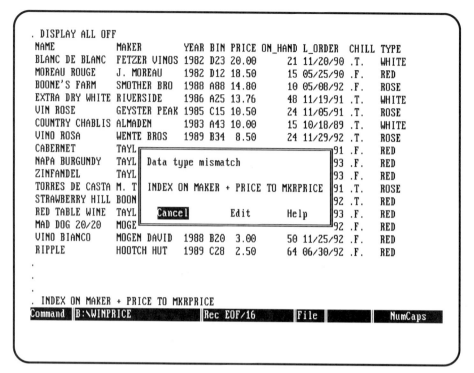

. DISPLAY ALL OFF
```
NAME              MAKER         YEAR BIN PRICE ON_HAND L_ORDER  CHILL TYPE
BLANC DE BLANC    FETZER VINOS  1982 D23 20.00      21 11/20/90 .T.   WHITE
MOREAU ROUGE      J. MOREAU     1982 D12 18.50      15 05/25/90 .F.   RED
BOONE'S FARM      SMOTHER BRO   1988 A88 14.80      10 05/08/92 .F.   ROSE
EXTRA DRY WHITE   RIVERSIDE     1986 A25 13.76      48 11/19/91 .T.   WHITE
VIN ROSE          GEYSTER PEAK  1985 C15 10.50      24 11/05/91 .T.   ROSE
COUNTRY CHABLIS   ALMADEN       1983 A43 10.00      15 10/18/89 .T.   WHITE
VINO ROSA         WENTE BROS    1989 B34  8.50      24 11/29/92 .T.   ROSE
CABERNET          TAYL┌──────────────────────────────────────┐91 .F.   RED
NAPA BURGUNDY     TAYL│ Data type mismatch                   │93 .F.   RED
ZINFANDEL         TAYL│                                      │93 .F.   RED
TORRES DE CASTA   M. T│  INDEX ON MAKER + PRICE TO MKRPRICE  │91 .T.   ROSE
STRAWBERRY HILL   BOON│                                      │92 .T.   RED
RED TABLE WINE    TAYL│ ▐Cancel▌       Edit        Help      │93 .F.   RED
MAD DOG 20/20     MOGE└──────────────────────────────────────┘92 .F.   RED
VINO BIANCO       MOGEN DAVID   1988 B20  3.00      50 11/25/92 .F.   RED
RIPPLE            HOOTCH HUT    1989 C28  2.50      64 06/30/92 .F.   RED
.
.
.
. INDEX ON MAKER + PRICE TO MKRPRICE
```
| Command | B:\WINPRICE | | Rec EOF/16 | File | | NumCaps |

FIGURE D.42. Data type mismatch detected in dBASE IV.

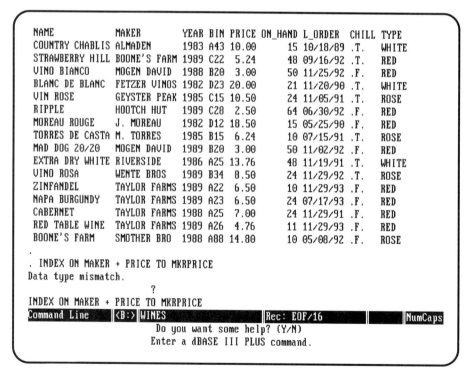

```
NAME              MAKER         YEAR BIN PRICE ON_HAND L_ORDER  CHILL TYPE
COUNTRY CHABLIS   ALMADEN       1983 A43 10.00      15 10/18/89 .T.   WHITE
STRAWBERRY HILL   BOONE'S FARM  1989 C22  5.24      48 09/16/92 .T.   RED
VINO BIANCO       MOGEN DAVID   1988 B20  3.00      50 11/25/92 .F.   RED
BLANC DE BLANC    FETZER VINOS  1982 D23 20.00      21 11/20/90 .T.   WHITE
VIN ROSE          GEYSTER PEAK  1985 C15 10.50      24 11/05/91 .T.   ROSE
RIPPLE            HOOTCH HUT    1989 C28  2.50      64 06/30/92 .F.   RED
MOREAU ROUGE      J. MOREAU     1982 D12 18.50      15 05/25/90 .F.   RED
TORRES DE CASTA   M. TORRES     1985 B15  6.24      10 07/15/91 .T.   ROSE
MAD DOG 20/20     MOGEN DAVID   1989 B20  3.00      50 11/02/92 .F.   RED
EXTRA DRY WHITE   RIVERSIDE     1986 A25 13.76      48 11/19/91 .T.   WHITE
VINO ROSA         WENTE BROS    1989 B34  8.50      24 11/29/92 .T.   ROSE
ZINFANDEL         TAYLOR FARMS  1989 A22  6.50      10 11/29/93 .F.   RED
NAPA BURGUNDY     TAYLOR FARMS  1989 A23  6.50      24 07/17/93 .F.   RED
CABERNET          TAYLOR FARMS  1988 A25  7.00      24 11/29/91 .F.   RED
RED TABLE WINE    TAYLOR FARMS  1989 A26  4.76      11 11/29/93 .F.   RED
BOONE'S FARM      SMOTHER BRO   1988 A88 14.80      10 05/08/92 .F.   ROSE
.
. INDEX ON MAKER + PRICE TO MKRPRICE
Data type mismatch.
                    ?
INDEX ON MAKER + PRICE TO MKRPRICE
```
| Command Line | <B:> WINES | | Rec: EOF/16 | | NumCaps |
```
             Do you want some help? (Y/N)
             Enter a dBASE III PLUS command.
```

FIGURE D.43. Data type mismatch detected in dBASE III+.

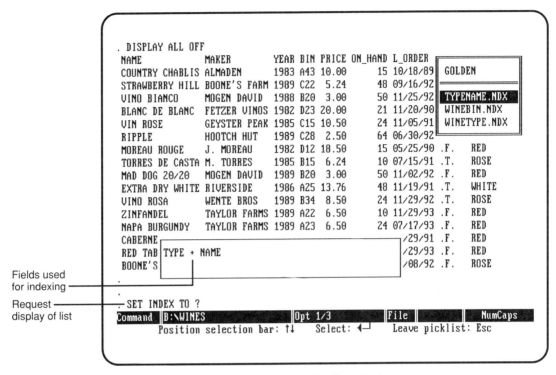

Fields used for indexing

Request display of list

FIGURE D.44. List of index files for selection.

b. **Move to:**	WINEBIN	Desired index file
Press:	Enter	Select index file
Press:	<left>	Leave the menu

version III+

The specified INDEX is thus activated. dBASE provides a message indicating this is the "Master" or active index. Your data are now available in the sequence of this "Master" index.

An alternative method of determining your available INDEX files is this:

To request a list of INDEX files

c. **Enter:**   DIR *.NDX   Request list of available INDEX files on *your entire DATA DISK*

This is a complete list of all NDX files on your data disk, regardless of the application with which they are used.

d. From the list, determine the INDEX file you want to activate.

e. Make use of the SET INDEX TO <index file> command to activate your desired INDEX.

Once you have activated the desired INDEX, you may then view your data in the desired sequence.

D.4.6   Lesson Summary

- The INDEX command facilitates displaying the records in a database in a different sequence than they were entered.

- A dBASE INDEX is stored in a separate file. Several different indexes may exist for the same database. The database is displayed in the sequence of only one "Master" index at a time.

- An index may be created by combining several fields. The additional fields act as tiebreakers when values in the prior fields are identical.
- The SET INDEX TO command activates an inactive INDEX file. When *no* INDEX file name is used, the index is turned off.
- The SORT command rearranges the records stored in a database file and places them in a second file. This results in a duplicate copy of the database file, except it is arranged in a different sequence.
- The combined application of the INDEX and LIST commands supports producing hard copy reports with selected fields and/or selected rows arranged in a specified sequence.
- The index for a database is updated when changes are made to a database file if the index(es) has been activated.
- If an index is *not* active when changes are made to a database, then the index needs to be recreated before displaying the database using the index.

D.4.7 Practice Tutorial

The database for the Wine Management System can be manipulated to construct several listings, as described in this Lesson. Generate these lists as a guided activity in a hands-on manner. Access the WINES database before you begin.

Task 1: Produce the listings identified as items 1 to 4.

Task 2: Create the Wine List, Serving List, and Order List for the Wine Management System.

Time Estimates

Novice: 60 minutes

Intermediate: 45 minutes

Advanced: 30 minutes

D.4.8 Practice Exercises

(1) **Case: Magnum Marketing**

Business Problem: Marketing Research
MIS Characteristics: Marketing
                                Strategic Planning

April Boulay is the director of market monitoring at Magnum Marketing. Magnum monitors the advertised price of grocery products, such as soft drinks and ketchup, in different market areas. Coding associates at Magnum scan daily newspapers recording the advertised price and advertisement size for each product. Also, they record whether or not it was a coop ad. A coop ad is typically a grocery store ad that combines advertising for a particular product together with that for other products. Both the store and the manufacture share in the cost of these coop advertisements. Once collected, these data are available for analysis and reporting to the product's manufacturer. Product manufacturers contract with Magnum for these price-monitoring services. To help with monitoring the advertised prices of products, April designed a database containing fields described by the following data dictionary definition:

Field Name	Description
UPC	Universal Produce Code (scanner bar code number)
PRODUCT	Product name
PACK	Package configuration or size
MARKET	Major city in market area of newspaper
ST	State location of MARKET
DATE	Date of newspaper containing the ad
PRICE	Price specified in ad
SIZE	Area of ad in newspaper in square inches
COOP	Indicator of whether or not this is a coop ad

Task 1: Access the MAGNUM.DBF database file in the EXERCISE catalog and review the structure and data. Produce a hard copy listing of the structure for documentation and reference. The dBASE commands are

- _____
- _____
- _____
- _____

Task 2: Create listings that organize the data in the MAGNUM database like this:

(1) List the products by SIZE from the smallest to largest advertisement sizes. The dBASE commands are

- _____
- _____

(2) List the products with PRODUCT as the primary key and the PACK as the secondary key. The dBASE commands are

- _____
- _____

(3) List the products by MARKET by PACK by PRODUCT. That is, arrange first by MARKET, second by PACK, and third by PRODUCT. The dBASE commands are

- _____
- _____

(4) List the products by PRICE so the higher priced products are listed first, followed by the lower priced products. The dBASE commands are

- _____
- _____

Task 3: Generate a Product Comparison List that contains only the fields PRODUCT, PACK, SIZE, PRICE, MARKET, and ST. This list is arranged by PRODUCT, PACK, and MARKET. The dBASE commands are

. _____

. _____

. _____

Task 4: Generate a Size Comparison List that contains only the fields SIZE, PRICE, PRODUCT, and PACK. This list is arranged by SIZE. The dBASE commands are

. _____

. _____

. _____

Time Estimates

Novice: 90 minutes

Intermediate: 60 minutes

Advanced: 45 minutes

(2) Case: PC Direct

Business Problem: Sales Order Processing
MIS Characteristics: Marketing
                                    Operational Control

PC Direct specializes in mail-order software for personal computers. Nikki Mojica, manager of order processing, is responsible for maintaining their product database. As customers phone in their orders, sales associates check the database to verify the availability and price of each product. Nikki has designed the database so that it contains three fields that are important in correctly filling a customer's order: disk size, disk density, and operating system. PC Direct stocks both DOS and Windows versions of software. The product database, which Nikki designed, contains fields described by the following data dictionary definition:

Field Name	Description
PN	Product number in advertisements and catalogs
DESCRIPT	Software product description or name
VENDOR	Manufacturer or publisher of software
VERSION	Version or release number of software
PRICE	Price charged for software
PROTECT	Indicator of whether or not the software is copy protected
SIZE	Size of disks containing software: 3.5 or 5.25 in.
DENSITY	Density of disks containing software: DD or HD
TYPE	Indicates operating system classified as DOS or WIN
QTY	Quantity of software stocked

Task 1: Access the PCDIRECT.DBF database file in the EXERCISE catalog and review the structure and data. Produce a hard copy listing of the database structure for documentation and reference. The dBASE commands are

· _____

· _____

Task 2: Create listings that organize the data in the PCDIRECT database in this manner:

(1) List the products by PRICE from the smallest to largest PRICE. The dBASE commands are

· _____

· _____

(2) List the products by VENDOR by DESCRIPT by VERSION, with VENDOR as the primary key, DESCRIPT as the secondary key, and VERSION as the third key. The dBASE commands are

· _____

· _____

(3) List the products by VENDOR by DESCRIPT by TYPE by VERSION. That is, arranged first by VENDOR, second by DESCRIPT, third by TYPE, and fourth by VERSION. The dBASE commands are

· _____

· _____

(4) List the products by PRICE so the higher priced products are listed first, followed by the lower priced products. The dBASE commands are

· _____

· _____

Task 3: Generate a Product Reference List that contains only the fields PN, DESCRIPT, VENDOR, VERSION, and TYPE. This list is arranged by PN. The dBASE commands are

· _____

· _____

· _____

Task 4: Generate a Catalog List that contains only the fields VENDOR, DESCRIPT, TYPE, VERSION, PRICE, and SIZE. This list is arranged by DESCRIPT, VENDOR, TYPE, and VERSION. The dBASE commands are

· _____

· _____

· _____

Time Estimates

Novice: 90 minutes

Intermediate: 60 minutes

Advanced: 45 minutes

D.4.9   Comprehensive Problems

(1)   Case: Yen To Travel (continued)

Sara and Ashley have defined several listings they want to generate from the database for their Tour Management System for Yen To Travel.

Task 1: Access the database file in your YENTO catalog.

· _____

· _____

Task 2: Produce listings that organize the tour data in this manner:

(1) List the tours by type—*all* air together, *all* sea, and so on.

· _____

· _____

(2) List the tours by tour code.

· _____

· _____

(3) List the tours arranged by tour type and tour name.

· _____

· _____

(4) List the tours by price so the higher priced tours are listed first, and then the lower priced tours.

· _____

· _____

Task 3: Create the Tour List, Representatives List, and Seat Request List. The fields included in each of these lists are as previously described in the Comprehensive Problem of Using dBASE Lesson D.1. The tours on the Seat Request List are those with fewer than 10 open seats, as specified in Using dBASE Lesson D.3. You may want to refer to these problem descriptions in producing the requested reports.

· _____

· _____

· _____

Time Estimates

Novice: 90 minutes

Intermediate: 60 minutes

Advanced: 30 minutes

(2)   Case: Silver Screen Video (continued)

At Silver Screen Video, Ernie and Amy have decided on several listings they want to assemble from the database for their Movie Management System.

Task 1: Access the database file in your SILVER catalog.

  • _____

  • _____

Task 2: Produce listings that arrange the movies data in this manner:

    (1) List the movies by type—all drama together, all suspense, and so on.

      • _____

      • _____

    (2) List the movies by location code.

      • _____

      • _____

    (3) List the movies arranged by movie type and movie name.

      • _____

      • _____

    (4) List the movies by price so the higher priced movies are listed first, and then the lower priced movies.

      • _____

      • _____

Task 3: Create the Movie List, Sales List, and Order List. The database fields included in each of these report listings are as previously described in the Comprehensive Problem of Using dBASE Lesson D.1. The movies to be reordered are those shown on TV with fewer than 7 units in inventory and those *not* on TV with fewer than 15 units, as specified as the exception condition in Using dBASE Lesson D.3. You may want to review those descriptions in determining the desired user requirements for these reports. [*Hint:* Use the .OR. logical operator and group the compound conditions to create one Order List containing the movies both on TV and *not* on TV.]

  • _____

  • _____

  • _____

Time Estimates

Novice: 90 minutes

Intermediate: 60 minutes

Advanced: 30 minutes

D.4.10 Application Case

(1)   **Case: Electronic Data Systems**

Business Problem: Skills Inventory
MIS Characteristics: Human Resources
                                    Managerial Control
Management Functions: Organizing
                                    Staffing
                                    Controlling
Tools Skills: Indexing
                    Sorting
                    Listing data

Electronic Data Systems (EDS) is a world leader in the computer and communications services industry. Headquartered in Dallas, Texas, EDS was founded in 1962 to design, develop, and implement large-scale business- and industry-specific applications. EDS pioneered the "facilities management" concept of service, in which EDS assumes all of the information processing responsibilities for its customers. EDS offers its customers, located in the United States and 27 foreign countries, cost-effective information services and business support. In order to meet the diverse and specific needs of the marketplace, EDS offers industry education, state-of-the-art communications, central systems support, recruiting and professional development, research, office automation, and financial and administrative skills. The customers of EDS include leading organizations in the automotive, government services, finance, insurance, communications, retail, distribution, transportation, utilities, and health care industries.

Examples of EDS involvement around the world are nearly limitless. General Motors (GM) receives computing and communications services to support their worldwide vehicle manufacturing. The U. S. Air Force has contracted with EDS to implement a Combat Ammunition System at virtually every Air Force base in the world. A five-year contract with California's Medi-Cal program supports the largest Medicare program in the nation. EDS recently extended it contract with Blue Shield of California for health insurance processing. "TradPro," a comprehensive multinational financial market trade processing system, was recently implemented for Shearson Lehman's United Kingdom operations. EDS supplies facilities management to Wilton-Fijenoord, the largest ship repair yard in the Netherlands. Shell Brasil SA, Brazil's second largest company, is provided computer and communications services. Other EDS commercial customers include Exxon, Kodak, Kmart, AT&T, and Western Union.

As described by Les Alberthal, President and Chief Executive Officer:

> EDS teams have created solution after solution to systems integration problems. Regardless of their magnitude. Regardless of their complexity. Our customers believe in us. And we believe in our ability to serve our customers. And we believe in performance delivered at a firm fixed price. Around the globe, for greater productivity, EDS is the team you can believe in. We do our job right, so you can do what you do best.

William D. "Bill" Stephenson, Vice President of the Systems Development Division (SDD), is concerned with the management of developing computer-based information systems for EDS customers. Within SDD, systems engineers (SEs) are assigned to the construction of integrated computer systems to solve a customer's business problems with information technology. The responsibility of managing each customer's project resides with a senior project manager. Konnie Goulding is a project manager who has been working with Bill on their Skill Inventory System (SIS). This system maintains information on the skills of systems engineers and their availability for assignment to projects. Konnie and Bill have established a maximum availability of a systems engineer at 1640 hours per year. Although EDS plans on a 2080-hour work year, the difference in hours is consumed with continuing education and other responsibilities. Some systems engineers have an even more limited availability, because of their management obligations. Working with Konnie, the senior project managers have defined several listings of information from the skills database of the SIS, which would assist them in identifying systems engineers with the appropriate skills and available time for assignment to their project. Each senior project manager is responsible for obtaining the required systems engineers from the pool of talent in the skill database of the SIS.

Konnie, working with Bill, the other senior project managers, and the human resource department, has developed the SIS skill database, which includes the following fields:

Field Name	Description
NAME	Systems engineer's (SE) name
SKILL_1	Primary system skill area
SKILL_2	Secondary system skill area
SKILL_3	Tertiary system skill area
EXP	Number of years of experience in systems engineering
BILL_RATE	Project hourly billing rate for systems engineer
HOUR_RATE	Wage rate paid to systems engineer
CDP	Whether or not systems engineer holds CDP certification
TOTAL	Total hours per year systems engineer can be assigned to development projects; excludes hours allowed for other, nonbillable activities
ASSGN	Hours systems engineer has been assigned to development projects

Tasks

1. Access the SKILL.DBF database of EDS's Skills Inventory System in the CASES catalog and review its structure and content. Obtain a hard copy of the structure.

2. Produce the following listings of information from the SIS database for use by the senior project managers:

   (a) A skill listing with the systems engineers (SEs) arranged by SKILL_1, SKILL_2, and SKILL_3, with SKILL_1 as the most important. The listing should contain the SE's name, each skill, experience, and CDP status.

   (b) A billing rate listing with the systems engineers organized by project hourly billing amount from the lowest billing rate to the highest billing rate. This listing should contain the SE's name, billing rate, total hours per year, and total assigned hours for the year.

   (c) An experience listing with systems engineers arranged by number of years of experience, with the most experienced listed first. This listing should contain the SE's name, years of experience, each skill, and hourly rate.

   (d) An availability listing with systems engineers arrayed by number of available hours for the year. This list should contain the SE's name, total hours per year, assigned hours for the year, available hours for the year, number of years experience, and primary skill. [*Hint:* Create a new field for available hours. Compute the available hours from the total hours and the assigned hours using the REPLACE command.]

3. The SKILL database does not include a social security number or personnel identification number. Should Bill and Konnie consider adding this to the database? Why or why not? What other listings could be produced from this database to assist in managing information systems development projects? Write a summary examining these questions.

Time Estimates

Novice: 120 minutes

Intermediate: 90 minutes

Advanced: 45 minutes

Creating Reports

CONTENT

- Designing Reports
- Defining dBASE Reports
- Producing dBASE Reports
- Quick Reports [dBASE IV]
- When Things Go Wrong

D.5.1 Designing Reports

Although the listings that Beth produced for the Golden Gourmet contained the desired information, Bert and Auggie have suggested that the appearance could be improved. Auggie would like a more impressive display of the Wine List for their customers. dBASE facilitates the creation of reports with a page heading, column headings, detail lines, field breaks, and totals. This permits more control over the appearance of a report than that which is available with the LIST command. A report for the Wine List can be produced as shown in Figure D.45, which also illustrates the three main logical pieces or areas of this report. To produce this dBASE report, a report format definition is created for use in displaying the data. dBASE stores these report format definitions in *separate files* with the .FRM extension.

A report format is a *description of the appearance of a final output report*, like that in Figure D.45. As shown in Figure D.46, the "final report" is produced when data from the database are output following the *description* contained in the report format definition. That is, a report format provides a description of how the data are to be displayed, but it is *not* the final report.

D.5.2 Defining dBASE Reports

Before Beth started entering the report format, she developed a plan for the report by sketching out a rough draft of the desired output, as illustrated in Figure D.47. This report sketch or layout is an example of how the report will appear when it is complete. Beth used X's to indicate character type data and 9's for numeric type data. These X's and 9's are merely place holders to indicate the location of these detail data when they are obtained from the database for the final report.

GOLDEN GOURMET
WINE LIST

— Page
Heading

WINES	VINEYARD	TYPE	YEAR	PRICE PER BOTTLE
STRAWBERRY HILL	BOONE'S FARM	RED	1989	5.24
VINO BIANCO	MOGEN DAVID	RED	1988	3.00
RIPPLE	HOOTCH HUT	RED	1989	2.50
MOREAU ROUGE	J. MOREAU	RED	1982	18.50
MAD DOG 20/20	MOGEN DAVID	RED	1988	3.00
ZINFANDEL	TAYLOR FARMS	RED	1988	6.50
NAPA BURGUNDY	TAYLOR FARMS	RED	1989	6.50
CABERNET	TAYLOR FARMS	RED	1986	7.00
RED TABLE WINE	TAYLOR FARMS	RED	1989	4.76
VIN ROSE	GEYSER PEAK	ROSE	1985	10.50
TORRES DE CASTA	M. TORRES	ROSE	1985	6.24
VINO ROSA	WENTE BROS	ROSE	1989	8.50
BOONE'S FARM	SMOTHERS BRO	ROSE	1988	14.80
COUNTRY CHABLIS	ALMADEN	WHITE	1983	10.00
BLANC DE BLANC	FETZER VINOS	WHITE	1982	20.00
EXTRA DRY WHITE	RIVERSIDE	WHITE	1986	13.76

— Column
Titles

— Detail
Lines

FIGURE D.45. Report Wine List.

Before you begin to create a report format, it is necessary to open the catalog for your application and to activate the database from which the report's data are obtained when the report is produced. This is accomplished with these commands:

Enter: SET CATALOG TO GOLDEN

Open catalog containing the database

Enter: USE WINES

Activate database containing data from which final report is to be produced

Keypoint!

An active database *must* be available for selecting the fields that are to be included in the report format definition. If an active database is *not* available, a report format *cannot* be created!

The process for fabricating the report format is initiated by entering the following command at the dot prompt:

To begin entering a REPORT format

Enter: CREATE REPORT WINELIST

Begin report format definition

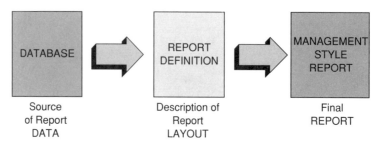

FIGURE D.46. Relationship among report writer components.

```
                    1111111111222222222233333333334444444444555555555566666
           12345678901234567890123456789012345678901234567890123456789012 34
 1
 2                                 GOLDEN  GOURMET
 3                                  WINE  LIST
 4
 5
 6                                                               PRICE
 7                                                                PER
 8            WINES               VINEYARD       TYPE    YEAR    BOTTLE
 9
10       XXXXXXXXXXXXXX       XXXXXXXXXXXX      XXXXX    XXXX     99.99
11       XXXXXXXXXXXXXX       XXXXXXXXXXXX      XXXXX    XXXX     99.99
12       XXXXXXXXXXXXXX       XXXXXXXXXXXX      XXXXX    XXXX     99.99
13       XXXXXXXXXXXXXX       XXXXXXXXXXXX      XXXXX    XXXX     99.99
                                     .
                                     .
                                     .
         XXXXXXXXXXXXXX       XXXXXXXXXXXX      XXXXX    XXXX     99.99
```

FIGURE D.47. Sketch of Wine List report layout.

The CREATE command is typically used for a brand new report format. Once a report format has been entered, it is changed by using the MODIFY REPORT command. If you want to change your report after it has been initially CREATEd, then use this MODIFY command.

All report formats are created under the CONTROL CENTER/ASSIST mode of operation with a "blackboard" or "report design work surface" provided for entering the page heading and column titles. A dot prompt option is *not* available for defining report formats.

One of the most significant differences between dBASE IV and dBASE III+ is the manner in which a report format is developed. dBASE IV provides you with more flexibility in creating report format definitions than dBASE III+. Because of the vast differences, the development of the report format definition is presented separately for each of the versions. Although the procedures for creating the report format definitions are different, the other commands employed to begin creating the report format definition and to produce the final output report are the same for both versions. Thus for developing the report format definition, your attention is directed to the version that is available for your use. You may want to read through the description of the other version to become familiar with the differences between these report format definition procedures.

D.5.2.1. Version III+ Report Format Definition

After the CREATE command has been entered, the screen shown in Figure D.48 appears for entering the report format. The report format of Figures D.45 and D.47 is input as described below:

To enter a report title or heading	**Move to:**	Options
	Move to:	Page Title
	Press:	<Enter> Select entry of the page title

A page heading or report title "blackboard" appears as shown in Figure D.49. The title is entered as follows:

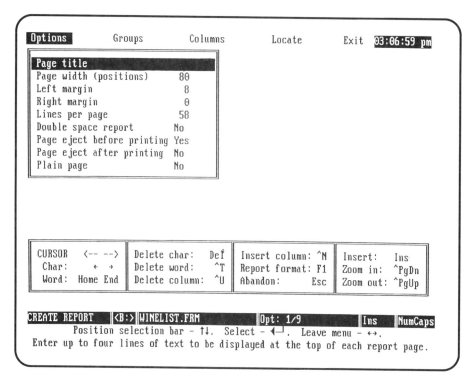

FIGURE D.48. Report format menu screen (version III+).

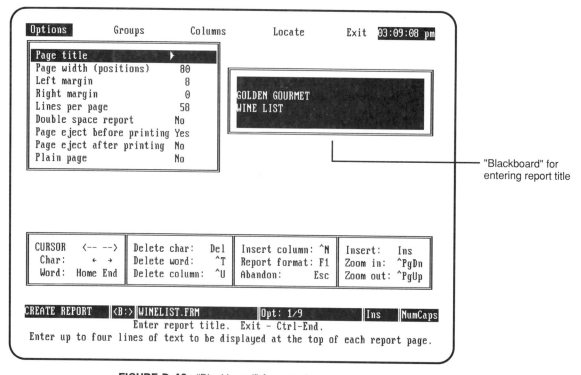

FIGURE D.49. "Blackboard" for entering page heading (version III+).

Type: `<Enter>`   Skip the top line
             `GOLDEN GOURMET<Enter>`
                                              First title line
             `WINE LIST<Enter>`   Second title line
             `<Enter>`   Terminate entry of the page title

To turn OFF the page eject *before* printing

Move to: `Page eject before printing`
Press: `<Enter>`   Toggle Yes to No

To request page eject *after* printing

Move to: `Page eject after printing`
Press: `<Enter>`   Toggle No to Yes

To request a plain page without a date or page number

Move to: `Plain page`
Press: `<Enter>`   Toggle No to Yes

A "plain page" is one without the current date and page number in the upper-left-hand corner of the page. Selecting this characteristic completes the specification of the report title and the page eject. dBASE will automatically center this heading over the width of the page as specified by the page margins. The size of the margins remains at the defaults.

Now, each of the columns or fields of data to be displayed in the report can be selected and a heading can be specified for each. Proceed in this manner:

To specify the first column included in the report

Move to: `Columns`
Press: `<Enter>`   Select column name entry
Press: `<F10>`   Display list of available columns or fields for the active database
Move to: `NAME`
Press: `<Enter>`   Select NAME
Press: `<Enter>`   Complete contents specification
Move to: `Heading`
Press: `<Enter>`   Select heading entry

A "blackboard" appears for entering the column heading similar to that in Figure D.49. Proceed as follows:

Type: `<Enter>`   First line is blank
             `<Enter>`   Second line is blank
             `<space><space>WINES<Enter>`
                                              Third line contains heading
             `<Enter>`   Terminate entry of this heading

Here, the column title is to appear on the third line. You may place the title on any of the four lines.

To specify the width of the first column

Move to: `Width`
Press: `<Enter>`   Select width specification
Enter: `17`   Desired column width
Press: `<PgDn>`   Go to next column in report format

MAKER is the next column in the report format. It is described in this manner:

Press:	`<Enter>`	Select column name entry
Press:	`<F10>`	Display list of available columns
Select:	`MAKER`	Desired field name
Press:	`<Enter>`	Complete contents specification
Move to:	`Heading`	
Press:	`<Enter>`	Select heading entry
Type:	`<Enter>`	Blank line
	`<Enter>`	Blank line
	`<space><space>VINEYARD<Enter>`	
		Desired column heading
	`<Enter>`	Terminate entry of this heading
Move to:	`Width`	
Press:	`<Enter>`	Select width specification
Enter:	`14`	Specify desired width
Press:	`<PgDn>`	Go to next column in report format

TYPE (that is the type of wine) is the next column in the report format. It is described in this manner:

Press:	`<Enter>`	Select column name entry
Press:	`<F10>`	Display list of available columns
Select:	`TYPE`	Desired field name
Press:	`<Enter>`	Complete contents specification
Move to:	`Heading`	
Press:	`<Enter>`	Select heading entry
Type:	`<Enter>`	Blank line
	`<Enter>`	Blank line
	`Type <Enter>`	Desired column heading
	`<Enter>`	Terminate entry of this heading
Move to:	`Width`	
Press:	`<Enter>`	Select width specification
Enter:	`7`	Specify desired width
Press:	`<PgDn>`	Go to next column in report format

YEAR is the next column in the report format. It is described in this manner:

Press:	`<Enter>`	Select column name entry
Press:	`<F10>`	Display list of available columns
Select:	`YEAR`	Desired field name
Press:	`<Enter>`	Complete contents specification
Move to:	`Heading`	
Press:	`<Enter>`	Select heading entry
Type:	`<Enter>`	Blank line
	`<Enter>`	Blank line
	`YEAR<Enter>`	Desired column heading
	`<Enter>`	Terminate entry of this heading

Move to:	Width	
Press:	<Enter>	Select width specification
Enter:	6	Specify desired width
Press:	<PgDn>	Go to next column in report format

PRICE is the next column in the report format. It is described in this manner:

Continue to specify report columns

Press:	<Enter>	Select column name entry
Press:	<F10>	Display list of available columns
Select:	PRICE	Desired field name
Press:	<Enter>	Complete contents specification
Move to:	Heading	
Press:	<Enter>	Select heading entry
Type:	PRICE<Enter>	Begin column heading
	PER<ENTER>	Continue column heading
	BOTTLE<Enter>	Third line of heading
	<Enter>	Terminate entry of this heading
Move to:	Width	
Press:	<Enter>	Select width specification
Enter:	8	Specify desired width
Move to:	Total this column	
Press:	<Enter>	Toggle off column total

This completes entry of the report format. Figure D.50 illustrates the completed report format. The format can now be saved to use in producing a report with the database.

To save the REPORT format and return to the dot prompt

Select:	Exit
Select:	Save

Keypoint!

- DELETE an *unwanted column* from a report format definition by using <PgUp> or <PgDn> to move to the desired column. Then, press <Ctrl>+<U> to remove the column. Any report columns that do *not* contain a database field are indicated by a question mark (?) in the REPORT FORMAT area. These empty fields should be removed from the report definition to avoid errors in producing the final report!

- INSERT an *additional column* in a report format definition by using <PgUp> or <PgDn> to move to the desired column *before* which the column will be inserted. Then, press <Ctrl>+<N> to insert the column!

- Obtain HELP with report format entries by pressing <F1> to toggle to the Help display!

D.5.2.2. Version IV Report Format Definition

After the CREATE command has been issued, the screen shown in Figure D.51 appears; it displays the report design work surface where the report format is entered. In general, the design work surface lets you enter the report by painting the layout in a manner similar to that of the sketch in Figure D.47. This report form definition template looks very much like the final report.

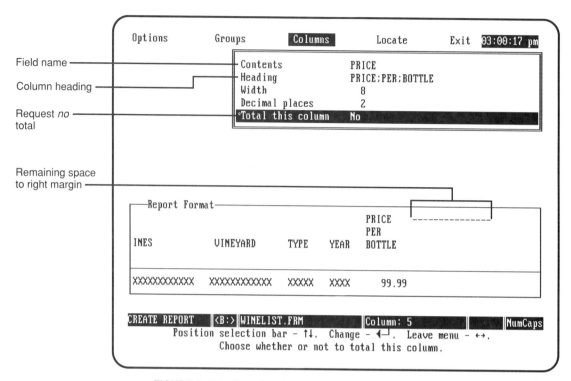

Field name
Column heading
Request *no* total
Remaining space to right margin
Options Groups Columns Locate Exit 03:00:17 pm
Contents PRICE
Heading PRICE;PER;BOTTLE
Width 8
Decimal places 2
Total this column No
Report Format
PRICE
PER
INES VINEYARD TYPE YEAR BOTTLE
XXXXXXXXXXXX XXXXXXXXXXXX XXXXX XXXX 99.99
CREATE REPORT <B:> WINELIST.FRM Column: 5 NumCaps
Position selection bar - ↑↓. Change - ◄┘. Leave menu - ↔.
Choose whether or not to total this column.

FIGURE D.50. Completed report format [version III+].

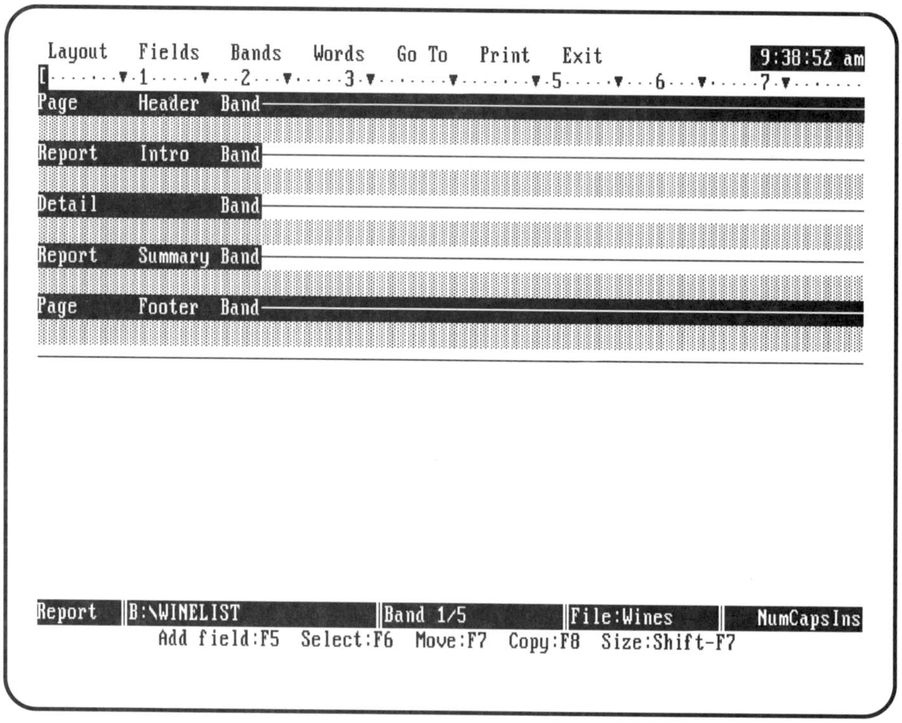

Layout Fields Bands Words Go To Print Exit 9:38:52 am
Page Header Band
Report Intro Band
Detail Band
Report Summary Band
Page Footer Band
Report B:\WINELIST Band 1/5 File:Wines NumCapsIns
Add field:F5 Select:F6 Move:F7 Copy:F8 Size:Shift-F7

FIGURE D.51. Report design work surface [version IV].

The design work surface is divided into six different report areas known as report "bands." Only five of these bands appear initially on the design surface shown in Figure D.51; the sixth is specified when it is required as a report option. The six report bands are as follows:

- *Page Header Band.* contains information that will be repeated at the *top of each page* that is printed. Typically, this would include the Page Heading and Column Titles shown in Figure D.45. In addition, this band may contain a report date and page number.

- *Report Intro Band.* contains information that appears only on the *first page* of the report. This might contain an explanation of the data appearing in the report.

- *Detail Band.* contains data values from records obtained from the database. These are the Detail Lines illustrated in Figure D.45.

- *Report Summary Band.* contains final summary totals that appear only at the *end of the report.* Concluding remarks and other narrative descriptions may be included here.

- *Page Footer Band.* contains information that is repeated at the *bottom of each page* that is printed. This might be a company name or running title or the report. If desired, this band may contain a page number or report date.

- *Group Bands.* when included, contain introductory and summary information for a set of records that make up the group. Each group is typically identified by a value in a selected field, such as grouping by the wine TYPEs of RED, ROSE, and WHITE. (Group bands are explored in the next lesson.)

On entering this dBASE IV report generator, the third or middle section of the Status Bar, shown in Figure D.51, specifies the location of the cursor. Initially, this value is **Band 1/5.** This indicates that the cursor is in the top band of the five available bands. As you move the cursor around on the design work surface, the current location of the cursor will continue to be displayed. The report format of Figures D.45 and D.47 is developed as described below.

In Version 1.5, you can use the mouse to position the cursor on the design work surface and make menu selections. These mouse operations are summarized in Figure D.52.

The Page Heading and Column Titles, sketched out in Figure D.45, are created in this manner:

| To insert space at top of report | **Press:** | <down> | Move cursor to Line 0, Col 0 in the Page Header Band |
| | **Press:** | <Enter> | Insert a blank line |

Yes, dBASE starts numbering the lines and columns in each band with zero (0), rather than one (1). The cursor movement keys <right>, <left>, <down>, and <up> are used to position the cursor at the desired location for typing the Page Heading and Column Titles.

To enter a report heading	**Move to:**	Line 1, Col 27	Position cursor for entering Page Heading
	Type:	GOLDEN GOURMET	First line of heading
	Press:	<Enter>	Insert another blank line
	Move to:	Line 2, Col 29	Position cursor for second heading line
	Type:	WINE LIST	Second line of heading
	Press:	<Enter>	Insert blank line
	Press:	<Enter>	One more line

Operation	Action
Move cursor to a location on the design work surface	Click the desired location
Add a field	Double-click the position where the field is to be added and use the fields list that appears to define the field. Or click **Addfield:F5** on the navigation line.
Modify a field	Double click the field
Highlight an item	Click the item
Move or copy text or a field	Highlight the item on the navigation line, choose **F6 Select**, and press <**Enter**>. On the navigation line, choose **F7 Move** or **F8 Copy**, move the item to the desired destination using the mouse, and click.
Create a box or line	Choose **Box** or **Line** from the **Layout** menu, click the starting position and drag to draw, and then release to complete drawing.
Size field template	Click the template. On the navigation line, select **Size:Shift-F7**, move mouse pointer to desired size, and click.
Open/close a report band	Double-click band border. (If the band is already highlighted, just click the band border.)
Open a menu on the menu bar	Click the menu name
Select from a menu	Click the menu item
Close menu	Click outside the menu

FIGURE D.52. Mouse actions with REPORT FORM.

Now the column titles can be entered for each of the fields displayed in the report.

To enter column titles as three lines	**Move to:**	Line 4, Col 56	Location for Column Title
	Type:	PRICE	Only column title in this line
	Press:	<Enter>	Advance to next line
	Move to:	Line 5, Col 58	Location for next piece of Column Title
	Type:	PER	Only column title in this line
	Press:	<Enter>	One more line
	Move to:	Line 6, Col 7	Location of next Column Title
	Type:	WINES	Column title for the NAME field
	Move to:	Line 6, Col 25	Next location
	Type:	VINEYARD	Column title for the MAKER field
	Move to:	Line 6, Col 39	
	Type:	TYPE	Include Column Title for the wine TYPE
	Move to:	Line 6, Col 46	
	Type:	YEAR	Next column title
	Move to:	Line 6, Col 55	
	Type:	BOTTLE	Complete the Column Titles
	Press:	<Enter>	Add one blank line after Column Titles

This completes entry of the report heading and column titles in the Page Header Band.

The Report Intro Band, which is not used since *no message* is to be included, is removed in this manner:

Press:	<down>	
Press:	<down>	Locate cursor on blank line in Report Intro Band
Press:	<Ctrl>+<Y>	Delete unwanted blank line

To remove blank lines from unused Report Intro Band

The Detail Lines, which contain the data for each record displayed in the report of Figure D.47, are set up as follows:

Press:	<down>	
Press:	<down>	Locate cursor on blank line in Detail Band

To position the cursor at the location of the first field

Move to:	Line 0, Col 5	Position of first data field
Press:	<F5>	Select "Add field"

To specify the first field in the Detail Line

A list of fields in the WINES database is displayed as illustrated in Figure D.53. The desired fields for each column in the report are selected from the list like this:

Move to:	NAME	Position selection bar on desired field name
Press:	<Enter>	Complete this field selection

Selecting the field results in a display of the template for this field, as shown in Figure D.54. Here, the X's are place holders that indicate the width of a character field. The

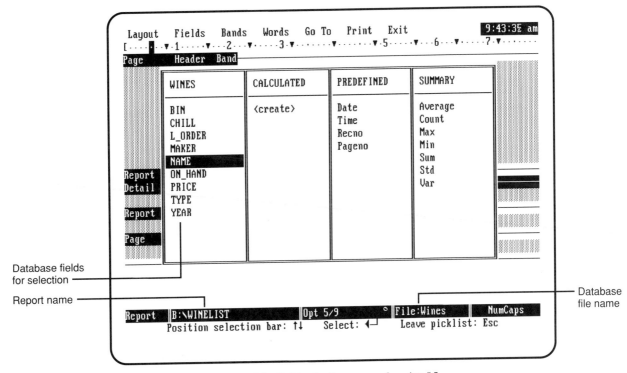

FIGURE D.53. Field selection screen [version IV].

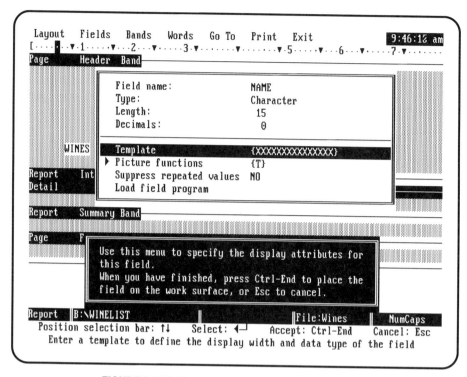

FIGURE D.54. Template definition screen [version IV].

width of the field is established from the field width of the currently active WINES database structure. Accept the suggested template and continue in this manner:

	Press:	<Ctrl>+<End>	Accept template definition

To specify the next field in the Detail Line

Move to:	Line 0, Col 23	Position of next field
Press:	<F5>	Select "Add field"
Select:	MAKER	Desired field
Press:	<Ctrl>+<End>	Accept template definition

To specify the next field

Move to:	Line 0, Col 38	Position of next field
Press:	<F5>	
Select:	TYPE	That is, the wine TYPE field
Press:	<Ctrl>+<End>	Accept template

To indicate the next field in the Detail Line

Move to:	Line 0, Col 46	
Press:	<F5>	
Select:	YEAR	Desired field
Press:	<Ctrl>+<End>	Complete field specification

To continue defining the Detail Line

Move to:	Line 0, Col 56	
Press:	<F5>	
Select:	PRICE	Next desired field
Press:	<Ctrl>+<End>	Accept numeric template

This completes the specification of the Detail Band.

The Report Summary Band and the Page Footer Band are not used for producing the report in Figure D.45. The blank lines produced by these bands may be removed in this manner:

To remove the blank lines of the unused Report Band	**Press:**	`<down><down>`	Position cursor at blank line in Report Summary Band

Press: `<Ctrl>+<Y>`   Remove unwanted line

Press: `<down><down>`   Position cursor in blank line in Page Footer Band

Press: `<Ctrl>+<End>`   Remove unwanted line

The finished report form definition appears as shown in Figure D.55.

Keypoint!   If an unwanted field has been accidentally included in the Detail Band of your report, this may be removed by placing the cursor on the unwanted field and pressing <Del>!

Caution Alert!   If the Detail Band contains one or more blank lines, these blank lines will be included for *each* detail line printed. This may cause your report to be double or triple spaced! Unwanted blank lines may be removed with the <Ctrl> + <Y> keys!

With dBASE IV, you may preview your report on the screen while you are creating your report format definition. The "Print" option in the Report Menu, at the top of the

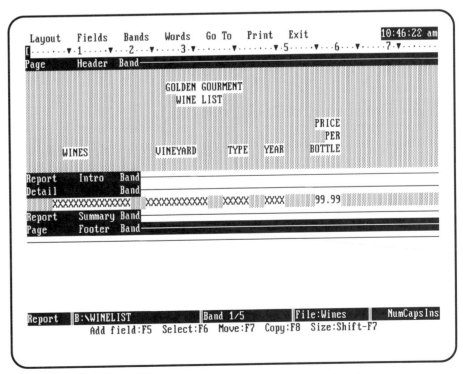

FIGURE D.55. Completed report format [version IV].

report format screen, allows you to carry out this action. Selecting the "Print" option may be accomplished in either of two ways as follows:

<table>
<tr><td>To PREVIEW a report before actually printing it</td><td>**Press:**</td><td><Alt>+<P></td><td>Selects "Print" from the Report Menu</td></tr>
<tr><td></td><td>or</td><td></td><td></td></tr>
<tr><td></td><td>**Press:**</td><td><F10></td><td>Access Report Menu Bar</td></tr>
<tr><td></td><td>**Move to:**</td><td>Print</td><td>Desired menu action</td></tr>
</table>

The screen preview can now be selected like this:

<table>
<tr><td>**Move to:**</td><td>View report on screen</td><td></td></tr>
<tr><td></td><td></td><td>Desire activity</td></tr>
<tr><td>**Press:**</td><td><Enter></td><td>Select action</td></tr>
</table>

If any modifications are required, they can be made immediately. After you have finished "viewing" the report, continue:

Press: <Esc>   Return to report format definition screen

When you have completed your report format definition, then exit and save the format in this manner:

<table>
<tr><td>To save the REPORT format and return to the dot prompt</td><td>**Press:**</td><td><Alt>+<E></td><td>Direct command selection</td></tr>
<tr><td></td><td>or</td><td></td><td></td></tr>
<tr><td></td><td>**Press:**</td><td><F10></td><td>Access menu for selection</td></tr>
<tr><td></td><td>**Move to:**</td><td>Exit</td><td></td></tr>
<tr><td></td><td>**Select:**</td><td>Save changes and exit</td><td>Select desired action</td></tr>
</table>

dBASE IV compiles your report definition into a more readily usable form as you are returned to the dot prompt, completing your report format definition.

D.5.3　Producing dBASE Reports

Once Beth has entered the report format definition, it is ready to be used in producing the Wine List. The report is generated for both versions III+ and IV in the same manner with this command:

<table>
<tr><td>To generate the final output report</td><td>**Enter:**</td><td>REPORT FORM WINELIST TO PRINT</td></tr>
</table>

A report containing data from the active database is produced by using the specified report format description.

If it is desired to have all of the wines grouped together on the report by type, then an INDEX can be used in generating the report. If the index WINETYPE has been produced that indexes on the TYPE of wine, then the report can be produced in this manner:

<table>
<tr><td>To generate a report with records arranged in INDEX sequence</td><td>**Enter:**</td><td>SET INDEX TO WINETYPE</td></tr>
<tr><td></td><td>**Enter:**</td><td>REPORT FORM WINELIST TO PRINT</td></tr>
</table>

1. Design report by sketching its layout.

2. Activate database containing report data.

3. Create report format definition.

   a. Enter: CREATE REPORT <report file name>

   b. Specify page heading

   c. Specify fields from the database and the associated column titles for display in each report column

4. Exit report format definition and save format.

5. Produce final report by using the report format definition and the active database.

   a. SET INDEX, if desired, to sequence final report output

   b. Enter: REPORT FORM <report file name> TO PRINT

6. Revise report definition, if necessary.

   a. Enter: MODIFY REPORT <report file name>

   b. Make desired changes

   c. Exit and produce report as indicated above

FIGURE D.56. Summary of producing dBASE reports.

The resulting report is shown in Figure D.45. The steps for producing a dBASE report are summarized in Figure D.56.

Caution Alert!

If the message "Syntax error in field expression" occurs, chances are you have created a column in your report form definition that does *not* contain a field name or valid expression. This column will be identified by the appearance of a question mark (?) in the heading area or in the column width image area of the dBASE III+ Report Format. Modify the report form either by editing the column contents or by removing the unwanted column!

dBASE III+

D.5.4   Quick Reports [dBASE IV]

dBASE Version IV provides a means for quickly developing a report format definition. This feature is *not* available in Version III+. Once developed, the report format can be used directly or it can be revised to produce a customized report from the initial "Quick Report." Figure D.57 is an example of a Quick Report produced from the WINES database. Key characteristics of this report:

- Includes all the fields of the database appearing from left to right in the same sequence as they are defined in the database structure.

- Displays a page number and date in the upper-left-hand corner that are generated by dBASE.

- Contains column titles that are the field names obtained from the database structure. Column titles for character, logical, and date field types are left-justified, and those for a numeric field type are right-justified above the contents of each column.

- Contains detail lines consisting of all of the fields in the database in the same sequences as they are defined in the database structure. The width of each field on the report is determined to be the larger of the field width specification or the name of the field from the structure. The width of numeric fields are increased to allow for summing these values.

- Displays a summary line that contains a total for each of the numeric fields defined in the database structure.

Page No.   1
2/13/92

NAME	MAKER	YEAR	BIN	PRICE	ON_HAND	L_ORDER	CHILL	TYPE
COUNTRY CHABLIS	ALMADEN	1983	A43	9.00	15	10/18/89	Y	WHITE
STRAWBERRY HILL	BOONE'S FARM	1989	C22	5.24	48	09/16/92	Y	RED
VINO BIANCO	MOGEN DAVID	1988	B20	3.00	50	11/25/92	N	RED
BLANC DE BLANC	FETZER VINOS	1982	D23	19.00	21	11/20/90	Y	WHITE
VIN ROSE	GEYSER PEAK	1985	C15	9.50	24	11/05/91	Y	ROSE
RIPPLE	HOOTCH NUT	1989	C28	2.50	64	06/30/92	N	RED
MOREAU ROUGE	J. MOREAU	1982	D12	18.50	15	05/25/90	N	RED
TORRES DE CASTA	M. TORRES	1985	B15	5.24	10	07/15/91	Y	ROSE
MAD DOG 20/20	MOGEN DAVID	1989	B20	3.00	50	11/02/92	N	RED
EXTRA DRY WHITE	RIVERSIDE	1986	A25	12.76	48	11/19/91	Y	WHITE
VINO ROSA	WENTE BROS	1989	B34	7.50	24	11/29/92	Y	ROSE
ZINFANDEL	TAYLOR FARMS	1989	A22	6.50	10	11/29/93	N	RED
NAPA BURGUNDY	TAYLOR FARMS	1989	A23	6.50	24	07/17/93	N	RED
CABERNET	TAYLOR FARMS	1988	A25	7.00	24	11/29/91	N	RED
RED TABLE WINE	TAYLOR FARMS	1989	A26	4.76	11	11/29/93	N	RED
BOONE'S FARM	SMOTHER BRO	1988	A88	13.80	10	05/08/92	N	ROSE
				133.80	448			

FIGURE D.57. Quick Report [version IV].

The report form definition for this Quick Report is described as shown in the report design work surface of Figure D.58. Notice how the column titles, detail line, and summary line are defined in each band of this report definition. The contents of the Report Intro Band have been completely eliminated, while the Page Footer Band contains a single blank line. This Quick Report form definition is produced, beginning from the dot prompt, in this manner:

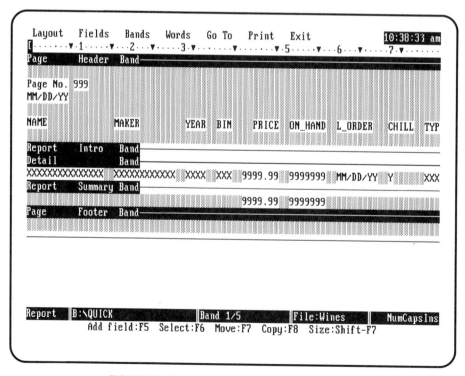

FIGURE D.58. Quick Report definition [version IV].

To create a Quick REPORT format	**Enter:**	CREATE REPORT QUICK	Begin report format definition

Of course, you may use any desired report file name. QUICK was used, since this reflects how the definition was created. The initiation of this report definition is the same as for developing any other report form definition in dBASE IV. Once the design work surface appears, then continue like this:

Press:	<F10>	Access Report Menu Bar
Move to:	Layout	If necessary
Select:	Quick layouts	Desired option
Select:	Column layout	Desired report arrangement

Figure D.59 illustrates these menu selections. Once you have selected the "Column layout," the report definition shown in Figure D.58 is automatically generated and ready for your immediate use or modification.

Action: Preview this Quick Report on your screen. The result should look like Figure D.60. Notice that the TYPE field is wider than the 80 characters that can be displayed on your screen. This causes the line to "wrap around" to the next line on the screen.

Action: Save this Quick Report definition and exit to the dot prompt. At the dot prompt, you are ready to produce a hard copy of this report, as described in the previous section of this lesson. Depending on your printer, "wrap around" may occur or the output line may be truncated. For now, just observe the results when you produce this report.

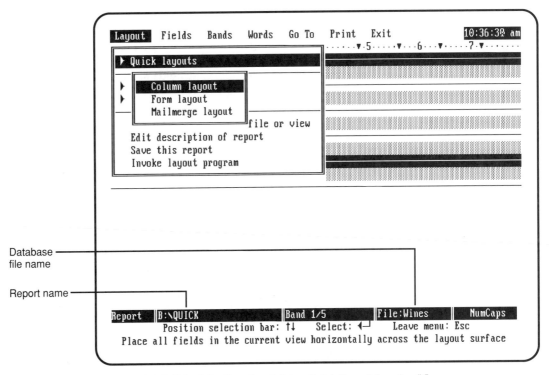

FIGURE D.59. Selections for defining Quick Report [version IV].

```
Page No.   1
04/08/93

NAME              MAKER         YEAR  BIN    PRICE  ON_HAND  L_ORDER   CHILL  TYP
E

COUNTRY CHABLIS   ALMADEN       1983  A43    10.00       15  10/18/89  Y      WHI
TE
STRAWBERRY HILL   BOONE'S FARM  1989  C22     5.24       48  09/16/92  Y      RED
VINO BIANCO       MOGEN DAVID   1988  B20     3.00       50  11/25/92  N      RED
BLANC DE BLANC    FETZER VINOS  1982  D23    20.00       21  11/20/90  Y      WHI
TE
VIN ROSE          GEYSTER PEAK  1985  C15    10.50       24  11/05/91  Y      ROS
E
RIPPLE            HOOTCH HUT    1989  C28     2.50       64  06/30/92  N      RED
MOREAU ROUGE      J. MOREAU     1982  D12    18.50       15  05/25/90  N      RED
TORRES DE CASTA   M. TORRES     1985  B15     6.24       10  07/15/91  Y      ROS
E
MAD DOG 20/20     MOGEN DAVID   1989  B20     3.00       50  11/02/92  N      RED
EXTRA DRY WHITE   RIVERSIDE     1986  A25    13.76       48  11/19/91  Y      WHI
TE
VINO ROSA         WENTE BROS    1989  B34     8.50       24  11/29/92  Y      ROS
E

         Cancel viewing: ESC,  Continue viewing: SPACEBAR
```

FIGURE D.60. Screen preview of Quick Report [version IV].

Once the "Quick layout" has produced the initial report definition of the design work surface, this definition may be revised. For example, the default column titles obtained from your database structure could be changed by deleting the current title and typing a new title. Or, an unwanted field might be removed from both the column titles and detail lines. This revision of the "Quick layout" is demonstrated by revising the report definition to produce the final report shown in Figure D.61. In this example, the column title for "ON_HAND" is changed and the width of the column is reduced. The remaining column titles and fields are then moved to the left; thus, the entire report will now fit into 80 characters.

Revision of the Quick Report is accomplished by proceeding from the dot prompt as follows:

To revise a report format created as a Quick Report		
Enter:	MODIFY REPORT QUICK	Since this has already been created, MODIFY is the appropriate action
Move to:	Page Header, Line 4, Col 51	Position cursor
Press:	<Del><Del><Del>	Remove "ON_"
Move to:	Page Header, Line 3, Col 52	
Type:	ON	Desired column title

The column title for ON_HAND has been revised.

Now the width of the column for the data values can be adjusted in this manner:

Move to:	Detail, Line 0, Col 51	Position cursor on field template for ON_HAND
Press:	<Shift>+<F7>	Select "Size" option

Page No.   1
2/13/92

| | | | | | ON | | | |
NAME	MAKER	YEAR	BIN	PRICE	HAND	L_ORDER	CHILL	TYPE
COUNTRY CHABLIS	ALMADEN	1983	A43	9.00	15	10/18/89	Y	WHITE
STRAWBERRY HILL	BOONE'S FARM	1989	C22	5.24	48	09/16/92	Y	RED
VINO BIANCO	MOGEN DAVID	1988	B20	3.00	50	11/25/92	N	RED
BLANC DE BLANC	FETZER VINOS	1982	D23	19.00	21	11/20/90	Y	WHITE
VIN ROSE	GEYSER PEAK	1985	C15	9.50	24	11/05/91	Y	ROSE
RIPPLE	HOOTCH NUT	1989	C28	2.50	64	06/30/92	N	RED
MOREAU ROUGE	J. MOREAU	1982	D12	18.50	15	05/25/90	N	RED
TORRES DE CASTA	M. TORRES	1985	B15	5.24	10	07/15/91	Y	ROSE
MAD DOG 20/20	MOGEN DAVID	1989	B20	3.00	50	11/02/92	N	RED
EXTRA DRY WHITE	RIVERSIDE	1986	A25	12.76	48	11/19/91	Y	WHITE
VINO ROSA	WENTE BROS	1989	B34	7.50	24	11/29/92	Y	ROSE
ZINFANDEL	TAYLOR FARMS	1989	A22	6.50	10	11/29/93	N	RED
NAPA BURGUNDY	TAYLOR FARMS	1989	A23	6.50	24	07/17/93	N	RED
CABERNET	TAYLOR FARMS	1988	A25	7.00	24	11/29/91	N	RED
RED TABLE WINE	TAYLOR FARMS	1989	A26	4.76	11	11/29/93	N	RED
BOONE'S FARM	SMOTHER BRO	1988	A88	13.80	10	05/08/92	N	ROSE
				133.80	448			

FIGURE D.61. Revised Quick Report [version IV].

When you select Size, the entire field template is highlighted and the cursor is placed in the rightmost position in the field. The size of the field is adjusted like this:

To adjust a report's display field size

Press: `<left><left><left>`   Preview size of revised field as cursor is moved

Press: `<enter>`   Complete action

And the new field Size has been established.

Next, the field Size for the summary is changed as follows:

Move to: Report Summary, Line 0, Col 51

Press: `<Shift>+<F7>`   Select Size

Press: `<left><left><left>`   Reduce field size

Press: `<Enter>`   Complete change

This completes the adjustments to the ON_HAND column, since three character positions have been removed from the column title, the detail data, and the summary data. Two changes remain to be made. The column titles for L_ORDER, CHILL, and TYPE need to be moved to the left, together with the detail line for these fields. This is accomplished in this manner:

To move or reposition column titles

Move to: Page Header, Line 4, Col 60
Position cursor on "L" of L_ORDER

Press: `<F6>`   Choose "Select"

Move to: Page Header, Line 4, Col 80
Highlight desired column titles

Press: `<Enter>`   Complete action

Press: `<F7>`   Choose "Move"

Move to: Page Header, Line 4, Col 57
Drag select column titles to desired location

Press: `<Enter>`   Complete command

Since the new location of the column titles overlaps the old location, this message appears:

Delete covered text and fields? (Y/N)

| **Press:** | <Y> | Yes, you want them to overlap |

The column titles are now in their desired location.
The detail templates are moved in this manner:

To move or relocate a field in the Detail Line

Move to:	Detail, Line 0, Col 60	Position cursor on leftmost "M" of MM/DD/YY
Press:	<F6>	Choose "Select"
Move to:	Detail, Line 0, Col 81	Highlight desired template fields
Press:	<Enter>	Complete action
Press:	<F7>	Choose "Move"
Move to:	Detail, Line 0, Col 57	Drag select templates to desired location
Press:	<Enter>	Complete command

Once again, the new location of the template fields overlaps the old location with this message appearing:

Delete covered text and fields? (Y/N)

| **Press:** | <Y> | Yes, you want them to overlap |

This revision of the "Quick layout" report definition is completed and can be used like the other report definitions.

Action: Preview this Quick Report on your screen. The result should look like Figure D.61. The entire final report will now fit within the 80 characters of your screen.

Action: Save this Quick Report definition and exit to the dot prompt. At the dot prompt, produce a hard copy of this report.

D.5.5   When Things Go Wrong

You may encounter several difficulties when you are creating your report definition and are producing the final output report. Some of the more common difficulties and how to approach them are as follows:

1. When displaying field names for selection in the report, strange names appear.
   a. Exit from the report definition screen.
   b. Use LIST STRUCTURE to confirm the fields contained in your active database.
   c. If you have the wrong database, activate the desired database with the USE command.
   d. Use MODIFY REPORT to return to your report definition screen.

2. A report heading or column title is incorrect.
   a. Use MODIFY REPORT to access the report definition.
   b. Change the heading or title as desired. The <Del> and <Ins> keys may be used in making these changes.

3. The data in your report do *not* appear in the desired sequence.
   a. Use the INDEX ON, SET INDEX TO, or SORT command to obtain the desired sequencing of your data.
   b. Reissue the REPORT FORM command.

4. You do not remember the name of your report format definition file.
   a. At the dot prompt, use the DIR *.FRM command to obtain a listing of your report format files.
   b. Access the desired report format to modify it, or use it with your active database to produce the desired report.

D.5.6   Lesson Summary

- A report format contains the description of the appearance of a final output report that is produced when data from the database are output following the instructions of the report format.
- A CREATE REPORT command is used to access the report format mode. MODIFY REPORT is used to change an existing report format.
- Report formats are created under the ASSIST/CONTROL CENTER mode of operation with a "blackboard" or "report design work surface" provided for sketching the report layout. The dot prompt mode of operation is *not* available for creating report formats.
- With the "blackboard" or "report design work surface," fields can be selected, column headings can be entered, column widths can be specified, and a report heading can be defined.
- A final output management report is produced with the command REPORT FORM <report-filename> TO PRINT.
- The sequence of data in a report can be controlled by issuing the INDEX command prior to the REPORT FORM command.

D.5.7   Practice Tutorial

A report format can be used to produce reports for the Wine Management System as described in this Lesson. Create a management style report as a guided activity in a hands-on manner. Access the WINES database before you initiate these tasks.

Task 1: Create the report format for the Wine List.

Task 2: Produce this report as illustrated in Figure D.45.

Time Estimates

Novice: 60 minutes

Intermediate: 45 minutes

Advanced: 30 minutes

D.5.8   Practice Exercises

(1)   **Case: Life Styles Financial Services**

Business Problem: Delinquent Account Reporting

MIS Characteristics: Finance

Managerial Control

Life Styles Financial Services provides consumer credit through its prestigious LifeCard credit card. The LifeCard is honored by thousands of merchants worldwide. For the best times of your life, never leave home without your LifeCard.

Mary Ann Moore is director of delinquent accounts at Life Styles Financial Services. She wants to produce an account status report from LifeCard's account database. Mary Ann has determined that this database contains the fields described by the following data dictionary definition:

Field Name	Description
ACCT	Customer account number
NAME	Customer name
YEAR	Year card was initially issued (member since year)
LIMIT	Credit limit
BALANCE	Previous account balance
PAYMENT	Minimum monthly payment
CHARGES	Current month's charges
PAID	Indicator of whether or not account payment has been received on time

Mary Ann sketched out a report design for her account status report as follows:

```
                    1111111111222222222233333333334444444444555555555566666
           12345678901234567890123456789012345678901234567890123456789001234

   1
   2                               LIFECARD
   3                         ACCOUNT STATUS REPORT
   4
   5
   6                                              PREVIOUS
   7           ACCOUNT                            ACCOUNT       CURRENT
   8           NUMBER          CUSTOMER NAME      BALANCE       CHARGES
   9
  10           XXXXXXXXXX      XXXXXXXXXXXXXXXX   99999.99      99999.99
  11           XXXXXXXXXX      XXXXXXXXXXXXXXXX   99999.99      99999.99
  12           XXXXXXXXXX      XXXXXXXXXXXXXXXX   99999.99      99999.99
  13           XXXXXXXXXX      XXXXXXXXXXXXXXXX   99999.99      99999.99
                                      .
                                      .
                                      .
               XXXXXXXXXX      XXXXXXXXXXXXXXXX   99999.99      99999.99
```

Task 1: Access the **LIFECARD.DBF** database file in the **EXERCISE** catalog and review the structure and data. Produce a hard copy listing of the database structure for documentation and reference.

_____

_____

_____

Task 2: Create a report form with the name of **LIFECARD.FRM** that defines the **ACCOUNT STATUS REPORT** as sketched out by Mary Ann.

_____

_____

_____

Task 3: Generate the ACCOUNT STATUS REPORT using the report form definition created in Task 2. Arrange this report in sequence by BALANCE.

_____

_____

_____

Task 4: (*Optional*)   Mary Ann wants you to use the same report form definition to produce an exception report that lists only those accounts that exceed their credit limit. That is, the report is to contain only those accounts where:

BALANCE + CHARGES > LIMIT

_____

_____

_____

Time Estimates

Novice: 90 minutes

Intermediate: 60 minutes

Advanced: 45 minutes

(2)   Case: Downlink Satellite

Business Problem: Service Fee Collection
MIS Characteristics: Finance
                           Operational Control

Downlink Satellite markets several combinations of satellite television programming services, which include HBO/Cinemax, Showtime, The Movie Channel, ESPN, CNN, Headline News, The Comedy Channel, The Family Channel, MTV, and Nickelodeon. Viewers with satellite dishes subscribe to these services through a Downlink Satellite connection. The programming services provided by Downlink are similar to those available with cable TV. Once viewers have paid their subscription fee, the videocipher decoder on their satellite receiver is activated so that they can view their selected program channels. Downlink offers several alternative arrangements of channels identified as the Prime Pak, the Super Pak, the Combo Pak, and the Basic Pak. These service packages include major network stations (ABC, NBC, and CBS) in those geographical areas where this programming cannot be clearly received with a regular TV antenna.

Margaret Rodriguez manages customer service at Downlink Satellite. To assist her in tracking the status of customer accounts, Margaret has developed a database that is described by the following data dictionary definition:

Field Name	Description
VCU	Videocipher unit number
PHONE	Customer's telephone number
LNAME	Customer's last name
FNAME	Customer's first name
ADDRESS	Street address
CITY	City name
ST	State
ZIP	Zip code
SERV	Service alternative selected: PRIME, SUPER, COMBO, or BASIC
EXPIRE	Expiration date of service
AMOUNT	Total price of programming services provided
NETWORK	Indicator of whether or not network channels are clearly received in the viewer's area

Margaret sketched out a report design for her customer account status report as follows:

```
                  111111111122222222223333333333444444444455555555556666
         1234567890123456789012345678901234567890123456789012345678901234
     ┌────────────────────────────────────────────────────────────────────┐
  1  │                                                                    │
  2  │                     DOWNLINK SATELLITE                              │
  3  │                 CUSTOMER ACCOUNT STATUS REPORT                      │
  4  │                                                                    │
  5  │                                                                    │
  6  │   VIDEO-                                                           │
  7  │   CIPHER                                                           │
  8  │   UNIT       LAST        FIRST    SERVICE  EXPIRE   AMOUNT NET-     │
  9  │   NUMBER     NUMBER      NAME     OPTION   DATE            WORK     │
 10  │                                                                    │
 11  │                                                                    │
 12  │   XXXXXXX   XXXXXXXXXX   XXXXXXXX XXXXX    MM/DD/YY 999.99 .L.      │
 13  │   XXXXXXX   XXXXXXXXXX   XXXXXXXX XXXXX    MM/DD/YY 999.99 .L.      │
 14  │   XXXXXXX   XXXXXXXXXX   XXXXXXXX XXXXX    MM/DD/YY 999.99 .L.      │
     │                                .                                   │
     │                                .                                   │
     │                                .                                   │
     │   XXXXXXX   XXXXXXXXXX   XXXXXXXX XXXXX    MM/DD/YY 999.99 .L.      │
     └────────────────────────────────────────────────────────────────────┘
```

Task 1: Access the DOWNLINK.DBF database file in the EXERCISE catalog and review the structure and data. Produce a hard copy listing of the database structure for documentation and reference.

  · _____

  · _____

  · _____

Task 2: Create a report form with the name of DOWNLINK.FRM that defines the CUSTOMER ACCOUNT STATUS REPORT as sketched out by Margaret.

  · _____

  · _____

  · _____

Task 3: Generate the CUSTOMER ACCOUNT STATUS REPORT using the report form definition created in Task 2. Arrange this report in sequence by SERV (service alternative), first, and LNAME, second.

  · _____

  · _____

  · _____

Task 4: (*Optional*) Margaret wants you to use the same report form definition to produce an exception report that lists only those viewer accounts that do *not* clearly receive network channels. That is, the report is to contain only those viewers who are:

.NOT. NETWORK

  · _____

  · _____

  · _____

Time Estimates

Novice: 90 minutes

Intermediate: 60 minutes

Advanced: 45 minutes

| D.5.9 | ## Comprehensive Problems |

(1)   Case: Yen To Travel (continued)

Sara and Brenda have reviewed the listings Ashley produced for the Tour Management System at Yen To Travel. They would like to improve the appearance of these listings, making them management-style reports. Brenda and Sara specified the fields contained in each report in the description of the TMS in Using dBASE, Lesson D.1. Refer to that lesson in producing these reports.

Task 1: Create a report format for the Tour List and the Representatives List. Each report should have a heading that includes the travel agency's name and the report name.

_____

_____

_____

Task 2: Produce the Tour List report with the tours arranged by type.

_____

_____

_____

Task 3: Generate the Representatives List with the tours prioritized by tour name.

_____

_____

_____

Time Estimates

Novice: 90 minutes

Intermediate: 60 minutes

Advanced: 45 minutes

(2)   Case: Silver Screen Video (continued)

Ernie and Amy have reviewed the listings for the Movie Management System at Silver Screen Video. After their discussions with Todd, they decided that the appearance of their listing should be improved, so they are management-style reports. Amy and Ernie specified the fields contained in the Movie List in the description of the MMS in Using dBASE, Lesson D.1. Refer to that lesson in developing this report.

Task 1: Create a report format for the Movie List. This report should have a heading that includes the store's name and the report name.

_____

_____

_____

Task 2: Produce the Movie List with the movies arranged in the desired sequence.

- _____
- _____
  _____
- _____

Time Estimates

Novice: 90 minutes

Intermediate: 60 minutes

Advanced: 45 minutes

D.5.10   Application Case

Case: Morrison-Kiewit Construction

Business Problem: Contract Tracking
MIS Characteristics: Marketing
                              Strategic Planning
Special Characteristic: International
Management Functions: Organizing
                                   Controlling
Tools Skills: Reporting
                 Indexing

Morrison-Kiewit Construction (MKC) was founded in 1921 by Robert Morrison and Peter Kiewit. Since then its operations have grown and expanded. MKC is now a multibillion dollar company that manages construction projects around the world. MKC's construction business is focused on large commercial and governmental projects, which include schools, hospitals, roads, manufacturing plants, and office buildings. The size of the majority of these projects exceeds $2 million. MKC has an outstanding reputation for quality construction throughout the world. In addition to MKC's 10,000 employees, they hire many construction workers from the local area where a project is being built. With many of the projects outside of the United States, they form a partnership with a local construction company. These business partnerships allow MKC to blend their construction expertise with the local companies' contacts and knowledge of conducting business in a different country. Often, the local partner makes the difference in MKC's ability to secure the necessary construction permits in a timely manner.

MKC's marketing efforts are directed by Christopher "Chris" Petz, Vice President of Project Development, from his Boise, Idaho, office. Chris's staff regularly monitors the *Commerce Business Daily* and other publications for construction projects for which MKC may prepare a construction bid proposal. Once a potential project has been identified, a bid proposal is prepared in the Project Development group for submission. Frequently, the deadline for submitting bid proposals is very short. Chris may only have a week or two for his staff to complete the bid proposal on a $20 million project. The Project Development group makes extensive use of spreadsheets and word processing in meeting these deadlines. Word processing files containing the "boilerplate" describing the qualifications of MKC have been created for use in proposal preparation. Depending on the particular proposal, the Project Development group selects the "boilerplate" narratives to be included. Spreadsheet templates have been established that encompass many of the costs of each type of project. These are applied to greatly reduce the effort in preparing the pricing for the proposal.

Once a proposal has been submitted and MKC is awaiting the bid selection, they continue the preliminary tasks for obtaining the required permits and for establishing any necessary business partnerships. A number of construction proposals are under consideration at any one time. To assist in better managing Project Development activities, Chris would like to set up a contract tracking system. This would contain information on the status of construction proposals.

Samantha "Sam" Derrick, Senior Development Engineer, and Chris met with the Project Development engineers to review the information requirements for a Contract Tracking Systems (CTS). After considerable discussion, they reached a consensus on maintaining the information described by the following data dictionary definitions:

Field Name	Description
NAME	Name of construction project
AMOUNT	Value of project in thousands of U.S. dollars
LOCATION	Geographical location of project identified by state or country
PERMIT	Indicator of whether or not the necessary permits have been obtained from the state or country in which the project is to be built
TYPE	General type of project classified as: HOSPITAL, OFFICE, PLANT, ROAD, or SCHOOL
STATUS	Project status of bid submitted or accepted delineated as BID or ACCEPT, respectively
START	Planned start date for construction project

Sam worked with Chris in sketching out the report design for the Contract Tracking report. A report design shows the layout of the report title, column titles, and location of data on the report. This mock-up of the report can be readily reviewed and revised before the actual report form definition is created. Sam used X's to sketch out the character fields and the L to signify a logical field. Sam's completed report design, as approved by Chris, is as follows:

```
                      MORRISON-KIEWIT CONSTRUCTION
                         PROJECT DEVELOPMENT
                          CONTRACT TRACKING


        PROJECT               TYPE      LOCATION      STATUS PERMIT

XXXXXXXXXXXXXXXXXXXX XXXXXXX XXXXXXXXXXXXXX XXXXXX .L.
XXXXXXXXXXXXXXXXXXXX XXXXXXX XXXXXXXXXXXXXX XXXXXX .L.
XXXXXXXXXXXXXXXXXXXX XXXXXXX XXXXXXXXXXXXXX XXXXXX .L.
                              .
                              .
                              .
XXXXXXXXXXXXXXXXXXXX XXXXXXX XXXXXXXXXXXXXX XXXXXX .L.
```

With the Contract Tracking database developed and the report design sketched out and approved, Sam was ready to embark on the fabrication of MKC's report.

Tasks

1. Access the PROJECT.DBF database for Morrison-Kiewit Construction's Contract Tracking System in the CASES catalog and review its structure and content. Obtain a hard copy of the structure.

2. Create the PROJECT report form definition for the Contract Tracking report as designed by Sam and approved by Chris.

3. Generate a Contract Tracking report using the PROJECT report form definition. Arrange the report alphabetically by TYPE and STATUS within TYPE.

4. Review the report and database. What other reports might be created from the Contract Tracking System? Prepare a report sketch for such a suggested report.

Time Estimates

Novice: 120 minutes

Intermediate: 90 minutes

Advanced: 60 minutes

LESSON

D.6

Producing Advanced Reports

CONTENT

- Reports for Wine Management System
- Numbering Pages and Dating Reports
- Summing Columns
- Grouping Data
- Computing Fields
- When Things Go Wrong

D.6.1 Reports for Wine Management System

For the Golden Gourmet, Bert, Beth, and Annie would like three management reports prepared by the Wine Management System (WMS). These reports are to replace the "plain" listings that were previously prepared. The dBASE report format permits headings, column titles, and other report writing features to be used in producing these management reports. The three reports desired for the Golden Gourmet are

1. Wine list
2. Serving list
3. Order list

The wine list was developed as described in the previous Lesson and as illustrated in Figure D.45. The reports for the serving list and the order list are produced as described here. The serving list report is shown in Figure D.62 and produced from the dBASE report format of Figure D.64 [version III+] or Figure D.65 [version IV]. The order listing in Figure D.63 is generated by using the report format of Figure D.66 [version III+] or Figure D.67 [version IV]. The serving list includes the report "housekeeping" feature of the page number and report date, and the order list incorporates the reporting feature of a total for the quantity ON_HAND column.

Page No. 1
03/21/92

GOLDEN GOURMET
SERVING LIST

BIN	NAME	VINEYARD	CHILL
A22	ZINFANDEL	TAYLOR FARMS	.F.
A23	NAPA BURGUNDY	TAYLOR FARMS	.F.
A25	EXTRA DRY WHITE	RIVERSIDE	.T.
A25	CABERNET	TAYLOR FARMS	.F.
A26	RED TABLE WINE	TAYLOR FARMS	.F.
A43	COUNTRY CHABLIS	ALMADEN	.T.
A88	BOONE'S FARM	SMOTHERS BRO	.F.
B15	TORRES DE CASTA	M. TORRES	.T.
B20	VINO BIANCO	MOGEN DAVID	.F.
B20	MAD DOG 20/20	MOGEN DAVID	.F.
B34	VINO ROSA	WENTE BROS	.T.
C15	VIN ROSE	GEYSER PEAK	.T.
C22	STRAWBERRY HILL	BOONE'S FARM	.T.
C28	RIPPLE	HOOTCH HUT	.F.
D12	MOREAU ROUGE	J. MOREAU	.F.
D23	BLANC DE BLANC	FETZER VINOS	.T.

FIGURE D.62. Serving LIST report.

D.6.2   Numbering Pages and Dating Reports

The page number and report generation date appear in the upper left-hand corner of the page for the Serving List illustrated in Figure D.62. The report format definition for this report is developed as described below for each dBASE version. In preparation for creating the SERVLIST format definition for this report, proceed as follows from the dot prompt:

To prepare for creating a REPORT format for the Serving List	**Enter:**	USE WINES	Activate desired database that contains the data to be included in the report
	Enter:	SET INDEX TO WINEBIN	Activate desired index to control sequence of final report

Page No. 1
03/21/92

GOLDEN GOURMET
ORDER LIST

NAME	MAKER	QUANTITY ON HAND
COUNTRY CHABLIS	ALMADEN	15
BLANC DE BLANC	FETZER VINOS	21
MOREAU ROUGE	J. MOREAU	15
TORRES DE CASTA	M. TORRES	10
ZINFANDEL	TAYLOR FARMS	10
RED TABLE WINE	TAYLOR FARMS	11
BOONE'S FARM	SMOTHERS BRO	10
*** Total ***		
		92

FIGURE D.63.   Order List report.

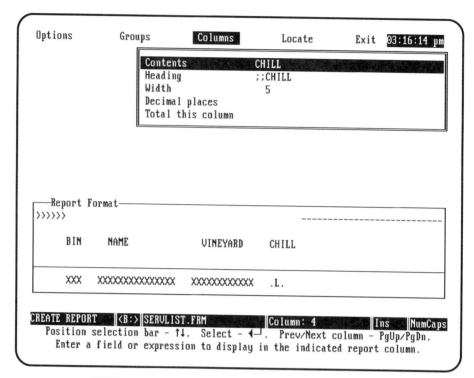

FIGURE D.64. Report format for Serving List [version III+].

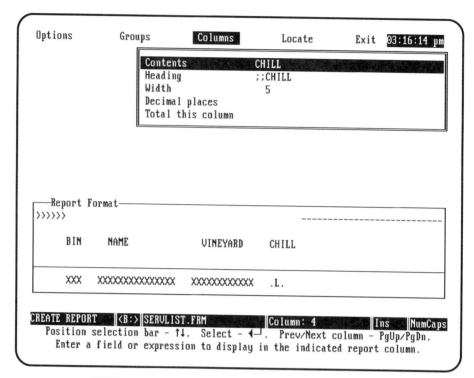

FIGURE D.65. Report format for Serving List [version IV].

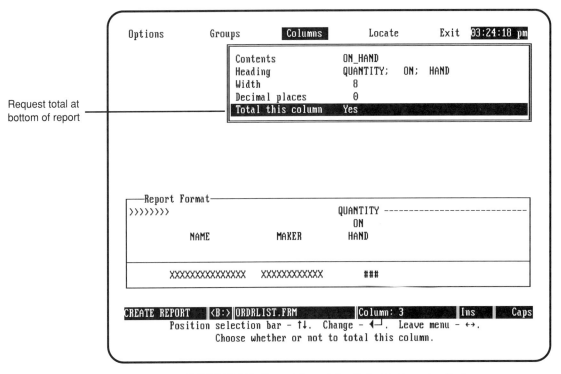

FIGURE D.66. Report format for Order List [version III+].

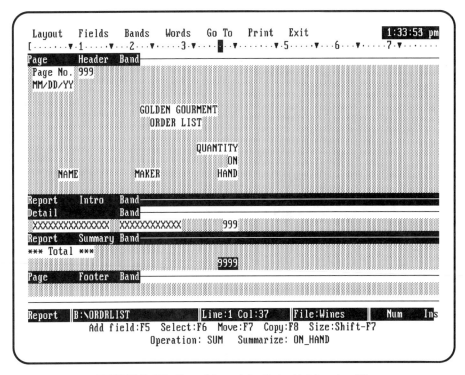

FIGURE D.67. Report format for Order List [version IV].

To create a REPORT format	**Enter:**	CREATE REPORT SERVLIST
		Begin report format definition

Now, you are ready to begin developing the report format definition for the version of dBASE that is available for your use. After you have completed this report format, the final output report is produced with the same commands, regardless of your dBASE version.

Caution Alert!   dBASE report format definitions are stored as separate DOS files. The report name is limited to eight characters!

D.6.2.1. Version III+ Page Numbers and Date Report Format

Specification of page numbers and a report date is made from the Option menu of the Report Format menu screen. Since this is the last option in the Options window, the report title and other options are frequently specified before the page numbers and date are selected. Continue to enter the SERVLIST report format in this manner:

Action: Enter the report heading as shown in Figure D.62. If necessary, review this procedure in the prior lesson.

The Plain page selection on the Option menu controls the appearance of the page number and report date appearing in the upper left-hand corner of the page, as illustrated in Figure D.62. "Plain page Yes" indicates that *no* page number and report date will appear, whereas "Plain page No" specifies printing of the page number and report date.

To display the page number and report date	**Move to:**	Plain Page	Option that controls page numbers and report date
	Press:	<Enter>	Toggle Plain page from yes to no, or from no to yes

If the "Plain page" is toggled to Yes, then:

	Press:	<Enter>	Toggle Plain page to *no*, the desired selection

Now, with the Plain page option toggled to *no,* you are ready to complete the SERVLIST for Beth and Bert.

Action: Complete the report format definition for the SERVLIST in Figure D.62. Define each column in the report by using the procedures presented in the prior lesson. Save this report definition as you exit to the dot prompt.

The completed report format definition is shown in Figure D.64. You are ready to produce the final output report, as described in Section D.6.2.3., "Generate Report with Page Numbers and Date."

D.6.2.2. Version IV Page Numbers and Date Report Format

The page number and report generation date are usually specified in the Page Header Band of the design work surface. This location is selected so that these report features will appear *at the top of each page* of your report, as illustrated in Figure D.62. However, with version IV, you could specify these to appear in the Page Footer Band if you wanted them at the bottom of each page. The page number and report date are placed in the desired position in the SERVLIST report format by proceeding in this manner with the work design surface:

To specify page number and report date	**Press:**	`<down>`	Locate cursor in Page Header Band
	Move to:	Line 0, Col 1	Position cursor for page number
	Type:	`Page No.`	Desired title to appear with page number
	Press:	`<right>`	Position cursor for location of page number
	Press:	`<F5>`	Select Add Field
	Move to:	`Pageno`	Pageno is a PREDEFINED option
	Press:	`<Enter>`	Select Pageno option

When you select the Pageno option, a Template window appears. dBASE provides a default Template of 999. Since this is satisfactory for this report, the Template is accepted in this manner:

Press:	`<Ctrl>+<End>`	Accept Template
Press:	`<Enter>`	Advance to next Page Header line
Move to:	Line 1, Col 1	Position cursor at desired location for the date
Press:	`<F5>`	Select Add Field
Select:	`Date`	Desired PREDEFINED option
Press:	`<Ctrl>+<End>`	Accept Template
Press:	`<Enter>`	Advance to next line

The page number and report date have been set up for the SERVLIST report format. The remainder of the report can now be defined.

Action: Complete the report format definition for the SERVLIST in Figure D.62. Preview your report on the screen, then Exit to the dot prompt and save your report definition.

The format definition for this report is shown in Figure D.65. You are ready to print the final output report, as described in the next section.

D.6.2.3.   Generate Report with Page Numbers and Date

Once the SERVLIST report format definition has been completed and saved, the final report can be produced using this definition. Since the index was previously set for the desired sequence, producing the report is accomplished as follows:

To produce the Serving List report	**Enter:**	`REPORT FORM SERVLIST TO PRINT`

The report shown in Figure D.62 is generated. In the event your report does *not* advance to the top of the next page, you may use the EJECT command to cause your report page to be advanced.

D.6.3   Summing Columns

The Order List Report for the Golden Gourmet shown in Figure D.63 is an exception report that contains only those wines with less than 24 bottles in stock. This order list makes use of the column total feature of dBASE reports with the report containing a "Total" for the number of bottles ON_HAND. That is, the ON_HAND column is summed and this total is displayed at the bottom of the report. Creation of the report format definition for each dBASE version of this report is described in the discussion that follows. Before you begin entering the report definition, be sure to activate the database from which the final report is to be produced.

Keypoint!

> Only NUMERIC fields may have a total computed and displayed. dBASE will total a field whether it makes business sense to do so or not. For example, PRICE PER BOTTLE may have a total computed, but the result has little meaning! You must be sure it makes sense to total a field!

To prepare for creating the Order List report

Action: Activate the WINES database, if necessary.

Enter: SET INDEX TO   Turn off all indexing

The use of SET INDEX TO without specifying the name of an index causes the index to be *turned off* and the records to be displayed in the sequence in which they were entered into the database.

To begin creating the Order List report format

Enter: CREATE REPORT ORDRLIST

Begin report format definition

You are ready to continue with the development of the report format definition by using your available version of dBASE. Once you finish this report format, the final output report is produced with the same command for both versions of dBASE.

D.6.3.1.   Version III+ Total Column Report Format

The summing of columns in the report is specified as each column containing numeric data is defined for the report format. Since this is part of the column selection, the other characteristics of the report are usually defined first. The ORDRLIST report format is created as follows:

Action: Enter the report heading and set the printing of the page number and date as shown in Figure D.63.

Action: Enter the definition of the NAME and MAKER columns in the report format as shown in Figure D.63.

Action: Enter the Contents and Heading for the ON_HAND column.

Action: Set the Width of the ON_HAND column to 8 characters.

The summing of a numeric column is controlled with the "Total this column" option of the column definition. This is toggled between "Yes" and "No."

To TOTAL a numeric field in a REPORT format

Action: Toggle the "Total this column" option to *Yes,* which is the desired action.

As indicated in Figure D.66 for the column ON_HAND, the "Total this column" specification is toggled to "Yes." This causes the quantity on hand to be summed and displayed at the bottom of the report, as shown in Figure D.63.

Action: Save this report format definition and return to the dot prompt.

In the completed report format shown in Figure D.66, notice that the "#" (pound symbol) indicates that the column is to be summed. The final output report can now be produced, as described in Section D.6.3.3, "Generate Report with Total Column."

D.6.3.2.   Version IV Total Column Report Format

The total for a report column is usually specified in the Report Summary Band of the design work surface. That is, only one total is to appear on the report for the selected column. This total is located at the bottom of the column on the last page of the report, as illustrated in Figure D.63. A column total is *not* displayed at the bottom of each page of the report. The ORDRLIST report format is produced in this manner:

Action: Enter the report format definition for the Page Header Band and the Detail Band of the report shown in Figure D.63. The column titled "QUANTITY ON HAND" contains the ON_HAND field.

Action:	Position your cursor at Line 0, Col 0 in the Report Summary Band.	
Type:	`*** Total ***`	Desired text to appear on total line of report
Press:	`<Enter>`	Advance to next line
Move to:	Line 1, Col 37	Position cursor at desired location for column total value
Press:	`<F5>`	Select Add Field
Select:	`Sum`	Desired SUMMARY option

To TOTAL a numeric field in the Report Summary Band of a report format

When you select this SUMMARY option, a Template window appears for specifying the field to be summed.

Move to:	`Field to summarize on`	Desired option
Press:	`<Enter>`	Select the option and display a list of fields
Move to:	`ON_HAND`	Desired field
Press:	`<Enter>`	Select the field
Move to:	`Template`	Desired option
Press:	`<Enter>`	Select Template
Action:	Use <backspace> to reduce the template to: 9999	
Press:	`<Enter>`	Complete Template specification
Press:	`<Ctrl>+<End>`	Complete summary specification
Action:	Preview your report on the screen. If necessary, make any revisions. Then, Exit to the dot prompt and save your report definition.	

The completed report format definition is shown in Figure D.67. You are ready to generate the final output report by using the command described in the next section.

D.6.3.3.   Generate Report with Total Column

After completing the ORDRLIST report format definition, the final report can be produced. This is an *exception report* because it contains only data for those wines with less than 24 bottles currently ON_HAND. That is, the exception reporting condition is to display only those records where the ON_HAND field contains a value that is less than 24. The final report is produced like this:

| To generate the Order List exception report | **Enter:** | `REPORT FORM ORDRLIST FOR ON_HAND < 24 TO PRINT` |

The FOR condition is used to select the desired database records with this REPORT FORM in the same manner as it is applied when using the DISPLAY and LIST commands.

The final output report shown in Figure D.63 is printed. Once again, in the event that your report does *not* advance to a new page as desired, use the EJECT command.

D.6.4 Grouping Data

dBASE permits data to be grouped by a value appearing in a field. For example, a break is inserted in the report between each grouping by wine TYPE, as portrayed in Figure D.68. With the "break on group" request, *the field wine TYPE does not need to be included as a column in the report,* since this value appears once at the beginning of each group break. Bert and Beth believe this report grouping will make the wine list easier for their customers to use. The format definition for this report is developed as described below for each dBASE version. Then, the generation of the report is described. Prepare to create the report format by proceeding as follows at the dot prompt:

Action: Make sure WINES is your active database.

Enter: `SET INDEX TO WINETYPE`

Activate desired index to control grouping

GOLDEN GOURMET
WINE LIST

BIN	WINES	VINEYARD	YEAR	PRICE PER BOTTLE
** WINE TYPE RED				
C22	STRAWBERRY HILL	BOONE'S FARM	1989	5.24
B20	VINO BIANCO	MOGEN DAVID	1988	3.00
C28	RIPPLE	HOOTCH HUT	1989	2.50
D12	MOREAU ROUGE	J. MOREAU	1982	18.50
B20	MAD DOG 20/20	MOGEN DAVID	1988	3.00
A22	ZINFANDEL	TAYLOR FARMS	1988	6.50
A23	NAPA BURGUNDY	TAYLOR FARMS	1989	6.50
A25	CABERNET	TAYLOR FARMS	1986	7.00
A26	RED TABLE WINE	TAYLOR FARMS	1989	4.76
** WINE TYPE ROSE				
C15	VIN ROSE	GEYSER PEAK	1985	10.50
B15	TORRES DE CASTA	M. TORRES	1985	6.24
B34	VINO ROSA	WENTE BROS	1989	8.50
A88	BOONE'S FARM	SMOTHERS BRO	1988	14.80
** WINE TYPE WHITE				
A43	COUNTRY CHABLIS	ALMADEN	1983	10.00
D23	BLANC DE BLANC	FETZER VINOS	1982	20.00
A25	EXTRA DRY WHITE	RIVERSIDE	1986	13.76

FIGURE D.68. Wine List grouped by wine type.

To begin creating the Wine List report format	**Enter:**	CREATE REPORT WINETYPE
		Begin report format definition

Proceed to develop your report format definition using the appropriate description for your version of dBASE.

Caution Alert!

Failure to arrange the data for a report before using a REPORT FORM with a "break on group" will cause the group break to appear *each time* a new value is encountered as the report is printed. If an INDEXED or SORTED file is *not* used, multiple group breaks for the *same* field value are likely to occur!

D.6.4.1.   Version III+ Groups Report Format

Grouping data is implemented from the Groups option of the Report Format Menu screen. This "break on group" is accomplished by specifying the group break, as shown in the report format of Figure D.69 for the WINETYPE report.

Action: Enter the report heading and define each column, as illustrated by Figure D.68.

To specify a "break on group" in a report format	**Move to:**	Groups	Report format option
	Move to:	Group on expression	Desired Groups option
	Press:	<Enter>	Select Group on expression option
	Press:	<F10>	Access list of available fields
	Select:	TYPE	Desired field for grouping
	Press:	<Enter>	Complete Group on expression
	Move to:	Group heading	Desired activity
	Press:	<Enter>	Select Group heading option
	Type:	WINE TYPE	Desired group heading text
	Press:	<Enter>	Complete group heading specification
	Action:	As necessary, toggle the "Summary report only" and "Page eject after each group" option to No. The <Enter> is used to toggle these options between yes and no.	
	Action:	Save this report format as you exit to the dot prompt.	

The finished report format definition with the grouping options is shown in Figure D.69. You are ready for producing the final report, as described in Section D.6.4.3, "Generate Report with Groups."

D.6.4.2.   Version IV Groups Report Format

A "break on group" request is implemented by adding a set of Group Bands to the report design work surface. These Group Bands enclose the Detail Band that is printed for each wine within a wine TYPE. The WINETYPE report format is developed like this:

Action: Enter the report format definition for the Page Header Band and the Detail Band for the report illustrated in Figure D.68. This portion of the report definition is shown in Figure D.70.

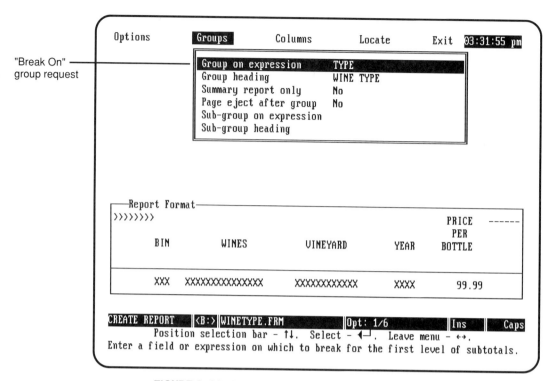

FIGURE D.69. Report format for grouped Wine List [version III+].

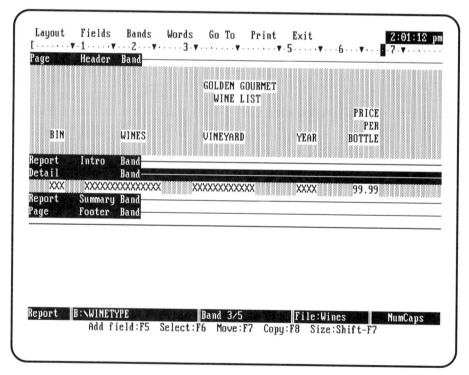

FIGURE D.70. Report format before grouping [version IV].

To specify a "break on group" in the Group Summary Band of a report format

Action: Position your cursor in the Page Header Band.

By placing your cursor in this location, you are ready to add the Group Summary Bands to your report design work surface.

Press:	`<Alt>+<B>`	Selects Bands from the Report Menu
or		
Press:	`<F10>`	Access Report Menu Bar
Move to:	`Bands`	Desired menu choice
Move to:	`Add a group band`	Desired action
Press:	`<Enter>`	Select action

A window appears with menu choices for specifying the "break on group."

Press:	`<Enter>`	Select Field value

A list of the fields in your database structure is now displayed.

Move to:	`TYPE`	Desired field for grouping
Press:	`<Enter>`	Select wine TYPE field

This selection causes a Group 1 Intro Band and a Group 1 Summary Band to be added to your report design work surface. A heading at the beginning of each group is added to the report format in this manner:

Move to:	`Group 1 Intro Band`	Band that will contain heading
Press:	`<down>`	Position cursor on blank line within the Group 1 Intro Band
Move to:	Line 0, Col 3	Location for Group heading
Type:	`** WINE TYPE`	Desired heading

As shown in Figure D.68, along with the group heading, the value for the wine TYPE is displayed, that is, a value of RED, ROSE, or WHITE. To have these values appear, the wine TYPE field needs to be requested for display with the group heading. This is accomplished as follows:

Move to:	Line 0, Col 16	Position cursor
Press:	`<F5>`	Select Add Field
Select:	`TYPE`	Wine TYPE is field containing desired values
Press:	`<Ctrl>+<End>`	Accept Template definition

This completes the description of the Group 1 Intro Band. Since *no* column totals are desired with each group, the Group 1 Summary Band contains only a single blank line. This blank line will appear between each group as shown in Figure D.68. If a column total was desired for each group, that summation could be included in this Group Summary Band.

Action: Preview this report on your screen; then Exit to the dot prompt and save your report definition.

The completed format definition is shown in Figure D.71. You may print the final output report as described in the following section.

D.6.4.3. Generate Report with Groups

Once the WINETYPE report format has been finished, the final report can be produced by using this definition. The report is printed with these commands:

To generate the Wine List report with Grouped data

Enter: REPORT FORM WINETYPE TO PRINT

The result is the report shown in Figure D.68. If your report is *not* advanced to the top of a new page, use the EJECT command to carry out this action.

D.6.5   Computing Fields

Bert is interested in producing a report that shows the investment in their wine inventory. However, he knows that the current database does *not* contain a field with an investment amount. But Bert knows that dBASE *allows new fields to be created in a report by calculating them from other fields.* For example, an INVESTMENT column could be computed by using the equation:

PRICE*ON_HAND

The calculation is performed at the moment when the columns are selected for display on the report. The investment amount would appear in the report but is *not* stored

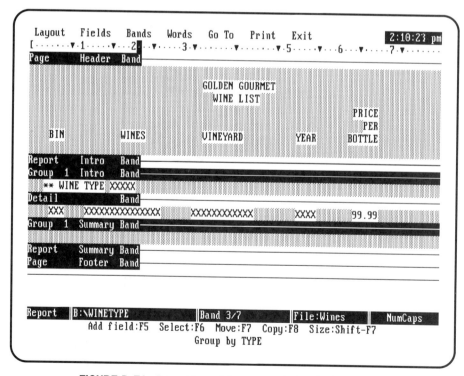

FIGURE D.71. Report format for grouped wine list [version IV].

as a separate column in the database. This saves data storage space. The computed column may also be summed and the total displayed. Figure D.72 illustrates the use of this calculated investment column for the WINES database. Develop an INVENTRY report format definition including this computation, using the description below for your particular version of dBASE.

Keypoint!

> New fields may be calculated and displayed in a REPORT FORM. Calculations are specified when the columns are selected for display! Only NUMERIC fields are used in these computations!

D.6.5.1.   Version III+ Computed Field Report Format

Calculated fields are implemented with the Columns option of the Report Format menu screen. Whenever a column is being defined for inclusion in your report, you have the option of specifying a computed value for the column. The INVENTRY report format is created in this manner:

Action: Enter the report heading and define each of the columns containing the BIN, NAME, MAKER, ON_HAND, and PRICE as illustrated in Figure D.72. Request the ON_HAND column to be summed, but do *not* total the PRICE column. ON_HAND contains data that make sense to add, whereas summing PRICE does *not* provide a meaningful result.

After you have entered the Columns definition for PRICE, then continue in this manner to define the INVESTMENT column:

To specify a calculated column in a REPORT format

Press:	`<PgDn>`	If necessary, advance to Column 6
Action:	Verify that the cursor is located on the Contents option under the Columns menu choice.	
Press:	`<Enter>`	Select Contents to begin entering column calculation
Press:	`<F10>`	Display list of available fields
Select:	`PRICE`	First field in equation
Press:	`*`	Insert arithmetic operator
Press:	`<F10>`	Display list again
Select:	`ON_Hand`	Second field in equation
Press:	`<Enter>`	Complete Contents specification
Move to:	`Heading`	Desired activity
Press:	`<Enter>`	Display "blackboard"
Action:	Enter the heading INVESTMENT on line three of the blackboard.	
Action:	Verify that the "Total this column" is toggled to Yes.	
Action:	Save this report format as you exit to the dot prompt.	

The INVENTRY report format definition is complete with the INVESTMENT column calculated from the PRICE and ON_HAND fields of the database, as portrayed in Figure D.73. The final output report can now be produced as described in Section 6.5.3, "Generate Report with Computed Field."

GOLDEN GOURMET
WINE INVENTORY LIST

BIN	WINE	MAKER	ON HAND	PRICE	INVESTMENT
A22	ZINFANDEL	TAYLOR FARMS	10	6.50	65.00
A23	NAPA BURGUNDY	TAYLOR FARMS	24	6.50	156.00
A25	EXTRA DRY WHITE	RIVERSIDE	48	13.76	660.48
A25	CABERNET	TAYLOR FARMS	24	7.00	168.00
A26	RED TABLE WINE	TAYLOR FARMS	11	4.76	52.36
A43	COUNTRY CHABLIS	ALMADEN	15	10.00	150.00
A88	BOONE'S FARM	SMOTHERS BRO	10	14.80	148.00
B15	TORRES DE CASTA	M. TORRES	10	6.24	62.40
B20	VINO BIANCO	MOGEN DAVID	50	3.00	150.00
B20	MAD DOG 20/20	MOGEN DAVID	50	3.00	150.00
B34	VINO ROSA	WENTE BROS	24	8.50	204.00
C15	VIN ROSE	GEYSER PEAK	24	10.50	252.00
C22	STRAWBERRY HILL	BOONE'S FARM	48	5.24	251.52
C28	RIPPLE	HOOTCH HUT	64	2.50	160.00
D12	MOREAU ROUGE	J. MOREAU	15	18.50	277.50
D23	BLANC DE BLANC	FETZER VINOS	21	20.00	420.00

*** Total ***

| | | | 448 | | 3327.26 |

FIGURE D.72.   Wine Inventory List with investment field computed.

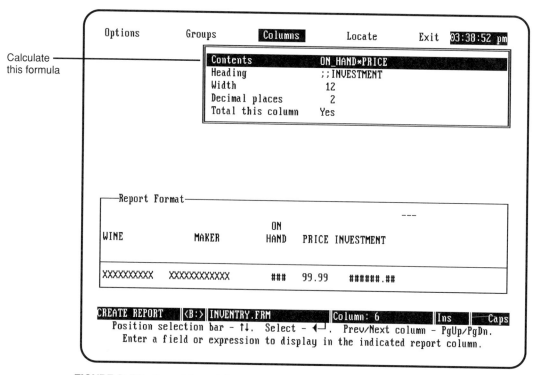

FIGURE D.73. Report format for computing investment column [version III+].

D.6.5.2.   Version IV Computed Field Report Format

Calculated columns are usually specified in the Detail Band of the report design work surface. That is, any column in the Detail Band could contain computed values for your report. The INVENTRY report format with the calculated INVESTMENT field is developed as follows:

Action: Enter the report format definition for the Page Header Band. Enter the BIN, NAME, MAKER, ON_HAND, and PRICE definitions in the Detail Band, as illustrated in Figure D.72. Enter the "*** Total ***" in the Report Summary Band. Then, enter the definition for summing the ON_HAND column in the Report Summary Band, but do *not* total the PRICE column.

To specify a calculated column in the Detail Band of a REPORT format

Action: Position your cursor at the desired location in the INVESTMENT column of the Detail Band where the calculated data value is to reside, such as Line 0, Col 62.

Press: `<F5>`   Select Add Field

Move to: `<create>` under CALCULATED
  Desired activity

Press: `<Enter>`   Select `<create>` option

A window appears for defining the calculated column. Three specifications are required for producing the INVENTRY report. A Name is specified for this computed column. This will be used in summing the column. The Expression specifies the arithmetic to be performed. The Template defines the appearance of the calculated value on the report. Continue defining the INVESTMENT column in this manner:

Action:	Verify that the cursor is located on Name.	
Press:	`<Enter>`	Select Name option
Type:	INVESTMENT	Desired name for calculated field
Press:	`<Enter>`	Complete Name specification
Move to:	Expression	Next desired option
Press:	`<Enter>`	Select option
Press:	`<Shift>+<F1>`	Request list of fields and operators
Move to:	PRICE	First field used in expression
Press:	`<Enter>`	Select PRICE
Press:	`<Shift>+<F1>`	Request list again
Move to:	*	Arithmetic operator
Press:	`<Enter>`	Select operator
Press:	`<Shift>+<F1>`	Request list
Move to:	ON_HAND	Second field used in expression
Press:	`<Enter>`	Select ON_HAND
Press:	`<Enter>`	Complete expression specification
Move to:	Template	Desired option
Press:	`<Enter>`	Select Template
Action:	Revise the template to be **9999.99** using `<left>`, `<backspace>`, and `<delete>`.	
Press:	`<Enter>`	Complete Template specification
Press:	`<Ctrl>+<End>`	Complete field specification

With the INVESTMENT column defined in the Detail Band, the total of this column can now be specified in the Report Summary Band as follows:

To total the calculated column in the Report Summary Band of the Report format

Action:	Position your cursor at the desired location in the INVESTMENT column of the Report Summary Band where the summarized value is to reside, such as Line 1, Col 61.	
Press:	<F5>	Select Add field
Move to:	Sum under SUMMARY	
		Desired SUMMARY option
Press:	<Enter>	Select Sum option
Move to:	Field to summarize on	
		Desired option
Press:	<Enter>	Select option and display list of fields
Move to:	INVESTMENT	Desired field
Press:	<Enter>	Select the field
Move to:	Template	Desired option
Press:	<Enter>	Select Template
Action:	Modify the template to **99999.99** using <left>, <backspace>, and <delete>.	
Press:	<Enter>	Complete Template specification
Press:	<Ctrl>+<End>	Complete summary specification
Action:	Preview your report on the screen. If required, make any revisions. Then, Exit to the dot prompt as you save this report definition.	

The complete INVENTRY report format definition is shown in Figure D.74. You are now ready to produce the final output report as described in the next section.

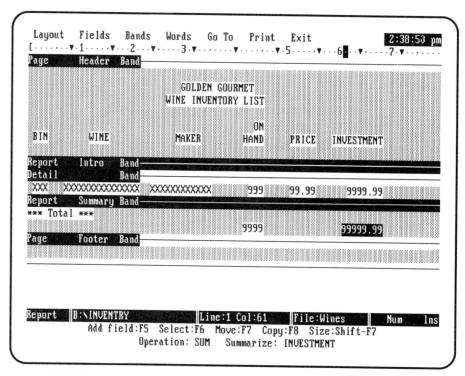

FIGURE D.74. Report format for computing investment column [version IV].

D.6.5.3. Generate Report with Computed Field

Once the report format has been defined, the report is produced in this manner:

To generate a Report that
contains a calculated field

Enter: REPORT FORM INVENTRY TO PRINT

The final output report is printed as illustrated in Figure D.72. Bert now has the desired report for evaluating their investment in wines.

D.6.6 When Things Go Wrong

In addition to the difficulties encountered in entering and producing reports described in Lesson D.5, several other conditions that may occur and how to approach them are described here:

1. An unwanted total column appears. This problem occurs most frequently with dBASE III+ report definitions.
   a. Use MODIFY REPORT to access the report definition.
   b. [VERSION III+] For the column with the unwanted total, toggle the "Total this column" to No.
      or
      [VERSION IV] Position your cursor on the unwanted total field in the Report Summary Band and delete the field specification.
2. A group on report has the group heading repeated at several locations throughout the report. This occurs when the data are *not in the appropriate sequence.*
   a. Use the SET INDEX TO command to obtain the desired sequencing of your data.
   b. Reissue the REPORT FORM command.

D.6.7 Lesson Summary

- A REPORT FORM permits a report heading and column headings to be arranged in preparing management style reports.
- A REPORT FORM can be used to produce a report with data arranged in a specified sequence by activating an INDEX or by reporting from a file that is SORTED.
- A FOR condition can be used with the REPORT FORM command to produce an exception report.
- NUMERIC fields can have a column total calculated and displayed with a dBASE report format.
- A report format permits data to be grouped based on the values contained in a field. Each time a different value is encountered for the specified field, a group subtitle may be printed. A database is usually sequenced on the field used for groups *before* a report is printed.
- New report columns can be computed in a report format. When selecting a column to be displayed, the equation to be calculated is specified. Calculated columns may be totaled.

D.6.8 Practice Tutorial

Report formats can be employed to complete the series of reports for the Wine Management System as described in this Lesson. Create these management-style reports as a guided activity in a hands-on manner. Access the WINES database before you begin developing these reports.

Task 1: Create the report formats for the Serving List, Order List, and Wine List, with the Wine List grouped by wine type.

Task 2: Produce each of these three reports, as shown in Figures D.62, D.63, and D.68.

Task 3: Produce the Wine Inventory List in Figure D.72.

Time Estimates

Novice: 90 minutes

Intermediate: 60 minutes

Advanced: 45 minutes

D.6.9 Practice Exercises

(1)   Case: Burgers and More

Business Problem: Payroll Processing

MIS Characteristics: Human Resources

Operational Control

As payroll manager at Burgers and More, Dominique Alvarez is responsible for preparing the biweekly payroll. To assist her with this record-keeping activity, Dominique has set up a database that contains the fields described by this data dictionary definition:

Field Name	Description
SSN	Social security number
LNAME	Last name
FNAME	First name
MI	Middle initial
RATE	Pay rate per hour
HOURS	Hours worked
EMP	A status indicator of whether or not the individual is currently employed

Dominique wants to improve the appearance of the report that she produces from this database. To accomplish this, she has completed the following report design:

```
              1111111111222222222233333333334444444444555555555566666
     12345678901234567890123456789012345678901234567890123456789012345

 1
 2                              BURGERS AND MORE
 3                              PAYROLL REPORT
 4
 5
 6                                           HOURS    PAY    GROSS
 7        SSN        LAST NAME    FIRST NAME  MI WORKED   RATE    PAY
 8
 9     XXXXXXXX    XXXXXXXXXX   XXXXXXXXXX   X  99.9   99.99   999.99
10     XXXXXXXX    XXXXXXXXXX   XXXXXXXXXX   X  99.9   99.99   999.99
11     XXXXXXXX    XXXXXXXXXX   XXXXXXXXXX   X  99.9   99.99   999.99
12     XXXXXXXX    XXXXXXXXXX   XXXXXXXXXX   X  99.9   99.99   999.99
                                    .
                                    .
                                    .
       XXXXXXXX    XXXXXXXXXX   XXXXXXXXXX   X  99.9   99.99   999.99
       XXXXXXXX    XXXXXXXXXX   XXXXXXXXXX   X  99.9   99.99   999.99

       *** TOTAL ***                           9999.9          9999.99
```

Task 1: Access the BURGERS.DBF database file in the EXERCISE catalog and review the structure and data. Produce a hard copy listing of the database structure for documentation and reference.

. _____

. _____

. _____

Task 2: Create a report form with the name of BURGPAY.FRM that defines the Payroll Report as sketched out by Dominique. The HOURS WORKED and GROSS PAY should be summed with the total printed at the bottom of the report, as illustrated. Dominique wants you to calculate the GROSS PAY field on this report as HOURS * RATE.

. _____

. _____

Task 3: Generate the Payroll Report by using the report form definition created in Task 2. Arrange this report in alphabetic sequence by last name.

. _____

. _____

Task 4: (*Optional*)   Dominique wants you to design and create a report form definition with columns for DEDUCTIONS and NET PAY. Give this report form the name BURGNET.FRM. Dominique computes deductions as 23 percent of GROSS PAY. In your report, the DEDUCTIONS field should be computed as **HOURS*RATE*.23** and the NET PAY field computed as **(HOURS*RATE) – (HOURS*RATE*.23)**. The HOURS WORKED, GROSS PAY, DEDUCTIONS, and NET PAY should all be summed and reported on the Total line. Produce this report arranged by social security number. Write a short paragraph describing why you cannot compute NET PAY as GROSS PAY – DEDUCTIONS in this report definition.

. _____

. _____

. _____

Time Estimates

Novice: 90 minutes

Intermediate: 60 minutes

Advanced: 45 minutes

(2)   Case: International Diversified Products

Business Problem: Sales Tracking

MIS Characteristics: Marketing

Managerial Control

International Diversified Products (IDP) is a manufacturer and distributor of a variety of consumer electronics and household appliances. John Porter is IDP's Vice President of Sales. John tracks sales by product family, country, and sales associate. A product family is a group of related products. John has organized IDP's products into three families: home appliances (APPL), sound and television (AUDIO) and health care (HEALTH). The home appliances product family includes refrigerators, washers, and dryers, and the health care family consists of hair dryers and dental care products.

Each of the sales associates at IDP receives a bonus at the end of the year that is computed as 2 percent of their annual sales. John is responsible for determining this bonus for each sales associate. To enable John to both track sales and calculate the annual bonus, he has set up a database containing the fields described by this data dictionary definition:

Field Name	Description
ASSOCIATE	Sales associate/representative
PRODUCT	Product family: APPL, AUDIO, HEALTH
COUNTRY	Country of sales
QTR1	Sales amount in thousands for first quarter
QTR2	Sales amount in thousands for second quarter
QTR3	Sales amount in thousands for third quarter
QTR4	Sales amount in thousands for fourth quarter

John has created a design for a Sales by Product Family Report that displays sales for the fourth quarter of the year (the most recent quarter), displays total sales for the year, and contains the bonus amount for each sales associate. The report design he sketched out is as follows:

```
            111111111122222222223333333333444444444455555555556666
   1234567890123456789012345678901234567890123456789012345678901234

1
2                   INTERNATIONAL DIVERSIFIED PRODUCTS
3                       SALES BY PRODUCT FAMILY
4                           FOURTH QUARTER
5
6
7                      SALES      FOURTH      ANNUAL      ANNUAL
8     COUNTRY        ASSOCIATE    QUARTER      TOTAL       BONUS
9
10
11  ** PRODUCT XXXXXXX
12     XXXXXXXXX     XXXXXXXXXXXX    999.9     99999.9     9999.9
13     XXXXXXXXX     XXXXXXXXXXXX    999.9     99999.9     9999.9
14     XXXXXXXXX     XXXXXXXXXXXX    999.9     99999.9     9999.9
                                       .
                                       .
                                       .
       XXXXXXXXX     XXXXXXXXXXXX    999.9     99999.9     9999.9
    ** SUBTOTAL **
                                   99999.9   9999999.9   999999.9

                    (Repeat above for each PRODUCT)

    *** TOTAL ***
                                   99999.9   9999999.9   999999.9
```

Task 1: Access the IDP.DBF database file in the EXERCISE catalog. Review the database structure and data.

- _____
- _____
- _____

Task 2: Create a report form with the name of IDPPROD.FRM that defines the Sales by Product Family as sketched out by John. The sales amounts for the four quarters are summed to obtain the ANNUAL TOTAL. The BONUS column is computed using this formula: **(QTR1 + QTR2 + QTR3 + QTR4) * .02.** The FOURTH QUARTER, ANNUAL TOTAL, and BONUS columns are summed to yield the subtotal for each product family and the grand total for all product families.

- _____
- _____
- _____

Task 3: Generate the IDPPROD report using the report form definition created in Task 2. Arrange this report in alphabetic sequence by product, country, and associate.

- _____
- _____
- _____

Task 4: (*Optional*)   John wants you to design and create a report form definition with the data grouped by country. This is the Sales by Country Report. Name this the IDPCNTRY.FRM report form. This report is to have subtotals for each country and a grand total, similar to the Sales by Product Family Report. Produce this report arranged by country, product, and associate. Write a brief paragraph describing why you cannot calculate BONUS as ANNUAL_TOTAL * .02 in this report definition.

- _____
- _____
- _____

Time Estimates

Novice: 90 minutes

Intermediate: 60 minutes

Advanced: 45 minutes

D.6.10   Comprehensive Problems

(1)   Case: Yen To Travel (continued)

At Yen To Travel, Brenda and Sara are ready to have you complete their series of management-style reports for their Tour Management System. Access the TOURS database and construct these reports.

Task 1: Create a report format for the Seat Request List. The report should have a total for the seats requested and should include a heading with the travel agency's name and the report name.

· _____

· _____

Task 2: Produce the Seat Request List arranged by tour code.

· _____

· _____

Task 3: Create a report format for the Tour List that groups the tours by type. This report should have a heading that includes the travel agency's name and the report name.

· _____

· _____

Task 4: Generate the Seat Request List with tours arranged in groups by tour type.

· _____

· _____

Task 5: Create a Tour Inventory Report that includes the tour code, tour name, tour agent, open seats, price per seat, and potential seat revenue. The *potential seat revenue* is the number of open seats times the price per seat. The report should include a total of the open seats and the potential revenue.

· _____

· _____

Task 6: Produce the Tour Inventory Report arranged by tour code.

· _____

· _____

Time Estimates

Novice: 90 minutes

Intermediate: 60 minutes

Advanced: 45 minutes

(2)   Case: Silver Screen Video (continued)

Amy, Ernie, and Todd want you to complete their series of management-style reports for the Movie Management System at Silver Screen Video. Access the MOVIES database and develop these reports.

Task 1: Create a report format for the Order List. The report should have a total for the movies on hand and should include a heading with the store's name and the report name.

· _____

· _____

Task 2: Produce the Order List arranged in the desired sequence.

· _____

· _____

Task 3: Create a report format for the Movie List that groups the movies by type. This report should have a heading that includes the store's name and the report name.

· _____

· _____

Task 4: Generate the Movie List with the movies grouped by type.

· _____

· _____

Task 5: Create a Movie Inventory Report that includes the movie, location code, movie name, filmmaker, quantity on hand, price per movie, and potential movie revenue or investment. The report should include a total of the movies on hand and the investment.

· _____

· _____

Task 6. Produce the Movie Inventory Report arranged by movie.

· _____

· _____

Time Estimates

Novice: 90 minutes

Intermediate: 60 minutes

Advanced: 45 minutes

D.6.11 Application Case

Case: SeaFirst Mutual Fund
         Business Problem: Portfolio Management
         MIS Characteristics: Finance
                             Managerial Control
         Management Functions: Planning
                             Controlling
         Tools Skills: Report generation
                 Indexing

Clay Chandler founded SeaFirst Mutual Fund in 1961 with an initial portfolio of $100 million. Since then SeaFirst's investment portfolio has grown to more than $2 billion under Clay's watchful guidance. As Chairman of the Board of Directors of SeaFirst, Clay is responsible for the overall direction of the investment portfolio. He works with SeaFirst's Investment Committee in establishing policy for the acquisition and disposition of investments each quarter. Clay and the Investment Committee are concerned with the composition of SeaFirst's stock portfolio. At each meeting, they review the current status of the stocks held by their mutual fund.

SeaFirst's Vice President and Senior Investment Analyst, Donna Carter, is a member of the Investment Committee. She oversees the day-to-day activities of the portfolio. With her direction, the general portfolio policies established by Clay and the Committee are transformed into guidelines for the individual investment advisors, like Martina Navistar. Martina follows the Drugs industry group of stocks recommending buy and sell decisions. Last month, one of her major recommendations was the purchase of Marion Merrell Dow (MKC).

Noralyn Luczak is SeaFirst's manager of their "back office" operations. The back office is responsible for the basic accounting functions, which support the operations of a mutual fund. This includes the record-keeping activities of collecting and dispersing funds, maintaining the securities database, and producing SeaFirst's financial statements for investors and regulators.

To fulfill the reporting requirements of investors and regulators, such as the Security and Exchange Commission (SEC), SeaFirst prepares reports of its current investment portfolio each quarter. This portfolio reporting requirement is satisfied by listing the shares of each stock, the total cost of the stock, and the current total market value of the stock.

Noralyn is in the process of improving SeaFirst's back office operations by enhancing the reports produced for the Investment Committee and generated to meet SEC and other reporting requirements. The data for these reporting requirements are stored in SeaFirst's Investment Tracking System (ITS) database. During the past several weeks, she has reviewed the SEC reporting requirements and refined their Portfolio Report, which can be generated from the ITS database. She is currently working with Clay and Donna to refine an Analysis Report for the Investment Committee to be produced from this same database.

In preparation for developing the Portfolio Report and the Analysis Report, Noralyn sketched out the report design for each of these two desired reports. A report design shows the layout of the report title, column titles, and location of data on the report. The report design can be readily reviewed and revised before the actual report is produced, since it is a mock-up of the report enabling an end-user like Clay or Donna to see how the report will appear. Noralyn used X's and 9's to sketch out the character and numeric fields. This illustrates the size of each field within the report mock-up. For numeric data, the location of the decimal would also be indicated. However, for the Portfolio Report, all numbers are displayed as integers. The report design for the quarterly Portfolio Report is as follows:

```
                         SEAFIRST MUTUAL FUND
                   SECOND QUARTER PORTFOLIO REPORT


   SHARES                                    COST            VALUE

   ** INDUSTRY XXXXXXXX
   99999999 XXXXXXXXXXXXXXXXXXXXXXXX 99999999999999 99999999999999
   99999999 XXXXXXXXXXXXXXXXXXXXXXXX 99999999999999 99999999999999
   99999999 XXXXXXXXXXXXXXXXXXXXXXXX 99999999999999 99999999999999
                                     .
                                     .
                                     .
   99999999 XXXXXXXXXXXXXXXXXXXXXXXX 99999999999999 99999999999999


   ** SUBTOTAL **
                                     99999999999999 99999999999999

                   (Repeat above for each INDUSTRY)

   *** TOTAL ***
                                     99999999999999 99999999999999
```

where: Report column COST is the number of SHARES multiplied by
       the COST per share and
       Report column VALUE is the number of SHARES multiplied by
       the PRICE per share

Noralyn reviewed this report design with Donna and obtained her approval to proceed with the implementation of the report.

After Noralyn completed the mock-up of the Analysis Report, she reviewed it with Clay, Donna, and the other member of the Investment Committee. They suggested several improvements in the arrangement of the columns on the report. Noralyn made these revisions and obtained the Committee's approval for implementing the report with the ITS database. The final Analysis Report sketch is as follows:

```
                         SEAFIRST MUTUAL FUND
                   SECOND QUARTER ANALYSIS REPORT


                                    COST    PRICE            PURCHASED
                                    PER     PER     PRICE    THIS
          STOCK          SYMBOL  SHARES   SHARE   SHARE   CHANGE   QUARTER

   XXXXXXXXXXXXXXXXXXXX XXXX   99999999  999.99  999.99  9999.99  .L.
   XXXXXXXXXXXXXXXXXXXX XXXX   99999999  999.99  999.99  9999.99  .L.
   XXXXXXXXXXXXXXXXXXXX XXXX   99999999  999.99  999.99  9999.99  .L.
                                     .
                                     .
                                     .
   XXXXXXXXXXXXXXXXXXXX XXXX   99999999  999.99  999.99  9999.99  .L.
```

Where report column PRICE CHANGE is the difference between the PRICE per share and the COST per share for each stock.

SeaFirst's ITS database contains fields that are described by the following data dictionary definitions:

Field Name	Description
NAME	Name of stock
SYMBOL	Stock exchange ticker symbol
SHARES	Number of shares of stock held in the Portfolio
COST	Cost or purchase price per share of the stock
PRICE	Current market price per share of the stock
INDUSTRY	Industry group to which the stock belongs
PTQ	Indicator of whether or not the stock was purchased during the current quarter

With the report designs completed and approved, Noralyn was ready to begin developing the reports for SeaFirst.

Tasks

1. Access the MUTUAL.DBF database for SeaFirst's Investment Tracking System in the CASES catalog and review its structure and content. Obtain a hard copy of the structure.

2. Create a report form for the quarterly Portfolio Report to investors.

3. Generate the quarterly Portfolio Report using the report form definition. Arrange the report alphabetically by industry group and company name within industry groups.

4. Develop a report form for the quarterly investment Analysis Report.

5. Produce the quarterly investment Analysis Report using the report form definition. Arrange the report by number of shares from the largest to the smallest number.

6. Produce a second investment Analysis Report using the report form definition that contains only the stocks *added* to the portfolio this quarter. Arrange the report by number of shares from the largest to the smallest number.

7. SeaFirst is considering expanding its Investment Tracking System. What additional data would you recommend they include in this database? Why should it be included? With these data other reports could be produced. Prepare a report sketch for such a suggested report.

Time Estimates

Novice: 120 minutes

Intermediate: 90 minutes

Advanced: 60 minutes

Joining Databases and Producing Labels

CONTENT

- A Second Database for Suppliers
- Joining Database Relations
- Producing Mailing Labels
- An Alternative for Joining Database Relations
- When Things Go Wrong

D.7.1 A Second Database for Suppliers

When Bert is reordering wines for the Golden Gourmet, he makes use of a second dBASE database file that contains the names and addresses of the maker of each wine. Data for each supplier are obtained from this database when it is time to place another order. Bert used this Database Planning Form in designing the SUPPLIER database:

DATABASE PLANNING FORM

Data Name	Data Type	Number of Characters for Largest Value	Dec(imal) Places
MAKER	Character	12	
ADDRESS	Character	20	
CITY	Character	14	
STATE	Character	2	
ZIP	Numeric	5	0

The structure of the SUPPLIER database relation, which Bert created, appears in Figure D.75. A list of the SUPPLIER records is provided in Figure D.76. SUPPLIER is a separate relation. Since Golden Gourmet references the producer of the wine as the MAKER in the WINES database, the same field name is used in the SUPPLIER

```
. display structure
Structure for database: A:supplier.dbf
Number of data records:     12
Date of last update   : 10/21/93
Field  Field Name  Type        Width    Dec
    1   MAKER       Character     12
    2   ADDRESS     Character     20
    3   CITY        Character     14
    4   STATE       Character      2
    5   ZIP         Numeric        5
** Total **                      54
```

FIGURE D.75. SUPPLIER database structure

database. When fields describing the same attribute are used in several different databases, it is usually desirable to assign them the same field name.

Of course, data can be entered and updated in the SUPPLIER database in the same manner as that illustrated with the WINES database. The suppliers can be displayed or listed, or reports can be created as desired.

Action: Create the SUPPLIER database file and enter the records from Figure D.76.

D.7.2 Joining Database Relations

Bert wants to expand the reorder report for the Golden Gourmet so it includes the supplier data for each wine that is to be ordered. This requires a list that contains the name and year of the wine from the WINES database and the address information from the SUPPLIER database. When information is contained in two separate database files, these files can be combined or joined by using a field that is common to both database files. In general, a field used in this manner to identify matching records is known as a *key field*.

In the WINES database file, the MAKER is repeated for each wine from the same vineyard. In the SUPPLIER database file, each supplier occurs only one time. Storing the address data in the SUPPLIER database file is more efficient, since these data are *not repeated for each wine*. Also, by storing the address data only one time, it needs to be changed in only one place.

For reordering wines, the database files will be joined as illustrated in Figure D.77. The wines that need to be reordered will be combined with the supplier names and addresses. In dBASE, this requires that both database files must be available or *open* at

```
. List all
```

Record#	MAKER	ADDRESS	CITY	STATE	ZIP
1	ALMADEN	4816 N. FORTY	WALNUT CREEK	CA	92001
2	BOONE'S FARM	14389 WIND ROAD	CULVER CITY	CA	93905
3	FETZER VINOS	7735 CLEAR CREEK RD	BATTLE CREEK	MI	48541
4	GEYSER PEAK	97882 FRONTAGE ROAD	FRESNO	CA	92211
5	HOOTCH HUT	88 GULCH WAY	SANTA CLARA	CA	91193
6	J. MOREAU	4782 AIRPORT DRIVE	SAN FRANCISCO	CA	94411
7	M. TORRES	RR 4, BOX 63	SAN MARCO	CA	93911
8	MOGEN DAVID	RR 3, BOX 98	SAN JOSE	CA	94089
9	RIVERSIDE	3006 CASA GRANDE	RIVERWOOD	CA	92299
10	SMOTHERS BRO	6798 SLUDGE WAY	FOUR CORNERS	NY	10177
11	TAYLOR FARMS	19 HILLSIDE ROAD	ROCHESTER	NY	10191
12	WENTE BROS	9800 S. MAIN	LIVERMORE	CA	94441

FIGURE D.76. SUPPLIER database list.

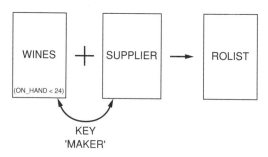

FIGURE D.77. General arrangement for joining databases.

the same time. A database file must be opened before any records can be read from it. To allow several database files to be accessed at one time, dBASE permits up to 10 databases to be "selected" or "opened" for use. As each database file is selected, it is assigned to what dBASE calls an "area." Fundamentally, this is a table within dBASE that keeps track of selected databases, any index used by the databases, and several other characteristics.

dBASE provides two different commands for joining the data stored in two separate database files. The JOIN command combines the data and produces a third database file, whereas the SET RELATION command makes the combined data available for your use, but does *not* create a separate database file. Because the JOIN command produces a file that you can access and look at, this command is explored first. Then the SET RELATION command is examined in the last section of this Lesson.

~~~~~~~~~
Caution Alert!
~~~~~~~~~

> Before embarking on the JOIN activity, enter the command:
>
> **CLOSE DATABASES**
>
> This will ensure that *all* your databases have been "closed" and will avoid potential difficulties when the SELECT is used to activate multiple database files for use with the JOIN command!

The desired JOIN is accomplished in this manner beginning with the CLOSE command:

To close all database files	**Enter:**	CLOSE DATABASES	Prepare for using multiple database files
To select or open a database file in an area	**Enter:**	SELECT 2	Choose area 2
	Enter:	USE SUPPLIER	Open database in area 2
To select or open another database file in a different area	**Enter:**	SELECT 1	Choose area 1
	Enter:	USE WINES	Open database in area 1

By using SELECT, both the SUPPLIER and WINES database files can be accessed in performing the join. Since WINES is the last database file SELECTed or opened, it is the *currently selected* database file, while SUPPLIER is available, but not currently selected. With the JOIN command, a *new* database file is created, containing rows formed when the data values in a specified field match. These fields serve as the key field for matching the records. For the reorder report, this is the MAKER field. The commands for performing the join are issued in this manner:

| To select desired records during the join process | **Enter:** | SET FILTER TO ON_HAND < 24 | |
| | | | Establish *exception* reporting criteria |

Keypoint! | The <F6> key or DISPLAY STATUS command may be used to check on the current assignment of database files to selected database areas!

To JOIN two database files using a key field

Enter: `JOIN WITH SUPPLIER TO ROLIST FOR MAKER=SUPPLIER->MAKER`

First, the SET FILTER TO command is used to specify that only those records in WINES that meet this condition are to be joined. Once again, this is the *exception reporting* condition of ON_HAND less than 24. In executing the JOIN command, WINES is the currently selected database file, while SUPPLIER is an available database. Both database files must be selected *before* the JOIN can be carried out. The JOIN WITH SUPPLIER indicates that the currently selected WINES database file is to be joined with the available SUPPLIER database file. ROLIST is the name of the output database file produced by the join. The MAKER=SUPPLIER->MAKER specifies that the MAKER field of WINES is to be matched with the MAKER field of SUPPLIER in performing the join. That is, "SUPPLIER->MAKER" specifies use of the MAKER field from the SUPPLIER database file. The "->" is an operator used in specifying the database file name of an available, but *not currently* selected, database.

Keypoint! | The *key fields* in the two database files should be the same *width* for the JOIN to be performed! If your field widths are *not* the same:

1. Use MODIFY STRUCTURE to change the width in one of the database files or
2. Use the TRIM function in the JOIN command! That is: TRIM(MAKER) = TRIM(SUPPLIER->MAKER)

Results of the join can now be viewed by using these commands:

To access the joined database file

Enter:	`SELECT 3`	Choose area 3
Enter:	`USE ROLIST`	Open database in area 3
Enter:	`LIST ALL`	Display contents of JOINed database

Results of the join are shown in Figure D.78. Since the number of characters in each record is greater than 80, display of the record continues (wraps around) on

Record#	NAME	MAKER	YEAR	BIN	PRICE	ON_HAND	L_ORDER
	CHILL TYPE	ADDRESS			CITY	STATE	ZIP
1	COUNTRY CHABLIS	ALMADEN	1983	A43	9.00	15	10/18/89
	.T. WHITE	4816 N. FORTY			WALNUT CREEK	CA	92001
1	BLANC DE BLANC	FETZER VINOS	1982	D23	20.00	21	11/20/89
	.T. WHITE	7735 CLEAR CREEK RD			BATTLE CREEK	MI	48541
3	MOREAU ROUGE	J. MOREAU	1982	D12	18.50	15	05/25/90
	.F. RED	4782 AIRPORT DRIVE			SAN FRANCISCO	CA	94411
4	TORRES DE CASTA	M. TORRES	1985	B15	5.24	10	07/15/90
	.T. RESE	RR 4, BOX 63			SAN MARCO	CA	93911
5	ZINFANDEL	TAYLOR FARMS	1988	122	6.50	10	11/29/91
	.F. RED	19 HILLSIDE ROAD			ROCHESTER	NY	10191
6	RED TABLE WINE	TAYLOR FARMS	1989	A26	4.76	11	11/29/92
	.F. RED	19 HILLSIDE ROAD			ROCHESTER	NY	10191
7	BOONE'S FARM	SMOTHERS BRO	1988	A88	13.80	10	05/08/90
	.F. ROSE	6798 SLUDGE WAY			FOUR CORNERS	NY	10177

FIGURE D.78. Database produced by JOIN on MAKER fields.

```
                        GOLDEN GOURMET
                        WINE ORDER LIST


                                                                              ZIP
MAKER             WINE              YEAR   ADDRESS             CITY      ST   CODE

ALMADEN           COUNTRY CHABLIS   1983   4816 N. FORTY       WALNUT CREEK    CA   92001
FETZER VINOS      BLANCE DE BLANCE  1982   7735 CLEAR CREEK RD BATTLE CREEK    MI   48541
J. MOREAU         MOREAU ROUGE      1982   4782 AIRPORT DRIVE  SAN FRANCISCO   CA   94411
M. TORRES         TORRES DE CASTA   1985   RR 4, BOX 63        SAN MARCO       CA   93911
TAYLOR FARMS      ZINFANDEL         1989   19 HILLSIDE ROAD    ROCHESTER       NY   10191
TAYLOR FARMS      RED TABLE WINE    1989   19 HILLSIDE ROAD    ROCHESTER       NY   10191
SMOTHERS BRO      BOONE'S FARM      1988   6798 SLUDGE WAY     FOUR CORNERS    NY   10177
```

FIGURE D.79. Wine Order List report for joined database.

the next line on your screen. Notice how records 5 and 6 for Taylor Farms have the address repeated. A reorder report as shown in Figure D.79 is produced by using the REPORT FORM ROLIST that appears as Figure D.80 [version III+] or Figure D.81 [version IV].

Keypoint!   The JOIN command produces a *separate* database file that takes up additional disk storage space. The SET RELATION TO command permits data to be accessed from two database files at one time similar to the JOIN, but without producing a separate database file!

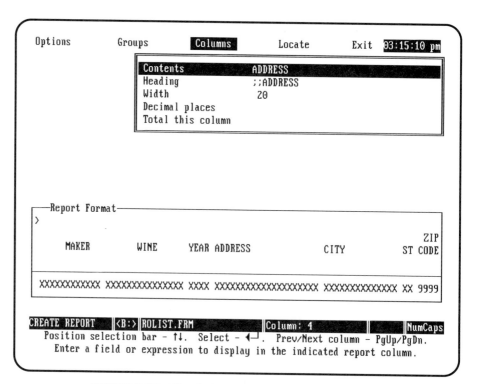

FIGURE D.80. Wine Order List report format [version III+].

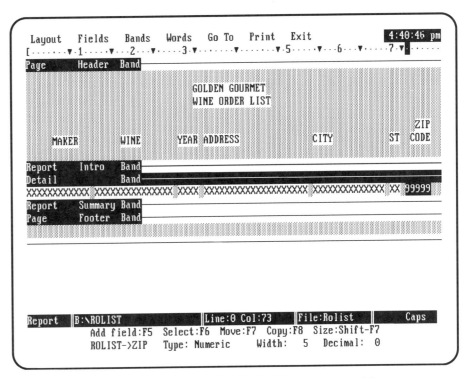

FIGURE D.81. Wine Order List report format [version IV].

D.7.3   Producing Mailing Labels

To expedite Bert's reorder processing, he wants to produce mailing labels as shown in Figure D.82. These mailing labels, produced in a "two-up" arrangement, appear in two columns. dBASE allows labels to be written in one, two, or three columns. The number of columns is selected as an option in creating the label format definition. Bert needs to create a LABEL FORM describing these labels. A LABEL FORM is similar to a REPORT FORM. The primary difference is that the output report is a mailing label. Since mailing labels are frequently produced from a database, dBASE provides a special Label Report for this purpose. Bert developed the LABEL FORM displayed in Figure D.83 [version III+] or Figure D.84 for printing these mailing labels.

Keypoint!   A dBASE LABEL FORM is used to produce mailing labels. This FORM is similar to the REPORT FORM!

ALMADEN
4816 N. FORTY
WALNUT CREEK CA 92001

FETZER VINOS
7735 CLEAR CREEK RD
BATTLE CREEK MI 48541

J. MOREAU
4782 AIRPORT DRIVE
SAN FRANCISCO CA 94411

M. TORRES
RR. 4, BOX 63
SAN MARCO CA 93911

SMOTHERS BRO
6798 SLUDGE WAY
FOUR CORNERS NY 10177

TAYLOR FARMS
19 HILLSIDE ROAD
ROCHESTER NY 10191

FIGURE D.82. "TWO-up" mailing labels.

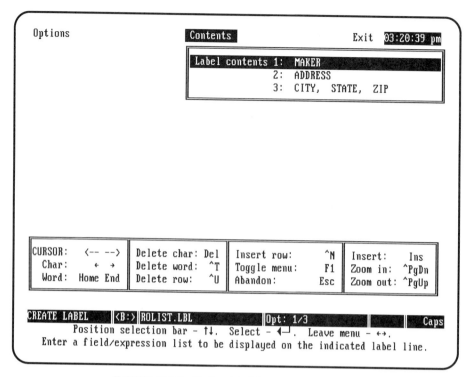

FIGURE D.83. Mailing label format [version III+].

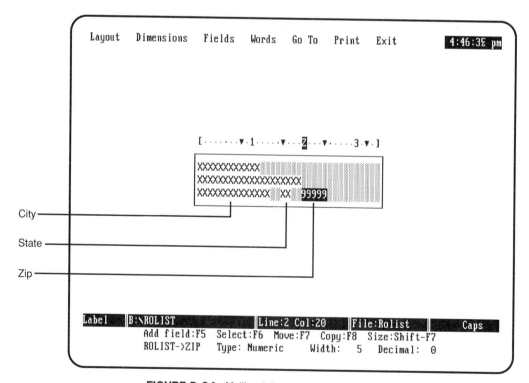

FIGURE D.84. Mailing label format [version IV].

The commands Bert used to initiate development of the mailing label format definition are as follows:

Action: Verify that ROLIST is your currently selected database.

| To create a LABEL format | **Enter:** | `CREATE LABEL ROLIST` Begin label format definition |

Once a mailing label format has been initially created, revisions to an existing labels format, such as ROLIST, are made by accessing it with the command MODIFY LABEL ROLIST.

Like the dBASE REPORT FORM, the LABEL FORM specification is different in version III+ than it is in version IV. Because of the differences in specifying the label format, the development of the definition is presented separately for each of the versions. You should follow the description that matches your available version of dBASE. You may want to read the description for the other version to gain an understanding of some of the differences and similarities in the label format definition process. However, once the LABEL FORM has been defined, the printing of the final mailing labels proceeds in exactly the same manner for both versions.

D.7.3.1. Version III+ Label Format

The CREATE LABEL command causes the screen shown in Figure D.83 to appear for describing the mailing label arrangement. Bert defined the mailing label format in this manner:

To specify a LABEL FORMAT	**Move to:**	Options	
	Move to:	Predefined size	
	Press:	<Enter>	Toggles the label size to $3\frac{1}{2}$ by $\frac{15}{16}$ by 2

Here, the "by 2" means two-up printing or side-by-side labels in two columns as in Figure D.82. If you continue pressing <Enter>, you toggle through the available predefined label sizes.

Move to:	Label height	Select option for revision
Press:	<Enter>	Select option for revision
Enter:	3	Label has only 3 lines
Move to:	Contents	Specify fields to appear on label
Press:	<Enter>	Select Label contents line 1
Press:	<F10>	Obtain a list of available field names
Move to:	MAKER	Desired field for this line
Press:	<Enter>	Select field name entry
Press:	<Enter>	Complete contents specification
Move to:	Label contents 2	Second line on label
Press:	<Enter>	Select Label contents line 2
Press:	<F10>	Display list of available field names
Move to:	ADDRESS	Desired field for this line
Press:	<Enter>	Select field name entry
Press:	<Enter>	Complete contents specification
Move to:	Label contents 3	Third line on label

Press:	\<Enter\>	Select Label contents line 3
Press:	\<F10\>	Display list of available field names
Move to:	CITY	Desired field for this line
Press:	\<Enter\>	Select field name entry
Type:	,	Separate field names with comma
Press:	\<F10\>	Display list of available field names
Move to:	STATE	Desired field for this line
Press:	\<Enter\>	Select field name entry
Type:	,	Separate field names with comma
Press:	\<F10\>	Display list of available field names
Move to:	ZIP	Desired field for this line
Press:	\<Enter\>	Select field name entry
Press:	\<Enter\>	Complete contents specification

To EXIT from the LABEL FORMAT specification and save this LABEL FORMAT file

Move to:	Exit
Select:	Save

The mailing label format has been completed and saved as a file with the *.LBL extension. You are ready to produce the mailing labels as described in Section D.7.3.3, "Generate Mailing Labels."

D.7.3.2.   Version IV Label Format

The CREATE LABEL command causes a label design work surface to appear, as shown in Figure D.84. This is similar to the report design work surface. However, label formats consist of only one print area. They do not have the Bands used in report formats.

Using a mouse to specify a LABEL format

Beginning with Version 1.5 of dBASE IV, you can use a mouse to position the cursor on the design work surface or to make menu selections. The mouse operations for a LABEL FORM are the same as those for the REPORT FORM as described in Figure D.52 in Lesson D.5.

Bert developed the mailing label format in the following manner:

To specify a label's size and arrangement

Press:	\<F10\>	
Move to:	Dimensions	Desired activity
Press:	\<Enter\>	Display list of available standard labels
Move to:	15/16 X 3 1/2 by 2	Desired label size and arrangement
Press:	\<Enter\>	Select label size

The "by 2" in the label size definition indicates that labels are to printed in a "two-up" or "side-by-side" arrangement in two columns, as is illustrated in Figure D.82. When you complete the selection of the label size, you are returned to the labels design work surface. dBASE provides a default label, which is five lines high. However, Bert only has three lines in his label. Continue defining the mailing label in this manner:

To specify the number of lines in the label

Press:	\<F10\>	
Move to:	Height of label	Desired Dimensions option
Press:	\<Enter\>	Select option

Type:	3	Desired label height
Press:	<Enter>	Complete specification
Press:	<Esc>	Return to label design work surface

The work surface now contains a label that is only three lines high. The cursor is positioned in Line 0, Col 0 of this work surface. Continue defining the label:

<table>
<tr><td>To specify the fields
contained on the label</td><td>**Press:**</td><td><F5></td><td>Select Add field</td></tr>
<tr><td></td><td>**Select:**</td><td>MAKER</td><td>Desired field for line 1</td></tr>
<tr><td></td><td>**Press:**</td><td><Ctrl>+<End></td><td>Accept Template</td></tr>
<tr><td></td><td>**Move to:**</td><td>Line 1, Col 0</td><td>Position cursor for line 2</td></tr>
<tr><td></td><td>**Press:**</td><td><F5></td><td>Select Add field</td></tr>
<tr><td></td><td>**Select:**</td><td>ADDRESS</td><td>Desired field for line 2</td></tr>
<tr><td></td><td>**Press:**</td><td><Ctrl>+<End></td><td>Accept Template</td></tr>
<tr><td></td><td>**Move to:**</td><td>Line 2, Col 0</td><td>Position cursor for line 3</td></tr>
<tr><td></td><td>**Action:**</td><td colspan="2">Place CITY field at this location.</td></tr>
<tr><td></td><td>**Move to:**</td><td colspan="2">Line 2, Col 16</td></tr>
<tr><td></td><td>**Action:**</td><td colspan="2">Place STATE field at this location.</td></tr>
<tr><td></td><td>**Move to:**</td><td colspan="2">Line 2, Col 20</td></tr>
<tr><td></td><td>**Action:**</td><td colspan="2">Place ZIP field at this location.</td></tr>
</table>

The ROLIST mailing label format definition is complete, as is illustrated in Figure D.84. This format file can be saved and the mailing labels can be produced. However, before exiting from the label form definition screen, the labels can be previewed like this:

<table>
<tr><td>To Preview the mailing label</td><td>**Press:**</td><td><Alt>+<P></td><td>Select Print from the Label Menu</td></tr>
<tr><td></td><td>or</td><td></td><td></td></tr>
<tr><td></td><td>**Press:**</td><td><F10></td><td>Access Label Menu Bar</td></tr>
<tr><td></td><td>**Move to:**</td><td>Print</td><td>Desired menu choice</td></tr>
<tr><td></td><td>**Move to:**</td><td>View labels on screen</td><td></td></tr>
<tr><td></td><td></td><td></td><td>Desired action</td></tr>
<tr><td></td><td>**Press:**</td><td><Enter></td><td>Select action</td></tr>
</table>

The mailing labels are generated on your screen like those portrayed in Figure D.82. After you have viewed your labels, then continue:

Action: Press any key as requested to return to the label design work surface.

Action: Exit to the dot prompt and save your label form definition.

The completed label definition is shown in Figure D.84. You may now proceed to print the labels as described in the following section.

D.7.3.3   Generate Mailing Labels

Once the ROLIST label format has been finished, the mailing labels can be produced by using this definition. Bert noticed that Taylor Farms is repeated in the Wine Order List in Figure D.79. However, he wants only *one label for each supplier*. By using a SET

UNIQUE command, he can produce just one mailing label for each supplier. He enters these commands:

Action: Verify that ROLIST is your active database file.

To eliminate the printing of duplicate Labels

Enter: `SET UNIQUE ON`   Command to eliminate duplicates

The SET UNIQUE ON command removes duplicates *when an index is created for a database file.* This is accomplished by continuing like this:

Enter: `INDEX ON MAKER TO MAKRLIST`
                                   Create index with duplicates removed

To generate the mailing label **Enter:**   `LABEL FORM ROLIST TO PRINT`
                                   Produce the mailing labels

The mailing labels shown in Figure D.82 are generated.

The command SET UNIQUE ON causes records with identical key fields to be displayed *only one time.* This command remains in effect until another database file is accessed or until the command SET UNIQUE OFF is issued.

Keypoint!

> SET UNIQUE ON eliminates the display of records with the same key value when an index is created!

In reviewing the mailing labels in Figure D.82, Bert noticed the absence of a comma between the city and state. Although the labels are quite satisfactory without this comma, he would like to include one to improve the label's appearance. He created the LABEL FORM ROLISTC with a revised third line, as is shown in Figure D.85 [version III+] or Figure D.86 [version IV]. The content of line 3 is defined in this manner:

To create a city, state, and zip code mailing label line TRIM(CITY)+", "+STATE+" "+STR(ZIP,5)

The TRIM function is used with the CITY field to remove the trailing blanks. This is concatenated to the character string enclosed in quotes, which contains the desired comma. The plus symbol indicates the concatenation here, in the same manner as that used in creating a compound field INDEX. The STATE and ZIP fields are concatenated after the comma following the CITY field with two spaces separating them, which are provided by the character string between STATE and ZIP. Since the ZIP field is a numeric data type, it is converted to character-type data with the STR function. By default the STR function converts a numeric data type into a character field with a width of 10. The 5 in the STR function specifies that the converted data is to have a width of 5, rather than the default value. The content of line 3 was entered in the same manner as previously described for each dBASE version. The field names could be obtained from a list as before. However, with this use of functions and concatenations, the easiest method of entering the contents is to just type it.

D.7.4   An Alternative for Joining Database Relations

The SET RELATION TO command can be used to produce a reorder list similar to that in Figure D.78. This command allows data from both database files to be accessed

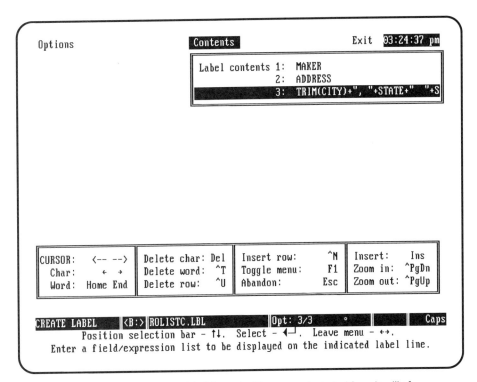

FIGURE D.85. Mailing label format with comma included [version III+].

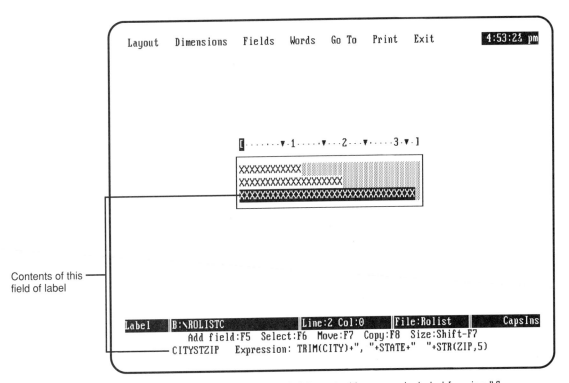

FIGURE D.86. Mailing label format with comma included [version IV].

and displayed *without* the need to produce a *separate* database file containing the joined data. This is accomplished in this manner:

| To close all database files | **Enter:** | CLOSE DATABASES | Prepare for using multiple database files |

| To select or open the child or secondary database file | **Enter:** | SELECT 2 | Choose area 2 |
| | **Enter:** | SUPPLIER | Open database in area 2 |

The key field MAKER in the SUPPLIER database file is used to link this file to the WINES database file. For this reason, the key field in SUPPLIER needs to be indexed to provide the required linkage. Since the SUPPLIER database file is an open file, but is *not the currently selected* file when doing the *SET RELATION,* this is known as the **child** database file. The field of the child file, which is used as the key to link this secondary file with the other primary database file, must be indexed. This is accomplished as follows:

| To establish the INDEX for linking database files | **Enter:** | INDEX ON MAKER TO SUPPMAKR | |
| | | | Index SUPPLIER on key field used to link database files |

Now the WINES database file may be opened.

| To open or select the parent or primary database file | **Enter:** | SELECT 1 | Choose area 1 |
| | **Enter:** | USE WINES | Open database in area 1 |

This database is the currently selected database, which contains the field used to control the linkage to the SUPPLIER database file. Because the *data values* in WINES are used to control the linkages, this is known as the **parent** database file.

The exception reporting condition of quantity ON_HAND < 24 is desired for any records that are to be displayed. This is established as follows:

| To select the desired records for exception reporting | **Enter:** | SET FILTER TO ON_HAND < 24 | |
| | | | Establish *exception* reporting criteria |

Because the mailing list of vineyards is being produced for reordering, only one entry of each is desired. Any duplicates need to be removed.

To eliminate duplicate records	**Enter:**	SET UNIQUE ON	Command to eliminate duplicate records when INDEX is used
	Enter:	INDEX ON MAKER TO WINEMAKR	
			Create INDEX with duplicates removed

Now the WINES database file is ready to be linked to the SUPPLIER database file to obtain the mailing address information for ordering more wines. This linkage is implemented with the SET RELATION TO command.

| To link the two database files using SET RELATION | **Enter:** | SET RELATION TO MAKER INTO SUPPLIER |

In this command, MAKER is the field in the currently selected WINES database file (the parent) that is used to link to the records in the SUPPLIER database file (the child). Because the INDEX of the SUPPLIER database file contains the name of the vineyard, these records are linked based on the data values in the MAKER fields of both database files.

Once the files are linked with the SET RELATION TO command, you may DISPLAY or LIST the records.

| To list fields in the database files linked with SET RELATION |

Enter: LIST OFF MAKER, SUPPLIER->ADDRESS, SUPPLIER->CITY,
               SUPPLIER->STATE, SUPPLIER->ZIP

Because the WINES database file is currently selected, the fields in the SUPPLIER database file require the specification of that database file name in requesting the fields to be listed. The result produced by executing the LIST command is shown in Figure D.87.

If the command,

Enter: LIST ALL OFF

is used with this SET RELATION command, only the fields in the WINES database file are displayed.

The data from the database files that are linked using the SET RELATION TO command can be displayed by using either a REPORT FORM or a LABEL FORM, like data from any other database file. To produce mailing labels from this relation, the fields from the SUPPLIER database file must have that file name included in specifying the field in the mailing label. This is specified in the same manner in the LABEL or REPORT FORM as that shown with the LIST command above, where the database file name precedes the field name, such as SUPPLIER->ADDRESS.

Action: (*Optional*)   Create a mailing label format SRLIST for producing the mailing labels by using the relation obtained from the SET RELATION command. Produce the mailing labels using this LABEL FORM. Your output should be the same as that shown previously, in Figure D.82.

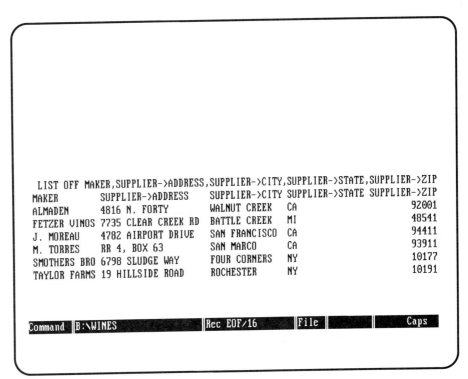

FIGURE D.87. Listing fields from database linked using the SET RELATION command.

Once you have finished using the data related with the SET RELATION command, this linkage is terminated by issuing this command:

To turn off a SET RELATION linkage

Enter: SET RELATION TO   Turn off the linkage to the second
                                             database file

The advantage of using the SET RELATION TO command is that another database file was *not* created, which occurs when you use the JOIN command. A limitation of the SET RELATION command is that the data in the child are linked by a field that may be *different* from the sequence in which you would like the data to be displayed. For example, with the SET RELATION TO for the WINES and SUPPLIER database files, the mailing labels could *not* be sequenced by the ZIP code, because this would require the use of a different INDEX in the SUPPLIER database file. On the other hand, once a database file is produced with JOIN, the resulting file can be easily displayed in any of a variety of desired arrangements. Overall, JOIN and SET RELATION perform the same activity in dBASE. Each has advantages and limitations. You should consider these as you pick the commands for use in your applications.

D.7.5   When Things Go Wrong

Several conditions may occur when you are trying to join databases and to produce mailing labels that can cause you difficulties. Some of the more common situations and the ways to recover from them are described here:

1. When performing the JOIN, you receive the message "No records joined." The most common cause of this error is when the fields being joined are not the same width or of the same data type.

   a. Use LIST STRUCTURE to verify the data type and width in characters of the key fields in each of the databases used in the JOIN.

   b. Pick one of the databases and use MODIFY STRUCTURE to change the field width or data type to exactly match the field definition in the other database. In modifying your structure, *be careful not to change the name of any of your data fields*.

   c. Exit from the STRUCTURE definition form and request the data to be rewritten.

   d. Repeat the JOIN command.

2. Error messages, such as "Variable not found," appear when you start to print your mailing labels. This may occur if the currently selected database does *not* contain the fields to be printed with the LABEL FORM.

   a. Make sure the currently selected database is the one from which you want to produce your mailing labels.

   b. USE or SELECT the database containing the data for the mailing labels.

   c. Reissue the LABEL FORM command to print your mailing labels.

3. You receive the message "File does not exit" when you try to print your labels. This usually occurs because the name of the LABEL FORM file was not correctly entered.

   a. Enter the command **DIR *.LBL** to obtain a list of your LABEL FORM files.

   b. Determine the correct name for your LABEL FORM file.

   c. Reissue the LABEL FORM command to print your labels using the correct file name.

D.7.6   Lesson Summary

- Several database files can be created with key fields that permit the data in the files to be joined.

- By using several database files, data can be *entered and stored only one time*. This makes it easier to enter and to update data in a database, and it reduces the storage space taken up by redundant data.

- The JOIN command facilitates creating a database file that is composed of the fields from two database files. Records are joined using a key field.

- When joining records, the key field should be the same size in both database files.

- The SELECT command makes database files available to dBASE so a JOIN can be performed.

- Mailing labels can be produced by using a LABEL FORM similar to a REPORT FORM, except that it is specifically designed for the special purpose of generating mailing labels.

- The command SET UNIQUE ON eliminates the *display* of duplicate records. It does *not* remove them from the database.

■ The SET RELATION TO command provides an alternative method of linking or joining data in two database files. An advantage of this command is that it *does not generate another database file.*

D.7.7   Practice Tutorial

A second database can be created for use with the Wine Management System at the Golden Gourmet. This database can be utilized in producing mailing labels as described in this Lesson. Create the SUPPLIER database and the mailing labels as a guided activity in a hands-on manner. Access the WINES database before you begin.

Task 1: Create the SUPPLIER database and enter the data that appear in Figure D.76.

Task 2: JOIN the WINES and SUPPLIER databases to produce the Wine Order List in Figure D.79.

Task 3: Create a LABEL FORM and produce the mailing labels in Figure D.82.

Time Estimates

Novice: 90 minutes

Expert: 45 minutes

Advanced: 60 minutes

D.7.8   Practice Exercises

(1)   **Case: High Yield Investments**

Business Problem: Investment Reporting

MIS Characteristics: Finance

Operational Control

High Yield Investments is a discount brokerage firm with multiple stock exchange floor locations strategically placed for fast executions. Each month High Yield produces a summary of their customers' accounts. Barry Lind, a senior partner in High Yield, prepares and sends a notice to their more speculative customers. High Yield had designated those stocks with a current market price of less than $10 as speculative.

To assist in these record-keeping activities, Barry has designed two database files. The first database file contains data on stock portfolios, while the second database file consists of their customers' names and addresses. The fields contained in these database files are described by the following data dictionary definitions:

HIGHYLD Database

Field Name	Description
ACCT	Customer's account number
SYMBOL	Stock exchange ticker symbol
SHARES	Security position in number of shares
COST	Purchase price per share
PRICE	Current market price per share
PUR_DATE	Purchase date of security
HOLD	Indicator of whether or not the certificate is held by the broker or by the customer. (Y=broker, N=customer)

HYICUST Database

Field Name	Description
ACCT	Customer's account number
NAME	Customer's name
ADDRESS	Customer's street address
CITY	Customer's city
ST	Customer's state
ZIP	Customer's zip code

Task 1: Access the HIGHYLD.DBF and HYICUST.DBF database files in the EXER-CISE catalog. Review the structure and data in each of these database files. Produce a hard copy listing of their database structures for documentation and reference.

· _____

· _____

· _____

Task 2: JOIN the HIGHYLD and HYICUST databases to produce a Speculative Stock List. This list contains only those customers with stocks that have a current market price per share that is less than $10. Place the joined database in the file named HYILIST.DBF. Use the ACCT field as the key field to carry out the JOIN of these database files. Review your joined database HYILIST with the DISPLAY command.

· _____

· _____

· _____

Task 3: Produce the Speculative Stock List from the joined database stored as the HYILIST.DBF file. Use the [version IV] HIGHYLD4 REPORT FORM or [version III+] HIGHYLD3 REPORT FORM for producing this report. Once you have completed the JOIN, you may want to review the REPORT FORM prior to generating this report. Notice the content of the group expression in the report definition.

· _____

· _____

· _____

Task 4: Produce mailing labels for the customers who own speculative stocks (those with a PRICE less than $10). First, create a LABEL FORM with the name HYIMAIL.LBL. Be sure to activate the HYILIST.DBF database before you begin to create this LABEL FORM. Then use your HYILIST.DBF database from the JOIN to produce these labels. This set of labels should *not* contain any duplicates.

· _____

· _____

· _____

Task 5: (*Optional*)   Perform a second JOIN and produce a set of mailing labels for the customers who HOLD their own securities (e.g., HOLD = N). Again, this set of labels should *not* contain any duplicates.

· _____

· _____

· _____

Time Estimates

Novice: 120 minutes

Intermediate: 90 minutes

Advanced: 45 minutes

(2)   Case: Modular Mansions

> Business Problem: Production Planning
> MIS Characteristics: Production/Operations
>   Managerial Control

Modular Mansions produces factory-built homes in its modern plant. A 20 percent down payment is required before materials are obtained and construction begins. Ken Woods, production manager, is responsible for scheduling the production of each home. In preparing his build schedule, Ken has developed a database to assist him with the necessary record-keeping activities. One of his primary concerns in scheduling production is to be sure the 20 percent down payment has been received for each order.

Ken set up two database files to satisfy his record-keeping requirements. The MODULAR database contains each order, while the CONTRACT database contains information on the contractor placing the order. The fields contained in these databases are described by the following data dictionary definitions:

MODULAR Database

Field Name	Description
ORDER	Order number
PLAN	House plan identification number
CTRID	Contractor identification number
CUSTOMER	Name of home purchaser
DUR	Estimated build duration in days
BLD_DATE	Planned start date for building
PRICE	Base price of house
OPTION	Option package
OPT_PR	Price of option package
DOWN	Indicator for receipt of down payment

CONTRACT Database:

Field Name	Description
CTRID	Contractor identification number
CONTRACTOR	Name of contractor or builder
ADDRESS	Contractor's street address
CITY	Contractor's city
ST	Contractor's state
ZIP	Contractor's zip code

Task 1: Access the MODULAR.DBF and CONTRACT.DBF database files in the EXERCISE catalog. Review the structure and data in each database file. Produce a hard copy listing of each database structure for documentation and reference. The dBASE commands are

. _____

. _____

. _____

Task 2: JOIN the MODULAR and CONTRACT databases to produce a Down Payment Required List. This list contains only those orders that require a down payment. That is, the DOWN payment is False (or *not* True). Place the joined database in the file named MODOWN.DBF. Use the CTRID field as the key field to JOIN these databases. Review your joined database MODOWN with the DISPLAY command. The dBASE commands are

. _____

. _____

. _____

Task 3: Produce the Down Payment Required List from the joined database stored as the MODOWN.DBF file. Use the [version IV] MODULAR4 REPORT FORM or [version III+] MODULAR3 REPORT FORM for producing this report. Once you have completed the JOIN, you may USE the resulting JOIN file and review the REPORT FORM prior to generating this report. The dBASE commands are

. _____

. _____

. _____

Task 4: Produce mailing labels for the contractors from whom a down payment is required on one or more of their orders. First, activate your MODOWN.DBF joined database and develop a LABEL FORM with the name MODMAIL.LBL. Then using your MODOWN.DBF database, produce these mailing labels. This set of labels should *not* contain any duplicates. The dBASE commands are

. _____

. _____

. _____

Time Estimates

Novice: 120 minutes

Intermediate: 90 minutes

Advanced: 45 minutes

D.7.9   Comprehensive Problems

(1)   Case: Yen To Travel (continued)

At Yen To Travel, Ashley works with independent tour agents in setting up tour packages. To assist her in this activity, she wants to establish an AGENT database. This database will enhance the Tour Management System so that additional tours can be requested from the tour agents.

Task 1: Design an AGENT database (a Database Planning Form is provided below).

Task 2: Enter this data in the AGENT database:

AGENT	ADDRESS	CITY	STATE	ZIP
WILD ADVENT	876 MAIN, SUITE 7	DALLAS	TX	72965
SNAKE RIVER	RR 3, BOX 77	SUTTER CREEK	ID	54701
SEA WATCH	1909 SEASHORE DR	SAN FRANCISCO	CA	90028
GRAY LINE	729 BLOSSOM BLVD	FRANKFORT	MI	48692
HMS TOURS	1559 MAJESTY LANE	HOMER	NY	10010

Task 3: JOIN the TOURS and AGENT databases to produce a Tour Request List that contains the tour name, tour agent, departure date, address, city, state and zip code. Use a report form to produce the final report after the databases have been joined. Additional seats are to be requested when the number of open seats is less than 10.

· _____

· _____

· _____

Task 4: Produce mailing labels for the agents from whom additional seats are being requested. This list should *not* contain any duplicate labels.

· _____

· _____

· _____

DATABASE PLANNING FORM

Data Name	Data Type	Number of Characters for Largest Value	Dec(imal) Places

Time Estimates

Novice: 120 minutes

Intermediate: 90 minutes

Advanced: 45 minutes

(2)   Case: Silver Screen Video (continued)

At the Silver Screen Video, Todd is responsible for the acquisition of new video tapes. This includes ordering additional copies of tapes currently in stock. To support him in this activity, he wants to develop a MAKER database. This database will improve on the Movie Management System so that movies can be readily requested from the video tape producers.

> *Task 1:* Design a film MAKER database (a Database Planning Form is provided below).

> *Task 2:* Enter this data for the MAKER database:

MAKER	ADDRESS	CITY	STATE	ZIP
LUCAS FILMS	RR 3, BOX 77	SUTTER CREEK	ID	54701
TRI STAR	56 ATLANTA PKWY	TALLAHASSEE	FLA	30627
UNITED ARTS	543 AUTUMN LANE	BANGOR	ME	20615
PARAMOUNT	427 CHARIOT WAY	BLACK HILLS	SD	32958
KING FILMS	695 MILL POND DR	PODUNK	NE	68526
TOUCH STONE	19562 MAYFEST RD	FREEPORT	TX	65217
HANKS FILMS	754 FIFTH AVE	NEW YORK	NY	10029
MGM FILMS	124 METRO LANE	HOLLYWOOD	CA	90029

> *Task 3:* JOIN the MOVIES and MAKER databases to produce a Movie Order List that contains the movie name, filmmaker, year produced, address, city, state, and zip code. Use a report form to produce the final report after the databases have been joined. Additional movies are to be ordered when the number on hand is less than seven.
>
> . _____
>
> . _____
>
> . _____

> *Task 4:* Produce mailing labels for the filmmakers from whom additional movies are being ordered. This list should *not* contain any duplicate labels.
>
> . _____
>
> . _____
>
> . _____

DATABASE PLANNING FORM

Data Name	Data Type	Number of Characters for Largest Value	Dec(imal) Places

Time Estimates

Novice: 120 minutes

Intermediate: 90 minutes

Advanced: 45 minutes

D.7.10 Application Case

Case: **Porsche Cars North America, Inc.**
        Business Problem: Advertising Media Schedule
        MIS Characteristics: Marketing
                            Managerial Control
        Management Functions: Planning
                            Organizing
        Tools Skills: Joining databases
                     Producing mailing labels
                     Indexing
                     Unique record selection

Porsche Cars North America, Inc., with corporate offices in Reno, Nevada, is preparing to introduce the Porsche 924SX model into the U. S. market. As a separate operating unit of Volkswagen AG, Porsche manufactures a line of very high performance, very expensive sports cars at their modern facility in Stuttgart, Germany. The suggested retail prices are as follows:

	PRICE	
Model	U.S. Dollars	Deutsche Mark
928S	$ 71,900	DM 108,700
911 TURBO	71,500	108,100
911 CABRIOLET	54,250	82,000
911 TARGA	49,500	74,800
911	46,750	70,700
944 TURBO	40,500	61,250
944S CABRIOLET	38,500	58,250
944S	34,500	52,250
944	31,250	47,250
NEW 924SX	24,250	36,750

The growing demand for two-seat sports cars has been one of the bright spots in automobile sales in the United States lately. However, most of the growth has been in the $16,000 to $25,000 price range. Mazda's RX7 and the Nissan ZX series are good examples. Thus, there existed a substantial price gap between Porsche's lowest price model and the top price of the (mostly) Japanese sports cars. Porsche intended the 924SX to reduce the gap and to get buyers from the top price end of the (mostly) Japanese sports cars to consider buying a Porsche.

The 924SX has the same drive train, brakes, running gear, and electrical system as the 944. John Cook, President of Porsche Cars of North America, summarized the new model by saying, "In effect, the 924SX provides Porsche fans with a car that is similar in performance to the 944 series, but with sleeker styling." In addition, 924s had been sold in Europe since 1976 and were sold in the United States between 1977 and 1983. They had a reputation as a reliable and thoroughly tested product. The improvements in the 924SX were a careful blend of refinements from its earlier predecessors with the 944 performance package.

Hans von Kluge, Porsche's Vice President for Sales and Marketing, met with Jean Cameron, Executive Vice President, Chiat/Day Advertising of Los Angeles, California, to discuss their advertising plan. Jean described to Hans how important it is to know exactly who your prospective customers are when you are working with a limited advertising budget. (Not that you can afford to waste money with larger budgets; they just have a little more "cushion.") Hans and Jean discussed how the target market of upper-end Japanese sports cars and European sport sedans were buyers 25 to 40 years of age with incomes of $55,000 or more. Interestingly, 35 percent were female. An analysis of this market segment indicated that a number of individuals wanted to own a "Porsche badge" and would be willing to "stretch" a little to achieve the status of that ownership. They were truly automobile enthusiasts.

Jean and Hans devised an advertising plan that recognized and dealt with the following issues:

- *Budgets.*   Sports car manufacturers in the lower price range sell a lot of units and can afford to spend a lot on advertising. Last year's budget for the RX7s was $16.2 million and that for the ZXs was $19.2 million. Both of these budgets vastly overshadowed Porsche's budget.

- *Attitudes.*   Prospective customers correctly perceived that the Japanese sports cars and the Porsches were in different classes.

- *Availability.*   Only a limited number of 924SXs were available, and so it was important that the 924SX sales were not simply substitutes for 944 sales, that is, the 924SX sales should not cannibalize those of 944s.

- *Image.*   The price of the 924SX should not "cheapen" the image of the 944. Porsche has never been a price brand, and there was no desire to change that fact.

In order to reach the prospective customers with exactly the right message, Hans worked with Jean on the production of a two-page, four-color ad that was scheduled to appear in *Car and Driver*, *Road and Track*, *Motor Trend*, and *Automobile* magazines during August and September.

Realizing the importance of its dealers, Porsche Cars North America wanted to develop a very complete dealer advertising program to support the national campaign at the local level. Plans were prepared for their major market areas. Chiat/Day produced four TV commercials for showing in the major markets. The TV commercials were filmed to allow a five second "tag" at the end of the commercial so the TV commercial could be individualized in different market areas to promote their dealers.

To support the TV marketing campaign for Porsche's introduction of the 924SX, Jean developed a database of the television advertising schedule. By using the database, she could revise and modify the schedule as the plan was developed. Since Chiat/Day handles many different TV advertising campaigns for different clients, Jean has also developed a database for the TV stations where the ads are to be placed. This facilitates her communications with the stations as the media campaign evolves.

The Television Schedule database for an advertising campaign contains fields that are described by the following data dictionary definitions:

Field Name	Description
AD_ID	Advertisement identification number
DESCRIPT	Description or name of the advertisement
DAY	Day of the week the advertisement is to appear
DATE	Date the advertisement is scheduled to appear
TIME	Time period during which the ad is shown
STATION	Call letters of TV station broadcasting the ad
PROGRAM	TV program during which the ad is shown

The Television Station database consists of data dictionary definitions as follows:

Field Name	Description
NAME	Name of advertising director at TV station
STATION	Call letters of TV station broadcasting the ad
ADDRESS	Street address of TV station
CITY	City for mailing address
STATE	State for mailing address
ZIP	Zip code

Tasks

1. Access the MEDIA.DBF for Porsche's 924SX advertising campaign in the CASES catalog and review its structure and content. Obtain a hard copy listing of its structure.

2. Generate a report of the Television Schedule using the [version VI] MEDIA4.FRM or [version III+] MEDIA3.FRM report form definition.

3. Access the STATION.DBF containing the TV station contact information in the CASES catalog and review its structure and data. Obtain a hard copy listing of the structure.

4. Produce a hard copy listing of the data contained in the STATION database. [*Hint:* Either use LIST or create a REPORT FORM, as desired.]

5. Jean needs to send a packet of information to those stations that are scheduled to run the BALLOON advertisement. For the BALLOON advertisement only, join records in the MEDIA and STATION relations. Save your resulting relation as the STATLIST.DBF file. Produce a hard copy listing of the resulting database file.

6. Create a "two-up" mailing label form definition (STATLIST.LBL) for the mailing labels that Jean will use in sending the necessary information to the station directors. Design the mailing label so the NAME is on the first line, the STATION is on the second line, and the last two lines contain the remainder of the mailing address.

7. Produce a unique set of mailing labels using the label form definition developed in (6) above. Arrange these mailing labels in order by zip code.

8. Write a summary describing why the MEDIA database should be maintained separately from the STATION database. What is accomplished by this organization as two separate databases?

Time Estimates

Novice: 120 minutes

Intermediate: 90 minutes

Advanced: 45 minutes

Programming with Command Files

CONTENT

- dBASE Programs
- Obtaining a Copy of a Command File
- Looking Up Information
- Processing a Missing Look Up
- When Things Go Wrong

D.8.1   dBASE Programs

The Wine Management System for the Golden Gourmet encompasses several different reports. An index is used with some of these reports and a second database may be used with the reorder list report. To make it easier to produce their reports, Bert and Beth would like to develop a dBASE program or command file.

A dBASE program contains a series of dBASE commands. They are stored in a file so that they can be reused on demand. This reduces the number of commands that must be remembered by the user for the WMS or any other dBASE system. You can envision your dBASE program as sitting on top of your database as illustrated in Figure D.88. The program contains dBASE data manipulation language (DML) commands that control processing actions on the database. Although a database has utility without any dBASE programs, there is usually little reason to have a dBASE program without a database.

In general, a dBASE program:

- Contains a series of dBASE commands for manipulating a database.
- Is stored in a file so that it can be reused as many times as desired.
- Can be readily reviewed and edited, which is usually easier than using a command entered interactively at the keyboard.
- Is deployed in developing customized applications for someone not familiar with details of operating dBASE, which is often the situation in most business applications.

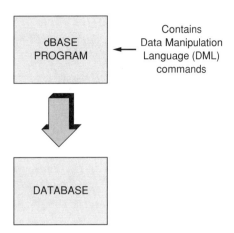

FIGURE D.88. Usual relationship between dBASE program and database.

- Provides documentation of how processing is to be performed so that some-one other than the person who developed the system can understand its op-eration.
- Automates frequently used dBASE commands sequences.
- Is about 10 times more efficient to use in developing data management applications than in developing them with other programming languages, such as Basic or C.
- Serves to automate applications to achieve ease of operation. (This advantage is similar to that obtained by using Lotus 1-2-3 macros.)

dBASE programs are developed and executed in *the same manner for both versions of dBASE.*

Bert developed a simple command file program that could be used to produce the WINELIST report. This command file appears in Figure D.89. You can begin to create or to revise a command file like this by issuing the MODIFY COMMAND command in this manner:

| To begin entering a dBASE program | **Enter:** | MODIFY COMMAND WINELIST |
| | | Initiate program entry |

Keypoint!

> The MODIFY COMMAND command is used for creating a *new* command file, as well as changing an *existing* command file!

Once this command has been entered, a full-screen text editor appears as your screen. You can move about the screen entering each command you want to have in your program for future execution. At the end of one line, use <Enter> to advance to the next line. <Ctrl>+<Y> is used to delete a line. <Ctrl>+<End> is used to exit from the command file editor and save your file. Characters can be inserted within a line by toggling the insert mode *on,* which is accomplished by pressing <Ins>. You can toggle back to the overtype mode by pressing <Ins> a second time. Some of the more frequently used special keys for creating and editing command files are described in Figure D.90. In Version 1.5 of dBASE IV, the mouse may also be used to locate the cursor or to make menu selections (Figure D.91).

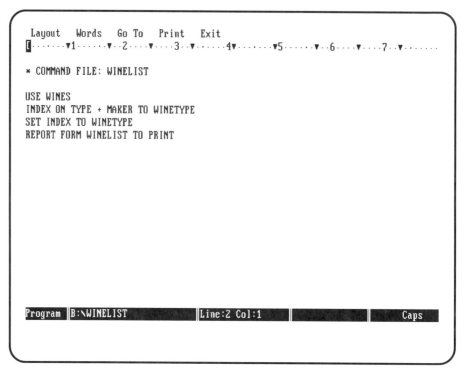

FIGURE D.89. WINELIST command file.

Caution Alert! A limitation of the dBASE III+ editor is that your file size must be less than 5000 characters! If you think that your program will be larger than this, you should use another editor such as WordPerfect and save your program as a DOS or ASCII file!

At any time, help is only a keystroke way. Pressing <F1> activates the help facility in the dBASE command file editor. In version III+, <F1> toggles the help screen on and off, whereas <Esc> is used to exit from the help screens in version IV.

| To examine a dBASE program that generates the Wine List

Action: Enter the commands shown in Figure D.89. Check them for any typing errors and make any necessary corrections.

Special Key	Action
<Ctrl>+<End> or <Ctrl>+<W>	Save work and exit editor
<Esc>	Abandon work and exit editor
<Ctrl>+<Enter>	Save work and stay in editor
<Ctrl>+<Y>	Delete current line containing cursor
<Enter> or <Ctrl>+<N>	Insert blank line
<Ins>	Toggle insert/overtype on or off
<Del>	Delete character at cursor location
<Backspace>	Delete character to left of cursor location

FIGURE D.90. Selected command file editing keys.

Operation	Action
Move cursor to a position on a program line	Click the position
Select a segment of text	Drag to highlight the text
Scroll program lines up or down	Drag and pull the mouse pointer toward the bottom or top of the screen
Open a menu on the menu bar	Click the menu name
Close menu	Click outside the menu

FIGURE D.91. Mouse actions in the program editor.

Let's leave the command file editor and save your file.

To exit from the dBASE program editor

Press: `<Ctrl>+<End>`   Exit and save command file

Once a command file has been created and saved, it can then be executed as desired in this manner:

To execute a dBASE program

Enter: `DO WINELIST`   Execute command file

Here, DO is the dBASE command that is used to execute the command file named WINELIST. Similar dBASE command files could be created for each of the reports produced from the Wine Management System.

All the commands for producing both the reorder report and the labels can be combined in one dBASE command file that appears as the ORDER program file in Figure D.92. The command file makes use of three new commands:

1. SET CONSOL OFF
2. SET SAFETY OFF
3. CLOSE DATABASE

To examine a dBASE program that performs a JOIN

```
*   GOLDEN GOURMET
*   WINE MANAGEMENT SYSTEM
*   COMMAND FILE:  ORDER
*   USE:  This command file is used to create the order reports.

SET CONSOL OFF
SET SAFETY OFF
CLOSE DATABASE

SELECT 2
USE SUPPLIER
SELECT 1
USE WINES
SET FILTER TO ON_HAND < 24
JOIN WITH SUPPLIER TO ROLIST FOR MAKER = SUPPLIER->MAKER
SELECT 3
USE ROLIST
REPORT FORM ROLIST TO PRINT
SET UNIQUE ON
INDEX ON MAKER TO MAKRLIST
LABEL FORM ROLIST TO PRINT
EJECT
SET FILTER TO
SELECT 1
RETURN
```

FIGURE D.92. ORDER command file.

These commands require an explanation:

SET CONSOL OFF— Eliminates the display of commands and reports on your screen when they are being executed or printed.

SET SAFETY OFF— Allows dBASE to create index files that are written *over* existing index files *without* pausing to ask. The "file already exists" message is suppressed, and you are not asked whether the existing file should be overwritten.

CLOSE DATABASE— Deactivates all of the currently open or active database files. In executing the following commands in this command file, any open database files should be closed before selecting files for use. This avoids accidentally accessing the wrong database file, just because it happened to be open prior to executing this command file.

Keypoint!

> CLOSE DATABASE is a good housekeeping command that helps ensure only the correct database files are active!

In Figure D.92, the commands that begin with an asterisk (*) are comment commands. They are used to provide descriptive information to any individual reading the file, but do *not* cause any processing action to take place. You should include sufficient comment commands in your program so that someone else can review the program and understand the purpose and activities performed by your program. Also, comment commands are useful in reminding you what your program does after several weeks have passed since you last looked at it.

D.8.2   Obtaining a Copy of a Command File

A hard copy listing of a command file may be obtained with the TYPE command in this manner:

To obtain a hard copy listing of a program file

Enter: TYPE ORDER.PRG TO PRINT

Request printing of command file

A command file is automatically given the extension PRG when it is created with the MODIFY COMMAND command. This extension must be included as part of the file name for printing. Once the command file has been printed, an EJECT command may be entered to advance the paper to the top of the next page.

D.8.3   Looking Up Information

Beth and the servers have a need to perform an on-line look up for an individual wine to check on the number of bottles that are currently in inventory. This inquiry can be performed for an individual wine at any time and does not require a report for all wines to be produced. The dBASE program CHECK1 shown in Figure D.93 has been created to satisfy this requirement. When executed, this program prompts the user for the name of the wine she wants to look up, as illustrated in Figure D.94. After the name has been input, the information illustrated is displayed for the requested wine.

In this dBASE program, ACCEPT and SEEK are the key commands that enable this processing to take place. The ACCEPT command causes command file processing to pause, while a server enters the name of the wine. So that this value can be used elsewhere in the program, it is placed into the memory variable mNAME. The "m" is

To examine a dBASE
program that performs a
look up

```
*   GOLDEN GOURMET
*   WINE MANAGEMENT SYSTEM
*   COMMAND FILE:  CHECK1
*   USE:  This command file is used to check the availability
*         of a wine.

SET SAFETY OFF
USE WINES
INDEX ON NAME TO WINENAME
SET INDEX TO WINENAME
CLEAR
@2,30 SAY "GOLDEN GOURMET"
@3,26 SAY "WINE MANAGEMENT SYSTEM"
@6,25 SAY " "
SET CONSOL ON
ACCEPT "      ENTER NAME OF WINE: " TO mNAME
@9,25 SAY " "
SEEK mNAME
DISPLAY OFF NAME, MAKER, YEAR, BIN, ON_HAND
WAIT
RETURN
```

FIGURE D.93. CHECK1 command file.

used as part of the memory variable name to help identify it as a memory variable. Although this is not required by dBASE, the "m" helps to distinguish a memory variable name from a database field name. The value stored in mNAME is then used with the SEEK command to locate the desired wine whose information is displayed on the screen. The SET CONSOL ON command is required to enable the ACCEPT command to display the message, which is enclosed in quotes, on the screen and allows a server to input a value for mNAME.

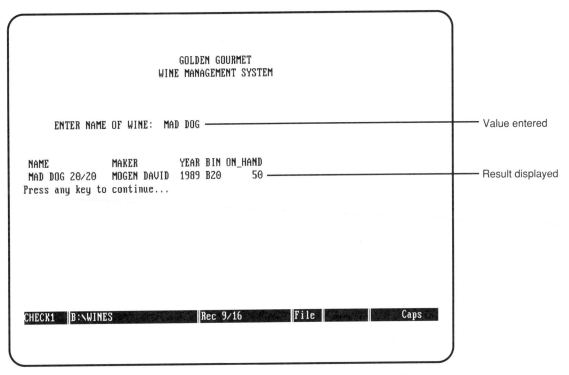

FIGURE D.94. Execution of CHECK1 to look up a wine.

Keypoint!

> The SEEK is performed using the currently active INDEX file. An INDEX *must* be SET *before* using the SEEK command!

Several other dBASE commands are shown in Figure D.93. The CLEAR command clears off the screen. The @..SAY command enables messages to be displayed on the screen. In the command,

@2,30 SAY "GOLDEN GOURMET"

The 2,30 is a cursor position on the screen. The 2 is the row position and the 30 is the column position. The message to be displayed is enclosed in quotes. An @..SAY with a blank as a message is used to position the cursor on the screen. The next output text is then displayed starting at that cursor location.

The WAIT command is used to stop processing until the user presses a key. In this program, it ensures that the information requested on the screen remains displayed until the user has had an opportunity to read it. Otherwise, the screen display usually occurs so fast that the output cannot be read.

Keypoint!

> The RETURN command should be used at the end of each command file. This ensures that the command file has completed its processing and helps prevent possible errors when several command files are executed one after another!

D.8.4 Processing a Missing Look Up

When checking on a wine, an incorrect response may be entered. Beth wants a more friendly message than "find not successful" or "no find" displayed for the servers. She wants the message to indicate that a particular wine is "not available." This requires the use of conditional programming logic that is implemented with the IF..ELSE..ENDIF commands. That is, IF the wine requested is a correct input, then you should display the information as illustrated in Figure D.94. ELSE the request is not correct and the desired message is displayed.

Command file CHECK2 in Figure D.95 performs this processing. When a database record is not found, the "not available" message is displayed, as illustrated in Figure D.96. In command file CHECK2, FOUND( ) is a dBASE function that has a value of true or yes if the SEEK was successful; otherwise it has a value of false or no. If the requested wine is located, FOUND( ) is true and the desired information is displayed. Otherwise, the value is false and the @..SAY message is displayed. The ENDIF is used to indicate the termination of the IF..ELSE commands. Figure D.97 illustrates the action of the IF..ELSE..ENDIF command. Either the commands in the "true" branch of the IF..ELSE..ENDIF are executed, or the commands in the "false" branch are performed. Both sets of commands will *not* be carried out during any single execution of this command file.

The general form of the IF..ELSE..ENDIF command set is as follows:

```
IF condition
    commands executed when condition is true
ELSE
    commands executed when condition is false
ENDIF
```

To examine a dBASE
program that displays a
message

```
*   GOLDEN GOURMET
*   WINE MANAGEMENT SYSTEM
*   COMMAND FILE:  CHECK2
*   USE:  This command file is used to check the availability of a
*         wine.  When a wine name is entered that is not in the
*         database, a friendly message is displayed for the server.

SET SAFETY OFF
USE WINES
INDEX ON NAME TO WINENAME
SET INDEX TO WINENAME
CLEAR
@2,30 SAY "GOLDEN GOURMET"
@3,26 SAY "WINE MANAGEMENT SYSTEM"
@6,25 SAY " "
SET CONSOL ON
ACCEPT "   ENTER NAME OF WINE: " TO mNAME
@9,25 SAY " "
SEEK mNAME
IF FOUND()
        DISPLAY OFF NAME, MAKER, YEAR, ON_HAND
ELSE
        @10,0 SAY"        WINE " + mNAME + " IS NOT AVAILABLE."
ENDIF
@20,0 SAY " "
WAIT
RETURN
```

FIGURE D.95. CHECK2 command file.

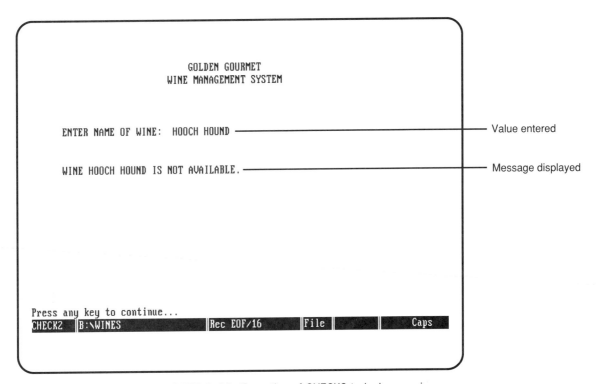

FIGURE D.96. Execution of CHECK2 to look up a wine.

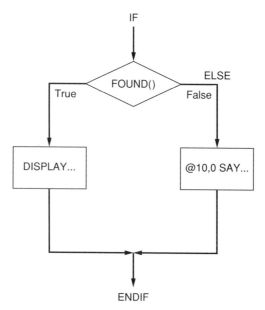

FIGURE D.97. IF..ELSE..ENDIF for command file CHECK2.

where the condition in this IF statement is specified in the same manner as that of the FOR condition used with other dBASE commands such as DISPLAY and LIST or that used with the SET FILTER TO command.

Merely knowing that a wine is "not available" is not as useful as being able to locate a wine. Perhaps the name of the wine was misspelled. When a wine is not found, the response can be expanded to allow Beth or the servers to request a list of available wines, as is indicated by the prompt shown in Figure D.98. This is accomplished by

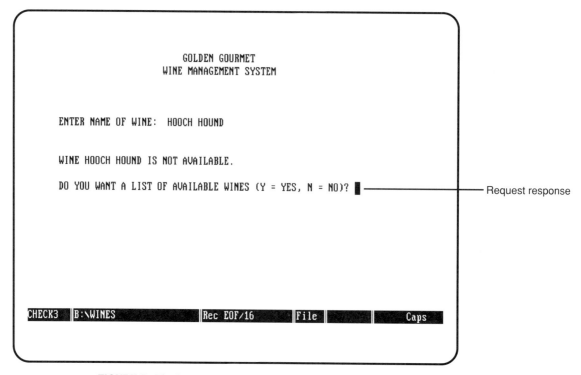

FIGURE D.98. Request for available list of wines from command file CHECK3.

using IF..ENDIF commands. IF the response is yes, the screen is cleared, and a list of wines is presented by using the DISPLAY command, as is shown in Figure D.99. Otherwise, the commands for displaying the list are skipped. That is, an IF *without* an ELSE is used, since no ELSE actions are required for a false condition, as is illustrated with command file CHECK3 in Figure D.100. The CHECK3 command file contains the revision with the IF..ENDIF command that permits the list of available wines to be displayed as requested by Beth or the servers. Both arrangements of the IF..ENDIF commands are summarized by the diagrams in Figure D.101.

The general form of the IF..ENDIF commands are as follows:

```
IF condition
    commands executed when condition is true
ENDIF
```

where the condition is the same as that of the FOR condition used with other dBASE commands.

This request to look up a wine is implemented with command file CHECK3, as is illustrated in Figure D.100. The memory variable mRESPONSE is used to keep track of the user's input response. The @..SAY..GET command and READ command are used to display the message prompting the user. The GET mRESPONSE permits the user to input a response. The READ command causes the mRESPONSE input by the user to be actually processed.

The @..SAY..GET and READ commands were used to obtain the user's response. An ACCEPT command could also be used. The ACCEPT command requires the SET CONSOL ON command to be in effect in order for the message to be displayed on your screen. The @..SAY..GET and READ commands are displayed on the screen regardless of whether the SET CONSOL is ON or OFF. In this situation, the application of SET CONSOL ON and ACCEPT versus the @SAY..GET and READ is a matter of

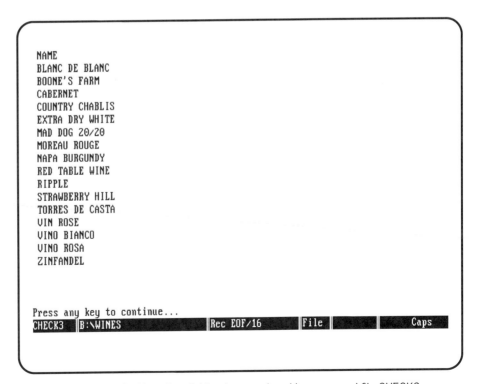

FIGURE D.99. List of available wines produced by command file CHECK3.

To examine a dBASE
program that displays an
optional list

```
*   GOLDEN GOURMET
*   WINE MANAGEMENT SYSTEM
*   COMMAND FILE:  CHECK3
*   USE:  This command file is used to check the availability of a
*         wine. When a wine name is entered that is not in the
*         database, a friendly message is displayed for the server.
*         The server then has the opportunity to request a list of
*         wines in the database.

SET SAFETY OFF
USE WINES
INDEX ON NAME TO WINENAME
SET INDEX TO WINENAME
CLEAR
@2,30 SAY "GOLDEN GOURMET"
@3,26 SAY "WINE MANAGEMENT SYSTEM"
@6,25 SAY " "
SET CONSOL ON
ACCEPT "      ENTER NAME OF WINE: " TO mNAME
@9,25 SAY " "
SEEK mNAME
IF FOUND()
      DISPLAY OFF NAME, MAKER, YEAR, BIN, ON_HAND
ELSE
      @10,0 SAY        WINE " + mNAME + " IS NOT AVAILABLE."
      @12,6 SAY "DO YOU WANT A LIST OF AVAILABLE WINES"
      mRESPONSE = " "
      @12,44 SAY "(Y = YES, N = NO)?" GET mRESPONSE
      READ
      IF mRESPONSE = "Y"
            CLEAR
            DISPLAY ALL OFF NAME
      ENDIF
ENDIF
@20,0 SAY " "
WAIT
RETURN
```

FIGURE D.100. CHECK3 command file.

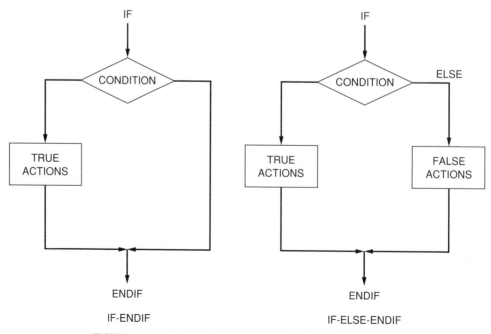

FIGURE D.101. General arrangement of IF..ENDIF commands.

your preference in creating the command file. The @SAY..GET and READ provide for *a more flexible data input* when several values are requested, rather than a single value.

In addition to the FOUND( ) function illustrated in these command files, dBASE contains many other functions that are useful in manipulating data. Numeric data can be changed to character data. Lowercase data can be converted to uppercase data. Other similar operations can be performed with other functions, which are described in the "Using dBASE Reference" section as well as the *dBASE Reference Manual.*

Keypoint!

The @..SAY..GET and READ commands are a team. The @..SAY..GET should be followed by the READ so the value entered with the @..SAY..GET is processed!

D.8.5   When Things Go Wrong

Entering dBASE programs with the command file editor is usually a straightforward process. You can cursor about the screen and make any desired changes. Most difficulties are encountered when you execute your dBASE programs. Some of the more frequently occurring situations and how to approach them are described here:

1. The error message "Unrecognized phrase/keyword in command" appears during command file execution. dBASE displays the command with version III+ using a "?" (question mark) to point to the location where the problem was detected or with version IV specifying the number of the line containing the command in error.

   a. Carefully inspect the command and determine the cause of the error.

   b. Use MODIFY COMMAND to access your dBASE program file.

   c. Correct the error using the appropriate editing keys.

   d. Exit from the command file editor and save your changes.

   e. Reissue the DO command to execute the command file.

2. A "file does not exist" error message is received when executing your program. This message could be caused by an incorrect file name for a database file, an index file, a report form file, a label form file, or any other file referenced in the program.

   a. Use the DIR command to determine the correct file name. You may need to include the extension for the kind of file, for instance, NDX, FRM, or LBL.

   b. Edit your program by changing the file name and save the correction.

   c. Reissue the DO command to execute the command file.

3. A "variable not found" error message is displayed during program execution. This message indicates that a field name has been incorrectly entered for your currently selected database.

   a. Use the LIST STRUCTURE command to verify the field names in your database. Determine the correct field and database file names.

   b. Edit the command file and save it with any corrected names.

   c. Reissue the DO command to execute the program.

4. Your program just does not work. You have correct dBASE commands since no error messages are displayed, but you do not get the desired results. For example, with a JOIN operation, the fields for the JOIN in the two databases may have a different width, causing no records to be joined. When this is executed at the dot prompt, the message "no records joined" is easily detected. However, when this occurs under program execution, the message may *not appear* on the screen or may *flash by* so quickly that you cannot read it.

   a. Carefully read through your command file to detect any wrong commands.

   b. If reading through your commands does not detect any wrong commands, then perform a "keyboard walkthrough." Other than your comment commands, enter each command at the dot prompt and carefully observe its action. Continue until you detect the wrong command or other difficulty.

   c. Edit your command file and save the revisions.

   d. Reissue the DO command.

D.8.6 ▬ Lesson Summary

- A dBASE command file is a series of dBASE commands that have been stored so that they can be reused on demand.
- A dBASE command file makes it easier for someone not familiar with dBASE to run a dBASE application.
- The MODIFY COMMAND is used to create and revise a command file.
- dBASE uses the extension PRG to identify a program command file.
- Special commands are often used with command files to control output to your display screen and to turn off interactive messages, such as SET CONSOL OFF.
- The TYPE command can be used to obtain a hard copy of a command file.
- The @..SAY command allows messages to be displayed on your screen.
- The RETURN command is used to terminate a command file and helps ensure that the execution of a command file has been completed.
- The ACCEPT command suspends execution of a command file so that a user can input a response that is frequently used to control processing.
- The SEEK command locates records in a database file that match the specified value.
- The FOUND( ) function is set to true when a SEEK has been successful; otherwise, it is set to false.
- IF..ELSE..ENDIF and IF..ENDIF commands control processing by allowing other dBASE commands to be selectively executed.
- The @..SAY..GET and READ commands are a team that allows a message to be displayed and input entered for processing.

D.8.7 ▬ Practice Tutorial

dBASE programs can be created for use with the Wine Management System at the Golden Gourmet. These command files can be used as described in this Lesson. Construct these command files as a guided activity in a hands-on manner.

Task 1: Create, execute, and list the WINELIST dBASE program command file.

Task 2: Create, execute, and list the ORDER command file of Figure D.92.

Task 3: Create, execute, and list the CHECK3 command file of Figure D.100.

Time Estimates

Novice: 90 minutes

Intermediate: 60 minutes

Advanced: 45 minutes

D.8.8 ▬ Practice Exercises

(1)   **Case: Kiddie Kampus**

Business Problem: Day Care Management
MIS Characteristics: Production/Operations
Operational Control

Kiddie Kampus provides child care with both preschool- and school age programs. Their services include a professionally planned curriculum to prepare preschool children and enrich school programs. Kiddie Kampus provides transportation to and from both home and elementary school. Nutritious hot meals and snacks are served to children at appropriate times throughout the day.

Brenda Merrihew manages the licensed trained professional staff of Kiddie Kampus. To assist her in running their operations, Brenda has created a database that contains the fields described by the following data dictionary definition:

Field Name	Description
LNAME	Last name
CFNAME	Child's first name
PFNAME	Parent's first name
ADDRESS	Street address
PHONE	Telephone number
DAYS	Days of week attending
HOURS	Hours of attendance
DOB	Date of birth
DIET	Special diet
TRANS	Transportation to/from home or school
AMOUNT	Current outstanding balance due

Brenda is currently concerned with two major activities while using this database: (1) producing weekly reports and (2) looking up information in response to parent inquiries. She has already set up three report definitions for reports that assist her in managing Kiddie Kampus: (1) Weekly Attendance List, (2) Transportation Report, and (3) Special Diet Report. Since generating reports and looking up information are actions she performs frequently, Brenda has decided that dBASE programs should be developed to support these efforts.

Task 1: Access the KIDDIE.DBF database file in the EXERCISE catalog. Review the structure and data in this database. Produce a hard copy listing of the database structure for your reference and documentation.

· _____

· _____

· _____

Task 2: Create and execute a dBASE program that produces the Weekly Attendance List, the Transportation Report, and the Special Diet Report by using the [version IV] KIDLIST4, KIDTRAN4, and KIDSPEC4 REPORT FORMS or [version III+] KIDLIST3, KIDTRAN3, and KIDSPEC3 REPORT FORMS, respectively, for generating these reports. The Weekly Attendance List is arranged by DAYS, as the primary key, and LNAME, as the secondary key. The Transportation Report and the Special Diet Report are arranged sequentially by LNAME, but only contain those children requiring transportation or special diets in the respective reports. [*Optional Action:* Before writing your dBASE program you may want to review each report definition and produce each report manually.]

· _____

· _____

· _____

Task 3: Create and execute a dBASE program that allows a child care associate to perform an on-line look up of information on a child. This program is to allow associates to enter the child's LNAME and displays the LNAME, CFNAME, PFNAME, PHONE, DAYS, HOURS, and AMOUNT fields when a match is found. Write this program so that a list of last names may be obtained when a match does not occur.

- _____
- _____
- _____

Task 4: Document your dBASE program command files by producing a listing of each file. Also, obtain a screen dump of the execution of the look up program.

Time Estimates

Novice: 90 minutes

Intermediate: 60 minutes

Advanced: 45 minutes

(2)   Case: Welcome Wagon Club of Waterloo

Business Problem: Fee Collection and Reporting
MIS Characteristics: Finance
                    Operational Control

Mary Jo Andrews is chairperson of the annual craft bazaar sponsored by the Welcome Wagon Club of Waterloo. This club greets new members of the community and provides a means for them to meet other individuals who have recently moved into the community. In addition to their monthly social activities, Welcome Wagon holds their annual craft bazaar as a fund-raising activity. Proceeds from this bazaar are used to support various community activities.

Sherman Crandell, programmer/analyst at Computer Solution Associates in Waterloo, has agreed to donate his time in developing a database system that will assist Mary Jo in tracking the participants of their craft bazaar. Mary Jo explained to Sherman how they desire to have a mix of different crafts represented at their bazaar, since this improves attendance. Mary Jo classifies the crafts into the groups: WOOD, CLOTH, FLOWERS, and JEWELRY. Each crafter pays a fee for table space at the bazaar. More than one space may be obtained. Working with Mary Jo, Sherman has determined that their database needs to contain the fields described by the following data dictionary definition:

Field Name	Description
LNAME	Participant's last name
FNAME	Participant's first name
ADDRESS	Street address
CITY	City name
ST	State
ZIP	Zip code
PHONE	Telephone number
TAX_ID	Tax identification number
YEAR	Year of initial participation
CRAFT	Type of craft: WOOD, CLOTH, FLOWERS, JEWELRY
SP	Number of spaces assigned
ID	Space identification number
FEE	Amount of space rental fee
PAID	Indicator of whether or not fee has been received
CK_NUM	Check number, when paid by check

Mary Jo's biggest task is assigning spaces to each of the crafters participating in the bazaar. Sherman developed a dBASE report form definition for her to use in producing the Annual Craft Bazaar Assignment Report.

Task 1: Access the WELCOME.DBF database file in the EXERCISE catalog. Review the structure and data of this database. Produce a hard copy listing of the database structure for documentation and reference.

. _____

. _____

. _____

Task 2: Create and execute a dBASE program that produces the Annual Craft Bazaar Assignment Report by using the [version IV] WELCOME4 REPORT FORM or [version III+] WELCOME3 REPORT FORM for producing this report. Three arrangements of the report should be produced by your program for Mary Jo. The first copy of the report is to be organized by LNAME; the second copy of the report is organized by ID; and the third copy is sequenced by LNAME but only contains those individuals who have NOT PAID their fee.

. _____

. _____

. _____

Task 3: Create and execute a dBASE program that allows Mary Jo to perform an on-line look up of information on a crafter. This program is to allow her to enter the crafter's LNAME and displays the LNAME, FNAME, SP, ID, and FEE fields when a match is found. Write this program so that a list of last names may be obtained when a match does not occur.

. _____

. _____

. _____

Task 4: Document your dBASE program command files by producing a listing of each file. Also, obtain a screen dump of the execution of the look up program.

Time Estimates

Novice: 90 minutes

Intermediate: 60 minutes

Advanced: 45 minutes

D.8.9 Comprehensive Problems

(1) Case: Yen To Travel (continued)

To assist Brenda and Ashley in operating the Tour Management System at Yen To Travel, Sara wants to create several dBASE programs. Then, all they will need to do is execute the desired program to obtain their information from the TOURS database.

Task 1: Create and execute a dBASE program to produce the Tour List report with tours grouped by type.

· _____

· _____

· _____

Task 2: Create and execute a dBASE program to produce the Tour Request List and the mailing labels. The mailing labels should start on a new page after the Tour Request List has been printed.

· _____

· _____

· _____

Task 3: Create and execute a dBASE program that allows a travel representative to look up a specified tour and determine the duration of the tour and the number of open seats. If the requested tour does not exist, display a list of the available tours.

· _____

· _____

· _____

Task 4: Document your command files by producing a listing of each one.

Time Estimates

Novice: 90 minutes

Intermediate: 60 minutes

Advanced: 45 minutes

(2)   Case: Silver Screen Video (continued)

At the Silver Screen Video, Ernie wants several dBASE programs developed to assist Amy and Todd in the operation of their Movie Management System. This will make it easier for them to produce the desired reports and obtain information from the MOVIES database. Moreover, Ernie won't need to remember all of the dBASE commands for printing their reports.

Task 1: Create and execute a dBASE program to produce the Movie List report.

_____

_____

_____

Task 2: Create and execute a dBASE program to produce the Movie Order List and the mailing labels. The mailing labels should start on a new page after the Movie Order List has been printed.

_____

_____

_____

Task 3: Create and execute a dBASE program that allows a sales person to look up a specified movie and determine the price, rating, and quantity on hand. If the requested movie does not exist, display a list of the available movies.

_____

_____

_____

Task 4: Document your command files by producing a listing of each one.

Time Estimates

Novice: 90 minutes

Intermediate: 60 minutes

Advanced: 45 minutes

D.8.10   Application Case

Case: Landon, Vandenwall & Reinmuth, P.C. Certified Public Accountants

Business Problem: Payroll

MIS Characteristics: Human Resources

Operational Control

Management Functions: Directing

Controlling

Tools Skills: Programs

Seeking information

Interactive data entry

Larry Landon opened his office as a certified public accountant (CPA) in 1973, after working for the regional accounting firm of Dutton & Associates for seven years. As Larry's CPA business expanded, he hired additional staff. Then, in 1987, he reorganized the company by bringing in two of his associates as partners. Steve Vandenwall had worked with Larry for the past six years, and Jessica Reinmuth had been with the firm for four years. Jessica had been with Goracke & Associates for several years before joining Larry and Steve, whereas Steve began working with Larry after completion of his accounting degree.

The number of clients served by Landon, Vandenwall & Reinmuth (LVR) has continued to grow. Several additional CPAs have been hired as associates, and a number of part-time people are employed during the peak tax season from January to April. In addition to tax work, the firm engages in auditing and management consulting, which provide a more evenly balanced work load throughout the year.

With LVR's heavy emphasis on tax work, they were a leader among smaller regional accounting firms in the application of personal computers to tax preparation. During the mid-1980s, they began using off-the-shelf tax preparation software. These programs generated the tax schedules in the appropriate form for direct submission to the Internal Revenue Service (IRS) and to the various state and local departments of revenue. Recently, Steve headed a project in which LVR installed electronic filing directly with the IRS. This speeds up the process of receiving tax refunds for their clients and has provided LVR with a competitive advantage over several competing accounting firms.

The back office operations of LVR have not shared the advances in automation that have occurred with their tax processing and filing. This is not because of the technical abilities of the LVR associates; rather, it has been a result of directing resources into the most profitable areas. However, as LVR has expanded its operations, the pressure has mounted to improve the back office operations. During tax season, when a number of part-time associates are employed, payroll processing has become an increasing burden on Imogene McGovern, LVR's office manager. Imogene suggested to Larry that they should consider automating their payroll process. At the October partners meeting last week, Larry, Steve, and Jessica discussed Imogene's proposal. They accepted her proposal, but wanted her to develop their payroll system before the beginning of the next tax season in January; otherwise, her work load would be too great to meet the demands of tax processing and of developing the payroll system at the same time.

Imogene considered several alternatives for LVR's payroll. Since their payroll processing requirements were not extremely complex and the number of employees has not exceeded 50, Imogene proposed the development of their payroll system using a database. She could enter payroll data into the database and have the payroll computations performed, including the generation of a payroll register report. The payroll register was to include the summary and total information required for the completion of the federal and state 941s. (A 941 is a form that is filed summarizing the payroll deduction tax deposits.)

The Payroll Register database that Imogene set up for LVR contains fields that are described by the following data dictionary definitions:

Field Name	Description
NAME	Employee name (first name and last name)
SSN	Employee social security number
PAY_RATE	Hourly rate of pay
REG_HOURS	Number of hours worked at regular rate of pay
OT_HOURS	Number of hour worked that qualify for overtime pay at 1.5 times the regular rate of pay
GROSS_PAY	Total pay for the weekly pay period
FED_TAX	Federal income tax withholding amount
ST_TAX	State income tax withholding amount
FICA	Social security contribution amount
HEALTH	Health insurance deduction amount
NET_PAY	Net pay for the weekly pay period after deductions from GROSS_PAY

Since the payroll register contains several fields whose values are computed, Imogene has organized the database fields into two groups in this manner:

NAME ... OT_HOURS	GROSS_PAY ... NET_PAY
←——— INPUT FIELDS ———→	←——— COMPUTED FIELDS ———→

Although this arrangement was not required, Imogene realized it would keep all the input data together and make data entry easier *without* the need to specify fields for processing with the EDIT and BROWSE commands. Imogene has determined the following methods of calculation for fields in the payroll register:

Weekly gross pay. Multiply the pay rate by the regular hours worked plus one and one-half times the overtime hours.

Federal withholding tax. 16 percent of the weekly gross pay for each employee.

State withholding tax. 6 percent of the weekly gross pay for each employee.

FICA. 7.5 percent of the weekly gross pay.

Health insurance. $25 per employee per week.

Tasks

1. Access the PAYROLL.DBF database file, which contains the input payroll data for the most recent pay period, in the CASES catalog and review its structure and data. Procure a hard copy listing of the database structure for documentation and reference.

2. Develop a command file program with the name of PAYROLL.PRG that calculates the computed fields from data in the input fields. This command file should produce the Payroll Register using the [version IV] PAYROLL4 or [version III+] PAYROLL3 REPORT FORM definition. Execute this command file and produce the Payroll Register. Produce a listing of the command file for inclusion in the system's documentation. [*Hint:* This program should make use of the REPLACE command in performing the required computations.]

3. Create a command file program with the name of RESET.PRG that sets the *computed fields* to zeros in preparation for entering the payroll data for the next pay period. Make a hard copy listing of the command file for inclusion in the systems documentation.

4. Occasionally Imogene needs to look up payroll information in the PAYROLL database. Construct a command file that assists her in looking up data for an individual employee in the Payroll Register. In this command file, include the capability for obtaining a list of employee names, if an incorrect name is entered. Execute this command file and use <Shift> + <PrtSc> to capture key screens in the processing sequence. Print a hard copy listing of the command file for inclusion in the system's documentation. [*Hint:* To facilitate the look up process, INDEX the PAYROLL database on the NAME field.]

5. Write a summary that includes end-user instructions for operating this Payroll Register system. These instructions should include how to enter data and execute the command file programs. Incorporate examples of the screens and sample reports in this user documentation. Use <Shift> + <PrtSc> to capture copies of the screens for inclusion in your documentation package.

6. (*Optional*)   Compare this database solution of the payroll register with the command file program to that developed in the Case Application of Using Lotus 1-2-3, Lesson L.3. Write a summary describing the similarities and differences between this application implemented in dBASE and that created in Lotus 1-2-3.

7. (*Optional*)   LVR's Payroll Register does *not* contain any year-to-date totals. Describe how the database could be modified to include this capability. Suggest how these year-to-date values could be computed. What problems, if any, do the year-to-date totals create when the data entered for one, and only one, employee needs to be revised, because of a data entry error, after the Payroll Register and year-to-date totals have been computed?

8. (*Optional*)   Develop a second version of the Payroll Register system with a database and the command file programs that include the year-to-date capability. Make copies of the database and command files before initiating this activity. Document this system as described in (5) above.

Time Estimates

Novice: 120 minutes

Intermediate: 75 minutes

Advanced: 60 minutes

LESSON

D.9

Processing with Menu Programs

CONTENT

- Menu Processing
- Continued Menu Processing
- Screen Painting in Menu Programs
- When Things Go Wrong

D.9.1 Menu Processing

By using a dBASE command file, a menu-driven application can be developed for the Golden Gourmet Wine Management System. Bert and Beth are excited about this approach, because they need to know only how to execute a single command file to handle all of their processing needs. This taps the real power of dBASE programs. The commands to produce each of the WMS reports can be combined in a single command file, and they can select the report to be produced from a menu, as shown in Figure D.102. The dBASE commands for this application are contained in the WINES command file, which appears as Figure D.103.

Most of the commands in the WINES command file are those that have been used in performing queries and producing reports. Several commands require additional explanation. mCHOICE is used as a memory variable for storing your menu selection. mCHOICE is given an initial value of zero. DO CASE allows the selected set of commands to be executed depending on the mCHOICE that you enter. The DOCASE..ENDCASE command is similar to an IF..ELSE..ENDIF. The IF command permits only two options to be processed, whereas the DO CASE allows a number of options to be considered for selected processing, as is illustrated by the diagram in Figure D.104. The mCHOICE alternatives correspond to the menu selections. The DO CASE is *terminated* with an ENDCASE.

Keypoint! The DO command, which causes a command file to be executed, is different from the DO CASE command, which permits several alternative sets of commands to be selected for execution *within an* individual command file!

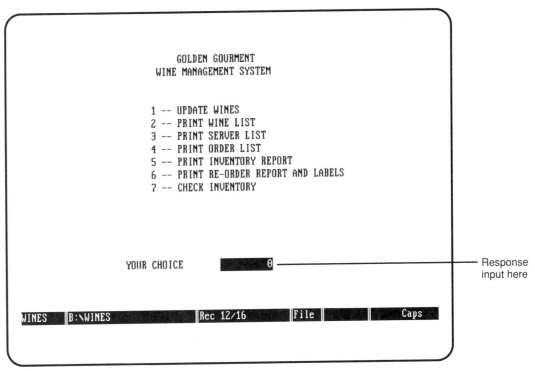

FIGURE D.102. Menu for Wine Management System.

The general form of the DO CASE..ENDCASE commands are as follows:

```
DO CASE
    CASE condition-1
        commands executed when condition-1 is true
    CASE condition-2
        commands executed when condition-2 is true
            .
            .
            .
    CASE condition-n
        commands executed when condition-n is true
ENDCASE
```

where the conditions are the same as those of the FOR condition used with other dBASE commands.

For menu choices 6 and 7 in the program in Figure D.103, another command file is *called* to be processed by including the DO command within the WINES command file. The command file ORDER, developed in the prior lesson, contains all of the commands for processing an order, whereas the command file CHECK3 contains the commands for looking up an individual wine. Although the commands from each of those command files could be repeated here, these two existing command files can be *called* for processing to implement menu choices 6 or 7. This arrangement of command files supports a *modular* approach to dBASE programming. A program, developed to implement a particular processing activity, is written and tested as a separate module. This program module is then called whenever its execution is desired. A modular approach like this allows you to write a number of smaller programs, where each module is usually easier to write and test than one large program.

The arrangement and interactions among the database files, the command file processes, and the reports and screen displays for the Wine Management System

To examine a dBASE
program with menu
processing

```
*  GOLDEN GOURMET
*  WINE MANAGEMENT SYSTEM
*  COMMAND FILE:  WINES
*  USE:  This command file presents a menu of update and report
*        options. The user then makes a desired menu choice.

SET CONSOL OFF
SET SAFETY OFF
SELECT 1
USE WINES
INDEX ON TYPE + MAKER TO WINETYPE
INDEX ON BIN + TYPE TO BINTYPE
mCHOICE = 0

CLEAR
@2,30 SAY "GOLDEN GOURMET"
@3,26 SAY "WINE MANAGEMENT SYSTEM"
@6,25 SAY "1 -- UPDATE WINES"
@7,25 SAY "2 -- PRINT WINE LIST"
@8,25 SAY "3 -- PRINT SERVER LIST"
@9,25 SAY "4 -- PRINT ORDER LIST"
@10,25 SAY "5 -- PRINT INVENTORY REPORT"
@11,25 SAY "6 -- PRINT REORDER REPORT AND LABELS"
@12,25 SAY "7 -- CHECK INVENTORY"
@18,20 SAY "YOUR CHOICE       " GET mCHOICE
READ

DO CASE
    CASE mCHOICE = 1
        SET INDEX TO
        APPEND
    CASE mCHOICE = 2
        SET INDEX TO WINETYPE
        REPORT FORM WINELIST TO PRINT
    CASE mCHOICE = 3
        SET INDEX TO BINTYPE
        REPORT FORM SERVLIST TO PRINT
    CASE mCHOICE = 4
        SET INDEX TO WINETYPE
        REPORT FORM ORDRLIST FOR ON_HAND < 24 TO PRINT
    CASE mCHOICE = 5
        SET INDEX TO BINTYPE
        REPORT FORM INVENTORY TO PRINT
    CASE mCHOICE = 6
        DO ORDER
    CASE mCHOICE = 7
        DO CHECK3
ENDCASE
RETURN
```

FIGURE D.103. Wines command file.

are shown in the *dataflow diagram* (DFD) of Figure D.105. The purpose of a DFD is to provide a graphical picture of the interrelationship among the major components of a system such as this. It furnishes a "big picture" look at the connections among the system's components.

The hierarchical manner in which one command file accesses or "calls" other command files is portrayed by the *structure chart* in Figure D.106. A structure chart is a graphical overview of the interactions among command files. The WINES command file, at the highest level, functions as the "presidential" level command file. By employing the existing ORDER and CHECK3 command files, the size of the WINES command file is reduced, and the commands in this file can be limited to those that

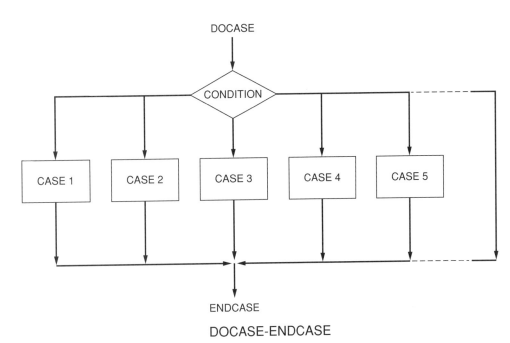

DOCASE-ENDCASE

FIGURE D.104. General arrangement of DO CASE..ENDCASE commands.

are used primarily to create the menu. Command files ORDER and CHECK3 each contain a number of commands that perform a specific processing function. When command files or programs are divided into modules like this, it represents a *structured approach* to programming. These DO commands, which call other command files, are a different command than the DO CASE..ENDCASE commands, which permit multiple options to be processed.

Keypoint!

A " call" from one dBASE program to another means that execution of the "calling" command file is suspended while the commands in the "called" command file are executed. Then, execution of the commands in the "calling" command file is continued at the command immediately following the DO command that initiated the call!

Caution Alert!

If you encounter the error message "Too many files open" when executing a command file, the DOS CONFIG.SYS file needs to be revised to allow for more open files. Each command file, database file, index file, and report format file that is being used is an "open file." The CONFIG.SYS file is modified as described in Section 0.2.4 of Using DOS. You must save your work in dBASE, exit dBASE, revise the CONFIG.SYS file, *reboot DOS*, and then execute dBASE again in order to correct this error!

D.9.2 Continued Menu Processing

Beth has been describing to Annie how the WINES command file is used. She demonstrated the manner in which Annie would enter the command DO WINES each time she wanted to make a menu selection. This happens because the WINES command file permits processing the menu only *one time*. Although this was certainly easier then executing a different command file for each activity on the menu, Annie thought it would be easier to be able to make several menu choices, one after another,

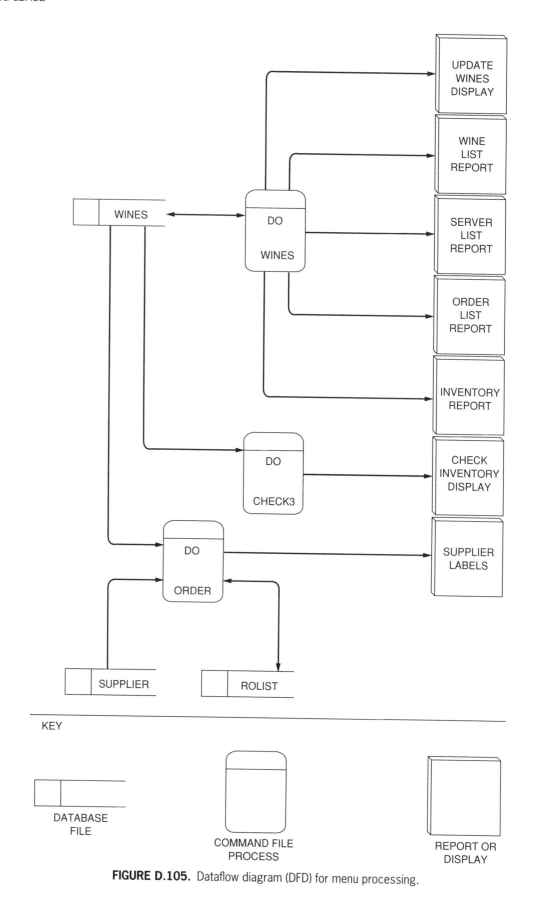

FIGURE D.105. Dataflow diagram (DFD) for menu processing.

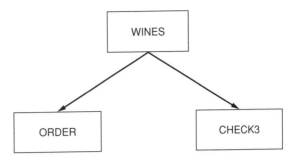

FIGURE D.106. Structure chart for menu processing illustrating "calling" arrangement of command files.

until they had completed all of their data entry and had processed all the desired reports. Annie pointed out to Beth that they would often want to process two or more menu selections during a single session. She emphasized that it would be necessary to execute the WINES command file for each selection. Beth thought that it would be a good idea to enhance the command file to permit processing as many menu selections as desired before leaving the command file.

Continued menu processing is accomplished by creating a loop that repeats until a menu selection is picked to terminate processing. As shown in Figure D.107, the selection 9 is used to terminate processing. This loop is implemented with a DO WHILE command, as is illustrated in Figure D.108. The DO WHILE is terminated with an ENDDO WHILE. The DO WHILE..ENDDO WHILE repeats processing, which displays the menu until a value of 9 is entered to select the *CANCEL* menu option. (dBASE has a CANCEL command that is different from this CANCEL menu option.)

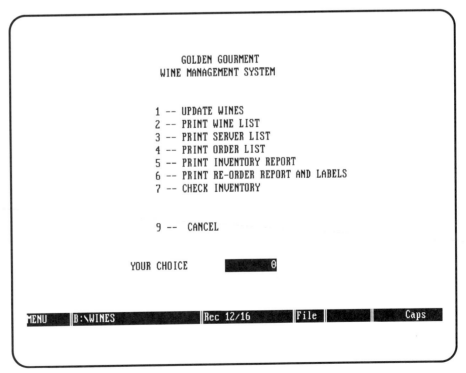

FIGURE D.107. Enhanced menu for Wine Management System.

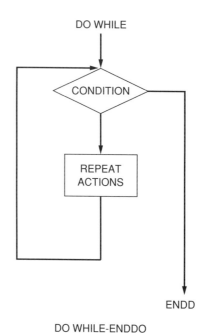

DO WHILE-ENDDO

FIGURE D.108.   General arrangement of DO WHILE..ENDDO WHILE commands.

The general form of the DO WHILE..ENDDO WHILE commands are as follows:

```
DO WHILE condition
     commands executed when condition is true
        (commands repeated in loop)
ENDDO WHILE optional comment
```

where the condition is the same as those of the FOR condition used with other dBASE commands. The optional comment is useful for indicating the ending point of a DO WHILE when several different DO WHILE loops are implemented in the same dBASE program.

The DO WHILE..ENDDO WHILE commands are deployed for continued menu processing, as is shown in the MENU command file in Figure D.109. Here, the @..SAY commands, which display the menu, and the DO CASE..ENDCASE commands, which perform the selected processing, are all contained within the DO WHILE..ENDDO WHILE commands. By placing them inside this loop, they are repeated until a value for mCHOICE is entered that is greater than 8. Notice that on the menu, "CANCEL" is specified as menu selection 9. CANCEL is applied here, since this is a commonly accepted word to indicate that you want to terminate processing. Also, the use of CANCEL rather that QUIT helps to avoid confusion for an end user, since QUIT is the command to exit from dBASE.

Keypoint!

CANCEL is employed as the menu choice to indicate that command file processing is to be terminated. CANCEL has been used because this is a commonly accepted word for indicating the termination of processing as defined under guidelines for Common User Access (CUA), which is part of the broader System Application Architecture (SAA) guidelines for computer systems. When creating dBASE programs, conventions for CUA should be followed whenever possible, since this assists users who operate *several different* computer applications!

To examine a dBASE
program with repeated menu
processing

```
*   GOLDEN GOURMET
*   WINE MANAGEMENT SYSTEM
*   COMMAND FILE:   MENU
*   USE:  This command file presents a menu of update and report
*         options. The user then makes a desired menu choice.

SET CONSOL OFF
SET SAFETY OFF
SELECT 1
USE WINES
INDEX ON TYPE + MAKER TO WINETYPE
INDEX ON BIN + TYPE TO BINTYPE
mCHOICE = 0
DO WHILE mCHOICE < 8
    CLEAR
    @2,30 SAY "GOLDEN GOURMET"
    @3,26 SAY "WINE MANAGEMENT SYSTEM"
    @6,25 SAY "1 -- UPDATE WINES"
    @7,25 SAY "2 -- PRINT WINE LIST"
    @8,25 SAY "3 -- PRINT SERVER LIST"
    @9,25 SAY "4 -- PRINT ORDER LIST"
    @10,25 SAY "5 -- PRINT INVENTORY REPORT"
    @11,25 SAY "6 -- PRINT REORDER REPORT AND LABELS"
    @12,25 SAY "7 -- CHECK INVENTORY"
    @15,25 SAY "9 -- CANCEL"
    @18,20 SAY "YOUR CHOICE        " GET mCHOICE
    READ
DO CASE
    CASE mCHOICE = 1
        SET INDEX TO
        APPEND
    CASE mCHOICE = 2
        SET INDEX TO WINETYPE
        REPORT FORM WINELIST TO PRINT
    CASE mCHOICE = 3
        SET INDEX TO BINTYPE
        REPORT FORM SERVLIST TO PRINT
    CASE mCHOICE = 4
        SET INDEX TO WINETYPE
        REPORT FORM ORDRLIST FOR ON_HAND < 24 TO PRINT
    CASE mCHOICE = 5
        SET INDEX TO BINTYPE
        REPORT FORM INVENTRY TO PRINT
    CASE mCHOICE = 6
        DO ORDER
    CASE mCHOICE = 7
        DO CHECK3
ENDCASE
ENDDO WHILE mCHOICE < 8
RETURN
```

FIGURE D.109. MENU command file.

D.9.3   Screen Painting in Menu Programs

As Beth developed the MENU command file, she discovered an alternative method for specifying the menu choices. Rather than using @..SAY commands, she could use the TEXT..ENDTEXT commands, as is illustrated in Figure D.110. With the TEXT..ENDTEXT commands, Beth entered or "painted" each line of the menu by including them in her command file *exactly* as she wanted them to appear on the screen when the program was executed. By "screen painting" this menu, Beth has a better idea of how the final menu will appear on the screen, because of the match between what is entered in the program and what is displayed on execution.

To use TEXT for screen
painting

```
*   GOLDEN GOURMET
*   WINE MANAGEMENT SYSTEM
*   COMMAND FILE:  MENU
*   USE:  This command file presents a menu of update and report
*         options. The user then makes a desired menu choice.
                                                          .
                                                          .
                                                          .

mCHOICE = 0
DO WHILE mCHOICE < 8
      CLEAR
      SET CONSOL ON
      TEXT


                              GOLDEN GOURMET
                         WINE MANAGEMENT SYSTEM


                         1 - UPDATE WINES
                         2 - PRINT WINE LIST
                         3 - PRINT SERVER LIST
                         4 - PRINT ORDER LIST
                         5 - PRINT INVENTORY REPORT
                         6 - PRINT REORDER REPORT AND LABELS
                         7 - CHECK INVENTORY


                         9 - CANCEL


      ENDTEXT
      SET CONSOL OFF
      @18,20 SAY "YOUR CHOICE      " GET mCHOICE
      READ
DO CASE
                              .
                              .
                              .


ENDCASE
ENDDO WHILE mCHOICE < 8
RETURN
```

FIGURE D.110. MENU command file.

To cause the screen display of the block of text enclosed within the
TEXT..ENDTEXT commands, Beth had to include the SET CONSOL ON command *before* the TEXT command and used the SET CONSOL OFF command *after* the
ENDTEXT command. The CONSOL must be set ON in order for the commands to be
displayed. The rest of the MENU program in Figure D.110 remains unchanged from
the version of the program in Figure D.109.

The general form of the TEXT..ENDTEXT commands are as follow:

TEXT
```
     block of text for display
```
ENDTEXT

where the block of text is entered in the command file program exactly as it is to be
displayed.

The purpose of these dBASE program examples is to illustrate how dBASE
command files can be used to create menu-driven user applications. As you can readily

see, these applications require the use of a number of dBASE commands that are very similar to those used in third-generation programming languages (3GLs), such as BASIC or C. The examples should also demonstrate that, if you want to become a dBASE programmer, there is a great deal to learn about the details of writing dBASE programs. It is beyond the scope of this introduction to expose you to all of the dBASE commands. Like most programming languages, dBASE often provides several different methods for performing the same activity, as is demonstrated with the @..SAY and TEXT..ENDTEXT commands. Another example is the JOIN command. This was explored as a means for combining data from two databases. The same reorder listing could be produced with a VIEW command. If you want to learn more about dBASE and its programming commands, see the *dBASE Reference Manual.*

D.9.4   When Things Go Wrong

The difficulties that may be encountered when executing dBASE programs for menu processing are similar to those encountered with any other dBASE program. More frequently occurring situations are as follows:

1. A "file does not exist" error message is encountered as you execute your menu program. In addition to those incorrect file name errors described in the prior lesson, this could be caused by specifying the wrong program file name in calling another program with the DO command.

   a. Terminate execution of the menu program by specifying "cancel" when prompted by dBASE.

   b. At the dot prompt, use the DIR *.PRG command to determine the correct program file name. Here, the PRG extension identifies dBASE program or command files.

   c. Edit your program, changing the file name, and save the corrected version of the program.

   d. Reissue the DO command to execute the command file.

2. The error message "too many files open" appears while executing your program. Each command file, database file, index file, and report file being used within a dBASE program is "opened" so it can be accessed. When a command file calls another command file, both files are "open." The number of files that can be "open" at any one time is controlled by DOS, not by dBASE, in the CONFIG.SYS file. This error most frequently occurs when several command files are being used with multiple database files, such as when a command file is called that performs a JOIN.

   a. Save your work in dBASE, as appropriate, and QUIT dBASE.

   b. Revise your CONFIG.SYS file, as described in the Using DOS, Lesson O.2.4 Set the number of FILES to, at least, 20. If your computer is connected to a network, be sure to have this change in the CONFIG.SYS file approved by your network manager!

   c. Re-boot DOS. This is the only way the CONFIG.SYS file is processed, and the number of files is set to the revised value.

   d. Access dBASE.

   e. Execute your dBASE program with the DO command.

D.9.5   Lesson Summary

- dBASE command files can be deployed to create menu-driven applications.
- The DO CASE..ENDCASE commands provide for the selection of a processing alternative from among a number of alternatives.
- The DO CASE command is different from the DO command, which causes another dBASE program to be executed.
- When a DO command is incorporated in a dBASE command file, it causes another command file to be "called" for processing.
- The DO WHILE..ENDDO WHILE commands facilitate creating a loop in which commands are executed repeatedly until a specified condition is no longer satisfied.
- A CANCEL menu selection alternative is the preferred method for specifying the termination of command file processing.
- The TEXT..ENDTEXT commands provide an alternative method for displaying a menu with screen painting.

- The dBASE command files, which have been explored, provide only an introduction into the capabilities of programming in dBASE.

D.9.6 Practice Tutorial

A dBASE program organized to present the end user with a menu can be developed for the Golden Gourmet's Wine Management System as described in this Lesson. Construct this command file as a guided activity in a hands-on manner.

Task 1: Create the MENU command file of Figure D.109.

Task 2: Execute this command file and test it by selecting several menu choices.

Task 3: Produce a listing of the command file.

Time Estimates

Novice: 90 minutes

Intermediate: 60 minutes

Advanced: 45 minutes

D.9.7 Practice Exercises

(1) **Case: State Employment Commission Job Bank**

Business Problem: Job Placement
MIS Characteristics: Human Resources
Operational Control

Graham Wampler manages the Job Bank at the State Employment Commission (SEC). To assist in tracking jobs and matching them with applicants, Graham has created two databases. The SECJOB database holds data about positions available, while the SECAPPL database consists of data about applicants. Graham has organized the positions into five major categories or types: (1) food service/restaurant (FOOD), (2) domestic/housekeeping (DOM), (3) clerical/office (CLER), (4) entertainment (ENT), and (5) health care (HEAL). The databases he has established contain fields as described by the following data dictionary definitions:

SECJOB Database:

Field Name	Description
JOB_ID	Position number
POSITION	Position title
TYPE	Position category: FOOD, DOM, CLER, ENT, HEAL
HOURS	Job hours
DAYS	Job days
RATE	Hourly pay rate
CONTACT	Employer's contact person
JPHONE	Job contact phone number
POSTED	Date job initially posted
FILL	Indicator of whether or not the job has been filled

SECAPPL Database:

Field Name	Description
JOB_ID	Position number
ANAME	Applicant's name
ADDRESS	Street address
CITY	Applicant's city
ST	Applicant's state
ZIP	Zip code
APHONE	Applicant's phone number

Graham has developed three dBASE programs to assist him in printing a job list, checking on job information, and printing mailing labels for communicating with job applicants. Each of these dBASE programs are identified as follows:

Program	Description
SECLIST	Produces the Job List report using the [version IV] SECLIST4 or [version III+] SECLIST3 REPORT FORM definition
SECCHECK	Supports looking up job information
SECMAIL	Generates mailing labels using the [version IV] SECMAIL4 or [version III+] SECMAIL3 LABEL FORM definition

Thus far, Graham has individually executed each of the programs. However, Beth Ming will begin assisting Graham with his job responsibilities next week. Graham wants to develop a menu-driven dBASE system that is easy for Beth to use. He sketched out the desired menu as follows:

```
                    STATE EMPLOYMENT COMMISSION
                      JOB PLACEMENT SYSTEM
1 -- ENTER/UPDATE JOBS
2 -- PRINT JOB LIST
3 -- CHECK POSITION INFORMATION
4 -- PRINT APPLICANT MAILING LABELS
9 -- CANCEL
ENTER YOUR SELECTION
```

Task 1: Access the SECJOB.DBF and SECAPPL.DBF database files in the EXER-CISE catalog. Review the structure and data in each of these database files. Produce a hard copy listing of these database structures for your reference and documentation.

. _____

. _____

. _____

Task 2: Access the SECLIST.PRG and SECMAIL.PRG dBASE programs. Mod-ify each program to use the desired REPORT or LABEL FORM for your version of dBASE. Execute each of the three dBASE programs and observe their operation. In addition to the printed output, obtain a screen dump from the execution of the look up program SECCHECK.

Task 3: Produce a hard copy listing, for your reference, of each of the three program files that Graham has developed.

· _____

· _____

· _____

Task 4: Create and execute a dBASE menu program that implements the menu sketched out by Graham. Create this menu program as the SEC.PRG command file. The "ENTER/UPDATE JOBS" menu choice is carried out by using the SET INDEX TO and APPEND commands. The other three menu choices are completed by calling the appropriate dBASE program, which Graham has already created.

Task 5: Complete the documentation of your dBASE system by obtaining a listing of your menu program command file SEC.PRG. Obtain a screen dump of the execution of the menu programs. Organize and assemble these outputs with those produced in Task 2 and Task 3 to finish your documentation package.

Time Estimates

Novice: 90 minutes

Intermediate: 60 minutes

Advanced: 45 minutes

(2)   Case: First General Building Maintenance

Business Problem: Accounts Receivable Aging
MIS Characteristics: Finance
                              Managerial Control

First General Building Maintenance (FGB) provides janitorial and related services to a number of customers. Each month FGB invoices their customers for the specific work performed the prior month. Some customers pay their invoices more quickly than others. To track their accounts receivable, Kieko Bang, an accountant at FGB, has created an accounts receivable aging system. This system contains two databases. One database contains the more permanent customer information, whereas the other contains the more temporary accounts receivable data. Kieko designed these database files containing the fields as described by the following data dictionary definitions:

FGBACCT Database:

Field Name	Description
ACCT	Customer's account number
AMT_DUE	Current month's amount due for 0 to 29 days
PAST_30	Amount outstanding from 30 to 59 days
PAST_60	Amount outstanding from 60 to 89 days
PAST_90	Amount outstanding 90 days or more
LATE	Amount of late penalty charges, if any
TOT_AMT	Total amount due
COLLECT	Indicator of whether or not account has been sent for credit collection
OPEN	Date account initially started
SREP	Sales representative identification of representative responsible for account

FGBCUST Database:

Field Name	Description
ACCT	Customer's account number
CNAME	Customer's name
ADDRESS	Street address
CITY	Customer's city
ST	Customer's state
ZIP	Zip code
CPHONE	Customer's phone number

Kieko has developed three dBASE programs to assist her in printing an accounts receivable aging report, checking on account past due amounts, and printing mailing labels for past due accounts. The three dBASE programs are described as follows:

Program	Description
FGBLIST	Produces the Accounts Receivable Aging Report using the [version IV] FGBLIST4 or [version III+] FGBLIST3 REPORT FORM definition
FGBCHECK	Supports looking up past due account information
FGBMAIL	Generates mailing labels for past due accounts using the [version IV] FGBMAIL4 or [version III+] FGBMAIL3 LABEL FORM definition

In operating the accounts receivable aging system, Kieko has been individually executing each of the programs. However, beginning next month, Brandon Wheeler will begin assisting Kieko with her job responsibilities. Kieko believes a menu-driven dBASE system will be easier and more convenient for both Brandon and her to use. She sketched out the proposed menu as follows:

```
                    FIRST GENERAL BUILDING MAINTENANCE
                    ACCOUNTS RECEIVABLE AGING SYSTEM
1 -- ENTER/UPDATE ACCOUNTS
2 -- PRINT AGING REPORT
3 -- CHECK PAST DUE ACCOUNT INFORMATION
4 -- PRINT PAST DUE MAILING LABELS
9 -- CANCEL
ENTER YOUR SELECTION
```

Task 1: Access the FGBACCT.DBF and FGBCUST.DBF database files in the EXERCISE catalog. Examine the structure and data in each database file. Produce a hard copy listing of the database structures for your reference and documentation.

· _____

· _____

· _____

Task 2: Access the FGBLIST.PRG and FGBMAIL.PRG dBASE programs. Modify each program to use the desired REPORT or LABEL FORM for your version of dBASE. Execute each of the three dBASE programs and observe their operation. In addition to the printed output, obtain screen dumps from the execution of the look up program FGBCHECK.

Task 3: Produce a hard copy listing, for your reference, of each of the three program files that Kieko has developed.

· _____

· _____

· _____

Task 4: Create and execute a dBASE menu program that produces the menu sketched out by Kieko. Create this menu program as the FGB.PRG command file. The "ENTER/UPDATE ACCOUNTS" menu choice should be implemented by using the SET INDEX TO and APPEND commands. The other three menu choices should cause the appropriate dBASE program that Kieko has already created to be called.

Task 5: Prepare the documentation of your dBASE system by obtaining a listing of your menu program command file FGB.PRG. Obtain a screen dump of the execution of the menu program. Organize and assemble these outputs with those produced in Task 2 and Task 3 to complete your documentation package.

Time Estimates

Novice: 90 minutes

Intermediate: 60 minutes

Advanced: 45 minutes

D.9.8   Comprehensive Problems

(1)   Case: Yen To Travel (continued)

To make it even easier for Ashley and Sara to interact with the Tour Management System at Yen To Travel, Brenda wants to create a dBASE program that displays a menu of processing options. All they would need to do is to select the desired options until their processing has been completed.

Task 1:   Create and execute a menu-driven dBASE program that selectively allows an individual to update the TOURS database, print the Tour List, print the Representatives List, print the Seat Request List, print the Tour Inventory Report, print the Tour Request List and mailing labels, and check on a specified tour.

Task 2:   Create a CLIENT database that contains the following information:
Client name (last and first as separate fields)
Client address
City, state, zip code
Telephone number
Tour code
Paid (a field that indicates if the client has paid for the selected tour)

Task 3:   Create your own data to populate this CLIENT database for at least six (6) of the tours. JOIN the CLIENT database with the TOURS database and prepare a Client Report that contains the client's name, the tour name, the departure date, the price of the tour, and whether payment has been made. Create a dBASE program to produce this report and execute the program.

Task 4:   Produce listing of each dBASE program to include in the systems documentation.

Time Estimates

Novice: 90 minutes

Intermediate: 60 minutes

Advanced: 45 minutes

DATABASE PLANNING FORM

Data Name	Data Type	Number of Characters for Largest Value	Dec(imal) Places

(2)   Case: Silver Screen Video (continued)

Amy has suggested to Ernie that a front-end menu should be added to the Silver Screen Video's Movie Management System. This would allow each of them merely to make menu selections for all of the desired processing that initiates execution of the command file for each request. Todd and Ernie definitely believe this would make the system even easier for them to use.

Task 1: Create and execute a menu-driven dBASE program that selectively allows an individual to update the movie database, print the Movie List, print the Sales List, print the Movie Order List, print the Movie Inventory Report, print the Movie Reorder List and mailing labels, and check on a specified movie.

Task 2: Create a CUSTOMER database that contains the following information:

Client name (last and first as separate fields)

Client address

City, state, zip code

Telephone number

Movie name

Task 3: Create your own data to populate this database for at least six (6) of the movies. JOIN the CUSTOMER database with the MOVIES database and prepare a Customer Report that contains the customer's name, the movie name, the year produced, the movie rating, and the price of the movie. Create a dBASE program to produce this report and to execute the program.

Task 4: Produce a listing of each dBASE program to include in the systems documentation.

Time Estimates

Novice: 90 minutes

Intermediate: 60 minutes

Advanced: 45 minutes

CUSTOMER DATABASE PLANNING FORM

Data Name	Data Type	Number of Characters for Largest Value	Dec(imal) Places

D.9.9　Application Case

Case:　Looart Creative Designs

Business Problem: Material Requirements Planning
MIS Characteristics: Production
　　　　　　　　　　Managerial Control
Management Functions: Planning
　　　　　　　　　　　Directing
　　　　　　　　　　　Controlling
Tools Skills: Programming
　　　　　　　Memory variables
　　　　　　　Menu processing
　　　　　　　Repetitive processing
　　　　　　　Modular programs
　　　　　　　User interfaces

Looart Creative Designs (LCD) was founded in 1951 by Charles and Herbert Loo to produce greeting cards that "celebrate life's special moments." Charles (Chuck) Loo serves as Chairman of the Board of Directors and Chief Executive Officer, while Herbert (Herbie) Loo is Looart's President and Chief Operating Officer. Last year Looart completed a major expansion and renovation of their printing plant in Colorado Springs, Colorado.

Looart supplies greeting cards to specialty and gift shops. As a franchised Looart dealer, a store is authorized to use Looart as part of its name, such as "Linda Lee's Looart" in Nashville, Tennessee. The success of Looart is founded on its close ties with its dealers. Looart has maintained its competitive market position with its dealers through the continuous development of new greeting card designs. Since Looart prints all of its own greeting cards, the time from the completion of a design to its shipment is minimized, providing Looart with a competitive advantage. Recently, Looart experienced difficulties in filling customer orders because of an out-of-stock situation with the silver foil paper that is used for printing some of Looart's best selling birthday and wedding cards. Looart had substituted similar greeting cards in filling customer orders. However, a number of these substitutes proved to be unacceptable and were subsequently returned. Chuck and Herbie were determined to avoid this predicament with future orders.

Looart uses several different papers in the production of greeting cards. They group their cards into the categories of birth announcements, birthday cards, wedding cards, and get well cards. For each category, a number of different designs are available that are described by the theme of the design. For each design, a kind of paper is selected that complements the design. Looart currently uses four different types of paper that are denoted as plain, linen, silver foil, and gold foil. The effect of the paper shortage was to curtail the production of all greeting cards made from the silver foil paper.

The Loo brothers' younger sister, Cassandra (Cassie) Loo-Snow, Vice President of Production and Operations, manages the printing and distribution of greeting cards. Cassie has maintained tight controls over Looart's production and inventory. She is quite concerned about the recent stockout, although this has not been a frequently occurring difficulty. However, to further improve Looart's performance and increase their effectiveness in responding to their customers, Cassie has given Shirlie Analist, a Senior Systems Engineer, the assignment of reviewing their production scheduling and material planning operations. Shirlie attended last month's dinner meeting of the local chapter of the American Production and Inventory Control Society (APICS), where Nicholas Aquilano, President of Aquilano and Associates, presented the benefits of material requirements planning (MRP) systems. He described how the production plan is coordinated with the materials needed for carrying out the manufacture of a product. To Shirlie, this appeared to provide the benefits Looart was seeking to better meet customers' needs. She decided to attend one of Aquilano's seminars on MRP to learn the details of its operation and implementation.

As explained by Nick, an MRP system creates production schedules that identify the specific materials required to produce end items and the exact number to be manufactured. For Looart, each different greeting card is an "end item." Nick described how MRP is used in a variety of industries where a number of products are made in batches using the same equipment, like Looart's greeting cards. He articulated that the main theme of MRP is "getting the right materials to the right place at the right time." The objectives of inventory management under an MRP system are to improve customer service, minimize inventory investment, and maximize production operating efficiency. Benefits of an MRP system include increased sales, reduced inventory, better customer service, better response to market demand, and reduced idle time. He spelled out the information needs for MRP that comprise customer orders, inventory records, and bill of material records, where a bill of material (BOM) file contains product descriptions, including the materials or components used in manufacturing a product. Shirlie was convinced that MRP could improve Looart's production operations and help avoid future stockout situations.

On returning from this seminar, Shirlie met with Cassie to discuss the implementation of an MRP system for Looart. Cassie encouraged Shirlie to develop a project proposal for the development and implementation of an MRP system. Cassie then discussed the benefits of the MRP project with Chuck and Herbie. They concurred with Cassie's recommendation to proceed with the project and authorized the necessary funding.

Shirlie has been working on Looart's new MRP system for several weeks. She first identified the system's requirements and then began to develop the system. As her design evolved, she periodically reviewed it with Cassie, obtaining an approval to continue the development effort with each critique. Her final system design consists of a series of main components, which are database files, command file processes, and report definitions. For Looart's MRP system, Shirlie established four databases delineated as follows:

Database	Description
ORDER	Customer orders with a record for each ITEM ordered
INVENT	Current inventory with a record for each ITEM produced
BOM	Bill of materials with a record for each ITEM produced
CUSTOMER	Customer name and address with a record for each customer

These four database files for Looart's MRP system contain data elements that are defined by these data dictionary entries:

ORDER Database:

Field Name	Description
ITEM	Item number of a greeting card design
QUANT	Number of boxes of greeting cards ordered by customer
CUSTOMER	Name of customer's business

INVENT (Inventory) Database:

Field Name	Description
ITEM	Item number of a greeting card design
ON_HAND	Number of boxes of greeting cards currently held in inventory
BIN	Bin identifier of storage bin containing greeting card
L_ORDER	Date of the last production run for the greeting card

BOM (Bill of Materials) Database:

Field Name	Description
ITEM	Item number of a greeting card design
DESCRIP	Description or name of a greeting card conveying the card's design
TYPE	Category of the greeting card: BIRTH ANC (Birth announcement), BIRTHDAY, GET WELL, and WEDDING
PAPER	Kind of paper on which the design is printed: GFOIL (gold foil), SFOIL (silver foil), PLAIN paper, and LINEN paper
FOLDS	Number of times paper is folded for a greeting card design
PRICE	Price per box of greeting cards

CUSTOMER Database:

Field Name	Description
CUSTOMER	Name of customer's business
ADDRESS	Customer's street address
CITY	City for shipping address
STATE	State for shipping address
ZIP	Zip or postal code

Shirlie has designed eight major processing activities for Looart's MRP system as follows:

Processing Activity	Description
UPDTORDR	Enter/update customer order data
UPDTBOM	Update bill of materials data for greeting cards
UPDTCUST	Enter/update customer data
INVNLIST	Produce the Inventory Report
MRPLIST	Generate the Production & Material Requirements Planning Report
CARDLIST	Create a Greeting Card List
CUSTLABL	Produce customer mailing labels for orders
CHCKINVN	Check the inventory status of a greeting card design

The MRP system produces three reports and a set of mailing labels. Each report uses a report form definition (*.FRM) file, whereas the mailing labels make use of a label form definition (*.LBL). The last or rightmost character of the REPORT or LABEL name specifies whether this is a dBASE version IV (4) or dBASE version III+ (3) file. These definitions are described as follows:

Report Form	Description	Organized by
INVNLIS	Inventory Report	Card TYPE
MRPLIST	Production & Material Requirements Planning Report	PAPER
CARDLIS	Card List Report	Card TYPE
CUSTLAB	Customer mailing labels	CUSTOMER name

Shirlie explained to Cassie that the Production & Material Requirements Planning (MRP) Report is the prominent report for determining their material requirements, since it specifies the total number of folds for each kind of PAPER material used in producing greeting cards. For Looart, the number of folds corresponds to the number of rolls of paper required to produce 50 boxes of greeting cards. Fifty boxes is Looart's standard production run for a particular greeting card design. Thus, by totaling the number of folds, the material requirement in number of rolls of paper is determined. Cassie and Shirlie met with Cheryl Quattro, Looart's director of purchasing, to review the report's content and to verify that it contains the information needed to support purchasing's actions. Cheryl indicated how she can use the material requirements from this report to order paper from their suppliers so that it will arrive on schedule to meet their production demands.

The other reports produced by the MRP system draw on the information in the MRP database files to support related activities. The Inventory Report contains the current inventory status of all greeting cards. In addition to Cassie's use of this report in monitoring inventory levels, the sales department uses the report when communicating with Looart's dealers. The Card List Report is Looart's catalog. This is used by the sales department and is sent to each dealer. The customer mailing labels are used for shipping each order to a customer. Although other reports may be included in an MRP system, Shirlie limited the scope of Looart's MRP system to encompass only these reports.

Shirlie prepared the dataflow diagram (DFD) shown in Figure D.111 to illustrate the interactions among these database files, their processing activities, and their reports and screen displays. She has developed most of the system and has been running it in the "unit test" mode to ensure that it is operating correctly. With a unit test, the command file for each processing activity is executed individually. Shirlie was careful to organize each processing activity as a separate dBASE command file to facilitate its development and unit testing. Shirlie has loaded test data in each of the databases to accommodate her testing endeavors.

Shirlie has developed an affiliation among the processing activities represented in the DFD. She has sketched out a structure chart that illustrates the "calling" arrangement among these dBASE command files, as shown in Figure D.112. With this "pancake" design, each processing activity is handled by a distinct dBASE command file that is "called" from the MRP "presidential" level command file. (Notice that a "structure chart" indicates the relationship among command files. A structure chart is a general system design tool. This is different from a dBASE structure that describes the fields contained in a dBASE database file!)

In the design Shirlie presented to Cassie, the MRP command file is to be a user-friendly menu that presents the processing alternatives for selection by the end user. Shirlie has sketched out the design for the screen display of the MRP command file as illustrated below.

Although Shirlie has completed most of Looart's MRP system, two processes remain to be developed: the UPDTBOM and MRP command files. The UPDTBOM command file controls the updating of the bill of materials (BOM) database, whereas the MRP command file contains the menu that is used to direct the overall processing activities. Because of an emergency with Looart's accounts receivable system, Shirlie had to postpone her development of the MRP system. Cassie has requested your assistance in completing Looart's MRP system.

```
                    LOOART CREATIVE DESIGNS
               MATERIAL REQUIREMENTS PLANNING SYSTEM
     1 -- ENTER/UPDATE CUSTOMER ORDER
     2 -- UPDATE BILL OF MATERIALS
     3 -- ENTER/UPDATE CUSTOMERS
     4 -- PRINT INVENTORY REPORT
     5 -- PRINT PRODUCTION & MRP REPORT
     6 -- PRINT CARD LIST
     7 -- PRINT CUSTOMER MAILING LABELS
     8 -- CHECK INVENTORY
     9 -- CANCEL
     ENTER PROCESSING CHOICE
```

Tasks

1. Access the ORDER.DBF, INVENT.DBF, BOM.DBF, and CUSTOMER.DBF database files in the CASES catalog and review their structures and data. Produce a hard copy listing of each database structure for documentation and reference.

2. Access the UPDTORDR.PRG, UPDTCUST.PRG, INVNLIST.PRG, MRP-LIST.PRG, CARDLIST.PRG, CUSTLABL.PRG, and CHCKINVN.PRG command files, and review these programs. Modify each program to use the desired REPORT or LABEL for your version of dBASE. Generate a hard copy listing

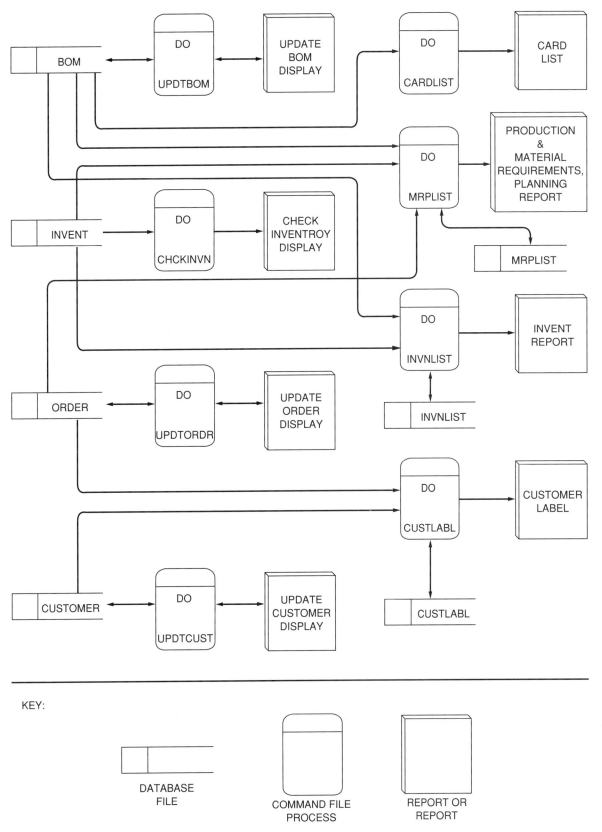

FIGURE D.111. Dataflow diagram (DFD) for MRP system.

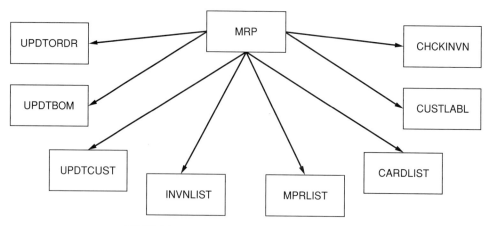

FIGURE D.112. Structure chart for MRP system.

of each program for documentation and reference. What is the programmed decision that determines that an ITEM is to be scheduled for production and included in the Production & Material Requirements Planning Report?

3. Write the UPDTBOM.PRG command file. Perform a unit test on this command file to verify its correct operation. Shirlie wants this command file to allow the end user to update the BOM.DBF database using the BROWSE command so that the data for several BOM records are displayed simultaneously on the screen. The records are to be displayed to the end user arranged by the ITEM field. Since the system Shirlie has developed uses each of the database files in a separate work area, she would like to have the BOM.DBF used in SELECT 3, which follows her other usage of the database.

4. Write the MRP.PRG command file that presents an end user with the menu that Shirlie and Cassie have designed for operating their MRP system. This command file should selectively "call" the other command files to perform the desired processing for each activity. Test each of the menu choices to ensure that the command file works correctly. Use <Shift> + <PrtSc> to capture the screen displays for those options that only display data on the screen. [*Hint:* If the message "File is already open" appears, then you need to include a USE command *without* specifying a database file name just before the RETURN command to close the database file before leaving the command file.]

5. What are the material requirements for the current production period? That is, how many rolls of each kind of paper are required?

6. Assemble the database structure listings, the output reports, the screen captures, and the command file listings as the MRP system documentation.

7. Write user instructions that describe how end users operate this MRP system. These should include instructions on how to access and initiate execution of the MRP system.

8. (*Optional*) Design and create a Picklist Report. This report is used by the associates filling each order. The report needs to contain the ITEM, BIN, QUANT, and CUSTOMER for each customer's order. It should be arranged with CUSTOMER as the primary key and BIN as the secondary key. The CUSTOMER should be used as a "group" for this report. The associate can then fill each order, proceeding in a systematic manner from one bin to the next as the customer's order is assembled for shipment. Develop a command

. file that produces this report. Modify the design of the MRP menu to include this "Print Picking List" Report and integrate this as a menu choice in the MRP.PRG command file.

9. (*Optional*)   Write a summary describing any enhancements you would suggest for Looart's MRP system.

Time Estimates

Novice: 120 minutes

Intermediate: 90 minutes

Advanced: 60 minutes

REFERENCE

CONTENT

- Starting dBASE
- Command Summary
- Function Summary

D.10.1 Starting dBASE

dBASE may be started in several different ways depending on your particular hardware configuration. When dBASE is installed on a local area network (LAN), a different start-up procedure may be used, which depends on your particular LAN arrangement. This section describes two of the more common methods of starting dBASE.

D.10.1.1. Two Floppy Drives

In preparation, obtain the dBASE SYSTEM Disk(s) (two disks for 5.25-in. format and one disk for 3.5-in. format) with DOS installed on it. If your disk is not set up with DOS, place the operating system on the disk by using the SYS command. With your disk(s) in hand, you are now ready to proceed:

1 Place dBASE SYSTEM Disk 1 in drive A:

2 Place your Data Disk in drive B:

    A   At the DOS prompt (usually, **A** >),

       Enter: DBASE

       or

    B   Perform a WARM BOOT by pressing <Ctrl>+<Alt>+<Del> all together. Enter the date and time, if requested. If the DOS A> prompt appears, enter: DBASE. Otherwise, skip this step.

       or

    C   Perform a COLD BOOT by turning on the power switch to your PC. Enter the date and time, if requested. If the DOS A> prompt appears, enter: DBASE. Otherwise, skip this step.

3 If you are using 5.25-in. disks, when requested place dBASE SYSTEM Disk 2 in drive A:

PRESS: \<Enter\>

You are now ready to begin using dBASE.

D.10.1.2. Hard Disk Drive

Before you are ready to start up dBASE, make sure that it has been installed on the hard disk. If the computer is not turned on, turn it on and enter the date and time, if requested.

Make sure you are at the DOS prompt (this is, **C** >). Drive C: is usually the default disk drive for a computer equipped with a hard disk. If you are accessing dBASE on a LAN, this may be a different disk drive. You should check on the drive for your particular computer configuration.

1 Place your Data Disk in drive A:

2 If dBASE is accessed from the root directory, at the DOS prompt (usually, **C** >),

Enter: DBASE

or

If dBASE is accessed from the DBASE directory, at the DOS prompt (usually, **C** >),

Enter: CD/DBASE   Change to DBASE directory

Enter: DBASE   Begin executing dBASE

You are now ready to begin using dBASE.

D.10.2 Command Summary

Many of the more frequently used dBASE commands are summarized in the following table. The purpose is to provide a quick reference review of these commands. The form of each command is a general form of the command that is most frequently used. Other, more advanced forms of the command may be available. The full syntax of each command may be reviewed in the *dBASE Reference Manuals*. A number of symbols are used to specify the syntax of these commands. They are described as the conventions for this command summary.

Conventions	Meaning
lowercase characters	User-supplied information
UPPERCASE CHARACTERS	dBASE key command words
< >	Indicates that the user-supplied information is required
[ ]	Specifies optional portion of dBASE command

Command	Action
@\<row\>,\<column\> SAY "\<message\>" **[GET memvar]**	Used to display a message at the specified location and optionally to indicate input of a value for a memory variable.
APPEND	Adds records to the bottom of the active dBASE relation, typing the data entered.

Command	Action
APPEND FROM <filename> [**TYPE**] <file type>]	Adds records to the bottom of the active dBASE relation from another dBASE database, Lotus 1-2-3 worksheet file, or ASCII text file.
	The <file type> options are:
	DELIMITED—comma delimited ASCII text file.
	SDF—Fixed formatted ASCII text file.
	WKS—Lotus 1-2-3 worksheet file.
AVERAGE [scope] [expression list] [**To memvar list**] [**FOR condition**]	Computes the average of the specified fields for the selected rows.
BROWSE <field list>	Enables full-screen viewing and editing for changing a database.
CLEAR	Clears the screen.
CLOSE DATABASE	Closes all open database files and index files.
COPY TO <new file> [**FIELDS** <fields list>] [**FOR condition**] [[**TYPE**] <file type>]	Copies records from the active database file to another dBASE database file, an ASCII text file, or a Lotus 1-2-3 worksheet file.
	The <file type> options are:
	DELIMITED—Comma delimited ASCII text file.
	SDF—Fixed formatted ASCII text file.
	WKS—Lotus 1-2-3 worksheet file.
COUNT [scope] [expression list] [**To memvar list**] [**FOR condition**]	Counts the number of rows or records in the database file.
CREATE <new file>	Allows a new database file to be created.
CREATE LABEL <filename>	Activates the full-screen menu for creating a label form file.
CREATE REPORT <filename>	Activates the full-screen menu for creating a report form file.
DELETE [<scope>] [**FOR condition**]	Marks the selected records for deletion.
DIR [<drive:>]	Displays the files on the specified disk drive.
DISPLAY [scope] [**ON/OFF**] [expression list] [**FOR condition**]	Displays the selected fields and records on the screen.
DISPLAY STATUS	Displays information about the active database and related files.
DISPLAY STRUCTURE [**TO PRINT**]	Displays the structure of the active database file.
DO <filename>	Initiates execution of the specified dBASE command file.
DO CASE . . . ENDCASE	A programming command that permits the selection of commands to be executed from a number of alternative sets of commands.
DO WHILE . . . ENDDO	A programming command that allows a set of commands to be repeated.
EDIT [<scope>]	Starts editing of the active database at the current or specified record.

Command	Action
EJECT	Causes printer to advance to the top of a new page.
FIND <character string>	Searches the active indexed database file for the first record that matches the specified character string.

[GO] <record number >
  GO TOP
  GO BOTTOM
  GOTO <record number >
	Positions the record pointed to the specified record number, top or bottom of the active database file.

IF...ELSE...ENDIF	A programming command that enables the conditional process of either one or two sets of commands.
INDEX ON [<key expression> **TO** <filename>]	Creates an index file from the current database and makes it active, or turns off the use of an index file.
JOIN WITH <file2> **TO** <file3> **FOR** <fields> = <file2> → <fields>	Creates a new database with file3 name by merging the specified records in the active database file with those of file2 name.

LABEL FORM <lbl filename>
  [**FOR** <condition>]
  [**TO PRINT/TO FILE** <filename>]
	Produces mailing labels using the specified label form. Output may be optionally directed to either the printer or a fixed formatted ASCII text file. dBASE appends TXT as the extension for this file.

LIST [scope] [**ON/OFF**]
  [expression list]
  [**FOR** <condition >]
  [**TO PRINT**]
	Produces a list of selected rows and columns from the active database.

LIST STATUS [**TO PRINT**]	Produces a listing of the status information about the active database and related files.
LIST STRUCTURE [**TO PRINT**]	Lists the structure of the active database file.
MODIFY COMMAND <filename>	Accesses the specified command file with the dBASE text editor for entry or modification.
MODIFY LABEL <filename>	Activates the full-screen menu for modifying a label form file.
MODIFY REPORT <filename>	Activates the full-screen menu for modifying a report form file.
MODIFY STRUCTURE	Allows the structure of the active database to be changed.
<memvar> = <expression>	Sets a memory variable to the value of the expression.
PACK	Removes the records marked for deletion.
QUIT	Terminates dBASE processing.
READ	Causes values to be obtained for the @...GET command.
RECALL [scope] [**FOR** <expression>]	Reinstates records marked for deletion.

REPLACE [scope] <field>
  WITH [expression]
  [**FOR** condition]
	Replaces the values in the specified field with the values from the expression.

REPORT FORM <filename>
  [**FOR** <condition>]
  [**TO PRINT/TO FILE** <filename>]
	Produces report using the specified report form. Output may be optionally directed to either the printer or a fixed formatted ASCII text file. dBASE places the TXT extension on this file.

Command	Action
SEEK <expression>	Searches the records in an indexed database for a key that matches the expression. The record pointer is positioned to the first record match.
SELECT <work area>	Specifies an active work area for a database file. Work areas may be numbered from 1 through 10.
SET ALTERNATE ON/OFF	Used to turn on/off the output of screen display to a designated ASCII text file.
SET ALTERNATE TO [<filename>]	Specify the name of the ASCII text file for recording output from the screen display. When *no* <filename> is specified, the output file is closed. dBASE places the TXT extension on this file.
SET CONSOL ON/OFF	Used to turn the screen display on/off during the execution of a dBASE command file.
SET DEFAULT TO <drive:>	Specifies the default disk drive for storing all files.
SET DELETED ON/OFF	Used to turn on/off the inclusion of records marked for deletion.
SET RELATION TO <field> **INTO** <file2>	Used to link two open database files according to a key expression common to both files where <field> is in the currently selected database file and <file2> is the name of the second or child file.
SET RELATION TO	Removes previously established relation links from currently selected work area.
SET SAFETY ON/OFF	Used to turn on/off the file overwrite message and response.
SET UNIQUE ON/OFF	Specifies whether records with the same key are included in an index file.
SORT ON <key field list> **[/A][/D]** **TO** <sort filename>	Sort the active database in ascending (/A) or descending (/D) order and write them to the specified database file.
SUM [scope] [expression list] **[TO memvar list]** **[FOR condition]**	Sums the specified fields in the selected rows of the database.
TEXT.. ENDTEXT	Specifies block of text in a command file that is to be displayed exactly as it appears in the command file.
TOTAL <key field> **TO** <filename> [<scope>] **[FIELDS** <field list>] **[FOR** <condition>]	Creates a new database with filename by summing the numeric fields of the active database file. The TO database file contains a single record for each key value in the original database with the totals for the numeric fields.
TYPE <filename> **TO PRINT**	Displays the contents of the specified ASCII-text file. This is frequently used with dBASE command files.
UPDATE ON <key field> **FROM** <filename> **REPLACE** <field> **WITH** <expression> **[RANDOM]**	Data values from the existing filename database are used to replace fields in the active database file. The field of the FROM database must be identified in the REPLACE expression as filename->field

Command	Action
USE	Closes the active database file and index files.
USE <filename> [INDEX <file list>]	Activates the specified database file and specified index files.
ZAP	Removes all records from the active database file.

D.10.3 Function Summary

Several of the available dBASE functions are summarized in the following table. dBASE functions provide a shortcut method for performing a number of more complex computations. Many of the dBASE functions enable data to be converted from one data type to another, such as converting from a number to a character string. The purpose of this summary is to provide a quick reference for some of the more regularly used functions. Each function is presented in a general form that is most frequently used. Other, more advanced forms of the function may be available. The full syntax and action performed by each function may be reviewed in the *dBASE Reference Manuals*.

Function	Action
CDOW(<date expression>)	Converts a date variable value to the name of the day of the week.
CMONTH(<date expression>)	Converts a date variable value to the name of the month.
CHR(<ASCII character number >)	Provides the ability to use an ASCII character for which there is no keyboard equivalent. Often used when sending control characters to a printer.
CTOD(<character string>)	Converts a date entered as a character string to a date variable value.
DATE ( )	Obtains the current date from the computer's clock.
DAY(<date expression>)	Converts a date variable value to the numeric day of the month.
DOW (<date expression>)	Converts a date variable value to a number of the day of the week, with Sunday being day 1.
DTOC(<date expression>)	Converts a date variable value to a character string. Often used with a multiple field INDEX that consists of a mix of character and date type fields.
EOF( )	Indicates the end-of-file with a logical value of true (.T.) when a command would cause the last record in the file to be passed.
EXP(<numeric expression>)	Computes e (2.7182818...) to the power of the expression.
FOUND ( )	Used with the FIND and SEEK commands. Contains a logical value of true (.T.) if the FIND or SEEK was successful.
INT(<numeric expression>)	Converts numeric expression to an integer.

Function	Action
LEN(<character string>)	Counts number of characters in string producing a numeric value.
LOG(<numeric expression>)	Common logarithm (base 10) of expression.
LOWER(<character string>)	Converts uppercase letters to lowercase letters.
MAX(<numeric exp1>, <numeric exp2>)	Finds maximum value of two expressions.
MIN(<numeric exp1>, <numeric exp2>)	Finds minimum value of two expressions.
MONTH(<date expression>)	Converts a date variable value to a number for the month.
RECNO ( )	Obtains the current record number in the active database file.
ROUND(<numeric expression>, <decimal expression>)	Rounds to the specified number of decimal places.
SQRT(<numeric expression>)	Computes the square root of a positive expression.
STR(<numeric expression> [, <length>] [, <decimal])	Converts a number to a character string of the specified length. A string length of 10 characters is used if the length is not specified. Decimal numbers are rounded to integers if no decimal places are specified. Often used with a multiple field INDEX that consists of a mix of character and numeric type fields.
SUBSTR(<character string>, <start position> [,<length>])	Extracts a specified number of characters from the character string, beginning with the start position.
TIME( )	Obtains the current time from the computer's clock as a character string.
TRIM(<character string>)	Removes the trailing blanks from the character string.
UPPER(<character string>)	Converts lowercase letters to uppercase letters.
VAL(<character string>)	Converts a character string of numbers to a numeric value.
YEAR(<date expression>)	Converts a date variable value to the numeric value of the year.

Using
WordPerfect

LESSON
W.1

Creating and Printing Documents

CONTENT

W.1.1 What Is WordPerfect?

WordPerfect is a word processing software package. Word processors are one of the most widely used personal computer software tools. There are a number of popular word processing programs other than WordPerfect, including WordStar, Microsoft Word, and Multimate. Word processing, also known as text processing, is such a widely employed application that word processing is available on nearly all hardware platforms, including mainframe and minicomputers.

The principal purpose of a word processor is to create documents like letters, memos, and reports. Fundamentally, a word processor has the ability to perform any activity that could be carried out with a typewriter. The application of a word processor in preparing typed documents is virtually unlimited.

Word processing software like WordPerfect can improve your ability to write. Because documents can be modified easily once they have been created, the quality of a word processing document's content is usually superior to that produced manually with a typewriter. The quality of writing is further improved with the assistance of a spelling checker and thesaurus, features included in WordPerfect.

With word processing software, such as WordPerfect, the computer's display screen allows you to enter and view your document. Because many documents are several pages long, the display screen becomes your window into an electronic copy of your document. Once you have the document displayed on your screen in the manner that you want it to appear on paper, the document can be printed. That is, with some limitations, WordPerfect operates under the WYSIWYG (What You See Is What You Get) principle. Paragraphs, paging, indenting, line spacing, underlining, and tables are all WYSIWYG characteristics of a document produced with WordPerfect. Many of these characteristics are *displayed immediately* as a document is entered. Some characteristics require the use of a *special preview display* so that you can see them before they are printed. These include features like large or small print, italics, and page numbers. Overall, the primary work you do with WordPerfect is entering a document as you want it to appear in printed form, and then printing it.

WordPerfect has evolved through a number of different versions. Each version has brought new features and increased WordPerfect's functional capabilities. For example, WordPerfect version 5.1 incorporates the use of pull-down and pop-out menus to assist in selecting desired commands and to permit the use of a mouse. This feature is not available in the earlier versions of WordPerfect. Currently, the most popular versions of WordPerfect are 5.0 and 5.1. Many of the commands used in these versions are identical, but there are some differences. Where differences occur among these two versions of WordPerfect, they are indicated throughout these Lessons. You should follow the description for the version you are using. However, in the event that you find yourself using another version of WordPerfect, you can readily review their operating and command differences in these Lessons.

W.1.2 Starting WordPerfect

The exact procedure for starting WordPerfect will vary depending on your particular hardware configuration and the manner in which WordPerfect has been installed on either floppy disks or the computer's fixed disk. The procedures will vary for floppy disk usage depending on whether DOS has been placed on the WordPerfect Program Disk and for fixed disk usage depending on whether WordPerfect is accessed by using a local area network (LAN). The floppy disk procedure may require the use of two disks, with the second disk inserted when a message is displayed on the screen. Some versions of WordPerfect, such as version 5.1, require high-density floppy disks for this medium to be used. The procedures described here are general procedures. You will need to check on the exact procedures for the computer and the version of WordPerfect you are using.

These procedures assume that you will be storing your WordPerfect document files on your own floppy disk. If your document files will be stored on the computer's fixed disk, you should investigate the specific procedures for this.

Before you begin, you will need a formatted floppy disk on which you will store your WordPerfect document files. This disk will be called your Data Disk. If you do not know how to format a new Data Disk, follow the procedure described in the Using DOS section.

The standard method to activate WordPerfect is to proceed at the DOS prompt:

To start WordPerfect   **Enter:**   WP

If your procedure is different, enter the instructions here:

My procedure to start WordPerfect:

_____

_____

_____

_____

W.1.3   The WordPerfect Document Screen

The WordPerfect screen is your electronic tablet on which you create and revise documents. A Status Line appears at the bottom of the screen, as illustrated in Figure W.1, and a menu can be displayed at the top for version 5.1. This menu is not available for earlier versions of WordPerfect and is most useful when using a mouse for selecting commands. Once you name a document file, the file name of your current document appears on the left side of the Status Line. The information on the right side indicates

```
                                              Doc 1 Pg 1 Ln 1" Pos 1"
```

FIGURE W.1. Arrangement of WordPerfect document screen with Status Line at the bottom.

the current position of the cursor designated by document number, page number, line number, and character position from the left as follows:

Doc. WordPerfect can hold two documents in memory simultaneously. Doc indicates the active Doc 1 or Doc 2.

Pg. Indicates the current page number within a multipage document.

Ln. Specifies the current cursor position from the top of a page (″ indicates measure in inches; otherwise, this is a measure of the number of character positions).

Pos. Registers the current position of the cursor from the left margin (″ indicates measure in inches). The position indicator serves a dual purpose. When it appears as "Pos," <Caps Lock> is turned off; "POS" indicates <Caps Lock> is turned on. The number of inches is highlighted or is underlined when a character is underlined, whereas this measurement changes color or intensity when a character is made bold. This indicator blinks when the <Num Lock> is toggled on.

When first entering WordPerfect, Ln is 1″ and Pos is 1″, indicating that the default margins have been established at 1 in. from the left and 1 in. from the top. The right and bottom margins of each page are originally set to the same 1 in. default, and WordPerfect assumes an 8.5-by-11 in. page size. The document screen displays only the portion of the page where you type information. That is, the margins are not shown on WordPerfect's document screen, although they are used when printing the document.

W.1.4   Entering Documents

Good Morning Products (GMP), an international bottler and distributor of the Liquid Gold brand of fresh orange juice, has applied to the Last National Bank (LNB) for a loan to finance a new juicing machine that would allow GMP to increase their production capacity by 25 percent and at the same time cut the cost of oranges used in each bottle by 10 percent. The cost of this equipment is $150,000. Christopher Frost, Treasurer of Good Morning Products, filed a loan application with Edward Z. Money, Senior Vice President of Commercial Lending, at Last Bank. Ed has reviewed the loan application and is in the process of preparing a letter notifying Good Morning Products of the approval of the loan. Since Ed usually composes loan notifications like this one directly in WordPerfect, he begins by creating the main response as shown in Figure W.2.

As words are typed, WordPerfect automatically begins a new line when the right margin of the current line is reached. This word processing feature of automatically advancing to the next line is known as **word wrap.** You should *not* press <Enter> at the end of a line to advance to the next line. <Enter> is used only at the end of a paragraph, to start a new paragraph.

If a word is initially typed incorrectly, you can correct it by using the <Backspace> to remove the error and then by typing the correct word. Other methods of correcting errors exist and will be presented in subsequent sections.

Enter Ed's initial response to the loan application in this manner:

Action: Activate WordPerfect, if necessary, and obtain the document screen.

Action: Type the paragraphs *exactly* as shown in Figure W.2. Remember to let word wrap move you to the next new line and to use <Enter> only at the end of each paragraph.

```
As chairperson of the Commercial Bending Loan Committee, I want to
let ya no that our huddled today to consider the loan request for
your new fangled machine.  After carefully reviewing your financial
plant for next year, the Loan Committee has recommended the
approval of your bippy.

Since the juicing machine will serve to secure the loan, we will
need the id goodies for this machine.  You should be able to obtain
this info from the manufacturer.  Please stop by my pad to complete
the necessary stuff and arrange to have the green transferred to
you whachamacallit.




                                            Doc 1 Pg 1 Ln 2.67" Pos 2.9"
```

FIGURE W.2. Initial draft of loan application response.

Initial entry of the document is complete.

Keypoint! | The initial rough draft of the letter in Figure W.2 contains numerous errors and bad writing. This should *not* be used as an example of how you should actually create your own documents. The purpose here is to show you only how errors and bad writing like this can be subsequently corrected in this and following Lessons using the various features of WordPerfect! When you create your own documents, use your best writing to minimize the number of corrections that you will need to make!

Keypoint! | Word wrap is the feature of WordPerfect that automatically advances the cursor to the next line in your document when the right margin is reached. You do *not* press <Enter> at the end of each line, but only at the end of each paragraph!

Keypoint! | Blank lines are placed in a document by pressing <Enter> for each blank line desired!

W.1.5 Revising Documents

A WordPerfect document can be revised by moving the cursor to the appropriate location in the document and by entering the desired correction. The cursor is moved about your screen using the cursor control keys: <left>, <right>, <up>, <down>, <PgUp>, <PgDn>, <Home>, <End>, <Ctrl>+<right>,<Ctrl>+<left>, and <Ctrl>+<Home>. The actions of special combinations of these keystrokes are summarized in Figure W.3.

Cursor Movement	Keystrokes
Word left	\<Ctrl\>+\<left\>
Word right	\<Ctrl\>+\<right\>
Beginning of line	\<Home\>\<left\>
End of line	\<Home\>\<right\> or \<End\>
Top of page	\<Ctrl\>+\<Home\>\<up\>
Bottom of page	\<Ctrl\>+\<Home\>\<down\>
Top of document	\<Home\>\<Home\>\<up\>
Bottom of document	\<Home\>\<Home\>\<down\>
Screen up	− (numeric keypad)
Screen down	+ (numeric keypad)

FIGURE W.3. Special cursor movement keystrokes.

Unwanted characters are removed from documents by using either the \<Backspace\> or \<Delete\>. The \<Backspace\> removes the character immediately to the left of the cursor, whereas the \<Delete\> removes the character located at the cursor.

Caution Alert!

The \<Backspace\> and \<Delete\> keys automatically repeat their actions while they continue to be depressed. Holding down these keys can very quickly wipe out many more characters than intended!

New text for a revision is entered by merely typing it. WordPerfect has two modes of text entry: (1) insert and (2) typeover. In the insert mode, text is added to the line with the current text moved to the right. The typeover mode causes the old character to be replaced with the newly typed character. The \<Insert\> key is used to toggle between these two modes of text entry. When the typeover mode is activated, "Typeover" appears at the left side of WordPerfect's Status Line.

Ed wants you to make several changes to the initial document by proceeding as follows:

Action: Make sure the initial document is still displayed on your screen.

To insert a word	**Move to:**	h in huddled	
	Type:	group\<space\>	Insert the word "group"
To typeover a word	**Move to:**	f in fangled	
	Press:	\<Insert\>	Toggle on typeover
	Type:	juicing	Replace the word
To remove an unwanted character	**Move to:**	t in plant	
	Press:	\<Delete\>	Remove the unwanted "t"
	Move to:	\<space\> following info	
	Press:	\<Insert\>	Toggle on insert
	Type:	rmation	Complete the word

These revisions are completed.

W.1.6   Saving Documents

A WordPerfect document is saved by storing it on your Data Disk. Until you save your document, you could lose it if your computer is turned off or if you exit from WordPerfect. Two situations occur in saving a document: (1) the document is newly created and has *not* been named, and (2) the document has been previously saved to disk. With a newly created document, you give it a file name when you save it for the first time. For an existing document, you may store it as a file with the same name or give it a new file name.

You can save Ed's newly created document file in this manner:

| To save a new document file | **Press:** | <F10> | Save and Resume function key |
| | **Enter:** | B:LETTER.DOC | Disk drive identifier for your Data Disk and a name for your file; if you are using a different disk drive for your Data Disk, be sure to use your disk drive identifier here and in the subsequent entries! |

The document is stored as the LETTER.DOC file. The document remains displayed on your screen so you can "Resume" or continuing working with it.

Keypoint!

> If something goes wrong, don't panic! Help is only a keystroke away. You can obtain information on many of WordPerfect's features!
>
> Press the <F3> function key and the WordPerfect help menu appears!
>
> Press the <F3> function key twice to display the WordPerfect function key template shown in Figure W.4! Use <Shift>+<PrtSc> to print out your own copy!
>
> Press <Enter> or <space> to exit Help!

WordPerfect does *not* require or automatically assign an extension in naming the file containing your document. The extension DOC is recommended as a convenient method to assist you in identifying your WordPerfect document files stored on your Data Disk. If you choose to use a different extension, the best situation is to be consistent, because this will help you identify your WordPerfect files from other files whenever a list of your file names is produced.

Once this document file has been saved, it becomes an existing file, which can be replaced in subsequent saves.

| To save an existing document file | **Press:** | <F10> | Save and Resume function key |

This message is displayed in the Status Line:

Document to be saved: B:\LETTER.DOC

| | **Press:** | <Enter> | Accept the current file name |

This prompt appears:

Replace B:\LETTER.DOC? No (Yes)

| | **Press:** | <Y> | Cause the file to be saved by replacing the old copy of the file with the current version |

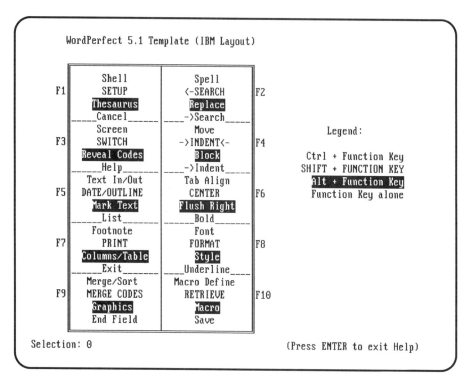

FIGURE W.4. Function key usage displayed from Help.

Once the file has been replaced, you are ready to continue working with your current document.

~~ *Caution Alert!* ~~~~~~~~	Replacing a file destroys the prior copy of the file. If you want to keep the old copy of the file, then enter a different file name when the old file name is displayed!

▬▬▬▬ *Keypoint!*	WordPerfect document file names must follow the DOS file-naming conventions, with up to eight characters for the filename and zero to three characters for the extension!

~~ *Caution Alert!* ~~~~~~~~	Save your document frequently, at least every 15 minutes. Then, if something goes wrong, you will not have lost all your work!

W.1.7 Printing Documents

A document is printed out by using WordPerfect's Print menu. This menu is accessed with the Print <Shift>+<F7> command. The menu appears as illustrated in Figure W.5. Several print actions and options are available. Those activities used in creating printed copies of your document are described as follows:

Full Document (Text). Prints all the pages of your currently active document.

Page. Prints the individual page where the cursor is currently located.

```
Print

        1 - Full Document
        2 - Page
        3 - Document on Disk
        4 - Control Printer
        5 - Multiple Pages
        6 - View Document
        7 - Initialize Printer


Options

        S - Select Printer                HP LaserJet Series II
        B - Binding Offset                0"
        N - Number of Copies              1
        U - Multiple Copies Generated by  WordPerfect
        G - Graphics Quality              Medium
        T - Text Quality                  High




Selection: 0
```

FIGURE W.5. Print menu.

Document on Disk. Prints a document from a file stored on disk. This does not need to be your currently active document.

Control Printer. Provides control over printing that includes terminating the printing of a document.

View Document (Preview). Displays a WYSIWYG preview of the layout of each page of a document prior to printing the document.

WYSIWYG, What You See Is What You Get, indicates that the image displayed on your screen is what will be printed. This means that you can actually see the various characteristics of your document before it is printed. If you don't like your document's appearance, you can change it before you actually print it.

As you learn more about WordPerfect, you may want to explore other print options that allow you to produce printed hard copy output.

Once the Print menu has been accessed, selections from the menu are made by

1. Typing the number or letter preceding each menu selection or
2. Typing the highlighted letter of the command name, which is usually the first letter of the command name.

Let's produce a printed copy of Ed's first draft of his letter.

To produce a printed copy of your document	**Action:**	Make sure your printer is attached to your computer and is turned on. If necessary, adjust the paper so printing will begin at the top of a new page.
	Press:	`<Shift>+<F7>` Access Print menu
	Press:	`<1>` or `<F>` Select Print the full document or text

The document is printed.

Action: Remove the printed document from your printer.

Keypoint!

> When your document is printed, the right margin appears justified with spaces added between words to enable this "full-justification." This is WordPerfect's default for printing documents. Your document is printed with full-justification, although it is *not* displayed on your screen that way. For now, accept your printed documents with full-justification. In later Lessons, you will learn how to change this!

Keypoint!

> WordPerfect menu selections are made by
>
> 1. Typing the number or letter preceding each menu selection
>
>   or
>
> 2. Typing the highlighted letter of the command name, which is usually the first letter of the command name
>
>   or
>
> 3. Using the mouse to click on the menu choice with the <left-button>.

W.1.8   Halting Document Printing

Once you have started printing a document, you may suddenly decide that you want to abandon the printing process. Ed's draft letter is so short a document that the entire document may be printed before termination is requested. However, this feature is quite useful for longer documents that you may create.

Printing is halted using the Print menu. To explore the interruption of printing Ed's draft letter, proceed in this manner: First, start printing the document:

Press: `<Shift>+<F7>`   Access Print menu

Select: `Full Document (text)`

Second, interrupt the document while it is being printed, as follows:

To terminate printing a document

Press: `<Shift>+<F7>`   Access Print menu

Select: `Control Printer`

Select: `Cancel Job`   Desired action

Follow the screen instructions and return to the document:

Press: `<F7>`   Exit the Control Printer menu and return to the document

The printing of the document is terminated, and you are ready to continue editing your document.

W.1.9 Menu Choices and Commands

The predominant WordPerfect commands are executed by using the function keys as previously illustrated in Figure W.4. For example, the SAVE command is executed with the <F10> function key. For WordPerfect 5.0, these commands must be executed by using these function keys. With WordPerfect version 5.1, a line menu, pull-down menus, and pop-out menus may be used to assist in the selection of commands, as illustrated in Figure W.6.

WordPerfect 5.1 menus can be operated with a mouse, if this device is available with your computer. Menu selections are made by pointing to the desired menu selection and then clicking a mouse button.

The rest of this section describes the use of menus in version 5.1. If you do not have this version, you may either skip this section and go to Section W.1.10; or, you may merely read this section to gain an understanding of this version of WordPerfect.

For WordPerfect 5.1, the main menu is accessed in this manner:

To access the version 5.1 main menu

Press: <Alt>+<=>   Selections can now be made from the menu

or

Click: <right-mouse-button>

If the main menu is not always displayed at the top of your WordPerfect screen, the <Alt>+<=> or <right-mouse-button> causes it to appear and allows menu selections to be made.

When the menu cursor is located in the main menu, you can return to the document mode by using the Cancel <F1> command or the <Esc>. With the menu displayed and the cursor in the main menu, return to the document mode:

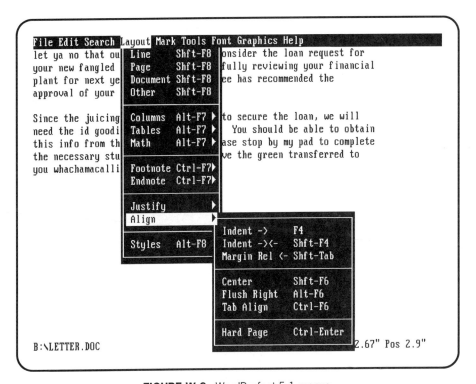

FIGURE W.6. WordPerfect 5.1 menus.

To return to the document mode from the main menu	**Press:**	Cancel <F1>	Return to document mode when menu cursor is located in the main menu
		or	
	Click:	<right-mouse-button>	

Once the main menu has been accessed, a pull-down menu is obtained (1) by typing the highlighted letter of the menu choice, usually the first letter, (2) by moving the menu cursor to the desired choice with the <left> or <right> cursor movement keys and then pressing <down> for the pull-down menu, or (3) by positioning the mouse pointer on the desired menu choice and clicking the <left-mouse-button>. The menu cursor can then be moved to the desired command, which is selected by pressing <Enter>. A menu choice with the arrowhead (▶) indicates the availability of a pop-out menu. This is accessed by using the <right> cursor key or clicking on the menu choice with the <left-mouse-button>. For each WordPerfect command that can be executed using the functions keys, these keys are specified on each pull-down or pop-out menu.

An example of using menus in WordPerfect 5.1 to save the current document file is as follows:

To save a document file using version 5.1 menu commands	**Press:**	<Alt>+<=>	Access the WordPerfect 5.1 menu
	Select:	File	Press <F> or press <down> since the menu cursor is located on File
	Move to:	Save	Use <down> to move menu cursor
	Press:	<Enter>	Select SAVE command

The message displayed on the Status Line is

Document to be saved: B:\LETTER.DOC

| | **Press:** | <Enter> | Accept the current file name |

The prompt on the Status Line is now

Replace B:\LETTER.DOC? No (Yes)

| | **Press:** | <Y> | Cause the file to be saved by replacing the old copy |

In this example with the WordPerfect 5.1 menu, once the SAVE command is selected, the remaining steps in executing the command are identical to those when the SAVE command is executed with the Save <F10> function key. This relationship between the version 5.1 menu and the function keys is the same for the other commands.

When selecting commands for execution for the examples that follow, you may use either the functions keys or the menus, depending on your version of WordPerfect and your preferences.

Keypoint!

WordPerfect commands may be selected for execution either by using the functions keys or by using menus with version 5.1. In the descriptions of WordPerfect that follow, the name of the command, such as SAVE or EXIT will be used in specifying the selection of a command for execution!

W.1.10 Reversing Menu Choices

The Cancel <F1> function key or the <Esc> key nullifies the current command and is used to "undo" or "back up" from the last menu selection or entry. In some situations, you may need to hit the <Esc> key twice. The Exit <F7> may be used to back out of menus in all versions of WordPerfect. For WordPerfect 5.1, the Exit <F7> terminates menu processing and returns to the document mode when using pull-down menus.

In general,

1. To back up one level in a menu structure, press Cancel <F1>, press <Esc>, or click the <right-mouse-button>. Each time you strike <F1> or <Esc>, you back up one level until you return to the document mode.

2. To get to the document mode from *anywhere* in the pull-down menu structure, press the Exit <F7> function key or click the <right-mouse-button>.

W.1.11 Previewing Documents

The layout of a document on a page can be previewed before printing. By performing a Preview (<Shift>+<F7> 6), you can determine whether you like the overall appearance of the document. A scaled-down view of each page of the document can be obtained as illustrated in Figure W.7. If the layout is not what you want, modify it before printing. This time-saving feature of WordPerfect lets you make sure that you like the appearance of a document before waiting for it to print. For longer documents, you can use <PgUp> and <PgDn> to move through the document, looking at each page layout. Also, you can preview a document from the Print menu by selecting Preview.

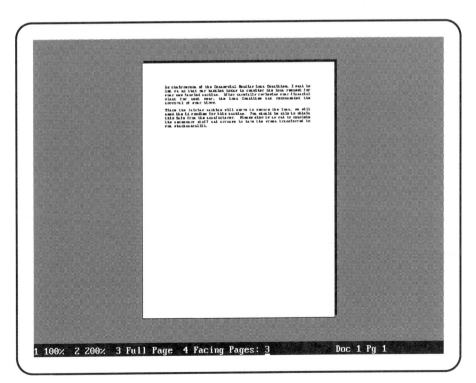

FIGURE W.7. View Document layout prior to printing.

You can preview Ed's draft letter by proceeding in this manner:

To preview a document	**Select:**	Print <Shift>+<F7>	Access the Print menu The PRINT command may be selected from the File pull-down menu in version 5.1
	Select:	View Document	Press <6> or <V>, the number or letter to make this menu selection
	Press:	<3>	Select Full Page display mode

The document appears in the "Full Page" mode, as illustrated in Figure W.7.

| | **Press:** | <1> | Select 100 percent display mode, which is an enlarged view of the document layout |

The document displayed with the VIEW DOCUMENT command is shown in its WYSIWYG form. This includes the "full-justification" for the right margin in the same manner as the ultimate printed output.

When you have completed your preview, then continue:

| | **Press:** | Exit <F7> | Exit from the View Document and Print menu |

Any desired changes in the layout of the document can now be made before printing it.

Caution Alert!   You *cannot* make changes to a document in the View mode. Use Exit <F7> to return to the Document mode to *correct* any errors detected while "viewing" the document!

Caution Alert!   If a graphics board is *not* installed in your computer, then these images may *not* be displayed in detail!

W.1.12 Leaving WordPerfect

When you have finished using WordPerfect, use the Exit <F7> command as described here. As you exit from WordPerfect, you are given the opportunity to save your current document, if desired. Let's exit and save your file.

| To exit and save your document file | **Select:** | Exit <F7> | Desired activity. Exit is reached from the File pull-down menu |

A message like this appears in the Status Line:

Save document? Yes (No)

| | **Press:** | <Enter> or <Y> | Select save document |

Then this prompt is displayed:

Document to be saved: B:\LETTER.DOC

| | **Press:** | <Enter> | Accept the suggested file name |

The following message results:

Replace B:\LETTER.DOC? No (Yes)

Press: <Y>   Select replace the file

This results in a display of the prompt:

Exit WP? No (Yes)

Press: <Y>   Select exit WordPerfect

You are now returned to the DOS prompt to continue any other activities.

Keypoint! Be sure to save your document file on your Data Disk before you leave WordPerfect. Once you exit WordPerfect, the electronic copy in the computer's memory is lost!

W.1.13 Retrieving WordPerfect Document Files

An existing WordPerfect document file can be retrieved from disk storage and loaded into WordPerfect for editing by one of two methods. The first method requires that you know the name of the document file, whereas the second method prompts you with a list of files from which you can make a selection. The Retrieve <Shift>+<F10> command is used to access a file when you know its name. The List Files <F5> command facilitates retrieving a file from a list generated by WordPerfect, as well as performing other operations on a file. An example of the List Files screen is shown in Figure W.8, and a description of each List Files operation is contained in the Help screen shown in Figure W.9.

Once a file has been saved to disk, it can be printed from the List Files screen. This provides an alternative for the printing of saved document files. Ed's draft letter can be loaded into WordPerfect directly with Retrieve <Shift>+<F10> command in this manner:

Action: Activate WordPerfect, if necessary.

To retrieve an existing document file

Select: Retrieve <Shift>+<F10>   Retrieve command. This command may be reached from the File pull-down menu

This message appears in the Status Line:

Document to be retrieved:

Enter: B:\LETTER.DOC   Name of the file to be retrieved including its disk drive identifier

The file LETTER.DOC is retrieved from the disk in drive B: and is ready for editing in the document mode.

Alternatively, you can retrieve Ed's file by using the List File command as follows:

To retrieve an existing document file using the File List command

Select: List Files <F5>   Access List Files. List Files is on the Files pull-down menu

A message is displayed in the Status Line indicating your default disk drive and directory, such as:

Dir C:\WP51*.*

```
10-21-94  10:51a              Directory B:\*.*
Document size:         0  Free:    361,472 Used:        993    Files:      1

 .     Current    <Dir>             | ..    Parent      <Dir>
LETTER   .DOC       993 10-21-94 10:50a














1 Retrieve; 2 Delete; 3 Move/Rename; 4 Print; 5 Short/Long Display;
6 Look; 7 Other Directory; 8 Copy; 9 Find; N Name Search: 6
```

FIGURE W.8. List Files screen.

```
List

    Displays a list of files or equation commands, depending on when you press
    this key.  Pressing List (F5) at the normal editing screen invokes the
    List Files feature which lists all files that match the filename template
    (pattern) given.  When WordPerfect displays the template (e.g.,
    c:\files\*.*), press Enter to display all the files in the current default
    directory, or edit the template to display the directory and files you
    wish to view.

    To perform an action on a file, move the cursor to the file before
    selecting the action.  To perform an action on several files at once, mark
    each of the files (i.e., move to each file and press *) and then select
    the action.  You can then delete, print, copy, or search the marked files.
    To print the directory listing, press Print (Shift-F7).

    Pressing List at a "Filename:" prompt (e.g., Graphics Box Definition,
    Style Definition) allows you to use List Files to find and retrieve a
    file.  Pressing List in the Equation Editor moves the cursor to the list
    of equation commands.

1 Retrieve; 2 Delete; 3 Move/Rename; 4 Print; 5 Short/Long Display;
6 Look; 7 Other Directory; 8 Copy; 9 Find; N Name Search

Selection: 0                                    (Press ENTER to exit Help)
```

FIGURE W.9. Help screen displaying List Files command actions.

Enter:	B:	Specify the disk drive
Move to:	LETTER.DOC	Select the desired file
Select:	Retrieve	Use number or first letter selection

This message is displayed on the Status Line:

Retrieve into current document? No (Yes)

Press:	<Y>	Request the retrieve to be performed

At this point, if your response was "No," then the document would *not* be retrieved, and the File List menu would continue to be displayed.

Caution Alert!

> *Never* retrieve any WordPerfect program files (those with a file name starting with WP or with an extension of COM or EXE), because you may damage them, and WordPerfect will no longer work!

What happened when you retrieved the document the second time? Instead of merely replacing the current document, it was added to the existing document at the location of your cursor. Whenever you have an existing document and retrieve another document, this will occur. The problem can be avoided by clearing your current document before retrieving another document as described in the next section.

W.1.14 Clearing a Document

Before you commence work on a new document or retrieve an existing document, you should clear the current document and obtain a blank document screen. This avoids the problem of scrambling documents together. The current document can be cleared by using the Exit <F7> command.

Let's clear Ed's document in preparation for working on another document.

To clear the current document

Press:	Exit <F7>	Desired command Available on the Files pull-down menu

A message appears, as before with Exit:

Save document? Yes (No)

Press:	<N>	Do *not* save the scrambled document

The prompt is displayed:

Exit WP? No (Yes)

Select:	No	Choose *not* to exit

You are thus returned to the document mode with a "clean screen" ready for your next activity.

Caution Alert!

> When you have been working on one document and want to switch to another document, be sure to save your file and then to clear the current document *before* you retrieve the other document!

W.1.15 When Things Go Wrong

Several situations may occur when you are initially entering your document into WordPerfect. Some of the more common difficulties and how to approach them are described here:

1. Unwanted text has been entered in your document. You want to get rid of it and replace it with different text.
   a. Position the cursor at the location of the unwanted text.
   b. Use <Delete> or <Backspace> to remove the unwanted text.
   c. Type the desired text. By toggling on the Overtype mode with <Insert>, you may be able to type over the unwanted text without first removing it. If you use Overtype, be sure to toggle it off so that you do *not* accidentally type over text that you do want.

2. You created and saved a document but you do not remember the file name you gave it. You want to retrieve the document to continue working with it.
   a. Make sure you have cleared the current document. If necessary, use Exit <F7> to do this, but do not exit from WordPerfect.
   b. Use Retrieve <Shift>+<F10> to initiate the file retrieval process, followed by List Files <F5>, or just press List Files <F5> twice, to obtain a list of existing files.
   c. When the current default directory is displayed, press <Enter> to accept this; otherwise, enter the disk drive identifier for the disk drive you want to access.
   d. A list of your existing files appears. Locate the desired name, move the cursor to it, and select Retrieve. The file is accessed as your current document and you can continue working with it.

W.1.16 Lesson Summary

- A WordPerfect document screen is the equivalent of electronic paper on which a document is typed.
- WordPerfect employs a limited WYSIWYG method of creating documents for printing; however, the Print View Document (Preview) command is required to see all of the characteristics of the final printed output.
- Word wrap automatically advances the entry of text to a new line when the right margin is encountered.
- <Enter> is used at the end of each paragraph and to insert blank lines in a document.
- <Backspace> and <Delete> can be used to make corrections as a document is initially entered.
- <F10>, the Save and Resume function key, is used to store a document as a disk file.
- A printed copy of a document is obtained with the Print <Shift>+<F7> command.
- The default in WordPerfect is to print a document with "full-justification" rather than a ragged right margin.
- The printing process can be terminated by using the CONTROL PRINTER and CANCEL JOB commands.
- The overall appearance of a document can be previewed prior to printing with the Print <Shift>+<F7> View Document (Preview) command, which displays the document in its final WYSIWYG form.

- The Exit <F7> command is used to exit from WordPerfect and return to DOS. When used with a menu, Exit <F7> returns processing to the document mode.
- A document can be retrieved with the Retrieve <Shift>+<F10> command or with the List Files <F5> command.
- An existing document must be cleared from WordPerfect's memory before beginning a new document or retrieving a different document to avoid scrambled documents.
- Always save your work on your Data Disk before you exit WordPerfect or retrieve a new document.

W.1.17 Practice Tutorial

Produce the draft LETTER document described in this Lesson as a guided activity in a hands-on manner. Clear your current WordPerfect document before you begin. Remember the utilization of the keywords as described in Lesson T.2 of the section Using Software Tools.

Task 1: Create the initial draft as illustrated in Figure W.2.

Task 2: Make the revisions to the draft described in Section W.1.5.

Task 3: Print the revised draft of the letter.

Task 4: Save this document as the file MYLETR.DOC.

Time Estimates

Novice: 60 minutes

Intermediate: 45 minutes

Advanced: 30 minutes

W.1.18 Practice Exercises

Keypoint!

> The first draft of the letters in these Practice Exercises contain numerous errors and bad writing. Do *not* use these as examples of how you should actually create your own documents. The intent is to show you how errors and bad writing like this can be corrected using the various features of WordPerfect in this and the next Lesson!

Case: Crazy River Canoe

Business Problem: Advertising Media Preparation

MIS Characteristics: Marketing

Operational Control

Harry Ross, a rugged outdoorsman, is Crazy River Canoe's director of marketing. He is in the process of preparing a draft copy of a letter to be sent to prospective canoeing enthusiasts. Harry hopes to convince them of the benefits of outdoor fun that comes from canoeing and of the virtues of owning a Crazy River. He wants you to create a draft copy of his document. Clear your current WordPerfect document before you begin. Make the requested changes as detailed below. Enter the following document:

Canoeing is a sport where you propel your own dinghy. Poorly designed equipment can prove to be a major hassle of great inconvenience in the pursuit of happiness paddling. You are the captain. It's your boot, and the adventure you quest is yours alone. A vessel allows you to experience the wilderness that faced our earlier frontier champions.

True adventure, rugged individualism, and self-reliance belong to an age in the past. They have given way to Kevlar, polypro, Gore-Tex, and goosedown boo ties. Today when we head for the out doors we rely on Jet-Age technology. Before you find yourself up a body of water without any means of transportation, consider the benefits of a Crazy River Canoe.

As paddlers, canoes provide a opportunity unique to get away from the handholds of civilization. Grab you propel, clean you flintlock, pack up you knapsack, and pay Lewis and Clark.

Task 1: Enter the initial draft of the document.

Task 2: Change "dinghy" to "boat." Change "body of water" to "creek."

Task 3: Delete "hassle of great."

Task 4: Insert "viable" between "without any" and "means of transportation."

Task 5: Save the document as file CANOE.DOC.

Task 6: Print the document.

Time Estimates

Novice: 60 minutes

Intermediate: 45 minutes

Advanced: 30 minutes

W.1.19   Comprehensive Problems

(1)   Case: Home Real Estate

Business Problem: Customer Inquiries
MIS Characteristics: Marketing
                                        Operational Control

Home Real Estate was founded as a full-service real estate company in 1953 by Ronald Burger. Since its founding, Home Real Estate has experienced significant growth and acquired several other smaller real estate firms. The current operation includes seven offices in the metropolitan area staffed by nearly 80 sales associates. Although Ron still provides general direction to the company by serving as the Chairman of the Board of Directors, the day-to-day operations are under the guidance of Warren Bridges, Home's President and Chief Operating Officer. As the business grew, Ron organized it into three divisions: residential sales, commercial sales, and property management. Residential sales are managed by Marge Mills, while Felix Rodriguez is in charge of commercial sales, and J. P. Morgan coordinates the property management of rental real estate.

Park Place Villas is a new development of rental units administered by J. P.'s staff in the Property Management Division. These townhomes are available as both standard and deluxe units with either two or three bedrooms. A standard two-bedroom unit rents for $410 per month, whereas the deluxe unit is $450 per month. For the three bedroom townhomes, a standard unit is $520 per month, and the deluxe is $570/month.

Krista Buffett, the resident manager of Park Place Villas, is responsible for the rental and maintenance of these townhomes. Krista receives a number of requests for rental information from prospective tenants. Many of these are telephone inquires. J. P. encourages Krista to follow up telephone inquiries with a letter describing the benefits of Park Place Villas. Krista met with J. P. to discuss her ideas for improving communications by developing a new letter for these follow-ups. She started the development of a letter that informs prospective tenants about the townhomes. The content of her initial draft of the letter is as follows:

Thank you for your asking about Park Place Villas. Our townhome apartments offer some of the finest in living modern for today's active group.

These apartments have the utmost in privacy, with entrances separate and individual attached garages. Other niceties of each unit include full carpeting, appliances, a private patio, and plenty of storage. In addition, our deluxe units include a microwave oven and whirlpool thing.

Krista wants you to use WordPerfect to assist in the development of this letter by completing the following tasks:

Task 1: Access WordPerfect and enter Krista's draft letter. [*Hint:* This letter consists of only two paragraphs. Use <Enter> only at the end of each paragraph and for the blank line between paragraphs. The word wrap feature should control the placement of the text on each line within a paragraph.]

Task 2: Review the letter for any typing errors that you may have made and correct them.

Task 3: Preview the letter on your screen.

Task 4: Print the letter.

Task 5: Save this document as file RENT.DOC.

Task 6: Edit the letter by making these changes:

    (1) In the first line of the first paragraph, change the word "asking" to "inquiry."

    (2) In the first line of the first paragraph, add an "s" to "townhome" and remove the word "apartments."

    (3) In the second paragraph, change the word "niceties" to "amenities."

Task 7: Preview your document and print it.

Task 8: Save this document as file RENT2.DOC.

Time Estimates

Novice: 75 minutes

Intermediate: 45 minutes

Advanced: 30 minutes

(2) Case: Pioneer Electric and Gas

    Business Problem: Customer Relations

    MIS Characteristics: Marketing

                       Operational Control

Pioneer Electric and Gas (PEG) is a publically owned utility serving the needs of more than 100,000 customers in the tricounty area. The customer relations division has experienced an increase in the number of complaints concerning changes in the service performed by PEG employees. This is partially owing to the economic growth and development of the tricounty region. The director of customer relations, Ramon Mora, is concerned. He called Mary Marshall, the manager of customer services, to his office to discuss their problem. Mary stated that the number of requests for service has been growing at the rate of 14 percent per year, although the number of employees processing these requests has not increased in the last three years.

Kelli Olsen, a customer service representative, handles customer inquires. A customer may request a repair, change, or connection for either gas or electric service. Kelli talks with each customer to determine the type of service desired. She explains PEG's fees for a service change or connection (there are no charges for repairs). A service change involves a change in billing for existing service, whereas a connection is concerned with the installation of new service. The primary activity performed for a service change is a meter reading and issuance of any final billing. A connection occurs when a new dwelling is constructed and the utility service initiated, which requires the installation of a gas or electric meter. PEG charges $35 for a change in electrical service and $25 for gas service. If both are changed at the same time, the fee is $50. PEG's connection fee for new service is $250 for gas service and $175 for electrical service.

When one customer requests a termination of service at an address, another customer does not always initiate service immediately. In this situation, the service to that address is turned off until a separate request is received to start it for the next customer. As part of processing these service requests, Kelli sends each customer an acknowledgment.

After Mary returned from her meeting with Ramon, she sat down with Kelli to discuss ways for improving operations in customer services. They believe that communications can be improved by developing a new letter that acknowledges the request for service. The content of their first draft of the letter is as follows:

Your appeal for service has been received and is being examined. As arranged by our customer service guy, technicians service are being scheduled to handle promptly your big deal. They will contact you by phone to notify you of the time they arriving at your humble deal.

All PEG employees carry a photo identification thing. Please don't hesitate to ask for identification before submitting an employee to your deal. If in doubt, phone 554-4100.

For thousands of PEG customers, a handy Level Payment Plan spreads the differences seasonal in utility service bills over an entire year. Each June PEG calculates the Level Payment Plan for the next 12 months, based on previous consumption, normal weather, and any planned rate adjustment. You pay the same amount each month, and you earn interest at the annual rate of 7% for each month your Level Payment results in a credit balance. All accounts are squared the following June. For customer greater convenience, the Level Payment Plan. Phone 554-PLAN.

Using WordPerfect, Mary wants you to prepare a first draft of the letter by completing these tasks:

Task 1: Activate WordPerfect and enter the letter as drafted by Mary and Kelli. [*Hint:* This letter consists of only three paragraphs. You should use the <Enter> only at the end of each paragraph and to provide the blank line between paragraphs. The word wrap feature should control the exact placement of the text on each line within a paragraph.]

Task 2: Review the letter for any typing errors you may have made while entering the letter and correct them.

Task 3: Preview the letter on your screen.

Task 4: Print this letter.

Task 5: Save this document as file PEG.DOC.

Task 6: Edit the letter by making these revisions:
  (a) In the first line of the first paragraph, change the word "appeal" to "request."
  (b) In the second sentence of the first paragraph, change "big deal" to "request."
  (c) In the last line of the first paragraph, remove the word "humble."
  (d) In the second paragraph, change the word "submitting" to "admitting."
  (e) In the third paragraph, add the word "out" following the word "spreads."

Task 7: Preview your document and print it.

Task 8: Save this document as file PEG2.DOC.

Time Estimates

Novice: 75 minutes

Intermediate: 45 minutes

Advanced: 30 minutes

W.1.20   Case Application

Case: Cutting Edge Equipment

Business Problem: Quality management system

MIS Characteristics: Production

Managerial Control

Special Characteristic: Information System Request

Management Functions: Planning

Organizing

Tools Skills: Entering text

Revising text

Saving documents

Printing documents

Cutting Edge Equipment (CEE) manufactures lawn mowers and other power equipment at its plant in Watsonville, North Carolina. CEE builds some of the world's finest walk-behind mowers. CEE Power Equipment associates carefully cast, machine, weld, paint, and assemble power mowers from the ground up. They even make their own four-stroke engines. After dozens of rigorous quality checks, every mower is started before it is shipped. Whether it's traveling across the country or being exported to destinations as distant as Germany or Japan, each American-made CEE is built to go the distance, because before any CEE lawn mower leaves Watsonville, CEE's manufacturing associates make sure it will cut grass.

Several years ago, Victor Zuberi, CEE's President, implemented Just-In-Time (JIT) production systems with total quality management (TQM). Vic explains TQM in this manner: "Total quality management is 'building in' product quality and not 'inspecting it in.' " With TQM, all Power Equipment associates are responsible for maintaining quality, not just "leaving it to the quality control department." With a TQM approach, a quality product is produced at each step in the manufacturing process. The other alternative is to build the entire product and then to check the quality. The mowers that do not pass the test are rejected as defective and must be reworked to correct their defects. Vic has learned that a better product can be fabricated at a lower cost by using the TQM approach. Repairing defective lawn mowers can significantly increase the total cost of manufacturing.

The JIT production system at CEE has allowed the company to minimize inventory investment, react faster to demand changes, and more quickly uncover quality problems. With JIT, every component part is expected to be correctly produced as that part arrives at the next stage in the manufacturing process, just as it is needed. Inventories are virtually eliminated.

To help ensure the smooth operation of their JIT production system, CEE makes use of quality circles. A quality circle is a group of employees who meet regularly to discuss their job functions and the problems they are encountering, to devise solutions to those problems, and to propose solutions to their management.

Karl Sharma works in the engine manufacturing cell, which is responsible for producing the completed mower engine. As engines are produced, they are tested to check their operation. Repairs are made on engines that are found to be defective. The number of engines that need to be repaired each day can vary because of the variability in the manufacturing processes. These "defects" are monitored to determine if changes are necessary in the manufacturing process.

Recently, Karl met with his quality circle to discuss defects. As part of CEE's TQM program, Karl monitors the number of defects each day by using a control chart like that shown in Figure W.10. As indicated by Karl, "the primary purpose of a control chart is to provide a basis for action. The control chart signals when a process requires action." He spends, at least, a half-hour preparing this chart at the end of each day. After considerable discussion, the members of the circle have suggested to management that this process be automated. Karl's quality circle would like to have an information system that prepares control charts installed on the computer located in their manufacturing cell. This computer is already used for production scheduling and other manufacturing reporting activities. However, members of Karl's quality circle think that adequate computer time may be available for the daily production of their control chart. This would provide more time for analyzing potential problems and improving their manufacturing operations.

At the recommendation of Karl's quality circle, Kendra Slade, Manager of Engine Fabrication, is preparing an information system request for a feasibility assessment study of this control charting system. A feasibility assessment determines the technical, economic, and operational feasibility of a system. Questions that would be addressed include: can the control system be developed by using available hardware and software, will it be cost effective, and will it work when it is installed? Also, the system might be used by other manufacturing cells. Kendra has started writing the information system request. However, she has been too busy to finish the final draft and would like your assistance in completing it.

Tasks

1. Access WordPerfect and enter the following paragraphs describing this information system request:

In their survey of the application of damage control charts to unique manufacturing, the quality circle determined that the automation of this analysis would greatly assist them in tracking and improving quality. Preliminary requirements that have been identified by the quality circle for the QMS are (1) the ability to prepare control charts for several different manufacturing and assembly processes, (2) the entry and editing of quality control data, and (3) the computations of the statistics for control charts.

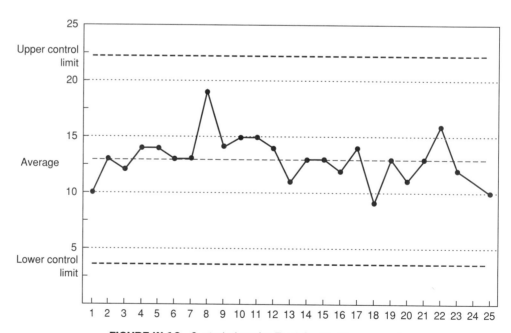

FIGURE W.10. Control chart for Total Quality Management.

The team's initial indicates that this system might be used in other manufacturing areas. Manufacturing departments already have computer stuff that supports production scheduling and other manufacturing reporting activities. It appears that this same equipment might be used for this proposed control chart quality management system.

Would you please undertake this here investigation. The quality round circle will meet with your staff to further discuss their ideas and provide additional information concerning the creation of control charts. Please contact Karl Sharma at extension 4357 to arrange a convenient meeting time with the entire quality circle team.

If you cannot proceed with the feasibility study, please contact me immediately to discuss our available alternatives. This system is important in meeting our quality improvement goals for the coming model year.

2. Review the document for any typing errors you may have made and correct them.

3. Preview the document on your screen. Print the document and save it as file REQUEST.DOC.

4. Edit the letter by making these changes:

   (a) In the first sentence of the first paragraph, change "survey" to "evaluation."

   (b) In the first sentence of the first paragraph, remove the word "damage."

   (c) In the first sentence of the first paragraph, change the word "unique" to "engine."

   (d) In the first sentence of the second paragraph, insert the word "review" following the word "initial."

   (e) In the second paragraph change the word "stuff" to "hardware."

   (f) In the first sentence of the third paragraph, delete the word "here."

   (g) In the second sentence of the third paragraph, delete the word "round."

   (h) In the second sentence of the third paragraph, change the word "staff" to "team of information services associates."

   (i) Make the changes necessary to add a fourth item to the end of the last sentence in the first paragraph, which is as follows:

   "(4) the printing of a completed chart for analysis."

5. Preview the document and save it as file REQUEST2.DOC.

6. Clear the current document from WordPerfect and retrieve the file QMS.DOC. Position your edit cursor at the bottom of this document and retrieve the document REQUEST2.DOC.

7. Review the combined document, which is the completed information system request. Print this document and save it as file REQUEST3.DOC.

Time Estimates

Novice: 90 minutes

Intermediate: 75 minutes

Advanced: 40 minutes

Modifying and Correcting Documents

CONTENT

- Adding to an Existing Document
- Checking and Correcting Spelling
- Deleting Text
- Undeleting Text
- Rearranging Text
- Searching for Text
- Searching for and Replacing Text
- Using the Thesaurus
- Revealing Codes
- Making Modifications
- When Things Go Wrong

W.2.1 Adding to Existing Documents

Documents are modified and corrected by adding text to existing documents and by replacing and rearranging text within a document. Ed wants to modify his draft letter by adding text as shown in Figure W.11. This includes the letter's date, inside address, salutation, additional text, closing, signature line, and title line. These changes are accomplished by moving the cursor to the desired location and inserting the desired text.

The changes to Ed's document are made in this manner:

Action: Access WordPerfect and retrieve the LETTER.DOC file from the prior Lesson.

To position the cursor at the top of your document	**Press:**	`<Home> <Home> <up>`	Position the cursor at the top of the document
	Press:	`<Enter>`	Add another blank line at the top of the document

Press:	`<up>`	Move the cursor to the newly created blank line
Enter:	`February 21, 1994`	Add the date as a paragraph and insert another line
Press:	`<Enter>`	Add one blank line as a paragraph
Action:	Enter three more blank lines between the date and inside address, as shown in Figure W.11.	
Action:	Enter the four lines for the inside address, with each line as a new paragraph, as shown in Figure W.11.	
Press:	`<Enter>`	Add another blank line
Enter:	`Dear Chris:`	Add the salutation
Press:	`<Enter>`	Add one more blank line

This completes the addition of the date, inside address, and salutation at the top of the document.

Now, let's add to the body of the document.

To add to the body of an existing document

Move to:	The end of the first paragraph of the body of the letter, that is, following the text, "`...the approval of your bippy.`"	
Action:	Enter the two new sentences in the same manner as the original text was entered. Remember, you do *not* press <Enter> when you reach the right margin.	

The text is added to the body of Ed's draft letter.

February 21, 1994

Mr. Chris Frost, Treasurer
Good Morning Products
911 Orange Blossom Lane
Citrus Grove Valley, CA 95941

Dear Chris:

As chairperson of the Commercial Bending Loan Committee, I want to let ya no that our group huddled today to consider the loan request for your new juicing machine. After carefully reviewing your financial plan for next year, the Loan Committee has recommended the approval of your bippy. **In addition, the loan carries with it the requirement to maintain a balance minimum of $5,000 in your checking account. The loan will have an interest rate of 11.5%.**

Since the juicing machine will serve to secure the loan, we will need the id goodies for this machine. You should be able to obtain this information from the manufacturer. Please stop by my pad to complete the necessary stuff and arrange to have the green transferred to you whachamacallit.

Sincerely,

Edward Z. Money, Vice President
Commercial Lending

FIGURE W.11. Revised document with added text.

Finally, add the closing as follows:

To position the cursor at the end of your document

Press: \<Home\> \<Home\> \<down\>

Position the cursor at the end of the document

Press: \<Enter\>   Insert a blank line

Enter: Sincerely,   Add the closing

Action: Insert three blank lines for the signature.

Action: Enter Ed's name and title in the signature and title lines.

The additions to the draft letter have been completed.

Action: Print the resulting draft of Ed's letter and save this as the document file LETTER2.DOC.

Keypoint!

> To add text to the top of a document, move your cursor to the top of the current document and press \<Enter\>, then move the cursor up to the newly created paragraph and begin adding text to your document!

W.2.2   Checking and Correcting Spelling

One of the functional features of WordPerfect is its spell checker, which helps you find your spelling and typographical errors. This is a powerful feature that greatly assists in producing high-quality finished documents. The nemesis of all spell checkers is that if you have used the wrong word, but it is correctly spelled (for example, using "and" when you wanted the word "any"), then the spell checker will not detect this error for you.

The WordPerfect spelling checker can be used to check:

- a word
- a page
- a document
- a block of text

When using the spell checker with a floppy disk system, you may need to use a separate Speller disk, depending on which WordPerfect version you are using. Some versions of WordPerfect, such as version 5.1, may only be installed on high-density 5.25-in. disks or 3.5-in. disks. Check on the requirements for your particular hardware configuration and your WordPerfect version. If you can use a separate disk for the spell checker, then remove your Data Disk and insert the Speller disk in the same drive, *before* performing the spelling check with the Spell \<Ctrl\>+\<F2\> command. Once you have completed the spelling check, replace the Speller disk with your Data Disk. If you are using WordPerfect on a hard disk system, it is not necessary to swap disks. If your procedure for using the Speller is different, enter the instructions here:

My procedure for using the WordPerfect Speller:

_____

_____

_____

_____

Once the Spell <Ctrl>+<F2> command has been initiated and an incorrectly spelled word located, the Speller menu is displayed for selecting the desired activity from this list of choices:

Skip Once. Accept the highlighted occurrence of the word as correct for this time only.

Skip. Accept this and all subsequent occurrences of the word throughout block, page, or document as correct.

Add Word. Include the word in the supplementary dictionary so it will be accepted as correct with future spell checks.

Edit. Change the spelling of the word as desired by modifying it.

Look Up. Search the dictionary for words that match a pattern and display them for possible selection.

With Look Up, a specific word can be checked or a search can be performed for a pattern. The DOS wild card characters of question mark (?) and asterisk (*) are used to enter a search pattern. A wild card indicates that any character may appear in the search pattern. A question mark specifies a wild card for a single letter, whereas an asterisk indicates one or more characters. For example, if you Look Up the character string ba?k, the words back, balk, bank, bark, and bask are displayed, whereas the character string br*ck produces the words brainsick, breakneck, brick, broomstick, and brunswick.

Keypoint!   If the spell checker is *not* available with your installation of WordPerfect, then make the following changes manually.

To check the spelling in Ed's draft letter, proceed in this manner:

Action: Verify that LETTER2.DOC is your currently active document in WordPerfect.

To spell check a document   **Select:**   Spell <Ctrl>+<F2>   Activate the Speller
The SPELL command may be reached from the Tools pull-down menu in version 5.1

Select: Document   Perform spelling check on entire document

Caution Alert!   In the event that you happened to create a few spelling errors of your own, then correct them at the same time by using the same procedure as described below!

The first spelling error detected is the given name, "Chris," which is highlighted. A list of possible replacement words appears on your screen, as illustrated in Figure W.12. Since this given name is correctly spelled, skip by this detected potential error by continuing in this manner:

<table>
<tr><td>To skip by a correctly spelled word not in the dictionary</td><td>**Select:**</td><td>Skip</td><td>Pass by this and all other occurrences of the word in the document</td></tr>
</table>

Now, the cursor moves to "ya," which is highlighted. Because a long list of replacement candidates exist, they extend to a second list. This additional list is accessed and the correct spelling selected like this:

Press:	\<Enter\>	Display the remainder of the list of possible words
Select:	you	Type the letter preceding "you" to select it for substitution into the document

Keypoint!   When the list of words exceeds a single screen, press \<Enter\> to continue viewing additional words!

The cursor moves to "bippy," which is highlighted as the next incorrect word. Proceed as follows:

Select:	Skip	This word is correctly spelled, but it is not contained in WordPerfect's dictionary

```
February 21, 1994

Mr. Chris Frost, Treasurer
Good Morning Products
911 Orange Blossom Lane
Citrus Grove Valley, CA  95941

Dear Chris:

As chairperson of the Commercial Bending Loan Committee, I want to
let ya no that our group huddled today to consider the loan request
                                       Doc 1 Pg 1 Ln 1.33" Pos 1.4"

   A. chrism        B. christ        C. crass
   D. craws         E. craze         F. crease
   G. crees         H. cres          I. cress
   J. crest         K. crews         L. cries
   M. cross         N. crows         O. cruise
   P. crus          Q. cruse         R. crust
   S. krause



Not Found: 1 Skip Once; 2 Skip; 3 Add; 4 Edit; 5 Look Up; 6 Ignore Numbers: 0
```

FIGURE W.12. List of potential substitute words.

The cursor moves down the document to "whachamacallit," which is now highlighted. There is only one suggested spelling correction. This is accepted as follows:

Select:	`whatchamacallit`	Type the letter preceding the only suggested spelling correction
Press:	`<Enter>`or `<any other key>`	Terminate the spelling check

You are returned to the document mode to continue working with the current document. If you are using floppy disks, remember to replace the Speller disk with your Data Disk.

Action: Print this corrected document and save it as file LETTER3.DOC.

Caution Alert! To stop the spell checking process, press the Cancel <F1> function key, and then press the Exit <F7> function key to return to your document!

W.2.3 Deleting Text

Deletion is the process of removing unwanted characters, words, sentences, paragraphs and control codes from a document. WordPerfect provides several methods for deleting text from a document:

- Single characters
- Individual words
- A line of text
- A block of text

A single character is removed with <Delete> or <Backspace>, as described in the previous Lesson. An individual word is removed at the location of the cursor with the <Ctrl>+<Backspace> or the <Ctrl>+<Delete>. The remainder of a line of text from the cursor to the right margin is removed with the <Ctrl>+<End>. A block of text is "marked" with the Block <Alt>+<F4> command and then removed with <Delete>. A marked block of text appears as the highlighted text in Figure W.13. As illustrated, a block of text is any contiguous group of characters. If the text is not contiguous, then separate blocks must be marked individually.

The deletion of text is explored with Ed's draft letter as follows:

Action: Clear your current document and retrieve LETTER3.DOC.

To delete an unwanted word	**Move to:**	`carefully`	Place the cursor on any character of this word, which is to be deleted
	Press:	`<Ctrl>+<Backspace>`	The word is deleted
		or	
		`<Ctrl>+<Delete>`	
To delete an unwanted line	**Move to:**	9 in "`911 Orange Blossom Lane`"	
	Press:	`<Ctrl>+<End>`	Delete the entire line

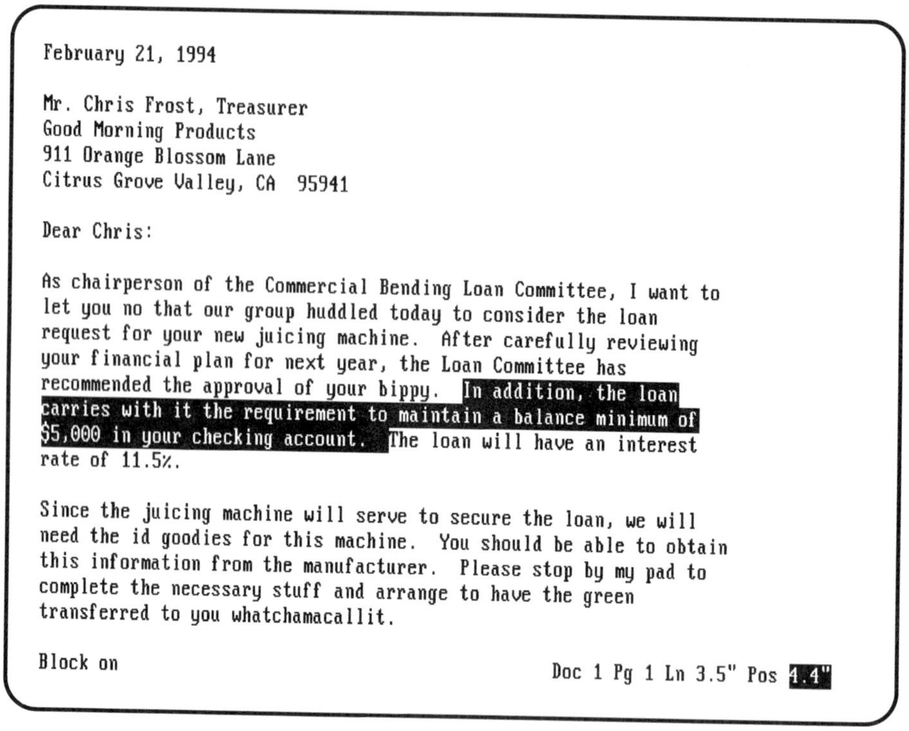

```
February 21, 1994

Mr. Chris Frost, Treasurer
Good Morning Products
911 Orange Blossom Lane
Citrus Grove Valley, CA  95941

Dear Chris:

As chairperson of the Commercial Bending Loan Committee, I want to
let you no that our group huddled today to consider the loan
request for your new juicing machine.  After carefully reviewing
your financial plan for next year, the Loan Committee has
recommended the approval of your bippy.  In addition, the loan
carries with it the requirement to maintain a balance minimum of
$5,000 in your checking account.  The loan will have an interest
rate of 11.5%.

Since the juicing machine will serve to secure the loan, we will
need the id goodies for this machine.  You should be able to obtain
this information from the manufacturer.  Please stop by my pad to
complete the necessary stuff and arrange to have the green
transferred to you whatchamacallit.

Block on                                    Doc 1 Pg 1 Ln 3.5" Pos 4.4"
```

FIGURE W.13. A marked block of text.

The text is removed, but a blank line remains; now continue:

Press:	<Backspace>	Remove the blank line by deleting the end of paragraph produced with <Enter>

To delete a block of text

Move to:	I in "In addition, the loan carries with it..."	
Select:	<Alt>+<F4>	Turn on the Block function to mark the block of text
Move to:	. (period) at end of sentence "...in your checking account."	This marks the block of text, which is highlighted on your screen
Press:	<Delete>	The deletion process is initiated

This message is displayed in the Status Line:

Delete Block? No (Yes)

Press:	<Y>	Carry out the deletion of the block

Action: Print the result and clear your screen *without* saving these revisions.

W.2.4 Undeleting Text

While you are deleting text, if you make a mistake and inadvertently delete the wrong text, you may be able to undo this error. As WordPerfect deletes text, the deleted text is temporarily stored in a scratchpad area of WordPerfect's memory, where it can be accessed with the Cancel <F1> function key. Up to three deletions are stored—the most recent and two prior deletions. However, just repeatedly pressing the <Delete> places the text in the same scratchpad area. You must move the cursor before your next deletion is placed in a different scratchpad area. In many situations, you move your cursor between deletions, resulting in each deletion being placed in a different scratchpad area. When undeleting, you have the option of obtaining previously deleted text from any of WordPerfect's three scratchpad areas. Hence, you may recover from a deletion error as long as it is within your last three deletions.

Caution Alert!
> A WordPerfect undelete should be performed as soon as possible, *before* additional deletions are performed!

Text can be undeleted from Ed's draft letter in the following manner:

Action:	Retrieve the document file LETTER3.DOC.	
Move to:	`carefully`	Position cursor on word to delete
Press:	`<Ctrl>+<Backspace>`	Delete the selected word
Press:	`<F1>`	Cancel the deletion; activate undelete operation

To undelete text just deleted

The text reappears in the document and is highlighted as shown in Figure W.14. An undelete menu is displayed for selecting the desired action from the choices:

Restore. Replace the most recently deleted text.

Previous Deletion. Show the second or third most recently deleted text for potential selection with the undelete.

```
February 21, 1994

Mr. Chris Frost, Treasurer
Good Morning Products
911 Orange Blossom Lane
Citrus Grove Valley, CA  95941

Dear Chris:

As chairperson of the Commercial Bending Loan Committee, I want to
let you no that our group huddled today to consider the loan
request for your new juicing machine.  After carefully reviewing
your financial plan for next year, the Loan Committee has
recommended the approval of your bippy.  In addition, the loan
carries with it the requirement to maintain a balance minimum of
$5,000 in your checking account.  The loan will have an interest
rate of 11.5%.

Since the juicing machine will serve to secure the loan, we will
need the id goodies for this machine.  You should be able to obtain
this information from the manufacturer.  Please stop by my pad to
complete the necessary stuff and arrange to have the green
transferred to you whatchamacallit.

Undelete: 1 Restore; 2 Previous Deletion: 0
```

FIGURE W.14. Suggested text to be undeleted.

Since WordPerfect "remembers" the most recent three deletions, the Previous Deletion selection or the cursor <down> or <up> can be used to have each deletion displayed as a candidate for undeletion in your document.

Continue with the undelete actions in this manner:

Select:	`Restore`	Text is replaced in the document
Action:	Using the Block <Alt>+<F4> command, mark the entire sentence "In addition, the loan carries with it...your checking account." and then delete it.	
Press:	`<F1>`	Cancel activates the undelete menu
Press:	`<up>`	Display Previous Deletion of "carefully"
Press:	`<down>`	Toggle back to most recent deletion

To place deleted text back into your document

〰〰〰〰〰
Caution Alert!
〰〰〰〰〰

If you have performed other deletions, this will be stored as your third choice and may be displayed if you happen to press <down> instead of <up>, or vice versa. If this happens, just use the cursor keys to display the desired text to be undeleted!

Select:	`Restore`	Text is replaced in the document

The resulting document should now be the same as when you retrieved the LETTER3.DOC file.

W.2.5 Rearranging Text

Text can be rearranged by moving a word, sentence, phrase, or paragraph from one location to another or by copying a portion of a document to another location. This feature of WordPerfect can enhance your abilities to write by assisting you in readily reorganizing your ideas. The Move feature is accessed with the <Ctrl> + <F4>. Text that can be rearranged within a document is

- A single sentence
- An individual paragraph
- A page of text
- A block of text

Keypoint!

The ability to easily rearrange text may help you improve the quality of your writing in documents prepared with a word processor!

Ed's letter can be improved by repositioning the sentence that contains the loan's interest rate, as follows:

Action: Make sure the current document has been cleared and then retrieve the LETTER3.DOC document file.

To move a block of text

Move to:	`T in "The loan will have an..."`	Position the cursor at the beginning of the block of text to be moved
Select:	Move `<Ctrl>+<F4>`	Select the MOVE command

A menu appears in the Status Line, which contains the choices as follows:

Sentence. Select the sentence at the location of the cursor to move.

Paragraph. Select the paragraph at the location of the cursor to move.

Page. Select the page containing the cursor to move.

Retrieve. Obtain text stored in the delete scratch pad by the last block delete command.

Select: `Sentence`   Desired activity

A second menu is displayed in the Status Line with the choices as follows:

Move. Move the marked text to a designated location.

Copy. Copy the marked text to a specified location and also leave the text at the original location.

Delete. Delete the marked text.

Append. Append the marked text to the end of a designated document file.

From this menu, you can see that an alternative method of deleting text from a document is provided with this Move <Ctrl>+<F4> command. Now, let's continue moving the sentence by inserting it at the desired location.

Select: `Move`   Desired action from the second menu

Move to: `<space> following "bippy"`
                                                  Position the cursor at the beginning of the desired destination

Press: `<Enter>`   Complete the Move operation

Press: `<space> <space>`   Add spaces between the two sentences

The move is completed with the sentence repositioned in the desired location.

Action: Print the result and save this document as LETTER4.DOC.

Besides the movement of text, the MOVE command provides the ability to copy text from one location to another location. This can be demonstrated with Ed's draft letter like this:

To copy a block of text			

Move to: `S in "Since the juicing machine will..."`

Select: `Move <Ctrl>+<F4>`   Initiate the Move operation

Select: `Paragraph`   Designate the text to be copied

Select: `Copy`   Desired action

Press: `<Home> <Home> <down>`
                                                  Position the cursor at the end of the document, the desired location

Press: `<Enter>`   Complete the Copy operation

The paragraph appears in both locations, illustrating the difference between the Copy and Move options within WordPerfect's Move <Ctrl>+<F4> command.

Action: Delete this copy of the second paragraph using the Move <Ctrl>+<F4> command.

In addition to sentences, paragraphs, and pages of text, any block of text can be moved or copied. This could be a word, a phrase, or several sentences. When rearranging a block of text, it is first necessary to identify the block by marking it using the Block <Alt>+<F4> command and then requesting the move operation with the Move <Ctrl>+<F4> command. This activity can be demonstrated with Ed's draft letter as follows:

To move a block of text

Move to:	I in "In addition, ..."	
		Position cursor at beginning of block of text to be moved or copied
Select:	Block <Alt>+<F4>	Turn on Block operation to mark block of text
Move to:	, in "In addition,"	
		Mark the block of text to move by using cursor movement keys
Select:	Move <Ctrl>+<F4>	Select the MOVE command
Select:	Block	A block of text is to be moved
Select:	Move	Desired action
Move to:	T in "The loan will have an..."	
		Position cursor at destination by using cursor movement keys
Press:	<Enter>	Complete the Move operation

The designated block of text has been relocated at the specified location.

Action: Insert the spaces and revise the capitalization necessary to complete the rearrangement of this text.

Action: Print the result of this move operation and then clear the document from your screen.

W.2.6   Searching for Text

WordPerfect provides the ability to search through a document looking for a text string. Here, a text string is any sequence of characters. This could be a word, a phrase, or a word fragment. Text searches are especially useful with longer documents. For example, rather than paging through a document, you could perform a search for a desired heading.

Your text search may proceed either forward or backward from the location of the cursor within your document. The Search <F2> command performs a forward search in your document, whereas the Search <Shift>+<F2> command conducts the search backwards from the current cursor position. Once an occurrence of the text string has been located, the cursor is positioned at the text string. The next occurrence of the text string in your document can be located by repeating the Search command. In the event that the text string does not reside in your document or the bottom or top of the document has been reached, the message "*Not found*" is displayed on the Status Line. When the text search is conducted, WordPerfect's default is to ignore uppercase and lowercase characters, so **LOAN, Loan,** and **loan** are all considered to be equivalent, if you specify the search for **loan.** But if you specify **LOAN,** WordPerfect will search only for the uppercase occurrence.

Ed wants you to review the use of the word "loan" in his draft letter. This is performed as follows:

Action: Retrieve the LETTER4.DOC document file and position the cursor at the upper left corner of the document.

To search forward for a text string	**Select:**	`Search <F2>`	Activate the Search down command Search is a main menu selection in version 5.1

A prompt appears on the Status Line requesting the text search character string. The "–>" indicates that a forward search down the document will be performed, whereas a "<–" signals a backward search up the document. Since this is a search down the document, the prompt displayed is

–>Srch:

Type:	`loan`	But do not press <Enter>; this is the character string for the search
Press:	`<F2>`	The second time you press <F2> the search is initiated

The cursor moves to the first occurrence of "loan" in the document, with the cursor positioned immediately to the right of "loan."

To search forward for the second occurrence of the same text string	**Press:**	`<F2> <F2>`	Cursor moves to the second occurrence of "loan"
	Press:	`<F2> <F2>`	And on to the third occurrence
	Action:		Continue with the <F2> <F2> Search command until the message "*Not found*" is displayed on the Status Line, signaling that the last occurrence of "loan" has been reached.

Now search up the document for the occurrence of the character string "rate" in this manner:

To search backwards through your document for a text string	**Press:**	`<Shift>+<F2>`	Activate the Search up command
	Type:	`rate`	Desired character string
	Press:	`<F2>`	Initiate the search

The cursor moves to the occurrence of the "rate" character string.

To search backwards for the second occurrence of the same text string	**Press:**	`<Shift>+<F2>`	Begin the search for the next occurrence of "rate"
	Press:	`<F2>`	Accept the suggested character string and initiate the search

Since "rate" occurs only once, the "*Not found*" message is displayed.
This completes the text searches for locating specified character strings.

W.2.7   Searching for and Replacing Text

In addition to searching for a desired character string, WordPerfect can also replace a specified set of characters with a new character string. Search and replace is initiated with the Replace <Alt>+<F2> command, which starts scanning for the text string beginning at the location of the cursor in your document and continuing until the end of the document. Character strings can be replaced either with or without confirmation. Under "with confirmation," at each replacement, you must indicate whether you want the replacement made; this helps avoid accidentally replacing an old text string that should not be changed. For "without confirmation," each occurrence of the search string is changed and you are returned to the document to continue processing.

Search and replace are applied in modifying Ed's draft letter as follows:

Action: Make sure your document is cleared and retrieve the LETTER4.DOC file.

To perform a search and replace of a text string	**Move to:** Top of document at left margin

Position the cursor at beginning of the document

Keypoint!

> Usually the best situation is to start searching for text from the top of a document. This helps to avoid missing any occurrences of your search text string!

Select: Replace <Alt>+<F2>   Initiate the Replace command
The Replace command is accessed from the Search pull-down menu in version 5.1

The following prompt appears on the Status Line:

w/Confirm? No (Yes)

Press: <Enter>   Accept the "without confirmation" replacement

The following message is displayed to prompt for input of the search or the "old text" string:

–> Srch:

Type: no   The text string "no" will be replaced
Press: <F2>   Accept the text string

The message appears requesting the replacement text string:

Replace with:

Type: know   "know" is the new text string
Press: <F2>   Accept the replacement text string

The replacement is made, and you are ready for the next activity.

Ed wants you to replace the "juicing machine" text string with the "crushing equipment" text string. This is accomplished as follows:

To perform a search and replace of a text string	**Action:** Position the cursor at the top of the document.

Select: Replace <Alt>+<F2>   Initiate the Replace command
Press: <Y>   Specify the "with confirmation" option
Type: juicing machine   Old text string

Press:	<F2>	Accept the text string
Type:	crushing equipment	New replacement text string
Press:	<F2>	Accept the replacement text string

The confirmation message is displayed on the Status Line in this manner:

Confirm? No (Yes)

Press:	<Y>	Accept the replacement
Press:	<Y>	Accept the second replacement

The replacement activities are completed.

Action: Print the resulting draft and save this as document file LETTER5.DOC.

Caution Alert!   Be careful in using replacement to avoid unwanted changes. For example, when attempting to replace "form" with "forum," consider the potential effect on other words, such as "conform" and "format," that could result. For this reason, replacement "with confirmation" is usually the safest method!

W.2.8   Using the Thesaurus

The quality of a document can be enhanced by using the thesaurus to select alternative words. Rather than using the same word repeatedly, the thesaurus offers "word relief" by providing a list of synonyms and, for some words, antonyms. You can then pick a different word for use in your document to improve readability. The thesaurus is activated with the Thesaurus <Alt>+<F1> command. WordPerfect allows the display of up to three columns of words and their alternatives on a single screen, arranged side by side, to assist you in choosing a more appropriate word.

When using the thesaurus with a floppy disk system, you may need to use a separate Thesaurus disk. If you need a separate disk, then remove your Data Disk and insert the Thesaurus disk in the same drive, before looking up a word with the Thesaurus <Alt>+<F1> command. Once you have finished with the thesaurus, replace the Thesaurus disk with your Data Disk. If you are using WordPerfect on a hard disk system, it is not necessary to swap disks. If your procedure for using the thesaurus is different, enter the instructions here:

My procedure for using the WordPerfect Thesaurus:

_____

_____

_____

_____

Keypoint!   If the thesaurus is *not* available with your installation of WordPerfect, then make the following changes manually.

Ed wants you to improve the draft letter by substituting alternative words for "huddled" and "stuff." This is accomplished as follows:

Action: Retrieve LETTER5.DOC as your active document.

<table>
<tr><td>To use the thesaurus to
select a different word</td><td>**Move to:**</td><td>huddled</td><td>Place the cursor on any character in this word</td></tr>
<tr><td></td><td>**Press:**</td><td>Thesaurus <Alt>+<F1></td><td>Initiate the THESAURUS command
The THESAURUS command may be accessed from the Tools pull-down menu</td></tr>
</table>

A window is opened on the screen displaying synonyms for "huddled," as shown in Figure W.15. These words are arranged in subgroups of words that have the same basic meaning. Each subgroup is indicated by its number, with the subgroups divided into nouns (n), verbs (v), adjectives (a), and antonyms (ant), as appropriate. Each word listed in the subgroup is a reference. References marked with a bullet (•) are those words contained in the thesaurus for which an additional look up can be performed to find other alternative word choices.

Select: Replace Word   One of the reference words will be picked

Select: gather   Enter the letter preceding the desired choice in the reference list

And, the selected word replaces the original one.

Since the replacement word does not contain the "ed" suffix, this remains to be added. You usually need to add "s" and "ed" to words selected from the thesaurus.

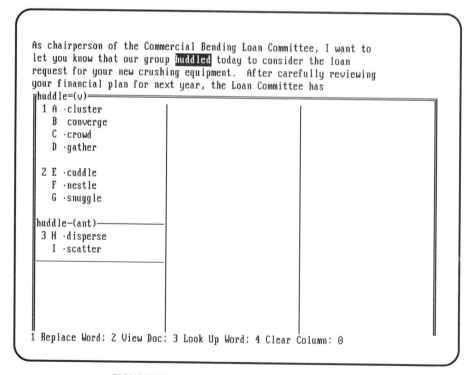

FIGURE W.15. Thesaurus display for single word.

When the replacement has been completed, WordPerfect positions the cursor at the right end of the word to assist in adding the needed suffix. Continue as follows:

Type: ed   The suffix is added to gather

This word replacement using the thesaurus is complete, and you are ready to look for an alternative for "stuff" by proceeding in this manner:

To use the thesaurus for selecting a different list of words

Move to:	stuff	Position the cursor on the word
Select:	Thesaurus <Alt>+<F1>	
		Issue the THESAURUS command
Select:	Look Up Word	Request additional words
Enter:	papers	Request a second list of alternative words
Select:	Look Up Word	Continue the quest for a better word
Enter:	A	Obtain a list of words for this reference
Action:	Using <left> and <right> move among the three words and their lists of references.	

Figure W.16 illustrates the three columns of reference lists. As you cursor from one column of words to the next, notice how the selection of letters appears in the column where your cursor is located. You may use <down> and <up> to inspect the list within a column when the list exceeds the room available on your screen.

Move to: papers   That is, the column with "papers" as the headword since this synonym will be selected from the list of reference words

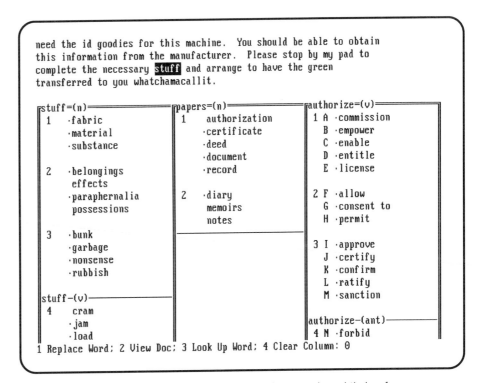

FIGURE W.16. Thesaurus display with the three words and their references.

| **Select:** | Replace Word | Your desired activity |
| **Select:** | authorization | Enter the letter preceding this desired substitute word |

Acceptable substitute words have been found and placed in Ed's draft letter. These new word choices together with the other modifications have improved the quality of Ed's draft letter.

Action: If you are using floppy disks, remember to replace the Thesaurus disk with your Data Disk.

Action: Print this draft of the letter and save it as LETTER6.DOC.

Caution Alert!   Once a word has been replaced using the thesaurus, any desired suffix must be added to the word!

W.2.9   Revealing Codes

In general, WordPerfect uses the WYSIWYG method of displaying a document on your screen, which appears, as closely as possible, to how the text will actually be printed. That is, you see each paragraph and other special characteristics such as indenting, bolding, and underlining. To control this display and to tell the printer how the document is to be printed, a number of special display control codes are used by WordPerfect. These *invisible* control codes are embedded within your document. Since the use of these codes can become complex, they can be displayed on request with the Reveal Codes <Alt>+<F3> command. This causes a split screen display of your document as illustrated in Figure W.17 with the original document in the upper window and the document with the embedded control codes in the lower window.

For Ed's letter, only two control codes have been included:

To understand hard and soft returns

[HRt]. A "hard return" placed in the document each time the <Enter> was used.

[SRt]. A "soft return" placed at the right end of each line in the document that does not contain a hard return.

Soft returns are automatically added to your document when word wrap occurs as you are typing, whereas hard returns are inserted when an <Enter> is used. Normally you use a hard return when you want to

- Start a new paragraph
- Insert a heading
- Insert a blank line

A soft return is temporary, because its insertion is automatically controlled by WordPerfect. With the insertion or deletion of text, the length of a line is changed and the locations of soft returns are automatically adjusted.

If you delete the hard return at the end of a paragraph, it will cause that paragraph to run together with the following paragraph. By inspecting the embedded codes, you could see that a hard return was missing. To correct this situation, all you need to do is place a [HRt] at the desired location by using the <Enter>.

The embedded codes in Ed's letter can be inspected by using the Reveal Codes <Alt>+<F3> command in this manner:

```
February 21, 1994

Mr. Chris Frost, Treasurer
Good Morning Products
911 Orange Blossom Lane
Citrus Grove Valley, CA  95941

Dear Chris:

As chairperson of the Commercial Bending Loan Committee, I want to
let you know that our group gathered today to consider the loan
B:\LETTER6.DOC                                    Doc 1 Pg 1 Ln 1" Pos 1"
{  ▲  ▲  ▲  ▲  ▲  ▲  ▲  ▲  ▲  ▲  ▲  }  ▲  ▲
February 21, 1994[HRt]
[HRt]
Mr. Chris Frost, Treasurer[HRt]
Good Morning Products[HRt]
911 Orange Blossom Lane[HRt]
Citrus Grove Valley, CA  95941[HRt]
[HRt]
Dear Chris:[HRt]
[HRt]
As chairperson of the Commercial Bending Loan Committee, I want to[SRt]

Press Reveal Codes to restore screen
```

FIGURE W.17. Revealing embedded control codes.

Action:	Verify that LETTER6.DOC is your current document; retrieve it, if necessary.	
Move to:	top of document	This is optional; it just positions the cursor so that the date, inside address, and salutation will be displayed

To toggle on the Reveal Control Codes display

Select:	Reveal Codes <Alt>+<F3>	Execute the REVEAL CODES command; the REVEAL CODES command appears on the Edit pull-down menu in version 5.1
Action:	Use the cursor <down> and <up> to move through the document and inspect the various embedded control codes.	
Move to:	End of the first paragraph of the body and position the cursor on the [HRt] hard return. The [HRt] hard return code is highlighted in the bottom window.	
Press:	<Delete>	The [HRt] is removed
Press:	<Delete>	Another [HRt] is removed and the two paragraphs run together

The two paragraphs run together with only soft returns at the end of each line.

Press:	<Enter>	Split the paragraph
Press:	<Enter>	Add the blank line

Ed's letter is returned to its original layout.

The Reveal Codes <Alt>+<F3> command is particularly useful when you are performing deletions, moves, and copies to ensure that control codes like these are not inadvertently scrambled.

~~~~~
*Caution Alert!*
~~~~~

Use the Reveal Codes <Alt>+<F3> command:

1. To ensure that embedded control codes are *not* scrambled when performing deletes, moves, and copies!

2. To locate errors any time your screen display is not what you expect. The codes will help you find what is wrong!

W.2.10 Making Modifications

The quality of Ed's letter has been improved by making a number of modifications and corrections. Ed has printed a draft copy of the letter and marked it with some additional revisions as shown in Figure W.18. Often, a printed copy provides a convenient method for recording revisions, rather than trying to make all of the changes interactively while the document is displayed within WordPerfect. Of course, this is a matter of personal preference. Some people like to do it all on the screen, whereas others feel more comfortable scratching their revisions on a paper copy before making the actual changes to their WordPerfect document.

In specifying his revisions, Ed made use of the proofreader's symbols shown in Figure W.19. These are some of the commonly used symbols for indicating changes on the paper copy of a document.

Action: Make sure that your screen has been cleared and retrieve LETTER6.DOC, Ed's most recent draft.

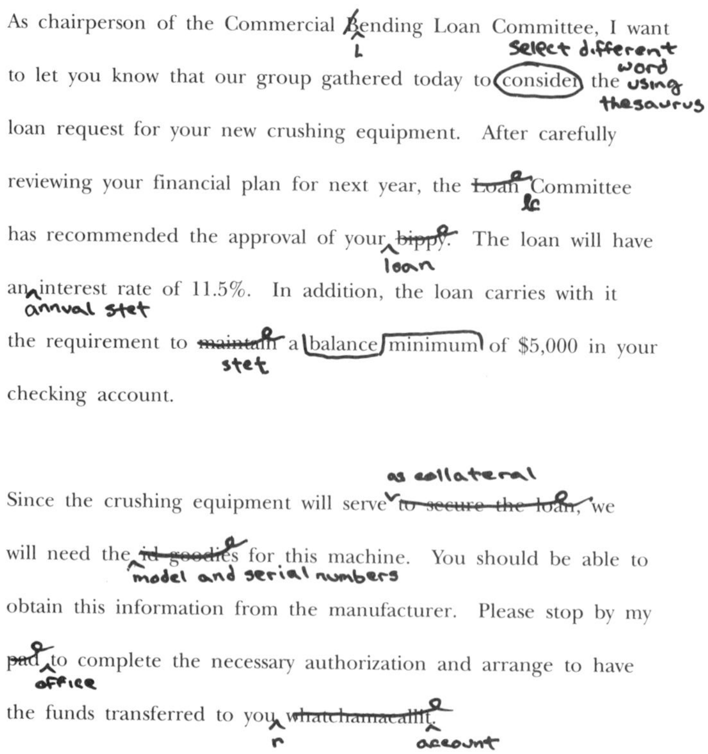

As chairperson of the Commercial Lending Loan Committee, I want
to let you know that our group gathered today to consider the
loan request for your new crushing equipment. After carefully
reviewing your financial plan for next year, the Loan Committee
has recommended the approval of your bippy. The loan will have
an interest rate of 11.5%. In addition, the loan carries with it
the requirement to maintain a balance minimum of $5,000 in your
checking account.

Since the crushing equipment will serve to secure the loan, we
will need the id-goodies for this machine. You should be able to
obtain this information from the manufacturer. Please stop by my
pad to complete the necessary authorization and arrange to have
the funds transferred to you whatchamacallit account.

FIGURE W.18. Ed's marked revisions.

FIGURE W.19. Selected proofreader's symbols.

Action: Make the changes indicated in Figure W.18. However, do not double space your document. This was done in Figure W.18 to accommodate the revisions. You will learn how to perform double spacing in the next lesson.

Action: Print the modified letter and save this as LETTER7.DOC.

The modifications have been completed, and Ed has his final version of the letter, which is ready for the mail.

W.2.11   When Things Go Wrong

Several difficulties may be encountered while you are modifying and correcting your document. Some of the more common situations and how to approach them are as follows:

1. You started to perform a Move <Ctrl>+<F4>, but decided the text should *not* be relocated. You want to terminate the move process.

   a. If you have already selected Move from the "Move, Copy, Delete, Append" menu, press <Enter> *before* you reposition your cursor.

   b. For all other selections, press Cancel <F1> or Exit <F7> to terminate the move process and return to editing your document.

2. You started using the spelling checker and want to terminate this processing.

   a. Use Cancel <F1> as the first step that causes the display of a message from the "Not Found:" menu or terminates the spelling check from the "Check:" menu.

   b. If the "Press any key to continue" message appears, press <F1>, <space>, or any other convenient key. This returns you to the "Check:" menu.

   c. At the "Check:" menu, use Cancel <F1> or Exit <F7> to return to editing your document. Depending on where you are in the spelling check process, pressing <F1> either once or three times will terminate spelling check.

3. You began a Replace <Alt>+<F2> *with* confirmation and discovered that you have specified the wrong Search or Replace text string. You want to terminate this replace command so that you can make your change with the desired text string.

   a. When the "Confirm? No (Yes)" message appears for the text replacement, press Cancel <F1> to terminate Replace and return to editing your document.

   b. Reinitiate the Replace <Alt>+<F2> and specify the desired Search and Replace text strings.

4. You performed a Replace <Alt>+<F2> *without* confirmation and discovered you specified the wrong text string. Usually this replacement will take place so fast that you cannot terminate it. Instead, you need to try to repair the damage after the unwanted replacement has been made.

   a. If you specified the wrong Search text string, use Replace <Alt>+<F2> and change this back to your original text string. Then use Replace <Alt>+<F2> to change the desired text string.

   b. If you specified the wrong Replace text string, use Replace <Alt> + <F2> and change this to your desired text string.

W.2.12   Lesson Summary

- You add new text to an existing document in the same manner as the text you entered when you first created your document.

- To add text to the top of an existing document, a blank line is inserted as a new paragraph with the <Enter>.

- The Spell <Ctrl>+<F2> command activates the spelling check feature. With a floppy disk system, the Speller disk may need to be swapped with your Data Disk.

- Characters, words, lines, and blocks of text can be deleted from a document. A block of text is selected by marking it with the Block <Alt>+<F4> command before performing a deletion.

- An entire word can be removed with the <Ctrl>+<Backspace> or the <Ctrl>+<Delete>, whereas a line of text is deleted with a <Ctrl>+<End>.

- Deleted text is stored in a scratchpad area that permits the text to be restored or undeleted if an error occurred in performing the deletion. The text is recalled with the Cancel <F1> command. Up to three deletions are available for restoration.

- A document can be rearranged by moving or copying sentences, paragraphs, pages, and blocks of text from one location in a document to another location. This feature helps improve the quality of your writing.

- The Search <F2> command is used to locate a word or phrase within a document. This feature makes it easy for you to position the cursor at a desired location for making edit revisions.

- The Replace <Alt>+<F2> command searches for a specified text string and replaces it with a new text string. Several occurrences of the same word are easily revised with this command.

- The Thesaurus <Alt>+<F1> command activates the thesaurus to assist you in finding a more appropriate word for your document. This may help improve the quality of your writing. With a floppy disk system, the Thesaurus disk may need to be swapped with your Data Disk.

- WordPerfect uses special embedded characters to control the printing of a document and its display on your screen. The Reveal Codes <Alt>+<F3> command displays these embedded control characters in a second window on your screen. This display is useful when performing deletions to ensure that these codes are not inadvertently deleted. In version 5.1, WordPerfect warns you before you delete the code (except for a [HRt]) if you are not in Reveal Codes.

- A [HRt] hard return is an embedded control code that is inserted into your document each time you press <Enter>.

- A [SRt] soft return is a temporary embedded control code inserted automatically at the end of each line as text is entered.

- Proofreader's symbols are useful in marking changes on a hard copy of a document in preparation for making the changes to the document with WordPerfect.

W.2.13 Practice Tutorial

Modify the initial draft of the LETTER document from Lesson W.1 to produce the LETTER7 document described in this Lesson as a guided activity in a hands-on manner. Clear your current WordPerfect document before you begin. Retrieve your MYLETR.DOC document file from the Practice Tutorial in Lesson W.1 as a starting point for this exercise.

Task 1: Make all the changes and modifications for the LETTER7.DOC version of this document.

Task 2: Print the final version of the letter.

Task 3: Save this document as the file MYLETR7.DOC.

Time Estimates

Novice: 60 minutes

Intermediate: 45 minutes

Advanced: 30 minutes

W.2.14 Practice Exercises

Case: Crazy River Canoe (continued)

After review of his first draft, Harry wants to make some changes to his letter. Retrieve your CANOE.DOC file, which contains Harry's draft, from the Practice Exercises in Lesson W.1 as the starting point for this exercise. Revise this document as described below.

Canoeing is a sport where you propel your own boat. Poorly designed equipment can prove to be a major inconvenience in the pursuit of happiness paddling. You are the captain. It's your boot, and the adventure you quest is yours alone. A vessel allows you to experience the wilderness that faced our earlier frontier champions.

[handwritten annotations: ship, challenges, seek, canoe, heros, select different word using thesaurus]

True adventure, rugged individualism, and self-reliance belong to an age in the past. They have given way to Kelvar, polypro, Gore-Tex, and goosedown boo ties. Today when we head for the out doors we rely on Jet-Age technology. Before you find yourself up a creek without any viable means of transportation consider the benefits of a Crazy River Canoe.

[handwritten annotations: exploration, more, select different word using thesaurus]

As paddlers, canoes provide a opportunity unique to get away from the handholds of civilization. Grab you propel, clean you flintlock, pack up you knapsack, and pay Lewis and Clark.

[handwritten annotations: select different word using thesaurus]

> *Task 1:* Make the revisions as marked.
>
> *Task 2:* Using the Replace command change every occurrence of "propel" to "paddle."
>
> *Task 3:* Use the Spell checker to make changes to any misspelled words. Be careful to accept correctly spelled words that are not in the dictionary.
>
> *Task 4:* Preview the document and print it.
>
> *Task 5:* Save this as the document file CANOE02.DOC.

Time Estimates

Novice: 60 minutes

Intermediate: 45 minutes

Advanced: 30 minutes

W.2.15 Comprehensive Problems

(1)   Case: Home Real Estate (continued)

At Home Real Estate, Krista has reviewed the initial draft of her follow-up letter to prospective tenants. After further discussions with J. P. and several other property managers, she wants to make these changes to the letter:

Thank you for your inquiry ~~about~~ concerning Park Place Villas. Our townhomes offer some of the finest in living modern for today's active ~~group~~ family.

These apartments have the (utmost) [select different word using thesaurus] in privacy, with entrances separate and individual attached garages. In addition, our deluxe units include a microwave oven and whirlpool ~~thing~~ spa. Other (amenities) of each unit include full carpeting, drapes, appliances, a private patio, and ~~plenty of~~ ample storage. [select different word using thesaurus] [move]

She has decided to add three more paragraphs to her letter as follows:

> Recreational facilities available to each tenant include a swimming pool, sauna, tennis courts, basketball court, recreation room, and exercise room with a variety of body building and other equipment. The recreation room can be scheduled for private parties. Our social person plans regular events such as dinner parties, craft clubs, and athletic events.

> We are centrally located, with easy access to shopping centers, medical facilities, schools, and several executive office complexes. Our People Mover station at the Villas provides convenient boarding of this modern high-speed train. Within 30 minutes, the train will take you to most downtown destinations and other key locations in the metroplex.

> For an appointment to view one of these excellent apartments and a tour of our facilities, please contact me at (817) 241-PARK or 1-800-4LIVING.

Krista wants you to carry out the following tasks to complete this second draft of her letter:

Task 1: Access the RENT2.DOC file from Lesson W.1.

Task 2: Complete the revisions that Krista has made for the initial draft of the letter. [*Caution:* Do *not* double space your changes. This was done only so Krista's edit symbols could be added for these revisions.] [*Hint:* If you do *not* have the thesaurus available with your installation of WordPerfect, then finish this part of your revision manually.]

Task 3: Add the three new paragraphs to the letter.

Task 4: Use the Spell Checker to make changes to any misspelled words. Accept "townhome," "metroplex," and "4LIVING" as correct spellings. [*Hint:* If you do *not* have the Spell Checker available with your installation of WordPerfect, then perform this activity manually.]

Task 5: Change "person" to "director" in the document. Use the Search command to locate the word "person." Begin your search from the top of your document.

Task 6: Change all the occurrences of "apartments" to "townhomes" for the entire document using the Replace command.

Task 7: Review your results and make any additional corrections for any other errors that may have accidentally crept into your letter. Check your use of hard and soft returns with the REVEAL CODES command.

Task 8: Print this completed draft of the letter.

Task 9: Save this document as file RENT3.DOC

Time Estimates

Novice: 75 minutes

Intermediate: 60 minutes

Advanced: 45 minutes

(2)   Case: Pioneer Electric and Gas (continued)

At Pioneer Electric and Gas, Kelli and Mary have reviewed the first draft of their customer service acknowledgment letter. They have formulated a number of revisions for their letter to improve its quality:

> Your request for service has been received and is being examined. As arranged by our customer service guy, technicians service are being scheduled to handle promptly your request. They will contact you by phone to notify you of the time they arriving at your deal.

> All PEG employees carry a photo identification thing. Please don't hesitate to ask for identification before admitting an employee to your deal. If in doubt, phone 554-4100.

> For thousands of PEG customers, a handy Level Payment Plan spreads out the differences seasonal in utility service bills over an entire year. Each June PEG calculates the Level Payment Plan for the next 12 months, based on previous consumption normal weather, and any planned rate adjustment. You pay the same amount each month, and you earn interest at the annual rate of 7% for each month your Level Payment results in a credit balance. All accounts are squared the following June. For customer greater convenience, the Level Payment Plan. Phone 554-PLAN.

At the suggestion of Ramon, they have decided to add two paragraphs to the letter reminding customers of PEG's automatic bill payment plan as follows:

> An Automatic Bill Payment Plan is a convenient service offered by PEG in cooperation with banks, savings and loans, or credit unions in PEG's service area. This program is designed to make bill paying as easy as possible for PEG customers. By signing up for this program, you save time, postage, and one check each month. It's an easy way to pay your utility service bill. Contact a PEG customer service guy for an authorization form.

> If you have any questions concerning the scheduled service request for your deal, please contact me at (409) 554-4107.

Kelli and Mary want you to perform these tasks to prepare a second draft of their letter:

> *Task 1:* Access the PEG2.DOC file from Lesson W.1.

Task 2: Complete the revisions that Kelli and Mary have made for the first draft of their letter. [*Caution:* Do *not* double space your changes. This was done only so Kelli's edit symbols could be added for these revisions.] [*Hint:* If you do *not* have the thesaurus available with your installation of WordPerfect, then finish this part of your revision manually.]

Task 3: Add the two new paragraphs to the letter.

Task 4: Use the Spell Checker to make changes to any misspelled words. [*Hint:* If you do *not* have the Spell Checker available with your installation of WordPerfect, then perform this activity manually.]

Task 5: Change "thing" to "card" in the document. Use the Search command to locate the word "thing." Begin your search from the top of your document.

Task 6: Change "guy" to "representative" in the letter. Use the SEARCH command to locate each occurrence of the word "guy." Begin your search from the bottom of your document.

Task 7: Change all the occurrences of "deal" to "dwelling" for the entire document using the Replace command.

Task 8: Review your results and make any additional corrections for any other errors that may have accidentally crept into your letter. Check your use of hard and soft returns with the REVEAL CODE command, making sure a hard return is used only at the end of each paragraph.

Task 9: Print this completed draft of the letter.

Task 10: Save this document as file PEG3.DOC

Time Estimates

Novice: 75 minutes

Intermediate: 60 minutes

Advanced: 45 minutes

W.2.16 Case Application

Case: Guardian Manufacturing International

Business Problem: Acquisition tender offer
MIS Characteristics: Finance
Strategic Planning
Management Functions: Planning
Directing
Tools Skills: Deleting text
Moving text
Search and replace text
Spell check
Thesaurus

Guardian Manufacturing International (GMI) produces a variety of specialty components for automobiles, trucks, buses, and airplanes. The company has experienced an average annual growth rate of 20 percent during the past five years. This growth has brought increased profits and a treasury flush with cash. The Board of Directors of GMI has been concerned about the possibility of a hostile takeover because of their current cash position.

Rover Industries is one of GMI's largest suppliers. A very close working relationship has been established with Rover, because it is an exclusive supplier for a number of items purchased by GMI. Recently, John Mott, the Chairman of the Board and Chief Executive Officer of GMI, met with Albert Sloan, the Chairman of the Board and Chief Executive Officer of Rover Industries. They had a preliminary discussion about the acquisition of part of Rover's common stock by GMI. John reviewed the long-standing relationship between the two companies. He assured Albert that the management of Rover would not change as a result of GMI's proposal. They laid the groundwork for a meeting of their company's boards of directors.

GMI's Board of Directors met with the management of Rover Industries to discuss GMI's desire to obtain a partial ownership in Rover. As a result of their long-standing and close working relationship, the managements of both companies agreed to GMI's purchase of stock in Rover Industries. With this arrangement, the relationship between the two companies would be strengthened. GMI would reduce its cash position and Rover's stock price would be increased. This would enable Rover to obtain additional financing to expand their plant capacity and improve their ability to supply GMI with high-quality products. With the consummation of the stock purchase acquisition, GMI would have a sufficient portion of Rover's common stock so GMI would control three seats on Rover's Board of Directors.

At their last meeting on Wednesday, GMI's Board of Directors voted unanimously to support the $38 per share common stock tender offer for 2,500,000 shares of Rover's stock as proposed by GMI's Finance Steering Committee. Since this purchase is approximately 30 percent of Rover's common stock, shareholders would have the opportunity to sell GMI 30 percent of their shares at the $38 per share price. This is a premium over Wednesday's $33.50 per share trading price, which should encourage stockholders to sell their shares to GMI.

Sharon Barncourt, GMI's treasurer, has the responsibility for carrying out this stock acquisition with the tender offer. She needs to inform each of Rover's stockholders of the offer so they can tender their shares in accordance with the agreement. Sharon is in the process of preparing a tender offer letter to send to the stockholders of Rover Industries. An initial draft of the letter has been formulated and a number of revisions have been specified. Sharon has assigned you the job of completing the letter by carrying out the following activities:

Tasks

1. Access the WordPerfect document file ROVER.DOC, which contains Sharon's initial draft. Print the document and review it.

2. Sharon has sketched out the revisions she wants you to make to the document as indicated. [*Caution:* Do not double space your changes. This was done only so edit symbols could be added for these revisions.] [*Hint:* If you do not have the thesaurus available with our installation of WordPerfect, then finish that part of your revision manually.]

Guardian Manufacturing International (GMI), a Delaware coporation, hereby offers

for purchase 2,500,000 Common Shares of Rover Industries, an Ohio corporation,

at $38 net to the seller in cash, subject to the conditions in the Offer to Purchase.

Shareholders tendering will not be obligated to pay broker commissions or transfer

taxes on the purchase of Shares by GMI.

The Company has pronounced a dividend quarterly of $0.50 per share, payable on December 10, 1992, to shareholders of record of November 16, 1992. Shareholders of retord on November 16, 1992, will be entitled to such quarterly divident whether or not they tender their shares pursuiant to the Offer.

GMI's obligation to Shares pursuiant to the Offer is conditioned, among other things, upon 2,500,000 Shares tendered being properly and not withdrawn prior to the spiration of the Offer. The Buyer holds teh right, however, to wave such deals.

The Company has advised the Buyer that asof June17, 1992, 7,865,906 Shares were reserved and an additional 317,330 Shares subject were to options issued in cinnection wiht employee various plans benefit. Based up on those numbers, follwing the purchse of 2,500,000 Shares pursuiant to Offer, the Buyer approximatly would own 30% of the total of the Shares reserved.

3. Sharon wants you to add the following as the fifth paragraph of the tender offer letter:

   GMI's Board of Directors has unanimously determined that the Offer is fair to the shareholders of Rover Industries, has consented to and approved the making of the Offer, and recommends acceptance of the Offer by shareholders of Rover Industries.

4. Correct any spelling errors using WordPerfect's Speller. [*Hint:* If you do not have the Spell Checker available with your installation of WordPerfect, then perform this activity manually.]

5. Change "total" to "aggregate" in the document. Use the Search command to locate the word "total." Begin your search from the top of the document.

6. Change all occurrences of "Buyer" to "Purchaser" in the document. Use the Replace command.

7. Change all occurrences of "reserved" to "outstanding" in the document. Use the Replace command.

8. Review your results and make any additional corrections for other errors that may have accidentally found their way into your document.

9. Print this completed draft of the letter and save it.

Time Estimates

Novice: 90 minutes

Intermediate: 60 minutes

Advanced: 45 minutes

Formatting Documents

CONTENT

W.3.1 What Is Formatting?

Formatting is the process of enhancing the appearance of text in a document. Characters can be emphasized with underlining and bolding. The placement of text on a page can be controlled by aligning and indenting paragraphs. The location of text on a line or within a table can be specified by using tab stops. Margins can be changed for the entire document or for a segment of a document. Page numbering can be added to a document, and header or footer lines can be used to identify groups of pages within a document. These formatting activities do not change the *content* of the text in a document—that is carried out by actions that revise and modify documents. Formatting merely arranges the location and appearance of text in a document.

A document's format can contribute to its ability to readily convey its message. Documents that are easy to read are more comprehensible and improve communications. You should select appropriately from among the formatting features explored in this Lesson when you create your own documents.

With WordPerfect, a few of the formatting features are WYSIWYG in the document mode, whereas others may be previewed with the Print View Document command. The manner in which formatting features, such as underlining and bolding, appear in the document mode depends on the particular version of WordPerfect, your hardware configuration, and how WordPerfect has been set up on your computer. The examples described in this Lesson are based on the standard, initial setup of WordPerfect. If your setup has been modified, your formatting features may appear differently.

W.3.2   Underlining Text

Underlining is a special printing effect that emphasizes text in a document. The Underline <F8> command is used to add this effect to text in your WordPerfect document. Underlined text may appear on your screen as highlighted in reverse video or with an actual underline. When previewed with the Print <Shift>+<F7> View Document command, underlining appears in its WYSIWYG form. Underlining can be included in your document (1) in the as-you-type mode or (2) by adding it to existing text. In the "as-you-type" mode, the Underline <F8> command is used to toggle underlining on and off. For the existing text method, a block of text is first marked with the Block <Alt>+<F4> or <F12> command (<F12> is an alternative function key that may be used with an enhanced keyboard) and then underlined with the Underline <F8> command. When text is inserted into a sentence or phrase that is already underlined, the new text is automatically underlined without toggling the Underline <F8> command.

To add underlining to Ed's letter, proceed in this manner:

Action: Verify that LETTER7.DOC is your current active document in WordPerfect.

To underline text as you type

Move to:	I in "In addition, the loan carries..."	
Select:	Underline <F8>	Activates Underline as you type

In the Status Line, the number of inches for the line position as specified following the "Pos" appears highlighted or underlined to indicate that Underline has been activated, as illustrated in Figure W.20.

Type:	Payments are to be made quarterly	
Select:	Underline <F8>	Turn off Underline
Type:	. (period)	Insert a period which is not underlined
Press:	<space> <space>	Place spaces between sentences
Press:	<left>	Reformat the line adjusting for the inserted text

The sentence has been added to the document with underlining included as the text was typed. Now, text will be added into this newly inserted line in the document.

Move to:	<space> following **s** in "Payments are..."	
Press:	<space>	Insert a space after "Payments"
Type:	on principal and interest	Additional text to be included in sentence
Press:	<right>	Reformat for inserted text

As this text is inserted into the document, it is automatically underlined because the text surrounding it was already underlined.

```
February 21, 1994

Mr. Chris Frost, Treasurer
Good Morning Products
911 Orange Blossom Lane
Citrus Grove Valley, CA  98924

Dear Chris:

As chairperson of the Commercial Lending Loan Committee, I want to
let you know that our group gathered today to deliberate the loan
request for your new crushing equipment.  After carefully reviewing
your financial plan for next year, the committee has recommended
the approval of your loan.  The loan will have an interest rate of
11.5%.  Payments on principal and interest are to be made
quarterly.  In addition, the loan carries with it the requirement
to maintain a minimum balance of $5,000 in your checking account.


Since the crushing equipment will serve as collateral, we will need
the model and serial numbers for this machine.  You should be able
to obtain this information from the manufacturer.  Please stop by
my office to complete the necessary authorization and arrange to
have the funds transferred to your account.
B:\LETTER7.DOC                              Doc 1 Pg 1 Ln 3.33" Pos 1.5"
```

FIGURE W.20. Completed underlining and status indicator for UNDERLINE command.

Existing text can be underlined by marking it and then executing the Underline <F8> command. This is performed for Ed's letter as follows:

To underline existing text

Move to: T in "The loan will have an..."
Select: Block <Alt>+<F4> or <F12>

Turn on the BLOCK command; <F12> may be used if you have an enhanced keyboard containing this function key

Move to: % in "11.5%"   Mark the desired block of text
Select: Underline <F8>   Execute the UNDERLINE command

The existing text is highlighted or underlined on your screen, demonstrating this WYSIWYG feature of WordPerfect.

Underlining inserts invisible control characters in the document. These can be observed with the REVEAL CODES command in this manner:

To reveal the underline codes

Select: Reveal Codes <Alt>+<F3> or <F11>

Turn on the Reveal Codes mode; <F11> may be used if you have an enhanced keyboard containing this function key

The resulting [UND] and [und] are "hidden" control codes that are included in the document, as illustrated in Figure W.21. Here, the uppercase control code, [UND], indicates the beginning of the underline, while the lowercase control code, [und], specifies the end of the underline. Two separate underlining activities were performed, and thus two sets of codes were inserted into the document.

```
911 Orange Blossom Lane
Citrus Grove Valley, CA  98924

Dear Chris:

As chairperson of the Commercial Lending Loan Committee, I want to
let you know that our group gathered today to deliberate the loan
request for your new crushing equipment.  After carefully reviewing
your financial plan for next year, the committee has recommended
the approval of your loan. The loan will have an interest rate of
11.5%. Payments on principal and interest are to be made
B:\LETTER7.DOC                                    Doc 1 Pg 1 Ln 3.33" Pos 1.5"
{    ▲    ▲    ▲    ▲    ▲    ▲    ▲    ▲    ▲    ▲    }    ▲    ▲
request for your new crushing equipment.  After carefully reviewing[SRt]
your financial plan for next year, the committee has recommended[SRt]
the approval of your loan.  [UND]The loan will have an interest rate of[SRt]
11.5%[und]  [UND]Payments on principal and interest are to be made[SRt]
quarterly[und].  In addition, the loan carries with it the requirement[SRt]
to maintain a minimum balance of $5,000 in your checking account. [SRt]
[HRt]
[HRt]
Since the crushing equipment will serve as collateral, we will need[SRt]
the model and serial numbers for this machine.  You should be able[SRt]

Press Reveal Codes to restore screen
```

FIGURE W.21. Embedded control codes for underlining.

Keypoint!	WordPerfect's hidden control codes are special instructions governing such matters as the format, style, and layout of characters and documents!

Underlining can be removed or deleted from a document by deleting the control codes. This activity is best performed with the Reveal Codes displayed to ensure that you are deleting the desired code.

To remove underlining

Move to: [UND] preceding "Payments on principle..."

Press: <Delete>   Remove the underline control code

The underlining of this sentence is removed and no longer appears in the document. Since the [UND] and [und] are included in pairs, known in WordPerfect as **paired control codes**, either underline control code may be deleted to remove the underlining.

Move to: [und] following "11.5%"

Press: <Delete>   Remove the underlining

To toggle off the reveal codes display

Select: Reveal Codes <Alt>+<F3> or <F11>
Turn off the Reveal Codes screen

Keypoint!	If you delete one of a set of paired control codes, both are deleted!

All the underlining has been removed from Ed's letter. However, he wants these two sentences underlined.

Action: Underline the two sentences, "The loan will have an...are to be made quarterly." Since this is now existing text, use the BLOCK command method of underlining.

Ed has the desired underlining in his letter.

Action: Preview the output as a WYSIWYG display with the Print and View Document at 100 percent commands. You may need to use <up> or <down> to position the document so you can view all the text at one time.

Action: Print the results and save this document as file LETTER8.DOC.

WordPerfect furnishes an alternative method for turning on/off underlining. This command may be accessed as the Font <Ctrl>+<F8> Appearance Underline command and may be selected from the Font Appearance pop-out menu, if available.

W.3.3 Bolding Text

Bolding provides a different method of emphasizing text. The Bold <F6> command is used to add this effect to text in your document. Bolding may appear as a WYSIWYG feature of WordPerfect in the document mode, depending on the version you are using. Other versions indicate bold text by using highlighting in reverse video or changing color or intensity. When previewed with the PRINT VIEW DOCUMENT command, bolding appears in its WYSIWYG form of characters that are darker than regular text. Like underlining, bolding can be included (1) by using the as-you-type mode, or (2) by adding it to existing text. In the as-you-type mode, the Bold <F6> command toggles bolding on and off. For existing text, a block of text is first marked with the Block <Alt>+<F4> command and then is bolded by using the Bold <F6> command. When additional text is inserted into a phrase that is already bolded, this new text is automatically bolded without toggling the Bold <F6> command.

The bolding of text is examined with Ed's letter as follows:

Action: Make sure LETTER8.DOC with the underlining added is your current document.

Move to: the end of the second paragraph
Place the cursor at the location where new text will be added

Press: <space> <space>   Add spaces between sentences

| To bold characters as you type

Select: Bold <F6>   Turn on Bold as you type

In the Status Line, the number of inches for the line position as specified following the "Pos" indicator changes color or intensity to signal that bold has been activated, similar to the indicator for underlining.

Type: I would like to meet with you before February 29th.
Desired text to be added with bolding

Select: Bold <F6>   Turn off bold

The sentence has been added to the document with bolding included as the text was typed. When additional text is inserted in the middle of bolded text, the text is automatically bolded as it is entered, as was done with underlined text.

Existing text can be boldfaced by marking it as a block and then executing the Bold <F6> command. This is carried out for Ed's letter in this manner:

To bold existing text

Move to: `P` in "`Please stop by my office...`"
                        Beginning of the block to be bolded

Select: `Block <Alt>+<F4>` or `<F12>`
                        Initiate the BLOCK command

Move to: . (period) at end of sentence following the word "`account`"
                        End of the block to be bolded

Select: `Bold <F6>`   Execute the BOLD command

The existing text is bolded. The text changes color or its intensity increases to indicate bolding. Like underlining, the BOLD command inserts [BOLD] and [bold] as embedded control characters in the document.

Action: Examine the insertion of the control characters for bolding by using the REVEAL CODES command.

To remove bolding

Action: Confirm you are in the REVEAL CODES mode.

Move to: `[BOLD]` preceding "`Please stop by my office...`"
                        Beginning of the sentence that will have the bolding removed

Press: `<Delete>`   Remove the bolding for this sentence

By deleting either the [BOLD] or [bold] embedded control commands, bolding is removed from a selected segment of text.

An alternative method for bolding is available with the Font <Ctrl>+<F8> Appearance Bold command and may be selected from the Font Appearance pop-out menu, if available.

Underlining and bolding can be used in combination. That is, a segment of text can be both bolded and underlined. Underlining and bolding can be turned on simultaneously when they are used in the "as-you-type" mode of applying these characteristics to the text in your document. That is, selecting Bold <F6> and then Underline <F8> activates both bolding and underlining, which is signaled by highlighting the inches specification following the "Pos" current position indicator in the Status Line. After the text has been typed, selecting Bold <F6> and Underline <F8> turns off these text editing characteristics. For existing text, underlining and bolding are performed as two separate activities. First underline the block of text and then bold it. This is demonstrated with Ed's letter as follows:

To underline and bold existing text

Move to: `m` at the beginning of "`...minimum balance of...`"
                        Position the cursor at the beginning of the block

Select: `Block <Alt>+<F4>` or `<F12>`
                        Turn on Block

Move to: last `0` (zero) at end of `$5,000`
                        End of Block

Select: `Underline <F8>`   Underline the block of text

Action: Mark the same block of text with the Block <Alt>+<F4> command.

Select: `Bold <F6>`   Add bold to the block of text

The specified phrase is both underlined and bolded.

Action: Review the embedded codes with the REVEAL CODES command.

The embedded control codes for both underline and bold appear at the beginning and ending of this selected segment of text.

Action: Preview the output as a WYSIWYG display, print the resulting document, and save this as file LETTER9.DOC.

The desired bolding and underlining have been completed in the body of Ed's response letter.

W.3.4 Centering Text

Centered text is positioned in the middle of a line on a page, an equal distance from the left and right margins of the page. Text can be centered as you type each paragraph or by requesting that a block of existing text be centered. Centering is performed with the Center <Shift>+<F6> command. (This command may be accessed from the Layout Align pop-out menu in version 5.1.)

Ed would like to add the bank's name and address as a heading to his letter, as shown in Figure W.22. This is accomplished as follows:

Action: Retrieve LETTER9.DOC as your currently active document.

Action: Position the cursor at the top-left corner of the document and insert a paragraph marker with the <return> to obtain a blank line for the first line of the bank's heading. Place the cursor on this newly created paragraph marker.

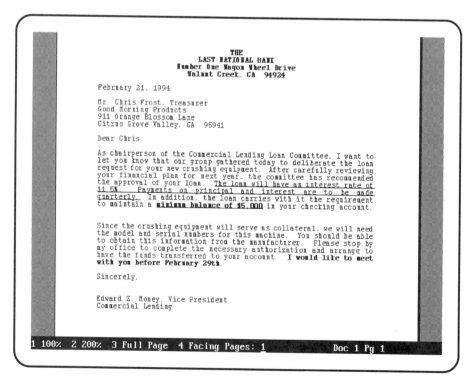

FIGURE W.22. Preview of letter with bank's heading.

| To center text as you type | **Select:** | `Center <Shift>+<F6>` | Perform a Center operation; Center resides on the Layout Align pop-out menu |

The cursor moves to the center of the line and is ready for entering the text.

| | **Enter:** | `THE` | Desired text |

When you press <Enter>, the cursor advances to the next line but is positioned at the left margin.

| | **Select:** | `Center <Shift>+<F6>` | Perform a Center operation for the second paragraph |
| | **Enter:** | `LAST NATIONAL BANK` | Desired text for the second line |

Again, the cursor is returned to the left margin. The next two lines of the bank's heading will be entered at the left margin and then is centered after it has been entered. Continue in this manner:

| To center existing text | **Enter:** | `Number One Wagon Wheel Drive` | |
| | **Enter:** | `Walnut Creek, CA 94924` | |

Since this is now existing text, centering is performed as follows:

| | **Action:** | Mark the block of text "Number One…CA 94924" using the Block <Alt>+<F4> command. |
| | **Select:** | `Center <Shift>+<F6>` Carry out the Center operation |

A message verifying the Center request is displayed in the Status Line like this:

[Just: Cntr]? No (Yes)

| | **Press:** | `<Y>` | Execute the CENTER command for the block of text |

The bank's heading has been added to the letter and is centered between the left and right margins.

~~~~~~~~
Caution Alert!
~~~~~~~~

> Be careful to execute the CENTER command (1) at the *left margin before* entering text in the as-you-type mode or (2) to mark the *entire* paragraph *before* executing the CENTER command. Otherwise, all your text will *not* be centered!

A second method of centering existing text is to center each line individually, regardless of whether the line ends with a [SRt], soft return, or a [HRt], hard return. The cursor is located at the left margin and the Center <Shift>+<F6> command is executed. This can be explored with Ed's letter as follows:

| To center a line of existing text | **Move to:** | `F in "February…"` | Locate cursor at the left margin |
| | **Select:** | `Center <Shift>+<F6>` | Perform a Center operation |

The line is centered. However, Ed really did not want to center the date. Once a line has been centered, this text formatting characteristic can be removed by deletion in this manner:

Action: Activate the Reveal Codes mode.

The [Cntr] or [Center] specifies the beginning of the line to be centered, whereas a [C/A/Flrt], if present, indicates the end of the text being centered. Here, "C" indicates Center, "A" designates Tab Align, and "Flrt" denotes Flush Right. Flush right is examined in the next section of this lesson. However, the ending of each of these specifications is delineated with the same [C/A/Flrt] embedded control characters in some versions of WordPerfect.

| To remove centering | **Move to:** | [Cntr] or [Center] preceding "February..." |
| | **Press:** | <Delete> Remove the [Cntr] or [Center] control code |

This line of text is now returned to its original position at the left margin. The bank's heading is complete.

Action: Bold the four lines of the bank's heading on Ed's letter.

Action: Preview the output as a WYSIWYG display, which should be similar to that shown in Figure W.22. Make any corrections, if necessary. Print the final document and save it as LETTER10.DOC.

W.3.5 Right-Aligning Text

Right alignment is an even or flush arrangement of text against the right margin, while the left margin is jagged or unaligned. The FLUSH RIGHT command is similar to the CENTER command. It can be applied to new text as it is typed or to existing text. For existing text, flush right can be performed for a block of text or on a line-by-line basis. The removal of a FLUSH RIGHT command proceeds in the same manner, using Reveal Codes, as for the CENTER command.

For Ed's letter, he wants the date to be located at the right margin. This is achieved as follows:

Action: Verify that LETTER10.DOC is the currently active document.

To align text against the right margin	**Move to:**	F in "February..." At the left margin of the desired line
	Select:	Flush Right <Alt>+<F6>
		Perform the Flush Right operation; Flush Right resides on the Layout Align pop-out menu of version 5.1

The line of text moves over with alignment at the right margin.

Action: Print this revised letter and save the document as file LETTER11.DOC.

W.3.6 Left-Aligning Text

The default in WordPerfect is to justify text. That is, both the left and right margins are justified (even), as described in Lesson W.1 and portrayed by each of the View Document illustrations, such as Figure W.22. You can make a document left-justified (with a ragged right margin) by changing the justification code in your document. Once the justification is changed, it remains changed until it is specifically changed to something else. If you turn off right or full justification *at the top* of a document, the entire document will be justified on the left side only. If full justification is turned off at the beginning of one paragraph and then turned on at the beginning of the next paragraph, only the one paragraph would not be left and right justified. The Center and Flush Right control codes are not affected by the justification. That is, Center and Flush Right are of a higher priority than justification and will remain regardless of the selected justification.

To left-justify Ed's letter and obtain a ragged right margin, proceed in the following manner:

Action: Verify that LETTER11.DOC is your currently active document.

To align text against the left margin with a ragged right margin	**Move to:**	left margin at beginning of first paragraph
	Select:	`Format <Shift>+<F8>` Initiate the FORMAT command; Format activities reside on the Layout pull-down menu, if available

This causes a menu to be displayed as illustrated in Figure W.23. The menu provides for formatting several characteristics of a document that control settings for a line, a page, an entire document, and other special characteristics, such as the style of underlining used. The Format menu in Figure W.23 contains a listing of each of the available choices once Line, Page, Document, or Other has been selected. A selection from this menu produces a second menu, like that for the Line selection shown in Figure W.24. Several of the formatting options are examined in the following sections.

The revisions to Ed's letter continue in this manner:

Select: `Line` Contains the Justification specification

Select: `Justification` Specification to be changed

```
Format

    1 - Line
            Hyphenation                     Line Spacing
            Justification                   Margins Left/Right
            Line Height                     Tab Set
            Line Numbering                  Widow/Orphan Protection

    2 - Page
            Center Page (top to bottom)     Page Numbering
            Force Odd/Even Page             Paper Size/Type
            Headers and Footers             Suppress
            Margins Top/Bottom

    3 - Document
            Display Pitch                   Redline Method
            Initial Codes/Font              Summary

    4 - Other
            Advance                         Overstrike
            Conditional End of Page         Printer Functions
            Decimal Characters              Underline Spaces/Tabs
            Language                        Border Options

    Selection: 0
```

FIGURE W.23. Format menu with alternatives for each choice.

```
Format: Line

    1 - Hyphenation                        No

    2 - Hyphenation Zone - Left            10%
                          Right            4%

    3 - Justification                      Left

    4 - Line Height                        Auto

    5 - Line Numbering                     No

    6 - Line Spacing                       1

    7 - Margins - Left                     1"
                  Right                    1"

    8 - Tab Set                            Rel: -1", every 0.5"

    9 - Widow/Orphan Protection            No


Selection: 0
```

FIGURE W.24. Line menu for justification selection.

[VERSION 5.0]

Select: No   Indicate desired justification

or

[VERSION 5.1]

Select: Left

Remember, in WordPerfect, Justification means that *both* the left and right margins are justified. Here, a response of "Yes" or "Full" would specify the justification of both margins. More recent versions of WordPerfect use the "Full" designation.

Press: Exit <F7>   Leave the Format menu and return to the document mode

Action: Preview the resulting document.

Action: Use Reveal Codes and inspect the insertion of [Just Off], or [Just:Left] as an embedded control code.

Action: Print the document and save this as the LETTER12.DOC.

W.3.7 Line Spacing

An entire document, a paragraph, or a section of a document may be single-spaced, double-spaced, or have any other desired spacing. The Format <Shift>+<F8> Line command is used to specify the desired line spacing. (The LINE command may be accessed from the Layout pull-down menu.) WordPerfect uses single-spacing as its default. Only if other spacing is desired is the Format <Shift>+<F8> Line command required. This command inserts an embedded control code of [Ln Spacing:2], for double-spacing, at the position of the cursor when the command is executed. This causes *all the following lines* in the document to have the selected spacing. If it is desired to double-space part of the document and then to have single-spacing follow the double-spacing, it is necessary to insert a single-spacing code, [Ln Spacing:1], where spacing switches from double- to single-spacing.

Consider the situation in which Ed wants to have the first paragraph of his document double-spaced, and the second paragraph single-spaced. This is accomplished as follows:

Action: Retrieve LETTER12.DOC as the currently active document.

To double-space lines of text		
Move to:	Beginning of first paragraph at the left margin	
Select:	`Format <Shift>+<F8>`	Select the FORMAT command; Format activities reside on the Layout pull-down menu
Select:	`Line`	Spacing is a Line activity
Select:	`Line Spacing`	Desired item to be specified
Enter:	`2`	Line spacing is changed to double-spacing
Press:	`<Enter>`	Return to Format menu
Press:	`<Enter>`	Return to document mode
or		
Select:	`Exit <F7>`	Alternative to returning directly to the document mode

The document is double-spaced from the beginning of the first paragraph to the end of the entire document.

Action: Review the double-spacing with the PRINT VIEW DOCUMENT command and inspect the control code with the REVEAL CODES command.

Now, change the spacing so only the first paragraph is double-spaced.

To single-space lines of text		
Move to:	Beginning of the second paragraph at the left margin	
Select:	`Format <Shift>+<F8>`	Select the FORMAT command
Select:	`Line`	Spacing is a Line activity
Select:	`Line Spacing`	Desired item to be specified
Enter:	`1`	Change the line spacing to singlespacing
Select:	`Exit <F7>`	Return to the document mode

The second paragraph and all following lines in the document are now single-spaced.

Action: Review the spacing with the PRINT VIEW DOCUMENT command and inspect the control codes for both the single- and double-spacing.

After reviewing the overall look of the letter, Ed thinks that single-spacing would be best. He wants to remove the double-spacing of the first paragraph. This is achieved as follows:

To remove double-spacing of text lines	
Action:	Make sure that the embedded codes are revealed and delete the [Ln Spacing:2] code at the beginning of the first paragraph. Then delete the [Ln Spacing:1] code at the beginning of the second paragraph.

The document is returned to its original single-spaced arrangement. Was it necessary to delete the [Ln Spacing:1] control code? Actually, this could remain in the document. However, since it is no longer needed, it was removed as a "good housekeeping" activity to avoid any future confusion with other control codes.

W.3.8 Indenting Paragraphs

With WordPerfect, three different types of indentation can be readily implemented:

- First line of a paragraph
- Left margin of an entire paragraph
- Left and right margins of an entire paragraph

Indenting the first line of a paragraph is performed with a [Tab], whereas the Indent <F4> command causes the entire left margin to be indented and the Indent <Shift>+<F4> command causes both the left and right margins to be indented. When indenting with the Indent <F4> and Indent <Shift>+<F4> commands (each time this command is executed at the beginning of a paragraph), the text is indented by one additional tab stop. Thus, by pressing Indent <F4> twice, the indentation would be two tab stops. The default tab stop settings in WordPerfect are at one-half-inch intervals. With the Reveal Codes display, WordPerfect indicates the location of each tab stop with the arrowhead or triangle (▲), which appears in the reverse video bar that splits the screen into the document area and the reveal codes area, as previously illustrated in Figure W.21.

Ed's letter can be revised to include indentation as follows:

Action: Retrieve LETTER12.DOC as the current document.

> To indent the first line of a paragraph

Move to: Beginning of first paragraph at the left margin

Press: `<Tab>` Indent the first line to the first tab stop

Action: Indent the first line of the second paragraph one-half inch.

Ed has decided to divide the first paragraph into two paragraphs so that the second one can be emphasized with indentation. The revisions continue in this manner:

Move to: `T` in "The loan will have an..."

Press: `<Enter>` Create a new paragraph

Press: `<Enter>` Place a blank line preceding the new paragraph

> To indent the left margin of the entire paragraph

Select: `Indent <F4>` Indent the left margin of the entire paragraph; Indent activities reside on the Layout Align pop-out menu

Select: `Indent <F4>` One more tab stop for the indentation

You see the changes on your screen.

Like other embedded control codes, those for indenting can be removed.

> To remove indenting

Action: Using Reveal Codes delete both of these left margin indentations, which are specified by the [—>Indent] control code.

Action: Verify that your cursor is located at the beginning of the paragraph.

To indent both the left and right margins

Select: `Indent <Shift>+<F4>`

Indent *both* margins by one tab stop; indent activities reside on the Layout Align pop-out menu

Select: `Indent <Shift>+<F4>` One more time

The Indent <Shift>+<F4> command inserts the [–>Indent<–] control code that indicates indentation from both margins. This indenting provides the emphasis Ed wants for the letter. However, he would like to change the closing line, signature line, and title line to a modified block style.

Action: Using <Tab> indent each of the closing, signature, and title lines by *five* tab stops to produce the desired modified block style closure for the letter.

Action: Review the embedded control codes for implementing this indentation.

Action: Preview the resulting letter, print it, and save this as file LETTER13.DOC.

Keypoint!

> Both the Indent <F4> and Indent <Shift>+<F4> commands are inserted in the document *at the location of the cursor*. If this is not at the beginning of a paragraph, then only the remainder of the paragraph is indented, often producing a strange and unwanted result. Should this occur, delete the indent control code and enter one at the desired location!

W.3.9 Setting Tabs

In WordPerfect, the default tab stops are set in one-half-inch intervals from the left edge of the page, *not* from the left margin of the page. The version 5.0 begins its tab setting measurements from the left edge of the page, whereas the version 5.1 begins the tab measurement one inch from the left edge of the page. For version 5.1, the default for the left edge of the page is a tab setting of -1 in. For indenting paragraphs and creating tables, these default tab settings meet many of the requirements for arranging text on each line. However, in a variety of situations, it is desirable to be able to modify the tab settings. Four different types of tab settings are available:

L (left). Aligns texts beginning at the tab stop and extending to the right. This provides an even left alignment of the text.

R (right). Aligns text ending at the tab stop and extending to the left. This provides an even right alignment of the text.

D (decimal). Aligns numeric values on the decimal point. The decimal is located at the tab stop and the number extends to the left and right based on the number of digits preceding or following the decimal.

C (center). Causes text to be centered on either side of the tab stop. This is similar to centering a paragraph, but with centering at a tab stop rather than the center of a line.

In addition to establishing tab stop locations, WordPerfect permits the use of a dot leader that causes a string of dots to occur between the text entered and the next tab stop. A dot leader can be used with left, right, and decimal tab stops.

A tab setting produces a control code that is inserted in a document. Once a tab setting has been inserted, that setting remains in effect for all the text that follows until another tab setting is inserted.

Ed used Lotus 1-2-3 to compute the loan payment for Good Morning Products crushing equipment and would like to include the following table in his letter to Chris:

```
Loan amount...........$140,000
Years.......................10
Interest rate..........11.5%
Quarterly payment.......$5,935
```

This table can be incorporated in Ed's letter as follows:

Action:	Retrieve LETTER13.DOC as the currently active document.	
Move to:	Blank line between the second and third paragraphs of the body of the letter	
Press:	`<Enter>`	Leave a blank line between the second paragraph and the table

To set tab stops

Select:	`Format <Shift>+<F8>`	Select Format in order to set the tab stops; Format activities reside on the Layout pull-down menu
Select:	`Line`	Setting tabs is a line activity
Select:	`Tab Set`	Tab Set menu appears

Tab stops are set from the Tab Set menu, as shown in Figure W.25. The "Ls" indicate the default tab setting for a left-justified tab at one-half-inch intervals.

FIGURE W.25. Tab Set menu.

	Press:	`<left>`	Display left end of the Tab Set menu and show how the tabs start at the left edge of the page
	Move to:	left edge of tab ruler	The <left> and <right> cursor keys control movement across this tab ruler
To remove all current tab settings	**Press:**	`<Ctrl>+<End>`	This is the EOL command, which removes all the tab settings from the line
To set a left-aligned tab stop	**Move to:**	the tab stop 2.0 in. from the left edge of the page	Use the cursor to locate the desired tab location
	Press:	`<L>`	An "L" appears on the tab ruler, signaling that a left-aligned tab now exists
To remove an individual tab stop	**Press:**	`<Delete>`	Individual tab stop is removed
To set a tab stop by typing the location [VERSION 5.0]	**Enter:**	`2.0`	Inches from *left* edge of page; Request a left-aligned tab stop by typing the desired location
	or		
[VERSION 5.1]	**Enter:**	`1.0`	Inches from left *margin* of page

WordPerfect provides the options of using the cursor to point to the location of a desired tab stop or specifying the location of a tab stop by entering the measurement from either the *left edge of the page* or the *left margin,* depending on the version.

To set a right-aligned tab stop with a dot leader	**Move to:**	the 5.5-in. position from the left *edge* of the page on the tab ruler	Specify the location for the next tab stop
	Press:	`<R>`	Numeric data in the table will be right-aligned
	Press:	`<.>`	A dot leader is desired, which is indicated by the appearance of the "R" as a highlighted tab stop
	Select:	`Exit <F7>`	Exit from the Tab Set
	Select:	`Exit <F7>`	Return to document mode

The period, < . >, serves as a toggle to turn the dot leader on or off for a left, right, or decimal tab stop.

This completes the specification of the tab stops for Ed's table. The text can now be entered for the table. Continue like this:

Action: Enter each of the four lines for Ed's table. Use <Tab> to move from the left margin to the location of the description and a second <Tab> to move to the location for entering the numeric values. Notice that the movement of the cursor to the right-aligned tab inserts the dot leader. Also notice the movement of the numbers to the left as they are typed at the right-aligned tab setting.

Action: Add a blank line after the table and before the third paragraph.

Action: Preview the resulting document. What is the difficulty with the third paragraph and the closing, signature, and title lines?

Keypoint!

> Once a tab setting has been inserted in a document, that setting remains in effect for all following paragraphs until another tab setting command is used!

The effect of the table's tab setting on the following paragraphs can be corrected in this manner:

To turn off the effect of a tab stop setting in following paragraphs

Move to: left margin at top of third paragraph

Position the cursor to enter another tab setting

Action: Create left-aligned tab settings at 0.5 in. and 1.0 in. from the *left margin* with these as the only two tab stops.

By setting these tabs immediately following Ed's table, you have established the desired tab settings for the rest of the body of Ed's letter. When using tab settings with tables like this, a good strategy for your WordPerfect document is to set the tabs you want to use for the main body of your letter at the beginning of your document *and* after each table. Once this tab setting has been established, you can easily position it as needed throughout your document. For Ed's letter, the tab setting is placed at the top of the document as follows:

Action: Use Reveal Codes to display the tab setting. Position the cursor on the tab setting at the beginning of paragraph three that follows Ed's table. Use <Del> to delete this code and then immediately restore it with <F1>. Move the cursor to the top of your document and again use <F1> to restore the tab setting code.

If your document contained additional tables, you could use the <Del> and <F1> to position the default tab setting for your document after each table.

A separate tab setting is desired for the closing of Ed's letter. This is created like this:

Move to: left margin of closing line

Position the cursor so a tab setting can be entered for this line

Action: Create a tab setting with a left aligned tab at 2.5 in. from the *left margin* as the only tab stop. Then, using the Reveal Codes screen, delete *four* [Tab] control codes for each of the closing, signature, and title lines.

Action: Preview this modified document, print the letter, and save the document as LETTER14.DOC.

These revisions, which added the table to Ed's letter, have been completed and corrections have been made to maintain the modified block style of the letter.

Caution Alert!

> If you make a mistake and reenter the Tab Set, be sure to delete the old one by using Reveal Codes, since a [Tab Set:...] is included in your document *each time* the Tab Set command is executed!

Keypoint!

> You can use delete <Del> and restore <F1> to place copies of a default tab setting for your document after each table or other section of your document that uses special tab settings!

W.3.10 Setting Margins

WordPerfect's margin settings control the size of the margins measured from the left, right, top, and bottom edges of the page. Default margins are set at one inch on all four edges of the page. Margins settings are control codes that are inserted into your document. As a result, changing the margin settings affects only your current document. Margins are set with the Format <Shift>+<F8> command. Because the changes in the left and right margins affect the length of a line, they are established with the FORMAT LINE command. (The LINE command may be accessed from the Layout pull-down menu.) Changes in the top and bottom margins affect the length of a page and are set by using the FORMAT PAGE command.

Keypoint!

> Left and right margins are changed to the new settings from the location of the cursor to the *end of your* document or the next margin control code! Several left and right margin settings can be inserted in one document to facilitate the use of different margins within the document!

Action: Retrieve LETTER14.DOC as your currently active document.

To change the left and right page margins

Action:		Move to top-left margin of the letter, since this is the location for inserting margin control codes that will apply to the entire document.
Select:	Format <Shift>+<F8>	Select the Format command; Format activities reside on the Layout pull-down menu
Select:	Line	Left/right margins is a Line activity
Select:	Margins Left/Right	The desired values to be specified
Enter:	2	Value for the left margin in inches
Enter:	2	Value for the right margin in inches from the right edge of the page
Select:	Exit <F7>	Return to the document mode

When specifying margins, it is necessary to enter values for both margins. If you want to use the default for one margin and change the other, then accept the suggested default value of one inch by merely pressing <Enter> for that margin, and enter the desired value for the other margin setting.

Keypoint!

> If you want to change only one margin, you must enter values for both margins. This can be accomplished by accepting the default value for the margin you do *not* want to revise!

Action: Preview the result with the PRINT VIEW DOCUMENT command. What problems are created with these margin settings?

Although Ed could make other revisions to the letter to avoid these difficulties, he believes that using a different left/right margin setting would be a better alternative.

Action: Using Reveal Codes, delete the left/right margin control code.

Action: Using the Format, LINE MARGINS LEFT/RIGHT commands, set the left and right margins at 1.25 in. each.

In a similar manner, the top and bottom margins can be adjusted for Ed's letter:

To change the top and
bottom page margins

Action:		Verify that the cursor is still located at the top-left margin of the letter.
Select:	`Format <Shift>+<F8>`	Select the FORMAT command
Select:	`Page`	Top/bottom margins is a Page activity
Select:	`Margins Top/Bottom`	Desired values to be specified
Enter:	`2`	Value for the top margin
Enter:	`2`	Value for the bottom margin
Select:	`Exit <F7>`	Return to the document mode

The top and bottom margins have been set.

Action: Preview the document with the PRINT VIEW DOCUMENT command. Use <PgDn> and <PgUp> to look at your document. What problem does this margin setting create?

By using these margins, the signature and title lines will not fit on one page. Word-Perfect starts a second page at the point indicated by a line of dashes or minus signs. Although Ed could place his letter on two pages, he would prefer to keep it on one page, which can be accomplished by using smaller top and bottom margins. Proceed to correct the letter in this manner:

Action: Using Reveal Codes, delete the top and bottom margin codes.

Action: Using the FORMAT PAGE MARGINS TOP/BOTTOM command, set the top and bottom margins at 1.5 in. each.

Action: Preview this document, print it, and save it as file LETTER15.DOC.

Ed has further improved the quality of his letter by modifying the margins.

W.3.11 Controlling Pages

New pages are controlled in WordPerfect similar to the manner in which new lines are created. The two options are as follows:

[SPg]. A soft page break. This is indicated by a horizontal line of dashes when the number of lines that will fit on a single page has been exceeded. This code is inserted automatically as you type the document.

[HPg]. A hard page break. This is indicated by a horizontal line of equal signs when you desire a new page in your document, regardless of the number of lines contained on the previous page. You create this control code with <Ctrl>+<Enter>.

Normally you use a hard page break when you want to force the beginning of a new page. For example, in writing a report, if you want to be sure that the summary and conclusion sections begin on a new page, insert a hard page break code.

Like hard returns, hard page breaks may be deleted from your document by using the Reveal Codes.

Ed's letter can be used to examine page breaks by adding double-spacing in this manner:

Action:	If necessary, retrieve the document file LETTER15.DOC.	
Move to:	D in "Dear Chris:"	
Select:	Format <Shift>+<F8>	Format activities reside on the Layout pull-down menu
Select:	Line	Type of formatting
Select:	Line Spacing	Desired activity
Enter:	2	Double-space the remainder of the document
Select:	Exit <F7>	Return to document mode

Double-spacing the letter causes it to occupy two pages. The soft page break is automatically inserted. This page break can be viewed as follows:

Press:	<PgDn>	Position the cursor at the top of the next page
Press:	<up>	Repeat this several times so the soft page break is in the middle of your screen

Figure W.26 illustrates this soft page break. For a document that has been divided into pages, the <PgDn> and <PgUp> keys provide a convenient means to move through the document one page at a time, and the "Pg" designator on the Status Line informs you of the page number where the cursor is currently located.

Action: Use the PRINT VIEW DOCUMENT command at 100 percent to look at the document layout for printing. Use <PgDn> and <PgUp> to move between the two pages of this document.

```
         addition, the loan carries with it the

         requirement to maintain a minimum

         balance of $5,000 in your checking

         account.


              Loan amount. . . . . .$140,000

---------------------------------------------------------------

              Years. . . . . . . . . . .10

              Interest rate. . . . . . 11.5%

              Quarterly payment. . . .$1,500


       Since the crushing equipment will serve as collateral, we
     will need the model and serial numbers for this machine.
 B:\LETTER15.DOC                            Doc 1 Pg 2 Ln 1.5" Pos 1.25"
```

FIGURE W.26. Soft page break inserted in letter.

As shown in Figure W.26, the soft page break may occur in the middle of the table. Rather than splitting the table between the two pages, a better arrangement is to have the entire table located on page 2. This is accomplished as follows:

Move to:	Left margin of the blank line between "account." in the second paragraph and the "Loan amount" in the table

To insert a hard page break

Press:	`<Ctrl>+<Enter>`	Insert a hard page break

The soft page break is no longer required. It disappears and the line of equal signs indicates the location of the hard page break.

Action: Preview the resulting letter using the Full Page selection and inspect both pages. Print the letter and save this document as file LETTER16.DOC.

Although Ed still prefers to use the single-spaced version of his letter, this arrangement has allowed you to investigate soft and hard page breaks.

W.3.12 Numbering Pages

WordPerfect allows page numbers to be located in several different positions on a page. Odd and even page numbers may be in different locations. The options for page number locations are illustrated with the Page Numbering menu shown in Figure W.27. The menu is accessed as a Format <Shift>+<F8> Page selection. (The Page command may be accessed from the Layout pull-down menu in version 5.1.) The PAGE NUMBERING command causes the pages *following* the command to be numbered. As a result, if you want all of the pages numbered, the PAGE NUMBERING command should be inserted at the top of the first page. However, if your first page was a title page and you want page numbering to begin with the second page, place the PAGE NUMBERING command somewhere below the top of page 1 and before the beginning of page 2. As shown by the menu of Figure W.27, Page Numbering can be turned off with the No Page Numbers menu selection.

Keypoint!

> When you need a title page, a better strategy is to create your title page as a separate document. This helps avoid page numbering problems, because your page number command can be located at the top of your document, where it is usually easy for you to enter and revise!

Page numbers can be added to Ed's letter with the page number centered at the bottom of each page in this manner:

Action: Retrieve the document file LETTER16.DOC.

To page number your document

Move to:	Top-left corner of the document.	
Select:	`Format <Shift>+<F8>`	Format activities reside on the Layout pull-down menu
Select:	`Page`	Numbering is a Page activity
Select:	`Page Numbering`	Desired activity

[VERSION 5.1]

Select:	`Page Number Position`	
		Desired option

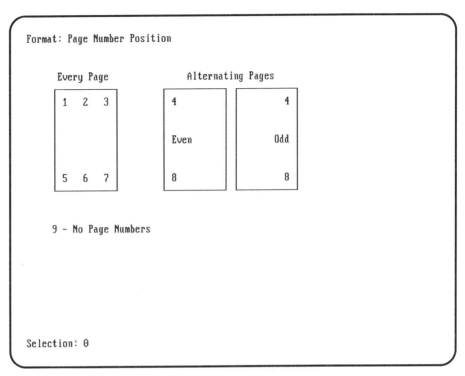

FIGURE W.27. Page numbering locations and selections.

[VERSIONS 5.0 and 5.1]	**Select:**	6	Choose bottom center location for the page numbers
	Select:	Exit <F7>	Exit for the menu

Page numbers are not immediately shown on the document screen. To see the pages numbers, preview or print your document.

Action: Preview the document with PRINT VIEW DOCUMENT FULL PAGE command and inspect the page numbers at the bottom center of each page.

Action: Print the document with the page numbers.

Page numbering can be removed by deleting the [Pg Numbering:Bottom Center] code.

Action: Delete the Page Numbering control code from this copy of Ed's letter.

W.3.13 Creating Headers and Footers

A header or footer is text that is repeated at the top or bottom of each page of a document. For example, suppose Ed wanted the phrase "The Last National Bank— Where Money Gets Down to Business" at the bottom of each page of his letters. A footer could be used to provide this text. Headers and footers are typically used with longer documents to assist in identifying sections or chapters. Headers and footers may also contain page numbers and dates as identifying information. Up to two different headers and footers are permitted. This allows one footer to be used on the even pages with a different one placed on the odd pages. Header and footer lines are placed *inside the margins* of the page and reduce the number of text lines on a page. When a header or footer is used, you can adjust the top/bottom margins and increase the page length to accommodate these special text lines.

The Header/Footer menu is accessed as a Format <Shift>+<F8> Page selection. (The PAGE command is located on the Layout pull-down menu.)

Since a header/footer control code is inserted in your document, header or footer lines begin on the page where the cursor is located when the header or footer is created. They remain in effect for *all* following pages until a different header or footer control code is encountered or until they are turned off with a DISCONTINUE command. When header and footer lines are added to a document, they do not appear on the screen with the main document. They can be inspected with the Reveal Codes display and appear when the document is previewed with the PRINT VIEW DOCUMENT command.

If you want a header to appear on the first page of your document, that header must be located *before* any text on page 1 including any [HRt] codes. Otherwise, the header will not appear on page 1. Also, if you are using header A and then add header B with the same page placement, both headers will appear on the page. A similar situation occurs for footers.

Keypoint!	When a header or footer is used for *all* pages in a document, it should be located at the top of the first page of the document before any text including [HRt] codes!

A footer can be added to Ed's letter like this:

Action: Retrieve LETTER16.DOC as your currently active document.

To add a footer to a document	**Move to:**	top left margin of the document	
	Select:	Format <Shift>+<F8>	Format activities reside on the Layout pull-down menu
	Select:	Page	Header/footer is a Page activity
	Select:	Footer	Desired activity

The Footer menu appears with the choices of

Footer A—the first footer
Footer B—a second footer

	Select:	Footer A	"A" is typically used when you have only one footer or header

The Header/Footer menu appears with these available selections:

Discontinue—turn off a header/footer
Every Page—display this header/footer on each page
Odd Page—include this header/footer on only the odd pages
Even Page—use this header/footer on only the even pages
Edit—revise an existing header/footer

	Select:	Every Page	Same footer will be used on both pages of the letter

A blank screen appears for entering the footer. Since headers and footers are separated from the main document, this separate screen is presented for their entry, as illustrated in Figure W.28. The Reveal Codes <Alt>+<F3> command may be used with this

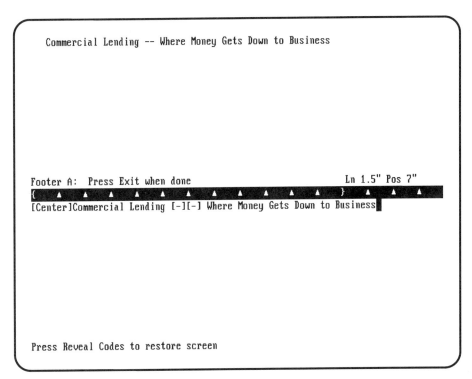

FIGURE W.28. Screen for entering footer.

screen to see any control codes that are included in your footer, like those to center or right-justify the footer.

Select:	Center <Shift>+<F6>	The CENTER command to place the footer
Type:	Commercial Lending--Where Money Gets Down to Business	Do *not* press <Enter>
Select:	Exit <F7>	Exit, entry of the footer
Select:	Exit <F7>	Return to document mode
Action:	Inspect the inclusion of the footer with the REVEAL CODES command, then preview the document with the PRINT VIEW DOCUMENT commands.	
Action:	Print this copy of Ed's letter and save the document as file LETTER17.DOC.	

Headers and footers can be removed from a document by deleting these codes using Reveal Codes.

Action: Reveal the control codes and delete the [Footer A: . . .] for this copy of Ed's letter.

Page numbering can be included with a header or footer. The <Ctrl>+<B> command is used to insert the characters ^**B** in a header or footer. These characters indicate that a page number is to be placed at that location in the header or footer when the page is viewed or printed.

Ed uses a footer with this letter for including his department's marketing slogan on each page. This provides him the ability to add his departmental identification to the bank's general stationery. A footer with page numbering can be placed in Ed's letter in this manner:

Action: If necessary, retrieve the document file LETTER16.DOC.

To add a footer with a page number to your document

Action:		Locate the cursor in the top-left corner of the document *before* the margin settings.
Select:	Format <Shift>+<F8>	Initiate the FORMAT command
Select:	Page	Footer is a Page activity
Select:	Footer	Desired activity
Select:	Footer A	Only one footer is used
Select:	Every Page	

Type (this command must be typed all on one line):

Commercial Lending--Where Money Gets Down to Business Page

Press:	<space> <space>	Add two spaces after "Page"

To specify page number location

Press:	<Ctrl>+<B>	Add the ˆ**B** to signal the location of the page number
Select:	Exit <F7>	Exit from specifying the footer
Select:	Exit <F7>	Return to the document mode
Action:		Preview the document, print it, and save it as file LETTER18.DOC.

The preview of the last page of Ed's letter with the footer containing the departmental slogan and page number is shown in Figure W.29.

This completes the development of Ed's letter to Chris and the exploration and demonstration of the more frequently used formatting features of WordPerfect. WordPerfect has many more commands that can be used to further enhance the appearance of your document. As you gain experience with WordPerfect, you may want to try some of these additional commands.

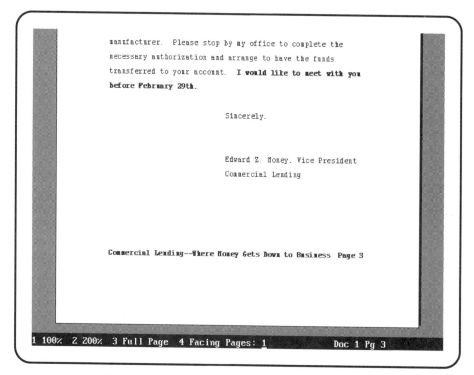

FIGURE W.29. Preview with footer containing page number.

W.3.14 When Things Go Wrong

Several situations may lead to difficulties when you are adding special formatting to your documents. Some of the more frequently occurring conditions and how to approach them are described here.

1. You have added special formatting to your document, but decide you want to use different formatting. For example, you have bolding where you want underlining or your margins are set at 2 in. when you want 1.5 in. margins.

   a. Use Reveal Codes <Alt>+<F3> to display the control codes currently embedded in your document.

   b. Move your cursor to the unwanted special formatting code and delete it.

   c. Add the desired formatting code to your document. If more than one special formatting feature is desired, add each feature individually.

2. You have included tab settings in your document. In establishing the desired tab settings, you used the Format <Shift>+<F8> command several times. As a result you now have several unwanted tab setting embedded in your document.

   a. Use Reveal Codes <Alt>+<F3> to display your current control codes.

   b. Locate the unwanted tab settings and delete them. Be careful not to delete the tab setting you still want.

3. You have used special formatting in your document, such as line spacing, margin settings, and tab settings. However, the formatting begins in the middle of your document rather than at the top of your document. This usually occurs because your cursor was located at the wrong location when you inserted the format control code in your document.

   a. Use Reveal Codes <Alt>+<F3> to display the current control codes.

   b. Locate the misplaced control code and use <Delete> to remove it.

   c. Position your cursor at the top of your document or other desired location for the control code.

   d. Use Cancel <F1> and Restore to insert the code at the desired position in your document.

W.3.15 Lesson Summary

- Formatting is used to enhance the appearance of a document and to assist in communicating its content.

- Text is underlined and/or bolded to emphasize it. Underlining and bolding can be added to text at the time it is typed or it can be added later to existing text.

- Control codes are inserted in a document to specify the occurrence of special effects such as bolding and underlining.

- The default in WordPerfect is to justify text with both an even left and right margin, rather than a ragged right edge.

- A paragraph of text can be centered, left-aligned, or right-aligned. Left alignment produces a ragged right margin.

- Single-spaced text is WordPerfect's default. This can be revised to any desired line spacing, such as double- or triple-spacing. A control code for spacing is inserted in a document at the location of the cursor when the Format <Shift>+<F8> Line command is applied to change the line spacing. This line spacing remains in effect until it is changed by another Format <Shift>+<F8> command.

- Paragraphs may be indented with the <Tab>, Indent <F4> (−>), or Indent <Shift>+<F4> (<−>) commands. <Tab> is used to indent the first line in a paragraph. The Indent <F4> command causes all the lines in a paragraph to be indented from the left margin. The Indent <Shift>+<F4> command causes both the left and right margins to be indented for an entire paragraph.

- Default tabs are set at one-half-inch intervals from the left edge of the page. Different tab settings can be made with the Format <Shift>+<F8> Line command. Tabs can be left-aligned, right-aligned, centered, or decimal-aligned. A dot leader can be used to precede a tab.

- Margins are set to a default of one inch from each side of the page. The left/right and top/bottom margins can be set to other values with the Format <Shift>+<F8> command for Line and Page, respectively.

- A document is automatically divided into pages with soft page breaks. A hard page break can be inserted in a document with the <Ctrl>+<Enter> command and forces the beginning of a new page.

- Page numbers can be placed in any of several different locations. The page numbers can have a different location for the odd and even pages. Page numbering commences from the location of the cursor when the Format <Shift>+<F8> Page command is executed.

- A header or footer can be added to each page of a document to assist in providing ongoing document identification. These headers and footers may contain page numbers if you use the <Ctrl>+<B> command.

- The Print <Shift>+<F7> View Document or PREVIEW command is useful in observing the WYSIWYG display of a document before printing.

- Special formatting codes, such as those for tabs, margins, line spacing, page numbering, and headers/footers are inserted in a document *at the location of the cursor* when the command is executed. These special formatting control codes remain in effect throughout the remainder of the document or until they are replaced by a subsequent control code.

- Many of the control codes have been revised from one version of WordPerfect to the next. Generally, control codes for different versions have similar syntax.

W.3.16 Practice Tutorial

(1)   Modify the draft of the LETTER7.DOC document from Lesson W.2 to produce the LETTER14.DOC document described in this Lesson as a guided activity in a hands-on manner. These activities add underlining, bolding, and other special effects to Ed's letter. Clear your current WordPerfect document before you begin. Retrieve your MYLETR7.DOC document file from the Practice Tutorial in Lesson W.2 as a starting point for this exercise.

Task 1: Make all the changes and modifications for the LETTER14.DOC version of this document.

Task 2: Print the final version of the letter.

Task 3: Save this document as the file MYLETR14.DOC.

Time Estimates

Novice: 60 minutes

Intermediate: 45 minutes

Advanced: 30 minutes

(2) Modify the draft of the LETTER14.DOC document from Practice Tutorial 1 to produce the LETTER18.DOC document described in this Lesson as a guided activity in a hands-on manner. These activities change margins, spacing, tab settings and footings for Ed's letter. Clear your current WordPerfect document before you begin. Retrieve your MYLETR14.DOC document file from Practice Tutorial 1 as a starting point for this exercise.

Task 1: Make all the changes and modifications for the LETTER14.DOC version of this document.

Task 2: Print the final version of the letter.

Task 3: Save this document as the file MYLETR18.DOC.

Time Estimates

Novice: 60 minutes

Intermediate: 45 minutes

Advanced: 30 minutes

W.3.17 Practice Exercises

(1) **Case: Crazy River Canoe (continued)**

Harry wants to improve the appearance of his marketing letter to prospective canoeing enthusiasts. Access the CANOE02.DOC document file from the Practice Exercise in Lesson W.2 as your starting point for making Harry's revisions. These operations integrate bolding, underlining, tab settings, and other special formatting effects into this document. Include the following revisions to your document as indicated in the tasks below:

(a) Opening:

>   Crazy River Canoe
>   4711 Shallow Brook
> Hungry Horse, MT 59873
>   Phone (406) 289-4724
>   Fax (406) 289-9453

(b) Closing enhancement:

> Crazy River Gives You a Wide Range of Choices. For Factory Direct Saving, Buy Direct From Our Factory or Selected Outlets!
>
> For more information, write or call.

(c) Table:

Model	Length	Weight	Price
Scout	11'4"	49 lb	$695
River Runner	12'3"	54 lb	$695
Adventurer	13'3"	56 lb	$715
Family	16'4"	63 lb	$725
Traveler	17'3"	67 lb	$750
Packer	18'1"	74 lb	$770

```
REFERENCE RULER:  12345678901234567890123456789012345678901234
                           1         2         3         4
```

Task 1: Add the heading in (a) at the top of your document. Be sure to center and bold this heading.

Task 2: Add the closing enhancement in (b) to the bottom of your document. Bold and underline this closing.

Task 3: Indent the first line of the first and third paragraphs by one-half inch.

Task 4: Indent the second paragraph one inch from both the left and right margins.

Task 5: Add the table in (c) between the second and third paragraphs. Include a blank line before and after this table. Use a dot leader between the Model and the Length columns in the table. Underline the column headings. Indent this table one inch from the left margin. Use the ruler to assist in setting up your tabs, but do *not* include the ruler in your document.

Task 6: Use "ragged right" margins for all the paragraphs that do not use other special formatting such as centering.

Task 7: Preview the document and print it.

Task 8: Save this as the document file CANOE03.DOC.

Time Estimates

Novice: 60 minutes

Intermediate: 45 minutes

Advanced: 30 minutes

(2)   Case: Crazy River Canoe (continued)

Harry wants to further modify the draft of the CANOE03.DOC document from Practice Exercise 1 to produce the CANOE04.DOC document described in this Lesson. These activities change margins and add a footer to the document. Start by retrieving your CANOE03.DOC document file from Practice Exercise 1.

Task 1: Change the left and right margins for the entire document to 1.5 inches.

Task 2: Add the following marketing slogan as a footer of the document and bold this footer:

Discover the Modern Frontier! Paddle a Crazy River!

Task 3: Preview the document and make any necessary corrections.

Task 4: Print the document.

Task 5: Save this document as the file CANOE04.DOC.

Time Estimates

Novice: 45 minutes

Intermediate: 30 minutes

Advanced: 20 minutes

W.3.18 Comprehensive Problems

(1)   Case: Park Place Villas (continued)

J.P. examined the most recent draft of Krista's letter to prospective tenants of Park Place Villas. He believes this should help the Property Management Division of Home Real Estate in attracting tenants. However, Krista still needs to add an opening and a closing to the letter. Also, J. P. has suggested that she include a table of the monthly rent for each type of townhome. The changes they would like to make to complete this letter are as follows:

(a)   Add this opening to the letter:

Park Place Villas
21400 Broomfield Boulevard
North Ridge, TX 75200

June 18, 1994

Ms. Heather Knapp
424 Pine Court
Riverside, OK 67891

Dear Heather:

(b)   Add this closing 3 inches from the left margin:

Sincerely,

Krista Buffett
Resident Manager

(c)   Add a paragraph with a table of rental prices:

The monthly rental for our townhomes is as follows:

```
                 Standard, two bedroom........................ $410
                 Deluxe, two bedroom.......................... $450
                 Standard, three bedroom...................... $520
                 Deluxe, three bedroom........................ $570

REFERENCE RULER:  12345678901234567890123456789012345678 90
                           1         2         3         4
```

(d)   Add a footer to the letter as follows:

Park Place Villas—The Good Life

Your tasks for incorporating these revisions into Krista's letter are as follows:

Task 1: Access the RENT3.DOC file from Lesson W.2.

Task 2: Add the opening in (a) to the letter. Center and bold the Park Place Villas letterhead. Right-align the date.

Task 3: Add the closing in (b) to the letter, located 3 in. from the left margin.

Task 4: Add the new paragraph in (c) that contains the rental prices. Make this the fifth paragraph in the letter, preceding the paragraph that begins, "For an appointment to view one of these..." Set up tabs for creating this table with the monthly rental amount right-aligned with a dot leader. Locate the table one inch from the left margin. Use the rule underneath the table to assist in locating your tabs, but do *not* include this in the table.

Task 5: Indent the first line of each paragraph one-half inch using tabs.

Task 6: Underline the phrase "within 30 minutes."

Task 7: Turn off the justification of the right margin of the letter so it has a ragged right margin.

Task 8: Add the footer in (d) to the letter. This footer is to be centered.

Task 9: Review your changes and make any additional corrections that may be necessary. Watch the use of indentation.

Task 10: Print the completed letter.

Task 11: Save this letter as file RENT4.DOC.

Time Estimates

Novice: 60 minutes

Intermediate: 45 minutes

Advanced: 30 minutes

(2)   Case: Pioneer Electric and Gas (continued)

Kelli and Mary inspected the most recent draft of their customer service acknowledgment letter for Pioneer Electric and Gas. Mary is confident that this will be helpful in addressing the problems she had discussed with Ramon. An opening and closing is still required for their letter. Also, Mary wants to include a table of the service change and connection fees. The revisions necessary to finish their letter are as follows:

(a)   Add this opening to the letter:

Pioneer Electric and Gas
One Energy Place
Broken Spring, MO 68127

July 1, 1994

Ms. Constance Ostland
4135 E. Lincoln Road
Blue Bell, MO 68122

Dear Ms. Ostland:

(b)   Add this closing 3 inches from the left margin:

Sincerely,

Kelli Olson
Customer Service

(c)   Add a paragraph with a table of service change and connection fees:

The fees for PEG's service changes and connections are as follows:

Service Type	Utility	Fee
Service Change	Electric	$25
	Gas	$35
	Both	$50
Connection	Electric	$175
	Gas	$250

REFERENCE RULER: 123456789012345678901234567890123456789012345
                        1   2   3   4

(d)   Add a footer to the letter as follows:

Pioneer Electric and Gas—We Light Up Your Life

Your tasks for including these modifications in Kelli's letter are as follows:

Task 1: Access the PEG3.DOC file from Lesson W.2.

Task 2: Add the opening in (a) to the letter. Center and bold the Pioneer Electric and Gas letterhead. Right-align the date.

Task 3: Add the closing in (b) located 3 inches from the left margin.

Task 4: Add the new paragraph in (c), containing the service change and connection fees. Make this the second paragraph in the letter, preceding the paragraph that begins, "All PEG employees carry . . . " Set up tabs for creating this table with the service fee amounts right aligned with the dot leader. Locate the table one inch from the left margin. Use underlining for the table headings. Use the ruler to help you determine your tab setting, but do *not* include it in your document.

Task 5: Indent the first line of each paragraph one-half inch using tabs.

Task 6: Underline the phrases "Level Payment Plan" and "Automatic Bill Payment Plan."

Task 7: Turn off the justification of the right margin of the letter so it has a ragged right margin. [*Hint:* begin this with the customer's name and address.]

Task 8: Add the footer in (d) to the letter. This footer is to be centered.

Task 9: Place the last paragraph and closing on page 2 of the letter. Include the following at the top of page 2 by typing it in your document:

Ms. Constance Ostland
Page 2
July 1, 1994

Obtain the page number using the <Ctrl>+<B> command, which inserts a ˆ**B.** The page number will appear instead of ˆ**B.**

Task 10: Review your changes and make any additional corrections that may be necessary. Watch the use of indentation.

Task 11: Print the completed letter.

Task 12: Save this letter as file PEG4.DOC.

Time Estimates

Novice: 60 minutes

Intermediate: 45 minutes

Advanced: 30 minutes

W.3.19 Case Application

Case: **State Fidelity Mutual**

Business Problem: Position information system
MIS Characteristics: Human Resources
Operational Control
Special Characteristic: Computer System Documentation
Management Functions: Directing
Controlling
Tools Skills: Underline and bold
Center and justify
Indent and tab
Tables
Line spacing
Page breaks
Page numbers
Footer
Forms

State Fidelity Mutual is a full-service health, life, property, and casualty insurance company that was founded in 1919. Since its early days of operation, State Fidelity has responded to the insurance needs of its customers. From its corporate headquarters in Broomfield, Indiana, State Fidelity delivers insurance coverage to its customers through more than 25,000 exclusive agents.

As described by Harry Walker, State Fidelity's President, "Insurance is a service. Information processing is the primary business activity of an insurance company like State Fidelity. Its modern computer facilities are the 'production line,' which processes premium collections and claim payments."

During the past two decades, State Fidelity has experienced moderate and continued growth averaging 10 percent per year. As a result, job vacancies occur continually throughout the company's headquarters and regional offices. Linda Schafer, Director of Human Resources, recently assigned Julie Scott, a Personnel Specialist, to a system development team charged with the implementation of a Position Information (PI) System that will monitor these job opportunities by keeping track of each position by job category, department, job requirements, and status of job opening. Julie served as the Human Resources Department user representative on the development team. Other team members included Jackie Felton and Alvin Bates, both information center consultants, from the Information Services Department.

An overview of the PI System developed by this team is provided by the dataflow diagram (DFD) in Figure W.30. A Completed-Position-Request is sent from the department manager, where the position is available, to the Director of Human Resources. Linda reviews the request (process M.1) and approves it or returns it to the department manager, as appropriate. The Approved-Position-Requests are entered into the Position Information System database (process P.1) each day by Julie or one of the other personnel specialists in the department. At the end of the day, Individual-Announcements are produced (process P.2) for duplicating and posting on company bulletin boards. A Summary-Report is also produced (process P.2) once a week for the Position Review Committee. If this Committee detects any problems with the posted positions, they contact the department managers and discuss the staffing requirements. The Review Committee looks for trends that may indicate that additional management attention is required for certain position categories.

Mary Baumgardner is the personnel specialist currently responsible for the operation of the PI System. Mary worked with Julie on the system's development and is familiar with the system's operation. However, its daily operation can be performed

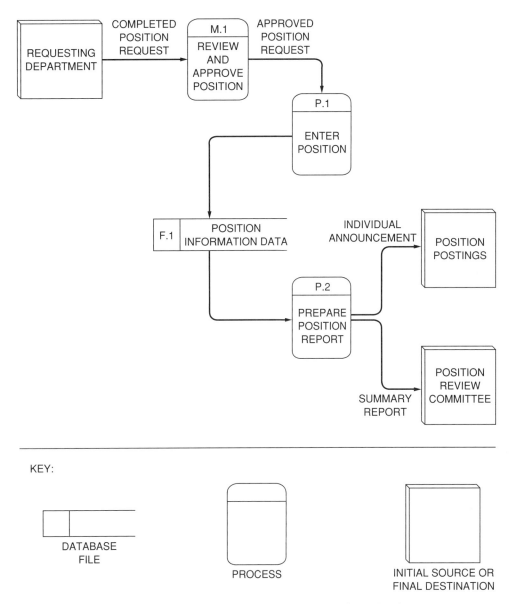

FIGURE W.30. Dataflow diagram (DFD) for Position Information System.

by several personnel specialists in the human resource department. The system was developed using a prototyping approach, where the system evolved through a series of revisions. Linda and Julie decided to place the system into operation before the documentation was completed. To assist the other personnel specialists in the operation of the PI System, Mary has been working with Julie and Jackie to develop documentation. Although the documentation is nearly complete, Mary has been busy with recent changes in the employees' health care plan and has not had time to finish the documentation. She is scheduled to start her annual vacation in two weeks and wants to complete the documentation so other personnel specialists can run the system while she is gone. She wants you to finish the documentation for the PI System.

Tasks

1. Access the POSINFO.DOC document file. Print the document and review its content. Notice that a blank "Position Information Description" form is included at the bottom of the document.

2. Change the justification of the *entire* document so it will have a ragged right margin.

3. Add blank lines to the document so each section title has one blank line before and after it. Section titles begin with a section number, such as 1.0, 3.0, or 5.2.

4. Bold the two lines of heading at the top of this system documentation and the top of the Position Information Description form.

5. Bold and underline each of the main section titles indicated as a **X.0** level, such as **1.0, 2.0,** and **6.0.**

6. Underline each of the lower level section titles, such as 5.1, 5.2, and 5.4. That is, all those *not* a level zero.

7. Indent the text in each section one-half inch.

8. Indent the lower level section titles one-half inch.

9. Indent the text within each lower level section by one inch. That is, an additional one-half inch from the main section indentation.

10. Indent the four menu choices 1.5 inches in the Operation section.

11. Place a blank line before each of the descriptions in the Edit Positions section, which are Enter New Position, Edit Existing Position, and Delete Position. Indent the left and right margins for these descriptions one-half inch. The total indentation for the left margin should now be 1.5 inches (one-half inch for the lower level section title, one-half inch for the text within this section, and one-half inch for these descriptions).

12. Add this table in the Processing Schedule section at the designated location:

Report	Schedule
Position Announcements	Daily @ 3:00 pm
Summary Report	Friday @ 4:00 pm

REFERENCE RULER: 12345678901234567890123456789012345678901234567890
                  1   2   3   4   5

The table is to be indented 1.5 inches from the left margin. Use the ruler underneath the table to assist in locating your tabs, but do not include the ruler in the table. Be sure to adjust any following tabs in your document to preserve the indentations created in the foregoing Tasks. Remove from the document the line that specifies the location of this table.

13. Add this table in the Department Listing section at the designated location:

Department	Number
Accounting	101
Claims	404
Finance	203
Human Resources	607
Information Services	301
Investments	297
Policy Development	501
Underwriting	402

REFERENCE RULER: 12345678901234567890123456789012345678901234567890
                  1   2   3   4

The table is to be indented 1.5 inches from the left margin. The department numbers are to be right-aligned with a dot leader. Use the ruler underneath the table to assist in locating your tabs, but do not include the ruler in the table. Again, be sure to adjust any following tabs in your document to preserve the indentations created by the earlier Tasks. Remove from the document the line that specifies the location of this table.

14. Add this footer to the document:

Position Information System—Page #

The footer is to appear on each page with the page number, is to be bolded and centered, and is to generate the correct page number as indicated by the # symbol.

15. (*Optional*) Complete the Position Information Description form by performing these activities:

   (a) Double-space the entire form.

   (b) Add underscores to create lines on which the desired information can be written.

16. Check all the spelling in the document and correct any errors.

17. Save the completed document.

18. Print the completed document.

19. Write a summary of any suggested changes that you would like to see included in this documentation. What could be added to this documentation to improve the ease of use in operating this system?

Time Estimates

Novice: 90 minutes

Intermediate: 60 minutes

Advanced: 45 minutes

Automating Documents

CONTENT

- What Are WordPerfect Macros?
- Creating Named Macros
- Executing Macros
- Editing Macros
- Fill-in-the-Form Documents
- Creating Form Documents
- Producing Form Documents
- What Is Mail Merge?
- Creating Mail Merge Documents
- Producing Mail Merge Documents
- When Things Go Wrong

W.4.1 What Are WordPerfect Macros?

A WordPerfect macro performs automatic typing. A sequence of keystrokes is saved in a special macro file so that it can be used repeatedly, whenever you want, by just entering the name of your macro file. Anytime you encounter a situation where you are continually duplicating the same series of commands, a phrase, or a paragraph, consider using a macro. The general concept behind WordPerfect macros is the same as that for Lotus 1-2-3 macros and dBASE programs. In each situation, a series of commands is executed repeatedly whenever desired. Macros allow automatic typing of any sequence of keystrokes in your WordPerfect document.

Although there are a number of situations where macros can be used to automate document preparation, several of the most common uses occur when the following arise:

1. Will you type the same sentence or paragraph in several different documents? If so, a macro may contain the desired text.

2. Do you use the same opening or closing for letters and memos? This can be stored in a macro for use on demand.

3. Do you use a special arrangement of margins and tab settings for your documents? New documents can be initially set up with a macro.

4. Will a merge be performed by someone not trained in this use of WordPerfect? A macro can be used to perform this operation.

Macros are most useful for situations such as

- Typing the same phrase
- Changing margins or spacing
- Setting tabs for special paragraphs and tables
- Reinstating previous tab settings
- Changing the directory

W.4.2 Creating Named Macros

There are two basic steps in using WordPerfect macros: (1) create the macro file of commands and (2) execute the macro. You should plan your macro before you begin to create it. What will the macro do? What sequence of keystrokes needs to be recorded in your macro to perform the desired action? To plan the steps in your macro, you may want to go through each keystroke manually, writing down each key as you press it. This is known as a "dry run," which is especially important for the WordPerfect commands and menu selections that may be included in your macro. Finally, verify that the sequence is correct before you begin to enter your macro. This planning should make it easier for you to create macros that perform your desired activities.

Begin creating a macro with the Macro Define <Ctrl>+<F10> command. When you issue this command, WordPerfect asks you to provide a name for your completed macro, and then asks you for a general description of the macro. Then, the keystrokes you enter are recorded in your macro file for subsequent playback and execution.

Sara Gould works with Ed at The Last National Bank. Like Ed, she is responsible for reviewing commercial loan applications and informing her customers of the loan's approval. As a Vice President of Commercial Lending, Sara generates a dozen or more letters each day. To assist her in the notification process, Sara decides to create a WordPerfect macro to generate a standard opening for her letters. She sketches out the opening of her letter, as shown in Figure W.31.

The macro for generating this opening for Sara's letters contains the keystrokes for bolding and centering the address, as well as entering the text in the document. The current date is obtained from the computer's clock with the Date <Shift>+<F5> command, so including the current date in the letter will be automatic.

The creation of Sara's macro proceeds as follows:

To create a WordPerfect macro		
Action:	Make sure you have cleared your WordPerfect screen with the Exit <F7> command.	
Select:	`Macro Define <Ctrl>+<F10>`	
	Initiate the entry of macro	
	Macro activities are accessed from the	
	Tools pull-down menu in version 5.1	

A message like this appears on the Status Line:

Define macro:

Although WordPerfect indicates you are to "Define" the macro, this is actually a request for you to enter the *name* of your macro.

THE
LAST NATIONAL BANK
Number One Wagon Wheel Drive
Walnut Creek, CA 94924

March 29, 1994

Dear

FIGURE W.31. Desired opening for letter.

Enter:	B:OPENING	The *name* of the macro with the disk drive identifier. The macro will be placed in the file OPENING.WPM on disk drive B:. WordPerfect automatically adds the extension **WPM**.

This message is displayed in the Status Line:

Description:

This request for the "Description" is prompting you to enter information about your use of the macro and *not* the actual macro commands.

Enter:	Opening for letter	Desired description, up to 39 characters

"Macro Def" flashes in the Status Line while you are entering the macro. *Every keystroke you enter,* from now until you press <Ctrl>+<F10> to turn off the macro recorder, is part of the macro.

Press:	<F6>	Activate Bold
Enter:	THE	Enter the bank's address
Enter:	LAST NATIONAL BANK	
Enter:	Number One Wagon Wheel Drive	
Enter:	Walnut Creek, CA 94924	
Press:	<F6>	Turn off Bold

Keypoint!

> Since each keystroke is recorded in the macro, WordPerfect commands in this example are selected directly with function keys. With version 5.1, pull-down menus could be used in selecting these commands, but this would increase the number of keystrokes recorded in the macro!

Press:	<Home> <Home> <up>	Return to upper-left corner
Press:	<Alt>+<F4>	Select Block
Press:	<down> <down> <down> <down>	Mark the block for centering
Press:	<Shift>+<F6>	Select Center

A message verifying that the Block Center request is displayed in the Status Line like this:

[Cntr]? No (Yes)

Press:	`<Y>`	Request centering of the block
Press:	`<right>`	Move cursor past [bold] termination
Press:	`<Enter> <Enter>`	Add two blank lines
Press:	`<Alt>+<F6>`	Select Flush Right
Press:	`<Shift>+<F5>`	Select Date
Select:	`Date Text`	Request text—not code—version of the current date
Press:	`<Enter> <Enter> <Enter>`	Add blank lines
Type:	`Dear`	Include this text
Press:	`<space>`	Add space following "Dear"

This completes the keystrokes Sara wants to include in her macro.

Press:	`<Ctrl>+<F10>`	Select Macro Define a second time to terminate the entry mode

The macro is written to the file B:OPENING.WPM. This file contains each of the keystrokes entered between the two Macro Define <Ctrl>+<F10> commands, as illustrated in Figure W.32. Once the macro is completed, it can then be executed when desired, as many times as desired.

If you made an error and then corrected it, these keystrokes are also included in the macro. In Figure W.32, the {DISPLAY OFF} macro command is automatically inserted to suppress the display of the macro commands as they are executed. This is the default condition in WordPerfect.

```
Macro: Action

    File            B:OPENING.WPM

    Description     Opening for letter

  ┌──────────────────────────────────────────────────────────────┐
  │ {DISPLAY OFF}{Bold}THE{Enter}                                  │
  │ LAST·NATIONAL·BANK{Enter}                                      │
  │ Number·One·Wagon·Wheel·Drive{Enter}                            │
  │ Walnut·Creek,·CA··94924{Enter}{Bold}                          │
  │ {Home}{Home}{Up}{Block}{Down}{Down}{Down}{Down}{Center}y{Right}{Enter}│
  │ {Enter}                                                        │
  │ {Flush Right}{Date/Outline}1{Enter}                           │
  │ {Enter}                                                        │
  │ {Enter}                                                        │
  │ Dear·                                                          │
  │                                                                │
  │                                                                │
  └──────────────────────────────────────────────────────────────┘

  Ctrl-PgUp for macro commands;  Press Exit when done
```

FIGURE W.32. Macro for generating opening for letter.

Keypoint!

> When some WordPerfect commands are included in macros, the selection of the command may terminate the entry of the macro. For example, including the Merge command (described later in this Lesson) in a macro causes the entry mode to be terminated without selecting the Macro Define <Ctrl>+<F10> a second time!

Keypoint!

> *Every* keystroke is recorded in the macro, including any errors and any corrections. Any such unwanted keystrokes may be removed by editing the macro!

W.4.3   Executing Macros

A macro is ready for execution, on demand, once it has been created and stored in a file. Each time the same keystrokes are desired, the macro is executed again with the Macro <Alt>+<F10> command.

Sara's macro for the opening of her letters is executed in this manner:

To execute a macro

Action: Clear your WordPerfect document mode screen.

Select: Macro <Alt>+<F10>   Initiate execution of the macro
Macro activities are reached from the
Tools pull-down menu

This prompt is displayed on the Status Line:

Macro:

Enter: B:OPENING   Name of the file containing the macro; the extension is *not* required

Sara's macro is executed and the letter's opening is placed in the document, as illustrated in Figure W.31. She is ready to continue with her letter.

Action: Preview the opening and print it.

W.4.4   Editing Macros

Once a macro has been created, it may be revised by editing it. WordPerfect has a built-in macro editor. The Define Macro <Ctrl>+<F10> command used to create a macro is also used to edit the macro. If a macro already exists, when the file name is entered in response to the "Define macro:" prompt, WordPerfect detects the existence of this file and provides the opportunity to (1) Replace or (2) Edit the macro. By selecting Replace, the old macro is erased and subsequently is replaced with the content of the new macro. By selecting Edit, you can revise the macro.

For Sara's macro, the opening to her letter can be modified as follows:

To revise an existing macro

Select: Define Macro <Ctrl>+<F10>   Initiate the Define Macro activity
Define Macro is accessed from the Tools
pull-down menu

Enter: B:OPENING   File name containing the macro

WordPerfect responds with a message on the Status Line indicating that this macro already exists and provides menu choices for replacing or making edit changes to it.

Select: Edit   Macro will be revised

The macro is displayed in the macro edit window.

Select: Action [if necessary]   Such as for version 5.0

The macro is revised by moving the cursor to the desired location and making edit changes, like editing a document. WordPerfect's special commands are enclosed in braces, {...}, as illustrated in Figure W.32. To remove these commands, place the cursor on the command and <Delete> it. Inserting commands in the macro requires additional steps, depending on whether you want to insert a single special command or a series of commands as follows:

Single command. Press <Ctrl>+<V>, the desired command.

Several commands. Press <Ctrl>+<F10>, enter the series of command key strokes, and then press <Ctrl>+<F10> to terminate entry of this series.

Sara would like to change the bolding of the address to underlining and the CA state designation to the state name. This is accomplished in the following manner:

Move to: {Bold}   The *command to be changed*
Press: <Delete>   Remove this unwanted command
Press: <Ctrl>+<V>   Only one new command will be entered
Press: <F8>   Select Underline
Action: In the same manner, change the other {Bold} keystroke to {Underline}.

The UNDERLINE command now replaces the BOLD command.

Move to: A in "CA"   The *text to be revised*
Press: <Delete>   Remove the unwanted character
Type: alifornia   New text

This completes these revisions.

Action: If you spot any other errors in your macro, correct them.
Select: Exit <F7>   Terminate the macro edit
Select: Exit <F7> [again, if necessary]
                                         Such as for version 5.0

When you exit from the macro edit process, the revised file is saved under the name of your macro. This completes the desired revisions to Sara's macro.

Caution Alert!

> Exercise care in making changes to WordPerfect commands. These commands *must be* in the correct sequence for their execution! For most changes to WordPerfect macros, usually the best alternative is to replace the macro rather than edit it!

W.4.5   Fill-in-the-Form Documents

Fill-in-the-form documents contain both fixed and variable information for a series of specific documents. The fixed or "standard" information, also known as "boiler plate," is the same for each letter, memo, proposal, legal contract, or other business document. The variable information is unique to each document generated, like that for personalized form letters (that is, to the extent you can personalize a form letter). To produce these documents in WordPerfect, fixed information is combined with variable information to yield the final finished document, as illustrated in Figure W.33. This combination of information is carried out with the Merge <Ctrl>+<F9> command in WordPerfect. To perform a merge, put the fixed information in a "primary file." This file can then be merged with variable information from either (1) the keyboard or (2) a secondary file. When the keyboard is used, the variable information is obtained interactively and is placed in the final document. When a secondary file is employed, the variable information is placed in a file for a subsequent merge with the primary file. Variable information, placed in a secondary file, may be edited and reused as desired. Interactive keyboard entry does not provide this reusability. The keyboard entry of variable information is presented first. This is followed by the discussion of using a secondary file.

As a Commercial Lending Vice President at The Last National Bank, Sara needs to write a number of letters to customers concerning their loan applications. She has created a standard fill-in-the form letter for this purpose, as illustrated in Figure W.34. In this figure, the variable information, to be entered from the keyboard, is identified for you by underlining. She has determined five pieces of variable information that she wants to include in each letter:

1. Current date
2. Customer name and address
3. Salutation
4. Loan use
5. Loan amount

The current date can be obtained from the computer's clock with a DATE MERGE command, whereas the other text is provided through FIELD MERGE commands. The fill-in-the-form letter is created as a regular WordPerfect document with special merge codes or commands inserted in those locations or fields where the variable information is to be obtained for each letter as input from the keyboard.

The dataflow diagram (DFD) in Figure W.35 indicates the processing to be performed. The fill-in-the-form letter is created as a document and is stored in a file. This document contains the special merge codes and commands that request the variable information from the keyboard. When merge processing is conducted, the merge combines keyboard input with the primary document to produce the completed letter.

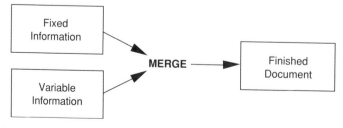

FIGURE W.33. Combining fixed and variable information for fill-in-the-form document processing.

THE
LAST NATIONAL BANK
Number One Wagon Wheel Drive
Walnut Creek, CA 94924

March 29, 1994

Ms. Susan Salem
Wente Brothers
9800 S. Main
Livermore, CA 94441

Dear Ms. Salem:

I am pleased to inform you that your loan for a high-speed bottler has been reviewed by our loan committee. Your loan in the amount of $198,000 has been approved.

Please stop by my office to complete the necessary authorization and arrange to have the funds transferred to your account.

Sincerely,

Sara S. Gould, Vice President
Commercial Lending

FIGURE W.34. Letter to be produced by merging the fill-in-the-form loan letter.

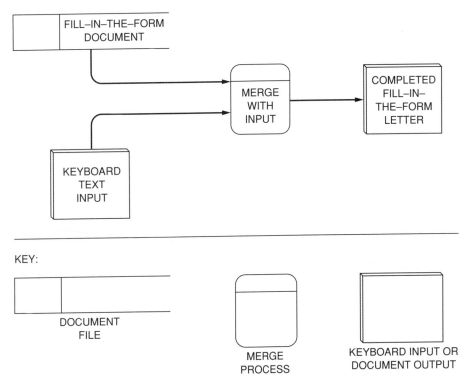

FIGURE W.35. Dataflow diagram (DFD) for interactive fill-in-the-form document processing.

W.4.6   Creating Form Documents

The fill-in-the-form document is created as a primary file that contains merge codes and commands at the field location where variable information will be inserted in a document. The merge codes used in WordPerfect version 5.0 are considerably different from those used in version 5.1. As a result, there are a number of differences in the creation of the primary files between these versions. The development of the primary file is presented separately for each version of WordPerfect. Read the information about the version available for your use. You may want to read through the procedure for the other version to become familiar with the differences between these two versions of WordPerfect.

W.4.6.1.   Version 5.0

For Sara's fill-in-the-form letter, the primary file in version 5.0 is created as follows:

To create a document containing merge codes		
Action:	Be sure to clear the WordPerfect screen with the Exit <F7> command.	
Action:	Enter the bank's name and address and bold it, as illustrated in Figure W.34, and include two blank lines after this.	
Select:	Flush Right <Alt>+<F6>	Date is to be right aligned
Select:	Merge Codes <Shift>+<F9>	Initiate entering a code for the date; obtain a menu of merge codes on the Status Line
Select:	^D	Date code, press: < **D** >
Press:	<Enter> <Enter>	Add two additional blank lines
Select:	Merge Codes <Shift>+<F9>	A code is needed for entering the customer name and address information
Select:	^C	Code for interactively entering text from the keyboard
Press:	<Enter> <Enter>	More blank lines
Type:	Dear	Standard text for salutation
Press:	<Space>	Place a space after "Dear"
Select:	Merge Codes <Shift>+<F9>	
Select:	^C	Permit salutation to be entered interactively
Action:	Enter the rest of Sara's loan approval form letter using the Merge Codes <Shift>+<F9> command and the ^C merge command for the loan use and loan amount in the locations shown in Figure W.36.	

Keypoint!

> The MERGE commands, such as ^C and ^D, *must* be inserted in your document using the Merge Codes <Shift>+<F9> command. You may *not* just type them into your document!

Action: Review the layout of this letter with the PRINT VIEW DOCUMENT command. Save this document as file LOANLET.PF. The extension **PF** is used to denote

```
                              THE
                       LAST NATIONAL BANK
                   Number One Wagon Wheel Drive
                    Walnut Creek, CA  94924
                                                          ^D


 ^C

 Dear ^C:

 I am pleased to inform you that your loan for a ^C has been
 reviewed by our loan committee.  Your loan in the amount of ^C has
 been approved.

 Please stop by my office to complete the necessary authorization
 and arrange to have the funds transferred to your account.

                         Sincerely,



                         Sara S. Gould, Vice President
                         Commercial Lending

 B:\LOANLET.PF                           Doc 1 Pg 1 Ln 1.5" POS 1"
```

FIGURE W.36. Fill-in-the-form loan letter with WordPerfect version 5.0 merge codes.

that this is a **P**rimary **F**ile. Of course, for this document file, you could use any extension. PF helps you identify this as a primary file for a WordPerfect merge operation.

W.4.6.2. Version 5.1

For Sara's fill-in-the-form letter, the primary file in version 5.1 is developed as follows:

To create a document containing merge codes	**Action:**	Be sure to clear your WordPerfect screen with the Exit <F7> command before you begin entering this new document.
	Action:	Enter the bank's name and address; center and bold it, as illustrated in Figure W.34; and include two blank lines after this.
	Select:	Flush Right <Alt>+<F6> Date is to be right aligned Align activities are accessed from the Layout pull-down menu
	Select:	Merge Codes <Shift>+<F9> Code is needed for the date Merge codes selections are reached from the Tools pull-down menu
	Select:	More The main merge codes menu does not contain the date merge code
	Select:	{DATE} Date code, also denoted with the ^**D** from earlier versions
	Press:	<Enter> <Enter> Add two more blank lines

Select:	Merge Codes <Shift>+<F9>	
		Code is needed for entering the customer name and address information
Select:	Input	Code for interactively entering text from the keyboard

A message is displayed on the Status Line requesting a name for this Input as follows:

Enter Message:

Enter:	Customer name and address	
		Your name for this input information
Press:	<Enter> <Enter>	More blank lines
Type:	Dear	Standard text for salutation
Press:	<Space>	Place a space after "Dear"
Select:	Merge Codes <Shift>+<F9>	
Select:	Input	Permit salutation to be entered interactively
Enter:	Salutation	Your name for this input information

The message with each {INPUT} identifies the information that is to be entered. The tilde (˜) is used to designate the end of this identification.

Keypoint!

> The tilde (˜) is placed in your document by the Merge Codes <Shift>+<F9> Input command. You do *not* type the tilde!

Action: Enter the rest of Sara's loan approval form letter by using the Merge Codes <Shift>+<F9> command and the INPUT MERGE command for the loan use and loan amount in the locations shown in Figure W.37.

Keypoint!

> The merge commands, such as {INPUT} and {DATE}, *must* be inserted in your document using the Merge Codes <Shift>+<F9> command. You may *not* just type them into your document!

Action: Review the layout of this letter with the PRINT VIEW DOCUMENT command. Save this document as file LOANLET.PF, where **PF** is used to denote the **P**rimary **F**ile. Of course, for this document file, you could use any extension. PF helps you identify this as a *Primary File* for a WordPerfect merge operation.

W.4.7   Producing Form Documents

The steps in generating a finished document from a fill-in-the-form document are the same for versions 5.0 and 5.1. This process involves merging your fill-in-the-form document file into your currently active document with the Merge <Ctrl>+<F9> command. As a result, your current document is usually cleared before performing the merge. During the merge operation, you enter the variable information by using your keyboard. The end of the variable information for each field is signaled with the Merge R <F9> command. When the variable information has been entered for one field, processing continues with the next field until information is input for all fields.

```
                             THE
                       LAST NATIONAL BANK
                   Number One Wagon Wheel Drive
                     Walnut Creek, CA  94924

                                              {DATE}

{INPUT}Customer name and address~

Dear {INPUT}Salutation~:

I am pleased to inform you that your loan for a {INPUT}Loan use~ has
been reviewed by our loan committee.  Your loan in the amount of
{INPUT}Loan amount~ has been approved.

Please stop by my office to complete the necessary authorization
and arrange to have the funds transferred to your account.

                        Sincerely,


                        Sara S. Gould, Vice President
                        Commercial Lending

B:\LOANLET.PF                           Doc 1 Pg 1 Ln 2" Pos 1"
```

FIGURE W.37. Fill-in-the-form loan letter with WordPerfect version 5.1 merge codes.

Sara's fill-in-the-form letter to Susan Salem is generated in this manner:

To use a document containing merge codes	**Action:** Clear the current document using Exit <F7>.

Keypoint! | The current document is usually cleared *before* performing a merge to avoid including the merged document with another document!

Select:	Merge <Ctrl>+<F9>	Initiate execution of merge operation, Merge resides on the Tools pull-down menu
Select:	Merge	Desired activity

A message appears on the Status Line prompting for the name of your document file like this:

Primary file:

Enter:	B:LOANLET.PF	Name of your document file, including the disk drive identifier, if necessary

Another message appears on the Status Line prompting for a second document file in this manner:

Secondary file:

Press:	<Enter>	No secondary file is used with this interactive fill-in-the-form document

When a fill-in-the-form document receives all of its input from the keyboard, no secondary document is used.

WordPerfect begins the merge operation of the document stored in your file with input from your keyboard. Continue in this manner:

Enter:	Ms. Susan Salem	Customer name and address are entered from the keyboard
Enter:	Wente Brothers	
Enter:	9800 S. Main	
Enter:	Livermore, CA 94441	
Press:	<F9>	Terminate the input of the customer name and address information

Keypoint!

> With version 5.1, the text following the {INPUT} is displayed on the Status Line, prompting your input from the keyboard!

Type:	Ms. Salem	The salutation
Press:	<F9>	Terminate this input
Type:	high-speed bottler	The loan use
Press:	<F9>	Terminate this input
Type:	$198,000	The loan amount
Press:	<F9>	Terminate the merge, since this is the last data item entered

The loan amount is the last information to be furnished, and then the merge is completed. The finished document now appears on your screen and is ready for any other WordPerfect activities.

Action: Preview the completed document with PRINT VIEW DOCUMENT, print the letter, and save this completed letter as the document file LOANLET.DOC.

This completes the use of Sara's fill-in-the-form letter for individual loan approvals. For each loan, Sara can execute the merge to produce a letter. These steps for creating and using a fill-in-the-form letter are summarized in Figure W.38. Once the merge is completed, if Sara needed to include any additional personal information in the letter, she could edit the letter as she would any other WordPerfect document.

1. Create the Primary File
    a. Type document
    b. Enter merge codes
        Select: Merge Codes <Shift>+<F9>
        Select: Interactive entry merge code (^C or {INPUT})
    c. Save <F10> the file with the .PF extension
    d. Clear the screen with Exit <F7>
2. Merge the File
    a. **Select:**   Merge/Sort <Ctrl>+<F9>
    b. **Select:**   Merge
    c. **Enter:**   Primary file name
    d. **Press:**   <Enter> [no secondary file]
    e. Type the text for each input and use <F9> to complete entry

FIGURE W.38. Summary of interactive fill-in-the-form processing.

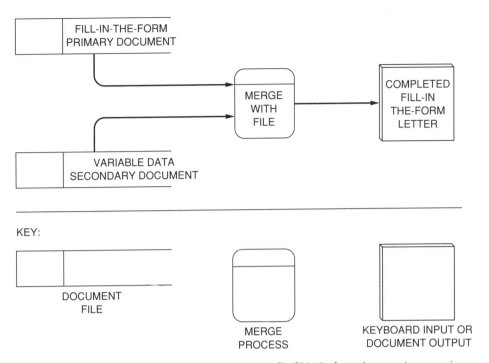

FIGURE W.39. Dataflow diagram (DFD) for secondary file fill-in-the-form document processing.

W.4.8   What Is Mail Merge?

A mail merge is a common business application in which a mailing list of variable information is combined with the fixed information of a standard document. The mailing list information is maintained in a separate file so that it may be used with a number of different standard documents. For example, a mail merge would be appropriate for a monthly letter sent to customers. Each month the content of the letter changes, but it is sent to the same customers. Mail merge is *not* limited to just name and address variable information. It encompasses all those business situations that make use of the general concept of combining files that contain fixed and variable information.

In WordPerfect, mail merge is implemented as a merge process with two document files. As illustrated in the dataflow diagram (DFD) in Figure W.39, the primary file is a fill-in-the-form document that contains the fixed information, and the secondary file holds the variable information. In addition to setting up the primary document with special merge codes and commands, the variable information in the secondary file must contain merge codes and commands that indicate the end of each item or field of variable information and the end of the information for each document in the series.

W.4.9   Creating Mail Merge Documents

The Merge Codes <Shift> + <F9> command is used to insert merge codes and commands into the primary document. A field is specified in the primary document for each item of variable information, such as a customer's name, similar to the manner in which the location for input information was identified for the interactive fill-in-the-form document preparation described previously. The value for each field resides in the secondary file. The fields in the primary document and the secondary document are matched up by a field number or name and the position of the variable information in the secondary file. Like the primary document, the secondary file contains special merge codes to indicate the end of each field and the end of the fields for a given record or final document.

Sara can produce her loan application letters by using a mail merge strategy with the variable information stored in a secondary file. With this arrangement, she might enter the information for each loan into the secondary file throughout the day. Then, at the end of the day, she could produce all of the letters at once in a single batch. Sara has defined seven fields of variable information that she wants to include in each letter. These fields will be stored in the secondary file as follows:

1. Customer's name
2. Company
3. Street
4. City–State–Zip
5. Salutation
6. Loan use
7. Loan amount

Since the Customer's name, Company, Street, and City-State-Zip are all on separate lines, she has defined them as separate fields. Although Sara could also define separate fields for City, State, and Zip, she has decided to treat these three fields as one, since they are all on the same line.

The special merge codes and commands are different in WordPerfect version 5.0 than the one used in version 5.1. You should explore the development of the primary and secondary files for your version of WordPerfect. You may want to examine the commands for the other version so that you are familiar with these differences between the versions of WordPerfect. Creation of the primary and secondary files is presented in the discussion that follows for each of the versions of WordPerfect. Sara created her secondary file first because this contains the field definitions she wants to use when she develops her primary file.

W.4.9.1. Version 5.0 Secondary File

In the secondary file, the variable information is entered in sequence for each field and each record. The end of field is marked with the ˆ**R** merge code, whereas the end of a record is indicated with ˆ**E**. The ˆ**R** merge code is produced by using the Merge R <F9> command, and the ˆ**E** is selected from the Merge Code <Shift>+<F9> menu.

A secondary file with the variable information for three of Sara's loan applications is created in this manner:

To create a mail merge secondary file of variable information	**Action:**	Clear the current document using Exit <F7>.
	Type:	`Ms. Susan Salem` First customer's name
	Press:	`Merge Return <F9>` Terminate the variable data for first field and advance to the next line
	Action:	Enter each of the other variable data field values for Susan Salem as follows:

> Wente Brothers
> 9800 S. Main
> Livermore, CA 94441
>
> Ms. Salem
> high-speed bottler
> $198,000

Press: `Merge Codes <Shift>+<F9>`

Initiate specifying the end of data for the first "record" or form letter

Select: `^E`   Enter the **^E** end of record marker

Action: Enter the variable data for the other two records as shown in Figure W.40. Review your data and correct any errors.

Action: Print this secondary document and save it as FORMLET.SF. Here, the extension **SF** is used to specify this as the **S**econdary **F**ile. Of course, you could use any desired extension.

W.4.9.2.   Version 5.0 Primary File

Variable information in the primary document file is specified with the ^Fn^ merge codes. The "F" indicates that this is a variable information "field," and the "n" specifies the "number" of the field. Each of the seven fields has been numbered in the sequence listed above, the same order in which they are encountered in the primary document, working from the document's top to its bottom.

```
Mr. Larry Thomas^R
Western Wind Farms^R
914 Executive Drive^R
Altamont, CA  92924^R
Mr. Thomas^R
performance monitoring computer system^R
$129,000^R
^E
==============================================================================
Ms. Marcella Scott^R
Boone's Farm^R
14389 Wind Road^R
Culver City, CA  93906^R
Ms. Scott^R
full color label printing machine^R
$147,000^R
^E
==============================================================================



B:\FORMLET.SF                                          Doc 1 Pg 2 Ln 1" POS 1"
```

FIGURE W.40. Variable information for fill-in-the-form loan letter with WordPerfect version 5.0 merge codes.

Sara's fill-in-the-form primary document for version 5.0 is developed as follows:

Action:	Retrieve the LOANLET.PF file as your currently active document.	
Action:	Erase all the ˆ**C** keyboard input merge codes.	
Move to:	Second blank line after the ˆ**D** date merge code	
		Location where customer name and address will be located
Select:	Merge Codes <Shift>+<F9>	
		Initiate entering a code for the name field and obtain a menu of merge codes on the Status Line
Select:	^F	Field code, press: <F>

A message is displayed on the Status Line requesting the field number in this manner:

Field:

Enter:	1	Each field is numbered, and this is the first one
Press:	<Enter>	Move to the next line for specifying the second field
Select:	Merge Codes <Shift>+<F9>	
		Initiate entering the next field
Select:	^F	Another field code, press: <F>
Enter:	2	Designate the second field
Action:	Enter field codes for the other five fields, resulting in the document illustrated in Figure W.41.	
Action:	Review your document to be sure you have entered all seven variable data field merge codes in the desired locations. Make any necessary corrections.	
Action:	Save this fill-in-the-form document as the primary file FORMLET.PF.	

W.4.9.3. Version 5.1 Secondary File

In the secondary file, the variable information is entered in sequence for each field and each record. An end of field is marked with the {END FIELD} merge command, whereas an end of record is indicated with {END RECORD}. The {END FIELD} merge command is produced by using the Merge R <F9> command, and the {END RECORD} is selected as a Merge Code <Shift>+<F9> command. A {FIELD NAMES} command is used to specify the name and sequence of each of the data items for each field.

The variable information for three of Sara's loan applications is placed in a secondary file like this:

Action:	Clear the current document using Exit <F7>	
Move to:	top-left margin of document	
		Position cursor at desired location for entering field name definitions
Select:	Merge Codes <Shift>+<F9>	

```
                            THE
                     LAST NATIONAL BANK
                  Number One Wagon Wheel Drive
                   Walnut Creek, CA  94924

                                                    ^D

   ^F1^
   ^F2^
   ^F3^
   ^F4^

   Dear ^F5^:

   I am pleased to inform you that your loan for a ^F6^ has been
   reviewed by our loan committee.  Your loan in the amount of ^F7^
   has been approved.

   Please stop by my office to complete the necessary authorization
   and arrange to have the funds transferred to your account.

                        Sincerely,



   B:\FORMLET.PF                         Doc 1 Pg 1 Ln 1.5" POS 1"
```

FIGURE W.41. Fill-in-the-form loan letter with WordPerfect version 5.0 variable data field merge codes.

Select:	More	Access next menu that contains desired command
Select:	{FIELD NAMES}name1~... name N~	Command that places field name definition in this secondary file

This message is displayed on the Status Line requesting the name for the first field:

Enter Field 1:

Enter:	Customer name	Name of the first field from the top of the document

The message now appears as

Enter Field 2:

Enter:	Company	Next field moving down the document
Action:	Enter the names for each of the other five fields. When the name is requested for the eighth field, continue like this:	
Press:	<Enter>	Terminate the specification of field names, because no field name is entered

By defining the field first, you are reminded of the variable information for each record. The variable information for each of Sara's letters is entered like this:

Type:	Ms. Susan Salem	First customer's name
Press:	Merge Return <F9>	Terminate the variable data for first field with the {END FIELD} merge code and advance to next line

Action: Using the Merge R <F9> command, enter each of the other variable data field values for Susan Salem as follows:

Wente Brothers
9800 S. Main
Livermore, CA 94441

Ms. Salem
high-speed bottler
$198,000

Select: Merge Codes <Shift>+<F9>

Initiate specifying the end of data for the first "record" or form letter; merge codes appear on the Tools pull-down menu

Select: End Record   Enter the {END RECORD} merge code with a hard page break

Action: Enter the variable data for the other two records as shown in Figure W.42. Review your data and correct any errors.

Action: Print this secondary document and save it as FORMLET.SF. Here, the extension **SF** is used to specify this as the **S**econdary **F**ile. Of course, you could use any desired extension.

W.4.9.4.   Version 5.1 Primary File

Fields for variable information in the primary document are specified with the {FIELD} merge command that includes the name of each field. The name of each of the seven fields identifies the information contained in that field. These field names are associated with a list of field names in the secondary file as a means of matching the information between the two files during the merge process.

```
Mr. Larry Thomas{END FIELD}
Western Wind Farms{END FIELD}
914 Executive Drive{END FIELD}
Altamont, CA  92924{END FIELD}
Mr. Thomas{END FIELD}
performance monitoring computer system{END FIELD}
$129,000{END FIELD}
{END RECORD}
===============================================================================
Ms. Marcella Scott{END FIELD}
Boone's Farm{END FIELD}
14389 Wind Road{END FIELD}
Culver City, CA  93906{END FIELD}
Ms. Scott{END FIELD}
full color label printing machine{END FIELD}
$147,000{END FIELD}
{END RECORD}
===============================================================================



Field: Customer name                          Doc 1 Pg 3 Ln 1" Pos 1"
```

FIGURE W.42. Variable information for fill-in-the-form loan letter with WordPerfect version 5.1 merge codes.

Sara's fill-in-the-form primary document for version 5.1 is developed in this manner:

To create a mail merge primary document containing merge codes with field names

Action:	Retrieve the LOANLET.PF file as your currently active document.	
Action:	Carefully erase all the **{INPUT}**... ~ keyboard input merge codes and their descriptions, including the tilde (~).	
Move to:	Second blank line after the {DATE} merge code	Location where customer name and address will be located
Select:	Merge Codes <Shift>+<F9>	Initiate entering a code for the variable data field; merge code selections are reached from the Tools pull-down menu
Select:	Field	Code for obtaining variable data from a file

A message is displayed on the Status Line requesting a name for the field like this:

Enter Field:

Enter:	Customer name	Each field is given a name; this could be a number, if desired, as required by earlier versions of WordPerfect
Press:	<Enter>	Move to the next line for specifying the second field
Select:	Merge Codes <Shift>+<F9>	Initiate specifying the next field
Select:	Field	Another field is specified
Enter:	Company	Name for the second field
Action:	Enter field codes and names for the other five fields resulting in the document illustrated in Figure W.43.	
Action:	Review your document to be sure you have entered all seven variable data field merge codes in the desired locations. Make any necessary corrections.	
Action:	Save this fill-in-the-form document as FORMLET.PF.	

W.4.10. Producing Mail Merge Documents

The final mail merge document is produced by merging the fill-in-the-form primary document file and the variable data secondary document file into the currently active document by using the Merge <Ctrl>+<F9> command. Normally, the current document is cleared before performing the merge operation. Since the variable data are obtained from the secondary file, once the merge has been started, it continues to completion *without* any keyboard entry. The procedure for carrying out a mail merge with the primary and secondary files is the same for both versions of WordPerfect.

Sara's group of loan approval form letters is produced as follows:

To perform the mail merge   **Action:** Clear the current document using Exit <F7>.

Keypoint!   The current document is usually cleared *before* performing a merge. This avoids mixing the merged documents with the current document!

```
                                        THE
                                 LAST NATIONAL BANK
                             Number One Wagon Wheel Drive
                              Walnut Creek, CA  94924

                                                        {DATE}

        {FIELD}Customer name~
        {FIELD}Company~
        {FIELD}Street~
        {FIELD}City State Zip~

        Dear {FIELD}Salutation~:

        I am pleased to inform you that your loan for a {FIELD}Loan use~ has
        been reviewed by our loan committee.  Your loan in the amount of
        {FIELD}Loan amount~ has been approved.

        Please stop by my office to complete the necessary authorization
        and arrange to have the funds transferred to your account.

                                Sincerely,


        B:\FORMLET.PF                              Doc 1 Pg 1 Ln 2" Pos 1"
```

FIGURE W.43. Fill-in-the-form loan letter with WordPerfect version 5.1 variable data field merge codes.

| **Select:** | Merge <Ctrl>+<F9> | Initiate execution of merge; merge resides on the Tools pull-down menu |
| **Select:** | Merge | Desired activity |

A message is displayed on the Status Line prompting for the name of the primary document file in this manner:

Primary file:

| **Enter:** | B:FORMLET.PF | Name of primary file, including the disk drive identifier, if necessary |

A message on the Status Line prompts for the second document file like this:

Secondary file:

| **Enter:** | B:LOANLET.SF | Name of secondary document file containing the variable data |

This message is displayed on the Status Line while the merge is carried out:

Merge

Once the merge is completed, the document cursor is positioned at the bottom of the combined document. Each letter has been placed on a different page. If desired, any other edit changes could be made to this combined document.

Action: Review the results of the merge by using <PgUp> and <PgDn> to move through the document.

The resulting letters are like that illustrated previously in Figure W.34.

Action: Print the resulting merged document.

Although you could save the merged document in a separate file, a merge can be performed whenever the combined results are desired. Therefore, there is usually no need to save the merged document.

Sara has used a mail merge approach (Figure W.44) to produce a batch of her loan application response letters. Once she has the primary fixed information document created, the secondary variable information document can be updated with the specific information for each loan. Then, periodically, batches of the letters can be produced. She has a system that supports her repetitive processing of loan applications.

1. Create the Secondary File
   a. Enter field names at top of file for each field [version 5.1 only]

Move to:	top,left corner
Press:	`<Shift>+<F9>`
Select:	`More`
Select:	`Field Names`
Enter:	Your field name

   Repeat entering field names for each field and terminate with <Enter> in blank field after the last one
   b. Enter data for each field

Type:	The variable data for the field
Press:	`<F9>`to end the field and advance to the next line

   c. Terminate each record

Press:	`Merge Codes <Shift>+<F9>`
Select:	`^E or {END RECORD}`

   d. Repeat entering field data and terminating each record
   e. Save <F10> the file with the SF extension
   f. Clear the screen with the Exit <F7>
2. Create the Primary File
   a. Type document
   b. Enter merge codes

Select:	`Merge Codes <Shift>+<F9>`
Select:	`Interactive entry merge code (^Fn^ or {Field})`

   c. Save <F10> the file with the .PF extension
   d. Clear the screen with Exit <F7>
3. Merge the Files

a. **Select:**	`Merge/Sort <Ctrl>+<F9>`
b. **Select:**	`Merge`
c. **Enter:**	Primary filename
d. **Enter:**	Secondary filename

   e. Wait for the merge to be completed
   f. As needed, edit your documents and rerun the merge.

FIGURE W.44. Summary of secondary file fill-in-the-form processing.

W.4.11 When Things Go Wrong

A variety of situations may occur when you create macros and perform mail merges. Some of the more common difficulties and how to approach them are described here:

1. When you created a macro, you used the <Backspace> and cursor movement keys to make corrections to the macro as you initially entered it, like those shown in Figure W.45. Each time you execute the macro, these errors and corrections are repeated. These mistakes can be removed from your macro so that they are not repeated with each execution.

   a. Use Macro Define <Ctrl>+<F10> and Edit to access your macro for making edit changes.

   b. Locate the unwanted keystrokes and carefully delete them. Be sure not to delete your good keystrokes.

2. You performed a mail merge and some of the fields that should have been filled with variable information from the secondary file appeared as blanks in your merged document. In version 5.0, this often occurs when the field number specified is greater than the number of fields entered in the secondary file. In version 5.1, this happens when the field name in the primary file is spelled differently from the field name in the secondary file.

   a. Clear the current document and access your secondary file. Verify the number of fields and, for version 5.1, the field names. If any field names are misspelled, correct them. Save your corrected secondary file.

   b. Clear the current document and access your primary file. Check the field numbers and, for version 5.1, the field names. Correct any field numbers or names that are in error. Save your corrected primary file.

   c. Clear the current document and reexecute your mail merge.

```
Macro: Action

    File            B:OPENING.WPM

    Description     Opening for letter


    {DISPLAY OFF}{Bold}THE{Enter}
    LAST·NATIONN{Backspace}AL·BANK{Enter}
    Number·On·{Backspace}e·Wagon{Left}{Right}·Wheel·Drive{Enter}
    Walnut·Creek,·CA··94924{Enter}{Bold}
    {Home}{Home}{Up}{Block}{Down}{Down}{Down}{Down}{Center}y{Right}{Enter}
    {Enter}
    {Flush Right}{Date/Outline}1{Enter}
    {Enter}
    {Enter}
    Dear·




Ctrl-PgUp for macro commands;   Press Exit when done
```

FIGURE W.45. Macro with unwanted error and correction keystrokes.

3. You performed a mail merge and the wrong variable information was placed in your merged document. This usually occurs when a wrong field number or name is specified in your primary file.

   a. Clear your current document and access your secondary file. Determine the appropriate field number or name for each variable information entry.

   b. Clear your current document and access your primary file. Review the field numbers and names you specified for each variable information entry. Determine the appropriate field number or name for the variable information at each designated location in your primary document and make the necessary correction. Save this revision of your primary file.

   c. Clear the current document and reexecute your mail merge.

W.4.12 Lesson Summary

- WordPerfect macros are like automatic typing for a repetitive series of commands, a phrase, or a paragraph.

- Macros are created one time and then executed as many times as desired.

- The Define Macro <Ctrl>+<F10> command is used to initiate the creation or editing of a macro, which is stored in a file with the extension WPM.

- The Macro <Alt>+<F10> command is used to execute a macro.

- Fill-in-the-form documents contain standard or fixed information that is combined with variable information when the document is processed with the Merge <Ctrl>+<F9> command. This feature supports the generation of "personalized form letters."

- Special merge commands are used to specify a document's fields, which receive values from either the keyboard or a secondary file during merge processing.

- Different versions of WordPerfect make use of different merge codes for fill-in-the-form documents and secondary files containing variable information (Figure W.46).

- Mail merge describes the general situation in which fixed information in one file is combined with variable information from another file to produce a batch of final documents.

- For mail merge processing, the sequence of fields in a primary document file needs to match the order of the data values in the secondary file. This is required to ensure that the data values from the secondary file are inserted at the correct location in the final document.

Version 5.0 Codes	Version 5.1 Commands	Meaning
^C	{KEYBOARD}	Pause for user input
^Omessage^O^C	{INPUT}message ~	Prompt input from keyboard
^D	{DATE}	Insert current date from computer's clock
^E	{END RECORD}	Specify end of record
^Fnumber^	{FIELD}name ~	Identify field in primary file
^T	{PRINT}	Send merged document to printer
^Q	{QUIT}	Terminate the merge
^R	{END FIELD}	Specify end of field

FIGURE W.46. Selected merge codes and commands.

W.4.13 Practice Tutorial

(1)   Create and execute the OPENING macro described in this Lesson as a guided activity in a hands-on manner. These activities produce the macro and execute it. Clear your current WordPerfect document before you begin.

Task 1: Create and save the OPENING macro.

Task 2: Produce a hard copy of the macro with <Shift>+<PrtSc>. Display the macro in the Macro Editor when you make this copy.

Task 3: Execute the macro and print the resulting document.

Time Estimates

Novice: 60 minutes

Intermediate: 45 minutes

Advanced: 30 minutes

(2)   Produce the LOANLET.PF form letter to Susan Salem described in this Lesson by creating and merging a fill-in-the-form document as a guided activity in a hands-on manner. Enter these data interactively from your keyboard when the merge is processed. Clear your current WordPerfect document before you begin.

Task 1: Create the fill-in-the-form primary document for the form letter placing Merge Codes in the letter for the interactive input of data.

Task 2: Print this version of the letter.

Task 3: Save this document as the file LOANLET.PF.

Task 4: Perform the merge and enter the variable data for Susan Salem interactively from the keyboard.

Task 5: Preview the final document and print it.

Time Estimates

Novice: 60 minutes

Intermediate: 45 minutes

Advanced: 30 minutes

(3)   Generate Sara's form letters described in this Lesson as a mail merge by creating the FORMLET.PF primary file and the FORMLET.SF secondary file as a guided activity. Merge these two files to produce the final documents. Clear your current WordPerfect document before you begin.

Task 1: Create the secondary file containing the variable information for the three letters.

Task 2: Print this file of variable information.

Task 3: Save this document as the file FORMLET.SF.

Task 4: Create the fill-in-the-form primary document for the form letter by placing merge codes in the letter for the fields that receive data from the secondary file.

Task 5: Print this version of the letter.

Task 6: Save this document as the file FORMLET.PF.

Task 7: Merge the primary and secondary file.

Task 8: Print the final letter for each of the customers.

Time Estimates

Novice: 60 minutes

Intermediate: 45 minutes

Advanced: 30 minutes

W.4.14 Practice Exercises

(1)   Case: Crazy River Canoe (second encounter)

Develop and execute a macro that contains the company name and address for Crazy River Canoe. Whenever this macro is executed, the information below will be inserted in the current document. The name, address, and associated information to be included in the macro are as follows:

Crazy River Canoe
Corporate Headquarters
4711 Shallow Brook
Hungry Horse, MT 59873

Phone (406) 289-4724
Toll Free 1-800-GO-CANOE
Fax (406) 289-9453

Task 1: Create this as the CRAZY macro. The name and address are to be bolded, but not the phone numbers. All lines generated by the macro are to be centered between the left and right margins. Clear your current WordPerfect document before you begin.

Task 2: Produce a hard copy of the macro with <Shift>+<PrtSc>. Display the macro in the Macro Editor when you make this copy.

Task 3: Save this macro.

Task 4: Execute the macro and print the resulting document.

Time Estimates

Novice: 60 minutes

Intermediate: 45 minutes

Advanced: 30 minutes

(2)   Case: Rocky Mountain Outfitters

Business Problem: Direct mail marketing
MIS Characteristics: Marketing
Operational Control

Produce a fill-in-the-form document that is completed by entering data interactively from the keyboard when a merge is performed. The document is sketched out as shown below, with the variable information denoted with underlining. Clear your current WordPerfect document before you begin.

Rocky Mountain Outfitters
770 Gunflint Trail
River-of-No-Return, ID 83117

[current date here]

[adventurer name here]
[street address here]
[city state zip here]

Dear Adventurer:

This letter will confirm the arrangements for your wild frontier adventure outing on the [name of outing here], departing on [date of departure here].

This adventure includes all equipment, food, and transportation. Please bring suitable clothing for both the cold and wet conditions that may be encountered during this adventure. If you have any questions, please contact me at (208)358-4357.

Warmest regards,

Lars North
Wild River Guide

Task 1: Plan the variable information fields to receive input data from the keyboard for this fill-in-the-form document with the adventurer's name and address designated as a single field. Use this table for your design:

Field
Content/Name

_____

_____

_____

_____

_____

_____

_____

_____

Task 2: Enter the letter as sketched out above. The heading is to be centered. The date is to be right-aligned and obtained from the computer's clock during the merge. For the inside address, you are to set up only one field. The name and date of the outing are separate fields. Each field is to be set up to receive data interactively during the merge.

Task 3: Print this letter, which contains the merge codes.

Task 4: Save this as the file ROCKY.PF.

Task 5: Perform a merge with these test data and print the resulting letter:

Adventurer's name and address:
Lila Orbach
3539 Sunset Lane
Moab, UT 84532

Outing information:
Flathead River Run
September 23, 1994

Time Estimates

Novice: 60 minutes

Intermediate: 45 minutes

Advanced: 30 minutes

(3) Case: PC Country

Business Problem: Consumer contest notification
MIS Characteristics: Marketing
                     Operational Control

Generate form letters from a mail merge by creating the MAIL.PF primary file and the MAIL.SF secondary file. Merge these two files to produce the final documents. The document is sketched out as shown here, with the variable information indicated by underlining. Clear your current WordPerfect document before you begin.

PC COUNTRY
444 Foothills Trail
Boulder, CO 80321

[current date here]

[customer's name here]
[street address here]
[city state zip here]

Dear [salutation here]:

Congratulations! Your name has been selected for entry in our super sweepstakes reader award program. You are eligible to win [award name here].

Please return the enclosed super sweepstakes response card to determine if you have won. Be sure to indicate on the card your desire to renew your subscription to PC COUNTRY at our special sweepstakes renewal price. To ensure your eligibility for an award, return the card to us immediately.

Sincerely,

Karla Miyashiro
Subscription Manager

Task 1: Plan the field names to be used with this fill-in-the-form document with each line of the customer's name and address designated as a separate field. Use this table for your design:

Field Number	Field Content/Name

Task 2: Create the secondary file containing the variable information for these customers:

Customer's name and address:
Ms. April Young
2001 Indian Trail
Santa Fe, NM 87505

Other data:
Ms. Young
a Cadillac Allante

Customer's name and address:
Mr. Irving Landry
350 Lincoln Lane
Springfield, IL 62707

Other data:
Mr. Landry
$25,000

Task 3: Print this file of variable information.

Task 4: Save this document as the file MAIL.SF.

Task 5: Create the fill-in-the-form primary document for the form letter by placing merge codes in the letter for the fields that will receive data from the secondary file.

Task 6: Print this version of the letter.

Task 7: Save this document as the file MAIL.PF.

Task 8: Merge the primary and secondary file.

Task 9: Print the final letter for each of the customers.

Time Estimates

Novice: 75 minutes

Intermediate: 60 minutes

Advanced: 45 minutes

W.4.15 Comprehensive Problems

(1) Case: Home Real Estate (second encounter)

As resident manager of Park Place Villas, Krista needs to write a variety of letters for Home Real Estate. To assist her with this process, she has decided that macros could be used to generate the opening and closing for these letters in this manner:

(a) Opening:

Home Real Estate
Property Management Division
1000 Bank of America Plaza
North Hills, TX 75410

July 10, 1994

Dear

(b) Closing:

Sincerely yours,

Krista Buffett
Property Management Associate

Krista wants you to create these macros for her use by completing the following task:

Task 1: Construct the macro in (a) for the opening. The company heading should be centered and bolded. The date is to be entered as text and right-aligned; you may use the current date.

Task 2: Save this as the macro file OPENLET.

Task 3: Access this macro for editing, make any corrections, if necessary, and produce a hard copy of it with <Shift>+<PrtSc>.

Task 4: Construct the macro in (b) for the closing. Be sure to indent this closing 3 in. from the left margin.

Task 5: Save this as the macro file CLOSELET.

Task 6: Access this macro for editing, correct it, if necessary, and produce a hard copy using <Shift>+<PrtSc>.

Task 7: Clear the current document and execute both macros.

Task 8: Preview the result and make any changes, as required.

Task 9: Print this test letter containing only the keystrokes generated by the opening and closing macros.

Time Estimates

Novice: 60 minutes

Intermediate: 45 minutes

Advanced: 30 minutes

(2)   Case: Pioneer Electric and Gas (second encounter)

As manager of customer services at Pioneer Electric and Gas, Mary Marshall prepares a number of memoranda for the service department. Frequently, she needs to include the fees for PEG's service changes and connections in a memo or letter. To assist her with these correspondence activities, she has concluded that macros could be developed to generate an opening for the memo and a table of the fees like this:

(a) Memo opening:

M E M O R A N D U M

Customer Service Department
Pioneer Electric and Gas
One Energy Place
Broken Spring, MO 68127

DATE: August 22, 1994

TO:

FROM: Mary Marshall
           Customer Service Manager

COPIES:

SUBJECT:

(b) Fee table:

Service Type	Utility	Fee
Service Change	Electric	$25
	Gas	$35
	Both	$50
Connection	Electric	$175
	Gas	$250

Mary wants you to create these macros for her by completing the following task:

Task 1: Construct the macro in (a) for the memo opening. The word "memorandum" and the company heading should be centered and bolded. The date is to be entered as text; you may use the current date.

Task 2: Save this as the macro file MEMO.

Task 3: Access this macro for editing, make any corrections, if necessary, and produce a hard copy of it with <Shift>+<PrtSc>.

Task 4: Construct the macro in (b) for the fee table. Be sure to indent the table 1 in. from the left margin and to use the dot leader between the utility name and the fee. Tab stops for utility name and fees are to be set at 3 in. and 5.5 in., respectively, with the tab for the fee right-aligned.

Task 5: Save this as the macro file FEES.

Task 6: Access this macro for editing, correct it, if necessary, and produce a hard copy using <Shift>+<PrtSc>.

Task 7: Clear the current document and execute both macros.

Task 8: Preview the result and make any changes, as required.

Task 9: Print this test letter, containing only the keystrokes generated by the memo opening and fee table macros.

Time Estimates

Novice: 60 minutes

Intermediate: 45 minutes

Advanced: 30 minutes

(3) Case: Home Real Estate (second encounter)

Diedra Robbins is a Home Real Estate associate responsible for organizing and directing the craft club activities at the various residential properties administered by the Property Management Division. She travels to each location and meets with the resident managers, including Krista at Park Place Villas, to plan each craft club event. The resident managers post and circulate lists of potential craft activities for their tenants to consider. Diedra compiles tenant responses and plans the most popular activities. Once arrangements have been made for an event, Diedra sends a confirmation letter to the resident manager. In analyzing her letters, Diedra found that most of the information in the letters was the same. The name of the craft activity, its scheduled time, and the fee for the activity comprise the variable information in each letter. Diedra has concluded that an interactive fill-in-the-blanks letter could be created to assist her with this confirmation process.

Diedra has sketched out the following fill-in-the-form letter for her confirmations. In her sketch, the variable information is specified with underlining. She wants you to complete the development of this letter and to test the fill-in-the-form processing with the test data she has provided.

Home Real Estate
Property Management Division
6300 Ward Parkway
North Hills, TX 75408

[current date here]

[resident manager's name here]
[property name here]
[street address here]
[city state zip here]

Dear [salutation here]:

This letter will confirm the arrangements for the meeting of the Handy Crafters for [name of craft here] on [date of meeting here] at [time of meeting here]. The fee for supplies for this craft is [amount of fee here].

Please advise each of your members of the Home Handy Crafters of this activity. If you have any questions, please contact me at 241-HOME, extension 4357.

Sincerely,

Diedra Robbins
Craft Club Coordinator

Diedra has detailed the following tasks for this project:

Task 1: Plan the variable information fields to receive input data from the keyboard for this fill-in-the-form document with the resident manager's name and address designated as a single field. Use this table for your design:

Field
Content/Name

_____

_____

_____

_____

_____

_____

_____

_____

Task 2: Enter the letter that Diedra has sketched out. The heading is to be centered and bolded. The date is to be right-aligned and obtained from the computer's clock during the merge. For the inside address, you are to set up only one field. The salutation, craft name, date of meeting, time of meeting, and amount of fee are separate fields. Each field is to be set up to receive data interactively during the merge.

Task 3: Print this letter, which contains the merge codes.

Task 4: Save this as the file CONFIRM.PF.

Task 5: Perform a merge with these test data and print the resulting letter:

Resident manager's name and address:
Ms. Krista Buffett
Park Place Villas
21400 Broomfield Boulevard
North Ridge, TX 75200

Other data:
Krista
basket weaving
Wednesday, September 23, 1994
7:30 P.M.
$15.00

Task 6: Perform a merge with these test data and print the resulting letter:

Resident manager's name and address:
Mr. Lucas Walker
Oak Wood Trail
7110 Fort Street
Dry Gulch, TX 76001

Other data:
Luke
advanced finger painting
Saturday, October 10, 1994
10:00 A.M.
$6.00

Time Estimates

Novice: 75 minutes

Intermediate: 60 minutes

Advanced: 45 minutes

(4)   Case: Pioneer Electric and Gas (second encounter)

Pioneer Electric and Gas provides a special service to the owners and managers of rental property. When a tenant vacates the premises, the utility services are automatically transferred to the property owner. This arrangement ensures that utilities continue while any maintenance activities, such as carpet cleaning, are performed between occupancies by different tenants. Also, during the winter, this automatic reversion of service prevents the termination of utilities, which might result in damage from environmental factors, such as water pipes bursting from freezing. For these rental properties, whenever a reversion of service occurs, a letter is sent notifying the owner of the change. Because the costs of final meter readings are reduced when a reversion of service occurs, the cost to the owner is considerably less than the usual service charge. PEG's fee for the reversion of service for either electric or gas service is only $12.

When a reversion of service takes place, Kelli Olson notifies Sharyl Tinman, the customer service representative responsible for this special service. Sharyl prepares a letter that is sent to the owner of the property advising of the reversion and the amount of the fee that will appear on the next utility bill.

Sharyl uses a standard letter for this change in service for rental property. The variable information in each letter consists of the owner's name and address, the customer's account number, the address of the utility service, the date of the final meter readings, and the cost of the service. Sharyl would like to create an interactive fill-in-the-blanks letter to assist her with this notification process.

Sharyl and Kelli have sketched out the following design for a fill-in-the-form letter for these notifications. In their sketch, the variable information is specified with underlining. Sharyl wants you to finish developing this letter and to test the fill-in-the-form processing with the test data she has furnished.

Pioneer Electric and Gas
One Energy Place
Broken Spring, MO 68127

[current date here]

[owner's name here]
[owner's company here]
[owner's street address here]
[owner's city state zip here]

Account Number: [owner's account number here]

Service Address: [service street address here]
[service city state zip here]

Dear Customer:

Your tenant has requested a final reading on [date of final reading here] for the utility services at the service address shown above.

According to your previous authorization, the utility services have been left on and transferred to your name for future billings. You will be billed for the service until a new tenant makes an application for the service. There is a [amount of fee] charge for this transfer of service.

We appreciate the opportunity to help you with utility service transfers. If you have any questions, please call us at 554-8876.

Sincerely,

Sharyl Tinman
Customer Service Representative

Sharyl and Kelli have enumerated the tasks for this project as follows:

Task 1: Plan the variable information fields to receive input data from the keyboard for this fill-in-the-form document with the owner's name and address and the service address each designated as a single field. Use this table for your design:

**Field
Content/Name**

_____
_____
_____
_____
_____
_____
_____

Task 2: Enter the letter that Kelli and Sharyl sketched out. The heading is to be centered and bolded. The date of the letter is to be right-aligned and obtained from the computer's clock during the merge. Each line of the owner's name and address and the service address should be set up as individual fields. The account number, date of final reading, and amount of fee are separate fields. Each field is to be set up to receive data interactively during the merge.

Task 3: Print the letter containing the merge codes.

Task 4: Save this as the file TRANSFER.PF.

Task 5: Perform a merge with these test data and print the resulting letter:

Owner's name and address:
Ms. Rebecca Rivera-Torres
Home Real Estate
14200 Bloomfield Court
North Woods, MO 58700

Account number:
4411-03045-1

Service address:
7701 West Beach
Gladstone, MO 58066

Other data:
July 31, 1994
$24.00

Task 6: Perform a merge with these test data and print the resulting letter:

Owner's name and address:
Mr. Brenden Watters
Watters Properties
411 Hiawatha Drive
Gladwin, MO 58700

Account number:
5419-06105-1

Service address:
5055 Marshall Drive
Overland, MO 58066

Other data:
August 29, 1994
$12.00

Time Estimates

Novice: 75 minutes

Intermediate: 60 minutes

Advanced: 45 minutes

(5)   Case: Home Real Estate (continued)

The Property Management Division of Home Real Estate manages nearly 300 residential properties in the metroplex area. Diedra Robbins schedules several hundred craft club activities each month. Dozens of confirmation letters are sent each week. After further analysis of her communication needs, Diedra has decided that a mail merge would provide her with a better method of producing a batch of confirmation letters each day.

In addition to the test data in Comprehensive Problem 3 above, Diedra has assembled the following test data for this mail merge:

Resident manager's name and address:
Ms. Margaret Yeung
Apple Creek
2100 Country Club Court
North Ridge, TX 75204

Other data:
Maggie
holiday bears deal
Tuesday, October 27, 1994
7:00 P.M.
$7.50

Resident manager's name and address:
Mr. Darin Matsura
Lake Forest North
3000 Lake Forest Drive
South Knoll, TX 77003

Other data:
Darin
dough art goodies
Saturday, November 14, 1994
1:00 P.M.
$11.00

Diedra is satisfied with the fill-in-the-form document she designed in Comprehensive Problem 3. This document can serve as a guide for developing the document for the mail merge. The tasks Diedra has identified for you for this project are as follows:

Task 1: Plan the field names to be used with this fill-in-the-form document with each line of the resident manager's name and address designated as a separate field. Use this table for your design:

Field Number	Field Content/Name

Task 2: Enter test data for four records into the secondary merge file CRAFT.SF. Use the two records provided above and those from Comprehensive Problem 3. [*Hint:* Remember to include the merge codes for these fields and records.]

Task 3: Print this document containing the variable data and merge codes.

Task 4: Access the CONFIRM.PF document file from Comprehensive Problem 3.

Task 5: Modify this fill-in-the-form document to receive data from a secondary WordPerfect file with each line of the resident manager's name and address as a separate field. The date is to be obtained from the computer's clock during the merge. Review the document and make any other required corrections. [*Note:* If you did not create the fill-in-the-form document for Comprehensive Problem 3, then create it for this problem and include the fields for the mail merge.]

Task 6: Print this letter with the merge codes.

Task 7: Save this as the document file CRAFT.PF.

Task 8: Perform the merge of the CRAFT.PF and the CRAFT.SF files.

Task 9: Preview the letters generated.

Task 10: Print the resulting letters.

Time Estimates

Novice: 75 minutes

Intermediate: 60 minutes

Advanced: 45 minutes

(6)   Case: Pioneer Electric and Gas (continued)

The Customer Services Department of Pioneer Electric and Gas processes several thousand reversions of service each year. Dozens of letters are prepared and mailed each week. Mary, Kelli, and Sharyl have analyzed their requirements for producing these letters to meet their communications needs. They have determined that a mail merge would provide Sharyl with a better method of generating a batch of transfer request letters each day.

In addition to the test data in Comprehensive Problem 4, Sharyl and Kelli have gathered the following test data for their mail merge:

Owner's name and address:
Ms. Lisa Hernandez
Property Management Limited
5656 Ravenswood Road
Elkhorn, MO 58700

Account number:
4319-04121-2

Service address:
7762 Seward Street
Elkhorn, MO 58066

Other data:
August 24, 1994
$24.00

Owner's name and address:
Mr. Kraig Kent
Old Kent Properties
200 Eastwood Avenue
Schoolcraft, MO 58700

Account number:
4604-01141-1

Service address:
16532 Fisher Road
Union, MO 58066

Other data:
August 24, 1994
$12.00

Kelli and Sharyl are pleased with the fill-in-the-form document they designed in Comprehensive Problem 4. That document can be used as the basis for developing the mail merge document. The following tasks have been defined for you for this project:

Task 1: Plan the field names to be used with this fill-in-the-form document, with each line of the owner's name and address and the service address designated as a separate field. Use this table for your design:

Field Number	Field Content/Name

Task 2: Enter test data for four records into the secondary merge file CHANGE.SF. Use the two records provided above and those from Comprehensive Problem 4. [*Hint:* Remember to include the merge codes for these fields and records.]

Task 3: Print the document containing the variable data and merge codes.

Task 4: Access the TRANSFER.PF document file from Comprehensive Problem 4.

Task 5: Modify this fill-in-the-form document to receive data from a secondary WordPerfect file, with each line of the owner's name and address and the service address as separate fields. The date is to be obtained from the computer's clock during the merge. Review the document and make any other required corrections. [*Note:* If you did not create the fill-in-the-form document for Comprehensive Problem 4, then create it for this problem and include the fields for the mail merge.]

Task 6: Print this letter with the merge codes.

Task 7: Save this as the document file CHANGE.PF.

Task 8: Perform the merge of the CHANGE.PF and CHANGE.SF files.

Task 9: Preview the letters generated.

Task 10: Print the resulting letters.

Time Estimates

Novice: 75 minutes

Intermediate: 60 minutes

Advanced: 45 minutes

W.4.16 Case Application

Case: Overland Steaks International

Business Problem: Personalized advertising
MIS Characteristics: Marketing
                Operational Control
Management Functions: Directing
                Controlling
Tools Skills: Merges
        Macros

Overland Steaks International (OSI) specializes in marketing and distributing meat products. As described by OSI's president Alan Simon, "We purchase boxed beef from meat packers, such as Iowa Prime Beef, and process it into single serving portions for sale directly to individual customers and restaurants. For example, we prepare an individual filet mignon from a beef loin. This is cut to the desired weight and individually wrapped to preserve freshness. If a restaurant sells one filet, they only open the package for that particular steak. The others remain sealed with their freshness preserved for future use."

Overland Steaks is a private, closely held corporation. It grew out of a family-run neighborhood meat market started in the early 1900s. As meat markets were merged with supermarkets, the Simon family expanded their business, specializing in preparing meats for restaurants and other institutional customers.

During the past 20 years, OSI has become a leader in mail-order gourmet steaks. They buy the finest meat, package it, freeze it, and guarantee its fresh delivery to a customer's door. From Maine to California and Seattle to Miami, Overland Steaks customers enjoy the quality and convenience of their gourmet steaks. Each steak arrives individually wrapped for freshness, frozen under dry ice, and expertly packed in a tough, totally reusable cooler.

Alan has organized OSI into three divisions: Gourmet, Institutional, and Production. The Gourmet Division, headed by Fred Simon, handles direct sales to customers. The Institutional Division, guided by Bruce Simon, is responsible for sales to restaurants and other wholesale customers. The Production Division, managed by Alyson Simon-Meijer, carries out the purchasing, packaging, and preparation of all orders. In addition to direct mail-order sales, the Gourmet Division also operates steak shops in several large department stores and at selected airport locations.

The Gourmet Division generates over one-half of its sales during the holiday season, because a box of gourmet steaks makes a wonderful holiday gift for friends, business associates, and family. Many holiday sales are from customers who believe a box of steaks usually make a better gift than a stinking cheese ball! However, Fred continues to expand their market during the rest of the year. One of the marketing strategies Fred utilizes is direct marketing with personalized letters. Fred has guided his staff in the development and maintenance of a select list of customers. OSI carefully protects this list from competitors because of the success OSI has with it.

Fred has found that summer is one of the slower times of the year for selling gourmet steaks. In purchasing boxed beef, Alyson has advised Fred that she expects increased supplies at lower prices during the next several months. To take advantage of these conditions, Fred has been working with the associates in the Gourmet Division on a personalized letter announcing a summer special. They anticipate that this will increase sales. Thus far, a fill-in-the-form letter has been created for entering the information for each customer individually from the keyboard. However, with OSI's mailing list, several thousand personalized letters will need to be produced. Fred is anxious to have you complete this project.

Tasks

1. Access the STEAKS50.PF [version 5.0] or STEAKS51.PF [version 5.1] document file. Print the document and review its content. Notice the location of the fill-in-the-blank fields.

2. Test the current fill-in-the-form letter by performing a merge and interactively entering the data from the keyboard. Use these data and print the resulting letter:

Customer's name:	Mr. Charles Bronson
Customer's address:	1621 Hickory Lane
Customer's city state zip:	Tupelo, MS 39209
Customer number:	76302-BK687
Salutation:	Mr. Bronson

   [*Hint:* Remember to use <F9> to complete the entry of *each* input field value, rather than pressing <Enter>.]

3. Continue testing by performing a second merge with data interactively entered from the keyboard. Use this data and print the resulting letter:

Customer's name:	Ms. Barbara Wahoo
Customer's address:	3431 Webster Street
Customer's city state zip:	Las Cruces, NM 88001
Customer number:	39406-GE364
Salutation:	Ms. Wahoo

4. Revise the fill-in-the-form primary document to perform a mail merge with the customer information obtained from a secondary file. Print your revised document and save this as the file OSIMAIL.PF. You may use this table to assist with your design prior to making the changes in your document:

Field Number	Field Content/Name

5. Now create a secondary document file OSIMAIL.SF containing the variable information for the mail merge. Include the data from Tasks 2 and 3 and the following test data in this file:

Customer's name:	Mr. Lampton Mitera
Customer's address:	1821 Northwest Radial Hwy
Customer's city state zip:	Roseburg, OR 97470
Customer number:	90621-TM391
Salutation:	Mr. Mitera

Customer's name:	Ms. Michelle Sweet
Customer's address:	818 River Road
Customer's city state zip:	Wilkes-Barre, PA 18704
Customer number:	39406-GE364
Salutation:	Ms. Sweet

[*Hint:* Remember to include the end-of-record markers.]

6. Produce the final letters by performing the mail merge with the primary and secondary document files. Print the letters.

7. Create an OSIMAIL macro that automatically performs the execution of the mail merge. This macro should clear the current document before performing the merge. [*Note:* The execution of a merge in the entry of your macro will terminate the creation of the macro. You will not need to use the <Ctrl>+<F10> to terminate the Macro entry mode.]

8. (*Optional*)   Review your macro using the Macro Editor. Make any corrections, if necessary. Use <Shift>+<PrtSc> to obtain a hard copy of your macro.

9. Complete your system test by executing the macro. Review the letters produced. Verify that they are the same as those produced in Task 6. Print this set of letters if you choose.

10. (*Optional*)   Other associates in the Gourmet Division will also be involved in operating this system. Write user documentation describing the procedures for the entry of customer information into the secondary file and the merging and printing of these letters.

Time Estimates

Novice: 120 minutes

Intermediate: 90 minutes

Advanced: 60 minutes

Reference

CONTENT

- Starting WordPerfect
- Command Summary
- Selected Hidden Codes

W.5.1 Starting WordPerfect

WordPerfect may be started in several different ways depending on your particular hardware configuration. When WordPerfect is installed on a local area network (LAN), a different startup procedure may be used. This section describes two of the more common methods of starting WordPerfect.

W.5.1.1. Two Floppy Drives

In preparation, obtain the WordPerfect Program Disk(s) (two disks for 5.25-in. format and one disk for 3.5-in. format) with DOS installed on it. If your disk is not set up with DOS, then you may place the operating system on the disk by using the SYS command, if you have permission to perform this activity at your site. With your disk(s) in hand, you are ready to proceed:

1 Place WordPerfect disk 1 in drive A:

2 Place your Data Disk in drive B:

   A At the DOS prompt (usually, **A>** or **A :\>**),

      Enter: WP

      or

   B Perform a warm boot by pressing <Ctrl>+<Alt>+<Del> all together. Enter the date and time, if requested.

      If the DOS A> prompt appears, enter: WP
      Otherwise, skip this step.

      or

C Perform a cold boot by turning on the power switch to your PC.
Enter the date and time, if requested.

If the DOS A> prompt appears, enter: WP
Otherwise, skip this step.

3 If you are using 5.25-in. disks, when requested, place the WordPerfect disk 2 in drive A:

Press: \<Enter>

You are now ready to use WordPerfect.

W.5.1.2. Hard Disk Drive

Before you are ready to start up WordPerfect, make sure that it has been installed on the hard disk. If the computer is not turned on, turn it on and enter the date and time, if requested.

Make sure that you are at the DOS prompt (this is, **C** > or **C** :\>). Drive C: is usually the default disk drive for a computer equipped with a hard disk. If you are accessing WordPerfect on a LAN, this may be a different disk drive.

1 Place your Data Disk in drive A:

2 If WordPerfect is accessed from the root directory, at the DOS prompt (usually, **C** > or **C** :\>),

Enter: WP

or

If WordPerfect is accessed from the WP directory, at the DOS prompt (usually, **C** > or **C** :\>),

Enter: CD\WP   Change to WP directory

Enter: WP   Begin executing WordPerfect

You are now ready to use WordPerfect.

W.5.2   Command Summary

Many of the more frequently used WordPerfect commands are summarized in the following table. The purpose is to provide a quick reference review of these commands. The form of each command is a general form of the command that is most frequently used; there may be other methods of achieving the same results. Many of the commands are implemented by selecting menu choices. The actual selection of the menu choice may be made by typing a number or letter for the menu item or, with version 5.1, by selecting the item from a pull-down or pop-out menu. The command word describing a menu choice has been included in the table rather than merely specifying the number of the menu selection. You need to use the method of menu selection available with your version of WordPerfect. For many commands, series of several menu selections are required. These series of menu choices are listed separated by commas. For example, to request the execution of the "Center Page" command, the menu choice sequence is

Format (\<Shift>+\<F8>), Page, Center Page, Yes/No

This means

Select:	Format (<Shift>+<F8>)	
Select:	Page	
Select:	Center Page	
Enter:	Y or N	Your desired Center Page action specified as Yes or No

The menu choices for some commands are different for the various versions of WordPerfect. Their usage within each version is indicated for your reference. Beyond these commands, additional commands are available that may be reviewed in the *WordPerfect Reference Manuals.*

Action	Version	Command
Align Right	5.x	Flush Right (<Alt>+<F6>)
Block Text	5.x	Block (<Alt>+<F4>)
Bold Text As-You-Type	5.x	Bold (<F6>)—turn on or off
Bold Existing Text	5.x	Block (<Alt>+<F4>), Bold (<F6>)
Cancel a Command	5.x	Cancel (<F1>)
Center Page	5.x	Format (<Shift> + <F8>), Page, Center Page, Yes/No
Center Block of Text	5.x	Block (<Alt> + <F4>), Center(<Shift>+<F6>)
Center Line of Text	5.x	Center (<Shift>+<F6>)
Clear Document	5.x	Exit (<F7>), No, No
Codes, Reveal	5.x	Reveal Codes (<Alt> + <F3>) •turn on or off
Copy Block of Text	5.x	Block (<Alt>+<F4>), Move (<Ctrl>+<F4>), Block, Copy
Copy File	5.x	File List (<F5>), (enter directory), Copy
Copy Rectangular Column of Text	5.x	Block (<Alt> + <F4>), Move (<Ctrl>+<F4>), Rectangle, Copy
Copy Page	5.x	Move (<Ctrl>+<F4>), Page, Copy
Copy Paragraph	5.x	Move (<Ctrl>+<F4>), Paragraph, Copy
Copy Sentence	5.x	Move (<Ctrl>+<F4>), Sentence, Copy
Cut (Move)	5.x	Move (<Ctrl>+<F4>) ...
Date, Insert Current Date	5.x	Date (<Shift>+<F5>), Date Text
Delete Character	5.x	Delete (<Delete> or <Backspace>)
Delete Block of Text	5.x	Block (<Alt>+<F4>), <Delete>
Delete File from List	5.x	List Files (<F5>), (enter directory), Delete
Delete Rectangular Column of Text	5.x	Block (<Ctrl> + <F4>), Move (<Alt> + <F4>), Rectangle, Delete
Delete to End of Line	5.x	EOL (<Ctrl>+<End>)
Delete Word	5.x	Delete Word (<Ctrl>+<Backspace>)
Directory, Change Default	5.x	List Files (<F5>), <=>, (enter default directory)
Double-Space Lines	5.x	Format (<Shift> + <F8>), Line, Line Spacing, 2

Action	Version	Command
End Field Merge Code	5.x	End Field (\<F9>)
Exit from Command	5.x	Exit (\<F7>)
Exit from WordPerfect	5.x	Exit (\<F7>), Yes/No, Yes
Flush Right	5.x	Flush Right (\<Alt>+\<F6>)
Footers	5.x	Format (\<Shift> + \<F8>), Page, Header/Footer, Footer
Footnote	5.x	Footnote (\<Ctrl>+\<F7>), Footnote, Create or Edit
Hard Page Break	5.x	Hard Page Break (\<Ctrl>+\<Enter>)
Hard Return	5.x	Hard Return (\<Enter>)
Headers	5.x	Format (\<Shift> + \<F8>), Page, Header/Footer, Header
Help Screens	5.x	Help (\<F3>)
Indent Paragraph from Left	5.x	Indent (\<F4>)
Indent Paragraph from Both	5.x	Indent (\<Shift>+\<F4>)
Insert ASCII Text From Another File	5.x	Text In/Out (\<Ctrl> + \<F5>), DOS Text, Retrieve
Justification, Full	5.1	Format (\<Shift> + \<F8>), Line, Justification, Full
	5.0	Format (\<Shift> + \<F8>), Line, Justification, Yes
Justification, Left	5.1	Format (\<Shift> + \<F8>), Line, Justification, Left
	5.0	Format (\<Shift> + \<F8>), Line, Justification, No
Line Spacing	5.x	Format (\<Shift> + \<F8>), Line, Line Spacing, #
List Files	5.x	List Files (\<F5>)
Macro, Define	5.x	Define Macro (\<Ctrl>+\<F10>)
Macro, Execute	5.x	Macro (\<Alt>+\<F10>)
Merge, Codes	5.x	Merge Codes (\<Shift>+\<F9>)
Merge, Execute	5.x	Merge (\<Ctrl>+\<F9>), Merge
Margin Set (left and right)	5.x	Format (\<Shift> + \<F8>), Line, Margins Left/Right
Margin Set (top and bottom)	5.x	Format (\<Shift> + \<F8>), Page, Margins Top/Bottom
Mail Merge	5.x	See "Merge,..."
Move Block	5.x	Block (\<Alt>+\<F4>), Move (\<Ctrl>+\<F4>), Block, Move
Move Page	5.x	Move (\<Ctrl>+\<F4>), Page, Move
Move Paragraph	5.x	Move (\<Ctrl>+\<F4>), Paragraph, Move
Move Sentence	5.x	Move (\<Ctrl>+\<F4>), Sentence, Move
Page Number	5.x	Format (\<Shift> + \<F8>), Page, Page Number
Preview Document	5.x	Print (\<Shift>+\<F7>), View Document
Print, Cancel	5.x	Print (\<Shift>+\<F7>), Printer Control, Cancel Job(s) or Stop
Print Current Document	5.x	Print (\<Shift>+\<F7>), Full Document
Print Any Document	5.x	List File (\<F5>), (enter directory), Print

Action	Version	Command
Replace Text	5.x	Replace (<Alt>+<F2>),...
Retrieve ASCII File	5.x	Text In/Out (<Ctrl> + <F5>), DOS Text, Retrieve
Retrieve Document	5.x	Retrieve (<Shift>+<F10>)
Retrieve Document from List	5.x	List Files (<F5>), (enter directory), Retrieve
Reveal Codes	5.x	Reveal Codes (<Alt>+<F3>)
Save ASCII File	5.x	Text In/Out (<Ctrl> + <F5>), DOS Text, Save
Save Current Document	5.x	Save (<F10>)
Save As Earlier WP Version	5.1	Text In/Out (<Ctrl> + <F5>), Save As (select WP version)
	5.0	Text In/Out (<Ctrl> + <F5>), Save As WP 4.2
Screen, Split	5.x	Screen (<Ctrl> + <F3>), Window, (window size)
Search for Text String Down Document	5.x	Search (<F2>),...
Search for Text String Up Document	5.x	Search (<Shift>+<F2>),...
Single-Space Lines	5.x	Format (<Shift> + <F8>), Line, Line Spacing, 1
Spell Check	5.x	Spell (<Ctrl>+<F2>)
Switch Between Documents	5.x	Switch (<Shift>+<F3>)
Tab Set	5.x	Format (<Shift>+<F8>), Line, Tab Set
Text In from Another WP Document	5.x	Retrieve (<Shift>+<F10>)
Thesaurus	5.x	Thesaurus (<Alt>+<F1>)
Typeover Characters	5.x	Insert (<Insert>)—toggle on or off
Undelete Text	5.x	Cancel (<F1>)
Underline Text As-You-Type	5.x	Underline (<F6>)—turn on or off
Underline Existing Text	5.x	Block (<Alt>+<F4>), Underline (<F6>)
View/Preview Document	5.x	Print (<Shift>+<F7>), View Document

W.5.3 Selected Hidden Codes

WordPerfect uses special hidden control codes embedded within a document to determine how the document is to be printed. These control codes are displayed with the Reveal Codes <Alt>+<F3> or <F11> command. Some of these control codes have been revised with the different versions of WordPerfect. Several of the more frequently used control codes are summarized in the following table with their usage within each version indicated for your reference. A complete listing of these control codes is available from the *WordPerfect Reference Manuals*.

Hidden Code	Version	Description
[-]	5.x	Hyphen
[Block]	5.x	Beginning of Block
[BOLD] [bold]	5.x	Bold (begin and end)

Hidden Code	Version	Description
[Center]	5.1	Center
[Cntr]	5.0	
[C/A/Flrt]	5.0	End of Tab Align or Flush Right
[Flsh Rt]	5.x	Flush Right
[Footer]	5.x	Footer
[Header]	5.x	Header
[HPg]	5.x	Hard Page Break
[HRt]	5.x	Hard Return
[–>Indent]	5.x	Indent
[–>Indent<–]	5.x	Left/Right Indent
[Just Off]	5.0	Left Justification
[Just On]	5.0	Full Justification
[Just:Full]	5.1	Full Justification (Just On)
[Just:Left]	5.1	Left Justification (Just Off)
[Just:Right]	5.1	Right Justification
[L/R Mar: . . .]	5.x	Left and Right Margins
[SPg]	5.x	Soft Page Break
[SRt]	5.x	Soft Return
[T/B Mar: . . .]	5.x	Top/Bottom Margin
[Tab]	5.x	Tab
[Tab Set: . . .]	5.x	Tab Settings
[UND] [und]	5.x	Underline (begin and end)

Integrating
Solutions

Exporting and Importing Results

CONTENT

- What Is Solution Integration?
- Reviewing Integrated Software Tools
- Applying ASCII Text Files
- Exporting Lotus 1-2-3 Results to WordPerfect
- Transferring Screen Display Results from dBASE to WordPerfect
- Transferring Report Results from dBASE to WordPerfect
- Creating Comma Delimited Files with WordPerfect
- Transferring Comma Delimited Files to Lotus 1-2-3
- Transferring Comma Delimited Files to dBASE
- When Things Go Wrong

I.1.1 What Is Solution Integration?

Solution integration is concerned with transferring results among software tool applications. For example, an initial analysis conducted in Lotus 1-2-3 could be transferred to WordPerfect to be incorporated in a more comprehensive management report. The worksheet is used to support the computations for the analysis, whereas the final document becomes a combination of both the text explaining the analysis and the worksheet analysis itself. With integrated solutions, each software tool is applied to perform those activities it does best, as summarized as follows:

Software Tool	Primary Function
Lotus 1-2-3	Formula-intensive business modeling
dBASE	Database development and maintenance
WordPerfect	Presentation quality text document preparation

Could you use Lotus 1-2-3 to prepare text documents? Of course. However, it does not include the functional features that permit the comprehensive word processing capabilities available in WordPerfect. If the only software tool you had was Lotus 1-2-3, you might use it, as some people have, to prepare simple memos or letters occasionally, but *not* more comprehensive reports. The ideal situation, then, is to use each software tool for the activities it does best.

When the results from one software tool need to be integrated with those in another software tool, the desired information can be selected for transfer to the second tool. These data are moved from a source application to a target application, such as from Lotus 1-2-3 (the source) to WordPerfect (the target).

If all software tools used the same format for storing data, this transfer of data would be easy. However, like most other software tools, Lotus 1-2-3, dBASE, and WordPerfect each store their files by using *special file formats*. Files are saved in these special coded formats to increase processing speed and to conserve disk space. Special format files make the information more easily accessible by a specific software tool, because the data are stored in the most convenient arrangement for that particular software tool. Unique characters and codes, like those that identify margins, bolding, and underlining in WordPerfect, are contained in special formatted files. Figure I.1 illustrates the appearance to DOS of special codes in a WordPerfect document file. Since WordPerfect uses its own distinct format, these files cannot be read directly into a Lotus 1-2-3 worksheet or dBASE database. Similar situations exist for Lotus 1-2-3 and dBASE files.

When information needs to be shared between two software tools, you have three choices:

1. Retype the information into the other application. This could introduce errors and require a significant amount of time.

2. Transfer the information as an ASCII text file. ASCII (American Standard Code for Information Interchange) is a universal method for transmitting and storing

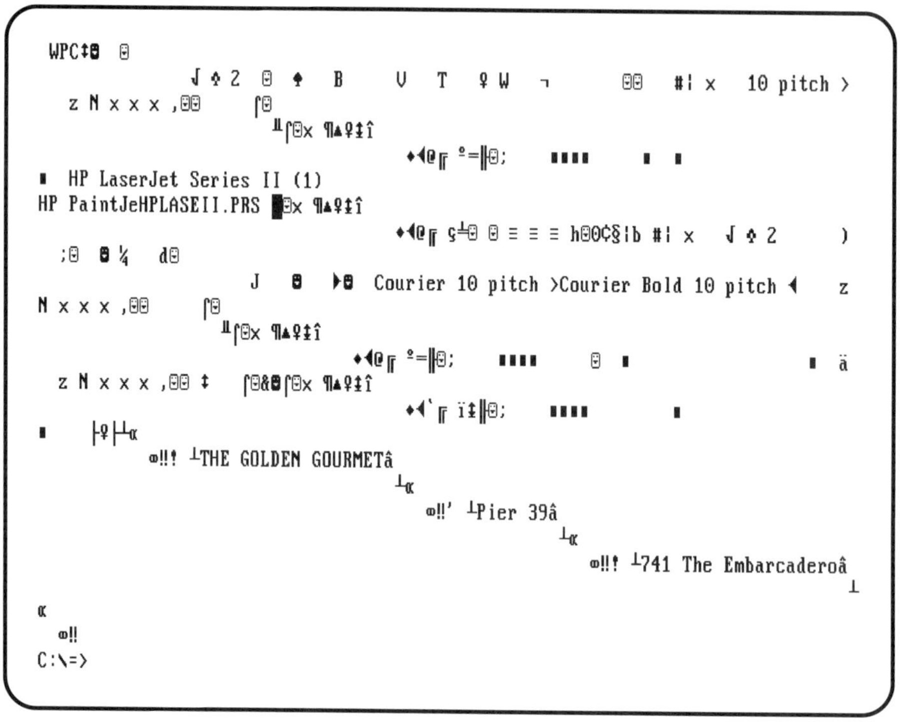

FIGURE I.1. WordPerfect special formatted file.

data, presented in more depth in Section I.1.3. An ASCII text file is written from the source application in a generic format that can be read directly by almost any DOS-based or WINDOWS-based target application.

3. Translate the special format of the source application into the special format of the target application. This translation may be performed by the source application tool, the target application tool, or a special-purpose translation utility. However, this translation is often less than perfect, with special codes and characters occasionally lost in the process.

Once you understand the file transfer techniques among Lotus 1-2-3, dBASE, and WordPerfect, you can extend these fundamental concepts to the transfer of data among a wide variety of applications, including the common accounting and other transaction processing applications used by most businesses. On a number of occasions, analysts have been observed retyping information from accounting reports produced on a company's mainframe computer into Lotus 1-2-3 for further analysis. However, this should be avoided, if possible, by performing the data transfers described in this Lesson.

Keypoint!

> Learning to transfer data among Lotus 1-2-3, dBASE, and WordPerfect serves as a foundation for transferring data among many different applications including common accounting and other transaction processing applications!

I.1.2 Reviewing Integrated Software Tools

Some software tools, such as Lotus Symphony, Lotus Works, Smart, Framework, and Microsoft Works, are integrated software tools. Each of these tools provide the ability to carry out word processing, spreadsheet modeling, and database management. Some integrated tools also support communications, graphics, and time management. An integrated software tool is like the ultimate Swiss Army knife. In addition to a knife blade, it also contains a spoon and a fork. It is convenient to take on a camping trip, but lacks the same capabilities as the separate pieces of tableware at home in your kitchen. Which would you prefer to use at your favorite gourmet restaurant? As you might expect, there are advantages and disadvantages to using integrated software tools.

The primary advantage of integrated software tools is a common user interface (CUI) for operating the tool within a single environment. All modules share a common screen format with menu selections and function key actions the same throughout the application modules. A CUI frequently appeals to the more casual end user of personal productivity software tools. Once an individual has learned one module of the software tool, the others are manipulated in a nearly identical manner. A CUI provides productivity gains from shorter training time and less switching among products, although a Microsoft Windows environment smooths out the transitions among individual software tools. Other advantages of integrated tools include the following:

- Easy movement of data among the spreadsheet, word processing, and database modules using the special formatted files of the software tool.

- The cost of a single integrated software tool is often less than that for separate tools that perform the same activities.

- Macros and command files are common to all application modules. A command file can be created to query a database, selectively retrieve data, send them to the word processing module for inclusion in a document, and print the completed document.

The chief disadvantage of integrated software tools is that the functional features available in each module are often a compromise. For instance, Symphony has a wonderful spreadsheet component, like that of Lotus 1-2-3; however, its word processor lacks many of the features supported by WordPerfect. Although Symphony has a better database capability than Lotus 1-2-3, it lacks the full capabilities furnished by dBASE. The Smart integrated software consists of a family of application modules that can be used independently as stand-alone tools, or integrated with the other modules. However, these Smart modules lack the same robust functional capabilities of Lotus 1-2-3, dBASE, and WordPerfect. Granted, the Smart spreadsheet, database, and word processing modules encompass a vast array of functional capabilities. But, in general, they are deficient in many of the advanced features included in Lotus 1-2-3, dBASE, and WordPerfect. The fundamental concept behind integrated software tools such as Smart and Symphony is that "the whole is greater than the sum of the individual parts," because of the convenience of the common user interface for the more casual user of the software. Other disadvantages of integrated software tools include the following:

- The differences that exist in operating each module; working in a spreadsheet is very different from doing word processing or developing databases.

- Processing speed and data storage efficiency, which are often sacrificed in providing the common user interface. For example, the amount of time required to calculate a Lotus 1-2-3 worksheet is usually less than that of an integrated software tool like the Smart spreadsheet.

- Size limitations, which may hamper the development and use of applications. For example, a Symphony database may only contain about 8000 records, whereas a dBASE database may hold several million records. Similar limitations may affect the size of a document, measured in number of pages, that can be handled by the word processing module.

- Special formatted files that still require translation for transfer to other applications outside the integrated software tool.

- All of the modules of the integrated software, which usually must be supported and maintained, although some end users may make use of only one or two of the modules. For example, in Symphony, if you used only the spreadsheet and word processing modules, the others would still require computer resources whether they are used or not.

Lotus 1-2-3, dBASE, and WordPerfect are among the most widely used personal productivity software tools and are generally accepted throughout business and industry. Most other spreadsheet and database management software tools interface with Lotus 1-2-3 and dBASE. For example, the Smart Integrated System can read and write ASCII, Lotus 1-2-3, and dBASE formatted files. Thus, knowing how to apply these popular software tools provides a foundation for using many different spreadsheet, database, and word processing software tools, whether they are stand-alone or integrated. Moreover, learning how to transfer data among these tools supplies the background for interfacing the solutions of many other common applications.

Keypoint! The primary advantage of an integrated software tool is the common user interface (CUI). Significant functional capabilities are usually sacrificed to obtain a CUI!

I.1.3 Applying ASCII Text Files

The trick to transferring data from one source application to another target application is to create a file that can be read by the *target* application. This situation is true not only for Lotus 1-2-3, dBASE, and WordPerfect but also for other applications, such as Peachtree or DacEasy, which provide general ledger, accounts receivable, accounts payable, inventory, order entry, payroll, and electronic mail modules. The common denominator in transferring data among applications is the use of an ASCII formatted file, as illustrated in Figure I.2. The popularity of the ASCII format is driven by the federal government's requirement that all of the computers it buys must be capable of storing data in this format. This requirement has contributed to establishing a standard method of storing data on both personal computers and mainframe computers.

A distinguishing feature of an ASCII file is that data are stored in the file in such a way that if the contents of the file are displayed or printed, you can read the file directly. The DOS TYPE and PRINT commands provide one method of directly displaying the contents of a file. If you display a file with these commands and it is readable, the file is an ASCII formatted file, also known as an ASCII text file, since any textual information may be stored in the file. Figure I.3 is one example of an ASCII text file. In addition to the text that you can read, each line in the text file is terminated with a carriage return and line feed (that is an <Enter>), as denoted by the paragraph symbol in this example. The special symbol ˆZ (<Ctrl>+<Z>) marks the end-of-file (EOF).

In general, the methods available for transferring data as ASCII text files among applications include the following:

File Structure	Description
Report Formatted	Contains text arranged as a report. Numbers may include edit characters, such as the currency symbol and commas as illustrated in Figure I.3.
Comma Delimited	Includes text with alphabetic or character labels enclosed in quotes and fields or columns separated or **delimited** by commas, as shown in Figure I.4. Numeric values do *not* include currency symbols and commas, but may include decimal points. In addition to comma delimited files, other characters, such as a blank, are also frequently used to delimit each of the fields in a record.
Fixed Formatted	Establishes text arranged in fields or columns of the *same width*. The position of data within a record determines its field designation, as illustrated in Figure I.5. Numeric values usually do *not* include currency symbols and commas, but may include decimal points.

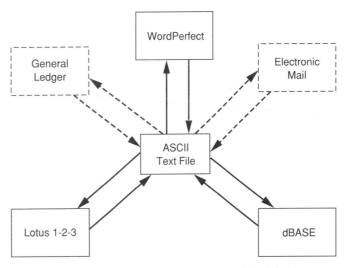

FIGURE I.2. ASCII text file as the common link in data transfer.

```
C:\=>TYPE B:PLAN17CP.DOC


                          GOOD MORNING PRODUCTS¶
                    PRO FORMA PROFIT AND LOSS STATEMENT¶
                    ------------------------------------¶
¶
Sales Growth Rate      0.08¶
Cost Percent           0.77¶
¶
                     1ST QTR   2ND QTR   3RD QTR   4TH QTR      TOTAL¶
                     -------   -------   -------   -------   ---------¶
Sales               $289,500  $312,660  $337,673  $364,687  $1,304,519¶
Cost of Sales       $222,915  $240,748  $260,008  $280,809  $1,004,480¶
                     -------   -------   -------   -------   ---------¶
Gross Profit         $66,585   $71,912   $77,665   $83,878    $300,039¶
                     =======   =======   =======   =======   =========¶
^Z



C:\=>
```

FIGURE I.3. Report formatted file structure.

```
C:\=>TYPE B:PLAN17CR.DOC

"Sales",289500,312660,337673,364687¶
"Cost of Sales",222915,240748,260008,280809¶
"Gross Profit",66585,71912,77665,83878¶
^Z


C:\=>
```

FIGURE I.4. Comma delimited file structure.

```
C:\=>TYPE B:PLAN17CQ.DOC


Sales              289500   312660   337673   346687¶
Cost of Sales      222915   240748   260008   280809¶
Gross Profit        66585    71912    77665    83878¶
^Z

C:\=>
```

FIGURE I.5. Fixed formatted file structure.

In general, even if an application does not directly support saving an ASCII format file, you may still be able to produce an ASCII text file if that application lets you print to a file. In most situations, the print file will be an ASCII format file.

With the prevalent use of ASCII formatted files across many different application tools, you might expect that Lotus 1-2-3, dBASE, and WordPerfect would each clearly identify file operations that involve ASCII files. Actually, all is not as expected, because they are *not identified directly as ASCII files*. Therefore, how are ASCII text files referenced for use with these software tools? The reference method depends on the software tool, with this notation frequently used:

Tool	ASCII Text File Designation
Lotus 1-2-3	Print File (*.PRN)
dBASE	SDF (System Data Format) (*.TXT)
WordPerfect	DOS Text File (*.ASC or any desired extension)

In integrating solutions, the key question to be addressed is: How can an ASCII text file be created by a *source* application in an appropriate format for direct input to a *target* application? This is the main focus of this and the next Lesson. The use of report formatted and comma delimited file structures is presented in this Lesson, and the use of fixed formatted file structures and special formatted files is examined in the next Lesson.

Keypoint!

ASCII text files are the most commonly used method of transferring data among a number of applications, including personal productivity software tools and common business applications!

I.1.4   Exporting Lotus 1-2-3 Results to WordPerfect

A report formatted file can be generated in Lotus 1-2-3 for transfer to WordPerfect, where it is subsequently included in a more comprehensive management report. In Lotus 1-2-3, the / Print File (/PF) command is used to create a report formatted file, which is an ASCII text file that can be directly accessed with the WordPerfect Retrieve <Shift>+<F10> command. When Lotus 1-2-3 writes this ASCII text file, it automatically adds the extension PRN to the filename. Since the file is being described with selections from the /Print File menu, the margins for the report need to be adjusted to avoid possible conflicts with the margin settings used in WordPerfect.

At Good Morning Products, Kim and Chris have completed the preparation of next year's budget. Kim wants Chris to produce a report of these results for submission to Frosty. The results are stored from their Lotus 1-2-3 worksheet in this manner:

Action: Access Lotus 1-2-3 and retrieve the worksheet file PLAN6.WK1, which is their complete budget for the California operations. (If you did not create the PLAN6.WK1 worksheet in prior lessons, create this by using Lotus 1-2-3 before you continue.)

Before storing the results, Chris wants to enhance the report's appearance by adding currency symbols and commas to the dollar amounts in their Pro Forma Statement. This is accomplished as follows:

Action: Change the format of the cells **B12** through **F13** and **B15** through **F15** to Currency with no decimal by using the /Range Format Currency command.

Action: Increase the width of the TOTAL column by two spaces to accommodate the newly formatted numbers by using the /Worksheet Column Set-Width command.

The report now appears in the desired form for inclusion in the report. Let us create a file containing this formatted report.

To create a report formatted file from Lotus 1-2-3			
Move to:	A2	Upper-left corner of the results that will be used in the management report
Press:	/	Access main menu
Select:	Print	Creating an output file is performed as a Print activity
Select:	File	Cause a *file* to be created rather than a paper copy
Enter:	PLAN18	Name of the ASCII text file; the extension PRN is automatically appended to this file name
Select:	Replace[if requested]	Replace an existing file with this name, if one exists
Select:	Range	Identify the section of the worksheet to be saved in the ASCII text file

Action: Specify the range **A2** through **F16** for storage.

Action: Set the margins like this:

Left = 0
Right = 78
Top = 0
Bottom = 0

Return to the Print menu when you have completed setting these margins.

Setting the margins in this manner helps to eliminate the additional indentation from the left-side margin in WordPerfect and reduces unwanted blank lines.

Select:	Go	Write selected report to the file
Select:	Quit	Exit from the Print menu and return to the READY mode. Do *not* use <Esc> to return to the Ready mode

Caution Alert!

Use the Quit command to exit from the Print menu and return to the Ready mode when writing results to a file. Quit causes the disk file to be "closed" or saved. If the <Esc> is used the file is *not* "closed." The file name you specified will exist, but it will be empty!

The results have been written to the file PLAN18.PRN for subsequent use in preparing a memorandum in WordPerfect.

Action: Save the worksheet as PLAN18. This will save the Print Setting for reuse, if you find it necessary to use the worksheet another time.

Action: Exit from Lotus 1-2-3 and return to the DOS prompt.

Action: Display the contents of the file PLAN18.PRN on your screen using the DOS TYPE command. Then, print a hard copy of this file by using the TYPE command with the ">" redirection to your printer (PRN). Here, the file extension PRN and the use of PRN to indicate the printer in redirection are purely coincidental. (Redirection with the TYPE command is discussed in Lesson D.1 of Using DOS.)

Chris has exported the data from Lotus 1-2-3 to an ASCII text file and is now ready to use the results in preparing the memo in WordPerfect. Let us continue with the preparation of Chris' memo.

To create a WordPerfect document that will receive the ASCII text file from Lotus 1-2-3

Action: Access WordPerfect and enter the preliminary memo, as illustrated in Figure I.6. "MEMORANDUM" is centered, whereas the date, to, from, and subject headings are located at tab stops. Save this as file MEMO17.DOC.

To get ready to insert the ASCII text file by positioning your cursor

Move to: the second blank line after "as follows:"

To add the ASCII text file from Lotus 1-2-3 to your current WordPerfect document

Action: Retrieve the PLAN18.PRN ASCII text file using the Retrieve <Shift>+<F10> command.

The ASCII text file, stored from the Lotus 1-2-3 worksheet, is inserted into the WordPerfect document at the location of the cursor. The importing of the results is completed.

MEMORANDUM

Date: October 12, 1994
To: Frosty
From: Crush

Subject: Next Year's Budget

Kimberly and Chris have analyzed our past sales and the current costs of producing Liquid Gold. Based on this analysis, they have formulated our budget for next year. The anticipated results are as follows:

Please review this projection and provide me with your assessment. Any required revision can be made prior to the Board of Directors meeting on the 21st.

FIGURE I.6. Preliminary draft of WordPerfect document.

Action: The default margins may cause the results to appear double-spaced. If this occurs, then revise the margins just above the table with Left = 1 in. and Right = 0.5 in. Change the margins below the table so that they are the same as those at the top of your document.

Keypoint!

> The margins may need to be adjusted in the source and/or target software tools, if there is *not* an appropriate match between them!

To remove any extra blank lines from the combined document

Action: If extra blank lines happened to occur in your report at the top or bottom of the imported Lotus 1-2-3 results, then use the Reveal Codes <Alt>+<F3> display and remove them.

Action: Enhance the appearance of the document by bolding "MEMORANDUM," the two lines of the report heading, and the amount of Gross Profit [Total].

Action: Preview the document, print the report, and save this as the MEMO18.DOC document file.

As Crush requested, Chris has completed the memo for next year's budget (Figure I.7) and is ready to submit it to Frosty. The procedures Chris used in preparing the document are summarized in Figure I.8.

I.1.5   Transferring Screen Display Results from dBASE to WordPerfect

Information displayed with dBASE from a database can be captured for transfer to WordPerfect, where text can be added to produce a complete management report. In dBASE, the DISPLAY and LIST commands are used to formulate database queries that appear on the screen. As this information is displayed, it can be directed to an ASCII text file for subsequent integration in a WordPerfect document. This capture of screen display information is carried out with the ALTERNATE commands in dBASE. The SET ALTERNATE TO command specifies a file to which a copy of the screen display is written. Once this file has been established, the SET ALTERNATE

MEMORANDUM

Date: October 12, 1994
To: Frosty
From: Crush

Subject: Next Year's Budget

Kimberly and Chris have analyzed our past sales and the current costs of producing Liquid Gold. Based on this analysis, they have formulated our budget for next year. The anticipated results are as follows:

GOOD MORNING PRODUCTS
PRO FORMA PROFIT AND LOSS STATEMENT

	1ST QTR	2ND QTR	3RD QTR	4TH QTR	TOTAL
Sales Growth Rate	0.08				
Cost Percent	0.77				
Sales	$289,500	$312,660	$337,673	$364,687	$1,304,519
Cost of Sales	$222,915	$240,748	$260,008	$280,809	$1,004,480
Gross Profit	$66,585	$71,912	$77,665	$83,878	**$300,039**

Please review this projection and provide me with your assessment. Any required revision can be made prior to the Board of Directors meeting on the 21st.

FIGURE I.7. Completed memo with integrated spreadsheet results.

1. Create the Lotus 1-2-3 Report File
   a. Use the / Print File command in Lotus 1-2-3 and specify a target file name.
   b. Select the print range and adjust the margins, as desired.
   c. Print the report in the text file and Quit the Print menu (a PRN extension is automatically added to the file name).
2. Transfer Text File to WordPerfect
   a. Access WordPerfect.
   b. If desired, retrieve the document to receive the report from Lotus 1-2-3.
   c. Position the cursor at desired location where the report from Lotus 1-2-3 is to be inserted.
   d. Retrieve <Shift>+<F10> the Lotus 1-2-3 text file with the PRN extension, inserting it into the current document.
   e. Remove any unwanted lines or special characters from the Lotus 1-2-3 report.
   f. Perform any other document additions or modifications.

FIGURE I.8. Summary of Lotus 1-2-3 report transfer to WordPerfect.

ON/OFF command is used to toggle on and off the storage of screen output in the designated file. This allows you to capture a segment of screen output, stop the capture while you perform other activities in dBASE, and then resume the capture of screen output, as desired. Once the SET ALTERNATE ON is activated, the screen capture continues for subsequent dBASE commands until the SET ALTERNATE OFF command is entered. Once established, the ALTERNATE file remains "open" to receive additional output until you either QUIT from dBASE or specify a different file with another SET ALTERNATE TO command. When dBASE generates this ALTERNATE file, it automatically appends the file extension TXT. dBASE uses the TXT extension to indicate that the file is an ASCII text file.

Once the ASCII text file has been created in dBASE, the file can be accessed immediately in WordPerfect for inclusion in a document file. This is achieved with the Retrieve <Shift>+<F10> command.

At the Golden Gourmet, Bert and Beth have received several suggestions from customers asking for the expansion of the restaurant's white wine selection. Since Auggie first opened the restaurant in 1957, customer satisfaction has been one of the cornerstones of the restaurant's operation. Recently, Bert had a conversation with Marc Fabiano at a Bay Area convention of restaurant owners. Marc suggested that Bert send him a list of his current selection of white wines. Marc would review it and would provide Bert with suggestions for expanding the white wine selections. The Golden Gourmet's wine management system (WMS) contains the information Bert needs to send Marc, and Bert knows that he can obtain this information by querying the database. Let's prepare Bert's response to Marc.

To create an ASCII text file for the screen display from dBASE	**Action:**	Access dBASE and load the WINES database with the TYPENAME index. (If you did not create the WINES database and the TYPENAME index as described in previous dBASE lessons, then create these before you continue.)

Enter: SET ALTERNATE TO MOREWINE

> Specify "MOREWINE" as the name of the ASCII text file for storing the results; the extension TXT is automatically appended to the name of this file

Enter: SET ALTERNATE ON   Toggle ON recording output of the display screen until it is toggled OFF

Enter (this command needs to be typed all on one line):

    LIST ALL OFF NAME, MAKER, YEAR, PRICE, ON_HAND FOR TYPE = "WHITE"

Enter: SET ALTERNATE OFF   Toggle OFF recording output to the display screen

If you wanted to store additional data in this ASCII text file, you could issue any other desired dBASE commands before you enter the SET ALTERNATE OFF command. You can use the SET ALTERNATE ON/OFF to toggle the recording on and off as many times as you want during your dBASE session, and the requested output information is stored in the designated file.

A general form of the SET ALTERNATE TO command is

SET ALTERNATE TO [<ASCII text filename>]

where **ASCII text filename** is the name of the file for storing the results. dBASE automatically appends the extension TXT to this file. If no filename is specified, an open ALTERNATE file is closed. This allows the use of several different ALTERNATE files during one dBASE session.

Action: Exit from dBASE and return to the DOS prompt.

Action: Use the TYPE command to display the MOREWINE.TXT ASCII text file on your screen and to obtain a hard copy of this output.

Bert has the information desired for his letter. This information has been obtained in a format arranged as a table for use with the letter. The letter can be prepared by continuing like this:

To create a WordPerfect document that will receive the ASCII text file from dBASE

Action: Access WordPerfect and enter the preliminary draft of Bert's letter, as shown in Figure I.9. Save this document as the MOREWINE.DOC file.

Move to: the second blank line after "is as follows:"

To add the ASCII text file from dBASE to your current WordPerfect document

Action: Retrieve the ASCII text file MOREWINE.TXT. The file is imported and inserted in the document at the current location of the cursor.

The LIST and the SET ALTERNATE OFF commands are included in the information obtained from recording the screen display.

THE GOLDEN GOURMET
Pier 39
741 The Embarcadero
San Francisco, California 94111

July 10, 1994

Mr. Marc Fabiano
Fabiano Brothers Distributing
8277 Barcelona Drive
Samona, California 96321

Dear Marc:

This will confirm our conversation concerning the white wines we currently include on our wine list. Since our customers are continually requesting additional choices, we would like to expand the white wines in our cellar. Our present selection of white wines is as follows:

After you have reviewed these selections, please advise me of your recommended additions to our wine list.

Sincerely,

Delbert Capriccio, General Manager

FIGURE I.9. Preliminary draft of WordPerfect document.

Action: Remove the LIST and the SET ALTERNATE OFF commands from the imported file. Add or delete blank lines so that there is one line before and one line after the table of information obtained from dBASE.

Action: (*Optional*) Enhance the appearance of the data in the table by underlining the column headings and adding space between each of the columns, similar to that shown in Figure I.10.

Action: Preview the final document, print it, and save it as the MOREWINE.DOC file.

Bert has created the desired letter, as illustrated in Figure I.10, by integrating selected information from the WINES database with his WordPerfect document.

WordPerfect provides an alternative method for retrieving an ASCII text file with the Text In/Out <Ctrl>+<F5> command. Instead of merely retrieving the file MOREWINE.TXT, Bert could have used another procedure. If you want, try out this alternate method for retrieving Bert's file.

Action: Delete the table of previously imported data from the MOREWINE.DOC document.

To use the TEXT IN/OUT method of retrieving ASCII text files in WordPerfect		

Move to: location where imported text is to be placed

Select: Text In/Out `<Ctrl>+<F5>`

Desired activity

Select: DOS Text Specify ASCII text

Select: Retrieve `(CR/LF to [HRt])`

[HRt] is usually desired for a table of information

Enter: `B:MOREWINE.TXT` Desired ASCII text file

The deleted table has again been inserted in the document.

THE GOLDEN GOURMET
Pier 39
741 The Embarcadero
San Francisco, California 94111

July 10, 1994

Mr. Marc Fabiano
Fabiano Brothers Distributing
8277 Barcelona Drive
Samona, California 96321

Dear Marc:

This will confirm our conversation concerning the white wines we currently include on our wine list. Since our customers are continually requesting additional choices, we would like to expand the white wines in our cellar. Our present selection of white wines is as follows:

NAME	MAKER	YEAR	PRICE	ON_HAND
BLANC DE BLANC	FETZER VINOS	1982	20.00	21
COUNTRY CHABLIS	ALMADEN	1983	10.00	15
EXTRA DRY WHITE	RIVERSIDE	1986	13.76	48

After you have reviewed these selections, please advise me of your recommended additions to our wine list.

Sincerely,

Delbert Capriccio, General Manager

FIGURE I.10. Completed letter with information from WINES database.

1. Create the dBASE Text File

   a. Use the SET ALTERNATE TO command in dBASE to open a target file to receive the screen display.

   b. Use SET ALTERNATE ON to turn on recording of screen display (a TXT extension is automatically added to the filename).

   c. Execute dBASE commands to produce desired screen display for recording in the target file.

   d. Use SET ALTERNATE OFF to turn off recording of screen displayed information.

2. Transfer Text File to WordPerfect

   a. Access WordPerfect.

   b. If desired, retrieve the document to receive the screen display results from dBASE.

   c. Position the cursor at desired location where the results obtained from dBASE are to be inserted.

   d. Retrieve <Shift>+<F10> the dBASE text file with the TXT extension, inserting it into the current document.

   e. Remove any unwanted lines from the dBASE results.

   f. Perform any other document changes.

FIGURE I.11. Summary of dBASE screen display transfer to WordPerfect.

The only difference between using Retrieve <Shift>+<F10> and Text In/Out <Ctrl>+<F5> with a dBASE "TXT" file is the occurrence of a "^Z" for a <Ctrl>+<Z> end-of-file (EOF) mark in WordPerfect version 5.0. Since this was included in the SET ALTERNATE OFF line, which was subsequently deleted, the method used for importing dBASE "TXT" files into WordPerfect becomes a matter of your preference.

I.1.6   Transferring Report Results from dBASE to WordPerfect

In addition to merely capturing screen displays in dBASE, a report produced by using the dBASE report writer can be saved as an ASCII text file for inclusion in a WordPerfect document. The dBASE report definition is prepared with the CREATE/MODIFY REPORT commands. The REPORT FORM command is then used to write the report directly to an ASCII text file. The main difference is that the report is written to a file rather than directed to your printer. dBASE identifies this output file as an ASCII text file by automatically appending the TXT extension to it. Although the ASCII text file is produced by using a REPORT FORM, it is the same as any other ASCII text file. In WordPerfect, the Retrieve <Shift>+<F10> command or the Text In/Out <Ctrl>+<F5> command is used to include the ASCII text file in the current document.

Bert and Beth, at the Golden Gourmet, would like to improve the appearance of their Wine List in hopes of bolstering their wine sales. This would include additional comments by their chef, Pierre von Kruger, describing the selection of wines and a recommended selection of the month. Beth realizes that the current Wine List is produced as a dBASE report that contains most of the desired information. She would like to improve the Wine List by adding the other information using WordPerfect. The enhanced Wine List can be produced in this manner:

Action: Access dBASE and load the WINES database with the TYPENAME index. Remember to set the default disk drive, if necessary.

Action: If you have not created the WINELIST report form as described in Using dBASE, Lesson D.5, then create this report definition now.

To create a report formatted file using a dBASE Report Form

Enter: REPORT FORM WINELIST **TO FILE** WINELIST

Generate the report and place the results in the ASCII file WINELIST.TXT

The desired report is produced and stored in the designated ASCII text file for use in WordPerfect. The general form of the REPORT FORM command is

REPORT FORM <report filename> [**FOR** <condition>]
[**TO PRINT/TO FILE** <ASCII text filename>]

The TO FILE option is the only difference between this command and the command used in directly printing a hard copy report.

With the REPORT FORM command, the actual dBASE commands are not included in the ASCII text file as they were with the SET ALTERNATE commands. However, SET ALTERNATE commands also could have been used to capture the WINELIST report as it was displayed. Hence, with dBASE reports, you may choose the method you prefer for capturing a report in an ASCII text file.

Bert wants Beth to enhance the appearance of the Wine List. This can be accomplished by importing the Wine List produced as a dBASE report into WordPerfect. Beth continues in this manner:

Action: Access WordPerfect and retrieve the WINELIST.TXT ASCII text file.

Action: Enhance the Wine List and add the text as illustrated in Figure I.12. If necessary, adjust the right margin to obtain single-spacing, and add or delete any blank lines.

Action: (*Optional*) Use the Screen <Ctrl>+<F3>, Line Draw, single line (|) command sequence to draw a box around the list of wines, as illustrated in Figure I.12. Be careful that you are in the typeover mode when you begin.

Action: Print the completed Wine List and save it as the WINELIST.DOC file.

Beth has completed the Wine List for the Golden Gourmet. WordPerfect provided a convenient method for enhancing the information obtained from the WINES database by using a dBASE report. The steps for this integration are summarized in Figure I.13.

GOLDEN GOURMET
WINE LIST

We are proud to present our wines, which have been specially selected by our chef, Pierre von Kruger, and our wine steward, Eric Frantz, to compliment our exquisite cuisine.

WINES	VINEYARD	TYPE	YEAR	PRICE PER BOTTLE
CABERNET	TAYLOR FARMS	RED	1986	7.00
MAD DOG 20/20	MOGEN DAVID	RED	1988	3.00
MOREAU ROUGE	J. MOREAU	RED	1982	18.50
NAPA BURGUNDY	TAYLOR FARMS	RED	1989	6.50
RED TABLE WINE	TAYLOR FARMS	RED	1989	4.76
RIPPLE	HOOTCH HUT	RED	1989	2.50
STRAWBERRY HILL	BOONE'S FARM	RED	1989	5.24
VINO BIANCO	MOGEN DAVID	RED	1988	3.00
ZINFANDEL	TAYLOR FARMS	RED	1988	6.50
BOONE'S FARM	SMOTHERS BRO	ROSE	1988	14.80
TORRES DE CASTA	M. TORRES	ROSE	1985	6.24
VIN ROSE	GEYSER PEAK	ROSE	1985	10.50
VINO ROSA	WENTE BROS	ROSE	1989	8.50
BLANC DE BLANC	FETZER VINOS	WHITE	1982	20.00
COUNTRY CHABLIS	ALMADEN	WHITE	1983	10.00
EXTRA DRY WHITE	RIVERSIDE	WHITE	1986	13.76

Eric has designated the Almaden Country Chablis as the premier wine of the month. For each dinner party with four or more individuals, this wine is included with your main entree selection.

FIGURE I.12. Wine List enhanced from dBASE report.

1. Create the dBASE Text File
   a. Create dBASE Report Form for the desired report.
   b. Use the REPORT FORM...TO FILE...command in dBASE to write the report to a target text file (a TXT extension is automatically added to the file name).
2. Transfer Text File to WordPerfect
   a. Access WordPerfect
   b. If desired, Retrieve the document that will receive the report from dBASE.
   c. Position the cursor at desired location where the report obtained from dBASE is to be inserted.
   d. Retrieve <Shift>+<F10> the dBASE text file with the TXT extension inserting it into the current document.
   e. Remove any unwanted lines from the dBASE results.
   f. Perform any other document changes.

FIGURE I.13. Summary of dBASE report results transfer to WordPerfect.

1.7 Creating Comma Delimited Files with WordPerfect

A comma delimited ASCII text file may be produced in a variety of ways. Word processor software like WordPerfect can produce a comma delimited file, as can any application program written in a programming language such as BASIC, Pascal, or C. This permits output to be obtained from a number of sources, including the common accounting and finance systems used by most businesses. With WordPerfect, comma delimited data are typed like any other text entered in a document. The resulting document is then saved as an ASCII text file by using the Text In/Out <Ctrl>+<F5> command and specifying the file as a "DOS Text" file. WordPerfect then writes the file in ASCII format rather than storing it in WordPerfect's special file format. All special format features such as bolding and underlining are lost when the file is saved as a "DOS Text" file. These comma delimited files can then be input into Lotus 1-2-3, dBASE, and many other applications.

Chris has been working on the development of Good Morning Products' financial reporting system. For selected expenses, each quarter Jennifer compiles the expense amounts for entry into their financial reports. Since Jennifer is primarily a user of WordPerfect, Chris is considering a prototype design that would permit her to enter the compiled actual expense data using WordPerfect. Further processing would take place in either Lotus 1-2-3 or dBASE. In evaluating the prototype design, Chris would like to experiment with both alternatives. The data to be imported consist of a combination of label or character data and numeric or value data. Chris believes that a comma delimited file would readily support the transfer of data from WordPerfect to either Lotus 1-2-3 or dBASE.

Using WordPerfect, Jennifer prepared the comma delimited file shown in Figure I.14 in this manner:

To create a WordPerfect document containing comma delimited data

Action: Access WordPerfect and enter the comma delimited data as shown in Figure I.14.

Action: Print the comma delimited data and save this as the ACTUAL.ASC document file.

Now the data can be saved as a plain ASCII text file without any special WordPerfect characters included in the file.

```
"Salaries",22314,23987,25621,29941
"Benefits",4261,4398,4801,5743
"Admin Expense",6361,7253,7892,8714
"Depreciation",2000,2000,2500,2500
"Interest",1423,1467,1492,1471
```

FIGURE I.14. Comma delimited ASCII text file.

Select:	Text In/Out `<Ctrl>+<F5>`	Desired file export activity, Text Out resides on the File pull-down menu
Select:	DOS Text	Type of file to be exported, DOS Text appears on the Text Out pop-out menu
Select:	Save	The specific action, if necessary
Enter:	`B:ACTUAL.ASC`	Disk drive identifier for your Data Disk and the name for your ASCII text file; if you are using a different disk drive, be sure to use your disk drive identifier
Action:	(*Optional*) If you are prompted to Replace the file, then a file with the designated name already exists on your Data Disk. Replace the file or enter a different file name, as appropriate.	
Action:	Exit from WordPerfect and return to the DOS prompt.	
Action:	Display the comma delimited file on your screen using the DOS TYPE command. Obtain a hard copy listing of this file.	

Jennifer has created the comma delimited file and written it to disk as an ASCII text file for transfer to the other software tools.

Keypoint!   Using WordPerfect is only one way to create a comma delimited file. Delimited files may be generated by other applications such as output from a general ledger or electronic mail!

I.1.8   Transferring Comma Delimited Files to Lotus 1-2-3

In Lotus 1-2-3, data in a comma delimited ASCII text file are transferred into the worksheet with the / File Import Numbers (/FIN) command. This command asks for the name of the source file containing the data. The / File Import command has two available options:

Command	Action
Text	Imports each line of text in the file as a *long label in a single cell*. Each successive line from the text file is placed in the same column, one cell below the other. Since this information is stored as labels, no numeric values are placed into these cells.
Numbers	Imports numbers and labels from a *comma delimited* file. Each line of numbers and labels from the text file is divided into a series of fields separated by the commas. The value for each field is *placed in a separate column in a row of adjacent cells*. Each line in the text file is placed in a separate row, one row below the other.

When a / File Import is carried out, the location of the incoming data is determined by *the position of the worksheet cursor*. This designates the upper-left corner of the range where the data will be located. If the cursor is *not* positioned correctly, the incoming data will not be placed in the desired location in the current worksheet.

Caution Alert!   The worksheet cursor *must* be carefully positioned in the upper-left-corner of the desired location for the incoming data!

At Good Morning Products, Chris was ready to test the prototype actual expense report preparation by importing the comma delimited file of expense data. This was accomplished as follows:

Action: Access Lotus 1-2-3.

<table>
<tr><td>**Move to:**</td><td>A3</td><td>Desired upper-left corner of the area where the results will be placed</td></tr>
<tr><td>**Press:**</td><td>/</td><td>Access main menu</td></tr>
<tr><td>**Select:**</td><td>File</td><td>Importing text is a File activity</td></tr>
<tr><td>**Select:**</td><td>Import</td><td>Specify this as an ASCII text file operation</td></tr>
<tr><td>**Select:**</td><td>Numbers</td><td>Specific action for a comma delimited text file</td></tr>
<tr><td>**Enter:**</td><td>B:ACTUAL.ASC</td><td>Name of comma delimited ASCII text file</td></tr>
</table>

To import comma delimited data into a Lotus 1-2-3 worksheet

The specified file is imported into the current worksheet and is ready for any other processing activities.

Action: Inspect the cell contents to verify that the account names in column **A** are *labels*, whereas the numbers in columns **B** through **E** are *values*.

Action: Add the column headings 1ST QTR, 2ND QTR, 3RD QTR, 4TH QTR, and TOTAL in columns **B** through **F** of row **1**.

Action: Add underlining to rows **2** and **8** in columns **B** through **F**.

Action: Add the account name "Total Expenses" in cell **A9**.

Action: Change the width of column **A** to 15 spaces.

Action: Add formulas to compute the "Total Expenses" in row **9** and the TOTAL in column **F** for each expense category. The completed worksheet should resemble Figure I.15.

Action: Print these results and save this as the ACTUAL worksheet file.

Action: (*Optional*)   Prepare a pie chart of the expenses by using the values in the TOTAL column. Only include the imported account categories in this graph, and *not* the Total Expenses category that was computed in the worksheet. Use appropriate titles and legends for this pie chart. Print a hard copy of the completed graph.

This completes the transfer of comma delimited ASCII text data into the Lotus 1-2-3 worksheet that is summarized in Figure I.16. Chris will compare this processing alternative to that available with dBASE.

I.1.9   Transferring Comma Delimited Files to dBASE

Before any data can be imported into a dBASE database, the database structure must be set up to specify the fields that make up the database. Of course, if the database already exists, then a structure has been defined. The target database is activated with the USE command. Then data from a comma delimited file can be included in the database with the APPEND FROM command that specifies the information is being appended from a DELIMITED type file.

Chris was ready to test Good Morning Product's prototype expense report preparation by transferring the comma delimited data into an ACTUAL expense database. This was completed as follows:

Action: Access dBASE and set the default disk drive, if necessary.

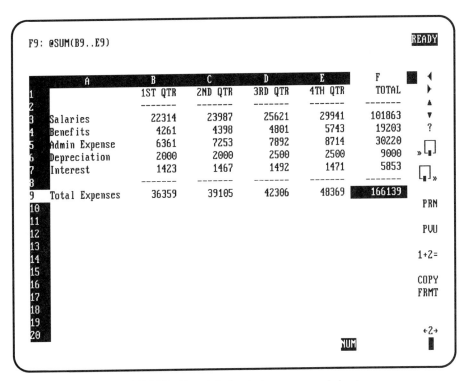

FIGURE I.15. Completed actual expense worksheet.

To create a dBASE database
file to receive data

Action: Create an ACTUAL database structure *without* any data entered during database creation. The structure of this ACTUAL database is described with a Database Planning Form as follows:

DATABASE PLANNING FORM

Data Name	Data Type	Width	Dec(imals)
ACCOUNT	Character	15	
QTR1	Numeric	9	0
QTR2	Numeric	9	0
QTR3	Numeric	9	0
QTR4	Numeric	9	0
TOTAL	Numeric	9	0

1. Create the Comma Delimited Text File
   a. Enter text in comma delimited form using WordPerfect.
   b. Use Text In/Out <Ctrl>+<F5> to save the text as a WordPerfect DOS Text File.
   c. Save the document file, if desired.
2. Transfer Text File to Lotus 1-2-3
   a. Access Lotus 1-2-3.
   b. If desired, retrieve the worksheet to receive the imported data.
   c. Position the cursor at upper-left corner of the range where the data are to be placed.
   d. Use the / File Import Numbers command to load the data from the text file into the current worksheet.
   e. Perform any other worksheet activities.

FIGURE I.16. Summary of comma delimited transfer to Lotus 1-2-3.

To import comma delimited
ASCII format data into a
dBASE database file

Enter: `APPEND FROM ACTUAL.ASC DELIMITED`

> Command for importing records from the
> designated comma delimited file

A general form of the APPEND FROM command is:

APPEND FROM <**filename**> [FOR <**condition**>] [<**file type**>]

where **filename** specifies the name of the *source* file and extension;
if an extension is not included, DBF is assumed,
file type designates the type of file with *no* file type
indicating a DBF file and DELIMITED specifying a comma
delimited file; dBASE also accommodates several other
special file types.

Enter: `DISPLAY ALL OFF`   View the database records

Notice that each line in the text file was loaded to a row in the database file while the
TOTAL field remained blank, because no values were provided for this field in the
ASCII text file.

Chris is now ready to compute the TOTAL expense for the year in this manner:

Enter: `REPLACE ALL TOTAL WITH QTR1+QTR2+QTR3+QTR4`

> Sum the data for the year and place the
> result in the TOTAL field

Enter: `DISPLAY ALL OFF`   View the database with values in the
TOTAL field

Action: Print the contents of this ACTUAL database.

The data that Chris asked Jennifer to prepare for Good Morning Products
have been successfully transferred from the ASCII text file created in WordPerfect
to the ACTUAL database file, as shown in Figure I.17, and the TOTAL field has
been computed. Of course, the quality of this output could be improved by using
a dBASE Report Form. However, for now, this output, obtained with the DISPLAY
command, meets Chris's requirement. The steps Chris used in transferring these data
are summarized in Figure I.18.

Keypoint!

> Each line in an ASCII text file is loaded as an individual record in a database. Each comma
> delimited value is placed in a separate field proceeding from left to right. If the database
> contains more fields than values supplied by the text file, the remaining fields in the
> database remain blank!

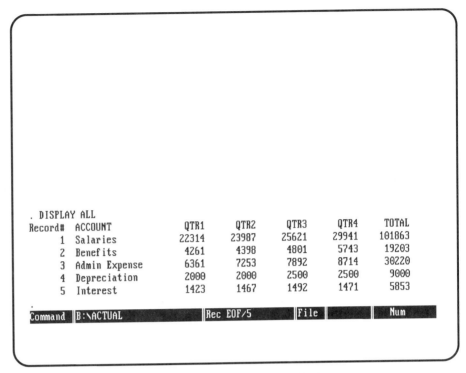

```
. DISPLAY ALL
Record#  ACCOUNT            QTR1     QTR2     QTR3     QTR4    TOTAL
      1  Salaries          22314    23987    25621    29941   101863
      2  Benefits           4261     4398     4801     5743    19203
      3  Admin Expense      6361     7253     7892     8714    30220
      4  Depreciation       2000     2000     2500     2500     9000
      5  Interest           1423     1467     1492     1471     5853
.
Command  B:\ACTUAL                   Rec EOF/5         File             Num
```

FIGURE I.17. Display of ACTUAL database.

1. Create the Comma Delimited Text File
   a. Enter text in comma delimited form using WordPerfect.
   b. Use Text In/Out <Ctrl>+<F5> to save the text as a WordPerfect DOS Text File.
   c. Save the document file, if desired.
2. Transfer Text File to dBASE
   a. Access dBASE.
   b. CREATE structure or USE existing database.
   c. APPEND FROM <ASCII text file> DELIMITED to load data from the text file into the current database.
   d. Use the REPLACE command to compute any desired fields.
   e. Perform any other database activities.

FIGURE I.18. Summary of comma delimited transfer to dBASE.

I.1.10   When Things Go Wrong

Several difficulties may be encountered when you are integrating information from the source application into your target application. Some of the more common situations and how to approach them are described here:

1. When you were integrating the results from a Lotus 1-2-3 *.PRN file or a dBASE *.TXT file into your WordPerfect document, you inserted the information at the *wrong location* in your current document.

   a. If you *saved* a copy of your initial WordPerfect document *just prior to* retrieving your Lotus 1-2-3 *.PRN file or your dBASE *.TXT file, then clear your WordPerfect document. This will allow you to repeat the integration by (1) retrieving the *saved* copy of your initial document, (2) carefully positioning the cursor at your desired location, and (3) retrieving the Lotus 1-2-3 *.PRN file or dBASE *.TXT file.

   b. If you did *not* save a copy of your initial WordPerfect document just prior to retrieving your *.PRN or *.TXT, then move the integrated text to a new location. This is achieved by (1) activating Reveal Codes <Alt>+<F3> to verify the beginning and ending of your text, (2) using Block <Alt>+<F4> to mark the block of text from the *.PRN or *.TXT file, (3) deleting the text, (4) positioning the cursor at your desired location, and (5) using Cancel <F1> to undelete the text, which places the text at your desired location.

2. When you imported a comma delimited file into Lotus 1-2-3, you placed the information at the wrong location in your worksheet.

   a. If your Lotus 1-2-3 worksheet contains information other than the imported values and if you saved your worksheet just prior to performing the / File Import, then perform a / File Retrieve to restore your initial worksheet content. Proceed to import the comma delimited data by (1) positioning the cursor at the upper-left-hand corner of the desired range and (2) redoing the / File Import to place the information at your desired location.

   b. If your worksheet does not contain information other than that you are importing, then do a / Worksheet Erase Yes to clear the misplaced information. This lets you repeat the integration by (1) positioning the cursor at your desired location and (2) redoing the / File Import. Alternatives to erasing the worksheet and redoing the import are to (1) use the Move command to reposition the imported range of cells or (2) use the Worksheet Insert or Delete command to add or remove blank rows or columns, causing the data to be positioned at your desired location.

3. When you integrated comma delimited data into dBASE, the wrong data ended up in your database fields. This usually occurs when the fields in the source file are not matched to those in the target database.

   a. Verify the location of each field in the comma delimited file. You may use the TYPE command to display the content of your source file from within dBASE. Be sure to include the file extension in your file specification for the TYPE command.

   b. Use ZAP to remove the records from your database.

   c. Do a MODIFY STRUCTURE to change the database structure so it *matches* the data fields in the comma delimited file.

   d. Use the APPEND FROM command to reload the data from your comma delimited file.

I.1.11   Lesson Summary

- An integrated solution is produced by transferring the results from one software tool to another tool for continued processing operations.

- Individual software tools store their worksheets, databases, and documents in special file formats that cannot be directly processed by other software tools. ASCII text files provide common file structures for transferring results among different software tools.

- The three choices in sharing data among software tools are to (1) retype the information into the other application, (2) transfer the information as an ASCII text file, and (3) translate the special file format of the source application into the special file format of the target application. Usually, retyping information should be avoided because of the time required and the potential introduction of errors.

- Integrated software tools usually include word processing, spreadsheet modeling, and database management in a single application program. These tools represent a trade-off in functional capabilities for a common user interface (CUI). In general, the capabilities of stand-alone software tools exceed those of the individual modules in integrated tools.

- Three common file structures used to transfer data as ASCII text files are (1) report formatted, (2) comma delimited, and (3) fixed formatted.

- A report formatted ASCII file is generated in Lotus 1-2-3 with the / Print File (/PF) command. The extension PRN is appended to this file to indicate that it is an ASCII file.

- A report formatted ASCII file is produced from a screen display in dBASE with the SET ALTERNATE commands, which cause displayed information to be captured in the specified file. The TXT extension is automatically appended to the file name to indicate that this is an ASCII file.

- A report formatted ASCII file is generated from a dBASE report definition by using the FILE option of the REPORT FORM command to direct the output to the specified file. dBASE identifies this ASCII file with the extension TXT.

- A report formatted ASCII file is imported into WordPerfect with either the Retrieve <Shift>+<F10> command or the Text In/Out <Ctrl>+<F5> command. Before executing either of these commands, position the cursor at the location where the file is to be inserted.

- A comma delimited file can be created with WordPerfect by typing the desired information. Character data should be enclosed in quotes, whereas numeric values should not be enclosed. Commas separate each of the respective fields or columns of data. The Text In/Out <Ctrl>+<F5> command is used to save the file as an ASCII text file. Special formatting characteristics, such as bolding and underlining, are lost when the ASCII file is written.

- A comma delimited file is transferred into Lotus 1-2-3 by using the / File Import Numbers (/FIN) command. The worksheet cursor is positioned at the upper-left corner of the range, where the incoming data are to be placed. Each of the comma delimited data items is placed in a separate cell with each line in the source comma delimited file becoming a row in the target worksheet.

- A comma delimited file is transferred into dBASE with the APPEND FROM command by using the DELIMITED option. Before a file can be appended, you must set up an active database file that has a structure that matches the incoming data in the comma delimited file.

I.1.12   Practice Tutorial

(1) Carry out the transfers of report formatted ASCII files from Lotus 1-2-3 and dBASE to WordPerfect as described in this Lesson in Sections I.1.4 through I.1.6 as a guided activity in a hands-on manner.

Task 1: Access Lotus 1-2-3 and retrieve the PLAN6 worksheet. If you did not develop this worksheet in the Using Lotus 1-2-3 section, create it before you continue with this activity.

Task 2: Revise the worksheet by using the / Range Format Currency command and print the results in the file PLAN18.PRN. Save the modified worksheet as PLAN18 and produce a hard copy output.

Task 3: Access WordPerfect and enter the draft memorandum.

Task 4: Integrate the results in the PLAN18.PRN into this document. Change the document's margins and print the completed document.

Task 5: Access dBASE and activate the WINES database. If you did not develop the WINES database in the Using dBASE section, then create this database, including entering the data.

Task 6: Store the information for the white wines in the MOREWINE.TXT file.

Task 7: Access WordPerfect and prepare the draft letter and integrate the MOREWINE.TXT file into this letter. Print the completed letter and save the combined results as the MOREWINE.DOC document file.

Task 8: Access dBASE and activate the WINES database. Use the WINELIST dBASE report format and the TYPENAME index to produce the WINELIST.TXT ASCII text file. If necessary, create the WINELIST report form and the TYPENAME index.

Task 9: Access WordPerfect and prepare the enhanced Wine List. Print this and save the document file.

Time Estimates

Novice: 90 minutes

Intermediate: 60 minutes

Advanced: 45 minutes

(2) Create a comma delimited ASCII text file using WordPerfect and integrate it into a Lotus 1-2-3 worksheet and a dBASE database as described in Sections I.1.7 through I.1.9 of this Lesson as a guided, hands-on activity as follows:

Task 1: Access WordPerfect and type the comma delimited file.

Task 2: Print this document and store it as an ASCII text file.

Task 3: Access Lotus 1-2-3 and import the comma delimited ASCII text file.

Task 4: Add the column headings, the TOTAL column, and the Total Expense account category to the worksheet.

Task 5: Print the completed worksheet and save the worksheet file.

Task 6: (*Optional*)   Prepare a pie chart of the imported account categories, using the summarized data in the TOTAL column.

Task 7: Access dBASE and create the structure for the ACTUAL database.

Task 8: Append the data from the comma delimited ASCII text file and compute the TOTAL field.

Task 9: Print the contents of the database.

Time Estimates

Novice: 60 minutes

Intermediate: 45 minutes

Advanced: 30 minutes

I.1.13   Comprehensive Problems

(1)   Case: Woodcraft Furniture (continued)

At Woodcraft Furniture, the quarterly projected income statement has been completed by using data provided by Herbert "Tall" Pine, Ray Jointer, and Martha Goodguess. They are ready to submit the report to Joe Birch for his review. Each quarter Joe meets with Sam Wyman at First America Bank to review Woodcraft's line of credit for the quarter. "Tall" wants Woodcraft's quarterly plan prepared in the form of a memorandum for submission to Joe. In addition to the data from the worksheet, "Tall" has sketched out the following memo:

MEMORANDUM

Date: April 11, 1995
To: Joe Birch
From: Herbert Pine

Subject: Third Quarter Budget

Next quarter's budget has been prepared using the market research data furnished by Martha Goodguess, the production cost data supplied by Ray Jointer, and the other revenue and expense data, which I compiled. For the quarter, Ray has estimated the raw materials cost as 26 percent of total sales. From our combined analysis, the anticipated results for the next quarter are as follows:

(projected income statement from worksheet WOOD2 goes here)

Please examine this projected income statement before our scheduled budget review meeting next Tuesday. If you require any additional information or have any suggested modifications, please contact me prior to our conference.

Your tasks in preparing the memo for "Tall" to submit to Joe Birch are as follows:

Task 1: Access the WOOD2 worksheet file from Comprehensive Problem 1 in Lesson L.3 of Using Lotus 1-2-3 and review its contents. If you have not already created this worksheet file, then create it from Lessons L.2 and L.3 of Using Lotus 1-2-3.

Task 2: Write the results as a report in an ASCII text file with the file name WOOD2.PRN. [*Hint:* Set the margins to eliminate unwanted spaces.]

Task 3: Access WordPerfect and enter "Tall's" draft copy of the memorandum.

Task 4: Import the projected quarterly income statement from the WOOD2.PRN file at the designated location in the memorandum.

Task 5: Remove the line containing the date from the report, because the memo already has a date. Remove any unwanted lines and adjust the margins, if necessary.

Task 6: Review the report and, if necessary, insert page breaks to improve the appearance of the document.

Task 7: Bold the report heading.

Task 8: Print the final document and save this as the WOOD2.DOC document file.

Time Estimates

Novice: 60 minutes

Intermediate: 45 minutes

Advanced: 30 minutes

(2) Case: Midwest Universal Gas (continued)

Each year Midwest Universal Gas (MUG) reviews its return on investment with the Public Utility Commission (PUC). Sam Wright, MUG's controller, has completed next year's forecast by using data supplied by Francis Foresight and Pete Newgas. He is ready to submit the forecast to Mary Derrick for her review prior to the annual meeting with the PUC. Sam wants MUG's annual forecast prepared in the form of a memorandum for submission to Mary. Besides the data from Sam's Lotus 1-2-3 worksheet, he has sketched out the following memo:

MEMORANDUM

Date: May 23, 1995
To: Mary Derrick
From: Sam Wright

Subject: Next Year's Forecast

The forecast for next year has been developed based on the demand analysis of 732 BCF, furnished by Francis. The breakout of Retail and Wholesale Gas Sold are as indicated in the Pro Forma Income Statement shown below. Pete Newgas expects the cost of gas to be 61 percent of total sales revenue. We anticipate that the total divisional investment will be $102,400,000. This investment is the basis for determining the return on investment for the PUC. Our combined analysis has resulted in the following anticipated performance for next year:

(pro forma income statement from worksheet MUG2 goes here)

A discussion of this forecast has been placed on the agenda for the Management Committee meeting on Wednesday. Please examine this forecast prior to our meeting. If you require any additional information or have any suggested revisions, please contact me.

Your tasks in composing the memo for Sam to forward to Mary Derrick are as follows:

Task 1: Access the MUG2 worksheet file from Comprehensive Problem 2 in Lesson L.3 of Using Lotus 1-2-3 and review its contents. If you have not already created this worksheet in the Using Lotus 1-2-3 lessons, then develop it before you continue with the next task.

Task 2: Write the results as a report in an ASCII text file with the file name MUG2.PRN. [*Hint:* Set the margins to eliminate unwanted spaces.]

Task 3: Access WordPerfect and enter Sam's draft copy of the memorandum.

Task 4: Import the projected income statement for next year from the MUG2.PRN file at the designated location in the memorandum.

Task 5: Remove any unwanted lines and adjust the margins, if necessary. If your worksheet report contains a date, remove the line containing the date from the report, because the memo already has a date.

Task 6: Review the report and, if necessary, insert page breaks to improve the appearance of the document.

Task 7: Bold the report heading and the line containing the return on investment.

Task 8: Print the final document and save this as the MUG2.DOC document file.

Time Estimates

Novice: 60 minutes

Intermediate: 45 minutes

Advanced: 30 minutes

(3)   Case: Yen To Travel (continued)

Meyer Laboratories Incorporated (MLI) arranges an outing for its sales associates each year as part of the sales and marketing meeting. In addition to informing associates of new products and sales campaigns, MLI uses the outing as a team-building activity. Julie Woodruff is MLI's associate responsible for arranging the outing. She has been in contact with Brenda at Yen To Travel. Julie asked Brenda to develop a list of outings from which MLI could make a selection. After further discussion with Julie, Brenda has determined that the tours conducted by the Wild Adventures (WILD ADVENT) agent most closely fit those desired by MLI. Brenda is excited about the opportunity to land a major contract with MLI. She has set out to prepare a letter to send to Julie, with a list of suggested tours. Her letter will make use of an ad hoc query of Yen To's Tour Management System to identify a list of potential tours. Brenda has outlined the following letter:

Ms. Julie Woodruff
Meyer Laboratories Incorporated
4100 Ward Parkway
Kansas City, MO 64118

Dear Ms. Woodruff:

Thank you for your inquiry regarding an exciting outing for your sales associates. In cooperation with our agent, Wild Adventures, we can offer you several thrilling tour packages for your annual sales and marketing meeting. I would like to suggest the following tour packages for your consideration:

(list of tours from TOURS database goes here)

A brochure describing each tour package is enclosed for your review. I will contact you next week to see if you need any additional information in considering these tour packages.

We appreciate this opportunity to serve you. If you have any questions, you may reach me by phone at 636-8687.

Sincerely,

Brenda Esprit
Travel Consultant

Enclosures

Your task is to complete the letter for Brenda to send to Julie as follows:

Task 1: Access the TOURS database from Comprehensive Problem (1) in Lessons D.1, D.2, and D.3 of Using dBASE. Review its contents. If you have not already created this database in the Using dBASE lessons, then develop it before you continue with the next task.

Task 2: Use the ALTERNATE commands to produce a list of the tours from the WILD ADVENT agent. The list should include only the TOUR, DAYS, and TYPE. Store this list in an ASCII text file with the name MLI.TXT.

Task 3: Access WordPerfect and enter Brenda's draft copy of the letter to Julie. Include the current date on your letter.

Task 4: Include the tour list in the MLI.TXT file at the designated location in the letter.

Task 5: Remove any unwanted lines and adjust the margins, if necessary.

Task 6: Review the letter and, if necessary, insert page breaks to improve the appearance of the document.

Task 7: Add extra spacing between the columns in the table of tours to improve its appearance.

Task 8: Underline the column title for the table of tours.

Task 9: Print the final document and save this as the MLI.DOC document file.

Time Estimates

Novice: 60 minutes

Intermediate: 45 minutes

Advanced: 30 minutes

(4)   Case: Silver Screen Video (continued)

WRAP TV in Miamisburg, Ohio, is a public broadcasting station managed by Thomas J. Hunt. Each year WRAP undertakes a fund-raising drive to solicit donations to support the station's operation. During the upcoming fund-raising drive, Tom is planning a comedy weekend. Beginning Friday evening and running through Sunday evening, the station will run a series of comedy movies as part of its fund-raising telethon. To assist with this project, Tom is soliciting comedy movies from several video sales and rental businesses. Tom phoned Amy Lighthart at Silver Screen Video and asked for her participation in the fund raiser. Amy explained that she could send Tom a list of available comedy movies and that Silver Screen could sponsor one of them. Since Silver Screen would need to contact the movie's maker to obtain permission for the showing, Amy would need to have, at least, three weeks' notice to accomplish all the arrangements for WRAP's use of the movies. In her conversation with Tom, Amy indicated that she would send him a list of the comedy movies she handles, so that Tom could specify his preference. She began preparing a letter to Tom containing a list of available movies. Her letter makes use of an ad hoc query to Silver Screen's Movie Management System to identify these potential movies. Amy outlined the following letter to Tom:

Mr. Thomas J. Hunt, Manager
WRAP TV
80 Timber Trail
Miamisburg, Ohio 45342

Dear Mr. Hunt:

Thank you for the opportunity to support your annual fund-raising drive. With the permission of the movie's maker, we can provide any of the following comedy movies:

(list of movies from MOVIES database goes here)

"Punchline" is one of my favorites. Please review this list and determine the most appropriate movie for your fund raiser. Once you have reached a decision, please contact me with your choice at 534-5653. Remember, we need at least three weeks to obtain the required permissions.

The staff at Silver Screen is looking forward to answering the phones on Saturday night during your fund drive.

Sincerely,

Amy Lighthart
Manager

Your task is to prepare the letter for Amy to send to Tom Hunt as follows:

Task 1: Access the MOVIES database from Comprehensive Problem 2 in Lessons D.1, D.2, and D.3 of Using dBASE. Review its contents. If you have not already created this database in the Using dBASE lessons, develop it before you continue with the next task.

Task 2: Use the ALTERNATE commands to produce a list of the comedy movies. The list should include only the fields MOVIE, YEAR, and RATE. Store this list in an ASCII text file with the name WRAP.TXT.

Task 3: Access WordPerfect and enter Amy's draft copy of the letter to Tom.

Task 4: Include the movie list in the WRAP.TXT file at the designated location in the letter.

Task 5: Remove any unwanted lines and adjust the margins, if necessary.

Task 6: Review the letter and, if necessary, insert page breaks to improve the appearance of the document.

Task 7: Add extra spacing between the columns in the table of movies to improve its appearance.

Task 8: Underline the column title for the table of movies.

Task 9: Print the final document and save this as the WRAP.DOC document file.

Time Estimates

Novice: 60 minutes

Intermediate: 45 minutes

Advanced: 30 minutes

(5) Case: Yen To Travel (continued)

At Yen To Travel, Brenda and Sara have reviewed the Tour List that Ashley prepared by using a dBASE Report Form. Although this report contains the information required for use with their customers, Brenda wants to improve the appearance of this Tour List before Yen To mails the list to its corporate clients and regular customers. Brenda believes that such a mailing at periodic intervals would help to increase the number of tour bookings. She wants you to carry out the following activities in preparing the enhanced Tour List:

Task 1: Access the TOURS database from Comprehensive Problem 2 in Lessons D.1, D.2, and D.3 of Using dBASE. Review its contents. If you have not already created this database in the Using dBASE lessons, develop it before you continue with the next task.

Task 2: Access the Tour List report form as developed in Using dBASE, Lesson D.5. Review the organization of this report. If you have not created this report form, develop it before you continue.

Task 3: Generate this report arranged by tour type with the output stored in the TOURLIST.TXT ASCII text file.

Task 4: Access WordPerfect and retrieve the TOURLIST.TXT file as the currently active document.

Task 5: Remove any unwanted lines and adjust the margins, if necessary.

Task 6: Bold the heading, which includes the travel agency's name and the report name.

Task 7: Underline the column titles for the table of tours.

Task 8: Leave one blank line after the heading and insert this text:

Yen To Travel is proud to announce its One-Two-Three-Free frequent traveler program. Purchase any three tour packages from Yen To during a two-year period and receive the fourth tour free. The amount of your free tour may not exceed the average value of the three tours you purchased. Yen To is committed to providing the finest travel programs available. Our One-Two-Three-Free program is our way of expressing our appreciation to you, our valued customer.

Leave two blank lines after this paragraph and before the column titles.

Task 9: At the bottom of the report, Brenda wants you to add this text:

This month's special is the Cherry Blossom tour. When you purchase a seat at the regular price, you can purchase a second seat for your traveling companion at a 50% discount. A limited number of seats are available under this special pricing arrangement. Make your reservation today!

Task 10: (*Optional*) Place a box around the list of tours. Be careful, because you are in the overtype mode and could wipe out text in your table.

Task 11: Print the final document and save this as the TOURLIST.DOC.

Time Estimates

Novice: 60 minutes

Intermediate: 45 minutes

Advanced: 30 minutes

(6) Case: Silver Screen Video (continued)

Amy Lighthart at Silver Screen Video reviewed the Movie List report with Ernie. They would like to improve the appearance of this report and make copies of it for distribution to their regular customers. Ernie has been working on the details of the Night Owl Viewers Club. Each customer would be issued a card that is punched every time a movie is rented. When a customer has 10 punches, the next movie is free. Ernie would like to include a description of the Club on the movie list. Amy wants you to prepare this improved Movie List by performing the following activities:

Task 1: Access the MOVIES database from Comprehensive Problem 2 in Lessons D.1, D.2, and D.3 of Using dBASE. Review its contents. If you have not already created this database in the Using dBASE lessons, develop it before you continue with the next task.

Task 2: Access the Movie List report form as developed in Using dBASE, Lesson D.5. Review the organization of this report. If you have not created this report form, create it before you continue.

Task 3: Generate this report arranged by movie type and movie name with the output stored in the MOVILIST.TXT ASCII text file.

Task 4: Access WordPerfect and retrieve the MOVILIST.TXT file as the currently active document.

Task 5: Remove any unwanted lines and adjust the margins, if necessary.

Task 6: Bold the heading, which includes the store's name and the report name.

Task 7: Underline the column titles for the table of movies.

Task 8: Leave one blank line after the heading and insert this text:

The Night Owl Viewers Club entitles you to free movies of your choice. Purchase 10 movies and the next one is free. Each time you buy a movie, have your Viewers Club card punched. The Night Owl Viewers Club is our way of thanking you for your continuing patronage.

Leave two blank lines after this paragraph and before the column titles.

Task 9: At the bottom of the document, Amy wants you to add this text:

> This month is designated as Suspense month. Each Suspense movie you rent qualifies for a 10% discount and a double punch on your Viewers Club card. If you like suspense movies, now is the time to add to your collection!

Task 10: (*Optional*) Place a box around the list of movies. Be careful because you are in the overtype mode and could wipe out text in your table.

Task 11: Print the final document and save this as the MOVILIST.DOC document file.

Time Estimates

Novice: 60 minutes

Intermediate: 45 minutes

Advanced: 30 minutes

(7)   Case: Woodcraft Furniture Company (second encounter)

At Woodcraft Furniture, Ray Jointer, the production manager, asked Amanda Drexeler, the production planner, to prepare a quarterly production report that details the actual number of units of each type of furniture produced every month. Larry King, Amanda's assistant, compiles this data for the report. Since Larry primarily works with WordPerfect, Amanda wants him to enter the data as a comma delimited file using the word processor. Amanda can then access the data in Lotus 1-2-3 and complete the required report. She wants you to develop a test system for this quarter to determine the feasibility of this processing and eliminate any bugs that may occur. Once they have debugged the system, Larry will enter the data for their report on a regular basis. The specific tasks she wants you to carry out in performing this system test are as follows:

Task 1: Access WordPerfect and enter the following data as a comma delimited file:

Tables	880	920	930
Chairs	4400	4400	4600
Sofas	590	600	600

[*Hint:* Remember that character data are enclosed in quotes, but numeric data are not.]

Task 2: Print a copy of these data and save them in the PRODSUM.ASC ASCII text file.

Task 3: Access Lotus 1-2-3 and import the PRODSUM.ASC file at cell location **A3.**

Task 4: Add column titles for the months of July, August, and September and underline these titles.

Task 5: Add a total column for the quarter. Use the @SUM function to compute the quarter total for each product. Include a "Total" title for this column and underline it.

Task 6: Print the resulting report.

Task 7: (*Optional*) Produce a bar chart that shows the production of each product for each month. Review the bar chart on your screen. Save this graph as the PRODSUM.PIC file and print it after you leave the main 1-2-3 worksheet program.

Task 8: Save this worksheet in the file PRODSUM.

Time Estimates

Novice: 60 minutes

Intermediate: 45 minutes

Advanced: 30 minutes

(8)   Case: Midwest Universal Gas (second encounter)

Sam Wright, the division comptroller for Midwest Universal Gas, needs to prepare a report of last year's actual revenues and expenses for Mary Derrick. He has asked Chad Eloff to collect the data for entry as a comma delimited file using WordPerfect. Sam knows that the data can be downloaded from MUG's general ledger system as a comma delimited file. However, for this report, he wants to test the use of a comma delimited file with Lotus 1-2-3. If this feasibility test is satisfactory, Sam will work with MUG's MIS department to set up a special report for use with the general ledger system. Hank Pletcher, MUG's director of MIS, has advised Sam that their general ledger system could produce comma delimited files regularly or by special request. In performing this feasibility test, Sam wants you to complete the following activities:

Task 1: Access WordPerfect and enter the following data as a comma delimited file:

Retail Sales	17452	14379	6411	17590
Wholesale Sales	51068	43921	19871	51022
Cost of Sales	42357	35791	14326	41099
Marketing and Selling	11927	7652	3743	9880
General and Admin	4629	3875	4107	4227
Depreciation	2202	2202	2202	2361

[*Hint:* Remember character data are enclosed in quotes, but numeric data are not.]

Task 2: Print a copy of these data and save them in the LASTYR.ASC ASCII text file.

Task 3: Access Lotus 1-2-3 and import the LASTYR.ASC file at cell location **A4.**

Task 4: Add column titles for each of the four quarters, beginning with the first quarter, and underline these titles.

Task 5: Add a total column for the year. Use the @SUM function to compute the annual total for each revenue or expense account. Include a "Total" title for this column and underline it.

Task 6: (*Optional*) Add the account "Total Sales" to the worksheet and compute these amounts by summing Retail Sales and Wholesale Sales. Include underlining above the quarterly amounts for Total Sales. Compute a "Total Expense" account in the same manner with the remaining accounts making up the Total Expenses.

Task 7: Print the resulting report.

Task 8: (*Optional*) Produce a line graph showing the revenue and expense data for each quarter. Review the graph on your screen. Save this graph in the LASTYR.PIC file and print it after you leave the main 1-2-3 worksheet program.

Task 9: Save this worksheet in the file LASTYR.

Time Estimates

Novice: 60 minutes

Intermediate: 45 minutes

Expert: 30 minutes

(9)   Case: Woodcraft Furniture Company (continued)

At Woodcraft Furniture, Amanda Drexeler, the production planner, would like to test the feasibility of another approach to preparing the quarterly production report. With this alternative, she still wants Larry King to enter the data as a comma delimited file using WordPerfect as explored in Comprehensive Problem 7 above. However, she wants to investigate the use of dBASE for producing the final report, rather than Lotus 1-2-3. Amanda believes that dBASE may provide more flexibility in storing the data for several different quarters so comparison reports for each product across several quarters might also be examined. Amanda has sketched out the following database plan:

DATABASE PLANNING FORM

Data Name	Data Type	Width	Dec(imals)
ACCOUNT	Character	12	
MONTH1	Numeric	9	0
MONTH2	Numeric	9	0
MONTH3	Numeric	9	0
TOTAL	Numeric	9	0
QUARTER	Numeric	2	0

For this design, the TOTAL field will be computed after the data are appended to the database. Also, the QUARTER field will contain the quarter number (1, 2, 3, or 4). The values for TOTAL and QUARTER will be calculated after the data are appended; therefore, they have been included as the last or rightmost fields in the database. The feasibility test of this processing should determine any shortcomings that need to be addressed before Larry begins entering the data on a regular basis. Amanda wants you to carry out the following activities in performing this system test:

Task 1: Access WordPerfect and retrieve the PRODSUM.ASC ASCII text file from Comprehensive Problem 7 containing the comma delimited data. If you did not create this comma delimited file for that problem, enter the data before you continue.

Task 2: Print a copy of this comma delimited data and exit WordPerfect.

Task 3: Access dBASE and create the structure in the foregoing Database Planning Form as the PRODSUM database.

Task 4: Import the comma delimited data in the PRODSUM.ASC database.

Task 5: Compute the TOTAL field and place "3" in the QUARTER field. [*Hint:* Use the same command to place the value in the QUARTER field as you used for computing the TOTAL field.]

Task 6: Produce a hard copy report of the results.

Task 7: (*Optional*)   Create a dBASE Report Form that can be used to produce this report. The report should contain all the fields except the TOTAL and QUARTER fields. Include a field in the report that contains the computed quarter total, rather than using the value stored in the database. Generate a hard copy of the report for the third quarter.

Task 8: (*Optional*)   Compare the Lotus 1-2-3 solution in Comprehensive Problem 7 to this dBASE solution. What do you consider to be the advantages and disadvantages of each? Why are they an advantage or disadvantage?

Time Estimates

Novice: 60 minutes

Intermediate: 45 minutes

Advanced: 30 minutes

(10)   Case: Midwest Universal Gas (continued)

At Midwest Universal Gas, Sam Wright would like to test the feasibility of a different method of preparing the report of last year's actual revenues and expenses for Mary Derrick. Under this option, Chad Eloff would collect the data and enter the data as a comma delimited file as described in Comprehensive Problem 8. However, dBASE would be used to produce the final report, rather than using Lotus 1-2-3. Hank Pletcher has indicated that MUG's general ledger system could produce a comma delimited file, and Sam realizes that he could use either dBASE or Lotus 1-2-3 for this special report for Mary. Sam has specified the following database design for use in this feasibility test:

DATABASE PLANNING FORM

Data Name	Data Type	Width	Dec(imals)
ACCOUNT	Character	22	
QTR1	Numeric	9	0
QTR2	Numeric	9	0
QTR3	Numeric	9	0
QTR4	Numeric	9	0
TOTAL	Numeric	9	0
CATEGORY	Character	2	

For this database design, the TOTAL field is computed after the data are appended from the comma delimited text file. Also, the CATEGORY field is used to identify the account as a revenue (R) account or an expense (X) account. Since the values for the TOTAL column are computed and the values for the CATEGORY field are assigned after the data have been appended, TOTAL and CATEGORY have been included in the database as the last or rightmost fields. This feasibility test should point out any limitations that need to be considered before Sam and Hank develop a direct extract from MUG's general ledger system. However, whenever any adjustments need to be made to the general ledger extract, Sam can still have Chad make them by using WordPerfect. Sam wants you to complete the following activities in performing the feasibility test:

Task 1: Access WordPerfect and retrieve the LASTYR.ASC ASCII text file from Comprehensive Problem 8, which contains the comma delimited data. If you did not create this file of comma delimited data for that problem, create it before you continue.

Task 2: Print a copy of this comma delimited data and exit WordPerfect.

Task 3: Access dBASE and create the structure defined by the Database Planning Form above. Name this the LASTYR database.

Task 4: Load the comma delimited data from the NEXTYR.ASC file.

Task 5: Compute the TOTAL field.

Task 6: Place an "R" in the CATEGORY field for revenues and an "X" in the CATEGORY field for expenses.

Task 7: Produce a hard copy output of the results arranged by CATEGORY.

Task 8: Describe another alternative for including the CATEGORY of account with each record in the database. What is the advantage/disadvantage of using that method?

Task 9: (*Optional*) Create a dBASE report form for producing this report. The report should contain all of the fields except TOTAL and CATEGORY. Include a field in the report that contains the computed annual total, rather than using the value stored in the database. Group the data in the report by CATEGORY with a total for each type. Generate a hard copy of the report with the data arranged by CATEGORY.

Task 10: (*Optional*) Compare the Lotus 1-2-3 solution in Comprehensive Problem 8 to this dBASE solution. What do you consider to be the advantages and disadvantages of each? Why are they an advantage or disadvantage?

Time Estimates

Novice: 60 minutes

Intermediate: 45 minutes

Advanced: 30 minutes

I.1.14 Case Application

Case 1: BioGen Laboratories

Business Problem: Work Center Analysis

MIS Characteristics: Production
Operational Control

Special Characteristic: Critical Success Factors

Management Functions: Directing
Controlling

Tools Skills: Creating ASCII report file from worksheet
Lotus 1-2-3 graphing
Integrating ASCII report file in document
Lotus 1-2-3 macro (optional)
WordPerfect graph integration (optional)

BioGen Laboratories (BGL) develops, manufactures, and markets genetically engineered and related pharmaceuticals. BGL was founded in 1968 by Wilson J. Freshwater, who continues to serve as the company's Chief Executive Officer and Chairman of the Board of Directors. Since the company's founding, it has experienced steady growth, with the development and introduction of a number of new products. Next year's sales are expected to exceed one billion dollars.

As indicated by BGL's corporate mission statement, the company promotes the following goals:

- Attain positions of product leadership through marketing and distribution of consumable and personal products of integrity and perceived differentiation in selected segments of health care.

- Attain a performance and people-oriented environment that stimulates integrity, entrepreneurial spirit, productivity, and a sense of responsibility to all BGL associates and society.

BGL has a solid line of more than 50 prescription and over-the-counter pharmaceuticals. Like some other pharmaceutical companies, it takes a human organ system approach to product discovery, development, licensing, and marketing. As a result, the company focuses on three key therapeutic areas: cardiovascular system, gastrointestinal system, and respiratory system. In addition, spin-off developments have led to the manufacture of a limited number of products for other disorders and ailments. Promotion of prescription products is directed primarily to physicians by BGL's sales associates. In addition, BGL promotes these products by advertising in medical journals and by selected distribution of samples and other information.

BGL maintains licenses for specific products and holds patents on a number of products, providing it with a unique marketing advantage. In the United States, the Federal Food, Drug, and Cosmetic Act and other federal statutes and regulations govern approval, testing, production, labeling, and advertising of most of BGL's products. The U. S. Food and Drug Administration (FDA) requires extensive preapproval testing for new products to demonstrate to the satisfaction of the FDA that such products are both safe and effective in treating the medical condition for which marketing approval is sought. BGL has several New Drug Applications (NDA) pending the approval of the FDA.

BGL manufactures all of its prescription products at its modern production facilities in Croton-on-Hudson, New York. Brandon Sequeira, Vice President of Manufacturing Operations, is responsible for the overall direction of BGL's production activities. Sabrina Rutkowski manages the Compound Preparation Division (CPD), which produces pharmaceuticals in tablet or capsule form.

Like BGL's other manufacturing divisions, CPD (also known as the "pill pushers") is organized as a series of work centers. A work center consists of one or more machines and the associates who operate the equipment. In general, each work center performs a defined job function, with jobs requiring the same type of work on the same equipment routed to the work center. Pharmaceuticals are manufactured in batches, with a batch moving from one work center to the next until the batch has been completed, tested, and packaged and is ready for shipment.

Work centers in the CPD operation include weighing and measuring, dry blending, encapsulating, and packaging. Each work center has a maximum available capacity for the number of batches it can produce. Based on a production schedule derived from the sales forecast and current orders, an actual load or number of batches is produced during the week. The difference between the available capacity and the actual load is defined as the slack capacity. Slack capacity is usually stated as the Percent Available, which is the slack capacity divided by the maximum available capacity. Sabrina and Brandon monitor the Percent Available as a critical success factor (CSF) in managing each work center. A normal Percent Available is between 5 and 15 percent. This provides for flexibility in meeting schedules while still maintaining an efficient production operation. A second CSF is labor efficiency. This is the number of standard labor hours divided by the actual labor hours. Sabrina has a target of 90 percent or better labor efficiency across all the work centers in the Compound Preparation Division. The standard hours are determined from a work standard for the number of hours per batch. This standard is established by industrial engineers and cost accountants in BGL's Work Standards Department.

Each week Sabrina prepares a work center analysis for Brandon. The analysis contains the Percent Available and Percent Labor Efficiency CSF's together with pertinent supporting information. With the numbers, Sabrina furnishes her interpretation and explanation of activities in the work center. Additionally, Sabrina includes a graph of the Percent Available and Percent Labor Efficiency as supporting exhibits. Sabrina frequently explains these graphs at the monthly production review meetings with Brandon.

For her weekly work center analysis, Sabrina has developed the WORKCEN worksheet with the following column usage:

Column	Use
A	Number of machines in work center
B	Work center identification number
C	Work center name
D	Available capacity in batches
E	Actual load in batches
F	Percent available
G	Standard labor hours per batch
H	Standard labor hours
I	Actual labor hours
J	Percent labor efficiency

She has sketched out this week's memo using WordPerfect and stored it as the WORKCEN.DOC document file, and she has entered the Actual Load and Actual Labor Hours for this week in the WORKCEN worksheet file. She needs to complete the memo by extracting two tables from the worksheet and obtaining two graphs. The first table, the Percent Available Table, is to include these columns: Work Center, Available Capacity, Actual Load, and Percent Available. The second table, the Percent Labor Efficiency Table, consists of the Work Center, Standard Labor Hours, Actual Labor Hours, and Percent Labor Efficiency. Sabrina wants you to finish the report for submission to Brandon.

Tasks

1. Access Lotus 1-2-3 and retrieve the WORKCEN worksheet file. Review the contents of the worksheet and examine the equations for computing Percent Available, Standard Hours, and Percent Labor Efficiency.

2. Print a hard copy report of the entire contents of the WORKCEN worksheet file.

3. Create an ASCII text file of the Percent Available Table consisting of the Work Center, Available Capacity, Actual Load, and Percent Available. Save this as the WORKCEN1.PRN file. [*Hint:* Be sure to adjust your margins before writing the report in the file. Remember that you must Quit the Print menu to cause this file to be permanently saved on your disk.]

4. Develop a bar chart of the Percent Available CSF data. Title the graph like this:

First Title	Exhibit 1
Second Title	Work Center Analysis
Y-Axis Title	Percent Available

Assign the work center names to the X-range of the graph. Preview this graph on your screen and save it in the WORKCEN1.PIC file. If desired, give this graph a name of AVAIL with the / Graph Name Create command. This saves the graph setting for future reference in the worksheet.

5. Rearrange and/or hide columns to produce the second table, the Labor Efficiency Table, consisting of the Work Center, Standard Labor Hours, Actual Labor Hours, and Percent Labor Efficiency. Create an ASCII text file containing this table and save it as the WORKCEN2.PRN file.

6. Produce a bar chart of the Percent Labor Efficiency CSF data. Title the graph in this manner:

First Title	Exhibit 2
Second Title	Work Center Analysis
Y-Axis Title	Percent Labor Efficiency

Assign the work center names to the *X* range of the graph. Preview the graph on your screen and save it in the WORKCEN2.PIC file. If you want, give this graph the name of LABOR with the /Graph Name Create command.

7. Save your worksheet as the WCRPT file.

8. Print the two graphs stored in the WORKCEN1.PIC and WORKCEN2.PIC file.

9. Access WordPerfect and retrieve the document file WORKCEN.DOC. Review the contents of this document.

10. At the designated location in the document, insert the Percent Available Table.

11. At the designated location in the document, insert the Percent Labor Efficiency Table.

12. Add the following sentences to the end of the last paragraph in to the document:

However, these changes still resulted in a decrease in the productivity of the division. Because the Percent Labor Efficiency was affected by the same problems as the Percent Available, and because these problems have been corrected, normal operations are anticipated for next week.

13. Review the page breaks and overall appearance of the document. Modify the page breaks, if necessary, so that a table is not split between two pages.

14. Print the completed document and save this as the document file WCRPT.DOC.

15. (*Optional*) Access Lotus 1-2-3 and retrieve the WCRPT worksheet file. Create a macro that produces both reports and graphs, saving them in the files specified above. The macro should include commands to make the changes for the Percent Labor Efficiency Table before it is written as an ASCII text file. This macro would allow Sabrina to change the Actual Load and Actual Labor Hours data and then execute the macro to output the ASCII report files and the graph files.

16. (*Optional*) Access WordPerfect and retrieve the WCRPT.DOC document file. Place a box around each of the two tables. Be careful, because you are in the overtype mode and could wipe out information in your table. Print the resulting document and save it in the same document file.

17. (*Optional*) Access the WCRPT.DOC document in WordPerfect. Instead of manually attaching the two graphs as separate exhibit pages, use the Graphics <Alt>+<F9> command to include the graphs in the WordPerfect document. Select Graphics <Alt>+<F9>, Figure, Create and define the graph, as shown in Figure I.19. When setting the graph's Size, use the Set Width/Auto Height option and specify the width as 6 in. Use hard returns in the document to provide sufficient space for each graph. Arrange the document with all the text on page 1, the WORKCEN1.PIC exhibit 1 at the top of page 2, and table 1 at the bottom of page 2. Place the WORKCEN2.PIC exhibit 2 at the top of page 3, and table 2 at the bottom of the page. Print the final document.

Time Estimates

Novice: 120 minutes

Intermediate: 90 minutes

Advanced: 60 minutes

```
Definition: Figure

    1 - Filename             WORKCEN1.PIC

    2 - Contents             Graphic

    3 - Caption

    4 - Anchor Type          Paragraph

    5 - Vertical Position    0"

    6 - Horizontal Position  Center

    7 - Size                 6" wide x 4.48" (high)

    8 - Wrap Text Around Box Yes

    9 - Edit




Selection: 0
```

FIGURE I.19. WordPerfect figure definition for graph.

BioGen Laboratories
MACRO PLANNING FORM

Macro Name	Macro Command	Descriptive Comment

Case 2: John Donnelly & Daughters
Business Problem: Bonus tracking
MIS Characteristics: Marketing
            Managerial Control
Management Functions: Staffing
            Controlling
Tools Skills: Comma delimited file creation
            Integrating comma delimited data in 1-2-3
            Integrating comma delimited data in dBASE
            Lotus 1-2-3 macro (optional)
            dBASE Program (optional)

John Donnelly & Daughters is a textbook publisher founded in 1937 by John and his two daughters, Miranda and Christine. Over the years, their business has flourished, and it is now one of the leading publishers in its market segment, which concentrates on publishing quality textbooks for engineering, technical reference, and college use. The company has been and remains a closely held, family-owned corporation.

Christine succeeded her father as the company's president in 1954. Three years ago, she turned over reins of the company to her daughter, Dawn Witham-Tate. John Donnelly, III, was recently promoted as the company's Vice President of Sales and Marketing. His father, John, Jr., had followed a career as a stock and bond mutual fund manager at a major New York brokerage. John, Jr., had no interest in publishing textbooks, because it lacked the electrifying atmosphere of Wall Street. However, John, Sr., had enticed his grandson to work for him during the summers while he was attending college. John, III, became enchanted with the excitement of the publishing business and decided to follow in his grandfather's footsteps.

Last week, Marti J. Ahlbrand, the Midwest Regional Sales Manager, visited with John, III, in his office in New York. Marti reviewed the company's current procedures for determining the bonuses paid to sales associates. Each associate is assigned a sales territory and calls on college faculty, bookstores, and librarians in selling publications. At the beginning of the year, each sales associate sits down with his or her regional manager and develops the associate's sales quota. A quota is established for both the first half and second half of the year. This facilitates paying a bonus for each six-month reporting period. The company's current sales bonus is 5 percent of the sales in excess of a sales associate's quota for that reporting period. Dawn and John, III, prefer a twice-a-year bonus payment because it has provided an incentive that has increased the productivity of their sales associates.

In Marti's meeting with John, III, she described the prototype of a bonus tracking system she wanted to develop. Marti would develop and test the system in her sales region. After she had used it for the next bonus payment calculations, she would review the results with John. If all went as expected, the bonus tracking system would then be phased in at the other sales regions. Marti would present the system at the annual sales meeting in August.

John expressed his concern about the data entry for bonus tracking. Not all of the office support associates were familiar with Lotus 1-2-3 or dBASE, although they used WordPerfect regularly in preparing correspondence. Marti assured John that the system would permit the entry of data by using WordPerfect. These data could then be transferred to Lotus 1-2-3 or dBASE for producing the bonus tracking report. An individual regional sales manager could choose either of these software tools for producing the final report.

After Marti returned to her office on Lake Shore Drive in Chicago, she began developing the bonus tracking system. She had Tom Black, her secretary, assemble the bonus tracking data for this reporting period and enter the data as a comma delimited file. Each record in the file would include the sales associate's name, employee identification number, current quota, and sales for each of the two quarters of the reporting period. Tom has entered most of the data using WordPerfect. Marti set up a Lotus 1-2-3 worksheet and developed a dBASE structure and report form for use with these data. However, because of the recent increase in sales activity, she has not had the time to test the system completely. John is pressing her for the results, because the annual sales meeting is rapidly approaching. She wants you to enter the remaining data and test the system's operation.

Tasks

1. Access WordPerfect and retrieve the TRACK.DOC document file. Review the contents of the document and the arrangement of the comma delimited fields.

2. Add the following records as comma delimited fields to the bottom of the current document:

Sehee, Tricia	3-5879	311000	177600	192400
Shishilla, Kerreck	4-3750	293000	167700	178400
Timko, Chanin	3-6675	289000	177400	153200
Zong, Justin	4-4273	275000	156600	143000

3. Print a hard copy report of the document and save it as the TRACK.DOC document file.

4. Create an ASCII text file of this comma delimited data with the file name of TRACK.ASC.

5. Access Lotus 1-2-3 and retrieve the TRACK worksheet file.

6. Examine the TRACK worksheet, reviewing the formulas that compute Total Sales and Bonus.

7. At cell location **A10,** import the comma delimited data from the TRACK.ASC file.

8. Review the completed worksheet and print the report as currently specified, with the report settings already included in the worksheet.

9. Preview the graph for the bonuses as defined by the current graph settings. Save this graph in the TRACK.PIC file for printing after you exit from the spreadsheet module of Lotus.

10. Print the TRACK.PIC graph.

11. Access dBASE and activate the TRACK database.

12. Obtain a hard copy listing of the structure (data definition) of this database.

13. Load the database with the comma delimited data in the TRACK.ASC file.

14. Obtain a hard copy of the data in this database.

15. Using the MODIFY command, review the [dBASE IV] TRACK4 or [dBASE III+] TRACK3 Report Form. Notice how the Total Sales and Bonus are computed with this report form. In this manner, Total Sales and Bonus amounts do not need to be stored in the database. This reduces the storage space needed for the database.

16. Produce a hard copy of the TRACK report.

17. Compare the Lotus 1-2-3 processing to that used with dBASE. Which method do you prefer? Why?

18. (*Optional*)   Create a Lotus Macro to automate the processing of the TRACK worksheet. This macro should erase any existing data in the worksheet, import the data from the ASCII text file, print the report, and save an updated graph file for printing.

19. (*Optional*)   Create a dBASE program that produces the bonus tracking report. This program should remove any existing data from the database, append the data from the ASCII text file and produce the report using the TRACK report form.

20. (*Optional*)   Draw a dataflow diagram (DFD) of the entry and processing of data to produce the reports using either Lotus 1-2-3 or dBASE.

Time Estimates

Novice: 90 minutes

Intermediate: 60 minutes

Advanced: 45 minutes

John Donnelly & Daughters
MACRO PLANNING FORM

Macro Name	Macro Command	Descriptive Comment

Performing Advanced Data Transfers

CONTENT

- What Are Advanced File Interfaces?
- Importing Lotus 1-2-3 Special Format Files to dBASE Databases
- Exporting dBASE Data to Lotus 1-2-3 Special Format Files
- Performing Special Format Files Translation with Lotus 1-2-3
- Preparing Fixed Format Records with WordPerfect
- Importing Fixed Format Records to dBASE Databases
- Importing Fixed Format Records to Lotus 1-2-3 Worksheets
- Composing dBASE Programs with WordPerfect
- Developing Special DOS Files with WordPerfect
- When Things Go Wrong

I.2.1   What Are Advanced File Interfaces?

In addition to the report formatted and comma delimited file transfers described in Lesson I.1, special formatted and fixed formatted file interfaces are other widespread methods of integrating solutions. Fixed formatted ASCII text files require more coordination to achieve successful integration than is necessary with comma delimited files. Special formatted files present a distinct challenge in performing the integration of solutions, since the special format of one software tool must be processed by the other software tool. Also, WordPerfect can be used to prepare a variety of ASCII text files in addition to those for dBASE and Lotus 1-2-3, which are explored in the preceding Lesson. Other applications of WordPerfect include creating special DOS files and entering dBASE programs. This Lesson examines (1) interfacing solutions with special formatted files and fixed formatted files and (2) preparing other special-purpose ASCII text files.

The movement of data between Lotus 1-2-3 and dBASE can be accomplished with either ASCII text files or special formatted files, as illustrated in Figure I.20. The integration of special formatted files is implemented by translating the special formatted file of the *source* application tool into that of the *target* application tool. This foreign file interface translation may be carried out by the source tool, the target tool, or a separate utility program. For example, when information from dBASE is being transferred to Lotus 1-2-3, a worksheet file in the Lotus 1-2-3 special file format can be

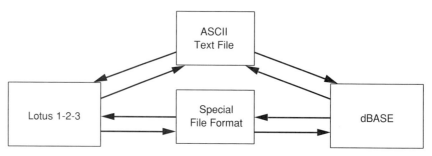

FIGURE I.20. Alternative Lotus 1-2-3 and dBASE data transfer interfaces.

written directly from dBASE. In addition, data residing in a Lotus 1-2-3 worksheet can be directly loaded to a dBASE database by translating the special Lotus 1-2-3 special file format as the data are brought into the database.

I.2.2   Importing Lotus 1-2-3 Special Format Files to dBASE Databases

Data from a Lotus 1-2-3 worksheet file can be imported directly into a dBASE database. Before this foreign file interface with the Lotus 1-2-3 worksheet is carried out, the structure of the dBASE database should be matched with the data residing in each row of the worksheet. In dBASE version IV, the IMPORT FROM command with the option TYPE WK1 reads the special formatted Lotus 1-2-3 worksheet file and loads the data to the active dBASE database. With dBASE version III+, the APPEND FROM command with the TYPE WKS is used to load the file. No intermediate file is required to temporarily store the Lotus 1-2-3 data, because a direct transfer occurs. However, because the *entire* worksheet file is translated, this file should contain only the data you want to transfer to dBASE. This would exclude any macros or other special ranges of data, such as an area of a worksheet containing assumption data.

At Good Morning Products, Chris prepared the ACTUAL worksheet containing the expense data by quarter for the last year. After discussing the content of the ACTUAL worksheet, Kim and Chris decided to transfer this Lotus 1-2-3 worksheet to a dBASE database, because Kim envisions including additional detailed expenses in this file. dBASE would provide a better environment for conducting queries on a larger database. Chris proceeded to carry out the Lotus 1-2-3 foreign file interface with dBASE like this:

To get ready to transfer 1-2-3 data to dBASE

Action: Access Lotus 1-2-3 and retrieve the ACTUAL worksheet file.

Action: Review the cell contents of the worksheet. Within Lotus 1-2-3, print a report of these results.

Action: Exit from Lotus 1-2-3.

Action: Access dBASE and load the ACTUAL database.

For convenience, Chris will use the same database for storing these data as he used previously with the comma delimited text file, since the same structure is used with these data. Of course, a different database with this structure could have been created in the same manner as that applied in loading the comma delimited data, as described in Lesson I.1. Before loading the Lotus 1-2-3 data, the existing data are removed from the database as follows:

Enter: ZAP   Remove all the records in the database

When requested to confirm this ZAP, then,

Press: <Y>   Yes, you want to ZAP it

The ACTUAL database can be loaded directly from the ACTUAL.WK1 Lotus 1-2-3 worksheet file. The IMPORT command is used for this activity in Version IV, whereas the APPEND command is used in Version III+. Directly loading the 1-2-3 worksheet is carried out in this manner:

To load 1-2-3 worksheet data directly into dBASE VERSION IV	**Enter:**	IMPORT FROM ACTUAL.WK1 TYPE **WK1**
		Specify loading data directly from a worksheet file into the database
	Select:	Overwrite — Request writing the records into the ACTUAL database file
	or	
VERSION III+	**Enter:**	APPEND FROM ACTUAL.WK1 TYPE **WKS**
		Specify loading data directly from a worksheet file and wait while the records are loaded

In this IMPORT/APPEND command, the type of "WK1" or "WKS" specifies the file is to be processed as a Lotus 1-2-3 worksheet file. *No other translation is required,* since dBASE is designed to read and process the special format of a Lotus 1-2-3 worksheet file.

Keypoint!

> The IMPORT or APPEND command with a TYPE of WK1 or WKS directly imports the labels and values from a Lotus 1-2-3 worksheet into the active dBASE database!

Enter: DISPLAY ALL OFF   Look at the records in the database

The resulting data appears as shown in Figure I.21. Notice how the labels for the column titles and underlining from the Lotus 1-2-3 worksheet appear in the numeric

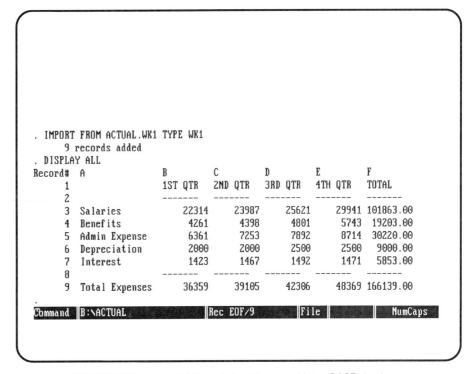

FIGURE I.21. Lotus 1-2-3 worksheet imported into dBASE database.

fields of the database. However, they do cause a record to be included in the database for each row in the source Lotus 1-2-3 worksheet file.

With dBASE version IV, the field names become the column letters from the worksheet. You need to change these to the desired field names for the ACTUAL database. This problem does not occur for version III+.

| VERSION IV |

Action: Use modify structure to change the field names from A, B, C, D, E, and F to the desired names of ACCOUNT, QTR1, QTR2, QTR3, QTR4, and TOTAL, respectively. The size of the fields do not need to be adjusted.

Now the unwanted records can be removed from the ACTUAL database. The database can be "cleaned up" like this:

| To remove unwanted records from the Imported or Appended 1-2-3 worksheet |

Enter: `DELETE ALL FOR ACCOUNT = " "`

Mark the records with a blank account field for deletion

Enter: `DELETE ALL FOR ACCOUNT = "Total Expenses"`

Mark this record for deletion, be careful to match the upper and lower case characters of the account name as it occurs in the database

Enter: `PACK`   Remove the records marked for deletion from the database

For version III+, the TOTAL column is not calculated. This is calculated for the ACTUAL database in this manner:

| VERSION III+ |

Enter: `REPLACE ALL TOTAL WITH QTR1+QTR2+QTR3+QTR4`

Compute the yearly total and store it in the TOTAL field

Enter: `DISPLAY ALL OFF`   Review the imported results

Action: Obtain a hard copy printout of the contents of the database.

The results from the Lotus 1-2-3 worksheet file have been transferred to a dBASE database for continued processing. If Kim and Chris decided they wanted a report with the Total Expenses, how could they readily produce this in dBASE? A dBASE REPORT FORM with a "Total this column" option set to Yes would compute the desired Total Expenses. As a result, records of summary accounts such as Total Expenses are not usually included in the data stored in the database.

Keypoint!

When importing data directly from a Lotus 1-2-3 worksheet file into dBASE, unwanted records may be included in the database. These records should be removed from the database before performing any other processing activities!

I.2.3   Exporting dBASE Data to Lotus 1-2-3 Special Format Files

Data in a dBASE database can be exported directly as a Lotus 1-2-3 special formatted file. This worksheet file can then be retrieved in Lotus 1-2-3 for continued use. No intermediate file is necessary in implementing the interface between dBASE and Lotus 1-2-3. The worksheet file is produced from inside dBASE with the COPY TO command

1. Create the Special Format Worksheet File

    a. Develop your Lotus 1-2-3 worksheet with labels, values and formulas.

    b. Save the results as a regular worksheet file.

2. Transfer Special Format File to dBASE

    a. Access dBASE.

    b. Activate a desired existing database or create a new database structure.

    c. Use the IMPORT FROM <filename> TYPE WK1 or APPEND FROM <filename> TYPE WKS command to load the data from the Lotus 1-2-3 special format worksheet file into the current database.

    d. Modify the structure obtained with the IMPORT command to establish the desired field names.

    e. Remove any unwanted database records, such as those caused by underlining.

    f. Perform any other database operations.

FIGURE I.22. Summary of special format transfer to dBASE.

using the TYPE WKS option. The WKI extension (or WKS extension for Lotus Release 1A) should be included in the name of the file written from dBASE to facilitate accessing it as a worksheet file within Lotus 1-2-3. You can retrieve the new file directly as a separate worksheet file or import the new file with / File Combine command to include it in the other worksheet. The field names from the database occupy the top row of the worksheet to help in identifying the data.

To explore this transfer of data from dBASE to Lotus 1-2-3 for the ACTUAL expense data at Good Morning Products, Kim suggested that Chris should export the expense data as a worksheet file. In the future, she may want Jennifer to enter the actual expense data in a dBASE database. Then, Chris could move it to Lotus 1-2-3 and prepare the graphs that Kim uses each quarter in her presentation to the Board of Directors. Chris transferred the data to a Lotus 1-2-3 worksheet in this manner:

Action: Access dBASE and load the existing ACTUAL database.

To produce a Lotus 1-2-3 worksheet file directly from dBASE

Enter: COPY TO NEXTYR.WK1 TYPE **WKS**

                    Create the NEXTYR.WK1 worksheet file

A general form of the COPY TO command is

COPY TO <**filename**> [FIELDS <**field list**>][FOR <condition>]
    [[TYPE] <file type>]

where **filename** specifies the name of the target Lotus 1-2-3 worksheet
                   file and extension,
      file type designates the type of the file with WKS specifying
                   the special Lotus 1-2-3 worksheet file format; dBASE
                   also accommodates several other special file types.

In this COPY TO command, the "TYPE WKS" designates the output as a Lotus 1-2-3 worksheet file. dBASE translates the character and numeric fields to labels and values, respectively, as the file is written in the special format of a Lotus 1-2-3 worksheet file.

Keypoint!

> The COPY TO command with a TYPE WKS directly exports data from the active dBASE database in the special format of a Lotus 1-2-3 worksheet file!

Action: Exit from dBASE.

Action: Access Lotus 1-2-3 and retrieve the NEXTYR.WK1 worksheet file.

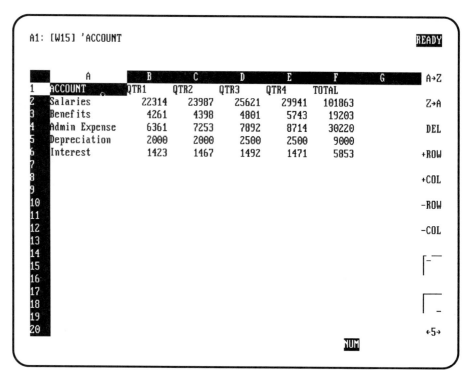

FIGURE I.23. dBASE database exported to Lotus 1-2-3 worksheet.

Notice that the field names have been included as the first row of the worksheet that was created from the database, as shown in Figure I.23.

Action: Review the contents of the worksheet and produce a hard copy of the results.

Retrieving the Lotus 1-2-3 worksheet places the data from dBASE beginning at cell location **A1,** as shown in Figure I.23. However, the data may be *placed at any desired location* in a worksheet. Move the cursor to the upper-left corner of the data area. The / File Combine Copy Entire-File (/FCCE) command loads the data at that designated location.

Keypoint!

> The / File Combine Copy Entire-File (/FCCE) command can be used to place data exported from a dBASE database into another Lotus 1-2-3 worksheet that already contains other labels, formulas, and values!

1. Transfer dBASE Data to Special Format File
   a. Construct or access a dBASE database file with the desired data.
   b. Use the COPY TO <filename> TYPE WKS command to save the data in the special format of a Lotus 1-2-3 worksheet file.
2. Load Special Format File
   a. Access Lotus 1-2-3.
   b. Retrieve the worksheet file.
   c. Perform any other worksheet activities.

FIGURE I.24. Summary of special format transfer to Lotus 1-2-3.

I.2.4   Performing Special Format Files Translation with Lotus 1-2-3

Lotus 1-2-3 supports the translation of data among several different special file formats. The Translation utility of Lotus 1-2-3 can translate to and from these software packages:

Source/Target Product	File Extension
Lotus 1-2-3 Release 1A	.WKS
Lotus 1-2-3 2 through 2.4	.WK1
Symphony 1.0 or 1.01	.WKK
Symphony 1.1 through 2.2	.WR1
dBASE II	.DBF
dBASE III	.DBF
Multiplan	.SLK
VisiCalc	.VC

The Translate utility is reached from the Lotus 1-2-3 Access System by selecting Translate from the menu or by entering TRANS from the DOS prompt. When used with a two-disk system, you may be asked to insert the Translate disk in drive A. This procedure is similar to that used when printing graphs with Lotus 1-2-3. The Translate utility is not available with some Student Editions of Lotus 1-2-3.

The Translate utility provides an interactive dialog of source file formats and target file formats. Execution of the translation is performed by selecting the source and target file format and specifying the filename of the source and target files. Figure I.25 shows the screen displayed for translating a dBASE III file to a Lotus 1-2-3 Release 2.4 file. Translations are carried out separately from the main Lotus 1-2-3 worksheet execution.

The Translate utility of Lotus 1-2-3 provides an alternative method for converting special file formats when data are transferred between Lotus 1-2-3 and dBASE. You may use this utility or the APPEND FROM and COPY TO command in dBASE.

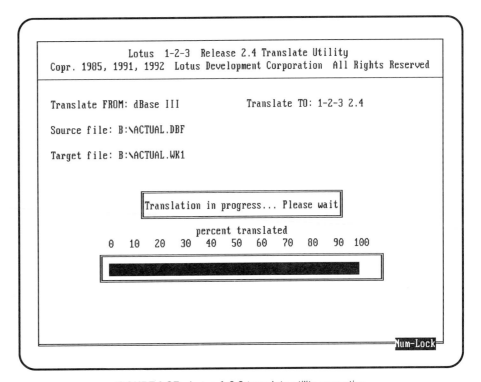

FIGURE I.25. Lotus 1-2-3 translate utility execution.

I.2.5 Preparing Fixed Format Records with WordPerfect

The data values contained in a fixed format record are identified by the character positions within the record. For example, consider the situation where a record contains an account name and data for four quarters, as illustrated in Figure I.26. The account name resides in positions 1 through 15, whereas the first quarter amount is in positions 16 through 24. Each field or column of data resides in the same character positions for all records in the file, as described by the data structure in Figure I.27. This definition of fields by their position is what makes this a **fixed format** record. When fixed format records are interfaced with other applications, numeric values do *not* contain any editing characters, such as currency symbols or commas, although decimals points are permitted.

In general, fixed formatted files are similar to report formatted files that consist of data arranged in columns. However, fixed formatted files do *not* include the headings, underlining, and other features that are usually contained in a report. Many application tools have a report-generator feature that supports writing a fixed formatted file like that illustrated in Figure I.26. Records can also be written from COBOL and BASIC language programs in a fixed formatted file. Whenever a report-generator capability is available, fixed formatted files can be produced directly from the *source* application.

WordPerfect can be used to create files of fixed formatted records. The key to typing these records is the use of tabs to designate each field. Usually, left-aligned tabs are used with fields containing character data, whereas right-aligned tabs work best for fields with numeric data. Figure I.28 shows the tab setting used with the fixed format data in Figure I.26.

At Good Morning Products, Jennifer discussed the entry of the quarterly expense data with Chris. Although the comma delimited method was straightforward, she would have preferred to enter the data in a table arrangement using tabs between each field. This would not only make entry of the data more efficient, but it would also help to eliminate errors because she could more easily review the data entered in a table arrangement to verify its accuracy. Chris realized that a table of WordPerfect data could be stored as a fixed formatted file and transferred to dBASE and Lotus 1-2-3. He encouraged Jennifer to try out this method of data entry. She proceeded in this manner:

To create fixed format data using WordPerfect

Action: Access WordPerfect and set the right-aligned tabs as specified in Figure I.28. Remember to use the <Home>+<left> to move to the left end of the tab ruler, and then to remove the initial tab settings with the EOL <Ctrl>+<End>.

Action: Type the expense data as displayed in Figure I.26. Remember to use the <Tab> to move to each of the numeric columns.

Action: Print the results and save this as the NEXTYR.DOC document file.

Action: Store the results in the ASCII text file NEXTYR.ASC.

Action: Exit WordPerfect and return to the DOS prompt.

Action: At the DOS prompt, display this ASCII text file using the DOS TYPE command.

```
                1         2         3         4         5         6
       12345678901234567890123456789012345678901234567890123456789 0

       Salaries        22314     23987     25621     29941
       Benefits         4261      4398      4801      5743
       Admin Expense    6361      7253      7892      8714
       Depreciation     2000      2000      2500      2500
       Interest         1423      1467      1492      1371
```

FIGURE I.26. Fixed format record.

Field	Type	Width
ACCOUNT	Character	15
QTR1	Numeric	9
QTR2	Numeric	9
QTR3	Numeric	9
QTR4	Numeric	9

FIGURE I.27. Data structure of formatted record.

Jennifer created a fixed format record that can be loaded directly into dBASE, Lotus 1-2-3, or any other application that can read fixed format records. Right-aligned tabs facilitated the entry of numeric data in the desired fixed format.

Keypoint! Using WordPerfect is only one way to create a fixed format file. Fixed format files may be generated by other applications, such as general ledger, payroll, and accounts receivable programs!

Keypoint! Fixed formatted files are frequently used to transfer data between applications that run on personal computers and mainframe computers. A fixed formatted file can be downloaded from a mainframe application for use with Lotus 1-2-3 or dBASE. Data generated as a fixed formatted file can be uploaded to a mainframe for use with a variety of applications. Because these are ASCII text files, they can be downloaded and uploaded readily with a communications program such as KERMIT, CrossTalk, or IRMA!

I.2.6 Importing Fixed Format Records to dBASE Databases

Data stored in a fixed formatted ASCII text file can be imported directly into a dBASE database. Prior to bringing the data into dBASE, you must set up a database structure that *exactly matches* the fixed formatted data records. For example, the data structure in Figure I.27 precisely matches the fixed formatted records of Figure I.26. This careful match is necessary because the position of characters within the record determines the field into which they are placed in the database. Once the matching database structure has been established, the APPEND FROM command with the option TYPE SDF causes the records from the fixed formatted file to be appended to the current database file. The TYPE SDF denotes a System Data Format ASCII file, which is the syntax option used by dBASE to specify a fixed formatted file.

Caution Alert! Before a fixed formatted ASCII text file can be appended to a dBASE database, the structure of the database must *exactly match* the fixed format arrangement of the data in the ASCII text file!

At Good Morning Products, Chris would like to transfer the fixed formatted ASCII text file created by Jennifer into his ACTUAL database. Jennifer prefers to enter the data as fixed formatted files because she finds it easier to type the data in a table arrangement using tabs rather than using the quotes and commas of a comma delimited file. Chris proceeded to transfer the data in this manner:

Version	Right-Aligned Tab Settings
5.0	3.4 in., 4.3 in., 5.2 in., 6.1 in.
5.1	2.4 in., 3.3 in., 4.2 in., 5.1 in.

FIGURE I.28. Tab settings in WordPerfect for data structure.

| To make another copy of a dBASE database file | **Action:** Access dBASE and make a backup copy of the entire ACTUAL database file using the command |

COPY FILE ACTUAL.DBF TO ACTUALBK.DBF

Chris wanted a backup copy of the database in case something would go wrong and he needed to access his old database. He did this because it is convenient to use the same ACTUAL database for storing the fixed formatted data that was used previously with both the comma delimited text file and the Lotus 1-2-3 worksheet file. He can do this because the structure remains the same. Of course, the structure could have been created in the same manner as that used in loading the comma delimited data, described in Lesson I.1. Before loading the fixed format records, the ACTUAL database is activated and the current records are removed from it as follows:

| **Action:** | Load the existing ACTUAL database. |
| **Enter:** | ZAP | Remove all the records in the database |

Now, the ACTUAL database can be loaded from the NEXTYR.ASC ASCII text file created with WordPerfect in this manner:

| To load fix format data directly into dBASE | **Enter:** | APPEND FROM NEXTYR.ASC TYPE **SDF** |
| | | Specify loading the data from a fixed formatted ASCII text file and wait while the records are loaded |

In this APPEND command, the "TYPE SDF" specifies that the file is to be processed as a fixed formatted ASCII text file. The column locations of data in each record are matched against the database structure to determine where the characters in each record will be placed in the database.

Enter:	DISPLAY ALL OFF	Look at the records in the database
Enter:	REPLACE ALL TOTAL WITH QTR1+QTR2+QTR3+QTR4
		Again, compute the values for the TOTAL field
Enter:	DISPLAY ALL OFF	View the records with the compute TOTAL field
Action:	Print the current contents of the ACTUAL database.

The data transfer from the fixed formatted ASCII text file has been successfully completed by using the procedure summarized in Figure I.29. Any other database processing activities could now be performed. Once again, a dBASE Report Form could be used to compute the "Total Expenses" whenever this information is required.

1. Create the Fixed Formatted Text File
    a. Specify tab settings in WordPerfect that match the data structure of the target database.
    b. Enter fixed formatted text using the <Tab> in WordPerfect to move from field to field.
    c. Save the text as a WordPerfect DOS Text File.
    d. Save the document file, if desired.
2. Transfer Fixed Formatted File to dBASE
    a. Access dBASE.
    b. Activate a desired existing database or create a new database structure.
    c. Use the APPEND FROM <filename> TYPE SDF command to load the data from the fixed formatted ASCII text file into the current database.
    d. Perform any other database operations.

FIGURE I.29. Summary of fixed formatted transfer to dBASE.

I.2.7   Importing Fixed Format Records to Lotus 1-2-3 Worksheets

The transfer of a fixed formatted file into a Lotus 1-2-3 worksheet is a two-step process that requires somewhat more effort than importing these data into dBASE. In Lotus 1-2-3, as a first step, data in fixed formatted records are transferred into the current worksheet with the / File Import Text (/FIT) command. With the Text option, each record becomes a *long label* with each successive record placed in the same column, one record below the other. Then, as a second step, the Data Parse command is used to separate the long labels into individual fields. The / Data Parse command has several options:

Command	Action
Format-Line	Creates or edits a specification that controls the way Lotus 1-2-3 separates a long label into individual cell entries.
Input-Column	Designates the column of long labels that is to be decomposed. The first cell in this range must contain the Format-Line.
Output-Range	Indicates the destination of the decomposed data. Only the upper-left cell needs to be specified.
Reset	Clears the Input-Column and Output-Range settings.
Go	Causes the Parse to be carried out as defined by the Parse Settings.

Chris wants to transfer the fixed formatted file, which Jennifer created using WordPerfect, into a 1-2-3 worksheet file. This would make it more convenient if he wanted to prepare any graphs using this data. Chris proceeded with the file interface as follows:

Action: Access Lotus 1-2-3.

To load fixed format data as long labels in a Lotus 1-2-3 worksheet

Move to: A1   Position the cursor in the upper-left corner for the imported data

The location of the incoming data is determined by *the position of the worksheet cursor*, when you begin the / File Import (/FI) command sequence. The cursor position specifies the upper-left corner of the range, where the data will be located.

Caution Alert!   Carefully position the worksheet cursor in the upper-left corner of the desired location for the incoming data!

Press: /   Access main menu

Select: File   Importing data is a File activity

Select: Import   Desired processing

Select: Text   Specify each record as a long label

Enter: NEXTYR.ASC   Name of the fixed formatted ASCII text file

The data in the designated file are transferred to the Lotus 1-2-3 worksheet file.

Action: Inspect the contents of the worksheet cells and confirm that each record of data from the fixed formatted ASCII text file is a long label residing in a cell in column **A** as illustrated in Figure I.30.

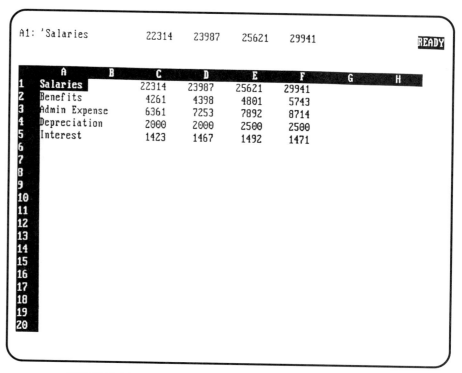

FIGURE I.30. Fixed format records as imported into Lotus 1-2-3.

This completes the first step in the integration of the fixed formatted data. Chris is ready to continue with the second step.

To create a Parse Format-Line for converting long labels into Lotus 1-2-3 cell entries			
Move to:	A1	Location of the first row of long labels
Press:	/	Access main menu
Select:	Data	Separating long labels is a Data operation
Select:	Parse	Desired procedure
Select:	Format-Line	Begin definition of decomposition
Select:	Create	Produce the initial Format-Line and insert it in the worksheet moving all data down the worksheet by one row

The symbols used in the Format-Line to define the data structure of each row of data to be parsed are described as follows:

Symbol	Description
L	Specifies the first character of a label data field.
V	Specifies the first character of a value data field.
D	Specifies the first character of a date type field.
S	Specifies the first character of a data field to be skipped during parsing.
>	Indicates the continued definition of a data field.
*	Indicates a blank space in the rows being parsed.

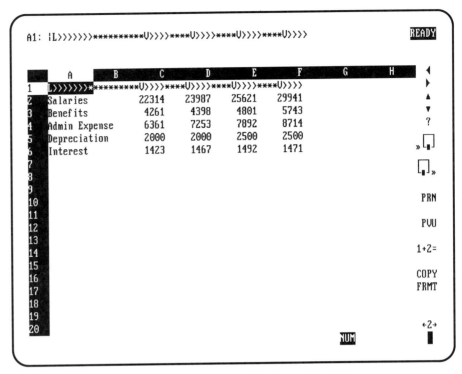

FIGURE I.31. Initial Format-Line for parsing data.

Next the Format-Line is modified so it matches the data structure.

Select:	Format-Line	Change the definition of the Format-Line to match the data structure
Select:	Edit	Initial format needs to be modified
Action:		Make edit changes to the Data Parse Format-Line by moving the cursor to the desired location and typing the characters to produce the Format-Line, as shown in Figure I.32. Press <Enter> to complete the edit of the Format-Line.

The revised Format-Line matches the data structure, as illustrated in Figure I.26 and defined in Figure I.27.

To perform the Data Parse creating individual Lotus 1-2-3 cell entries

Select:	Input-Column	Specify the range of long labels to be decomposed by parsing with the Format-Line as the first cell in the range
Action:		Define the range **A1** through **A6** as the input range. The Format-Line is contained in the topmost cell in the range.
Select:	Output-Range	Specify the range where the decomposed data will be placed
Move to:	A11	Point to the upper-left corner of this cell range
Press:	<Enter>	Complete the range specification
Select:	Go	Perform the Parse procedure
Action:		Inspect the cell contents in the Output-Range by moving the cursor within that range of cells, as shown in Figure I.32.

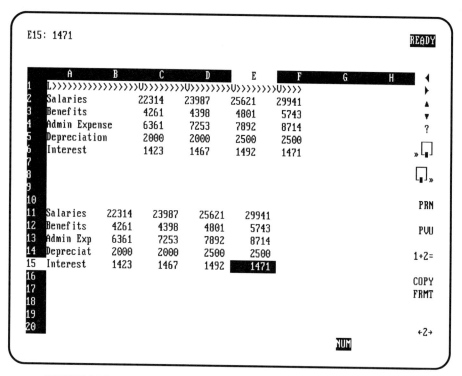

FIGURE I.32. Format-Line matching data structure and parsed output data.

The long labels of the fixed format records have been converted to individual labels and values for further use in the worksheet.

Action: Set the width of column **A** to 15 characters to match the data structure.

Action: Print the resulting worksheet and save this as the FIXED worksheet file.

The fixed formatted file has been transferred to Lotus 1-2-3 and converted to a form that supports continued processing activities by using the procedure summarized in Figure I.33. Chris has the data he wants in the desired cells.

1. Create the Fixed Formatted Text File
   a. Enter fixed formatted text using WordPerfect with tab setting to indicate the field locations.
   b. Save the text as a WordPerfect DOS Text File.
   c. Save the document file, if desired.
2. Transfer Fixed Formatted Text File to Lotus 1-2-3
   a. Access Lotus 1-2-3.
   b. If desired, Retrieve a worksheet that is to receive the imported data.
   c. Position the cursor at upper-left corner of the range where the data are to be placed.
   d. Use the / File Import Text command to load the data from the text file into the current worksheet
   e. Use the / Data Parse command to describe the data to be decomposed and to perform the parse operation
   f. Perform any other worksheet activities

FIGURE I.33. Summary of fixed formatted transfer to Lotus 1-2-3.

I.2.8 Composing dBASE Programs with WordPerfect

WordPerfect can be used to develop dBASE programs, since they are plain ASCII text files. One advantage of using WordPerfect is *the ability to edit larger programs than you can with the dBASE editor.* Another advantage of using WordPerfect in creating these files includes the ability to employ features such as Search, Replace, Block Copy, and Block Move. By performing a Block Copy, a segment of a program can be duplicated for use at another location. Once copied, the program segment could be modified by using the REPLACE command. The BLOCK MOVE command is convenient in rearranging commands within a program when they are not in the desired sequence. The completed program is stored as a DOS Text File with the file extension PRG. dBASE uses this extension to identify its programs.

For the Golden Gourmet's Wine Management System, Beth prefers to use Word-Perfect in developing dBASE programs because it saves her time in rearranging dBASE commands as she writes a program. She used WordPerfect to create the WINELIST program in this manner:

Action: Access WordPerfect.

To create a dBASE program using WordPerfect

Action: Type the WINELIST program as shown in Figure I.34. Use WordPerfect's editing capabilities to correct any errors you detect as you type this program.

Action: Save this as an ASCII text file using the Text In/Out <Ctrl>+<F5> command and the DOS Text File option. Name the file WINELIST.PRG.

Action: Access dBASE. If necessary, change the default disk drive.

Action: Execute the WINELIST program.

WordPerfect furnishes a convenient method for developing dBASE programs. Revisions can be readily performed without the significant retyping that might be required with the dBASE program text editor.

I.2.9 Developing Special DOS Files with WordPerfect

Special DOS files, such as the CONFIG.SYS and AUTOEXEC.BAT files, can be created with WordPerfect rather than by using the DOS COPY CON command, the EDLIN text editor, or the DOS EDIT program. These are plain ASCII text files that can be created and modified by using WordPerfect. The advantage of using WordPerfect for these files is the same as for employing WordPerfect to create dBASE programs. WordPerfect's features, such as Search, Replace, Block Copy, and Block Move, can be used to produce the desired ASCII text file.

At the Golden Gourmet, Bert used WordPerfect to create a CONFIG.SYS file and AUTOEXEC.BAT file for use with the Wine Management System. Bert knew that if his system did not have a CONFIG.SYS with a sufficient number of "files," then the "Too

```
*   COMMAND FILE:  WINELIST

USE WINES
INDEX ON TYPE + MAKER TO WINETYPE
SET INDEX TO WINETYPE
REPORT FORM WINELIST TO PRINT
```

FIGURE I.34. dBASE program WINELIST.PRG created with WordPerfect.

many files open" error message would occur when Beth ran the system. He created a new CONFIG.SYS file using WordPerfect in this manner:

Action: Access WordPerfect.

To create a special DOS file using WordPerfect

Action: Type the CONFIG.SYS in Figure I.35. Use WordPerfect's editing capabilities to correct any errors.

or

If you already have a CONFIG.SYS file on your disk containing DOS, access your existing CONFIG.SYS file and use WordPerfect to make these changes in the number of FILES and BUFFERS.

Action: Save your newly created or modified CONFIG.SYS file on your Data Disk. Because this needs to be an ASCII text file, use the Text In/Out <Ctrl>+<F5> command and the DOS Text File option when you save the file.

Action: Exit from WordPerfect.

Action: (*Optional*)   If you already have a CONFIG.SYS file on your disk containing DOS, make a backup copy of this as the file CONFIG.BAK on your Data Disk. Copy your CONFIG.SYS file from your Data Disk to the root directory of your disk containing DOS. Reboot your computer to use the newly created CONFIG.SYS file.

Action: (*Optional*)   If necessary, replace the modified CONFIG.SYS file on your disk containing DOS with your backup copy so it contains the original configuration settings.

The CONFIG.SYS file was readily developed with WordPerfect. An AUTO-EXEC.BAT file can be created following the same procedure as that employed with the CONFIG.SYS file. WordPerfect provides a convenient way to create or modify plain ASCII text files such as these special DOS files.

```
FILES = 20
BUFFERS = 20
```

FIGURE I.35. CONFIG.SYS file created with WordPerfect for use with dBASE.

I.2.10   When Things Go Wrong

A variety of different conditions may occur while you are integrating information from a source application into your target application by using direct translation or by using fixed formatted records. Some of the more common difficulties and how to approach them are presented here:

1. When you are moving data from a Lotus 1-2-3 worksheet directly to a dBASE database, the information received by dBASE is correct, but it resides in the wrong fields. This happens when there is a mismatch between the columns of your 1-2-3 worksheet and the fields of your dBASE database.

   a. In Lotus 1-2-3, access your source worksheet and verify the content of each column.

   b. In dBASE, access the target database.

   c. Use COPY FILE to make a backup copy of this database file, in case you need to return to your original copy.

   d. Use ZAP to remove the incorrect information from your database file.

   e. Check the definition of each field by using the MODIFY STRUCTURE command. Determine the mismatch between the worksheet columns and each database field.

   f. Modify the structure of your database to match the content of each column in your worksheet.

   g. Use the IMPORT/APPEND FROM command to reload your database from your 1-2-3 worksheet.

2. When you transferred your Lotus 1-2-3 worksheet to your dBASE database, numeric fields in several of your database records contained blanks, instead of the values from your worksheet. This usually occurs when the cells in your worksheet contained formulas instead of data values.

   a. In Lotus 1-2-3, access your source worksheet file.

   b. Use the /File Xtract Values (/FXV) command to create a second Lotus worksheet that contains only labels and numeric constants.

   c. In dBASE, access your target database.

   d. Use either ZAP to remove all the records from the database or use DELETE and PACK to remove selected records from the database.

   e. Use the IMPORT/APPEND FROM command to reload your database from your 1-2-3 worksheet that was created with the /File Xtract processing.

3. When you were integrating a 1-2-3 worksheet file output directly from dBASE into another worksheet file, you inserted the information at the wrong location in your target worksheet. This usually occurs because the worksheet cursor was not positioned at the desired location when integrating the worksheet file produced with dBASE.

   a. Use /Range Erase to remove the unwanted information, position the worksheet cursor at the desired location and reissue the / File Combine Copy Entire-File (/FCCE) command.

   b. Or use the /Move command to relocate the information at the desired position in your worksheet.

4. When you integrated information from a fixed formatted file into your dBASE database, some of the fields contained values that were split between two different fields, rather than residing in the desired field. This usually occurs when the size of fields in your fixed formatted file is different from the size of the fields as defined in your dBASE structure.

a. Verify the location of each field in your fixed formatted record. You may use the TYPE command to display the content of your source file from within dBASE. Be sure to include the file extension in your file specification for the TYPE command.

b. Use ZAP to remove the unwanted records from your database.

c. Use MODIFY STRUCTURE to revise the database definition so that it matches the data fields in your fixed formatted records.

d. Reissue the IMPORT/APPEND FROM command to reload the data from your fixed formatted file.

I.2.11   Lesson Summary

- Special formatted files store data in a unique arrangement for a particular software tool. Several processing options support the direct translation from the special file format of one application to that of another application, such as a Lotus 1-2-3 to dBASE translation.

- In dBASE, the IMPORT/APPEND FROM command with the TYPE WKS option reads a Lotus 1-2-3 special formatted worksheet file into dBASE, with the incoming data placed in the current database. Records containing report features, such as headings and underlining, may be transferred to the dBASE database. Usually, these report features are unwanted records that need to be deleted from the database.

- In dBASE, data can be written to a Lotus 1-2-3 formatted worksheet file for immediate access within 1-2-3. The dBASE COPY TO command with the TYPE WKS option produces this worksheet file. Usually, the WK1 extension is applied in naming the worksheet file. In Lotus 1-2-3, either the /File Retrieve (/FR) command or the /File Combine Copy Entire-File (/FCCE) command can be used to access the worksheet file. The /FCCE command allows the incoming worksheet data to be integrated with that in another worksheet.

- Lotus 1-2-3 has a separate Translate utility that converts special file formats. This Translate is reached from the Lotus 1-2-3 Access System, rather than from within the 1-2-3 worksheet component. An interactive dialog guides the process of translation among the various special file formats that include translations between Lotus 1-2-3 and dBASE.

- Fixed format records are arranged with fields of data residing in specified positions within record. All records in a file consist of data arranged in the same positions. Fixed formatted files can be used to transfer data between applications on personal computers and mainframe computers, as well as among applications on either size computer.

- Fixed format records can readily be produced by using tab settings in WordPerfect and saving the file as a DOS Text File.

- In dBASE, records in a fixed formatted ASCII text file can be incorporated in the active database with the APPEND FROM command using the TYPE SDF option. Here, SDF specifies the incoming file as System Data Format, which is the method dBASE employs to denote a fixed formatted ASCII text file. The fixed format of incoming records must be carefully matched to the structure of the database.

- In Lotus 1-2-3, the integration of fixed formatted records is a two-step process. First, the /File Import Text (/FIT) command is used to bring in the records as long labels. Second, the / Data Parse (/DP) commands are used to decompose the long labels into individual cell contents in separate columns. A Format-Line specifies a template for decomposing the long labels into the individual fields.

- WordPerfect can be used to develop dBASE programs, which are plain ASCII text files. This allows you to make use of the more advanced features of WordPerfect in entering and revising these programs. The Text In/Out <Ctrl> + <F5> command with the DOS Text File selection saves the file in the appropriate ASCII format. A dBASE program needs the file extension PRG.

- Special DOS files, such as CONFIG.SYS and AUTOEXEC.BAT, can be created with WordPerfect and saved as DOS Text Files with the Text In/Out <Ctrl> + <F5> command.

I.2.12   Practice Tutorial

(1)   Perform the special formatted file transfers between Lotus 1-2-3 and dBASE as described in this Lesson in Sections I.2.2 and I.2.3 as a guided hands-on activity in this manner:

Task 1: Access dBASE and load the ACTUAL database.

Task 2: Remove any existing records from the database and load the data from the ACTUAL.WK1 Lotus 1-2-3 file.

Task 3: Delete the unwanted records and obtain a hard copy of the contents of the database.

Task 4: Store the contents of the database in the NEXTYR.WK1 worksheet file.

Task 5: Access Lotus 1-2-3 and retrieve the NEXTYR.WK1 worksheet file.

Task 6: Print a hard copy report of the worksheet.

Time Estimates

Novice: 60 minutes

Intermediate: 45 minutes

Advanced: 30 minutes

(2)   Devise a fixed formatted ASCII text file using WordPerfect and integrate it into a dBASE database and a Lotus 1-2-3 worksheet as described in Sections I.2.5 through I.2.7 of this Lesson as a guided hands-on activity as follows:

Task 1: Access WordPerfect and set up the tabs for the fixed formatted file.

Task 2: Type the data using the tabs to position each entry and store this file as an ASCII text file.

Task 3: Access dBASE and load the ACTUAL database.

Task 4: Remove the existing data from the database and load the records contained in the fixed formatted file.

Task 5: Produce a hard copy report of the contents of the database.

Task 6: Access Lotus 1-2-3 and import the fixed formatted ASCII text file as long labels.

Task 7: Parse the long labels, converting each field in the record into an individual column of data.

Task 8: Print a hard copy report of the worksheet and save this file.

Time Estimates

Novice: 60 minutes

Intermediate: 45 minutes

Advanced: 30 minutes

I.2.13   Comprehensive Problems

(1)   Case: Woodcraft Furniture Company (continued)

At Woodcraft Furniture, "Tall" Pine would like to explore moving the quarterly forecast from Lotus 1-2-3 to dBASE. This would permit the data for several different forecasts to be stored, with any one forecast retrievable on demand. Also, he could formulate queries that would compare selected accounts for different forecasts. He is anxious to test the feasibility of transferring the data by using only the most recent forecast. If this proves to be satisfactory, then, as additional versions of the forecast are prepared, he will include them in the database. "Tall" has sketched out the following design for the database:

DATABASE PLANNING FORM

Data Name	Data Type	Width	Dec(imals)
ACCOUNT	Character	20	
MONTH1	Numeric	12	0
MONTH2	Numeric	12	0
MONTH3	Numeric	12	0
TOTAL	Numeric	12	0
VERSION	Character	5	

"Tall" wants you to test the feasibility of using dBASE for his intended purpose by performing the following activities:

Task 1: Access the WOOD2 worksheet file from Comprehensive Problem 1 in Lessons L.2 and L.3 of Using Lotus 1-2-3 and review its contents. If you have not already created this worksheet, do so before you continue.

Task 2: Make sure there are *no* blank columns in the worksheet. Columns **A** through **E** should contain the account name, the three months' data, and the total. If you have any blank columns, delete them before you continue.

Task 3: The Pro Forma Income Statement contains numerous equations so that their *values* must be stored before the data are moved to dBASE. Otherwise, every formula would end up as a blank in the dBASE database. Use the /File Extract Values (/FXV) command in Lotus 1-2-3 to save this as the WOOD2XTV.WK1 file. [*Hint:* Specify the range to be saved as all the cells of the entire forecast.]

Task 4: Access dBASE and create the WOOD2 database as described in the foregoing Database Planning Form.

Task 5: Load the data from the WOOD2XTV.WK1 file to this database.

Task 6: Remove the records with a blank account name and with blanks or zeros for the data values for all quarters.

Task 7: Identify this VERSION as the "MOSTP" (most probable) version by entering "MOSTP" in the VERSION field of each record loaded to the database.

Task 8: Generate a hard copy listing of the data for the MOSTP VERSION.

Task 9: (*Optional*)   Create a dBASE report form for producing a report of these data and generate this report.

Task 10: (*Optional*)   Write a description of how the VERSION name might be obtained as data from the Lotus 1-2-3 worksheet. Compare this 1-2-3 method to that of providing the VERSION name in dBASE.

Task 11: (Optional)   Prepare system documentation by drawing a dataflow diagram (DFD) of the processing that generates the final dBASE report.

Time Estimates

Novice: 90 minutes

Intermediate: 60 minutes

Advanced: 45 minutes

(2)   Case: Midwest Universal Gas (continued)

Each year, as Sam Wright develops the next year's budget for Midwest Universal Gas (MUG), a number of planning alternatives are explored. Mary Derrick has suggested that preferred plans should be stored so that selected revenues and expenses can be compared. Sam believes that a dBASE database would provide the best ability to formulate queries for these comparisons. As each Pro Forma Income Statement alternative is produced by using Lotus 1-2-3, these data are transferred to the dBASE database for future queries. Sam has sketched out the following database design for storing these data:

DATABASE PLANNING FORM

Data Name	Data Type	Width	Dec(imals)
ACCOUNT	Character	22	
QTR1	Numeric	10	0
QTR2	Numeric	10	0
QTR3	Numeric	10	0
QTR4	Numeric	10	0
TOTAL	Numeric	10	0
VERSION	Character	5	

Sam wants you to set up this database and load the data for MUG's most recently developed plan by performing the following activities:

Task 1: Access the MUG2 worksheet file from Comprehensive Problem 1 in Lessons L.2 and L.3 of Using Lotus 1-2-3 and review its contents. If you have not already created this worksheet, do so before you continue.

Task 2: Make sure that there are *no* blank columns in the worksheet. Columns **A** through **F** should contain the account name, the four quarters' data, and the total. If you have any blank columns, delete them before you continue.

Task 3: The Pro Forma Income Statement contains numerous equations, and their *values* must be stored before the data are moved to dBASE. Otherwise, every formula would become a blank in the dBASE database. Use the / File Extract Values (/FXV) command in Lotus 1-2-3 to save this as the MUG2XTV.WK1 file. [*Hint:* Specify the range to be saved as all of the cells of the entire forecast.]

Task 4: Access dBASE and create the MUG2 database as described in the foregoing Database Planning Form.

Task 5: Load the data from the MUG2XTV.WK1 file to this database.

Task 6: Remove the records with a blank account name and with blanks or zeros for the data values for all quarters.

Task 7: Identify this VERSION as the "BEST" version by entering "BEST" in the VERSION field of each record loaded to the database.

Task 8: Generate a hard copy listing of the data for the BEST VERSION.

Task 9: (*Optional*)   Create a dBASE report form for producing a report of these data and generate this report.

Task 10: (*Optional*)   Write a description of how the Version name might be directly obtained as data from the Lotus 1-2-3 worksheet. Compare this 1-2-3 method to that of providing the VERSION name in dBASE.

Task 11: (*Optional*)   Draw a dataflow diagram (DFD) of the processing that results in producing the final dBASE report.

Time Estimates

Novice: 90 minutes

Intermediate: 60 minutes

Advanced: 45 minutes

(3)   Case: Yen To Travel (continued)

At Yen To Travel, Brenda Esprit and Sara McGill would like to conduct an analysis of the SOLD and OPEN seats for each TOUR and for the AIR tours. Brenda would like to have a report that includes both the number of SOLD and OPEN seats and the percentage of the total number for each of the two categories of seats. Sara believes that a pie chart would help focus on the tours that should be emphasized to customers based on the number of available seats. To compute these percentages and prepare the pie chart, Sara believes that Lotus 1-2-3 should be used. She wants you to produce these for Yen To by carrying out these activities:

Task 1: Access the TOURS database from Comprehensive Problem 1 in Lessons D.1, D.2 and D.3 of Using dBASE. Review the contents of the database. If you have not already created this database, do so before you continue.

Task 2: Activate or create an INDEX that causes the database to be displayed arranged by tour TYPE.

Task 3: Use the COPY TO command to store the TOUR, AGENT, SOLD, and OPEN fields in the TOURS.WK1 worksheet file. [*Hint:* Use the FIELDS option of the COPY TO command to specify a subset (or subschema) of the database fields.]

Task 4: Use the COPY TO command to store the TOUR, AGENT, SOLD, and OPEN fields for only the AIR tours in the AIR.WK1 worksheet file. [*Hint:* Use the FOR option to select a subset of rows from the database.]

Task 5: Access Lotus 1-2-3 and retrieve the TOURS worksheet file. Review the contents of this worksheet.

Task 6: Add cell formulas to compute the total number of OPEN and the total number of SOLD seats at the bottom of the columns of data transferred from the database.

Task 7: Add two columns on the right side of the worksheet, columns **E** and **F,** which compute the percentage of total SOLD seats and the percentage of total OPEN seats, respectively. Format these two columns as Percent 2. The general layout of the resulting worksheet is shown here:

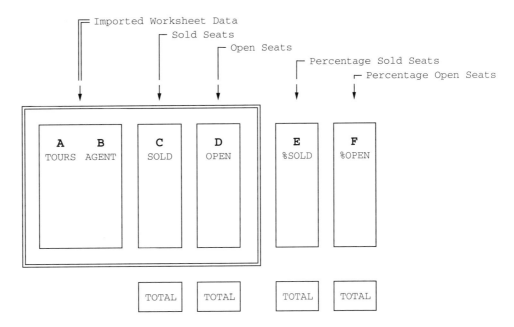

Task 8: Prepare a pie chart of the OPEN seats. Crosshatch and explode the slices of the pie chart. You may use the same cross-hatching for each TYPE of tour. Save this in the TOURS.PIC file for printing after you exit from the 1-2-3 worksheet module.

Task 9: Print the resulting report and save the modified TOURS worksheet file.

Task 10: Retrieve the AIR worksheet file and review its contents.

Task 11: Add cells with the totals for the OPEN and SOLD seats in the same manner as that described in Task 6.

Task 12: Add columns **E** and **F** with the percentage of total SOLD and percentage of total OPEN seats in the same manner as described in Task 7.

Task 13: Develop a pie chart of the OPEN seats for the AIR tours similar to that described in Task 8. Save the graph in the AIR.PIC file for printing.

Task 14: Print the results and save the modified AIR worksheet.

Task 15: Print the TOURS and AIR graphs.

Task 16: (*Optional*)   Describe how the two percentage columns might be created in dBASE. Could this be performed by using a dBASE program? What would be the advantage of using such a program?

Task 17: (*Optional*)   Prepare a dataflow diagram (DFD) of the processing that yields the final worksheet report.

Time Estimates

Novice: 90 minutes
Intermediate: 60 minutes
Advanced: 45 minutes

(4)   Case: Silver Screen Video (continued)

Amy Lighthart at Silver Screen Video would like to analyze the company's investment in movies with a separate analysis for the horror movies. Amy wants to review this analysis of the inventory with Ernie and Todd. For the review, she would like to include a pie chart to highlight movies that are candidates for the monthly special. The analysis is to include both the investment in each movie (PRICE * QTY) and the percentage that each movie is of the total inventory investment. To prepare this analysis, Amy would like you to use Lotus 1-2-3. She wants you to complete the analysis by performing these activities:

Task 1: Access the MOVIES database from Comprehensive Problem 1 in Lessons D.1, D.2, and D.3 of Using dBASE. Review the contents of the database. If you have not already created this database, do so before you continue.

Task 2: Activate or create an INDEX that causes the database to be displayed arranged by movie TYPE.

Task 3: Use the COPY TO command to store the MOVIE, MAKER, PRICE, and QTY in the MOVIES.WK1 worksheet file. [*Hint:* Use the FIELDS option of the COPY TO command to specify a subset (or subschema) of the database fields.]

Task 4: Use the COPY TO command to store the MOVIE, MAKER, PRICE, and QTY fields for only the HOR movies in the HORROR.WK1 worksheet file. [*Hint:* Use the FOR option to select a subset of rows from the database.]

Task 5: Access Lotus 1-2-3 and retrieve the MOVIES worksheet file. Review the contents of this worksheet.

Task 6: Add two columns on the right side of the worksheet, columns **E** and **F,** with the investment in each movie computed in column **E** and the percentage of the total investment in each movie computed in column **F.** Set up a separate cell to compute the total investment and use it in the percentage of total investment computation. Format the percentage of total investment column as Percent 2. The general layout of the resulting worksheet is

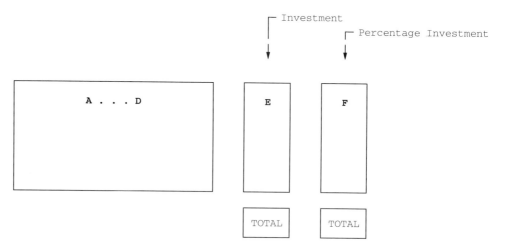

Task 7: Prepare a pie chart of the percentage investment in each movie. Crosshatch and explode the slices of the pie chart. You may use the same cross-hatching for each TYPE of movie. Save this in the MOVIE.PIC file for printing after you exit from the 1-2-3 worksheet module.

Task 8: Print the resulting report and save the revised MOVIES worksheet file.

Task 9: Retrieve the HORROR worksheet file and review its contents.

Task 10: Add columns **E** and **F** with the investment in each movie and the percentage investment in each movie in the same manner as described in Task 6.

Task 11: Develop a pie chart of the percentage investment in HORROR movies similar to that described in Task 7. Save the graph in the HORROR.PIC file for printing.

Task 12: Print the results and save the revised HORROR worksheet.

Task 13: Print the MOVIES and HORROR graphs.

Task 14: (*Optional*)   Describe how the investment and percentage investment columns might be created in dBASE. Could this be performed using a dBASE program? What would be the advantage of using such a program?

Task 15: (*Optional*)   Draw a dataflow diagram (DFD) of these processing activities for producing the final worksheet report.

Time Estimates

Novice: 90 minutes

Intermediate: 60 minutes

Advanced: 45 minutes

(5)   Case: Woodcraft Furniture Company (second encounter)

At Woodcraft Furniture, Larry King, Amanda Drexeler's assistant for production planning, has found that missing quotes and commas sometimes create errors when typing comma delimited files. Also, proofreading or "sight verifying" data in comma delimited form requires extra effort when trying to determine in which monthly columns the data belong. A more orderly arrangement of the data would assist in the sight verification and help reduce data-entry errors.

Ray Jointer, the production manager, would like Amanda to store the data for several different quarters so that comparison reports could be more easily produced. Amanda believes that dBASE would let her easily implement this system requirement. She has drawn up the following database plan:

DATABASE PLANNING FORM

Data Name	Data Type	Width	Dec(imals)
ACCOUNT	Character	12	
MONTH1	Numeric	9	0
MONTH2	Numeric	9	0
MONTH3	Numeric	9	0
TOTAL	Numeric	9	0
QUARTER	Numeric	2	0

For this design, the TOTAL field will be computed *after* the data are transferred to the database. Also, the QUARTER field will contain a designator for the quarter number (1, 2, 3, or 4). Since the values for TOTAL and QUARTER are determined after the data are appended, they have been included as the last or rightmost fields in the database design (or schema).

A feasibility test of this processing should determine any limitations and difficulties that need to be addressed before Larry begins operating the system routinely. Amanda is anxious to explore a less error-prone method of data entry and wants you to carry out the following activities in performing this system feasibility test:

Task 1: Access WordPerfect and enter the following data as a fixed formatted file:

```
              1         2         3         4         5
     12345678901234567890123456789012345678901234567890


     Tables          880       920       930
     Chairs         4400      4400      4600
     Sofas           590       600       600
```

[*Hint:* Remember to use right-aligned tabs for the numeric data values.]

Task 2: Print a copy of these data and save them in the PRODUCT.ASC ASCII text file.

Task 3: Access dBASE and create the structure shown above as the database file called PRODUCT.

Task 4: Load the fixed formatted data in the PRODUCT.ASC database.

Task 5: Compute the TOTAL field and place "3" in the QUARTER field. [*Hint:* Use the same command to place the value in the QUARTER field that you used for computing the TOTAL field.]

Task 6: Produce a hard copy report of the results.

Task 7: (*Optional*)   Develop a dBASE Report Form that can be used to produce this report. The report should contain all the fields except the TOTAL and QUARTER fields. Include a field in the report that contains a computed quarter total, rather than using the value stored in the TOTAL field of the database. For a dBASE report, a total column can be computed and stored in the database or calculated "on the fly" as needed in a report. Output a hard copy of the report for the third quarter. Describe the advantages of computing the total in the report, rather than obtaining it from the TOTAL field.

Task 8: (*Optional*)   Sketch a dataflow diagram (DFD) of the entry and processing of data that result in producing the final dBASE report.

Time Estimates

Novice: 90 minutes

Intermediate: 60 minutes

Advanced: 45 minutes

(6)   Case: Midwest Universal Gas (second encounter)

At Midwest Universal Gas (MUG), Sam Wright and Chad Eloff met with Hank Pletcher, MUG's Director of MIS, to discuss the difficulties Chad had encountered in entering and verifying last year's actual revenues and expenses as a comma delimited file. After Chad entered the data, he would proofread or "sight verify" the values entered. Because the account names and amount contained different numbers of characters, they did not line up in columns. This made it more difficult for Chad to perform the verification. In the meeting, Hank explained that comma delimited data worked well when they were produced by a BASIC language program and that fixed formatted records were easier to produce with COBOL language programs, such as the program for their general ledger. Hank described how Chad could create and verify a fixed formatted file. Sam perceives that a fixed formatted file would simplify Chad's job and would still pave the way for future automation of this activity by having the data downloaded directly from the general ledger. Sam wants the data placed in a dBASE database so that he can conduct ad hoc queries. He has outlined the following database design (or schema) for use with this system:

DATABASE PLANNING FORM

Data Name	Data Type	Width	Dec(imals)
ACCOUNT	Character	22	
QTR1	Numeric	9	0
QTR2	Numeric	9	0
QTR3	Numeric	9	0
QTR4	Numeric	9	0
TOTAL	Numeric	9	0
CATEGORY	Character	2	

For this database design, the TOTAL field is computed after the data are obtained from the fixed formatted ASCII text file. Also, the TYPE CATEGORY field is used to identify the account as a revenue (R) account or an expense (X) account. Since the values for the TOTAL column are computed and the values for the CATEGORY field are assigned after the data have been transferred, they have been included in the database as the last or rightmost fields.

This system feasibility test should point out any remaining issues and limitations that need to be considered in either the manual entry of the data or the future direct extract from MUG's general ledger system. In the event that any adjustments need to be made to a general ledger extract, Sam can still have Chad take care of them by using WordPerfect. Sam wants you to tackle the following activities in completing the feasibility test:

Task 1: Access WordPerfect and enter the following data as a fixed formatted file:

```
         1         2         3         4         5         6
1234567890123456789012345678901234567890123456789012345678901234567890
                       |         |         |         |         |

Retail Sales           17452     14379      6411     17590
Wholesale Sales        51068     43921     19871     51022
Cost of Sales          42357     35791     14326     41099
Marketing and Selling  11927      7652      3743      9880
General and Admin       4629      3875      4107      4227
Depreciation            2202      2202      2202      2361
```

[*Hint:* Remember to use right-aligned tabs for the numeric data values.]

Task 2: Print a copy of these data and save them in the THISYR.ASC ASCII text file.

Task 3: Access dBASE and create the structure defined by the Database Planning Form above. Name this the THISYR database.

Task 4: Load the comma delimited data from the THISYR.ASC file.

Task 5: Compute the TOTAL field.

Task 6: Place an "R" in the CATEGORY field for revenues and an "X" in the CATEGORY field for expenses.

Task 7: Produce a hard copy output of the results arranged by CATEGORY.

Task 8: Describe another alternative for including the CATEGORY of account with each record in the database. What is the advantage/disadvantage of using that method?

Task 9: (*Optional*)   Develop a dBASE Report Form for generating this report. The report should contain all the fields except TOTAL and CATEGORY. Include a field in the report that contains the calculated annual total, rather than using the value stored in the TOTAL column of the database. For a dBASE report, a total column can be calculated and stored in the database or calculated "on the fly" as needed in a report. Group the data in the report by CATEGORY with a total for each category. Output a hard copy of the report with the data arranged by CATEGORY. Describe any advantages of calculating the total column in the report, rather than obtaining it from the TOTAL field in the database.

Task 10: (*Optional*)   Prepare a dataflow diagram (DFD) of the entry and processing of data to generate the final dBASE report.

Time Estimates

Novice: 90 minutes

Intermediate: 60 minutes

Advanced: 45 minutes

(7)   Case: Woodcraft Furniture Company (continued)

At Woodcraft Furniture, Amanda Drexeler, the production planner, would like to test the feasibility of one more technique for generating the quarterly production report. For this alternative, she still wants Larry King to enter the data as a fixed formatted file using WordPerfect, as explored in Comprehensive Problem 5. This will facilitate the proofreading or "sight verification" of the data. However, she wants to investigate the use of Lotus 1-2-3 for computing the total column and preparing a graph. Amanda anticipates that 1-2-3 has more flexibility in computing special ratios and graphing selected data. This processing should yield an assessment of the feasibility of using fixed formatted records before Larry begins entering the data on a periodic basis. Amanda wants you to complete the following activities in doing this system test:

Task 1: Access WordPerfect and retrieve the PRODUCT.ASC ASCII text file from Comprehensive Problem 5 that holds the fixed formatted data. If you did not produce this fixed formatted file for that problem, enter the data before you continue.

Task 2: Print a copy of this fixed formatted data and exit WordPerfect.

Task 3: Access Lotus 1-2-3 and import the PRODUCT.ASC file as a series of long labels beginning at the cell location **A1.**

Task 4: Parse the imported long labels, dividing them into the account name and monthly data for each month. Store this parsed data beginning at cell location **A10.**

Task 5: Add column titles for the months of July, August, and September and underline these titles.

Task 6: Add a total column for the quarter. Use the @SUM function to compute the quarter total for each product. Include a "Total" title for this column and underline it.

Task 7: Print the resulting report.

Task 8: (*Optional*)   Produce a stacked bar chart showing the production by month. Review the bar chart on your screen. Save this graph as the PRODUCT.PIC file and print it after you leave the main 1-2-3 worksheet program.

Task 9: Save this worksheet in the file PRODUCT.

Task 10: (*Optional*)   Draw a dataflow diagram (DFD) of the entry and processing of data to produce this final worksheet report.

Time Estimates

Novice: 90 minutes

Intermediate: 60 minutes

Advanced: 45 minutes

(8)   Case: Midwest Universal Gas (continued)

At Midwest Universal Gas, Sam Wright, would like to test the feasibility of one other alternative for generating the report of last year's actual revenues and expenses for Mary Derrick. Chad Eloff would still collect the data and enter them as a fixed formatted file as described in Comprehensive Problem 6. Lotus 1-2-3 would be employed to develop the final report, rather than using dBASE. This would give Sam increased flexibility in computing special ratios and producing plots of selected data. With the satisfactory completion of this test, either Sam could have Chad enter a fixed formatted file or Sam could obtain one directly from the general ledger system. Sam could use Lotus 1-2-3 for his formula-intensive and graphing needs while dBASE stored the data for conducting queries and printing standard reports. Sam wants you to carry out the following activities in performing this feasibility test:

Task 1: Access WordPerfect and retrieve the THISYR.ASC ASCII text file from Comprehensive Problem 6, which contains the fixed formatted data. If you did not create this file of fixed formatted data for that problem, create it before you continue.

Task 2: Print a copy of this fixed formatted data and exit WordPerfect.

Task 3: Access Lotus 1-2-3 and import the THISYR.ASC file as a series of long labels, starting at the cell location **A1.**

Task 4: Parse the imported long labels, arranging them into the account name and the data for each of the four quarters. Place this parsed data in the worksheet, beginning at cell location **A10.**

Task 5: Add column titles for each of the four quarters, beginning with the first quarter, and underline these titles.

Task 6: Add a total column for the year. Use the @SUM function to calculate the annual total for each revenue or expense account. Include a "Total" title for this column and underline it.

Task 7: (*Optional*)   Add the line item "Total Sales" to the worksheet and calculate these amounts by summing Retail Sales and Wholesale Sales. Place underlining above each of the quarterly data values for the Total Sales. Compute a "Total Expense" line item in the same manner. This line item should be the sum of all the remaining accounts that make up the Total Expenses.

Task 8: Print the resulting report.

Task 9: (*Optional*)   Produce a line graph showing the revenue and expense data for each quarter. Review the graph on your screen. Save this graph in the THISYR.PIC file and print it after you leave the main 1-2-3 worksheet program.

Task 10: Save this worksheet in the file THISYR.

Task 11: (*Optional*)   Draw a dataflow diagram (DFD) of the entry and processing of data to produce the final worksheet report.

Time Estimates

Novice: 90 minutes

Intermediate: 60 minutes

Advanced: 45 minutes

I.2.14   Case Application

Case 1: Amedus Angstrom Consulting

    Business Problem: Wage and salary administration
    MIS Characteristics: Human Resources
                        Managerial Control
    Management Functions: Planning
                            Staffing
    Tools Skills: dBASE reports
               Special file formats
               dBASE program (optional)
               Lotus 1-2-3 macros
               Combining worksheet files
               Lotus 1-2-3 regression analysis
               Lotus 1-2-3 graphing

Amedus Angstrom Consulting (AA) is an engineering design and development company. The kinds of projects undertaken are described by AA's president, Torrance K. ("TK") Brogan "Some of our typical projects have been the design of a refuse-fired electrical generating plant in Boca Raton, Florida, and a 500-bed hospital in Jidda, Saudi Arabia. Our efforts included all the design and supervision of the construction of both of these projects." TK received his mechanical engineering degree from General Motors Institute in 1961. After building cars for several years, he obtained a Master of Business Administration from the University of Michigan and joined AA. During the past 20 years, TK has held a number of engineering and management positions within the firm.

Last week TK met with Tammie Bucholtz, AA's Vice President of Human Resources, to discuss a review of the company's wage and salary structure. It seems that a number of AA's most productive employees have recently left for jobs at other engineering companies in the area. Tammie described how she wants to examine the current wage structure to determine if inequities exist that might be addressed through salary adjustments or promotions. TK encouraged Tammie to proceed with her analysis.

After Tammie returned to her office, she phoned Alice Ottarski and arranged for a 1:00 P.M. meeting. Alice's responsibilities in the Human Resources Department include compensation administration, which is concerned with determining comparable wage and salary rates both within an organization and in relation to other businesses. AA uses the "comparable norm" concept of wage determination, which is based on setting general wage levels that neither fall substantially behind nor greatly exceed those of other comparable businesses.

At AA, a job evaluation method is used to determine the relationship among wages and salary rates. Systematic judgment is applied in carrying out job evaluations. The completion of a job evaluation often leads to some increases in a company's total wages; normally, no one get his or her wages cut. If the rates that are finally set for the jobs are out of line with prevailing rates for that job in the community, the job-evaluation program may result in adjustments to a company's wage rates.

A point system is one of the most common systems of job evaluation, and is the one used by AA. This system evaluates a job based on a set of factors that describe the job requirements and difficulty. A point system does not compare one job directly to another one, nor does it evaluate a whole job. Instead, it defines factors for which jobs will be compensated and then assigns points to each job according to the degree to which the job contains each factor. Degrees are the basic unit in measuring the importance of any one factor in a given job. That is, factors are divided into a number of degrees, each degree receiving a point score to differentiate it from other degrees.

The point values for a particular position are added to determine the relative standing of the job. The point system applied at AA is as follows:

Factors	Degree and Points				
	1	2	3	4	5
Education	20	40	60	80	100
Experience	25	50	75	100	125
Complexity	20	40	60	80	100
Responsibility	10	20	40	60	80
Contact	10	20	30	50	80
Environment	10	20	30	40	60
Supervision	10	20	40	60	100

For AA's professional employees, salaries are determined based on an employee's pay grade and step. Considering the points assigned to a job, the department manager recommends a pay grade and step to Alice and Tammie in Human Resources. They meet with the department manager and arrive at the appropriate pay grade and step from the following table:

Step	Pay Grade			
	14	15	16	17
1	25000	28940	33510	38800
2	26250	30390	35190	40740
3	27560	31910	36950	42780
4	28940	33510	38800	44920
5	30390	35190	40740	47170
6	31910	36950	42780	49530

To ensure consistency between wage rates and job requirements, Alice, like other wage and salary administrators, constructs a two-dimensional graph on which actual or proposed wage rates are plotted against job evaluation points. This assists in identifying those positions that warrant a closer analysis. Overpaid employees are identified as those with "red circle" pay rates.

When a job evaluation is conducted, AA, like other companies, guarantees that overpaid employees will continue to receive the same pay rate as long as they personally continue to hold the job. However, anyone who subsequently replaces a "red circle" rate employee will receive only the rate established by the job evaluation. Employees with a "red circle" rate may find their salaries frozen at present levels until, at some later date, it falls within the correct range for the pay grade. One option for employees with "red circle" rates is to be promoted into positions consistent with their current salary.

After meeting with Tammie, Alice examined her dataflow diagram (DFD) of the wage and salary analysis reporting system, as shown in Figure I.36. WAGES.DBF (F.1) is a database containing salary and job evaluation data for the professional employees. Alice uses the database to produce a number of ad hoc reports on current salaries. It contains the data she needs for the wage and salary analysis. Alice has already created the COMPEN.WK1 (F.3) Lotus 1-2-3 worksheet, which she uses to determine the relationship between job points and salaries. The worksheet is designed to perform curve fitting using regression analysis and to graph the results for visual evaluation. Alice wants to obtain two reports and a graph, as indicated in the DFD. Since the database is maintained in dBASE and the curve fitting and graphing are carried out in Lotus 1-2-3, Alice needs to move the data from the database file to the worksheet file. Howard Ling, an Analyst I in the MIS department, served as an information center

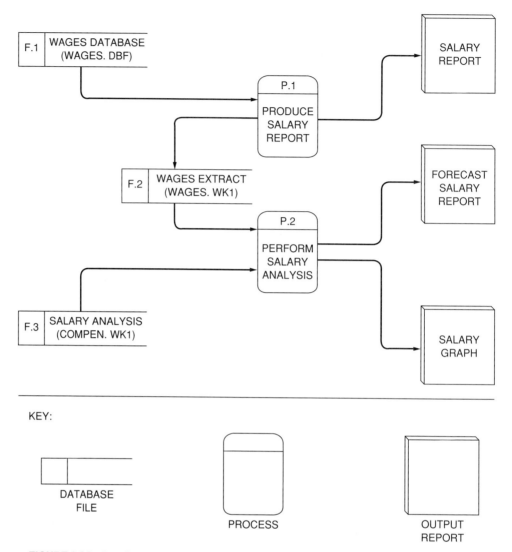

FIGURE I.36. Dataflow Diagram (DFD) of AA Consulting's wage and salary analysis system.

consultant to assist Alice in developing her analysis system. However, Howard has been assigned to another project, and Alice needs to complete her wage and salary analysis for a review meeting on Monday. You are to produce Alice's reports and to generate the graph while she continues to review the wage survey she recently obtained from Robert Half and Associates, a professional placement company.

Tasks

1. Access dBASE and activate the WAGES database. Review the content and structure of this database. Obtain a hard copy of the structure for your future reference.

2. Add the following records to the bottom of the current database:

LNAME	FNAME	EMPID	DEPT	POSITION	SEX	PAY GRADE	STEP	POINTS	SALARY
Talbot	Lawrence	22-374	Mech Eng	Analyst I	M	15	4	477	33510
Thompson	James	20-521	Elec Eng	Sr Engr	M	17	2	580	40740
Trevino	Mercedes	19-257	Chem Eng	Engr II	F	16	3	464	36950
Zapata	Nevins	20-748	Elec Eng	Engr II	M	16	2	464	35190

3. Produce a hard copy listing of the database. List all of the fields by using compressed print, if available on your printer; otherwise, generate a listing containing these fields: LNAME, DEPT, POSITION, PAYGRADE, STEP, POINTS, and SALARY.

4. Alice has developed a dBASE Report Form, [dBASE IV] WAGES4.FRM or [dBASE III+] WAGES3.FRM, for producing the Salary Report organized by position classification. Index the database on POSITION, DEPT, and LNAME, with POSITION as the primary key, and generate a hard copy of the WAGES report.

5. Turn off all indexes. Convert the file from dBASE to a 1-2-3 worksheet; call the new file WAGES.WK1. Exit from dBASE.

6. (*Optional*)   Create a dBASE program that produces the WAGES report and stores the WAGES data in a Lotus 1-2-3 worksheet file. Execute this program, which should output another copy of the dBASE report and write over the existing WAGES.WK1 file.

7. Access Lotus 1-2-3 and retrieve the COMPEN.WK1 worksheet file. This worksheet is designed to accept data from dBASE for further analysis. Besides the input area, the worksheet contains a column for computing a Forecast Salary, an area for the regression analysis, which computes a "best fit" line from the actual data, and a macro for combining the data from dBASE into this analysis worksheet. Using <Tab>, page to the right on the worksheet and inspect each of these pieces of the worksheet. Carefully review the \R macro.

8. Execute the \R macro and examine the results.

9. Inspect the graph that is produced. The graph is set up for 30 employees. If you have more or fewer employees for your analysis, adjust the X, A, and B ranges for the graph. [(*Optional,* Release 2.2 or higher)   Execute the \G macro to adjust the ranges for you, but do *not* repeat the execution of this macro.] After viewing the graph, save its image in the WAGES.PIC file for printing after you exit from the 1-2-3 worksheet module.

10. Print a report containing these fields: LNAME, DEPT, POSITION, PAYGRADE, STEP, POINTS, ACTUAL SALARY, and FORECAST SALARY. [*Hint:* In creating this report from 1-2-3, either hide the unwanted columns or use another area on your worksheet to lay out the desired report. Also, watch your page margins.]

11. Save the worksheet as the COMPFCST.WK1 file and exit from the worksheet module. [*Hint:* If you need to repeat this process for any reason, the COMPEN.WK1 worksheet should remain unchanged and can be reused readily.]

12. Print the WAGES.PIC graph.

13. Examine the reports and graph. Write a report identifying three employees whose salaries appear to be too high or too low and are candidates for determining if a salary adjustment is appropriate. Explain your choices. Select those employees that you evaluate as having "red circle" salaries.

Time Estimates

Novice: 90 minutes

Intermediate: 60 minutes

Advanced: 45 minutes

Case 2: Northland Corporation

Business Problem: Performance reporting
MIS Characteristics: Finance
                    Managerial Control
Special Characteristic: Executive Information System
Management Functions: Directing
                      Controlling
Tools Skills: Fixed formatted files
              dBASE reports
              dBASE program (optional)
              Lotus 1-2-3 text importing
              Lotus 1-2-3 data parsing
              Lotus 1-2-3 graphing

Northland Corporation (NLC) is a hospitality management company that holds franchises for two dozen Leisure Inns in the Midwest. Founded by Louis (Lou) LeBlanc in 1964 with the first Leisure Inn located in Fairborn, the Northland Corporation has experienced steady growth. A typical Leisure Inn is a moderately priced motel with a restaurant, lounge, swimming pool and spa, and exercise facility. Leisure Inns cater to both business and family travelers. Each motel has a convention area with individual meeting rooms and a large ballroom. During the week, business travelers are the primary source of revenues, while families constitute most of the weekend guests.

The Leisure Inn franchise provides NLC with access to the LeisureNet worldwide reservation system. Each Leisure Inn has a computer terminal connected to this network for continually receiving and placing reservations. Leisure Inn operates LeisureNet from its worldwide reservation headquarters in Omaha. Twenty-four hours a day, operators are on duty to receive phone reservations at 1-800-LEISURE. Leisure Inn, like several other major hotel/motel franchises, located its reservation center in Omaha because of the central geographical location and reduced cost of operation for their 800 number. Lou has been extremely satisfied with the service provided by the LeisureNet centralized computer reservation system. This network was a key factor in Lou's selection of the Leisure Inn franchise. Other franchises do not provide the same level of reservation service.

Leisure Inns do not provide centralized computing for the business and account-ing operations of franchisees. Each franchisee is responsible for the acquisition and operation of its own financial reporting and performance monitoring systems. As Northland Corporation expanded, Lou hired David Schwinn as the company's man-ager of management information services (MIS). Dave and Lou have established a decentralized system of operation and management. Each inn has its own on-site com-puter system that handles the day-to-day processing activities. Dave coordinated these systems so that they all run the same accounting and finance software. He was able to negotiate special pricing on multiple copies of this software. This decentralization of NLC's computer operations provides each manager with an increased responsibility for an inn's performance. Lou believes that this is an important ingredient in the growth and profitability of Northland's business.

To maintain control over the operations of Northland's two dozen inns, Dave and Lou have set up an executive information system (EIS) that monitors the monthly financial performance of their inns. No later than the fifth business day of the month, each inn submits its financial results for the prior month to Northland's corporate headquarters for entry into the EIS. These data are reported as dollars in thousands. Since only a minimum amount of data are transmitted each month, the data are communicated by phoning the office of Liz Clayborn, Northland's accountant, or by faxing the data to the company's headquarters. In this manner, Lou can have the financial performance report on his desk by the sixth business day of each month, and the data in the EIS can be manipulated to answer Lou's questions. If any change in managing an inn appears appropriate, Lou can immediately initiate corrective action. The EIS provides Lou with this ability to monitor performance in controlling operations.

The financial performance data for the EIS are described by the data dictionary definitions that Dave and Liz developed for each inn as follows:

Field Name	Description
INN	Name of inn identified by location
ROOMS	Room occupancy revenues
REST	Restaurant sales revenues
LOUNGE	Lounge sales revenues
WAGES	Wages expenses including benefits
FOOD	Food expenses of restaurant
BEV	Beverage expenses of lounge
MAINT	Maintenance expenses, such as minor repairs and grounds-keeping
OTHER	Other expenses, such as employee training and courtesy transportation

Dave has organized these data in a dBASE database using the following structure:

Field	Type	Width
INN	Character	12
ROOMS	Numeric	7
REST	Numeric	7
LOUNGE	Numeric	7
WAGES	Numeric	7
FOOD	Numeric	7
BEV	Numeric	7
MAINT	Numeric	7
OTHER	Numeric	7

Jessica Cervantes, Lou's executive secretary, compiles the financial performance data and enters them as a fixed formatted data file using WordPerfect. Dave developed a WordPerfect document file with the desired tabs set for entering the financial data from each inn. All Jessica needs to do is retrieve the document file, and she is ready to begin entering the data in the correct format. Dave prefers the fixed formatted file because he is exploring the electronic transmission of these data. Northland's accounting software at each inn can readily produce a file in this desired format. By switching to this feature, operation of their current EIS could be continued without modification, and the manual entry of data would be eliminated.

Once Jessica has entered the data in a fixed format file, the data are transferred to dBASE for generating queries and reports. Dave and Liz perform other special analyses and prepare graphs of the data by transferring the fixed formatted file to Lotus 1-2-3.

Dave wants to enhance the EIS by adding a dBASE report produced with a dBASE Report Form. A report form is preferred, since this is a periodic report containing the critical success factors (CSF) for each inn. Dave has sketched out the following report design:

```
NORTHLAND CORPORATION
MONTHLY REPORT


                                                      RETURN
                    TOTAL        TOTAL        NET        ON
    INN            REVENUE      EXPENSE      INCOME     SALES


XXXXXXXXXXX    ##########   ##########   ##########   9999999.99
XXXXXXXXXXX    ##########   ##########   ##########   9999999.99
XXXXXXXXXXX    ##########   ##########   ##########   9999999.99
XXXXXXXXXXX    ##########   ##########   ##########   9999999.99
                                  .
                                  .
                                  .
*** Total ***
               ##########   ##########   ##########
```

where the columns are computed as follows:

```
TOTAL REVENUE    = ROOMS + REST + LOUNGE

TOTAL EXPENSE    = WAGES + FOOD + BEV + MAINT + OTHER

NET INCOME       = (ROOMS + REST + LOUNGE) -
                   (WAGES + FOOD + BEV + MAINT + OTHER)



RETURN ON SALES = ((ROOMS + REST + LOUNGE) -
                  (WAGES + FOOD + BEV + MAINT + OTHER)) /
                  (ROOMS + REST + LOUNGE) * 100
```

The columns for **TOTAL REVENUE**, **TOTAL EXPENSE**, and **NET INCOME** are summed to obtain a total for the company. **RETURN ON SALES** is not summed since this is a ratio that does *not* make sense when it is added.

For this month, Jessica has received and entered the data for 20 of NLC's inns. The other data have just arrived but have not been entered. Dave had planned to complete the dBASE report before he left to handle a special problem at the Okemos Inn. Since he will be gone for a couple days, he wants you to produce the monthly report and analysis for Lou. The data will then be ready for any other queries that Lou might request from the EIS.

Tasks

1. Access WordPerfect and retrieve the NORTH.DOC document file. Review the contents of the document and the layout of the fixed formatted file. Inspect the right-aligned tabs that have been used for entering data in the desired columns.

2. Add the following records as fixed formatted fields to the bottom of the current document:

```
          1         2         3         4         5         6
1234567890123456789012345678901234567890123456789012345678901234567
+        +         +         +         +         +         +        +
Inn            Rooms   Rest  Lounge   Wages    Food    Bev   Maint   Other

Royal Oak        140     24      44      75       5     14      37      27
Speedway         112     36      46      76       8     16      37      29
Troy              85     29      43      57       6     13      31      27
Woodland          88     28      46      57       6     13      31      28
```

3. Print a hard copy report of the document and save it as the NORTH.DOC document file.

4. Create an ASCII text file of this fixed formatted data with the file name of NORTH.ASC.

5. Access dBASE and activate the NORTH.DBF database file, which is structured as defined by Dave.

6. Load the fixed formatted data in the NORTH.ASC file to this database.

7. Examine the contents of the database using the BROWSE command.

8. Remove the first record in the database, which contains the column headings included in the ASCII text file produced with WordPerfect.

9. Create the NORTH.FRM dBASE Report Form to produce the report as sketched out and defined by Dave for Lou.

10. Generate a hard copy output of this month's results using the NORTH.FRM report form.

11. (*Optional*)   Create a dBASE program to ZAP the records from the current database, load the fixed formatted ASCII text file from WordPerfect, remove the unwanted column title record, and generate the NORTH.FRM report. Execute this program and produce a second copy of the report.

12. Access Lotus 1-2-3 and position the worksheet cursor at cell **A1.** Import the NORTH.ASC fixed formatted ASCII text file as long labels.

13. Parse only the long label containing the field names and create a single row with these column headings beginning at cell location **A41.** Be sure you parse *only* the field names and not the other rows containing data values.

14. Parse the long labels containing the *data values* and place the results in the rows immediately below the field names obtained in the foregoing task.

15. Change the width of column **A** to 14 spaces.

16. Add columns to compute the Total Revenue, Total Expense, Net Income, and Return On Sales for each inn.

17. Print a report with the field names as column headings. The report is to contain these fields: INN, ROOMS, REST, LOUNGE, TOTAL REVENUE, TOTAL EXPENSE, NET INCOME, and RETURN ON SALES. Format the RETURN ON SALES cells holding the data values as Percent 2. [*Hint:* These columns may be computed using the same formulas you used with the dBASE Report Form.]

18. Create two graphs. The first graph is to be a bar chart of the Total Revenue for the Inns. The second graph is to be a bar chart of the Return on Sales for the Inns. Display the inn names on the X-axis. Place a title on each graph and label both the Y-axis and the X-axis. Save the first graph in the REVENUE.PIC file, and the second graph in the RETURN.PIC file.

19. Save the entire analysis as the NORTH worksheet file, and then print the two graphs.

20. (*Optional*)   Draw a dataflow diagram (DFD) of the entry and processing of data to produce the report from dBASE, the report from Lotus 1-2-3, and the two bar charts.

21. Examine the reports and graphs. Write an analysis identifying the three "best" inns and the three "worst" ones. Explain the Critical Success Factors (CSF) that you have used to determine "best" and "worst."

22. (*Optional*)   Dave wants you to prepare end user documentation that covers entering data and producing the monthly report using the dBASE Report Form. This documentation should be designed for an end user like Jessica.

Time Estimates

Novice: 180 minutes

Intermediate: 150 minutes

Advanced: 120 minutes

Software Tool Perspective

CONTENT

- Developing Solutions
- Selecting Software Tools
- Beyond Today's Software Tools
- Strategy for Continued Learning

I.3.1 Developing Solutions

Now that you have gained an understanding of the application and operation of several software tools, an overall approach for developing solutions to everyday business problems can be examined. You need to avoid the trap encountered by some end users: (1) turn on the computer, (2) access Lotus 1-2-3, (3) start typing, (4) think about the problem, (5) discover the need to use WordPerfect or dBASE, (6) exit from Lotus 1-2-3, and (7) start over. A potential difficulty with starting over is that you may not have enough time to complete your analysis.

In producing a solution to your business problem, you need to sufficiently understand your situation so that you can determine a feasible approach to producing the required information. Only after obtaining a fundamental understanding of your problem can you select the most appropriate software tool and begin developing your solution to produce the required information. The information you generate with a chosen software tool is *not* an end in itself, but merely a means of producing information that helps resolve your problem.

Keypoint!

> The information you generate by applying a software tool to a business problem is *not* an *end*, but a *means* to solving the problem!

Business problems do not occur in nice neat categories wearing signs identifying themselves as spreadsheet problems, database problems, or word processing problems. You must size up each business situation and determine the most appropriate course of action. This includes determining whether a software tool should be used and, if so, which tool is most appropriate.

What is an appropriate approach to follow in developing a solution? A system development life cycle (SDLC) describes a process for creating a solution that consists of these steps:

1. *Initiate.* Identify a business need or opportunity that exists. Determine that a feasible solution can be obtained by using a software tool to generate information addressing the business problem.

2. *Analyze.* Examine the situation to determine the end user's information requirements that need to be satisfied. Does the solution require a narrative description, or are data required that describe the characteristics of an entity such as a customer, a product, or a planning account? Collect and prepare examples of data that are entered in tables or background material for narratives.

3. *Design.* Develop a sketch or outline of the results to be produced. Determine the specific inputs, outputs, and calculations required. Layout a rough draft of the final report to be generated. Does the desired report contain data organized as a table or does it consist of textual information arranged in sections? You can obtain ideas for your design from (a) manually created workpapers, (b) a form selected from a set of standardized forms, (c) a purchased template application, or (d) a previously created application that might be adapted to the current problem.

4. *Implement.* Build the application by actually creating the spreadsheet, database, or document:

   a. *Choose the software tool.* Review your design and select the most appropriate software tool or set of tools.

   b. *Enter data, formulas, text, and/or queries.* Actually create your spreadsheet, database, or document using the selected software tool.

   c. *Verify logic, content, and/or database lookups.* Check your work and determine if any changes are required. Make the necessary corrections and/or additions.

   d. *Prepare user documentation.* Document your application for future reference. This may include listing cell formulas for a spreadsheet, listing the database structure and any programs, and identifying the content of any document file.

5. *Operate.* Produce the final output that is needed to meet the information requirements that support the end user's business activities:

   a. *Produce final reports and/or graphs.* Generate the final copy of your desired outputs.

   b. *Review completed results.* Perform the final quality check on your output to determine that the desired information is included in your format. Proofread your document. Check spreadsheet and database output for reasonableness, that is, do any numbers, such as totals, seem unreasonable because they are too large or small? If any input data may have changed during the time you were constructing your solution, make sure you included the most recent data.

   c. *Accept results and/or obtain approval.* Use the results to support management decision making. If the results were prepared for use by another business associate, obtain that associate's approval of the final output and documentation.

Software tool selection is only one part of the overall SDLC followed to produce a solution to a business problem. In this process, software selection occurs in the Implement stage at Step 4, as emphasized in Figure I.37. This emphasizes the need to determine your information requirements and design your solutions before selecting the software tool to be used.

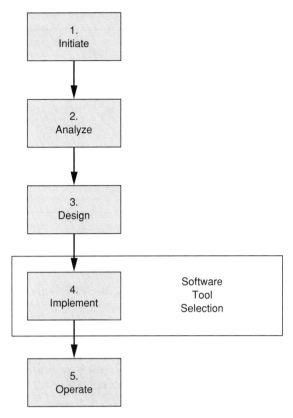

FIGURE I.37. Software tool selection in SDLC.

The information required to solve some business problems is more obvious than for other problems. For this reason, the effort expended across the SDLC can vary considerably. In some situations, the Initiate, Analyze, and Design Steps are so evident that they require little effort. In other situations, the most time-consuming activity is determining what information is required and what layout is desired for the report. However, in each situation, you need to be sure that you have a sufficient understanding of the problem at hand so that you can select the most appropriate software tool.

Keypoint!

> Software tool selection occurs in the Implement stage at Step 4 of the SDLC. An understanding of your business problem and its information requirements are necessary before selecting the most appropriate software tool!

I.3.2   Selecting Software Tools

In this book, you have been guided in learning the fundamentals of operating Lotus 1-2-3, dBASE, and WordPerfect. This provided you with the opportunity to gain an understanding of common applications of these software tools. Because business problems do not identify themselves by software tool, you must select the tool for each of your own problems. Using a "selection by example" approach, the problems presented in each lesson illustrate common applications for the three different software tools. This look in the "rearview mirror" lets you compare your current business problems to these examples in determining where each software tool appeared as the appropriate tool. Figure I.38 is an overview of the Tutorial Problems and software tool applications

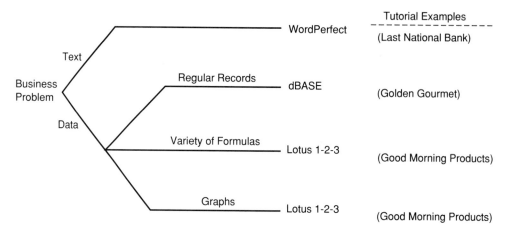

FIGURE I.38. Overview of software tool selection.

explored in this book. You should review the Practice Tutorials, Practice Exercises, Comprehensive Problems, and Case Applications as a guide when selecting a software tool for use with your own problems. In many situations, problems with similar characteristics can be tackled with the same type of software tool.

The main characteristic of the problems approached with each of the three productivity software tools are indicated in Figure I.39. The general characteristics of these problems are described as follows:

Lotus 1-2-3

- Results obtained from many different formulas with a different formula used in nearly every row and column.
- Tables of numeric data are primarily *calculated using formulas.*
- Numeric data are graphed, such as a line graph or pie chart.
- The Practice Tutorials for Good Morning Products and the Comprehensive Problems for Woodcraft Furniture Company and Midwest Universal Gas illustrated the formula-intensive application situation for applying Lotus 1-2-3.

dBASE

- Record-keeping activities are performed where the primary activities consist of entering, updating, selecting, and displaying data.
- Database queries involve the "slicing and dicing" or arranging and selecting of information by a variety of data values, such as selecting by location or product specified with a FOR Condition.
- When computations are performed, the same computation is applied to an entire field in the database, such as computing an INVEST field as PRICE * QTY.
- The Practice Tutorials for the Golden Gourmet and the Comprehensive Problems for Yen To Travel and Silver Screen Video demonstrated the record-keeping activities typically performed with a database management system.

WordPerfect

- Text-processing activities used in preparing written (narrative) documents.
- Tables are limited in scope and consist primarily of data that are typed directly into the table, rather than being calculated by formulas or selected by conditions from a much larger table.

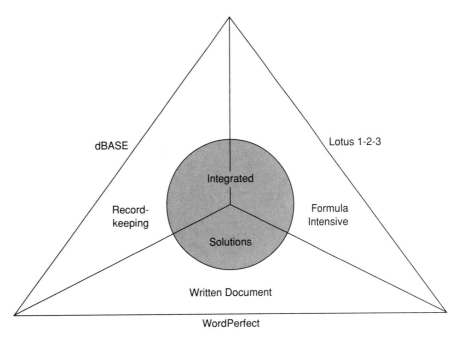

FIGURE I.39. Software tool main characteristics.

- The Practice Tutorials for Last National Bank and the Comprehensive Problems for Home Real Estate and Pioneer Electric and Gas explored text processing activities with a word processor.

Integration

- A situation in which the problem being solved requires a combination of formula-intensive computations, record-keeping activities, and/or written document preparation.
- Each tool is selected and applied based on the most appropriate use of that tool.
- The final solution is obtained by combining results produced with the individual tools, often using ASCII text files or translating directly special formatted files.

The choice of WordPerfect for text processing is often the most straightforward software tool selection. If you are preparing a written document, such as a letter or narrative report, consisting mainly of words, WordPerfect is usually the appropriate tool for this application.

The choice between Lotus 1-2-3 and dBASE is not as easy. These software tools are used to develop data processing applications that consist of fields or columns of numeric and/or character data that describe entities such as products, customers, accounts, and budget line items. As you have observed in prior lessons, the final results generated with both tools are often organized as a report that is a table of rows and columns. In choosing between Lotus 1-2-3 and dBASE, two key characteristics of your business problem that guide your selection are (1) the formula intensity and (2) the data editing requirements. Formula intensity is the number and variety of equations versus directly input data values in your solution, whereas data editing is checking the validity of your input data as they are entered.

Figure I.40 highlights the formula versus data intensity of your application as a selection characteristic. When your application consists of nearly all formulas, a Lotus 1-2-3 spreadsheet is usually the best solution, whereas if your application is all user-entered data values, a dBASE database is usually the most appropriate solution.

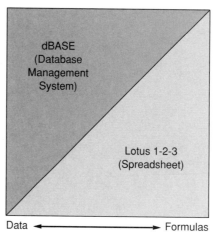

FIGURE I.40. Tool selection consideration between Lotus 1-2-3 and dBASE.

Selection is straightforward when the characteristics of your data processing activities place your application at either end of the formula versus data distinction. The most difficult situation is using judgment in those applications where you have a mix of formulas and data values.

When a solution is a combination of formulas and data values, Lotus 1-2-3 supports a more "free-form" arrangement or "scrambled-egg" approach to developing an application, whereas dBASE forces a "regular" arrangement or "sunny-side-up" approach. The *scrambled* approach of Lotus 1-2-3 lets you place labels, data values, and

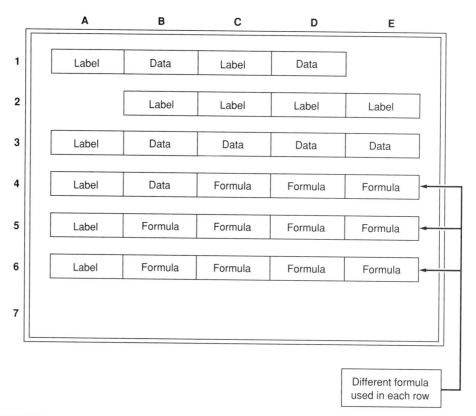

FIGURE I.41. Scrambled arrangement of data values and formulas in spreadsheet application.

formulas wherever you want them in the cells of your spreadsheet, as shown in Figure I.41. As you have experienced in prior lessons, this provides you with considerable flexibility in the use of a worksheet to develop your application. dBASE requires a *regular* arrangement of data as records organized with a common set of fields, where *all fields* are included in each record. When formulas are used with dBASE's arrangement of data, the formulas are applied to all or selected records in computing either another field or a summary, in the manner illustrated in Figure I.42. These convenient dBASE computations are performed with commands such as AVERAGE, COUNT, SUM, and REPLACE. They do not require the copying of formulas like a spreadsheet solution would. In general, the "free-form" arrangement of a Lotus 1-2-3 solution works best with problems requiring smaller spreadsheets, whereas dBASE handles a regular arrangement of data that is better for very large databases.

Data editing is concerned with detecting and correcting errors for input data values. An objective of data editing is to have the computer determine if a data-entry error exists so that you can immediately correct it. Data editing is important because it increases the quality of the input data, which should improve the quality of decisions made by using the information obtained from your application. The best designed output report is of little value if it contains erroneous data. dBASE is better at editing data than Lotus 1-2-3 because dBASE supports checks for numeric, date, and logical data input. With dBASE, you cannot enter character data in a numeric field. Lotus 1-2-3, on the other hand, accepts any data as input directly into a cell regardless of whether it is character (a label) or numeric (a value). If you have a large volume of data that are manually input, the built-in data editing feature of dBASE can help reduce data-entry errors. As a result, if your business problem could be addressed with either dBASE or Lotus 1-2-3, dBASE is the preferred software tool because it helps ensure data integrity through its increased data editing capabilities. The data editing capabilities of Lotus 1-2-3 and dBASE are summarized in Figure I.43 to help you with your software tool selection decision.

Like eggs, a "sunny-side-up" design of formulas and data values is more easily "scrambled" than it is to create a regular arrangement of fields from a scrambled

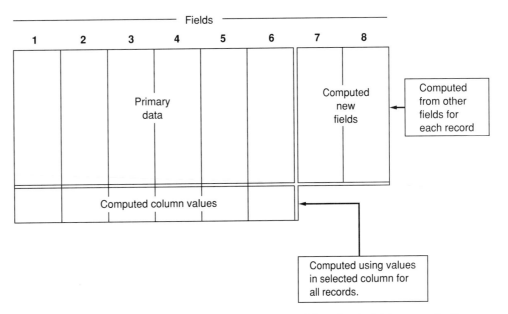

FIGURE I.42. Regular arrangement of data values and formulas in database application.

Software Tool	Data Editing Capability

Lotus 1-2-3	• Very limited editing by first character typed to determine if entry is
	  • Label
	  • Value (or Formula)
	• NO edit checking for type of data entered directly into cell
	• Macro commands required for data editing
	  • /XN {GETNUMBER}
	  • /XL {GETLABEL}
	• Length of data entry tested only against maximum of 240 characters

dBASE	• Data editing implemented by field type
	  • Character
	  • Numeric
	  • Date
	  • Logical
	• Field length established by database structure and monitored with bell ("beep")

FIGURE I.43. Summary of input data editing capabilities.

organization of cells. Furthermore, it is usually easier for another business associate to understand the regular arrangement of fields and the data editing forced with a dBASE application than it is to make sense of a helter-skelter use of cells in a Lotus 1-2-3 application. Whereas dBASE forces the organization of your solution, Lotus 1-2-3 requires any organization to come from you, not Lotus 1-2-3, as you design the application. The Lotus 1-2-3 examples in this book demonstrate typical approaches to the organizing of cells. With Lotus 1-2-3, examples of design features that *you* must implement are (1) placing your macros below and to the right of the rest of your worksheet and (2) organizing the cells as input, computation, and output areas.

If your problem is data intensive and matches the regular arrangement of data values for a database approach, then dBASE is usually the tool of choice. dBASE has no Copy or Move command like Lotus 1-2-3 to reproduce cells formulas or re-arrange columns for display. This feature is simply not necessary in dBASE, because when formulas are used they are applied across all or a specified group of records (rows). dBASE does not use the WYSIWYG method of displaying data on your screen—arranged like your final output report—when you are entering and revising your database. Because of this, dBASE does not require a Copy or Move command. Database fields are easily rearranged for display without permanently relocating them.

Although Lotus 1-2-3 has a data management capability, dBASE provides considerably more power for undertaking the development and operation of data intensive record-keeping applications, as summarized in Figure I.44. For some reason, if you initially selected Lotus 1-2-3 to develop a simple database application, keep the capabilities of dBASE in mind. If the scope or complexity of your application increases, you can move it from Lotus 1-2-3 to dBASE using the procedures described in the Integrating Solutions, Lessons I.1 and I.2.

Overall, WordPerfect is readily selected for text processing applications. Lotus 1-2-3 and dBASE are selected for data processing applications that often consist of a mix of formulas and input data values. Lotus 1-2-3 is a more general- purpose tool than dBASE. This means you can more readily apply Lotus 1-2-3 to a larger variety of business problems. However, the flexibility of Lotus 1-2-3 is a trade-off in obtaining data integrity when the complexity of your application requires large volumes of input data. When the business problem characteristics match those of a database solution, dBASE is usually preferred to Lotus 1-2-3 for your data processing applications. Figure I.45 summarizes selection conditions for choosing software tools.

Software Tool	Data Management Capability
Lotus 1-2-3	• A relatively small number of rows or records are stored and manipulated, usually less than several thousand records. • Simple queries are performed in selecting desired records. • A variety of different formulas may be used in various fields or columns of the solution table. • Values for some columns in the solution table are computed from data values not stored in the table, but provided by equations placed at a separate location within the spreadsheet. • A scrambled arrangement of data and formulas in the table may be used with problems requiring smaller spreadsheets. • A single output report is usually the only report produced with the application. • The application is not shared with other end users or sharing is limited with only one user at a time. • Multiple user access is not required.
dBASE	• A large number of records are stored and manipulated with the potential number exceeding several million. • Multiple tables or relations may be used that are linked by a common data element, such as customer identification number. • When field values are calculated, the same formula is used for all records or large groups of records. • A regular arrangement of rows and columns as fields and records is required that is usually better for very large databases. • Complex queries may involve a number of conditional tests. • Developed application may use several processing menus and different report definitions. • Applications may be readily shared with other end users. • Multiple access is available when required by several end users.

FIGURE I.44. Summary of data management capabilities.

Software Tool	Selection Conditions
Lotus 1-2-3	• Formulas are used to compute values in cells at a number of different locations. • A mixed arrangement of input data values and cells values derived with formulas is required for the application.
dBASE	• Data are entered in regular arrangement for a large number of entities. • When formulas are used, the same formula is applied to all or large groups of records (rows).
WordPerfect	• A document is produced that contains only narrative text. • A text document is desired that includes some small tables containing data values that are entered directly into the table.
Lotus 1-2-3 and WordPerfect Integrated Solution	• A text document is created with a narrative that includes comprehensive tables containing values obtained from complex formulas.
dBASE and WordPerfect Integrated Solution	• A text document is developed with a narrative that contains tables obtained by selecting information from a much larger table of data.
dBASE and Lotus 1-2-3 Integrated Solution	• Large tables of data (1) are used to produce graphs or (2) have complex computations performed on information selected from one or more databases.

FIGURE I.45. Summary of software tool selection.

I.3.3   Beyond Today's Software Tools

As computer technology has advanced with more memory, more disk storage, and faster processing time, software capabilities have expanded, supplying more powerful tools that are easier to use. For example, hardware advances have led to enhancements that permit desktop publishing with WordPerfect and spreadsheet publishing with Lotus 1-2-3. With continued advances like these, the software tools of tomorrow are likely to be different than those of today, whereas many of the business problems faced by tomorrow's managers are likely to be similar to those of today.

As the IBM personal computer entered the business environment more than a decade ago, VisiCalc, dBASE II, and WordStar became the most popular personal productivity software tools. VisiCalc has disappeared completely, to be supplanted by Lotus 1-2-3. dBASE has changed considerably through several versions. WordStar has been displaced by WordPerfect in popularity. Clearly, the "hot" software tool of today is likely to give way to an improved product in the future. However, the fundamental business problems and the management information obtained by using software tools are nearly identical to that obtained with the first personal computers. A major difference with current software tools is that more people are using personal computers in their business and the software has become easier to use.

New versions or releases of software tools have occurred every one or two years. Will the next release of Lotus 1-2-3, dBASE, or WordPerfect make your knowledge of the operation and application of software tools obsolete? When General Motors rolls out next year's Chevrolet, is last year's model obsolete and of no further use? If you learned how to drive last year's model, do your driving skills carry over to the new model? Although the new model may have sleek new styling, an improved engine, or an advanced braking system, last year's model is still likely to provide many trouble-free miles. A similar situation exists for software tools. The next version or release improves on the previous one, providing enhanced capabilities that make them even easier for you to use. If you learned how to operate and to apply the old version, you can use most, if not all, of that knowledge in operating and applying the new version. For example, users of VisiCalc readily moved to Lotus 1-2-3 and began applying its advanced features without the need to completely relearn the operation of a spreadsheet tool.

A new version may have a sleek new user interface with icons that are selected using a mouse or pen, but the fundamental activities performed with the tool remain the same. For example, with Lotus 1-2-3, the same activity is performed regardless of whether you directly type an equation or cell range or whether you use a mouse to specify it. Although the user interface may change, the fundamental operation of the software tool is not likely to become obsolete. For example, the organization of a spreadsheet tool as an accountant's worksheet, with a series of cells that are arranged in rows and columns, continues to endure changes in software operation. As document preparation has progressed from pen and quill to typewriters to word processors, the documents created by using advanced technology have remained virtually the same.

For each version of a software tool, its features can be classified as (1) leading edge, (2) advanced, and (3) fundamental, which can be defined as follows:

- *Leading edge.* New features introduced in the most recent versions of the software tool. These are often enhancements that add entirely new capabilities to the tool and may be a unique feature not available in competitive software tools.

- *Advanced.* Features available for several versions that support more complex activities. These features are usually available in similar competitive tools.

- *Fundamental.* Features included in nearly all software tools of the same type. That is, most of the available spreadsheets, database management systems, or word processors would have these capabilities.

Feature Category	Software Tool		
	Lotus 1-2-3	dBASE	WordPerfect
Leading Edge	Backsolver Spreadsheet publishing Map view	User-defined pop-up menus Users-defined windows Rollback	Desktop publishing Grammar checking
Advanced	Macro programming Regression analysis	dBASE programming Data views Multiple user access	Macros Imbedded graphics Spell checker Thesaurus
Fundamental	Cell layout arrangement Formulas and data values "As Displayed" reporting Graphing	Database definition Data entry Queries Report writer	Document creation Document formatting Cut and paste

FIGURE I.46. Example software tool features.

Examples of software tool features for these three categories are indicated in Figure I.46. In general, new versions of software tools result in "trickle down": the leading-edge features become the advanced features, which are accepted as fundamental capabilities. This reinforces the idea that the best of the latest features added to a particular software tool will, after several versions, become a "standard" found in nearly all software tools of the same type. If Lotus 1-2-3 does not contain a leading-edge feature found in a competitive tool like Microsoft Excel, often you need only to wait for the next upgraded release of Lotus 1-2-3 for the feature to become available.

The techniques for integrating results between software tools are likely to be enhanced in future versions, with capabilities that go beyond the ASCII text files and special formatted file conversions described in the previous Integrating Solutions Lessons. For example, object linking and embedding (OLE) and dynamic data exchange (DDE) are newer methods of passing data between software tools that let a change made in your spreadsheet automatically update a table in your word processing document. Once the link is established, the document is updated with current spreadsheet values as the document is retrieved. Although OLE and DDE have not been implemented among Lotus 1-2-3 version 2.4, dBASE IV version 1.5, and WordPerfect 5.1, these capabilities have been implemented with other software tools and appear as a possible future direction for integrating results.

This book has focused on the fundamental operation of software tools. By learning these fundamentals, you will be prepared to master future product enhancements. These changes will, in general, help you become more effective and efficient in applying the software tools to your business problems.

I.3.4   Strategy for Continued Learning

By working your way through this book, you have experienced a strategy for continued learning about new versions of software tools or advanced features of the current versions and for the application of these tools in solving common business problems. The learning method appropriate for mastering a software tool is as follows:

1. Read a description of the use of the software tool's features and understand their operation and application.

2. Explore the operation of the features, using an example from the software's reference manual or a trial example you have constructed to gain experience.

3. Apply the features in obtaining information to solve your own business problem.

By mastering the operation and understanding the application of each software tool presented in this book, you have obtained a strong foundation for continued learning with these tools. You should apply this method in learning about new and advanced features as you employ these tools or their successors in preparing management information to solve tomorrow's business problems.

I.3.5   Lesson Summary

- The steps for developing a solution with a software tool are (1) initiate, (2) analyze, (3) design, (4) implement, and (5) operate.

- Selection of a software tool should occur in the implement stage at Step 4. You need to understand your business problem with sufficient detail before choosing the software tool you will use.

- Text processing is usually performed using WordPerfect.

- Data processing activities are carried out with either Lotus 1-2-3 or dBASE. Lotus 1-2-3 is better at formula intensive applications than dBASE. dBASE has better data editing capabilities than Lotus 1-2-3.

- Applications with a large number of input data that follow a regular arrangement of fields are often best suited to the use of dBASE.

- Solutions involving a combination of formula intensive computations, record-keeping activities, and written document preparation frequently require an integrated solution, with the most appropriate tool selected for each part of the application.

- Software tools are continually enhanced through upgraded versions.

- Learning how to use a current version of a software tool prepares you for learning to apply enhanced features of a new version.

- You should feel comfortable with learning new and advanced features of a software tool by exploring these features with a trial example and then applying the features in solving your current business problem.

Index